PREFACE TO THE THIRD EDITION

The Revised edition of the book "MATHEMATICS FOR CLASS VIII" has been written strictly according to the latest syllabus prescribed by the NCERT.

Keeping in mind the mental level of a child, every effort has been made to introduce new concepts in a simple language so that the child understands them easily. Basic concepts have been explained through attractive illustrations relating to our day-to-day life experiences.

The book has been divided into 27 Chapters. The text has been re-written in a lucid manner. The difficulty level of the problems has been reduced and mathematical concepts have been explained in the simplest possible way. Each chapter contains a large number of illustrative examples to understand the applications of concepts. In each section, illustrative examples are followed by an exercise containing an adequate number of unsolved problems. The difficulty level of problms in exercises has also been reduced.

Students are advised to read the theory carefully and solve Illustrative Examples on their own before attempting the Exercises.

I hope that this book will be useful to the students and teachers alike.

I avail this opportunity to convey my sincere thanks to Sh. Ish Kapur of Dhanpat Rai Publications (P) Ltd. for this encouragement and painstaking efforts in bringing out this book in such an excellent form.

Inspite of my best efforts to make this edition error free, some printed errors might have gone un-noticed. I shall be grateful to the teachers and students if the same are brought to my notice. You may send your valuable suggestions, feedback or queries by post or through e-mail to **ish.dhanpat@gmail.com** which would be verified by me and the corrections would be incorporated in the subsequent editions.

Any suggestion/criticism to enhance the quality of the book will be gratefully acknowledged.

Dr. R.D. SHARMA

CONTENTS

1

RATIONAL NUMBERS

1.1 INTRODUCTION

In class VI, we began our study of numbers with counting numbers or natural numbers i.e., 1, 2, 3, 4, ... By including 0 to natural numbers, we got whole numbers i.e., 0, 1, 2, 3, 4, ... The negative of natural numbers were put together with whole numbers to get integers i.e., ... –4, –3, –2, –1, 0, 1, 2, 3, 4, ... Addition, subtraction, multiplication and division operations were defined on integers and various properties (closure property, commutativity, associativity, existence of identity, existence of inverse) of these operations were discussed. In class VII, the concept of rational numbers was introduced and addition, subtraction, multiplication and division operations on rational numbers were defined. In this chapter, we will learn about various properties of these operations on rational numbers.

Let us first recall, in brief, what we have learnt about rational numbers in class VII.

1.2 RECAPITULATION

RATIONAL NUMBER *A number of the form* $\frac{p}{q}$ *or a number which can be expressed in the form* $\frac{p}{q}$, *where p and q are integers and* $q \neq 0$, *is called a rational number.*

In other words, a rational number is any number that can be expressed as the quotient of two integers with the condition that the divisor is not zero.

Each of the numbers $\frac{7}{9}, \frac{-2}{11}, \frac{-3}{-2}, \frac{15}{-7}$ is a rational number.

It should be noted that every integer is a rational number.

In the rational number $\frac{p}{q}$, integer p is known as the numerator and non-zero integer q is called the denominator.

If the numerator and denominator of a rational number are of the same sign, then it is said to be positive. Otherwise, it is negative.

Rational numbers $\frac{7}{11}$ and $\frac{-25}{-9}$ are positive whereas $\frac{-11}{7}$ and $\frac{4}{-15}$ are negative rational numbers.

If $\frac{p}{q}$ is a rational number and m is a non-zero integer, then

$$\frac{p}{q} = \frac{p \times m}{q \times m}$$

Rational number $\frac{p \times m}{q \times m}$ is a rational number *equivalent* to $\frac{p}{q}$.

If $\frac{p}{q}$ is a rational number and m is a common divisor of p and q, then

$$\frac{p}{q}=\frac{p\div m}{q\div m}$$

LOWEST FORM OF A RATIONAL NUMBER *A rational number $\frac{p}{q}$ is said to be in the lowest form or simplest form if p and q have no common factor other than1.*

Rational number $\frac{5}{7}$ is in the lowest form, but $\frac{15}{21}$ is not in the lowest form. In order to reduce a rational number $\frac{p}{q}$ in the lowest form, we divide its numerator p and denominator q by the HCF of p and q.

A rational number $\frac{p}{q}$ is said to be in standard form, if its denominator q is a positive integer and p and q have no common divisor other than 1.

EQUALITY OF RATIONAL NUMBERS Two rational numbers $\frac{p}{q}$ and $\frac{r}{s}$ are equal iff $p\times s=q\times r$.

i.e., $\frac{p}{q}=\frac{r}{s}$

$\Leftrightarrow$ $p\times s=q\times r$ $\begin{matrix} p & & r \\ & \times & \\ q & & s \end{matrix}$

$\Leftrightarrow$ Numerator of first $\times$ Denominator of second = Numerator of second $\times$ Denominator of first

For example , $\frac{-7}{21}=\frac{3}{-9}$ and $\frac{5}{7}=\frac{20}{28}$, because $(-7)\times(-9)=21\times3$ and $5\times28=7\times20$.

1.3 ADDITION OF RATIONAL NUMBERS

In class VII, we have defined the operation of addition of rational numbers. The addition of rational numbers is carried out in the same way as that of addition of fractions which we have learnt in earlier classes. If two rational numbers are to be added, we first express each one of them as rational numbers with positive denominator. For addition purpose, we divide the rational numbers into the following two categories:

1.3.1 RATIONAL NUMBERS WITH SAME DENOMINATORS

In order to add two rational numbers having the same denominator, we follow the following steps:

<u>Step I</u> *Obtain the numerators of the two given rational numbers and their common denominator.*

<u>Step II</u> *Add the numerators obtained in step I*

<u>Step III</u> *Write a rational number whose numerator is the sum obtained in step II, and whose denominator is the common denominator of the given rational numbers.*

It follows from the above steps that if $\frac{p}{q}$ *and* $\frac{r}{q}$ *are two rational numbers with the same denominator, then*

$$\frac{p}{q}+\frac{r}{q}=\frac{p+r}{q}$$

Following examples will illustrate the above procedure for the addition of two rational numbers with the same denominator.

ILLUSTRATIVE EXAMPLES

Example 1 Add $\frac{3}{5}$ and $\frac{13}{5}$.

Solution We have,

$$\frac{3}{5}+\frac{13}{5}=\frac{3+13}{5}=\frac{16}{5} \qquad [\because 3+13=16]$$

Example 2 Add $\frac{7}{9}$ and $\frac{-12}{9}$.

Solution We have,

$$\frac{7}{9}+\frac{-12}{9}=\frac{7+(-12)}{9}=\frac{-5}{9} \qquad [\because 7+(-12)=-5]$$

Example 3 Add $\frac{-5}{9}$ and $\frac{-17}{9}$.

Solution We have,

$$\frac{-5}{9}+\frac{-17}{9}=\frac{(-5)+(-17)}{9}=\frac{-22}{9} \qquad [\because (-5)+(-17)=-22]$$

Example 4 Add $\frac{4}{-11}$ and $\frac{7}{11}$.

Solution We first express $\frac{4}{-11}$ as a rational number with positive denominator.

We have, $\frac{4}{-11}=\frac{4\times(-1)}{(-11)\times(-1)}=\frac{-4}{11}$

$$\therefore \quad \frac{4}{-11}+\frac{7}{11}=\frac{-4}{11}+\frac{7}{11}=\frac{(-4)+7}{11}=\frac{3}{11} \qquad [\because (-4)+7=3]$$

1.3.2 NUMBERS WITH DISTINCT DENOMINATORS

To find the sum of two rational numbers which do not have the same denominator, we follow the following steps:

<u>Step I</u> *Obtain the rational numbers and see whether their denominators are positive or not. If the denominator of one (or both) of the numbers is negative, re-write it so that the denominator becomes positive.*

<u>Step II</u> *Obtain the denominators of the rational numbers in step I.*

<u>Step III</u> *Find the LCM of the denominators obtained in step II.*

<u>Step IV</u> *Express each one of the rational numbers in step I so that the LCM obtained in step III becomes their common denominator.*

<u>Step V</u> *Write a rational number whose numerator is equal to the sum of the numerators of rational numbers obtained in step IV and denominator as the LCM obtained in step III.*

<u>Step VI</u> *The rational number obtained in step V is the required sum.*

Following examples will illustrate the above procedure.

ILLUSTRATIVE EXAMPLES

Example 1 Add $\frac{5}{12}$ and $\frac{3}{8}$.

Solution Clearly, denominators of the given numbers are positive.

The LCM of denominators 12 and 8 is 24.

Now, we express $\frac{5}{12}$ and $\frac{3}{8}$ into forms in which both of them have the same denominator 24.

We have,

$$\frac{5}{12}=\frac{5\times2}{12\times2}=\frac{10}{24} \text{ and, } \frac{3}{8}=\frac{3\times3}{8\times3}=\frac{9}{24}$$

$$\therefore \quad \frac{5}{12}+\frac{3}{8}=\frac{10}{24}+\frac{9}{24}=\frac{10+9}{24}=\frac{19}{24}$$

Example 2 Add $\frac{7}{9}$ and 4.

Solution We have, $4=\frac{4}{1}$.

Clearly, denominators of the two rational numbers are positive. We now re-write them so that they have a common denominator equal to the LCM of the denominators.

LCM of 9 and 1 is 9.

We have, $\frac{4}{1}=\frac{4\times9}{1\times9}=\frac{36}{9}$

$$\therefore \quad \frac{7}{9}+4=\frac{7}{9}+\frac{4}{1}=\frac{7}{9}+\frac{36}{9}=\frac{7+36}{9}=\frac{43}{9}$$

Example 3 Add $\frac{3}{8}$ and $\frac{-5}{12}$.

Solution The denominators of the given rational numbers are 8 and 12 respectively. The LCM of 8 and 12 is 24.

Now we re-write the given rational numbers into forms in which both of them have the same denominator.

It follows from the above steps that if $\frac{p}{q}$ *and* $\frac{r}{q}$ *are two rational numbers with the same denominator, then*

$$\frac{p}{q}+\frac{r}{q}=\frac{p+r}{q}$$

Following examples will illustrate the above procedure for the addition of two rational numbers with the same denominator.

ILLUSTRATIVE EXAMPLES

Example 1 Add $\frac{3}{5}$ and $\frac{13}{5}$.

Solution We have,

$$\frac{3}{5}+\frac{13}{5}=\frac{3+13}{5}=\frac{16}{5} \qquad [\because 3+13=16]$$

Example 2 Add $\frac{7}{9}$ and $\frac{-12}{9}$.

Solution We have,

$$\frac{7}{9}+\frac{-12}{9}=\frac{7+(-12)}{9}=\frac{-5}{9} \qquad [\because 7+(-12)=-5]$$

Example 3 Add $\frac{-5}{9}$ and $\frac{-17}{9}$.

Solution We have,

$$\frac{-5}{9}+\frac{-17}{9}=\frac{(-5)+(-17)}{9}=\frac{-22}{9} \qquad [\because (-5)+(-17)=-22]$$

Example 4 Add $\frac{4}{-11}$ and $\frac{7}{11}$.

Solution We first express $\frac{4}{-11}$ as a rational number with positive denominator.

We have, $\frac{4}{-11}=\frac{4\times(-1)}{(-11)\times(-1)}=\frac{-4}{11}$

$$\therefore \frac{4}{-11}+\frac{7}{11}=\frac{-4}{11}+\frac{7}{11}=\frac{(-4)+7}{11}=\frac{3}{11} \qquad [\because (-4)+7=3]$$

1.3.2 NUMBERS WITH DISTINCT DENOMINATORS

To find the sum of two rational numbers which do not have the same denominator, we follow the following steps:

Step I *Obtain the rational numbers and see whether their denominators are positive or not. If the denominator of one (or both) of the numbers is negative, re-write it so that the denominator becomes positive.*

Step II *Obtain the denominators of the rational numbers in step I.*

<u>Step III</u> *Find the LCM of the denominators obtained in step II.*

<u>Step IV</u> *Express each one of the rational numbers in step I so that the LCM obtained in step III becomes their common denominator.*

<u>Step V</u> *Write a rational number whose numerator is equal to the sum of the numerators of rational numbers obtained in step IV and denominator as the LCM obtained in step III.*

<u>Step VI</u> *The rational number obtained in step V is the required sum.*

Following examples will illustrate the above procedure.

ILLUSTRATIVE EXAMPLES

Example 1 Add $\frac{5}{12}$ and $\frac{3}{8}$.

Solution Clearly, denominators of the given numbers are positive.

The LCM of denominators 12 and 8 is 24.

Now, we express $\frac{5}{12}$ and $\frac{3}{8}$ into forms in which both of them have the same denominator 24.

We have,

$$\frac{5}{12} = \frac{5 \times 2}{12 \times 2} = \frac{10}{24} \text{ and, } \frac{3}{8} = \frac{3 \times 3}{8 \times 3} = \frac{9}{24}$$

$$\therefore \quad \frac{5}{12} + \frac{3}{8} = \frac{10}{24} + \frac{9}{24} = \frac{10+9}{24} = \frac{19}{24}$$

Example 2 Add $\frac{7}{9}$ and 4.

Solution We have, $4 = \frac{4}{1}$.

Clearly, denominators of the two rational numbers are positive. We now re-write them so that they have a common denominator equal to the LCM of the denominators.

LCM of 9 and 1 is 9.

We have, $\frac{4}{1} = \frac{4 \times 9}{1 \times 9} = \frac{36}{9}$

$$\therefore \quad \frac{7}{9} + 4 = \frac{7}{9} + \frac{4}{1} = \frac{7}{9} + \frac{36}{9} = \frac{7+36}{9} = \frac{43}{9}$$

Example 3 Add $\frac{3}{8}$ and $\frac{-5}{12}$.

Solution The denominators of the given rational numbers are 8 and 12 respectively. The LCM of 8 and 12 is 24.

Now we re-write the given rational numbers into forms in which both of them have the same denominator.

$$\frac{3}{8}=\frac{3\times 3}{8\times 3}=\frac{9}{24} \text{ and, } \frac{-5}{12}=\frac{-5\times 2}{12\times 2}=\frac{-10}{24}$$

$$\therefore \quad \frac{3}{8}+\frac{-5}{12}=\frac{9}{24}+\frac{(-10)}{24}=\frac{9-10}{24}=\frac{-1}{24}$$

Example 4 Simplify: $\frac{8}{-15}+\frac{4}{-3}$.

Solution We have,

$$\frac{8}{-15}+\frac{4}{-3}=\frac{-8}{15}+\frac{-4}{3} \qquad \left[\because \frac{8}{-15}=\frac{8\times -1}{(-15)\times(-1)}=\frac{-8}{15} \text{ and } \frac{4}{-3}=\frac{4\times -1}{(-3)\times(-1)}=\frac{-4}{3}\right]$$

LCM of 15 and 3 is 15.

Re-writing $\frac{-4}{3}$ in the form in which it has denominator 15, we get

$$\frac{-4}{3}=\frac{-4\times 5}{3+5}=\frac{-20}{15}$$

$$\therefore \quad \frac{8}{-15}+\frac{4}{-3}=\frac{-8}{15}+\frac{-4}{3}$$

$$=\frac{-8}{15}+\frac{-20}{15} \qquad \left[\because \frac{-4}{3}=\frac{-20}{15}\right]$$

$$=\frac{(-8)+(-20)}{15}=\frac{-28}{15}$$

Example 5 Simplify: $\frac{7}{-26}+\frac{16}{39}$.

Solution We have,

$$\frac{7}{-26}+\frac{16}{39}=\frac{-7}{26}+\frac{16}{39} \qquad \left[\because \frac{7}{-26}=\frac{7\times -1}{(-26)\times(-1)}=\frac{-7}{26}\right]$$

LCM of 26 and 39 is 78.

Re-writing $\frac{-7}{26}$ and $\frac{16}{39}$ in forms having the same denominator 78, we get

$$\frac{-7}{26}=\frac{-7\times 3}{26\times 3}=\frac{-21}{78}, \frac{16}{39}=\frac{16\times 2}{39\times 2}=\frac{32}{78}$$

$$\therefore \quad \frac{7}{-26}+\frac{16}{39}=\frac{-7}{26}+\frac{16}{39}=\frac{-21}{78}+\frac{32}{78}=\frac{11}{78}$$

EXERCISE 1.1

1. Add the following rational numbers:

(i) $\frac{-5}{7}$ and $\frac{3}{7}$ (ii) $\frac{-15}{4}$ and $\frac{7}{4}$ (iii) $\frac{-8}{11}$ and $\frac{-4}{11}$ (iv) $\frac{6}{13}$ and $\frac{-9}{13}$

2. Add the following rational numbers:

(i) $\frac{3}{4}$ and $\frac{-5}{8}$ (ii) $\frac{5}{-9}$ and $\frac{7}{3}$ (iii) -3 and $\frac{3}{5}$ (iv) $\frac{-7}{27}$ and $\frac{11}{18}$

(v) $\frac{31}{-4}$ and $\frac{-5}{8}$ (vi) $\frac{5}{36}$ and $\frac{-7}{12}$ (vii) $\frac{-5}{16}$ and $\frac{7}{24}$ (viii) $\frac{7}{-18}$ and $\frac{8}{27}$

3. Simplify:

(i) $\frac{8}{9}+\frac{-11}{6}$ (ii) $3+\frac{5}{-7}$ (iii) $\frac{1}{-12}+\frac{2}{-15}$ (iv) $\frac{-8}{19}+\frac{-4}{57}$

(v) $\frac{7}{9}+\frac{3}{-4}$ (vi) $\frac{5}{26}+\frac{11}{-39}$ (vii) $\frac{-16}{9}+\frac{-5}{12}$ (viii) $\frac{-13}{8}+\frac{5}{36}$

(ix) $0+\frac{-3}{5}$ (x) $1+\frac{-4}{5}$

4. Add and express the sum as a mixed fraction:

(i) $\frac{-12}{5}$ and $\frac{43}{10}$ (ii) $\frac{24}{7}$ and $\frac{-11}{4}$ (iii) $\frac{-31}{6}$ and $\frac{-27}{8}$ (iv) $\frac{101}{6}$ and $\frac{7}{8}$

ANSWERS

1. (i) $\frac{-2}{7}$ (ii) -2 (iii) $\frac{-12}{11}$ (iv) $\frac{-3}{13}$

2. (i) $\frac{1}{8}$ (ii) $\frac{16}{9}$ (iii) $\frac{-12}{5}$ (iv) $\frac{19}{54}$ (v) $\frac{-67}{8}$ (vi) $\frac{-4}{9}$

(vii) $\frac{-1}{48}$ (viii) $\frac{-5}{54}$

3. (i) $\frac{-17}{18}$ (ii) $\frac{16}{7}$ (iii) $\frac{-13}{60}$ (iv) $\frac{-28}{57}$ (v) $\frac{1}{36}$ (vi) $\frac{-7}{78}$

(vii) $\frac{-79}{36}$ (viii) $\frac{-107}{72}$ (ix) $\frac{-3}{5}$ (x) $\frac{1}{5}$

4. (i) $1\frac{9}{10}$ (ii) $\frac{19}{28}$ (iii) $-8\frac{13}{24}$ (iv) $17\frac{17}{24}$

1.4 PROPERTIES OF ADDITION OF RATIONAL NUMBERS

In this section, we shall learn some properties of addition of rational numbers. These properties are similar to those of addition of integers which we have learnt in the previous class.

CLOSURE PROPERTY *The sum of any two rational numbers is always a rational number.*

Thus, if $\frac{a}{b}$ and $\frac{c}{d}$ are any two rational numbers, then $\left(\frac{a}{b}+\frac{c}{d}\right)$ is also a rational number.

Verification: In order to verify this property. Let us consider the following:

(i) $\frac{1}{4}+\frac{2}{3}=\frac{3}{12}+\frac{8}{12}=\frac{3+8}{12}=\frac{11}{12}$, which is a rational number.

(ii) $\frac{-3}{4}+\frac{5}{6}=\frac{-9}{12}+\frac{10}{12}=\frac{-9+10}{12}=\frac{1}{12}$, which is a rational number.

(iii) $\frac{-5}{4}+\frac{-1}{24}=\frac{-30}{24}+\frac{-1}{24}=\frac{-30-1}{24}=\frac{-31}{24}$, which is a rational number.

COMMUTATIVITY *The addition of rational numbers is commutative i.e., if* $\frac{a}{b}$ *and* $\frac{c}{d}$ *are any two rational numbers, then*

$$\frac{a}{b}+\frac{c}{d}=\frac{c}{d},+\frac{a}{b}$$

Verification: In order to verify this property, let us consider two expressions

$$\frac{5}{6}+\frac{-4}{9} \text{ and } \frac{-4}{9}+\frac{5}{6}$$

We have,

$$\frac{-4}{9}+\frac{5}{6}=\frac{-8}{18}+\frac{15}{18}=\frac{-8+15}{18}=\frac{7}{18} \text{ and, } \frac{5}{6}+\frac{-4}{9}=\frac{15}{18}+\frac{-8}{18}=\frac{15+(-8)}{18}=\frac{7}{18}$$

$$\therefore \quad \frac{5}{6}+\frac{-4}{9}=\frac{-4}{9}+\frac{5}{6}$$

Similarly, it can be verified for other pairs of rational numbers.

ASSOCIATIVITY *The addition of rational numbers is associative i.e. if* $\frac{a}{b}, \frac{c}{d}$ *and* $\frac{e}{f}$ *are any three rational numbers, then*

$$\frac{a}{b}+\left(\frac{c}{d}+\frac{e}{f}\right)=\left(\frac{a}{b}+\frac{c}{d}\right)+\frac{e}{f}$$

Verification: In order to verify this property, let us consider the following expressions

$$\frac{-3}{4}+\left(\frac{5}{6}+\frac{-4}{9}\right) \text{and} \left(\frac{-3}{4}+\frac{5}{6}\right)+\frac{-4}{9}$$

We have,

$$\frac{-3}{4}+\left(\frac{5}{6}+\frac{-4}{9}\right)=\frac{-3}{4}+\left(\frac{15}{18}+\frac{-8}{18}\right)$$

$$=\frac{-3}{4}+\frac{15-8}{18}$$

$$=\frac{-3}{4}+\frac{7}{18}=\frac{-27}{36}+\frac{14}{36}=\frac{-27+14}{36}=\frac{-13}{36}$$

and, $\left(\frac{-3}{4}+\frac{5}{6}\right)+\frac{-4}{9}=\left(\frac{-9}{12}+\frac{10}{12}\right)+\frac{-4}{9}$

$$=\frac{-9+10}{12}+\frac{-4}{9}$$

$$=\frac{1}{12}+\frac{-4}{9}=\frac{3}{36}+\frac{-16}{36}=\frac{3+(-16)}{36}=\frac{-13}{36}$$

$$\therefore \quad \frac{-3}{4}+\left(\frac{5}{6}+\frac{-4}{9}\right)=\left(\frac{-3}{4}+\frac{5}{6}\right)+\frac{-4}{9}$$

Similarly, it can be verified for other rational numbers.

Remark 1 *From the associativity of addition of rational numbers, we find that three or more rational numbers can be added without using parentheses and from the commutativity of addition of rational numbers we observe that the order in which the numbers are arranged before addition does not affect the sum. It follows from these two properties that while adding three or more rational numbers, we can re-arrange the numbers in any order before adding them and the use of paraentheses is not essential.*

Remark 2 *While adding three or more rational numbers we re-arrange and group them in such a way that each group contains a pair of numbers either with a common denominator or their denominators have a common divisor. The following illustrations will illustrate the sum.*

ILLUSTRATION 1 Simplify: $\frac{4}{3}+\frac{3}{5}+\frac{-2}{3}+\frac{-11}{5}$.

Solution We find that out of the four rational numbers to be added, two have the same denominator 3 and the remaining two have the same denominator 5. So, we re-arrange and group them in such a way that each group contains a pair of numbers with a common denomiator.

$$\therefore \quad \frac{4}{3}+\frac{3}{5}+\frac{-2}{3}+\frac{-11}{5}=\left(\frac{4}{3}+\frac{-2}{3}\right)+\left(\frac{3}{5}+\frac{-11}{5}\right)$$

$$=\frac{4+(-2)}{3}+\frac{3+(-11)}{5}$$

$$=\frac{2}{3}+\frac{-8}{5}$$

$$=\frac{2\times 5}{3\times 5}+\frac{(-8)\times 3}{5\times 3} \quad \left[\begin{array}{l}\because \text{LCM of 3 and 5 is 15} \\ \therefore \text{Each rational number is} \\ \text{expressed with denominator 15}\end{array}\right]$$

$$=\frac{10}{15}+\frac{-24}{15}=\frac{10+(-24)}{15}=\frac{-14}{15}$$

ILLUSTRATION 2 Simplify: $\frac{3}{8}+\frac{7}{2}+\frac{-3}{5}+\frac{9}{8}+\frac{-3}{2}+\frac{6}{5}$.

Solution Re-arranging and grouping the numbers in pairs in such a way that each group contains a pair of rational numbers with a common denominator, we have

$$\frac{3}{8}+\frac{7}{2}+\frac{-3}{5}+\frac{9}{8}+\frac{-3}{2}+\frac{6}{5}$$

$$=\left(\frac{3}{8}+\frac{9}{8}\right)+\left(\frac{7}{2}+\frac{-3}{2}\right)+\left(\frac{-3}{5}+\frac{6}{5}\right)$$

$$=\frac{3+9}{8}+\frac{7+(-3)}{2}+\frac{(-3)+6}{5}$$

$$=\frac{12}{8}+\frac{4}{2}+\frac{3}{5}$$

$$=\frac{3}{2}+2+\frac{3}{5}$$

$$=\frac{3\times5}{2\times5}+\frac{2\times10}{1\times10}+\frac{3\times2}{5\times2}=\frac{15}{10}+\frac{20}{10}+\frac{6}{10}=\frac{15+20+6}{10}=\frac{41}{10}$$

ILLUSTRATION 3 Simplify: $\frac{-3}{10}+\frac{7}{15}+\frac{3}{-20}+\frac{-9}{10}+\frac{13}{15}+\frac{13}{-20}$

Solution Re-arranging and grouping the numbers in pairs such that each group contains a pair of rational numbers with equal denominators, we have

$$\frac{-3}{10}+\frac{7}{15}+\frac{3}{-20}+\frac{-9}{10}+\frac{13}{15}+\frac{13}{-20}$$

$$=\left(\frac{-3}{10}+\frac{-9}{10}\right)+\left(\frac{7}{15}+\frac{13}{15}\right)+\left(\frac{3}{-20}+\frac{13}{-20}\right)$$

$$=\left(\frac{-3}{10}+\frac{-9}{10}\right)+\left(\frac{7}{15}+\frac{13}{15}\right)+\left(\frac{-3}{20}+\frac{-13}{20}\right)$$

$$=\frac{(-3)+(-9)}{10}+\frac{7+13}{15}+\frac{(-3)+(-13)}{20}$$

$$=\frac{-12}{10}+\frac{20}{15}+\frac{-16}{20}$$

$$=\frac{-6}{5}+\frac{4}{3}+\frac{-4}{5}$$ [Expressing each rational in lowest terms]

$$=\left(\frac{-6}{5}+\frac{-4}{5}\right)+\frac{4}{3}$$

$$=\frac{(-6)+(-4)}{5}+\frac{4}{3}=\frac{-10}{5}+\frac{4}{3}=-2+\frac{4}{3}=\frac{-6+4}{3}=\frac{-2}{3}$$

EXISTENCE OF ADDITIVE IDENTITY (ZERO) *The sum of any rational number and zero (0) is the national number itself.*

In other words, if $\frac{a}{b}$ *is any rational number, then*

$$\frac{a}{b}+0=\frac{a}{b}=0+\frac{a}{b}$$

Verification: We have,

(i) $\frac{2}{3}+0=\frac{2}{3}+\frac{0}{3}=\frac{2+0}{3}=\frac{2}{3}$ and, $0+\frac{2}{3}=\frac{0}{3}+\frac{2}{3}=\frac{0+2}{3}=\frac{2}{3}$

$\therefore \quad \frac{2}{3}+0=\frac{2}{3}=0+\frac{2}{3}$

(ii) $\frac{-4}{5}+0=\frac{-4}{5}+\frac{0}{5}=\frac{-4+0}{5}=\frac{-4}{5}$ and, $0+\frac{-4}{5}=\frac{0}{5}+\frac{-4}{5}=\frac{0+(-4)}{5}=\frac{-4}{5}$

$\therefore \quad \frac{-4}{5}+0=\frac{-4}{5}=0+\frac{-4}{5}$

Similarly, it can be verified for other rational numbers.

<u>Remark</u> *The rational number 0 is called the identity element for the addition of rational numbers.*

EXISTENCE OF NEGATIVE (ADDITIVE INVERSE) OF A RATIONAL NUMBER *For every rational number $\frac{a}{b}$ there is a rational number $\frac{c}{d}$ such that*

$$\frac{a}{b}+\frac{c}{d}=0=\frac{c}{d}+\frac{a}{b}$$

The rational numbers $\frac{a}{b}$ and $\frac{c}{d}$ satisfying the above property are called additive inverse or negative of each other. The additive inverse of $\frac{a}{b}$ is written as $-\frac{a}{b}$.

Verification: We have,

$$\frac{3}{5}+\frac{-3}{5}=\frac{3+(-3)}{5}=\frac{0}{5}=0$$

and, $\frac{-3}{5}+\frac{3}{5}=\frac{(-3)+3}{5}=\frac{0}{5}=0$

$\therefore \quad \frac{3}{5}+\frac{-3}{5}=0=\frac{-3}{5}+\frac{3}{5}$

It follows from this that the additive inverse (negative) of $\frac{3}{5}$ is $\frac{-3}{5}$ and the additive inverse of $\frac{-3}{5}$ is $\frac{3}{5}$. But, the additive inverse (negative) of $\frac{3}{5}$ is written as $-\frac{3}{5}$ and that of $\frac{-3}{5}$ is written as $-\left(\frac{-3}{5}\right)$. Therefore, $\frac{-3}{5}$ and $-\frac{3}{5}$ represent the same rational number, that is,

$$\frac{-3}{5}=-\frac{3}{5}$$

Also, $\frac{3}{5}$ and $-\frac{-3}{5}$ represent the same rational number, that is

$$-\left(\frac{-3}{5}\right)=\frac{3}{5} \Rightarrow -\left(-\frac{3}{5}\right)=\frac{3}{5} \qquad \left[\because \frac{-3}{5}=-\frac{3}{5}\right]$$

Similarly, we have

$$-\left(-\frac{5}{7}\right)=\frac{5}{7},-\left(-\frac{15}{13}\right)=\frac{15}{13},-\left(-\frac{7}{12}\right) \text{ and so on.}$$

Thus for any rational number $\frac{a}{b}$, *we have*

$$-\left(-\frac{a}{b}\right)=\frac{a}{b}$$

Remark *We have,* $0+0=0=0+0$

$\therefore$ *0 is the additive inverse of itself, that is,* $0=0$.

NOTE: *It should be noted that 0 is the only rational number which is its own negative.*

ILLUSTRATION 4 Write the additive inverse of each of the following rational numbers:

(i) $\frac{4}{9}$ (ii) $\frac{-13}{7}$ (iii) $\frac{5}{-11}$ (iv) $\frac{-11}{-14}$

Solution (i) The additive inverse of $\frac{4}{9}$ is $-\frac{4}{9}=\frac{-4}{9}$

(ii) The additive inverse of $\frac{-13}{7}$ is $-\left(\frac{-13}{7}\right)=-\left(-\frac{13}{7}\right)=\frac{13}{7}$

(iii) We have, $\frac{5}{-11}=\frac{-5}{11}$

The additive inverse of $\frac{-5}{11}$ is $-\left(\frac{-5}{11}\right)=-\left(-\frac{5}{11}\right)=\frac{5}{11}$

(iv) We have, $\frac{-11}{-14}=\frac{11}{14}$

The additive inverse of $\frac{11}{14}$ is $-\left(\frac{11}{14}\right)=\frac{-11}{14}$

ILLUSTRATIVE EXAMPLES

Example 1 Verify: $\left(\frac{a}{b}+\frac{c}{d}\right)+\frac{e}{f}=\frac{a}{b}+\left(\frac{c}{d}+\frac{e}{f}\right)$ for $\frac{a}{b}=\frac{-2}{3}, \frac{c}{d}=\frac{5}{7}$ and $\frac{e}{f}=\frac{-1}{6}$.

Solution We have,

$$\left(\frac{a}{b}+\frac{c}{d}\right)+\frac{e}{f}$$

$$=\left(\frac{-2}{3}+\frac{5}{7}\right)+\frac{-1}{6}$$

$$=\frac{(-2)\times 7+3\times 5}{21}+\frac{-1}{6}$$

$$=\frac{(-14)+15}{21}+\frac{-1}{6}$$

$$=\frac{1}{21}+\frac{(-1)}{6}=\frac{1\times 2+(-1)\times 7}{42}=\frac{2+(-7)}{42}=\frac{(-5)}{42}=\frac{-5}{42}$$

and, $\frac{a}{b}+\left(\frac{c}{d}+\frac{e}{f}\right)$

$$=\frac{-2}{3}+\left(\frac{5}{7}+\frac{-1}{6}\right)$$

$$=\frac{-2}{3}+\frac{5\times 6+7\times(-1)}{42}$$

$$=\frac{-2}{3}+\frac{30+(-7)}{42}$$

$$=\frac{(-2)}{3}+\frac{23}{42}=\frac{(-2)\times 14+23\times 1}{42}=\frac{(-28)+(23)}{42}=\frac{(-5)}{42}=\frac{-5}{42}$$

$$\therefore \quad \left(\frac{a}{b}+\frac{c}{d}\right)+\frac{e}{f}=\frac{a}{b}+\left(\frac{c}{d}+\frac{e}{f}\right)$$

Example 2 Using commutativity and associativity of addition of rational numbers, express each of the following as a rational number:

(i) $\frac{3}{5}+\frac{-7}{6}+\frac{2}{5}+\frac{-5}{6}$ (ii) $\frac{4}{3}+\frac{-4}{5}+\frac{-2}{3}+\frac{7}{5}-2$

Solution (i) Re-arranging and grouping the numbers in pairs in such a way that each group contains a pair of rational numbers with equal denominators, we have

$$\frac{3}{5}+\frac{-7}{6}+\frac{2}{5}+\frac{-5}{6}$$

$$=\left(\frac{3}{5}+\frac{2}{5}\right)+\left(\frac{-7}{6}+\frac{-5}{6}\right)$$

$$=\left(\frac{3}{5}+\frac{2}{5}\right)+\left\{\frac{(-7)}{6}+\frac{(-5)}{6}\right\}$$

$$=\frac{3+2}{5}+\frac{(-7)+(-5)}{6}=\frac{5}{5}+\frac{(-12)}{6}=1+(-2)=1-2=-1$$

(ii) Re-arranging and grouping the numbers in pairs in such a way that each group contains a pair of rational numbers with equal denominators, we have

$$\frac{4}{3}+\frac{-4}{5}+\frac{-2}{3}+\frac{7}{5}-2$$

$$=\left(\frac{4}{3}+\frac{-2}{3}\right)+\left(\frac{-4}{5}+\frac{7}{5}\right)-2$$

$$=\left(\frac{4}{3}+\frac{(-2)}{3}\right)+\left(\frac{(-4)}{5}+\frac{7}{5}\right)-2$$

$$=\frac{4+(-2)}{3}+\frac{(-4)+7}{5}-2$$

$$=\frac{2}{3}+\frac{3}{5}-2$$

$$=\left(\frac{2}{3}+\frac{3}{5}\right)-2$$

$$=\frac{2\times5+3\times3}{15}+(-2)$$

$$=\frac{10+9}{15}+(-2)=\frac{19}{15}+\frac{(-2)}{1}=\frac{19+(-2)\times15}{15}=\frac{19+(-30)}{15}=\frac{-11}{15}$$

Example 3 Re-arrange suitably and find the sum in each of the following:

(i) $\frac{5}{3}+\frac{11}{2}+\frac{-9}{4}+\frac{-8}{3}+\frac{-7}{2}$ (ii) $\frac{-4}{7}+\frac{7}{6}+\frac{2}{7}+3+\frac{-11}{6}$

Solution (i) Re-arranging and grouping the numbers in pairs in such a way that each group contains a pair of rational numbers with equal denominators, we have

$$\frac{5}{3}+\frac{11}{2}+\frac{-9}{4}+\frac{-8}{3}+\frac{-7}{2}$$

$$=\left(\frac{5}{3}+\frac{-8}{3}\right)+\left(\frac{11}{2}+\frac{-7}{2}\right)+\frac{-9}{4}$$

$$=\frac{5+(-8)}{3}+\frac{11+(-7)}{2}+\frac{(-9)}{4}$$

$$=\frac{-3}{3}+\frac{4}{2}+\frac{(-9)}{4}$$

$$=-1+2+\frac{(-9)}{4}$$

$$=(-1+2)+\frac{(-9)}{4}$$

$$=1+\frac{(-9)}{4}=\frac{1}{1}+\frac{(-9)}{4}=\frac{1\times4+(-9)}{4}=\frac{4+(-9)}{4}=\frac{-5}{4}$$

(ii) Re-arranging and grouping the numbers in pairs in such a way that each group contains a pair of rational numbers with equal denominators, we have

$$\frac{-4}{7}+\frac{7}{6}+\frac{2}{7}+3+\frac{-11}{6}$$

$$=\left(\frac{-4}{7}+\frac{2}{7}\right)+\left(\frac{7}{6}+\frac{-11}{6}\right)+3$$

$$=\frac{(-4)+2}{7}+\frac{7+(-11)}{6}+3$$

$$=\frac{-2}{7}+\frac{(-4)}{6}+3$$

$$=\frac{(-2)}{7}+\frac{(-2)}{3}+3 \qquad \left[\because \frac{-4}{6}=\frac{-2}{3}\right]$$

$$= \left(\frac{(-2)}{7} + \frac{(-2)}{3}\right) + 3$$

$$= \frac{(-2)\times 3 + (-2)\times 7}{21} + 3$$

$$= \frac{(-6)+(-14)}{21} + 3$$

$$= \frac{(-20)}{21} + \frac{3}{1} = \frac{(-20)+3\times 21}{21} = \frac{(-20)+63}{21} = \frac{43}{21}$$

EXERCISE 1.2

1. Verify commutativity of addition of rational numbers for each of the following pairs of rational numbers:

   (i) $\frac{-11}{5}$ and $\frac{4}{7}$ (ii) $\frac{4}{9}$ and $\frac{7}{-12}$ (iii) $\frac{-3}{5}$ and $\frac{-2}{-15}$ (iv) $\frac{2}{-7}$ and $\frac{12}{-35}$

   (v) 4 and $\frac{-3}{5}$ (vi) -4 and $\frac{4}{-7}$

2. Verify associativity of addition of rational numbers i.e., $(x+y)+z = x+(y+z)$, when:

   (i) $x = \frac{1}{2}, y = \frac{2}{3}, z = -\frac{1}{5}$ (ii) $x = \frac{-2}{5}, y = \frac{4}{3}, z = \frac{-7}{10}$

   (iii) $x = \frac{-7}{11}, y = \frac{2}{-5}, z = \frac{-3}{22}$ (iv) $x = -2, y = \frac{3}{5}, z = \frac{-4}{3}$

3. Write the additive inverse of each of the following rational numbers:

   (i) $\frac{-2}{17}$ (ii) $\frac{3}{-11}$ (iii) $\frac{-17}{5}$ (iv) $\frac{-11}{-25}$

4. Write the negative (additive inverse) of each of the following:

   (i) $\frac{-2}{5}$ (ii) $\frac{7}{-9}$ (iii) $\frac{-16}{13}$ (iv) $\frac{-5}{1}$

   (v) 0 (vi) 1 (vii) -1

5. Using commutativity and associativity of addition of rational numbers, express each of the following as a rational number:

   (i) $\frac{2}{5} + \frac{7}{3} + \frac{-4}{5} + \frac{-1}{3}$ (ii) $\frac{3}{7} + \frac{-4}{9} + \frac{-11}{7} + \frac{7}{9}$

   (iii) $\frac{2}{5} + \frac{8}{3} + \frac{-11}{15} + \frac{4}{5} + \frac{-2}{3}$ (iv) $\frac{4}{7} + 0 + \frac{-8}{9} + \frac{-13}{7} + \frac{17}{21}$

6. Re-arrange suitably and find the sum in each of the following:

   (i) $\frac{11}{12} + \frac{-17}{3} + \frac{11}{2} + \frac{-25}{2}$ (ii) $\frac{-6}{7} + \frac{-5}{6} + \frac{-4}{9} + \frac{-15}{7}$

   (iii) $\frac{3}{5} + \frac{7}{3} + \frac{9}{5} + \frac{-13}{15} + \frac{-7}{3}$ (iv) $\frac{4}{13} + \frac{-5}{8} + \frac{-8}{13} + \frac{9}{13}$

   (v) $\frac{2}{3} + \frac{-4}{5} + \frac{1}{3} + \frac{2}{5}$ (vi) $\frac{1}{8} + \frac{5}{12} + \frac{2}{7} + \frac{7}{12} + \frac{9}{7} + \frac{-5}{16}$

ANSWERS

3. (i) $\frac{2}{17}$ (ii) $\frac{3}{11}$ (iii) $\frac{17}{5}$ (iv) $\frac{-11}{25}$

4. (i) $\frac{2}{5}$ (ii) $\frac{7}{9}$ (iii) $\frac{16}{13}$ (iv) 5 (v) 0
(vi) −1 (vii) 1

5. (i) $\frac{8}{5}$ (ii) $\frac{-17}{21}$ (iii) $\frac{37}{15}$ (iv) $\frac{-86}{63}$

6. (i) $\frac{-141}{12}$ (ii) $\frac{-77}{18}$ (iii) $\frac{23}{15}$ (iv) $\frac{-25}{104}$ (v) $\frac{3}{5}$
(vi) $\frac{267}{112}$

1.5 SUBTRACTION OF RATIONAL NUMBERS

If $\frac{a}{b}$ and $\frac{c}{d}$ are two rational numbers, then subtracting $\frac{c}{d}$ from $\frac{a}{b}$ means adding additive inverse (negative) of $\frac{c}{d}$ to $\frac{a}{b}$.

The subtraction of $\frac{c}{d}$ from $\frac{a}{b}$ is written as $\frac{a}{b}-\frac{c}{d}$.

Thus, we have

$$\frac{a}{b}-\frac{c}{d}=\frac{a}{b}+\left(\frac{-c}{d}\right) \qquad \left[\because \text{Additive inverse of } \frac{c}{d} \text{ is } \frac{-c}{d}\right]$$

ILLUSTRATIVE EXAMPLES

Example 1 Subtract $\frac{3}{4}$ from $\frac{5}{6}$.

Solution The additive inverse of $\frac{3}{4}$ is $\frac{-3}{4}$.

$$\therefore \quad \frac{5}{6}-\frac{3}{4}=\frac{5}{6}+\frac{-3}{4}=\frac{5\times2}{6\times2}+\frac{-3\times3}{4\times3}=\frac{10}{12}+\frac{-9}{12}=\frac{10+(-9)}{12}=\frac{1}{12}$$

Example 2 Subtract $\frac{-3}{8}$ from $\frac{-5}{7}$.

Solution The additive inverse of $\frac{-3}{8}$ is $\frac{3}{8}$.

$$\therefore \quad \frac{-5}{7}-\left(\frac{-3}{8}\right)=\frac{-5}{7}+\frac{3}{8} \qquad \left[\because -\left(\frac{-3}{8}\right)=\frac{3}{8}\right]$$

$$=\frac{(-5)\times8+3\times7}{56}=\frac{-40+21}{56}=-\frac{19}{56}$$

Example 3 Subtract $\frac{-3}{5}$ from $\frac{9}{10}$.

Solution The additive inverse of $\frac{-3}{5}$ is $-\left(\frac{-3}{5}\right)=\frac{3}{5}$.

$$\therefore \quad \frac{9}{10}-\left(\frac{-3}{5}\right)=\frac{9}{10}+\frac{3}{5}=\frac{9+3\times 2}{10}=\frac{9+6}{10}=\frac{15}{10}=\frac{3}{2}$$

Example 4 The sum of two rational numbers is $\frac{-3}{5}$. If one of the number is $\frac{-9}{20}$, find the other.

Solution It is given that

Sum of the numbers $=\frac{-3}{5}$ and, One of the numbers $=\frac{-9}{20}$

Suppose the other rational number is x. Since the sum is $\frac{-3}{5}$

$$\therefore \quad x+\left(\frac{-9}{20}\right)=\frac{-3}{5}$$

$$\Rightarrow \quad x=\frac{-3}{5}-\left(\frac{-9}{20}\right)$$

$$\Rightarrow \quad x=\frac{-3}{5}+\frac{9}{20} \qquad \left[\because -\left(\frac{-9}{20}\right)=\frac{9}{20}\right]$$

$$\Rightarrow \quad x=\frac{(-3)\times 4+9\times 1}{20}$$

$$\Rightarrow \quad x=\frac{(-3)\times 4+9\times 1}{20}=\frac{-12+9}{20}=\frac{-3}{20}$$

Example 5 What number should be added to $\frac{-5}{8}$ so as to get $\frac{5}{9}$?

Solution Suppose x is the rational number to be added to $\frac{-5}{8}$ to get $\frac{5}{9}$. Then,

$$\frac{-5}{8}+x=\frac{5}{9}$$

$$\Rightarrow \quad x=\frac{5}{9}-\left(\frac{-5}{8}\right) \qquad \left[\text{Transposing } \frac{-5}{8} \text{ to RHS}\right]$$

$$\Rightarrow \quad x=\frac{5}{9}+\frac{5}{8}$$

$$\Rightarrow \quad x=\frac{5\times 8+5\times 9}{72}=\frac{40+45}{72}=\frac{85}{72}$$

Example 6 What should be subtracted from $\frac{-3}{4}$ so as to get $\frac{5}{6}$?

Solution Suppose x is the rational number to be subtracted from $\frac{-3}{4}$ to get $\frac{5}{6}$. Then,

$$\frac{-3}{4} - x = \frac{5}{6}$$

$$\Rightarrow \frac{-3}{4} - \frac{5}{6} = x \qquad \left[\text{Transposing } x \text{ to RHS and } \frac{5}{6} \text{ to LHS}\right]$$

$$\Rightarrow x = \frac{-3}{4} - \frac{5}{6}$$

$$\Rightarrow x = \frac{-3}{4} + \frac{-5}{6} \qquad \left[\because -\frac{5}{6} = \frac{-5}{6}\right]$$

$$\Rightarrow x = \frac{(-3)\times 3 + (-5)\times 2}{12} \qquad [\because \text{LCM of 4 and 6 is 12}]$$

$$\Rightarrow x = \frac{(-9)+(-10)}{12} = \frac{-19}{12}$$

1.6 PROPERTIES OF SUBTRACTION

CLOSURE PROPERTY *If $\frac{a}{b}$ and $\frac{c}{d}$ are any two rational numbers, then $\frac{a}{b} - \frac{c}{d}$ is a rational number.*

COMMUTATIVITY *The subtraction of rational numbers is not always commutative. That is, for any two rational numbers $\frac{a}{b}$ and $\frac{c}{d}$, we have*

$$\frac{a}{b} - \frac{c}{d} \neq \frac{c}{d} - \frac{a}{b}$$

For example, $\frac{2}{3} - \frac{1}{6} = \frac{2}{3} + \frac{-1}{6} = \frac{2\times 2 + (-1)\times 1}{6} = \frac{4-1}{6} = \frac{3}{6} = \frac{1}{2}$

and, $\frac{1}{6} - \frac{2}{3} = \frac{1}{6} + \frac{-2}{3} = \frac{1 + (-2)\times 2}{6} = \frac{1-4}{6} = \frac{-3}{6} = \frac{-1}{2}$

$\therefore \quad \frac{2}{3} - \frac{1}{6} \neq \frac{1}{6} - \frac{2}{3}$

ASSOCIATIVITY *The subtraction of rational numbers is not associative, i.e. for any three rational numbers $\frac{a}{b}, \frac{c}{d}$ and $\frac{e}{f}$, we have*

$$\left(\frac{a}{b} - \frac{c}{d}\right) - \frac{e}{f} \neq \frac{a}{b} - \left(\frac{c}{d} - \frac{e}{f}\right)$$

EXISTENCE OF RIGHT IDENTITY *The rational number 0 is the right identity. That is, for any rational number $\frac{a}{b}$, we have*

$$\frac{a}{b} - 0 = \frac{a}{b}$$

EXERCISE 1.3

1. Subtract the first rational number from the second in each of the following:

(i) $\frac{3}{8}, \frac{5}{8}$ (ii) $\frac{-7}{9}, \frac{4}{9}$ (iii) $\frac{-2}{11}, \frac{-9}{11}$ (iv) $\frac{11}{13}, \frac{-4}{13}$

(v) $\frac{1}{4}, \frac{-3}{8}$ (vi) $\frac{-2}{3}, \frac{5}{6}$ (vii) $\frac{-6}{7}, \frac{-13}{14}$ (viii) $\frac{-8}{33}, \frac{-7}{22}$

2. Evaluate each of the following:

(i) $\frac{2}{3} - \frac{3}{5}$ (ii) $-\frac{4}{7} - \frac{2}{-3}$ (iii) $\frac{4}{7} - \frac{-5}{-7}$ (iv) $-2 - \frac{5}{9}$

(v) $\frac{-3}{-8} - \frac{-2}{7}$ (vi) $\frac{-4}{13} - \frac{-5}{26}$ (vii) $\frac{-5}{14} - \frac{-2}{7}$ (viii) $\frac{13}{15} - \frac{12}{25}$

(ix) $\frac{-6}{13} - \frac{-7}{13}$ (x) $\frac{7}{24} - \frac{19}{36}$ (xi) $\frac{5}{63} - \frac{-8}{21}$

3. The sum of the two numbers is $\frac{5}{9}$. If one of the numbers is $\frac{1}{3}$, find the other.

4. The sum of two numbers is $\frac{-1}{3}$. If one of the numbers is $\frac{-12}{3}$, find the other.

5. The sum of two numbers is $\frac{-4}{3}$. If one of the numbers is -5, find the other.

6. The sum of two rational numbers is -8. If one of the numbers is $\frac{-15}{7}$, find the other.

7. What should be added to $\frac{-7}{8}$ so as to get $\frac{5}{9}$?

8. What number should be added to $\frac{-5}{11}$ so as to get $\frac{26}{33}$?

9. What number should be added to $\frac{-5}{7}$ to get $\frac{-2}{3}$?

10. What number should be subtracted from $\frac{-5}{3}$ to get $\frac{5}{6}$?

11. What number should be subtracted from $\frac{3}{7}$ to get $\frac{5}{4}$?

12. What should be added to $\left(\frac{2}{3}+\frac{3}{5}\right)$ to get $\frac{-2}{15}$?

13. What should be added to $\left(\frac{1}{2}+\frac{1}{3}+\frac{1}{5}\right)$ to get 3?

14. What should be subtracted from $\left(\frac{3}{4}-\frac{2}{3}\right)$ to get $\frac{-1}{6}$?

15. Fill in the blanks:

(i) $\frac{-4}{13}-\frac{-3}{26}=\ldots$ (ii) $\frac{-9}{14}+\ldots=-1$ (iii) $\frac{-7}{9}+\ldots=3$ (iv) $\ldots+\frac{15}{23}=4$

ANSWERS

1. (i) $\frac{1}{4}$ (ii) $\frac{11}{9}$ (iii) $\frac{-7}{11}$ (iv) $\frac{-15}{13}$

(v) $\frac{-5}{8}$ (vi) $\frac{3}{2}$ (vii) $\frac{-1}{14}$ (viii) $\frac{-5}{66}$

2. (i) $\frac{1}{15}$ (ii) $\frac{2}{21}$ (iii) $\frac{-1}{7}$ (iv) $\frac{-23}{9}$

(v) $\frac{37}{56}$ (vi) $\frac{-3}{26}$ (vii) $\frac{-1}{14}$ (viii) $\frac{29}{75}$

(ix) $\frac{1}{13}$ (x) $\frac{-17}{72}$ (xi) $\frac{29}{63}$

3. $\frac{2}{9}$

4. $\frac{11}{3}$ 5. $\frac{11}{3}$ 6. $\frac{-41}{7}$ 7. $\frac{103}{72}$

8. $\frac{41}{33}$ 9. $\frac{1}{21}$ 10. $\frac{-5}{2}$ 11. $\frac{-23}{28}$

12. $\frac{-7}{5}$ 13. $\frac{59}{30}$ 14. $\frac{1}{4}$

15. (i) $\frac{-5}{26}$ (ii) $\frac{-5}{14}$ (iii) $\frac{34}{9}$ (iv) $\frac{77}{23}$

1.7 SIMPLIFICATION OF EXPRESSIONS INVOLVING ADDITION AND SUBTRACTION OF RATIONAL NUMBERS

Uptill now, we have been simplifying rational expressions involving addition and subtraction of more than two rational numbers by making groups of pairs of rational numbers having either the same denominator or having some common factor in their denominators, by using commutativity and associativity of addition (see illustrations 1, 2 and 3 on pages 1.8 – 1.9). We may simplify expressions involving addition and subtraction more easily by using the following algorithm.

ALGORITHM

<u>Step I</u> *Find the LCM of the denominators of all the numbers involved.*

<u>Step II</u> *Divide the LCM by the denominator of the first rational number and get a quotient.*

<u>Step III</u> *Multiply the first numerator by the quotient obtained in step II and get an integer.*

<u>Step IV</u> *Repeat steps II and III for the remaining rational numbers in the sum and obtain integers.*

<u>Step V</u> *Retain the given symbols of addition and subtraction between the given rationals and get an expression involving integers. Simplify this expression and get an integer.*

<u>Step VI</u> *Obtain the required sum equal to the rational number whose numerator is equal to the integer obtained in step V and denominator equal to the LCM obtained in step I. Reduce this number to the lowest form if it is not already so.*

ILLUSTRATION

Suppose, we wish to simplify

$$\frac{2}{5}+\frac{8}{3}-\frac{12}{15}+\frac{4}{5}-\frac{2}{3}$$

<u>Step I</u> *LCM of denominators* 5, 3, 15, 5 *and* 3 *is* 15.

<u>Step II</u> $15 \div 5 = 3$ (*Quotient*)

<u>Step III</u> *First numerator*

$= \textit{Numerator of } \frac{2}{3} = 2$

$\therefore$ *First numerator* $\times$ *Quotient*

$= 2 \times 3 = 6$

<u>Step IV</u> *Integers obtained are:*

$8\times5,\ 12\times1,\ 4\times3,\ 2\times5$

<u>Step V</u> $2\times3+8\times5-12\times1+4\times3-2\times5$

$=6+40-12+12-10$

$=58-22=36$

<u>Step VI</u> *Required sum* $= \frac{\overset{12}{\cancel{36}}}{\underset{5}{\cancel{15}}} = \frac{12}{5}$

i.e., $\frac{2}{5}+\frac{8}{3}-\frac{12}{15}+\frac{4}{5}-\frac{2}{3}=\frac{12}{5}$

The above procedure, in shorter form, may be written as follows:

$$\frac{2}{5}+\frac{8}{3}-\frac{12}{15}+\frac{4}{5}-\frac{2}{3}$$

$$=\frac{(2\times3)+(8\times5)-(12\times1)+(4\times3)-(2\times5)}{15}$$

$$=\frac{6+40-12+12-10}{15}=\frac{58-22}{15}=\frac{36}{15}=\frac{12}{5}$$

In order to understand the above procedure properly, let us discuss some more examples.

ILLUSTRATIVE EXAMPLES

Example 1 Find: $\frac{3}{7}+\left(-\frac{6}{11}\right)+\frac{8}{21}+\left(\frac{-5}{22}\right)$

Solution We have,

$$\frac{3}{7}+\left(-\frac{6}{11}\right)+\frac{8}{21}+\left(\frac{-5}{22}\right)$$

$$= \frac{3}{7} + \frac{-6}{11} + \frac{8}{21} + \frac{-5}{22} \qquad \left[\because -\frac{6}{11} = \frac{-6}{11}\right]$$

$$= \frac{(3\times 66) + ((-6)\times 42) + (8\times 22) + ((-5)\times 21)}{462}$$

$$= \frac{198 + (-252) + 176 + (-105)}{462}$$

$$= \frac{374 - 357}{462} = \frac{17}{462}$$

7	7,	11,	21,	22
11	1,	11,	3,	22
	1,	1,	3,	2

∴ LCM of 7, 11, 21, 22 is $7\times 11\times 3\times 2 = 462$

Example 2 Find: $\frac{-7}{4} + \frac{5}{3} + \frac{-5}{6} + \frac{1}{3} + \frac{-1}{2}$

Solution LCM of 4, 3, 6, 3 and 2 is 12

$$\therefore \quad \frac{-7}{4} + \frac{5}{3} + \frac{-5}{6} + \frac{1}{3} + \frac{-1}{2}$$

$$= \frac{((-7)\times 3) + (5\times 4) + ((-5)\times 2) + (1\times 4) + ((-1)\times 6)}{12}$$

$$= \frac{(-21) + 20 + (-10) + 4 + (-6)}{12}$$

$$= \frac{(-37) + 24}{12} = \frac{-13}{12}$$

2	4,	3,	6,	2
2	2,	3,	3,	1
3	1,	3,	3,	1
	1,	1,	1,	1

∴ LCM of 4, 3, 6, 3, 2 is $2\times 2\times 3 = 12$

Example 3 Evaluate: $\frac{-12}{5} + \frac{-7}{20} + \frac{3}{14} + \frac{1}{7} + \frac{-1}{10}$

Solution LCM of 5, 20, 14, 7, 10 is 140

$$\therefore \quad \frac{-12}{5} + \frac{-7}{20} + \frac{3}{14} + \frac{1}{7} + \frac{-1}{10}$$

$$= \frac{(-12)\times(28) + (-7)\times 7 + 3\times 10 + 1\times 20 + (-1)\times 14}{140}$$

$$= \frac{(-336) + (-49) + 30 + 20 + (-14)}{140}$$

$$= \frac{(-399) + 50}{140} = \frac{-349}{140}$$

2	5,	20,	14,	7,	10
5	5,	10,	7,	7,	5
7	1,	2,	7,	7,	1
	1,	2,	1,	1,	1

∴ LCM $= 2\times 5\times 7\times 2 = 140$

Example 4 Find: $\frac{3}{4} + \left(\frac{-3}{5}\right) + \left(\frac{-2}{3}\right) + \frac{5}{8} + \left(\frac{-4}{15}\right)$

Solution LCM of 4, 5, 3, 8, 15 is 120

$$\therefore \quad \frac{3}{4} + \frac{(-3)}{5} + \frac{(-2)}{3} + \frac{5}{8} + \frac{(-4)}{15}$$

$$= \frac{3\times 30 + (-3)\times 24 + (-2)\times 40 + 5\times 15 + (-4)\times 8}{120}$$

4	4,	5,	3,	8,	15
5	1,	5,	3,	2,	15
3	1,	1,	3,	2,	3
	1,	1,	1,	2,	1

∴ LCM $= 4\times 5\times 3\times 2 = 120$

$$= \frac{90 + (-72) + (-80) + 75 + (-32)}{120}$$

$$= \frac{(-184) + 165}{120} = \frac{-19}{120}$$

Example 5 Evaluate: $\frac{6}{7} - 2 + \frac{-7}{9} + \frac{19}{21}$

Solution We have,

$$\frac{6}{7} - 2 + \frac{-7}{9} + \frac{19}{21}$$

$$= \frac{6}{7} + \frac{(-2)}{1} + \frac{(-7)}{9} + \frac{19}{21}$$

$$= \frac{6 \times 9 + (-2) \times 63 + (-7) \times 7 + 19 \times 3}{63}$$

$$= \frac{54 + (-126) + (-49) + 57}{63} = \frac{111 + (-175)}{63} = \frac{-64}{63}$$

7	7, 1, 9, 21
3	1, 1, 9, 3
	1, 1, 3, 1

$\therefore$ LCM $= 7 \times 3 \times 3 = 63$

Example 6 Simplify:

(i) $\frac{-2}{3} + \frac{5}{9} - \frac{-7}{6}$ (ii) $\frac{5}{12} + \frac{-5}{18} - \frac{7}{24}$

Solution (i) We have,

$$\frac{-2}{3} + \frac{5}{9} - \frac{-7}{6}$$

$$= \frac{-2}{3} + \frac{5}{9} + \frac{7}{6} \quad \left[\because -\left(\frac{-7}{6}\right) = \frac{7}{6}\right]$$

$$= \frac{(-2) \times 6 + 5 \times 2 + 7 \times 3}{18} \quad [\because \text{LCM of 3, 9 and 6 is 18}]$$

$$= \frac{-12 + 10 + 21}{18} = \frac{-12 + 31}{18} = \frac{19}{18}$$

(ii) We have,

$$\frac{5}{12} + \frac{-5}{18} - \frac{7}{24}$$

$$= \frac{5}{12} + \frac{-5}{18} + \frac{-7}{24} \quad \left[\because -\frac{7}{24} = \frac{-7}{24}\right]$$

$$= \frac{5 \times 6 + (-5) \times 4 + (-7) \times 3}{72} \quad [\because \text{LCM of 12, 18 and 24 is 72}]$$

$$= \frac{30 + (-20) + (-21)}{72} = \frac{30 + (-41)}{72} = \frac{-11}{72}$$

EXERCISE 1.4

1. Simplify each of the following and write as a rational number of the the form $\frac{p}{q}$:

(i) $\frac{3}{4} + \frac{5}{6} + \frac{-7}{8}$ (ii) $\frac{2}{3} + \frac{-5}{6} + \frac{-7}{9}$ (iii) $\frac{-11}{2} + \frac{7}{6} + \frac{-5}{8}$

(iv) $\frac{-4}{5}+\frac{-7}{10}+\frac{-8}{15}$ (v) $\frac{-9}{10}+\frac{22}{15}+\frac{13}{-20}$ (vi) $\frac{5}{3}+\frac{3}{-2}+\frac{-7}{3}+3$

2. Express each of the following as a rational number of the form $\frac{p}{q}$:

(i) $\frac{-8}{3}+\frac{-1}{4}+\frac{-11}{6}+\frac{3}{8}-3$ (ii) $\frac{6}{7}+1+\frac{-7}{9}+\frac{19}{21}+\frac{-12}{7}$ (iii) $\frac{15}{2}+\frac{9}{8}+\frac{-11}{3}+6+\frac{-7}{6}$

(iv) $\frac{-7}{4}+0+\frac{-9}{5}+\frac{19}{10}+\frac{11}{14}$ (v) $\frac{-7}{4}+\frac{5}{3}+\frac{-1}{2}+\frac{-5}{6}+2$

3. Simplify:

(i) $\frac{-3}{2}+\frac{5}{4}-\frac{7}{4}$ (ii) $\frac{5}{3}-\frac{7}{6}+\frac{-2}{3}$ (iii) $\frac{5}{4}-\frac{7}{6}-\frac{-2}{3}$

(iv) $\frac{-2}{5}-\frac{-3}{10}-\frac{-4}{7}$ (v) $\frac{5}{6}+\frac{-2}{5}-\frac{-2}{15}$ (vi) $\frac{3}{8}-\frac{-2}{9}+\frac{-5}{36}$

ANSWERS

1. (i) $\frac{17}{24}$ (ii) $\frac{-17}{18}$ (iii) $\frac{-119}{24}$ (iv) $\frac{-61}{30}$ (v) $\frac{-1}{12}$ (vi) $\frac{5}{6}$

2. (i) $\frac{-59}{8}$ (ii) $\frac{17}{63}$ (iii) $\frac{235}{24}$ (iv) $\frac{-121}{140}$ (v) $\frac{7}{12}$

3. (i) -2 (ii) $\frac{-1}{6}$ (iii) $\frac{3}{4}$ (iv) $\frac{33}{70}$ (v) $\frac{17}{30}$ (vi) $\frac{11}{24}$

1.8 MULTIPLICATION OF RATIONAL NUMBERS

In earlier classes, we have learnt how to multiply two fractions. Recall that the product of two given fractions is a fraction whose numerator is the product of the numerators of the given fractions and whose denominator is the product of the denominators of the given fractions. In other words,

$$\text{Product of two given fractions} = \frac{\text{Product of their numerators}}{\text{Product of their denominators}}$$

This rule is also true for the product of rational numbers.

$$\therefore \quad \text{Product of two rational numbers} = \frac{\text{Product of their numerators}}{\text{Product of their denominators}}$$

Thus, if $\frac{a}{b}$ and $\frac{c}{d}$ are any two rational numbers, then

$$\frac{a}{b}\times\frac{c}{d}=\frac{a\times c}{b\times d}$$

ILLUSTRATIVE EXAMPLES

Example 1 Multiply:

(i) $\frac{3}{4}$ by $\frac{5}{7}$ (ii) $\frac{3}{7}$ by $\left(\frac{-4}{5}\right)$ (iii) $\left(\frac{-5}{9}\right)$ by 4

(iv) $\left(\frac{-36}{7}\right)$ by $\left(-\frac{28}{9}\right)$

Solution We have,

(i) $\frac{3}{4}\times\frac{5}{7}=\frac{3\times5}{4\times7}=\frac{15}{28}$

(ii) $\frac{3}{7}\times\left(\frac{-4}{5}\right)=\frac{3\times-4}{7\times5}=\frac{-12}{35}$

(iii) $\left(\frac{-5}{9}\right)\times4=\frac{-5}{9}\times\frac{4}{1}=\frac{(-5)\times4}{9\times1}=\frac{-20}{9}$

(iv) $\left(\frac{-36}{7}\right)\times\left(-\frac{28}{9}\right)=\left(\frac{-36}{7}\right)\times\left(\frac{-28}{9}\right)$ $\left[\because -\frac{28}{9}=\frac{-28}{9}\right]$

$=\frac{(-36)\times(-28)}{7\times9}=\frac{1008}{63}=16$

Example 2 Simplify:

(i) $\frac{-8}{7}\times\frac{14}{5}$ (ii) $\frac{13}{6}\times\frac{-18}{91}$ (iii) $\frac{-5}{9}\times\frac{72}{-125}$ (iv) $\frac{-22}{9}+\frac{-51}{-88}$

Solution (i) $\frac{-8}{7}\times\frac{14}{5}=\frac{-8\times14}{7\times5}=\frac{-8\times2}{1\times5}=\frac{-16}{5}$

(ii) $\frac{13}{6}\times\frac{-18}{91}=\frac{13\times(-18)}{6\times91}=\frac{1\times-3}{1\times7}=\frac{-3}{7}$

(iii) $\frac{-5}{9}\times\frac{72}{-125}=\frac{(-5)\times72}{9\times(-125)}=\frac{-1\times8}{1\times-25}=\frac{-8}{-25}=\frac{8}{25}$

(iv) $\frac{-22}{9}\times\frac{-51}{-88}=\frac{-22}{9}\times\frac{51}{88}$ $\left[\because \frac{-51}{-98}=\frac{51}{88}\right]$

$=\frac{-22\times51}{9\times88}=\frac{-1\times17}{3\times4}=\frac{-17}{12}$

Example 3 Simplify:

(i) $\left(\frac{-16}{5}\times\frac{20}{8}\right)-\left(\frac{15}{5}\times\frac{-35}{3}\right)$ (ii) $\left(\frac{-3}{2}\times\frac{4}{5}\right)+\left(\frac{9}{5}\times\frac{-10}{3}\right)-\left(\frac{1}{2}\times\frac{3}{4}\right)$

(iii) $\left(\frac{-7}{18}\times\frac{15}{-7}\right)-\left(1\times\frac{1}{4}\right)+\left(\frac{1}{2}\times\frac{1}{4}\right)$

Solution (i) $\left(\frac{-16}{5}\times\frac{20}{8}\right)-\left(\frac{15}{5}\times\frac{-35}{3}\right)$

$=\left(\frac{-16\times20}{5\times8}\right)-\left(\frac{15\times-35}{5\times3}\right)$

$=\left(\frac{-2\times4}{1\times1}\right)-\left(\frac{5\times-7}{1\times1}\right)=\frac{-8}{1}-\frac{-35}{1}=-8-(-35)=-8+35=27$

(ii) $\left(\frac{-3}{2}\times\frac{4}{5}\right)+\left(\frac{9}{5}\times\frac{-10}{3}\right)-\left(\frac{1}{2}\times\frac{3}{4}\right)$

$$=\frac{-3\times4}{2\times5}+\frac{9\times-10}{5\times3}-\frac{1\times3}{2\times4}$$

$$=\frac{-3\times2}{1\times5}+\frac{3\times-2}{1\times1}-\frac{3}{8}$$

$$=\frac{-6}{5}+\frac{-6}{1}-\frac{3}{8}$$

$$=\frac{-6}{5}+\frac{-6}{1}+\frac{-3}{8}$$

$$=\frac{(-6)\times8+(-6)\times40+(-3)\times5}{40}=\frac{-48+(-240)+(-15)}{40}=\frac{-303}{40}$$

(iii) $\left(\frac{-7}{18}\times\frac{15}{-7}\right)-\left(1\times\frac{1}{4}\right)+\left(\frac{1}{2}\times\frac{1}{4}\right)$

$$=\left(\frac{-7}{18}\times\frac{15}{-7}\right)-\left(\frac{1}{1}\times\frac{1}{4}\right)+\left(\frac{1}{2}\times\frac{1}{4}\right)$$

$$=\frac{-7\times15}{18\times-7}-\frac{1\times1}{1\times4}+\frac{1\times1}{2\times4}$$

$$=\frac{1\times5}{6\times1}-\frac{1\times1}{1\times4}+\frac{1\times1}{2\times4}$$

$$=\frac{5}{6}-\frac{1}{4}+\frac{1}{8}$$

$$=\frac{5}{6}+\frac{-1}{4}+\frac{1}{8} \qquad \left[\because -\frac{1}{4}=\frac{-1}{4}\right]$$

$$=\frac{5\times4+(-1)\times6+1\times3}{24}=\frac{20+(-6)+3}{24}=\frac{17}{24}$$

EXERCISE 1.5

1. Multiply:

(i) $\frac{7}{11}$ by $\frac{5}{4}$ (ii) $\frac{5}{7}$ by $\frac{-3}{4}$ (iii) $\frac{-2}{9}$ by $\frac{5}{11}$ (iv) $\frac{-3}{17}$ by $\frac{-5}{-4}$

(v) $\frac{9}{-7}$ by $\frac{36}{-11}$ (vi) $\frac{-11}{13}$ by $\frac{-21}{7}$ (vii) $-\frac{3}{5}$ by $-\frac{4}{7}$ (viii) $-\frac{15}{11}$ by 7

2. Multiply:

(i) $\frac{-5}{17}$ by $\frac{51}{-60}$ (ii) $\frac{-6}{11}$ by $\frac{-55}{36}$ (iii) $\frac{-8}{25}$ by $\frac{-5}{16}$ (iv) $\frac{6}{7}$ by $\frac{-49}{36}$

(v) $\frac{8}{-9}$ by $\frac{-7}{-16}$ (vi) $\frac{-8}{9}$ by $\frac{3}{64}$

3. Simplify each of the following and express the result as a rational number in standard form:

(i) $\frac{-16}{21} \times \frac{14}{5}$ (ii) $\frac{7}{6} \times \frac{-3}{28}$ (iii) $\frac{-19}{36} \times 16$ (iv) $\frac{-13}{9} \times \frac{27}{-26}$

(v) $\frac{-9}{16} \times \frac{-64}{-27}$ (vi) $\frac{-50}{7} \times \frac{14}{3}$ (vii) $\frac{-11}{9} \times \frac{-81}{-88}$ (viii) $\frac{-5}{9} \times \frac{72}{-25}$

4. Simplify:

(i) $\left(\frac{25}{8} \times \frac{2}{5}\right) - \left(\frac{3}{5} \times \frac{-10}{9}\right)$ (ii) $\left(\frac{1}{2} \times \frac{1}{4}\right) + \left(\frac{1}{2} \times 6\right)$

(iii) $\left(-5 \times \frac{2}{15}\right) - \left(-6 \times \frac{2}{9}\right)$ (iv) $\left(\frac{-9}{4} \times \frac{5}{3}\right) + \left(\frac{13}{2} \times \frac{5}{6}\right)$

(v) $\left(\frac{-4}{3} \times \frac{12}{-5}\right) + \left(\frac{3}{7} \times \frac{21}{15}\right)$ (vi) $\left(\frac{13}{5} \times \frac{8}{3}\right) - \left(\frac{-5}{2} \times \frac{11}{3}\right)$

(vii) $\left(\frac{13}{7} \times \frac{11}{26}\right) - \left(\frac{-4}{3} \times \frac{5}{6}\right)$ (viii) $\left(\frac{8}{5} \times \frac{-3}{2}\right) + \left(\frac{-3}{10} \times \frac{11}{16}\right)$

5. Simplify:

(i) $\left(\frac{3}{2} \times \frac{1}{6}\right) + \left(\frac{5}{3} \times \frac{7}{2}\right) - \left(\frac{13}{8} \times \frac{4}{3}\right)$ (ii) $\left(\frac{1}{4} \times \frac{2}{7}\right) - \left(\frac{5}{14} \times \frac{-2}{3}\right) + \left(\frac{3}{7} \times \frac{9}{2}\right)$

(iii) $\left(\frac{13}{9} \times \frac{-15}{2}\right) + \left(\frac{7}{3} \times \frac{8}{5}\right) + \left(\frac{3}{5} \times \frac{1}{2}\right)$ (iv) $\left(\frac{3}{11} \times \frac{5}{6}\right) - \left(\frac{9}{12} \times \frac{4}{3}\right) + \left(\frac{5}{13} \times \frac{6}{15}\right)$

ANSWERS

1. (i) $\frac{35}{44}$ (ii) $\frac{-15}{28}$ (iii) $\frac{-10}{99}$ (iv) $\frac{-15}{68}$ (v) $\frac{324}{77}$ (vi) $\frac{33}{13}$ (vii) $\frac{12}{35}$ (viii) $\frac{-105}{11}$

2. (i) $\frac{1}{4}$ (ii) $\frac{5}{6}$ (iii) $\frac{1}{10}$ (iv) $\frac{-7}{6}$ (v) $\frac{-7}{18}$ (vi) $\frac{-1}{24}$

3. (i) $\frac{-32}{15}$ (ii) $\frac{-1}{8}$ (iii) $\frac{-76}{9}$ (iv) $\frac{3}{2}$ (v) $\frac{-4}{3}$ (vi) $\frac{-100}{3}$ (vii) $\frac{-9}{8}$ (viii) $\frac{8}{5}$

4. (i) $\frac{23}{12}$ (ii) $\frac{25}{8}$ (iii) $\frac{2}{3}$ (iv) $\frac{5}{3}$ (v) $\frac{19}{5}$ (vi) $\frac{483}{30}$ (vii) $\frac{239}{126}$ (viii) $\frac{-417}{160}$

5. (i) $\frac{47}{12}$ (ii) $\frac{47}{21}$ (iii) $\frac{-102}{15}$ (iv) $\frac{-177}{286}$

1.9 PROPERTIES OF MULTIPLICATION OF RATIONAL NUMBERS

In this section, we shall learn some properties of multiplication of rational numbers. These properties are similar to those of multiplication of integers which we have learnt in earlier classes.

The multiplication of rational numbers possesses the following properties:

CLOSURE PROPERTY *The product or multiplication of any two rational numbers is always a rational number.*

Verification: We have,

(i) $\frac{3}{2} \times \frac{5}{7} = \frac{3 \times 5}{7 \times 2} = \frac{15}{14}$, which is a rational number.

(ii) $\frac{-4}{7} \times \frac{3}{5} = \frac{-4 \times 3}{7 \times 5} = \frac{-12}{35}$, which is a rational number.

(iii) $\frac{-15}{4} \times \frac{-12}{9} = \frac{(-15) \times (-12)}{4 \times 9} = \frac{180}{36} = \frac{5}{1}$, which is a rational number.

COMMUTATIVITY *The multiplication of rational numbers is commutative. That is, if $\frac{a}{b}$ and $\frac{c}{d}$ are any two rational numbers, then*

$$\frac{a}{b} \times \frac{c}{d} = \frac{c}{d} \times \frac{a}{b}$$

Verification: We have,

(i) $\frac{3}{4} \times \frac{5}{7} = \frac{3 \times 5}{4 \times 7} = \frac{15}{28}$ and, $\frac{5}{7} \times \frac{3}{4} = \frac{5 \times 3}{7 \times 4} = \frac{15}{28}$

$\therefore \quad \frac{3}{4} \times \frac{5}{7} = \frac{5}{7} \times \frac{3}{4}$

(ii) $\frac{-5}{12} \times \frac{-3}{4} = \frac{-5 \times -3}{12 \times 4} = \frac{15}{48} = \frac{5}{16}$ and, $\frac{-3}{4} \times \frac{-5}{12} = \frac{-3 \times -5}{4 \times 12} = \frac{15}{48} = \frac{5}{16}$

$\therefore \quad \frac{-5}{12} \times \frac{-3}{4} = \frac{-3}{4} \times \frac{-5}{12}$

ASSOCIATIVITY *The multiplication of rational numbers is associative. That is, if $\frac{a}{b}, \frac{c}{d}$ and $\frac{e}{f}$ are three rational numbers, then*

$$\left(\frac{a}{b} \times \frac{c}{d}\right) \times \frac{e}{f} = \frac{a}{b} \times \left(\frac{c}{d} \times \frac{e}{f}\right)$$

Verification: We have,

$$\left(\frac{-5}{4}\right) \times \left(\frac{-6}{11} \times \frac{2}{7}\right) = \frac{-5}{4} \times \left(\frac{-6 \times 2}{11 \times 7}\right)$$

$$= \frac{-5}{4} \times \frac{-12}{77} = \frac{(-5) \times (-12)}{4 \times 77} = \frac{(-5) \times (-3)}{1 \times 77} = \frac{15}{77}$$

and,

$$\left(\frac{-5}{4} \times \frac{-6}{11}\right) \times \frac{2}{7} = \left\{\frac{(-5) \times (-6)}{4 \times 11}\right\} \times \frac{2}{7}$$

$$=\left\{\frac{(-5)\times(-3)}{2\times 11}\right\}\times\frac{2}{7}=\frac{15}{22}\times\frac{2}{7}=\frac{15\times 2}{22\times 7}=\frac{15}{77}$$

$$\therefore \quad \frac{-5}{4}\times\left(\frac{-6}{11}\times\frac{2}{7}\right)=\left(\frac{-5}{4}\times\frac{-6}{11}\right)\times\frac{2}{7}$$

Remark *We have seen that the multiplication of rational numbers is an operation on a pair of fractions. But, as a consequence of associativity of multiplication of rational numbers, three or more rational numbers can be multiplied without using parentheses.*

ILLUSTRATION 1 Simplify: $\frac{-3}{5}\times\left(-\frac{10}{9}\right)\times\left(\frac{21}{-4}\right)\times(-6)$

Solution We have,

$$\frac{-3}{5}\times\left(-\frac{10}{9}\right)\times\left(\frac{21}{-4}\right)\times(-6)$$

$$=\frac{-3}{5}\times\frac{-10}{9}\times\frac{21}{-4}\times\frac{-6}{1}$$

$$=\frac{(-3)\times(-10)\times 21\times(-6)}{5\times 9\times(-4)\times 1}$$

$$=\frac{-(3\times 10\times 21\times 6)}{-(5\times 9\times 4\times 1)}=\frac{3\times 10\times 21\times 6}{5\times 9\times 4}=\frac{1\times 5\times 21\times 6}{5\times 3\times 2}=\frac{1\times 1\times 7\times 3}{1\times 1\times 1}=21$$

ILLUSTRATION 2 Simplify: $\frac{3}{11}\times\frac{-5}{6}\times\left(-\frac{22}{9}\right)\times\left(-\frac{9}{5}\right)$

Solution We have,

$$\frac{3}{11}\times\frac{-5}{6}\times\left(\frac{-22}{9}\right)\times\left(\frac{-9}{5}\right)$$

$$=\frac{3}{11}\times\frac{-5}{6}\times\frac{-22}{9}\times\frac{-9}{5}$$

$$=\frac{3\times -5\times -22\times -9}{11\times 6\times 9\times 5}=\frac{-(3\times 5\times 22\times 9)}{11\times 6\times 9\times 5}=\frac{-(1\times 1\times 2\times 1)}{1\times 2\times 1\times 1}=\frac{-2}{2}=-1.$$

EXISTENCE OF MULTIPLICATIVE IDENTITY *If $\frac{a}{b}$ is any rational number, then*

$$\frac{a}{b}\times 1=\frac{a}{b}=1\times\frac{a}{b}$$

1 is called the multiplicative identity for rational numbers.

Verification: We have,

(i) $\frac{2}{5}\times 1=\frac{2}{5}\times\frac{1}{1}=\frac{2\times 1}{5\times 1}=\frac{2}{5}$ and, $1\times\frac{2}{5}=\frac{1}{1}\times\frac{2}{5}=\frac{1\times 2}{1\times 5}=\frac{2}{5}$

$\therefore \quad \frac{2}{5}\times 1=\frac{2}{5}=1\times\frac{2}{5}$

(ii) $\frac{-3}{7}\times 1=\frac{-3}{7}\times\frac{1}{1}=\frac{-3\times 1}{7\times 1}=\frac{-3}{7}$ and, $1\times\frac{-3}{7}=\frac{1}{1}\times\frac{-3}{7}=\frac{1\times -3}{1\times 7}=\frac{-3}{7}$

$\therefore \quad \frac{-3}{7}\times 1=\frac{-3}{7}=1\times\frac{-3}{7}$

MULTIPLICATION BY 0 *Every rational number when multiplied with 0 gives 0.*

That is, if $\frac{a}{b}$ *is any rational number, then*

$$\frac{a}{b}\times 0=0=0\times\frac{a}{b}$$

Verification: We have,

(i) $\frac{5}{7}\times 0=\frac{5}{7}\times\frac{0}{1}=\frac{5\times 0}{7\times 1}=\frac{0}{7}=0$ and, $0\times\frac{5}{7}=\frac{0}{1}\times\frac{5}{7}=\frac{0\times 5}{1\times 7}=\frac{0}{7}=0$

$\therefore \quad \frac{5}{7}\times 0=0=0\times\frac{5}{7}$

(ii) $\frac{-9}{13}\times 0=\frac{-9}{13}\times\frac{0}{1}=\frac{-9\times 0}{13\times 1}=\frac{0}{13}=0$ and, $0\times\frac{-9}{13}=\frac{0}{1}\times\frac{-9}{13}=\frac{0\times -9}{1\times 13}=\frac{0}{13}=0$

$\therefore \quad \frac{-9}{13}\times 0=0=0\times\frac{-9}{13}$

DISTRIBUTIVITY OF MULTIPLICATION OVER ADDITION *The multiplication of rational numbers is distributive over their addition.*

That is, if $\frac{a}{b}, \frac{c}{d}$ *and* $\frac{e}{f}$ *are any three rational numbers, then*

$$\frac{a}{b}\times\left(\frac{c}{d}+\frac{e}{f}\right)=\frac{a}{b}\times\frac{c}{d}+\frac{a}{b}\times\frac{e}{f}$$

Verification: Consider any three rational numbers, say, $\frac{2}{3}, \frac{-3}{5}$ and $\frac{7}{10}$.

We have,

$$\frac{2}{3}\times\left(\frac{-3}{5}+\frac{7}{10}\right)=\frac{2}{3}\times\left(\frac{-3\times 2+7}{10}\right)=\frac{2}{3}\times\left(\frac{-6+7}{10}\right)=\frac{2}{3}\times\frac{1}{10}=\frac{2\times 1}{3\times 10}=\frac{1}{15}$$

and, $\frac{2}{3}\times\frac{-3}{5}+\frac{2}{3}\times\frac{7}{10}$

$=\frac{2\times -3}{3\times 5}+\frac{2\times 7}{3\times 10}$

$=\frac{2\times -1}{1\times 5}+\frac{1\times 7}{3\times 5}=\frac{-2}{5}+\frac{7}{15}=\frac{-2\times 3+7}{15}=\frac{-6+7}{15}=\frac{1}{15}$

$\therefore \quad \frac{2}{3}\times\left(\frac{-2}{5}+\frac{7}{10}\right)=\frac{2}{3}\times\frac{-3}{5}+\frac{2}{3}\times\frac{7}{10}$

EXISTENCE OF MULTIPLICATIVE INVERSE OR RECIPROCAL OF A NON-ZERO RATIONAL NUMBER *For every non-zero rational number* $\frac{a}{b}$ *there exists a rational number* $\frac{c}{d}$ *such that* $\frac{a}{b}\times\frac{c}{d}=1=\frac{c}{d}\times\frac{a}{b}$

The rational number $\frac{c}{d}$ *is called the multiplicative inverse or reciprocal of a denoted be* $\left(\frac{a}{b}\right)^{-1}$

For any non-zero rational number $\frac{a}{b}$, *we have*

$$\frac{a}{b}\times\frac{b}{a}=\frac{a\times b}{b\times a}=\frac{ab}{ba}=\frac{ab}{ab}=1 \text{ and, } \frac{b}{a}\times\frac{a}{b}=\frac{b\times a}{a\times b}=\frac{ba}{ab}=\frac{ab}{ab}=1$$

$$\therefore \quad \frac{a}{b}\times\frac{b}{a}=1=\frac{b}{a}\times\frac{a}{b}$$

It follows from this result that the multiplicative inverse or reciprocal of $\frac{a}{b}$ *is* $\frac{b}{a}$.

That is, $\left(\frac{a}{b}\right)^{-1}=\frac{b}{a}$

It also follows from the result (i) that the multiplicative inverse of $\frac{b}{a}$ *is* $\frac{a}{b}$.

That is, $\left(\frac{b}{a}\right)^{-1}=\frac{a}{b}$. *But,* $\frac{b}{a}=\left(\frac{a}{b}\right)^{-1}$

$$\therefore \quad \left\{\left(\frac{a}{b}\right)^{-1}\right\}^{-1}=\frac{a}{b}$$

In other words, the reciprocal of the reciprocal of a rational number is the number itself. Thus, we have

The reciprocal of $\frac{5}{12}$ is $\frac{12}{5}$ i.e., $\left(\frac{5}{12}\right)^{-1}=\frac{12}{5}$

The reciprocal of $\frac{-3}{7}$ is $\frac{7}{-3}$ i.e., $\left(\frac{-3}{7}\right)^{-1}=\frac{7}{-3}$

The reciprocal of -5 is $\frac{1}{-5}$, since $-5\times\frac{1}{-5}=\frac{-5}{1}\times\frac{1}{-5}=\frac{-5\times1}{-5\times1}=1$

<u>NOTE:</u> *The reciprocal of 1 is 1 and the reciprocal of – 1 is – 1. Also, 1 and – 1 are the only rational numbers which are their own reciprocals. No other rational number is its own reciprocal.*

<u>Remark</u> *We know that there is no rational number which when multiplied with 0, gives 1. Therefore, rational number 0 has no reciprocal or multiplicative inverse.*

ILLUSTRATIVE EXAMPLES

Example 1 Write the reciprocal of each of the following rational numbers:

(i) 7 (ii) -11 (iii) $\frac{2}{5}$ (iv) $\frac{-7}{15}$ (v) $\frac{5}{-12}$

Solution (i) Reciprocal of 7 is $\frac{1}{7}$ i.e., $7^{-1} = \frac{1}{7}$

(ii) Reciprocal of -11 is $\frac{1}{-11}$ i.e., $(-11)^{-1} = \frac{1}{-11}$

(iii) Reciprocal of $\frac{2}{5}$ is $\frac{5}{2}$ i.e., $\left(\frac{2}{5}\right)^{-1} = \frac{5}{2}$

(iv) Reciprocal of $\frac{-7}{15}$ is $\frac{15}{-7}$ i.e., $\left(\frac{-7}{15}\right)^{-1} = \frac{15}{-7}$

(v) Reciprocal of $\frac{5}{-12}$ is $\frac{-12}{5}$ i.e., $\left(\frac{5}{-12}\right)^{-1} = \frac{-12}{5}$

Example 2 Find the reciprocal of

(i) $\frac{2}{5} \times \frac{4}{9}$ (ii) $\frac{-3}{8} \times \frac{-7}{13}$

Solution (i) We have,

$$\frac{2}{5} \times \frac{4}{9} = \frac{2 \times 4}{5 \times 9} = \frac{8}{45}$$

$\therefore$ The reciprocal of $\frac{2}{5} \times \frac{4}{9} = \left(\text{Reciprocal of } \frac{8}{45}\right) = \frac{45}{8}$

(ii) We have,

$$\frac{-3}{8} \times \frac{-7}{13} = \frac{(-3) \times (-7)}{8 \times 13} = \frac{21}{104}$$

$\therefore$ The reciprocal of $\frac{-3}{8} \times \frac{-7}{13} = \left(\text{Reciprocal of } \frac{21}{104}\right) = \frac{104}{21}$

EXERCISE 1.6

1. Verify the property: $x \times y = y \times x$ by taking:

(i) $x = -\frac{1}{3}, y = \frac{2}{7}$ (ii) $x = \frac{-3}{5}, y = \frac{-11}{13}$ (iii) $x = 2, y = \frac{7}{-8}$ (iv) $x = 0, y = \frac{-15}{8}$

2. Verify the property: $x \times (y \times z) = (x \times y) \times z$ by taking:

(i) $x = \frac{-7}{3}, y = \frac{12}{5}, z = \frac{4}{9}$ (ii) $x = 0, y = \frac{-3}{5}, z = \frac{-9}{4}$

(iii) $x = \frac{1}{2}, y = \frac{5}{-4}, z = \frac{-7}{5}$ (iv) $x = \frac{5}{7}, y = \frac{-12}{13}, z = \frac{-7}{18}$

3. Verify the property: $x \times (y+z) = x \times y + x \times z$ by taking:

(i) $x = \frac{-3}{7}, y = \frac{12}{13}, z = \frac{-5}{6}$ (ii) $x = \frac{-12}{5}, y = \frac{-15}{4}, z = \frac{8}{3}$

(iii) $x = \frac{-8}{3}, y = \frac{5}{6}, z = \frac{-13}{12}$ (iv) $x = \frac{-3}{4}, y = \frac{-5}{2}, z = \frac{7}{6}$

4. Use the distributivity of multiplication of rational numbers over their addition to simplify:

(i) $\frac{3}{5} \times \left(\frac{35}{24} + \frac{10}{1}\right)$ (ii) $\frac{-5}{4} \times \left(\frac{8}{5} + \frac{16}{5}\right)$ (iii) $\frac{2}{7} \times \left(\frac{7}{16} - \frac{21}{4}\right)$ (iv) $\frac{3}{4} \times \left(\frac{8}{9} - 40\right)$

5. Find the multiplicative inverse (reciprocal) of each of the following rational numbers:

(i) 9 (ii) -7 (iii) $\frac{12}{5}$ (iv) $\frac{-7}{9}$

(v) $\frac{-3}{-5}$ (vi) $\frac{2}{3} \times \frac{9}{4}$ (vii) $\frac{-5}{8} \times \frac{16}{15}$ (viii) $-2 \times \frac{-3}{5}$

(ix) -1 (x) $\frac{0}{3}$ (xi) 1

6. Name the property of multiplication of rational numbers illustrated by the following statements:

(i) $\frac{-5}{16} \times \frac{8}{15} = \frac{8}{15} \times \frac{-5}{16}$ (ii) $\frac{-17}{5} \times 9 = 9 \times \frac{-17}{5}$

(iii) $\frac{7}{4} \times \left(\frac{-8}{3} + \frac{-13}{12}\right) = \frac{7}{4} \times \frac{-8}{3} + \frac{7}{4} \times \frac{-13}{12}$ (iv) $\frac{-5}{9} \times \left(\frac{4}{15} \times \frac{-9}{8}\right) = \left(\frac{-5}{9} \times \frac{4}{15}\right) \times \frac{-9}{8}$

(v) $\frac{13}{-17} \times 1 = \frac{13}{-17} = 1 \times \frac{13}{-17}$ (vi) $\frac{-11}{16} \times \frac{16}{-11} = 1$

(vii) $\frac{2}{13} \times 0 = 0 = 0 \times \frac{2}{13}$ (viii) $\frac{-3}{2} \times \frac{5}{4} + \frac{-3}{2} \times \frac{-7}{6} = \frac{-3}{2} \times \left(\frac{5}{4} + \frac{-7}{6}\right)$

7. Fill in the blanks:

(i) The product of two positive rational numbers is always ......
(ii) The product of a positive rational number and a negative rational number is always ......
(iii) The product of two negative rational numbers is always ......
(iv) The reciprocal of a positive rational number is ......
(v) The reciprocal of a negative rational number is ......
(vi) Zero has ...... reciprocal.
(vii) The product of a rational number and its reciprocal is ......
(viii) The numbers ...... and ...... are their own reciprocals.
(ix) If a is reciprocal of b, then the reciprocal of b is ......
(x) The number 0 is ...... the reciprocal of any number.
(xi) Reciprocal of $\frac{1}{a}, a \neq 0$ is ......
(xii) $(17 \times 12)^{-1} = 17^{-1} \times$......

8. Fill in the blanks:

(i) $-4 \times \frac{7}{9} = \frac{7}{9} \times \ldots\ldots$ (ii) $\frac{5}{11} \times \frac{-3}{8} = \frac{-3}{8} \times \ldots\ldots$

(iii) $\frac{1}{2} \times \left(\frac{3}{4} + \frac{-5}{12}\right) = \frac{1}{2} \times \ldots\ldots + \ldots\ldots \times \frac{-5}{12}$ (iv) $\frac{-4}{5} \times \left(\frac{5}{7} + \frac{-8}{9}\right) = \left(\frac{-4}{5} \times \ldots\ldots\right) + \frac{-4}{5} \times \frac{-8}{9}$

ANSWERS

4. (i) $\frac{55}{8}$ (ii) -6 (iii) $\frac{-11}{8}$ (iv) $\frac{-88}{3}$

5. (i) $\frac{1}{9}$ (ii) $\frac{-1}{7}$ (iii) $\frac{5}{12}$ (iv) $\frac{9}{-7}$ (v) $\frac{5}{3}$ (vi) $\frac{2}{3}$
(vii) $\frac{-3}{2}$ (viii) $\frac{5}{6}$ (ix) -1 (x) Does not exist (xi) 1

6. (i) Commutativity (ii) Commutativity
(iii) Distributivity of multiplication over addition
(iv) Associativity of multiplication
(v) Existence of identity for multiplication
(vi) Existence of multiplication inverse
(vii) Multiplication by 0 (viii) Distributivity

7. (i) Positive (ii) Negative (iii) Positive (iv) Positive (v) Negative (vi) No
(vii) 1 (viii) 1, -1 (ix) a (x) not (xi) a (xii) 12^{-1}

8. (i) -4 (ii) $\frac{5}{11}$ (iii) $\frac{1}{2} \times \frac{3}{4} + \frac{1}{2} \times \frac{-5}{12}$ (iv) $\frac{5}{7}$

1.10 DIVISION OF RATIONAL NUMBERS

In earlier classes, we have learnt how to divide a fraction by another fraction. Recall that division of fractions is the inverse of multiplication. In case of rational number also, division is the inverse of multiplication as defined below:

DIVISION *If x and y are two rational numbers such that $y \neq 0$, then the result of dividing x by y is the rational number obtained on multiplying x by the reciprocal of y.*

When x is divided by y, we write $x \div y$.

Thus, we have $x \div y = x \times \frac{1}{y}$

If $\frac{a}{b}$ and $\frac{c}{d}$ are two rational numbers such that $\frac{c}{d} \neq 0$, then

$$\frac{a}{b} \div \frac{c}{d} = \frac{a}{b} \times \left(\frac{c}{d}\right)^{-1} = \frac{a}{b} \times \frac{d}{c}$$

DIVIDEND *The number to be divided is called the dividend.*

DIVISOR *The number which divides the dividend is called the divisor.*

QUOTIENT *When dividend is divided by the divisor, the result of the division is called the quotient.*

If $\frac{a}{b}$ is divided by $\frac{c}{d}$, then $\frac{a}{b}$ is the dividend, $\frac{c}{d}$ is the divisor, and

$\frac{a}{b} \div \frac{c}{d} = \frac{a}{b} \times \left(\frac{c}{d}\right)^{-1} = \frac{a}{b} \times \frac{d}{c}$ *is the quotient.*

NOTE: *It should be noted that division by 0 is not defined.*

ILLUSTRATIVE EXAMPLES

Example 1 Divide:

(i) $\frac{3}{5}$ by $\frac{4}{25}$ (ii) $\frac{-8}{9}$ by $\frac{4}{3}$ (iii) $\frac{-16}{21}$ by $\frac{-4}{3}$ (iv) $\frac{-8}{13}$ by $\frac{3}{-26}$

Solution (i) $\frac{3}{5} \div \frac{4}{25} = \frac{3}{5} \times \frac{25}{4} = \frac{3 \times 25}{5 \times 4} = \frac{3 \times 5}{1 \times 4} = \frac{15}{4}$

(ii) $\frac{-8}{9} \div \frac{4}{3} = \frac{-8}{9} \times \frac{3}{4} = \frac{-8 \times 3}{9 \times 4} = \frac{-2 \times 1}{3 \times 1} = \frac{-2}{3}$

(iii) $\frac{-16}{21} \div \frac{-4}{3} = \frac{-16}{21} \times \frac{3}{-4} = \frac{-16 \times 3}{21 \times (-4)} = \frac{4 \times 1}{7 \times 1} = \frac{4}{7}$

(iv) $\frac{-8}{13} \div \frac{3}{-26} = \frac{-8}{13} \times \frac{-26}{3} = \frac{(-8) \times (-26)}{13 \times 3} = \frac{8 \times 26}{13 \times 3} = \frac{8 \times 2}{1 \times 3} = \frac{16}{3}$

Example 2 The product of two rational numbers is $\frac{-28}{81}$. If one of the number is $\frac{14}{27}$, find the other.

Solution We have,

Product of two numbers $= \frac{-28}{81}$, One number $= \frac{14}{27}$

So, the other number is obtained by dividing the product by the given number.

$\therefore$ Other number $= \frac{-28}{81} \div \frac{14}{27}$

$$= \frac{-28}{81} \times \frac{27}{14} = \frac{-28 \times 27}{81 \times 14} = \frac{-(28 \times 27)}{81 \times 14} = \frac{-(2 \times 1)}{3 \times 1} = \frac{-2}{3}$$

<u>Aliter</u> Let the other number be x. Then,

$$\frac{14}{27} \times x = \frac{-28}{81}$$

$$\Rightarrow \quad x = \frac{-28}{81} \div \frac{14}{27}$$

$$\Rightarrow \quad x = \frac{-28}{81} \times \frac{27}{14} = \frac{-28 \times 27}{81 \times 14} = \frac{-(\overset{2}{\cancel{28}} \times \overset{1}{\cancel{27}})}{\underset{3}{\cancel{81}} \times \underset{1}{\cancel{14}}} = \frac{-(2 \times 1)}{3 \times 1} = \frac{-2}{3}$$

Example 3 By what number should we multiply $\frac{3}{-14}$, so that the product may be $\frac{5}{12}$.

Solution We have,

Product of two numbers $= \frac{5}{12}$, One number $= \frac{3}{-14}$

$\therefore$ The other number $= \frac{5}{12} \div \frac{3}{-14}$

$$= \frac{5}{12} \times \frac{-14}{3}$$

$$= \frac{5\times(-14)}{12\times3} = \frac{-(5\times14)}{12\times3} = \frac{-(5\times7)}{6\times3} = \frac{-35}{18}.$$

Aliter Let the required number be x. Then,

$$x \times \frac{3}{-14} = \frac{5}{12}$$

$$\Rightarrow \quad x = \frac{5}{12} \div \frac{3}{-14}$$

$$\Rightarrow \quad x = \frac{5}{12} \times \frac{-14}{3}$$

$$\Rightarrow \quad x = \frac{5\times-14}{12\times3} = \frac{-(5\times\overset{7}{\cancel{14}})}{\underset{6}{\cancel{12}}\times3} = \frac{-(5\times7)}{6\times3} = \frac{-35}{18}$$

Hence, required number is $\frac{-35}{18}$.

1.10.1 PROPERTIES OF DIVISION OF RATIONAL NUMBERS

Properties I *If $\frac{a}{b}$ and $\frac{c}{d}$ are two rational numbers such that $\frac{c}{d} \neq 0$, then $\frac{a}{b} \div \frac{c}{d}$ is always a rational number.*

That is, the set of all non-zero rational numbers is closed under division.

Properties II *For any rational number $\frac{a}{b}$, we have*

$$\frac{a}{b} \div 1 = \frac{a}{b} \text{ and } \frac{a}{b} \div (-1) = -\frac{a}{b} = \frac{-a}{b}$$

Properties III *For every non-zero rational number $\frac{a}{b}$, we have*

(i) $\frac{a}{b} \div \frac{a}{b} = 1$ (ii) $\frac{a}{b} \div \left(-\frac{a}{b}\right) = -1$ (iii) $\left(\frac{-a}{b}\right) \div \frac{a}{b} = -1$

Remark *The division of rational numbers is neither commutative nor associative.*

EXERCISE 1.7

1. Divide:

(i) 1 by $\frac{1}{2}$ (ii) 5 by $\frac{-5}{7}$ (iii) $\frac{-3}{4}$ by $\frac{9}{-16}$ (iv) $\frac{-7}{8}$ by $\frac{-21}{16}$

(v) $\frac{7}{-4}$ by $\frac{63}{64}$ (vi) 0 by $\frac{-7}{5}$ (vii) $\frac{-3}{4}$ by -6 (viii) $\frac{2}{3}$ by $\frac{-7}{12}$

(ix) -4 by $\frac{-3}{5}$ (x) $\frac{-3}{13}$ by $\frac{-4}{65}$

2. Find the value and express as a rational number in standard form:

(i) $\frac{2}{5} \div \frac{26}{15}$ (ii) $\frac{10}{3} \div \frac{-35}{12}$ (iii) $-6 \div \left(\frac{-8}{17}\right)$ (iv) $\frac{-40}{99} \div (-20)$

(v) $\frac{-22}{27} \div \frac{-110}{18}$ (vi) $\frac{-36}{125} \div \frac{-3}{75}$

3. The product of two rational numbers is 15. If one of the numbers is – 10, find the other.

4. The product of two rational numbers is $\frac{-8}{9}$. If one of the numbers is $\frac{-4}{15}$, find the other.

5. By what number should we multiply $\frac{-1}{6}$ so that the product may be $\frac{-23}{9}$?

6. By what number should we multiply $\frac{-15}{28}$ so that the product may be $\frac{-5}{7}$?

7. By what number should we multiply $\frac{-8}{13}$ so that the product may be 24?

8. By what number should $\frac{-3}{4}$ be multiplied in order to produce $\frac{2}{3}$?

9. Find $(x + y) \div (x - y)$, if

(i) $x = \frac{2}{3}, y = \frac{3}{2}$ (ii) $x = \frac{2}{5}, y = \frac{1}{2}$ (iii) $x = \frac{5}{4}, y = \frac{-1}{3}$ (iv) $x = \frac{2}{7}, y = \frac{4}{3}$

(v) $x = \frac{1}{4}, y = \frac{3}{2}$

10. The cost of $7\frac{2}{3}$ metres of rope is Rs $12\frac{3}{4}$. Find its cost per metre.

11. The cost of $2\frac{1}{3}$ metres of cloth is Rs $75\frac{1}{4}$. Find the cost of cloth per metre.

12. By what number should $\frac{-33}{16}$ be divided to get $\frac{-11}{4}$?

13. Divide the sum of $\frac{-13}{5}$ and $\frac{12}{7}$ by the product of $\frac{-31}{7}$ and $\frac{-1}{2}$.

14. Divide the sum of $\frac{65}{12}$ and $\frac{12}{7}$ by their difference.

15. If 24 trousers of equal size can be prepared in 54 metres of cloth, what length of cloth is required for each trouser?

ANSWERS

1. (i) 2 (ii) −7 (iii) $\frac{4}{3}$ (iv) $\frac{2}{3}$ (v) $\frac{-16}{9}$ (vi) 0

(vii) $\frac{1}{8}$ (viii) $\frac{-8}{7}$ (ix) $\frac{20}{3}$ (x) $\frac{15}{4}$

2. (i) $\frac{3}{13}$ (ii) $\frac{-8}{7}$ (iii) $\frac{51}{4}$ (iv) $\frac{2}{99}$ (v) $\frac{2}{15}$ (vi) $\frac{36}{5}$

3. (i) $\frac{-3}{2}$ 4. $\frac{10}{3}$ 5. $\frac{46}{3}$ 6. $\frac{4}{3}$ 7. -39 8. $\frac{-8}{9}$

9. (i) $\frac{-13}{5}$ (ii) -9 (iii) $\frac{11}{19}$ (iv) $\frac{-17}{11}$ (v) $\frac{-7}{5}$

10. (i) Rs $1\frac{61}{92}$ 11. Rs 32.25 12. $\frac{3}{4}$ 13. $\frac{-2}{5}$ 14. $\frac{599}{311}$ 15. $\frac{9}{4}$ metres

1.11 REPRESENTATION OF RATIONAL NUMBERS ON THE NUMBER LINE

In earlier classes, we have learnt how to represent natural numbers, whole numbers, integers and rational numbers on a number line. To represent the integers on a number line, we draw a line and mark a point 'O' on it corresponding to the number 'zero'. Starting from O, we mark on it points at equal distances on right as well as on left of O. Let A, B, C, D etc. be the points of division on the right of O and A', B', C', D' etc. be the points of division on the left of O as shown in Fig. 1.1. If we take $OA = 1$ unit, then points A, B, C, D, etc. represent the integers 1, 2, 3, 4, etc respectively and the points A', B', C', D', etc. represent the integers –1 , –2 , –3, –4, etc. respectively.

–4 –3 –2 –1 0 1 2 3 4

D′ C′ B′ A′ O A B C D

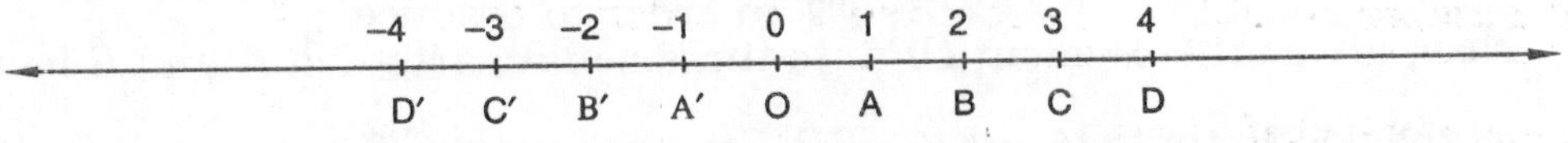

Fig. 1.1

The point O represents integer 0.

Clearly, every positive integer lies to the right of O and every negative integer lies to the left of O.

Rational numbers can also be represented on the number line in the same way. In order to represent rational numbers on the number line, we draw a line and mark a point O on it to represent the rational number zero. The positive rational numbers will be represented by points on the line lying to the right of O and negative rational numbers will be represented by points on the line lying to the left of O. If we mark a point A on the line to the right of O to represent 1, then $OA = 1$ unit. Similarly, if we choose a point A' on the line to the left of O to represent –1, then $OA' = 1$ unit.

Now, suppose we wish to represent the rational number $\frac{1}{2}$ on the number line. For this, we divide the segment OA into two equal parts. Let P be the mid-point of segment OA. Then, $OP = PA = \frac{1}{2}$. Since O represents 0 and, A represents 1. Therefore, P represents the rational number $\frac{1}{2}$ as shown in Fig 1.2.

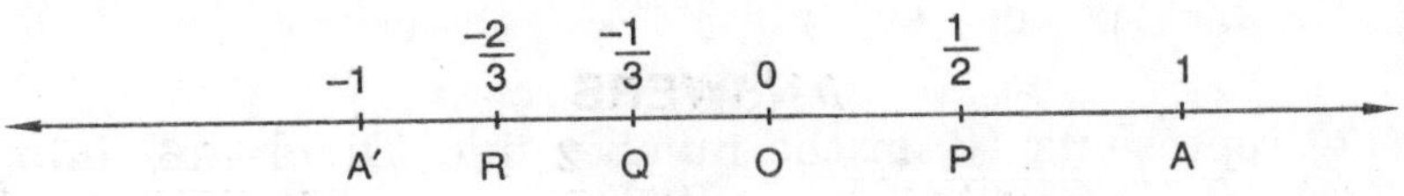

–1 $\frac{-2}{3}$ $\frac{-1}{3}$ 0 $\frac{1}{2}$ 1

A′ R Q O P A

Fig. 1.2

Similarly, if we want to represent the rational numbers $\frac{-1}{3}$ and $\frac{-2}{3}$ on the number line, we divide the segment OA' into three equal parts. Let Q and R be the points dividing segment OA' into three equal parts. Then, $OQ = QR = RA' = \frac{1}{3}$. Since O represents 0 and A' represents –1. Therefore, Q and R represent $\frac{-1}{3}$ and $\frac{-2}{3}$ respectively.

Following illustrations will illustrate the representation of more rational numbers on the number line.

ILLUSTRATION 1 Represent $\frac{5}{3}$ and $\frac{-5}{3}$ on the number line.

Solution In order to represent $\frac{5}{3}$ and $\frac{-5}{3}$ on the number line, we first draw a number line and mark a point O on it to represent zero. Now, we find the points P and Q on the number line representing the positive integers 5 and –5 respectively as shown in Fig. 1.3.

Fig. 1.3

Now, divide the segment OP into three equal parts. Let A and B be the points of division so that $OA = AB = BP$. By construction, OA is one-third of OP.

Therefore, A represents the rational number $\frac{5}{3}$.

Point Q represents –5 on the number line. Now, divide OQ into three equal parts OC, CD and DQ. The point C is such that OC is one third of OQ. Since Q represents the number –5. Therefore, C represents the rational number $\frac{-5}{3}$.

ILLUSTRATION 2 Represent $\frac{8}{5}$ and $\frac{-8}{5}$ on the number line.

Solution To represent $\frac{8}{5}$ and $\frac{-8}{5}$ on the number line, draw a number line and mark a point O on it to represent zero. Now, mark two points P and Q representing integers 8 and –8 respectively on the number line. Divide the segment OP into five equal parts. Let A, B, C, D be the points of division so that $OA = AB = BC = CD = DP$. By consturction, OA is one-fifth of OP. So, A represents the rational number $\frac{8}{5}$.

Fig. 1.4

Now, Q represents –8 on the number line. Divide OQ into five equal parts OA', $A'B'$, $B'C'$, $C'D'$ and $D'Q$. Since Q represents –8. Therefore, A' represents the rational number $\frac{-8}{5}$.

1.12 RATIONAL NUMBERS BETWEEN TWO RATIONAL NUMBERS

In earlier class, we have learnt, by using the procedure of insertion of rational numbers between two given rational numbers, that there are countless rational numbers between any two given rational numbers. This property of rational numbers is known as the *dense property*. In this section, we will study an alternative method of inserting rational numbers between two given rational numbers. Let us first recall what we have learnt in the previous class.

Suppose we wish to find two rational numbers between $\frac{3}{7}$ and $\frac{6}{7}$. Since these two numbers have the same denominator. So, we choose their numerators 3 and 6. Integers between 3 and 6 are 4 and 5. Therefore, $\frac{4}{7}$ and $\frac{5}{7}$ are two rational numbers between $\frac{3}{7}$ and $\frac{6}{7}$ such that

$$\frac{3}{7} < \frac{4}{7} < \frac{5}{7} < \frac{6}{7}$$

Let us now choose two rational numbers having distinct denominators. Let the numbers be $\frac{1}{4}$ and $\frac{2}{3}$ and we wish to find two rational numbers between these two. First we find equivalent rational numbers having a common denominator equal to the LCM of the denominators 4 and 3 i.e., 12. Thus, we write

$$\frac{1}{4} = \frac{3}{12} \text{ and } \frac{2}{3} = \frac{8}{12}$$

Now, we choose integers between the numerators 3 and 8 of these equivalent rational numbers. Clearly, 4, 5, 6 and 7 are four integers between 3 and 8. Therefore, $\frac{4}{12}, \frac{5}{12}, \frac{6}{12}$ and $\frac{7}{12}$ are rational numbers between $\frac{3}{12}$ and $\frac{8}{12}$ such that

$$\frac{3}{12} < \frac{4}{12} < \frac{5}{12} < \frac{6}{12} < \frac{7}{12} < \frac{8}{12}$$

$$\text{i.e., } \frac{1}{4} < \frac{4}{12} < \frac{5}{12} < \frac{6}{12} < \frac{7}{12} < \frac{2}{3}$$

We can choose any two rational numbers out of these four rational numbers.

Between 3 and 8 there are only four integers. So, we can find only four rational numbers between $\frac{1}{4}$ and $\frac{2}{3}$ by using this method. If we were to find, more number of rational numbers between $\frac{1}{4}$ and $\frac{2}{3}$, then we proceed as follows:

We replace numbers $\frac{1}{4}$ and $\frac{2}{3}$ by equivalent rational numbers having sufficiently large common denominator. For example, we write

$$\frac{1}{4} = \frac{3}{12} = \frac{30}{120} = \frac{300}{1200} = \frac{3000}{12000} \text{ etc. and, } \quad \frac{2}{3} = \frac{8}{12} = \frac{80}{120} = \frac{800}{1200} = \frac{8000}{12000} \text{ etc.}$$

Now, choosing $\frac{30}{120}$ for $\frac{1}{4}$ and $\frac{80}{120}$ for $\frac{2}{3}$ and finding integers 31, 32, ..., 79 between 30 and 80, we find 49 rational numbers $\frac{31}{120}, \frac{32}{120}, \cdots, \frac{79}{120}$ between $\frac{30}{120}$ and $\frac{80}{120}$ such that

$$\frac{1}{4} = \frac{30}{120} < \frac{31}{120} < \frac{32}{120} < \cdots < \frac{79}{120} < \frac{80}{120} = \frac{2}{3}$$

To find more number of rational numbers between $\frac{1}{4}$ and $\frac{2}{3}$, we may take the equivalent rational numbers as $\frac{300}{1200}$ and $\frac{800}{1200}$.

Continuing in this manner, we can insert as many rational numbers between $\frac{1}{3}$ and $\frac{2}{4}$ as we wish.

ILLUSTRATIVE EXAMPLES

Example 1 Write any three rational numbers between –2 and 0.

Solution We can write

$$-2 = \frac{-2}{1} = \frac{-2\times5}{1\times5} = \frac{-10}{5} \text{ and } 0 = \frac{0}{5}$$

Integers between –10 and 0 are –9, – 8, – 7, – 6, – 5, ···, – 1.

$\therefore$ $\frac{-9}{5}, \frac{-8}{5}, \frac{-7}{5}, \cdots, \frac{-2}{5}, \frac{-1}{5}$ are rational numbers between –2 and 0.

We can choose any three of these rational numbers.

Example 2 Find four rational numbers between $\frac{2}{3}$ and $\frac{4}{5}$.

Solution First we convert given rational numbers to rational numbers with the same denominator equal to the LCM of their denominators. The LCM of denominators 3 and 5 is 15.

$$\therefore \quad \frac{2}{3} = \frac{2\times5}{3\times5} = \frac{10}{15} \text{ and } \frac{4}{5} = \frac{4\times3}{5\times3} = \frac{12}{15}$$

Between the numerators 10 and 12 of these equivalent rational numbers there is only one integer. So, we replace these numbers by equivalent rational numbers having a sufficiently large common denominator.

We write

$$\frac{2}{3} = \frac{10}{15} = \frac{40}{60} \text{ and } \frac{4}{5} = \frac{12}{15} = \frac{48}{60}$$

Between 40 and 48 there are seven integers 41, 42, 43, ..., 47. Therefore,

$\frac{41}{60}, \frac{42}{60}, \cdots, \frac{47}{60}$ are seven rational numbers between $\frac{40}{60}\left(=\frac{2}{3}\right)$ and $\frac{48}{60}\left(=\frac{4}{5}\right)$.

We can take any four of these rational numbers.

Example 3 Find five rational numbers between $\frac{-3}{2}$ and $\frac{5}{3}$.

Solution The LCM of denominators 2 and 3 is 6. Converting given rational numbers to equivalent rational numbers having common denominator 6, we get

$$\frac{-3}{2}=\frac{-3\times3}{2\times3}=\frac{-9}{6} \text{ and } \frac{5}{3}=\frac{5\times2}{3\times2}=\frac{10}{6}$$

Clearly, $-8,-7,\cdots,7,8,9$ are integers between numerators -9 and 10 of these equivalent rational numbers. Thus, we have

$$\frac{-8}{6},\frac{-7}{6},\frac{-6}{6},\frac{-5}{6},\dots,\frac{7}{6},\frac{8}{6},\frac{9}{6}$$

as rational numbers between $\frac{-9}{6}\left(=\frac{-3}{2}\right)$ and $\frac{10}{6}\left(=\frac{5}{3}\right)$.

We can take any four of these as required rational numbers.

AN ALTERNATIVE METHOD TO FIND RATIONAL NUMBERS BETWEEN TWO RATIONAL NUMBERS

In the above discussion, we have learnt how to find rational numbers between two distinct rational numbers. We did this by using the property that between two non-consecutive integers, there are integers lying between them. In the previous sections, we have learnt various operations and their properties on the set of rational numbers. By using these properties we obtain the following result which will help us to find rational numbers between two distinct rational numbers.

RESULT *If x and y are any two rational numbers such that $x<y$, then*

$$x<\frac{x\times y}{2}<y \text{ or, } x<\frac{1}{2}(x+y)<y$$

In other words, the rational number $\frac{x+y}{2}=(x+y)\div 2$ *lies between x and y.*

The rational number $\frac{x+y}{2}$ is called the mean of x and y.

Following examples will illustrate the use of the above result to find rational numbers between two given rational numbers.

ILLUSTRATIVE EXAMPLES

Example 1 Find a rational number between -2 and 6.

Solution We know that between two rational numbers x and y such that $x<y$ there is a rational number $\frac{x+y}{2}$.

i.e., $x<\frac{x+y}{2}<y$

So, a rational number between -2 and 6 is $\frac{-2+6}{2}=\frac{4}{2}=2$

Thus, we have $-2<2<6$.

Example 2 Find a rational number between $\frac{-2}{3}$ and $\frac{1}{4}$.

Solution The rational number $\left(\frac{-2}{3}+\frac{1}{4}\right)\div 2$ lies between $\frac{-2}{3}$ and $\frac{1}{4}$

Now,

$$\left(\frac{-2}{3}+\frac{1}{4}\right)=\frac{(-2)\times 4+3\times 1}{12}=\frac{-8+3}{12}=\frac{-5}{12}$$

$$\therefore \quad \left(\frac{-2}{3}+\frac{1}{4}\right)\div 2=\frac{-5}{12}\div 2=\frac{-5}{12}\times\frac{1}{2}=\frac{-5}{24}$$

Thus, the required rational number is $\frac{-5}{24}$.

i.e, $\frac{-2}{3}<\frac{-5}{24}<\frac{1}{4}$

Example 3 Find three rational between – 2 and 5.

Solution A rational number lying between – 2 and 5 is

$$(-2+5)\div 2=3\div 2=\frac{3}{2}$$

$$\therefore \quad -2<\frac{3}{2}<5$$

Now, a rational number lying between – 2 and $\frac{3}{2}$ is

$$\left(-2+\frac{3}{2}\right)\div 2=\left(\frac{-2\times 2+3}{2}\right)\div 2=\left(\frac{-4+3}{2}\right)\div 2=\left(\frac{-1}{2}\right)\div 2=\frac{-1}{2}\times\frac{1}{2}=\frac{-1}{4}$$

$$\therefore \quad -2<\frac{-1}{4}<\frac{3}{2}<5$$

A rational number lying between $\frac{3}{2}$ and 5 is

$$\left(\frac{3}{2}+5\right)\div 2=\left(\frac{3+5\times 2}{2}\right)\div 2=\left(\frac{3+10}{2}\right)\div 2=\frac{13}{2}\div 2=\frac{13}{2}\times\frac{1}{2}=\frac{13}{4}$$

$$\therefore \quad \frac{3}{2}<\frac{13}{4}<5$$

Thus, we have

$$-2<\frac{-1}{4}<\frac{3}{2}<\frac{13}{4}<5$$

Hence, $\frac{-1}{4},\frac{3}{2},\frac{13}{4}$ are three rational numbers between –2 and 5.

EXERCISE 1.8

1. Find a rational number between -3 and 1.
2. Find any five rational numbers less than 2.
3. Find two rational numbers between $\frac{-2}{9}$ and $\frac{5}{9}$.
4. Find two rational numbers between $\frac{1}{5}$ and $\frac{1}{2}$.
5. Find ten rational numbers between $\frac{1}{4}$ and $\frac{1}{2}$.
6. Find ten rational numbers between $\frac{-2}{5}$ and $\frac{1}{2}$.
7. Find ten rational numbers between $\frac{3}{5}$ and $\frac{3}{4}$.

ANSWERS

1. -1
2. $0, \frac{1}{5}, \frac{2}{5}, \frac{3}{5}, \frac{4}{5}$
3. $\frac{-1}{9}, 0, \frac{1}{9}, \frac{2}{9}$
4. $\frac{3}{10}, \frac{4}{10}$
5. $\frac{21}{80}, \frac{22}{80}, \frac{23}{80}, \ldots, \frac{39}{80}$
6. $\frac{-7}{20}, \frac{-6}{20}, \frac{-5}{20}, \ldots, \frac{9}{20}$
7. $\frac{61}{100}, \frac{62}{100}, \ldots, \frac{74}{100}$

THINGS TO REMEMBER

1. *The operation of addition of rational numbers has the following properties:*
   (i) *Closure property: The addition of any two rational numbers is always a rational number.*
   (ii) *Commutativity: The addition of rational numbers is commutative i.e. $x + y = y + x$ for any two rational numbers x and y.*
   (iii) *Associativity: The addition of rational numbers is associative i.e. $(x + y) + z = x + (y + z)$ for all rational numbers x, y, z*
   (iv) *Existence of additive identity: The rational number 0 is the additive identity i.e. $x + 0 = 0 + x = x$ for all rational numbers x.*
   (v) *Existence of additive inverse: For every rational number x there exists $-x$ (additive inverse of x) such that $(-x) + x = 0 = x + (-x)$*
2. *The multiplication of rational numbers has the following properties:*
   (i) *Closure property: The multiplication of any two rational numbers is always a rational number.*
   (ii) *Commutativity: The multiplication of rational numbers is commutative i.e. $x \times y = y \times x$ for any two rational numbers x and y.*
   (iii) *Associativity: The multiplication of rational numbers is associative i.e. $(x \times y) \times z = x \times (y \times z)$ for all rational numbers x, y, and z.*
   (iv) *Existence of identity: The rational number 1 is the identity element for multiplication i.e. $x \times 1 = x = 1 \times x$ for all rational numbers x.*
   (v) *Existence of multiplicative inverse: For every non-zero rational number x, there exists a rational number $\frac{1}{x}$ (reciprocal of x) such that*
   $$x \times \frac{1}{x} = 1 = \frac{1}{x} \times x$$
   (vi) *Multiplication by zero: For any rational number x, we have*
   $$x \times 0 = 0 = 0 \times x$$
   (vii) *Distributivity of Multiplication over addition: For any three rational numbers x, y, z, we have*
   $$x(y + z) = xy + xz$$
3. *Subtraction of rational numbers has the following properties:*
   (i) *Closure property: The subtraction of any two rational numbers is a rational number i.e. $x - y$ is a rational number for all rational numbers x, y.*
   (ii) *The subtraction of rational numbers is neither commutative nor associative.*
4. *Division of rational numbers has the following properties:*
   (i) *The division of any two rational numbers is a rational number: provided that divisor is a non-zero rational number.*
   (ii) *Division of rational numbers is neither commutative nor associative.*
5. *Between two rational numbers x and y, there is a rational number $\frac{x+y}{2}$.*
6. *We can find as many rational numbers between x and y as we want.*

2

POWERS

2.1 INTRODUCTION

In earlier class, we have learnt about powers and exponents of rational numbers. We have learnt that for any non-zero rational number '*a*' and a natural number *n*, the product $\underbrace{a\times a\times a\times\cdots\times a}_{n\text{-times}}$ i.e. the continued product of '*a*' multiplied with itself *n*-times, is written as a^n. It is known as the *n*th power of '*a*' and is read as "*a* raised to the power *n*". The rational number '*a*' is called the base and *n* is called the exponent or index. This notation of writing the product of a rational number by itself several times is called the exponential notation or power notation.

We have learnt the following laws of exponents:

(i) $a^m \times a^n = a^{m+n}$ (First law)

(ii) $\dfrac{a^m}{a^n} = a^{m-n},\ m > n$ (Second law)

(iii) $(a^m)^n = a^{mn} = (a^n)^m$ (Third law)

(iv) $(ab)^n = a^n b^n$ (Fourth law)

(v) $\left(\dfrac{a}{b}\right)^n = \dfrac{a^n}{b^n}$ (Fifth law)

(vi) $a^1 = a$ and $a^0 = 1$,

where *a* and *b* are non-zero rational numbers and *m*, *n* are whole numbers.

In this chapter, we shall learn the laws of integral (positive and negative both) exponents of rational numbers. As we have already learnt the laws of positive integral exponents of rational numbers, so let us know about negative integral exponents.

2.2 NEGATIVE INTEGRAL EXPONENTS

In class VII, we have learnt that

$10^0 = 1$

$10^1 = 10$

$10^2 = 100$

$10^3 = 1000$

$10^4 = 10000$ and so on.

We know that

$$\frac{10000}{10} = 1000$$

$$\frac{1000}{10} = 100$$

$$\frac{100}{10} = 10$$

$$\frac{10}{10} = 1$$

In exponential notation these results can be written as follows:

$$\frac{10^4}{10} = 10^3 \text{ or, } 10^3 = \frac{10^4}{10}$$

$$\frac{10^3}{10} = 10^2 \text{ or, } 10^2 = \frac{10^3}{10}$$

$$\frac{10^2}{10} = 10^1 \text{ or, } 10^1 = \frac{10^2}{10}$$

$$\frac{10^1}{10} = 1\,(= 10^0) \text{ or, } 10^0 = 1 = \frac{10^1}{10}$$

These results exhibit a pattern that as the exponent of 10 decreases by 1, the value becomes one-tenth of the previous value. So, if the same pattern is continued, we must have

$$10^{-1} = \frac{1}{10}$$

$$10^{-2} = \frac{1}{10} \div 10 = \frac{1}{10} \times \frac{1}{10} = \frac{1}{100} = \frac{1}{10^2}$$

$$10^{-3} = \frac{1}{100} \div 10 = \frac{1}{10} \times \frac{1}{100} = \frac{1}{1000} = \frac{1}{10^3}$$

$$10^{-4} = \frac{1}{1000} \div 10 = \frac{1}{10} \times \frac{1}{1000} = \frac{1}{10000} = \frac{1}{10^4} \text{ and so on.}$$

This suggests us the following definition for negative integral exponents of a non-zero rational number.

NEGATIVE INTEGRAL EXPONENT *For any non-zero rational number 'a' and a positive integer, we define*

$$a^{-n} = \frac{1}{a^n}$$

i.e., a^{-n} *is the reciprocal of* a^n.

For example,

(i) $2^{-4} = \frac{1}{2^4}$ (ii) $7^{-3} = \frac{1}{7^3}$ (iii) $5^{-4} = \frac{1}{5^4}$

(iv) $10^{-15} = \frac{1}{10^{15}}$ (v) $\left(\frac{2}{3}\right)^{-3} = \frac{1}{\left(\frac{2}{3}\right)^3}$ etc.

ILLUSTRATIVE EXAMPLES

Example 1 Express each of the following as a rational number of the form $\frac{p}{q}$:

(i) 5^{-3} (ii) $(-2)^{-5}$ (iii) $\left(\frac{4}{3}\right)^{-3}$ (iv) $\left(\frac{-2}{5}\right)^{-4}$ (v) $\frac{1}{2^{-3}}$

Solution We know that, if a is a non-zero rational number and n is a positive integer, then

$$a^{-n} = \frac{1}{a^n}$$

Thus, we have

(i) $5^{-3} = \frac{1}{5^3}$

$= \frac{1}{125}$ $\left[\because a^{-n} = \frac{1}{a^n}\right]$

(ii) $(-2)^{-5} = \frac{1}{(-2)^5}$ $\left[\because a^{-n} = \frac{1}{a^n}\right]$

$= \frac{1}{-32} = -\frac{1}{32}$

(iii) $\left(\frac{4}{3}\right)^{-3} = \frac{1}{\left(\frac{4}{3}\right)^3} = \frac{1}{\frac{4^3}{3^3}}$ $\left[\because \left(\frac{a}{b}\right)^n = \frac{a^n}{b^n} \text{ when } n \text{ is a whole number}\right]$

$= \frac{1}{\frac{64}{27}} = \frac{27}{64}$

(iv) $\left(\frac{-2}{5}\right)^{-4} = \frac{1}{\left(\frac{-2}{5}\right)^4}$ $\left[\because a^{-n} = \frac{1}{a^n}\right]$

$= \frac{1}{\frac{(-2)^4}{5^4}} = \frac{1}{\frac{16}{625}} = \frac{625}{16}$ $\left[\because \left(\frac{a}{b}\right)^n = \frac{a^n}{b^n} \text{ for } n > 0\right]$

(v) $\dfrac{1}{2^{-3}} = \dfrac{1}{\dfrac{1}{2^3}}$ $\left[\because a^{-n} = \dfrac{1}{a^n}\right]$

$= \dfrac{2^3}{1} = \dfrac{8}{1} = 8$

Example 2 Express each of the following as a rational number of the form $\dfrac{p}{q}$:

(i) $\left(\dfrac{3}{8}\right)^{-2} \times \left(\dfrac{4}{5}\right)^{-3}$ (ii) $\left(\dfrac{-2}{7}\right)^{-4} \times \left(\dfrac{-7}{5}\right)^{2}$

Solution (i) We have,

$$\left(\frac{3}{8}\right)^{-2} \times \left(\frac{4}{5}\right)^{-3} = \frac{1}{\left(\frac{3}{8}\right)^2} \times \frac{1}{\left(\frac{4}{5}\right)^3} \qquad \left[\because a^{-n} = \frac{1}{a^n}\right]$$

$$= \frac{1}{\frac{3^2}{8^2}} \times \frac{1}{\frac{4^3}{5^3}} \qquad \left[\because \left(\frac{a}{b}\right)^n = \left(\frac{a^n}{b^n}\right)\right]$$

$$= \frac{1}{\frac{9}{64}} \times \frac{1}{\frac{64}{125}} = \frac{64}{9} \times \frac{125}{64} = \frac{125}{9}$$

(ii) We have,

$$\left(\frac{-2}{7}\right)^{-4} \times \left(\frac{-7}{5}\right)^{2}$$

$$= \frac{1}{\left(\frac{-2}{7}\right)^4} \times \left(\frac{-7}{5}\right)^2 = \frac{1}{\frac{(-2)^4}{7^4}} \times \frac{(-7)^2}{5^2}$$

$$= \frac{7^4}{(-2)^4} \times \frac{(-7)^2}{5^2} = \frac{7\times7\times7\times7}{16} \times \frac{-7\times-7}{25} = \frac{7^6}{16\times25} = \frac{7^6}{400} = \frac{117649}{400}$$

Example 3 Express each of the following as power of a rational number with positive exponent:

(i) $\left(\dfrac{1}{4}\right)^{-3}$ (ii) $5^{-3} \times 5^{-6}$ (iii) $\left(\dfrac{-1}{4}\right)^{-5} \times \left(\dfrac{-1}{4}\right)^{-7}$

Solution (i) We have,

$$\left(\frac{1}{4}\right)^{-3} = \frac{1}{\left(\frac{1}{4}\right)^3} = \frac{1}{\frac{1^3}{4^3}} = \frac{4^3}{1^3} = 4^3$$

(ii) We have,

$$5^{-3} \times 5^{-6} = \frac{1}{5^3} \times \frac{1}{5^6} = \frac{1\times1}{5^3\times5^6} = \frac{1}{5^{3+6}} = \frac{1}{5^9} = \frac{1^9}{5^9} = \left(\frac{1}{5}\right)^9$$

(iii) We have,

$$\left(\frac{-1}{4}\right)^{-5}\times\left(\frac{-1}{4}\right)^{-7}$$

$$=\frac{1}{\left(\frac{-1}{4}\right)^{5}}\times\frac{1}{\left(\frac{-1}{4}\right)^{7}}=\frac{1}{\frac{(-1)^5}{4^5}}\times\frac{1}{\frac{(-1)^7}{4^7}}=\frac{1}{\frac{-1}{4^5}}\times\frac{1}{\frac{-1}{4^7}}=\frac{4^5}{-1}\times\frac{4^7}{-1}=\frac{4^5\times4^7}{(-1)\times(-1)}=\frac{4^{5+7}}{1}=4^{12}$$

Example 4 Simplify:

(i) $\left(2^{-1}\div5^{-1}\right)^2\times\left(\frac{-5}{8}\right)^{-1}$ (ii) $\left(6^{-1}-8^{-1}\right)^{-1}+\left(2^{-1}-3^{-1}\right)^{-1}$

(iii) $\left(5^{-1}\times3^{-1}\right)^{-1}\div6^{-1}$ (iv) $\left(4^{-1}+8^{-1}\right)\div\left(\frac{2}{3}\right)^{-1}$

Solution (i) We have,

$$\left(2^{-1}\div5^{-1}\right)^2\times\left(\frac{-5}{8}\right)^{-1}$$

$$=\left(\frac{1}{2}\div\frac{1}{5}\right)^2\times\frac{1}{\left(\frac{-5}{8}\right)} \qquad \left[\because a^{-1}=\frac{1}{a}\right]$$

$$=\left(\frac{1}{2}\times\frac{5}{1}\right)^2\times\left(\frac{8}{-5}\right)$$

$$=\left(\frac{5}{2}\right)^2\times\left(\frac{8}{-5}\right)=\frac{5^2}{2^2}\times\frac{8}{-5}=\frac{5}{4}\times\frac{8}{-1}=\frac{5}{1}\times\frac{2}{-1}=-10$$

(ii) We have,

$$\left(6^{-1}-8^{-1}\right)^{-1}+\left(2^{-1}-3^{-1}\right)^{-1}$$

$$=\left(\frac{1}{6}-\frac{1}{8}\right)^{-1}+\left(\frac{1}{2}-\frac{1}{3}\right)^{-1}$$

$$=\left(\frac{4-3}{24}\right)^{-1}+\left(\frac{3-2}{6}\right)^{-1}$$

$$=\left(\frac{1}{24}\right)^{-1}+\left(\frac{1}{6}\right)^{-1}=\frac{1}{\frac{1}{24}}+\frac{1}{\frac{1}{6}}=\frac{24}{1}+\frac{6}{1}=30 \qquad \left[\because a^{-1}=\frac{1}{a}\right]$$

(iii) We have,

$$\left(5^{-1}\times3^{-1}\right)^{-1}\div6^{-1}$$

$$=\left(\frac{1}{5}\times\frac{1}{3}\right)^{-1}\div\frac{1}{6}$$

$$=\left(\frac{1}{15}\right)^{-1}\div\frac{1}{6}=\frac{1}{\frac{1}{15}}\div\frac{1}{6}=15\div\frac{1}{6}=15\times\frac{6}{1}=90$$

(iv) We have,

$$\left(4^{-1}+8^{-1}\right)\div\left(\frac{2}{3}\right)^{-1}$$

$$=\left(\frac{1}{4}+\frac{1}{8}\right)\div\frac{1}{\frac{2}{3}}=\left(\frac{2+1}{8}\right)\div\left(\frac{3}{2}\right)=\frac{3}{8}\div\frac{3}{2}=\frac{3}{8}\times\frac{2}{3}=\frac{1}{4}$$

Example 5 Simplify:

(i) $\left(\frac{1}{4}\right)^{-2}+\left(\frac{1}{2}\right)^{-2}+\left(\frac{1}{3}\right)^{-2}$ (ii) $\left\{6^{-1}+\left(\frac{3}{2}\right)^{-1}\right\}^{-1}$

Solution (i) We have,

$$\left(\frac{1}{4}\right)^{-2}+\left(\frac{1}{2}\right)^{-2}+\left(\frac{1}{3}\right)^{-2}$$

$$=\frac{1}{\left(\frac{1}{4}\right)^{2}}+\frac{1}{\left(\frac{1}{2}\right)^{2}}+\frac{1}{\left(\frac{1}{3}\right)^{2}} \qquad \left[\because a^{-n}=\frac{1}{a^{n}}\right]$$

$$=\frac{1}{\frac{1^2}{4^2}}+\frac{1}{\frac{1^2}{2^2}}+\frac{1}{\frac{1^2}{3^2}}=\frac{4^2}{1^2}+\frac{2^2}{1^2}+\frac{3^2}{1^2}=\frac{4^2}{1}+\frac{2^2}{1}+\frac{3^2}{1}$$

$$=4^2+2^2+3^2=16+4+9=29$$

(ii) We have,

$$\left\{6^{-1}+\left(\frac{3}{2}\right)^{-1}\right\}^{-1}$$

$$=\left\{\frac{1}{6}+\frac{1}{\frac{3}{2}}\right\}^{-1}=\left(\frac{1}{6}+\frac{2}{3}\right)^{-1}=\left(\frac{1+2\times2}{6}\right)^{-1}=\left(\frac{5}{6}\right)^{-1}=\frac{1}{\frac{5}{6}}=\frac{6}{5}$$

Example 6 Express each of the following as a rational number of the form $\frac{p}{q}$:

(i) $\left(2^{-1}+3^{-1}\right)^2$ (ii) $\left(2^{-1}-4^{-1}\right)^2$ (iii) $\left\{\left(\frac{3}{4}\right)^{-1}-\left(\frac{1}{4}\right)^{-1}\right\}^{-1}$

Solution We know that for any positive integer n and any rational number a, $a^{-n}=\frac{1}{a^n}$. Thus, we have

(i) $\left(2^{-1}+3^{-1}\right)^2=\left(\frac{1}{2}+\frac{1}{3}\right)^2=\left(\frac{3+2}{6}\right)^2=\left(\frac{5}{6}\right)^2=\frac{5^2}{6^2}=\frac{25}{36}$

(ii) $\left(2^{-1}-4^{-1}\right)^2=\left(\frac{1}{2}-\frac{1}{4}\right)^2=\left(\frac{2-1}{4}\right)^2=\left(\frac{1}{4}\right)^2=\frac{1^2}{4^2}=\frac{1}{16}$

(iii) $\left\{\left(\frac{3}{4}\right)^{-1}-\left(\frac{1}{4}\right)^{-1}\right\}^{-1}$

$$=\left(\frac{1}{\frac{3}{4}}-\frac{1}{\frac{1}{4}}\right)^{-1}=\left(\frac{4}{3}-\frac{4}{1}\right)^{-1}=\left(\frac{4-3\times4}{3}\right)^{-1}=\left(\frac{-8}{3}\right)^{-1}=\frac{1}{\frac{-8}{3}}=\frac{3}{-8}=-\frac{3}{8}$$

Example 7 By what number should $(-8)^{-1}$ be multiplied so that the product may be equal to 10^{-1}?

Solution Let $(-8)^{-1}$ be multiplied by x to get 10^{-1}. Then,

$$x\times(-8)^{-1}=10^{-1}$$

$$\Rightarrow\quad x=10^{-1}\div(-8)^{-1}$$

$$\Rightarrow\quad x=\frac{1}{10}\div\frac{1}{-8}\qquad\left[\because a^{-1}=\frac{1}{a}\right]$$

$$\Rightarrow\quad x=\frac{1}{10}\times\frac{-8}{1}=\frac{-8}{10}=\frac{-4}{5}$$

Hence, the required number is $\frac{-4}{5}$.

Example 8 By what number should $(-24)^{-1}$ be divided so that the quotient may be 3^{-1}?

Solution Let the required number be x. Then,

$$(-24)^{-1}\div x=3^{-1}$$

$$\Rightarrow\quad \frac{(-24)^{-1}}{x}=3^{-1}$$

$$\Rightarrow\quad \frac{\frac{1}{-24}}{x}=\frac{1}{3}\qquad\left[\because a^{-1}=\frac{1}{a}\right]$$

$$\Rightarrow\quad \frac{1}{-24x}=\frac{1}{3}\Rightarrow 3=-24x\Rightarrow x=\frac{3}{-24}\Rightarrow x=\frac{-3}{24}=-\frac{1}{8}$$

Aliter We know that

Dividend = Quotient × Divisor

or, Divisor = Dividend ÷ Quotient

Here, Dividend = $(-24)^{-1}$ and Quotient = 3^{-1}

$$\therefore\quad \text{Divisor}=(-24)^{-1}\div 3^{-1}=\left(\frac{1}{-24}\right)\div\left(\frac{1}{3}\right)=\frac{1}{-24}\times\frac{3}{1}=\frac{1}{-8}=(-8)^{-1}$$

EXERCISE 2.1

1. Express each of the following as a rational number of the form $\frac{p}{q}$, where p and q are integers and $q \neq 0$:

(i) 2^{-3} (ii) $(-4)^{-2}$ (iii) $\frac{1}{3^{-2}}$ (iv) $\left(\frac{1}{2}\right)^{-5}$ (v) $\left(\frac{2}{3}\right)^{-2}$

2. Find the values of each of the following:

(i) $3^{-1}+4^{-1}$ (ii) $(3^0+4^{-1})\times 2^2$

(iii) $(3^{-1}+4^{-1}+5^{-1})^0$ (iv) $\left\{\left(\frac{1}{3}\right)^{-1}-\left(\frac{1}{4}\right)^{-1}\right\}^{-1}$

3. Find the values of each of the following:

(i) $\left(\frac{1}{2}\right)^{-1}+\left(\frac{1}{3}\right)^{-1}+\left(\frac{1}{4}\right)^{-1}$ (ii) $\left(\frac{1}{2}\right)^{-2}+\left(\frac{1}{3}\right)^{-2}+\left(\frac{1}{4}\right)^{-2}$

(iii) $(2^{-1}\times 4^{-1})\div 2^{-2}$ (iv) $(5^{-1}\times 2^{-1})\div 6^{-1}$

4. Simplify:

(i) $\left(4^{-1}\times 3^{-1}\right)^2$ (ii) $\left(5^{-1}\div 6^{-1}\right)^3$

(iii) $\left(2^{-1}+3^{-1}\right)^{-1}$ (iv) $\left(3^{-1}\times 4^{-1}\right)^{-1}\times 5^{-1}$

5. Simplify:

(i) $\left(3^2+2^2\right)\times\left(\frac{1}{2}\right)^3$ (ii) $\left(3^2-2^2\right)\times\left(\frac{2}{3}\right)^{-3}$

(iii) $\left[\left(\frac{1}{3}\right)^{-3}-\left(\frac{1}{2}\right)^{-3}\right]\div\left(\frac{1}{4}\right)^{-3}$ (iv) $\left(2^2+3^2-4^2\right)\div\left(\frac{3}{2}\right)^2$

6. By what number should 5^{-1} be multiplied so that the product may be equal to $(-7)^{-1}$?

7. By what number should $\left(\frac{1}{2}\right)^{-1}$ be multiplied so that the product may be equal to $\left(-\frac{4}{7}\right)^{-1}$?

8. By what number should $(-15)^{-1}$ be divided so that the quotient may be equal to $(-5)^{-1}$?

ANSWERS

1. (i) $\frac{1}{8}$ (ii) $\frac{1}{16}$ (iii) 9 (iv) 32 (v) $\frac{9}{4}$

2. (i) $\frac{7}{12}$ (ii) 5 (iii) 1 (iv) –1

3. (i) 9 (ii) 29 (iii) $\frac{1}{2}$ (iv) $\frac{3}{5}$

4. (i) $\frac{1}{144}$ (ii) $\frac{216}{125}$ (iii) $\frac{6}{5}$ (iv) $\frac{12}{5}$

5. (i) $\frac{13}{8}$ (ii) $\frac{135}{8}$ (iii) $\frac{19}{64}$ (iv) $\frac{-4}{3}$

6. $\frac{-5}{7}$ 7. $\frac{-7}{8}$ 8. $\frac{1}{3}$

2.3 DECIMAL NUMBER SYSTEM

In earlier classes, we have learnt how to express decimal numbers in the expanded form. For example, 5473.35 can be expressed in the following form:

$$5473.35 = 5\times1000 + 4\times100 + 7\times10 + 3\times1 + \frac{3}{10} + \frac{5}{100}$$

Similarly, we have

$$0.273 = 0\times1 + \frac{2}{10} + \frac{7}{100} + \frac{3}{1000}$$

$$15.235 = 1\times10 + 5\times1 + \frac{2}{10} + \frac{3}{100} + \frac{5}{1000}$$

Using exponents, we have

$$10000 = 10^4,\ 1000 = 10^3,\ 100 = 10^2,\ 10 = 10^1$$

$$1 = 10^0,\ 10^{-1} = \frac{1}{10},\ 10^{-2} = \frac{1}{100},\ 10^{-3} = \frac{1}{1000},\ 10^{-4} = \frac{1}{10000} \text{ etc.}$$

$$\therefore\quad 5473.35 = 5\times10^3 + 4\times10^2 + 7\times10^1 + 3\times10^0 + 3\times10^{-1} + 5\times10^{-2}$$

$$0.273 = 2\times10^{-1} + 7\times10^{-2} + 3\times10^{-3}$$

and, $15.235 = 1\times10^1 + 5\times10^0 + 2\times10^{-1} + 3\times10^{-2} + 5\times10^{-3}$

Thus, any decimal number can be written in expanded form by using integral exponents of 10.

2.4 LAWS OF INTEGRAL EXPONENTS

In this section, we shall discuss laws of integral exponents of rational numbers. In earlier class, we have learnt following laws of exponents of rational numbers when exponents are whole numbers.

If m, n are whole numbers and a, b are non-zero rational numbers, then

(i) $a^m \times a^n = a^{m+n}$ (First law)

(ii) $\frac{a^m}{a^n} = a^{m-n},\ m > n$ (Second law)

(iii) $(a^m)^n = a^{mn} = (a^n)^m$ (Third law)

(iv) $(ab)^n = a^n b^n$ (Fourth law)

(v) $\left(\frac{a}{b}\right)^n = \frac{a^n}{b^n}$ (Fifth law)

These laws also hold good for negative integral exponents. Let us discuss the proof of one of these laws for negative integral exponents. Other laws can be proved on the same lines.

FIRST LAW *If a is a non-zero rational number and m, n are integers, then*

$$a^m\, a^n = a^{m+n}$$

Proof: For positive integral exponents, we have studied in class VII. So, let us discuss the following cases:

CASE I *When m and n are negative integers:*

Since m and n are negative integers. Therefore, there exist positive integers p and q such that $m = -p$ and $n = -q$.

$$\therefore \quad a^m \times a^n = a^{-p} \times a^{-q}$$

$$= \frac{1}{a^p} \times \frac{1}{a^q} \qquad \left[\because a^{-k} = \frac{1}{a^k} \text{ for positive integer } k\right]$$

$$= \frac{1 \times 1}{a^p \times a^q} \qquad \text{[Using multiplication of rational numbers]}$$

$$= \frac{1}{a^{p+q}} \qquad \text{[Using first law of exponents for whole numbers]}$$

$$= a^{-(p+q)} \qquad \left[\because a^{-k} = \frac{1}{a^k}\right]$$

$$= a^{(-p)+(-q)}$$

$$= a^{m+n}$$

CASE II *When m is a postive integer and n is a negative integer.*

Since n is a negative integer. Therefore, there exists a positive integer p such that $n = -p$.

$$\therefore \quad a^m \times a^n = a^m \times a^{-p}$$

$$= a^m \times \frac{1}{a^p} \qquad \left[\because a^{-p} = \frac{1}{a^p}\right]$$

$$= \frac{a^m}{a^p}$$

$$= \begin{cases} a^{m-p} & \text{, if } m > p \\ \dfrac{1}{a^{p-m}} & \text{, if } m < p \end{cases} \qquad \left[\begin{array}{l}\text{Using second law of exponents} \\ \text{for whole numbers}\end{array}\right]$$

$$= \begin{cases} a^{m-p} & \text{, if } m > p \\ a^{-(p-m)} & \text{, if } m < p \end{cases} \qquad \left[\because \frac{1}{a^k} = a^{-k}\right]$$

$$= a^{m-p}$$

$$= a^{m+(-p)} = a^{m+n} \qquad [\because n = -p]$$

When m is a negative integer and n is a positive integer, we proceed as in case II.

Hence, $a^m \times a^n = a^{m+n}$ for all integers m, n.

SECOND LAW *If a is a non-zero rational number and m, n are integers, then*

$$a^m \div a^n = a^{m-n} \quad \text{or,} \quad \frac{a^m}{a^n} = a^{m-n}$$

Proof: Proceed as in first law.

THIRD LAW *If a is a non-zero rational number and m, n are integers, then*

$$(a^m)^n = a^{mn} = (a^n)^m$$

Proof: Proceed as in first law.

FOURTH LAW *If a, b are non-zero rational numbers and n is an integer, then*

$$(ab)^n = a^n b^n$$

Proof: Proceed as in first law.

FIFTH LAW *If a, b are non-zero rational numbers and n is an integer, then*

$$\left(\frac{a}{b}\right)^n = \frac{a^n}{b^n}$$

Proof: Proceed as in first law.

SIXTH LAW *If a, b are non-zero rational numbers and n is a positive integer, then*

$$\left(\frac{a}{b}\right)^{-n} = \left(\frac{b}{a}\right)^n$$

Proof: We have,

$$\left(\frac{a}{b}\right)^{-n} = \frac{1}{\left(\frac{a}{b}\right)^n} \qquad \left[\because x^{-n} = \frac{1}{x^n}\right]$$

$$\Rightarrow \quad \left(\frac{a}{b}\right)^{-n} = \frac{1}{\frac{a^n}{b^n}} \qquad \left[\because \left(\frac{a}{b}\right)^n = \frac{a^n}{b^n}\right]$$

$$\Rightarrow \quad \left(\frac{a}{b}\right)^{-n} = \frac{b^n}{a^n} = \left(\frac{b}{a}\right)^n$$

Let us now solve some examples by using the above laws of exponents.

ILLUSTRATIVE EXAMPLES

Example 1 Using the laws of exponents, simplify each of the following and express in exponential form:

(i) $3^7 \times 3^{-2}$ (ii) $2^{-7} \div 2^{-3}$ (iii) $(5^2)^{-3}$ (iv) $2^{-3} \times (-7)^{-3}$ (v) $\frac{3^{-5}}{4^{-5}}$

Solution Using laws of exponents, we have

(i) $3^7 \times 3^{-2} = 3^{7+(-2)} = 3^5$ $\quad [\because a^m \times a^n = a^{m+n}]$

(ii) $2^{-7} \div 2^{-3} = \frac{2^{-7}}{2^{-3}} = 2^{-7-(-3)}$

$= 2^{-7+3} = 2^{-4}$ $\quad \left[\because \frac{a^m}{a^n} = a^{m-n}\right]$

(iii) $(5^2)^{-3} = 5^{2 \times -3} = 5^{-6}$ $\quad [\because (a^m)^n = a^{mn}]$

(iv) $2^{-3} \times (-7)^{-3} = (2 \times (-7))^{-3}$ $\quad [\because a^n \times b^n = (ab)^n]$

$= (-14)^{-3}$

(v) $\frac{3^{-5}}{4^{-5}} = \left(\frac{3}{4}\right)^{-5}$ $\quad \left[\because \frac{a^n}{b^n} = \left(\frac{a}{b}\right)^n\right]$

Example 2 Using the laws of exponents simplify and express each of the following in exponential form with positive exponent:

(i) $(-4)^4 \times (-4)^{-10}$ (ii) $2^{-5} \div 2^2$ (iii) $3^{-4} \times 2^{-4}$

(iv) $\left(\frac{1}{2^3}\right)^2$ (v) $(3^{-7} \div 3^{-10}) \times 3^{-5}$ (vi) $(-3)^4 \times \left(\frac{5}{3}\right)^4$

Solution (i) We have,

$$(-4)^4 \times (-4)^{-10} = (-4)^{4+(-10)} \qquad [\because a^m \times a^n = a^{m+n}]$$

$$= (-4)^{-6}$$

$$= \frac{1}{(-4)^6} \qquad \left[\because a^{-n} = \frac{1}{a^n}\right]$$

$$= \frac{1^6}{(-4)^6} \qquad [\because 1^6 = 1]$$

$$= \left(\frac{1}{-4}\right)^6 \qquad \left[\because \frac{a^n}{b^n} = \left(\frac{a}{b}\right)^n\right]$$

$$= \left(\frac{-1}{4}\right)^6 \qquad \left[\because \frac{1}{-4} = \frac{-1}{4}\right]$$

(ii) We have,

$$2^{-5} \div 2^2 = \frac{2^{-5}}{2^2} = 2^{-5-2} \qquad \left[\because \frac{a^m}{a^n} = a^{m-n}\right]$$

$$= 2^{-7} = \frac{1}{2^7} \qquad \left[\because a^{-n} = \frac{1}{a^n}\right]$$

$$= \frac{1^7}{2^7} = \left(\frac{1}{2}\right)^7$$

(iii) We have,

$$3^{-4} \times 2^{-4} = (3 \times 2)^{-4} \qquad [\because a^n \times b^n = (ab)^n]$$

$$= 6^{-4}$$

$$= \frac{1}{6^4} \qquad \left[\because a^{-n} = \frac{1}{a^n}\right]$$

$$= \frac{1^4}{6^4} \qquad [\because 1^4 = 1]$$

$$= \left(\frac{1}{6}\right)^4 \qquad \left[\because \frac{a^n}{b^n} = \left(\frac{a}{b}\right)^n\right]$$

(iv) We have,

$$\left(\frac{1}{2^3}\right)^2 = \left(\frac{1^3}{2^3}\right)^2 = \left\{\left(\frac{1}{2}\right)^3\right\}^2 = \left(\frac{1}{2}\right)^{3 \times 2} = \left(\frac{1}{2}\right)^6$$

(v) We have,

$$(3^{-7} \div 3^{-10}) \times 3^{-5} = \left(\frac{3^{-7}}{3^{-10}}\right) \times 3^{-5} = 3^{-7-(-10)} \times 3^{-5}$$

$$= 3^{-7+10} \times 3^{-5} = 3^3 \times 3^{-5} = 3^{3+(-5)} = 3^{-2}$$

$$= \frac{1}{3^2} = \frac{1^2}{3^2} = \left(\frac{1}{3}\right)^2$$

(vi) We have,

$$(-3)^4 \times \left(\frac{5}{3}\right)^4 = (-1 \times 3)^4 \times \left(\frac{5}{3}\right)^4 \qquad [\because -3 = -1 \times 3]$$

$$= \left\{(-1)^4 \times 3^4\right\} \times \frac{5^4}{3^4} \qquad \left[\because (ab)^n = a^n b^n \text{ and } \left(\frac{a}{b}\right)^n = \frac{a^n}{b^n}\right]$$

$$= (1 \times 3^4) \times \frac{5^4}{3^4} \qquad \left[\because (-1)^4 = 1\right]$$

$$= 3^4 \times \frac{5^4}{3^4} = 3^{4-4} \times 5^4 = 3^0 \times 5^4 = 1 \times 5^4 = 5^4$$

Example 3 Simplify and write the answer in the exponential form:

(i) $\left(2^5 \div 2^8\right)^5 \times 2^{-5}$ (ii) $(-4)^3 \times (5)^{-3} \times (-5)^{-3}$ (iii) $\frac{1}{8} \times 3^{-3}$

Solution (i) We have,

$$\left(2^5 \div 2^8\right)^5 \times 2^{-5}$$

$$= \left(\frac{2^5}{2^8}\right)^5 \times 2^{-5} = \left(2^{5-8}\right)^5 \times 2^{-5} = \left(2^{-3}\right)^5 \times 2^{-5} = 2^{-3 \times 5} \times 2^{-5}$$

$$= 2^{-15} \times 2^{-5} = 2^{-15-5} = 2^{-20}$$

(ii) We have,

$$(-4)^{-3} \times 5^{-3} \times (-5)^{-3}$$

$$= \{-4 \times 5 \times (-5)\}^{-3} \qquad \left[\because a^n \times b^n \times c^n = (abc)^n\right]$$

$$= (100)^{-3} = \left(10^2\right)^{-3} = 10^{2 \times -3} = 10^{-6}$$

(iii) We have,

$$\frac{1}{8} \times 3^{-3} = \frac{1}{2^3} \times 3^{-3} = 2^{-3} \times 3^{-3} = (2 \times 3)^{-3} = 6^{-3}$$

Example 4 Simplify each of the following:

(i) $\left[\left\{\left(\frac{-1}{5}\right)^{-2}\right\}^2\right]^{-1}$ (ii) $\left\{\left(\frac{1}{3}\right)^{-2} - \left(\frac{1}{2}\right)^{-3}\right\} \div \left(\frac{1}{4}\right)^{-2}$

Solution (i) We have,

$$\left[\left\{\left(\frac{-1}{5}\right)^{-2}\right\}^{2}\right]^{-1} = \left\{\left(\frac{-1}{5}\right)^{-2}\right\}^{2\times -1} \qquad [\because (a^m)^n = a^{mn}]$$

$$= \left\{\left(\frac{-1}{5}\right)^{-2}\right\}^{-2} = \left(\frac{-1}{5}\right)^{(-2)\times(-2)}$$

$$= \left(\frac{-1}{5}\right)^{4} = \frac{(-1)^4}{5^4} = \frac{1}{625}$$

(ii) We have,

$$\left\{\left(\frac{1}{3}\right)^{-2} - \left(\frac{1}{2}\right)^{-3}\right\} \div \left(\frac{1}{4}\right)^{-2}$$

$$\left\{\left(\frac{3}{1}\right)^{2} - \left(\frac{2}{1}\right)^{3}\right\} \div \left(\frac{4}{1}\right)^{2} \qquad \left[\because \left(\frac{a}{b}\right)^{-n} = \left(\frac{b}{a}\right)^{n}\right]$$

$$= \left\{\frac{3^2}{1^2} - \frac{2^3}{1^3}\right\} \div \frac{4^2}{1^2} = (9-8) \div 16 = 1 \div 16 = \frac{1}{16}$$

Example 5 Simplify:

(i) $\left(\frac{5}{8}\right)^{-7} \times \left(\frac{8}{5}\right)^{-5}$ (ii) $\left(\frac{-2}{3}\right)^{-2} \times \left(\frac{4}{5}\right)^{-3}$

(iii) $\left(\frac{3}{4}\right)^{-4} \div \left(\frac{3}{2}\right)^{-3}$ (iv) $\left(\frac{3}{7}\right)^{-2} \times \left(\frac{7}{6}\right)^{-3}$

Solution (i) We have,

$$\left(\frac{5}{8}\right)^{-7} \times \left(\frac{8}{5}\right)^{-5} = \frac{5^{-7}}{8^{-7}} \times \frac{8^{-5}}{5^{-5}} = \frac{5^{-7}}{5^{-5}} \times \frac{8^{-5}}{8^{-7}} = 5^{-7-(-5)} \times 8^{-5-(-7)}$$

$$= 5^{-7+5} \times 8^{-5+7} = 5^{-2} \times 8^{2} = \frac{8^2}{5^2} = \frac{64}{25}$$

(ii) We have,

$$\left(\frac{-2}{3}\right)^{-2} \times \left(\frac{4}{5}\right)^{-3} = \frac{(-2)^{-2}}{3^{-2}} \times \frac{4^{-3}}{5^{-3}} = \frac{3^2}{(-2)^2} \times \frac{5^3}{4^3} = \frac{9}{4} \times \frac{125}{64} = \frac{9\times 125}{4\times 64} = \frac{1125}{256}$$

(iii) We have,

$$\left(\frac{3}{4}\right)^{-4} \div \left(\frac{3}{2}\right)^{-3} = \left(\frac{3}{4}\right)^{-4} \times \frac{1}{\left(\frac{3}{2}\right)^{-3}} = \left(\frac{3}{4}\right)^{-4} \times \left(\frac{3}{2}\right)^{3} = \frac{3^{-4}}{4^{-4}} \times \frac{3^3}{2^3}$$

$$= \frac{3^{-4} \times 3^3}{(2^2)^{-4} \times 2^3} = \frac{3^{-4} \times 3^3}{2^{-8} \times 2^3} = \frac{3^{-4+3}}{2^{-8+3}} = \frac{3^{-1}}{2^{-5}} = \frac{2^5}{3^1} = \frac{32}{3}$$

(iv) We have,

$$\left(\frac{3}{7}\right)^{-2}\times\left(\frac{7}{6}\right)^{-3}=\frac{3^{-2}}{7^{-2}}\times\frac{7^{-3}}{6^{-3}} \qquad \left[\because \left(\frac{a}{b}\right)^n=\frac{a^n}{b^n}\right]$$

$$=\frac{3^{-2}}{7^{-2}}\times\frac{7^{-3}}{(2\times3)^{-3}}$$

$$=\frac{3^{-2}}{7^{-2}}\times\frac{7^{-3}}{2^{-3}\times3^{-3}} \qquad \left[\because (ab)^n=a^n\,b^n\right]$$

$$=\frac{3^{-2}}{3^{-3}}\times\frac{7^{-3}}{7^{-2}}\times\frac{1}{2^{-3}}$$

$$=3^{-2+3}\times7^{-3+2}\times2^3$$

$$=3\times7^{-1}\times2^3=3\times\frac{1}{7}\times8=\frac{24}{7}$$

Example 6 Evaluate: $\dfrac{8^{-1}\times5^3}{2^{-4}}$

Solution We have,

$$\frac{8^{-1}\times5^3}{2^{-4}}=\frac{(2^3)^{-1}\times5^3}{2^{-4}}=\frac{2^{3\times-1}\times5^3}{2^{-4}}=\frac{2^{-3}\times5^3}{2^{-4}}=2^{-3+4}\times5^3$$

$$=2^1\times5^3=2\times125=250$$

Example 7 Simplify:

(i) $\dfrac{25\times a^{-4}}{5^{-3}\times10\times a^{-8}}$ (ii) $\dfrac{3^{-5}\times10^{-5}\times125}{5^{-7}\times6^{-5}}$

Solution (i) We have,

$$\frac{25\times a^{-4}}{5^{-3}\times10\times a^{-8}}=\frac{5^2\times a^{-4}}{5^{-3}\times(2\times5)\times a^{-8}}=\frac{5^2\times a^{-4}}{5^{-3+1}\times2\times a^{-8}}$$

$$=\frac{5^2\times a^{-4}}{5^{-2}\times2\times a^{-8}}=\frac{5^{2-(-2)}\times a^{-4+8}}{2}=\frac{5^4\times a^4}{2}=\frac{5^4}{2}\times a^4=\frac{625}{2}a^4$$

(ii) We have,

$$\frac{3^{-5}\times10^{-5}\times125}{5^{-7}\times6^{-5}}=\frac{3^{-5}\times(2\times5)^{-5}\times5^3}{5^{-7}\times(2\times3)^{-5}}$$

$$=\frac{3^{-5}\times2^{-5}\times5^{-5}\times5^3}{5^{-7}\times2^{-5}\times3^{-5}}$$

$$=3^{-5-(-5)}\times2^{-5-(-5)}\times5^{-5+3-(-7)}$$

$$=3^0\times2^0\times5^{-5+3+7}=1\times1\times5^5=5^5$$

Example 8 By what number should $(-4)^{-2}$ be multiplied so that the product may be equal to 10^{-2}?

Solution Let $(-4)^{-2}$ be multiplied by x to get 10^{-2}. Then,

$$x \times (-4)^{-2} = 10^{-2}$$

$$\Rightarrow \quad x = 10^{-2} \div (-4)^{-2}$$

$$\Rightarrow \quad x = 10^{-2} \times \frac{1}{(-4)^{-2}}$$

$$\Rightarrow \quad x = \frac{10^{-2}}{(-4)^{-2}}$$

$$\Rightarrow \quad x = \frac{(-4)^2}{10^2} = \frac{16}{100} = \frac{4}{25}$$

Hence, required number is $\frac{4}{25}$.

Example 9 By what number should $(-12)^{-1}$ be divided so that the quotient may be $\left(\frac{2}{3}\right)^{-1}$?

Solution Let the required number be x. Then,

$$(-12)^{-1} \div x = \left(\frac{2}{3}\right)^{-1}$$

$$\Rightarrow \quad \frac{(-12)^{-1}}{x} = \left(\frac{2}{3}\right)^{-1}$$

$$\Rightarrow \quad x = (-12)^{-1} \div \left(\frac{2}{3}\right)^{-1}$$

$$\Rightarrow \quad x = \frac{1}{-12} \div \left(\frac{3}{2}\right) \qquad \left[\because a^{-1} = \frac{1}{a} \text{ and } \left(\frac{a}{b}\right)^{-1} = \frac{b}{a}\right]$$

$$\Rightarrow \quad x = \frac{1}{-12} \times \frac{2}{3} = \frac{1}{-18} = \frac{-1}{18}$$

Example 10 By what number should $\left(\frac{-3}{2}\right)^{-3}$ be divided so that the quotient may be $\left(\frac{4}{27}\right)^{-2}$?

Solution Let the required number be x. Then,

$$\left(\frac{-3}{2}\right)^{-3} \div x = \left(\frac{4}{27}\right)^{-2}$$

$$\Rightarrow \quad \left(\frac{-3}{2}\right)^{-3} \times \frac{1}{x} = \left(\frac{4}{27}\right)^{-2}$$

$$\Rightarrow \quad x = \left(\frac{-3}{2}\right)^{-3} \div \left(\frac{4}{27}\right)^{-2}$$

$$\Rightarrow \quad x = \left(\frac{2}{-3}\right)^{3} \div \left(\frac{27}{4}\right)^{2} \qquad \left[\because \left(\frac{a}{b}\right)^{-n} = \left(\frac{b}{a}\right)^{n}\right]$$

$$\Rightarrow \quad x = \left(\frac{2}{-3}\right)^{3} \times \frac{1}{\left(\frac{27}{4}\right)^{2}}$$

$$\Rightarrow \quad x = \frac{2^3}{(-3)^3} \times \frac{1}{\frac{27^2}{4^2}}$$

$$\Rightarrow \quad x = \frac{8}{-27} \times \frac{4^2}{27^2} = \frac{-8}{27} \times \frac{4^2}{27^2} = \frac{-2 \times 4^3}{27^3} = -2 \times \left(\frac{4}{27}\right)^{3}$$

Example 11 Find x so that $\left(\frac{5}{3}\right)^{-5} \times \left(\frac{5}{3}\right)^{-11} = \left(\frac{5}{3}\right)^{8x}$

Solution We have,

$$\left(\frac{5}{3}\right)^{-5} \times \left(\frac{5}{3}\right)^{-11} = \left(\frac{5}{3}\right)^{8x}$$

$$\Rightarrow \quad \left(\frac{5}{3}\right)^{-5-11} = \left(\frac{5}{3}\right)^{8x}$$

$$\Rightarrow \quad \left(\frac{5}{3}\right)^{-16} = \left(\frac{5}{3}\right)^{8x}$$

$$\Rightarrow \quad 8x = -16$$

$$\Rightarrow \quad x = -\frac{16}{8} = -2$$

Example 12 Find m so that $\left(\frac{2}{9}\right)^{3} \times \left(\frac{2}{9}\right)^{-6} = \left(\frac{2}{9}\right)^{2m-1}$

Solution We have,

$$\left(\frac{2}{9}\right)^{3} \times \left(\frac{2}{9}\right)^{-6} = \left(\frac{2}{9}\right)^{2m-1}$$

$$\Rightarrow \quad \left(\frac{2}{9}\right)^{3-6} = \left(\frac{2}{9}\right)^{2m-1}$$

$$\Rightarrow \quad \left(\frac{2}{9}\right)^{-3} = \left(\frac{2}{9}\right)^{2m-1}$$

$\Rightarrow \quad 2m - 1 = -3$

$\Rightarrow \quad 2m = -3 + 1$

$\Rightarrow \quad 2m = -2$

$\Rightarrow \quad m = -1$

Example 13 If $x = \left(\frac{3}{2}\right)^2 \times \left(\frac{2}{3}\right)^{-4}$, find the value of x^{-2}.

Solution We have,

$$x = \left(\frac{3}{2}\right)^2 \times \left(\frac{2}{3}\right)^{-4}$$

$$\Rightarrow \quad x = \left(\frac{3}{2}\right)^2 \times \left(\frac{3}{2}\right)^4 \qquad \left[\because \left(\frac{a}{b}\right)^{-n} = \left(\frac{b}{a}\right)^n\right]$$

$$\Rightarrow \quad x = \left(\frac{3}{2}\right)^{2+4} = \left(\frac{3}{2}\right)^6$$

$$\therefore \quad x^{-2} = \left\{\left(\frac{3}{2}\right)^6\right\}^{-2} = \left(\frac{3}{2}\right)^{6\times -2} = \left(\frac{3}{2}\right)^{-12} = \left(\frac{2}{3}\right)^{12}$$

EXERCISE 2.2

1. Write each of the following in exponential form:

   (i) $\left(\frac{3}{2}\right)^{-1} \times \left(\frac{3}{2}\right)^{-1} \times \left(\frac{3}{2}\right)^{-1} \times \left(\frac{3}{2}\right)^{-1}$ (ii) $\left(\frac{2}{5}\right)^{-2} \times \left(\frac{2}{5}\right)^{-2} \times \left(\frac{2}{5}\right)^{-2}$

2. Evaluate:

   (i) 5^{-2} (ii) $(-3)^{-2}$ (iii) $\left(\frac{1}{3}\right)^{-4}$ (iv) $\left(\frac{-1}{2}\right)^{-1}$

3. Express each of the following as a rational number in the form $\frac{p}{q}$:

   (i) 6^{-1} (ii) $(-7)^{-1}$ (iii) $\left(\frac{1}{4}\right)^{-1}$ (iv) $(-4)^{-1} \times \left(\frac{-3}{2}\right)^{-1}$

   (v) $\left(\frac{3}{5}\right)^{-1} \times \left(\frac{5}{2}\right)^{-1}$

4. Simplify:

   (i) $\{4^{-1} \times 3^{-1}\}^2$ (ii) $\{5^{-1} \div 6^{-1}\}^3$ (iii) $(2^{-1} + 3^{-1})^{-1}$ (iv) $\{3^{-1} \times 4^{-1}\}^{-1} \times 5^{-1}$

   (v) $(4^{-1} - 5^{-1}) \div 3^{-1}$

5. Express each of the following rational numbers with a negative exponent:

   (i) $\left(\frac{1}{4}\right)^3$ (ii) 3^5 (iii) $\left(\frac{3}{5}\right)^4$ (iv) $\left\{\left(\frac{3}{2}\right)^4\right\}^{-3}$

   (v) $\left\{\left(\frac{7}{3}\right)^4\right\}^{-3}$

6. Express each of the following rational numbers with a positive exponent:

(i) $\left(\frac{3}{4}\right)^{-2}$ (ii) $\left(\frac{5}{4}\right)^{-3}$ (iii) $4^3 \times 4^{-9}$ (iv) $\left\{\left(\frac{4}{3}\right)^{-3}\right\}^{-4}$

(v) $\left\{\left(\frac{3}{2}\right)^{4}\right\}^{-2}$

7. Simplify:

(i) $\left\{\left(\frac{1}{3}\right)^{-3} - \left(\frac{1}{2}\right)^{-3}\right\} \div \left(\frac{1}{4}\right)^{-3}$ (ii) $\left(3^2 - 2^2\right) \times \left(\frac{2}{3}\right)^{-3}$

(iii) $\left\{\left(\frac{1}{2}\right)^{-1} \times (-4)^{-1}\right\}^{-1}$ (iv) $\left[\left\{\left(\frac{-1}{4}\right)^{2}\right\}^{-2}\right]^{-1}$

(v) $\left\{\left(\frac{2}{3}\right)^{2}\right\}^{3} \times \left(\frac{1}{3}\right)^{-4} \times 3^{-1} \times 6^{-1}$

8. By what number should 5^{-1} be multiplied so that the product may be equal to $(-7)^{-1}$?

9. By what number should $\left(\frac{1}{2}\right)^{-1}$ be multiplied so that the product may be equal to $\left(\frac{-4}{7}\right)^{-1}$?

10. By what number should $(-15)^{-1}$ be divided so that the quotient may be equal to $(-5)^{-1}$?

11. By what number should $\left(\frac{5}{3}\right)^{-2}$ be multiplied so that the product may be $\left(\frac{7}{3}\right)^{-1}$?

12. Find x, if

(i) $\left(\frac{1}{4}\right)^{-4} \times \left(\frac{1}{4}\right)^{-8} = \left(\frac{1}{4}\right)^{-4x}$ (ii) $\left(\frac{-1}{2}\right)^{-19} \div \left(\frac{-1}{2}\right)^{8} = \left(\frac{-1}{2}\right)^{-2x+1}$

(iii) $\left(\frac{3}{2}\right)^{-3} \times \left(\frac{3}{2}\right)^{5} = \left(\frac{3}{2}\right)^{2x+1}$ (iv) $\left(\frac{2}{5}\right)^{-3} \times \left(\frac{2}{5}\right)^{15} = \left(\frac{2}{5}\right)^{2+3x}$

(v) $\left(\frac{5}{4}\right)^{-x} \div \left(\frac{5}{4}\right)^{-4} = \left(\frac{5}{4}\right)^{5}$ (vi) $\left(\frac{8}{3}\right)^{2x+1} \times \left(\frac{8}{3}\right)^{5} = \left(\frac{8}{3}\right)^{x+2}$

13. (i) If $x = \left(\frac{3}{2}\right)^{2} \times \left(\frac{2}{3}\right)^{-4}$, find the value of x^{-2}.

(ii) If $x = \left(\frac{4}{5}\right)^{-2} \div \left(\frac{1}{4}\right)^{2}$, find the value of x^{-1}.

14. Find the value of x for which $5^{2x} \div 5^{-3} = 5^5$.

ANSWERS

1. (i) $\left(\frac{3}{2}\right)^{-4}$ (ii) $\left(\frac{2}{5}\right)^{-6}$
2. (i) $\frac{1}{25}$ (ii) $\frac{1}{9}$ (iii) 81 (iv) −2
3. (i) $\frac{1}{6}$ (ii) $\frac{-1}{7}$ (iii) 4 (iv) $\frac{1}{6}$ (v) $\frac{2}{3}$
4. (i) $\frac{1}{144}$ (ii) $\frac{216}{125}$ (iii) $\frac{6}{5}$ (iv) $\frac{12}{5}$ (v) $\frac{3}{20}$
5. (i) 4^{-3} (ii) $\left(\frac{1}{3}\right)^{-5}$ (iii) $\left(\frac{5}{3}\right)^{-4}$ (iv) $\left(\frac{3}{2}\right)^{-12}$ (v) $\left(\frac{7}{3}\right)^{-12}$
6. (i) $\left(\frac{4}{3}\right)^{2}$ (ii) $\left(\frac{4}{5}\right)^{3}$ (iii) $\left(\frac{1}{4}\right)^{6}$ (iv) $\left(\frac{4}{3}\right)^{12}$ (v) $\left(\frac{2}{3}\right)^{8}$
7. (i) $\frac{19}{64}$ (ii) $\frac{135}{8}$ (iii) −2 (iv) $\frac{1}{256}$ (v) $\frac{32}{81}$

2.5 USE OF EXPONENTS TO EXPRESS SMALL NUMBERS IN STANDARD FORM

In the previous class, we have learnt how to express very large numbers in standard form by using exponents of 10. Let us now see how can we write very small numbers in standard form. We may use following steps to do so:

Step I *Obtain the number and see whether the number is between 1 and 10 or it is less than 1.*

Step II *If the number is between 1 and 10, then write it as the product of the number itself and 10^0.*

Step III *If the number is less than one, then move the decimal point to the right so that there is just one digit on the left side of the decimal point. Write the given number as the product of the number so obtained and 10^{-n}, where n is the number of places the decimal point has been moved to the right. The number so obtained is the standard form of the given number.*

Following examples will illustrate the above procedure.

ILLUSTRATIVE EXAMPLES

Example 1 Write the following numbers in standard form:

(i) 0.4579 (ii) 0.000007 (iii) 0.000000564 (iv) 0.0000021

(v) 216000000 (vi) 0.0000529×10^4 (vii) 9573×10^{-4}

Solution (i) To express 0.4579 in standard form the decimal point is moved through one place only to the right so that there is just one digit on the left of the decimal point.

$\therefore$ $0.4579 = 4.579 \times 10^{-1}$ is in the standard form.

(ii) $0.000007 = 7 \times 10^{-6}$ [$\because$ The decimal point is moved 6 places to the right]

(iiii) $0.000000564 = 5.64 \times 10^{-7}$ [∵ The decimal point is moved 7 places to the right]

(iv) $0.0000021 = 2.1 \times 10^{-6}$ [∵ The decimal point is moved 6 places to the right]

(v) $216000000 = 2.16 \times 10^{8}$ [∵ The decimal point is moved 8 places to the left]

(vi) $0.0000529 \times 10^4 = 5.29 \times 10^{-5} \times 10^4 = 5.29 \times 10^{-5+4} = 5.29 \times 10^{-1}$

(vii) $9573 \times 10^{-4} = 9.573 \times 10^3 \times 10^{-4} = 9.573 \times 10^{3+(-4)} = 9.573 \times 10^{-1}$

Example 2 Express the following numbers in usual form:

(i) 3.52×10^5 (ii) 7.54×10^{-4} (iii) 3×10^{-5}

Solution We have,

(i) $3.52 \times 10^5 = 3.52 \times 100000 = 352000$

(ii) $7.54 \times 10^{-4} = \dfrac{7.54}{10^4} = \dfrac{7.54}{10000} = 0.000754$

(iii) $3 \times 10^{-5} = \dfrac{3}{10^5} = \dfrac{3}{100000} = 0.00003$

Example 3 Express the number appearing in the following statements in standard form:

(i) 1 micron is equal to $\dfrac{1}{1000000}$ metre.

(ii) Charge of an electron is 0.0000000000000000016 coloumbs.

(iii) Size of a bacteria is 0.0000005 metre.

(iv) Size of a plant cell is 0.00001275 metre.

(v) Thickness of a normal paper is 0.07 mm.

Solution (i) 1 micron is equal to $\dfrac{1}{1000000}$ metre = 10^{-6} metre

(ii) Charge of an electron is 0.0000000000000000016 coloumbs = 1.6×10^{-18} columbs

(iii) Size of a bacteria is 0.0000005 metre = 5×10^{-7} metre

(iv) Size of a plant cell is 0.00001275 metre = 1.275×10^{-5} metre

(v) The thickness of a normal paper is 0.07 mm = 7×10^{-2} mm

Example 4 If the diameters of the Sun and the Earth are 1.4×10^9 metres and 1.275×10^7 metres respectively. Compare these two.

Solution We have,

$$\frac{\text{Dia. of the Sun}}{\text{Dia. of the Earth}} = \frac{1.4 \times 10^9}{1.275 \times 10^7} = \frac{1.4 \times 10^2 \times 10^7}{1.275 \times 10^7}$$

$$= \frac{1.4}{1.275} \times 100 = \frac{1.4}{1.3} \times 100 \simeq 100 \qquad \left[\because 1.275 \simeq 1.3 \text{ and } \frac{1.4}{1.3} \simeq 1\right]$$

So, the diameter of the Sun is about 100 times the diameter of the Earth.

Example 5 The size of a red blood cell is 0.000007 m and the size of a plant cell is 0.00001275 m. Compare thses two.

Solution We have,

Size of red blood cell = 0.000007 m = 7×10^{-6} m

Size of plant cell = 0.00001275 = 1.275×10^{-5} m

$$\therefore \quad \frac{\text{Size of red blood cell}}{\text{Size of plant cell}} = \frac{7 \times 10^{-6}}{1.275 \times 10^{-5}} = \frac{7 \times 10^{-6+5}}{1.275} = \frac{7 \times 10^{-1}}{1.275}$$

$$= \frac{0.7}{1.275} \simeq \frac{0.7}{1.3} \simeq \frac{1}{2}$$

So, a red blood cell is approximately half of a plant cell in size.

EXERCISE 2.3

1. Express the following numbers in standard form:
   (i) 602000000000000000 (ii) 0.000000000000942
   (iii) 0.00000000085 (iv) 846×10^7
   (v) 3759×10^{-4} (vi) 0.00072984
   (vii) 0.000437×10^4 (viii) $4 \div 100000$

2. Write the following numbers in the usual form:
   (i) 4.83×10^7 (ii) 3.02×10^{-6}
   (iii) 4.5×10^4 (iv) 3×10^{-8}
   (v) 1.0001×10^9 (vi) 5.8×10^2
   (vii) 3.61492×10^6 (viii) 3.25×10^{-7}

ANSWERS

1. (i) 6.02×10^{15} (ii) 9.42×10^{-12} (iii) 8.5×10^{-10} (iv) 8.46×10^9 (v) 3.759×10^{-1}
   (vi) 7.2984×10^{-4} (vii) 4.37 (viii) 4×10^{-5}
2. (i) 48300000 (ii) 0.00000302 (iii) 45000 (iv) 0.00000003 (v) 1000100000
   (vi) 580 (vii) 3614920 (viii) 0.000000325

EXERCISE (MCQs)

Choose the correct alternative in each of the following:

1. Square of $\left(\frac{-2}{3}\right)$ is

   (a) $-\frac{2}{3}$ (b) $\frac{2}{3}$ (c) $-\frac{4}{9}$ (d) $\frac{4}{9}$

2. Cube of $\frac{-1}{2}$ is

   (a) $\frac{1}{8}$ (b) $\frac{1}{16}$ (c) $-\frac{1}{8}$ (d) $\frac{-1}{16}$

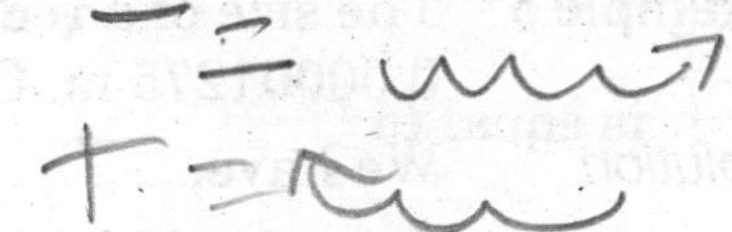

3. Which of the following is not equal to $\left(\frac{-3}{5}\right)^4$?

(a) $\frac{(-3)^4}{5^4}$ (b) $\frac{3^4}{(-5)^4}$ (c) $-\frac{3^4}{5^4}$ (d) $\frac{-3}{5}\times\frac{-3}{5}\times\frac{-3}{5}\times\frac{-3}{5}$

4. Which of the following is not reciprocal of $\left(\frac{2}{3}\right)^4$?

(a) $\left(\frac{3}{2}\right)^4$ (b) $\left(\frac{2}{3}\right)^{-4}$ (c) $\left(\frac{3}{2}\right)^{-4}$ (d) $\frac{3^4}{2^4}$

5. Which of the following numbers is not equal to $\frac{-8}{27}$?

(a) $\left(\frac{2}{3}\right)^{-3}$ (b) $-\left(\frac{2}{3}\right)^3$ (c) $\left(-\frac{2}{3}\right)^3$ (d) $\left(\frac{-2}{3}\right)\times\left(\frac{-2}{3}\right)\times\left(\frac{-2}{3}\right)$

6. $\left(\frac{2}{3}\right)^{-5}$ is equal to

(a) $\left(\frac{-2}{3}\right)^5$ (b) $\left(\frac{3}{2}\right)^5$ (c) $\frac{2x-5}{3}$ (d) $\frac{2}{3\times5}$

7. $\left(\frac{-1}{2}\right)^5\times\left(\frac{-1}{2}\right)^3$ is equal to

(a) $\left(\frac{-1}{2}\right)^8$ (b) $-\left(\frac{1}{2}\right)^8$ (c) $\left(\frac{1}{4}\right)^8$ (d) $\left(-\frac{1}{2}\right)^{15}$

8. $\left(\frac{-1}{5}\right)^3\div\left(\frac{-1}{5}\right)^8$ is equal to

(a) $\left(-\frac{1}{5}\right)^5$ (b) $\left(-\frac{1}{5}\right)^{11}$ (c) $(-5)^5$ (d) $\left(\frac{1}{5}\right)^5$

9. $\left(\frac{-2}{5}\right)^7\div\left(\frac{-2}{5}\right)^5$ is equal to

(a) $\frac{4}{25}$ (b) $\frac{-4}{25}$ (c) $\left(\frac{-2}{5}\right)^{12}$ (d) $\frac{25}{4}$

10. $\left\{\left(\frac{1}{3}\right)^2\right\}^4$ is equal to

(a) $\left(\frac{1}{3}\right)^6$ (b) $\left(\frac{1}{3}\right)^8$ (c) $\left(\frac{1}{3}\right)^{24}$ (d) $\left(\frac{1}{3}\right)^{16}$

11. $\left(\frac{1}{5}\right)^0$ is equal to

(a) 0 (b) $\frac{1}{5}$ (c) 1 (d) 5

12. $\left(\frac{-3}{2}\right)^{-1}$ is equal to

(a) $\frac{2}{3}$ (b) $-\frac{2}{3}$ (c) $\frac{3}{2}$ (d) none of these

13. $\left(\frac{2}{3}\right)^{-5} \times \left(\frac{5}{7}\right)^{-5}$ is equal to

(a) $\left(\frac{2}{3}\times\frac{5}{7}\right)^{-10}$ (b) $\left(\frac{2}{3}\times\frac{5}{7}\right)^{-5}$ (c) $\left(\frac{2}{3}\times\frac{5}{7}\right)^{25}$ (d) $\left(\frac{2}{3}\times\frac{5}{7}\right)^{-25}$

14. $\left(\frac{3}{4}\right)^5 \div \left(\frac{5}{3}\right)^5$ is equal to

(a) $\left(\frac{3}{4}\div\frac{5}{3}\right)^5$ (b) $\left(\frac{3}{4}\div\frac{5}{3}\right)^1$ (c) $\left(\frac{3}{4}\div\frac{5}{3}\right)^0$ (d) $\left(\frac{3}{4}\div\frac{5}{3}\right)^{10}$

15. For any two non-zero rational numbers a and b, $a^4 \div b^4$ is equal to

(a) $(a \div b)^1$ (b) $(a \div b)^0$ (c) $(a \div b)^4$ (d) $(a \div b)^8$

16. For any two rational numbers a and b, $a^5 \times b^5$ *is equal to*

(a) $(a\times b)^0$ (b) $(a\times b)^{10}$ (c) $(a\times b)^5$ (d) $(a\times b)^{25}$

17. For a non-zero rational number a, $a^7 \div a^{12}$ is equal to

(a) a^5 (b) a^{-19} (c) a^{-5} (d) a^{19}

18. For a non zero rational number a, $(a^3)^{-2}$ is equal to

(a) a^6 (b) a^{-6} (c) a^{-9} (d) a^1

ANSWERS

1. (d)	2. (c)	3. (c)	4. (c)	5. (a)	6. (b)	7. (a)
8. (c)	9. (a)	10. (b)	11. (c)	12. (b)	13. (b)	14. (a)
15. (c)	16. (c)	17. (c)	18. (b)			

THINGS TO REMEMBER

1. *If a is a non-zero rational number and n is a positive integer, then*

   (i) $a^n = a \times a \times a \times \cdots \times a$ (*n times*)

   (ii) $a^{-n} = \dfrac{1}{a^n}$

   (iii) $a^0 = 1$

2. *If a, b are non-zero rational numbers and m, n are integers, then*

   (i) $a^m \times a^n = a^{m+n}$

   (ii) $\dfrac{a^m}{a^n} = a^{m-n}$

   (iii) $(a^m)^n = a^{mn} = (a^n)^m$

   (iv) $\left(\dfrac{a}{b}\right)^n = \dfrac{a^n}{b^n}$

   (v) $(ab)^n = a^n \times b^n$

3. *If* $\dfrac{a}{b}$ *is any non-zero rational number and n is a positive integer, then*

$$\left(\frac{a}{b}\right)^{-n} = \left(\frac{b}{a}\right)^n = \frac{b^n}{a^n}$$

3

SQUARES AND SQUARE ROOTS

3.1 INTRODUCTION

In earlier classes, we have learnt about integral exponents of rational numbers. When the exponent of a natural number is 2, the number obtained is called a square number or a perfect square. For example, $2^2, 3^2, 9^2$ etc. are the square numbers or perfect squares. In this chapter, we will discuss various techniques to determine whether a given natural number is a perfect square or not. These techniques are suggested by the properties and patterns followed by square numbers. So, we will first study some properties and patterns of square numbers. These properties and patterns will also be used to find the squares of two and three digit numbers by using some short-cuts. In the end of the chapter, we will study various methods for finding the square roots of square numbers. We will also try to find the square roots of numbers which are not perfect squares.

3.2 SQUARE OF A NUMBER AND SQUARE NUMBERS

The square of a number is that number raised to the power 2.

Thus, if 'a' is a number, then the square of a is written as a^2 and is given by

$$a^2 = a \times a$$

That is, the square of a number is obtained by multiplying it by itself

If $a \times a = b$ i.e. $a^2 = b$, then we say that the square of number a is number b or the number b is the square of number a.

For example,

$2^2 = 2 \times 2 = 4$, so we say that the square of 2 is 4

$3^2 = 3 \times 3 = 9$, so we say that the square of 3 is 9

$12^2 = 12 \times 12 = 144$, so we say that the square of 12 is 144 etc.

The following table contains the squares of first thirty natural numbers. Students are advised to commit these to memory.

Table 3.1

Number	*Square*	*Number*	*Square*
1	$1^2 = 1 \times 1 = 1$	16	$16^2 = 16 \times 16 = 256$
2	$2^2 = 2 \times 2 = 4$	17	$17^2 = 17 \times 17 = 289$
3	$3^2 = 3 \times 3 = 9$	18	$18^2 = 18 \times 18 = 324$
4	$4^2 = 4 \times 4 = 16$	19	$19^2 = 19 \times 19 = 361$
5	$5^2 = 5 \times 5 = 25$	20	$20^2 = 20 \times 20 = 400$
6	$6^2 = 6 \times 6 = 36$	21	$21^2 = 21 \times 21 = 441$
7	$7^2 = 7 \times 7 = 49$	22	$22^2 = 22 \times 22 = 484$
8	$8^2 = 8 \times 8 = 64$	23	$23^2 = 23 \times 23 = 529$

Number	*Square*	*Number*	*Square*
9	$9^2 = 9\times 9 = 81$	24	$24^2 = 24\times 24 = 576$
10	$10^2 = 10\times 10 = 100$	25	$25^2 = 25\times 25 = 625$
11	$11^2 = 11\times 11 = 121$	26	$26^2 = 26\times 26 = 676$
12	$12^2 = 12\times 12 = 144$	27	$27^2 = 27\times 27 = 729$
13	$13^2 = 13\times 13 = 169$	28	$28^2 = 28\times 28 = 784$
14	$14^2 = 14\times 14 = 196$	29	$29^2 = 29\times 29 = 841$
15	$15^2 = 15\times 15 = 225$	30	$30^2 = 30\times 30 = 900$

It is evident from the above table that the numbers 1, 4, 9, 16, ..., 841, 900 are squares of the numbers 1, 2, 3, ..., 30. Such numbers are called perfect squares or square numbers as defined below.

PERFECT SQUARE OR SQUARE NUMBER *A natural number n is called a perfect square or a square number if there exists a natural number m such that* $n = m^2$.

In other words, a natural number is a perfect square if it is the square of some natural number.

Since $4 = 2\times 2 = 2^2$. Therefore, 4 is a square number.

Also,

$25 = 5\times 5 = 5^2$, so 25 is a square number or a perfect square.

$144 = 12\times 12 = 12^2$, so 144 is a square number or a perfect square etc.

Remark *The perfect squares 1, 4, 9, 16, ... can be represented geometrically by dots forming a square as shown below:*

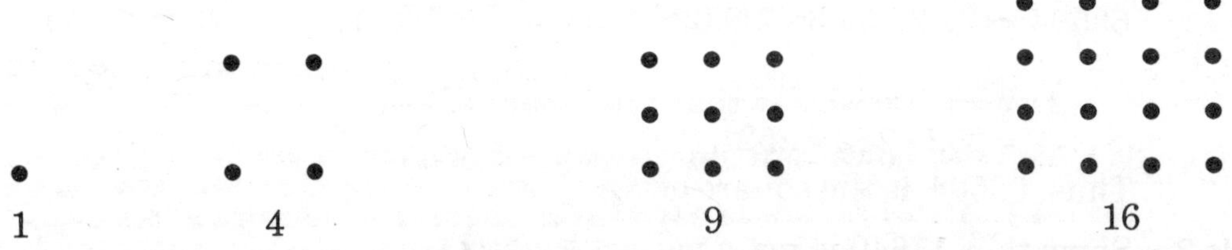

Hence, the name 'perfect squares' or square numbers is assigned to these numbers.

In order to check whether a given natural number is a perfect square or not, we follow the following steps:

Step I *Obtain the natural number.*

Step II *Write the number as a product of prime factors.*

Step III *Group the factors in pairs in such a way that both the factors in each pair are equal.*

Step IV *See whether some factor is left over or not. If no factor is left over in grouping, then the given number is a perfect square. Otherwise, it is not a perfect square.*

Step V *To obtain the number whose square is the given number take one factor from each group and multiply them.*

Following examples will illustrate the above procedure:

ILLUSTRATIVE EXAMPLES

Example 1 Is 225 a perfect square? if so, find the number whose square is 225.

Solution Resolving 225 into prime factors, we obtain

$$225 = 3 \times 3 \times 5 \times 5$$

Grouping the factors in pairs in such a way that both the factors in each pair are equal, we have

$$225 = (3 \times 3) \times (5 \times 5)$$

Clearly, 225 can be grouped into pairs of equal factors and no factor is left over. Hence, 225 is a perfect square.

3	225
3	75
5	25
5	5
	1

Again, $225 = (3 \times 5) \times (3 \times 5)$

$$= 15 \times 15 = 15^2$$

So, 225 is the square of 15.

Example 2 Show that 63504 is a perfect square. Also, find the number whose square is 63504.

Solution Resolving 63504 into prime factors, we obtain

2	63504
2	31752
2	15876
2	7938
3	3969
3	1323
3	441
3	147
7	49
7	7
	1

$$63504 = 2 \times 2 \times 2 \times 2 \times 3 \times 3 \times 3 \times 3 \times 7 \times 7$$

Grouping the factors in pairs of equal factors, we obtain

$$63504 = (2 \times 2) \times (2 \times 2) \times (3 \times 3) \times (3 \times 3) \times (7 \times 7)$$

Clearly, no factor is left over in grouping the factors in pairs of equal factors, So, 63504 is a perfect square.

Again,

$$63504 = (2 \times 2 \times 3 \times 3 \times 7) \times (2 \times 2 \times 3 \times 3 \times 7)$$

[Grouping first factors in each group]

$$= 252 \times 252 = 252^2$$

Thus, 63504 is the square of 252.

Example 3 Show that 17640 is not a perfect square.

Solution Resolving 17640 into prime factors, we have

2	17640
2	8820
2	4410
3	2205
3	735
5	245
7	49
7	7
	1

$$17640 = 2 \times 2 \times 2 \times 3 \times 3 \times 5 \times 7 \times 7$$

Grouping the factors into pairs of equal factors, we get

$$17640 = (2 \times 2) \times (3 \times 3) \times (7 \times 7) \times (2 \times 5)$$

Clearly, on grouping into pairs of equal factors, we are left with two factors 2 and 5 which cannot be paired.

Hence, 17640 is not a perfect square.

Example 4 Find the smallest number by which 180 must be multiplied so that the product is a perfect square.

Solution Resolving 180 into prime factors, we get

$$180 = 2 \times 2 \times 3 \times 3 \times 5$$

Grouping the factors into pairs of equal factors, we get

$180 = (2\times 2)\times(3\times 3)\times 5$

For a number to be a perfect square, it should be possible to pair all its prime factors. In this case, 5 is without a pair.

Thus, we must multiply the number by 5 so that the product is a perfect square.

Hence, the smallest number by which 180 should be multiplied is 5.

2	180
2	90
3	45
3	15
5	5
	1

Example 5 Find the smallest number by which 25200 should be divided so that the result is a perfect square.

Solution Resolving 25200 into prime factors, we get

$25200 = 2\times 2\times 2\times 2\times 3\times 3\times 5\times 5\times 7$

Now, grouping the factors into pairs of equal factors, we get

$25200 = (2\times 2)\times(2\times 2)\times(3\times 3)\times(5\times 5)\times 7$

We observe that 7 cannot be paired. Thus, if we divide 25200 by 7 the quotient will be a perfect square.

Hence, the smallest number by which 25200 must be divided to make the result a perfect square is 7.

2	25200
2	12600
2	6300
2	3150
3	1575
3	525
5	175
5	35
7	7
	1

EXERCISE 3.1

1. Which of the following numbers are perfect squares?
   (i) 484 (ii) 625 (iii) 576 (iv) 941 (v) 961 (vi) 2500
2. Show that each of the following numbers is a perfect square. Also, find the number whose square is the given number in each case:
   (i) 1156 (ii) 2025 (iii) 14641 (iv) 4761
3. Find the smallest number by which the given number must be multiplied so that the product is a perfect square:
   (i) 23805 (ii) 12150 (iii) 7688
4. Find the smallest number by which the given number must be divided so that the resulting number is a perfect square:
   (i) 14283 (ii) 1800 (iii) 2904
5. Which of the following numbers are perfect squares?
   11, 12, 16, 32, 36, 50, 64, 79, 81, 111, 121
6. Using prime factorization method, find which of the following numbers are perfect squares?
   189, 225, 2048, 343, 441, 2916, 11025, 3549
7. By what number should each of the following numbers be multiplied to get a perfect square in each case? Also, find the number whose square is the new number.
   (i) 8820 (ii) 3675 (iii) 605 (iv) 2880 (v) 4056 (vi) 3468
   (vii) 7776
8. By what numbers should each of the following be divided to get a perfect square in each case? Also, find the number whose square is the new number.
   (i) 16562 (ii) 3698 (iii) 5103 (iv) 3174 (v) 1575
9. Find the greatest number of two digits which is a perfect square.
10. Find the least number of three digits which is perfect square.

11. Find the smallest number by which 4851 must be multiplied so that the product becomes a perfect square.
12. Find the smallest number by which 28812 must be divided so that the quotient becomes a perfect square.
13. Find the smallest number by which 1152 must be divided so that it becomes a perfect square. Also, find the number whose square is the resulting number.

ANSWERS

1. (i), (ii), (iii), (v), (vi)
2. (i) 34 (ii) 45 (iii) 121 (iv) 69
3. (i) 5 (ii) 6 (iii) 2
4. (i) 3 (ii) 2 (iii) 6
5. 16, 36, 64, 81, 121
6. 225, 441, 2916, 11025
7. (i) 5, 210 (ii) 3, 105 (iii) 5, 55 (iv) 5, 120 (v) 6, 156 (vi) 3, 102 (vii) 6, 216
8. (i) 2, 91 (ii) 2, 43 (iii) 7, 27 (iv) 6, 23 (v) 7, 15
9. 81
10. 100
11. 11
12. 3
13. 2, 24

3.3 PROPERTIES AND PATTERNS OF SOME SQUARE NUMBERS

In the previous section, we have learnt about the method by which we can check whether a given natural number is a perfect square or not. We can also check the same by using some properties and patterns followed by square numbers. So, let us first discuss the same. There are several interesting properties and patterns about the squares of natural numbers. In this section, we will discuss some of them and the same will be applied to check whether a given natural number is a perfect square or not.

3.3.1 PROPERTIES OF SQUARE NUMBERS

Property 1 *A number having 2, 3, 7 or 8 at unit's place is never a perfect square. In other words, no square number ends in 2, 3, 7 or 8.*

Verification: On page 3.1-3.2, the table gives us the squares of first 30 natural numbers. If we have a glance at the unit's place of these squares, we observe that they have 0, 1, 4, 5, 6 or 9 at unit's place. Thus, the square of a number cannot have 2, 3, 7 or 8 at unit's place.

Application: Check the digit at unit's place of the given number. If it is one of the digits 2, 3, 7 and 8, then the given number is not a perfect square.

ILLUSTRATION 1 None of the numbers 152, 7693, 14357, 88888, 798328 is a perfect square.

Remark 1 *The phrase "number ends in a" means that the unit's digit of the number is a.*

Remark 2 *It should be noted that a number having unit's digit other than the digits 2, 3, 7 and 8 is not necessarily a perfect square. It may or may not be a perfect square. For example, 71, 124, 1500 etc. are not perfect squares.*

Property 2 *The number of zeros at the end of a perfect square is always even.*

In other words, a number ending in an odd number of zeros is never a perfect square.

Verification: Consider the following tables:

Table 3.2

Number	*Number of zeros at unit's place*	*Square of the number*	*Number of zeros at the unit's place of the square number*
10	1	100	2
20	1	400	2
200	2	40000	4
2500	2	6250000	4
5000	3	25000000	6
20000	4	400000000	8

It is evident from the above table that the number of zeros at the end of the square of a number is twice the number of zeros at the end of the given number.

Application: By just looking at a number which ends in an odd number of zeros, we can say that it cannot be perfect square. For example, 45000, 16000, 90 etc. are not perfect square.

Remark *It should be noted that numbers ending in an even number of zeros may or may not be a perfect square. For example, 2500 is a perfect square but, 2600, 44700 etc. are not perfect squares.*

Property 3 *Squares of even numbers are always even numbers and squares of odd numbers are always odd numbers.*

Verification: This fact can be easily verified from table 3.1 for natural numbers upto 30. However, the result is true in general.

Property 4 *The square of a natural number other than one is either a multiple of 3 or exceeds a multiple of 3 by 1.*

In other words, a perfect square leaves remainder 0 or 1 on division by 3.

Verification: The above property can be easily verified from the following computations:

Square number	Remainder when divided by 3
$2^2 = 4 = 3\times1+1$	1
$3^2 = 9 = 3\times3+0$	0
$4^2 = 16 = 3\times5+1$	1
$5^2 = 25 = 3\times8+1$	1
$6^2 = 36 = 3\times12+0$	0
$7^2 = 49 = 3\times16+1$	1
$8^2 = 64 = 3\times21+1$	1

Application: If a number when divided by 3 leaves remainder 2, then it is not a perfect square.

ILLUSTRATION 2 635, 98, 122 are not perfect squares as they leave remainder 2 when divided by 3.

Remark *If a number leaves remainder 0 or 1 when divided by 3, it is not necessarily a perfect square. However, when it leaves remainder other than 0 and 1, it is not a perfect square.*

Property 5 *The square of a natural number other than one is either a multiple of 4 or exceeds a multiple of 4 by 1.*

In other words, a perfect square leaves remainder 0 or 1 on division by 4.

Verification: The above property can be easily verified from the following computations:

Square number	Remainder when divided by 4
$2^2 = 4 = 4 \times 1 + 0$	0
$3^2 = 9 = 4 \times 2 + 1$	1
$4^2 = 16 = 4 \times 4 + 0$	0
$5^2 = 25 = 4 \times 6 + 1$	1
$6^2 = 36 = 4 \times 9 + 0$	0
$7^2 = 49 = 4 \times 12 + 1$	1
$8^2 = 64 = 4 \times 16 + 0$	0
$9^2 = 81 = 4 \times 20 + 1$	1 etc.

Application: If a number when divided by 4 leaves remainder 2 or 3, it cannot be a perfect square.

ILLUSTRATION 3 67, 146, 363, 10003 are not perfect squares as they leave remainder 3, 2, 3 and 3 respectively, when divided by 4.

Remark *If a number leaves remainder 0 or 1 when divided by 4, it is not necessarily a perfect square. However, when it leaves remainder other than 0 and 1, it is not a perfect square.*

The following table gives the possible remainders when a perfect square (or square number) is divided by some prime numbers:

Table 3.3

Divisor	*Possible remainders*
3	0, 1
5	0, 1, 4
7	0, 1, 2, 4
11	0, 1, 3, 4, 5, 9
13	0, 1, 3, 4, 9, 10, 12

This table is helpful when a number is not a perfect square. For example, if we divide a number by 5 and get the remainder 3, then the number is not a perfect square.

Property 6 *The unit's digit of the square of a natural number is the unit's digit of the square of the digit at unit's place of the given natural number.*

Table 3.4

Unit's digit of the number	*Unit's digit of the square of the number*
0	0
1 or 9	1
2 or 8	4
3 or 7	9
4 or 6	6
5	5

Verification: The above property can be easily verified from the table given on page 3.1-3.2.

Property 7 *There are no natural numbers p and q such that* $p^2 = 2q^2$.

Proof: We have the following four cases:

CASE I *When p and q both are odd:*

Since the square of an odd natural number is odd and that of an even natural number is even.

$\therefore$ p and q are odd

$\Rightarrow$ p^2 and q^2 are odd

$\Rightarrow$ p^2 is odd and $2q^2$ is even

$\Rightarrow$ $p^2 = 2q^2$ is not possible.

Thus, $p^2 = 2q^2$ is not possible when p and q both are odd natural numbers.

CASE II *When p is odd and q is even:*

Since the square of an odd natural number is an odd natural number and that of an even natural number is even. Therefore,

p is odd and q is even

$\Rightarrow$ p^2 is odd and q^2 is even

$\Rightarrow$ p^2 is odd and $2q^2$ is even

$\Rightarrow$ $p^2 = 2q^2$ is not possible.

Thus, $p^2 = 2q^2$ is not possible when p is odd and q is even.

CASE III *When p is even and q is odd:*

In this case,

p is even

$\Rightarrow$ p contains 2 as a factor

$\Rightarrow$ p^2 contains $2^2 (= 4)$ as a factor

q is odd

$\Rightarrow$ q^2 is odd

$\Rightarrow$ $2q^2$ contains 2 as the only even factor.

Thus, p^2 contains 4 as the smallest even factor and $2q^2$ contains only 2 as the even factor. So, $p^2 = 2q^2$ is not possible.

Thus, $p^2 = 2q^2$ is not possible when p is even and q is odd.

CASE IV *When p and q both are even:*

In this case,

p and q both are even $\Rightarrow$ p and q both contain 2 as a factor

Let d = H C F of p and q. Then,

$p = dx$ and $q = dy$ for some natural numbers x and y having one common factor other than 1.

Now, $p^2 = 2q^2$

$\Rightarrow \quad (dx)^2 = 2(dy)^2$

$\Rightarrow \quad d^2x^2 = 2d^2y^2$

$\Rightarrow \quad x^2 = 2y^2$

Since x and y have no common factor other than 1, therefore at least one of them is odd.

Thus, $p^2 = 2q^2 \Rightarrow x^2 = 2y^2$, where at least one of x and y is odd.

But, this is not possible, because $x^2 = 2y^2$ reduces to one of the first three cases which are not possible.

Hence, there can be no natural numbers p and q such that $p^2 = 2q^2$.

Remark *It follows from the above property that if n is a perfect square, then 2n can never be a perfect square.*

Property 8 *For every natural number n,*

$$(n+1)^2 - n^2 = (n+1) + n$$

i.e., the difference of squares of two consecutive natural numbers is equal to their sum

Proof: For any natural number n, we have

$$(n+1)^2 - n^2 = (n+1+n)(n+1-n) \quad \left[\text{Using} : a^2 - b^2 = (a+b)(a-b)\right]$$
$$= (n+1+n)$$

ILLUSTRATION 4 $9^2 - 8^2 = 9 + 8 = 17$

$19^2 - 18^2 = 19 + 18 = 37$

$28^2 - 27^2 = 28 + 27 = 55$

$136^2 - 135^2 = 136 + 135 = 271$ etc.

Property 9 *The square of a natural number n is equal to the sum of first n odd natural numbers.*

We have,

$1^2 = 1 =$ Sum of first 1 odd natural number;

$2^2 = 1 + 3 =$ Sum of first 2 odd natural numbers;

$3^2 = 1 + 3 + 5 =$ Sum of first 3 odd natural numbers;

$4^2 = 1 + 3 + 5 + 7 =$ Sum of first 4 odd natural numbers;

and so on.

In general, for any natural number n, we have

$n^2 =$ Sum of first n odd natural numbers

i.e., $n^2 = 1 + 3 + 5 + 7 + \ldots + (2n - 1)$

PYTHAGOREAN TRIPLETS *A triplet (m, n, p) of three natural numbers m, n and p is called a Pythagorean triplet, if* $m^2 + n^2 = p^2$.

ILLUSTRATION 5 (3, 4, 5), (5, 12, 13), (8, 15, 17) etc. are Pythagorean triplets, because

$$3^2 + 4^2 = 25 = 5^2$$

$$5^2 + 12^2 = 169 = 13^2$$

and, $$8^2 + 15^2 = 289 = 17^2$$

Property 10 *For any natural number m greater than* $1, (2m, m^2 - 1, m^2 + 1)$ *is a Pythagorean triplet.*

Proof: In order to prove that $(2m, m^2-1, m^2+1)$ is a Pythagorean triplet, it is sufficient to prove that

$$(2m)^2 + (m^2-1)^2 = (m^2+1)^2$$

We have, $(2m^2) + (m^2-1)^2 = 4m^2 + m^4 - 2m^2 + 1^2$

$$= m^4 + 2m^2 + 1^2$$

$$= (m^2+1)^2$$

Hence, $(2m, m^2-1, m^2+1)$ is Pythagorean triplet for any natural number $m > 1$.

Remark *If m and n are relatively prime natural numbers such that m > n and exactly one of them is even and other is odd, then* $(2mn, m^2-n^2, m^2+n^2)$ *is a primitive Pythagorean triple.*

Here, the word 'primitive' means that the three numbers contain no common factor.

ILLUSTRATION 6 Write a Pythagorean triplet whose one member is:

(i) 6 (ii) 18

Solution For any natural number $m > 1$, we have

$2m, m^2-1, m^2+1$ as a Pythagorean triplet.

(i) Here,

$2m = 6 \Rightarrow m = 3.$

$\therefore$ $m^2 - 1 = 3^2 - 1 = 9 - 1 = 8$ and $m^2 + 1 = 3^2 + 1 = 9 + 1 = 10$

So, Pythagorean triplet is 6, 8, 10

(ii) Here,

$2m = 18 \Rightarrow m = 9$

$\therefore$ $m^2 - 1 = 9^2 - 1 = 81 - 1 = 80$ and $m^2 + 1 = 9^2 + 1 = 81 + 1 = 82$

So, Pythagorean triple is 18, 80, 82.

3.3.2 SOME INTERESTING PATTERNS OF SQUARE NUMBERS

PATTERN 1 *The sum of two consecutive triangular numbers is a square number.*

Explanation: In class VI, we have learnt that whole numbers can be represented by triangles and squares. Numbers whose dot patterns can be arranged as triangles are known as triangular numbers. 1, 3, 6, 10, 15, 21, ... are triangular numbers. These numbers can be represented by triangles as shown below:

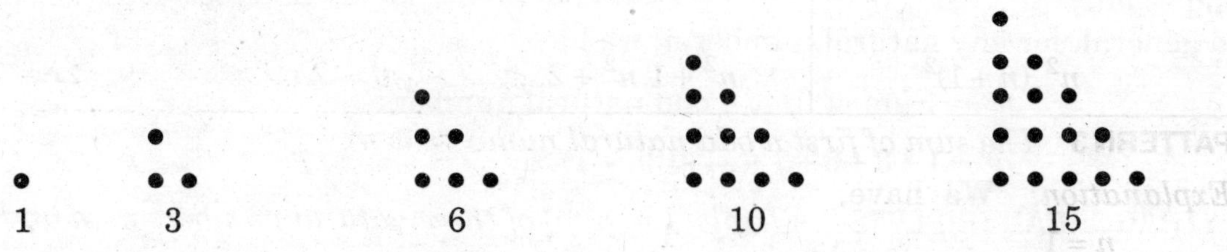

n^{th} triangular number is given by $\frac{n(n+1)}{2}$.

Numbers whose dot patterns can be arranged to form squares are known as square numbers. Square numbers 1,4,9,16, ... have following dot patterns:

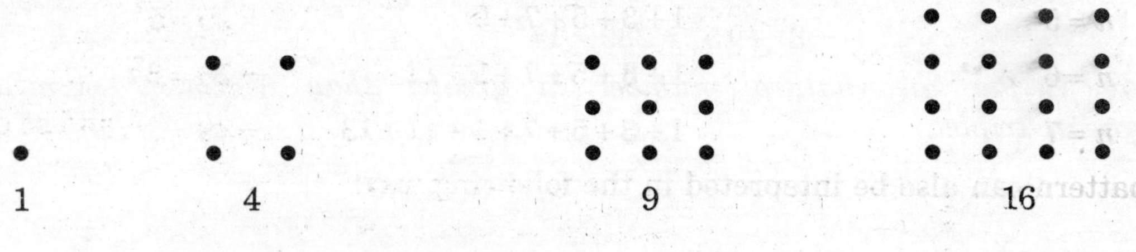

Let us now try to observe some characteristic of triangular numbers 1, 3, 6, 10, 15, 21, ... We observe that

$$1 = 1^2$$
$$1 + 3 = 4 = 2^2$$
$$3 + 6 = 9 = 3^2$$
$$6 + 10 = 16 = 4^2$$
$$10 + 15 = 25 = 5^2$$
$$15 + 21 = 36 = 6^2 \text{ etc.}$$

Clearly, the sum of two consecutive triangular numbers is a square number. This fact can also be observed from the dot patterns. If we combine two consecutive triangular patterns, we get a dot pattern representing a square number as shown below:

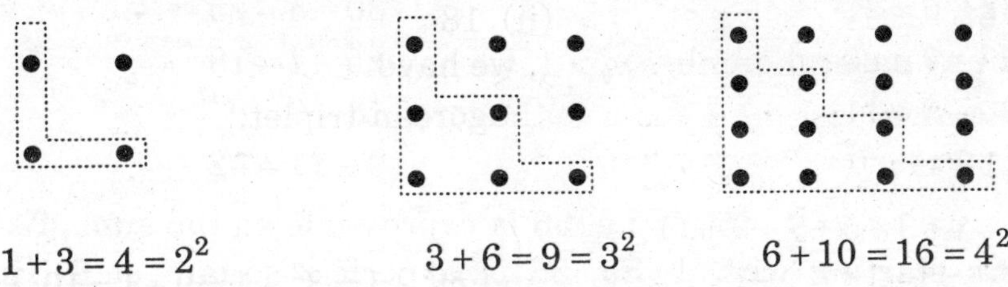

$1 + 3 = 4 = 2^2$ $\quad$ $3 + 6 = 9 = 3^2$ $\quad$ $6 + 10 = 16 = 4^2$

PATTERN 2 *There are 2n non-perfect square numbers between two consecutive square numbers n^2 and $(n + 1)^2$.*

Explanation: Square numbers are $1^2, 2^2, 3^2, 4^2$, ...

Consecutive Square numbers	*Non-perfect-square numbers between two consecutive square number*	*Number of non-perfect square numbers*
$1^2, 2^2$	2, 3	$2 = 2 \times 1$
$2^2, 3^2$	5, 6, 7, 8	$4 = 2 \times 2$
$3^2, 4^2$	10, 11, 12, 13, 14, 15	$6 = 2 \times 3$
$4^2, 5^2$	17, 18, 19, 20, 21, 22, 23, 24	$8 = 2 \times 4$
$\vdots$	$\vdots$	$\vdots$
$n^2, (n+1)^2$	$n^2 + 1, n^2 + 2, \ldots\ldots\ldots\ldots, n^2 + 2n$	$2n = 2 \times n$

PATTERN 3 *The sum of first n odd natural numbers is n^2*

Explanation: We have,

$n = 1$	1	$= 1 = 1^2$
$n = 2$	$1 + 3$	$= 4 = 2^2$
$n = 3$	$1 + 3 + 5$	$= 9 = 3^2$
$n = 4$	$1 + 3 + 5 + 7$	$= 16 = 4^2$
$n = 5$	$1 + 3 + 5 + 7 + 9$	$= 25 = 5^2$
$n = 6$	$1 + 3 + 5 + 7 + 9 + 11$	$= 36 = 6^2$
$n = 7$	$1 + 3 + 5 + 7 + 9 + 11 + 13$	$= 49 = 7^2$ and so on

This pattern can also be intepreted in the following way:

If a number is a square number, it has to be the sum of consecutive odd numbers starting from 1.

This means that if a number is not equal to the sum of successive odd natural numbers starting with 1, then it is not a perfect square.

We may use this result to find whether a number is perfect square or not. For this, we successively subtract 1,3,5,7,9,........... from the given number till we get 0 or a negative number. If we get 0, then the number is a perfect square, otherwise not.

For example, consider the numbers 36 and 34.

Let us subtract successively 1, 3, 5, 7, 9, ... from 36 and 34

We have,

$36-1=35$	$34-1=33$
$35-3=32$	$33-3=30$
$32-5=27$	$30-5=25$
$27-7=20$	$25-7=18$
$20-9=11$	$18-9=9$
$11-11=0$	$9-11=-2$

This means $36=1+3+5+7+9+11$ i.e. 36 is expressible as the sum of six consecutive odd natural numbers starting with 1. So, 36 is a perfect square of 6. However, 34 is not expressible as the sum of the squares of consecutive odd natural numbers starting with 1. So, 34 is not a perfect square.

PATTERN 4 *If 1 is added to the product of two consecutive odd natural numbers, it is equal to the square of the only even natural number between them.*

Explanation: We have,

$$1\times3+1=4=2^2$$
$$3\times5+1=16=4^2$$
$$5\times7+1=36=6^2$$
$$7\times9+1=64=8^2$$
$$9\times11+1=100=10^2 \text{ etc.}$$

In general,

$$(2n-1)\times(2n+1)+1=4n^2=(2n)^2$$

PATTERN 5 *If 1 is added to the product of two consecutive even natural numbers, it is equal to the square of the only odd natural number between them.*

Explanation: We have,

$$2\times4+1=9=3^2$$
$$4\times6+1=25=5^2$$
$$6\times8+1=49=7^2$$
$$8\times10+1=81=9^2$$
$$10\times12+1=121=11^2 \text{ etc.}$$

In general,

$$2n\times(2n+2)+1=4n^2+4n+1=(2n+1)^2.$$

PATTERN 6 *The square of any odd natural number other than 1 can be expressed as the sum of two consecutive natural numbers.*

Explanation: We have,

$$3^2 = 9 = 4 + 5$$
$$5^2 = 25 = 12 + 13$$
$$7^2 = 49 = 24 + 25$$
$$9^2 = 81 = 40 + 41$$
$$11^2 = 121 = 60 + 61$$
$$13^2 = 169 = 84 + 85$$
$$15^2 = 225 = 112 + 113 \text{ etc.}$$

In general,

$$(2n+1)^2 = 4n^2 + 4n + 1 = (2n^2 + 2n) + (2n^2 + 2n + 1)$$

PATTERN 7 *Squares of natural numbers having all digits 1 follow the following pattern:*

$$11^2 = 1\underline{2}1$$
$$111^2 = 12\underline{3}21$$
$$1111^2 = 123\underline{4}321$$
$$11111^2 = 1234\underline{5}4321$$
$$111111^2 = 12345\underline{6}54321$$
$$1111111^2 = 123456\underline{7}654321$$
$$11111111^2 = 1234567\underline{8}7654321$$
$$111111111^2 = 12345678\underline{9}87654321$$

In this pattern the sum of the digits of every number on the right hand side is a perfect square as given below.

$$1+2+1 = 4 = 2^2$$
$$1+2+3+2+1 = 9 = 3^2$$
$$1+2+3+4+3+2+1 = 16 = 4^2$$
$$1+2+3+4+5+4+3+2+1 = 25 = 5^2$$
$$1+2+3+4+5+6+7+6+5+4+3+2+1 = 49 = 7^2$$
$$1+2+3+4+5+6+7+8+7+6+5+4+3+2+1 = 64 = 8^2$$
$$1+2+3+4+5+6+7+8+9+8+7+6+5+4+3+2+1 = 81 = 9^2$$

Also, in the above pattern the digits on RHS are symmetrical about the middle digit.

PATTERN 8 *The squares of the natural numbers like 11, 111, ... etc. have a nice pattern as shown below:*

$$121 \times (1+2+1) = 484 = 22^2$$

i.e., $11^2 \times (\text{Sum of digits in } 11^2) = (2 \times 11)^2$

$$12321 \times (1+2+3+2+1) = 110889 = 333^2$$

i.e., $111^2 \times (\text{Sum of the digits in } 111^2) = (3 \times 111)^2$

$$1234321 \times (1+2+3+4+3+2+1) = 19749136 = (4444)^2$$

i.e., $1111^2 \times (\text{Sum of the digits in } 1111^2) = (4 \times 1111)^2$

$\vdots \qquad \vdots \qquad \vdots$

PATTERN 9 *Observe the following pattern:*

$$7^2 = 49$$
$$67^2 = 4489$$
$$667^2 = 444889$$
$$6667^2 = 44448889$$
$$66667^2 = 4444488889$$
$$666667^2 = 444444888889$$
$$6666667^2 = 44444448888889$$

Using the above pattern find the squares of the following numbers:

(i) 66666667 (ii) 666666667

It is evident from the above pattern that

(i) $66666667^2 = 4444444488888889$

(ii) $666666667^2 = 444444444888888889$

Following examples will illustrate the applications of these properties in determining whether a given number is a perfect square.

ILLUSTRATIVE EXAMPLES

Example 1 The following numbers are not perfect squares. Give reason.

(i) 1057 (ii) 23453 (iii) 7928 (iv) 222222

Solution We know that the natural numbers ending in the digits 2, 3, 7 or 8 are not perfect squares.

Therefore, 1057, 23453, 7928 and 222222 are not perfect squares.

Example 2 What will be the unit's digit of the squares of the following numbers?

(i) 71 (ii) 599 (iii) 2783 (iv) 1234

Solution We know that the unit's digit of the square of a number having digit at unit's place as 1 or 9 is 1. Therefore, unit's digit of the squares of numbers 71 and 599 are each equal to 1. Since the unit's digit of the square of a number having 3 as unit's digit is 9. So, the unit's digit of the square of the number 2783 is 9.

The unit's digit of the square of the number 1234 is 6, because the unit's digit of the square of a number having 4 or 6 at units place is 6.

Example 3 Which of the following end with digit 1?

$$123^2, 77^2, 82^2, 161^2, 109^2$$

Solution By property 6, we know that the unit's digit of the square of a natural number is the unit's digit of the square of the digit at unit's place of the given natural number.

$\therefore$ Unit's digit of 123^2 is 9. [$\because 3^2 = 9$]

Unit's digit of 77^2 is 9. [$\because$ Unit's digit of 7^2 is 9]

Unit's digit of 82^2 is 4. [$\because 2^2 = 4$]

Unit's digit of 161^2 is 1 [$\because 1^2 = 1$]

and, Unit's digit of 109^2 is 1. [$\because$ Unit's digit of 9^2 is 1]

Example 4 Determine whether squares of the following numbers are even or odd.

(i) 213 (ii) 3824 (iii) 9777 (iv) 40028

Solution We know that the square of an even number is even and that of an odd number is odd. Therefore,

(i) The square of 213 is an odd number.

(ii) The square of 3284 is an even number.

(iii) The square of 9777 is an odd number.

(iv) The square of 40028 is an even number.

Example 5 The following numbers are not perfect squares. Give reason.

(i) 64000 (ii) 89722 (iii) 222000 (iv) 505050

Solution We know that the numbers ending in an odd number of consecutive zeros are not perfect squares. Therefore, 64000, 222000 and 505050 are not perfect squares.

Also, a number having 2 at unit's place cannot be a perfect square. Therefore, 89722 is not a perfect square.

Example 6 Write a pythagorean triplet whose one member is

(i) 14 (ii) 16

Solution For any natural number m, we know that

$$2m, m^2-1, m^2+1$$

is a pythagorean triplet.

(i) Here, $2m = 14 \Rightarrow m = 7$.

$\therefore$ $m^2-1 = 7^2-1 = 49-1 = 48$ and $m^2+1 = 7^2+1 = 49+1 = 50$

So, Pythagorean triplet is 14, 48, 50.

(ii) Here, $2m = 16 \Rightarrow m = 8$.

$\therefore$ $m^2-1 = 64-1 = 63$ and $m^2+1 = 64+1 = 65$

So, Pythagorean triplet is 16, 63, 65.

Example 7 Without adding, find the sum:

(i) $1+3+5+7+9$ (ii) $1+3+5+7+9+11+13+15+17+19$

(iii) $1+3+5+7+9+11+13+15+17+19+21+23$

Solution We know that the sum of first n odd natural numbers is n^2.

(i) Since $1+3+5+7+9$ is the sum of first five odd natural numbers.

$\therefore$ $1+3+5+7+9 = 5^2 = 25$

(ii) Given sum is the sum of first-ten odd natural numbers.

$\therefore$ $1+3+5+7+9+11+13+15+17+19 = 10^2 = 100$

(iii) Given sum is the sum of first twelve odd natural numbers.

$\therefore$ $1+3+5+7+9+11+13+15+17+19+21+23 = 12^2 = 144$

Example 8 Express:

(i) 49 as the sum of 7 odd natural numbers.

(ii) 121 as the sum of 11 odd natural numbers.

Solution (i) We know that the sum of first n odd natural numbers is n^2.

Since $49 = 7^2$

$\therefore$ 49 = Sum of first 7 odd natural numbers $= 1+3+5+7+9+11+13$

(ii) Since $121 = 11^2$

$\therefore$ 121 = Sum of first 11 odd natural numbers

$= 1+3+5+7+9+11+13+15+17+19+21$

Example 9 How many natural numbers lie between squares of the following natural numbers?

(i) 12 and 13 (ii) 25 and 26 (iii) 89 and 100

Solution We know that between n^2 and $(n+1)^2$ there are $2n$ non-perfect square numbers (see pattern 2). Therefore,

(i) between 12^2 and 13^2 there are $2\times 12 = 24$ natural numbers.

(ii) between 25^2 and 26^2 there are $2\times 25 = 50$ natural numbers.

(iii) between 99^2 and 100^2 there are $2\times 99 = 198$ natural numbers.

Example 10 Express each of the following as the sum of two consecutive natural numbers:

(i) 21^2 (ii) 13^2 (iii) 19^2

Solution We know that the square of an odd natural number $2n+1$ is the sum of two consecutive natural numbers $2n^2 + 2n$ and $2n^2 + 2n + 1$.

(i) Here, $2n+1 = 21$

$\therefore$ $n = 10$.

Hence, $(2n+1)^2 = (2n^2+2n)+(2n^2+2n+1)$

$21^2 = (2\times 10^2 + 2\times 10) + (2\times 10^2 + 2\times 10 + 1)$ [Putting $n = 10$]

$\Rightarrow$ $21^2 = 220 + 221$

(ii) Here, $2n+1 = 13$

$\therefore$ $n = 6$

$\therefore$ $(2n+1)^2 = (2n^2+2n)+(2n^2+2n+1)$

$\Rightarrow$ $13^2 = (2\times 6^2 + 2\times 6) + (2\times 6^2 + 2\times 6 + 1)$ [Putting $n = 6$]

$\Rightarrow$ $13^2 = 84 + 85$

(iii) Proceeding as above, we have

$19^2 = 180 + 181$

Example 11 Find whether 55 is a perfect square or not?

Solution In order to check whether 55 is a perfect square or not, we successively subtract 1,3,5,7,9, ..., from it.

We have,

$55 - 1 = 54$

$54 - 3 = 51$

$51 - 5 = 46$

$46 - 7 = 39$

$39 - 9 = 30$

$30 - 11 = 19$

$19 - 13 = 6$

$6 - 13 = -7$

This shows that 55 cannot be expressed as the sum of consecutive odd numbers starting with 1.

Hence, it is not a perfect square.

Example 12 Observe the following pattern and find the missing digits:

$$11^2 = 121$$
$$101^2 = 10201$$
$$1001^2 = 1002001$$
$$10001^2 = 100020001$$
$$100001^2 = 1 \ldots 2 \ldots 1$$
$$10000001^2 = \ldots\ldots\ldots\ldots\ldots$$

Solution We observe that the square of the number on RHS of the equality has an odd number of digits such that the middle digit is 2 and first and last digit are both equal to 1. Also, the number of zeros between left-most digit 1 and the middle digit 2 or between the middle digit 2 and the right-most digit 1 is same as the number of zeros in the given number. Therefore,

$$100001^2 = 10000200001$$

and, $10000001^2 = 100000020000001$.

Example 13 Observe the following pattern and supply the missing numbers:

$$11^2 = 121$$
$$101^2 = 10201$$
$$10101^2 = 102030201$$
$$1010101^2 = \ldots\ldots\ldots\ldots\ldots$$
$$\ldots\ldots\ldots\ldots\ldots = 10203040504030201$$

Solution We observe that the middle digit in the square of the given number is equal to the number of one's in the number. Also, the square is symmetric about the middle digit. If the middle digit is 4 (say), then the number to be squared is 1010101 and its square is 1020304030201. Similarly, by observing the pattern, we have

$$101010101^2 = 10203040504030201$$
$$10101010101^2 = 102030405060504030201 \text{ etc.}$$

Hence,

$$1010101^2 = 1020304030201$$

and, $101010101^2 = 10203040504030201$

Example 14 Using the given pattern, find the missing numbers:

$$1^2 + 2^2 + 2^2 = 3^2$$
$$2^2 + 3^2 + 6^2 = 7^2$$
$$3^2 + 4^2 + 12^2 = 13^2$$
$$4^2 + 5^2 + (\ldots)^2 = 21^2$$
$$5^2 + (\ldots)^2 + 30^2 = 31^2$$
$$6^2 + 7^2 + (\ldots)^2 = (\ldots)^2$$

Solution We have,

$$1^2 + 2^2 + 2^2 = 3^2$$

i.e., $1^2 + 2^2 + (1\times 2)^2 = (1^2 + 2^2 - 1\times 2)^2$

$$2^2 + 3^2 + 6^2 = 7^2$$

i.e., $2^2 + 3^2 + (2\times 3)^2 = (2^2 + 3^2 - 2\times 3)^2$

$$3^2 + 4^2 + 12^2 = 13^2$$

i.e., $3^2 + 4^2 + (3\times 4)^2 = (3^2 + 4^2 - 3\times 4)^2$

$\therefore$ $4^2 + 5^2 + (4\times 5)^2 = (4^2 + 5^2 - 4\times 5)^2$

$$5^2 + 6^2 + (5\times 6)^2 = (5^2 + 6^2 - 5\times 6)^2$$

and, $6^2 + 7^2 + (6\times 7)^2 = (6^2 + 7^2 - 6\times 7)^2$

or, $6^2 + 7^2 + 42^2 = 43^2$

Example 15 Using suitable patterns, compute the following:

(i) $\dfrac{333^2}{12321} = \ldots$ (ii) $\dfrac{666666^2}{12345654321} = \ldots$

Solution We have the following pattern:

$$11^2 = 121$$

$$111^2 = 12321 \quad \ldots\text{(i)}$$

$$1111^2 = 1234321$$

$$11111^2 = 123454321$$

$$111111^2 = 12345654321 \text{ etc.} \quad \ldots\text{(ii)}$$

(i) $\dfrac{333^2}{12321} = \dfrac{(3\times 111)^2}{(111)^2}$ [Using (i)]

$$= \frac{3^2 \times 111^2}{111^2} = 9$$

(ii) $\dfrac{666666^2}{12345654321} = \dfrac{(6\times 111111)^2}{(111111)^2}$ [Using (ii)]

$$= \frac{6^2 \times 111111^2}{111111^2} = 6^2 = 36$$

EXERCISE 3.2

1. The following numbers are not perfect squares. Give reason.
   (i) 1547 (ii) 45743 (iii) 8948 (iv) 333333
2. Show that the following numbers are not perfect squares:
   (i) 9327 (ii) 4058 (iii) 22453 (iv) 743522
3. The square of which of the following numbers would be an odd number?
   (i) 731 (ii) 3456 (iii) 5559 (iv) 42008

4. What will be the units digit of the squares of the following numbers?

(i) 52 (ii) 977 (iii) 4583 (iv) 78367 (v) 52698
(vi) 99880 (vii) 12796 (viii) 55555 (ix) 53924

5. Observe the following pattern

$$1+3=2^2$$
$$1+3+5=3^2$$
$$1+3+5+7=4^2$$

and write the value of $1+3+5+7+9+\cdots$ upto n terms.

6. Observe the following pattern

$$2^2-1^2 = 2+1$$
$$3^2-2^2 = 3+2$$
$$4^2-3^2 = 4+3$$
$$5^2-4^2 = 5+4$$

and find the value of

(i) 100^2-99^2 (ii) 111^2-109^2 (iii) 99^2-96^2

7. Which of the following triplets are Pythagorean?

(i) (8, 15, 17) (ii) (18, 80, 82) (iii) (14, 48, 51) (iv) (10, 24, 26)
(v) (16, 63, 65) (vi) (12, 35, 38)

8. Observe the following pattern

$$(1\times 2)+(2\times 3)=\frac{2\times 3\times 4}{3}$$
$$(1\times 2)+(2\times 3)+(3\times 4)=\frac{3\times 4\times 5}{3}$$
$$(1\times 2)+(2\times 3)+(3\times 4)+(4\times 5)=\frac{4\times 5\times 6}{3}$$

and find the value of

$$(1\times 2)+(2\times 3)+(3\times 4)+(4\times 5)+(5\times 6)$$

9. Observe the following pattern

$$1 =\frac{1}{2}\{1\times(1+1)\}$$
$$1+2 =\frac{1}{2}\{2\times(2+1)\}$$
$$1+2+3 =\frac{1}{2}\{3\times(3+1)\}$$
$$1+2+3+4 =\frac{1}{2}\{4\times(4+1)\}$$

and find the values of each of the following:

(i) $1+2+3+4+5+\ldots+50$

(ii) $31+32+\ldots+50$

10. Observe the following pattern

$$1^2 = \frac{1}{6}[1\times(1+1)\times(2\times1+1)]$$

$$1^2+2^2 = \frac{1}{6}[2\times(2+1)\times(2\times2+1)]$$

$$1^2+2^2+3^2 = \frac{1}{6}[3\times(3+1)\times(2\times3+1)]$$

$$1^2+2^2+3^2+4^2 = \frac{1}{6}[4\times(4+1)\times(2\times4+1)]$$

and find the values of each of the following:

(i) $1^2+2^2+3^2+4^2+\ldots+10^2$

(ii) $5^2+6^2+7^2+8^2+9^2+10^2+11^2+12^2$

11. Which of the following numbers are squares of even numbers?

121, 225, 256, 324, 1296, 6561, 5476, 4489, 373758

12. By just examining the units digits, can you tell which of the following cannot be whole squares?

(i) 1026 (ii) 1028 (iii) 1024 (iv) 1022 (v) 1023
(vi) 1027

13. Write five numbers for which you cannot decide whether they are squares.

14. Write five numbers which you cannot decide whether they are square just by looking at the unit's digit.

15. Write true (T) or false (F) for the following statements.

(i) The number of digits in a square number is even.
(ii) The square of a prime number is prime.
(iii) The sum of two square numbers is a square number.
(iv) The difference of two square numbers is a square number.
(v) The product of two square numbers is a square number.
(vi) No square number is negative.
(vii) There is no square number between 50 and 60.
(viii) There are fourteen square number upto 200.

ANSWERS

5. n^2 6. (i) 199 (ii) 440 (iii) 585
7. (i), (ii), (iv) and (v) 8. 70 9. (i) 1275 (ii) 810
10. (i) 385 (ii) 620 11. 256, 324, 1296, 5476
12. (ii), (iv), (v), (vi) 15. (i) F (ii) F (iii) F
(iv) F (v) T (vi) T (vii) T (viii) T

HINTS TO SELECTED PROBLEMS

6. (ii) $111^2-109^2=(111^2-110^2)+(110^2-109)^2=(111+110)+(110+109)$

(iii) $99^2-96^2=(99^2-98^2)+(98^2-97^2)+(97^2-96^2)=(99+98)+(98+97)+(97+96)$

7. (i) Equate first number of each triplet by $2m$, obtain m from it and find $(2m, m^2-1, m^2+1)$. If you get the triplet, it is Pythagorean otherwise not.
9. (ii) We have,

$$31+32+\ldots+50$$
$$=(1+2+3+\ldots+30+31+\ldots+50-(1+2+3+\ldots+30)$$
$$=\frac{1}{2}\{50\times(50+1)\}-\frac{1}{2}\{30\times(30+1)\}$$

12. Write any five numbers not having 2, 3, 7 or 8 at unit's place.
13. Write any five numbers not having 2, 3, 7 or 8 at unit's place.

3.4 SOME SHORT-CUTS TO FIND SQUARES

In order to find the square of a number, we multiply the given number by itself. The multiplication is convenient for small numbers only. For large numbers, multiplication may be laborious and time-consuming. In this section, we shall discuss some short methods for finding the squares of natural numbers without using actual multiplication.

3.4.1 COLUMN METHOD

This method is based upon an old Indian method of multiplying two numbers. It is convenient for finding squares of two digit numbers only. As the number of digits increases, this method becomes difficult and time-consuming. So, we shall discuss it for two digit numbers only.

This method uses the identity $(a+b)^2 = a^2 = 2ab + b^2$ for finding the square of a two digit number ab (where a is the tens digit and b is the units digit). We follow the following steps to find the square of a two digit number ab (where a is the tens digit and b is the units digit).

<u>Step I</u> *Make three columns and write the value of a^2, $2\times a\times b$ and b^2 respectively in these columns as follows:*

As an illustration let us take ab = 57.

$\therefore$ $a=5$ *and* $b=7$.

Column I	*Column II*	*Column III*
a^2	$2\times a\times b$	b^2
25	70	49

<u>Step II</u> *Underline the units digit of b^2 (in column III) and add its tens digit, if any, to $2\times a\times b$ (in column II).*

Column I a^2	*Column II* $2\times a\times b$	*Column III* b^2
25	70 +4 74	4<u>9</u>

<u>Step III</u> *Underline the units digit in column II and add the number formed by tens and other digit, if any, to a^2 in column I.*

Column I	*Column II*	*Column III*
a^2	$2\times a\times b$	b^2
25 + 7	70 + 4	4$\underline{9}$
32	7$\underline{4}$	

Step IV *Under the number in column I*

Column I	*Column II*	*Column III*
a^2	$2\times a\times b$	b^2
25 + 7 $\underline{32}$	70 + 4 7$\underline{4}$	4$\underline{9}$
32	4	9

Step V *Write the underlined digits at the bottom of each column to obtain the square of the given number.*

In this case, we have $57^2 = 3249$

ILLUSTRATIVE EXAMPLES

Example 1 Find the squares of the following numbers using column method:
(i) 25 (ii) 96

Solution (i) Here, $a = 2$ and $b = 5$.
We have,

Column I	*Column II*	*Column III*
a^2	$2\times a\times b$	b^2
4 + 2 $\underline{6}$	20 + 2 2$\underline{2}$	2$\underline{5}$
6	2	5

$\therefore$ $25^2 = 625$.

(ii) Here, $a = 9$ and $b = 6$.
We have,

Column I	*Column II*	*Column III*
a^2	$2\times a\times b$	b^2
81 + 11 $\underline{92}$	108 + 3 11$\underline{1}$	3$\underline{6}$
92	1	6

$\therefore$ $96^2 = 9216$

Example 2 Find the squares of the following numbers using column method:

(i) 99 (ii) 89

Solution (i) Here, $a = 9$ and $b = 9$.

We have,

Column I	*Column II*	*Column III*
a^2	$2\times a\times b$	b^2
81	162	$8\underline{1}$
$+17$	$+8$	
$\underline{98}$	$17\underline{0}$	
98	0	1

$\therefore \quad 99^2 = 9801.$

(ii) Here, $a = 8$ and $b = 9$

We have,

Column I	*Column II*	*Column III*
a^2	$2\times a\times b$	b^2
64	144	$8\underline{1}$
$+15$	$+8$	
$\underline{79}$	$15\underline{2}$	
79	2	1

$\therefore \quad 89^2 = 7921.$

3.4.2 VISUAL METHOD

In the column method we have used the algebraic identity $(a+b)^2 = a^2 + 2ab + b^2$ to compute the square of a two digit number. The square of a positive integer can also be computed by closely following the visual representation of $(a+b)^2$. In order to represent $(a+b)^2$, we draw a square of side $a+b$ and divide it into two rectangles of size $a\times(a+b)$ and $b\times(a+b)$ by drawing a vertical line as shown in Fig. 1 We also draw a horizontal line to divide the square into two rectangles of size $(a+b)\times b$ and $(a+b)\times a$ as shown in Fig. 3.1. These two lines divide the square into four parts, namely, two squares of size $a\times a$ and $b\times b$ and two rectangles of size $a\times b$ and $b\times a$. The sum of the areas of these four parts is

$$a\times a + a\times b + b\times a + b\times b = a^2 + 2ab + b^2 = (a+b)^2$$

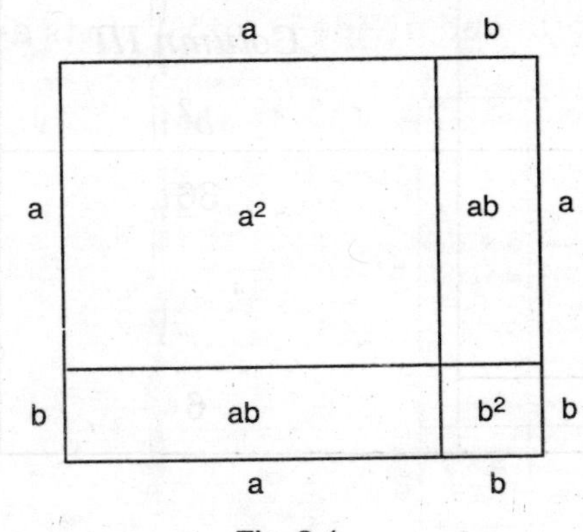

Fig. 3.1

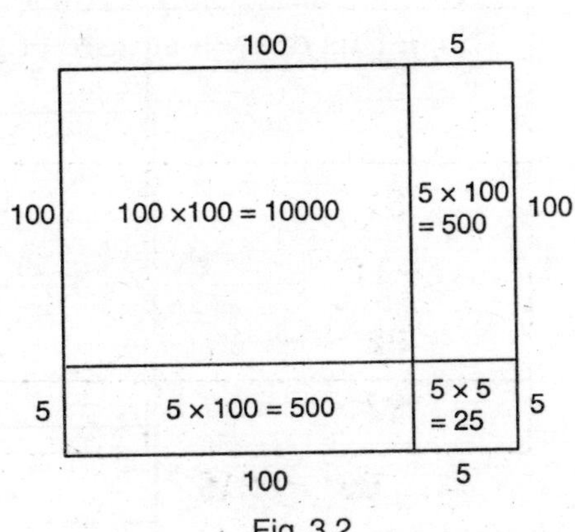

Fig. 3.2

We use this visual representation of $(a+b)^2$ to find the square of a number.

Suppose we wish to find the square of 105.

We have, $105 = 100 + 5$

So, we draw a square of side 105 units and divide it into four parts as shown in Fig. 3.2. The sum of the areas of these four parts is the square of 105.

$\therefore \quad 105^2 = 10000 + 500 + 500 + 25 = 11025$

Following examples will illustrate the above method.

ILLUSTRATIVE EXAMPLES

Example 1 Find the square of the following numbers by Visual method:

(i) 54 (ii) 97

Solution (i) We have, $54 = 50 + 4$

So, we draw a square of side 54 units and divide it into parts as shown in Fig. 3.3

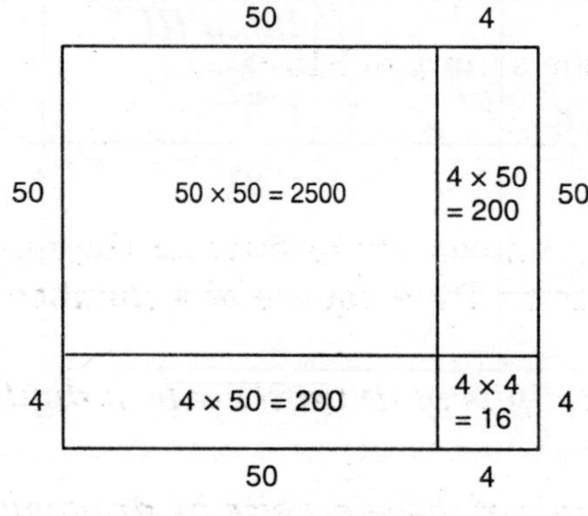

Fig. 3.3

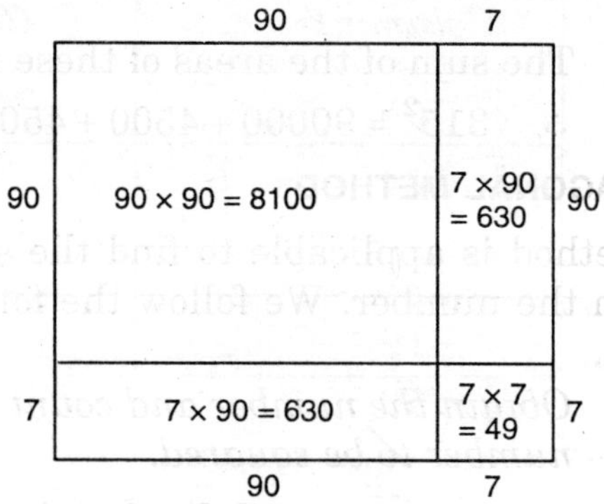

Fig. 3.4

The sum of the areas of these four parts is the square of 54.

$\therefore \quad 54^2 = 2500 + 200 + 200 + 16 = 2916$

(ii) We have, $97 = 90 + 7$

So, we draw a square of side 97 units and divide it into parts as shown in Fig. 3.4

The sum of the areas of these four parts is the square of 97.

$\therefore \quad 97^2 = 8100 + 630 + 630 + 49 = 9409$

Example 2 Find the square of the following numbers by Visual method:

(i) 205 (ii) 315

Solution (i) We have, $205 = 200 + 5$

So, let us draw a square of side 205 units and divide it into 4 parts as shown in Fig. 3.5

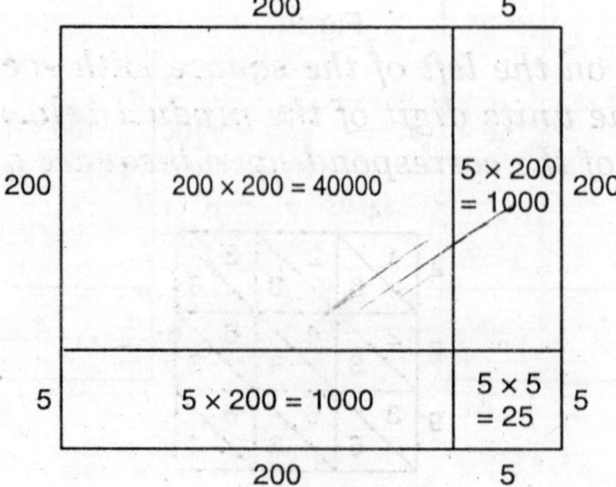

Fig. 3.5

$\therefore \quad 205^2 = 40000 + 1000 + 1000 + 25 = 41025$

(ii) We have, $315 = 300 + 15$

So, let us draw a square of side 315 units and divide it into parts as shown in Fig. 3.6.

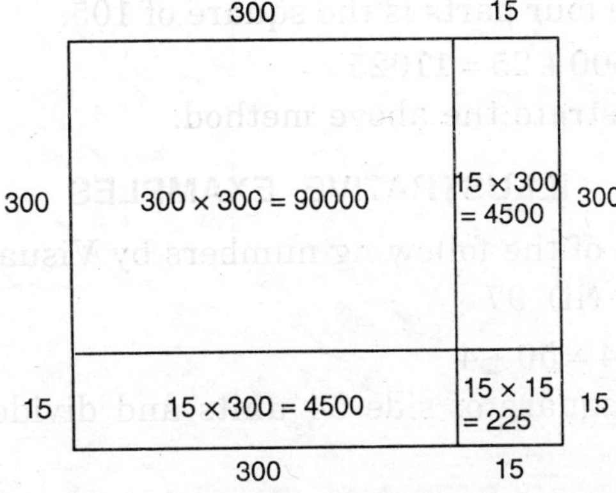

Fig. 3.6

The sum of the areas of these four parts is the square of 315.

$\therefore \quad 315^2 = 90000 + 4500 + 4500 + 225 = 99225$

3.4.3 DIAGONAL METHOD

This method is applicable to find the square of any number irrespective of the number of digits in the number. We follow the following steps to find the square of a number by this method.

Step I *Obtain the number and count the number of digits in it. Let there be n digits in the number to be squared.*

Step II *Draw square and divide it into n^2 sub-squares of the same size by drawing $(n-1)$ horizontal and $(n-1)$ vertical lines.*

Step III *Draw the diagonals of each sub-square. As an illustration, let the number to be squared be 479.*

Step IV *Write the digits of the number to be squared along left vertical side and top horizontal side of the squares as shown below.*

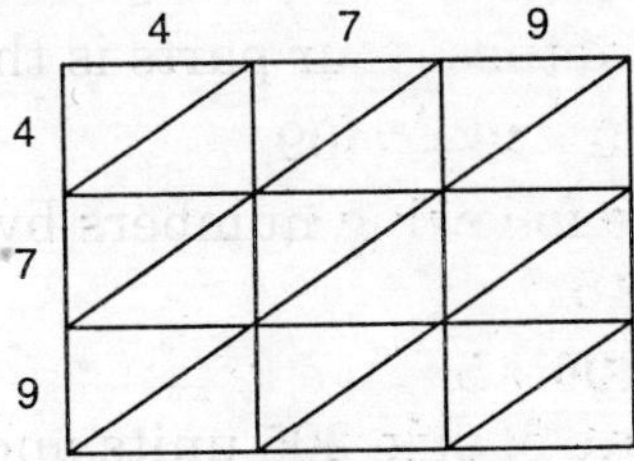

Fig. 3.7

Step V *Multiply each digit on the left of the square with each digit on top of the column one-by-one. Write the units digit of the product below the diagonal and tens digit above the diagonal of the corresponding sub-square as shown below.*

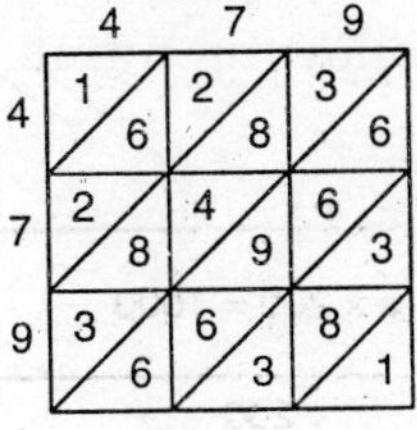

Fig. 3.8

Step VI *Starting below the lowest diagonal sum the digits along the diagonals so obtained. Write the units digit of the sum and take carry, the tens digit (if any) to the diagonal above as shown below.*

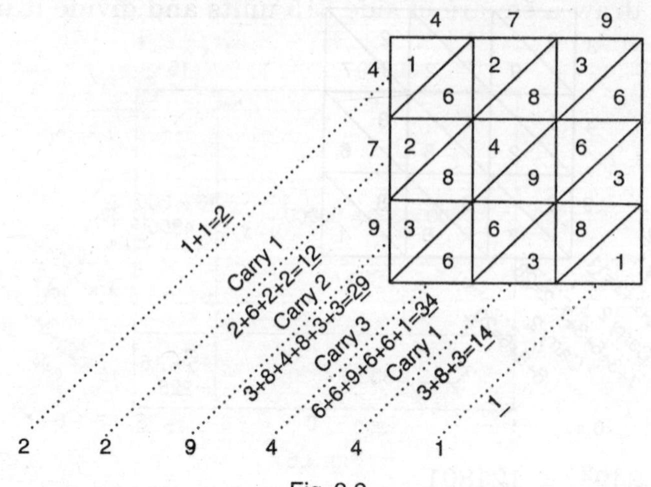

Fig. 3.9

Step VII *Obtain the required square by writing the digits from the left-most side.*

$\therefore \quad 479^2 = 229441.$

ILLUSTRATIVE EXAMPLES

Example 1 Find the squares of the following using diogonal method:

(i) 89 (ii) 68

Solution (i) Using diagonal method, we have (ii) Using diagonal method, we have

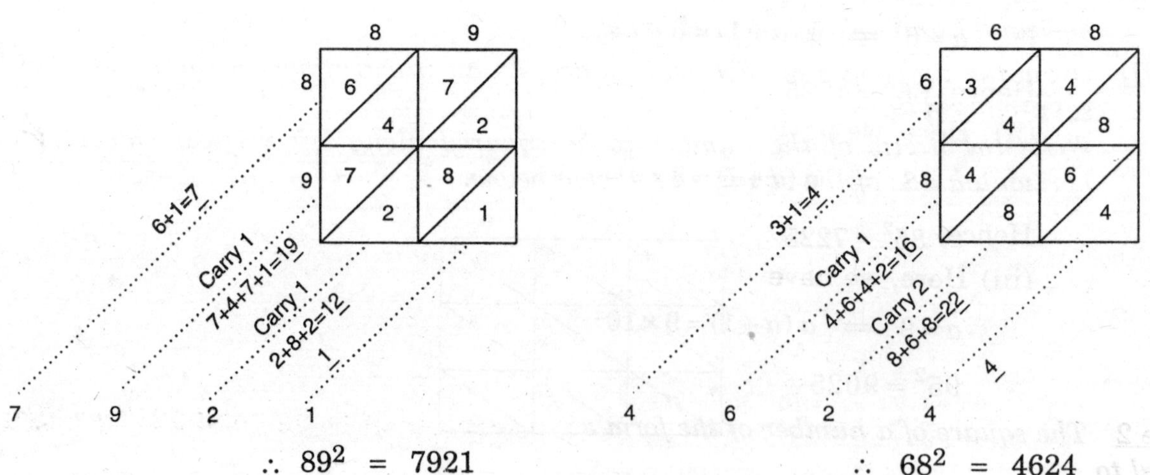

$\therefore \; 89^2 = 7921$ $\therefore \; 68^2 = 4624$

Fig. 3.10 Fig. 3.11

Example 2 Find the square of the following numbers by diagonal method:

(i) 349 (ii) 293

Solution (i) Using diagonal method, we have (ii) Using diagonal method, we have

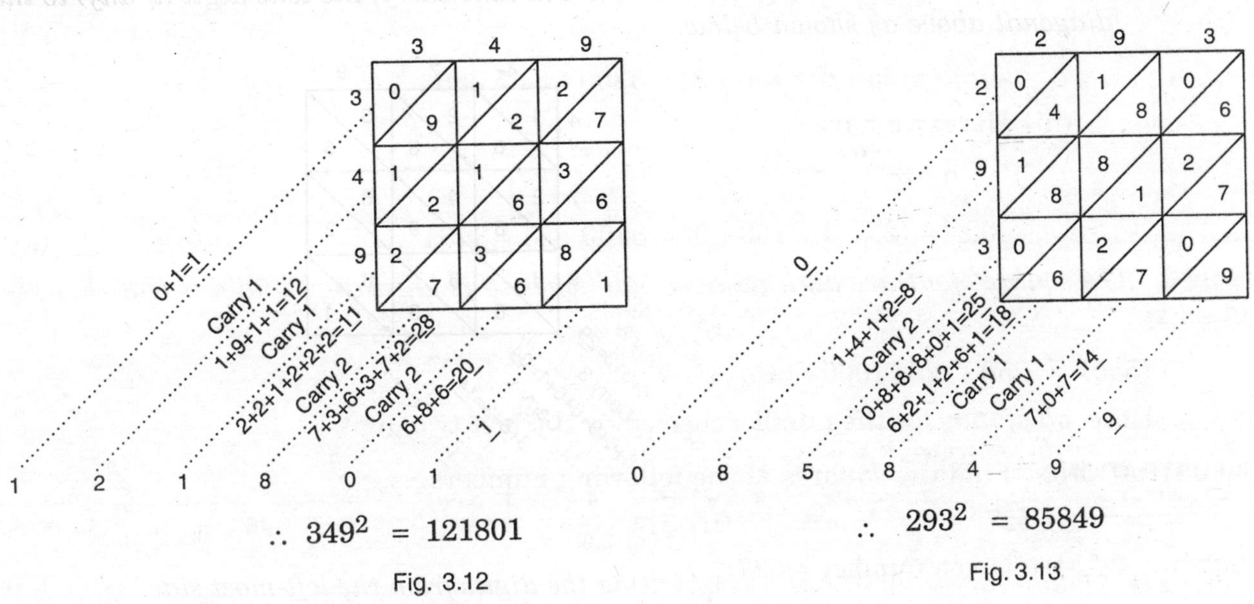

$\therefore\ 349^2 = 121801$ $\therefore\ 293^2 = 85849$

Fig. 3.12 Fig. 3.13

3.4.4 SOME PARTICULAR METHODS

Rule 1 *The square of a number of the form a5 (where a is tens digit and 5 is units digit) is the number which ends in 25 and has the number* $a(a+1)$ *before 25.*

ILLUSTRATION 1 Find the squares of the following numbers:

(i) 65 (ii) 85 (iii) 95

Solution (i) Here, we have

$$a = 6 \Rightarrow a(a+1) = 6\times 7 = 42$$

Hence, $65^2 = 4225$

(ii) Here, we have

$$a = 8 \Rightarrow a(a+1) = 8\times 9 = 72$$

Hence, $85^2 = 7225$

(iii) Here, we have

$$a = 9 \Rightarrow a(a+1) = 9\times 10 = 90$$

$\therefore\ 95^2 = 9025$

Rule 2 *The square of a number of the form 5a (where a is units digit and 5 is tens digit) is equal to*

$$(25+a)\times 100 + a^2$$

i.e.,

$$(5a)^2 = (25+a)\times 100 + a^2$$

ILLUSTRATION 2 Find the squares of the following numbers:

(i) 56 (ii) 58 (iii) 59

Solution (i) Here, we have

$$a = 6$$

$$\therefore\ (56)^2 = (25+6)\times 100 + 6^2 = 3100 + 36 = 3136$$

(ii) Here, we have

$a = 8$

$\therefore \quad (58)^2 = (25+8)\times 100 + 8^2 = 3300 + 64 = 3364$

(iii) Here, we have

$a = 9$

$\therefore \quad (59)^2 = (25+9)\times 100 + 9^2 = 3400 + 81 = 3481$

Rule 3 *The square of a three digit number 5ab (where b is units digit and a is tens digit) is given by*

$$(5ab)^2 = (250 + ab)\times 1000 + (ab)^2$$

Here, ab stands for the number formed by the last two digits.

ILLUSTRATION 3 Find the squares of the following numbers:

(i) 527 (ii) 514 (iii) 525

Solution (i) Given number = 527

$\therefore \quad a = 2$ and $b = 7$

Hence, $(527)^2 = (250+27)\times 1000 + (27)^2 = 277000 + 729 = 277729$

(ii) Given number = 514

$\therefore \quad a = 1$ and $b = 4$

Hence, $(514)^2 = (250+14)\times 1000 + (14)^2 = 264000 + 196 = 264196$

(iii) Given number = 525

$\therefore \quad a = 2$ and $b = 5$

Hence, $(525)^2 = (250+25)\times 1000 + (25)^2 = 275000 + 625 = 275625$

Rule 4 *The square of a number abc ... 5 (i.e. a number having 5 at unit's place is obtained by affixing 25 to the right of the number n (n + 1), where n = abc ...*

ILLUSTRATION 4 Find the square of the following numbers:

(i) 125 (ii) 215 (iii) 1235

Solution (i) Here $n = 12$

$\therefore \quad n(n+1) = 12\times 13 = 156$

Hence, $125^2 = 15625$

(ii) Here, $n = 21$

$\therefore \quad n(n+1) = 21\times 22 = 462$

Hence, $215^2 = 46225$

(iii) Here, $n = 123$

$\therefore \quad n(n+1) = 123\times 124 = 15252$

Hence, $1235^2 = 1525225$

ILLUSTRATIVE EXAMPLES

Example 1 Find the square of 87 by using column method and diagonal method.

Solution *Column method:*

We have, $a = 8$ and $b = 7$

Column I	Column II	Column III
a^2	$2 \times a \times b$	b^2
64 +11	112 +4	4$\underline{9}$
$\underline{75}$	11$\underline{6}$	
75	6	9

$\therefore \quad 87^2 = 7569$

Diagonal method: Using diagonal method, we have

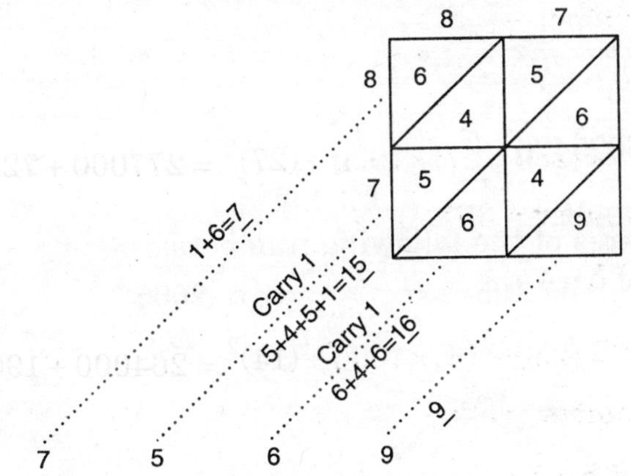

$\therefore \quad 87^2 = 7569$

Fig. 3.14

Example 2 Find the squares of the following numbers by diagonal method:

(i) 854 (ii) 2576

Solution (i) Using diagonal method, we have

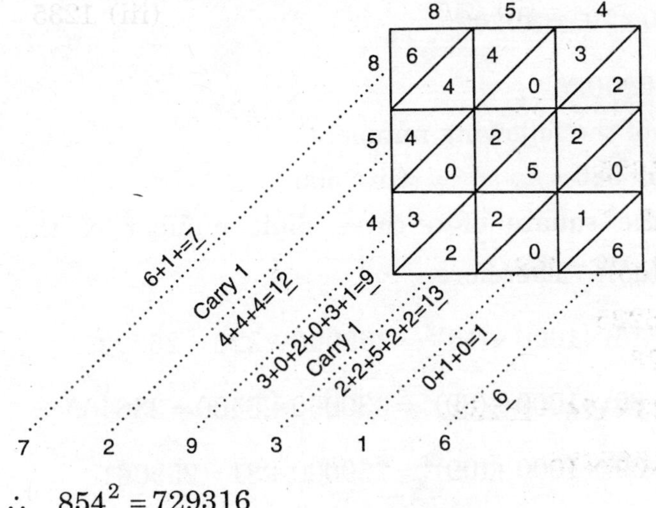

$\therefore \quad 854^2 = 729316$

Fig. 3.15

(ii) Using diagonal method, we have

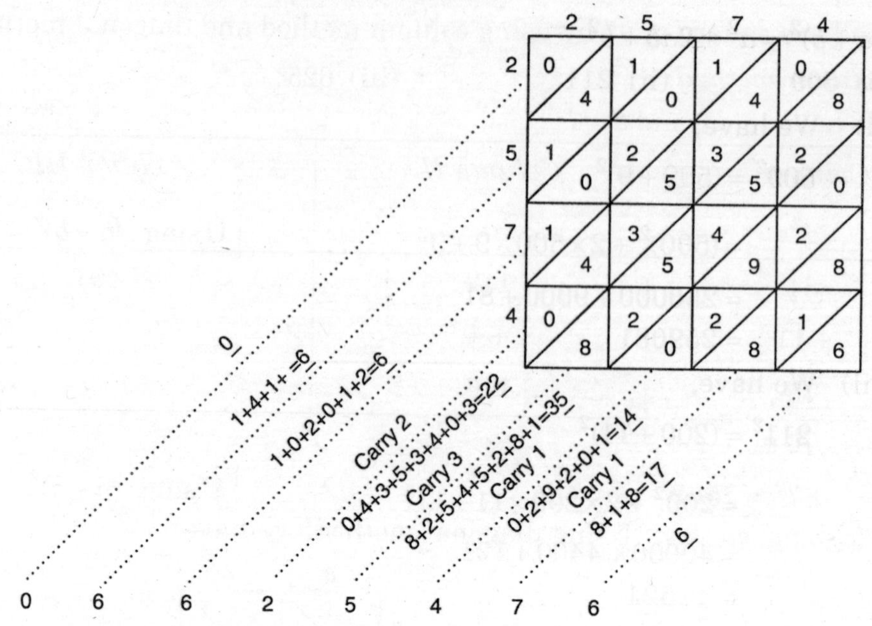

$\therefore \quad 2574^2 = 6625476$

Fig. 3.16

Example 3 Find the squares of the following numbers:

(i) 35 (ii) 105 (iii) 2005

Solution (i) Here, $n = 3$

$\therefore \quad n(n+1) = 3 \times 4 = 12$

Hence, $35^2 = 1225$

(ii) Here, $n = 10$

$\therefore \quad n(n+1) = 10 \times 11 = 110$

Hence, $105^2 = 11025$

(iii) Here, $n = 200$

$\therefore \quad n(n+1) = 200 \times 201 = 40200$

Hence, $2005^2 = 4020025$

Example 4 Find the squares of the following numbers:

(i) 515 (ii) 580 (iii) 509

Solution We know that the square of a three digit number of the form $5ab$ is $(250 + ab) \times 100 + (ab)^2$. Therefore,

(i) $515^2 = (250 + 15) \times 1000 + (15)^2 = 265000 + 225 = 265225$

(ii) $580^2 = (250 + 80) \times 1000 + (80)^2 = 330000 + 6400 = 336400$

(iii) $509^2 = (250 + 09) \times 1000 + (09)^2 = 259000 + 81 = 259081$

Example 5 Find the square of the following numbers using the identity

$(a+b)^2 = a^2 + 2ab + b^2$

(i) 509 (ii) 211 (iii) 625

Solution (i) We have,

$509^2 = (509+9)^2$

$= (500)^2 + 2\times 500\times 9 + 9^2$ $\left[\text{Using}: (a+b)^2 = a^2 + 2ab + b^2\right]$

$= 250000 + 9000 + 81$

$= 259081$

(ii) We have,

$211^2 = (200+11)^2$

$= 200^2 + 2\times 200\times 11 + 11^2$ $\left[\text{Using}: (a+b)^2 = a^2 + 2ab + b^2\right]$

$= 40000 + 4400 + 121$

$= 44521$

(iii) We have,

$625^2 = (600+25)^2$

$= 600^2 + 2\times 600\times 25 + 25^2$

$= 360000 + 30000 + 625$

$= 390625$

Example 6 Find the square of the following numbers using the identity

$(a-b)^2 = a^2 - 2ab + b^2$:

(i) 491 (ii) 189 (iii) 575

Solution (i) We have,

$491^2 = (500-9)^2$

$= 500^2 - 2\times 500\times 9 + 9^2$

$= 250000 - 9000 + 81$

$= 241081.$

(ii) We have,

$189 = (200-11)^2$

$= 40000 - 2\times 200\times 11 + 11^2$

$= 40000 - 4400 + 121$

$= 35721$

(iii) We have,

$575^2 = (600-25)^2$

$= 600^2 - 2\times 600\times 25 + 25^2$

$= 360000 - 30000 + 625$

$= 330625$

EXERCISE 3.3

1. Find the squares of the following numbers using column method. Verify the result by finding the square using the usual multiplication:

   (i) 25 (ii) 37 (iii) 54 (iv) 71 (v) 96

2. Find the squares of the following numbers using diagonal method:

   (i) 98 (ii) 273 (iii) 348 (iv) 295 (v) 171

3. Find the squares of the following numbers:

   (i) 127 (ii) 503 (iii) 451 (iv) 862 (v) 265

4. Find the squares of the following numbers:

   (i) 425 (ii) 575 (iii) 405 (iv) 205 (v) 95
   (vi) 745 (vii) 512 (viii) 995

5. Find the squares of the following numbers using the identity $(a+b)^2 = a^2 + 2ab + b^2$:

   (i) 405 (ii) 510 (iii) 1001 (iv) 209 (v) 605

6. Find the squares of the following numbers using the identity $(a-b)^2 = a^2 - 2ab + b^2$:

   (i) 395 (ii) 995 (iii) 495 (iv) 498 (v) 99
   (vi) 999 (vii) 599

7. Find the squares of the following numbers by visual method:

   (i) 52 (ii) 95 (iii) 505 (iv) 702 (v) 99

ANSWERS

1. (i) 625 (ii) 1369 (iii) 2916 (iv) 5041 (v) 9216
2. (i) 9604 (ii) 74529 (iii) 121104 (iv) 9025 (v) 29241
3. (i) 16129 (ii) 253009 (iii) 203401 (iv) 743044 (v) 70225
4. (i) 180625 (ii) 330625 (iii) 164025 (iv) 42025 (v) 9025
   (vi) 555025 (vii) 262144 (viii) 990025
5. (i) 164025 (ii) 260100 (iii) 1002001 (iv) 43681 (v) 366025
6. (i) 156025 (ii) 990025 (iii) 245025 (iv) 248004 (v) 9801
   (vi) 998001 (vii) 358801.
7. (i) 2704 (ii) 9025 (iii) 255025 (iv) 492804 (v) 9801

3.5 SQUARE ROOTS

SQUARE ROOT *The square root of a number a is that number which when multiplied by itself gives a as the product.*

Thus, if b is the square root of a number a, then

$$b \times b = a \text{ or, } b^2 = a$$

The square root of a number a is denoted by $\sqrt{a}$.

It follows from this that

$$b = \sqrt{a} \Leftrightarrow b^2 = a.$$

i.e., b is the square root of a if and only if a is the square of b.

ILLUSTRATION 1 (i) $\sqrt{4} = 2$, because $2^2 = 4$.

(ii) $\sqrt{9} = 3$, because $3^2 = 9$.

(iii) $\sqrt{324} = 18$, because $18^2 = 324$.

Remark *Since* $4 = 2^2 = (-2)^2$, *therefore* 2 *and* -2 *can both be the square roots of* 4. *However, we agree that the square root of a number will be taken to be positive square root only . Thus, we have* $\sqrt{4} = 2$.

3.5.1 PROPERTIES OF SQUARE ROOTS

Based upon the properties of square number discussed in section 3.3, we have the following properties of square roots

Property 1 *If the units digit of a number is 2, 3, 7 or 8, then it does not have a square root in N (the set of natural numbers).*

Explanation: By property 1 in section 3.3.1, a number having 2, 3, 7 or 8 at unit's place cannot be a perfect square. Hence, a number having 2, 3, 7 or 8 at units place does not have a square root in N.

Property 2 *If a number ends in an odd number of zeros, then it does not have a square root. If a square number is followed by an even number of zeros, it has a square root in which the number of zeros in the end is half the number of zeros in the number.*

Explanation: By property 2, in section 3.3.1, the number of zeros at the end of a perfect square is always even and is twice the number of zeros at the end of the number.

Property 3 *The square root of an even square number is even and that square root of an odd square number is odd.*

Explanation: By property 3, in section 3.3.1, the squares of even numbers are even numbers and that of odd numbers are odd numbers.

Property 4 *If a number has a square root in N, then its units digit must be 0, 1, 4, 5 or 9.*

Explanation By property 6, in section 3.3.1, the units digits of the square and square root are related as below:

Units digit of square:	0	1	4	5	6	9
Units digit of square root:	0	1 or 9	2 or 8	5	4 or 6	3 or 7

Property 5 *Negative numbers have no square root in the system of rational numbers.*

Explanation: We have, $2^2 = 4, 3^2 = 9, 4^2 = 16$ and so on. Also, $(-2)^2 = (-2)\times(-2) = 4$, $(-3)^2 = (-3)\times(-3) = 9, (-4)^2 = (-4)\times(-4) = 16$ and so on. This means that the square of a number whether positive or negative is always positive. Consequently, negative numbers are not perfect squares. Hence, negative numbers have no square roots.

Property 6 *The sum of first n odd natural numbers is* n^2 *i.e.*

$$1 + 3 + 5 + 7 + \ldots + (2n-1) = n^2.$$

FINDING SQUARE ROOT THROUGH REPEATED SUBTRACTION

The above property of natural numbers can be used to find the square roots of small natural numbers.

In order to determine the number of odd natural numbers whose sum is the given natural number, we subtract from it successively 1, 3, 5, 7, 9, ... The number of times we have to perform subtraction to arrive at zero will be the number of natural numbers whose sum is the given natural number.

Thus, to find the square root of a small perfect square, we can use the following procedure:

Step I *Obtain the given perfect square whose square root is to be calculated. Let the number be a.*

Step II *Subtract from it successively 1, 3, 5, 7, 9, ... till you get zero.*

Step III *Count the number of times the subtraction is performed to arrive at zero. Let the number be n*

Step IV *Write* $\sqrt{a} = n$.

ILLUSTRATION 2 Find the square root of 36 by successive subtractions.

Solution We have,

$$36 - 1 = 35$$
$$35 - 3 = 32$$
$$32 - 5 = 27$$
$$27 - 7 = 20$$
$$20 - 9 = 11$$
$$11 - 11 = 0$$

Clearly, we have performed subtraction six times

$\therefore \quad \sqrt{36} = 6$

This is the simplest method of finding the square root of a perfect square. But, it is convenient for small numbers only as it is lengthy and time-consuming for large numbers. In the following sections we shall discuss other more efficient methods for extracting square roots.

3.6 SQUARE ROOT OF A PERFECT SQUARE BY PRIME FACTORIZATION

In order to find the square root of a perfect square by prime factorization, we follow the following steps.

Step I *Obtain the given number.*

Step II *Resolve the given number into prime factors by successive division.*

Step III Make pairs of prime factors such that both the factors in each pair are equal. Since the number is a perfect square, you will be able to make an exact number of pairs of prime factors.

Step IV *Take one factor from each pair.*

Step V *Find the product of factors obtained in step IV.*

Step VI *The product obtained in step V is the required square root.*

Following examples will illustrate the above procedure.

ILLUSTRATIVE EXAMPLES

Example 1 Find the square root of 11025 by prime factorization.

Solution Resolving 11025 into prime factors, we have

3	11025
3	3675
5	1225
5	245
7	49
	7

$$11025 = 3 \times 3 \times 5 \times 5 \times 7 \times 7$$

Grouping the factors into pairs of equal factors, we get

$$11025 = (3 \times 3) \times (5 \times 5) \times (7 \times 7)$$

Taking one factor from each pair, we get

$$\sqrt{11025} = 3 \times 5 \times 7 = 105$$

Example 2 Find the square root of 7744 by prime factorization.

Solution Resolving 7744 into prime factors, we get

2	7744
2	3872
2	1936
2	968
2	484
2	242
11	121
	11

$$7744 = 2 \times 2 \times 2 \times 2 \times 2 \times 2 \times 11 \times 11$$

Now, grouping the factors into pairs of equal factors, we get

$$7744 = (2 \times 2) \times (2 \times 2) \times (2 \times 2) \times (11 \times 11)$$

Now, taking one factor from each pair, we obtain

$$\sqrt{7744} = 2 \times 2 \times 2 \times 11 = 88.$$

Example 3 Find the square root of 298116 by prime factorization.

Solution Resolving 298116 into prime factors, we get

2	298116
2	149058
3	74529
3	24843
7	8281
7	1183
13	169
	13

$$298116 = 2 \times 2 \times 3 \times 3 \times 7 \times 7 \times 13 \times 13$$

Now, grouping the factors into pairs of equal factors, we get

$$298116 = (2 \times 2) \times (3 \times 3) \times (7 \times 7) \times (13 \times 13)$$

Taking one factor from each pair, we obtain

$$\sqrt{298116} = 2 \times 3 \times 7 \times 13 = 546$$

Example 4 Find the smallest number by which 1100 must be multiplied so that the product becomes a perfect square. Also, in each case find the square root of the perfect square so obtained.

Solution Resolving 1100 into prime factors, we get

2	1100
2	550
5	275
5	55
	11

$$1100 = 2 \times 2 \times 5 \times 5 \times 11$$

Grouping the factors into pairs of equal factors, we get

$$1100 = (2 \times 2) \times (5 \times 5) \times 11$$

We find that the prime factors 2 and 5 occur in pairs, but there is no prime factor to form a pair with 11. Therefore, we must multiply the number by 11 so that it becomes a perfect square.

If we multiply the number by 11, then

New number $= 1100 \times 11$

$= 12100$

$= (2 \times 2) \times (5 \times 5) \times (11 \times 11)$

Taking one factor from each pair, we get

Square root of the new number $= 2 \times 5 \times 11 = 110.$

Example 5 Find the smallest number by which 9408 must be divided so that it becomes a perfect square. Also, find the square root of the perfect square so obtained.

Solution Resolving 9408 into prime factors. we get

$9408 = 2\times2\times2\times2\times2\times2\times3\times7\times7$

2	9408
2	4704
2	2352
2	1176
2	588
2	294
3	147
7	49
	7

Grouping the factors into pairs of equal factors, we get

$9408 = (2\times2)\times(2\times2)\times(2\times2)\times(7\times7)\times3$

We find that there is no prime factor to form a pair with 3. Therefore, we must divide the number by 3 so that the quotient becomes a perfect square.

If we divide the given number by 3, we get

$$\text{New number} = \frac{9408}{3}$$

$$= 3136$$

$$= (2\times2)\times(2\times2)\times(2\times2)\times(7\times7)$$

Taking one factor from each pair, we get

Square root of new number $= 2\times2\times2\times7 = 56$.

Example 6 5929 students are sitting in an auditorium in such a manner that there are as many students in a row as there are rows in the auditorium. How many rows are there in the auditorium ?

Solution Let there be 'a' rows in the auditorium.

7	5929
7	847
11	121
	11

Since the number of students in a row is same as the number of rows in the auditorium.

$\therefore$ Number of students in a row $= a$

$\Rightarrow$ Number of students in 'a' rows $= a\times a = a^2$

It is given that the total number of students in the auditorium = 5929.

$\therefore \quad a^2 = 5929$

$\Rightarrow \quad a = \sqrt{5929}$

$\Rightarrow \quad a = \sqrt{(7\times7)\times(11\times11)}$ [By prime factorization]

$\Rightarrow \quad a = 7\times11$ [Taking one factor in each pair]

$\Rightarrow \quad a = 77$

Hence, there are 77 rows in the auditorium.

Example 7 A general wishing to arrange his men, who were 335250 in number in the form of a square found that there were 9 men left over. How many were there in each row ?

Solution Let there were 'a' men in each row. Then,

Number of rows $= a$

$\therefore$ Total number of men in a rows $= a\times a = a^2$

It is given that after arranging men in the form of a square, 9 men were left over.

$\therefore$ Total number of men $= a^2 + 9$

But the total number of men was 335250

$\Rightarrow \quad a^2 = 335250 - 9$

$\Rightarrow \quad a^2 = 335241$

$\Rightarrow \quad a = \sqrt{335241}$

$\Rightarrow \quad a = \sqrt{3 \times 3 \times 193 \times 193}$ [By prime factorization]

$\Rightarrow \quad a = 3 \times 193$ [Taking one factor from each pair]

$\Rightarrow a = 579.$

Hence, there were 579 men in each row.

Example 8 The product of two numbers is 1575 and their quotient is $\frac{9}{7}$. Find the numbers.

Solution Let one of the two numbers be a. Since the product of numbers is 1575.

$\therefore \quad$ Other number $= \frac{1575}{a}$

It is given that the quotient of the two numbers is $\frac{9}{7}$.

$$\therefore \quad \frac{a}{\frac{1575}{a}} = \frac{9}{7}$$

$$\Rightarrow \quad \frac{a^2}{1575} = \frac{9}{7}$$

$$\Rightarrow \quad a^2 = \frac{9 \times 1575}{7}$$

$$\Rightarrow \quad a^2 = 2025$$

$$\Rightarrow \quad a^2 = (5 \times 5) \times (3 \times 3)^2$$

$$\Rightarrow \quad a = \sqrt{(5 \times 5) \times (3 \times 3)^2}$$

$$\Rightarrow \quad a = 5 \times 3^2 = 45$$

Hence, the numbers are 45 and $\frac{1575}{45} = 35$.

Example 9 Find the smallest square number divisible by each one of the numbers 8, 9 and 10.

Solution The smallest number divisible by each one of the numbers 8, 9, 10 is their L.C.M.

Clearly, the L. C. M of 8, 9, 10 is $(2 \times 4 \times 9 \times 5) = 360$.

Now, resolving 360 into prime factors, we obtain

$$360 = 2 \times 2 \times 2 \times 3 \times 3 \times 5$$

Grouping the factors into pairs of equal factors, we have

$$360 = (2 \times 2) \times (3 \times 3) \times 2 \times 5$$

Clearly, there is no factor to form pairs with 2 and 5. Thus, to make 360 a perfect square, we must multiply it by 2×5 i.e. 10.

Hence, the smallest square number divisible by 8, 9 and 10 is 3600.

EXERCISE 3.4

1. Write the possible unit's digits of the square root of the following numbers. Which of these numbers are odd square roots?
   (i) 9801 (ii) 99856 (iii) 998001 (iv) 657666025
2. Find the square root of each of the following by prime factorization.
   (i) 441 (ii) 196 (iii) 529 (iv) 1764 (v) 1156
   (vi) 4096 (vii) 7056 (viii) 8281 (ix) 11664 (x) 47089
   (xi) 24336 (xii) 190969 (xiii) 586756 (xiv) 27225 (xv) 3013696
3. Find the smallest number by which 180 must be multiplied so that it becomes a perfect square. Also, find the square root of the perfect square so obtained.
4. Find the smallest number by which 147 must be multiplied so that it becomes a perfect square. Also, find the square root of the number so obtained.
5. Find the smallest number by which 3645 must be divided so that it becomes a perfect square. Also, find the square root of the resulting number.
6. Find the smallest number by which 1152 must be divided so that it becomes a perfect square. Also, find the square root of the number so obtained.
7. The product of two numbers is 1296. If one number is 16 times the other, find the numbers.
8. A welfare association collected Rs 202500 as donation from the residents. If each paid as many rupees as there were residents, find the number of residents.
9. A society collected Rs 92.16. Each member collected as many paise as there were members. How many members were there and how much did each contribute ?
10. A school collected Rs 2304 as fees from its students. If each student paid as many paise as there were students in the school, how many students were there in the school ?
11. The area of a square field is 5184 m^2. A rectangular field, whose length is twice its breadth has its perimeter equal to the perimeter of the square field. Find the area of the rectangular field.
12. Find the least square number, exactly divisible by each one of the numbers:
    (i) 6, 9, 15 and 20 (ii) 8, 12, 15 and 20
13. Find the square roots of 121 and 169 by the method of repeated subtraction.
14. Write the prime factorization of the following numbers and hence find their square roots.
    (i) 7744 (ii) 9604 (iii) 5929 (iv) 7056
15. The students of class VIII of a school donated Rs 2401 for PM's National Relief Fund. Each student donated as many rupees as the number of students in the class. Find the number of students in the class.
16. A PT teacher wants to arrange maximum possible number of 6000 students in a field such that the number of rows is equal to the number of columns. Find the number of rows if 71 were left out after arrangement.

ANSWERS

1. (i) 1 or 9, odd (ii) 4 or 6 (iii) 10 or 9, odd (iv) 5, odd
2. (i) 21 (ii) 14 (iii) 23 (iv) 42 (v) 34
   (vi) 64 (vii) 84 (viii) 91 (ix) 108 (x) 217
   (xi) 156 (xii) 437 (xiii) 766 (xiv) 165 (xv) 1736

3. 5, 30 4. 3, 21 5. 5, 27 6. 2, 24
7. 144, 9 8. 450 9. 96, 96 paise 10. 48 students
11. 4608 m^2 12. (i) 900 (ii) 3600 13. 11, 13
14. (i) 88 (ii) 98 (iii) 77 (iv) 84
15. 49 students 16. 77 rows

3.7 RELATION BETWEEN THE DIGITS OF A PERFECT SQUARE AND ITS SQUARE ROOT

In order to find the number of digits in the square root of a natural number, we follow the following steps:

<u>Step I</u> *Obtain the number.*

<u>Step II</u> *Place a bar over every pair of digits starting with the units digit. Each pair and remaining one digit (if any) on the extreme left is called a period. For example (i) 2809 will be written as* $\overline{28}\,\overline{09}$. *In this 28 is called the first period and 09 is called the second period. (ii) 39204 will be written as* $\overline{3}\,\overline{92}\,\overline{02}$. *Here, 3 is the first period, 92 is the second period and 04 is the third period.*

<u>Step III</u> *Count the number of bars. The number of bars is the number of digits in the square root of the given number. For example, the square root of 2809 has two digits and the square root of 39204 has three digits.*

ILLUSTRATION 1 Find the number of digits in the square roots of each of the following perfect squares:

(i) 390625 (ii) 1758276 (iii) 152399025

Solution Placing a bar over pair of digits starting with the units digits, we have

(i) $\overline{39}\,\overline{06}\,\overline{25}$. So, the square root of 390625 has three digits.

(ii) $\overline{1}\,\overline{75}\,\overline{82}\,\overline{76}$. So, 1758276 has four digits.

(iii) $\overline{1}\,\overline{52}\,\overline{39}\,\overline{90}\,\overline{25}$. So, 152399025 has five digits.

It follows from the above discussion that:

If the number of digits in a square number is n, then

(i) the number of digits in its square root is $\frac{n}{2}$, when n is even.

(ii) the number of digits in its square root is $\left(\frac{n+1}{2}\right)$, When n is odd.

3.8 SQUARE ROOTS OF PERFECT SQUARES BY THE METHOD OF LONG DIVISION

In section 3.5, we have learnt the method of finding the square root of perfect squares by prime factorization. When the square numbers are very large, the method of finding their square roots by prime factorization becomes very lengthy and difficult also. In such cases, we use the method of long division to find the square root. We follow the following stepwise procedure to find the square root of squares by long division method.

PROCEDURE

<u>*Step I*</u> *Obtain the number whose square root is to be computed.*

<u>*Step II*</u> *Place bars over every pair of digits starting with the units digit. Also, place a bar on one digit (if any) not forming a pair on the extreme left. Each pair and the remaining one digit (if any) on the extreme left is called a period.*

<u>*Step III*</u> *Think of the largest number whose square is less than or equal to the first period. Take this number as the divisor and the quotient.*

<u>*Step IV*</u> *Put the quotient above the period and write the product of divisor and quotient just below the first period.*

<u>*Step V*</u> *Subtract the product of divisor and quotient from the first period and bring down the next period to the right of the remainder. This becomes the new dividend.*

<u>*Step VI*</u> *Double the quotient as it appears and enter it with a blank on the right for the next digit, as the next possible divisor.*

<u>*Step VII*</u> *Think of a digit, to fill the blank in step VI, in such a way that the product of new divisor and this digit is equal to or just less than the new dividend obtained in step V.*

<u>*Step VIII*</u> *Subtract the product of the digit chosen in step VII and the new divisor from the dividend obtained in step V and bring down the next period to the right of the remainder. This becomes new dividend.*

<u>*Step IX*</u> *Repeat steps VI, VII and VIII till all periods have been taken up.*

<u>*Step X*</u> *Obtain the quotient as the square root of the given number.*

Following examples will illustrate the above procedure.

ILLUSTRATIVE EXAMPLES

Example 1 Find the square root of each of the following numbers by long division method:

(i) 54756 (ii) 390625 (iii) 4937284

Solution

	234
2	$\overline{5}\ \overline{47}\ \overline{56}$
	4
43	147
	129
464	1856
	1856
	0

$\therefore \quad \sqrt{54756} = 234.$

Explanation: The given number is 54756. Placing bars over every pair of digits starting with the units digit, we find that there are three periods. The first period has only one digit 5. Clearly, the largest number whose square is just less than 5 is 2. So, we take 2 as the divisor and quotient both and put the quotient above the first period i.e. 5.

Subtracting the product of divisor and quotient from the first period, we get 1 as the remainder. Bringing down the next period i.e. 47 to the right of the remainder, we obtain 147 as the new dividend.

For the next divisor double the quotient 2 i.e. take 4 as the left most digit of the new divisior. Now, 3 is the largest digit such that $43 \times 3 = 129$ which is just less than the new dividend 147. So, take 43 as the new divisor and 23 as the new quotient.

Now, subtract 129 from 147 to get 18 as the remainder.

Bring down the next period 56 to the right of 18 to get 1856 as the new dividend.

For the next divisor double the quotient 23 to get 46. Take 46 as the left two digits of the new divisor. Now 4 is the largest digit such that $464 \times 4 = 1856$. So, take 464 as the new divisor and 4 as the new digit of the quotient.

Subtract 1856 from the new dividend 1856 to get 0 as the remainder.

The last quotient is 234.

Hence, $\sqrt{54756} = 234$.

(ii)

	625
6	$\overline{39}\ \overline{06}\ \overline{25}$
	36
122	306
	244
1245	6225
	6225
	0

$\therefore \quad \sqrt{390625} = 625$

(iii)

	2222
2	$\overline{4}\ \overline{93}\ \overline{72}\ \overline{84}$
	4
42	093
	84
442	972
	884
4442	8884
	8884
	0

$\because \quad \sqrt{4937284} = 2222$

Example 2 Find the least number which must be subtracted from 18265 to make it a perfect square. Also, find the square root of the resulting number.

Solution Let us work out the process of finding the square root of 18265 by long division method.

```
         135
   1 | 1 82 65
     | 1
     |--------
  23 |   82
     |   69
     |--------
 265 |   1365
     |   1325
     |--------
     |     40
```

We find that in the process of working out the square root of 18265 by long division method, the remainder in the last step is 40. This means that if 40 be subtracted from the given number, the remainder will be zero and the new number will be a perfect square.

Hence, the required least number = 40

and, required square number = 18265 – 40 = 18225

Also, $\sqrt{18225} = 135$

Example 3 Find the least number which must be added to 306452 to make it a perfect square.

Solution Let us first work out the process of finding the square root by the division method:

```
          553                       554
    5 | 30 64 52             5 | 30 64 52
      | 25                       | 25
      |---------                 |---------
  105 |   564              105   |   564
      |   525                    |   525
      |---------                 |---------
 1103 |    3952            1104  |    3952
      |    3309                  |    4416
```

It is evident from the above working that $(553)^2 < 306452 < (554)^2$. Also, 306452 is (4416 – 3952) = 464 less than $(554)^2$. Thus, if we add 464 to 306452, it will be a perfect square.

Hence, the required least number is 464

Example 4 Find the greatest number of six digits which is a perfect square.

Solution We know that the greatest number of six digits is 999999. In order to find the greatest number of six digits which is a perfect square, we must first find the smallest number that must be subtracted from 999999 to make it a perfect square. For this, we work out the process of finding the square root of 999999 by long division method as given below.

```
          999
     ┌──────────
   9 │ 99 99 99
     │ 81
     ├──────────
 189 │ 1899
     │ 1701
     ├──────────
1989 │  19899
     │  17901
     ├──────────
     │   1998
```

It follows from this, that we must subtract 1998 from 999999 to make it a perfect square.

$\therefore$ Required number = 999999 – 1998 = 998001.

Example 5 Find the least number of four digits which is a perfect square.

Solution We know that the least number of 4 digits is 1000.

In order to find the least number of four digits which is a perfect square, we must first find the smallest number that must be added to 1000 to make it a perfect square. For this, we work out the process of finding the square root by long division method as given below.

```
       31                    32
   ┌──────               ┌──────
 3 │ 10 00             3 │ 10 00
   │  9                  │  9
   ├──────               ├──────
61 │  100             62 │  100
   │   61                │  124
   ├──────
   │   39
```

It follows from this that 1000 is (124 – 100) = 24 less than $(32)^2$. Thus, if we add 24 to 1000, it becomes a perfect square.

Hence, the smallest number of four digits which is a perfect square is (1000 + 24) = 1024.

EXERCISE 3.5

1. Find the square root of each of the following by long division method:

   (i) 12544 (ii) 97344 (iii) 286225 (iv) 390625 (v) 363609

   (vi) 974169 (vii) 120409 (viii) 1471369 (ix) 291600 (x) 9653449

   (xi) 1745041 (xii) 4008004 (xiii) 20657025 (xiv) 152547201 (xv) 20421361

   (xvi) 62504836 (xvii) 82264900 (xviii) 3226694416 (xix) 6407522209 (xx) 3915380329

2. Find the least number which must be subtracted from the following numbers to make them a perfect square:

   (i) 2361 (ii) 194491 (iii) 26535 (iv) 16160 (v) 4401624

3. Find the least number which must be added to the following numbers to make them a perfect square:

   (i) 5607 (ii) 4931 (iii) 4515600 (iv) 37460 (v) 506900

4. Find the greatest number of 5 digits which is a perfect square.

5. Find the least number of 4 digits which is a perfect square.

6. Find the least number of six digits which is a perfect square.

7. Find the greatest number of 4 digits which is a perfect square.
8. A General arranges his soldiers in rows to form a perfect square. He finds that in doing so, 60 soldiers are left out. If the total number of soldiers be 8160, find the number of soldiers in each row.
9. The area of a square field is 60025 m^2. A man cycles along its boundary at 18 km/hr. In how much time will he return at the starting point ?
10. The cost of levelling and turfing a square lawn at Rs 2.50 per m^2 is Rs 13322.50. Find the cost of fencing it at Rs 5 per metre.
11. Find the greatest number of three digits which is a perfect square.
12. Find the smallest number which must be added to 2300 so that it becomes a perfect square.

ANSWERS

1. (i) 112 (ii) 312 (iii) 535 (iv) 625 (v) 603 (vi) 987 (vii) 347 (viii) 1213 (ix) 540 (x) 3107 (xi) 1321 (xii) 2002 (xiii) 4545 (xiv) 12351 (xv) 4519 (xvi) 7906 (xvii) 9070 (xviii) 56804 (xix) 80047 (xx) 62573
2. (i) 57 (ii) 10 (iii) 291 (iv) 31 (v) 20
3. (i) 18 (ii) 110 (iii) 25 (iv) 176 (v) 44
4. 99856 5. 1024 6. 100489 7. 9801 8. 90 soldiers 9. 3 min 16 sec
10. Rs 1460 11. 961 12. 4

3.9 SQUARE ROOTS OF RATIONAL NUMBERS IN THE FORM OF FRACTIONS

Up till now, we have learnt about the square roots of natural numbers which were perfect squares. In this section, we shall discuss about the square root of a rational number which can be written as the square of a rational number.

SQUARE ROOT OF A RATIONAL NUMBER *The square root of a rational number x is that rational number y which when multiplied by itself gives the number x.*

Thus, $y = \sqrt{x}$ if and only if $y^2 = x$

For example, $\left(\frac{3}{4}\right)^2 = \frac{9}{16} \Rightarrow \sqrt{\frac{9}{16}} = \frac{3}{4}$

$\left(\frac{9}{25}\right)^2 = \frac{81}{625} \Rightarrow \sqrt{\frac{81}{625}} = \frac{9}{25}$ and so on.

<u>Remark 1</u> *Since* $\frac{9}{16} = \left(\frac{3}{4}\right)^2 = \left(-\frac{3}{4}\right)^2$. *Therefore,* $\frac{3}{4}$ *and* $-\frac{3}{4}$ *can be both as the square roots of* $\frac{9}{16}$. *But, we shall be finding only the positive square roots of rational numbers. Thus, we have*

$$\sqrt{\frac{9}{16}} = \frac{3}{4} \text{ and } \sqrt{\frac{9}{16}} \neq -\frac{3}{4}$$

Remark 2 *The square root of a negative number is not possible, because there is no number x such that x^2 is negative.*

Result *If a and b are squares of some numbers, then* $\sqrt{\frac{a}{b}} = \frac{\sqrt{a}}{\sqrt{b}}$

This result will be used to find the square roots of rational numbers.

In order to find the square roots of rational numbers by factorization, we follow the following steps:

Step I *Obtain the fraction.*

Step II *If the given fraction is a mixed fraction, then convert it into an improper fraction.*

Step III *Find the square root of the numerator and the denominator separately.*

Step IV *Obtain the fraction whose numerator and denominator are the square roots of numerator and denominator respectively of the given fraction.*

Step V *The fraction obtained in step IV is the square root of the given fraction.*

Following examples will illustrate the above procedure.

ILLUSTRATIVE EXAMPLES

Example 1 Find the square root of $\frac{256}{441}$.

Solution We have, $\sqrt{\frac{256}{441}} = \frac{\sqrt{256}}{\sqrt{441}}$

Now, we find the square roots of 256 and 441 separately as shown below:

$$\begin{array}{r|l} & 16 \\ \hline 1 & \overline{2}\,\overline{56} \\ & 1 \\ \hline 26 & 156 \\ & 156 \\ \hline & 0 \end{array} \qquad \begin{array}{r|l} & 21 \\ \hline 2 & \overline{4}\,\overline{41} \\ & 4 \\ \hline 41 & 41 \\ & 41 \\ \hline & 0 \end{array}$$

Thus, $\sqrt{256} = 16$ and $\sqrt{441} = 21$

Hence, $\sqrt{\frac{256}{441}} = \frac{\sqrt{256}}{\sqrt{441}} = \frac{16}{21}$

Example 2 Find the square root of $\frac{625}{1296}$.

Solution We have, $\sqrt{\frac{625}{1296}} = \frac{\sqrt{625}}{\sqrt{1296}}$

Now, we find the square roots of 625 and 1296 separately as shown below:

$$\begin{array}{r|l} & 25 \\ \hline 2 & \overline{6}\;\overline{25} \\ & 4 \\ \hline 45 & 225 \\ & 225 \\ \hline & 0 \end{array} \qquad \begin{array}{r|l} & 36 \\ \hline 3 & \overline{12}\;\overline{96} \\ & 9 \\ \hline 66 & 396 \\ & 396 \\ \hline & 0 \end{array}$$

Thus, $\sqrt{625} = 25$ and $\sqrt{1296} = 36$

Hence, $\sqrt{\dfrac{625}{1296}} = \dfrac{\sqrt{625}}{\sqrt{1296}} = \dfrac{25}{36}$

Example 3 Find the square root of $52\dfrac{857}{2116}$.

Solution We have $\sqrt{52\dfrac{857}{2116}} = \sqrt{\dfrac{110889}{2116}}$

Now, we find the square roots of 110889 and 2116 separately as given below:

$$\begin{array}{r|l} & 333 \\ \hline 3 & \overline{11}\;\overline{08}\;\overline{89} \\ & 9 \\ \hline 63 & 208 \\ & 189 \\ \hline 663 & 1989 \\ & 1989 \\ \hline & 0 \end{array} \qquad \begin{array}{r|l} & 46 \\ \hline 2 & \overline{21}\;\overline{16} \\ & 16 \\ \hline 40 & 516 \\ & 516 \\ \hline & 0 \end{array}$$

Thus, $\sqrt{110889} = 333$ and $\sqrt{2116} = 46$

$\therefore \quad \dfrac{\sqrt{110889}}{\sqrt{2116}} = \dfrac{333}{46}$

Hence, $\sqrt{52\dfrac{857}{2116}} = \dfrac{333}{46}$

Example 4 The area of a square field is $101\dfrac{1}{400}$ square metres. Find the length of one side of the field.

Solution Let the length of one side of the square field be x metres. Then,

Area of the field $= x^2$

But, area of the field $= 101\frac{1}{400}\,m^2 = \frac{40401}{400}\,m^2$

$\therefore \quad x^2 = \frac{40401}{400}$

$\Rightarrow \quad x = \sqrt{\frac{40401}{400}} = \frac{\sqrt{40401}}{\sqrt{400}}$

Now, we shall find the square roots of 40401 and 400 separately, as given below:

	201
3	$\overline{4}\,\overline{04}\,\overline{01}$
	4
401	0401
	401
	0

	20
3	$\overline{4}\,\overline{00}$
	4
40	000
	000
	0

Thus, $\sqrt{40401} = 201$ and $\sqrt{400} = 20$

$\therefore \quad x = \frac{\sqrt{40401}}{\sqrt{400}} = \frac{201}{20}$

Hence, the length of one side of the field is $\frac{201}{20}$ metres.

Example 5 Find the value of

(i) $\frac{\sqrt{243}}{\sqrt{867}}$ (ii) $\frac{\sqrt{1183}}{\sqrt{2023}}$ (iii) $\sqrt{0.0196}$ (iv) $\sqrt{37.0881}$

Solution (i) We have,

$\frac{\sqrt{243}}{\sqrt{867}} = \sqrt{\frac{243}{867}}$ $\left[\because \frac{\sqrt{a}}{\sqrt{b}} = \sqrt{\frac{a}{b}}\right]$

$= \sqrt{\frac{81}{289}}$ [Cancelling common factor 3 from numerator and denominator]

$= \frac{\sqrt{81}}{\sqrt{289}} = \frac{9}{17}$ $[\because \sqrt{81} = 9$ and $\sqrt{289} = 17]$

(ii) We have,

$\frac{\sqrt{1183}}{\sqrt{2023}} = \sqrt{\frac{1183}{2023}}$ $\left[\because \frac{\sqrt{a}}{\sqrt{b}} = \sqrt{\frac{a}{b}}\right]$

$= \sqrt{\frac{169}{289}}$ [Cancelling common factor 7 from numerator and denominator]

$= \frac{\sqrt{169}}{\sqrt{289}} = \frac{13}{17}$ $[\because \sqrt{169} = 13$ and $\sqrt{289} = 17]$

(iii) We have,

$$\sqrt{0.0196} = \sqrt{\frac{196}{10000}}$$

$$= \frac{\sqrt{196}}{\sqrt{10000}} = \frac{\sqrt{2\times2\times7\times7}}{\sqrt{100\times100}} = \frac{2\times7}{100} = 0.14$$

(iv) We have,

$$\sqrt{37.0881} = \sqrt{\frac{370881}{10000}}$$

$$= \frac{\sqrt{370881}}{\sqrt{10000}} = \frac{609}{100} = 6.09 \quad \left[\because \sqrt{370881} = 609 \text{ and } \sqrt{10000} = 100\right]$$

Example 6 Find the value of

(i) $\sqrt{99}\times\sqrt{396}$ (ii) $\sqrt{147}\times\sqrt{243}$

Solution (i) We have,

$$\sqrt{99}\times\sqrt{396} = \sqrt{99\times396} \qquad \left[\because \sqrt{a}\times\sqrt{b} = \sqrt{ab}\right]$$

$$= \sqrt{3\times3\times11\times2\times2\times3\times3\times11}$$

$$= \sqrt{3\times3\times3\times3\times2\times2\times11\times11}$$

$$= 3\times3\times2\times11 = 198$$

(ii) We have,

$$\sqrt{147}\times\sqrt{243} = \sqrt{147\times243} \qquad \left[\because \sqrt{a}\times\sqrt{b} = \sqrt{ab}\right]$$

$$= \sqrt{3\times7\times7\times3\times3\times3\times3\times3}$$

$$= \sqrt{3\times3\times3\times3\times3\times3\times7\times7} = 3\times3\times3\times7 = 189$$

EXERCISE 3.6

1. Find the square root of:

(i) $\frac{441}{961}$ (ii) $\frac{324}{841}$ (iii) $4\frac{29}{29}$ (iv) $2\frac{14}{25}$ (v) $2\frac{137}{196}$

(vi) $23\frac{26}{121}$ (vii) $25\frac{544}{729}$ (viii) $75\frac{46}{49}$ (ix) $3\frac{942}{2209}$ (x) $3\frac{334}{3025}$

(xi) $21\frac{2797}{3364}$ (xii) $38\frac{11}{25}$ (xiii) $23\frac{394}{729}$ (xiv) $21\frac{51}{169}$ (xv) $10\frac{151}{225}$

2. Find the value of:

(i) $\frac{\sqrt{80}}{\sqrt{405}}$ (ii) $\frac{\sqrt{441}}{\sqrt{625}}$ (iii) $\frac{\sqrt{1587}}{\sqrt{1728}}$ (iv) $\sqrt{72}\times\sqrt{338}$ (v) $\sqrt{45}\times\sqrt{20}$

3. The area of a square field is $80\frac{244}{729}$ square metres. Find the length of each side of the field.

4. The area of a square field is $30\frac{1}{4}$ m^2. Calculate the length of the side of the square.

5. Find the length of a side of a square playground whose area is equal to the area of a rectangular field of dimensions 72 m and 338 m.

ANSWERS

1. (i) $\frac{21}{31}$ (ii) $\frac{18}{29}$ (iii) $\frac{15}{7}$ (iv) $\frac{8}{5}$ (v) $\frac{23}{14}$ (vi) $\frac{53}{11}$
(vii) $\frac{137}{27}$ (viii) $\frac{61}{7}$ (ix) $\frac{87}{47}$ (x) $\frac{97}{55}$ (xi) $\frac{271}{58}$ (xii) $\frac{31}{5}$
(xiii) $4\frac{23}{27}$ (xiv) $4\frac{8}{13}$ (xv) $3\frac{4}{15}$

2. (i) $\frac{4}{9}$ (ii) $\frac{21}{25}$ (iii) $\frac{23}{24}$ (iv) 156 (v) 30

3. $8\frac{26}{27}$ m 4. $5\frac{1}{2}$ m 5. 156 m

3.10 SQUARE ROOTS OF RATIONAL NUMBERS IN DECIMAL FORM

Recall that the square root of a rational number x is that rational number y which when multiplied by itself gives the number x. That is,

$$y^2 = x \quad \Rightarrow \sqrt{x} = y.$$

$$\therefore \quad (0.4)^2 = 0.16 \quad \Rightarrow \sqrt{0.16} = 0.4$$
$$(0.41)^2 = 0.1681 \quad \Rightarrow \sqrt{0.1681} = 0.41$$
$$(0.411)^2 = 0.168921 \quad \Rightarrow \sqrt{0.168921} = 0.411$$
$$(2.1)^2 = 4.41 \quad \Rightarrow \sqrt{4.41} = 2.1$$
$$(2.11)^2 = 4.4521 \quad \Rightarrow \sqrt{4.4521} = 2.11 \text{ and so on.}$$

It is evident from the above calculations that the square of a decimal fraction consists of twice as many decimal places as given in the number. Consequently, the number of decimal places in the square root of a given decimal fraction is half of the number of decimal places in the given number. Therefore, the tenth's digit of the square root comes from the first two decimal places to the right, hundredth's from the third and fourth places and so on.

In view of the above observations, we have the following step-wise procedure to find the square root of a decimal fraction.

PROCEDURE

Step I *Obtain the number in the decimal form.*

Step II *Place bars on the integral part as we do in the process of finding the square root of a perfect square of some natural number.*

Step III *Make even number of decimal places by affixing a zero on the extreme right of decimal part, if necessary.*

Step IV *Place bars on the decimal part on every pair of digits beginning with the first decimal place.*

Step V *Start finding the square root by the long division method and put the decimal point in the square root as soon as the integral part is exhausted.*

Following examples will illustrate the above procedure.

ILLUSTRATIVE EXAMPLES

Example 1 Find the square root of 477. 4225.

Solution Here, the number of decimal places is already even. So, we place bars on the integral and decimal parts and proceed as given below:

	21.85
2	$\overline{4}\,\overline{77}.\overline{42}\,\overline{25}$
	4
41	77
	41
428	3642
	3424
4365	21825
	21825
	0

Thus, we have $\sqrt{477.4225} = 21.85$

Example 2 Find the square root of 0.00008281.

Solution Here, the number of decimal places is even. So, we place the bars and find the square root as shown below:

	0.0091
	$0.\overline{00}\,\overline{00}\,\overline{82}\,\overline{81}$
	0
9	00 00 82
	81
181	181
	181
	0

Thus, $\sqrt{0.00008281} = 0.0091$

Example 3 Find the square root of 0.053361.

Solution Here, the number of decimal places is even. So, we mark off periods and find the square root as given below:

	0.231
2	$0.\overline{05}\,\overline{33}\,\overline{61}$
	4
43	133
	129
461	461
	461
	0

Thus, $\sqrt{0.053361} = 0.231$

Example 4 A decimal fraction is multiplied by itself. If the product is 251953.8025, find the fraction.

Solution Let the required fraction be x. Then,

$$x \times x = 251953.8025$$

$$\Rightarrow \quad x^2 = 251953.8025$$

$$\Rightarrow \quad x = \sqrt{251953.8025}$$

Now, we mark off the periods and find the square root of 251953.8025 as given below.

```
              501.95
        5 | 25 19 53 . 80 25
          | 25
          |-----------------
     1001 |    1953
          |    1001
          |-----------------
    10029 |     95280
          |     90261
          |-----------------
   100385 |     501925
          |     501925
          |-----------------
          |          0
```

Hence, $x = \sqrt{251953.8025} = 501.95$

Example 5 Find the value of $\sqrt{15625}$ and the use it to find the value of $\sqrt{156.25} + \sqrt{1.5625}$.

Solution We first find the value of $\sqrt{15625}$ by long division method as given below:

```
          125
     1 | 1 56 25
       | 1
       |--------
    22 |   56
       |   44
       |--------
   245 |   1225
       |   1225
       |--------
       |      0
```

$\therefore \quad \sqrt{15625} = 125$

Now,

$$\sqrt{156.25} + \sqrt{1.5625}$$

$$= \sqrt{\frac{15625}{100}} + \sqrt{\frac{15625}{10000}}$$

$$= \frac{\sqrt{15625}}{\sqrt{100}} + \frac{\sqrt{15625}}{\sqrt{10000}} = \frac{125}{10} + \frac{125}{100} = 12.5 + 1.25 = 13.75$$

Example 6 Find the square roots of 2304 and 1764 and hence find the value of

$$\frac{\sqrt{0.2304} + \sqrt{0.1764}}{\sqrt{0.2304} - \sqrt{0.1764}}$$

Solution First we find the square roots of 2304 and 1764 as given below:

$$\begin{array}{r|l} & 48 \\ \hline 2 & \overline{23}\ \overline{04} \\ & 16 \\ \hline 88 & 704 \\ & 704 \\ \hline & 0 \end{array} \qquad \begin{array}{r|l} & 42 \\ \hline 4 & \overline{17}\ \overline{64} \\ & 16 \\ \hline 82 & 164 \\ & 164 \\ \hline & 0 \end{array}$$

$\therefore$ $\sqrt{2304} = 48$ and $\sqrt{1764} = 42$

Now, $\sqrt{0.2304} = \sqrt{\dfrac{2304}{10000}} = \dfrac{\sqrt{2340}}{\sqrt{10000}} = \dfrac{48}{100}$

and, $\sqrt{0.1764} = \sqrt{\dfrac{1764}{10000}} = \dfrac{\sqrt{1764}}{\sqrt{10000}} = \dfrac{42}{100}$

$$\therefore \quad \frac{\sqrt{0.2304}+\sqrt{0.1764}}{\sqrt{0.2304}-\sqrt{0.1764}} = \frac{\frac{48}{100}+\frac{42}{100}}{\frac{48}{100}-\frac{42}{100}} = \frac{\frac{48+42}{100}}{\frac{48-42}{100}} = \frac{48+42}{48-42} = \frac{90}{6} = 15$$

EXERCISE 3.7

Find the square root of the following numbers in decimal form:

1. 84.8241
2. 0.7225
3. 0.813604
4. 0.00002025
5. 150.0625
6. 225.6004
7. 3600.720036
8. 236.144689
9. 0.00059049
10. 176.252176
11. 9998.0001
12. 0.00038809
13. What is that fraction which when multiplied by itself gives 227.798649?
14. The area of a square playground is 256.6404 square metres. Find the length of one side of the playground.
15. What is the fraction which when multiplied by itself gives 0.00053361?
16. Simplify: (i) $\dfrac{\sqrt{59.29}-\sqrt{5.29}}{\sqrt{59.29}+\sqrt{5.29}}$ (ii) $\dfrac{\sqrt{0.2304}+\sqrt{0.1764}}{\sqrt{0.2304}-\sqrt{0.1764}}$
17. Evaluate $\sqrt{50625}$ and hence find the value of $\sqrt{506.25}+\sqrt{5.0625}$
18. Find the value of $\sqrt{103.0225}$ and hence find the value of
(i) $\sqrt{10302.25}$ (ii) $\sqrt{1.030225}$

ANSWERS

1. 9.21 2. 0.85 3. 0.902 4. 0.0045 5. 12.25 6. 15.02
7. 60.006 8. 15.367 9. 0.0243 10. 13.276 11. 99.99 12. 0.0197
13. 15.093 14. 16.02 metres 15. 0.0231 16. (i) 0.54 (ii) 15
17. 225, 24.75 18. 10.15 (i) 101.5 (ii) 1.015

3.11 APPROXIMATE VALUES OF SQUARE ROOTS BY THE METHOD OF LONG DIVISION

In this section, we shall use the method of long division to find the square roots correct to certain decimal places. We use the following stepwise procedure to do the same.

PROCEDURE

Step I *Obtain the number whose square root is to be computed.*

Step II *Determine the number of decimal places to which the square root of the number is to be computed.*

Suppose the square root of the given number is to be computed correct to n places of decimal.

Step III *Count the number of digits in the decimal part. If the number of digits is less than 2n, then affix a suitable number of zeros at the extreme right of the decimal part so that the number of digits in decimal part becomes 2n.*

Step IV *Use the method of long division to find the square root upto (n + 1) places of decimal.*

Step V *Check the digit at (n + 1)th decimal place, if it is less than 5, then delete it to get the answer correct to n decimal places. If the digit at (n + 1)th decimal place is 5 or more than, then increase the digit at nth decimal place by one and delete the digit at (n + 1)th place to obtain the square root correct upto n decimal places.*

The above procedure is illustrated by means of the following examples.

ILLUSTRATIVE EXAMPLES

Example 1 Find the square root of 2 correct to three places of decimal.

Solution Since we have to find the square root of 2 correct to three places of decimal, we shall first find the square root of 2 upto four places of decimal. For this purpose, we affix 8 zeros to the right of the decimal point. So, we write

$$2 = 2.00000000$$

Now, mark off periods and proceed as under:

```
          1.4142
      1 | 2.00 00 00 00
        | 1
     24 | 100
        |  96
    281 |   400
        |   281
   2824 |   11900
        |   11296
  28282 |   60400
        |   56564
        |    3856
```

$\therefore$ $\sqrt{2} = 1.4142$ upto four places of decimal.

$\Rightarrow$ $\sqrt{2} = 1.414$ correct upto three places of decimal.

Hence, $\sqrt{2} = 1.414$

Example 2 Find the square root of 3 correct to three places of decimal.

Solution Since we have to find the square root of 3 correct to three places of decimal, we shall first find the square root of 3 upto four places of decimal. For this purpose, we must add 8 zeros to the right of the decimal point. Thus, we write

$$3 = 3.00000000$$

Now, we mark off periods and compute square root by long division method as given below:

$$\begin{array}{r|l} & 1.7320 \\ \hline 1 & \overline{3}.\overline{00}\,\overline{00}\,\overline{00}\,\overline{00} \\ & 1 \\ \hline 27 & 200 \\ & 189 \\ \hline 343 & \quad 1100 \\ & \quad 1029 \\ \hline 3462 & \qquad 7100 \\ & \qquad 6924 \\ \hline 34640 & \qquad\quad 17600 \end{array}$$

$\therefore$ $\sqrt{3} = 1.7320$ upto four places of decimal.

$\Rightarrow$ $\sqrt{3} = 1.732$ correct upto three places of decimal.

Hence, $\sqrt{3} = 1.732$

Example 3 Find the square root of 237.615 correct to three places of decimal.

Solution Since we have to find the square root of 237.615 correct to three places of decimal. Therefore, we first find the square root upto four decimal places. For this, we require 8 digits in the decimal part. So, we affix 5 zeros to the right of decimal part. That is, we write

$$237.615 = 237.61500000$$

Now, we mark off periods and proceed as under:

$$\begin{array}{r|l} & 15.4147 \\ \hline 1 & \overline{2}\,\overline{37}.\overline{61}\,\overline{50}\,\overline{00}\,\overline{00} \\ & 1 \\ \hline 25 & 137 \\ & 125 \\ \hline 304 & \quad 1261 \\ & \quad 1216 \\ \hline 3081 & \qquad 4550 \\ & \qquad 3081 \\ \hline 30824 & \qquad 146900 \\ & \qquad 123296 \\ \hline 308287 & \qquad\quad 2360400 \\ & \qquad\quad 2158009 \\ \hline & \qquad\qquad 202391 \end{array}$$

$\therefore \quad \sqrt{237.615} = 15.4147$ upto four places of decimal

$\Rightarrow \quad \sqrt{237.615} = 15.415$ correct to three places of decimal.

Example 4 Find the square root of $10\frac{2}{3}$ correct to three places of decimal.

Solution Since we have to find the square root of $10\frac{2}{3}$ correct to three places of decimal. So, we first find the square root upto four places of decimal. For this purpose, we convert the mixed fraction into improper fraction and then we write it in the decimal form in such a way that there are eight digits to the right of the decimal point.

Thus, we write

$$10\frac{2}{3} = 10.66666666$$

Now, we mark off periods and proceed as under:

	3.2659
3	$\overline{10}.\overline{66}\,\overline{66}\,\overline{66}\,\overline{66}$
	9
62	166
	124
646	4266
	3876
6525	39066
	32625
65309	644166
	587781
	56385

$\therefore \quad \sqrt{10\frac{2}{3}} = 3.2659$ upto four places of decimal.

$\Rightarrow \quad \sqrt{10\frac{2}{3}} = 3.266$ correct to three places of decimal.

Example 5 Find the square root of $\frac{3}{7}$ correct to four places of decimal.

Solution Since we have to find the square root of $\frac{3}{7}$ correct to four places of decimal. So, we first find its square root upto five places of decimal. For this, we write $\frac{3}{7}$ in decimal form such that there are 10 digits after the decimal point. That is,

$$\frac{3}{7} = 0.4285714285$$

Now, we mark off the periods and proceed to find the square root by long division method as given below:

	0.65465
6	$0.\overline{42}\,\overline{85}\,\overline{71}\,\overline{42}\,\overline{85}$
	36
125	685
	625
1304	6071
	5216
13086	85542
	78516
130925	702685
	654625
	48060

$\therefore \quad \sqrt{\frac{3}{7}} = 0.65465$ upto five decimal places

$\Rightarrow \quad \sqrt{\frac{3}{7}} = 0.6547$ correct to three places of decimal.

Example 6 Given that $\sqrt{2} = 1.414$ and $\sqrt{5} = 2.236$, evaluate each of the following:

(i) $\sqrt{\frac{36}{5}}$ (ii) $\sqrt{\frac{625}{98}}$

Solution (i) $\sqrt{\frac{36}{5}} = \frac{\sqrt{36}}{\sqrt{5}} = \frac{6}{\sqrt{5}} = \frac{6}{\sqrt{5}} \times \frac{\sqrt{5}}{\sqrt{5}} = \frac{6\sqrt{5}}{5}$

$\Rightarrow \sqrt{\frac{36}{5}} = \frac{6 \times 2.236}{5} = \frac{13.416}{5} = 2.6832$

(ii) $\sqrt{\frac{625}{98}} = \frac{\sqrt{625}}{\sqrt{98}} = \frac{\sqrt{25 \times 25}}{\sqrt{49 \times 2}} = \frac{25}{7 \times \sqrt{2}} = \frac{25}{7 \times \sqrt{2}} \times \frac{\sqrt{2}}{\sqrt{2}} = \frac{25\sqrt{2}}{7 \times 2} = \frac{25\sqrt{2}}{14}$

$\Rightarrow \sqrt{\frac{625}{98}} = \frac{25 \times 1.414}{14} = \frac{35.35}{14} = 2.525$

EXERCISE 3.8

1. Find the square root of each of the following correct to three places of decimal.

(i) 5 (ii) 7 (iii) 17 (iv) 20 (v) 66
(vi) 427 (vii) 1.7 (viii) 23.1 (ix) 2.5 (x) 237.615

(xi) 15.3215 (xii) 0.9 (xiii) 0.1 (xiv) 0.016 (xv) 0.00064

(xvi) 0.019 (xvii) $\frac{7}{8}$ (xviii) $\frac{5}{12}$ (xix) $2\frac{1}{2}$ (xx) $287\frac{5}{8}$

2. Find the square root of 12.0068 correct to four decimal places.

3. Find the square root of 11 correct to five decimal places.

4. Given that: $\sqrt{2} = 1.414$, $\sqrt{3} = 1.732$, $\sqrt{5} = 2.236$ and $\sqrt{7} = 2.646$, evaluate each of the following:

(i) $\sqrt{\frac{144}{7}}$ (ii) $\sqrt{\frac{2500}{3}}$

5. Given that $\sqrt{2} = 1.414$, $\sqrt{3} = 1.732$, $\sqrt{5} = 2.236$ and $\sqrt{7} = 2.646$, find the square roots of the following:

(i) $\frac{196}{75}$ (ii) $\frac{400}{63}$ (iii) $\frac{150}{7}$ (iv) $\frac{256}{5}$ (v) $\frac{27}{50}$

ANSWERS

1. (i) 2.236 (ii) 2.646 (iii) 4.123 (iv) 4.472 (v) 8.124 (vi) 20.664
(vii) 1.304 (viii) 4.806 (ix) 1.581 (x) 15.415 (xi) 3.914 (xii) 0.949
(xiii) 0.316 (xiv) 0.126 (xv) 0.025 (xvi) 0.138 (xvii) 0.935 (xviii) 0.645
(xix) 1.581 (xx) 16.960 2. 3.4651 3. 3.31662
4. (i) 4.536 (ii) 28.867 5. (i) 1.617 (ii) 2.520 (iii) 4.628 (iv) 7.155 (v) 0.735

HINTS TO SELECTED PROBLEMS

4. (i) $\sqrt{\frac{144}{7}} = \frac{\sqrt{144}}{\sqrt{7}} = \frac{12}{\sqrt{7}} = \frac{12\sqrt{7}}{\sqrt{7}\times\sqrt{7}} = \frac{12\sqrt{7}}{7} = \frac{12\times 2.646}{7}$

(ii) $\sqrt{\frac{2500}{3}} = \frac{\sqrt{2500}}{\sqrt{3}} = \frac{50}{\sqrt{3}} = \frac{50\sqrt{3}}{\sqrt{3}\times\sqrt{3}} = \frac{50\sqrt{3}}{3} = \frac{50\times 1.732}{3}$

3.12 APPROXIMATE VALUES OF SQUARE ROOTS BY USING SQUARE ROOT TABLES

In many practical problems, we need the square roots of numbers and finding approximate values of square roots of numbers by the method of long division is very time consuming and combursome. For this reason, tables have been prepared which provide the approximate values of square roots of different numbers correct to a certain decimal place. With the help of these tables the square roots of most of the numbers can be written down.

The following table gives values of square roots of all natural numbers from 1 to 99.

x	$\sqrt{x}$	x	$\sqrt{x}$	x	$\sqrt{x}$	x	$\sqrt{x}$
1	1.000	26	5.999	51	7.141	76	8.718
2	1.414	27	5.196	52	7.211	77	8.775
3	1.732	28	5.292	53	7.208	78	8.832
4	2.000	29	5.385	54	7.348	79	8.888
5	2.236	30	5.447	55	7.416	80	8.944
6	2.449	31	5.568	56	7.483	81	9.000
7	2.646	32	5.657	57	7.550	82	9.055
8	2.828	33	5.745	58	7.616	83	9.110
9	3.000	34	5.831	59	5.681	84	9.165
10	3.162	35	5.916	60	7.746	85	9.220
11	3.317	36	6.000	61	7.810	86	9.274
12	3.464	37	6.083	62	7.874	87	9.327
13	3.606	38	6.164	63	7.937	88	9.381
14	3.742	39	6.245	64	8.000	89	9.434
15	3.873	40	6.325	65	8.062	90	9.487
16	4.000	41	6.403	66	8.124	91	9.539
17	4.123	42	6.481	67	8.185	92	9.592
18	4.243	43	6.557	68	8.246	93	9.644
19	4.359	44	6.633	69	8.307	94	9.695
20	4.472	45	6.708	70	8.367	95	9.747
21	4.583	46	6.782	71	8.426	96	9.798
22	4.690	47	6.856	72	8.485	97	9.849
23	4.796	48	6.928	73	8.544	98	9.899
24	4.899	49	7.000	74	8.602	99	9.950
25	5.000	50	7.071	75	8.660		

Using this table, we can find the square roots of numbers, larger than 100 also, as illustrated in the following examples.

ILLUSTRATIVE EXAMPLES

Example 1 By using the table for square roots, find the values of:

(i) $\sqrt{7}$ (ii) $\sqrt{26}$ (iii) $\sqrt{432}$ (iv) $\sqrt{1280}$

Solution (i) Let $x = 7$. Look at the row containing 7. We find that the entry in the column of $\sqrt{x}$ is 2.646

$\therefore \quad \sqrt{x} = \sqrt{7} = 2.646$

(ii) Let $x = 26$. In the table containing square roots, we find that the entry in the column of $\sqrt{x}$ is 5.009

Hence, $\sqrt{x} = \sqrt{26} = 5.009$

(iii) $\sqrt{432} = \sqrt{2\times 2\times 2\times 2\times 3\times 3\times 3}$

$= 2\times 2\times 3\times \sqrt{3}$

$= 12\sqrt{3}$

$= 12\times 1.732$ [Using table for $\sqrt{3}$]

$= 20.784$

(iv) $\sqrt{1280} = \sqrt{2\times 2\times 2\times 2\times 2\times 2\times 2\times 2\times 5}$

$= 2\times 2\times 2\times 2\times \sqrt{5}$

$= 16\times (2.236)$ [Using table for $\sqrt{5}$]

$= 35.776$

Example 2 Find the value of each of the following by using the square root table:

(i) $\sqrt{13.32}$ (ii) $\sqrt{3.1428}$ (iii) $\dfrac{\sqrt{37}}{64}$

Solution (i) $\sqrt{13.32} = \sqrt{\dfrac{1332}{100}}$

$= \dfrac{\sqrt{1332}}{\sqrt{100}}$

$= \dfrac{\sqrt{2^2\times 3^2\times 37}}{\sqrt{10^2}}$

$= \dfrac{2\times 3\times \sqrt{37}}{10}$

$= \dfrac{6\sqrt{37}}{10}$

$= \dfrac{6\times 6.083}{10} = 3.6498$ [Using table: $\sqrt{37} = 6.083$]

(ii) $\sqrt{3.1428} = \sqrt{\dfrac{31428}{10000}}$

$= \dfrac{\sqrt{2^2\times 9^2\times 97}}{\sqrt{10000}}$

$= \dfrac{2\times 9\times \sqrt{97}}{100}$

$= \dfrac{18\times 9.849}{100} = 1.77282$ [Using table: $\sqrt{97} = 9.849$]

(iii) $\sqrt{\frac{37}{64}} = \frac{\sqrt{37}}{\sqrt{64}} = \frac{\sqrt{37}}{8} = \frac{6.083}{8}$ [Using table: $\sqrt{37} = 6.083$]

$= 0.7604$

Example 3 Using the square root able, find the value of each of the following:

(i) 71.79 (ii) 6.328 (iii) 55.62

Solution (i) From the square root table, we have

$\sqrt{71} = 8.426$ and $\sqrt{72} = 8.485$

$\therefore$ Difference in the values of $\sqrt{72}$ and $\sqrt{71}$ is 0.059

Thus, for the difference of $(72-71)=1$, the difference in the values of their square roots is 0.059.

$\therefore$ For the difference of 0.79, the difference in the values of their square roots is

$0.059 \times 0.79 = 0.04661$

$= 0.047$ (Upto 3 decimal places)

$\therefore$ $\sqrt{71.79} = 8.426 + 0.047 = 8.473$

(ii) From the square root table, we have

$\sqrt{6} = 2.449$ and $\sqrt{7} = 2.646$

$\therefore$ Difference in the values of $\sqrt{7}$ and $\sqrt{6}$ is $(2.646 - 2.449) = 0.197$

Thus, for the difference of $(7-6)=1$, the difference in the values of the square roots is 0.197

$\therefore$ For the difference of 0.328, the difference in the values their square roots

$= 0.328 \times 0.197 = 0.064616 = 0.065$ (upto 3 places)

$\therefore$ $\sqrt{6.328} = 2.449 + 0.065 = 2.514$

(iii) From the square root table, we have

$\sqrt{55} = 7.416$ and $\sqrt{56} = 7.483$

Difference in the values of $\sqrt{56}$ and $\sqrt{55} = 0.067$

Thus, for the difference of $(56-55)=1$, the difference in the values of their square roots is 0.067.

$\therefore$ For the difference of 0.62, the difference in the values of square roots

$= 0.067 \times 0.62$

$= 0.04154$

$= 0.042$ [Upto 3 decimal places]

$\therefore$ $\sqrt{55.62} = 7.416 + 0.042 = 7.458$

EXERCISE 3.9

Using square root table, find the square roots of the following:

1. 7	2. 15	3. 74	4. 82	5. 198
6. 540	7. 8700	8. 3509	9. 6929	10. 25725
11. 1312	12. 4192	13. 4955	14. $\frac{99}{144}$	15. $\frac{57}{169}$
16. $\frac{101}{169}$	17. 13.21	18. 21.97	19. 110	20. 1110

21. 11.11

22. The area of a square field is 325 m^2. Find the approximate length of one side of the field.

23. Find the length of a side of a square, whose area is equal to the area of a rectangle with sides 240 m and 70 m.

ANSWERS

1. 2.646	2. 3.873	3. 8.602	4. 9.055	5. 14.070	6. 23.24
7. 93.27	8. 59.235	9. 83.239	10. 160.41	11. 36.22	12. 64.75
13. 70.39	14. 0.829	15. 0.581	16. 0.773	17. 3.635	18. 4.6827
19. 10.488	20. 33.317	21. 3.333	22. 18.030 m	23. 129.60 m	

THINGS TO REMEMBER

1. *A natural number x is a perfect square if there exists a natural number y such that* $x = y^2$.

   In other words, a natural number x is a perfect square, if it is equal to the product of a number with itself.

2. *A number ending in 2, 3, 7, or 8 is never a perfect square.*

3. *The number of zeros in the end of a perfect square is never odd. So, a number ending in an odd number of zeros is never a perfect square.*

4. *(i) Squares of even numbers are always even.*

   (ii) Squares of odd numbers are always odd.

5. *For any natural number n, we have*

   n^2 = *(Sum of first n odd natural numbers)*

6. *The square of a natural number, other than 1, is either a multiple of 3 or exceeds a multiple of 3 by 1.*

7. *The square of a natural number, other than 1, is either a multiple of 4 or exceeds a multiple of 4 by 1.*

8. *There are no natural numbers p and q such that* $p^2 = 2q^2$.

9. *For any natural number n greater than 1,* $(2n, n^2 - 1, n^2 + 1)$ *is a Pythagorean triplet.*

10. *The square root of a given natural number n is that natural number which when multiplied by itself gives n as the product and we denote the square root of n by* $\sqrt{n}$. *Thus,* $\sqrt{n} = m \Leftrightarrow n = m^2$.

11. *In order to find the square root of a perfect square, resolve it into prime factors; make pairs of similar factors and take the product of prime factors, choosing one out of every pair.*

12. *For finding the square root of a decimal fraction, make even number of decimal places by affixing a zero, if necessary; mark off periods and extract the square root; putting the decimal point in the square root as soon as the integral part is exhausted.*

13. *For positive numbers a and b, we have*

    (i) $\sqrt{ab} = \sqrt{a} \times \sqrt{b}$ *(ii)* $\sqrt{\frac{a}{b}} = \frac{\sqrt{a}}{\sqrt{b}}$

4

CUBES AND CUBE ROOTS

4.1 INTRODUCTION

In the earlier chapters, we have learnt about square and square roots. We extend the idea of square and square roots to cubes and cube roots in this chapter. As we have seen that the square roots of positive real numbers can be found only. However, cube roots are defined for positive as well as negative numbers. In fact, cube root of a negative number is negative of the cube root of its absolute value.

4.2 CUBES

CUBE *The cube of a number is that number raised to the power 3.*

Thus, if a is a number, then the cube of a is a^3.

That is, $$a^3 = a \times a \times a$$

For example,

$$2^3 = 2 \times 2 \times 2 = 8, \text{ that is the cube of 2 is 8}$$

$$3^3 = 3 \times 3 \times 3 = 27, \text{ that is the cube of 3 is 27}$$

$$4^3 = 4 \times 4 \times 4 = 64, \text{ that is the cube of 4 is 64}$$

$$(1.2)^3 = 1.2 \times 1.2 \times 1.2 = 1.728, \text{ that is the cube of 1.2 is 1.728}$$

$$\left(\frac{2}{3}\right)^3 = \frac{2}{3} \times \frac{2}{3} \times \frac{2}{3} = \frac{8}{27}, \text{ that is the cube of } \frac{2}{3} \text{ is } \frac{8}{27}.$$

4.3 CUBES OF NATURAL NUMBERS AND PERFECT CUBE NUMBERS

CUBE OF A NATURAL NUMBER *The cube of a natural number is that natural number raised to the power 3.*

Thus, if m is a natural number, then m^3 is the cube of m and we have

$$m^3 = m \times m \times m$$

PERFECT CUBE *A natural number is said to be a perfect cube, if it is the cube of some natural number.*

In other words, a natural number n is a perfect cube if there exists a natural number m whose cube is n i.e., $n = m^3$

ILLUSTRATION 1 8 is a perfect cube, because there is natural number 2 such that $8 = 2 \times 2 \times 2 = 2^3$. But, 12 is not a perfect cube, because there is no natural number whose cube is 12.

ILLUSTRATION 2 We have,

$3^3 = 3\times3\times3 = 27,\ 4^3 = 4\times4\times4 = 64,\ 5^3 = 5\times5\times5 = 125.$

So, 27, 64 and 125 are perfect cubes of natural numbers 3, 4 and 5 respectively.

If a prime p divides m, then $p\times p\times p$ will divide $m\times m\times m$ i.e., p^3 will divide m^3

Thus, if a prime p divides a perfect cube, then p^3 also divides this perfect cube.

In order to check whether a given natural number is a perfect cube or not, we follow the following procedure:

PROCEDURE

Step I *Obtain the natural number.*

Step II *Express the given natural number as a product of prime factors.*

Step III *Group the factors in triples in such a way that all the three factors in each triple are equal.*

Step IV *If no factor is left over in grouping in step III, then the number is a perfect cube, otherwise not.*

To find the natural number whose cube is the given number, take one factor from each triple and multiply them. The cube of the number so obtained will be the given number.

The above procedure is illustrated in the following examples:

ILLUSTRATIVE EXAMPLES

Example 1 Is 256 a perfect cube?

Solution Resolving 256 into prime factors, we have

$$256 = 2\times2\times2\times2\times2\times2\times2\times2$$

Grouping the factors in triplets of equal factors, we get

$$256 = \{2\times2\times2\}\times\{2\times2\times2\}\times2\times2$$

Clearly, in grouping the factors in triples of equal factors, we are left with two factors 2×2.

Therefore, 256 is not a perfect cube.

2	256
2	128
2	64
2	32
2	16
2	8
2	4
2	2
	1

Example 2 Is 216 a perfect cube? What is that number whose cube is 216?

Solution Resolving 216 into prime factors, we get

$$216 = 2\times2\times2\times3\times3\times3$$

Grouping the factors in triples of equal factors, we get

$$216 = \{2\times2\times2\}\times\{3\times3\times3\}$$

We find that the prime factors of 216 can be grouped into triples of equal factors and no factor is left over.

$\therefore$ 216 is a perfect cube.

Taking one factor from each triple, we obtain

$$2\times3 = 6$$

Hence, 216 is the cube of 6.

2	216
2	108
2	54
3	27
3	9
3	3
	1

Example 3 Is 27000 a perfect cube? What is the number whose cube is 27000?

Solution Resolving 27000 into prime factors, we get

2	27000
2	13500
2	6750
3	3375
3	1125
3	375
5	125
5	25
5	5

$$27000 = 2\times2\times2\times3\times3\times3\times5\times5\times5$$

Grouping the factors in triplets of equal factors, we get

$$27000 = \{2\times2\times2\}\times\{3\times3\times3\}\times\{5\times5\times5\}$$

We find that the prime factors of 27000 can be grouped into triples of equal factor and no factor is left over. Therefore, 27000 is a perfect cube.

To determine the number whose cube is 27000, we collect one factor from each group.

Taking one factor from each triple, we obtain

$$2\times3\times5 = 30$$

Thus, 27000 is the cube of 30.

Example 4 What is the smallest number by which 392 must be multiplied so that the product is a perfect cube?

Solution Resolving 392 into prime factors, we get

2	392
2	196
2	98
7	49
7	7
	1

$$392 = \{2\times2\times2\}\times7\times7$$

Grouping the factors in triplets of equal factors, we get

$$392 = \{2\times2\times2\}\times7\times7$$

We find that 2 occurs as a prime factors of 392 thrice but 7 occurs as a prime factor only twice. Thus, if we multiply 392 by 7, 7 will also occur as a prime factor thrice and the product will be $2\times2\times2\times7\times7\times7$, which is a perfect cube.

Hence, we must multiply 392 by 7 so that the product becomes a perfect cube.

Example 5 What is the smallest number by which 3087 must be divided so that the quotient is a perfect cube?

Solution Resolving 3087 into prime factors, we get

3	3087
3	1029
7	343
7	49
7	7
	1

$$3087 = 3\times3\times7\times7\times7$$

Grouping the factors in triplets of equal factors, we get

$$3087 = 3\times3\times\{7\times7\times7\}$$

Clearly, if we divide 3087 by $3\times3 = 9$, the quotient would be $7\times7\times7$ which is a perfect cube. Therefore, we must divide 3087 by 9 so that the quotient is a perfect cube.

Example 6 Prove that if a number is doubled, then its cube is eight times the cube of the given number.

Solution Let the given number be a. Let b denote the double of a i.e., $b = 2a$. Then,

$$b^3 = b\times b\times b = 2a\times2a\times2a = 2\times2\times2\times a\times a\times a = 8\times a\times a\times a = 8\times a^3$$

$$\Rightarrow\ b^3 = 8\times(\text{Cube of } a)$$

Example 7 Evaluate the following:

(i) $\left\{(24^2+7^2)^{1/2}\right\}^3$ (ii) $\left\{\sqrt{15^2+8^2}\right\}^3$

Solution (i) We have,

$$\left\{(24^2+7^2)^{1/2}\right\}^3=\left\{(576+49)^{1/2}\right\}^3$$
$$=\left\{\sqrt{625}\right\}^3$$
$$=\left\{\sqrt{25\times25}\right\}^3$$
$$=25^3 \qquad [\because \sqrt{25\times25}=25]$$
$$=25\times25\times25=15625$$

(ii) We have,

$$\left\{\sqrt{15^2+8^2}\right\}^3=\left\{\sqrt{225+64}\right\}^3$$
$$=\left(\sqrt{289}\right)^3=\left(\sqrt{17\times17}\right)^3=17^3=17\times17\times17=4913$$

Example 8 Find the volume of a cube whose surface area is 150 m^2.

Solution Let the length of each edge of the given cube be x metres. Then,

Surface area $=150\ m^2$

$\Rightarrow\ 6x^2=150$

$\Rightarrow\ x^2=\frac{150}{6}=25 \qquad [\because \text{Surface area}=6x^2]$

$\Rightarrow\ x=\sqrt{25}=\sqrt{5\times5}=5$

$\therefore$ Volume of the cube $=x^3$ cubic metres

$=5^3$ cubic metres

$=(5\times5\times5)$ cubic metres $=125$ cubic metres.

4.3.1 SOME PROPERTIES OF CUBES OF NATURAL NUMBERS

The cubes of natural numbers have the following interesting properties:

Property 1 *Cubes of all even natural numbers are even.*

Property 2 *Cubes of all odd natural numbers are odd.*

Property 3 *The sum of the cubes of first n natural numbers is equal to the square of their sum. That is,*

$$1^3+2^3+3^3+\ldots+n^3=(1+2+3+\ldots+n)^2$$

Property 4 *Cubes of the numbers ending in digits 1, 4, 5, 6 and 9 are the numbers ending in the same digit. Cubes of numbers ending in digit 2 ends in digit 8 and the cube of numbers ending in digit 8 ends in digit 2. The cubes of the numbers ending in digits 3 and 7 ends in digit 7 and 3 respectively.*

Explanation: The cubes of first 10 natural numbers are given in the following table.

Number x	Cube x^3	Number x	Cube x^3
1	1	11	1331
2	8	12	1728
3	27	13	2197
4	64	14	2744
5	125	15	3375
6	216	16	4096
7	343	17	4913
8	512	18	5832
9	729	19	6059
10	1000	20	8000

It is evident from the above table that the cubes of the digits 1, 4, 5, 6 and 9 are numbers ending in the same digits 1, 4, 5, 6 and 9 respectively. The cube of 2 ends in 8 and the cube of 8 ends in 2. Similarly, the cube of 3 ends in 7 and the cube of 7 ends in 3. Also, if a number ends in 0, then its cube will end in three zeros.

4.4 FINDING CUBE OF A TWO DIGIT NUMBER BY COLUMN METHOD

In the previous chapter, we have learnt about the column method for finding the square of a natural number. In this section, we will discuss column method for finding the cubes of two digit natural numbers. Let $x = ab$ (where a is the tens digit and b is the units digit) be a two digit natural number. Recall that for finding $x^2 = (ab)^2$, we formed three columns containing $a^2, 2 \times a \times b$ and b^2, because $(a+b)^2 = a^2 + 2 \times a \times b + b^2$. Since $(a+b)^3 = a^3 + 3a^2b + 3ab^2 + b^3$. Therefore, for finding $x^3 = (ab)^3$ we will form four columns containing $a^3, 3 \times a^2 \times b, 3 \times a \times b^2$ and b^3. The remaining procedure is exactly indentical to the method of finding the square of a two digit natural numbers.

Following examples will illustrate the procedure.

ILLUSTRATIVE EXAMPLES

Example 1 Find the cube of 24^3 by using column method.

Solution Here, $a = 2$ and $b = 4$.

By using column method, we have

Column I a^3	Column II $3 \times a^2 \times b$	Column III $3 \times a \times b^2$	Column IV b^3
$2^3 = 8$ $+5$	$3 \times 2^2 \times 4 = 48$ $+10$	$3 \times 2 \times 4^2 = 96$ $+6$	$4^3 = 6\underline{4}$
$\underline{13}$	$5\underline{8}$	$10\underline{2}$	
13	8	2	4

$\therefore\ 24^3 = 13824.$

Example 2 Using column method find the cubes of the following natural numbers.

(i) 42 (ii) 45 (iii) 87

Solution (i) Here, $a = 4$ and $b = 2$.

Using column method, we have

Column I a^3	Column II $3 \times a^2 \times b$	Column III $3 \times a \times b^2$	Column IV b^3
$4^3 = 64$ $+10$	$3 \times 4^2 \times 2 = 96$ $+4$	$3 \times 4 \times 2^2 = 48$ $+0$	$2^3 = \underline{8}$
$\underline{74}$	$10\underline{0}$	$4\underline{8}$	
74	0	8	8

$\therefore \quad 42^3 = 74088$

(ii) Here, $a = 4$ and $b = 5$.

Using column method, we have

Column I a^3	Column II $3 \times a^2 \times b$	Column III $3 \times a \times b^2$	Column IV b^3
$4^3 = 64$ $+27$	$3 \times 4^2 \times 5 = 240$ $+31$	$3 \times 4 \times 25 = 300$ $+12$	$5^3 = 12\underline{5}$
$\underline{91}$	$27\underline{1}$	$31\underline{2}$	
91	1	2	5

$\therefore \quad 45^3 = 91125$

(iii) Here, $a = 8$ and $b = 7$.

Using column method, we have

Column I a^3	Column II $3 \times a^2 \times b$	Column III $3 \times a \times b^2$	Column IV b^3
$8^3 = 512$ $+146$	$3 \times 8^2 \times 7 = 1344$ $+121$	$3 \times 8 \times 7^2 = 1176$ $+34$	$7^3 = 34\underline{3}$
$\underline{658}$	$146\underline{5}$	$121\underline{0}$	
658	5	0	3

$\therefore \quad 87^3 = 658503$

Example 3 Using column method find the cubes of the following numbers:

(i) 98 (ii) 99 (iii) 85

Solution (i) Here, $a = 9$ and $b = 8$.

Using column method, we have

Column I a^3	Column II $3\times a^2\times b$	Column III $3\times a\times b^2$	Column IV b^3
$9^3 = 729$ $+212$	$3\times 9^2\times 8 = 1944$ $+177$	$3\times 9\times 8^2 = 1728$ $+51$	$8^3 = 51\underline{2}$
$\underline{941}$	$212\underline{1}$	$177\underline{9}$	
941	1	9	2

$\therefore \quad 98^3 = 941192$

(ii) Here, $a = 9$ and $b = 9$.

Using column method, we have

Column I a^3	Column II $3\times a^2\times b$	Column III $3\times a\times b^2$	Column IV b^3
$9^3 = 729$ $+241$	$3\times 9^2\times 9 = 2187$ $+225$	$3\times 9\times 9^2 = 2187$ $+72$	$9^3 = 72\underline{9}$
$\underline{970}$	$241\underline{2}$	$225\underline{9}$	
970	2	9	9

$\therefore \quad 99^3 = 970299$

(iii) Here, $a = 8$ and $b = 5$.

Using column method, we have

Column I a^3	Column II $3\times a^2\times b$	Column III $3\times a\times b^2$	Column IV b^3
$8^3 = 512$ $+102$	$3\times 8^2\times 5 = 960$ $+61$	$3\times 8\times 5^2 = 600$ $+12$	$5^3 = 12\underline{5}$
$\underline{614}$	$102\underline{1}$	$61\underline{2}$	
614	1	2	5

$\therefore \quad 85^3 = 614125$

EXERCISE 4.1

1. Find the cubes of the following numbers:

(i) 7 (ii) 12 (iii) 16 (iv) 21 (v) 40 (vi) 55

(vii) 100 (viii) 302 (ix) 301

2. Write the cubes of all natural numbers between 1 and 10 and verify the following statements:
   (i) Cubes of all odd natural numbers are odd.
   (ii) Cubes of all even natural numbers are even.
3. Observe the following pattern:
$$1^3 = 1$$
$$1^3 + 2^3 = (1+2)^2$$
$$1^3 + 2^3 + 3^3 = (1+2+3)^2$$
Write the next three rows and calculate the value of $1^3 + 2^3 + 3^3 + \ldots + 9^3 + 10^3$ by the above pattern.
4. Write the cubes of 5 natural numbers which are multiples of 3 and verify the followings:
'The cube of a natural number which is a multiple of 3 is a multiple of 27'
5. Write the cubes of 5 natural numbers which are of the form $3n + 1$ (e.g. 4, 7, 10, ...) and verify the following:
'The cube of a natural number of the form $3n + 1$ is a natural number of the same form i.e. when divided by 3 it leaves the remainder 1'.
6. Write the cubes of 5 natural numbers of the form $3n + 2$ (i.e. 5, 8, 11, ...) and verify the following:
'The cube of a natural number of the form $3n + 2$ is a natural number of the same form i.e. when it is dividend by 3 the remainder is 2'.
7. Write the cubes of 5 natural numbers of which are multiples of 7 and verify the following:
'The cube of a multiple of 7 is a multiple of 7^3'.
8. Which of the following are perfect cubes?
(i) 64 (ii) 216 (iii) 243 (iv) 1000 (v) 1728 (vi) 3087
(vii) 4608 (viii) 106480 (ix) 166375 (x) 456533
9. Which of the following are cubes of even natural numbers?
216, 512, 729, 1000, 3375, 13824
10. Which of the following are cubes of odd natural numbers?
125, 343, 1728, 4096, 32768, 6859
11. What is the smallest number by which the following numbers must be multiplied, so that the products are perfect cubes?
(i) 675 (ii) 1323 (iii) 2560 (iv) 7803 (v) 107811 (vi) 35721
12. By which smallest number must the following numbers be divided so that the quotient is a perfect cube?
(i) 675 (ii) 8640 (iii) 1600 (iv) 8788 (v) 7803 (vi) 107811
(vii) 35721 (viii) 243000
13. Prove that if a number is trebled then its cube is 27 times the cube of the given number.
14. What happens to the cube of a number if the number is multiplied by
(i) 3? (ii) 4? (iii) 5?

15. Find the volume of a cube, one face of which has an area of 64 m^2.
16. Find the volume of a cube whose surface area is 384 m^2.
17. Evaluate the following:

    (i) $\left\{(5^2+12^2)^{1/2}\right\}^3$ (ii) $\left\{(6^2+8^2)^{1/2}\right\}^3$

18. Write the units digit of the cube of each of the following numbers:

    31, 109, 388, 833, 4276, 5922, 77774, 44447, 125125125

19. Find the cubes of the following numbers by column method:

    (i) 35 (ii) 56 (iii) 72

20. Which of the following numbers are not perfect cubes?

    (i) 64 (ii) 216 (iii) 243 (iv) 1728

21. For each of the non-perfect cubes in Q. No. 20 find the smallest number by which it must be
    (a) multiplied so that the product is a perfect cube.
    (b) divided so that the quotient is a perfect cube.
22. By taking three different values of n verify the truth of the following statements:
    (i) If n is even, then n^3 is also even.
    (ii) if n is odd, then n^3 is also odd.
    (iii) If n leaves remainder 1 when divided by 3, then n^3 also leaves 1 as remainder when divided by 3.
    (iv) If a natural number n is of the form $3p + 2$ then n^3 also a number of the same type.
23. Write true (T) or false (F) for the following statements:
    (i) 392 is a perfect cube.
    (ii) 8640 is not a perfect cube.
    (iii) No cube can end with exactly two zeros.
    (iv) There is no perfect cube which ends in 4.
    (v) For an integer a, a^3 is always greater than a^2.
    (vi) If a and b are integers such that $a^2 > b^2$, then $a^3 > b^3$.
    (vii) If a divides b, then a^3 divides b^3.
    (viii) If a^2 ends in 9, then a^3 ends in 7.
    (ix) If a^2 ends in 5, then a^3 ends in 25.
    (x) If a^2 ends in an even number of zeros, then a^3 ends in an odd number of zeros.

ANSWERS

1. (i) 343 (ii) 1728 (iii) 4096 (iv) 9261 (v) 64000 (vi) 166375 (vii) 1000000 (viii) 27543608 (ix) 27270901
3. (i), (ii), (iv), (v), (ix), (x)
9. 216, 1000, 512, 13824
10. 125, 343, 6859
11. (i) 5 (ii) 7 (iii) 25 (iv) 17 (v) 9 (vi) 7
12. (i) 25 (ii) 5 (iii) 25 (iv) 4 (v) 289 (vi) 3 (vii) 49 (viii) 9
14. (i) 27 times the cube of the number. (ii). 64 times the cube of the number (iii) 125 times the cube of the given number
15. 512 m3
16. 512m3
17. (i) 2197 (ii) 1000
18. 1, 9, 2, 7, 6, 8, 4, 3, 5
19. (i) 42875 (ii) 175616 (iii) 373248
20. (iii)
21. (a) (ii), 3 (b) (iii), 9
23. (i) F (ii) T (iii) T (iv) F (v) F (vi) F (vii) T (viii) F (ix) F (x) F

4.5 CUBES OF NEGATIVE INTEGERS

In the previous section, we have learnt about cubes of natural numbers. We have seen that the cubes of natural numbers are also natural numbers. Now, we shall learn about the cubes of negative integers.

We have,

$(-1)^3 = -1 \times -1 \times -1 = -1$

$\therefore$ -1 is the cube of itself.

Similarly,

$(-2)^3 = -2 \times -2 \times -2 = -8$

$\therefore$ -8 is the cube of -2.

$(-3)^3 = -3 \times -3 \times -3 = -27$

$\therefore$ -27 is the cube of -3 and so on.

In general, if m is a positive integer, then

$(-m)^3 = -m \times -m \times -m = -m^3$

Thus, for any positive integer $m, -m^3$ is the cube of $-m$.

ILLUSTRATIVE EXAMPLES

Example 1 Show that – 1331 is a perfect cube. What is the number whose cube is – 1331?

Solution Resolving 1331 into prime factors, we get

11	1331
11	121
11	11
	1

$1331 = 11 \times 11 \times 11$

Grouping the factors in triples of equal factors, we get

$1331 = \{11 \times 11 \times 11\}$

Clearly, 1331, can be grouped into triples of equal factors. So, it is a perfect cube of 11

We know that $-m^3$ is the cube of $-m$ for any positive integer m

$\therefore$ 1331 is the cube of $\Rightarrow -1331$ is the cube of -11

Hence, -1331 is a perfect cube and it is perfect cube of -11

Example 2 Which of the following numbers are cubes of negative integers?

(i) -1728 (ii) -3888

Solution In order to check whether a negative integer is a perfect cube or not, we first check whether the corresponding positive integer is a perfect cube or not.

2	1728
2	864
2	432
2	216
2	108
2	54
3	27
3	9
3	3
	1

(i) Resolving 1728 into prime factors, we get

$1728 = 2 \times 2 \times 2 \times 2 \times 2 \times 2 \times 3 \times 3 \times 3$

Clearly, 1728 can be grouped into triplets of equal factors as given below.

$1728 = \{2 \times 2 \times 2\} \times \{2 \times 2 \times 2\} \times \{3 \times 3 \times 3\}$

So, 1728 is a perfect cube. Thus, – 1728 is also a perfect cube.

Collecting one factor from each triple, we find that 1728 is the cube of $2 \times 2 \times 3 = 12$

Hence, -1728 is the cube of -12

(ii) Resolving 3888 into prime factors, we get

2	3888
2	1944
2	972
2	486
3	243
3	81
3	27
3	9
3	3
	1

$$3888 = 2 \times 2 \times 2 \times 2 \times 3 \times 3 \times 3 \times 3 \times 3$$

Clearly, 3888 cannot be grouped into triples of equal factors as shown below.

$$3888 = \{2 \times 2 \times 2\} \times \{3 \times 3 \times 3\} \times 2 \times 3 \times 3$$

So, 3888 is not a perfect cube.

Hence, -3888 is not a perfect cube.

Example 3 Show that -17576 is a perfect cube. Also, find the number whose cube is -17576.

Solution Resolving 17576 into prime factors, we get

2	17576
2	8788
2	4394
13	2197
13	169
13	13
	1

$$17576 = 2 \times 2 \times 2 \times 13 \times 13 \times 13$$

Grouping the factors into triples of equal factors, we get

$$17576 = \{2 \times 2 \times 2\} \times \{13 \times 13 \times 13\}$$

Clearly, 17576 can be grouped into triples of equal factors and no factor is left over.

So, 17576 is a perfect cube.

Thus, -17576 is also a perfect cube.

Taking one factor from each group, we find that 17576 is a perfect cube of $2 \times 13 = 26$

Hence, -17576 is a perfect cube of -26.

4.6 CUBES OF RATIONAL NUMBERS

In the previous sections, we have learnt about the cubes of natural numbers and negative integers. Similarly, we define the cube of a rational number which is not an integer as given below.

CUBE OF A RATIONAL NUMBER *Let $a = \frac{m}{n}$ be a rational number (m, n are non-zero integers such that $n \neq \pm 1$) other than an integer, then the cube of a is defined as $a^3 = a \times a \times a$*

or, $$\left(\frac{m}{n}\right)^3 = \frac{m}{n} \times \frac{m}{n} \times \frac{m}{n} = \frac{m^3}{n^3}$$

ILLUSTRATIVE EXAMPLES

Example 1 Find the cube of $\frac{2}{3}$.

Solution We have,

$$\left(\frac{2}{3}\right)^3 = \frac{2^3}{3^3} = \frac{2 \times 2 \times 2}{3 \times 3 \times 3} = \frac{8}{27} \qquad \left[\because \left(\frac{m}{n}\right)^3 = \frac{m^3}{n^3}\right]$$

Example 2 Find the cube of $5\frac{2}{7}$.

Solution We have, $5\frac{2}{7} = \frac{37}{2}$

$$\therefore \quad \left(5\frac{2}{7}\right)^3 = \left(\frac{37}{7}\right)^3 = \frac{37^3}{7^3} = \frac{37\times37\times37}{7\times7\times7} = \frac{50653}{343}$$

Example 3 Is $\frac{27}{125}$ a cube of a rational number?

Solution We have, $\frac{27}{125} = \frac{3\times3\times3}{5\times5\times5}$ [Resolving 27 and 125 into prime factors]

$$\Rightarrow \quad \frac{27}{125} = \frac{3^3}{5^3} = \left(\frac{3}{5}\right)^3$$

$\therefore \quad \frac{27}{125}$ is cube of $\frac{3}{5}$.

Example 4 Show that $\frac{-216}{42875}$ is the cube of a rational number. Also, find that rational number.

Solution Resolving 216 and 42875 into prime factors, we get

$216 = 2\times2\times2\times3\times3\times3$ and $42875 = 5\times5\times5\times7\times7\times7$

2	216
2	108
2	54
3	27
3	9
3	3
	1

5	42875
5	8675
5	1715
7	343
7	49
7	7
	1

Clearly, 216 and 42875 can be grouped into triples of equal factors.

$\therefore \quad 216 = (2\times3)^3$ and $42875 = (5\times7)^3$

$\Rightarrow \quad 216 = 6^3$ and $42875 = 35^3$

Now, $\frac{-216}{42875} = \frac{(-6)^3}{35^3} = \left(\frac{-6}{35}\right)^3$

Thus, $\frac{-216}{42875}$ is the cube of a rational number $\frac{-6}{35}$.

Example 5 Find the cube of rational number 3.1.

Solution We have,

$$(3.1)^3 = 3.1 \times 3.1 \times 3.1 = 29.791$$

Example 6 Show that 0.001728 is the cube of a rational number.

Solution We have,

$$0.001728 = \frac{1728}{1000000} = \frac{2\times2\times2\times2\times2\times2\times3\times3\times3}{2\times2\times2\times2\times2\times2\times5\times5\times5\times5\times5\times5}$$

$$\Rightarrow \quad 0.001728 = \frac{(2\times2\times3)^3}{(2\times2\times5\times5)^3} = \left(\frac{12}{100}\right)^3 = \left(\frac{3}{25}\right)^3$$

Hence, 0.001728 is the cube of the rational number $\frac{3}{25}$.

EXERCISE 4.2

1. Find the cubes of:
   (i) -11 (ii) -12 (iii) -21
2. Which of the following numbers are cubes of negative integers
   (i) -64 (ii) -1056 (iii) -2197 (iv) -2744 (v) -42875
3. Show that the following integers are cubes of negative integers. Also, find the integer whose cube is the given integer.
   (i) -5832 (ii) -2744000
4. Find the cube of:
   (i) $\frac{7}{9}$ (ii) $-\frac{8}{11}$ (iii) $\frac{12}{7}$ (iv) $-\frac{13}{8}$ (v) $2\frac{2}{5}$ (vi) $3\frac{1}{4}$
   (vii) 0.3 (viii) 1.5 (ix) 0.08 (x) 2.1
5. Find which of the following numbers are cubes of rational numbers:
   (i) $\frac{27}{64}$ (ii) $\frac{125}{128}$ (iii) 0.001331 (iv) 0.04

ANSWERS

1. (i) -1331 (ii) -1728 (iii) -9261 2. (i), (iii), (iv), (v)

3. (i) -18 (ii) -140 4. (i) $\frac{343}{729}$ (ii) $\frac{-512}{1331}$ (iii) $\frac{1728}{343}$ (iv) $\frac{-2197}{512}$

(v) $\frac{1728}{125}$ (vi) $\frac{2197}{64}$ (vii) 0.027 (viii) 3.375 (ix) 0.000512 (x) 9.261

5.(i), (iii)

4.7 CUBE ROOTS

CUBE ROOT *A number m is the cube root of a number n if $n = m^3$.*

In other words, the cube root of a number n is that number m whose cube gives n.

The cube root of a number n is denoted by $\sqrt[3]{n}$. $\sqrt[3]{n}$ is also called a radical, n is called the radicand and 3 is called the index of the radical.

We have,

$8 = 2^3 \quad \therefore \quad \sqrt[3]{8} = 2$

$27 = 3^3 \quad \therefore \quad \sqrt[3]{27} = 3$

$343 = 7^3 \quad \therefore \quad \sqrt[3]{343} = 7$

$1331 = 11^3 \quad \therefore \quad \sqrt[3]{1331} = 11$

$-125 = (-5)^3 \quad \therefore \quad \sqrt[3]{-125} = -5$

$\frac{64}{125} = \left(\frac{4}{5}\right)^3 \quad \therefore \quad \sqrt[3]{\frac{64}{125}} = \frac{4}{5}$

$0.008 = (0.2)^3 \quad \therefore \quad \sqrt[3]{0.008} = 0.2$

Following tables provide all the perfect cubes upto 1000 and their cube roots.

m	1	2	3	4	5	6	7	8	9	10
m^3	1	8	27	64	125	216	343	512	729	1000

n	1	8	27	64	125	216	343	512	729	1000
$\sqrt[3]{n}$	1	2	3	4	5	6	7	8	9	10

<u>Remark</u> *The symbol $\sqrt[3]{\ }$ for the cube root is very much similar to the symbol for square root. The only difference is that whereas in the case of square root, we use the symbol '$\sqrt{\ }$' for the cube root we use the same symbol '$\sqrt{\ }$' but with a '3' which indicates that we are taking a cube root.*

4.8 CUBE ROOT OF A NATURAL NUMBER

A natural number m is the cube root of a natural number n if $n = m^3$ and we write $\sqrt[3]{n} = m$.

Thus, $\sqrt[3]{n} = m \Leftrightarrow n = m^3$

4.8.1 COMPUTATION OF CUBE ROOT THROUGH A PATTERN

In order to calculate cube roots of small numbers which are perfect cubes of natural numbers, we can use the following method:

We know that

$$1^3 = 1 \qquad \text{... (i)}$$

$$\Rightarrow \quad 1^3 - 0^3 = 1 = 1 + 0 \times 6 = 1 + \frac{1 \times 0}{2} \times 6$$

$$2^3 - 1^3 = 8 - 1 = 7 \qquad \text{... (ii)}$$

$$\Rightarrow \quad 2^3 - 1^3 = 7 = 1 + 1 \times 6 = 1 + \frac{2 \times 1}{2} \times 6$$

$$3^3 - 2^3 = 27 - 8 = 19 \qquad \text{... (iii)}$$

$$\Rightarrow \quad 3^3 - 2^3 = 19 = 1 + 1\times6 + 2\times6 = 1 + \frac{3\times2}{2}\times6 \quad \text{... (iv)}$$

$$4^3 - 3^3 = 64 - 27 = 37$$

$$\Rightarrow \quad 4^3 - 3^3 = 37 = 1 + 1\times6 + 2\times6 + 3\times6 = 1 + \frac{4\times3}{2}\times6 \quad \text{... (v)}$$

$$5^3 - 4^3 = 125 - 64 = 61$$

$$\Rightarrow \quad 5^3 - 4^3 = 61 = 1 + 1\times6 + 2\times6 + 3\times6 + 4\times6 = 1 + \frac{5\times4}{2}\times6 \quad \text{... (vi)}$$

$$6^3 - 5^3 = 216 - 125 = 91$$

$$\Rightarrow \quad 6^3 - 5^3 = 91 = 1 + 1\times6 + 2\times6 + 3\times6 + 4\times6 + 5\times6 = 1 + \frac{6\times5}{2}\times6$$

$$\vdots \quad \vdots \quad \vdots \quad \vdots$$

$$9^3 - 8^3 = 729 - 512 = 217$$

$$\Rightarrow \quad 9^3 - 8^3 = 217 = 1 + 1\times6 + 2\times6 + 3\times6 + 4\times6 + 5\times6 + 6\times6 = 1 + \frac{9\times8}{2}\times6 \text{ etc.}$$

Also,

$1^3 = 1$

$2^3 = 1 + 7$ [Adding (i) and (ii)]

$3^3 = 1 + 7 + 19$ [Adding (i) — (iii)]

$4^3 = 1 + 7 + 19 + 37$ [Adding (i) — (iv)]

$5^3 = 1 + 7 + 19 + 37 + 61$ [Adding (i) — (v)]

$6^3 = 1 + 7 + 19 + 61 + 91$ etc. [Adding (i) — (vi)]

The above pattern suggests the following method to find the cube root of a perfect cube of natural number:

PROCEDURE

Step I *Obtain the natural number.*

Step II *Subtract 1 from it. If you get zero as the result, then the cube root of the number is 1. Otherwise go to next step.*

Step III *Subtract* $7\left(=1+\frac{2\times1}{2}\times6\right)$ *from the resulting number obtained in step II. If the result is zero, then the cube root of the given number is 2. Otherwise go to next step.*

Step IV *Subtract* $19\left(=1+\frac{3\times2}{2}\times6\right)$ *from the number obtained in step III. Do you get 0 as the result. If yes, the cube root of the given number is 3. Otherwise, go to next step*

Step V *Subtract* $37\left(=1+\frac{4\times3}{2}\times6\right)$ *from the number obtained in the previous step. Do you get 0 as the result. If yes, the cube root of the given number is 4. Otherwise, go to next step.*

<u>Step VI</u> *Subtract* $61\left(=1+\frac{5\times4}{2}\times6\right)$ *from the number obtained in the previous step. Do you get 0 as the result. If yes, the cube root of the given number is 5. Otherwise, go to next step.*

Continue this process till you get 0. The cube root of the given number will be equal to the number of times the subtraction is performed.

<u>Remark</u> *The above procedure is suitable to find the cube roots of small natural numbers only. Also, one should remember the sequence* 1, $1+\frac{2\times1}{2}\times6=7$, $1+\frac{3\times2}{2}\times6=19$,

$1+\frac{4\times3}{2}\times6=37, 1+\frac{5\times4}{2}\times6=61, 1+\frac{6\times5}{2}\times6=91, 1+\frac{7\times6}{2}\times6=127, 1+\frac{8\times7}{2}\times6=169,$

of the numbers which are to be subtracted in succession from the given number.

ILLUSTRATIVE EXAMPLES

Example 1 Find the cube root of 216

Solution We have,

$$\begin{array}{r} 216 \\ 1 \\ \hline 215 \\ 7 \\ \hline 208 \\ 19 \\ \hline 189 \\ 37 \\ \hline 152 \\ 61 \\ \hline 91 \\ 91 \\ \hline 0 \end{array}$$

Clearly, the subtraction is performed six times to get 0.

$\therefore \quad \sqrt[3]{216}=6$

Example 2 Find the cube root of 343.

Solution We have,

$$\begin{array}{r} 343 \\ \underline{1} \\ 342 \\ \underline{7} \\ 335 \\ \underline{19} \\ 316 \\ \underline{37} \\ 279 \\ \underline{61} \\ 218 \\ \underline{91} \\ 127 \\ \underline{127} \\ 0 \end{array}$$

Since the subtraction is performed seven times.

$\therefore \quad \sqrt[3]{343} = 7.$

4.8.2 CUBE ROOT OF A NUMBER BY USING ITS UNITS DIGIT

In property 4 of the cubes of natural numbers, we have seen that the units digit of cube of a natural number depends upon the units digit of the given number. Following table gives the units digit of cube root of a number corresponding to units digit of the number.

Units digit of the number n	*Units digit of the cube root of the number* $\sqrt[3]{n}$
0	0
1	1
2	8
3	7
4	4
5	5
6	6
7	3
8	2
9	9

Thus by looking at the units digit of a perfect cube number, we can determine the units digit of its cube root.

We shall now describe a method that can be used to find cube roots of the perfect cubes having at most 6 digits.

Since the least seven digit number is 1000000 $(=100^3)$ and its cube root is 100 (the smallest three digit number). Therefore, if a perfect cube number has at the most 6 digits, then its cube root has at the most two digits. The method of finding the cube root of a number having at the most 6 digits depends upon this logic.

In order to find the cube root, we follow the following steps:

PROCEDURE

Step I *Look at the digit at the units place and determine the digit at the units place in the cube root by using the table given above.*

Step II *Strike out from the right, last three digits (units, tens and hundreds) of the number. If no digit(s) is (are) left, then the digit obtained in step I is the required cube root. Otherwise go to next step.*

Step III *Consider the number left from step II. Find the largest single digit number whose cube root is less than or equal to this left over number. This number is the tens digit of the cube root.*

Step IV *Obtain the required cube root by forming a number whose units digit is the number obtained in step I and tens digit is the number obtained in step III.*

The above procedure is illustrated in the following examples.

ILLUSTRATIVE EXAMPLES

Example 1 Find the cube roots of the following numbers:

(i) 64 (ii) 343 (iii) 729

Solution (i) The units digit of 64 is 4. Therefore, the digit at the units place in the cube root is 4. Since no number is left after striking out the units and tens digits of the number. Therefore, the required cube root is 4 i.e.,

$$\sqrt[3]{64} = 4$$

(ii) The given number is 343.

Here, units digit is 3. Therefore, the units digit of the cube root is 7. Since no number is left after striking out the units, tens, and hundreds digits of the given number. Therefore, the cube root of 343 is 7 i.e.,

$$\sqrt[3]{343} = 7$$

(iii) The given number is 729.

We observe that the units digit of 729 is 9. Therefore, units digit of its cube root is also 9. As no number is left after striking out the units, tens and hundreds digits of the given number. Therefore, the cube root of 729 is 9 i.e.,

$$\sqrt[3]{729} = 9$$

Example 2 Find the cube roots of the following numbers.

(i) 2197 (ii) 389017 (iii) 91125

Solution (i) The given number is 2197

Here, units digit of 2197 is 7. Therefore, the units digit of the cube root of the given number is 3. After striking out the units, tens and hundreds digits of the given number, we are left with the number 2. Now, 1 is the largest number whose cube is less than 2. Therefore, tens digit of the cube root of 2197 is 1.

Hence, $\sqrt[3]{2197} = 13$

(ii) The given number is 389017

Clearly, units digit of this number is 7. Therefore, units digit of its cube root is also 3. After striking out the last three digit from the right, we are left with the number 389.

Now,

$7^3 = 343 < 389$ and $8^3 = 512 > 389$.

$\therefore$ Tens digit of the cube root of the given number is 7.

Hence, $\sqrt[3]{389017} = 73$

(iii) The given number is 91125

Since units digit of this number is 5. Therefore, units digit of its cube root is also 5.

After striking out the last three digits from the right, the number left is 91.

$\because$ $4^3 < 91 < 5^3$

$\therefore$ Tens digit of the cube root of 91125 is 4.

Hence, $\sqrt[3]{91125} = 45$.

Example 3 Find the cube root of given number = 4.

(i) 46656 (ii) 175616 (iii) 571787

Solution (i) Given number = 46656

Units digit of given number = 6

$\Rightarrow$ Units digit of cube root = 6

Number obtained by striking out units, tens and hundreds digits is 46

$\because$ $3^3 < 46 < 4^3$

$\therefore$ Tens digit of cube root = 3

Hence, $\sqrt[3]{46656} = 36$

(ii) Given number = 175616.

Units digit of given number = 6

$\Rightarrow$ Units digit of cube root = 6

Number obtained by striking out units, tens and hundreds digit is 175

$\because$ $5^3 < 175 < 6^3$

$\therefore$ Tens digit of cube root = 5

Hence, $\sqrt[3]{175616} = 56$

(iii) Given number = 571787

Units digit of given number = 7

$\Rightarrow$ Units digit of its cube root = 3

Number obtained by striking out units, tens and hundreds digits = 571

$\because$ $8^3 < 571 < 9^3$

$\therefore$ Tens digit of the cube root of the given number = 8

Hence, $\sqrt[3]{571787} = 83$

4.8.3 CUBE ROOT OF A PERFECT CUBE BY FACTORS

In order to find the cube root of a perfect cube by factors, we follow the following procedure:

Step I *Obtain the given number.*

Step II *Resolve it into prime factors.*

Step III *Group the factors in triples such that all the three factors in each triple are equal.*

<u>Step IV</u> *Take one factor from each triple formed in step III.*

<u>Step V</u> *Find the product of factors obtained in step IV. This product is the required cube root.*

The above procedure is illustrated in the following examples.

ILLUSTRATIVE EXAMPLES

Example 1 Find the cube root of 13824.

Solution Resolving the given number into prime factors, we get

$13824 = \{2\times2\times2\}\times\{2\times2\times2\}\times\{2\times2\times2\}\times\{3\times3\times3\}$

Grouping the factors in triples of equal factors, we get

$13824 = 2\times2\times2\times2\times2\times2\times2\times2\times2\times3\times3\times3$

Taking one factor from each triple, we get

$\sqrt[3]{13824} = 2\times2\times2\times3 = 24$

2	13824
2	6912
2	3456
2	1728
2	864
2	432
2	216
2	108
2	54
3	27
3	9
3	3
	1

Example 2 Find the cube root of 91125.

Solution Resolving the given number into prime factors, we get

$91125 = 5\times5\times5\times3\times3\times3\times3\times3\times3$

Grouping the factors in triples of equal factors, we get

$91125 = \{5\times5\times5\}\times\{3\times3\times3\}\times\{3\times3\times3\}$

Taking one factor from each triple, we get

$\sqrt[3]{91125} = 5\times3\times3 = 45$

5	91125
5	18225
5	3645
3	729
3	243
3	81
3	27
3	9
3	3
	1

Example 3 Find the smallest number which when multiplied with 137592 will make the product a perfect cube. Further, find the cube root of the product.

Solution Resolving 137592 into prime factors, we get

$137592 = 2\times2\times2\times3\times3\times3\times7\times7\times13$

Grouping the factors in triples of equal factors, we get

$137592 = \{2\times2\times2\}\times\{3\times3\times3\}\times7\times7\times13$

We know that if a number is to be a perfect cube then each of its prime factors must occur thrice. We find that 7 occurs twice and 13 occurs once only. Hence, the smallest number by which the given number must be multiplied in order that the product is a perfect cube is

$7\times13\times13 = 1183$

Also, the product $= 137592\times1183 = 162771336$

Now, arranging into triples of equal prime factors, we have

$162771336 = \{2\times2\times2\}\times\{3\times3\times3\}\times\{7\times7\times7\}\times\{13\times13\times13\}$

Taking one factor from each triple, we get

$\sqrt[3]{162771336} = 2\times3\times7\times13 = 546$

2	137592
2	68796
2	34398
3	17199
3	5733
3	1911
7	637
7	91
13	13
	1

Example 4 Divide the number 26244 by the smallest number so that the quotient is a perfect cube. Also, find the cube root of the quotient.

Solution Resolving 26244 into prime factors, we get

$$26244 = 2\times2\times3\times3\times3\times3\times3\times3\times3\times3$$

2	26244
2	13122
3	6561
3	2187
3	729
3	243
3	81
3	27
3	9
3	3
	1

Grouping the factors in triples of equal factors, we get

$$26244 = 2\times2\times\{3\times3\times3\}\times\{3\times3\times3\}\times3\times3$$

For a number to be a perfect cube each of its prime factors must occur thrice. Therefore, the smallest number by which the given number must be divided in order that the quotient is a perfect cube is

$$2\times2\times3\times3 = 36$$

Also, the quotient $= \dfrac{26244}{36} = 729 = 3\times3\times3\times3\times3\times3$

Arranging into triples of equal prime factors, we get

$$729 = \{3\times3\times3\}\times\{3\times3\times3\}$$

Taking one factor from each triple, we get

$$\sqrt[3]{729} = 3\times3 = 9$$

Example 5 Three numbers are to one another 2 : 3 : 4. The sum of their cubes is 33957. Find the numbers.

Solution Let the numbers be $2x$, $3x$ and $4x$. Then,

$$(2x)^3 + (3x)^3 + (4x)^3 = 33957$$

$$\Rightarrow \quad 8x^3 + 27x^3 + 64x^3 = 33957$$

$$\Rightarrow \quad 99x^3 = 33957$$

$$\Rightarrow \quad x^3 = \frac{33957}{99} = 343$$

$$\Rightarrow \quad x^3 = 7\times7\times7 \qquad \text{[Resolving 343 into prime factors]}$$

$$\Rightarrow \quad x = \sqrt[3]{7\times7\times7} = 7$$

Hence, the numbers are: $2x = 2\times7 = 14$, $3x = 3\times7 = 21$ and $4x = 4\times7 = 28$

EXERCISE 4.3

1. Find the cube roots of the following numbers by successive subtraction of numbers:

   1, 7, 19, 37, 61, 91, 127, 169, 217, 271, 331, 397, ...

   (i) 64 (ii) 512 (iii) 1728

2. Using the method of successive subtraction examine whether or not the following numbers are perfect cubes:

   (i) 130 (ii) 345 (iii) 792 (iv) 1331

3. Find the smallest number that must be subtracted from those of the numbers in question 2 which are not perfect cubes, to make them perfect cubes. What are the corresponding cube roots?

4. Find the cube root of each of the following natural numbers:
   (i) 343 (ii) 2744 (iii) 4913 (iv) 1728 (v) 35937 (vi) 17576
   (vii) 134217728 (viii) 48228544 (ix) 74088000 (x) 157464
   (xi) 1157625 (xii) 33698267
5. Find the smallest number which when multiplied with 3600 will make the product a perfect cube. Further, find the cube root of the product.
6. Multiply 210125 by the smallest number so that the product is a perfect cube. Also, find out the cube root of the product.
7. What is the smallest number by which 8192 must be divided so that quotient is a perfect cube? Also, find the cube root of the quotient so obtained.
8. Three numbers are in the ratio 1 : 2 : 3. The sum of their cubes is 98784. Find the numbers.
9. The volume of a cube is 9261000 m^3. Find the side of the cube.

ANSWERS

1. (i) 4 (ii) 8 (iii) 12
2. (i) No (ii) No (iii) No (iv) Yes
3. (i) 5; 5 (ii) 2; 7 (iii) 63; 9
4. (i) 7 (ii) 14 (iii) 17 (iv) 12 (v) 33 (vi) 26
   (vii) 512 (viii) 364 (ix) 420 (x) 54 (xi) 105 (xii) 323
5. 60, 60 6. 41, 205 7. 2, 16 8. 14, 28, 42 9. 210 m

4.9 CUBE ROOT OF A NEGATIVE INTEGERAL PERFECT CUBE

We know that for any positive integer x, $-x$ is a negative integer such that

$$(-x)^3 = (-x)\times(-x)\times(-x) = -x^3$$

$$\therefore \quad \sqrt[3]{-x^3} = -x \qquad [\because m^3 = n \Rightarrow \sqrt[3]{n} = m]$$

$$\Rightarrow \quad \sqrt[3]{-x^3} = -\sqrt[3]{x^3} \qquad [\because \sqrt[3]{x^3} = x]$$

Thus, the cube root of a negative perfect cube is negative of the cube root of its absolute value.

In other words, to find the cube root of a negative perfect cube, we find the cube root of its absolute value and multiply it by – 1.

ILLUSTRATIVE EXAMPLES

Example 1 Find the cube root of – 1728.

Solution We have, $\sqrt[3]{-1728} = -\sqrt[3]{1728}$

Now, resolving 1728 into prime factors, we get

2	1728
2	864
2	432
2	216
2	168
2	54
3	27
3	9
3	3
	1

$$1728 = \{2\times2\times2\}\times\{2\times2\times2\}\times\{3\times3\times3\}$$

$$\therefore \quad \sqrt[3]{1728} = 2\times2\times3 = 12$$

Hence, $\sqrt[3]{-1728} = -\sqrt[3]{1728} = -12$

Example 2 Find the cube root of -5832.

Solution We have, $\sqrt[3]{-5832} = -\sqrt[3]{5832}$

Now, resolving 5832 into prime factors, we get

$$5832 = \{2\times2\times2\}\times\{3\times3\times3\}\times\{3\times3\times3\}$$

$$\therefore \sqrt[3]{5832} = 2\times3\times3 = 18$$

Hence, $\sqrt[3]{-5832} = -\sqrt[3]{5832} = -18$

Example 3 Find the cube roots of the following numbers:

(i) -226981 (ii) -571787 (iii) -175616

Solution (i) We have, $\sqrt[3]{-226981} = -\sqrt[3]{226981}$

Consider the number 226981

Since unit's digit of 226981 is 1. Therefore, units digit of its cube root is also 1

Now,

Number obtained by striking out units, tens and hundreds digits = 226

$\because$ $6^3 < 226 < 7^3$

$\therefore$ Tens digit of the cube root of 226981 is 6.

Hence, $\sqrt[3]{226981} = 61$

$\therefore$ $\sqrt[3]{-226981} = -61$

(ii) We have,

$$\sqrt[3]{-571787} = -\sqrt[3]{571787}$$

Now,

Unit's digit of 571787 is 7

$\therefore$ Unit digit of its cube root = 3.

Number obtained by striking out units, tens and hundreds digits of 571787 is 571.

$\because$ $8^3 < 571 < 9^3$

$\therefore$ Tens digit of the cube root of 571787 is 8

Hence, $\sqrt[3]{571787} = 83$

$\therefore$ $\sqrt[3]{-571787} = -83$

(iii) We have,

$$\sqrt[3]{-175616} = -\sqrt[3]{175616}$$

Now,

Units digit of 175616 is 6

$\therefore$ Units digit of its cube root = 6

Number obtained by striking out units, tens and hundreds digits of 175616 is 175.

$\because \quad 5^3 < 175 < 6^3$

$\therefore$ Tens digit of the cube root of 175616 is 5

Hence, $\sqrt[3]{175616} = 56$

$\therefore \quad \sqrt[3]{-175616} = -56$

4.10 CUBE ROOT OF PRODUCT OF INTEGERS

In order to find the cube root of the product of two integers, we use the following result:

Result *For any two integers a and b, we have*

$$\sqrt[3]{ab} = \sqrt[3]{a} \times \sqrt[3]{b}$$

Following examples will illustrate the applications of the above result.

ILLUSTRATIVE EXAMPLES

Example 1 Find the cube root of each of the following:

(i) -216×1728 (ii) -125×-3375

Solution We have,

(i) $\sqrt[3]{-216 \times 1728} = \sqrt[3]{-216} \times \sqrt[3]{1728}$ [Using: $\sqrt[3]{ab} = \sqrt[3]{a} . \sqrt[3]{b}$]

$= -\sqrt[3]{216} \times \sqrt[3]{1728}$ [$\because \sqrt[3]{-x} = -\sqrt[3]{x}$]

Now, resolving 216 and 1728 into prime factors:

2	216
2	108
2	54
3	27
3	9
3	3
	1

2	1728
2	864
2	432
2	216
2	108
2	54
3	27
3	9
3	3
	1

$\therefore \quad 216 = \underbrace{2 \times 2 \times 2} \times \underbrace{3 \times 3 \times 3}$ and $1728 = \underbrace{2 \times 2 \times 2} \times \underbrace{2 \times 2 \times 2} \times \underbrace{3 \times 3 \times 3}$

$\therefore \quad \sqrt[3]{216} = 2 \times 3 = 6$ and $\sqrt[3]{1728} = 2 \times 2 \times 3 = 12$

Hence, $\sqrt[3]{-216 \times 1728} = -\sqrt[3]{216}\ \sqrt[3]{1728} = -6 \times 12 = -72$

(ii) We have,

$$\sqrt[3]{-125 \times -3375} = \sqrt[3]{-125} \times \sqrt[3]{-3375} = -\sqrt[3]{125} \times -\sqrt[3]{3375} = \sqrt[3]{125} \times \sqrt[3]{3375}$$

Now, resolving 125 and 3375 into prime factors:

5	125
5	25
5	5
	1

5	3375
5	675
5	135
3	27
3	9
3	3
	1

$\therefore \quad 125 = \underbrace{5\times5\times5}$ and $3375 = \underbrace{5\times5\times5}\times\underbrace{3\times3\times3}$

$\Rightarrow \sqrt[3]{125} = 5$ and $\sqrt[3]{3375} = 5\times3 = 15$

Hence, $\sqrt[3]{-125\times-3375} = \sqrt[3]{125}\times\sqrt[3]{3375} = 5\times15 = 75$

Example 2 Find the cube root of each of the following numbers:

(i) 140×2450 (ii) -2300×5290

Solution (i) We have,

$$\sqrt[3]{140\times2450} = \sqrt[3]{343000}$$

$$= \sqrt[3]{343\times1000}$$

$$= \sqrt[3]{343}\times\sqrt[3]{1000} \qquad [\because \sqrt[3]{ab} = \sqrt[3]{a}\,.\sqrt[3]{b}]$$

$$= \sqrt[3]{7\times7\times7}\times\sqrt[3]{10\times10\times10} = 7\times10 = 70$$

(ii) We have,

$$\sqrt[3]{-2300\times5290}$$

$$= -\sqrt{2300\times5290} \qquad [\because \sqrt[3]{-a} = -\sqrt[3]{a}]$$

$$= -\sqrt[3]{23\times529\times1000}$$

$$= -\sqrt[3]{23\times529}\,.\sqrt[3]{1000}$$

$$= -\sqrt[3]{23\times23\times23}\,.\sqrt[3]{10\times10\times10} = -23\times10 = -230$$

Example 3 Evaluate: $\sqrt[3]{1372}\times\sqrt[3]{1458}$.

Solution We observe that 1372 and 1458 both are not perfect cubes. Therefore, we factorize them and use the property $\sqrt[3]{a}\,\sqrt[3]{b} = \sqrt[3]{ab}$.

Thus, we have

$$\sqrt[3]{1372}\;\sqrt[3]{1458} = \sqrt[3]{1372\times1458}$$

Now, resolving 1372 and 1458 into prime factors

$$\begin{array}{r|r} 2 & 1372 \\ \hline 2 & 686 \\ \hline 7 & 343 \\ \hline 7 & 49 \\ \hline 7 & 7 \\ \hline & 1 \end{array} \qquad \begin{array}{r|r} 2 & 1458 \\ \hline 3 & 729 \\ \hline 3 & 243 \\ \hline 3 & 81 \\ \hline 3 & 27 \\ \hline 3 & 9 \\ \hline 3 & 3 \\ \hline & 1 \end{array}$$

$\therefore \quad \sqrt[3]{1372}\ \sqrt[3]{1458} = \sqrt[3]{2\times2\times7\times7\times7\times2\times3\times3\times3\times3\times3\times3}$

$= \sqrt[3]{2\times2\times2\times7\times7\times7\times3\times3\times3\times3\times3\times3} = 2\times7\times3\times3 = 126.$

4.11 CUBE ROOT OF A RATIONAL NUMBER

DEFINITION *If x and a are two rational numbers such that $x^3 = a$, then we say that x is the cube root of a and we write $\sqrt[3]{a} = x$.*

We know that $\left(\frac{3}{4}\right)^3 = \frac{27}{64} \quad \therefore \quad \sqrt[3]{\frac{27}{64}} = \frac{3}{4}$

Similarly, $\left(-\frac{4}{11}\right)^3 = \frac{-64}{1331} \quad \therefore \quad \sqrt[3]{\frac{-64}{1331}} = -\frac{4}{11}$

In order to find the cube root of a rational number we use the following result:

Result *For any rational number $\frac{a}{b}$, we have*

$$\sqrt[3]{\frac{a}{b}} = \frac{\sqrt[3]{a}}{\sqrt[3]{b}}$$

Following examples will illustrate the use of the above result in finding the cube roots of rational numbers.

ILLUSTRATIVE EXAMPLES

Example 1 Find the cube root of each of the following numbers:

(i) $\frac{1331}{4096}$ (ii) $\frac{-2197}{9261}$ (iii) $\frac{4096}{-2197}$ (iv) $\frac{-3375}{-2744}$

Solution (i) We have,

$$\sqrt[3]{\frac{1331}{4096}} = \frac{\sqrt[3]{1331}}{\sqrt[3]{4096}} \qquad \left[\text{Using: } \sqrt[3]{\frac{a}{b}} = \frac{\sqrt[3]{a}}{\sqrt[3]{b}}\right]$$

Now, resolving 1331 and 4096 into prime factors, we have

11	1311
11	121
11	11
	1

2	4096
2	2048
2	1024
2	512
2	256
2	188
2	64
2	32
2	16
2	8
2	4
2	2
	1

$\therefore \quad 1311 = 11\times11\times11$ and $4096 = \underbrace{2\times2\times2}\times\underbrace{2\times2\times2}\times\underbrace{2\times2\times2}\times\underbrace{2\times2\times2}$

$\Rightarrow \quad \sqrt[3]{1331} = 11$ and $\sqrt[3]{4096} = 2\times2\times2\times2 = 16$

Hence, $\sqrt[3]{\dfrac{1331}{4096}} = \dfrac{\sqrt[3]{1331}}{\sqrt[3]{4096}} = \dfrac{11}{16}$

(ii) $\sqrt[3]{\dfrac{-2197}{9261}} = \dfrac{\sqrt[3]{-2197}}{\sqrt[3]{9261}}$ $\left[\text{Using: } \sqrt[3]{\dfrac{a}{b}} = \dfrac{\sqrt[3]{a}}{\sqrt[3]{b}}\right]$

$= -\dfrac{\sqrt[3]{2197}}{\sqrt[3]{9261}}$ $[\because \sqrt[3]{-a} = -\sqrt[3]{a}]$

Now, resolving 2197 and 9261 into prime factors, we get

13	2197
13	169
13	13
	1

3	9261
3	3087
3	1029
7	343
7	49
7	7
	1

$\therefore \quad 2197 = \underbrace{13\times13\times13}$ and $9261 = \underbrace{3\times3\times3}\times\underbrace{7\times7\times7}$

$\Rightarrow \quad \sqrt[3]{2197} = 13$ and $\sqrt[3]{9261} = 3\times7 = 21$

Hence, $\sqrt[3]{\dfrac{-2197}{9261}} = -\dfrac{\sqrt[3]{2197}}{\sqrt[3]{9261}} = -\dfrac{13}{21}$

(iii) We have,

$$\sqrt[3]{\frac{4096}{-2197}} = \frac{\sqrt[3]{4096}}{\sqrt[3]{-2197}} \qquad \left[\text{Using: } \sqrt[3]{\frac{a}{b}} = \frac{\sqrt[3]{a}}{\sqrt[3]{b}}\right]$$

$$= \frac{\sqrt[3]{4096}}{-\sqrt[3]{2197}} \qquad [\text{Using: } \sqrt[3]{-a} = -\sqrt[3]{a}]$$

$$= \frac{16}{-13} \qquad [\text{See (i) and (ii)}]$$

(iv) We have,

$$\sqrt[3]{\frac{-3375}{-2744}} = \frac{\sqrt[3]{-3375}}{\sqrt[3]{-2744}} \qquad \left[\text{Using: } \sqrt[3]{\frac{a}{b}} = \frac{\sqrt[3]{a}}{\sqrt[3]{b}}\right]$$

$$= \frac{-\sqrt[3]{3375}}{-\sqrt[3]{2744}} = \frac{\sqrt[3]{3375}}{\sqrt[3]{2744}} \qquad [\because \sqrt[3]{-a} = -\sqrt[3]{a}]$$

Now, resolving 3375 and 2744 into prime factors, we get

5	3375
5	675
5	135
3	27
3	9
3	3
	1

2	2744
2	1372
2	686
7	343
7	49
7	7
	1

$$3375 = \underbrace{5\times5\times5}\times\underbrace{3\times3\times3} \text{ and } 2744 = \underbrace{2\times2\times2}\times\underbrace{7\times7\times7}$$

$$\therefore \quad \sqrt[3]{3375} = 5\times3 = 15 \text{ and } \sqrt[3]{2744} = 2\times7 = 14$$

Hence, $\sqrt[3]{\frac{-3375}{-2744}} = \frac{\sqrt[3]{3375}}{\sqrt[3]{2744}} = \frac{15}{14}$

Example 2 Find the cube root 1.331.

Solution We have,

$$1.331 = \frac{1.331\times1000}{1000} = \frac{1331}{1000}$$

$$\therefore \quad \sqrt[3]{1331} = \sqrt[3]{\frac{1331}{1000}} = \frac{\sqrt[3]{1331}}{\sqrt[3]{1000}} \qquad \left[\text{Using: } \sqrt[3]{\frac{a}{b}} = \frac{\sqrt[3]{a}}{\sqrt[3]{b}}\right]$$

$$= \frac{11}{10} = 1.1 \qquad [\because \sqrt[3]{1331} = 11 \text{ and } \sqrt[3]{1000} = 10]$$

Example 3 Find the cube root of 0.003375.

Solution We have,

$$0.003375 = \frac{3375}{1000000}$$

$$\therefore \quad \sqrt[3]{0.003375} = \sqrt[3]{\frac{3375}{1000000}} = \frac{\sqrt[3]{3375}}{\sqrt[3]{1000000}}$$

$$= \frac{15}{100} \qquad \left[\because 3375 = 3^3 \times 5^3 \text{ and } 1000000 = (100)^3\right]$$

$$= 0.15 \qquad \left[\therefore \sqrt[3]{3375} = 3 \times 5 = 15 \text{ and, } \sqrt[3]{1000000} = 100\right]$$

Example 4 The volume of a cubical box is 32.768 cubic metres. Find the length of a side of the box.

Solution Let the length of a side of the box be x metres. Then, its volume is x^3 cubic meters. But, the volume is given as 32.768 cubic metres.

$$\therefore \quad x^3 = 32.768$$

$$\Rightarrow \quad x = \sqrt[3]{32.768} = \sqrt[3]{\frac{32768}{1000}} = \frac{\sqrt[3]{32768}}{\sqrt[3]{1000}}$$

Now, resolving 32768 and 1000 in prime factors, we have

2	32768
2	16384
2	8192
2	4096
2	2048
2	1024
2	512
2	256
2	128
2	64
2	32
2	16
2	8
2	4
2	2
	1

2	1000
2	500
2	250
5	125
5	25
5	5
	1

$$\therefore \quad 32768 = \underbrace{2\times2\times2}\times\underbrace{2\times2\times2}\times\underbrace{2\times2\times2}\times\underbrace{2\times2\times2}\times\underbrace{2\times2\times2}$$

$$\text{and, } \quad 1000 = \underbrace{2\times2\times2}\times\underbrace{5\times5\times5}$$

$$\therefore \quad \sqrt[3]{32768} = \underbrace{2\times2\times2}\times\underbrace{2\times2\times2} = 32 \text{ and } \sqrt[3]{1000} = 2\times5 = 10$$

$$\text{Hence, } x = \frac{\sqrt[3]{32768}}{\sqrt[3]{1000}} = \frac{32}{10} = \frac{16}{5} = 3.2 \text{ metres}$$

EXERCISE 4.4

1. Find the cube roots of each of the following integers:
   (i) -125 (ii) -5832 (iii) -2744000 (iv) -753571 (v) -32768
2. Show that:
   (i) $\sqrt[3]{27}\times\sqrt[3]{64}=\sqrt[3]{27\times 64}$ (ii) $\sqrt[3]{64\times 729}=\sqrt[3]{64}\times\sqrt[3]{729}$
   (iii) $\sqrt[3]{-125\times 216}=\sqrt[3]{-125}\times\sqrt[3]{216}$ (iv) $\sqrt[3]{-125\times -1000}=\sqrt[3]{-125}\times\sqrt[3]{-1000}$
3. Find the cube root of each of the following numbers:
   (i) 8×125 (ii) -1728×216 (iii) -27×2744 (iv) -729×-15625
4. Evaluate:
   (i) $\sqrt[3]{4^3\times 6^3}$ (ii) $\sqrt[3]{8\times 17\times 17\times 17}$ (iii) $\sqrt[3]{700\times 2\times 49\times 5}$ (iv) $125\sqrt[3]{a^6}-\sqrt[3]{125a^6}$
5. Find the cube root of each of the following rational numbers:
   (i) $\frac{-125}{729}$ (ii) $\frac{10648}{12167}$ (iii) $\frac{-19683}{24389}$ (iv) $\frac{686}{-3456}$ (v) $\frac{-39304}{-42875}$
6. Find the cube root of each of the following rational numbers:
   (i) 0.001728 (ii) 0.003375 (iii) 0.001 (iv) 1.331
7. Evaluate each of the following:
   (i) $\sqrt[3]{27}+\sqrt[3]{0.008}+\sqrt[3]{0.064}$ (ii) $\sqrt[3]{1000}+\sqrt[3]{0.008}-\sqrt[3]{0.125}$ (iii) $\sqrt[3]{\frac{729}{216}}\times\frac{6}{9}$
   (iv) $\sqrt[3]{\frac{0.027}{0.008}}\div\sqrt{\frac{0.09}{0.04}}-1$ (v) $\sqrt[3]{0.1\times 0.1\times 0.1\times 13\times 13\times 13}$
8. Show that:
   (i) $\frac{\sqrt[3]{729}}{\sqrt[3]{1000}}=\sqrt[3]{\frac{729}{1000}}$ (ii) $\frac{\sqrt[3]{-512}}{\sqrt[3]{343}}=\sqrt[3]{\frac{-512}{343}}$
9. Fill in the blanks:
   (i) $\sqrt[3]{125\times 27}=3\times\ldots$ (ii) $\sqrt[3]{8\times\ldots}=8$ (iii) $\sqrt[3]{1728}=4\times\ldots$
   (iv) $\sqrt[3]{480}=\sqrt[3]{3}\times 2\times\sqrt[3]{\ldots}$ (v) $\sqrt[3]{\ldots}=\sqrt[3]{7}\times\sqrt[3]{8}$ (vi) $\sqrt[3]{\ldots}=\sqrt[3]{4}\times\sqrt[3]{5}\times\sqrt[3]{6}$
   (vii) $\sqrt[3]{\frac{27}{125}}=\frac{\ldots}{5}$ (viii) $\sqrt[3]{\frac{729}{1331}}=\frac{9}{\ldots}$ (ix) $\sqrt[3]{\frac{512}{\ldots}}=\frac{8}{13}$
10. The volume of a cubical box is 474.552 cubic metres. Find the length of each side of the box.
11. Three numbers are to one another 2 : 3 : 4. The sum of their cubes is 0.334125. Find the numbers.
12. Find the side of a cube whose volume is $\frac{24389}{216}\text{ m}^3$.

13. Evaluate:

(i) $\sqrt[3]{36} \times \sqrt[3]{384}$ (ii) $\sqrt[3]{96} \times \sqrt[3]{144}$ (iii) $\sqrt[3]{100} \times \sqrt[3]{270}$ (iv) $\sqrt[3]{121} \times \sqrt[3]{297}$

14. Find the cube roots of the numbers 3048625, 20346417, 210644875, 57066625 using the fact that

(i) $3048625 = 3375 \times 729$ (ii) $20346417 = 9261 \times 2197$

(iii) $210644875 = 42875 \times 4913$ (iv) $57066625 = 166375 \times 343$

15. Find the units digit of the cube root of the following numbers:

(i) 226981 (ii) 13824 (iii) 571787 (iv) 175616

16. Find the tens digit of the cube root of each of the numbers in Q. No. 15.

ANSWERS

1. (i) −5 (ii) −18 (iii) −140 (iv) −91 (v) −32
3. (i) 10 (ii) −72 (iii) −42 (iv) 225
4. (i) 24 (ii) 34 (iii) 70 (iv) $120a^2$
5. (i) $-\frac{5}{9}$ (ii) $\frac{22}{23}$ (iii) $\frac{-27}{29}$ (iv) $\frac{-7}{12}$ (v) $\frac{34}{35}$
6. (i) 0.12 (ii) 0.15 (iii) 0.1 (iv) 1.1
7. (i) 3.6 (ii) 9.7 (iii) 1 (iv) 0 (v) 1.3
9. (i) 5 (ii) 64 (iii) 3 (iv) 20 (v) 56 (vi) 120 (vii) 3 (viii) 11 (ix) 2197
10. 7.8 m
11. 0.3, 0.45, 0.6
12. $\frac{29}{6}$ m
13. (i) 24 (ii) 24 (iii) 30 (iv) 33
14. (i) 135 (ii) 273 (iii) 595 (iv) 385
15. (i) 1 (ii) 4 (iii) 7 (iv) 6
16. (i) 6 (ii) 2 (iii) 8 (iv) 5

4.12 CUBE ROOT TABLES

In the previous sections, we have seen that all numbers are not perfect cubes. In fact, there are only ten numbers between 1 and 1000 which are perfect cubes. Thus, there are only 10 numbers, namely, 1, 8, 27, 64, 125, 216, 343, 512, 729, and 1000 whose cube roots are whole numbers. The remaining natural numbers are not perfect cubes. Consequently, their cube roots are not whole numbers and they cannot be found exactly. These cube roots are non-terminating and non-recurring decimals and are therefore irrational numbers. Only approximate values of the cube roots of these numbers can be found. Approximate cube roots of numbers can be found using cube root tables as given above:

The second column consists of cube root of natural numbers between 1 and 100 multiplied by 10.

The third column gives the cube roots of all natural numbers between 1 and 100 multiplied by 100.

All the cube roots are correct to four significant places.

x	$\sqrt[3]{x}$	$\sqrt[3]{10x}$	$\sqrt[3]{100x}$	x	$\sqrt[3]{x}$	$\sqrt[3]{10x}$	$\sqrt[3]{100x}$
1	1.000	2.154	4.642	51	3.708	7.990	17.21
2	1.260	2.714	5.848	52	3.733	8.041	17.32
3	1.442	3.107	6.694	53	3.756	8.093	17.44
4	1.587	3.420	7.368	54	3.780	8.143	17.54
5	1.710	3.684	7.937	55	3.803	8.193	17.65
6	1.817	3.915	8.434	56	3.826	8.243	17.76
7	1.913	4.121	8.879	57	3.849	8.291	17.86
8	2.000	4.309	9.283	58	3.871	8.340	17.97
9	2.080	4.481	9.655	59	3.893	8.387	18.07
10	2.154	4.642	10.00	60	3.915	8.434	18.17
11	2.224	4.791	10.32	61	3.936	8.481	18.27
12	2.289	4.932	10.63	62	3.958	8.527	18.37
13	2.351	5.066	10.91	63	3.979	8.573	18.47
14	2.410	5.192	11.19	64	4.000	8.618	18.57
15	2.466	5.313	11.45	65	4.021	8.662	18.66
16	2.520	5.429	11.70	66	4.041	8.707	18.76
17	2.571	5.540	11.93	67	4.062	8.750	18.85
18	2.621	5.646	12.16	68	4.082	8.794	18.95
19	2.668	5.749	12.39	69	4.102	8.837	19.04
20	2.714	5.848	12.60	70	4.121	8.879	19.13
21	2.759	5.944	12.81	71	4.141	8.921	19.22
22	2.802	6.037	13.01	72	4.160	8.963	19.31
23	2.844	6.127	13.20	73	4.179	9.004	19.40
24	2.884	6.214	13.39	74	4.198	9.045	19.49
25	2.924	6.300	13.57	75	4.217	9.086	19.57
26	2.962	6.383	13.75	76	4.236	9.126	19.66
27	3.000	6.463	13.92	77	4.254	9.166	19.75
28	3.037	6.542	14.09	78	4.273	9.205	19.83
29	3.072	6.619	14.26	79	4.291	9.244	19.92
30	3.107	6.694	14.42	80	4.309	9.283	20.00
31	3.141	6.768	14.58	81	4.327	9.322	20.08
32	3.175	6.840	14.74	82	4.344	9.360	20.17
33	3.208	6.910	14.89	83	4.362	9.398	20.25
34	3.240	6.980	15.04	84	4.380	9.435	20.33
35	3.271	7.047	15.18	85	4.397	9.473	20.41
36	3.302	7.114	15.33	86	4.414	9.510	20.49
37	3.332	7.179	15.47	87	4.431	9.546	20.57
38	3.362	7.243	15.60	88	4.448	9.583	20.65
39	3.391	7.306	15.74	89	4.465	9.619	20.72
40	3.420	7.368	15.87	90	4.481	9.655	20.80
41	3.448	7.429	16.01	91	4.498	9.691	20.88
42	3.476	7.489	16.13	92	4.514	9.726	20.95
43	3.503	7.548	16.26	93	4.531	9.761	21.03
44	3.530	7.606	16.39	94	4.547	9.796	21.10
45	3.557	7.663	16.51	95	4.563	9.830	21.18
46	3.583	7.719	16.63	96	4.579	9.865	21.25
47	3.609	7.775	16.75	97	4.595	9.899	21.33
48	3.634	7.830	16.87	98	4.610	9.933	21.40
49	3.659	7.884	16.98	99	4.626	9.967	21.47
50	3.684	7.937	17.10				

The above table consists of cube roots in three columns. The first column gives the cube roots of natural numbers between 1 and 100.

4.13 FINDING CUBE ROOTS USING CUBE ROOT TABLES

Following examples will illustrate the procedure for finding the cube root of a number by using cube root tables.

ILLUSTRATIVE EXAMPLES

Example 1 Using cube root tables, find the cube root of

(i) 62 (ii) 620 (iii) 6200

Solution (i) Clearly, 62 lies between 1 and 100. So, to find the cube root of 62, we look at the row containing 62 in the column of x. From the table, we find that

$$\sqrt[3]{62} = 3.958$$

(ii) We have,

$$620 = 62 \times 10$$

Therefore, the cube root of the 620 is the column of $\sqrt[3]{10x}$ against 62. From the cube root table, we find that

$$\sqrt[3]{620} = 8.527$$

(iii) We have,

$$6200 = 62 \times 100$$

Therefore, the cube root of 6200 is found in the column of $\sqrt[3]{100x}$ against 62. From the cube root table, we get

$$\sqrt[3]{620} = 18.370$$

Example 2 Find the cube root of 448.

Solution Resolving 448 into prime factors, we get

$$\begin{array}{r|r} 2 & 448 \\ \hline 2 & 224 \\ \hline 2 & 112 \\ \hline 2 & 56 \\ \hline 2 & 28 \\ \hline 2 & 14 \\ \hline 7 & 7 \\ \hline & 1 \end{array}$$

$$448 = \underbrace{2 \times 2 \times 2} \times \underbrace{2 \times 2 \times 2} \times 7$$

$$\therefore \quad \sqrt[3]{448} = \sqrt{\underbrace{2 \times 2 \times 2} \times \underbrace{2 \times 2 \times 2} \times 7}$$

$$= 2 \times 2 \times \sqrt[3]{7} = 4\sqrt[3]{7}$$

$$= 4 \times 1.913 \qquad \text{[From cube root table } \sqrt[3]{7} = 1.913\text{]}$$

$$= 7.652$$

Example 3 Find the cube root of 17064.

Solution Resolving 17064 into prime factors, we have

$$\begin{array}{r|r} 2 & 17064 \\ \hline 2 & 8532 \\ \hline 2 & 4266 \\ \hline 3 & 2133 \\ \hline 3 & 711 \\ \hline 3 & 237 \\ \hline & 79 \end{array}$$

$$17064 = \underbrace{2 \times 2 \times 2} \times \underbrace{3 \times 3 \times 3} \times 79$$

$$\therefore \quad \sqrt[3]{17064} = \sqrt[3]{\underbrace{2 \times 2 \times 2} \times \underbrace{3 \times 3 \times 3} \times 79}$$

$$= 2 \times 3 \times \sqrt[3]{79}$$

$$= 6 \times 4.291 \qquad \text{[From cube root table } \sqrt[3]{79} = 4.291\text{]}$$

$$= 25.746$$

Example 4 Using cube root table, find the value of $\sqrt[3]{\frac{51}{125000}}$.

Solution We have,

$$\sqrt[3]{\frac{51}{125000}} = \frac{\sqrt[3]{51}}{\sqrt[3]{125000}}$$

$$= \frac{\sqrt[3]{51}}{\sqrt[3]{50\times 50\times 50}} \quad [\because 125000 = 50\times 50\times 50]$$

$$= \frac{\sqrt[3]{51}}{50} = \frac{3.708}{50} \quad \text{[Using cube root table]}$$

$$= 0.07416$$

Example 5 Using cube root tables, find the cube root of 85.9.

Solution We have,

$$85 < 85.9 < 86$$

$$\Rightarrow \sqrt[3]{85} < \sqrt[3]{85.9} < \sqrt[3]{86}$$

From the cube root table, we have

$$\sqrt[3]{85} = 4.397 \text{ and } \sqrt[3]{86} = 4.414$$

Thus, for the difference $(86-85)$, i.e. 1, the difference in the values

$$= (4.414 - 4.397) = 0.017$$

$\therefore$ For the difference of (85.9 – 85) i.e. 0.9, the difference in the values

$$= \frac{0.017}{1}\times 0.9$$

$$= 0.0153 = 0.015 \quad \text{[Upto three decimal places]}$$

Hence, $\sqrt[3]{85.9} = 4.397 + 0.015 = 4.412$

Example 6 Using cube root table, find the cube root of 953.

Solution We have,

$$950 < 953 < 960$$

$$\Rightarrow \sqrt[3]{950} < \sqrt[3]{953} < \sqrt[3]{960}$$

From the cube root table, we have

$$\sqrt[3]{950} = 9.830 \text{ and } \sqrt[3]{960} = 9.865$$

Thus, for the difference of (960 – 950) i.e. 10, the difference in the values

$$= (9.865 - 9.830) = 0.035$$

$\therefore$ For the difference of (953 – 950) i.e. 3, the difference in the values

$$= \left(\frac{0.035}{10}\times 3\right)$$

$$= 0.0105 = 0.010 \quad \text{[Upto three decimal places]}$$

Hence, $\sqrt[3]{953} = 9.830 + 0.010 = 9.840$

Example 7 Using cube root table, find the cube root of 5319.

Solution We have, $5300 < 5319 < 5400$

$\Rightarrow \quad \sqrt[3]{5300} < \sqrt[3]{5319} < \sqrt[3]{5400}$

From the cube root table, we have

$\sqrt[3]{5300} = 17.44$ and $\sqrt[3]{5400} = 17.54$

Thus, for the difference of (5400 – 5300) i.e. 100, we have

The difference in the values = 17.54 – 17.44 = 0.10

$\therefore$ For the difference of 19, we have

The difference in the values $= \frac{0.10}{100} \times 19 = 0.019$

Hence, $\sqrt[3]{5319} = 17.44 + 0.019 = 17.459$

Example 8 Using cube root table, find the cube root of 309400.

Solution The cube root table gives cube roots of natural numbers upto 9900.

Clearly, 309400 is greater than 9900.

So, we write

$309400 = 1547 \times 200$

$\therefore \quad \sqrt[3]{309400} = \sqrt[3]{1547 \times 200}$

$= \sqrt[3]{1547} \times \sqrt[3]{200}$

Now, $1500 < 1547 < 1600$

$\therefore \quad \sqrt[3]{1500} < \sqrt[3]{1547} < \sqrt[3]{1600}$

From the cube root table, we have

$\sqrt[3]{1500} = 11.45$ and $\sqrt[3]{1600} = 11.70$

Thus, for the difference of (1600 – 1500) i.e. 100, we have,

The difference in the values = 11.70 – 11.45 = 0.25

$\therefore$ For the difference of (1547 – 1500) i.e. 47, we have

The difference in the values $= \frac{0.25}{100} \times 47$

$= 0.1175 = 0.117$ [Upto three decimal places]

$\therefore \quad \sqrt[3]{1547} = 11.45 + 0.117 = 11.567$

Also, from the cube root table, we have

$\sqrt[3]{200} = 5.848$

$\therefore \quad \sqrt[3]{309400} = \sqrt[3]{1547} \times \sqrt[3]{200} = 11.567 \times 5.848 = 67.643$

EXERCISE 4.5

Making use of the cube root table, find the cube roots of the following (correct to three decimal places) : (1 - 22)

1. 7	2. 70	3. 700	4. 7000	5. 1100	6. 780
7. 7800	8. 1346	9. 250	10. 5112	11. 9800	12. 732
13. 7342	14. 133100	15. 37800	16. 0.27	17. 8.6	18. 0.86
19. 8.65	20. 7532	21. 833	22. 34.2		

23. What is the length of the side of a cube whose volume is 275 cm^3. Make use of the table for the cube root.

ANSWERS

1. 1.913	2. 4.121	3. 8.879	4. 19.13	5. 10.32	6. 9.205
7. 19.83	8. 11.04	9. 6.3	10. 17.223	11. 21.40	12. 9.012
13. 19.4378	14. 51.062	15. 33.56	16. 0.646	17. 2.049	18. 0.951
19. 2.053	20. 19.60	21. 9.409	22. 3.246	23. 6.504 cm	

THINGS TO REMEMBER

1. *The cube of a number is that number raised to the power 3.*

   Thus, if a is a number, then $a^3 = a \times a \times a$.
2. *A natural number is a perfect cube, if it is cube of some natural number.*

   Thus, a natural number n is a perfect cube. If $n = m^3$ *for some natural number m.*
3. *The cube of an even natural number is even.*
4. *The cube of an odd natural number is odd.*
5. *A number m is the cube root of a natural number n, if* $n = m^3$. *In other words, a cube root of a number n is the number whose cube is n. The cube root of n is denoted by* $\sqrt[3]{n}$
6. *For any positive integer, we have*

   $$\sqrt[3]{-n} = -\sqrt[3]{n}$$
7. *For any two integers a and b, we have*

   (i) $\sqrt[3]{ab} = \sqrt[3]{a} \times \sqrt[3]{b}$ (ii) $\sqrt[3]{\frac{a}{b}} = \frac{\sqrt[3]{a}}{\sqrt[3]{b}}, b \neq 0$

5

PLAYING WITH NUMBERS

5.1 INTRODUCTION

In class VI, we have learnt about various tests of divisibility without knowing how they work. In this chapter, we shall go into the details of the reason of validity of these tests. We shall also see how we frame puzzles on numbers by using place values of digits.

5.2 GENERALIZED FORM OF NUMBERS

In earlier classes, we have learnt about the method of writing a number in expanded form by using the place values of its digits. In chapter 2 on powers, we have seen that a natural number can be expressed in exponential form by using powers of 10 and the digits of the number. For example,

Expanded Form		*Exponential form*
$57 = 10\times5+7$	or,	$57 = 10^1\times5+10^0\times7$
$975 = 100\times9+10\times7+5$	or,	$975 = 10^2\times9+10^1\times7+10^0\times5$
$5498 = 1000\times5+4\times100+9\times10+8$	or,	$5498 = 10^3\times5+10^2\times4+10^1\times9+10^0\times8$ etc.

Let us now consider a two digit number having a and b respectively as tens and units digits. Using the above notations the number can be written as

$10\times a+b$ or, $10^1\times a+10^0\times b$

Let us use the notation $\overline{ab}$ to denote this number.

i.e., $\overline{ab}=10\times a+b$ or, $\overline{ab}=10^1\times a+10^0\times b$

Here, we have put a line over ab to distinguish it from the expression ab, which means "a multiplied by b".

Thus, any two digit number can be written as $\overline{ab}$, where a and b are whole numbers taking values from 0 to 9 such that $a\neq0$. This is known as the generalized form of a two digit number.

Similarly, if a, b, c denote numbers taking values from 0 to 9, then $\overline{abc}$, where $a\neq0$, is the generalized form of a three digit number whose ones, tens and hundreds digits are c, b and a respectively.

In general any natural number can be written as $\overline{\ldots cba}$ in which ones digits is a, tens digit is b, hundreds digit is c and so on. Here, dots mean that there may be more digits to the left of c.

In expanded form, we have

$$\overline{ab}=10a+b,\ \overline{abc}=100a+10b+c \text{ and, } \overline{\ldots cba}=\ldots+100c+10b+a.$$

5.3 INTERCHANGING THE DIGITS OF A NUMBER

Consider a two digit number $\overline{ab}$ having ones and tens digits as b and a respectively. On reversing the digits of this number, we obtain a two digit number $\overline{ba}$.

In expanded form, we have

$$\overline{ab} = 10a + b \quad \text{... (i)}$$

and, $$\overline{ba} = 10b + a \quad \text{... (ii)}$$

Adding (i) and (ii), we get

$$\overline{ab} + \overline{ba} = (10a + b) + (10b + a)$$

$$\Rightarrow \quad \overline{ab} + \overline{ba} = 11a + 11b$$

$$\Rightarrow \quad \overline{ab} + \overline{ba} = 11(a + b)$$

$$\Rightarrow \quad \frac{\overline{ab} + \overline{ba}}{11} = a + b \text{ and } \frac{\overline{ab} + \overline{ba}}{a + b} = 11$$

Thus, $\overline{ab} + \overline{ba}$ is completely divisible by 11 and the quotient is $a + b$.
Also, it is divisible by $a + b$ and in that case the quotient is 11.

In other words, the sum of any two digit number $\overline{ab}$ and the number $\overline{ba}$ by reversing its digits is completely divisible by

(i) *the sum $a + b$ of its digits and the quotient is 11.*

(ii) *11 and the quotient is $a + b$ i.e. the sum of its digits.*

Subtracting (ii) from (i), we get

$$\overline{ab} - \overline{ba} = (10a + b) - (10b + a)$$

$$\Rightarrow \quad \overline{ab} - \overline{ba} = 9a - 9b$$

$$\Rightarrow \quad \overline{ab} - \overline{ba} = 9(a - b)$$

$$\Rightarrow \quad \frac{\overline{ab} - \overline{ba}}{9} = a - b \text{ and } \frac{\overline{ab} - \overline{ba}}{a - b} = 9 \quad \text{[Assuming that } a > b\text{]}$$

Thus, $\overline{ab} - \overline{ba}$ is exactly divisible by 9 and the quotient is $a - b$ i.e. the difference of the digits. Also, $\overline{ab} - \overline{ba}$ is exactly divisible by $a - b$ (difference of digits) and the quotient is 9.

In other words, the difference of any two digit number $\overline{ab}$ and the number $\overline{ba}$ by reversing its digits is exactly divisible by

(i) *the difference $a - b$ of its digits and the quotient is 9.*

(ii) *9 and the quotient is $a - b$ i.e. the difference of its digits.*

The following are some illustrations for the above assertions.

ILLUSTRATION 1 Without performing actual addition and division write the quotient when the sum of 79 and 97 is divided by (i) 16 (ii) 11.

Solution Clearly, 79 and 97 are two numbers such that one can be obtained by reversing the digits of the other. Therefore, their sum when divided by the sum of the digits i.e. 7 + 9 = 16, we obtain 11 as the quotient. If the sum of these two numbers is divided by 11, we get 7 + 9 (sum of the digits) = 16 as the quotient.

ILLUSTRATION 2 Without performing actual computations. Find the quotient when 92 – 29 is divided by (i) 9 (ii) 7.

Solution (i) We know that

$\overline{ab} - \overline{ba}$ when divided by 9, the quotient is $a - b$

$\therefore$ $92 - 29$ when divided by 9, the quotient is $9 - 2 = 7$.

(ii) We know that

$\overline{ab} - \overline{ba}$ when divided by $a - b$, the quotient is 9.

$\therefore$ $92 - 29$ when divided by $9 - 2 = 7$, the quotient is 9.

Let us now take a three digit number $\overline{abc}$. By changing the order of its digits in cyclic order, we obtain numbers $\overline{bca}$ and $\overline{cab}$.

These numbers in expanded form can be written as

$$\overline{abc} = 100a + 10b + c$$

$$\overline{bca} = 100b + 10c + a$$

$$\overline{cab} = 100c + 10a + b$$

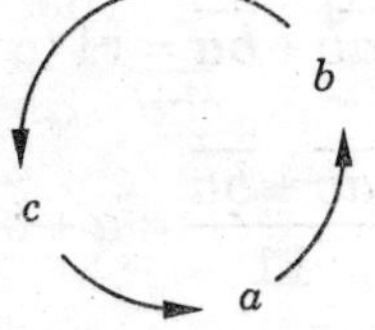

Fig. 5.1

On adding these three numbers, we get

$$\begin{aligned}\overline{abc} + \overline{bca} + \overline{cab} &= (100a + 10b + c) + (100b + 10c + a) + (100c + 10a + b)\\ &= 111a + 111b + 111c\\ &= 111\,(a + b + c)\\ &= 3 \times 37 \times (a + b + c)\end{aligned}$$

It follows from the above expression that the sum $\overline{abc} + \overline{bca} + \overline{cab}$ is exactly divisible by 3, 37, $a + b + c$, 111, $3\,(a + b + c)$ and $37\,(a + b + c)$.

The quotients in each case are listed below:

Number	*Divisior*	*Quotient*
$\overline{abc} + \overline{bca} + \overline{cab}$	111	$a + b + c$
	$a + b + c$	111
	37	$3\,(a + b + c)$
	3	$37\,(a + b + c)$
	$3\,(a + b + c)$	37
	$37\,(a + b + c)$	3

ILLUSTRATION 3 Without performing actual addition, find the quotient when 237 + 372 + 723 is divided by (i) 111 (ii) 12 (iii) 37 (iv) 3 (v) 36 (vi) 444

Solution If digits 2, 3 and 7 are arranged in cyclic order, we get three numbers 237, 372 and 723. The sum of these numbers i.e. 237 + 372 + 723 when divided by

(i) 111 gives quotient 2 + 3 + 7 = 12
(ii) 12 i.e. 2 + 3 + 7 gives quotient 111.
(iii) 37 gives quotient 3 (2 + 3 + 7) = 36
(iv) 3 gives quotient 37 (2 + 3 + 7) = 444
(v) 36 gives quotient 37.
(vi) 444 gives quotient 3.

Again, let us take the number $\overline{abc}$. Interchanging its ones and hundreds digits, we get the number $\overline{cba}$.

Now,

$$\overline{abc} = 100a + 10b + c \text{ and, } \overline{cba} = 100c + 10b + a$$

If $a > c$, then $\overline{abc} > \overline{cba}$. Therefore, the difference between these two numbers is

$$\begin{aligned}\overline{abc} - \overline{cba} &= (100a + 10b + c) - (100c + 10b + a) \\ &= 99a - 99c \\ &= 99\,(a - c) = 3^2 \times 11 \times (a - c)\end{aligned}$$

If $c > a$, then $\overline{cba} > \overline{abc}$. Therefore, the difference between the numbers is

$$\begin{aligned}\overline{cba} - \overline{abc} &= (100c + 10b + a) - (100a + 10b + c) \\ &= 99c - 99a \\ &= 99(c - a) = 3^2 \times 11 \times (c - a)\end{aligned}$$

If $a = c$, then $\overline{abc} = \overline{cba}$. Therefore, the diffrence between the numbers is zero.

It follows from this that the difference of the numbers $\overline{abc}$ and $\overline{cba}$ is equal to $3^2 \times 11 \times$ difference between hundreds digit and ones digit of the number

So, the difference will always be a multiple of 99 and the quotient will always be equal to the difference between the hundreds digit and the once digit of the number.

Thus, the difference of a three digit number $\overline{abc}$ and the number obtained by interchanging its ones and hundreds digits i.e. $\overline{cba}$ is always a multiple of 99 and the quotient is always equal to the difference between the hundreds and ones digit of the number.

Various divisors and the corresponding quotients of the difference $\overline{abc} - \overline{cba}$ are as follows:

Divisor	*Quotient*
99	$a - c$
$a - c$	99
3	$33\,(a - c)$
$33\,(a - c)$	3
$3\,(a - c)$	33
33	$3\,(a - c)$
9	$11\,(a - c)$
$11\,(a - c)$	9
11	$9\,(a - c)$
$9\,(a - c)$	11

ILLUSTRATION 4 Write the quotients when the difference of 985 and the number obtained by interchanging its ones and hundreds digits is divided by

(i) 99 (ii) 4 (iii) 33 (iv) 3 (v) 44

Solution We have,

$$\overline{abc} - \overline{cba} = 99\,(a - c) \text{ or, } \overline{abc} - \overline{cba} = 3^2 \times 11 \times (a - c)$$

Here, $a = 9, b = 8$ and $c = 5$.

$$\therefore \quad 985 - 589 = 3^2 \times 11 \times 4 \qquad \text{... (i)}$$

(i) We know that

$\overline{abc} - \overline{cba}$ when divided by 99, the quotient is $a - c$.

$\therefore$ 985 – 589 when divided by 99, the quotient is 4

(ii) We know that

$\overline{abc} - \overline{cba}$ when divided by $a - c$, the quotient is 99.

$\therefore$ 985 – 589 when divided by 9 – 5 i.e. 4, the quotient is 99.

(iii) From (i), we have

$$\frac{985-589}{33} = \frac{3^2 \times 11 \times 4}{33} = 12$$

(iv) From (i), we have

$$\frac{985-589}{3} = \frac{3^2 \times 11 \times 4}{3} = 132$$

(v) From (i), we have

$$\frac{985-589}{3} = \frac{3^2 \times 11 \times 4}{44} = 9$$

Now, consider three digit numbers $\overline{abc}$ and $\overline{acb}$ i.e. three digit numbers whose ones and tens digits are interchanged.

We have,

$\overline{abc} = 100a + 10b + c$ and, $\overline{acb} = 100a + 10c + b$

$\therefore$ $\overline{abc} - \overline{acb} = (100a + 10b + c) - (100a + 10c + b) = 9\,(b - c)$

This shows that $\overline{abc} - \overline{acb}$ is exactly divisible by 9 and the quotient is $b - c$.

EXERCISE 5.1

1. Without performing actual addition and division write the quotient when the sum of 69 and 96 is divided by

   (i) 11 (ii) 15

2. Without performing actual computations, find the quotient when 94 – 49 is divided by

   (i) 9 (ii) 5

3. If sum of the number 985 and two other numbers obtained by arranging the digits of 985 in cyclic order is divided by 111, 22 and 37 respectively. Find the quotient in each case.

4. Find the quotient when the difference of 985 and 958 is divided by 9.

ANSWERS

1. (i) 15 (ii) 11 2. (i) 15 (ii) 9 3. (i) 22 (ii) 66 4. 3

5.4 TESTS OF DIVISIBILITY

In class VI, we have learnt about various test to check the divisibility by following divisors:

2, 3, 4, 5, 6, 8, 9, 10, and 11.

In this section, we shall see how these tests work. Also, we will discuss some more problems on divisibility of the above mentioned divisors.

5.4.1 DIVISIBILITY BY 10

Let $\overline{...cba}$ be an arbitrary number whose ones digit is a, tens digit is b, hundreds digit is c and so on. Then,

$$\overline{...cba} = ... + 100c + 10b + a$$

$\Rightarrow$ $\overline{...cba} = 10(... + 10c + b) + a$

$\Rightarrow$ $\overline{...cba} = 10k + a$, where $k = ... + 10c + b$ ... (i)

$\Rightarrow$ $\overline{...cba}$ is divisible by 10 if and only if $a = 0$.

$\Rightarrow$ $\overline{...cba}$ is divisibli by 10 if and only if its units digit is 0.

It follows from the above discussion that a number is divisible by 10 if and only if its units digit is zero. So, we have following test of divisibility by 10.

TEST OF DIVISIBILITY BY 10 *A number is divisible by 10, if its units digit is zero.*

<u>Remark 1</u> *It is evident from (i) that any number having, its units digit 'a' can be written as $10k + a$.*

<u>Remark 2</u> *From (i), we have*

$$\overline{...cba} - a = 10k$$

Thus, if we subtract the ones digit of a number from that number, the number left over is divisible by 10.

ILLUSTRATION Write the following numbers in the form $10b + a$.

(i) 231 (ii) 542 (iii) 908 (iv) 1234

Solution (i) We know that if units digit of a number is subtracted from the number then the left over number is divisible by 10.

$\therefore$ $231 - 1$ is divisible by 10.

We have,

$231 - 1 = 230$

$\Rightarrow$ $231 - 1 = 10 \times 23$

$\Rightarrow$ $231 = 10 \times 23 + 1$

$\Rightarrow$ $231 = 10b + a$, where $a = 1$ and $b = 23$.

(ii) We have,

$542 - 2 = 540$

$\Rightarrow$ $542 - 2 = 10 \times 54$

$\Rightarrow$ $542 = 10 \times 54 + 2$

$\Rightarrow$ $542 = 10b + a$, where $b = 54$ and $a = 2$

(iii) We have,

$908 - 8 = 900$

$\Rightarrow$ $908 - 8 = 10 \times 90$

$\Rightarrow$ $908 = 10 \times 90 + 8$

$\Rightarrow$ $908 = 10b + a$, where $a = 8$ and $b = 90$

(iv) We have,

$1234 - 4 = 1230$

$\Rightarrow$ $1234 - 4 = 10 \times 123$

$\Rightarrow$ $1234 = 10 \times 123 + 4$

$\Rightarrow$ $1234 = 10b + a$, where $a = 4$ and $b = 123$.

5.4.2 DIVISIBILITY BY 5

In subsection 5.4.1, we have shown that any integer can be written as $10a + b$, where b is the ones digit.

Clearly, 10 is a multiple of 5. Therefore, $10a$ is also a multiple of 5. Since the sum of any two multiples of 5 is a multiple of 5. Therefore, $10a + b$ will be a multiple of 5, if b is a multiple of 5. Thus, an integer is divisible by 5, if its units digit is a multiple of 5. That is its units digit is either 0 or 5.

So, we have the following test of divisibility by 5.

TEST OF DIVISIBILITY BY 5 *A number is divisible by 5, if its units digit is 0 or 5.*

It also follows from the above discussion that if the units digit of a number is not 0 or 5, then it is not divisible by 5.

Let n be any natural number. Then, n can be wirtten as

$n = 10a + b$, where b is the units digit of n

Since $10a$ is a multiple of 5. Therefore, when $10a + b$ is divided by 5, the remainder will be equal to the remainder when b is divided by 5.

Thus, the remainder when an integer is divided by 5 is equal to the remainder when its units digit is divided by 5.

For example, if

521 is divided by 5, the remainder is 1.

294 is divided by 5, the remainder is 4.

928 is divided by 5, the remainder is equal to the remainder when 8 is divided by 5. i.e. equal to 3.

2587 is divided by 5, the remainder is equal to 2.

ILLUSTRATION If the division of a natural number n by 5 leaves a remainder of

(i) 3, what might be the ones digit of n?

(ii) 1, what might be the ones digit of n?

(iii) 4, what might be the ones digit of n?

Solution (i) If n is divided by 5, then the remainder is equal to the remainder when its ones digit is divided by 5. Therefore, units digit of n when divided by 5, must leave remainder of 3. Consequently, the units digit of n must be 3 or 8.

(ii) If the division of n by 5 leaves a remainder of 1, then the units digit must also leave the same remainder when divided by 5. So, the units digit of n is 1 or 6.

(iii) If the division of n by 5 leaves a remainder of 4, then the units digit must also leave the same remainder when divided by 5. So, the units digit of n must be 4 or 9.

5.4.3 DIVISIBILITY BY 2

Let n be any natural number. Then,

$$n = 10a + b, \text{ where } b \text{ is units digit of } n.$$

Since $10a$ is an even number and the sum of two even numbers is an even number and the sum of an even number and an odd number is an odd number. Therefore, $n = 10a + b$ is even, if b is an even digit. Thus, we have the following test of divisibility by 2.

TEST OF DIVISIBILITY BY 2 *A number is divisible by 2, if its units digit is an even digit i.e. 0, 2, 4, 6, or 8.*

Since $10a$ is divisible by 2. Therefore, when $n = 10a + b$ is divided by 2, the remainder is equal to the remainder when the units digit b is divided by 2. Infact, when n is divided by 2, the remainder is zero if n is even, otherwise the remainder is 1.

ILLUSTRATION 1 Let n be a natural number. If the division $n \div 2$ leaves a remaineder of 1, what might be the units digit of n?

Solution Since the division $n \div 2$ leaves a remainder of 1. So, n must be an odd natural number. Hence, its units digit can be 1, 3, 5, 7, or 9.

ILLUSTRATION 2 Let n be a natural number. If the division $n \div 2$ leaves no remainder, what might be the units digit of n?

Solution Since the division $n \div 2$ leaves no remainder. So, n must be an even natural number. Hence, its units digit can be 0, 2, 4, 6, or 8.

ILLUSTRATION 3 Let n be a natural number such that the division $n \div 5$ leaves a remaineder of 4, and the division $n \div 2$ leaves a remainder of 1. What must be the units digit of n?

Solution It is given that the division of n by 5 leaves a remainder of 4. Therefore, the division of units digit of n by 5 must leave a remainder of 4. So, the units digit of n is either 4 or 9.

It is also given that the division of n by 2 leaves a remainder of 1. Therefore, n must be an odd number. So, its units digit can be 1, 3, 5, 7 or 9.

Clearly, 9 is the common value of units digit in two cases.

Hence, the units digit of n is 9.

Uptill now, we have studied three tests of divisibility. In all the three tests the divisibility is decided just by the units digit. So, we have used only the units digit of the given number without even bothering about the rest of the number. This has happened because 10, 5, and 2 are divisors of 10, which is the key number in our place value system.

Let us now discuss some more tests of divisibility in which all digits of the given number will be used to test the divisibility.

5.4.4 DIVISIBILITY BY 9

Let $n = \overline{ab}$ be a two digit number. Then, n can be written as

$$n = 10a + b, \text{ where } b \text{ is units digit of } n.$$

$\Rightarrow \quad n = 9a + a + b$

$\Rightarrow \quad n = 9a + (a + b)$

$\Rightarrow \quad n = \text{a multiple of } 9 + (a + b)$

$\Rightarrow \quad n$ is a multiple of 9, if $(a + b)$ is a multiple of 9

$\Rightarrow \quad \overline{ab}$ is a multiple of 9, if $(a + b)$ is a multiple of 9

Thus, a two digit number is divisible by 9, if the sum of its digits is divisible by 9.

Consider now a three digit number $\overline{abc}$.

We have,

$$\overline{abc} = 100a + 10b + c$$

$\Rightarrow \quad \overline{abc} = 99a + a + 9b + b + c$

$\Rightarrow \quad \overline{abc} = 99a + 9b + (a + b + c)$

$\Rightarrow \quad \overline{abc} = 9(11a + b) + (a + b + c)$

$\Rightarrow \quad \overline{abc} = \text{a multiple of } 9 + (a + b + c)$

$\Rightarrow \quad \overline{abc}$ is a multiple of 9, if $(a + b + c)$ is a multiple of 9

Thus, a three digit number is divisible by 9, if the sum of its digits is divisible by 9.

This is true for any digit number. Thus, we have following test of divisibility by 9.

TEST OF DIVISIBILITY BY 9 *If the sum of the digits of a natural number is divisible by 9, then the number is divisible by 9.*

It should be noted that a number is not divisible by 9 when the sum of its digits is not divisible by 9.

It is evident from the above discussion that the remainder obtained by dividing a number by 9 is equal to the remainder when the sum of its digits is divided by 9.

Consider the number $n = 24163785$. The sum of the digits of n is $2+4+1+6+3+7+8+5=36$. This number is divisible by 9. So, n is divisible by 9. Let us now check the divisibility of $m = 187525$. The sum of the digits of m is $1+8+7+5+2+5=28$, which is not divisible by 9. So, m is not divisible by 9.

Let us now discuss more illustrations on divisibility by 9.

ILLUSTRATION 1 If $\overline{24a}$ is divisible by 9, find the value of a.

Solution Since $\overline{24a}$ is divisible by 9.

$\therefore \quad 2 + 4 + a$ is a multiple of 9

$\Rightarrow \quad 6 + a$ is a multiple of 9

$\Rightarrow \quad 6 + a = 0$, or 9, or 18, or 27, $\cdots$ ...(i)

But, a is a digit. So, it can take values 0, 1, 2, 3, 4, ..., 9.

And hence, $6 + a$ can take values 6, 7, 8, 9, 10, ..., 15. ...(ii)

From (i) and (ii), we get

$$6 + a = 9 \Rightarrow a = 3$$

Hence, $a = 3$.

ILLUSTRATION 2 If $\overline{21y5}$ is a multiple of 9, where y is a digit, what is the value of y?

Solution Since $\overline{21y5}$ is a multiple of 9. Therefore, the sum of its digits is a multiple of 9.

i.e. $2 + 1 + y + 5$ is a multiple of 9

$\Rightarrow$ $y + 8$ is a multiple of 9

$\Rightarrow$ $y + 8 = 0$, or 9, or 18, or 27, 36, ...(i)

But, y is a digit. So, y can take values 0, 1, 2, ..., 9.

$\therefore$ $y + 8$ can take values 8, 9, 10, 11, ..., 17. ...(ii)

From (i) and (ii), we get

$$y + 8 = 9 \Rightarrow y = 9 - 8 = 1$$

Hence, $y = 1$.

ILLUSTRATION 3 If $\overline{2a25}$ is a multiple of 9, where a is a digit, what is the values of a?

Solution It is given that the number $\overline{2a25}$ is a multiple of 9. Therefore, the sum of its digits is a multiple of 9.

$\therefore$ $2 + a + 2 + 5$ is a multiple of 9

$\Rightarrow$ $a + 9$ is a multiple of 9.

$\Rightarrow$ $a + 9 = 0$, or 9, or 18, or 27, ...(i)

But, a is a digit. So, a can take values 0, 1, 2, ..., 8, 9.

$\therefore$ $a + 9$ can take values 9, 10, 11, ..., 18. ...(ii)

From (i) and (ii), we get

$$a + 9 = 9 \text{ or, } 18$$

$\Rightarrow$ $a + 9 = 9$ or, $a + 9 = 18$

$\Rightarrow$ $a = 0$ or, $a = 9$

Hence, $a = 0, 9$.

5.4.5 DIVISIBILITY BY 3

In the previous sub-section, we have seen that

$$\overline{ab} = \text{a multiple of } 9 + (a + b)$$

$$\overline{abc} = \text{a multiple of } 9 + (a + b + c)$$

In general,

$$\overline{\cdots cba} = \text{a multiple of } 9 + (\cdots + c + b + a)$$

That is, every natural number can be written as the sum of a multiple of 9 and the sum of its digits. Since a multiple of 9 is also a multiple of 3. So, a natural number is divisible by 3 if the sum of its digits is also divisible by 3.

Thus, we have the following test of divisibility by 3.

TEST OF DIVISIBILITY BY 3 *A number is divisible by 3, if the sum of its digits is divisible by 3.*

Also, if the sum of the digits of a number is not divisible by 3, then the number is not divisible by 3. The remainder obtained by dividing the number by 3 is same as the remainder obtained by dividing the sum of its digits by 3.

Consider the number $n = 7856421$. The sum of the digits of n is $7+8+5+6+4+2+1=33$, which is divisible by 3. So, n is divisible by 3. Let us now consider another number $m = 78215$. The sum of its digits is $7+8+2+1+5=23$, which is not divisible by 3. So, m is not divisible by 3. This can also be verified by the actual division of 78215 by 3. The remainder obtained by dividing m by 3 is equal the remainder when 23 is divided by 3. Clearly, it is 2.

Hence, the remainder when $m = 78215$ is divided by 3, is equal to 2. Let us now discuss some more problems on divisibility by 3.

ILLUSTRATIVE EXAMPLES

Example 1 If $\overline{24x}$ is a multiple of 3, where x is a digit, what is the value of x?

Solution It is given that $\overline{24x}$ is a multiple of 3

$\therefore$ $2+4+x$ is a multiple of 3

$\Rightarrow$ $6+x$ is a multiple of 3.

$\Rightarrow$ $6+x=0, 3, 6, 9, 12, 15, 18, 21, \cdots$ ...(i)

But, x is a digit of the number $\overline{24x}$.

$\therefore$ x can take values 0, 1, 2, 3, ..., 9

$\Rightarrow$ $6+x$ can take values 6, 7, 8, 9, 10, ..., 15 ...(ii)

From (i) and (ii), we get

$6+x=6$ or, 9 or, 12 or, 15

$\Rightarrow$ $6+x=6$ or, $6+x=9$ or, $6+x=12$ or, $6+x=15$

$\Rightarrow$ $x=0$ or, $x=3$ or, $x=6$ or, $x=9$

Hence, $x=0, 3, 6, 9$.

Example 2 If $\overline{24y5}$ is a multiple of 3, where y is a digit, what might be the value of y?

Solution Since $\overline{24y5}$ is a multiple of 3.

$\therefore$ $2+4+y+5$ is a multiple of 5.

$\Rightarrow$ $11+y$ is a multiple of 3.

$\Rightarrow$ $11+y=0, 3, 6, 9, 12, 15, 18, 21, \cdots$. ...(i)

But, y is a digit of the number $\overline{24y5}$. So, y can take values 0, 1, 2, ..., 9.

$\therefore$ $11+y$ can take values 11, 12, 13, ... 22. ...(ii)

From (i) and (ii), we get

$11+y=15$ or, 18

$\Rightarrow$ $11+y=15$ or, $11+y=18$

$\Rightarrow \quad y = 4$ or, $y = 7$

Hence, $y = 4$ or, 7.

Example 3 If $\overline{31z5}$ is a multiple of 3, where z is a digit, what might be the value of z?

Solution Since $\overline{31z5}$ is a multiple of 3.

$\therefore \quad 3+1+z+5$ is a multiple of 3.

$\Rightarrow \quad z+9$ is a multiple of 3.

$\Rightarrow \quad z+9 = 0, 3, 6, 9, 12, 15, 18, \cdots$ ...(i)

But, z is a digit of the number $\overline{31z5}$. So, z can take values 0, 1, 2, 3, ..., 9

$\Rightarrow \quad z+9$ can take values 9, 10, 11, 12, ..., 18 ...(ii)

From (i) and (ii), we get

$z+9$ can take values 9 or, 12 or, 15 or, 18

$\Rightarrow \quad z+9 = 9$ or, $z+9 = 12$ or, $z+9 = 15$ or, $z+9 = 18$

$\Rightarrow \quad z = 0, 3, 6, 9$

Hence, z can take values 0, 3, 6, 9.

Example 4 Without actual division find the remainder when 379843 is divided by 3.

Solution The remainder obtained by dividing 379843 by 3 is same as the remainder obtained by dividing the sum of its digits by 3.

We have,

Sum of the digits $= 3+7+9+8+4+3 = 34$

When 34 is divided by 3, we get 1 as the remainder.

Hence, division of 379843 by 3 leaves remainder of 1.

5.4.6 DIVISIBILITY BY 6

We have, $6 = 2 \times 3$

So, if a number n is divisible by 6. Then, it must be divisible by both 2 and 3. Thus, we have the following test of divisibility by 6.

TEST OF DIVISIBILITY BY 6 *A number is divisible by 6, if it is divisible by 2 as well as 3.*

Also, if a number is not divisible by either 2 or by 3 or by both, then it is not divisible by 6.

Consider the number $n = 87540$. Clearly, n is an even natural number as its units digit is an even number. The sum of the digits of n is $8+7+5+4+0 = 24$, which is divisible by 3. So, n is divisible by 3. Thus, n is divisible by both 2 and 3. Hence, n is divisible by 6.

Let us now take the number $m = 23678772$. Its units digit is 2, which is even. So, m is divisible by 2. The sum of the digits of m is $2+3+6+7+8+7+7+2 = 42$, which is divisible by 3. So, m is divisible by both 2 and 3. Hence, m is divisible by 6.

Finally, let us take the number $p = 37868$. Its units digit is 8, which is even. So, p is divisible by 2. The sum of the digits of p is $3+7+8+6+8 = 32$, which is not divisible by 3. So, p is not divisible by 6.

It also follows from the above discussion that any odd natural number is not divisible by 6 and all even natural numbers which are divisible by 3 are also divisible by 6.

Following examples will illustrate some applications of divisibility by 6.

ILLUSTRATIVE EXAMPLES

Example 1 If $\overline{24x}$ is a multiple of 6, where x is a digit, what is the value of x?

Solution It is given that the number $\overline{24x}$ is a multiple of 6. Therefore, it is a multiple of both 2 and 3.

Now,

$\overline{24x}$ is a multiple of 3

$\Rightarrow$ $2+4+x$ is a multiple of 3

$\Rightarrow$ $6+x$ is a multiple of 3

$\Rightarrow$ $6+x=0, 3, 6, 9, 12, 15, 18, \cdots$ ...(i)

and,

$\overline{24x}$ is a multiple of 2

$\Rightarrow$ x is an even digit

$\Rightarrow$ $x=0, 2, 4, 6, 8$

$\Rightarrow$ $6+x=6, 8, 10, 12, 14$ ...(ii)

From (i) and (ii), we have

$6+x=6$ or, $6+x=12 \Rightarrow x=0$ or, $x=6$

Hence, $x=0$ or, $x=6$.

Example 2 If $\overline{21y8}$ is a multiple of 6, where y is a digit, what might be the value of y?

Solution Clearly, $\overline{21y8}$ has an even digit at units place. So, it is a multiple of 2.

Now,

$\overline{21y8}$ will be a multiple of 3, if the sum of its digits is a multiple of 3.

$\Rightarrow$ $2+1+y+8$ is a multiple of 3

$\Rightarrow$ $y+11$ is a multiple of 3

$\Rightarrow$ $y+11=0, 3, 6, 9, 12, \cdots$ ...(i)

But, y is a digit. So, y can take values $0, 1, 2, 3, \cdots, 9$

$\Rightarrow$ $y+11=11, 12, 13, \cdots, 20$ ...(ii)

From (i) and (ii), we have

$y+11=12$ or, 15 or, 18

$\Rightarrow$ $y+11=12$ or, $y+11=15$ or, $y+11=18$

$\Rightarrow$ $y=1$ or, $y=4$ or, $y=7$

$\Rightarrow$ $y=1, 4, 7$

Hence, y can take values 1 or, 4 or, 7.

Example 3 If $\overline{13z4}$ is a multiple of 6, where z is a digit, what might be the value of z?

Solution Clearly, units digit of $\overline{13z4}$ is 4. So, it is an even number and hence a multiple of 2.

Now,

$\overline{13z4}$ will be a multiple of 3, if the sum of its digits is a multiple 3.

$\Rightarrow$ $1+3+z+4$ must be a multiple of 3

$\Rightarrow$ $z+8$ must be a multiple of 3

$\Rightarrow$ $z+8=3,6,9,12,15,\cdots$ ...(i)

But, z is a digit. So, z can take values $0,1,2,3,4,\cdots,9$

$\Rightarrow$ $z+8=8,9,10,\cdots,17$ ...(ii)

From (i) and (ii), we have

$z+8=9,12,15$

$\Rightarrow$ $z+8=9$ or, $z+8=12$ or, $z+8=15$

$\Rightarrow$ $z=1$ or, $z=4$ or, $z=7$

Hence, z can take 3 values 1 or, 4 or, 7.

5.4.7 DIVISIBILITY BY 11

Consider a two digit number $\overline{ab}$.

We have,

$\overline{ab}=10a+b$

$\Rightarrow$ $\overline{ab}=11a+b-a$

$\Rightarrow$ $\overline{ab}=$ a multiple of $11+(b-a)$

$\Rightarrow$ $\overline{ab}$ is a multiple of 11, if $b-a$ is a multiple of 11

$\Rightarrow$ $\overline{ab}$ is a multiple of 11, if $b-a=0$ $\left[\begin{array}{l}\because a \text{ and } b \text{ take values from 0 to 9}\\ \text{So, } a-b \text{ or } b-a \text{ take values from 0 to 9}\end{array}\right]$

$\Rightarrow$ $\overline{ab}$ is a multiple of 11, if $a=b$.

Thus, a two digit number is divisible by 11 if its two digits are equal.

Also, if the digits of a two digit number are unequal, then it is not divisible by 11.

Let $\overline{abc}$ be a three digit number. Then,

$\overline{abc}=100a+10b+c$

$\Rightarrow$ $\overline{abc}=99a+a+11b-b+c$

$\Rightarrow$ $\overline{abc}=99a+11b+a-b+c$

$\Rightarrow$ $\overline{abc}=11(9a+b)+a-b+c$

$\Rightarrow$ $\overline{abc}=$ a multiple of $11+(a-b+c)$

$\Rightarrow$ $\overline{abc}$ is a multiple of 11, if $a-b+c$ is a multiple of 11.

Thus, a 3-digit number is divisible by 11 if the sum of its odd digits minus the sum of its middle digit is a multiple of 11.

Also, if the sum of odd digits of a three digit number minus the middle digit is not a multiple of 11, then the number is not divisible by 11.

Let us now take a four digit number $\overline{abcd}$.

We have,

$$\overline{abcd} = 1000a + 100b + 10c + d$$

$$\Rightarrow \quad \overline{abcd} = 1001a - a + 99b + b + 11c - c + d$$

$$\Rightarrow \quad \overline{abcd} = 1001a + 99b + 11c - a + b - c + d$$

$$\Rightarrow \quad \overline{abcd} = 11(91a + 9b + c) + (b + d) - (a + c)$$

$$\Rightarrow \quad \overline{abcd} = \text{a multiple of } 11 + (b + d) - (a + c)$$

$\Rightarrow$ $\overline{abcd}$ is divisible by 11, if $(b + d) - (a + c)$ is a multiple of 11.

Thus, a four digit number is divisible by 11, if the difference of the sum of its digits in even places and the sum of its digits in odd places is a multiple of 11.

It follows from the above discussion that:

An odd digit number = a multiple of 11 + Sum of its digit in odd places – Sum of its digits in even places

An even digit number = a multiple of 11 + Sum of its digit in even places – Sum of its digits in odd places

The above argument is applicable to any digit number, and the conclusion is the same. Thus, we have the following test of divisibility by 11.

TEST OF DIVISIBILITY BY 11 *A number is divisible by 11, if the difference of its digits in odd places and the sum of its digits in even places is either 0 or a multiple of 11.*

Consider three-digit number 264. For this number, we have

Sum of the digits in odd places – Sum of the digits in even places

$= (2 + 4) - 6 = 0$

So, 264 is divisible by 11.

Let us now take the number 61809. For this number, we have

Sum of the digits in odd places – Sum of the digits in even places

$= (6 + 8 + 9) - (1 + 0) = 23 - 1 = 22$, which is a multiple of 11.

So, 61809 is divisible by 11.

Let us now take some problems on divisibility by 11.

ILLUSTRATIVE EXAMPLES

Example 1 If $\overline{24x}$ is a multiple of 11, where x is a digit, what is the value of x?

Solution We have,

Sum of the digits in even places = 4, Sum of the digits in odd places $= 2 + x$

$\therefore$ Difference of the sum of the digits in odd places and the sum of the digits in even places $= (2 + x) - 4 = x - 2$.

Now,

$\overline{24x}$ will be a multiple of 11, if

$x-2$ is a multiple of 11

$\Rightarrow \quad x-2=0$ or, 11 or, 22, ⋯

$\Rightarrow \quad x=2$ or, 13 or, 24, ⋯ ...(i)

But, x is a digit of the number $\overline{24x}$. So,

$x=0, 1, 2, 3, \cdots, 9$ ...(ii)

From (i) and (ii), we get $x=2$.

Example 2 If $\overline{2y5}$ is divisible by 11, where y is a digit, what is the value of y?

Solution We have,

Sum of the digits in odd places $=2+5=7$, Sum of the digits in evenplaces $=y$.

$\therefore$ Sum of the digits in even places – Sum of the digits in odd places $=y-7$.

If $\overline{2y5}$ is divisible by 11, then

$y-7$ must be a multiple of 11.

$\Rightarrow \quad y-7=0$ or, 11 or, 22 or, 33, ⋯

$\Rightarrow \quad y=7$ or, 18 or, 29, ⋯ ...(i)

But, y is a digit. So, y can take values 0, 1, 2, 3, ..., 9 ...(ii)

From (i) and (ii), we get $y=7$.

Example 3 If $\overline{31z}$ is a multiple of 11, where z is a digit, what is the value of z?

Solution If $\overline{31z}$ is a multiple of 11, then

$(3+z)-1$ is a multiple of 11

$\Rightarrow \quad z+2$ is a multiple of 11

$\Rightarrow \quad z+2=0$ or, 11 or, 22, ⋯

$\Rightarrow \quad z=-2$ or, 9 or, 20, ⋯ ...(i)

But, z is a digit. So, z can take values 0, 1, 2, 3, ..., 9 ...(ii)

From (i) and (ii), we get $z=9$

Example 4 Given that the number $\overline{148101a095}$ is divisible by 11, where a is some digit, what are the possible values of a?

Solution If $\overline{148101a095}$ is divisible by 11, then

$(1+8+0+a+9)-(4+1+1+0+5)$ is a multiple of 11.

$\Rightarrow \quad (a+18)-11$ is a multiple of 11

$\Rightarrow \quad a+7$ is a multiple of 11

$\Rightarrow \quad a+7=0$ or, 11 or, 22 or, 33, $\cdots$ ...(i)

But, a is a digit of some number. So, a can take one of the values from 0 to 9.

Therefore, $a + 7$ can take values 7, 8, 9, ..., 16 ...(ii)

From (i) and (ii), we get

$$a+7=11 \Rightarrow a=4$$

5.4.8 DIVISIBILITY BY 4

Consider a three digit number $\overline{abc}$.

We have,

$$\overline{abc}=100a+10b+c$$

$$\Rightarrow \quad \overline{abc}=100a+(10b+c)$$

$$\Rightarrow \quad \overline{abc}=100a+\overline{bc} \qquad [\because \overline{bc}=10b+c]$$

$$\Rightarrow \quad \overline{abc}=(4\times 25a)+\overline{bc}$$

$\Rightarrow \quad \overline{abc}=$ a multiple of $4+\overline{bc}$

$\Rightarrow \quad \overline{abc}$ is divisible by 4, if $\overline{bc}$ i.e. the number formed by digits in units and tens places is divisible by 4.

Consider now a four digit number $\overline{abcd}$.

We have,

$$\overline{abcd}=1000a+100b+10c+d$$

$$\Rightarrow \quad \overline{abcd}=100(10a+b)+10c+d$$

$$\Rightarrow \quad \overline{abcd}=100\,(10a+b)+\overline{cd} \qquad [\because \overline{cd}=10c+d]$$

$\Rightarrow \quad \overline{abcd}=$ a multiple of $4+\overline{cd}$

$\Rightarrow \quad \overline{abcd}$ is divisible by 4, if $\overline{cd}$ i.e. the number formed by its digits in units and tens places, is divisible by 4.

This argument applies to any digit number. Thus, we have the following test of divisibility by 4.

TEST OF DIVISIBILITY BY 4 *A natural number is divisible by 4, if the number formed by its digits in units and tens places is divisible by 4.*

Also, if the number formed by its digits in units and tens places is not divisible by 4, then the given number is not divisible by 4.

Consider the number 79812. Since 12 is a multiple of 4. So, 79812 is divisible by 4.

Consider now the number $n=23472392$. Since, 92 is a multiple of 4. So, n is divisible by 4. The number $m=23798531$ is not divisible by 4, because 31 is not a multiple of 4.

ILLUSTRATIVE EXAMPLES

Example 1 Given that the number $\overline{59142a}$ is divisible by 4, where a is a digit, what are the possible values of a?

Solution Given number is divisible by 4. Therefore, the number formed by its digits in units and tens places must be divisible by 4 i.e. $\overline{2a}$ must be divisible by 4. So, a can take values 0, 4 and 8.

Example 2 Given that the number $\overline{7713a8}$ is divisible by 4, where a is a digit, what are the possible values of a?

Solution If $\overline{7713a8}$ is divisible by 4, then the number $\overline{a8}$ must be divisible by 4.

We have,

$$\overline{a8} = 10a + 8, \text{ where } a = 0, 1, 2, 3, \cdots, 9$$

$$\Rightarrow \quad \overline{a8} = 8, 18, 28, 38, 48, 58, 68, 78, 88, 98$$

Clearly, out of these values of $\overline{a8}$ only 8, 28, 48, 68 and 88 are divisible by 4.

Hence, possible values of a are 0, 2, 4, 6, and 8.

Example 3 Given that the number $\overline{1735538a05}$ is divisible by 9, where 'a' is a digit, what are the possible values of a?

Solution If the number $\overline{1735538a05}$ is divisible by 9, then

$$1+7+3+5+5+3+8+a+0+5 \text{ is a multiple of } 9$$

$$\Rightarrow \quad a+37 \text{ is a multiple of } 9 \quad \ldots(i)$$

But, a is some digit of a number. So, a can take values 0, 1, 2, 4, ..., 9.

$$\therefore \quad a+37 = 37, 38, 39, 40, \cdots, 46 \quad \ldots(ii)$$

From (i) and (ii), we have

$$a+37 = 45 \Rightarrow a = 8$$

Hence, a can take only one value equal to 8.

Example 4 Given that the number $\overline{60ab57377}$ is divisible by 99, where a and b are digits, what are the values of a and b?

Solution Since a and b are digits of a number. So, a and b can take values from 0 to 9.

It is given that $\overline{60ab57377}$ is divisible by 99 which is divisible by both 9 and 11.

$$\therefore \quad \overline{60ab57377} \text{ is divisible by both 9 and 11}$$

$$\Rightarrow \quad 6+0+a+b+5+7+3+7+7 \text{ is a multiple of } 9$$

and,

$$(6+a+5+3+7)-(0+b+7+7) \text{ is a multiple of } 11.$$

$$\Rightarrow \quad a+b+35 \text{ is a multiple of } 9$$

and,

$$(a+21)-(b+14) \text{ is a multiple of } 11$$

$$\Rightarrow \quad a+b+35 \text{ is a multiple of } 9$$

and,

$$a-b+7 \text{ is a multiple of } 11$$

Since a and b can take values from 0 to 9. Therefore, $a+b$ can take values from 0 to 18 and hence, $a+b+35$ can take values from 35 to 53.

Also, $a+b+35$ is a multiple of 9.

$\therefore$ either $a+b+35=36$ or, $a+b+35=45$

$\Rightarrow$ $a+b=1$ or, $a+b=10$

Now,

$a-b+7$ is a multiple of 11

$\Rightarrow$ $a-b+7=0$ or, $a-b+7=11$ $\left[\because 0 \leq a, b \leq 9 \therefore -9 \leq a-b \leq 9 \Rightarrow -2 \leq a-b+7 \leq 16\right]$

$\Rightarrow$ $a-b=-7$ or, $a-b=4$

Thus, we have following equations giving values of a and b.

$a+b=1$ or, $a+b=10$

$a-b=-7$ or, $a-b=4$

These equations give the following pairs of equations in a and b.

$a+b=1$ and $a-b=-7$ ...(i)

$a+b=1$ and $a-b=4$ ...(ii)

$a+b=10$ and $a-b=-7$ ...(iii)

$a+b=10$ and $a-b=4$ ...(iv)

Adding and subtracting equations in (iv), we get

$2a=14$ and $2b=6 \Rightarrow a=7$ and $b=3$

Other pairs of equations do not give non-negative integral values of a and b.

Hence, $a=7$ and $b=3$.

Example 5 Without performing actual division, find the remainders left when 192837465 is divided by

(i) 9 (ii) 11

Solution (i) In sub-section 5.4.4, we have seen that any natural number n, can be written as

$n=$ a multiple of 9 + Sum of the digits of n

$\therefore$ $192837465=$ a multiple of $9+(1+9+2+8+3+7+4+6+5)$

$\Rightarrow$ $192837465=$ a multiple of $9+45$

$\Rightarrow$ $192837465=$ a multiple of $9+9\times 5$

$\Rightarrow$ $192837465=$ a multiple of 9

So, the remainder left when 192837465 is divided by 9 is zero.

(ii) In sub-section 5.4.7, we have seen that any odd digit natural numbr n can be written as

$n=$a multiple of 11 + Sum of its digits in odd places – Sum of its digits in even places

$\Rightarrow$ $192837465=$ a multiple of $11+(1+2+3+4+5)-(9+8+7+6)$

$\Rightarrow$ $192837465=$ a multiple of $11+15-30$

$\Rightarrow$ 192837465 = a multiple of 11 − 15

$\Rightarrow$ 192837465 = a multiple of 11 − 22 + 7

$\Rightarrow$ 192837465 = a multiple of 11 − 2×11 + 7

$\Rightarrow$ 192837465 = (a multiple of 11) + 7

So, the remainder left when 192837465 is divided by 11 is 7.

Example 6 Without performing actual division, find the remainder when 28735429 is divided by 11.

Solution Since 28735429 is an even digit number.

$\therefore$ 28735429 = a multiple of 11 + Sum of its digits in even places − Sum of its digits in odd places

= a multiple of 11 + (8 + 3 + 4 + 9) − (2 + 7 + 5 + 2)

= a multiple of 11 + 24 − 16

= a multiple of 11 + 8

Hence, required remainder is 8.

EXERCISE 5.2

1. Given that the number $\overline{35a64}$ is divisible by 3, where a is a digit, what are the possible values of a?
2. If x is a digit such that the number $\overline{18x71}$ is divisible by 3, find possible values of x.
3. If x is a digit of the number $\overline{66784x}$ such that it is divisible by 9, find possible values of x.
4. Given that the number $\overline{67y19}$ is divisible by 9, where y is a digit, what are the possible values of y?
5. If $\overline{3x2}$ is a multiple of 11, where x is a digit, what is the value of x?
6. If $\overline{98215x2}$ is a number with x as its tens digit such that it is divisible by 4. Find all possible values of x.
7. If x denotes the digit at hundreds place of the number $\overline{67x19}$ such that the number is divisible by 11. Find all possible values of x.
8. Find the remainder when 981547 is divided by 5. Do this without doing actual division.
9. Find the remainder when 51439786 is divided by 3. Do this without performing actual division.
10. Find the remainder, without performing actual division, when 798 is divided by 11.
11. Without performing actual division, find the remainder when 928174653 is divided by 11.
12. Given an example of a number which is divisible by
    (i) 2 but not by 4. (ii) 3 but not by 6.
    (iii) 4 but not by 8. (iv) both 4 and 8 but not by 32.
13. Which of the following statements are true?
    (i) If a number is divisible by 3, it must be divisible by 9.

(ii) If a number is divisible by 9, it must be divisible by 3.

(iii) If a number is divisible by 4, it must be divisible by 8.

(iv) If a number is divisible by 8, it must be divisible by 4.

(v) A number is divisible by 18, if it is divisible by both 3 and 6.

(vi) If a number is divisible by both 9 and 10, it must be divisible by 90.

(vii) If a number exactly divides the sum of two numbers, it must exactly divide the numbers separately.

(viii) If a number divides three numbers exactly, it must divide their sum exactly.

(ix) If two numbers are co-prime, at least one of them must be a prime number.

(x) The sum of two consecutive odd numbers is always divisible by 4.

ANSWERS

1. 0, 3, 6, 9 2. 1, 4, 7 3. 5 4. 4 5. 5 6. 1, 3, 5, 7, 9
7. 4 8. 2 9. 1 10. 6 11. 10
12. (i) 10 (ii) 15 (iii) 28 (iv) 48
13. (i) F (ii) T (iii) F (iv) T (v) F (vi) T (vii) F (viii) T (ix) F (x) T

5.5 CRYPTARITHMS

Cryptarithms are puzzles, on various operations on numbers, in which letters take the place of digits and one has to find out which letter represents which digit. In this section, we shall discuss problems on addition and multiplication only. While solving cryptarithms involving addition and multiplication, we assume that each letter in a puzzle stands for just one digit and each digit is represented by just one letter. We also assume that the first digit of a number cannot be zero. For example, thirty four will be written as 34 not as 034 or 0034.

Let us now discuss some cryptarithms on addition and multiplication to illustrate the procedure of solving cryptarithms.

ILLUSTRATIVE EXAMPLES

Example 1 Solve the following cryptarithms:

(i) $\begin{array}{r} 3\ 1\ A \\ +1\ A\ 3 \\ \hline 5\ 0\ 1 \end{array}$ (ii) $\begin{array}{r} B\ 9 \\ +4\ A \\ \hline 6\ 5 \end{array}$ (iii) $\begin{array}{r} A \\ +A \\ +A \\ \hline BA \end{array}$ (iv) $\begin{array}{r} 8\ A\ 5 \\ +9\ 4\ A \\ \hline 1A\ 3\ 3 \end{array}$

Solution (i) We have,

$$\begin{array}{r} 3\ 1\ A \\ +1\ A\ 3 \\ \hline 5\ 0\ 1 \end{array}$$

Here, we have to find the value of A which can take values from 0 to 9.

As A takes values from 0 to 9. Therefore, $A+3$ can take values from 3 to 12. Since digit at the units place of the sum of two digits A and 3 is 1. Therefore, either $A+3$ is equal to 1 or $A+3$ is a number between 3 and 12 whose units digit is 1. Clearly, such a number between 3 and 12 is 11.

$\therefore \quad A+3=11 \Rightarrow A=8$

This value of A satisfies the addition in tens and hundreds columns.

Hence, $A = 8$.

(ii) We have,

$$\begin{array}{r} B\ 9 \\ +4\ A \\ \hline A\ 5 \end{array}$$

Clearly, $9 + A$ is a number taking values from 9 to 18. Also, either $9 + A$ is 5 or it is a two digit number whose units digit is 5. But, $9 + A$ is greater than or equal to 9.

$\therefore \quad 9 + A = 15 \Rightarrow A = 6$

Now, considering tens column, we have

$B + 4 + 1 = A \Rightarrow B + 5 = 6 \Rightarrow B = 1$

Hence, $A = 6$ and $B = 1$.

(iii) We have,

$$\begin{array}{r} A \\ +A \\ +A \\ \hline BA \end{array}$$

Here, valeus of two letters A and B are to be found.

In ones column the sum of three A's is a number whose ones digit is A, which is possible only when the units digit of the sum of two A's is 0. This happens only for $A = 0$ and $A = 5$.

If $A = 0$, then the sum of three A's is 0.

Since $A + A + A = \overline{BA}$. Therefore, $B = 0$.

This is not possible as $\overline{BA}$ is a two digit number. So, $A = 5$.

$\because \quad A + A + A = \overline{BA}$

$\therefore \quad 3A = \overline{BA} \Rightarrow 3 \times A = 10B + A \Rightarrow 15 = 10B + 5 \Rightarrow 10B = 10 \Rightarrow B = 1$

Hence, $A = 5$ and $B = 1$.

(iv) We have,

$$\begin{array}{r} 8\ A\ 5 \\ +9\ 4\ A \\ \hline 1A\ 3\ 3 \end{array}$$

In the ones column the sum of 5 and A is 3. This means that the sum of 5 and A is a two digit number between 10 and 19 whose units digit is 3. Clearly, such a number is 13.

$\therefore \quad 5 + A = 13 \Rightarrow A = 8$

Clearly, this value of A satisfies the addition in tens and hundreds columns.

Example 2 Solve the cryptarithm: $\overline{AB}+\overline{BA}=\overline{DAD}$

Solution Clearly, $\overline{AB}$ and $\overline{BA}$ are two digit numbers. So, maximum value of their sum is $99+99+198$. This means that the number $\overline{DAD}$ is at most equal to 198. So, D must be equal to 1. Note that D can not be zero as $\overline{DAD}$ is a three digit number.

Now,

$$\overline{AB}+\overline{BA}=\overline{DAD}$$

$$\Rightarrow \quad (10A+B)+(10B+A)=\overline{1A1}$$

$$\Rightarrow \quad 11A+11B=\overline{1A1}$$

$$\Rightarrow \quad 11(A+B)=\overline{1A1} \qquad \ldots(i)$$

Clearly, LHS of this equation is a multiple of 11. So, RHS must be a multiple of 11 having digits at units and hundreds place as unity. RHS can take ten values viz. 101, 111, 121, 131, ..., 191. Out of these values only 121 is a multiple of 11. Therefore, $A=2$.

Substituting $A=2$ in (i), we get

$$11(2+B)=121 \Rightarrow 2+B=11 \Rightarrow B=9$$

Hence, $A=2, B=9$ and $D=1$.

Example 3 Solve the cryptarithm: $\overline{ON}+\overline{ON}=\overline{GO}$ or, $2\times\overline{ON}=\overline{GO}$.

Solution We have,

$$\overline{ON}+\overline{ON}=\overline{GO} \text{ or, } 2\times\overline{ON}=\overline{GO} \qquad \ldots(i)$$

Clearly, $\overline{GO}$ is a two digit number whose maximum value can be 99. Therefore, maximum value of $\overline{ON}$ can be 49. So, the maximum value of digit O can be 4.

Since LHS of (i) is an even number. So, $\overline{GO}$ is also an even number.

Consequently, O can take even values only.

$\therefore$ Digit O can take values 2 or 4.

CASE I *When digit O takes value 2.*

Substituting 2 in place of digit O in equation (i), we get

$$2\times\overline{2N}=\overline{G2} \qquad \ldots(ii)$$

$\Rightarrow$ Multiplication of 2 and N must be either 2 or a two digit number between 10 and 19 having 2 at ones place.

$\Rightarrow$ $N=1$ or, $N=6$

When $N=1$, equation (ii) gives

$$2\times 21=\overline{G2} \Rightarrow 42=\overline{G2} \Rightarrow G=4$$

When $N=6$, equation (ii) gives

$$2\times 26=\overline{G2} \Rightarrow 52=\overline{G2} \Rightarrow G=5$$

Thus, we have

$$O=2, G=4 \text{ and } N=1 \text{ or, } O=2, G=5 \text{ and } N=6.$$

CASE II *When digit O takes value* 4:

Putting $O=4$ in (i), we get

$$2\times\overline{4N}=\overline{G4} \quad \text{...(iii)}$$

$\Rightarrow$ $2\times N$ is either equal to 4 or, $2\times N=14$

$\Rightarrow$ $N=2$ or, $N=7$

When $N=2$, equation (iii) gives

$$2\times 42=\overline{G4} \Rightarrow 84=\overline{G4} \Rightarrow G=8$$

When $N=7$, equation (iii) gives

$$2\times\overline{47}=\overline{G4} \Rightarrow 94=\overline{G4} \Rightarrow G=9$$

Thus, we have

$$O=4, G=8 \text{ and } N=2 \text{ or, } O=4, G=9 \text{ and } N=7$$

Hence, the solutions of the given cryptarithms are:

	O	G	N
(i)	2	4	1
(ii)	2	5	6
(iii)	4	8	2
(iv)	4	9	7

Example 4 Solve the Cryptarithm: $\overline{ON}+\overline{ON}+\overline{ON}=\overline{GO}$ or, $3\times\overline{ON}=\overline{GO}$

Solution We have,

$$3\times\overline{ON}=\overline{GO} \quad \text{...(i)}$$

Since $\overline{GO}$ is a two digit number. So, it can have maximum value equal to 99.

$\therefore$ $3\times\overline{ON}=\overline{GO}$

$\Rightarrow$ $3\times\overline{ON}$ is at most equal to 99

$\Rightarrow$ $\overline{ON}$ is at most equal to 33

$\Rightarrow$ O is at most equal to 3

$\Rightarrow$ O is equal to 1 or 2 or 3 [$\because$ O can not be zero as $\overline{ON}$ is a two digit number]

CASE I *When* $O=1$

Putting $O=1$ in (i), we get

$$3\times\overline{1N}=\overline{G1} \quad \text{...(ii)}$$

$\Rightarrow$ $3\times N=1$ or, $3\times N=$ a two digit number having 1 at units place

$\Rightarrow$ $N=7$

Putting $N=7$ in (ii), we get

$$3\times 17=\overline{G1} \Rightarrow \overline{G1}=51 \Rightarrow G=5$$

$\therefore$ $O=1, G=5$ and $N=7$

CASE II *When* $O = 2$

Putting $O = 2$ in (i), we get

$$3 \times \overline{2N} = \overline{G2} \quad \text{...(iii)}$$

$\Rightarrow$ $3 \times N =$ a two digit number having 2 at units place

$\Rightarrow$ $N = 4$

Putting $N = 4$ in (iii), we get

$$3 \times 24 = \overline{G2} \Rightarrow \overline{G2} = 72 \Rightarrow G = 7$$

$\therefore$ $O = 2, G = 7$ and $N = 4$

CASE III *When* $O = 3$

Putting $O = 3$ in (i), we get

$$3 \times \overline{3N} = \overline{G3} \quad \text{...(iv)}$$

$\Rightarrow$ $3 \times N = 3$

$\Rightarrow$ $N = 1$

Putting $N = 1$ in (iv), we get

$$3 \times 31 = \overline{G3} \Rightarrow \overline{G3} = 93 \Rightarrow G = 9$$

$\therefore$ $O = 3, G = 9$ and $N = 1$

Thus, we have following solutions of equation (i):

	O	G	N
(i)	1	5	7
(ii)	2	7	4
(iii)	3	9	1.

Example 5 Solve the Cryptarithm: $\overline{ON} + \overline{ON} + \overline{ON} + \overline{ON} = \overline{GO}$ or, $4 \times \overline{ON} = \overline{GO}$

Solution We have,

$$4 \times \overline{ON} = \overline{GO} \quad \text{...(i)}$$

Since $\overline{GO}$ is a two digit number. So, it can have maximum value 99. Therefore, $\overline{ON}$ can have maximum value 24. This means that O can have maximum value 2.

Also, LHS of equation (i) is an even number (being a multiple of 4). So, RHS is also a two digit even number. Thus, O can take values 2, 4, 6, 8. Note that O can not be zero as $\overline{ON}$ is a two digit number.

$\therefore$ O is an even number whose maximum value is 2.

Hence, $O = 2$.

Putting $O = 2$ in (i), we have

$$4 \times \overline{2N} = \overline{G2} \quad \text{...(ii)}$$

$\Rightarrow$ $4 \times N$ is either 2 or a two digit number between 10 and 19 having 2 at units place

$\Rightarrow \quad 4 \times N = 12$ $\quad [\because \ 4 \times N$ is greater than 4]

$\Rightarrow \quad N = 3$

Putting $N = 3$ in (ii), we get

$$4 \times 23 = \overline{G2} \Rightarrow 92 = \overline{G2} \Rightarrow G = 9$$

Hence, $O = 2, G = 9$ and $N = 3$.

Example 6 Solve the following Cryptarithms:

(i)
$$\begin{array}{r} 1 \ A \\ \times \ A \\ \hline 9 \ A \end{array}$$

(ii)
$$\begin{array}{r} A \ B \\ \times \ 6 \\ \hline BBB \end{array}$$

(iii)
$$\begin{array}{r} A \ B \\ \times \ 5 \\ \hline CAB \end{array}$$

Solution (i) We have,

$$\begin{array}{r} 1 \ A \\ \times \ A \\ \hline 9 \ A \end{array}$$

This means that the product of A with itself is either A or it has units digit as A. Since $A = 1$ satisfies $A \times A = 1$ but it is not possible as the product is 9A. The other value of A is 6 whose product with itself is a number having 6 at units place.

Taking $A = 6$, we have

$$\begin{array}{r} 1 \ 6 \\ \times \ 6 \\ \hline 9 \ 6 \end{array}$$

Clearly, it satisfies the given product.

Hence, $A = 6$.

(ii) We have,

$$\begin{array}{r} A \ B \\ \times \ 6 \\ \hline BBB \end{array}$$

This means that $6 \times B$ is a number having its ones digit as B. Such values of B are 2, 4, 6 and 8, because $6 \times 2 = 12$, $6 \times 4 = 24$, $6 \times 6 = 36$ and $6 \times 8 = 48$. So, we have following cases:

CASE I *When* $B = 2$

In this case, we have

$$\overline{AB} \times 6 = \overline{BBB}$$

$\Rightarrow \quad \overline{A2} \times 6 = 222$

$\Rightarrow \quad (10A + 2) \times 6 = 222$

$\Rightarrow \quad 60A+12=222$

$\Rightarrow \quad 60A=210$

$\Rightarrow \quad 2A=7$

$\Rightarrow \quad A=\frac{7}{2}$, which is not possible.

CASE II *When* $B=4$

In this case, we have

$\overline{AB}\times 6=\overline{BBB}$

$\Rightarrow \quad \overline{A4}\times 6=444$

$\Rightarrow \quad (10A+4)\times 6=444$

$\Rightarrow \quad 10A+4=\frac{444}{6}$

$\Rightarrow \quad 10A+4=74$

$\Rightarrow \quad 10A=70$

$\Rightarrow \quad A=7$

$\therefore \quad A=7$ and $B=4$ is the required solution.

CASE III *When* $B=6$

In this case, we have

$\overline{A6}\times 6=666$

$\Rightarrow \quad \overline{A6}=111$

This is not possible as LHS is a two digit number and RHS is a three digit number.

CASE IV *When* $B=8$

In this case, we have

$\overline{AB}\times 6=\overline{BBB}$

$\Rightarrow \quad \overline{A8}\times 6=888$

$\Rightarrow \quad \overline{A8}=148$

This is not possible as LHS is a two digit number and RHS is a three digit number.

(iii) We have,

$$\begin{array}{r} A\ \ B \\ \times\ \ 5 \\ \hline C\,A\,B \end{array}$$

This means that $5\times B$ is a number whose units digit is B. Clearly, B can take value 5.

Taking $B=5$, we have

$\overline{A5}\times 5=\overline{CA5}$

$\Rightarrow \quad (10A+5)\times 5 = 100C + 10A + 5$

$\Rightarrow \quad 10A+5 = 20C + 2A + 1$

$\Rightarrow \quad 8A + 4 = 20C$

$\Rightarrow \quad 2A+1 = 5C$ ...(i)

$\Rightarrow \quad 2A+1$ is an odd multiple of 5 [$\because$ $2A+1$ is odd]

$\Rightarrow \quad 2A+1 = 5, 2A+1 = 15$ [$\because$ $O < A \le 9$]

$\Rightarrow \quad A = 2, A = 7$

Putting $A = 2$ in (i), we get $C = 1$

$\therefore \quad A = 2, B = 5$ and $C = 1$.

Putting $A = 7$ in (i), we get $C = 3$

$\therefore \quad A = 7, B = 5$ and $C = 3$.

Example 7 Show that the following cryptarithms does not have any solution:

(i)
$$\begin{array}{r} A\ \ B \\ \times\ \ 3 \\ \hline CAB \end{array}$$

(ii)
$$\begin{array}{r} A\ \ B \\ \times\ \ 4 \\ \hline CAB \end{array}$$

Solution We have,

$$\begin{array}{r} A\ \ B \\ \times\ \ 3 \\ \hline CAB \end{array}$$

This means that $3\times B$ is a number whose ones digit is B. Clearly, such a number is 5. Therefore, $B = 5$.

Taking $B = 5$, we have

$$\begin{array}{r} A\ \ 5 \\ \times\ \ 3 \\ \hline CA\ 5 \end{array}$$

$\Rightarrow \quad \overline{A5}\times 3 = \overline{CA5}$

$\Rightarrow \quad (10A+5)\times 3 = 100C + 10A + 5$

$\Rightarrow \quad 30A + 15 = 100C + 10A + 5$

$\Rightarrow \quad 20A + 10 = 100C$

$\Rightarrow \quad 2A + 1 = 10C$

This is not possible as LHS is an odd integer and RHS is an even integer.

Hence, given Cryptarithm has no solution.

(ii) We have,

$$\begin{array}{r} A\ \ B \\ \times\ \ 4 \\ \hline CAB \end{array}$$

This means that $4 \times B$ is a number whose units digit is B. Clearly, there is no such digit. Hence, the given cryptarithm has no solution.

Example 8 Solve the Cryptarithm:

$$\begin{array}{r} B\ A \\ \times\ B\ 3 \\ \hline 5\ 7\ A \\ \hline \end{array}$$

Solution Here, we have to find the values of A and B.

Since ones digit of $3 \times A$ is A. Therefore, $A = 0$ or $A = 5$.

Now, $\overline{BA} \times \overline{B3} = \overline{57A}$ ...(i)

$\Rightarrow$ $\overline{BA} \times \overline{B3}$ is a three digit number between 500 and 600.

If $B = 1$, then $\overline{BA} \times \overline{B3}$ can have maximum value $19 \times 13 = 247$. Therefore, $B \neq 1$. If $B = 3$, then $\overline{BA} \times \overline{B3}$ can have minimum value $30 \times 33 = 990$. Therefore, $B \neq 3$. Thus, we have $B = 2$.

Putting $B = 2$ in (i), we get

$$\overline{2A} \times 23 = \overline{57A}$$

$$\Rightarrow \quad (20 + A) \times 23 = 500 + 70 + A$$

$$\Rightarrow \quad 460 + 23A = 570 + A$$

$$\Rightarrow \quad 22A = 110$$

$$\Rightarrow \quad A = 5$$

Hence, $A = 5$ and $B = 2$ and, $\begin{array}{r} 25 \\ \times\ 23 \\ \hline 575 \end{array}$

Example 9 Solve the Cryptarithm: $\overline{AB} \times \overline{AB} = \overline{ACB}$

Solution We have,

$$\overline{AB} \times \overline{AB} = \overline{ACB} \quad \text{...(i)}$$

This means that the units digit of $B \times B$ is B. Therefore, $B = 1$ or $B = 6$.

Again, $\overline{AB} \times \overline{AB} = \overline{ACB}$

$\Rightarrow$ The square of a two digit number is a three digit number.

So, A can take values 1, 2 and 3.

We find that $A = 1, B = 1$ satisfies equation (i). For these values of A and B, we have

$$11 \times 11 = 121$$

$$\therefore \quad C = 2$$

No other pairs of values of A and B satisfy equation (i).

Hence, $A = 1, B = 1$ and $C = 2$.

EXERCISE 5.3

Solve each of the following Cryptarithms:

1. $$\begin{array}{r} 3\ \ 7 \\ +A\ \ B \\ \hline 9\ \ A \end{array}$$

2. $$\begin{array}{r} A\ \ B \\ +\ 3\ \ 7 \\ \hline 9\ \ A \end{array}$$

3. $$\begin{array}{r} A\ \ 1 \\ +\ 1\ \ B \\ \hline B\ \ 0 \end{array}$$

4. $$\begin{array}{r} 2\ \ A\ \ B \\ +A\ \ B\ \ 1 \\ \hline B\ \ 1\ \ 8 \end{array}$$

5. $$\begin{array}{r} 1\ \ 2\ \ A \\ +6\ \ A\ \ B \\ \hline A\ \ 0\ \ 9 \end{array}$$

6. $$\begin{array}{r} A\ \ B\ \ 7 \\ +7\ \ A\ \ B \\ \hline 9\ \ 8\ \ A \end{array}$$

7. Show that the Cryptarithm $4 \times \overline{AB} = \overline{CAB}$ does not have any solution.

ANSWERS

1. $A = 5, B = 8$
2. $A = 2, B = 5$
3. $A = 7, B = 9$
4. $A = 4, B = 7$
5. $A = 8, B = 1$
6. $A = 2, B = 5$

THINGS TO REMEMBER

1. *Any two digit number can be written as* $\overline{ab}$, *where a and b are its tens and ones digit respectively.*
2. *If a, b, c denote respectively hundreds, tens and ones digit of a number then the number can be written as* $\overline{abc}$.
3. $\overline{ab} + \overline{ba}$ *is always a multiple of 11.*
4. $\overline{ab} - \overline{ba}$ *is always a multiple of 9.*
5. $\overline{abc} + \overline{bca} + \overline{cab}$ *is always a multiple of 111.*
6. $\overline{abc} + \overline{cba}$ *is always a multiple of 99.*
7. $\overline{abc} - \overline{cba}$ *is always a multiple of 9.*
8. *A number is divisible by 10, if its units digit is zero.*
9. *A number is divisible by 5, if its ones digit is 0 or 5.*
10. *If we subtract the ones digit of a number from that number, the remainder is divisible by 10.*
11. *If a number is divided by 5, then the remainder is equal to the remainder when its ones digit is divided by 5.*
12. *A number is even or odd according as its ones digit is even or odd.*
13. *A number is divisible by 9, if the sum of its digits is divisible by 9.*
14. *Any number n can be written as*

    n = *a multiple of 9 + Sum of the digits of n*
15. *If a number is divided by 9, then the remainder is equal to the remainder when the sum of its digits is divided by 9.*
16. *A number is divisible by 3, if the sum of its digits is divisible by 3.*
17. *Any number n can be written as*

    n = *a multiple of 3 + Sum of the digits of n*
18. *If a number is divided by 3, then the remainder is equal to the remainder when the sum of its digits is divided by 3.*
19. *A number is divisible by 6, if it is divisible by both 2 and 3.*
20. *A number is divisible by 4, if the number formed by its last two digits is divisible by 4.*
21. *If a number is divided by 4, then the remainder is equal to the remainder when the number formed by its last two digits is divided by 4.*
22. *If* $\overline{ab}$ *is a two digit number, then*

    $\overline{ab}$ = *a multiple of* $11 + (-a + b)$

    Thus, a two digit number $\overline{ab}$ *is divisible by 11, if* $a = b$.
23. *If* $\overline{abc}$ *is a three digit number, then*

    $\overline{abc}$ = *a multiple of* $11 + (a - b + c)$

    Thus, a three digit number $\overline{abc}$ *is divisible by 11, if* $a - b + c$ *is a multiple of 11.*
24. *If* $\overline{abcd}$ *is a four digit number, then*

    $\overline{abcd}$ = *a multiple of* $11 + (-a + b - c + d)$

    Thus, a four digit number $\overline{abcd}$ *is divisible by 11, if* $-a + b - c + d$ *is a multiple of 11.*
25. *Cryptarithms are puzzles in which letters take the place of digits in an arithmetic sum.*

6

ALGEBRAIC EXPRESSIONS AND IDENTITIES

6.1 INTRODUCTION

In the previous class, we have learnt about algebraic expressions and their addition and subtraction. Most of the expressions that we worked with had integer coefficients. In this chapter, we shall study multiplication of algebraic expressions in the form of monomials and binomials etc. Also, we shall learn to work with algebraic expressions that contain both integer and fractional coefficients. In other words, we shall work with algebraic expressions containing rational numbers as the coefficients of various terms. We shall also learn how to factorize algebraic expressions. But before all these things, we review here what we have learnt earlier.

6.2 REVIEW OF CONCEPTS AND DEFINITIONS

In algebra, we generally come across two types of symbols, namely constants and variables.

CONSTANT *A symbol having a fixed numerical value is called a constant.*

VARIABLE *A symbol which takes various numerical values is called a variable.*

ILLUSTRATION 1 We know that the perimeter P of a square of side s is given by $P = 4 \times s$. Here, 4 is a constant and P and s are variables.

ILLUSTRATION 2 The perimeter P of a rectangle of sides l and b is given by $P = 2(l + b)$. Here, 2 is a constant and l and b are variables.

ALGEBRAIC EXPRESSIONS *A combination of constants and variables connected by the signs of fundamental operations of addition, subtraction, multiplication and division is called an algebraic expression.*

TERMS *Various parts of an algebraic expression which are separated by the signs of + or − are called the 'terms' of the expression.*

ILLUSTRATION 3 $2x^2 - 3xy + 5y^2$ is an algebraic expression consisting of three terms, namely, $2x^2, -3xy$ and $5y^2$.

ILLUSTRATION 4 The expression $2x^3 - 3x^2 + 4x - 7$ is an algebraic expression consisting of four terms, namely, $2x^3, -3x^2, 4x$ and -7.

MONOMIAL *An algebraic expression containing only one term is called a monomial.*

ILLUSTRATION 5 $-5, 3y, 7xy, \frac{2}{3}x^2yz, \frac{5}{3}a^2bc^3$ etc. are all monomials.

Two monomials containing unlike terms when added give a binomial as defined below.

BINOMIAL *An algebraic expression containing two terms is called a binomial.*

ILLUSTRATION 6 The expressions $2x - 3$, $3x + 2y$, $xyz - 5$ etc. are all binomials.

Note that $3x + 7x$ is not a binomial, because $3x + 7x = 10x$, which is a monomial.

TRINOMIAL *An algebraic expression containing three terms is called a trinomial.*

In other words, if three monomials are such that no two contain like terms, then their sum is a trinomial.

ILLUSTRATION 7 The expressions $a-b+2x^2+y^2-xy, x^3-2y^3-3x^2y^2z$ etc. are trinomials.

FACTORS *Each term in an algebraic expression is a product of one or more numbers (s) and / or literal(s). These number(s) and / or literal(s) are known as the factors of that term.*

A constant factor is called a numerical factor, while a variable factor is known as a literal factor.

COEFFICIENT *In a term of an algebraic expression any of the factors with the sign of the term is called the coefficient of the product of the other factors.*

ILLUSTRATION 8 In $-5xy$, the coefficient of x is $-5y$; the coefficient of y is $-5x$ and the coefficient of xy is -5.

ILLUSTRATION 9 In $-x$, the coefficient of x is -1.

ILLUSTRATION 10 In $3a^2bc$, the coefficient of a^2 is $3bc$, the coefficient of b is $3a^2c$ and the coefficient of c is $3a^2b$.

CONSTANT TERM *A term of the expression having no literal factor is called a constant term.*

ILLUSTRATION 11 In the algebraic expression $x^2-xy+yz-4$, the constant term is -4.

LIKE AND UNLIKE TERMS *The terms having the same literal factors are called like or similar terms, otherwise they are called unlike terms.*

ILLUSTRATION 12 In the algebraic expression $2a^2b+3ab^2-7ab-4ba^2$, we have $2a^2b$ and $-4ba^2$ as like terms, whereas $3ab^2$ and $-7ab$ are unlike terms.

EXERCISE 6.1

1. Identify the terms, their coefficients for each of the following expressions:

(i) $7x^2yz-5xy$ (ii) x^2+x+1 (iii) $3x^2y^2-5x^2y^2z^2+z^2$

(iv) $9-ab+bc-ca$ (v) $\frac{a}{2}+\frac{b}{2}-ab$ (vi) $0.2x-0.3xy+0.5y$

2. Classify the following polynomials as monomials, binomials, trinomials. Which polynomials do not fit in any category?

(i) $x+y$ (ii) 1000 (iii) $x+x^2+x^3+x^4$

(iv) $7+a+5b$ (v) $2b-3b^2$ (vi) $2y-3y^2+4y^3$

(vii) $5x-4y+3x$ (viii) $4a-15a^2$ (ix) $xy+yz+zt+tx$

(x) pqr (xi) p^2q+pq^2 (xii) $2p+2q$

ANSWERS

1.

	Terms	Coefficients		Terms	Coefficients
(i)	$7x^2yz$	7	(ii)	x^2	1
	$-5xy$	-5		x	1
				1	1
(iii)	$3x^2y^2$	3	(iv)	$-ab$	-1
	$-5x^2y^2z^2$	-5		bc	1
	z^2	1		$-ca$	-1
				9	9

(v)	$\frac{a}{2}$	$\frac{1}{2}$	(vi)	$0.2x$	0.2
	$\frac{b}{2}$	$\frac{1}{2}$		$-0.3xy$	-0.3
	$-ab$	-1		$0.5y$	0.5

2. Monomial	Binomial	Trinomial	None of these
(ii), (x)	(i), (v), (vii), (viii) (xi), (xii)	(iv), (vi)	(iii), (ix)

6.2.1 ADDITION OF ALGEBRAIC EXPRESSIONS

In adding algebraic expressions, we collect different groups of like terms and find the sum of like terms in each group. Note that the sum of several like terms is another like term whose coefficient is the sum of the coefficients of those like terms.

Following examples will illustrate the same.

ILLUSTRATIVE EXAMPLES

Example 1 Add: $7x^2 - 4x + 5, -3x^2 + 2x - 1$ and $5x^2 - x + 9$.

Solution We have,

Required sum

$$= (7x^2 - 4x + 5) + (-3x^2 + 2x - 1) + (5x^2 - x + 9)$$

$$= 7x^2 - 3x^2 + 5x^2 - 4x + 2x - x + 5 - 1 + 9 \quad \text{[Collecting like terms]}$$

$$= (7 - 3 + 5)x^2 + (-4 + 2 - 1)x + (5 - 1 + 9) \quad \text{[Adding like terms]}$$

$$= 9x^2 - 3x + 13$$

Example 2 Add: $5x^2 - \frac{1}{3}x + \frac{5}{2}, -\frac{1}{2}x^2 + \frac{1}{2}x - \frac{1}{3}$ and $-2x^2 + \frac{1}{5}x - \frac{1}{6}$.

Solution Required sum

$$= \left(5x^2 - \frac{1}{3}x + \frac{5}{2}\right) + \left(-\frac{1}{2}x^2 + \frac{1}{2}x - \frac{1}{3}\right) + \left(-2x^2 + \frac{1}{5}x - \frac{1}{6}\right)$$

$$= 5x^2 - \frac{1}{2}x^2 - 2x^2 - \frac{1}{3}x + \frac{1}{2}x + \frac{1}{5}x + \frac{5}{2} - \frac{1}{3} - \frac{1}{6} \quad \text{[Collecting like terms]}$$

$$= \left(5 - \frac{1}{2} - 2\right)x^2 + \left(-\frac{1}{3} + \frac{1}{2} + \frac{1}{5}\right)x + \left(\frac{5}{2} - \frac{1}{3} - \frac{1}{6}\right) \quad \text{[Adding like terms]}$$

$$= \left(\frac{10 - 1 - 4}{2}\right)x^2 + \left(\frac{-10 + 15 + 6}{30}\right)x + \left(\frac{15 - 2 - 1}{6}\right)$$

$$= \frac{5}{2}x^2 + \frac{11}{30}x + 2$$

Example 3 Add the following algebraic expressions:

$$2, \frac{2y}{3} - \frac{5y^2}{3} + \frac{5y^3}{2}, -\frac{4}{3} + \frac{2y^2}{3} - \frac{y}{2}, \frac{5y^3}{3} + 3y^2 + 3y + \frac{6}{5}$$

Solution Required sum

$$= 2 + \frac{2y}{3} - \frac{5y^2}{3} + \frac{5y^3}{2} - \frac{4}{3} + \frac{2y^2}{3} - \frac{y}{2} + \frac{5y^3}{3} + 3y^2 + 3y + \frac{6}{5}$$

$$= 2 - \frac{4}{3} + \frac{6}{5} + \frac{2y}{3} - \frac{y}{2} + 3y - \frac{5y^2}{3} + \frac{2y^2}{3} + 3y^2 + \frac{5y^3}{2} + \frac{5y^3}{3}$$

$$= \left(2 - \frac{4}{3} + \frac{6}{5}\right) + \left(\frac{2}{3} - \frac{1}{2} + 3\right)y + \left(-\frac{5}{3} + \frac{2}{3} + 3\right)y^2 + \left(\frac{5}{2} + \frac{5}{3}\right)y^3$$

$$= \left(\frac{30 - 20 + 18}{15}\right) + \left(\frac{4 - 3 + 18}{6}\right)y + \left(\frac{-5 + 2 + 9}{3}\right)y^2 + \left(\frac{15 + 10}{6}\right)y^3$$

$$= \frac{28}{15} + \frac{19}{6}y + 2y^2 + \frac{25}{6}y^3$$

6.2.2 SUBTRACTION OF ALGEBRAIC EXPRESSIONS

In order to subtract an algebraic expression from another, we change the signs (from '+' to '–' or from '–' to '+') of all the terms of the expression which is to be subtracted and then the two expressions are added.

Following examples will illustrate the procedure.

ILLUSTRATIVE EXAMPLES

Example 1 Subtract : $\left(-2y^2 + \frac{1}{2}y - 3\right)$ from $7y^2 - 2y + 10$.

Solution The required difference is given by

$$(7y^2 - 2y + 10) - \left(-2y^2 + \frac{1}{2}y - 3\right)$$

$$= 7y^2 - 2y + 10 + 2y^2 - \frac{1}{2}y + 3$$

$$= 7y^2 + 2y^2 - 2y - \frac{1}{2}y + 10 + 3 \quad \text{[Grouping like terms]}$$

$$= (7 + 2)y^2 + \left(-2 - \frac{1}{2}\right)y + 13$$

$$= 9y^2 - \frac{5}{2}y + 13$$

Example 2 Subtract : $\frac{3}{2}x^2y + \frac{4}{5}y - \frac{1}{3}x^2yz$ from $\frac{12}{5}x^2yz - \frac{3}{5}xyz + \frac{2}{3}x^2y$.

Solution We have,

$$\left(\frac{12}{5}x^2yz - \frac{3}{5}xyz + \frac{2}{3}x^2y\right) - \left(\frac{3}{2}x^2y + \frac{4}{5}y - \frac{1}{3}x^2yz\right)$$

$$= \frac{12}{5}x^2yz - \frac{3}{5}xyz + \frac{2}{3}x^2y - \frac{3}{2}x^2y - \frac{4}{5}y + \frac{1}{3}x^2yz$$

$$= \frac{12}{5}x^2yz + \frac{1}{3}x^2yz + \frac{2}{3}x^2y - \frac{3}{2}x^2y - \frac{3}{5}xyz - \frac{4}{5}y \quad \text{[Grouping like terms]}$$

$$= \left(\frac{12}{5} + \frac{1}{3}\right)x^2yz + \left(\frac{2}{3} - \frac{3}{2}\right)x^2y - \frac{3}{5}xyz - \frac{4}{5}y$$

$$= \frac{41}{15}x^2yz - \frac{5}{6}x^2y - \frac{3}{5}xyz - \frac{4}{5}y$$

Example 3 Take away $\frac{9}{2} + \frac{x}{2} + \frac{3}{5}x^2 + \frac{7}{4}x^3$ from $\frac{7}{2} - \frac{x}{3} - \frac{x^2}{5}$.

Solution We have,

$$\left(\frac{7}{2}-\frac{x}{3}-\frac{x^2}{5}\right)-\left(\frac{9}{2}+\frac{x}{2}+\frac{3}{5}x^2+\frac{7}{4}x^3\right)$$

$$=\frac{7}{2}-\frac{x}{3}-\frac{x^2}{5}-\frac{9}{2}-\frac{x}{2}-\frac{3}{5}x^2-\frac{7}{4}x^3$$

$$=\frac{7}{2}-\frac{9}{2}-\frac{x}{3}-\frac{x}{2}-\frac{x^2}{5}-\frac{3}{5}x^2-\frac{7}{4}x^3 \quad \text{[Grouping like terms]}$$

$$=\left(\frac{7-9}{2}\right)+\left(-\frac{1}{3}-\frac{1}{2}\right)x+\left(-\frac{1}{5}-\frac{3}{5}\right)x^2-\frac{7}{4}x^3$$

$$=-1-\frac{5}{6}x-\frac{4}{5}x^2-\frac{7}{4}x^3$$

EXERCISE 6.2

1. Add the following algebraic expressions:
   (i) $3a^2b, -4a^2b, 9a^2b$
   (ii) $\frac{2}{3}a, \frac{3}{5}a, -\frac{6}{5}a$
   (iii) $4xy^2-7x^2y,\ 12x^2y-6xy^2,\ -3x^2y+5xy^2$
   (iv) $\frac{3}{2}a-\frac{5}{4}b+\frac{2}{5}c, \frac{2}{3}a-\frac{7}{2}b+\frac{7}{2}c, \frac{5}{3}a+\frac{5}{2}b-\frac{5}{4}c$
   (v) $\frac{11}{2}xy+\frac{12}{5}y+\frac{13}{7}x, -\frac{11}{2}y-\frac{12}{5}x-\frac{13}{7}xy$
   (vi) $\frac{7}{2}x^3-\frac{1}{2}x^2+\frac{5}{3}, \frac{3}{2}x^3+\frac{7}{4}x^2-x+\frac{1}{3}, \frac{3}{2}x^2-\frac{5}{2}x-2$

2. Subtract:
   (i) $-5xy$ from $12xy$
   (ii) $2a^2$ from $-7a^2$
   (iii) $2a-b$ from $3a-5b$
   (iv) $2x^3-4x^2+3x+5$ from $4x^3+x^2+x+6$
   (v) $\frac{2}{3}y^3-\frac{2}{7}y^2-5$ from $\frac{1}{3}y^3+\frac{5}{7}y^2+y-2$
   (vi) $\frac{3}{2}x-\frac{5}{4}y-\frac{7}{2}z$ from $\frac{2}{3}x+\frac{3}{2}y-\frac{4}{3}z$
   (vii) $x^2y-\frac{4}{5}xy^2+\frac{4}{3}xy$ from $\frac{2}{3}x^2y+\frac{3}{2}xy^2-\frac{1}{3}xy$
   (viii) $\frac{ab}{7}-\frac{35}{3}bc+\frac{6}{5}ac$ from $\frac{3}{5}bc-\frac{4}{5}ac$

3. Take away:
   (i) $\frac{6}{5}x^2-\frac{4}{5}x^3+\frac{5}{6}+\frac{3}{2}x$ from $\frac{x^3}{3}-\frac{5}{2}x^2+\frac{3}{5}x+\frac{1}{4}$

(ii) $\frac{5a^2}{2}+\frac{3a^3}{2}+\frac{a}{3}-\frac{6}{5}$ from $\frac{1}{3}a^3-\frac{3}{4}a^2-\frac{5}{2}$

(iii) $\frac{7}{4}x^3+\frac{3}{5}x^2+\frac{1}{2}x+\frac{9}{2}$ from $\frac{7}{2}-\frac{x}{3}-\frac{x^2}{5}$

(iv) $\frac{y^3}{3}+\frac{7}{3}y^2+\frac{1}{2}y+\frac{1}{2}$ from $\frac{1}{3}-\frac{5}{3}y^2$

(v) $\frac{2}{3}ac-\frac{5}{7}ab+\frac{2}{3}bc$ from $\frac{3}{2}ab-\frac{7}{4}ac-\frac{5}{6}bc$

4. Subtract $3x-4y-7z$ from the sum of $x-3y+2z$ and $-4x+9y-11z$.
5. Subtract the sum of $3l-4m-7n^2$ and $2l+3m-4n^2$ from the sum of $9l+2m-3n^2$ and $-3l+m+4n^2$.....
6. Subtract the sum of $2x-x^2+5$ and $-4x-3+7x^2$ from 5.
7. Simplify each of the following:

(i) $x^2-3x+5-\frac{1}{2}(3x^2-5x+7)$

(ii) $[5-3x+2y-(2x-y)]-(3x-7y+9)$

(iii) $\frac{11}{2}x^2y-\frac{9}{4}xy^2+\frac{1}{4}xy-\frac{1}{14}y^2x+\frac{1}{15}yx^2+\frac{1}{2}xy$

(iv) $\left(\frac{1}{3}y^2-\frac{4}{7}y+11\right)-\left(\frac{1}{7}y-3+2y^2\right)-\left(\frac{2}{7}y-\frac{2}{3}y^2+2\right)$

(v) $-\frac{1}{2}a^2b^2c+\frac{1}{3}ab^2c-\frac{1}{4}abc^2-\frac{1}{5}cb^2a^2+\frac{1}{6}cb^2a-\frac{1}{7}c^2ab+\frac{1}{8}ca^2b.$

ANSWERS

1. (i) $8a^2b$ (ii) $\frac{1}{15}a$ (iii) $3xy^2+2x^2y$ (iv) $\frac{23a}{6}-\frac{9b}{4}+\frac{53c}{20}$

(v) $\frac{51}{14}xy-\frac{19}{35}x-\frac{31}{10}y$ (vi) $5x^3+\frac{11x^2}{4}-\frac{7x}{2}$

2. (i) $17xy$ (ii) $-9a^2$ (iii) $a-4b$ (iv) $2x^3+5x^2-2x+1$

(v) $-\frac{1}{3}y^3+y^2+y+3$ (vi) $-\frac{5}{6}x+\frac{11}{4}y+\frac{13}{6}z$ (vii) $-\frac{1}{3}x^2y+\frac{23}{10}xy^2-\frac{5}{3}xy$

(viii) $-\frac{1}{7}ab+\frac{184}{15}bc-2ac$

3. (i) $\frac{17}{15}x^3-\frac{37}{10}x^2-\frac{9}{10}x-\frac{7}{12}$ (ii) $-\frac{7}{6}a^3-\frac{13}{4}a^2-\frac{a}{3}-\frac{13}{10}$ (iii) $-\frac{7}{4}x^3-\frac{4}{5}x^2-\frac{5}{6}x-1$

(iv) $-\frac{1}{3}y^3-4y^2-\frac{1}{2}y-\frac{1}{6}$ (v) $\frac{31}{14}ab-\frac{29}{12}ac-\frac{3}{2}bc$

4. $-6x+10y-2z$ 5. $l+4m+12n^2$ 6. $3+2x-6x^2$

7. (i) $-\frac{1}{2}x^2-\frac{1}{2}x+\frac{3}{2}$ (ii) $-4-8x+10y$ (iii) $\frac{167}{30}x^2y-\frac{65}{28}xy^2+\frac{3}{4}xy$

(iv) $-y^2-y+12$ (v) $-\frac{7}{10}a^2b^2c+\frac{1}{2}ab^2c-\frac{11}{28}abc^2+\frac{1}{8}a^2bc$

6.3 MULTIPLICATION OF ALGEBRAIC EXPRESSIONS

In the previous section, we have studied the addition and subtraction of algebraic expressions. In this section, we shall study the multiplication of algebraic expressions. In the multiplication of algebraic expressions, we shall be using the following rules of signs:

(i) *The product of two factors with like signs is positive and the product of two factors with unlike signs is negative*

i.e., (*a*) $(+)\times(+)=+$

(*b*) $(+)\times(-)=-$

(*c*) $(-)\times(+)=-$

and, (*d*) $(-)\times(-)=+$

(ii) *If a is any variable and m, n are positive integers, then*

$$a^m\times a^n=a^{m+n}$$

For example, $a^3\times a^5=a^{3+5}=a^8, y^4\times y=y^{4+1}=y^5$ etc.

When two algebraic expressions are multiplied, the result is called the product and the two expressions making up the product are called factors or multiplicands. The multiplicands in a multiplication operation may be two monomials, one monomial and one binomial, two binomials or two polynomials.

The simplest case of multiplication is the multiplication of one monomial with another monomial. So, we first discuss the multiplication of two monomials.

6.3.1 MULTIPLICATION OF TWO MONOMIALS

Consider the multiplication of two monomials, say, $3ab$ and $5b$. We shall perform the multiplication of these two monomials by the repeated use of commutativity and associativity of multiplication.

We have,

$(3ab)\times(5b)=(3ab)\times(5\times b)$

$=(3ab)\times(b\times 5)$ [By commutativity of multiplication we have, $5\times b=b\times 5$]

$=(3ab\times b)\times 5$ [By associativity of multiplication]

$=[(3a\times b)\times b]\times 5$ [$\because\ 3ab=3a\times b$]

$=[3a\times(b\times b)]\times 5$ [By commutativity of multiplication we have, $(3a\times b)\times b=3a\times(b\times b)$]

$=(3ab^2)\times 5$

$=5\times 3ab^2$ [By commutativity of multiplication]

$=(5\times 3)\times ab^2$ [By associativity of multiplication]

$=15\times ab^2=15ab^2$

Thus, the product of monomials $3ab$ and $5b$ is $15ab^2$. Clearly, the coefficient 15 of the product $15ab^2$ is equal to the product of the coefficients in $3ab$ and $5b$. Also, the variable ab^2 in the product $15ab^2$ is equal to the product of the variable parts ab and b in monomials $3ab$ and $5b$ respectively.

Thus, we have the following two rules for the multiplication of two monomials.

Rule 1 *The coefficient of the product of two monomials is equal to the product of their coefficients.*

Rule 2 *The variable part in the product of two monomials is equal to the product of the variable parts in the given monomials.*

These two rules are also applicable for the product of three or more monomials.

Following examples will illustrate the use of these two rules in the product of two or more monomials.

ILLUSTRATIVE EXAMPLES

Example 1 Find the product of the following pairs of polynomials:

(i) $4, 7x$ (ii) $-4a, 7a$ (iii) $-4x, 7xy$ (iv) $4x^3, -3xy$ (v) $4x, 0$

Solution We have,

(i) $4 \times 7x = (4 \times 7) \times x = 28 \times x = 28x$

(ii) $(-4a) \times (7a) = (-4 \times 7) \times (a \times a) = -28a^2$

(iii) $(-4x) \times (7xy) = (-4 \times 7) \times (x \times xy) = -28x^{1+1}y = -28x^2y$

(iv) $(4x^3) \times (-3xy) = (4 \times -3) \times (x^3 \times xy) = -12\left(x^{3+1}y\right) = -12x^4y$

(v) $4x \times 0 = (4 \times 0) \times x = 0 \times x = 0$

Example 2 Find the areas of rectangles with the following pairs of monomials as their length and breadth respectively:

(i) (x, y) (ii) $(10x, 5y)$ (iii) $(2x^2, 5y^2)$ (iv) $(4a, 3a^2)$ (v) $(3mn, 4np)$

Solution We know that the area of a rectangle is the product of its length and breadth.

	Length	Breadth	Area = Length × Breadth
(i)	x	y	$x \times y = xy$
(ii)	$10x$	$5y$	$10x \times 5y = 50\,xy$
(iii)	$2x^2$	$5y^2$	$2x^2 \times 5y^2 = (2 \times 5) \times (x^2 \times y^2) = 10x^2y^2$
(iv)	$4a$	$3a^2$	$4a \times 3a^2 = (4 \times 3) \times (a \times a^2) = 12a^3$
(v)	$3mn$	$4np$	$3mn \times 4np = (3 \times 4) \times (m \times n \times n \times p) = 12mn^2p$

Example 3 Multiply:

(i) $3ab^2c^3$ by $5a^3b^2c$ (ii) $4x^2yz$ by $-\frac{3}{2}x^2yz^2$ (iii) $-\frac{8}{5}x^2yz^3$ *by* $-\frac{3}{4}xy^2z$

(iv) $\frac{3}{14}x^2y$ by $\frac{7}{2}x^4y$ (v) $2.1a^2bc$ by $4ab^2$

Solution (i) We have,

$(3ab^2c^3) \times (5a^3b^2c)$

$= (3 \times 5) \times (a \times a^3 \times b^2 \times b^2 \times c^3 \times c)$

$$= 15a^{1+3}b^{2+2}c^{3+1}$$

$$= 15a^4b^4c^4$$

(ii) We have,

$$(4x^2yz) \times \left(-\frac{3}{2}x^2yz^2\right)$$

$$= \left(4 \times -\frac{3}{2}\right) \times (x^2 \times x^2 \times y \times y \times z \times z^2)$$

$$= -6x^{2+2}y^{1+1}z^{1+2} = -6x^4y^2z^3$$

(iii) We have,

$$\left(-\frac{8}{5}x^2yz^3\right) \times \left(-\frac{3}{4}xy^2z\right)$$

$$= \left(-\frac{8}{5} \times -\frac{3}{4}\right) \times (x^2 \times x \times y \times y^2 \times z^3 \times z)$$

$$= \frac{6}{5}x^{2+1}y^{1+2}z^{3+1} = \frac{6}{5}x^3y^3z^4$$

(iv) We have,

$$\left(\frac{3}{14}x^2y\right) \times \left(\frac{7}{2}x^4y\right)$$

$$= \left(\frac{3}{14} \times \frac{7}{2}\right) \times (x^2 \times x^4 \times y \times y)$$

$$= \frac{3}{4}x^{2+4}y^{1+1} = \frac{3}{4}x^6y^2$$

(v) We have,

$$(2.1a^2bc) \times (4ab^2)$$

$$= (2.1 \times 4) \times (a^2 \times a \times b \times b^2 \times c)$$

$$= 8.4a^{2+1}b^{1+2}c = 8.4a^3b^3c$$

Example 4 Find the volume of the rectangular boxes with following length, breadth and height:

	Length	Breadth	Height
(i)	$2ax$	$3by$	$5cz$
(ii)	m^2n	n^2p	p^2m
(iii)	$2q$	$4q^2$	$8q^3$

Solution We know that the volume of a rectangular box is given by

Volume = Length × Breadth × Height

(i) Volume $= 2ax \times 3by \times 5\,cz$

$= (2 \times 3 \times 5) \times (ax \times by \times cz)$

$= 30\ abcxyz$

(ii) Volume $= m^2n \times n^2p \times p^2m = m^{2+1}n^{1+2}p^{1+2} = m^3n^3p^3$

(iii) Volume $= 2q \times 4q^2 \times 8q^3 = (2 \times 4 \times 8)\,q^{1+2+3} = 64q^6$

Example 5 Multiply:

(i) $-6a^2bc, 2a^2b$ and $-\frac{1}{4}$ (ii) $\frac{4}{9}a^5b^2, 10a^3b$ and 6

(iii) 3.15x and $-23x^2y$ (iv) $-x$, x^2yz and $-\frac{3}{7}xyz^2$

Solution (i) We have,

$$(-6a^2bc)\times(2a^2b)\times\left(-\frac{1}{4}\right)$$
$$=\left(-6\times2\times-\frac{1}{4}\right)\times(a^2\times a^2\times b\times b\times c)$$
$$=3a^{2+2}b^{1+1}c = 3a^4b^2c$$

(ii) We have,

$$\left(\frac{4}{9}a^5b^2\right)\times(10a^3b)\times(6)$$
$$=\left(\frac{4}{9}\times10\times6\right)\times(a^5\times a^3\times b^2\times b)$$
$$=\frac{80}{3}a^{5+3}b^{2+1} = \frac{80}{3}a^8b^3$$

(iii) We have,

$$(3)\times(15x)\times(-23x^2y)$$
$$=(3\times15\times-23)\times(x\times x^2\times y)$$
$$=-1035x^{1+2}y = -1035x^3y.$$

(iv) We have,

$$(-x)\times(x^2yz)\times\left(\frac{-3}{7}xyz^2\right)$$
$$=\left(-1\times\frac{-3}{7}\right)\times(x\times x^2\times x\times y\times y\times z\times z^2)$$
$$=\frac{3}{7}x^{1+2+1}y^{1+1}z^{1+2} = \frac{3}{7}x^4y^2z^3$$

Example 6 Find each of the following products:

(i) $(-2x^2)\times(7a^2x^7)\times(6a^5x^5)$ (ii) $(4s^2t)\times(3s^3t^3)\times(2st^4)\times(-2)$

(iii) $(5x^6)\times(-10xy^4)\times(-2x^6y^6)\times(10xy)$

Solution (i) We have,

$$(-2x^2)\times(7a^2x^7)\times(6a^5x^5)$$
$$=(-2\times7\times6)\times(x^2\times x^7\times x^5\times a^2\times a^5)$$
$$=-84x^{2+7+5}a^{2+5} = -84x^{14}a^7$$

(ii) We have,

$$(4s^2t)\times(3s^3t^3)\times(2st^4)\times(-2)$$
$$=(4\times3\times2\times-2)\times(s^2\times s^3\times s\times t\times t^3\times t^4)$$
$$=-48s^{2+3+1}t^{1+3+4} = -48s^6t^8$$

(iii) We have,

$$(5x^6)\times(-10xy^4)\times(-2x^6y^6)\times(10xy)$$
$$=(5\times-10\times-2\times10)\times(x^6\times x\times x^6\times x\times y^4\times y^6\times y)$$
$$=1000x^{6+1+6+1}y^{4+6+1}=1000x^{14}y^{11}$$

Example 7 Multiply each of the following monomials:

(i) $3xyz, 5x, 0$ (ii) $\frac{6}{5}ab, \frac{5}{6}bc, \frac{12}{9}abc$

(iii) $\frac{3}{4}x^2yz^2, 0.5xy^2z^2, 1.16x^2yz^3, 2xyz$ (iv) $20x^{10}y^{20}z^{30}, (10xyz)^2$

(v) $(-3x^2y), (4xy^2z), (-xy^2z^2)$ and $\left(\frac{4}{5}z\right)$

Solution (i) We have,

$$(3xyz)\times(5x)\times0$$
$$=(3\times5\times0)\times(x\times x\times y\times z)$$
$$=0\times x^2yz=0$$

(ii) We have,

$$\left(\frac{6}{5}ab\right)\times\left(\frac{5}{6}bc\right)\times\left(\frac{12}{9}abc\right)$$
$$=\left(\frac{6}{5}\times\frac{5}{6}\times\frac{12}{9}\right)+(a\times a\times b\times b\times b\times c\times c)$$
$$=\frac{12}{9}a^{1+1}b^{1+1+1}c^{1+1}=\frac{4}{3}a^2b^3c^2$$

(iii) We have,

$$\left(\frac{3}{4}x^2yz^2\right)\times(0.5xy^2z^2)\times(1.16x^2yz^3)\times(2xyz)$$
$$=\left(\frac{3}{4}\times0.5\times1.16\times2\right)\times(x^2\times x\times x^2\times x\times y\times y^2\times y\times y\times z^2\times z^2\times z^3\times z)$$
$$=\left(\frac{3}{4}\times\frac{5}{10}\times\frac{116}{100}\times2\right)\times(x^{2+1+2+1}\times y^{1+2+1+1}\times z^{2+2+3+1})$$
$$=\frac{87}{100}x^6y^5z^8$$

(iv) We have,

$$(20x^{10}y^{20}z^{30})\times(10xyz)^2$$
$$=(20x^{10}y^{20}z^{30})\times(10xyz)\times(10xyz)$$
$$=(20\times10\times10)\times(x^{10}\times x\times x\times y^{20}\times y\times y\times z^{30}\times z\times z)$$
$$=2000x^{10+1+1}y^{20+1+1}z^{30+1+1}$$
$$=2000x^{12}y^{22}z^{32}$$

(v) We have,

$$(-3x^2y)\times(4xy^2z)\times(-xy^2z^2)\times\left(\frac{4}{5}z\right)$$

$$= \left(-3\times4\times-1\times\frac{4}{5}\right)\times(x^2\times x\times x\times y\times y^2\times y^2\times z\times z^2\times z)$$

$$= \frac{48}{5}x^{2+1+1}y^{1+2+2}z^{1+2+1} = \frac{48}{5}x^4y^5z^4$$

Example 8 Express the following product as a monomial:

$$(x^3)\times(7x^5)\times\left(\frac{1}{5}x^2\right)\times(-6x^4)$$

Verify the product for $x = 1$.

Solution We have,

$$(x^3)\times(7x^5)\times\left(\frac{1}{5}x^2\right)\times(-6x^4)$$

$$= \left(1\times7\times\frac{1}{5}\times-6\right)\times(x^3\times x^5\times x^2\times x^4) = -\frac{42}{5}x^{3+5+2+4} = -\frac{42}{5}x^{14}$$

Verification: For $x = 1$, we have

$$\text{L.H.S.} = (x^3)\times(7x^5)\times\left(\frac{1}{5}x^2\right)\times(-6x^4)$$

$$= (1)^3\times\{7\times(1^5)\}\times\left\{\frac{1}{5}\times(1)^2\right\}\times\{-6\times(1)^4\}$$

$$= 1\times7\times\frac{1}{5}\times-6 = -\frac{42}{5}$$

and,

$$\text{R.H.S.} = -\frac{42}{5}\times(1)^{14} = -\frac{42}{5}$$

$\therefore$ L.H.S. = R.H.S.

Example 9 Multiply $-\frac{4}{3}xy^3$ by $\frac{6}{7}x^2y$ and verify your result for $x = 2$ and $y = 1$.

Solution We have,

$$\left(-\frac{4}{3}xy^3\right)\times\left(\frac{6}{7}x^2y\right) = \left(-\frac{4}{3}\times\frac{6}{7}\right)\times(x\times x^2\times y^3\times y)$$

$$= -\frac{8}{7}x^{1+2}y^{3+1} = -\frac{8}{7}x^3y^4$$

Verification: For $x = 2$ and $y = 1$, we have

$$\text{L.H.S.} = \left(-\frac{4}{3}xy^3\right)\times\left(\frac{6}{7}x^2y\right)$$

$$= \left(-\frac{4}{3}\times2\times(1)^3\right)\times\left(\frac{6}{7}\times(2)^2\times1\right) = -\frac{8}{3}\times\frac{24}{7} = -\frac{64}{7}$$

and,

$$\text{R.H.S.} = -\frac{8}{7}x^3y^4 = -\frac{8}{7}\times2^3\times(1)^4 = -\frac{64}{7}$$

Hence, for $x = 2$ and $y = 1$, we have L.H.S. = R.H.S.

Example 10 Find the product of $-5x^2y, -\frac{2}{3}xy^2z, \frac{8}{15}xyz^2$ and $-\frac{1}{4}z$. Verify the result when $x = 1, y = 2$ and $z = 3$.

Solution We have,

$$(-5x^2y)\times\left(-\frac{2}{3}xy^2z\right)\times\left(\frac{8}{15}xyz^2\right)\times\left(-\frac{1}{4}z\right)$$

$$=\left(-5\times-\frac{2}{3}\times\frac{8}{15}\times-\frac{1}{4}\right)\times(x^2\times x\times x\times y\times y^2\times y\times z\times z^2\times z)$$

$$=-\frac{4}{9}x^4y^4z^4$$

Verification: For $x = 1, y = 2$ and $z = 3$, we have

$$\text{L.H.S.} =(-5\times(1)^2\times2)\times\left(-\frac{2}{3}\times1\times(2)^2\times3\right)\times\left(\frac{8}{15}\times1\times2\times(3)^2\right)\times\left(-\frac{1}{4}\times3\right)$$

$$=(-5\times1\times2)\times\left(-\frac{2}{3}\times1\times4\times3\right)\times\left(\frac{8}{15}\times1\times2\times9\right)\times\left(-\frac{3}{4}\right)$$

$$=(-10)\times(-8)\times\left(\frac{48}{5}\right)\times\left(-\frac{3}{4}\right) =-576$$

and, $\text{R.H.S.} =-\frac{4}{9}\times(1)^4\times2^4\times3^4 =-\frac{4}{9}\times1\times16\times81 =-576$

$\therefore$ L.H.S. = R.H.S.

Example 11 Find the value of $(5a^6)\times(-10ab^2)\times(-2.1a^2b^3)$ for $a = 1$ and $b = \frac{1}{2}$.

Solution We have,

$$(5a^6)\times(-10ab^2)\times(-2.1a^2b^3)$$

$$=(5\times-10\times-2.1)\times(a^6\times a\times a^2\times b^2\times b^3)$$

$$=\left(5\times-10\times-\frac{21}{10}\right)\times(a^6\times a\times a^2\times b^2\times b^3)$$

$$=105a^{6+1+2}b^{2+3} =105a^9b^5$$

Putting $a = 1$ and $b=\frac{1}{2}$, we have

$$105a^9b^5 =105\times(1)^9\times\left(\frac{1}{2}\right)^5 =105\times1\times\frac{1}{32} =\frac{105}{32}$$

EXERCISE 6.3

Find each of the following products: (1–8)

1. $5x^2\times4x^3$
2. $-3a^2\times4b^4$
3. $(-5xy)\times(-3x^2yz)$
4. $\frac{1}{2}xy\times\frac{2}{3}x^2yz^2$

5. $\left(-\frac{7}{5}xy^2z\right)\times\left(\frac{13}{3}x^2yz^2\right)$

6. $\left(\frac{-24}{25}x^3z\right)\times\left(-\frac{15}{16}xz^2y\right)$

7. $\left(-\frac{1}{27}a^2b^2\right)\times\left(\frac{9}{2}a^3b^2c^2\right)$

8. $(-7xy)\times\left(\frac{1}{4}x^2yz\right)$

Find each of the following products: (9–17)

9. $(7ab)\times(-5ab^2c)\times(6abc^2)$

10. $(-5a)\times(-10a^2)\times(-2a^3)$

11. $(-4x^2)\times(-6xy^2)\times(-3yz^2)$

12. $\left(-\frac{2}{7}a^4\right)\times\left(-\frac{3}{4}a^2b\right)\times\left(-\frac{14}{5}b^2\right)$

13. $\left(\frac{7}{9}ab^2\right)\times\left(\frac{15}{7}ac^2b\right)\times\left(-\frac{3}{5}a^2c\right)$

14. $\left(\frac{4}{3}u^2vw\right)\times(-5uvw^2)\times\left(\frac{1}{3}v^2wu\right)$

15. $(0.5x)\times\left(\frac{1}{3}xy^2z^4\right)\times(24x^2yz)$

16. $\left(\frac{4}{3}pq^2\right)\times\left(-\frac{1}{4}p^2r\right)\times(16p^2q^2r^2)$

17. $(2.3xy)\times(0.1x)\times(0.16)$

Express each of the following products as a monomials and verify the result in each case for x = 1: (18–26)

18. $(3x)\times(4x)\times(-5x)$

19. $(4x^2)\times(-3x)\times\left(\frac{4}{5}x^3\right)$

20. $(5x^4)\times(x^2)^3\times(2x)^2$

21. $(x^2)^3\times(2x)\times(-4x)\times(5)$

22. Write down the product of $-8x^2y^6$ and $-20xy$. Verify the product for $x = 2.5$, $y = 1$.

23. Evaluate $(3.2x^6y^3)\times(2.1x^2y^2)$ when $x = 1$ and $y = 0.5$

24. Find the value of $(5x^6)\times(-1.5x^2y^3)\times(-12xy^2)$ when $x = 1$, $y = 0.5$.

25. Evaluate $(2.3a^5b^2)\times(1.2a^2b^2)$ when $a = 1$ and $b = 0.5$.

26. Evaluate $(-8x^2y^6)\times(-20xy)$ for $x = 2.5$ and $y = 1$.

Express each of the following products as a monomials and verify the result for x = 1, y = 2: (27–31)

27. $(-xy^3)\times(yx^3)\times(xy)$

28. $\left(\frac{1}{8}x^2y^4\right)\times\left(\frac{1}{4}x^4y^2\right)\times(xy)\times5$

29. $\left(\frac{2}{5}a^2b\right)\times(-15b^2ac)\times\left(-\frac{1}{2}c^2\right)$

30. $\left(-\frac{4}{7}a^2b\right)\times\left(-\frac{2}{3}b^2c\right)\times\left(-\frac{7}{6}c^2a\right)$

31. $\left(\frac{4}{9}abc^3\right)\times\left(-\frac{27}{5}a^3b^2\right)\times(-8b^3c)$

Evaluate each of the following when x = 2, y = – 1.

32. $(2xy)\times\left(\frac{x^2y}{4}\right)\times(x^2)\times(y^2)$

33. $\left(\frac{3}{5}x^2y\right)\times\left(-\frac{15}{4}xy^2\right)\times\left(\frac{7}{9}x^2y^2\right)$

ANSWERS

1. $20x^5$ 2. $-12a^2b^4$ 3. $15x^3y^2z$ 4. $\frac{1}{3}x^3y^2z^2$ 5. $\frac{-91}{15}x^3y^3z^3$

6. $\frac{9}{10}x^4yz^3$ 7. $\frac{-1}{6}a^5b^4c^2$ 8. $\frac{-7}{4}x^3y^2z$ 9. $-210a^3b^4c^3$ 10. $-100a^6$

11. $-72x^3y^3z^2$ 12. $\frac{-3}{5}a^6b^3$ 13. $-a^4b^3c^3$ 14. $\frac{-20}{9}u^4v^4w^4$ 15. $4x^4y^3z^5$

16. $\frac{-16}{3}p^5q^4r^3$ 17. $0.0368x^2y$ 18. $-60x^3$ 19. $\frac{-48}{5}x^6$ 20. $20x^{12}$

21. $-40x^8$ 22. $160x^3y^7$ 23. 0.21 24. $\frac{45}{16}$ 25. $\frac{6.9}{40}$

26. 2500 27. $-x^5y^5$ 28 $\frac{5}{32}x^7y^7$ 29. $3a^3b^3c^3$ 30. $\frac{-4}{9}a^3b^3c^3$

31. $\frac{96}{5}a^4b^6c^4$ 32. 16 33. 56

6.4 MULTIPLICATION OF A MONOMIAL AND A BINOMIAL

In the chapter on operations on rational numbers, we have learnt the distributivity of multiplication over addition. This property helps us to simplify the expressions of the form $3\times(2+7)$. In the previous class, we have studied that multiplication of literals is also distributive over their addition i.e., $a\times(b+c)=a\times b+a\times c$. We shall use this property to multiply a monomial and a binomial.

Thus, if P,Q and R are three monomials, then we have

(i) $P\times(Q+R)=(P\times Q)+(P\times R)$ (ii) $(Q+R)\times P=Q\times P+R\times P$

In other words, we multiply each term of the binomial $Q + R$ by the monomial P and add the products to get the required result.

Also, $P\times(Q-R)=(P\times Q)-(P\times R)$ and, $(Q-R)\times P=(Q\times P)-(R\times P)$

Following examples will illustrate the multiplication of a monomial and a binomial.

ILLUSTRATIVE EXAMPLES

Example 1 Multiply: $2x$ by $(3x + 5y)$

Solution We have,

$$2x\times(3x+5y) = 2x\times 3x+2x\times 5y = 6x^2+10xy$$

Example 2 Multiply: $(7xy + 5y)$ by $3xy$

Solution We have,

$$(7xy+5y)\times 3xy$$
$$=7xy\times 3xy+5y\times 3xy$$
$$=21x^{1+1}y^{1+1}+15xy^{1+1} = 21x^2y^2+15xy^2$$

Example 3 Multiply: $-\frac{3ab^2}{5}$ by $\left(\frac{2a}{3}-b\right)$

Solution We have,

$$\left(-\frac{3ab^2}{5}\right)\times\left(\frac{2a}{3}-b\right)$$

$$= \left(-\frac{3ab^2}{5}\right) \times \frac{2a}{3} - \left(-\frac{3ab^2}{5}\right) \times b$$

$$= -\frac{3}{5} \times \frac{2}{3} a^{1+1} b^2 + \frac{3}{5} ab^{2+1} = -\frac{2}{5} a^2 b^2 + \frac{3}{5} ab^3$$

Example 4 Find the product of $\frac{7}{2}s^2t$ and $s+t$. Verify the result for $s = \frac{1}{2}$ and $t = 5$.

Solution We have,

$$\frac{7s^2t}{2} \times (s+t) = \frac{7}{2}s^2t \times s + \frac{7}{2}s^2t \times t = \frac{7}{2}s^3t + \frac{7}{2}s^2t^2$$

Verification: When $s = \frac{1}{2}$ and $t = 5$, we have

L.H.S. $= \frac{7}{2}s^2t \times (s+t)$

$$= \left\{\frac{7}{2} \times \left(\frac{1}{2}\right)^2 \times 5\right\} \times \left(\frac{1}{2} + 5\right) = \left(\frac{7}{2} \times \frac{1}{4} \times 5\right) \times \frac{11}{2} = \frac{35}{8} \times \frac{11}{2} = \frac{385}{16}$$

R.H.S. $= \frac{7}{2}s^3t + \frac{7}{2}s^2t^2$

$$= \frac{7}{2} \times \left(\frac{1}{2}\right)^3 \times 5 + \frac{7}{2} \times \left(\frac{1}{2}\right)^2 \times (5)^2$$

$$= \frac{7}{2} \times \frac{1}{8} \times 5 + \frac{7}{2} \times \frac{1}{4} \times 25 = \frac{35}{16} + \frac{175}{8} = \frac{35+350}{16} = \frac{385}{16}$$

$\therefore$ L.H.S. = R.H.S.

<u>Remark</u> *The method used to multiply a monomial and a binomial in the above four examples is generally known as horizontal method. However, the multiplication can also be performed column-wise as given in the following examples.*

Example 5 Multiply: $\left(3x - \frac{4}{5}y^2x\right)$ by $\frac{1}{2}xy$.

Solution *Horizontal method*

We have,

$$\left(3x - \frac{4}{5}y^2x\right) \times \frac{1}{2}xy$$

$$= 3x \times \frac{1}{2}xy - \frac{4}{5}y^2x \times \frac{1}{2}xy$$

$$= \left(3 \times \frac{1}{2}\right) \times x \times x \times y - \left(\frac{4}{5} \times \frac{1}{2}\right) \times y^2 \times y \times x \times x$$

$$= \frac{3}{2}x^2y - \frac{2}{5}y^3x^2 = \frac{3}{2}x^2y - \frac{2}{5}x^2y^3$$

Column method

We have,

$$\begin{array}{r} 3x - \frac{4}{5}y^2x \\ \times \frac{1}{2}xy \\ \hline \frac{3}{2}x^2y - \frac{2}{5}x^2y^3 \end{array}$$

Example 6 Find the following products:

(i) $100x \times (0.01x^4 - 0.01x^2)$ (ii) $121.5ab \times \left(ac + \frac{b}{10}\right)$

(iii) $0.1a \times (0.01a \times 0.001b)$

Solution (i) We have,

$$100x \times (0.01x^4 - 0.01x^2)$$
$$= 100x \times 0.01x^4 - 100x \times 0.01x^2$$
$$= (100 \times 0.01)x^5 - (100 \times 0.01)x^3$$
$$= \left(100 \times \frac{1}{100}\right)x^5 - \left(100 \times \frac{1}{100}\right)x^3 = x^5 - x^3$$

(ii) We have,

$$121.5ab \times \left(ac + \frac{b}{10}\right)$$
$$= 121.5ab \times ac + 121.5ab \times \frac{b}{10}$$
$$= 121.5a^2bc + 12.15ab^2$$

(iii) We have,

$$0.1a \times (0.01a + 0.001b)$$
$$= 0.1a \times 0.01a + 0.1a \times 0.001b = 0.001a^2 + 0.0001ab$$

Example 7 Determine each of the following products and find the value of each for $x = 2$, $y = 1.15$, $z = 0.01$.

(i) $27x^2(1 - 3x)$ (ii) $xz\,(x^2 + y^2)$ (iii) $z^2(x - y)$ (iv) $(2z - 3x) \times (-4y)$

Solution (i) We have,

$$27x^2(1 - 3x)$$
$$= 27x^2 \times (1 - 3x)$$
$$= 27x^2 \times 1 - 27x^2 \times 3x \quad \text{[Expanding the bracket]}$$
$$= 27x^2 - 81x^3$$

Putting $x = 2$, we have

$$27x^2(1 - 3x)$$
$$= 27 \times (2)^2 \times (1 - 3 \times 2) = 27 \times 4 \times (1 - 6) = 27 \times 4 \times -5 = -540$$

(ii) We have,

$$xz\,(x^2 + y^2)$$
$$= xz \times (x^2 + y^2)$$
$$= xz \times x^2 + xz \times y^2 = x^3z + xy^2z$$

Putting $x = 2$, $y = 1.15$ and $z = 0.01$, we get

$$xz\,(x^2 + y^2)$$

$= 2 \times 0.01 \times \{(2)^2 + (1.15)^2\}$

$= 0.02 \times (4 + 1.3225) \ = 0.02 \times 5.3225 \ = 0.106450$

(iii) We have,

$z^2(x - y)$

$= z^2 \times (x - y)$

$= z^2 \times x - z^2 \times y \ = z^2x - z^2y$

Putting $x = 2, y = 1.15$ and $z = 0.01$, we get

$z^2(x - y)$

$= (0.01)^2 \times (2 - 1.15)$

$= (0.0001) \times (0.85) \ = 0.000085$

(iv) We have,

$(2z - 3x) \times (-4y)$

$= (2z) \times (-4y) - 3x \times (-4y) \ = -8zy + 12xy$

Putting $x = 2, y = 1.15$ and $z = 0.01$, we have

$(2z - 3x) \times -4y$

$= [(2 \times 0.01) - (3 \times 2)] \times (-4 \times 1.15)$

$= (0.02 - 6) \times (-4.6) \ = -5.98 \times -4.6 = 27.508$

Example 8 Simplify the expression and evaluate them as directed:

(i) $x(x - 3) + 2$ for $x = 1$ (ii) $3y\,(2y - 7) - 3(y - 4) - 63$ for $y = -2$

Solution (i) We have,

$x\,(x - 3) + 2 = x^2 - 3x + 2$

For $x = 1$, we have,

$x^2 - 3x + 2 = (1)^2 - 3 \times 1 + 2 = 1 - 3 + 2 = 3 - 3 = 0$

(ii) We have,

$3y\,(2y - 6) - 3\,(y - 4) - 63$

$= (6y^2 - 21y) - (3y - 12) - 63$

$= 6y^2 - 21y - 3y + 12 - 63$

$= 6y^2 - 24y - 51$

For $y = -2$, we have

$6y^2 - 24y - 51 = 6 \times (-2)^2 - 24\,(-2) - 51$

$= 6 \times 4 + 24 \times 2 - 51 = 24 + 48 - 51 = 72 - 51 = 21$

Example 9 Add:

(i) $5m\,(3 - m)$ and $6m^2 - 13m$ (ii) $4y\,(3y^2 + 5y - 7)$ and $2\,(y^3 - 4y^2 + 5)$

Solution (i) We have,

$5m\,(3 - m) = 5m \times 3 - 5m \times m = 15m - 5m^2$

$\therefore$ $5m\,(3 - m) + 6m^2 - 13m$

$= 15m - 5m^2 + 6m^2 - 13m$

$= (15m - 13m) + (6m^2 - 5m^2)$

$= 2m + m^2$

(ii) We have,

$4y(3y^2 + 5y - 7) = 4y \times 3y^2 + 4y \times 5y - 4y \times 7$

$= 12y^3 + 20y^2 - 28y$

$2(y^3 - 4y^2 + 5) = 2 \times y^3 + 2(-4y^2) + 2 \times 5$

$= 2y^3 - 8y^2 + 10$

Adding the two expressions

$$\begin{array}{r} 12y^3 + 20y^2 - 28y \\ +\ 2y^3 - 8y^2 + 10 \\ \hline 14y^3 + 12y^2 - 28y + 10 \end{array}$$

Example 10 Subtract $3pq(p - q)$ from $2pq(p + q)$

Solution (i) We have,

$3pq(p - q) = 3p^2q - 3pq^2$

and, $2pq(p + q) = 2p^2q + 2pq^2$

Subtraction:

$$\begin{array}{r} 2p^2q + 2pq^2 \\ 3p^2q - 3pq^2 \\ - \quad\quad + \\ \hline -p^2q + 5pq^2 \end{array}$$

Aliter We have to find

$2pq(p + q) - 3pq(p - q)$

$= 2p^2q + 2pq^2 - 3p^2q + 3pq^2$

$= 2p^2q - 3p^2q + 2pq^2 + 3pq^2$

$= -p^2q + 5pq^2$

Example 11 Add: (i) $p(p - q)$, $q(q - r)$ and $r(r - p)$ (ii) $2x(z - x - y)$ and $2y(z - y - x)$

Solution (i) We have,

$p(p - q) + q(q - r) + r(r - p)$

$= p^2 - pq + q^2 - qr + r^2 - rp$

$= p^2 + q^2 + r^2 - pq - qr - rp$

(ii) We have,

$2x(z - x - y) + 2y(z - y - x)$

$= 2xz - 2x^2 - 2xy + 2yz - 2y^2 - 2xy$

$= 2xz - 2x^2 - 4xy + 2yz - 2y^2$

Example 12 (i) Subtract: $3l(l-4m+5n)$ from $4l(10n-3m+2l)$

(ii) Subtract: $3a(a+b+c)-2b(a-b+c)$ from $4c(-a+b+c)$

Solution (i) We have,

Required difference

$= 4l(10n-3m+2l)-3l(l-4m+5n)$

$= (40ln-12lm+8l^2)-(3l^2-12lm+15ln)$

$= 40ln-12lm+8l^2-3l^2+12lm-15ln$

$= 25ln+5l^2$

(ii) We have,

Required difference

$= 4c(-a+b+c)-\{3a(a+b+c)-2b(a-b+c)\}$

$= -4ac+4bc+4c^2-\left\{3a^2+3ab+3ac-2ab+2b^2-2bc\right\}$

$= -4ac+4bc+4c^2-\left\{3a^2+ab+3ac+2b^2-2bc\right\}$

$= -4ac+4bc+4c^2-3a^2-ab-3ac-2b^2+2bc$

$= -7ac+6bc+4c^2-3a^2-ab-2b^2$

Example 13 Simplify each of the following expressions:

(i) $15a^2-6a(a-2)+a(3+7a)$

(ii) $x^2(1-3y^2)+x(xy^2-2x)-3y(y-4x^2y)$

(iii) $4st(s-t)-6s^2(t-t^2)-3t^2(2s^2-s)+2st(s-t)$

Solution (i) We have,

$15a^2-6a(a-2)+a(3+7a)$

$= 15a^2-6a^2+12a+3a+7a^2$

$= 15a^2-6a^2+7a^2+12a+3a$

$= 16a^2+15a$

(ii) We have,

$x^2(1-3y^2)+x(xy^2-2x)-3y(y-4x^2y)$

$= x^2\times 1-3y^2\times x^2+x\times xy^2-x\times 2x-3y\times y+3y\times 4x^2y$

$= x^2-3x^2y^2+x^2y^2-2x^2-3y^2+12x^2y^2$

$= (x^2-2x^2)+(-3x^2y^2+x^2y^2+12x^2y^2)-3y^2$

$= -x^2+10x^2y^2-3y^2$

(iii) We have,

$4st(s-t)-6s^2(t-t^2)-3t^2(2s^2-s)+2st(s-t)$

$= 4st\times s-4st\times t-6s^2\times t+6s^2\times t^2-3t^2\times 2s^2+3t^2\times s+2st\times s-2st\times t$

$$= 4s^2t - 4st^2 - 6s^2t + 6s^2t^2 - 6s^2t^2 + 3st^2 + 2s^2t - 2st^2$$
$$= (4s^2t - 6s^2t + 2s^2t) + (-4st^2 + 3st^2 - 2st^2) + (6s^2t^2 - 6s^2t^2)$$
$$= (4 - 6 + 2)s^2t + (-4 + 3 - 2)st^2 + (6 - 6)s^2t^2$$
$$= -3st^2$$

EXERCISE 6.4

Find the following products: (1-15)

1. $2a^3(3a+5b)$
2. $-11a(3a+2b)$
3. $-5a(7a-2b)$
4. $-11y^2(3y+7)$
5. $\frac{6x}{5}(x^3+y^3)$
6. $xy(x^3-y^3)$
7. $0.1y(0.1x^5+0.1y)$
8. $\left(-\frac{7}{4}ab^2c-\frac{6}{25}a^2c^2\right)(-50a^2b^2c^2)$
9. $-\frac{8}{27}xyz\left(\frac{3}{2}xyz^2-\frac{9}{4}xy^2z^3\right)$
10. $-\frac{4}{27}xyz\left(\frac{9}{2}x^2yz-\frac{3}{4}xyz^2\right)$
11. $1.5x(10x^2y-100xy^2)$
12. $4.1xy(1.1x-y)$
13. $250.5xy\left(xz+\frac{y}{10}\right)$
14. $\frac{7}{5}x^2y\left(\frac{3}{5}xy^2+\frac{2}{5}x\right)$
15. $\frac{4}{3}a(a^2+b^2-3c^2)$
16. Find the product $24x^2(1-2x)$ and evaluate its value for $x = 3$.
17. Find the product $-3y(xy+y^2)$ and find its value for $x = 4$ and $y = 5$.
18. Multiply $-\frac{3}{2}x^2y^3$ by $(2x-y)$ and verify the answer for $x = 1$ and $y = 2$.
19. Multiply the monomial by the binomial and find the value of each for $x = -1$, $y = 0.25$ and $z = 0.05$:

    (i) $15y^2(2-3x)$ (ii) $-3x(y^2+z^2)$ (iii) $z^2(x-y)$ (iv) $xz(x^2+y^2)$
20. Simplify:

    (i) $2x^2(x^3-x)-3x(x^4+2x)-2(x^4-3x^2)$

    (ii) $x^3y(x^2-2x)+2xy(x^3-x^4)$

    (iii) $3a^2+2(a+2)-3a(2a+1)$

    (iv) $x(x+4)+3x(2x^2-1)+4x^2+4$

    (v) $a(b-c)-b(c-a)-c(a-b)$

    (vi) $a(b-c)+b(c-a)+c(a-b)$

    (vii) $4ab(a-b)-6a^2(b-b^2)-3b^2(2a^2-a)+2ab(b-a)$

(viii) $x^2(x^2+1)-x^3(x+1)-x(x^3-x)$

(ix) $2a^2+3a(1-2a^3)+a(a+1)$

(x) $a^2(2a-1)+3a+a^3-8$

(xi) $\frac{3}{2}x^2(x^2-1)+\frac{1}{4}x^2(x^2+x)-\frac{3}{4}x(x^3-1)$

(xii) $a^2b(a-b^2)+ab^2(4ab-2a^2)-a^3b(1-2b)$

(xiii) $a^2b(a^3-a+1)-ab(a^4-2a^2+2a)-b(a^3-a^2-1)$

ANSWERS

1. $6a^4+10a^3b$ 2. $-33a^2-22ab$ 3. $-35a^2+10ab$ 4. $-33y^3-77y^2$

5. $\frac{6}{5}x^4+\frac{6}{5}xy^3$ 6. x^4y-xy^4 7. $0.01x^5y+0.01y^2$

8. $\frac{175}{2}a^3b^4c^3+12a^4b^2c^4$ 9. $\frac{-4}{9}x^2y^2z^3+\frac{2}{3}x^2y^3z^4$

10. $\frac{-2}{3}x^3y^2z^2+\frac{1}{9}x^2y^2z^3$ 11. $15x^3y-150x^2y^2$

12. $4.51x^2y-4.1xy^2$ 13. $250.5x^2yz+25.05xy^2$

14. $\frac{21}{25}x^3y^3+\frac{14}{25}x^3y$ 15. $\frac{4}{3}a^3+\frac{4}{3}ab^2-4ac^2$

16. $24x^2-48x^3, -1080$ 17. $-3xy^2-3y^3-675$

18. $-3x^3y^3+\frac{3}{2}x^2y^4, 0$ 19. (i) $30y^2-45xy^2, \frac{75}{16}$

(ii) $-3xy^2-3xz^2, \frac{39}{200}$ (iii) $z^2x-z^2y, -\frac{1}{320}$ (iv) $x^2z+xy^2z, \frac{17}{320}$

20. (i) $-x^5-2x^4-2x^3$ (ii) $-x^5y$ (iii) $-3a^2-a+4$ (iv) $6x^3+5x^2+x+4$

(v) $2ab-2ac$ (vi) 0 (vii) $-4a^2b+ab^2$ (viii) $-x^4+2x^2-x^3$

(ix) $-6a^4+3a^2+4a$ (x) $3a^3-a^2+3a-8$ (xi) $x^4+\frac{1}{4}x^3-\frac{3}{2}x^2+\frac{3}{4}x$

(xii) $3a^2b^3$ (xiii) b

6.5 MULTIPLICATION OF TWO BINOMIALS

In the previous section, we have studied multiplication of a monomial and a binomial. In this section, we shall study multiplication of two binomials. In the multiplication of two binomials, we will use the distributive property of multiplication of literals over their addition as discussed below.

Consider two binomials, say $(a+b)$ and $(c+d)$. By using the distributive property of multiplication of literals over their addition, we have

$$(a+b)\times(c+d)=a\times(c+d)+b\times(c+d)$$
$$=(a\times c+a\times d)+(b\times c+b\times d)$$
$$=ac+ad+bc+bd$$

It follows from the above result that to multiply any two binomials, we multiply each term of one binomial by each term of the other and add the products.

The procedure is illustrated by following examples.

ILLUSTRATIVE EXAMPLES

Example 1 Multiply $(3x+2y)$ and $(5x+3y)$.

Solution We have,

$$(3x+2y)\times(5x+3y)$$
$$=3x\times(5x+3y)+2y\times(5x+3y)$$
$$=(3x\times 5x+3x\times 3y)+(2y\times 5x+2y\times 3y)$$
$$=(15x^2+9xy)+(10xy+6y^2)$$
$$=15x^2+9xy+10xy+6y^2$$
$$=15x^2+19xy+6y^2$$

Example 2 Multiply $(2x+3y)$ and $(4x-5y)$

Solution We have,

$$(2x+3y)\times(4x-5y)$$
$$=2x\times(4x-5y)+3y\times(4x-5y)$$
$$=(2x\times 4x-2x\times 5y)+(3y\times 4x-3y\times 5y)$$
$$=(8x^2-10xy)+(12xy-15y^2)$$
$$=8x^2-10xy+12xy-15y^2$$
$$=8x^2+2xy-15y^2$$

Example 3 Multiply $\left(\frac{1}{5}x-\frac{1}{4}y\right)$ and $(5x^2-4y^2)$.

Solution We have,

$$\left(\frac{1}{5}x-\frac{1}{4}y\right)\times(5x^2-4y^2)$$
$$=\frac{1}{5}x\times(5x^2-4y^2)-\frac{1}{4}y\times(5x^2-4y^2)$$
$$=\frac{1}{5}x\times 5x^2-\frac{1}{5}x\times 4y^2-\frac{1}{4}y\times 5x^2+\frac{1}{4}y\times 4y^2$$
$$=x^3-\frac{4}{5}xy^2-\frac{5}{4}x^2y+y^3$$

Remark *The above procedure of multiplying two binomials is known as horizontal method. There is another way of multiplying each term of one binomial with each term of another binomial and arranging these products so that like terms are combined column-wise. This method is known as the column method of multiplication of two binomials. This method is very similar to long multiplication of two whole numbers. Note that the column method of multiplication is useful when the binomials being multiplied contain terms with the same base so that the product contains like terms. These like terms when arranged in columns can be easily simplified.*

Following examples will illustrate the column method.

Example 4 Multiply $(7a+3b)$ and $(2a+3b)$ by column method.

Solution We have,

$$\begin{array}{rl} & 7a+3b \\ \times & 2a+3b \\ \hline & 14a^2+6ab \\ & \quad +21ab+9b^2 \\ \hline & 14a^2+27ab+9b^2 \end{array}$$

Multiplying $7a+3b$ by $2a$

Multiplying $7a+3b$ by $3b$

Adding the like terms

Example 5 Multiply $(7x-3y)$ by $(4x-5y)$ by column method.

Solution We have,

$$\begin{array}{rl} & 7x-3y \\ \times & 4x-5y \\ \hline & 28x^2-12xy \\ & \quad -35xy+15y^2 \\ \hline & 28x^2-47xy+15y^2 \end{array}$$

Multiplying $7x-3y$ by $4x$

Multiplying $7x-3y$ by $-5y$

Adding the like terms

Example 6 Multiply $(3x^2+y^2)$ by (x^2+2y^2).

Solution *Column method:*

We have,

$$\begin{array}{rl} & 3x^2+y^2 \\ \times & x^2+2y^2 \\ \hline & 3x^4+x^2y^2 \\ & \quad +6x^2y^2+2y^4 \\ \hline & 3x^4+7x^2y^2+2y^4 \end{array}$$

Multiplying $3x^2+y^2$ by x^2

Multiplying $3x^2+y^2$ by $2y^2$

Adding the like terms

Horizontal Method:

We have,

$(3x^2+y^2)(x^2+2y^2)$

$=3x^2\times(x^2+2y^2)+y^2\times(x^2+2y^2)$

$=3x^2\times x^2+3x^2\times 2y^2+y^2\times x^2+y^2\times 2y^2$

$=3x^4+6x^2y^2+x^2y^2+2y^4$

$=3x^4+7x^2y^2+2y^4$

Example 7 Multiply $(0.5x-y)$ by $(0.5x+y)$

Solution *Horizontal Method:*

We have,

$(0.5x-y)\times(0.5x+y)$

$=0.5x\,(0.5x+y)-y\,(0.5x+y)$

$= 0.5x \times 0.5x + 0.5x \times y - y \times 0.5x - y \times y$

$= 0.25x^2 + 0.5xy - 0.5xy - y^2$

$= 0.25x^2 - y^2$

Column method:

We have,

$$\begin{array}{rl} & 0.5x - y \\ \times & 0.5x + y \\ \hline & 0.25x^2 - 0.5xy \\ & \qquad +0.5xy - y^2 \\ \hline & 0.25x^2 - y^2 \end{array}$$

Multiplying $0.5x - y$ by $0.5x$

Multiplying $0.5x - y$ by y

Adding the like terms

Example 8 Multiply $\left(4x + \frac{3y}{5}\right)$ and $\left(3x - \frac{4y}{5}\right)$

Solution *Horizontal Method:*

We have,

$\left(4x + \frac{3y}{5}\right) \times \left(3x - \frac{4y}{5}\right)$

$= 4x \times \left(3x - \frac{4y}{5}\right) + \frac{3y}{5} \times \left(3x - \frac{4y}{5}\right)$

$= 4x \times 3x - 4x \times \frac{4y}{5} + \frac{3y}{5} \times 3x - \frac{3y}{5} \times \frac{4y}{5}$

$= 12x^2 - \frac{16}{5}xy + \frac{9}{5}xy - \frac{12}{25}y^2$

$= 12x^2 - \frac{7}{5}xy - \frac{12}{25}y^2$

Column method:

We have,

$$\begin{array}{rl} & 4x + \frac{3y}{5} \\ \times & 3x - \frac{4y}{5} \\ \hline & 12x^2 + \frac{9}{5}xy \\ & \qquad -\frac{16}{5}xy - \frac{12}{25}y^2 \\ \hline & 12x^2 - \frac{7}{5}xy - \frac{12}{25}y^2 \end{array}$$

Multiplying $4x + \frac{3y}{5}$ by $3x$.

Multiplying $4x + \frac{3y}{5}$ by $-\frac{4y}{5}$

Adding the like terms

Example 9 Multiply: $\{2m+(-n)\}$ by $\{-3m+(-5)\}$

Solution *Horizontal Method:*

We have,

$$\{2m+(-n)\}\times\{-3m+(-5)\}$$
$$=(2m-n)\times(-3m-5)$$
$$=2m\times(-3m-5)-n\times(-3m-5)$$
$$=-6m^2-10m+3mn+5n$$

Column method:

We have, $2m+(-n)=2m-n$ and $-3m+(-5)=-3m-5$

$\therefore$ $\quad 2m-n$

$\times\ -3m-5$

$-6m^2+3mn$	Multiplying $2m-n$ by $-3m$
$-10m+5n$	Multiplying $2m-n$ by -5
$-6m^2+3mn-10m+5n$	Adding the like terms

Example 10 Find the product of $\left(y+\frac{2}{7}y^2\right)$ and $(7y-y^2)$ and verify the result for $y=3$.

Solution We have,

$$\left(y+\frac{2}{7}y^2\right)\times(7y-y^2)$$
$$=y\times(7y-y^2)+\frac{2}{7}y^2\times(7y-y^2)$$
$$=y\times7y-y\times y^2+\frac{2}{7}y^2\times7y-\frac{2}{7}y^2\times y^2$$
$$=7y^2-y^3+2y^3-\frac{2}{7}y^4$$
$$=7y^2+y^3-\frac{2}{7}y^4$$

Verification: When $y=3$, we have

$$\text{L.H.S.}=\left(y+\frac{2}{7}y^2\right)\times(7y-y^2)$$
$$=\left(3+\frac{2}{7}\times(3)^2\right)\times(7\times3-(3)^2)$$
$$=\left(3+\frac{2}{7}\times9\right)\times(21-9)$$
$$=\left(3+\frac{18}{7}\right)\times12=\left(\frac{21+18}{7}\right)\times12=\frac{39}{7}\times12=\frac{468}{7}$$

$$\text{R.H.S.}=7y^2+y^3-\frac{2}{7}y^4$$
$$=7\times(3)^2+(3)^3-\frac{2}{7}\times(3)^4$$

$$= 7 \times 9 + 27 - \frac{2}{7} \times 81$$

$$= 63 + 27 - \frac{162}{7} = 90 - \frac{162}{7} = \frac{630 - 162}{7} = \frac{468}{7}$$

$\therefore$ L.H.S. = R.H.S.

Example 11 Find the value of the following products:

(i) $(x + 2y)(x - 2y)$ at $x = 1, y = 0$

(ii) $(3m - 2n)(2m - 3n)$ at $m = 1, n = -1$

(iii) $(4a^2 + 3b)(4a^2 + 3b)$ at $a = 1, b = 2$

Solution (i) We have,

$(x + 2y)(x - 2y)$
$= x(x - 2y) + 2y(x - 2y)$
$= x \times x - x \times 2y + 2y \times x - 2y \times 2y$
$= x^2 - 2xy + 2yx - 4y^2$
$= x^2 - 4y^2$

When $x = 1, y = 0$, we get

$(x + 2y)(x - 2y)$
$= x^2 - 4y^2 = (1)^2 - 4 \times (0)^2 = 1 - 0 = 1.$

(ii) We have,

$(3m - 2n)(2m - 3n)$
$= 3m(2m - 3n) - 2n(2m - 3n)$
$= 3m \times 2m - 3m \times 3n - 2n \times 2m + 2n \times 3n$
$= 6m^2 - 9mn - 4mn + 6n^2$
$= 6m^2 - 13mn + 6n^2$

When $m = 1, n = -1$, we get

$(3m - 2n)(2m - 3n)$
$= 6m^2 - 13mn + 6n^2$
$= 6 \times (1)^2 - 13 \times 1 \times (-1) + 6 \times (-1)^2 = 6 + 13 + 6 = 25$

(iii) We have,

$(4a^2 + 3b)(4a^2 + 3b)$
$= 4a^2 \times (4a^2 + 3b) + 3b \times (4a^2 + 3b)$
$= 4a^2 \times 4a^2 + 4a^2 \times 3b + 3b \times 4a^2 + 3b \times 3b$
$= 16a^4 + 12a^2b + 12a^2b + 9b^2$
$= 16a^4 + 24a^2b + 9b^2$

When, $a = 1, b = 2$, we get

$(4a^2 + 3b)(4a^2 + 3b)$
$= 16a^4 + 24a^2b + 9b^2$

$= 16 \times (1)^4 + 24 \times (1)^2 \times 2 + 9 \times (2)^2$

$= 16 + 48 + 36 = 100$

Example 12 Simplify the following:

(i) $\frac{1}{3}(6x^2 + 15y^2)(6x^2 - 15y^2)$ (ii) $9x^4(2x^3 - 5x^4) \times 5x^6(x^4 - 3x^2)$

Solution (i) We have,

$\frac{1}{3}(6x^2 + 15y^2)(6x^2 - 15y^2)$

$= \left\{\frac{1}{3} \times (6x^2 + 15y^2)\right\} \times (6x^2 - 15y^2)$ [By using associativity of multiplication]

$= \left(\frac{1}{3} \times 6x^2 + \frac{1}{3} \times 15y^2\right) \times (6x^2 - 15y^2)$ [By using distributivity of multiplication over addition]

$= (2x^2 + 5y^2) \times (6x^2 - 15y^2)$

$= 2x^2 \times (6x^2 - 15y^2) + 5y^2 \times (6x^2 - 15y^2)$

$= 2x^2 \times 6x^2 - 2x^2 \times 15y^2 + 5y^2 \times 6x^2 - 5y^2 \times 15y^2$

$= 12x^4 - 30x^2y^2 + 30x^2y^2 - 75y^4$

$= 12x^4 - 75y^4$

(ii) We have,

$9x^4(2x^3 - 5x^4) \times 5x^6(x^4 - 3x^2)$

$= 9x^4 \times (2x^3 - 5x^4) \times 5x^6 \times (x^4 - 3x^2)$

$= \{9x^4 \times (2x^3 - 5x^4)\} \times \{5x^6 \times (x^4 - 3x^2)\}$ [By using associativity of multiplication]

$= (9x^4 \times 2x^3 - 9x^4 \times 5x^4) \times (5x^6 \times x^4 - 5x^6 \times 3x^2)$

$= (18x^7 - 45x^8) \times (5x^{10} - 15x^8)$

$= 18x^7 \times (5x^{10} - 15x^8) - 45x^8(5x^{10} - 15x^8)$

$= 18x^7 \times 5x^{10} - 18x^7 \times 15x^8 - 45x^8 \times 5x^{10} + 45x^8 \times 15x^8$

$= 90x^{17} - 270x^{15} - 225x^{18} + 675x^{16}$

$= -225x^{18} + 90x^{17} + 675x^{16} - 270x^{15}$

Example 13 Simplify the following:

(i) $(2x + 5)(3x - 2) + (x + 2)(2x - 3)$

(ii) $(3x + 2)(2x + 3) - (4x - 3)(2x - 1)$

(iii) $(2x + 3y)(3x + 4y) - (7x + 3y)(x + 2y)$

Solution (i) We have,

$(2x + 5)(3x - 2) + (x + 2)(2x - 3)$

$= 2x(3x - 2) + 5(3x - 2) + x(2x - 3) + 2(2x - 3)$

$= 6x^2 - 4x + 15x - 10 + 2x^2 - 3x + 4x - 6$

$= (6x^2 + 2x^2) + (-4x + 15x - 3x + 4x) + (-10 - 6)$

$= 8x^2 + 12x - 16$

(ii) We have,

$$(3x+2)(2x+3)-(4x-3)(2x-1)$$
$$=\{3x(2x+3)+2(2x+3)\}-\{4x(2x-1)-3(2x-1)\}$$
$$=(6x^2+9x+4x+6)-(8x^2-4x-6x+3)$$
$$=(6x^2+13x+6)-(8x^2-10x+3)$$
$$6x^2+13x+6-8x^2+10x-3$$
$$=-2x^2+23x+3$$

(iii) We have,

$$(2x+3y)(3x+4y)-(7x+3y)(x+2y)$$
$$=\{2x(3x+4y)+3y(3x+4y)-\{7x(x+2y)+3y(x+2y)\}$$
$$=(6x^2+8xy+9xy+12y^2)-(7x^2+14xy+3xy+6y^2)$$
$$=(6x^2+17xy+12y^2)-(7x^2+17xy+6y^2)$$
$$=6x^2+17xy+12y^2-7x^2-17xy-6y^2$$
$$=6x^2-7x^2+17xy-17xy+12y^2-6y^2$$
$$=-x^2+6y^2.$$

Remark *The distributivity of multiplication of literals can be extended to the product of algebraic expressions containing any number of terms, as shown in the following examples.*

Example 14 Multiply: $(2x^2-3x+5)$ by $(5x+2)$.

Solution *Horizontal method:*

We have,

$$(2x^3-3x+5)\times(5x+2)$$
$$=(2x^2-3x+5)\times 5x+(2x^2-3x+5)\times 2$$
$$=(10x^3-15x^2+25x)+(4x^2-6x+10)$$
$$=10x^3-11x^2+19x+10$$

Column Method:

We have,

$$\begin{array}{lrrrr} & & 2x^2 & -3x & +5 \\ \times & & & 5x & +2 \\ \hline & 10x^3 & -15x^2 & +25x & \\ & & +4x^2 & -6x & +10 \\ \hline & 10x^3 & -11x^2 & +19x & +10 \end{array}$$

Multiplying $2x^2-3x+5$ by $5x$

Multiplying $2x^2-3x+5$ by 2

Adding the like terms

Example 15 Multiply: $(2x^2-4x+5)$ by (x^2+3x-7)

Solution *Horizontal method:*

We have,

$$(2x^2-4x+5)\times(x^2+3x-7)$$
$$=2x^2(x^2+3x-7)-4x(x^2+3x-7)+5(x^2+3x-7)$$

$= (2x^4 + 6x^3 - 14x^2) + (-4x^3 - 12x^2 + 28x) + (5x^2 + 15x - 35)$
$= 2x^4 + 6x^3 - 4x^3 - 14x^2 - 12x^2 + 5x^2 + 28x + 15x - 35$
$= 2x^4 + 2x^3 - 21x^2 + 43x - 35$

Column Method:

We have,

$$\begin{array}{rl} 2x^2 - 4x + 5 & \\ \times \quad x^2 + 3x - 7 & \\ \hline 2x^4 - 4x^3 + 5x^2 \qquad\qquad & \text{Multiplying } 2x^2 - 4x + 5 \text{ by } x^2 \\ +6x^3 - 12x^2 + 15x \qquad & \text{Multiplying } 2x^2 - 4x + 5 \text{ by } 3x \\ -14x^2 + 28x - 35 & \text{Multiplying } 2x^2 - 4x + 5 \text{ by } -7 \\ \hline 2x^4 + 2x^3 - 21x^2 + 43x - 35 & \text{Adding the like terms} \end{array}$$

Example 16 Simplify:

(i) $(3x - 2)(x - 1)(3x + 5)$ (ii) $(5 - x)(3 - 2x)(4 - 3x)$

Solution (i) We have,

$(3x - 2)(x - 1)(3x + 5)$
$= \{(3x - 2)(x - 1)\} \times (3x + 5)$ [By Associativity of Multiplication]
$= \{3x(x - 1) - 2(x - 1)\} \times (3x + 5)$
$= (3x^2 - 3x - 2x + 2) \times (3x + 5)$
$= (3x^2 - 5x + 2) \times (3x + 5)$
$= 3x^2 \times (3x + 5) - 5x(3x + 5) + 2 \times (3x + 5)$
$= (9x^3 + 15x^2) + (-15x^2 - 25x) + (6x + 10)$
$= 9x^3 + 15x^2 - 15x^2 - 25x + 6x + 10$
$= 9x^3 - 19x + 10$

(ii) We have,

$(5 - x)(3 - 2x)(4 - 3x)$
$= \{(5 - x)(3 - 2x)\} \times (4 - 3x)$
$= \{5(3 - 2x) - x(3 - 2x)\} \times (4 - 3x)$
$= (15 - 10x - 3x + 2x^2) \times (4 - 3x)$
$= (2x^2 - 13x + 15) \times (4 - 3x)$
$= 2x^2 \times (4 - 3x) - 13x \times (4 - 3x) + 15 \times (4 - 3x)$
$= 8x^2 - 6x^3 - 52x + 39x^2 + 60 - 45x$
$= -6x^3 + 47x^2 - 97x + 60$

EXERCISE 6.5

Multiply:

1. $(5x + 3)$ by $(7x + 2)$
2. $(2x + 8)$ by $(x - 3)$
3. $(7x + y)$ by $(x + 5y)$
4. $(a - 1)$ by $(0.1a^2 + 3)$
5. $(3x^2 + y^2)$ by $(2x^2 + 3y^2)$
6. $\left(\frac{3}{5}x + \frac{1}{2}y\right)$ by $\left(\frac{5}{6}x + 4y\right)$

7. $(x^6 - y^6)$ by $(x^2 + y^2)$

8. $(x^2 + y^2)$ by $(3a + 2b)$

9. $[-3d + (-7f)]$ by $(5d + f)$

10. $(0.8a - 0.5b)$ by $(1.5a - 3b)$

11. $(2x^2y^2 - 5xy^2)$ by $(x^2 - y^2)$

12. $\left(\frac{x}{7} + \frac{x^2}{2}\right)$ by $\left(\frac{2}{5} + \frac{9x}{4}\right)$

13. $\left(-\frac{a}{7} + \frac{a^2}{9}\right)$ by $\left(\frac{b}{2} - \frac{b^2}{3}\right)$

14. $(3x^2y - 5xy^2)$ by $\left(\frac{1}{5}x^2 + \frac{1}{3}y^2\right)$

15. $(2x^2 - 1)$ by $(4x^3 + 5x^2)$

16. $(2xy + 3y^2)(3y^2 - 2)$

Find the following products and verify the result for $x = -1$, $y = -2$:

17. $(3x - 5y)(x + y)$

18. $(x^2y - 1)(3 - 2x^2y)$

19. $\left(\frac{1}{3}x - \frac{y^2}{5}\right)\left(\frac{1}{3}x + \frac{y^2}{5}\right)$

Simplify:

20. $x^2(x + 2y)(x - 3y)$

21. $(x^2 - 2y^2)(x + 4y)x^2y^2$

22. $a^2b^2(a + 2b)(3a + b)$

23. $x^2(x - y)y^2(x + 2y)$

24. $(x^3 - 2x^2 + 5x - 7)(2x - 3)$

25. $(5x + 3)(x - 1)(3x - 2)$

26. $(5 - x)(6 - 5x)(2 - x)$

27. $(2x^2 + 3x - 5)(3x^2 - 5x + 4)$

28. $(3x - 2)(2x - 3) + (5x - 3)(x + 1)$

29. $(5x - 3)(x + 2) - (2x + 5)(4x - 3)$

30. $(3x + 2y)(4x + 3y) - (2x - y)(7x - 3y)$

31. $(x^2 - 3x + 2)(5x - 2) - (3x^2 + 4x - 5)(2x - 1)$

32. $(x^3 - 2x^2 + 3x - 4)(x - 1) - (2x - 3)(x^2 - x + 1)$

ANSWERS

1. $35x^2 + 31x + 6$

2. $2x^2 + 2x - 24$

3. $7x^2 + 36xy + 5y^2$

4. $0.1a^3 - 0.1a^2 + 3a - 3$

5. $6x^4 + 11x^2y^2 + 3y^4$

6. $\frac{1}{2}x^2 + \frac{169}{60}xy + 2y^2$

7. $x^8 + x^6y^2 - x^2y^6 - y^8$

8. $3ax^2 + 3ay^2 + 2bx^2 + 2by^2$

9. $-15d^2 - 38df - 7f^2$

10. $1.2a^2 - 3.15ab + 1.5b^2$

11. $2x^4y^2 - 5x^3y^2 - 2x^2y^4 + 5xy^4$

12. $\frac{9}{8}x^3 + \frac{73}{140}x^2 + \frac{2}{35}x$

13. $-\frac{1}{14}ab + \frac{1}{21}ab^2 + \frac{1}{18}a^2b - \frac{1}{27}a^2b^2$

14. $\frac{3}{5}x^4y - x^3y^2 + x^2y^3 - \frac{5}{3}xy^4$

15. $8x^5 + 10x^4 - 4x^3 - 5x^2$

16. $6xy^3 - 4xy + 9y^4 - 6y^2$

17. $3x^2 - 2xy - 5y^2$

18. $5x^2y - 2x^4y^2 - 3$

19. $\frac{1}{9}x^2 - \frac{1}{25}y^4$

20. $x^4 - x^3y - 6x^2y^2$

21. $x^5y^2 + 4x^4y^3 - 2x^3y^4 - 8x^2y^5$

22. $3a^4b^2 + 7a^3b^3 + 2a^2b^4$

23. $x^4y^2 + x^3y^3 - 2x^2y^4$
24. $2x^4 - 7x^3 + 16x^2 - 29x + 21$
25. $15x^3 - 16x^2 - 5x + 6$
26. $60 - 92x + 41x^2 - 5x^3$
27. $6x^4 - x^3 - 22x^2 + 37x - 20$
28. $11x^2 - 11x + 3$
29. $-3x^2 - 7x + 9$
30. $-2x^2 + 3y^2 + 30xy$
31. $-x^3 - 22x^2 + 30x - 9$
32. $x^4 - 5x^3 + 10x^2 - 12x + 7$

6.6 IDENTITIES

In the previous class, we have studied linear equations in one variable. We have also learnt that an equation contains two algebraic expressions on either side of the equality sign ('='). Consider the equation $3x + 2 = 11$. For $x = 3$, we have, L.H.S. $= 3 \times 3 + 2 = 11$ and R.H.S. $= 11$. Thus, L.H.S. = R.H.S. when $x = 3$. In other words, the equation $3x + 2 = 11$ is true when $x = 3$. Also, it does not hold good for any other value of x. On the other hand, the equality $x + 2x = 3x$ is true for all values of x. This type of equalities are known as identities as defined below.

IDENTITY *An identity is an equality which is true for all values of the variale (s).*

Clearly, an identity implies that the expressions on either side of the equality sign (=) are identical.

6.6.1 STANDARD IDENTITIES

We shall now study three standard identities. These identities are very useful in factorization and simplification of algebraic expressions.

IDENTITY 1 $(a+b)^2 = a^2 + 2ab + b^2$

or, $(a+b)^2 = a^2 + b^2 + 2ab$

i.e., *Square of the sum of two terms*

$=$ *(Square of the first term) + (Square of the second term)*

$+ 2 \times$ *(First term)* $\times$ *(Second term)*

Proof: We have,

$(a+b)^2 = (a+b)(a+b)$ $[\because x^2 = x \times x]$

$\Rightarrow$ $(a+b)^2 = a(a+b) + b(a+b)$ [By distributivity of multiplication over addition]

$\Rightarrow$ $(a+b)^2 = a^2 + ab + ba + b^2$ [By distributivity of multiplication over addition]

$\Rightarrow$ $(a+b)^2 = a^2 + ab + ab + b^2$ $[\because ab = ba]$

$\Rightarrow$ $(a+b)^2 = a^2 + 2ab + b^2$

$\Rightarrow$ $(a+b)^2 = a^2 + b^2 + 2ab$

IDENTITY 2 $(a-b)^2 = a^2 - 2ab + b^2$

or, $(a-b)^2 = a^2 + b^2 - 2ab$

i.e., *Square of the difference of two terms*

$=$ *(Square of the first term) + (Square of the second term)*

$- 2 \times$ *(First term)* $\times$ *(Second term)*

Proof: We have,

$(a-b)^2 = (a-b)(a-b)$ $[\because x^2 = x \times x]$

$\Rightarrow$ $(a-b)^2 = a(a-b) - b(a-b)$ [By distributivity of multiplication over addition]

$\Rightarrow \quad (a-b)^2 = a^2 - ab - ba + b^2$ [By distributivity of multiplication over addition]

$\Rightarrow \quad (a-b)^2 = a^2 - ab - ab + b^2$ $[\because ab = ba]$

$\Rightarrow \quad (a-b)^2 = a^2 - 2ab + b^2$

$\Rightarrow \quad (a-b)^2 = a^2 + b^2 - 2ab$

IDENTITY 3 $(a+b)(a-b) = a^2 - b^2$

i.e., (First term + Second term) (First term – Second term) = (First term)^2 – (Second term)^2

Proof: We have,

$(a+b)(a-b) = a(a-b) + b(a-b)$ [By distributivity of multiplication over addition]

$\Rightarrow \quad (a+b)(a-b) = a^2 - ab + ba - b^2$

$\Rightarrow \quad (a+b)(a-b) = a^2 - ab + ab - b^2$ $[\because ab = ba]$

$\Rightarrow \quad (a+b)(a-b) = a^2 - b^2$

Following examples will illustrate the applications of these identities.

ILLUSTRATIVE EXAMPLES

Example 1 Evaluate: (i) $(2x+3y)^2$ (ii) $(2x-3y)^2$ (iii) $(2x+3y)(2x-3y)$.

Solution (i) We have,

$$(2x^2+3y)^2 = (2x)^2 + 2\times(2x)\times(3y) + (3y)^2 \quad [\text{Using} : (a+b)^2 = a^2+2ab+b^2]$$
$$= 4x^2 + 12xy + 9y^2$$

(ii) We have,

$$(2x-3y)^2 = (2x)^2 - 2\times(2x)\times(3y) + (3y)^2 \quad [\text{Using} : (a-b)^2 = a^2-2ab+b^2]$$
$$= 4x^2 - 12xy + 9y^2$$

(iii) We have,

$$(2x+3y)(2x-3y) = (2x)^2 - (3y)^2 \quad [\text{Using} : (a+b)(a-b) = a^2-b^2]$$
$$= 4x^2 - 9y^2.$$

Example 2 Write down the squares of each of the following binomials:

(i) $\left(x+\frac{a}{2}\right)$ (ii) $\left(5b-\frac{1}{2}\right)$ (iii) $\left(y+\frac{y^2}{2}\right)$

Solution (i) We have,

$$\left(x+\frac{a}{2}\right)^2 = x^2 + 2\times x\times\frac{a}{2} + \left(\frac{a}{2}\right)^2 \quad [\text{Using} : (a+b)^2 = a^2+2ab+b^2]$$
$$= x^2 + xa + \frac{a^2}{4}$$

(ii) We have,

$$\left(5b-\frac{1}{2}\right)^2 = (5b)^2 - 2\times 5b\times\frac{1}{2} + \left(\frac{1}{2}\right)^2 \quad [\text{Using} : (a-b)^2 = a^2-2ab+b^2]$$
$$= 25b^2 - 5b + \frac{1}{4}$$

(iii) We have,

$$\left(y+\frac{y^2}{2}\right)^2 = y^2 + 2\times y\times\frac{y^2}{2}+\left(\frac{y^2}{2}\right)^2$$

$$= y^2 + y^3 + \frac{y^4}{4}$$

Example 3 Find the product of the following binomials:

(i) $\left(\frac{4}{3}x^2+3\right)\left(\frac{4}{3}x^2+3\right)$ (ii) $\left(\frac{2}{3}x^2+5y^2\right)\left(\frac{2}{3}x^2+5y^2\right)$

Solution (i) We have,

$$\left(\frac{4}{3}x^2+3\right)\left(\frac{4}{3}x^2+3\right)$$

$$=\left(\frac{4}{3}x^2+3\right)^2 \qquad [\because a.a=a^2]$$

$$=\left(\frac{4}{3}x^2\right)^2+2\times\frac{4}{3}x^2\times3+(3)^2 \qquad [\text{Using}: (a+b)^2=a^2+2ab+b^2]$$

$$=\frac{16}{9}x^4+8x^2+9$$

(ii) We have,

$$\left(\frac{2}{3}x^2+5y^2\right)\left(\frac{2}{3}x^2+5y^2\right)$$

$$=\left(\frac{2}{3}x^2+5y^2\right)^2 \qquad [\because a.a=a^2]$$

$$=\left(\frac{2}{3}x^2\right)^2+2\times\frac{2}{3}x^2\times5y^2+(5y^2)^2 \qquad [\text{Using}: (a+b)^2=a^2+2ab+b^2]$$

$$=\frac{4}{9}x^4+\frac{20}{3}x^2y^2+25y^4$$

Example 4 Find the product of the following binomials:

(i) $(6x^2-7y^2)(6x^2-7y^2)$ (ii) $\left(\frac{1}{2}x-\frac{1}{5}y\right)\left(\frac{1}{2}x-\frac{1}{5}y\right)$

Solution (i) We have,

$$(6x^2-7y^2)(6y^2-7y^2)$$

$$=(6x^2-7y^2)^2 \qquad [\because a.a=a^2]$$

$$=(6x^2)^2-2\times6x^2\times7y^2+(7y^2)^2$$

$$=36x^4-84x^2y^2+49y^4.$$

Example 5 Find the product of the following binomials:

(i) $\left(\frac{3}{4}x+\frac{5}{6}y\right)\left(\frac{3}{4}x-\frac{5}{6}y\right)$ (ii) $\left(2a+\frac{3}{b}\right)\left(2a-\frac{3}{b}\right)$

(iii) $(a^2+b^2)(-a^2+b^2)$ (iv) $(-a+c)(-a-c)$

Solution (i) We have,

$$\left(\frac{3}{4}x+\frac{5}{6}y\right)\left(\frac{3}{4}x-\frac{5}{6}y\right)$$

$$=\left(\frac{3}{4}x\right)^2-\left(\frac{5}{6}y\right)^2 \qquad [\text{Using}:(a+b)(a-b)=a^2-b^2]$$

$$=\frac{9}{16}x^2-\frac{25}{36}y^2$$

(ii) We have,

$$\left(2a+\frac{3}{b}\right)\left(2a-\frac{3}{b}\right)$$

$$=(2a)^2-\left(\frac{3}{b}\right)^2 \qquad [\text{Using}:(a+b)(a-b)=a^2-b^2]$$

$$=4a^2-\frac{9}{b^2}$$

(iii) We have,

$$(a^2+b^2)(-a^2+b^2)$$

$$=(a^2+b^2)\left\{-(a^2-b^2)\right\}$$

$$=-(a^2+b^2)(a^2-b^2)$$

$$=-\left\{(a^2)^2-(b^2)^2\right\}=-(a^4-b^4)=-a^4+b^4=b^4-a^4$$

(iv) We have,

$$(-a+c)(-a-c)$$

$$=\{-(a-c)\}\{-(a+c)\}$$

$$=(a-c)(a+c)=a^2-c^2$$

Example 6 If $x+\frac{1}{x}=4$, find the values of

(i) $x^2+\frac{1}{x^2}$ (ii) $x^4+\frac{1}{x^4}$

Solution (i) We have,

$$x+\frac{1}{x}=4$$

On squaring both sides, we get

$$\left(x+\frac{1}{x}\right)^2=4^2$$

$$\Rightarrow \quad x^2+2\times x\times\frac{1}{x}+\left(\frac{1}{x}\right)^2=16$$

$$\Rightarrow \quad x^2+2+\frac{1}{x^2}=16$$

$$\Rightarrow \quad x^2+\frac{1}{x^2}=16-2 \qquad [\text{On transposing 2 on RHS}]$$

$$\Rightarrow \quad x^2+\frac{1}{x^2}=14$$

(ii) We have,

$$x^2 + \frac{1}{x^2} = 14$$

On squaring both sides, we get

$$\left(x^2 + \frac{1}{x^2}\right)^2 = 14^2$$

$$\Rightarrow \quad (x^2)^2 + \left(\frac{1}{x^2}\right)^2 + 2 \times x^2 \times \frac{1}{x^2} = 196$$

$$\Rightarrow \quad x^4 + \frac{1}{x^4} + 2 = 196$$

$$\Rightarrow \quad x^4 + \frac{1}{x^4} = 196 - 2$$ [On transposing 2 on RHS]

$$\Rightarrow \quad x^4 + \frac{1}{x^4} = 194$$

Example 7 If $x - \frac{1}{x} = 9$, find the value of $x^2 + \frac{1}{x^2}$.

Solution We have,

$$x - \frac{1}{x} = 9$$

On squaring both sides, we get

$$\left(x - \frac{1}{x}\right)^2 = 81$$

$$\Rightarrow \quad x^2 - 2 \times x \times \frac{1}{x} + \left(\frac{1}{x}\right)^2 = 81$$

$$\Rightarrow \quad x^2 - 2 + \frac{1}{x^2} = 81$$

$$\Rightarrow \quad x^2 + \frac{1}{x^2} = 81 + 2$$ [On transposing – 2 on RHS]

$$\Rightarrow \quad x^2 + \frac{1}{x^2} = 83$$

Example 8 If $x - \frac{1}{x} = 9$, find $x + \frac{1}{x}$.

Solution We have,

$$x - \frac{1}{x} = 9$$

$$\Rightarrow \quad \left(x - \frac{1}{x}\right)^2 = 9^2$$ [On squaring both sides]

$$\Rightarrow \quad x^2 + \frac{1}{x^2} - 2x \times \frac{1}{x} = 81$$

$$\Rightarrow \quad x^2 + \frac{1}{x^2} - 2 = 81$$

$$\Rightarrow \quad x^2 + \frac{1}{x^2} = 83 \quad \text{...(i)}$$

Now, $$\left(x + \frac{1}{x}\right)^2 = x^2 + \frac{1}{x^2} + 2x \times \frac{1}{x}$$

$$\Rightarrow \quad \left(x + \frac{1}{x}\right)^2 = 83 + 2 \quad \text{[Using (i)]}$$

$$\Rightarrow \quad \left(x + \frac{1}{x}\right)^2 = 85$$

$$\Rightarrow \quad x + \frac{1}{x} = \pm\sqrt{85}$$

Example 9 If $x^2 + \frac{1}{x^2} = 27$, find the values of each of the following:

(i) $x + \frac{1}{x}$ (ii) $x - \frac{1}{x}$

Solution (i) We have,

$$\left(x + \frac{1}{x}\right)^2 = x^2 + 2 \times x \times \frac{1}{x} + \frac{1}{x^2}$$

$$\Rightarrow \quad \left(x + \frac{1}{x}\right)^2 = x^2 + 2 + \frac{1}{x^2}$$

$$\Rightarrow \quad \left(x + \frac{1}{x}\right)^2 = x^2 + \frac{1}{x^2} + 2$$

$$\Rightarrow \quad \left(x + \frac{1}{x}\right)^2 = 27 + 2 \quad \left[\because x^2 + \frac{1}{x^2} = 27 \text{ (given)}\right]$$

$$\Rightarrow \quad \left(x + \frac{1}{x}\right)^2 = 29$$

$$\Rightarrow \quad x + \frac{1}{x} = \pm\sqrt{29} \quad \text{[Taking square root of both sides]}$$

(ii) We have,

$$\left(x - \frac{1}{x}\right)^2 = x^2 - 2 \times x \times \frac{1}{x} + \left(\frac{1}{x}\right)^2$$

$$\Rightarrow \quad \left(x - \frac{1}{x}\right)^2 = x^2 - 2 + \frac{1}{x}$$

$$\Rightarrow \quad \left(x - \frac{1}{x}\right)^2 = x^2 + \frac{1}{x^2} - 2$$

$\Rightarrow \quad \left(x - \frac{1}{x}\right)^2 = 27 - 2$ $\quad \left[\because x^2 + \frac{1}{x^2} = 27 \text{ (given)}\right]$

$\Rightarrow \quad \left(x - \frac{1}{x}\right)^2 = 25$

$\Rightarrow \quad \left(x - \frac{1}{x}\right)^2 = 5^2$

$\Rightarrow \quad x - \frac{1}{x} = \pm 5$ [Taking square root of both sides]

Example 10 If $x + y = 12$ and $xy = 14$, find the value of $x^2 + y^2$.

Solution We have,

$(x + y)^2 = x^2 + y^2 + 2xy$

Putting the values of $x + y$ and xy, we obtain

$12^2 = x^2 + y^2 + 2 \times 14$

$\Rightarrow \quad 144 = x^2 + y^2 + 28$

$\Rightarrow \quad 144 - 28 = x^2 + y^2$

$\Rightarrow \quad x^2 + y^2 = 116$

Example 11 If $3x + 2y = 12$ and $xy = 6$, find the value of $9x^2 + 4y^2$.

Solution We have,

$(3x + 2y)^2 = (3x)^2 + (2y)^2 + 2 \times 3x \times 2y$

$\Rightarrow \quad (3x + 2y)^2 = 9x^2 + 4y^2 + 12xy$

$\Rightarrow \quad 12^2 = 9x^2 + 4y^2 + 12 \times 6$ [Putting $3x + 2y = 12$ and $xy = 6$]

$\Rightarrow \quad 144 = 9x^2 + 4y^2 + 72$

$\Rightarrow \quad 144 - 72 = 9x^2 + 4y^2$

$\Rightarrow \quad 9x^2 + 4y^2 = 72$

Example 12 If $4x^2 + y^2 = 40$ and $xy = 6$, find the value of $2x + y$.

Solution We have,

$(2x + y)^2 = (2x)^2 + y^2 + 2 \times 2x \times y$

$\Rightarrow \quad (2x + y)^2 = (4x^2 + y^2) + 4xy$

$\Rightarrow \quad (2x + y)^2 = 40 + 4 \times 6$ [Using $4x^2 + y^2 = 40$ and $xy = 6$]

$\Rightarrow \quad (2x + y)^2 = 64$

$\Rightarrow \quad 2x + y = \pm\sqrt{64}$

$\Rightarrow \quad 2x + y = \pm 8$ [Taking square root of both sides]

Example 13 Find the continued product:

(i) $(x + 2)(x - 2)(x^2 + 4)$

(ii) $(2x + 3y)(2x - 3y)(4x^2 + 9y^2)$

(iii) $(x - 1)(x + 1)(x^2 + 1)(x^4 + 1)$

(iv) $\left(x - \frac{1}{x}\right)\left(x + \frac{1}{x}\right)\left(x^2 + \frac{1}{x^2}\right)\left(x^4 + \frac{1}{x^4}\right)$

(v) $\left(x - \frac{y}{5} - 1\right)\left(x + \frac{y}{5} + 1\right)$

Solution (i) We have,

$(x+2)(x-2)(x^2+4)$

$=\{(x+2)(x-2)\}(x^2+4)$ [By associativity of multiplication]

$=(x^2-2^2)(x^2+4)$ [$\because (a+b)(a-b)=a^2-b^2$]

$=(x^2-4)(x^2+4)$

$=(x^2)^2-4^2$ [$\because (a+b)(a-b)=a^2-b^2$]

$=x^4-16$

(ii) We have,

$(2x+3y)(2x-3y)(4x^2+9y^2)$

$=\{(2x+3y)(2x-3y)\}(4x^2+9y^2)$

$=\{(2x+3y)(2x-3y)\}(4x^2+9y^2)$

$=\left\{(2x)^2-(3y)^2\right\}(4x^2+9y^2)$ [Using :$(a+b)(a-b)=a^2-b^2$]

$=(4x^2-9y^2)(4x^2+9y^2)$

$=(4x^2)^2-(9y^2)^2$ [Using :$(a+b)(a-b)=a^2-b^2$]

$=16x^4-81y^4.$

(iii) We have,

$(x-1)(x+1)(x^2+1)(x^4+1)$

$=\left\{(x-1)(x+1)\right\}(x^2+1)(x^4+1)$

$=(x^2-1)(x^2+1)(x^4+1)$

$=\left\{(x^2-1)(x^2+1)\right\}(x^4+1)$

$=\left\{(x^2)^2-1^2\right\}(x^4+1)$

$=(x^4-1)(x^4+1)$

$=\left\{(x^4)^2-1^2\right\}$

$=x^8-1$

(iv) We have

$\left(x-\frac{1}{x}\right)\left(x+\frac{1}{x}\right)\left(x^2+\frac{1}{x^2}\right)\left(x^4+\frac{1}{x^4}\right)$

$=\left\{\left(x-\frac{1}{x}\right)\left(x+\frac{1}{x}\right)\right\}\left(x^2+\frac{1}{x^2}\right)\left(x^4+\frac{1}{x^4}\right)$

$=\left(x^2-\frac{1}{x^2}\right)\left(x^2+\frac{1}{x^2}\right)\left(x^4+\frac{1}{x^4}\right)$

$=\left\{(x^2)^2-\left(\frac{1}{x^2}\right)^2\right\}\left(x^4+\frac{1}{x^4}\right)$

$=\left(x^4-\frac{1}{x^4}\right)\left(x^4+\frac{1}{x^4}\right)$

$=(x^4)^2-\left(\frac{1}{x^4}\right)^2$

$=x^8-\frac{1}{x^8}$

(v) We have,

$$\left(x-\frac{y}{5}-1\right)\left(x+\frac{y}{5}+1\right)$$

$$=\left\{x-\left(\frac{y}{5}+1\right)\right\}\left\{x+\left(\frac{y}{5}+1\right)\right\}$$

$$=x^2-\left(\frac{y}{5}+1\right)^2$$

$$=x^2-\left(\frac{y^2}{25}+\frac{2y}{5}+1\right)$$

$$=x^2-\frac{y^2}{25}-\frac{2y}{5}-1$$

Example 14 Simplify the following products:

(i) $(x^2+x+1)(x^2-x+1)$ (ii) $(x^2+2x+2)(x^2-2x+2)$

Solution (i) We have,

$$(x^2+x+1)(x^2-x+1)$$

$$=\{(x^2+1)+x\}\{(x^2+1)-x\}$$

$$=(x^2+1)^2-x^2$$

$$=x^4+2x^2+1-x^2$$

$$=x^4+x^2+1$$

(ii) We have,

$$(x^2+2x+2)(x^2-2x+2)$$

$$=\{(x^2+2)+2x\}\{(x^2+2)-2x\}$$

$$=(x^2+2)^2-(2x)^2$$

$$=x^4+2x^2+4-4x^2$$

$$=x^4-2x^2+4$$

Example 15 Prove that:

$$2a^2+2b^2+2c^2-2ab-2bc-2ca=(a-b)^2+(b-c)^2+c-a)^2$$

Solution We have,

$$\text{LHS}=2a^2+2b^2+2c^2-2ab-2bc-2ca$$

$$=(a^2-2ab+b^2)+(b^2-2bc+c^2)+(c^2-2ca+a^2) \quad \text{[Re-arranging the terms]}$$

$$=(a-b)^2+(b-c)^2+(c-a)^2$$

$$=\text{R.H.S.}$$

Hence, $2a^2+2b^2+2c^2-2ab-2bc-2ca=(a-b)^2+(b-c)^2+(c-a)^2$

Example 16 If $a^2+b^2+c^2-ab-bc-ca=0$, prove that $a=b=c$.

Solution We have,

$$a^2+b^2+c^2-ab-bc-ca=0$$

$$\Rightarrow \quad 2a^2+2b^2+2c^2-2ab-2bc-2ca=2\times 0 \quad \text{[Multiplying both sides by 2]}$$

$$\Rightarrow \quad (a^2-2b+b^2)+(b^2-2bc+c^2)+(c^2-2ac+a^2)=0$$

$\Rightarrow \quad (a-b)^2+(b-c)^2+(c-a)^2=0$

$\Rightarrow \quad a-b=0, b-c=0, c-a=0$ [∵ Sum of positive quantities is zero if and only if each quantity is zero]

$\Rightarrow \quad a=b, b=c$ and $c=a$

$\Rightarrow \quad a=b=c.$

Example 17 Using the formulae for squaring a binomial, evaluate the following:

(i) $(101)^2$ (ii) $(99)^2$ (iii) $(93)^2$

Solution We have,

(i) $(101)^2 = (100+1)^2$

$= (100)^2 + 2\times100\times1+(1)^2$ [Using : $(a+b)^2 = a^2+2ab+b^2$]

$= 10000+200+1$

$= 10201$

(ii) $(99)^2 = (100-1)^2$

$= (100)^2 - 2\times100\times1+(1)^2$ [Using : $(a-b)^2 = a^2-2ab+b^2$]

$= 10000-200+1$

$= 9801$

(iii) $(93)^2 = (90+3)^2$

$= (90)^2+2\times90\times3+(3)^2$

$= 8100+540+9$

$= 8649$

Example 18 Simplify the following by using: $(a+b)(a-b)=a^2-b^2$.

(i) 68×72 (ii) 101×99 (iii) 67×73 (iv) 128^2-77^2

Solution (i) We have,

$$\frac{68+72}{2}=70$$

So, we express 68 and 72 in terms of 70.

$\therefore \quad 68\times72 = (70-2)\times(70+2) = (70)^2-2^2 = 4900-4 = 4896$

(ii) We have,

$$\frac{101+99}{2}=100$$

So, we express 101 and 99 in terms of 100.

$101\times99 = (100+1)\times(100-1) = (100)^2-1^2 = 10000-1 = 9999$

(iii) We have,

$$\frac{67+73}{2}=70$$

So, we express 67 and 73 in terms of 70.

$67\times73 = (70-3)\times(70+3) = (70)^2-(3)^2 = 4900-9 = 4891$

(iv) We have,

$128^2-77^2 = (128+77)\times(128-77) = 205\times51 = 10455$

Example 19 Find the value of x, if

(i) $6x = 23^2 - 17^2$ (ii) $4x = 98^2 - 88^2$ (iii) $25x = 536^2 - 136^2$

Solution (i) We have,

$6x = 23^2 - 17^2$

$\Rightarrow\ 6x = (23+17)\times(23-17)$ [Using : $a^2 - b^2 = (a+b)(a-b)$]

$\Rightarrow\ 6x = 40\times 6$

$\Rightarrow\ \frac{6x}{6} = \frac{40\times 6}{6}$ [Dividing both sides by 6]

$\Rightarrow\ x = 40$

(ii) We have,

$4x = 98^2 - 88^2$

$\Rightarrow\ 4x = (98+88)\times(98-88)$ [Using : $a^2 - b^2 = (a+b)(a-b)$]

$\Rightarrow\ 4x = 186\times 10$

$\Rightarrow\ \frac{4x}{4} = \frac{186\times 10}{4}$ [Dividing both sides by 4]

$\Rightarrow\ x = \frac{1860}{4}$

$\Rightarrow\ x = 465$

(iii) We have,

$25x = 536^2 - 136^2$

$\Rightarrow\ 25x = (536+136)\times(536-136)$ [Using : $a^2 - b^2 = (a+b)(a-b)$]

$\Rightarrow\ 25x = 672\times 400$

$\Rightarrow\ \frac{25x}{25} = \frac{672\times 400}{25}$ [Dividing both sides by 25]

$\Rightarrow\ x = 672\times 16$

$\Rightarrow\ x = 10752$

Example 20 What must be added to $9x^2 - 24x + 10$ to make it a whole square?

Solution We have,

$9x^2 - 24x + 10 = (3x)^2 - 2\times 3x\times 4 + 10$

It is evident from the above expression that

First term = $3x$ and, Second term = 4

To make the given expression a whole square, we must have $(4)^2 = 16$ in place of 10.

Hence, we must add 6 to it to make a perfect square.

Adding and subtracting 6, we get

$$9x^2 - 24x + 10 + 6 - 6 = 9x^2 - 24x + 16 - 6$$

$$= (3x-4)^2 - 6$$

EXERCISE 6.6

1. Write the following squares of binomials as trinomials:

(i) $(x+2)^2$ (ii) $(8a+3b)^2$ (iii) $(2m+1)^2$ (iv) $\left(9a+\frac{1}{6}\right)^2$

(v) $\left(x+\frac{x^2}{2}\right)^2$ (vi) $\left(\frac{x}{4}-\frac{y}{3}\right)^2$ (vii) $\left(3x-\frac{1}{3x}\right)^2$ (viii) $\left(\frac{x}{y}-\frac{y}{x}\right)^2$

(ix) $\left(\frac{3a}{2}-\frac{5b}{4}\right)^2$ (x) $(a^2b-bc^2)^2$ (xi) $\left(\frac{2a}{3b}+\frac{2b}{3a}\right)^2$ (xii) $(x^2-ay)^2$

2. Find the product of the following binomials:

(i) $(2x+y)(2x+y)$ (ii) $(a+2b)(a-2b)$ (iii) $(a^2+bc)(a^2-bc)$

(iv) $\left(\frac{4x}{5}-\frac{3y}{4}\right)\left(\frac{4x}{5}+\frac{3y}{4}\right)$ (v) $\left(2x+\frac{3}{y}\right)\left(2x-\frac{3}{y}\right)$ (vi) $(2a^3+b^3)(2a^3-b^3)$

(vii) $\left(x^4+\frac{2}{x^2}\right)\left(x^4-\frac{2}{x^2}\right)$ (viii) $\left(x^3+\frac{1}{x^3}\right)\left(x^3-\frac{1}{x^3}\right)$

3. Using the formula for squaring a binomial, evaluate the following:

(i) $(102)^2$ (ii) $(99)^2$ (iii) $(1001)^2$ (iv) $(999)^2$ (v) $(703)^2$

4. Simplify the following using the formula: $(a-b)(a+b)=a^2-b^2$:

(i) $(82)^2-(18)^2$ (ii) $(467)^2-(33)^2$ (iii) $(79)^2-(69)^2$ (iv) 197×203

(v) 113×87 (vi) 95×105 (vii) 1.8×2.2 (viii) 9.8×10.2

5. Simplify the following using the identities:

(i) $\frac{58^2-42^2}{16}$ (ii) $178\times 178-22\times 22$ (iii) $\frac{198\times 198-102\times 102}{96}$

(iv) $1.73\times 1.73-0.27\times 0.27$ (v) $\frac{8.63\times 8.63-1.37\times 1.37}{0.726}$

6. Find the value of x, if:

(i) $4x=(52)^2-(48)^2$ (ii) $14x=(47)^2-(33)^2$ (iii) $5x=(50)^2-(40)^2$

7. If $x+\frac{1}{x}=20$, find the value of $x^2+\frac{1}{x^2}$.

8. If $x-\frac{1}{x}=3$, find the values of $x^2+\frac{1}{x^2}$ and $x^4+\frac{1}{x^4}$.

9. If $x^2+\frac{1}{x^2}=18$, find the values of $x+\frac{1}{x}$ and $x-\frac{1}{x}$.

10. If $x+y=4$ and $xy=2$, find the value of x^2+y^2

11. If $x-y=7$ and $xy=9$, find the value of x^2+y^2

12. If $3x + 5y = 11$ and $xy = 2$, find the value of $9x^2 + 25y^2$

13. Find the values of the following expressions:

 (i) $16x^2 + 24x + 9$, when $x = \frac{7}{4}$

 (ii) $64x^2 + 81y^2 + 144xy$, when $x = 11$ and $y = \frac{4}{3}$

 (iii) $81x^2 + 16y^2 - 72xy$, when $x = \frac{2}{3}$ and $y = \frac{3}{4}$

14. If $x + \frac{1}{x} = 9$, find the value of $x^4 + \frac{1}{x^4}$.

15. If $x + \frac{1}{x} = 12$, find the value of $x - \frac{1}{x}$.

16. If $2x + 3y = 14$ and $2x - 3y = 2$, find the value of xy.

 [Hint: Use $(2x + 3y)^2 - (2x - 3y)^2 = 24xy$]

17. If $x^2 + y^2 = 29$ and $xy = 2$, find the value of

 (i) $x + y$ (ii) $x - y$ (iii) $x^4 + y^4$

18. What must be added to each of the following expressions to make it a whole square?

 (i) $4x^2 - 12x + 7$ (ii) $4x^2 - 20x + 20$

19. Simplify:

 (i) $(x - y)(x + y)(x^2 + y^2)(x^4 + y^4)$ (ii) $(2x - 1)(2x + 1)(4x^2 + 1)(16x^4 + 1)$

 (iii) $(7m - 8n)^2 + (7m + 8n)^2$ (iv) $(2.5p - 1.5q)^2 - (1.5p - 2.5q)^2$

 (v) $(m^2 - n^2m)^2 + 2m^3n^2$

20. Show that:

 (i) $(3x + 7)^2 - 84x = (3x - 7)^2$ (ii) $(9a - 5b)^2 + 180ab = (9a + 5b)^2$

 (iii) $\left(\frac{4m}{3} - \frac{3n}{4}\right)^2 + 2mn = \frac{16m^2}{9} + \frac{9n^2}{16}$ (iv) $(4pq + 3q)^2 - (4pq - 3q)^2 = 48pq^2$

 (v) $(a - b)(a + b) + (b - c)(b + c) + (c - a)(c + a) = 0$

ANSWERS

1. (i) $x^2 + 4x + 4$ (ii) $64a^2 + 48ab + 9b^2$ (iii) $4m^2 + 4m + 1$ (iv) $81a^2 + 3a + \frac{1}{36}$

 (v) $x^2 + x^3 + \frac{x^4}{4}$ (vi) $\frac{x^2}{16} - \frac{xy}{6} + \frac{y^2}{9}$ (vii) $9x^2 - 2 + \frac{1}{9x^2}$ (viii) $\frac{x^2}{y^2} - 2 + \frac{y^2}{x^2}$

 (ix) $\frac{9a^2}{4} - \frac{15}{4}ab + \frac{25}{16}b^2$ (x) $a^4b^2 - 2a^2b^2c^2 + b^2c^4$

 (xi) $\frac{4a^2}{9b^2} + \frac{8}{9} + \frac{4b^2}{9a^2}$ (xii) $x^4 - 2x^2ay + a^2y^2$

2. (i) $4x^2+4xy+y^2$ (ii) a^2-4b^2 (iii) $a^4-b^2c^2$ (iv) $\frac{16}{25}x^2-\frac{9}{16}y^2$
(v) $4x^2-\frac{9}{y^2}$ (vi) $4a^6-b^6$ (vii) $x^8-\frac{4}{x^4}$ (viii) $x^6-\frac{1}{x^6}$

3. (i) 10404 (ii) 9801 (iii) 1002001 (iv) 998001 (v) 494209

4. (i) 6400 (ii) 217000 (iii) 1480 (iv) 39991 (v) 9831 (vi) 9975
(vii) 3.96 (viii) 99.96

5. (i) 100 (ii) 31200 (iii) 300 (iv) 2.92 (v) 100

6. (i) 100 (ii) 80 (iii) 180

7. 398 8. (i) 11, 119 9. $\sqrt{20}, 4$ 10. 12 11. 67 12. 61

13. (i) 100 (ii) 10000 (iii) 9

14. 6239 15. $\pm\sqrt{140}$ 16. 8 17. (i) $\pm\sqrt{33}$ (ii) ± 5 (iii) 833

18. (i) 2 (ii) 5 19. (i) x^8-y^8 (ii) $256x^8-1$ (iii) $98m^2+128n^2$ (iv) $4(p^2-q^2)$
(v) $m^4+m^2n^4$

6.6.2 A SPECIAL PRODUCT

We have,

$$\begin{aligned}(x+a)(x+b) &= x(x+b)+a(x+b) && \text{[By distributitivity]}\\ &= x^2+xb+ax+ab && \text{[By distributitivity]}\\ &= x^2+bx+ax+ab && [\because xb = bx]\\ &= x^2+ax+bx+ab && [\because bx+ax = ax+bx]\\ &= x^2+(a+b)x+ab\end{aligned}$$

Thus, we have the following identity:

$$(x+a)(x+b) = x^2+(a+b)x+ab$$

Using this identity, we can derive the following results:

(i) $$\begin{aligned}(x+a)(x-b) &= (x+a)\{x+(-b)\}\\ &= x^2+\{a+(-b)\}x+a(-b)\\ &= x^2+(a-b)x-ab\end{aligned}$$

$\therefore$ $(x+a)(x-b) = x^2+(a-b)x-ab$

(ii) $$\begin{aligned}(x-a)(x+b) &= \{x+(-a)\}(x+b)\\ &= x^2+\{(-a)+b\}x+(-a)b\\ &= x^2+(b-a)x-ab\end{aligned}$$

$\therefore$ $(x-a)(x+b) = x^2+(b-a)x-ab$

(iii) $$\begin{aligned}(x-a)(x-b) &= \{x+(-a)\}\{x-(-b)\}\\ &= x^2+\{(-a)+(-b)\}x+(-a)(-b)\end{aligned}$$

$\therefore$ $(x-a)(x-b) = x^2-(a+b)x+ab$

Following examples exhibit the use of these identities in simplifying and evaluating algebraic expressions.

ILLUSTRATIVE EXAMPLES

Example 1 Find the following products:

(i) $(x+2)(x+3)$ (ii) $(x+7)(x-2)$ (iii) $(y-4)(y-3)$

(iv) $(y-7)(y+3)$ (v) $(2x-3)(2x+5)$ (iv) $(3x+4)(3x-5)$

Solution Using the identity: $(x+a)(x+b)=x^2+(a+b)x+ab$, we have

(i) $(x+2)(x+3)=x^2+(2+3)x+2\times 3$

$=x^2+5x+6$

(ii) $(x+7)(x-2)=(x+7)\{x+(-2)\}$

$=x^2+\{7+(-2)\}x+7\times -2$

$=x^2+5x-14$

(iii) $(y-4)(y-3)=\{y+(-4)\}\{y+(-3)\}$

$=y^2+\{(-4)+(-3)\}y+(-4)\times(-3)$

$=y^2-7y+12$

(iv) $(y-7)(y+3)=\{y+(-7)\}(y+3)$

$=y^2+\{(-7)+3\}y+(-7)\times 3$

$=y^2-4y-21$

(v) $(2x-3)(2x+5)=(y-3)(y+5)$, where $y=2x$

$=\{y+(-3)\}(y+5)$

$=y^2+\{(-3)+5\}y+(-3)\times 5$

$=y^2-y-20$

$=(3x)^2-3x-20$

$=9x^2-3x-20.$

Example 2 Evaluate the following:

(i) 107×103 (ii) 56×48 (iii) 95×97

Solution Using the identity: $(x+a)(x+b)=x^2+(a+b)x+ab$ we have

(i) $107\times 103=(100+7)\times(100+3)$

$=(100)^2+(7+3)\times 100+7\times 3$

$=10000+10\times 100+21$

$=10000+1000+21$

$=11021$

(ii) $56\times 48=(50+6)\times(50-2)$

$=(50+6)\times\{50+(-2)\}$

$=(50)^2+\{6+(-2)\}\times 50+6\times -2$

$=2500+4\times 50-12$

$=2500+200-12$

$=2700-12$

$=2688$

(iii) $95 \times 97 = (100-5) \times (100-3)$

$= \{100+(-5)\} \times \{100+(-3)\}$

$= (100)^2 + \{(-5)+(-3)\} \times 100 + (-5) \times (-3)$

$= 10000 - 8 \times 100 + 15$

$= 10000 - 800 + 15$

$= 9215$

EXERCISE 6.7

1. Find the following products:

(i) $(x+4)(x+7)$ (ii) $(x-11)(x+4)$ (iii) $(x+7)(x-5)$

(iv) $(x-3)(x-2)$ (v) $(y^2-4)(y^2-3)$ (vi) $\left(x+\frac{4}{3}\right)\left(x+\frac{3}{4}\right)$

(vii) $(3x+5)(3x+11)$ (viii) $(2x^2-3)(2x^2+5)$

(ix) $(z^2+2)(z^2-3)$ (x) $(3x-4y)(2x-4y)$

(xi) $(3x^2-4xy)(3x^2-3xy)$ (xii) $\left(x+\frac{1}{5}\right)(x+5)$

(xiii) $\left(z+\frac{3}{4}\right)\left(z+\frac{4}{3}\right)$ (xiv) $(x^2+4)(x^2+9)$

(xv) $(y^2+12)(y^2+6)$ (xvi) $\left(y^2+\frac{5}{7}\right)\left(y^2-\frac{14}{5}\right)$

(xvii) $(p^2+16)\left(p^2-\frac{1}{4}\right)$

2. Evaluate the following:

(i) 102×106 (ii) 109×107 (iii) 35×37 (iv) 53×55

(v) 103×96 (vi) 34×36 (vii) 994×1006

ANSWERS

1. (i) $x^2+11x+28$ (ii) $x^2-7x-44$ (iii) $x^2+2x-35$ (iv) x^2-5x+6

(v) y^4-y^2-12 (vi) $x^2+\frac{25}{12}x+1$ (vii) $9x^2+48x+55$ (viii) $4x^4+4x^2-15$

(ix) z^4-z^2-6 (x) $6x^2-20xy+16y^2$ (xi) $9x^4-21x^3y+12x^2y^2$ (xii) $x^2+\frac{26}{5}x+1$

(xiii) $z^2+\frac{25}{12}z+1$ (xiv) x^4+13x^2+36 (xv) y^4+18y^2+72 (xvi) $y^4-\frac{73}{35}y^2-2$

(xvii) $p^4+\frac{63}{4}p^2-4$

2. (i) 10812 (ii) 11663 (iii) 1295 (iv) 2915

(v) 9888 (vi) 1224 (vii) 999964

6.7 ACTIVITIES FOR VERIFYING THE IDENTITIES

As we know that the area of a square is the square of its side and that of a rectangle is the product of its length and breadth. We use these results to represent algebraic terms geometrically. If x is the length of a side of a square, then its area is x^2. So, geometrically the term x^2 is represented by the area of a square of side x units.

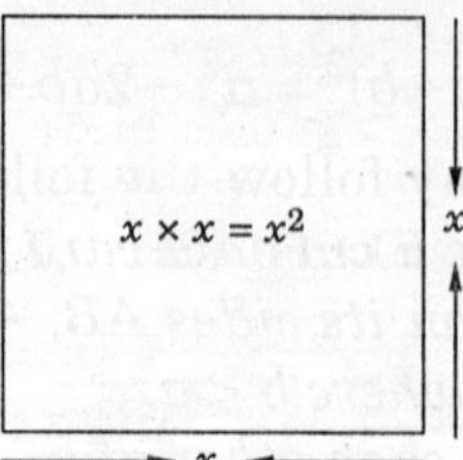

If length and breadth of a rectangle are x and y, then its area is xy. So, term xy is represented geometrically by a rectangle of dimensions x and y units.

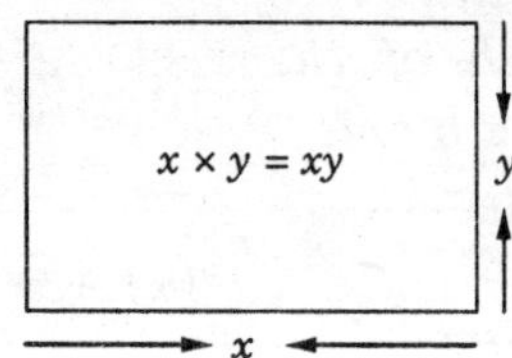

Let us now see how these results help us in verifying algebraic identities.

ACTIVITY1 *Verification of identity:* $(a+b)^2 = a^2 + 2ab + b^2$

In order to verify the identity $(a+b)^2 = a^2 + 2ab + b^2$, we follow the following steps:

<u>Step I</u> *Draw a square ABCD of side a cm on a card board paper.*

<u>Step II</u> *Extend the sides AB and AD by b cms, to get the points E and F.*

Clearly, BE = DF = b cm.

<u>Step III</u> *Complete the square AEGF.*

<u>Step IV</u> *Produce BC and DC to intersect sides FG and EG at H and I respectively.*

<u>Step V</u> *Cut the square along BH and DI to get two squares ABCD and CIGH of sides a cm and b cm respectively and two rectangles BCIE and DFHC each of dimensions a cm and b cm.*

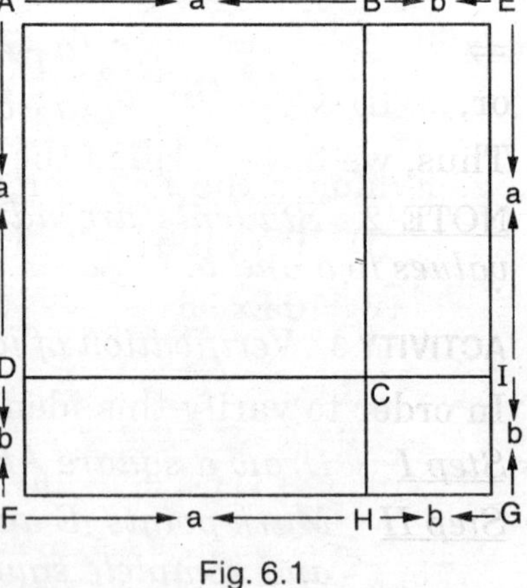

Fig. 6.1

Clearly,

Area of square $ABCD = a^2$, Area of square $CIGH = b^2$

Area of rectangle $BCIE = ab$, Area of rectangle $DFHC = ab$

and, Area of square $AEGF = (a + b)^2$

Since square $AEGF$ is cut into four pieces (two squares and two rectangles.

$\therefore$ Area of square $AEGF$ = Area of square $ABCD$ + Area of rectangle $BCIE$ + Area of square $CIGH$ + Area of rectangle $DFHC$

$$\Rightarrow \quad (a+b)^2 = a^2 + ab + b^2 + ab$$

or, $(a+b)^2 = a^2 + 2ab + b^2$

Thus we have verified the identity $(a+b)^2 = a^2 + 2ab + b^2$ through an activity.

NOTE 1 *Students are advised to take any numeric values of a and b and verify the above identity for those values.*

ACTIVITY 2 *Verification of identity:* $(a-b)^2 = a^2 - 2ab + b^2$

In order to verify this identity, we may follow the following steps:

Step I *Draw a square ABCD of side a cm on a card board paper.*

Step II *Mark points E, F, G and H on its sides AB, AD, CD and CB respectively such that $BE = DF = CG = CH = b$ cm, where $b < a$.*

Step III *Join EG and FH to intersect each other at I.*

Step IV *Cut out the square AEIF.*

Clearly, $AE = AB - BE = (a-b)$ cm.

So, length of each side of square AEIF is $(a-b)$ cm and dimensions of each of the rectangles BCGE and CDFH are a cm × b cm.

$\therefore$ *Area of square AEIF* $= (a-b)^2$

Area of square ABCD $= a^2$

and, *Area of L-shaped shaded part*

$= BC \times BE + DG \times DF$

$= ab + (a-b)\,b$

$= ab + ab - b^2$

$= 2ab - b^2$

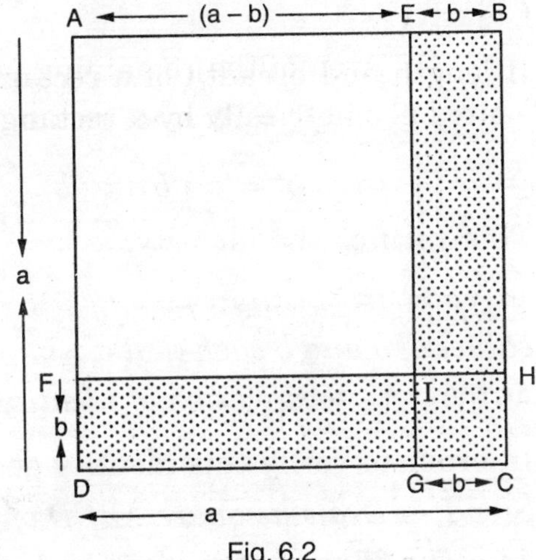

Fig. 6.2

Clearly,

Area of square *AEIF* = Area of square *ABCD* – Area of *L*-shaped shaded part

$\Rightarrow$ $(a-b)^2 = a^2 - (2ab - b^2)$

or, $(a-b)^2 = a^2 - 2ab + b^2$

Thus, we have verified the identity through an activity.

NOTE 2 *Students are advised to verify the identity by giving different sets of numeric values to a and b.*

ACTIVITY 3 *Verification of identity:* $a^2 - b^2 = (a+b)(a-b)$

In order to varify this identity, we may follow following steps:

Step I *Draw a square ABCD of side a cm on a card-board paper.*

Step II *Mark points, E and G on sides AB and AD such that $AE = AG = b$ cm, where $b < a$ and complete square AEFG.*

Step III *Cut out the square AEFG.*

Clearly,

Area of the remaining portion = Area of square ABCD – Area of square AEFG

$= a^2 - b^2$

Step IV *Cut out the remaining portion of the square along CF and put the portion CDFG in such a way that the positions of C and F are interchanged as shown in Fig. 6.3. This gives us a rectangle BEDG as shown in Fig. 6.3 such that $BE = a - b$ and $BG = BC + FG = a + b$.*

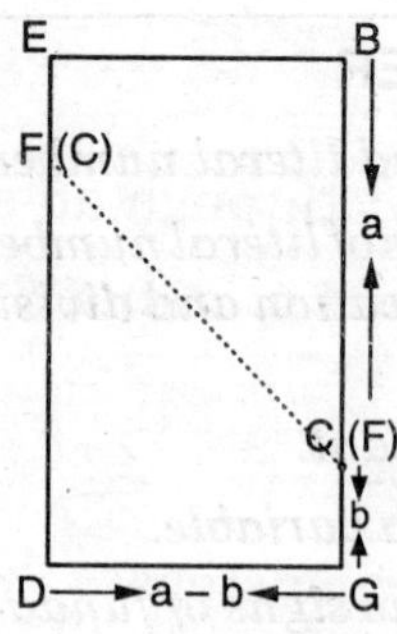

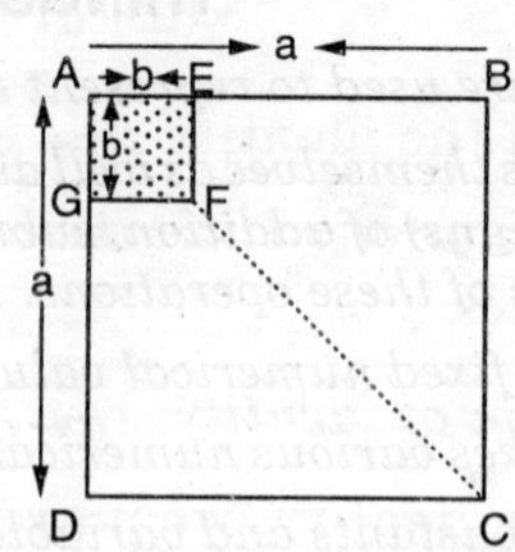

Fig. 6.3

$\therefore$ *Area of rectangle BEDG* = $(a+b)(a-b)$

Clearly,

Area of the remaining portion of square $ABCD$ (unshaded area)

= Area of rectangle $BEDG$.

$\Rightarrow$ $a^2 - b^2 = (a+b)(a-b)$

This verifies the identity.

NOTE 3 *Students are advised to verify the above identity by giving different numeric values of a and b such that* $a > b$.

ACTIVITY 4 *Verification of identity:* $(x+a)(x+b) = x^2 + x(a+b) + ab$

In order to verify this identity geometrically, let us follow the following steps:

Step I *Draw a square ABCD of side x cm on a card board paper.*

Step II *Extend sides AB and AD to E and F respectively such that BE = a cm and DF = b cm.*

Step III *Complete rectangle AEGF with two adjacent sides AE and AF.*

Step IV *Produce BC to meet FG at H. Also, produce DC to meet EG at I.*

Step V *Cut out rectangle AEGF along BH and DI to get one square ABCD and three rectangles BCIE, DCHF and CHGI.*

Step VI *Compute the areas of square and rectangles obtained in step V.*

Area of square ABCD = x^2

Area of rectangle BEIC = xa

Area of rectangle CDFH = xb

Area of rectangle CHGI = ab

Area of rectangle AEGF = $(x+a)(x+b)$

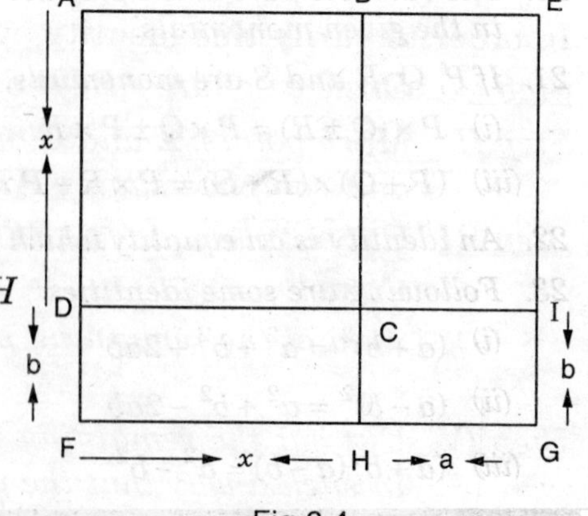

Fig.6.4

Clearly,

Area of rectangle $AEGF$ = Area of square $ABCD$

+ Area of rectangle $BEIC$

+ Area of rectangle $CDFH$

+ Area of rectangle $CHGI$

$\therefore$ $(x+a)(x+b) = x^2 + xa + xb + ab$

or, $(x+a)(x+b) = x^2 + x(a+b) + ab$

This verifies the identity.

NOTE: *Students are advised to verify the above identity by giving different numeric values to x, a and b.*

THINGS TO REMEMBER

1. *The letters which are used to represent numbers are called literal numbers or literals.*
2. *The literal numbers themselves as well as the combinations of literal numbers and numbers obey all the rules (and signs) of addition, subtraction, multiplication and division of numbers along with the properties of these operations.*
3. *A symbol having a fixed numerical value is called a constant.*
4. *A symbol which takes various numerical values is called a variable.*
5. *A combination of constants and variables connected by the signs of fundamental operations of addition, subtraction, multiplication and division is called an algebraic expression.*
6. *Various parts of an algebraic expression which are separated by the signs of ' + ' or ' – ' are called the terms of the expression.*
7. *An algebraic expression is called a monomial, a binomial, a trinomial, a quadrinomial according as it contains one term, two terms, three terms and four terms respectively.*
8. *Each term in an algebraic expression is a product of one or more number(s) and/or literal number(s). These number(s) and/or literal number(s) are known as the factors of that term.*
9. *A term of the expression having no literal factor is called a constant term.*
10. *In a term of an algebraic expression any of the factors with the sign of the term is called the coefficient of the product of the factors.*
11. *The terms having the same literal factors are called like or similar terms.*
12. *The terms not having same literal factors are called unlike or dissimilar terms.*
13. *The sum or difference of several like terms is another like term whose coefficient is the sum or difference of those like terms.*
14. *In adding or subtracting algebraic expressions, we collect different groups of like terms and find the sum or difference of like terms in each group.*
15. *To subtract an expression from another, we change the sign (from ' + ' to ' – ' and from ' – ' to ' + ') of each term of the expression to be subtracted and then add the two expressions.*
16. *When a grouping symbol preceded by ' – ' sign is removed or inserted, then the sign of each term of the corresponding expression is changed (from ' + ' to ' – ' and from ' – ' to ' + ').*
17. *The product of two factors with like signs is positive and the product of two factors with unlike signs is negative.*
18. *If a is a variable and m, n are positive integers, then* $a^m \times a^n = a^{m+n}$
19. *The coefficient of the product of monomials is equal to the product of their coefficients.*
20. *The variable part in the product of two monomials is equal to the product of the variable parts in the given monomials.*
21. *If P, Q, R and S are monomials, then we have*

    (i) $P \times (Q \pm R) = P \times Q \pm P \times R$ (ii) $(Q \pm R) \times P = Q \times P \pm R \times P$

    (iii) $(P+Q) \times (R+S) = P \times R + P \times S + Q \times R + Q \times S$
22. *An identity is an equality which is true for all values of the variable (s).*
23. *Following are some identities:*

    (i) $(a+b)^2 = a^2 + b^2 + 2ab$

    (ii) $(a-b)^2 = a^2 + b^2 - 2ab$

    (iii) $(a+b)(a-b) = a^2 - b^2$

7

FACTORIZATION

7.1 INTRODUCTION

In the previous chapter, we have learnt multiplication of algebraic expressions. The multiplication of algebraic expressions gives us a new algebraic expression. In this chapter, we shall do the other way round, that is, we shall find two or more algebraic expressions whose product is equal to the given expression. The process of writing a given algebraic expression as the product of two expressions will be known as the factorization of the expression.

7.2 FACTORS

In the previous class, we have studied factors and multiples of a given positive integer. We have also learnt that a given positive integer can always be expressed as the product of prime factors. For example, 30 can be written as $30 = 2 \times 3 \times 5$. Each of the numbers 2, 3 and 5 are known as the factors of 30 and the process of expressing an integer as the product of two or more integers is called factorization. Now the question arises : What is meant by a factor of an algebraic expression and how do we find the factors of an algebraic expression. To understand this, let us consider a monomial, say, $5xy$. This monomial can be expressed as the product of two or more monomials in the following possible ways:

$$5xy = 1 \times 5xy = 5 \times xy = 5x \times y = 5y \times x = 5 \times x \times y$$

It follows from the above that the possible factors of $5xy$ are:

$$1, 5xy, 5, xy, 5x, y, 5y, x$$

Thus, we may define the term *'factor'* as follows:

FACTORS *If an algebraic expression is written as the product of numbers or algebraic expressions, then each of these numbers and expressions are called the factors of the given algebraic expression and the algebraic expression is called the product of these expressions.*

FACTORIZATION *The process of writing a given algebraic expression as the product of two or more factors is called factorization.*

7.3 FACTORS OF A MONOMIAL

In this section, we shall discuss some examples on factors of a monomial. Note that the factors of a monomial consist of every literal, their product and number that will divide it exactly.

ILLUSTRATION 1 Write down all possible factors of $3x^2y$.

Solution We have,

$$3x^2y = 1 \times 3x^2y = 3 \times x^2y = 3x \times xy = 3xy \times x = x^2 \times 3y = y \times 3x^2$$

Thus, the possible factors of $3x^2y$ are

$$1, 3x^2 y, 3, x^2 y, 3x, xy, 3xy, x, x^2, 3y, y, 3x^2$$

ILLUSTRATION 2 Write down all possible factors of $12x^2$.

Solution We have,

$$12x^2 = 1 \times 12x^2 = 12 \times x^2 = 3 \times 4x^2 = 4 \times 3x^2 = 2 \times 6x^2 = 6 \times 2x^2$$
$$= 3x \times 4x = 6x \times 2x = 2 \times 3x \times 2x = 3 \times 2x \times 2x$$

Thus, the possible factors of $12x^2$ are

$$1, 12x^2, 12, x^2, 3, 4x^2, 4, 3x^2, 2, 6x^2, 6, 2x^2, 3x, 4x, 6x, 2x$$

7.4 COMMON FACTORS AND GREATEST COMMON FACTOR OF MONOMIALS

In this section, we shall first discuss the common factors of two or more monomials and then we shall define and obtain the greatest common factor of two or more monomials.

To understand the meaning of the term 'common factors', let us consider the monomials $3xy$ and $7x$. We find that:

The possible factors of $3xy$ are: $1, 3xy, 3, xy, 3x, y, 3y, x$

and,

The possible factors of $7x$ are: $1, 7x, 7, x$

Clearly, 1 and x are common factors of both the monomials $3xy$ and $7x$.

Now, consider three monomials $3x$, $21x^2$ and $15xy$.

We observe that:

The possible factors of $3x$ are: $1, 3x, 3, x$

The possible factors of $21x^2$ are: $1, 21x^2, 21, x^2, 3, 7, 3x^2, 7x, 3x, x, 7x^2, 21x$

and,

The possible factors of $15xy$ are: $1, 15xy, 15, xy, 15x, y, 15y, x, 3, 3x, 3y, 3xy, 5, 5x, 5y, 5xy$.

Clearly, 1, x, 3 and $3x$ are common factors of all the three monomials. Out of these common factors, the common factor having greatest coefficient and highest power of the variable is $3x$. This common factor is called the greatest common factor (GCF) or highest common factor (HCF) of the given monomials.

Thus, we define the greatest common factor (GCF) or highest common factor (HCF) of monomials as follows:

GREATEST COMMON FACTOR (GCF) OR HIGHEST COMMON FACTOR (HCF) *The greatest common factor of given monomials is the common factor having greatest coefficient and highest power of the variables.*

The following step-wise procedure will be helpful to find the GCF of two or more monomials.

Step I *Obtain the given monomials.*

Step II *Find the numerical coefficient of each monomial and their greatest common factor (GCF/HCF).*

Step III *Find the common literals appearing in the given monomials.*

Step IV *Find the smallest power of each common literal.*

Step V *Write a monomial of common literals with smallest powers obtained in step IV.*

Step VI *The required GCF is the product of the coefficient obtained in step II and the monomial obtained in step V.*

Following examples will illustrate the above procedure.

ILLUSTRATIVE EXAMPLES

Example 1 Find the greatest common factors of the monomials $21a^3b^7$ and $35\,a^5b^5$.

Solution The numerical coefficients of the given monomials are 21 and 35

The greatest common factor of 21 and 35 is 7

The common literals appearing in the given monomials are a and b

The smallest power of 'a' in the two monomials $= 3$

The smallest power of 'b' in the two monomials $= 5$

The monomial of common literals with smallest powers $= a^3b^5$

$\therefore$ The greatest common factor $= 7a^3b^5$

Example 2 Find the greatest common factors of the monomials $14x^2y^3, 21x^2y^2, 35x^4y^5\,z$.

Solution The numerical coefficients of the given monomials are 14, 21 and 35

The greatest common factor of 14, 21 and 35 is 7

The common literals appearing in the three monomials are x and y

The smallest power of 'x' in the three monomials $= 2$

The smallest power of 'y' in the three monomials $= 2$

The monomial of common literals with smallest powers $= x^2y^2$

Hence, the greatest common factor $= 7x^2y^2$

Example 3 Find the greatest common factor of the monomials $6x^3a^2b^2c, 8x^2\,ab^3\,c^3$ and $12a^3\,b^2\,c^2$.

Solution The numerical coefficients of the given monomials are 6, 8 and 12.

The greatest common factor of 6, 8 and 12 is 2.

The common literals appearing in the given monomials are a, b and c.

The smallest power of 'a' in the three monomials $= 1$

The smallest power of 'b' in the three monomials $= 2$

The smallest power of 'c' in the three monomials $= 1$

The monomial of common literals with smallest powers $= a^1b^2c^1 = ab^2c$

Hence, the greatest common factor $= 2ab^2c$

EXERCISE 7.1

Find the greatest common factor (GCF/HCF) of the following polynomials: (1-14)

1. $2x^2$ and $12x^2$
2. $6x^3y$ and $18x^2y^3$
3. $7x, 21x^2$ and $14xy^2$
4. $42x^2yz$ and $63x^3y^2z^3$
5. $12ax^2, 6a^2x^3$ and $2a^3x^5$
6. $9x^2, 15x^2y^3, 6xy^2$ and $21x^2y^2$
7. $4a^2b^3, -12a^3b, 18a^4b^3$
8. $6x^2y^2, 9xy^3, 3x^3y^2$

9. a^2b^3, a^3b^2

10. $36a^2b^2c^4, 54a^5c^2, 90a^4b^2c^2$

11. $x^3, -yx^2$

12. $15a^3, -45a^2, -150a$

13. $2x^3y^2, 10x^2y^3, 14xy$

14. $14x^3y^5, 10x^5y^3, 2x^2y^2$

Find the greatest common factor of the terms in each of the following expressions:

15. $5a^4 + 10a^3 - 15a^2$

16. $2xyz + 3x^2y + 4y^2$

17. $3a^2b^2 + 4b^2c^2 + 12a^2b^2c^2$

ANSWERS

1. $2x^2$ 2. $6x^2y$ 3. $7x$ 4. $21x^2yz$
5. $2ax^2$ 6. $3x$ 7. $2a^2b$ 8. $3xy^2$
9. a^2b^2 10. $18a^2c^2$ 11. x^2 12. $15a$
13. $2xy$ 14. $2x^2y^2$ 15. $5a^2$ 16. y
17. b^2

7.5 FACTORIZATION OF ALGEBRAIC EXPRESSIONS WHEN A COMMON MONOMIAL FACTOR OCCURS IN EACH TERM

In order to factorize algebraic expressions consisting of a common monomial factors of each term we use the following step-wise procedure:

Step I *Obtain the algebraic expression.*

Step II *Find the greatest common factor (GCF/HCF) of its terms.*

Step III *Express each term of the given expression as the product of the GCF and the quotient when it is divided by the GCF.*

Step IV *Use the distributive property of multiplication over addition to express the given algebraic expression as the product of the GCF and the quotient of the given expression by the GCF.*

Following examples will illustrate the above procedure.

ILLUSTRATIVE EXAMPLES

Example 1 Factorize each of the following algebraic expressions:

(i) $3x + 15$ (ii) $2x^2 + 5x$ (iii) $3x^2y - 6xy^2$ (iv) $6x^3 + 8x^2y$

Solution (i) The greatest common factor of the two terms namely, $3x$ and 15 of the expression $3x + 15$ is 3. Also, $3x = 3 \times x$ and $15 = 3 \times 5$.

$\therefore \quad 3x + 15 = 3(x + 5)$

(ii) The greatest common factor of the terms $2x^2$ and $5x$ of the expression $2x^2 + 5x$ is x. Also, $2x^2 = 2x \times x$ and $5x = 5 \times x$.

$$\therefore \quad 2x^2 + 5x = 2x \times x + 5 \times x$$
$$= (2x + 5)\, x$$

(iii) Clearly, $3xy$ is the greatest common factor of the terms $3x^2y$ and $6xy^2$ of the binomial $3x^2y - 6xy^2$. Also, $3x^2y = 3xy \times x$ and $6xy^2 = 3xy \times 2y$

$\therefore \quad 3x^2y - 6xy^2 = 3xy \times x - 3xy \times 2y$

$= 3xy(x - 2y)$

(iv) Clearly, $2x^2$ is the GCF of the terms $6x^3$ and $8x^2y$ of the given binomial $6x^3 + 8x^2y$. Also, $6x^3 = 2x^2 \times 3x$ and $8x^2y = 2x^2 \times 4y$.

$\therefore \quad 6x^3 + 8x^2y = 2x^2 \times 3x + 2x^2 \times 4y$

$= 2x^2(3x + 4y)$

Example 2 Factorize:

(i) $12x^3y^4 + 16x^2y^5 - 4x^5y^2$ (ii) $18a^3b^2 + 36ab^4 - 24a^2b^3$

Solution (i) The greatest common factor of the terms $12x^3y^4, 16x^2y^5$ and $4x^5y^2$ of the expression $12x^3y^4 + 16x^2y^5 - 4x^5y^2$ is $4x^2y^2$.

Also, we can write

$12x^3y^4 = 4x^2y^2 \times 3xy^2, 16x^2y^5 = 4x^2y^2 \times 4y^3$ and, $4x^5y^2 = 4x^2y^2 \times x^3$

$\therefore \quad 12x^3y^4 + 16x^2y^5 - 4x^5y^2 = 4x^2y^2 \times 3xy^2 + 4x^2y^2 \times 4y^3 - 4x^2y^2 \times x^3$

$= 4x^2y^2(3xy^2 + 4y^3 - x^3)$

(ii) We have, $18a^3b^2 + 36ab^4 - 24a^2b^3$

The greatest common factor of the terms $18a^3b^2, 36ab^4$ and $24a^2b^2$ is $6ab^2$.

Also, we can write $18a^3b^2 = 6ab^2 \times 3a^2, 36ab^4 = 6ab^2 \times 6b^2$ and, $24a^2b^2 = 6ab^2 \times 4ab$

$\therefore \quad 18a^3b^2 + 36ab^4 - 24a^2b^3 = 6ab^2 \times 3a^2 + 6ab^2 \times 6b^2 - 6ab^2 \times 4ab$

$= 6ab^2(3a^2 + 6b^2 - 4ab)$

EXERCISE 7.2

Factorize the following:

1. $3x - 9$
2. $5x - 15x^2$
3. $20a^{12}b^2 - 15a^8b^4$
4. $72x^6y^7 - 96x^7y^6$
5. $20x^3 - 40x^2 + 80x$
6. $2x^3y^2 - 4x^2y^3 + 8xy^4$
7. $10m^3n^2 + 15m^4n - 20m^2n^3$
8. $2a^4b^4 - 3a^3b^5 + 4a^2b^5$
9. $28a^2 + 14a^2b^2 - 21a^4$
10. $a^4b - 3a^2b^2 - 6ab^3$
11. $2l^2mn - 3lm^2n + 4lmn^2$
12. $x^4y^2 - x^2y^4 - x^4y^4$
13. $9x^2y + 3axy$
14. $16m - 4m^2$
15. $-4a^2 + 4ab - 4ca$
16. $x^2yz + xy^2z + xyz^2$
17. $ax^2y + bxy^2 + cxyz$

ANSWERS

1. $3(x-3)$
2. $5x(1-3x)$
3. $5a^8b^2(4a^4-3b^2)$
4. $24x^6y^6(3y-4x)$
5. $20x(x^2-2x+4)$
6. $2xy^2(x^2-2xy+4y^2)$
7. $5m^2n(2mn+3m^2-4n^2)$
8. $a^2b^4(2a^2-3ab+4b)$
9. $7a^2(a+2b^2-3a^2)$
10. $ab(a^3-3ab-6b^2)$
11. $lmn(21-3m+4n)$
12. $x^2y^2(x^2-y^2-x^2y^2)$
13. $3xy(3x+a)$
14. $4m(4-m)$
15. $-4a(a-b+c)$
16. $xyz(x+y+z)$
17. $xy(ax+by+cz)$

7.6 FACTORIZATION OF ALGEBRAIC EXPRESSIONS WHEN A BINOMIAL IS A COMMON FACTOR

In order to factorize algebraic expressions containing a binomial as a common factor, we write the expression as the product of the binomial and the quotient obtained by dividing the given expression by this binomial.

Following examples will illustrate the procedure.

ILLUSTRATIVE EXAMPLES

Example 1 Factorize:

(i) $7(2x+5)+3(2x+5)$ (ii) $(x+2)y+(x+2)x$

(iii) $5a(2x+3y)-2b(2x+3y)$ (iv) $8(5x+9y)^2+12(5x+9y)$

Solution We have,

(i) $7(2x+5)+3(2x+5)=(7+3)(2x+5)$ [Taking $(2x+5)$ common]

$=10(2x+5)$

(ii) $(x+2)y+(x+2)x=(x+2)(y+x)$ [Taking $(x+2)$ common]

(iii) $5a(2x+3y)-2b(2x+3y)=(2x+3y)(5a-2b)$ [Taking $(2x+3y)$ common]

(iv) $8(5x+9y)^2+12(5x+9y)=4(5x+9y)\{2(5x+9y)+3\}$

$=4(5x+9y)(10x+18y+3)$

Example 2 Factorize:

(i) $(y-x)a+(x-y)b$ (ii) $9(a-2b)^2+6(2b-a)$

(iii) $(x-2y)^2-4x+8y$ (iv) $2a+6b-3(a+3b)^2$

Solution We have,

(i) $(y-x)a+(x-y)b=-(x-y)a+(x-y)b$ [Taking (-1) common from $(y-x)$]

$=(x-y)(-a+b)$ [Taking $(x-y)$ common]

$=(x-y)(b-a)$ [$\because -a+b=b-a$]

(ii) $9(a-2b)^2+6(2b-a)$

$$=9(a-2b)^2-6(a-2b) \quad [\because 2b-a=-(a-2b)]$$

$$=3(a-2b)\{3(a-2b)-2\} \quad [\text{Taking } 3(a-2b) \text{ common}]$$

$$=3(a-2b)(3a-6b-2)$$

(iii) $(x-2y)^2-4x+8y=(x-2y)^2-4(x-2y)$ [Taking -4 common from $-4x+8y$]

$$=(x-2y)\{(x-2y)-4\} \quad [\text{Taking } (x-2y) \text{ common}]$$

$$=(x-2y)(x-2y-4)$$

(iv) $2a+6b-3(a+3b)^2=2(a+3b)-3(a+3b)^2$ [Taking 2 common from $2a+6b$]

$$=(a+3b)\{2-3(a+3b)\} \quad [\text{Taking } (a-3b) \text{ common}]$$

$$=(a+3b)(2-3a-9b)$$

Example 3 Factorize:

(i) $(x+y)(2x+3y)-(x+y)(x+1)$ (ii) $(x+y)(2a+b)-(3x-2y)(2a+b)$

Solution We have,

(i) $(x+y)(2x+3y)-(x+y)(x+1)$

$$=(x+y)\{(2x+3y)-(x+1)\} \quad [\text{Taking } (x+y) \text{ common}]$$

$$=(x+y)(2x+3y-x-1)$$

$$=(x+y)(x+3y-1)$$

(ii) $(x+y)(2a+b)-(3x-2y)(2a+b)$

$$=\{(x+y)-(3x-2y)\}(2a+b) \quad [\text{Taking } (2a+b) \text{ common}]$$

$$=(x+y-3x+2y)(2a+b)$$

$$=(-2x+3y)(2a+b)$$

EXERCISE 7.3

Factorize each of the following algebraic expressions:

1. $6x(2x-y)+7y(2x-y)$
2. $2r(y-x)+s(x-y)$
3. $7a(2x-3)+3b(2x-3)$
4. $9a(6a-5b)-12a^2(6a-5b)$
5. $5(x-2y)^2+3(x-2y)$
6. $16(2l-3m)^2-12(3m-2l)$
7. $3a(x-2y)-b(x-2y)$
8. $a^2(x+y)+b^2(x+y)+c^2(x+y)$
9. $(x-y)^2+(x-y)$
10. $6(a+2b)-4(a+2b)^2$
11. $a(x-y)+2b(y-x)+c(x-y)^2$
12. $-4(x-2y)^2+8(x-2y)$
13. $x^3(a-2b)+x^2(a-2b)$
14. $(2x-3y)(a+b)+(3x-2y)(a+b)$
15. $4(x+y)(3a-b)+6(x+y)(2b-3a)$

ANSWERS

1. $(2x-y)(6x+7y)$
2. $(x-y)(s-2r)$
3. $(2x-3)(7a+3b)$
4. $3a(3-4a)(6a-5b)$
5. $(x-2y)(5x-10y+3)$
6. $4(2l-3m)(8l-12m+3)$
7. $(x-2y)(3a-b)$
8. $(x+y)(a^2+b^2+c^2)$
9. $(x-y)(x-y+1)$
10. $2(a+2b)(3-2a-4b)$
11. $(x-y)(a-2b+cx-cy)$
12. $4(x-2y)(2-x+2y)$
13. $x^2(a-2b)(x+1)$
14. $5(a+b)(x-y)$
15. $2(x+y)(4b-3a)$

7.7 FACTORIZATION BY GROUPING THE TERMS

Look at the expression $3xy - 3y + 7x - 7$. We observe that all terms of this expression do not have any common factor neither a monomial nor a binomial. But, we find that first two terms have monomial $3y$ as a common factor and the last two terms have a monomial 7 as common factor. Also, by taking $3y$ common from first two terms, we have

$$3xy-3y=3y\,(x-1)$$

Taking 7 common from the last two terms, we have

$$7x-7=7\,(x-1)$$

We also notice that the binomial $(x-1)$ is common from these two groups of terms.

Thus, by grouping the terms of $3xy-3y+7x-7$, we have

$$\begin{aligned}3xy-3y+7x-7&=(3xy-3y)+(7x-7)\\&=3y\,(x-1)+7\,(x-1)\\&=(3y+7)\,(x-1)\end{aligned}$$

It follows from the above discussion that grouping of the terms of an algebraic expression may lead to its factorization. Also, grouping of terms is not unique. That is terms can be grouped in different ways. For example, the same algebraic expression can also be grouped as follows:

$$\begin{aligned}3xy-3y+7x-7&=(3xy+7x)-3y-7\\&=(3y+7)\,x-1\,(3y+7)\\&=(3y+7)\,(x-1)\end{aligned}$$

Let us now discuss, some more examples to illustrate the grouping of terms to factorize algebraic expressions.

LLUSTRATIVE EXAMPLES

Example 1 Factorize:

(i) $x^2+xy+8x+8y$ (ii) $15xy-6x+10y-4$

(iii) $15ab+15+9b+25a$ (iv) $n-7+7lm-lmn$

Solution (i) We observe that there is no common factor among all terms. Also, there are four terms.

So, let us think of grouping the terms in pairs in such a way that there are some factors common to them and after taking factors common from each pair same binomial is left inside the two brackets. We observe that first two terms have x as a common factor. Taking x common from them, we have

$$x^2 + xy = x(x + y)$$

Also, 8 is a common factor from the last two terms. Taking 8 common from the last two terms, we have

$$8x + 8y = 8(x + y)$$

Clearly, $x + y$ is common from the two groups.

Thus, we group the terms as follows:

$$x^2 + xy + 8x + 8y = (x^2 + xy) + (8x + 8y)$$
$$= x(x + y) + 8(x + y)$$
$$= (x + 8)(x + y)$$

(ii) We have, $15xy - 6x + 10y - 4$

Clearly, there is no common factor among all the terms. Also, there are four terms. So, let us think of grouping the terms in pairs in such a way that there are some factors common to the terms in each pair and after taking factors common from each pair same binomial is left inside the two brackets.

We observe that first two terms have $3x$ as a common factor. Taking $3x$ common from them, we have

$$15xy - 6x = 3x(5y - 2)$$

Last two terms have 2 as the common factor. Taking 2 common from these two, we have

$$10y - 4 = 2(5y - 2)$$

Clearly, $(5y - 2)$ is the binomial common from these two groups. Thus, we group the terms as follows:

$$15xy - 6x + 10y - 4 = 3x(5y - 2) + 2(5y - 2)$$
$$= (3x + 2)(5y - 2)$$

(iii) We have, $15ab + 15 + 9b + 25a$

Clearly, all terms of the expression do not have any common factor. We notice that first two terms have a common factor but the last two terms do not have a common factor. So, we think of re-grouping the terms. We observe that if we group first and third terms, $3b$ is a common factor. By taking $3b$ common from these two terms, we have

$$15ab + 9b = 3b(5a + 3)$$

Taking 5 common from second and fourth terms, we have

$$15 + 25a = 5(3 + 5a) = 5(5a + 3)$$

Clearly, $(5a + 3)$ is common from these two groups.

So, we re-group the terms as follows:

$$15ab + 15 + 9b + 25a = (15ab + 9b) + (15 + 25a)$$
$$= 3b\,(5a + 3) + 5\,(3 + 5a)$$
$$= 3b\,(5a + 3) + 5\,(5a + 3)$$
$$= (3b + 5)\,(5a + 3)$$

(iv) We have,

$$n - 7 + 7lm - lmn = (n - 7) + (7lm - lmn)$$
$$= (n - 7) + (7 - n)\,lm$$
$$= (n - 7) - (n - 7)\,lm$$
$$= (n - 7)\,(1 - lm)$$

Example 2 Factorize:

(i) $ax + bx + ay + by$ (ii) $ax^2 + by^2 + bx^2 + ay^2$

(iii) $a^2 + bc + ab + ac$ (iv) $ax - ay + bx - by$

Solution We have,

(i) $ax + bx + ay + by = (ax + bx) + (ay + by)$ [Grouping the terms]
$= (a + b)x + (a + b)y$
$= (a + b)(x + y)$ [Taking $(a + b)$ common]

(ii) $ax^2 + by^2 + bx^2 + ay^2 = ax^2 + bx^2 + ay^2 + by^2$ [Re-arranging the terms]
$= (a + b)\,x^2 + (a + b)y^2$
$= (a + b)(x^2 + y^2)$ [Taking $(a + b)$ common]

(iii) $a^2 + bc + ab + ac = (a^2 + ab) + (ac + bc)$ [Re-grouping the terms]
$= a(a + b) + (a + b)\,c$
$= (a + b)(a + c)$ [Taking $(a + b)$ common]

(iv) $ax - ay + bx - by = a(x - y) + b(x - y)$
$= (a + b)(x - y)$ [Taking $(x - y)$ common]

Example 3 Factorize:

(i) $a^2 + 2a + ab + 2b$ (ii) $x^2 - xz + xy - xz$

Solution We have,

(i) $a^2 + 2a + ab + 2b = (a^2 + 2a) + (ab + 2b)$ [Grouping the terms]
$= a\,(a + 2) + (a + 2)\,b$
$= (a + 2)(a + b)$ [Taking $(a + 2)$ common]

(ii) $x^2 - xz + xy - yz = (x^2 - xz) + (xy - yz)$ [Grouping the terms]
$= x(x - z) + y(x - z)$
$= (x + y)(x - z)$ [Taking $(x - z)$ common]

Example 4 Factorize each of the following expressions:

(i) $a^2 - b + ab - a$ (ii) $xy - ab + bx - ay$

(iii) $6ab - b^2 + 12ac - 2bc$ (iv) $a\,(a + b - c) - bc$

(v) $a^2x^2 + (ax^2 + 1)\,x + a$ (vi) $3ax - 6ay - 8by + 4bx$

Solution (i) We have,

$$a^2 - b + ab - a = a^2 + ab - b - a$$
$$= (a^2 + ab) - (b + a)$$
$$= a(a + b) - (a + b)$$
$$= (a + b)(a - 1)$$

(ii) $$xy - ab + bx - ay = xy + bx - ab - ay$$
$$= x(y + b) - a(b + y)$$
$$= x(y + b) - a(y + b)$$
$$= (y + b)(x - a)$$

(iii) $$6ab - b^2 + 12ac - 2bc = 6ab + 12ac - b^2 - 2bc$$
$$= 6a(b + 2c) - b(b + 2c)$$
$$= (b + 2c)(6a - b)$$

(iv) $$a(a + b - c) - bc = a^2 + ab - ac - bc$$
$$= (a^2 + ab) - (ac + bc)$$
$$= a(a + b) - c(a + b)$$
$$= (a + b)(a - c)$$

(v) $$a^2x^2 + (ax^2 + 1)x + a = a^2x^2 + ax^3 + x + a$$
$$= ax^2(x + a) + (x + a)$$
$$= (x + a)(ax^2 + 1)$$

(vi) $$3ax - 6ay - 8by + 4bx = 3ax + 4bx - 6ay - 8by$$
$$= (3ax + 4bx) - (6ay + 8by)$$
$$= x(3a + 4b) - 2y(3a + 4b)$$
$$= (3a + 4b)(x - 2y)$$

Example 5 Factorize each of the following expressions:

(i) $a^3x + a^2(x - y) - a(y + z) - z$

(ii) $(x^2 + 3x)^2 - 5(x^2 + 3x) - y(x^2 + 3x) + 5y$

Solution (i) We have,

$$a^3x + a^2(x - y) - a(y + z) - z$$
$$= a^3x + a^2x - a^2y - ay - az - z$$
$$= (a^3x + a^2x) - (a^2y + ay) - (az + z)$$
$$= a^2x(a + 1) - ay(a + 1) - z(a + 1)$$
$$= (a + 1)(a^2x - ay - z)$$

(ii) $$(x^2 + 3x)^2 - 5(x^2 + 3x) - y(x^2 + 3x) + 5y$$
$$= (x^2 + 3x)\left\{(x^2 + 3x) - 5\right\} - y\left\{(x^2 + 3x) - 5\right\}$$
$$= (x^2 + 3x - 5)(x^2 + 3x - y)$$

Example 6 Factorize:

(i) $x^3 - 2x^2y + 3xy^2 - 6y^3$ (ii) $6ab - b^2 + 12ac - 2bc$

Solution (i) We have,

$$x^3 - 2x^2y + 3xy^2 - 6y^3 = (x^3 - 2x^2y) + (3xy^2 - 6y^3)$$
$$= x^2(x - 2y) + 3y^2(x - 2y)$$
$$= (x - 2y)(x^2 + 3y^2)$$

(ii) We have,

$$6ab - b^2 + 12ac - 2bc = b(6a - b) + 2c(6a - b) = (6a - b)(b + 2c)$$

EXERCISE 7.4

Factorize each of the following expressions:

1. $qr - pr + qs - ps$
2. $p^2q - pr^2 - pq + r^2$
3. $1 + x + xy + x^2y$
4. $ax + ay - bx - by$
5. $xa^2 + xb^2 - ya^2 - yb^2$
6. $x^2 + xy + xz + yz$
7. $2ax + bx + 2ay + by$
8. $ab - by - ay + y^2$
9. $axy + bcxy - az - bcz$
10. $lm^2 - mn^2 - lm + n^2$
11. $x^3 - y^2 + x - x^2y^2$
12. $6xy + 6 - 9y - 4x$
13. $x^2 - 2ax - 2ab + bx$
14. $x^3 - 2x^2y + 3xy^2 - 6y^3$
15. $abx^2 + (ay - b)x - y$
16. $(ax + by)^2 + (bx - ay)^2$
17. $16(a - b)^3 - 24(a - b)^2$
18. $ab(x^2 + 1) + x(a^2 + b^2)$
19. $a^2x^2 + (ax^2 + 1)x + a$
20. $a(a - 2b - c) + 2bc$
21. $a(a + b - c) - bc$
22. $x^2 - 11xy - x + 11y$
23. $ab - a - b + 1$
24. $x^2 + y - xy - x$

ANSWERS

1. $(q - p)(r + s)$
2. $(p - 1)(pq - r^2)$
3. $(1 + x)(1 + xy)$
4. $(x + y)(a - b)$
5. $(x - y)(a^2 + b^2)$
6. $(x + y)(x + z)$
7. $(2a + b)(x + y)$
8. $(a - y)(b - y)$
9. $(xy - z)(a + bc)$
10. $(lm - n^2)(m - 1)$
11. $(x - y^2)(x^2 + 1)$
12. $(2x - 3)(3y - 2)$
13. $(x - 2a)(x + b)$
14. $(x - 2y)(x^2 + 3y^2)$
15. $(bx + y)(ax - 1)$
16. $(x^2 + y^2)(a^2 + b^2)$
17. $8(a - b)^2(2a - 2b - 3)$
18. $(ax + b)(bx + a)$
19. $(x + a)(ax^2 + 1)$
20. $(a - 2b)(a - c)$

21. $(a+b)(a-c)$

22. $(x-11y)(x-1)$

23. $(a-1)(b-1)$

24. $(x-1)(x-y)$

7.8 FACTORIZATION OF BINOMIAL EXPRESSIONS EXPRESSIBLE AS THE DIFFERENCE OF TWO SQUARES

To factorize binomial expressions expressible as the difference of two squares, we use the following identity:

$$a^2-b^2=(a+b)(a-b)$$

Following examples will illustrate the application of the above formula.

ILLUSTRATIVE EXAMPLES

Example 1 Factorize:

(i) $9a^2-16b^2$ (ii) $36a^2-(x-y)^2$

(iii) $80a^2-45b^2$ (iv) $(3a-b)^2-9c^2$

Solution We have,

(i) $9a^2-16b^2=(3a)^2-(4b)^2$

$=(3a+4b)(3a-4b)$ [Using: $(a^2-b^2)=(a+b)(a-b)$]

(ii) $36a^2-(x-y)^2=(6a)^2-(x-y)^2$

$=\{6a+(x-y)\}\{6a-(x-y)\}$ [Using: $a^2-b^2=(a+b)(a-b)$]

$=(6a+x-y)(6a-x+y)$

(iii) $80a^2-45b^2=5(16a^2-9b^2)$

$=5\{(4a)^2-(3b)^2\}$

$=5(4a+3b)(4a-3b)$ [Using: $a^2-b^2=(a+b)(a-b)$]

(iv) $(3a-b)^2-9c^2=(3a-b)^2-(3c)^2$

$=\{(3a-b)+3c\}\{(3a-b)-3c\}$

$=(3a-b+3c)(3a-b-3c)$

Example 2 Factorize:

(i) x^4-y^4 (ii) $16x^4-81$ (iii) $x^4-(y+z)^4$

(iv) $2x-32x^5$ (v) $3a^4-48b^4$ (vi) $81x^4-121x^2$

Solution We have,

(i) $x^4-y^4=(x^2)^2-(y^2)^2$

$=(x^2-y^2)(x^2+y^2)$ [Using: $a^2-b^2=(a-b)(a+b)$]

$=(x-y)(x+y)(x^2+y^2)$ [Using: $a^2-b^2=(a-b)(a+b)$]

(ii) $16x^4-81=(4x^2)^2-(9)^2$

$=(4x^2-9)(4x^2+9)$ [Using: $a^2-b^2=(a-b)(a+b)$]

$=\{(2x)^2-(3)^2\}(4x^2+9)$

$=(2x-3)(2x+3)(4x^2+9)$ [Using: $a^2-b^2=(a-b)(a+b)$]

(iii) $x^4-(y+z)^4=(x^2)^2-\left\{(y+z)^2\right\}^2$

$=\left\{x^2-(y+z)^2\right\}\left\{x^2+(y+z)^2\right\}$

$=\{x-(y+z)\}\{x+(y+z)\}\left\{x^2+(y+z)^2\right\}$

$=(x-y-z)(x+y+z)\left\{x^2+(y+z)^2\right\}$

(iv) $2x-32x^5=2x(1-16x^4)$

$=2x\{1^2-(4x^2)^2\}$

$=2x(1+4x^2)(1-4x^2)$

$=2x(1+4x^2)\left\{1-(2x)^2\right\}$

$=2x(1+4x^2)(1-2x)(1+2x)$

(v) $3a^4-48b^4=3(a^4-16b^4)$

$=3\{(a^2)^2-(4b^2)^2\}$

$=3(a^2-4b^2)(a^2+4b^2)$

$=3\{a^2-(2b)^2\}(a^2+4b^2)$

$=3(a-2b)(a+2b)(a^2+4b^2)$

(vi) $81x^4-121x^2=x^2(81x^2-121)$

$=x^2\left\{(9x)^2-(11)^2\right\}$

$=x^2(9x-11)(9x+11)$

Example 3 Factorize:

(i) $16a^2-\dfrac{25}{4a^2}$ (ii) $16a^2b-\dfrac{b}{16a^2}$

(iii) $100(x+y)^2-81(a+b)^2$ (iv) $(x-1)^2-(x-2)^2$

Solution We have,

(i) $16a^2-\dfrac{25}{4a^2}=(4a)^2-\left(\dfrac{5}{2a}\right)^2=\left(4a+\dfrac{5}{2a}\right)\left(4a-\dfrac{5}{2a}\right)$

(ii) $16a^2b-\dfrac{b}{16a^2}=b\left(16a^2-\dfrac{1}{16a^2}\right)$

$=b\left\{(4a)^2-\left(\dfrac{1}{4a}\right)^2\right\}=b\left(4a+\dfrac{1}{4a}\right)\left(4a-\dfrac{1}{4a}\right)$

(iii) $100(x+y)^2-81(a+b)^2=\{10(x+y)\}^2-\{9(a+b)\}^2$

$=\{10(x+y)+9(a+b)\}\{10(x+y)-9(a+b)\}$

$=(10x+10y+9a+9b)(10x+10y-9a-9b)$

(iv) $(x-1)^2-(x-2)^2 = \{(x-1)+(x-2)\}\{(x-1)-(x-2)\}$

$= (2x-3)(x-1-x+2)$

$= (2x-3)\times 1$

$= 2x-3$

Example 4 Factorize each of the following algebraic expressions:

(i) x^4-81y^4 (ii) $2x^5-2x$ (iii) $3x^4-243$

(iv) $2-50x^2$ (v) x^8-y^8 (vi) $a^{12}x^4-a^4x^{12}$

Solution (i) $x^4-81y^4 = (x^2)^2-(9y^2)^2$

$= (x^2-9y^2)(x^2+9y^2)$

$= \left\{x^2-(3y)^2\right\}(x^2+9y^2)$

$= (x-3y)(x+3y)(x^2+9y^2)$

(ii) $2x^5-2x = 2x(x^4-1)]$

$= 2x\left\{(x^2)^2-1^2\right\}$

$= 2x(x^2-1)(x^2+1)$

$= 2x(x-1)(x+1)(x^2+1)$

(iii) $3x^4-243 = 3(x^4-81)$

$= 3\left\{(x^2)^2-9^2\right\}$

$= 3(x^2-9)(x^2+9)$

$= 3(x^2-3^2)(x^2+9)$

$= 3(x+3)(x+3)(x^2+9)$

(iv) $2-50x^2 = 2\{1-25x^2\}$

$= 2\left\{1^2-(5x)^2\right\}$

$= 2(1-5x)(1+5x)$

(v) $x^8-y^8 = \left\{(x^4)^2-(y^4)^2\right\}$

$= (x^4-y^4)(x^4+y^4)$

$= \left\{(x^2)^2-(y^2)^2\right\}(x^4+y^4)$

$= (x^2-y^2)(x^2+y^2)(x^4+y^4)$

$= (x-y)(x+y)(x^2+y^2)(x^4+y^4)$

$= (x-y)(x+y)(x^2+y^2)\left\{(x^2)^2+(y^2)^2+2x^2y^2-2x^2y^2\right\}$.

$= (x-y)(x+y)(x^2+y^2)\left\{(x^2+y^2)^2-\left(\sqrt{2}xy\right)^2\right\}$

$= (x-y)(x+y)(x^2+y^2)\left(x^2+y^2-\sqrt{2}xy\right)\left(x^2+y^2+\sqrt{2}xy\right)$

(vi) $a^{12}x^4 - a^4x^{12} = a^4x^4\left(a^8 - x^8\right)$

$= a^4x^4\left\{(a^4)^2 - (x^4)^2\right\}$

$= a^4x^4\left(a^4 + x^4\right)\left(a^4 - x^4\right)$

$= a^4x^4\left(a^4 + x^4\right)\left\{(a^2)^2 - (x^2)^2\right\}$

$= a^4x^4\left(a^4 + x^4\right)\left(a^2 + x^2\right)\left(a^2 - x^2\right)$

$= a^4x^4\left(a^4 + x^4\right)\left(a^2 + x^2\right)(a + x)(a - x)$

Example 5 Factorize each of the following algebraic expressions:

(i) $16\,(2x-1)^2 - 25z^2$ (ii) $4a^2 - 9b^2 - 2a - 3b$

(iii) $x^2 - 4x + 4y - y^2$ (iv) $3 - 12\,(a-b)^2$

(v) $x\,(x+z) - y\,(y+z)$ (vi) $a^2 - b^2 - a - b$

Solution (i) $16\,(2x-1)^2 - 25z^2 = \{4\,(2x-1)\}^2 - (5z)^2$

$= \{4\,(2x-1) - 5z\}\,\{4\,(2x-1) + 5z\}$

$= (8x - 4 - 5z)\,(8x - 4 + 5z)$

$= (8x - 5z - 4)\,(8x + 5z - 4)$

(ii) $4a^2 - 9b^2 - 2a - 3b = \left\{(2a)^2 - (3b)^2\right\} - (2a + 3b)$

$= (2a - 3b)\,(2a + 3b) - (2a + 3b)$

$= (2a + 3b)\,\{(2a - 3b) - 1\}$

$= (2a + 3b)\,(2a - 3b - 1)$

(iii) $x^2 - 4x + 4y - y^2 = (x^2 - y^2) - (4x - 4y)$

$= (x - y)\,(x + y) - 4\,(x - y)$

$= (x - y)\,\{(x + y) - 4\}$

$= (x - y)\,(x + y - 4)$

(iv) $3 - 12\,(a-b)^2 = 3\left\{1 - 4\,(a-b)^2\right\}$

$= 3\left[1^2 - \{2\,(a-b)\}^2\right]$

$= 3\left[\{1 + 2\,(a-b)\}\,\{1 - 2\,(a-b)\}\right]$

$= 3\,(1 + 2a - 2b)\,(1 - 2a + 2b)$

(v) $x\,(x+z) - y\,(y+z) = x^2 + xz - y^2 - yz$

$= (x^2 - y^2) + (xz - yz)$

$= (x - y)\,(x + y) + z\,(x - y)$

$= (x - y)\,\{(x + y) + z\}$

$= (x - y)\,(x + y + z)$

(vi) $a^2 - b^2 - a - b = (a^2 - b^2) - (a + b)$

$$= (a - b)(a + b) - (a + b)$$

$$= (a + b)\{(a - b) - 1\}$$

EXERCISE 7.5

Factorize each of the following expressions:

1. $16x^2 - 25y^2$
2. $27x^2 - 12y^2$
3. $144a^2 - 289b^2$
4. $12m^2 - 27$
5. $125x^2 - 45y^2$
6. $144a^2 - 169b^2$
7. $(2a - b)^2 - 16c^2$
8. $(x + 2y)^2 - 4(2x - y)^2$
9. $3a^5 - 48a^3$
10. $a^4 - 16b^4$
11. $x^8 - 1$
12. $64 - (a + 1)^2$
13. $36l^2 - (m + n)^2$
14. $25x^4y^4 - 1$
15. $a^4 - \frac{1}{b^4}$
16. $x^3 - 144x$
17. $(x - 4y)^2 - 625$
18. $9(a - b)^2 - 100(x - y)^2$
19. $(3 + 2a)^2 - 25a^2$
20. $(x + y)^2 - (a - b)^2$
21. $\frac{1}{16}x^2y^2 - \frac{4}{49}y^2z^2$
22. $75a^3b^2 - 108ab^4$
23. $x^5 - 16x^3$
24. $\frac{50}{x^2} - \frac{2x^2}{81}$
25. $256x^5 - 81x$
26. $a^4 - (2b + c)^4$
27. $(3x + 4y)^4 - x^4$
28. $p^2q^2 - p^4q^4$
29. $3x^3y - 243xy^3$
30. $a^4b^4 - 16c^4$
31. $x^4 - 625$
32. $x^4 - 1$
33. $49(a - b)^2 - 25(a + b)^2$
34. $x - y - x^2 + y^2$
35. $16(2x - 1)^2 - 25y^2$
36. $4(xy + 1)^2 - 9(x - 1)^2$
37. $(2x + 1)^2 - 9x^4$
38. $x^4 - (2y - 3z)^2$
39. $a^2 - b^2 + a - b$
40. $16a^4 - b^4$
41. $a^4 - 16(b - c)^4$
42. $2a^5 - 32a$
43. $a^4b^4 - 81c^4$
44. $xy^9 - yx^9$
45. $x^3 - x$
46. $18a^2x^2 - 32$

ANSWERS

1. $(4x + 5y)(4x - 5y)$
2. $3(3x - 2y)(3x + 2y)$
3. $(12a - 17b)(12a + 17b)$
4. $3(2m - 3)(2m + 3)$
5. $5(5x - 3y)(5x + 3y)$
6. $(12a + 13x)(12a - 13x)$
7. $(2a - b + 4c)(2a - b - 4c)$
8. $5x(-3x + 4y)$
9. $3a^3(a - 4)(a + 4)$
10. $(a + 2b)(a - 2b)(a^2 + 4b^2)$
11. $(x - 1)(x + 1)(x^2 + 1)(x^4 + 1)$
12. $-(a + 9)(a - 7)$
13. $(6l + m + n)(6l - m - n)$
14. $(5x^2y^2 - 1)(5x^2y^2 + 1)$

15. $\left(a-\frac{1}{b}\right)\left(a+\frac{1}{b}\right)\left(a^2+\frac{1}{b^2}\right)$
16. $x(x-12)(x+12)$
17. $(x-4y+25)(x-4y-25)$
18. $(3a-3b+10x-10y)(3a-3b-10x+10y)$
19. $3(1-a)(3+7a)$
20. $(x+y+a-b)(x+y-a+b)$
21. $y^2\left(\frac{x}{4}-\frac{2}{7}z\right)\left(\frac{x}{4}+\frac{2}{7}z\right)$
22. $3ab^2(5a+6b)(5a-6b)$
23. $x^3(x-4)(x+4)$
24. $2\left(\frac{5}{x}+\frac{x}{9}\right)\left(\frac{5}{x}-\frac{x}{9}\right)$
25. $x(4x+3)(4x-3)(16x^2+9)$
26. $(a-2b-c)(a+2b+c)(a^2+(2b+c)^2)$
27. $8(x+2y)(x+y)[(3x+4y)^2+x^2]$
28. $p^2q^2(1+pq)(1-pq)$
29. $3xy(x-3y)(x+3y)$
30. $(ab-2c)(ab+2c)(a^2b^2+4c^2)$
31. $(x-5)(x+5)(x^2+25)$
32. $(x-1)(x+1)(x^2+1)$
33. $4(a-6b)(6a-b)$
34. $(x-y)(1-x-y)$
35. $(8x+5y-4)(8x-5y-4)$
36. $(2xy+3x-1)(2xy-3x+5)$
37. $(3x^2+2x+1)(-3x^2+2x+1)$
38. $(x^2+2y-3z)(x^2-2y+3z)$
39. $(a-b)(a+b+1)$
40. $(2a+b)(2a-b)(4a^2+b^2)$
41. $(a+2b-2c)(a-2b+2c)\left(a^2+4(b-c)^2\right)$
42. $2a(a-2)(a+2)(a^2+4)$
43. $(ab+3c)(ab-3c)(a^2b^2+9c^2)$
44. $-xy(x^2+y^2)(x+y)(x-y)(x^4+y^4)$
45. $x(x+1)(x-1)$
46. $2(3ax+4)(3ax-4)$

7.9 FACTORIZATION OF ALGEBRAIC EXPRESSIONS EXPRESSIBLE AS A PERFECT SQUARE

In order to factorize algebraic expressions expressible as a perfect square, we use the following expressions.

(i) $a^2+2ab+b^2=(a+b)^2=(a+b)(a+b)$

(ii) $a^2-2ab+b^2=(a-b)^2=(a-b)(a-b)$

Following examples will illustrate the use of these formulae in the factorization of algebraic expressions.

ILLUSTRATIVE EXAMPLES

Example 1 Factorize:

(i) $x^2+8x+16$ (ii) $4a^2-4a+1$

Solution We have,

(i) $x^2+8x+16=x^2+2\times x\times 4+4^2$

$=(x+4)^2$ [Using: $a^2+2ab+b^2=(a+b)^2$]

$=(x+4)(x+4)$

(ii) $4a^2-4a+1=(2a)^2-2\times 2a\times 1+(1)^2$

$=(2a-1)^2$ [Using: $a^2-2ab+b^2=(a-b)^2$]

$=(2a-1)(2a-1)$

Example 2 Factorize:

(i) $4x^2 + 12xy + 9y^2$ (ii) $x^4 - 10x^2y^2 + 25y^4$ (iii) $a^4 - 2a^2b^2 + b^4$

Solution We have,

(i) $4x^2 + 12xy + 9y^2 = (2x)^2 + 2 \times 2x \times 3y + (3y)^2$

$= (2x + 3y)^2$

$= (2x + 3y)(2x + 3y)$

(ii) $x^4 - 10x^2y^2 + 25y^4 = (x^2)^2 - 2 \times x^2 \times 5y^2 + (5y^2)^2$

$= (x^2 - 5y^2)^2$

$= (x^2 - 5y^2)(x^2 - 5y^2)$

(iii) $a^4 - 2a^2b^2 + b^4 = (a^2)^2 - 2 \times a^2 \times b^2 + (b^2)^2$

$= (a^2 - b^2)^2$

$= \{(a - b)(a + b)\}^2 = (a - b)^2 (a + b)^2$

Example 3 Factorize:

(i) $4x^2 - 4xy + y^2 - 9z^2$ (ii) $16 - x^2 - 2xy - y^2$ (iii) $x^4 - (x - z)^4$

Solution We have,

(i) $4x^2 - 4xy + y^2 - 9z^2 = (4x^2 - 4xy + y^2) - 9z^2$

$= \{(2x)^2 - 2 \times 2x \times y + y^2\} - (3z)^2$

$= (2x - y)^2 - (3z)^2$

$= (2x - y + 3z)(2x - y - 3z)$

(ii) $16 - x^2 - 2xy - y^2 = 16 - (x^2 + 2xy + y^2)$

$= 4^2 - (x + y)^2$

$= \{4 + (x + y)\}\{4 - (x + y)\}$

$= (4 + x + y)(4 - x - y)$

(iii) $x^4 - (x - z)^4 = (x^2)^2 - \{(x - z)^2\}^2$

$= \{x^2 + (x - z)^2\}\{x^2 - (x - z)^2\}$

$= (x^2 + x^2 - 2xz + z^2)[\{x + (x - z)\}\{x - (x - z)\}]$

$= (2x^2 - 2xz + z^2)(x + x - z)(x - x + z)$

$= (2x^2 - 2xz + z^2)(2x - z)z$

Example 4 Factorize:

(i) $(a^4 - 8a^2b^2 + 16b^4) - 256$ (ii) $a^4 - 6a^2b^2 + 9b^4 - 81$

Solution We have,

(i) $(a^4 - 8a^2b^2 + 16b^4) - 256 = \{(a^2)^2 - 2 \times a^2 \times 4b^2 + (4b^2)^2\} - 16^2$

$$= (a^2 - 4b^2)^2 - 16^2$$

$$= (a^2 - 4b^2 + 16)(a^2 - 4b^2 - 16)$$

(ii) $a^4 - 6a^2b^2 + 9b^4 - 81 = (a^4 - 6a^2b^2 + 9b^4) - 81$

$$= \{(a^2)^2 - 2 \times a^2 \times 3b^2 + (3b^2)^2\} - 9^2$$

$$= (a^2 - 3b^2)^2 - 9^2$$

$$= (a^2 - 3b^2 + 9)(a^2 - 3b^2 - 9)$$

Example 5 Factorize each of the following expressions:

(i) $x^2 - 2xy + y^2 - x + y$ (ii) $4a^2 + 12ab + 9b^2 - 8a - 12b$

(iii) $a^2 + b^2 - 2(ab - ac + bc)$

Solution (i) $x^2 - 2xy + y^2 - x + y = (x^2 - 2xy + y^2) - (x - y)$

$$= (x - y)^2 - (x - y)$$

$$= (x - y)\{(x - y) - 1\}$$

$$= (x - y)(x - y - 1)$$

(ii) $4a^2 + 12ab + 9b^2 - 8a - 12b = (2a)^2 + 2 \times 2a \times 3b + (3b)^2 - 4(2a + 3b)$

$$= (2a + 3b)^2 - 4(2a + 3b)$$

$$= (2a + 3b)(2a + 3b - 4)$$

(iii) $a^2 + b^2 - 2(ab - ac + bc) = a^2 + b^2 - 2ab + 2ac - 2bc$

$$= (a - b)^2 + 2c(a - b)$$

$$= (a - b)\{(a - b) + 2c\}$$

$$= (a - b)(a - b + 2c)$$

Example 6 Factorize:

(i) $4(x + y)^2 - 28y(x + y) + 49y^2$

(ii) $(2a + 3b)^2 + 2(2a + 3b)(2a - 3b) + (2a - 3b)^2$

Solution (i) $4(x + y)^2 - 28y(x + y) + 49y^2$

$$= \{2(x + y)\}^2 - 2 \times 2(x + y) \times 7y + (7y)^2$$

$$= \{2(x + y) - 7y\}^2 = (2x + 2y - 7y)^2 = (2x - 5y)^2$$

(ii) $(2a + 3b)^2 + 2(2a + 3b)(2a - 3b) + (2a - 3b)^2$

$$= [(2a + 3b) + (2a - 3b)]^2 = (4a)^2 = 16a^2$$

Example 7 Factorize each of the following expressions:

(i) $9x^2 - 4y^2$ (ii) $36x^2 - 12x + 1 - 25y^2$ (iii) $a^2 - 1 + 2x - x^2$

Solution (i) $9x^2 - 4y^2 = (3x)^2 - (2y)^2 = (3x + 2y)(3x - 2y)$

(ii) $36x^2 - 12x + 1 - 25y^2$

$$= (6x)^2 - 2 \times 6x \times 1 + 1^2 - (5y)^2$$
$$= (6x - 1)^2 - (5y)^2$$
$$= \{(6x - 1) - 5y\}\{(6x - 1) + 5y\}$$
$$= (6x - 1 - 5y)(6x - 1 + 5y)$$
$$= (6x - 5y - 1)(6x + 5y - 1)$$

(iii) $a^2 - 1 + 2x - x^2 = a^2 - (1 - 2x + x^2)$

$$= a^2 - \left(1^2 - 2 \times 1 \times x + (x)^2\right)$$
$$= a^2 - (1 - x)^2$$
$$= \{a - (1 - x)\}\{a + (1 - x)\}$$
$$= (a - 1 + x)(a + 1 - x)$$

Example 8 Factorize each of the following expressions:

(i) $x^2 + 2xy + y^2 - a^2 + 2ab - b^2$ (ii) $25x^2 - 10x + 1 - 36y^2$

(iii) $1 - 2ab - (a^2 + b^2)$

Solution (i) $x^2 + 2xy + y^2 - a^2 + 2ab - b^2 = (x^2 + 2xy + y^2) - (a^2 - 2ab + b^2)$

$$= (x + y)^2 - (a - b)^2$$
$$= \{(x + y) + (a - b)\}\{(x + y) - (a - b)\}$$
$$= (x + y + a - b)(x + y - a + b)$$

(ii) $25x^2 - 10x + 1 - 36y^2 = (5x)^2 - 2 \times 5x \times 1 + 1^2 - (6y)^2$

$$= (5x - 1)^2 - (6y)^2$$
$$= (5x - 1 + 6y)(5x - 1 - 6y)$$

(iii) $1 - 2ab - (a^2 + b^2) = 1 - (2ab + a^2 + b^2)$

$$= 1 - (a + b)^2$$
$$= \{1 + (a + b)\}\{1 - (a + b)\}$$
$$= (1 + a + b)(1 - a - b)$$

Example 9 Factorize:

(i) $x^2 + 8x + 15$ (ii) $x^4 + x^2 + 1$ (iii) $x^4 + 4$

Solution We have,

(i) $x^2 + 8x + 15 = (x^2 + 8x + 16) - 1$ [Replacing 15 by 16 – 1]

$$= \{(x)^2 + 2 \times x \times 4 + 4^2\} - 1$$
$$= (x + 4)^2 - 1^2$$
$$= \{(x + 4 + 1\}\{(x + 4) - 1\}$$
$$= (x + 5)(x + 3)$$

(ii) $x^4+x^2+1 = x^4+2x^2+1-x^2$ [Adding and subtracting x^2]

$= (x^4+2x^2+1)-x^2$

$= \left((x^2)^2+2\times x^2\times 1+1^2\right)-x^2$

$= (x^2+1)^2-x^2$

$= \{(x^2+1)+x\}\{(x^2+1)-x\}$

$= (x^2+x+1)(x^2-x+1)$

(iii) $x^4+4 = x^4+4x^2+4-4x^2$ [Adding and subtracting $4x^2$]

$= \{(x^2)^2+2\times x^2\times 2+2^2\}-4x^2$

$= (x^2+2)^2-(2x)^2$

$= \{(x^2+2)+2x\}\{(x^2+2)-2x\}$

$= (x^2+2x+2)(x^2-2x+2)$

Example 10 Factorize:

(i) $9-a^6+2a^3b^3-b^6$ (ii) $x^{16}-y^{16}+x^8+y^8$

(iii) $(p+q)^2-(a-b)^2+p+q-a+b$

Solution We have,

(i) $9-a^6+2a^3b^3-b^6 = 9-(a^6-2a^3b^3+b^6)$

$= 3^2-\{(a^3)^2-2\times a^3\times b^3+(b^3)^2\}$

$= 3^2-(a^3-b^3)^2$

$= \{3+(a^3-b^3)\}\{3-(a^3-b^3)\}$

$= (3+a^3-b^3)(3-a^3+b^3) = (a^3-b^3+3)(-a^3+b^3+3)$

(ii) $x^{16}-y^{16}+x^8+y^8 = \{(x^8)^2-(y^8)^2\}+(x^8+y^8)$

$= (x^8-y^8)(x^8+y^8)+(x^8+y^8)$

$= (x^8+y^8)(x^8-y^8+1)$

(iii) $(p+q)^2-(a-b)^2+p+q-a+b$

$= \left\{(p+q)^2-(a-b)^2\right\}+(p+q)-(a-b)$

$= \{(p+q)+(a-b)\}\{(p+q)-(a-b)\}+\{(p+q)-(a-b)\}$

$= (p+q+a-b)(p+q-a+b)+(p+q-a+b)$

$= (p+q-a+b)(p+q+a-b+1)$

EXERCISE 7.6

Factorize each of the following algebraic expressions:

1. $4x^2+12xy+9y^2$
2. $9a^2-24ab+16b^2$
3. $p^2q^2-6pqr+9r^2$
4. $36a^2+36a+9$

5. $a^2 + 2ab + b^2 - 16$

6. $9z^2 - x^2 + 4xy - 4y^2$

7. $9a^4 - 24a^2b^2 + 16b^4 - 256$

8. $16 - a^6 + 4a^3b^3 - 4b^6$

9. $a^2 - 2ab + b^2 - c^2$

10. $x^2 + 2x + 1 - 9y^2$

11. $a^2 + 4ab + 3b^2$

12. $96 - 4x - x^2$

13. $a^4 + 3a^2 + 4$

14. $4x^4 + 1$

15. $4x^4 + y^4$

16. $(x + 2)^2 - 6(x + 2) + 9$

17. $25 - p^2 - q^2 - 2pq$

18. $x^2 + 9y^2 - 6xy - 25a^2$

19. $49 - a^2 + 8ab - 16b^2$

20. $a^2 - 8ab + 16b^2 - 25c^2$

21. $x^2 - y^2 + 6y - 9$

22. $25x^2 - 10x + 1 - 36y^2$

23. $a^2 - b^2 + 2bc - c^2$

24. $a^2 + 2ab + b^2 - c^2$

25. $49 - x^2 - y^2 + 2xy$

26. $a^2 + 4b^2 - 4ab - 4c^2$

27. $x^2 - y^2 - 4xz + 4z^2$

ANSWERS

1. $(2x + 3y)(2x + 3y)$

2. $(3a - 4b)(3a - 4b)$

3. $(pq - 3r)(pq - 3r)$

4. $9(2a + 1)(2a + 1)$

5. $(a + b + 4)(a + b - 4)$

6. $(x - 2y + 3z)(-x + 2y + 3z)$

7. $(3a^2 - 4b^2 + 16)(3a^2 - 4b^2 - 16)$

8. $(a^3 - 2b^3 + 4)(-a^3 + 2b^3 + 4)$

9. $(a - b - c)(a - b + c)$

10. $(x + 3y + 1)(x - 3y + 1)$

11. $(a + 3b)(a + b)$

12. $(x + 12)(-x + 8)$

13. $(a^2 + a + 2)(a^2 - a + 2)$

14. $(2x^2 + 2x + 1)(2x^2 - 2x + 1)$

15. $(2x^2 + 2xy + y^2)(2x^2 - 2xy + y^2)$

16. $(x - 1)(x - 1)$

17. $-(p + q + 5)(p + q - 5)$

18. $(x - 3y + 5a)(x - 3y - 5a)$

19. $-(a - 4b + 7)(a - 4b - 7)$

20. $(a - 4b + 5c)(a - 4b - 5c)$

21. $(x + y - 3)(x - y + 3)$

22. $(5x - 6y - 1)(5x + 6y - 1)$

23. $(a + b - c)(a - b + c)$

24. $(a + b + c)(a + b - c)$

25. $(x - y + 7)(y - x + 7)$

26. $(a - 2b + 2c)(a - 2b - 2c)$

27. $(x + y - 2z)(x - y - 2z)$

7.10 POLYNOMIALS

We have studied that an algebraic expression consisting of just one term is called a monomial, a sum of exactly two monomials is called a binomial and a trinomial is a sum of exactly three monomials. In all the algebraic expressions which we have discussed so far the variables (x, y, z, a, b etc) occurred with exponents (or indices) as 0, 1, 2, 3, ... (whole numbers). This type of algebraic expressions are known as polynomials. We have never dealt with an expression having variable in the denominator or in which variable has fractional exponents. Note that the exponent (or index) of a variable in a polynomial cannot be a negative integer or a fraction. Also, a polynomial is a sum of monomials in which variables always occur in indices 0, 1, 2, 3, ... etc. Following algebraic expressions are polynomials:

(i) $2xy - 3y + 5$ (ii) $x + y + z + 2$ (iii) $2x + 3$

(iv) $xy + yz + zx$ (v) $a + b + c + 7$ (vi) $2x^2 - x + 6$

None of the following algebraic expressions is a polynomial:

$$\frac{3}{x}, \frac{1}{x} - 2, \frac{2}{4-3x}, 2\sqrt{x} + 5, x^2 - \sqrt{x} + 2, xy + \frac{1}{z} - 2$$

A polynomial may consist of more than one variable. For example,

$$2xy - 3x + 4y - 1, \quad xy + yz - 3xyz + 1, \quad a^2b^2 - 5ab + 6$$

etc. are polynomials in two or more variables.

Let us now talk about polynomials with one variable only. Clearly, $3x + 2, -4y + 1, 2z - 5$ etc are polynomials in one variable such that the highest power of the variable in each term is 1. Such polynomials are known as *linear* polynomials.

Consider now the following polynomials:

$$x^2 - 3x + 2, \ 2y^2 - 1, \ -z^2 + 2z, \ t^2 - 5t + 6$$

In these polynomials the highest power of the variable in each term is 2. Such polynomials are called quadratic polynomials. If the highest power of the variable in a polynomial is three, it is known as a cubic polynomial.

In the remaining part of this chapter, we will discuss quadratic polynomials in one variable only.

7.11 FACTORIZATION OF QUADRATIC POLYNOMIALS IN ONE VARIABLE

In this section, we will discuss how we can factorize quadratic polynomials in one variable, like $x^2 + 5x + 4$, $y^2 - 5y + 6$, $z^2 - 4z - 12$, $t^2 + 3t + 2$, etc. These polynomials are of the type $x^2 + (a + b)x + ab$. Therefore, we will use the identity $x^2 + x(a + b) + ab = (x + a)(x + b)$ to factorize such polynomials.

Consider the polynomial $x^2 + 7x + 12$.

Comparing this polynomial with $x^2 + (a + b)x + ab$, we find that $a + b = 7$ and $ab = 12$.

From these two equations, we have to find the values of a and b. The factors then are $(x + a)(x + b)$.

We have, $a + b = 7$ and $ab = 12$.

Note that $ab = 12$ means that a and b are factors of 12. Also, ab is positive, therefore a and b are of the same sign. But, $a + b = 7$ is positive. Therefore, a and b both are positive. Thus, we have to find positive factors of 12 whose sum is 7. Clearly, such factors are 3 and 4.

$\therefore$ $(a = 3$ and $b = 4)$ or $(a = 4$ and $b = 3)$

The factors of $x^2 + 7x + 12$ corresponding to $a = 3$ and $b = 4$ are : $(x + 3)(x + 4)$.

The factors of $x^2 + 7x + 12$ corresponding to $a = 4$ and $b = 3$ are: $(x + 4)(x + 3)$.

In other words, we get the same factors in both cases. So, we should consider only one pair of values of a and b.

Let us now consider the polynomial $y^2 - 7y + 12$.

Comparing this with the polynomial $y^2 + (a + b)y + ab$, we get $a + b = -7$ and $ab = 12$.

Now, we have to find factors of 12 whose sum is -7.

Since $a + b$ is negative and ab is positive. Therefore, a and b both must negative.

Clearly, such factors are – 3 and – 4.

Hence, the factors of $y^2 - 7y + 12$ are $(y - 3)$ and $(y - 4)$.

$\therefore \quad y^2 - 7y + 12 = (y - 3)(y - 4)$.

Finally, let us take the polynomial $z^2 - 4z - 12$.

Comparing this with the polynomial $z^2 + (a + b)z + ab$, we get

$$a + b = -4 \text{ and } ab = -12.$$

Since $a + b$ and ab both are negative. Therefore, one of a and b is positive and the other is negative. As $a + b$ is negative, therefore the number with greater magnitude must be negative. Clearly, – 6 and 2 are factors of – 12 such that their sum is – 4.

$\therefore \quad a = -6$ and $b = 2$

Hence, factors of $z^2 - 4z - 12$ are $(z - 6)$ and $(z + 2)$.

Hence, $z^2 - 4z - 12 = (z - 6)(z + 2)$.

Above discussion suggests the following algorithm to factorize quadratic polynomials of the form $x^2 + px + q$.

ALGORITHM

Step I *Obtain the quadratic polynomial $x^2 + px + q$.*

Step II *Obtain p = coefficient of x and, q = constant term.*

Step III *Find two numbers a and b such that a + b = p and ab = q.*

Step IV *Split up the middle term as the sum of two terms ax and bx.*

Step V *Factorize the expression obtained in step IV by grouping the terms.*

Following examples will illustrate the above algorithm.

ILLUSTRATIVE EXAMPLES

Example 1 Factorize each of the following expressions:

(i) $x^2 + 6x + 8$ (ii) $x^2 + 4x - 21$ (iii) $x^2 - 7x + 12$

Solution (i) In order to factorize $x^2 + 6x + 8$, we find two numbers p and q such that $p + q = 6$ and $pq = 8$.

Clearly, $2 + 4 = 6$ and $2 \times 4 = 8$.

We now split the middle term $6x$ in the given quadratic as $2x + 4x$.

$$\begin{aligned} \therefore \quad x^2 + 6x + 8 &= x^2 + 2x + 4x + 8 \\ &= (x^2 + 2x) + (4x + 8) \\ &= x(x + 2) + 4(x + 2) \\ &= (x + 2)(x + 4) \end{aligned}$$

(ii) In order to factorize $x^2 + 4x - 21$, we have to find two numbers p and q such that

$$p + q = 4 \text{ and } pq = -21$$

Clearly, $7 + (-3) = 4$ and $7 \times -3 = -21$.

We now split the middle term $4x$ of $x^2 + 4x - 21$ as $7x - 3x$.

$$\therefore \quad x^2 + 4x - 21 = x^2 + 7x - 3x - 21$$
$$= (x^2 + 7x) - (3x + 21)$$
$$= x(x + 7) - 3(x + 7)$$
$$= (x + 7)(x - 3)$$

(iii) In order to factorize $x^2 - 7x + 12$ we have to find two numbers p and q such that $p + q = -7$ and $pq = 12$.

Clearly, $-3 - 4 = -7$ and $-3 \times -4 = 12$.

We now split the middle term $-7x$ of the given quadratic as $-3x - 4x$.

$$\therefore \quad x^2 - 7x + 12 = x^2 - 3x - 4x + 12$$
$$= (x^2 - 3x) - (4x - 12)$$
$$= x(x - 3) - 4(x - 3)$$
$$= (x - 3)(x - 4)$$

Example 2 Factorize each of the following quadratic polynomials:

(i) $x^2 - 23x + 132$ (ii) $x^2 - 21x + 108$ (iii) $x^2 + 5x - 36$

Solution (i) In order to factorize $x^2 - 23x + 132$, we have to find two numbers p and q such that $p + q = -23$ and $pq = 132$.

Clearly, $-12 - 11 = -23$ and $-12 \times -11 = 132$.

We now split the middle term $-23x$ of $x^2 - 23x + 132$ as $-12x - 11x$

$$\therefore \quad x^2 - 23x + 132 = x^2 - 12x - 11x + 132$$
$$= (x^2 - 12x) - (11x - 132)$$
$$= x(x - 12) - 11(x - 12)$$
$$= (x - 12)(x - 11)$$

(ii) In order to factorize $x^2 - 21x + 108$, we have to find two numbers such that their sum is -21 and the product 108.

Clearly, $-21 = -12 - 9$ and $-12 \times -9 = 108$

So, we split the middle term $-21x$ as $-12x - 9x$

$$\therefore \quad x^2 - 21x + 108 = x^2 - 12x - 9x + 108$$
$$= (x^2 - 12x) - (9x - 108)$$
$$= x(x - 12) - 9(x - 12)$$
$$= (x - 12)(x - 9)$$

(iii) In order to factorize $x^2 + 5x - 36$, we have to find two numbers p and q such that $p + q = 5$ and $pq = -36$.

Clearly, $9 + (-4) = 5$ and $9 \times -4 = -36$.

So, we write the middle term $5x$ of $x^2 + 5x - 36$ as $9x - 4x$.

$$\therefore \quad x^2 - 5x - 36 = x^2 + 9x - 4x - 36$$
$$= (x^2 + 9x) - (4x + 36)$$
$$= x(x + 9) - 4(x + 9)$$
$$= (x + 9)(x - 4)$$

EXERCISE 7.7

Factorize each of the following algebraic expressions:

1. $x^2+12x-45$
2. $40+3x-x^2$
3. $a^2+3a-88$
4. $a^2-14a-51$
5. $x^2+14x+45$
6. $x^2-22x+120$
7. $x^2-11x-42$
8. a^2+2a-3
9. $a^2+14a+48$
10. $x^2-4x-21$
11. $y^2+5y-36$
12. $(a^2-5a)^2-36$
13. $(a+7)(a-10)+16$

ANSWERS

1. $(x+15)(x-3)$
2. $(x+5)(-x+8)$
3. $(a+11)(a-8)$
4. $(a-17)(a+3)$
5. $(x+9)(x+5)$
6. $(x-12)(x-10)$
7. $(x-14)(x+3)$
8. $(a+3)(a-1)$
9. $(a+6)\,a+8)$
10. $(x-7)(x+3)$
11. $(y+9)(y-4)$
12. $(a+1)(a-2)(a-3)(a-6)$
13. $(a-9)(a+6)$

7.11.1 FACTORIZATION OF QUADRATIC POLYNOMIALS OF THEOREM $ax^2+bx+c, a\neq 1$

We have learnt about the factorization of quadratic polynomials of the form x^2+ax+b. Following stepwise procedure will be useful to factorize polynomials of the form ax^2+bx+c, where $a\neq 1$.

PROCEDURE

Step I *Obtain the quadratic trinomial $ax^2 + bx + c$*

Step II *Obtain a = coefficient of x^2, b = coefficient of x and c = constant term.*

Step III *Find the product of the coefficient of x^2 and the constant term i.e. ac.*

Step IV *Split up the coefficient of x i.e. b into two parts whose sum is b and product ac and write the middle term as the sum of two terms.*

Step V *Factorize the expression obtained in step IV by grouping the terms. Factors so obtained will be the required factors of the given quadratic trinomial.*

Following examples will illustrate the above procedure.

ILLUSTRATIVE EXAMPLES

Example 1 Factorize:

(i) $2x^2+5x+3$ (ii) $6x^2+5x-6$ (iii) $6x^2-13x+6$ (iv) $-2x^2-3x+2$

Solution (i) The given expression is $2x^2+5x+3$

Here, coefficient of $x^2=2$, coefficient of x = 5, and constant term = 3.

We shall now split up the coeffcient of the middle term i.e. 5 into two parts such that their sum is 5 and product equal to the product of coefficient of x^2 and constant term i.e. $2\times 3=6$. Clearly, $2+3=5$ and $2\times 3=6$. So, we replace the middle term $5x$ by $2x + 3x$.

Thus, we have

$$2x^2 + 5x + 3 = 2x^2 + 2x + 3x + 3$$
$$= (2x^2 + 2x) + (3x + 3)$$
$$= 2x(x + 1) + 3(x + 1)$$
$$= (x + 1)(2x + 3)$$

(ii) The given expression is $6x^2 + 5x - 6$

Here, coefficient of $x^2 = 6$, coefficient of $x = 5$, constant term $= -6$

We shall now split up the coefficient of x i.e., 5 into two parts such that their sum is equal to coefficient of x i.e., 5 and product equal to the product of coefficient of x^2 and constant term i.e., $6 \times -6 = -36$.

Clearly, $9 + (-4) = 5$ and $9 \times -4 = -36$. So, we replace the middle term $5x$ by $9x - 4x$.

Thus, we have

$$6x^2 + 5x - 6 = 6x^2 + 9x - 4x - 6$$
$$= 3x(2x + 3) - 2(2x + 3)$$
$$= (2x + 3)(3x - 2)$$

(iii) The given expression is $6x^2 - 13x + 6$.

Here, coefficient of $x^2 = 6$, coefficient of $x = -13$, and constant term $= 6$.

We shall now split up the coefficient of x i.e. -13 into two parts whose sum is -13 and product equal to the product of the coefficient of x^2 and constant term i.e., $6 \times 6 = 36$. Clearly, $-4 - 9 = -13$ and $-4 \times -9 = 36$. So, we write the middle term $-13x$ as $-4x - 9x$

Thus, we have

$$6x^2 - 13x + 6 = 6x^2 - 4x - 9x + 6$$
$$= 2x(3x - 2) - 3(3x - 2)$$
$$= (3x - 2)(2x - 3)$$

(iv) The given expression is $-2x^2 - 3x + 2$.

Here, coefficient of $x^2 = -2$, coefficient of $x = -3$ and constant term $= 2$.

We shall now split up the coefficient of the middle term i.e. -3 into two parts such that their sum is -2 and the product is equal to the product of the coefficient of x^2 and constant term i.e. $-2 \times 2 = -4$.

Clearly, $-4 + 1 = -3$ and $-4 \times 1 = -4$.

So, we write the middle term $-3x$ as $-4x + x$.

Thus, we have

$$-2x^2 - 3x + 2 = -2x^2 - 4x + x + 2$$
$$= -2x(x + 2) + 1(x + 2)$$
$$= (x + 2)(-2x + 1)$$

Example 2 Factorize:

(i) $12x^2 - 23xy + 10y^2$ (ii) $12x^2 + 7xy - 10y^2$ (iii) $6x^2 + 35xy - 6y^2$

Solution (i) The given expression is $12x^2 - 23xy + 10y^2$

Here, coefficient of $x^2 = 12$, coefficient of $x = -23y$, and constant term $= 10y^2$.

Now, we split up the coefficient of the middle term i.e., $-23y$ into two parts whose sum is $-23y$ and product equal to the product of the coefficient of x^2 and constant term i.e., $12 \times 10y^2 = 120y^2$.

Clearly, $-15y - 8y = -23y$ and $-15y \times -8y = 120y^2$

So, we replace the middle term $-23xy$ by $-15xy - 8xy$.

Thus, we have

$$\begin{aligned} 12x^2 - 23xy + 10y^2 &= 12x^2 - 15xy - 8xy + 10y^2 \\ &= 3x(4x - 5y) - 2y(4x - 5y) \\ &= (4x - 5y)(3x - 2y) \end{aligned}$$

(ii) The given expression is $12x^2 + 7xy - 10y^2$

Here, coefficient of $x^2 = 12$, coefficient of $x = 7y$ and constant term $= -10y^2$.

We shall now split up the coefficient of the middle term i.e. $7y$ into two parts whose sum is $7y$ and product equal to the product of the coefficient of x^2 and constant term i.e. $12 \times -10y^2 = -120y^2$.

Clearly, $15y - 8y = 7y$ and $15y \times -8y = -120y^2$

So, we replace the middle term $7xy$ by $15xy - 8xy$

Thus, we have

$$\begin{aligned} 12x^2 + 7xy - 10y^2 &= 12x^2 + 15xy - 8xy - 10y^2 \\ &= 3x(4x + 5y) - 2y(4x + 5y) \\ &= (4x + 5y)(3x - 2y) \end{aligned}$$

(iii) The given expression is $6x^2 + 35xy - 6y^2$.

Here, coefficient of $x^2 = 6$, coefficient of $x = 35y$ and constant term $= -6y^2$.

We shall now split up the coefficient of x i.e., $35y$ into two parts whose sum is $35y$ and product equal to the product of the coefficient of x^2 and constant term i.e., $6 \times -6y^2 = -36y^2$. Clearly, $36y - y = 35y$ and $36y \times -y = -36y^2$.

So, we replace the middle term $35xy$ by $36\,xy - xy$.

Thus, we have

$$\begin{aligned} 6x^2 + 35xy - 6y^2 &= 6x^2 + 36xy - xy - 6y^2 \\ &= 6x(x + 6y) - y(x + 6y) \\ &= (6x - y)(x + 6y) \end{aligned}$$

Example 3 Factorize: $(2x + 3y)^2 - 5(2x + 3y) - 14$

Solution The given expression is $(2x + 3y)^2 - 5(2x + 3y) - 14$

Let $2x + 3y = a$. Then,

$$\begin{aligned} (2x + 3y)^2 - 5(2x + 3y) - 14 &= a^2 - 5a - 14 \\ &= a^2 - 7a + 2a - 14 \\ &= a(a - 7) + 2(a - 7) \\ &= (a - 7)(a + 2) \\ &= (2x + 3y - 7)(2x + 3y + 2) \end{aligned}$$

EXERCISE 7.8

Resolve each of the following quadratic trinomials into factors:

1. $2x^2+5x+3$
2. $2x^2-3x-2$
3. $3x^2+10x+3$
4. $7x-6-2x^2$
5. $7x^2-19x-6$
6. $28-31x-5x^2$
7. $3+23y-8y^2$
8. $11x^2-54x+63$
9. $7x-6x^2+20$
10. $3x^2+22x+35$
11. $12x^2-17xy+6y^2$
12. $6x^2-5xy-6y^2$
13. $6x^2-13xy+2y^2$
14. $14x^2+11xy-15y^2$
15. $6a^2+17ab-3b^2$
16. $36a^2+12abc-15b^2c^2$
17. $15x^2-16xyz-15y^2z^2$
18. $(x-2y)^2-5(x-2y)+6$
19. $(2a-b)^2+2(2a-b)-8$

ANSWERS

1. $(2x+3)(x+1)$
2. $(2x+1)(x-2)$
3. $(3x+1)(x+3)$
4. $(2-x)(2x-3)$
5. $(x-3)(7x+2)$
6. $(4-5x)(x+7)$
7. $(1+8y)(3-y)$
8. $(x-3)(11x-21)$
9. $(3x+4)(5-2x)$
10. $(x+5)(3x+7)$
11. $(3x-2y)(4x-3y)$
12. $(2x-3y)(3x+2y)$
13. $(x-2y)(6x-y)$
14. $(2x+3y)(7x-5y)$
15. $(a+3b)(6a-b)$
16. $3(6a+5bc)(2a-bc)$
17. $(5x+3yz)(3x-5yz)$
18. $(x-2y-2)(x-2y-3)$
19. $(2a-b+4)(2a-b-2)$

7.11.2 FACTORIZATION OF QUADRATIC POLYNOMIALS BY USING THE METHOD OF COMPLETING THE PERFECT SQUARE

In order to factorize quadratic polynomials by using the method of completing the square, we may use the following stepwise procedure.

PROCEDURE

<u>Step I</u> *Obtain the quadratic polynomial. Let the polynomial be* ax^2+bx+c, *where* $a \neq 0$.

<u>Step II</u> *Make the coefficient of* x^2 *unity by dividing and multiplying throughout by it, if it is not unity i.e., write*

$$ax^2+bx+c = a\left(x^2+\frac{b}{a}x+\frac{c}{a}\right)$$

<u>Step III</u> *Add and subtract square of half of the coefficient of x i.e., write*

$$ax^2+bx+c = a\left(x^2+\frac{b}{a}x+\frac{c}{a}\right)$$

$$= a\left\{x^2+2\left(\frac{b}{2a}\right)x+\left(\frac{b}{2a}\right)^2-\left(\frac{b}{2a}\right)^2+\frac{c}{a}\right\}$$

<u>Step IV</u> *Write first three terms as the square of a binomial and simplify last two terms i.e., write*

$$ax^2+bx+c = a\left\{x^2+2\left(\frac{b}{2a}\right)x+\left(\frac{b}{2a}\right)^2-\left(\frac{b}{2a}\right)^2+\frac{c}{a}\right\}$$

$$= a\left\{\left(x+\frac{b}{2a}\right)^2-\left(\frac{b^2-4ac}{4a^2}\right)\right\}$$

<u>*Step V*</u> *Factorize last step obtained in step IV by using* $a^2 - b^2 = (a-b)(a+b)$ *to get desired factors.*

Following examples will illustrate the above procedure.

ILLUSTRATIVE EXAMPLES

Example 1 Factorize $y^2 + 6y + 8$ by using the method of completing the square.

Solution Here, coefficient of y^2 is unity. So, we add and subtract the square of the half of coefficient of y.

$$\therefore \quad y^2 + 6y + 8 = y^2 + 6y + 3^2 - 3^2 + 8 \qquad \left[\text{Adding and subtracting} \left(\frac{6}{2}\right)^2 = 3^2\right]$$

$$= (y^2 + 6y + 3^2) - 1$$

$$= (y+3)^2 - 1^2 \qquad \text{[By completing the square]}$$

$$= \{(y+3) - 1\}\{(y+3) + 1\} \qquad \left[\text{Using} : a^2 - b^2 = (a-b)(a+b)\right]$$

$$= (y+2)(y+4)$$

Example 2 Factorize: $3m^2 + 24m + 36$

Solution We have,

$$3m^2 + 24m + 36$$

$$= 3(m^2 + 8m + 12) \qquad \text{[Making coefficient of } m^2 \text{ as 1]}$$

$$= 3\{m^2 + 8m + 4^2 - 4^2 + 12\} \qquad \left[\text{Adding and subtracting} \left(\frac{8}{2}\right)^2 = 4^2\right]$$

$$= 3\{m^2 + 2 \times m \times 4 + 4^2 - 4\}$$

$$= 3\{(m+4)^2 - 2^2\} \qquad \text{[Completing the square]}$$

$$= 3\{(m+4) - 2\}\{(m+4) + 2\}$$

$$= 3(m + 4 - 2)(m + 4 + 2)$$

$$= 3(m+2)(m+6)$$

Example 3 Factorize: $4y^2 - 8y + 3$

Solution We have,

$$4y^2 - 8y + 3$$

$$= 4\left\{y^2 - 2y + \frac{3}{4}\right\} \qquad \text{[Making coefficient of } y^2 \text{ as 1]}$$

$$= 4\left\{y^2 - 2y + 1^2 - 1^2 + \frac{3}{4}\right\} \qquad \left[\text{Adding and subtracting} \left(\frac{1}{2} \text{Coeff. of } y\right)^2 \text{ i.e., } 1^2\right]$$

$$= 4\left\{(y^2 - 2y + 1^2) - \frac{1}{4}\right\}$$

$$= 4\left\{(y-1)^2 - \left(\frac{1}{2}\right)^2\right\} \qquad \text{[Completing the square]}$$

$$= 4\left[\left\{(y-1)-\frac{1}{2}\right\}\left\{(y-1)+\frac{1}{2}\right\}\right] \qquad \left[\text{Using } a^2-b^2=(a-b)(a+b)\right]$$

$$= 4\left(y-1-\frac{1}{2}\right)\left(y-1+\frac{1}{2}\right)$$

$$= 4\left(y-\frac{3}{2}\right)\left(y-\frac{1}{2}\right)$$

$$= 4\left(\frac{2y-3}{2}\right)\left(\frac{2y-1}{2}\right)$$

$$= (2y-3)(2y-1).$$

Example 4 Factorize: $6-x-2x^2$

Solution We have,

$$6-x-2x^2$$

$$= -2x^2-x+6$$

$$= -2\left(x^2+\frac{1}{2}x-3\right) \qquad [\text{Dividing and multiplying by } -2 \text{ i.e., the coeff. of } x^2]$$

$$= -2\left\{x^2+\frac{1}{2}x+\left(\frac{1}{4}\right)^2-\left(\frac{1}{4}\right)^2-3\right\} \qquad \left[\begin{array}{l}\text{Adding and subtracting}\left(\frac{1}{2}\text{Coeff. of } x\right)^2\\ \text{i.e.,}\left(\frac{1}{4}\right)^2\end{array}\right]$$

$$= -2\left[\left\{x^2+2\times\frac{1}{4}\times x+\left(\frac{1}{4}\right)^2\right\}-\left\{\frac{1}{16}+3\right\}\right]$$

$$= -2\left\{\left(x+\frac{1}{4}\right)^2-\frac{49}{16}\right\}$$

$$= -2\left\{\left(x+\frac{1}{4}\right)^2-\left(\frac{7}{4}\right)^2\right\}$$

$$= -2\left\{\left(x+\frac{1}{4}\right)-\frac{7}{4}\right\}\left\{\left(x+\frac{1}{4}\right)+\frac{7}{4}\right\}$$

$$= -2\left(x+\frac{1}{4}-\frac{7}{4}\right)\left(x+\frac{1}{4}+\frac{7}{4}\right)$$

$$= -2\left(x-\frac{3}{2}\right)(x+2)$$

$$= (-2x+3)(x+2)$$

EXERCISE 7.9

Factorize each of the following quadratic polynomials by using the method of completing the square:

1. p^2+6p+8
2. $q^2-10q+21$
3. $4y^2+12y+5$
4. $p^2+6p-16$
5. $x^2+12x+20$
6. $a^2-14a-51$

7. $a^2 + 2a - 3$
8. $4x^2 - 12x + 5$
9. $y^2 - 7y + 12$
10. $z^2 - 4z - 12$

ANSWERS

1. $(p+2)(p+4)$
2. $(q-3)(q-7)$
3. $(2y+1)(2y+5)$
4. $(p+8)(p-2)$
5. $(x+2)(x+10)$
6. $(a-17)(a+3)$
7. $(a+3)(a-1)$
8. $(2x-5)(2x-1)$
9. $(y-3)(y-4)$
10. $(z-6)(z+2)$

THINGS TO REMEMBER

1. *When an expression is the product of two or more expressions then each of these expressions is called a factor of the given expression.*
2. *The process of writing a given expression as the product of two or more factors is called factorization.*
3. *The greatest common factor of two or more monomials is the product of the greatest common factors of the numerical coefficients and the common letters with smallest powers.*
4. *When a common monomial factor occurs in each term of an algebraic expression then it can be expressed as a product of the greatest common factor of its terms and the quotient of the given expression by the greatest common factor of its terms.*
5. *When a binomial is a common factor, we write the given expression as the product of this binomial and the quotient of this given expression by this binomial.*
6. *If the given expression is the difference of two squares, then to factorize it, we use the formula:*

$$(a^2 - b^2) = (a+b)(a-b)$$

7. *If the given expression is a complete square, we use one of the following formulae to factorize it :*

   (i) $a^2 + 2ab + b^2 = (a+b)^2 = (a+b)(a+b)$

   (ii) $a^2 - 2ab + b^2 = (a-b)^2 = (a-b)(a-b)$

8. *If the given expression is in the form* $x^2 + x(a+b) + ab$, *then we factorize, it in the form* $(x+a)(x+b)$.

8

DIVISION OF ALGEBRAIC EXPRESSIONS

8.1 INTRODUCTION

We have been using four fundamental operations of addition, subtraction, multiplication and division on numbers since primary classes. About addition and subtraction of algebraic expressions we have studied in class VII and multipliation of algebraic expressions have been discussed in chapter 6. In this chapter, we shall study about division of algebraic expressions and the same will be extended to division of polynomials.

8.2 POLYNOMIALS

In the previous chapter, we have introduced the concept of a polynomial. Let us recall some useful terms and definitions.

POLYNOMIALS *An algebraic expression in which the variables involved have only non-negative integral powers, is called a polynomial.*

ILLUSTRATION 1 $\frac{2}{3}x^2 - \frac{3}{2}x^2 + x - 5$ is a polynomial in variables x whereas $\frac{1}{2}x^3 - 3x^2 + 5x^{1/2} + x - 1$ is not a polynomial, because it contains a term $5x^{1/2}$ which contains $\frac{1}{2}$ as the power of variable x, which is not a non-negative integer.

ILLUSTRATION 2 $3 - 2x^2 + 4x^2y + 8y - \frac{5}{3}xy^2$ is a polynomial in two variables x and y.

DEGREE OF A POLYNOMIAL IN ONE VARIABLE *In a polynomial in one variable, the highest power of the variable is called its degree.*

ILLUSTRATION 3 (i) $2x + 3$ is a polynomial in x of degree 1.

(ii) $2x^2 - 3x + \frac{7}{5}$ is a polynomial in x of degree 2.

(iii) $\frac{2}{3}a^3 - \frac{7}{2}a^2 + 4$ is a polynomial in a of degree 3.

DEGREE OF A POLYNOMIAL IN TWO VARIABLES *In a polynomial in more than one variable the sum of the powers of the variables in each term is computed and the highest sum so obtained is called the degree of the polynomial.*

ILLUSTRATION 4 $3x^4 - 2x^3y^2 + 7xy^3 - 9x + 5y + 4$ is a polynomial in x and y of degree 5, whereas $\frac{1}{2} - 3x + 7x^2y - \frac{3}{4}x^2y^2$ is a polynomial of degree 4 in x and y.

CONSTANT POLYNOMIAL *A polynomial consisting of a constant term only is called a constant polynomial. The degree of a constant polynomial is zero.*

LINEAR POLYNOMIAL *A polynomial of degree 1 is called a linear polynomial.*

ILLUSTRATION 5 $2-\frac{3}{4}x, \frac{1}{2}+\frac{3}{5}y, 2+3a$ etc. are linear polynomials.

QUADRATIC POLYNOMIAL *A polynomial of degree 2 is called a quadratic polynomial.*

ILLUSTRATION 6 $2x^2-3x+4, 2-x+x^2, 2y^2-\frac{3}{2}y+\frac{1}{4}$ are quadratic polynomials.

CUBIC POLYNOMIAL *A polynomial of degree 3 is called a cubic polynomial.*

ILLUSTRATION 7 $x^3-7x^2+2x-3, 2+\frac{1}{2}y-\frac{3}{2}y^2+4y^3$ are cubic polynomials.

BIQUADRATIC POLYNOMIALS *A polynomial of degree 4 is called a biquadratic polynomial.*

ILLUSTRATION 8 $3x^4-7x^3+x^2-x+9, 4-\frac{2}{3}x^2+\frac{3}{5}x^4$ are biquadratic polynomials.

A polynomial is said to be a monomial, a binomial or a trinomial according as it contains 1 term, 2 terms or 3 terms respectively.

Every polynomial is an algebraic expression but an algebraic expression need not be a polynomial. So, the addition, subtraction and multiplication of polynomials are performed exactly in the same way as we have done in case of algebraic expressions.

EXERCISE 8.1

1. Write the degree of each of the following polynomials:

(i) $2x^3+5x^2-7$ (ii) $5x^2-3x+2$

(iii) $2x+x^2-8$ (iv) $\frac{1}{2}y^7-12y^6+48y^5-10$

(v) $3x^3+1$ (vi) 5

(vii) $20x^3+12x^2y^2-10y^2+20$

2. Which of the following expressions are not polynomials?

(i) x^2+2x^{-2} (ii) $\sqrt{ax}+x^2-x^3$

(iii) $3y^3-\sqrt{5}y+9$ (iv) $ax^{1/2}+ax+9x^2+4$

(v) $3x^{-2}+2x^{-1}+4x+5$

3. Write each of the following polynomials in the standard form. Also, write their degree:

(i) $x^2+3+6x+5x^4$ (ii) a^2+4+5a^6

(iii) $(x^3-1)(x^3-4)$ (iv) $(y^3-2)(y^3+11)$

(v) $\left(a^3-\frac{3}{8}\right)\left(a^3+\frac{16}{17}\right)$ (vi) $\left(a+\frac{3}{4}\right)\left(a+\frac{4}{3}\right)$

ANSWERS

1. (i) 3 (ii) 2 (iii) 2 (iv) 7
   (v) 3 (vi) 0 (vii) 4
2. (i), (iv), (v)

3. (i) $3+6x+x^2+5x^4$ or, $5x^4+x^2+6x+3$ (ii) $4+a^2+5a^6$ or, $5a^6+a^2+4$

(iii) x^6-5x^3+4 or, $4-5x^3+x^6$ (iv) y^6+9y^3-22 or, $-22+9y^3+y^6$

(v) $a^6+\frac{27}{136}a^3-\frac{48}{136}$ or, $-\frac{48}{136}+\frac{27}{136}a^3+a^6$ (vi) $a^2+\frac{25}{12}a+1$ or, $1+\frac{25}{12}a+a^2$

8.3 DIVISION OF A MONOMIAL BY A MONOMIAL

In arithmetic, we have learnt that dividing a number 24 (say) by a number 4 (say) means determining a number such that when it is multiplied by 4 the product is equal to 24. Clearly, such a number is 6 and we write

$$24 \div 4 = 6 \text{ or, } \frac{24}{4} = 6$$

The division of a monomial by a monomial is also defined in a similar manner.

In fact, dividing a monomial X (say) by a monomial Y (say) means finding a monomial Z such that $X = YZ$ and we write

$$X \div Z \text{ or, } \frac{X}{Y} = Z$$

Here, X is called the *dividend*, Y is called the *divisor* and Z is known as the *quotient.*

While dividing a monomial by a monomial, we follow the following two rules:

Rule 1 *The coefficient of the quotient of two monomials is equal to the quotient of their coefficients.*

Rule 2 *The variable part in the quotient of two monomials is equal to the quotient of the variables in the given monomials.*

As the variables in a monomial represent numbers, so they follow all the laws of exponents that are valid for numbers.

Thus, in determining the variable part of the quotient of two monomials, we use the laws of exponents.

Following examples will illustrate the division of a monomial by a monomial.

ILLUSTRATIVE EXAMPLES

Example 1 Divide:

(i) $12x^3y^3$ by $3x^2y$ (ii) $-15a^2bc^3$ by $3ab$

Solution We have,

$$\frac{12x^3y^2}{3x^2y} = \frac{12\times x\times x\times x\times y\times y}{3\times x\times x\times y} = 4\times x\times y = 4xy$$

Aliter $$\frac{12x^3y^2}{3x^2y} = \frac{12}{3}x^{3-2}y^{2-1} = 4xy$$

(ii) We have,

$$\frac{-15a^2bc^3}{3ab} = \frac{-15\times a\times a\times b\times c\times c\times c}{3\times a\times b} = -5ac^3$$

Aliter $$\frac{-15a^2bc^3}{3ab} = -\frac{15}{3}a^{2-1}b^{1-1}c^3 = -5ab^0c^3 = -5ac^3$$

Example 2 Divide:

(i) $25x^3y^2$ by $-15x^2y$ (ii) $-72x^2yz$ by $-12xyz$

Solution (i) We have,

$$\frac{25x^3y^2}{-15x^2y} = \frac{25 \times x \times x \times x \times y \times y}{-15 \times x \times x \times y} = -\frac{5}{3}xy$$

Aliter $$\frac{25x^3y^2}{-15x^2y} = -\frac{25}{15}x^{3-2}\,y^{2-1} = -\frac{5}{3}xy$$

(ii) We have,

$$\frac{-72x^2yz}{-12xyz} = \frac{-72 \times x \times x \times y \times z}{-12 \times x \times y \times z} = 6x$$

Aliter $$\frac{-72x^2yz}{-12xyz} = \frac{-72}{-12}x^{2-1}\,y^{1-1}\,z^{1-1} = 6x\,y^0\,z^0 = 6x$$

Remark *In the above examples, if we look carefully at the monomials in numerator and denominator, we find that in each case the monomial in the denominator did not have different variables from those in the numerator. Further, for those variables which were common to both, the numerator and, the denominator, the exponent in the denominator was not greater than that in the numerator. Let us now consider the following divisions of monomials:*

(i) $6x^2y \div 9xy^2 = \dfrac{6x^2y}{9xy^2} = \dfrac{2x}{3y}$ (ii) $4x \div 12x^3 = \dfrac{4x}{12x^3} = \dfrac{1}{3x^2}$

(iii) $2x^2yz \div 3xyz^2 = \dfrac{2x^2yz}{3xyz^2} = \dfrac{2x}{3z}$

In these divisions of monomials, we are getting expressions with variables in the denominator. These are also algebraic expressions, since they are formed from powers of variables, but they are not monomials. Let us call them as terms. Thus, $\dfrac{2x}{3y}, \dfrac{1}{3x^2}, \dfrac{2x}{3z}$ etc. are terms. Note that every monomial is also a term but a term need not be a monomial. Also, multiplication of monomials is a monomial, but division of one monomial by the another is not necessarily a monomial. In fact, it is a term.

EXERCISE 8.2

Divide:

1. $6x^3y^2z^2$ by $3x^2yz$
2. $15m^2n^3$ by $5m^2n^2$
3. $24a^3b^3$ by $-8ab$
4. $-21abc^2$ by $7abc$
5. $72xyz^2$ by $-9xz$
6. $-72a^4b^5c^8$ by $-9a^2b^2c^3$

Simplify:

7. $\dfrac{16m^3y^2}{4m^2y}$
8. $\dfrac{32m^2n^3p^2}{4mnp}$

ANSWERS

1. $2xyz$ 2. $3n$ 3. $-3a^2b^2$ 4. $-3c$ 5. $-8yz$ 6. $8a^2b^3c^5$
7. $4my$ 8. $8mn^2p$

8.4 ALGEBRAIC EXPRESSIONS WHICH ARE NOT POLYNOMIALS

In the above section, we have seen that the division of a monomial by another monomial may give an algebraic expression which is not a monomial. Such expressions are known as terms.

Consider following algebraic expressions:

$$x+\frac{1}{x},\quad 3x^2-\frac{2}{x}+\frac{4}{x^2}\quad 2xy+\frac{3}{2}$$

These expressions are not polynomials as they have the variables in the denominator. Expressions in which variables occur under the square root sign are also not polynomials. For example, $\sqrt{x}$, $3-2\sqrt{xy}$, $(1+\sqrt{x})$, $\sqrt{x}+\sqrt{y}$, $x^2+2\sqrt{x}+1$ etc are not polynomials.

Consider the expression $2x+\frac{3}{x}$. In this expression there are two terms, one is $2x$ which is a monomial and the other is $\frac{3}{x}$ which is not a monomial. The expression $\frac{x}{x+5}$ consists of a single term but it is not a monomial. It is also not a binomial, although it is formed by dividing a monomial x by a binomial $x + 5$.

8.5 DIVISION OF POLYNOMIALS IN ONE VARIABLE

In this section, we shall first discuss the division of a polynomial in one variable by a monomial and utilize this knowledge in the division of a polynomial by a binomial and also by a polynomial.

8.5.1 DIVISION OF A POLYNOMIAL BY A MONOMIAL

For dividing a polynomial in one variable by a monomial in the same variable, we perform the following steps :

Step I *Obtain the polynomial (dividend) and the monomial (divisor).*

Step II *Arrange the terms of the dividend in descending order of their degrees.*

For example, write $7x^2+4x-3+5x^3$ *as* $5x^3+7x^2+4x-3$.

Step III *Divide each term of the polynomial by the given monomial by using the rules of division of a monomial by a monomial.*

The above procedure is illustrated by the following examples.

ILLUSTRATIVE EXAMPLES

Example 1 Divide:

(i) $9m^5+12m^4-6m^2$ by $3m^2$ (ii) $24x^3y+20x^2y^2-4xy$ by $2xy$

Solution (i) We have,

$$\frac{9m^5+12m^4-6m^2}{3m^2}=\frac{9m^5}{3m^2}+\frac{12m^4}{3m^2}-\frac{6m^2}{3m^2}=3m^3+4m^2-2$$

(ii) We have,

$$\frac{24x^3y+20x^2y^2-4xy}{2xy}=\frac{24x^3y}{2xy}+\frac{20x^2y^2}{2xy}-\frac{4xy}{2xy}=12x^2+10xy-2$$

Example 2 Divide:

(i) $6x^4yz-3xy^3z+8x^2yz^4$ by $2xyz$ (ii) $\frac{2}{3}a^2b^2c^2+\frac{4}{3}ab^2c^3-\frac{1}{5}ab^3c^2$ by $\frac{1}{2}abc$

Solution (i) We have,

$$\frac{6x^4yz - 3xy^3z + 8x^2yz^4}{2xyz} = \frac{6x^4yz}{2xyz} - \frac{3xy^3z}{2xyz} + \frac{8x^2yz^4}{2xyz} = 3x^3 - \frac{3}{2}y^2 + 4xz^3$$

(ii) We have,

$$\frac{\frac{2}{3}a^2b^2c^2 + \frac{4}{3}ab^2c^3 - \frac{1}{5}ab^3c^2}{\frac{1}{2}abc} = \frac{\frac{2}{3}a^2b^2c^2}{\frac{1}{2}abc} + \frac{\frac{4}{3}ab^2c^3}{\frac{1}{2}abc} - \frac{\frac{1}{5}ab^3c^2}{\frac{1}{2}abc} = \frac{4}{3}abc + \frac{8}{3}bc^2 - \frac{2}{5}b^2c$$

EXERCISE 8.3

Divide:

1. $x + 2x^2 + 3x^4 - x^5$ by $2x$
2. $y^4 - 3y^3 + \frac{1}{2}y^2$ by $3y$
3. $-4a^3 + 4a^2 + a$ by $2a$
4. $-x^6 + 2x^4 + 4x^3 + 2x^2$ by $\sqrt{2}\,x^2$
5. $5z^3 - 6z^2 + 7z$ by $2z$
6. $\sqrt{3}\,a^4 + 2\sqrt{3}\,a^3 + 3a^2 - 6a$ by $3a$

ANSWERS

1. $\frac{1}{2} + x + \frac{3}{2}x^3 - \frac{1}{2}x^4$
2. $\frac{1}{3}y^3 - y^2 + \frac{1}{6}y$
3. $-2a^2 + 2a + \frac{1}{2}$
4. $-\frac{1}{\sqrt{2}}x^4 + \sqrt{2}\,x^2 + 2\sqrt{2}\,x + \sqrt{2}$
5. $\frac{5}{2}z^2 - 3z + \frac{7}{2}$
6. $\frac{1}{\sqrt{3}}a^3 + \frac{2}{\sqrt{3}}a^2 + a - 2$

8.5.2 DIVISION OF A POLYNOMIAL BY A BINOMIAL BY USING LONG DIVISION

For dividing a polynomial by a binomial, we may follow the following steps:

Step I *Arrange the terms of the dividend and divisor in descending order of their degrees.*

Step II *Divide the first term of the dividend by the first term of the divisor to obtain the first term of the quotient.*

Step III *Multiply the divisor by the first term of the quotient and subtract the result from the dividend to obtain the remainder.*

Step IV *Consider the remainder (if any) as dividend and repeat step II to obtain the second term of the quotient.*

Step V *Repeat the above process till we obtain a remainder which is either zero or a polynomial of degree less than that of the divisor.*

Following examples will illustrate the above procedure.

ILLUSTRATIVE EXAMPLES

Example 1 Divide $6 + x - 4x^2 + x^3$ by $x - 3$.

Solution We go through the following steps to perform the division:

Step I We write the terms of the dividend as well as of divisor in descending order of their degrees. Thus, we write

$6 + x - 4x^2 + x^3$ *as* $x^3 - 4x^2 + x + 6$ and $x - 3$ as $x - 3$

Step II We divide the first term x^3 of the dividend by the first term x of the divisor and obtain $\frac{x^3}{x} = x^2$ as the first term of the quotient.

Step III We multiply the divisor $x - 3$ by the first term x of the quotient and subtract the result from the dividend $x^3 - 4x^2 + x + 6$. We obtain $-x^2 + x + 6$ as the remainder.

Step IV We take $-x^2 + x + 6$ as the new dividend and repeat step II to obtain the second term $\left(-\frac{x^2}{x} = \right) - x$ of the quotient.

Step V We multiply the divisor $x - 3$ by the second term $-x$ of the quotient and subtract the result $-x^2 + 3x$ from the new dividend. We obtain $-2x + 6$ as the remainder.

Step VI Now we treat $-2x + 6$ as the new dividend and divide its first term $-2x$ by the first term x of the divisor to obtain $\frac{-2x}{x} = -2$ as the third term of the quotient.

$$
\begin{array}{r|l}
 & x^2 - x - 2 \\
\hline
x-3 & x^3 - 4x^2 + x + 6 \\
 & x^3 - 3x^2 \\
 & - \quad + \\
\hline
 & -x^2 + x + 6 \\
 & -x^2 + 3x \\
 & + \quad - \\
\hline
 & -2x + 6 \\
 & -2x + 6 \\
 & + \quad - \\
\hline
 & 0
\end{array}
$$

Step VII We multiply the divisor $x - 3$ and the third term -2 of the quotient and subtract the result $-2x + 6$ from the new dividend. We obtain 0 as the remainder.

Thus, we can say that

$$(6 + x - 4x^2 + x^3) \div (x - 3) = x^2 - x - 2$$

or,
$$\frac{6 + x - 4x^2 + x^3}{x - 3} = x^2 - x - 2$$

The above procedure is displayed on the right side of the above steps.

<u>NOTE:</u> *In the above example, the remainder is zero. So, we can say that $(x - 3)$ is a factor of* $6 + x - 4x^2 + x^3$.

Example 2 Divide the polynomial $2x^4 + 8x^3 + 7x^2 + 4x + 3$ by $x + 3$.

Solution Using the procedure learnt in the previous example, we have

$$
\begin{array}{r|l}
 & 2x^3 + 2x^2 + x + 1 \\
\hline
x+3 & 2x^4 + 8x^3 + 7x^2 + 4x + 3 \\
 & 2x^4 + 6x^3 \\
 & - \quad - \\
\hline
 & 2x^3 + 7x^2 + 4x + 3 \\
 & 2x^3 + 6x^2 \\
 & - \quad - \\
\hline
 & x^2 + 4x + 3 \\
 & x^2 + 3x \\
 & - \quad - \\
\hline
 & x + 3 \\
 & x + 3 \\
 & - \quad - \\
\hline
 & 0
\end{array}
$$

First term of quotient $\frac{2x^4}{x} = 2x^3$

New dividend is $2x^3 + 7x^2 + 4x + 3$

Second term of quotient $= \frac{2x^3}{x} = 2x^2$

New dividend is $x^2 + 4x + 3$

Third term of quotient $= \frac{x^2}{x} = x$

New dividend is $x + 3$

Fourth term of quotient $= \frac{x}{x} = 1$

As the remainder is zero, we can say that $x + 3$ is a factor of the given polynomial $2x^4 + 8x^3 + 7x^2 + 4x + 3$.

$\therefore \quad 2x^4 + 8x^3 + 7x^2 + 4x + 3 = (x + 3)(2x^3 + 2x^2 + x + 1)$

Remark *In the above two examples, we are getting 0 as the remainder. In fact, if on dividing a polynomial (dividend) by another polynomial (divisor), we obtain a zero remainder, then the second polynomial (divisor) is called a factor of the first polynomial (dividend). Also, the quotient is a factor of the dividend.*

We know that if on dividing a number by another number, we obtain a zero remainder, then we can write

Dividend = Divisor × Quotient

In the same way, if on dividing a polynomial by another polynomial we obtain a zero remainder, then we write

Dividend = Divisor × Quotient

Example 3 Divide: $x^3 - 6x^2 + 11x - 6$ by $x^2 - 4x + 3$

Solution On dividing, we get

$$\begin{array}{r|l} & x - 2 \\ \hline x^2 - 4x + 3 & x^3 - 6x^2 + 11x - 6 \\ & x^3 - 4x^2 + 3x \\ & - \quad + \quad - \\ \hline & -2x^2 + 8x - 6 \\ & -2x^2 + 8x - 6 \\ & + \quad - \quad + \\ \hline & 0 \end{array}$$

$\therefore \quad x^3 - 6x^2 + 11x - 6 = (x - 2)(x^2 - 4x + 3)$

Example 4 Divide: $10x^4 + 17x^3 - 62x^2 + 30x - 3$ by $2x^2 + 7x - 1$

Solution On dividing, we get

$$\begin{array}{r|l} & 5x^2 - 9x + 3 \\ \hline 2x^2 + 7x - 1 & 10x^4 + 17x^3 - 62x^2 + 30x - 3 \\ & 10x^4 + 35x^3 - 5x^2 \\ & - \quad - \quad + \\ \hline & -18x^3 - 57x^2 + 30x - 3 \\ & -18x^3 - 63x^2 + 9x \\ & + \quad + \quad - \\ \hline & 6x^2 + 21x - 3 \\ & 6x^2 + 21x - 3 \\ & - \quad - \quad + \\ \hline & 0 \end{array}$$

$\therefore \quad 10x^4 + 17x^3 - 62x^2 + 30x - 3 = (2x^2 + 7x - 1)(5x^2 - 9x + 3)$

Example 5 Using division show that $3y^2+5$ is factor of $6y^5+15y^4+16y^3+4y^2+10y-35$.

Solution On dividing $6y^5+15y^4+16y^3+4y^2+10y-35$ by $3y^2+5$, we obtain

$$\begin{array}{r|l}
 & 2y^3+5y^2+2y-7 \\
\hline
3y^2+5 & 6y^5+15y^4+16y^3+4y^2+10y-35 \\
 & 6y^5 \qquad\quad +10y^3 \\
 & - \qquad\quad\; - \\
\hline
 & 15y^4+6y^3+4y^2+10y-35 \\
 & 15y^4 \qquad +25y^2 \\
 & - \qquad\quad - \\
\hline
 & 6y^3-21y^2+10y-35 \\
 & 6y^3 \qquad +10y \\
 & - \qquad\quad - \\
\hline
 & -21y^2-35 \\
 & -21y^2-35 \\
 & + \qquad + \\
\hline
 & 0
\end{array}$$

Since the remainder is zero. Therefore, $3y^2+5$ is a factor of $6y^5+15y^4+16y^3+4y^2+10y-35$.

DIVISION ALGORITHM We know that if a number is divided by another number, then

Dividend = Divisor × Quotient + Remainder

Similarly, if a polynomial is divided by another polynomial, then

Dividend = Divisor × Quotient + Remainder

This is generally known as the division algorithm.

Example 6 Divide $3y^5+6y^4+6y^3+7y^2+8y+9$ by $3y^3+1$ and verify that

Dividend = Divisor × Quotient + Remainder

Solution On dividing, we get

$$\begin{array}{r|l}
 & y^2+2y+2 \\
\hline
3y^3+1 & 3y^5+6y^4+6y^3+7y^2+8y+9 \\
 & 3y^5 \qquad\qquad + y^2 \\
 & - \qquad\qquad\; - \\
\hline
 & 6y^4+6y^3+6y^2+8y+9 \\
 & 6y^4 \qquad\qquad +2y \\
 & - \qquad\qquad\; - \\
\hline
 & 6y^3+6y^2+6y+9 \\
 & 6y^3 \qquad\qquad +2 \\
 & - \qquad\qquad\; - \\
\hline
 & 6y^2+6y+7
\end{array}$$

Clearly, the degree of the remainder $6y^2+6y+7$ is 2, which is less than the degree of the divisor $3y^3+1$. So, division process stops at this step and we have,

$$\text{Quotient} = y^2+2y+2 \text{ and, Remainder} = 6y^2+6y+7$$

Verification: We have,

Divisor × Quotient + Remainder

$= (3y^3+1)(y^2+2y+2)+6y^2+6y+7$

$= 3y^3(y^2+2y+2)+1(y^2+2y+2)+6y^2+6y+7$

$= 3y^5+6y^4+6y^3+y^2+2y+2+6y^2+6y+7$

$= 3y^5+6y^4+6y^3+7y^2+8y+9$ = Dividend

Example 7 What must be subtracted from $8x^4+14x^3-2x^2+7x-8$ so that the resulting polynomial is exactly divisible by $4x^2+3x-2$.

Solution We know that

Dividend = Quotient × Divisor + Remainder

⇒ Dividend – Remainder = Quotient × Divisor

Clearly, R.H.S. of the above result is divisible by the divisor. Therefore, L.H.S. is also divisible by the divisor. Thus, if we subtract remainder from the dividend, then it will be exactly divisible by the divisor.

Dividing $8x^4+14x^3-2x^2+7x-8$ by $4x^2+3x-2$, we get

$$\begin{array}{r|l}
 & 2x^2+2x-1 \\ \hline
4x^2+3x-2 & 8x^4+14x^3-2x^2+7x-8 \\
 & 8x^4+6x^3-4x^2 \\
 & -\quad -\quad + \\ \hline
 & 8x^3+2x^2+7x-8 \\
 & 8x^3+6x^2-4x \\
 & -\quad -\quad + \\ \hline
 & -4x^2+11x-8 \\
 & -4x^2-3x+2 \\
 & +\quad +\quad - \\ \hline
 & 14x-10
\end{array}$$

∴ Quotient $= 2x^2+2x-1$ and, Remainder $= 14x-10$

Thus, if we subtract the remainder $14x-10$ from $8x^4+14x^3-2x^2+7x-8$, it will be divisible by $4x^2+3x-2$.

Example 8 Find the values of a and b so that $x^4+x^3+8x^2+ax+b$ is divisible by x^2+1.

Solution If $x^4+x^3+8x^2+ax+b$ is exactly divisible by x^2+1, then the remainder should be zero.

On dividing, we get

$$
\begin{array}{r|l}
 & x^2 + x + 7 \\
\hline
x^2+1 & x^4 + x^3 + 8x^2 + ax + b \\
 & x^4 \quad + x^2 \\
 & - \quad\quad - \\
\hline
 & x^3 + 7x^2 + ax + b \\
 & x^3 \quad\quad + x \\
 & - \quad\quad - \\
\hline
 & 7x^2 + x(a-1) + b \\
 & 7x^2 \quad\quad + 7 \\
 & - \quad\quad - \\
\hline
 & x(a-1) + b - 7
\end{array}
$$

$\therefore$ Quotient $= x^2 + x + 7$ and, Remainder $= x(a-1) + b - 7$

Now, Remainder $= 0$

$\Rightarrow \quad x(a-1) + (b-7) = 0$

$\Rightarrow \quad x(a-1) + (b-7) = 0x + 0$

$\Rightarrow \quad a - 1 = 0$ and $b - 7 = 0$ [Comparing coefficients of x and constant terms]

$\Rightarrow \quad a = 1$ and $b = 7$

EXERCISE 8.4

Divide:

1. $5x^3 - 15x^2 + 25x$ by $5x$
2. $4z^3 + 6z^2 - z$ by $-\frac{1}{2}z$
3. $9x^2y - 6xy + 12xy^2$ by $-\frac{3}{2}xy$
4. $3x^3y^2 + 2x^2y + 15xy$ by $3xy$
5. $x^2 + 7x + 12$ by $x + 4$
6. $4y^2 + 3y + \frac{1}{2}$ by $2y + 1$
7. $3x^3 + 4x^2 + 5x + 18$ by $x + 2$
8. $14x^2 - 53x + 45$ by $7x - 9$
9. $-21 + 71x - 31x^2 - 24x^3$ by $3 - 8x$
10. $3y^4 - 3y^3 - 4y^2 - 4y$ by $y^2 - 2y$
11. $2y^5 + 10y^4 + 6y^3 + y^2 + 5y + 3$ by $2y^3 + 1$
12. $x^4 - 2x^3 + 2x^2 + x + 4$ by $x^2 + x + 1$
13. $m^3 - 14m^2 + 37m - 26$ by $m^2 - 12m + 13$
14. $x^4 + x^2 + 1$ by $x^2 + x + 1$
15. $x^5 + x^4 + x^3 + x^2 + x + 1$ by $x^3 + 1$

Divide each of the following and find the quotient and remainder:

16. $14x^3 - 5x^2 + 9x - 1$ by $2x - 1$
17. $6x^3 - x^2 - 10x - 3$ by $2x - 3$
18. $6x^3 + 11x^2 - 39x - 65$ by $3x^2 + 13x + 13$

19. $30x^4 + 11x^3 - 82x^2 - 12x + 48$ by $3x^2 + 2x - 4$

20. $9x^4 - 4x^2 + 4$ by $3x^2 - 4x + 2$

21. Verify division algorithm i.e., Dividend = Divisor × Quotient + Remainder, in each of the following. Also, write the quotient and remainder:

	Dividend	Divisor
(i)	$14x^2 + 13x - 15$	$7x - 4$
(ii)	$15z^3 - 20z^2 + 13z - 12$	$3z - 6$
(iii)	$6y^5 - 28y^3 + 3y^2 + 30y - 9$	$2y^2 - 6$
(iv)	$34x - 22x^3 - 12x^4 - 10x^2 - 75$	$3x + 7$
(v)	$15y^4 - 16y^3 + 9y^2 - \frac{10}{3}y + 6$	$3y - 2$
(vi)	$4y^3 + 8y + 8y^2 + 7$	$2y^2 - y + 1$
(vii)	$6y^5 + 4y^4 + 4y^3 + 7y^2 + 27y + 6$	$2y^3 + 1$

22. Divide $15y^4 + 16y^3 + \frac{10}{3}y - 9y^2 - 6$ by $3y - 2$. Write down the coefficients of the terms in the quotient.

23. Using division of polynomials state whether

(i) $x + 6$ is a factor of $x^2 - x - 42$

(ii) $4x - 1$ is a factor of $4x^2 - 13x - 12$

(iii) $2y - 5$ is a factor of $4y^4 - 10y^3 - 10y^2 + 30y - 15$

(iv) $3y^2 + 5$ is a factor of $6y^5 + 15y^4 + 16y^3 + 4y^2 + 10y - 35$

(v) $z^2 + 3$ is a factor of $z^5 - 9z$

(vi) $2x^2 - x + 3$ is a factor of $6x^5 - x^4 + 4x^3 - 5x^2 - x - 15$

24. Find the value of a, if $x + 2$ is a factor of $4x^4 + 2x^3 - 3x^2 + 8x + 5a$.

25. What must be added to $x^4 + 2x^3 - 2x^2 + x - 1$ so that the resulting polynomial is exactly divisible by $x^2 + 2x - 3$.

ANSWERS

1. $x^2 - 3x + 5$
2. $-8z^2 - 12z + 2$
3. $-6x + 4 - 8y$
4. $x^2y + \frac{2}{3}x + 5$
5. $x + 3$
6. $2y + \frac{1}{2}$
7. $3x^2 - 2x + 9$
8. $2x - 5$
9. $3x^2 + 5x - 7$
10. $3y^2 + 3y + 2$
11. $y^2 + 5y + 3$
12. $x^2 - 3x + 4$
13. $m - 2$
14. $x^2 - x + 1$
15. $x^2 + x + 1$
16. $Q = 7x^2 + x + 5, R = 4$
17. $Q = 3x^2 + 4x + 1, R = 0$
18. $Q = 2x - 5$, $R = 0$
19. $Q = 10x^2 - 3x - 12$, $R = 0$

20. $Q = 3x^2 + 4x + 2$, $R = 0$

21. (i) $Q = 2x + 3$, $R = -3$ (ii) $Q = 5z^2 + \frac{10}{3}z + 11$, $R = 54$

(iii) $Q = 3y^3 - 5y + \frac{3}{2}$, $R = 0$ (iv) $Q = -4x^3 + 2x^2 - 8x + 30$, $R = -285$

(v) $Q = 5y^3 - 2y^2 + \frac{5}{3}y$, $R = 6$ (vi) $Q = 2y + 5$, $R = 11y + 2$

(vii) $Q = 3y^3 + 2y + 2$, $R = 4y^2 + 25y + 4$

22. Quotient $= 5y^3 + \frac{26}{3}y^2 + \frac{25}{9}y + \frac{80}{27}$, Coefficients of $y^3 = 5$, Coefficient of $y^2 = \frac{26}{3}$

Coefficient of $y = \frac{25}{9}$, Constant term $= \frac{80}{27}$

23. (i) Yes (ii) No (iii) No (iv) Yes (v) Yes (vi) Yes

24. -4 25. $x - 2$

8.5.3 AN ALTERNATIVE AND SHORTER FORM OF LONG DIVISION

As we have seen that the long division method is quite lengthy and time consuming. In this section, we will discuss an alternative form of long division method. This form is very short and easy to use.

Suppose we wish to divide $x^3 - 4x^2 + 7x - 2$ by $(x - 2)$. Let us illustrate the division by following steps:

<u>Step I</u> *Divide the first term of dividend i.e., x^3 by the first term of divisor i.e., x to get* $\frac{x^3}{x} = x^2$.

<u>Step II</u> *Write the given polynomial on LHS of the equality sign and on the right hand side write the product of x^2 obtained in step I and divisor $(x - 2)$ i.e., $x^2 (x - 2)$*

$$x^3 - 4x^2 + 7x - 2 = x^2 (x - 2) + \cdots$$

<u>Step III</u> *Since $x^2 (x - 2) = x^3 - 2x^2$. So, we get the first term of the dividend and an additional term $-2x^2$. On the LHS of the equality, we need $-4x^2$. To get $-4x^2$, we require $-4x^2 - (-2x^2) = -2x^2$ on RHS. So, we write $-2x (x - 2)$ as the second term on RHS.*

$$x^3 - 4x^2 + 7x - 2 = x^2 (x - 2) - 2x (x - 2) + \cdots$$

<u>Step IV</u> *Since $-2x (x - 2) = -2x^2 + 4x$. This adjusts the second term on LHS and give an additional term $4x$. We required $7x$ on LHS. To get $7x$, on LHS, we require $7x - 4x = 3x$ on RHS. So, we write $3 (x - 2)$ as the third term on RHS.*

$$x^3 - 4x^2 + 7x - 2$$
$$= x^2(x - 2) - 2x (x - 2) + 3 (x - 2) + \cdots$$

Step V	*Since 3 (x – 2) = 3x – 6. This adjusts the third term on LHS and gives an additional term – 6 on RHS. We require – 2 on LHS. So, we write –2 – (– 6) = 4 on RHS.*	$x^3 - 4x^2 + 7x - 2$ $= x^2(x-2) - 2x(x-2) + 3(x-2) + 4$
Step VI	*Take (x – 2) common from first three terms to obtain $x^2 - 2x + 3$ as the quotient and 4 as the remainder.*	$x^3 - 4x^2 + 7x - 2$ $= (x-2)(x^2 - 2x + 3) + 4$

Hence, quotient $= x^2 - 2x + 3$ and remainder = 4.

Let us now illustrate the above method by more examples.

ILLUSTRATIVE EXAMPLES

Example 1 Divide $x^4 - x^3 + x^2 + 5$ by $(x+1)$ and write the quotient and remainder.

Solution We have,

$$x^4 - x^3 + x^2 + 5 = x^3(x+1) - 2x^2(x+1) + 3x(x+1) - 3(x+1) + 8$$
$$= (x+1)(x^3 - 2x^2 + 3x - 3) + 8$$

Hence, Quotient $= x^3 - 2x^2 + 3x - 3$ and, Remainder = 8.

Example 2 Divide $16x^4 + 12x^3 - 10x^2 + 8x + 20$ by $4x - 3$. Also, write the quotient and remainder.

Solution We have,

$$16x^4 + 12x^3 - 10x^2 + 8x + 20$$
$$= 4x^3(4x-3) + 6x^2(4x-3) + 2x(4x-3) + \frac{7}{2}(4x-3) + \frac{61}{2}$$
$$= (4x-3)\left(4x^3 + 6x^2 + 2x + \frac{7}{2}\right) + \frac{61}{2}$$

Hence, Quotient $= 4x^3 + 6x^2 + 2x + \frac{7}{2}$ and, Remainder $= \frac{61}{2}$

Example 3 Divide $12x^3 - 8x^2 - 6x + 10$ by $(3x - 2)$. Also, write the quotient and the remainder.

Solution We have,

$$12x^3 - 8x^2 - 6x + 10$$
$$= 4x^2(3x-2) - 2(3x-2) + 6$$
$$= \left\{4x^2(3x-2) - 2(3x-2)\right\} + 6$$
$$= (3x-2)(4x^2 - 2) + 6$$

Hence, Quotient $= 4x^2 - 2$ and, Remainder = 6.

Example 4 Divide $8y^3 - 6y^2 + 4y - 1$ by $4y + 2$. Also, write the quotient and the remainder.

Solution We have,

$$8y^3 - 6y^2 + 4y - 1$$

$$= 2y^2(4y+2) - \frac{5}{2}y(4y+2) + \frac{9}{4}(4y+2) - \frac{11}{2}$$

$$= \left\{2y^2(4y+2) - \frac{5}{2}y(4y+2) + \frac{9}{4}(4y+2)\right\} - \frac{11}{2}$$

$$= (4y+2)\left(2y^2 - \frac{5}{2}y + \frac{9}{4}\right) - \frac{11}{2}$$

Hence, Quotient $= 2y^2 - \frac{5}{2}y + \frac{9}{4}$ and, Remainder $= -\frac{11}{2}$.

Example 5 Divide $6x^3 - x^2 - 10x - 3$ by $(2x - 3)$.

Solution We have,

$$6x^3 - x^2 - 10x - 3$$

$$= 3x^2(2x-3) + 4x(2x-3) - 1(2x-3) - 6$$

$$= \{3x^2(2x-3) + 4x(2x-3) - 1(2x-3)\} - 6$$

$$= (2x-3)(3x^2+4x-1) - 6$$

Hence, Quotient $= 3x^2 + 4x - 1$ and, Remainder $= -6$.

EXERCISE 8.5

1. Divide the first polynomial by the second polynomial in each of the following. Also, write the quotient and remainder:

(i) $3x^2 + 4x + 5,\ x - 2$ (ii) $10x^2 - 7x + 8,\ 5x - 3$

(iii) $5y^3 - 6y^2 + 6y - 1,\ 5y - 1$ (iv) $x^4 - x^3 + 5x,\ x - 1$

(v) $y^4 + y^2,\ y^2 - 2$

2. Find, whether or not the first polynomial is a factor of the second:

(i) $x + 1,\ 2x^2 + 5x + 4$ (ii) $y - 2,\ 3y^3 + 5y^2 + 5y + 2$

(iii) $4x^2 - 5,\ 4x^4 + 7x^2 + 15$ (iv) $4 - z,\ 3z^2 - 13z + 4$

(v) $2a - 3,\ 10a^2 - 9a - 5$ (v) $4y + 1,\ 8y^2 - 2y + 1$

ANSWERS

	Quotient	Remainder		Quotient	Remainder
1.	(i) $3x + 10$	25		(iii) $y^2 - y + 1$	0
	(ii) $2x - \frac{1}{5}$	$\frac{47}{5}$		(iv) $x^3 + 5$	5
				(v) $y^2 + 3$	6

2. (i) No (ii) No (iii) No (iv) Yes (v) No (vi) No

8.6 DIVISION OF POLYNOMIALS BY USING FACTORIZATION

In this section, we shall learn division of polynomials in one and two variables by factorizing the dividend and divisor and then cancelling out the common factors from the numerator and denominator. Following examples will illustrate the procedure:

ILLUSTRATIVE EXAMPLES

Example 1 Divide:

(i) $35a^2 + 32a - 99$ by $7a - 9$ (ii) $ax^2 + (b + ac)x + bc$ by $x + c$

Solution (i) We have,

$35a^2 + 32a - 99$

$= 35a^2 + 77a - 45a - 99$

$= 7a(5a + 11) - 9(5a + 11) = (5a + 11)(7a - 9)$ ...(i)

$\therefore$ $(35a^2 + 32a - 99) \div (7a - 9)$

$= \dfrac{35a^2 + 32a - 99}{7a - 9}$

$= \dfrac{(5a + 11)(7a - 9)}{(7a - 9)}$ [Using (i)]

$= 5a + 11$ [Just as numbers, we cancel common factor $(7a - 9)$ in numerator and denominator]

(ii) We have,

$ax^2 + (b + ac)x + bc$

$= (ax^2 + bx) + (acx + bc)$

$= x(ax + b) + c(ax + b) = (ax + b)(x + c)$ ...(i)

$\therefore$ $\left(ax^2 + (b + ac)x + bc\right) \div (x + c)$

$= \dfrac{ax^2 + (b + ac)x + bc}{x + c}$

$= \dfrac{(ax + b)(x + c)}{(x + c)}$ [Using (i)]

$= ax + b$ [Cancelling common factor $(x + c)$ in numerator and denominator]

Example 2 Divide: $a^4 - b^4$ by $a - b$

Solution We have,

$a^4 - b^4 = (a^2)^2 - (b^2)^2$

$\Rightarrow$ $a^4 - b^4 = (a^2 - b^2)(a^2 + b^2)$ [Using : $x^2 - y^2 = (x + y)(x - y)$]

$\Rightarrow$ $a^4 - b^4 = (a - b)(a + b)(a^2 + b^2)$ ...(i)

$\therefore$ $(a^4 - b^4) \div (a - b)$

$= \dfrac{a^4 - b^4}{a - b}$

$= \dfrac{(a - b)(a + b)(a^2 + b^2)}{(a - b)}$ [Using (i)]

$= (a + b)(a^2 + b^2)$ [Cancelling common factor $(a - b)$ in N^r and D^r]

Example 3 Divide: $a^{12} + a^6 b^6 + b^{12}$ by $a^6 - a^3 b^3 + b^6$

Solution We have,

$$a^{12} + a^6 b^6 + b^{12}$$

$$= a^{12} + 2a^6 b^6 + b^{12} - a^6 b^6 \quad \text{[Adding and subtracting } a^6 b^6\text{]}$$

$$= (a^6 + b^6)^2 - (a^3 b^3)^2$$

$$= (a^6 + b^6 - a^3 b^3)(a^6 + b^6 + a^3 b^3) = (a^6 - a^3 b^3 + b^6)(a^6 + a^3 b^3 + b^6) \quad \ldots\text{(i)}$$

$$\therefore \quad \frac{a^{12} + a^6 b^6 + b^{12}}{a^6 - a^3 b^3 + b^6}$$

$$= \frac{(a^6 - a^3 b^3 + b^6)(a^6 + a^3 b^3 + b^6)}{(a^6 - a^3 b^3 + b^6)}$$

$$= a^6 + a^3 b^3 + b^6 \quad \left[\text{Cancelling } a^6 - a^3 b^3 + b^6 \text{ from } N^r \text{ and } D^r\right]$$

Example 4 Divide: $x^{4a} + x^{2a} y^{2b} + y^{4b}$ by $x^{2a} + x^a y^b + y^{2b}$

Solution We have,

$$x^{4a} + x^{2a} y^{2b} + y^{4b}$$

$$= (x^{2a})^2 + x^{2a} y^{2b} + (y^{2b})^2$$

$$= (x^{2a})^2 + 2x^{2a} y^{2b} + (y^{2b})^2 - x^{2a} y^{2b}$$

$$= (x^{2a} + y^{2b})^2 - (x^a y^b)^2$$

$$= (x^{2a} + y^{2b} + x^a y^b)(x^{2a} + y^{2b} - x^a y^b) = (x^{2a} + x^a y^a + y^{2b})(x^{2a} - x^a y^b + y^{2b})$$

$$\therefore \quad \frac{x^{4a} + x^{2a} y^{2b} + y^{4b}}{x^{2a} + x^a y^b + y^{2b}} = \frac{(x^{2a} + x^a y^b + y^{2b})(x^{2a} - x^a y^b + y^{2b})}{(x^{2a} + x^a y^b + y^{2b})} = x^{2a} - x^a y^b + y^{2b}$$

EXERCISE 8.6

Divide:

1. $x^2 - 5x + 6$ by $x - 3$
2. $ax^2 - ay^2$ by $ax + ay$
3. $x^4 - y^4$ by $x^2 - y^2$
4. $acx^2 + (bc + ad)x + bd$ by $(ax + b)$
5. $(a^2 + 2ab + b^2) - (a^2 + 2ac + c^2)$ by $2a + b + c$
6. $\frac{1}{4}x^2 - \frac{1}{2}x - 12$ by $\frac{1}{2}x - 4$

ANSWERS

1. $x - 2$
2. $(x - y)$
3. $x^2 + y^2$
4. $cx + d$
5. $(b - c)$
6. $\frac{1}{2}x + 3$

THINGS TO REMEMBER

1. *An algebraic expression in which the variables involved have only non-negative integral powers, is called a polynomial.*
2. *In a polynomial in one variable, the highest power of the variable is called its degree.*
3. *A polynomial consisting of a constant term only is called a constant polynomial. The degree of a constant polynomial is zero.*
4. *A polynomial of degree 1 is called a linear polynomial.*

   $ax + b$, *where* $a \neq 0$, *is a linear polynomial.*

5. *A polynomial of degree 2 is called a quadratic polynomial.*

   $ax^2 + bx + c$, $a \neq 0$, *is the general form of a quadratic polynomial.*

6. *A polynomial of degree 3 is called a cubic polynomial.*

   $ax^3 + bx^2 + cx + d$, $a \neq 0$, *is the general form of a cubic polynomial.*

7. *A polynomial of degree 4 is called a biquadratic polynomial.*
8. *While dividing a monomial by a monomial, we follow the following two rules:*

   Rule 1 *The coefficient of the quotient of two monomials is equal to the quotient of their coefficients.*

   Rule 2 *The variable part in the quotient of two monomials is equal to the quotient of the variables in the given monomials.*

9. *For dividing a polynomial in one variable by a monomial in the same variable, we divide each term of the polynomial by the given monomial by using the rules of division of a monomial by a monomial.*
10. *If a polynomial is divided by another polynomial, then*

    Dividend = Divisor × Quotient + Remainder

    This is generally known as the division algorithm.

9

LINEAR EQUATION IN ONE VARIABLE

9.1 INTRODUCTION

In class VII, we have learnt the meaning of an equation and its solution. Most of the equations that we have worked with had integer coefficients and integer solutions. In this chapter, we shall deal with equations involving rational numbers as the coefficients and their solutions can also be rational numbers.

9.2 LINEAR EQUATION

EQUATION *A statement of equality which contains one or more unknown quantity or variable (literals) is called an equation.*

ILLUSTRATION 1 $3x+7=12$, $\frac{5}{2}x-9=1$, $x^2+1=5$ and $\frac{x}{3}+5=\frac{x}{2}-3$ are equations in one variable x.

ILLUSTRATION 2 $2x+3y=15$, $7x-\frac{y}{3}=3$ are equations in two variables x and y.

LINEAR EQUATION *An equation involving only linear polynomials is called a linear equation.*

ILLUSTRATION 3 $3x-2=7$, $\frac{3}{2}x+9=\frac{1}{2}$, $\frac{y}{3}+\frac{y-2}{4}=5$ are linear equations in one variable, because the highest power of the variable in each equation is one whereas the equations $3x^2-2x+1=0$, $y^2-1=8$ are not linear equations, because the highest power of the variable in each equation is not one.

In this chapter, we shall study linear equations in one variable only.

9.3 SOLUTION OF A LINEAR EQUATION

SOLUTION *A value of the variable which when substituted for the variable in an equation, makes L.H.S. = R.H.S. is said to satisfy the equation and is called a solution or a root of the equation.*

In other words, a value of the variable which makes the equation a true statement, is called a solution or a root of 2the equation.

ILLUSTRATION 1 Verify that $x=4$ is a root of the equation $2x-3=5$.

Solution Substituting $x=4$ in the given equation, we get

$$\text{L.H.S.} = 2x-3 = 2\times4-3 = 8-3 = 5 = \text{R.H.S.}$$

Hence, $x=4$ is a root of the equation $2x-3=5$

ILLUSTRATION 2 Verify that $x=8$ is a solution of the equation $\frac{5x-4}{8}-\frac{x-3}{5}=\frac{x+6}{5}$

Solution Substituting $x=8$ in the given equation, we get

$$\text{L.H.S} = \frac{5x-4}{8} - \frac{x-3}{5} = \frac{5\times 8-4}{8} - \frac{8-3}{5} = \frac{36}{8} - \frac{5}{5} = \frac{9}{2} - 1 = \frac{9-2}{2} = \frac{7}{2}$$

$$\text{and,} \quad \text{R.H.S} = \frac{x+6}{4} = \frac{8+6}{4} = \frac{7}{2}$$

Thus, for $x = 8$, we have

L.H.S. = R.H.S.

Hence, $x = 8$ is a solution of the given equation.

SOLVING AN EQUATION *Solving an equation means determining its roots i.e., determining the value of the variable which satisfies it.*

RULES FOR SOLVING LINEAR EQUATIONS IN ONE VARIABLE

We have learnt the rules for solving an equation in one variable. Let us recall them. They are:

Rule 1 *Same quantity (number) can be added to both sides of an equation without changing the equality.*

Rule 2 *Same quantity can be subtracted from both sides of an equation without changing the equality.*

Rule 3 *Both sides of an equation may be multiplied by the same non-zero number without changing the equality.*

Rule 4 *Both sides of an equation may be divided by the same non-zero number without changing the equality.*

It should be noted that some complicated equations can be solved by using two or more of these rules together.

9.4 SOLVING EQUATIONS HAVING VARIABLE TERMS ON ONE SIDE AND NUMBER(S) ON THE OTHER SIDE

Following examples will illustrate the method of solving linear equations in one variable having variable terms on one side and numbers on the other side.

ILLUSTRATIVE EXAMPLES

Example 1 Solve the equation : $\frac{x}{5} + 11 = \frac{1}{15}$ and check the result.

Solution We have,

$$\frac{x}{5} + 11 = \frac{1}{15}$$

$$\Rightarrow \frac{x}{5} + 11 - 11 = \frac{1}{15} - 11 \quad \text{[Subtracting 11 from both sides]}$$

$$\Rightarrow \frac{x}{5} = \frac{1}{15} - 11$$

$$\Rightarrow \frac{x}{5} = \frac{1-165}{15}$$

$$\Rightarrow \frac{x}{5} = -\frac{164}{15}$$

$\Rightarrow \quad 5 \times \frac{x}{5} = 5 \times -\frac{164}{15}$ [Multiplying both sides by 5]

$\Rightarrow \quad x = -\frac{164}{3}$

Thus, $x = -\frac{164}{3}$ is the solution of the given equation.

Check Substituting $x = \frac{-164}{3}$ in the given equation, we get

$$\text{L.H.S.} = \frac{x}{5} + 11 = \frac{-164}{3} \times \frac{1}{5} + 11 = \frac{-164}{15} + 11 = \frac{-164+165}{15} = \frac{1}{15}$$

and,

$$\text{R.H.S} = \frac{1}{15}$$

$\therefore$ L.H.S. = R.H.S. for $x = \frac{-164}{3}$

Hence, $x = \frac{-164}{3}$ is the solution of the given equation.

Example 2 Solve: $\frac{1}{3}x - \frac{5}{2} = 6$

Solution We have,

$\frac{1}{3}x - \frac{5}{2} = 6$

$\Rightarrow \quad \frac{1}{3}x - \frac{5}{2} + \frac{5}{2} = 6 + \frac{5}{2}$ [Adding $\frac{5}{2}$ on both sides]

$\Rightarrow \quad \frac{1}{3}x = 6 + \frac{5}{2}$

$\Rightarrow \quad \frac{1}{3}x = \frac{12+5}{2}$

$\Rightarrow \quad \frac{1}{3}x = \frac{17}{2}$

$\Rightarrow \quad 3 \times \frac{1}{3}x = 3 \times \frac{17}{2}$ [Multiplying both sides by 3]

$\Rightarrow \quad x = \frac{51}{2}$

Thus, $x = \frac{51}{2}$ is the solution of the given equation.

Check Substituting $x = \frac{51}{2}$ in the given equation, we get

$$\text{L.H.S.} = \frac{1}{3}x - \frac{5}{2} = \frac{1}{3} \times \frac{51}{2} - \frac{5}{2} = \frac{17}{2} - \frac{5}{2} = \frac{17-5}{2} = \frac{12}{2} = 6$$

and,

$$\text{R.H.S.} = 6$$

$\therefore$ L.H.S. = R.H.S. for $x = \frac{51}{2}$

Hence, $x = \frac{51}{2}$ is the solution of the given equation.

Example 3 Solve: $\frac{x}{2} - \frac{x}{3} = 8$

Solution We have, $\frac{x}{2} - \frac{x}{3} = 8$

LCM of denominators 2 and 3 on L.H.S. is 6.

Multiplying both sides by 6, we get

$\Rightarrow \quad 3x - 2x = 6 \times 8$

$\Rightarrow \quad x = 48$

Check Substituting $x = 48$ in the given equation, we get

$$\text{L.H.S.} = \frac{x}{2} - \frac{x}{3} = \frac{48}{2} - \frac{48}{3} = 24 - 16 = 8 \text{ and, R.H.S.} = 8$$

$\therefore$ L.H.S. = R.H.S. for $x = 48$

Hence, $x = 48$ is the solution of the given equation.

Example 4 Solve: $\frac{x}{2} + \frac{x}{3} - \frac{x}{4} = 7$

Solution We have, $\frac{x}{2} + \frac{x}{3} - \frac{x}{4} = 7$

LCM of denominators 2, 3, 4 on L.H.S. is 12. Multiplying both sides by 12, we get

$6x + 4x - 3x = 7 \times 12$

$\Rightarrow \quad 7x = 7 \times 12$

$\Rightarrow \quad 7x = 84$

$\Rightarrow \quad \frac{7x}{7} = \frac{84}{7}$ [Dividing both sides by 7]

$\Rightarrow \quad x = 12$

Check Substituting $x = 12$ in the given equation, we get

$$\text{L.H.S.} = \frac{12}{2} + \frac{12}{3} - \frac{12}{4} = 6 + 4 - 3 = 7 \text{ and, R.H.S.} = 7$$

$\therefore$ L.H.S. = R.H.S. for $x = 12$.

Hence, $x = 12$ is the solution of the given equation.

Example 5 Solve: $\frac{y-1}{3} - \frac{y-2}{4} = 1$

Solution We have, $\frac{y-1}{3} - \frac{y-2}{4} = 1$

LCM of denominators 3 and 4 on L.H.S. is 12.

Multiplying both sides by 12, we get

$$12\times\left(\frac{y-1}{3}\right)-12\times\left(\frac{y-2}{4}\right)=12\times1$$

$\Rightarrow\quad 4(y-1)-3(y-2)=12$

$\Rightarrow\quad 4y-4-3y+6=12$

$\Rightarrow\quad 4y-3y-4+6=12$

$\Rightarrow\quad y+2=12$

$\Rightarrow\quad y+2-2=12-2$ [Subtracting 2 from both sides]

$\Rightarrow\quad y=10$

Thus, $y = 10$ is the solution of the given equation.

Check Substituting $y = 10$ in the given equation, we get

$$\text{L.H.S.} = \frac{10-1}{3}-\frac{10-2}{4}=\frac{9}{3}-\frac{8}{4}=3-2=1 \text{ and, R.H.S.} =1$$

$\therefore$ L.H.S. = R.H.S. for $y = 10$.

Hence, $y = 10$ is the solution of the given equation.

EXERCISE 9.1

Solve each of the following equations and also verify your solution:

1. $9\frac{1}{4}=y-1\frac{1}{3}$
2. $\frac{5x}{3}+\frac{2}{5}=1$
3. $\frac{x}{2}+\frac{x}{3}+\frac{x}{4}=13$
4. $\frac{x}{2}+\frac{x}{8}=\frac{1}{8}$
5. $\frac{2x}{3}-\frac{3x}{8}=\frac{7}{12}$
6. $(x+2)(x+3)+(x-3)(x-2)-2x(x+1)=0$
7. $\frac{x}{2}-\frac{4}{5}+\frac{x}{5}+\frac{3x}{10}=\frac{1}{5}$
8. $\frac{7}{x}+35=\frac{1}{10}$
9. $\frac{2x-1}{3}-\frac{6x-2}{5}=\frac{1}{3}$
10. $13(y-4)-3(y-9)-5(y+4)=0$
11. $\frac{2}{3}(x-5)-\frac{1}{4}(x-2)=\frac{9}{2}$

ANSWERS

1. $\frac{127}{12}$ 2. $\frac{9}{25}$ 3. 12 4. $\frac{1}{5}$ 5. 2 6. 6

7. 1 8. $\frac{-70}{349}$ 9. $\frac{-1}{2}$ 10. 9 11. $\frac{88}{5}$

9.5 TRANSPOSITION METHOD FOR SOLVING LINEAR EQUATIONS IN ONE VARIABLE

Sometimes the two sides of an equation contain both variable (unknown quantity) and constants (numerals). In such cases, we first simplify two sides in their simplest forms and then transpose (shift) terms containing variable on R.H.S. to L.H.S and constant terms on L.H.S to R.H.S. By transposing a term from one side to the other side, we mean changing its sign and carrying it to the other side. In transposition the plus sign of the term changes into minus sign on the other side and vice-versa.

The transposition method involves the following steps:

Step I *Obtain the linear equation.*

Step II *Identify the variable (unknown quantity) and constants (numerals).*

Step III *Simplify the L.H.S. and R.H.S. to their simplest forms by removing brackets.*

Step IV *Transpose all terms containing variable on L.H.S. and constant terms on R.H.S. Note that the sign of the terms will change in shifting them from L.H.S. to R.H.S. and vice-versa.*

Step V *Simplify L.H.S. and R.H.S. in the simplest form so that each side contains just one term.*

Step VI *Solve the equation obtained in step V by dividing both sides by the coefficient of the variable on L.H.S.*

Following examples will illustrate the above procedure.

ILLUSTRATIVE EXAMPLES

Example 1 Solve: $\frac{x}{2}-\frac{1}{5}=\frac{x}{3}+\frac{1}{4}$

Solution We have,

$$\frac{x}{2}-\frac{1}{5}=\frac{x}{3}+\frac{1}{4}$$

The denominators on two sides are 2,5,3, and 4. Their LCM is 60.

Multiplying both sides of the given equation by 60, we get

$$60\times\left(\frac{x}{2}-\frac{1}{5}\right)=60\left(\frac{x}{3}+\frac{1}{4}\right)$$

$$\Rightarrow\quad 60\times\frac{x}{2}-60\times\frac{1}{5}=60\times\frac{x}{3}+60\times\frac{1}{4}$$

$$\Rightarrow\quad 30x-12=20x+15$$

$$\Rightarrow\quad 30x-20x=15+12 \qquad \text{[On transposing } 20x \text{ to LHS and } -12 \text{ to RHS]}$$

$$\Rightarrow\quad 10x=27$$

$$\Rightarrow\quad x=\frac{27}{10} \qquad \text{[On dividing both sides by 10]}$$

Hence, $x=\frac{27}{10}$ is the solution of the given equation.

Check Substituting $x=\frac{27}{10}$ in the given equation, we get

$$\text{L.H.S.}=\frac{x}{2}-\frac{1}{5}=\frac{27}{10}\times\frac{1}{2}-\frac{1}{5}=\frac{27}{20}-\frac{1}{5}=\frac{27-1\times4}{20}=\frac{27-4}{20}=\frac{23}{20}$$

and,

$$\text{R.H.S.}=\frac{x}{3}+\frac{1}{4}=\frac{27}{10}\times\frac{1}{3}+\frac{1}{4}=\frac{9}{10}+\frac{1}{4}=\frac{9\times2+1\times5}{20}=\frac{18+5}{20}=\frac{23}{20}$$

Thus, for $x=\frac{27}{10}$, we have L.H.S. = R.H.S.

Example 2 Solve: $x+7-\frac{8x}{3}=\frac{17}{6}-\frac{5x}{8}$

Solution We have,

$$x+7-\frac{8x}{3}=\frac{17}{6}-\frac{5x}{8}$$

The denominators on two sides are 3, 6 and 8. Their LCM is 24.

Multiplying both sides of the given equation by 24, we get

$$24\left(x+7-\frac{8x}{3}\right)=24\left(\frac{17}{6}-\frac{5x}{8}\right)$$

$$\Rightarrow \quad 24x+24\times7-24\times\frac{8x}{3}=24\times\frac{17}{6}-24\times\frac{5x}{8}$$

$$\Rightarrow \quad 24x+168-64x=68-15x$$

$$\Rightarrow \quad 168-40x=68-15x$$

$$\Rightarrow \quad -40x+15x=68-168 \qquad \text{[Transposing } -15x \text{ to LHS and 168 to RHS]}$$

$$\Rightarrow \quad -25x=-100$$

$$\Rightarrow \quad 25x=100$$

$$\Rightarrow \quad x=\frac{100}{25} \qquad \text{[Dividing both sides by 25]}$$

$$\Rightarrow \quad x=4$$

Thus, $x=4$ is the solution of the given equation.

Check Substituting $x=4$ in the given equation, we get

$$\text{L.H.S.}=x+7-\frac{8x}{3}=4+7-\frac{8\times4}{3}=11-\frac{32}{3}=\frac{33-32}{3}=\frac{1}{3}$$

and,

$$\text{R.H.S.}=\frac{17}{6}-\frac{5x}{8}=\frac{17}{6}-\frac{5\times4}{8}=\frac{17}{6}-\frac{5}{2}=\frac{17-15}{6}=\frac{2}{6}=\frac{1}{3}$$

Thus, for $x=4$, we have L.H.S. = R.H.S.

Example 3 Solve: $\frac{3t-2}{4}-\frac{2t+3}{3}=\frac{2}{3}-t$

Solution We have,

$$\frac{3t-2}{4}-\frac{2t+3}{3}=\frac{2}{3}-t$$

The denominators on two sides are 4, 3 and 3. Their LCM is 12.

Multiplying both sides of the given equation by 12, we get

$$12\left(\frac{3t-2}{4}\right)-12\left(\frac{2t+3}{3}\right)=12\left(\frac{2}{3}-t\right)$$

$$\Rightarrow \quad 3(3t-2)-4(2t+3)=12\left(\frac{2}{3}-t\right)$$

$$\Rightarrow \quad 9t-6-8t-12=12\times\frac{2}{3}-12t$$

$\Rightarrow \quad 9t-6-8t-12=8-12t$

$\Rightarrow \quad t-18=8-12t$

$\Rightarrow \quad t+12t=8+18$ [Transposing $-12t$ to LHS and -18 to RHS]

$\Rightarrow \quad 13t=26$

$\Rightarrow \quad t=\frac{26}{13}$ [Dividing both sides by 13]

$\Rightarrow \quad t=2$

Check Substituting $t=2$ on both sides of the given equation, we get

$$\text{L.H.S.}=\frac{3t-2}{4}-\frac{2t+3}{3}$$

$$=\frac{3\times2-2}{4}-\frac{2\times2+3}{3}=\frac{6-2}{4}-\frac{4+3}{3}=\frac{4}{4}-\frac{7}{3}=1-\frac{7}{3}=\frac{3-7}{3}=\frac{-4}{3}$$

and,

$$\text{R.H.S.}=\frac{2}{3}-t=\frac{2}{3}-2=\frac{2-6}{4}=\frac{-4}{3}$$

Thus, for $t=2$, we have L.H.S. = R.H.S.

Example 4 Solve: $\frac{x+2}{6}-\left(\frac{11-x}{3}-\frac{1}{4}\right)=\frac{3x-4}{12}$

Solution We have,

$$\frac{x+2}{6}-\left(\frac{11-x}{3}-\frac{1}{4}\right)=\frac{3x-4}{12}$$

The denominators on two sides of the given equation are 6, 3, 4 and 12. Their LCM is 24. Multiplying both sides of the given equation by 24, we get

$$24\left(\frac{x+2}{6}\right)-24\left(\frac{11-x}{3}-\frac{1}{4}\right)=24\left(\frac{3x-4}{12}\right)$$

$\Rightarrow \quad 4(x+2)-24\left(\frac{11-x}{3}\right)+24\times\frac{1}{4}=2(3x-4)$

$\Rightarrow \quad 4(x+2)-8(11-x)+6=2(3x-4)$

$\Rightarrow \quad 4x+8-88+8x+6=6x-8$

$\Rightarrow \quad 12x-74=6x-8$

$\Rightarrow \quad 12x-6x=74-8$ [Transposing $6x$ to LHS and -74 to RHS]

$\Rightarrow \quad 6x=66$

$\Rightarrow \quad x=\frac{66}{6}$ [Dividing both sides by 6]

$\Rightarrow \quad x=11$

Check Substituting $x = 11$ on both sides of the given equation, we get

$$\text{L.H.S.} = \frac{x+2}{6} - \left(\frac{11-x}{3} - \frac{1}{4}\right)$$

$$= \frac{11+2}{6} - \left(\frac{11-11}{3} - \frac{1}{4}\right) = \frac{13}{6} - \left(0 - \frac{1}{4}\right) = \frac{13}{6} + \frac{1}{4} = \frac{26+3}{12} = \frac{29}{12}$$

and,

$$\text{R.H.S.} = \frac{3x-4}{12} = \frac{3\times 11-4}{12} = \frac{33-4}{12} = \frac{29}{12}$$

Thus, for $x = 11$, we have L.H.S. = R.H.S.

Example 5 Solve: $x - \frac{2x+8}{3} = \frac{1}{4}\left(x - \frac{2-x}{6}\right) - 3$

Solution We have,

$$x - \frac{2x+8}{3} = \frac{1}{4}\left(x - \frac{2-x}{6}\right) - 3$$

$$\Rightarrow \quad x - \frac{2x+8}{3} = \frac{x}{4} - \frac{2-x}{24} - 3$$

The denominators on the two sides of this equation are 3, 4 and 24. Their LCM. is 24.

Multiplying both sides of this equation by 24, we get

$$24x - 24\left(\frac{2x+8}{3}\right) = 24\times\frac{x}{4} - 24\left(\frac{2-x}{24}\right) - 3\times 24$$

$$\Rightarrow \quad 24x - 8(2x+8) = 6x - (2-x) - 72$$

$$\Rightarrow \quad 24x - 16x - 64 = 6x - 2 + x - 72$$

$$\Rightarrow \quad 8x - 64 = 7x - 74$$

$$\Rightarrow \quad 8x - 7x = 64 - 74 \qquad \text{[Transposing } 7x \text{ to LHS and } -64 \text{ to RHS]}$$

$$\Rightarrow \quad x = -10$$

Thus, $x = -10$ is the solution of the given equation.

Check Putting $x = -10$ in the given equation, we get

$$\text{L.H.S.} = x - \frac{2x+8}{3} = -10 - \frac{2\times -10+8}{3} = -10 - \frac{-20+8}{3} = -10 - \left(\frac{-12}{3}\right) = -10 + 4 = -6$$

and,

$$\text{R.H.S.} = \frac{1}{4}\left(x - \frac{2-x}{6}\right) - 3 = \frac{1}{4}\left(-10 - \frac{2+10}{6}\right) - 3 = \frac{1}{4}(-10-2) - 3 = -3 - 3 = -6$$

Thus, L.H.S. = R.H.S. for $x = -10$.

Example 6 Solve: $0.16(5x-2)=0.4x+7$

Solution We have,

$$0.16(5x-2)=0.4x+7$$

$\Rightarrow 0.8x-0.32=0.4x+7$ [Expanding the bracket on LHS]

$\Rightarrow 0.8x-0.4x=0.32+7$ [Transposing $0.4x$ to LHS and -0.32 to RHS]

$\Rightarrow 0.4x=7.32$

$\Rightarrow \dfrac{0.4x}{0.4}=\dfrac{7.32}{0.4}$ [Dividing both sides by 0.4]

$\Rightarrow x=\dfrac{732}{40}\Rightarrow x=\dfrac{183}{10}=18.3$

Hence, $x=18.3$ is the solution of the given equation.

Example 7 Solve: $\dfrac{2}{5x}-\dfrac{5}{3x}=\dfrac{1}{15}$

Solution We have,

$$\frac{2}{5x}-\frac{5}{3x}=\frac{1}{15}$$

Multiplying both sides by $15x$, the LCM of $5x$ and $3x$, we get

$$15x\times\frac{2}{5x}-15x\times\frac{5}{3x}=15x\times\frac{1}{15}$$

$\Rightarrow 6-25=x\Rightarrow -19=x\Rightarrow x=-19$

Hence, $x=-19$ is the solution of the given equation.

Example 8 Solve: $\dfrac{17-3x}{5}-\dfrac{4x+2}{3}=5-6x+\dfrac{7x+14}{3}$

Solution Multiplying both sides by 15 i.e. the LCM of 5 and 3, we get

$$3(17-3x)-5(4x+2)=15(5-6x)+5(7x+14)$$

$\Rightarrow 51-9x-20x-10=75-90x+35x+70$

$\Rightarrow 41-29x=145-55x$

$\Rightarrow -29x+55x=145-41$

$\Rightarrow 26x=104$

$\Rightarrow \dfrac{26x}{26}=\dfrac{104}{26}$

$\Rightarrow x=4$

Thus, $x=4$ is the solution of the given equation.

Example 9 Solve: $\dfrac{x+2}{3}-\dfrac{x+1}{5}=\dfrac{x-3}{4}-1$

Solution Multiplying both sides by 60 i.e. the LCM of 3, 5, and 4, we get

$$20(x+2)-12(x+1)=15(x-3)-1\times 60$$

$\Rightarrow 20x+40-12x-12=15x-45-60$

$\Rightarrow 8x+28=15x-105$

$\Rightarrow \quad 8x - 15x = -105 - 28$

$\Rightarrow \quad -7x = -133$

$\Rightarrow \quad \frac{-7x}{-7} = \frac{-133}{-7}$ [Dividing both sides by – 7]

$\Rightarrow \quad x = \frac{133}{7} = 19$

Thus, $x = 19$ is the solution of the given equation.

Example 10 Solve: $(2x+3)^2 + (2x-3)^2 = (8x+6)(x-1) + 22$

Solution We have,

$(2x+3)^2 + (2x-3)^2 = (8x+6)(x-1) + 22$

$\Rightarrow \quad 2\{(2x)^2 + 3^2\} = x(8x+6) - (8x+6) + 22$ $\left[\text{Using}: (a+b)^2 + (a-b)^2 = 2(a^2+b^2) \text{ on LHS}\right]$

$\Rightarrow \quad 2(4x^2+9) = 8x^2 + 6x - 8x - 6 + 22$

$\Rightarrow \quad 8x^2 + 18 = 8x^2 - 2x + 16$

$\Rightarrow \quad 8x^2 - 8x^2 + 2x = 16 - 18$

$\Rightarrow \quad 2x = -2$

$\Rightarrow \quad x = -1$

Hence, $x = -1$ is the solution of the given equation.

EXERCISE 9.2

Solve each of the following equations and also check your result in each case:

1. $\frac{2x+5}{3} = 3x - 10$
2. $\frac{a-8}{3} = \frac{a-3}{2}$
3. $\frac{7y+2}{5} = \frac{6y-5}{11}$
4. $x - 2x + 2 - \frac{16}{3}x + 5 = 3 - \frac{7}{2}x$
5. $\frac{1}{2}x + 7x - 6 = 7x + \frac{1}{4}$
6. $\frac{3}{4}x + 4x = \frac{7}{8} + 6x - 6$
7. $\frac{7}{2}x - \frac{5}{2}x = \frac{20}{3}x + 10$
8. $\frac{6x+1}{2} + 1 = \frac{7x-3}{3}$
9. $\frac{3a-2}{3} + \frac{2a+3}{2} = a + \frac{7}{6}$
10. $x - \frac{(x-1)}{2} = 1 - \frac{(x-2)}{3}$
11. $\frac{3x}{4} - \frac{(x-1)}{2} = \frac{(x-2)}{3}$
12. $\frac{5x}{3} - \frac{(x-1)}{4} = \frac{(x-3)}{5}$
13. $\frac{(3x+1)}{16} + \frac{(2x-3)}{7} = \frac{(x+3)}{8} + \frac{(3x-1)}{14}$
14. $\frac{(1-2x)}{7} - \frac{(2-3x)}{8} = \frac{3}{2} + \frac{x}{4}$
15. $\frac{9x+7}{2} - \left(x - \frac{x-2}{7}\right) = 36$
16. $0.18(5x-4) = 0.5x + 0.8$
17. $\frac{2}{3x} - \frac{3}{2x} = \frac{1}{12}$
18. $\frac{4x}{9} + \frac{1}{3} + \frac{13}{108}x = \frac{8x+19}{18}$

19. $\frac{(45-2x)}{15} - \frac{(4x+10)}{5} = \frac{(15-14x)}{9}$

20. $5\left(\frac{7x+5}{3}\right) - \frac{23}{3} = 13 - \frac{4x-2}{3}$

21. $\frac{7x-1}{4} - \frac{1}{3}\left(2x - \frac{1-x}{2}\right) = \frac{10}{3}$

22. $\frac{0.5(x-0.4)}{0.35} - \frac{0.6(x-2.71)}{0.42} = x+6.1$

23. $6.5x + \frac{19.5x-32.5}{2} = 6.5x+13+\left(\frac{13x-26}{2}\right)$

24. $(3x-8)(3x+2)-(4x-11)(2x+1) = (x-3)(x+7)$

25. $[(2x+3)+(x+5)]^2 + [(2x+3)-(x+5)]^2 = 10x^2+92$

ANSWERS

1. 5	2. −7	3. −1	4. $\frac{24}{17}$	5. $\frac{25}{2}$	6. $\frac{41}{10}$	
7. $\frac{-30}{17}$	8. $\frac{-15}{4}$	9. $\frac{1}{3}$	10. $\frac{7}{5}$	11. 14	12. $\frac{-51}{73}$	
13. 5	14. −10	15. 9	16. 3.8	17. −10	18. 6	
19. $\frac{15}{14}$	20. 1	21. $\frac{41}{11}$	22. −2.8	23. 5	24. 4	25. $\frac{6}{11}$

9.6 CROSS-MULTIPLICATION METHOD FOR SOLVING EQUATIONS OF THE FORM $\frac{ax+b}{cx+d} = \frac{m}{n}$

Consider the equation $\frac{2x+5}{3x+7} = \frac{3}{5}$.

Clearly, it is an equation of the form

$$\frac{ax+b}{cx+d} = \frac{m}{n}, \text{ where } a=2, b=5, c=3, d=7, m=3 \text{ and } n=5.$$

Evidently, it is an equation in one variable x but it is not a linear equation, because the LHS is not a linear polynomial. However, it can be converted into a linear equation by applying the rules for solving an equation as discussed below.

We have, $\frac{2x+5}{3x+7} = \frac{3}{5}$ ... (i)

As x represents a number, so $3x + 7$ also represents a number. Multiplying both sides of (i) by $(3x + 7) \times 5$ i.e., the product of numbers in the denominators on LHS and RHS, we get

$$(3x+7)\times 5\times\left(\frac{2x+5}{3x+7}\right) = \frac{3}{5}\times(3x+7)\times 5$$

$\Rightarrow\quad 5\times(2x+5) = 3\times(3x+7)$ ... (ii)

$\Rightarrow\quad 10x+25 = 9x+21$

$\Rightarrow\quad 10x-9x = 21-25$

$\Rightarrow\quad x = -4$

This is the required solution of equation $\frac{2x+5}{3x+7} = \frac{3}{5}$.

Note that in solving this equation, we have first converted it into a linear equation given in (ii) by applying the rules of solving equations. Equation (ii) can also be obtained directly from equation (i) by equating the product of numerator of L.H.S. and denominator of R.H.S. to the product of denominator of L.H.S. and numerator of R.H.S. This can be exhibited as follow:

$$\frac{2x+5}{3x+7} \times \frac{3}{5}$$

This process of multiplying the numerator on L.H.S. with the denominator on R.H.S. and equating it to the product of the denominator on L.H.S. with the numerator on R.H.S. is called cross-multiplication.

It is evident from the above discussion that by using cross-multiplication we can convert an equation of the form

$$\frac{ax+b}{cx+d} = \frac{m}{n}$$

to a linear equation $n(ax+b) = m(cx+d)$.

This equation can now be solved by using the rules for solving equations.

Following examples will illustrate the use of cross-multiplication in solving equations.

ILLUSTRATIVE EXAMPLES

Example 1 Solve: $\frac{2x+1}{3x-2} = \frac{9}{10}$

Solution We have,

$$\frac{2x+1}{3x-2} = \frac{9}{10}$$

$\Rightarrow \quad 10 \times (2x+1) = 9 \times (3x-2)$ [By cross-multiplication]

$\Rightarrow \quad 20x + 10 = 27x - 18$

$\Rightarrow \quad 20x - 27x = -18 - 10$ [Using transposition]

$\Rightarrow \quad -7x = -28$

$\Rightarrow \quad \frac{-7x}{-7} = \frac{-28}{-7}$ [Dividing both sides by -7]

$\Rightarrow \quad x = 4$

Hence, $x = 4$ is the solution of the given equation.

Example 2 Solve: $\frac{3x+5}{2x+7} = 4$

Solution We have,

$$\frac{3x+5}{2x+7} = 4$$

$\Rightarrow \quad \frac{3x+5}{2x+7} = \frac{4}{1}$

$\Rightarrow \quad 1 \times (3x+5) = 4 \times (2x+7)$ [By cross-multiplication]

$\Rightarrow \quad 3x+5=8x+28$

$\Rightarrow \quad 3x-8x=28-5$ [Using transposition]

$\Rightarrow \quad -5x=23$

$\Rightarrow \quad \frac{-5x}{-5}=\frac{23}{-5}$ [Dividing both sides by -5]

$\Rightarrow \quad x=-\frac{23}{5}$

Hence, $x=-\frac{23}{5}$ is the solution of the given equation.

Example 3 Solve: $\frac{17(2-x)-5(x+12)}{1-7x}=8$

Solution We have,

$$\frac{17(2-x)-5(x+12)}{1-7x}=8$$

$\Rightarrow \quad \frac{34-17x-5x-60}{1-7x}=\frac{8}{1}$

$\Rightarrow \quad \frac{-22x-26}{1-7x}=\frac{8}{1}$

$\Rightarrow \quad 1\times(-22x-26)=8\times(1-7x)$ [By cross-multiplication]

$\Rightarrow \quad -22x-26=8-56x$

$\Rightarrow \quad -22x+56x=8+26$

$\Rightarrow \quad 34x=34$

$\Rightarrow \quad \frac{34x}{34}=\frac{34}{34}$ [Dividing both sides by 34]

$\Rightarrow \quad x=1$

Hence, $x=1$ is the solution of the given equation.

Example 4 Solve: $\frac{x+b}{a-b}=\frac{x-b}{a+b}$

Solution We have,

$$\frac{x+b}{a-b}=\frac{x-b}{a+b}$$

$\Rightarrow \quad (x+b)\times(a+b)=(x-b)\times(a-b)$ [By cross-multiplication]

$\Rightarrow \quad x(a+b)+b(a+b)=x(a-b)-b(a-b)$

$\Rightarrow \quad ax+bx+ba+b^2=ax-bx-ba+b^2$

$\Rightarrow \quad ax+bx-ax+bx=-ba+b^2-ba-b^2$

$\Rightarrow \quad 2bx = -2ba$

$\Rightarrow \quad \frac{2bx}{2b} = -\frac{2ab}{2b}$

$\Rightarrow \quad x = -a$

Hence, $x = -a$ is the solution of the given equation.

Example 5 Solve: $\frac{(4+x)(5-x)}{(2+x)(7-x)} = 1$

Solution We have,

$$\frac{(4+x)(5-x)}{(2+x)(7-x)} = 1$$

$\Rightarrow \quad \frac{20-4x+5x-x^2}{14-2x+7x-x^2} = 1$

$\Rightarrow \quad \frac{20+x-x^2}{14+5x-x^2} = 1$

$\Rightarrow \quad 20+x-x^2 = 14+5x-x^2$ [By cross-multiplication]

$\Rightarrow \quad x-x^2-5x+x^2 = 14-20$

$\Rightarrow \quad -4x = -6$

$\Rightarrow \quad \frac{-4x}{-4} = \frac{-6}{-4}$

$\Rightarrow \quad x = \frac{3}{2}$

Hence, $x = \frac{3}{2}$ is the solution of the given equation.

Example 6 Solve: $\frac{1}{x+1} + \frac{1}{x+2} = \frac{2}{x+10}$

Solution We have,

$$\frac{1}{x+1} + \frac{1}{x+2} = \frac{2}{x+10}$$

Multiplying both sides by $(x+1)(x+2)(x+10)$ i.e., the LCM of $x+1$, $x+2$ and $x+10$, we get

$$\frac{(x+1)(x+2)(x+10)}{x+1} + \frac{(x+1)(x+2)(x+10)}{x+2} = \frac{2(x+1)(x+2)(x+10)}{x+10}$$

$\Rightarrow \quad (x+2)(x+10)+(x+1)(x+10) = 2(x+1)(x+2)$

$\Rightarrow \quad x^2+2x+10x+20+x^2+10x+x+10 = 2(x^2+x+2x+2)$

$\Rightarrow \quad 2x^2+23x+30 = 2(x^2+3x+2)$

$\Rightarrow \quad 2x^2+23x+30 = 2x^2+6x+4$

$\Rightarrow \quad 2x^2+23x-2x^2-6x = 4-30$

$\Rightarrow \quad 17x = -26$

$\Rightarrow \quad x = -\dfrac{26}{17}$

Hence, $x = -\dfrac{26}{17}$ is the solution of the given equation.

Example 7 Solve: $\dfrac{6x^2+13x-4}{2x+5} = \dfrac{12x^2+5x-2}{4x+3}$

Solution We have,

$$\frac{6x^2+13x-4}{2x+5} = \frac{12x^2+5x-2}{4x+3}$$

$\Rightarrow \quad (6x^2+13x-4)(4x+3) = (12x^2+5x-2)(2x+5)$ [By cross-multiplication]

$\Rightarrow \quad (6x^2+13x-4)\times 4x + (6x^2+13x-4)\times 3 = (12x^2+5x-2)\times 2x + (12x^2+5x-2)\times 5$

$\Rightarrow \quad 24x^3+52x^2-16x+18x^2+39x-12 = 24x^3+10x^2-4x+60x^2+25x-10$

$\Rightarrow \quad 24x^3+70x^2+23x-12 = 24x^3+70x^2+21x-10$

$\Rightarrow \quad 24x^3+70x^2+23x-24x^3-70x^2-21x = -10+12$

$\Rightarrow \quad 2x = 2$

$\Rightarrow \quad x = 1$

Hence, $x = 1$ is the solution of the given equation.

Example 8 Solve: $\dfrac{4x+17}{18} - \dfrac{13x-2}{17x-32} + \dfrac{x}{3} = \dfrac{7x}{12} - \dfrac{x+16}{36}$

Solution We have,

$$\frac{4x+17}{18} - \frac{13x-2}{17x-32} + \frac{x}{3} = \frac{7x}{12} - \frac{x+16}{36}$$

$\Rightarrow \quad \dfrac{4x+17}{18} - \dfrac{7x}{12} + \dfrac{x+16}{36} + \dfrac{x}{3} = \dfrac{13x-2}{17x-32}$

Multiplying both sides by 36 i.e., the LCM of 18, 12, 36 and 3, we get

$$36\times\frac{4x+17}{18} - 36\times\frac{7x}{12} + 36\times\frac{x+16}{36} + 36\times\frac{x}{3} = 36\times\left(\frac{13x-2}{17x-32}\right)$$

$\Rightarrow \quad 2(4x+17) - 3\times 7x + x + 16 + 12x = 36\times\left(\dfrac{13x-2}{17x-32}\right)$

$\Rightarrow \quad 8x+34-21x+x+16+12x = 36\times\left(\dfrac{13x-2}{17x-32}\right)$

$\Rightarrow \quad 50 = 36\times\left(\dfrac{13x-2}{17x-32}\right)$ [By cross-multiplication]

$\Rightarrow \quad 50\times(17x-32) = 36(13x-2)$

$\Rightarrow \quad 850x-1600 = 468x-72$

$\Rightarrow \quad 850x-468x = 1600-72$

$\Rightarrow \quad 382x = 1528$

$\Rightarrow \quad x = \dfrac{1528}{382} = 4$

Hence, $x = 4$, is the solution of the given equation.

EXERCISE 9.3

Solve the following equations and verify your answer:

1. $\dfrac{2x-3}{3x+2}=-\dfrac{2}{3}$
2. $\dfrac{2-y}{y+7}=\dfrac{3}{5}$
3. $\dfrac{5x-7}{3x}=2$
4. $\dfrac{3x+5}{2x+7}=4$
5. $\dfrac{2y+5}{y+4}=1$
6. $\dfrac{2x+1}{3x-2}=\dfrac{5}{9}$
7. $\dfrac{1-9y}{19-3y}=\dfrac{5}{8}$
8. $\dfrac{2x}{3x+1}=-3$
9. $\dfrac{y-(7-8y)}{9y-(3+4y)}=\dfrac{2}{3}$
10. $\dfrac{6}{2x-(3-4x)}=\dfrac{2}{3}$
11. $\dfrac{2}{3x}-\dfrac{3}{2x}=\dfrac{1}{12}$
12. $\dfrac{3x+5}{4x+2}=\dfrac{3x+4}{4x+7}$
13. $\dfrac{7x-2}{5x-1}=\dfrac{7x+3}{5x+4}$
14. $\left(\dfrac{x+1}{x+2}\right)^2=\dfrac{x+2}{x+4}$
15. $\left(\dfrac{x+1}{x-4}\right)^2=\dfrac{x+8}{x-2}$
16. $\dfrac{9x-7}{3x+5}=\dfrac{3x-4}{x+6}$
17. $\dfrac{x+2}{x+5}=\dfrac{x}{x+6}$
18. $\dfrac{2x-(7-5x)}{9x-(3+4x)}=\dfrac{7}{6}$
19. $\dfrac{15(2-x)-5(x+6)}{1-3x}=10$
20. $\dfrac{x+3}{x-3}+\dfrac{x+2}{x-2}=2$
21. $\dfrac{(x+2)(2x-3)-2x^2+6}{x-5}=2$
22. $\dfrac{x^2-(x+1)(x+2)}{5x+1}=6$
23. $\dfrac{(2x+3)-(5x-7)}{6x+11}=-\dfrac{8}{3}$
24. Find a positive value of x for which the given equation is satisfied:

    (i) $\dfrac{x^2-9}{5+x^2}=-\dfrac{5}{9}$ (ii) $\dfrac{y^2+4}{3y^2+7}=\dfrac{1}{2}$

ANSWERS

1. $\dfrac{5}{12}$ 2. $\dfrac{-11}{8}$ 3. -7 4. $\dfrac{-23}{5}$ 5. -1 6. $\dfrac{-19}{3}$

7. $\dfrac{-29}{19}$ 8. $\dfrac{-3}{11}$ 9. $\dfrac{15}{17}$ 10. 2 11. -10 12. $\dfrac{-27}{19}$

13. $\dfrac{1}{2}$ 14. $\dfrac{-4}{3}$ 15. $\dfrac{26}{9}$ 16. $\dfrac{1}{2}$ 17. -4 18. 3

19. 1 20. $\dfrac{12}{5}$ 21. 10 22. $-\dfrac{8}{33}$ 23. $-\dfrac{118}{39}$ 24. (i) 2 (ii) 1

9.7 APPLICATIONS OF LINEAR EQUATIONS TO PRACTICAL PROBLEMS

In this section, we will study formulation and solution of some practical problems. These problems involve relations among unkown quantities (variables) and known quantities (numbers) and are often stated in words. That is why we often refer to these problems as word problems. A word problem is first translated in the form of an equation containing unknown quantities (variables) and known quantities (numbers or constants) and then we solve it by using any one of the methods discussed in the earlier section. The procedure to translate a word problem in the form of an equation is known as the formulation of the problem. Thus, the process of solving a word problem consists of two parts, namely, formulation and solution.

The following steps should be followed to solve a word problem:

Step I Read the problem carefully and note what is given and what is required.

Step II Denote the unknown quantity by some letters, say x, y, z, etc.

Step III Translate the statements of the problem into mathematical statements.

Step IV Using the condition (s) given in the problem, form the equation.

Step V Solve the equation for the unknown.

Step VI Check whether the solution satisfies the equation.

Following examples will illustrate these steps.

ILLUSTRATIVE EXAMPLES

Example 1 A number is such that it is as much greater than 84 as it is less than 108. Find it.

Solution Let the number be x. Then, the number is greater than 84 by $x - 84$ and it is less than 108 by $108 - x$.

$\therefore \quad x - 84 = 108 - x$ [Given]

$\Rightarrow \quad x + x = 108 + 84$

$\Rightarrow \quad 2x = 192$

$\Rightarrow \quad \frac{2x}{2} = \frac{192}{2}$

$\Rightarrow \quad x = 96$

Hence, the number is 96.

Example 2 A number is 56 greater than the average of its third, quarter and one-twelfth. Find it.

Solution Let the number be x. Then,

One third of x is $= \frac{1}{3}x$, Quarter of x is $= \frac{x}{4}$, One-twelfth of x is $= \frac{x}{12}$

Average of third, quarter and one-twelfth of x is $= \frac{\left(\frac{x}{3} + \frac{x}{4} + \frac{x}{12}\right)}{3} = \frac{1}{3}\left(\frac{x}{3} + \frac{x}{4} + \frac{x}{12}\right)$

It is given that the number x is 56 greater than the average of the third, quarter and one-twelfth of x.

$\therefore \quad x = \frac{1}{3}\left(\frac{x}{3} + \frac{x}{4} + \frac{x}{12}\right) + 56$

$\Rightarrow \quad x = \frac{x}{9} + \frac{x}{12} + \frac{x}{36} + 56$

$\Rightarrow \quad x - \frac{x}{9} - \frac{x}{12} - \frac{x}{36} = 56$

$\Rightarrow \quad 36x - 4x - 3x - x = 36 \times 56$ [Multiplying both sides by 36 i.e., the L.C.M. of 9, 12 and 36]

$\Rightarrow \quad 36 - 8x = 36 \times 56$

$\Rightarrow \quad 28x = 36 \times 56$

$\Rightarrow \quad \frac{28x}{28} = \frac{36 \times 56}{28}$ [Dividing both sides by 28]

$\Rightarrow \quad x = 36 \times 2$

$\Rightarrow \quad x = 72$

Hence, the number is 72.

Example 3 A number consists of two digits whose sum is 8. If 18 is added to the number its digits are reversed. Find the number.

Solution Let one's digit be x.

Since the sum of the digits is 8. Therefore, ten's digit = $8 - x$.

$\therefore \quad \text{Number} = 10 \times (8 - x) + x = 80 - 10x + x = 80 - 9x$ ... (i)

Now,

Number obtained by reversing the digit $= 10 \times x + (8 - x) = 10x + 8 - x = 9x + 8$.

It is given that if 18 is added to the number its digits are reversed.

$\therefore$ Number + 18 = Number obtained by reversing the digits

$\Rightarrow \quad 80 - 9x + 18 = 9x + 8$

$\Rightarrow \quad 98 - 9x = 9x + 8$

$\Rightarrow \quad 98 - 8 = 9x + 9x$

$\Rightarrow \quad 90 = 18x$

$\Rightarrow \quad \frac{18x}{18} = \frac{90}{18}$

$\Rightarrow \quad x = 5$

Putting the value of x in (i), we get

Number $= 80 - 9 \times 5 = 80 - 45 = 35$

Example 4 Divide 34 into two parts in such a way that $\left(\frac{4}{7}\right)^{th}$ of one part is equal to $\left(\frac{2}{5}\right)^{th}$ of the other.

Solution Let one part be x. Then, other part is $(34 - x)$. It is given that

$\left(\frac{4}{7}\right)^{th}$ of one part $= \left(\frac{2}{5}\right)^{th}$ of the other part

$\Rightarrow \quad \frac{4}{7}x = \frac{2}{5}(34 - x)$

$\Rightarrow \quad 20x = 14(34 - x)$ [Multiplying both sides by 35, the LCM of 7 and 5]

$\Rightarrow \quad 20x = 14 \times 34 - 14x$

$\Rightarrow \quad 20x + 14x = 14 \times 34$

$\Rightarrow \quad 34x = 14 \times 34$

$\Rightarrow \quad \frac{34x}{34} = \frac{14 \times 34}{34}$ [Dividing both sides by 34]

$\Rightarrow \quad x = 14$

Hence, the two parts are 14 and $34 - 14 = 20$

Example 5 The numerator of a fraction is 4 less than the denominator. If 1 is added to both its numerator and denominator, it becomes 1/2. Find the fraction.

Solution Let the denominator of the fraction be x. Then,

Numerator of the fraction $= x - 4$

$\therefore$ Fraction $= \dfrac{x-4}{x}$ ...(i)

If 1 is added to both its numerator and denominator, the fraction becomes $\dfrac{1}{2}$.

$\therefore \quad \dfrac{x-4+1}{x+1} = \dfrac{1}{2}$

$\Rightarrow \quad \dfrac{x-3}{x+1} = \dfrac{1}{2}$

$\Rightarrow \quad 2(x-3) = x+1$ [Using cross- multiplication]

$\Rightarrow \quad 2x-6 = x+1$

$\Rightarrow \quad 2x-x = 6+1$

$\Rightarrow \quad x = 7$

Putting $x = 7$ in (i), we get

Fraction $= \dfrac{7-4}{7} = \dfrac{3}{7}$. Hence, the given fraction is $\dfrac{3}{7}$.

Example 6 Saurabh has Rs 34 fifty paise and twenty-five paise coins. If the number of 25-paise coins be twice the number of 50-paise coins, how many coins of each kind does he have?

Solution Let the number of 50-paise coins be x. Then,

Number of 25-paise coins $= 2x$

$\therefore$ Value of x fifty-paise coins $= 50 \times x$ paise $=$ Rs $\dfrac{50 \times x}{100} =$ Rs $\dfrac{x}{2}$

Value of $2x$ twenty-five paise coins $= 25 \times 2x$ paise $= 50x$ paise $=$ Rs $\dfrac{50x}{100} =$ Rs $\dfrac{x}{2}$

$\therefore$ Total value of all coins $=$ Rs $\left(\dfrac{x}{2} + \dfrac{x}{2}\right) =$ Rs x

But, the total value of the money is Rs 34

$\therefore \quad x = 34$

Thus, number of 50-paise coins $= 34$

Number of twenty-five paise coins $= 2x = 2 \times 34 = 68$

Example 7 Arvind has Piggy bank. It is full of one-rupee and fifty-paise coins. It contains 3 times as many fifty paise coins as one rupee coins. The total amount of the money in the bank is Rs 35. How many coins of each kind are there in the bank?

Solution Let there be x one rupee coins in the bank. Then,

Number of 50-paise coins $= 3x$

$\therefore$ Value of x one rupee coins $=$ Rs x

Value of $3x$ fifty-paise coins $= 50 \times 3x$ paise

$= 150\, x$ paise $=$ Rs $\dfrac{150}{100} x =$ Rs $\dfrac{3x}{2}$

$\therefore$ Total value of all the coins $=$ Rs $\left(x + \dfrac{3x}{2}\right)$

But, the total amount of the money in the bank is given as Rs 35.

$$\therefore \quad x+\frac{3x}{2}=35$$

$$\Rightarrow \quad 2x+3x=70 \qquad \text{[Multiplying both sides by 2]}$$

$$\Rightarrow \quad 5x=70 \Rightarrow \frac{5x}{5}=\frac{70}{5} \Rightarrow x=14$$

$\therefore$ Number of one rupee coins $=$ 14, Number of 50 paise coins $=3x=3\times14=42$.

Example 8 Kanwar is three years older than Anima. Six years ago, Kanwar's age was four times Anima's age. Find the ages of Knawar and Anima.

Solution Let Anima's age be x years. Then, Kanwar's age is $(x + 3)$ years.

Six years ago, Anima's age was $(x - 6)$ years

Kanwar's age was $(x + 3 - 6)$ years $=$ $(x - 3)$ years.

It is given that six years ago kanwar's age was four times Anima's age.

$$\therefore \quad x-3=4(x-6)$$

$$\Rightarrow \quad x-3=4x-24$$

$$\Rightarrow \quad x-4x=-24+3$$

$$\Rightarrow \quad -3x=-21$$

$$\Rightarrow \quad \frac{-3x}{-3}=\frac{-21}{-3}$$

$$\Rightarrow \quad x=7$$

Hence, Anima's age $=$ 7 years

Kanwar's age $= (x + 3)$ years $= (7 + 3)$ years $=$ 10 Years.

Example 9 After 12 years I shall be 3 times as old as I was 4 years ago. Find my present age.

Solution Let my present age be x years. After 12 years my age will be $(x + 12)$ years.

4 years ago my age was $(x - 4)$ years.

It is given that after 12 years I shall be 3 times as old as I was 4 years ago.

$$\therefore \quad x+12=3(x-4)$$

$$\Rightarrow \quad x+12=3x-12$$

$$\Rightarrow \quad x-3x=-12-12$$

$$\Rightarrow \quad -2x=-24$$

$$\Rightarrow \quad \frac{-2x}{-2}=\frac{-24}{-2}$$

$$\Rightarrow \quad x=12$$

Thus, my present age is 12 years.

Example 10 My age is four times the difference of my age after four years and my age three years back. How old am I ?

Solution Let my present age be x years. Then, after four years I will be $(x+4)$ years old. and, three years ago my age was $(x-3)$ years.

It is given that my present age is four times the difference of my age after four years and my age three years back.

$\therefore \quad x = 4\{(x+4)-(x-3)\}$

$\Rightarrow \quad x = 4(x+4-x+3)$

$\Rightarrow \quad x = 4\times 7$

$\Rightarrow \quad x = 28$

Hence, I am 28 years old now.

Example 11 Hamid has three boxes of different fruits. Box A weighs $2\frac{1}{2}$ kg more than Box B and Box C weighs $10\frac{1}{4}$ kg more than Box B. The total weight of the boxes is $48\frac{3}{4}$ How many kg does Box A weigh?

Solution Suppose the box B weights x kg.

Since box A weighs $2\frac{1}{2}$ kg more than box B and C weighs $10\frac{1}{4}$ kg more than box B.

$$\therefore \quad \text{Weight of box } A = \left(x+2\frac{1}{2}\right)\text{kg} = \left(x+\frac{5}{2}\right)\text{kg} \qquad \text{... (i)}$$

$$\text{Weight of box } C = \left(x+10\frac{1}{4}\right)\text{kg} = \left(x+\frac{41}{4}\right)\text{kg}$$

$$\therefore \quad \text{Total weight of all the boxes} = \left(x+\frac{5}{2}+x+x+\frac{41}{4}\right)\text{kg}$$

But, the total weight of the boxes is given as $48\frac{3}{4}\text{ kg} = \frac{195}{4}\text{ kg}$

$\therefore \quad x+\frac{5}{2}+x+x+\frac{41}{4} = \frac{195}{4}$

$\Rightarrow \quad 4x+10+4x+4x+41 = 195$ [Multiplying both sides by 4]

$\Rightarrow \quad 12x+51 = 195$

$\Rightarrow \quad 12x = 195-51$

$\Rightarrow \quad 12x = 144$

$\Rightarrow \quad \frac{12x}{12} = \frac{144}{12}$

$\Rightarrow \quad x = 12$

Putting $x = 12$ in (i), we get

$$\text{Weight of box } A = \left(12+\frac{5}{2}\right)\text{kg} = \frac{29}{2}\text{ kg} = 14\frac{1}{2}\text{ kg}$$

Example 12 There are 90 multiple choice questions in a test. Suppose you get two marks for every correct answer and for every question you leave unattempted or answer wrongly, one mark is deducted from your total score of correct answers. If you get 60 marks in the test, then how may questions did you answer correctly?

Solution Suppose I answered x questions correctly. Then,

Number of wrong answers and unattempted questions = $(90 - x)$

Since for every correct answer 2 marks are awarded and for every wrong answer or unattempted question one mark is deducted.

$\therefore$ Total score $= 2x - (90 - x) \times 1 = 2x - (90 - x)$

But, the total score is given as 60

$$\therefore \quad 2x - (90 - x) = 60$$
$$\Rightarrow \quad 2x - 90 + x = 60$$
$$\Rightarrow \quad 3x - 90 = 60$$
$$\Rightarrow \quad 3x = 60 + 90$$
$$\Rightarrow \quad 3x = 150$$
$$\Rightarrow \quad \frac{3x}{3} = \frac{150}{3}$$
$$\Rightarrow \quad x = 50$$

$\therefore$ Number of correct answer = Rs 50.

Example 13 A man sold an artical for Rs 495 and gained 10% on it. Find the cost price of the article.

Solution Let the cost price of the article be Rs x

It is given that the man gained 10%. This means that:

On Rs 100 gain = Rs 10

$\therefore$ On Re 1 gain = Rs $\frac{10}{100}$

On Rs x gain = Rs $\frac{10}{100} \times x$ = Rs $\frac{x}{10}$

We know that

S.P. = C.P. + Gain

$$\therefore \quad 495 = x + \frac{x}{10}$$
$$\Rightarrow \quad 495 \times 10 = 10x + x \quad \text{[Multiplying both sides by 10]}$$
$$\Rightarrow \quad 4950 = 11x$$
$$\Rightarrow \quad \frac{11x}{11} = \frac{4950}{11}$$
$$\Rightarrow \quad x = 450$$

Hence, cost price of the article = Rs 450.

Example 14 How much pure alcohol be added to 400 ml of a 15% solution to make its strength 32%?

Solution Let x ml pure alcohol be added to 400 ml of a 15% solution to make its strength 32%. Here, 15% solution means that there is 15 ml pure alcohol in a solution of 100 ml.

Now, Quantity of alcohol in 100 ml solution = 15 ml

$\therefore$ Quantity of alcohol in one ml solution $= \frac{15}{100}$ ml

Quantity of alcohol in 400 ml solution $= \frac{15}{100} \times 400 \text{ ml} = 60 \text{ ml}$

Total quantity of the solution $= (400 + x)$ ml

Total quantity of alcohol in $(400 + x)$ ml solution $= (60 + x)$ ml

$\therefore$ Quantity of alcohol in one ml $= \dfrac{60 + x}{400 + x}$ ml

Quantity of alcohol in 100 ml $= \dfrac{60 + x}{400 + x} \times 100$ ml

$\Rightarrow$ Strength of the solution $= \left(\dfrac{60 + x}{400 + x}\right) \times 100\%$

But, the strength of the solution is given as 32%.

$$\therefore \quad \frac{60 + x}{400 + x} \times 100 = 32$$

$$\Rightarrow \quad 100(60 + x) = 32(400 + x) \qquad \text{[Multiplying both sides by } (400 + x)]$$

$$\Rightarrow \quad 6000 + 100x = 12800 + 32x$$

$$\Rightarrow \quad 100x - 32x = 12800 - 6000$$

$$\Rightarrow \quad 68x = 6800$$

$$\Rightarrow \quad \frac{68x}{68} = \frac{6800}{68}$$

$$\Rightarrow \quad x = 100$$

Thus, 100 ml alcohol must be added to make 32% strength of the solution.

Example 15 50 kg of an alloy of lead and tin contains 60% lead. How much lead must be melted into it to make an alloy containing 75% lead?

Solution Lean contents in 100 kg alloy $= 60$ kg

$\therefore$ Lead contents in 50 kg alloy $= \left(\dfrac{60}{100} \times 50\right)$ kg $= 30$ kg

Let x kg of lead be melted into the alloy to make it an alloy containing 75% lead. Then,

Weight of the new alloy $= (50 + x)$ kg

Weight of lead in the new alloy $= (30 + x)$ kg

Now,

Lead contents in $(50 + x)$ kg alloy $= (30 + x)$ kg

$\therefore$ Lead contents in one kg alloy $= \left(\dfrac{30 + x}{50 + x}\right)$ kg

Lead contents in 100 kg alloy $= \left(\dfrac{30 + x}{50 + x}\right) \times 100$ kg

$\Rightarrow$ Percentage of lead in new alloy $= \left(\dfrac{30 + x}{50 + x} \times 100\right)\%$

But, the percentage of lead in the new alloy is given as 75%.

$$\therefore \quad \frac{30 + x}{50 + x} \times 100 = 75$$

$\Rightarrow \quad (30+x)\times 100 = 75\times(50+x)$ [Using cross-multiplication]

$\Rightarrow \quad 3000+100x = 3750+75x$

$\Rightarrow \quad 100x-75x = 3750-3000$

$\Rightarrow \quad 25x = 750$

$\Rightarrow \quad \frac{25x}{25} = \frac{750}{25}$

$\Rightarrow \quad x = 30$

Hence, required lead to be added = 30 kg.

Example 16 The sum of two numbers is 2490. If 6.5% of one number is equal to 8.5% of the other, find the numbers.

Solution Let the first number be x. Then,

Second number $= 2490 - x$ [$\therefore$ Sum of the numbers is given to be 2490]

Now,

$$6.5\% \text{ of the first number} = \frac{6.5}{100}\times x = \frac{65x}{1000}$$

and,

$$8.5\% \text{ of the second number} = \frac{8.5}{100}\times(2490-x) = \frac{85}{1000}(2490-x)$$

It is given that 6.5% of the first number is equal to 8.5% of the other.

$\therefore \quad \frac{65x}{1000} = \frac{85}{1000}(2490-x)$

$\Rightarrow \quad 65x = 85(2490-x)$ [Multiplying both sides by 1000]

$\Rightarrow \quad 65x = 2490\times 85 - 85x$

$\Rightarrow \quad 65x+85x = 2490\times 85$

$\Rightarrow \quad 150x = 2490\times 85$

$\Rightarrow \quad x = \frac{2490\times 85}{150}$

$\Rightarrow \quad x = 1411$

$\therefore$ First number $= 1411$, Second number $= 2490-1411 = 1079$

Check We have,

$$6.5\% \text{ of first number} = \frac{6.5}{100}\times 1411 = \frac{91715}{1000}$$

$$8.5\% \text{ of the socond number} = \frac{8.5}{100}\times 1079 = \frac{91715}{1000}$$

Clearly, 6.5% of the first number is equal to 8.5% of the second number, which is the same as given in the problem.

Example 17 The sum of two numbers is 45 and their ratio is 7 : 8. Find the numbers.

Solution Let one of the numbers be x. Since the sum of the two numbers is 45. Therefore, the other number will be $45-x$.

It is given that the ratio of the numbers is 7 : 8.

$\therefore \quad \dfrac{x}{45-x}=\dfrac{7}{8}$

$\Rightarrow \quad 8\times x=7\times(45-x)$ [By cross-multiplication]

$\Rightarrow \quad 8x=315-7x$

$\Rightarrow \quad 8x+7x=315$

$\Rightarrow \quad 15x=315$

$\Rightarrow \quad x=\dfrac{315}{15}=21$

Thus, one number is 21 and, Other number $=45-x=45-21=24$

Check Clearly, sum of the numbers $=21+24=45$, which is same as given in the problem.

Ratio of the numbers $=\dfrac{21}{24}=\dfrac{7}{8}$, which is same as given in the problem.

Thus, our solution is correct.

Example 18 Two numbers are such that the ratio between them is 3:5. If each is increased by 10, the ratio between the new numbers so formed is 5:7. Find the original numbers.

Solution Since the ratio between the numbers is 3 : 5. So, let the two numbers be $3x$ and $5x$.

If each number is increased by 10, the new numbers are $3x+10$ and $5x+10$.

It is given that the ratio between the new numbers is 5 : 7.

$\therefore \quad \dfrac{3x+10}{5x+10}=\dfrac{5}{7}$

$\Rightarrow \quad 7\times(3x+10)=5\times(5x+10)$ [By cross-multiplication]

$\Rightarrow \quad 21x+70=25x+50$

$\Rightarrow \quad 21x-25x=50-70$

$\Rightarrow \quad -4x=-20$

$\Rightarrow \quad x=\dfrac{-20}{-4}=5$

Hence, the two numbers are $3x=3\times5=15$ and $5x=5\times5=25$.

Example 19 Three prizes are to be distributed in a quiz contest. The value of the second prize is five-sixths the value of the first prize and the value of the third prize is four-fifths that of the second prize. If the total value of three prizes is Rs 150, find the value of each prize.

Solution Let the value of the first prize be Rs x. Then,

Value of second prize $=\text{Rs}\ \dfrac{5}{6}x$

Value of third prize = Four-fifths the value of second prize

$$=\text{Rs}\ \frac{4}{5}\times\left(\frac{5}{6}x\right)=\text{Rs}\ \frac{4}{6}x=\text{Rs}\ \frac{2}{3}x$$

$\therefore \quad$ Total value of three prizes $=\text{Rs}\left(x+\dfrac{5}{6}x+\dfrac{2}{3}x\right)$

But, the total value of three prizes is given as Rs 150.

$\therefore \quad x+\frac{5}{6}x+\frac{2}{3}x=150$

$\Rightarrow \quad 6x+5x+2\times 2x=6\times 150$ [Multiplying both sides by 6 i.e., the L.C.M. of 6 and 3]

$\Rightarrow \quad 15x=900$

$\Rightarrow \quad x=\frac{900}{15}=60$

$\therefore$ Value of first prize = Rs 60, Value of second prize $=\text{Rs}\left(\frac{5}{6}\times 60\right)=\text{Rs } 50$,

Value of third prize $=\text{Rs}\left(\frac{2}{3}\times 60\right)=\text{Rs } 40$.

Example 20 Divide Rs 1380 among Ahmed, John and Babita so that the amount Ahmed receives is 5 times as much as Babita's share and is 3 times as much as John's share.

Solution Let Babita's share be Rs x. Then,

Ahmed's share = Rs $5x$

$\therefore$ John's share = Total amount − (Babita's share + Ahmed's share)

$= \text{Rs }[1380-(x+5x)] = \text{Rs }(1380-6x)$

It is given that Ahmed's share is three times John's share.

$\therefore \quad 5x=3(1380-6x)$

$\Rightarrow \quad 5x=4140-18x$

$\Rightarrow \quad 5x+18x=4140$

$\Rightarrow \quad 23x=4140$

$\Rightarrow \quad x=\frac{4140}{23}=180$

$\therefore$ Babita's share = Rs 180, Ahmed's share = Rs (5×180) = Rs 900

John's share = Rs $(1380-6\times 180)$ = Rs 300

Example 21 The length of a rectangle exceeds its breadth by 4 cm. If length and breadth are each increased by 3 cm, the area of the new rectangle will be 81 cm^2 more than that of the given rectangle. Find the length and breadth of the given rectangle.

Solution Let the breadth of the given rectangle be x cm. Then, Length $=(x+4)$ cm

$\therefore$ Area = Length × Breadth $=(x+4)\,x=x^2+4x$.

When length and breadth are each increased by 3 cm.

New length $=(x+4+3)$ cm $=(x+7)$ cm, New breadth $=(x+3)$ cm

$\therefore$ Area of new rectangle = Length × Breadth

$=(x+7)(x+3)$

$=x(x+3)+7(x+3)$

$=x^2+3x+7x+21=x^2+10x+21$

It is given that the area of new rectangle is 81 cm^2 more than the given rectangle.

$\therefore \quad x^2+10x+21=x^2+4x+81$

$\Rightarrow \quad x^2+10x-x^2-4x=81-21$

$\Rightarrow \quad 6x=60$

$\Rightarrow \quad x=\frac{60}{6}=10$

Thus,

Length of the given rectangle $=(x+4)$ cm $=(10+4)$ cm $=14$ cm

Breadth of the given rectangle = 10 cm

Check Area of the given rectangle $=(x^2+4x)\text{ cm}^2$

$$=(10^2+4\times 10)\text{cm}^2=140\text{ cm}^2$$

Area of the new rectangle $=(x^2+10x+21)\text{ cm}^2=(10^2+10\times 10+21)\text{cm}^2=221\text{cm}^2$

Clearly, area of the new rectangle is 81 cm^2 more than that of the given rectangle, which is the same as given in the problem.

Hence, our answer is correct.

Example 22 An altitutde of a triangle is five-thirds the length of its corresponding base. If the altitude were increased by 4 cm and the base be decreased by 2 cm, the area of the triangle would remain the same. Find the base and the altitude of the triangle.

Solution Let the length of the base of the triangle be x cm. Then,

$$\text{Altitude}=\left(\frac{5}{3}\times x\right)\text{cm}=\frac{5x}{3}\text{ cm}$$

$$\therefore \quad \text{Area}=\frac{1}{2}(\text{Base}\times\text{Altitude})\text{ cm}^2=\frac{1}{2}\left(x\times\frac{5x}{3}\right)\text{cm}^2=\frac{5x^2}{6}\text{cm}^2$$

When the altitude is increased by 4 cm and the base is decreased by 2 cm, we have

$$\text{New base}=(x-2)\text{ cm, New altitude}=\left(\frac{5x}{3}+4\right)\text{cm}$$

$$\therefore \quad \text{Area of the new triangle}=\frac{1}{2}(\text{Base}\times\text{Altitude})$$

$$=\frac{1}{2}\left\{\left(\frac{5x}{3}+4\right)\times(x-2)\right\}\text{cm}^2$$

$$=\frac{1}{2}\left\{(x-2)\times\left(\frac{5x}{3}+4\right)\right\}\text{cm}^2$$

$$=\frac{1}{2}\left\{\frac{5x}{3}(x-2)+4(x-2)\right\}\text{cm}^2$$

$$=\frac{1}{2}\left\{\frac{5x^2}{3}-\frac{10x}{3}+4x-8\right\}\text{cm}^2$$

$$=\left(\frac{5x^2}{6}-\frac{5x}{3}+2x-4\right)\text{cm}^2$$

It is given that the area of the given triangle is same as the area of the new triangle.

$$\therefore \quad \frac{5x^2}{6} = \frac{5x^2}{6} - \frac{5x}{3} + 2x - 4$$

$$\Rightarrow \quad \frac{5x^2}{6} - \frac{5x^2}{6} + \frac{5x}{3} - 2x = -4$$

$$\Rightarrow \quad \frac{5x}{3} - 2x = -4$$

$$\Rightarrow \quad 5x - 6x = -12 \qquad \text{[Multiplying both sides by 3]}$$

$$\Rightarrow \quad -x = -12$$

$$\Rightarrow \quad x = 12\,\text{cm}$$

Hence, base of the triangle = 12 cm.

Altitude of the triangle $= \left(\frac{5}{3} \times 12\right) \text{cm} = 20\,\text{cm}$

Check We have,

Area of the given triangle $= \left(\frac{5}{6} \times 12^2\right) \text{cm}^2 = 120\,\text{cm}^2$

Area of the new triangle $= \left(\frac{5}{6} \times 12^2 - \frac{5}{3} \times 12 + 2 \times 12 - 4\right) \text{cm}^2$

$= (120 - 20 + 24 - 4)\,\text{cm}^2 = 120\,\text{cm}^2$

Therefore, area of the given triangle is the same as that of the new triangle, which is the same as given in the problem. Thus, our answer is correct.

EXERCISE 9.4

1. Four-fifth of a number is more than three-fourth of the number by 4. Find the number.
2. The difference between the squares of two consecutive numbers is 31. Find the numbers.
3. Find a number whose double is 45 greater than its half.
4. Find a number such that when 5 is subtracted from 5 times the number, the result is 4 more than twice the number.
5. A number whose fifth part increased by 5 is equal to its fourth part diminished by 5. Find the number.
6. A number consists of two digits whose sum is 9. If 27 is subtracted from the number, its digits are reversed. Find the number.
7. Divide 184 into two parts such that one-third of one part may exceed one-seventh of another part by 8.
8. The numerator of a fraction is 6 less than the denominator. If 3 is added to the numerator, the fraction is equal to $\frac{2}{3}$. What is the original fraction equal to?
9. A sum of Rs 800 is in the form of denominations of Rs 10 and Rs 20. If the total number of notes be 50, find the number of notes of each type.
10. Seeta Devi has Rs 9 in fifty-paise and twenty five-paise coins. She has twice as many twenty-five paise coins as she has fifty-paise coins. How many coins of each kind does she have?

11. Sunita is twice as old as Ashima. If six years is subtracted from Ashima's age and four years added to Sunita's age, then Sunita will be four times Ashima's age. How old were they two years ago?
12. The ages of Sonu and Monu are in the ratio 7 : 5. Ten years hence, the ratio of their ages will be 9 : 7. Find their present ages.
13. Five years ago a man was seven times as old as his son. Five years hence, the father will be three times as old as his son. Find their present ages.
14. I am currently 5 times as old as my son. In 6 years time I will be three times as old as he will be then. What are our ages now?
15. I have Rs 1000 in ten and five rupee notes. If the number of ten rupee notes that I have is ten more than the number of five rupee notes, how many notes do I have in each denomination?
16. At a party, colas, squash and fruit juice were offered to guests. A fourth of the guests drank colas, a third drank squash, two fifths drank fruit juice and just three did not drink any thing. How many guests were in all?
17. There are 180 multiple choice questions in a test. If a candidate gets 4 marks for every correct answer and for every unattempted or wrongly answered question one mark is deducted from the total score of correct answers. If a candidate scored 450 marks in the test, how many questions did he answer correctly?
18. A labourer is engaged for 20 days on the condition that he will receive Rs 60 for each day, he works and he will be fined Rs 5 for each day, he is absent. If he receives Rs 745 in all, for how many days he remained absent?
19. Ravish has three boxes whose total weight is $60\frac{1}{2}$ kg. Box B weighs $3\frac{1}{2}$ kg more than box A and box C weighs $5\frac{1}{3}$ kg more than box B. Find the weight of box A.
20. The numerator of a rational number is 3 less than the denominator. If the denominator is increased by 5 and the numerator by 2, we get the rational number 1/2. Find the rational number.
21. In a rational number, twice the numerator is 2 more than the denominator. If 3 is added to each, the numerator and the denominator, the new fraction is 2/3. Find the original number.
22. The distance between two stations is 340 km. Two trains start simultaneously from these stations on parallel tracks to cross each other. The speed of one of them is greater than that of the other by 5 km/hr. If the distance between the two trains after 2 hours of their start is 30 km, find the speed of each train.
23. A steamer goes downstream from one point to another in 9 hours. It covers the same distance upstream in 10 hours. If the speed of the stream be 1 km/hr, find the speed of the steamer in still water and the distance between the ports.
24. Bhagwanti inherited Rs 12000.00. She invested part of it as 10% and the rest at 12%. Her annual income from these investments is Rs 1280.00. How much did she invest at each rate?
25. The length of a rectangle exceeds its breadth by 9 cm. If length and breadth are each increased by 3 cm, the area of the new rectangle will be 84 cm^2 more than that of the given rectangle. Find the length and breadth of the given rectangle.

26. The sum of the ages of Anup and his father is 100. When Anup is as old as his father now, he will be five times as old as his son Anuj is now. Anuj will be eight years older than Anup is now, when Anup is as old as his father. What are their ages now?

27. A lady went shopping and spent half of what she had on buying hankies and gave a rupee to a begger waiting outside the shop. She spent half of what was left on a lunch and followed that up with a two rupee tip. She spent half of the remaining amount on a book and three rupees on bus fare. When she reached home, she found that she had exactly one rupee left. How much money did she start with?

ANSWERS

1. 80
2. 15, 16
3. 30
4. $\frac{3}{8}$
5. 200
6. 63
7. 72, 112
8. $\frac{1}{3}$
9. Number of 10 rupee notes = 20, Number of 20 rupee notes = 30
10. 50 paise coins = 9, 25 paise coins = 18
11. Sunita is 26 years, Ashima is 12 years
12. 35 years, 25 years
13. Son's age = 10 years, Father's age = 40 years
14. 30 years, 6 years
15. Five rupee notes : 60, Ten rupee notes : 70
16. 180
17. 126
18. 7 days
19. $\frac{289}{18}$ kg
20. $\frac{4}{7}$
21. $\frac{7}{12}$
22. 75 km/hr, 80 km/hr
23. 19 km/hr, 180 km
24. Rs 8000 at 10% and Rs 4000 at 12%
25. 17 cm, 8 cm
26. Anup's Father's age = 65 years, Anup's age = 35 years, Anuj's age = 13 years
27. Rs 42

HINTS TO SELECTED PROBLEMS

26. Let Anup's present age be x years. His father's present age = $100 - x$ years

$\therefore$ Anup's present age $= \dfrac{100-x}{5}$ years.

Anup becomes as old as his father is now after $(100 - 2x)$ years.

$\therefore$ After $100 - 2x$ years, we have

$$\text{Anup's age} = \left(\frac{100-x}{5} + 100 - 2x\right) \text{ years} = \frac{600-11x}{5} \text{ years}$$

It is given that after $(100 - 2x)$ years, Anuj is 8 years older than his father Anup is now.

$$\therefore \quad \frac{600-11x}{5} = x + 8 \Rightarrow 600 - 11x = 5(x+8) \Rightarrow 600 - 11x = 5x + 40 \Rightarrow 16x = 560 \Rightarrow x = 35$$

THINGS TO REMEMBER

1. *An equation is a statement of equality which contains one or more unknown quantity (or variable) is called an equation.*
2. *An equation involving only linear polynomials is called a linear equation.*
3. *Rules for solving a linear equation:*

Rule 1 *Same quantity (number) can be added to both sides of an equation without changing the equality.*

Rule 2 *Same quantity can be subtracted from both sides of an equation without changing the equality.*

Rule 3 *Both sides of an equation may be multiplied by the same non-zero number without changing the equality.*

Rule 4 *Both sides of an equation may be divided by the same non-zero number without changing the equality.*

Rule 5 *(Transposition) Any term of an equation may be taken to the other side with the sign changed. This process is called transposition.*

For example, $7x - 3 = 2x + 7 \Leftrightarrow 7x - 2x = 3 + 7$

It should be noted that some complicated equations can be solved by using two or more of these rules together as discussed below.

4. *If* $\frac{ax+b}{cx+d} = \frac{m}{n}$ *is an equation in variable x, then*

$\frac{ax+b}{cx+d} = \frac{m}{n} \Leftrightarrow n(ax+b) = m(cx+d)$, *which is a linear equation.*

The process of obtaining the above linear equation from $\frac{ax+b}{cx+d} = \frac{m}{n}$ *is called cross-multiplication.*

10

DIRECT AND INVERSE VARIATIONS

10.1 INTRODUCTION

In this chapter, we shall learn the concepts of direct and inverse variations which are very useful in many walks of life. The applications of the same will be discussed in the subsequent chapters.

10.2 VARIATIONS

If the values of two quantities depend on each other in such a way that a change in one results in a corresponding change in the other, then the two quantities are said to be in variation.

Let us consider the distance travelled by a car in a given interval of time and its speed. We observe that if the speed is more, the car will travel more distance in a given period of time. So, we can say that the speed of a car and distance covered by it, in a given period of time are in variation.

Now, if we consider the speed of the moving car and the time taken by it to cover a certain distance, we observe that the time taken by the car to travel a given distance will be less, if the speed is more. In other words, as the speed increases, the time taken to cover a given distance decreases. Thus, we can say that the speed of a car and the time taken by it to cover a given distance are also in variation.

10.3 TYPES OF VARIATIONS

In the above discussion, we have seen that the two quantities may be linked in such a way that both increase or decrease together. Also, the two quantities may vary in such a way that if one increases, the other decreases and vice-versa. So, there are two types of variations : direct and inverse as defined below.

DIRECT VARIATION *If two quantities are linked in such a way that an increase in one quantity leads to a corresponding increase in the other and vice-versa, then such a variation is called a direct variation.*

If two quantities are in direct variation, then we also say that they are proportional to each other.

ILLUSTRATION 1 Consider the number of articles bought by a person and the amount paid. We find that the larger the number of articles, the greater the amount paid. So, the number of articles bought by a person and the amount paid are in direct variation.

ILLUSTRATION 2 Consider a money lender who lends money on interest. We observe that if he lends more money on a certain rate of interest, the interest earned will be more. In other words, if the money invested increases, the interest earned also increases and vice-versa. Thus, the money invested and the interest earned on it are in direct variation.

ILLUSTRATION 3 If we consider the pressure and volume of a gas at a specific temperature we find that the increase in pressure leads to decrease in volume and if the pressure is reduced, the volume will increase. Thus, the pressure and volume of a gas at a given temperature are not in direct variation.

INVERSE VARIATION *If two quantities are linked in such a way that an increase in one causes a corresponding decrease in the other and vice-versa, then such a variation is called an inverse variation.*

If two quantities are in inverse variation, then we also say that they are inversely proportional to each other.

ILLUSTRATION 4 Consider the number of workers working on a project and the time taken by them to complete the work. We observe that the time taken to complete the work reduces if we increase the number of workers and the decrease in the number of workers lead to increase in the time of completion. Thus, the number of workers working on a project and the time taken to complete it are in inverse variation.

As discussed in Illustration 3, the pressure and volume of a gas at a given temperature are also in inverse variation.

10.4 DIRECT VARIATION

In class VI, you have learnt unitary method. By using it we can find the cost of any number of articles if we are given the cost of one article. For example, if one ball pen costs Rs 8, then the cost of 2 ball pens of the same type is Rs 16; the cost of 3 ball pens of the same type is Rs 24 and so on. Let a denote the number of ball pens and b denote the corresponding cost. Then, the following table exhibits some values of a and the corresponding values of b.

Number of ball pens (a):	1	2	3	6	8	15
Cost in Rupees (b):	8	16	24	48	64	120

It is evident from the above table that as the values of a increase, the values of b also increase. Also, in all the above cases the ratio $\frac{a}{b}$ is constant and is equal to $\frac{1}{8}$. So, we may also define direct variation in mathematical form as follows :

DIRECT VARIATION *If two quantities a and b vary with each other in such a manner that the ratio* $\frac{a}{b}$ *remains constant and is positive, then we say that a and b vary directly with each other or a and b are in direct variation.*

Thus, if two quantities a and b are in direct variation, then the ratio $\frac{a}{b}$ *is always constant. This constant is called the constant of variation.*

If two quantities a and b are in direct variation and a_1 and b_1 are the corresponding values that the quantities take at one point, then

$$\frac{a_1}{b_1} = \text{Constant } (= k, \text{ say}) \qquad \ldots \text{(i)}$$

Similarly, if a_2 and b_2 are the corresponding values at another point, then

$$\frac{a^2}{b^2} = k \qquad \ldots \text{(ii)}$$

From (i) and (ii), we get

$$\frac{a_1}{b_1} = \frac{a_2}{b_2}$$

$\Rightarrow \quad a_1 b_2 = a_2 b_1$ [By cross-multiplication]

$\Rightarrow \quad \frac{a_1}{a_2} = \frac{b_1}{b_2}$

$\Rightarrow \quad a_1 : a_2 :: b_1 : b_2$

or, $\quad a_1 : a_2 = b_1 : b_2$

Thus, we obtain the following rule:

Rule *If two quantities a and b are in direct variation, the ratio of any two values of a is equal to the ratio of the corresponding values of b.*

This result is very useful in solving problems which we had solved in class VI by unitary method.

ILLUSTRATIVE EXAMPLES

Example 1 In which of the following tables, a and b vary directly. Also, find the constant of variation if a and b are in direct variation.

(i)

a	4	7	21	28
b	12	21	63	84

(ii)

a	2.5	5	7.5	10	15
b	10	20	30	40	60

(iii)

a	1	2	3	4	5
b	2	1	6	3	2/5

Solution (i) We have,

$$\frac{4}{12} = \frac{7}{21} = \frac{21}{63} = \frac{28}{84} = \frac{1}{3}.$$

Thus, the ratio of the corresponding values of a and b is constant and is equal to $\frac{1}{3}$.

Hence, a and b are in direct variation with the constant of variation equal to $\frac{1}{3}$.

(ii) We have,

$$\frac{2.5}{10} = \frac{5}{20} = \frac{7.5}{30} = \frac{10}{40} = \frac{15}{60} = \frac{1}{4}$$

This shows that the ratio of the corresponding values of a and b is constant and is equal to $\frac{1}{4}$. Thus, a and b vary directly. The constant of variation is $\frac{1}{4}$.

(iii) It is evident from the table that the ratio of the corresponding values of a and b is not constant. So, a and b are not in direct variation i.e. they do not vary directly.

Example 2 If x and y vary directly, find the missing entries in the following table:

(i)

x	2.5	...	...	21
y	5	8	24	...

(ii)

x	...	9	15	...
y	3	4.5	7.5	13.25

Solution (i) It is given that x and y are in direct variation. Therefore, the ratio of the corresponding values of x and y remain constant.

We have,

$$\frac{2.5}{5} = \frac{1}{2}$$

So, x and y are in direct variation with the constant of variation equal to $\frac{1}{2}$. This means that x is half of y or y is twice of x. Thus, the required entries are $\frac{8}{2}, \frac{24}{2}$ and 21×2 i.e., 4, 12 and 42.

(ii) We have,

$$\frac{9}{4.5} = \frac{15}{7.5} = 2$$

So, x and y are in direct variation such that x is twice of y.

Thus, the missing entries are $3 \times 2 = 6$ and $13.25 \times 2 = 26.5$.

Example 3 A car travels 432 km on 48 litres of petrol. How far would it travel on 20 litres of petrol?

Solution Suppose the car travels x km on 20 litres of petrol. Then, the above information can be put in the following tabular form:

Petrol (in litres)	48	20
Distance (in km)	432	x

We observe that the lesser the petrol consumed, the smaller the number of kilometres travelled. So, it is a case of direct variation.

$\therefore$ Ratio of petrol consumed = Ratio of distance travelled

$\Rightarrow$ $48:20 = 432:x$

$\Rightarrow$ $\frac{48}{20} = \frac{432}{x}$

$\Rightarrow$ $48 \times x = 20 \times 432$ [By cross-multiplication]

$\Rightarrow$ $x = \frac{20 \times 432}{48} = 180.$

Hence, the car would travel 180 km on 20 litres of petrol.

Example 4 If 40 metres of a cloth costs Rs 1940, how many metres can be bought for Rs 727.5?

Solution Let x metres of cloth be bought for Rs 727.5. Then, the given information can be exhibited in the following tabular form.

Money (in rupees) :	1940	727.5
Length of the cloth (in metres) :	40	x

Clearly, less money will fetch less metres of cloth. So, it is a case of direct variation. Therefore,

Ratio of number of rupees = Ratio of number of metres

$$\Rightarrow \quad \frac{1940}{727.5} = \frac{40}{x}$$

$$\Rightarrow \quad x = \frac{40 \times 727.5}{1940} = 15$$

Hence, 15 metres of cloth can be bought for Rs 727.50.

Example 5 A private taxi charges a fare of Rs 260 for a Journey of 200 km. How much would it travel for Rs 279.50 ?

Solution Suppose the taxi travels x km for Rs 279.50. Then, the given information can be exhibited in the following tabular form.

Fare (in rupees) :	260	279.50
Distance travelled (in km) :	200	x

Clearly, the taxi will travel more for more money. So, it is a case of direct variation.

∴ Ratio of number of rupees = Ratio of distance travelled

$$\Rightarrow \quad \frac{260}{279.50} = \frac{200}{x}$$

$$\Rightarrow \quad x = \frac{200 \times 279.50}{260} = 215$$

Hence, the taxi will travel 215 km for Rs 279.50.

Example 6 Reema types 540 words during half an hour. How many words would she type in 6 minutes?

Solution Suppose she types x words in 6 minutes. Then, the given information can be exhibited in the following tabular form.

Number of words :	540	x
Time (inminutes) :	30	6

Since in more time more words can be typed. So, it is a case of direct variation.

∴ Ratio of number of words = Ratio of number of minutes

$$\Rightarrow \quad \frac{540}{x} = \frac{30}{6}$$

$$\Rightarrow \quad x = \frac{6 \times 540}{30}$$

$$\Rightarrow \quad x = 108$$

Hence, she types 108 words in 6 minutes.

Example 7 The amount of extension in an elastic spring varies directly as the weight hung on it. If a weight of 150 gm produces an extension of 2.9 cm, then what weight would produce an extension of 17.4 cm?

Solution Let the required weight be x gram. Then, the above information can be exhibited in the following tabular form.

Weight (in gram):	150	x
Extension (in cm):	2.9	17.4

It is given that the amount of extension in the spring varies directly as the weight hung on it. So, it is a case of direct variation.

$\therefore$ Ratio of weights = Ratio of extensions

$$\Rightarrow \quad 150 : x = 2.9 : 17.4$$

$$\Rightarrow \quad \frac{150}{x} = \frac{2.9}{17.4}$$

$$\Rightarrow \quad \frac{150}{x} = \frac{1}{6}$$

$$\Rightarrow \quad 150 \times 6 = 1 \times x$$

$$\Rightarrow \quad x = 900$$

Hence, a weight of 900 gram would produce an extension of 17.4 cm.

EXERCISE 10.1

1. Explain the concept of direct variation.
2. Which of the following quantities vary directly with each other?
   (i) Number of articles (x) and their price (y).
   (ii) Weight of articles (x) and their cost (y).
   (iii) Distance x and time y, speed remaining the same.
   (iv) Wages (y) and number of hours (x) of work.
   (v) Speed (x) and time (y) (distance covered remaining the same).
   (vi) Area of a land (x) and its cost (y).
3. In which of the following tables x and y vary directly?

(i)

a	7	9	13	21	25
b	21	27	39	63	75

(ii)

a	10	20	30	40	46
b	5	10	15	20	23

(iii)

a	2	3	4	5	6
b	6	9	12	17	20

(iv)

a	1^2	2^2	3^2	4^2	5^2
b	1^3	2^3	3^3	4^3	5^3

4. Fill in the blanks in each of the following so as to make the statement true :
   (i) Two quantities are said to vary.... with each other if they increase (decrease) together in such a way that the ratio of the corresponding values remains same.
   (ii) x and y are said to vary directly with each other if for some positive number k, ...$= k$.
   (iii) If $u = 3v$, then u and v vary .... with each other.
5. Complite the following tables given that x varies directly as y.

(i)

x	2.5	...	...	15
y	5	8	12	...

(ii)

x	5	...	10	35	25	...
y	8	12	...	...	...	32

(iii)

x	6	8	10	...	20
y	15	20	...	40	...

(iv)

x	4	9	...	...	3	...
y	16	...	48	36	...	4

(v)

x	3	5	7	9
y	...	20	28	...

6. Find the constant of variation from the table given below:

x	3	5	7	9
y	12	20	28	36

Set up a table and solve the following problems. Use unitary method to verify the answer.

7. Rohit bought 12 registers for Rs 156, find the cost of 7 such registers.
8. Anupama takes 125 minutes in walking a distance of 100 metre. What distance would she cover in 315 minutes ?
9. If the cost of 93 m of a certain kind of plastic sheet is Rs 1395, then what would it cost to buy 105 m of such plastic sheet?
10. Suneeta types 1080 words in one hour. What is her GWAM (gross words a minute rate) ?
11. A car is travelling at the average speed of 50 km/hr. How much distance would it travel in 12 minutes?
12. 68 boxes of a certain commodity require a shelf-length of 13.6 m. How many boxes of the same commodity would occupy a shelf length of 20.4 m?
13. In a library 136 copies of a certain book require a shelf-length of 3.4 metre. How many copies of the same book would occupy a shelf-length of 5.1 metres?
14. The second class railway fare for 240 km of Journey is Rs 15.00. What would be the fare for a journey of 139.2 km?
15. If the thickness of a pile of 12 cardboards is 35 mm, find the thickness of a pile of 294 cardboards.
16. The cost of 97 metre of cloth is Rs 242.50. What length of this can be purchased for Rs 302.50?
17. 11 men can dig $6\frac{3}{4}$ metre long trench in one day. How many men should be employed for digging 27 metre long trench of the same type in one day?
18. A worker is paid Rs 210 for 6 days work. If his total income of the month is Rs 875, for how many days did he work?
19. A woker is paid Rs 200 for 8 days work. If he works for 20 days, how much will he get?
20. The amount of extension in an elastic string varies directly as the weight hung on it. If a weight of 150 gm produces an extension of 2.9 cm, then what weight would produce an extension of 17.4 cm?

21. The amount of extension in an elastic spring varies directly with the weight hung on it. If a weight of 250 gm produces an extension of 3.5 cm, find the extension produced by the weight of 700 gm.

22. In 10 days, the earth picks up 2.6×10^8 pounds of dust from the atmosphere. How much dust will it pick up in 45 days?

23. In 15 days, the earth picks up 1.2×10^8 kg of dust from the atmosphere. In how many days it will pick up 4.8×10^8 kg of dust?

ANSWERS

2. (i), (ii), (iv) (vi) 3. (i), (ii), 4. (i) directly (ii) $\frac{x}{y}$ (iii) directly

5. (i) 4, 6, 30 (ii) $\frac{15}{2}$, 16, 56, 40, 20 (iii) 25, 16, 50 (iv) 36, 12, 9, 12, 1 (v) 12, 36

10. 18 6. $\frac{1}{4}$ 7. Rs 91 8. 252 metre 9. Rs 1575 10. 18 11. 10 km

12. 102 13. 204 14. Rs 8.70 15. 85.75 cm 16. 121 metre 17. 44 men

18. 25 days 19. Rs 500 20. 900 gram 21. 9.8 cm 22. 11.7×10^8 pound 23.60 days.

10.5 INVERSE VARIATION

In the previous section, we have learnt about direct variation. We have seen that in the case of direct variation, the two quantities increase or decrease together in the same ratio. In section 10.3, we have seen that in the case of inverse variation, the two quantities are linked in such a way that an increase in one causes a corresponding decrease in the other and vice-versa. For example, if 2 men can do a job in 12 days, then if we put only one man on the same job, he would take (2×12) days $=$ 24 days to complete the same job. Clearly, 4 men will do the job in 6 days ; 6 men will do it in 4 days ; 12 men will do it in 2 days and 24 men will complete the job in one day.

The above information can be put in the following tabular form:

Number of men (a):	2	4	6	12	24
Number of days required to finish the work (b):	12	6	4	2	1

It is evident from the above table that as the number of men increases, the number of days decreases and as the number of men decreases, the number of days increases. Also, in all the above cases, the product ab is constant and is equal to 24. So, we may define inverse variation in the following mathematical form:

INVERSE VARIATION *If two quantities x and y vary with each other in such a manner that the product ab remains constant and is positive, then we say that a and b vary inversely as each other or a varies inversely as b and b varies inversely as a.*

Thus, if two quantities a and b vary inversely as each other, then the product ab always remains constant. The product ab is called the constant of variation.

If two quantities a and b vary inversely as each other and b_1, b_2 are the values of b corresponding to the values a_1, a_2 of a respectively, then

$a_1 b_1 = \text{Constant} (= k, \text{say})$ and, $a_2 b_2 = k$

$\therefore \quad a_2 b_2 = a_2 b_2$

$$\Rightarrow \quad \frac{a_1}{a_2} = \frac{b_2}{b_1}$$

$$\Rightarrow \quad a_1 : a_2 = b_2 : b_1 \text{ or, } a_1 : a_2 :: b_2 : b_1$$

Thus, we obtain the following rule:

Rule *If two quantities a and b vary inversely as each other, then the ratio of any two values of a is equal to the inverse ratio of the corresponding values of b.*

Following examples will illustrate the use of this rule in solving problems.

ILLUSTRATIVE EXAMPLES

Example 1 In which of the following tables a and b vary inversely:

(i)

a	8	16	32	256
b	32	16	8	1

(ii)

a	9	18	2	12
b	8	4	30	6

(iii)

a	2	16	8	4
b	40	5	10	20

Solution We know that if a and b vary inversely, then the product ab remains same for all values of a and b.

(i) Here,

$8 \times 32 = 256,\ 16 \times 16 = 256,\ 32 \times 8 = 256$ *and* $256 \times 1 = 256$.

Clearly, the products of the values of a and the corresponding values of b are fixed. So, a and b vary inversely.

(ii) We have,

$9 \times 8 = 72, 18 \times 4 = 72, 2 \times 30 = 60$ and $12 \times 6 = 72$.

Since the products of the values of a and the corresponding values of b are not fixed. So, a and b do not vary inversely.

(iii) We have,

$2 \times 40 = 80, 16 \times 5 = 80, 8 \times 10 = 80$ and $4 \times 20 = 80$.

Clearly, the products of the values of a and the corresponding values of b are fixed. So, a and b vary inversely.

Example 2 If a and b vary inversely, fill in the blanks:

(i)

a	8	2	...	5	1
b	10	...	20	...	80

(ii)

a	16	32	8	128
b	4	...	...	0.5

Solution (i) Since a and b vary inversely, so the product ab remains constant and is equal to $8 \times 10 = 80$.

$\therefore$ First blank space is to be filled by $\frac{80}{2} = 40$

Second blank space is to be filled by $\frac{80}{20}=4$

Third blank space is to be filled by $\frac{80}{5}=16$.

(ii) Proceeding as in (i), we find that

First blank space is to be filled by $\frac{64}{32}=2$

Second blank space is to be filled by $\frac{64}{8}=8$

Example 3 If 52 men can do a piece of work in 35 days, in how many days 28 men will do it?

Solution Suppose 28 men will do the piece of work in x days. The given information can be exhibited in the following tabular form.

Number of men	52	28
Number of days	35	x

Clearly, less is the number of men, more will be the number of days to finish the work. It is therefore, the case of inverse variation.

$\therefore$ Ratio of number of men = Inverse ratio of number of days

$\Rightarrow$ $52:28 = x:35$

$\Rightarrow$ $\frac{52}{28}=\frac{x}{35}$

$\Rightarrow$ $52\times 35 = 28\times x$

$\Rightarrow$ $x = \frac{52\times 35}{28}=65$

Hence, 28 men will do the work in 65 days.

Example 4 If 56 men can do a piece of work in 42 days. How many men will do it in 14 days?

Solution Suppose x men will do the given piece of work in 14 days. The given information can be put in the following tabular form.

Number of men	56	x
Number of days	42	14

We note that more the number of men, less will be the number of days to finish the work. It is, therefore, a case of inverse variation.

$\therefore$ Ratio of number of men = Ratio of number of days

$\Rightarrow$ $56:x = 14:42$

$\Rightarrow$ $\frac{56}{x}=\frac{14}{42}$

$\Rightarrow$ $14\times x = 56\times 42$

$\Rightarrow$ $x = \frac{56\times 42}{14}$

$\Rightarrow$ $x = 168$

Hence, 168 men will finish the given piece of work in 14 days.

Example 5 Shalu cycles to her school at an average speed of 12 km/hr. It takes her 20 minutes to reach the school. If she wants to reach her school in 15 minutes, what should be her average speed?

Solution Let the required speed be x km/hr. Then, the given information may be presented in the following tabular form.

Speed (in km / hr)	12	x
Time (in minutes)	20	15

We note that more the speed, less will be the time taken to cover the given distance. So, it is a case of inverse variation.

$\therefore$ Ratio of speeds = Inverse ratio of time taken

$\Rightarrow \quad 12 : x = 15 : 20$

$\Rightarrow \quad \frac{12}{x} = \frac{15}{20}$

$\Rightarrow \quad 15 \times x = 12 \times 20$

$\Rightarrow \quad x = \frac{12 \times 20}{15} = 16$

Hence, Shalu's average speed should be 16 km/hr.

Example 6 1000 soldiers in a fort had enough food for 20 days. But some soldiers were transferred to another fort and the food lasted for 25 days. How many soldiers were transferred?

Solution Suppose x soldiers were left in the fort after transferring some soldiers. Then,

Number of transferred soldiers $= 1000 - x$.

The given information may be put in the following tabular form.

Number of soldiers	1000	x
Number of days	20	25

Since more soldiers will finish the food in less days.

So, it is a case of inverse variation.

$\therefore$ Ratio of number of soldiers = Inverse ratio of number of days.

$\Rightarrow \quad 1000 : x = 25 : 20$

$\Rightarrow \quad \frac{1000}{x} = \frac{25}{20}$

$\Rightarrow \quad 25 \times x = 1000 \times 20$

$\Rightarrow \quad x = \frac{1000 \times 20}{25}$

$\Rightarrow \quad x = 800$

Hence, the number of transferred soldiers = 1000 − 800 = 200.

Example 7 120 men had food provision for 200 days. After 5 days, 30 men died due to an epidemic. How long will the remaining food last?

Solution Since 30 men die after 5 days. Therefore, the remaining food is sufficient for 120 men for 195 days.

Suppose the remaining food lasts for x days for the remaining 90 men.

Thus, we have the following table:

Number of men	120	90
Number of days	195	x

We note that more men will consume the food in less number of days and less number of men will consume the food in more number of days. So, it is a case of inverse variation.

$\therefore$ Ratio of number of men = Inverse ratio of number of days

$\Rightarrow$ $120:90 = x:195$

$$\Rightarrow \quad \frac{120}{90} = \frac{x}{195}$$

$$\Rightarrow \quad x = \frac{120 \times 195}{90} = 260$$

Hence, the remaining men will consume the food in 260 days.

Example 8 If x and y vary inversely as each other, and $x = 10$ when $y = 6$. Find y when $x = 15$.

Solution Since x and y vary inversely as each other, therefore the product xy always remains constant.

$\therefore$ $10 \times 6 = 15 \times y$

$\Rightarrow$ $60 = 15y$

$$\Rightarrow \quad \frac{60}{15} = y$$

$\Rightarrow$ $y = 4$

EXERCISE 10.2

1. In which of the following tables x and y vary inversely:

(i)

x	4	3	12	1
y	6	8	2	24

(ii)

x	5	20	10	4
y	20	5	10	25

(iii)

x	4	3	6	1
y	9	12	8	36

(iv)

x	9	24	15	3
y	8	3	4	25

2. It x and y vary inversely, fill in the following blanks:

(i)

x	12	16	...	8	...
y	...	6	4	...	0.25

(ii)

x	16	32	8	128
y	4	...	...	0.25

(iii)

x	9	...	81	243
y	27	9	...	1

3. Which of the following quantities vary inversely as each other?
   (i) The number of x men hired to construct a wall and the time y taken to finish the job.
   (ii) The length x of a journey by bus and price y of the ticket.
   (iii) Journey (x km) undertaken by a car and the petrol (y litres) consumed by it.
4. It is known that for a given mass of gas, the volume v varies inversely as the pressure p. Fill in the missing entries in the following table :

v *(in* cm^3*)*	...	48	60	...	100	...	200
p *(in atmospheres)*	2	...	3/2	1	...	1/2	...

5. If 36 men can do a piece of work in 25 days, in how many days will 15 men do it ?
6. A work force of 50 men with a contractor can finish a piece of work in 5 months. In how many months the same work can be completed by 125 men?
7. A work-force of 420 men with a contractor can finish a certain piece of work in 9 months. How many extra men must he employ to complete the job in 7 months?
8. 1200 men can finish a stock of food in 35 days. How many more men should join them so that the same stock may last for 25 days?
9. In a hostel of 50 girls, there are food provisions for 40 days. If 30 more girls join the hostel, how long will these provisions last?
10. A car can finish a certain journey in 10 hours at the speed of 48 km/hr. By how much should its speed be increased so that it may take only 8 hours to cover the same distance?
11. 1200 soldiers in a fort had enough food for 28 days. After 4 days, some soldiers were transferred to another fort and thus the food lasted now for 32 more days. How many soldiers left the fort?
12. Three spraying machines working together can finish painting a house in 60 minutes. How long will it take for 5 machines of the same capacity to do the same job?
13. A group of 3 friends staying together, consume 54 kg of wheat every month. Some more friends join this group and they find that the same amount of wheat lasts for 18 days. How many new members are there in this group now?
14. 55 cows can graze a field in 16 days. How many cows will graze the same field in 10 days?
15. 18 men can reap a field in 35 days. For reaping the same field in 15 days, how many men are required?
16. A person has money to buy 25 cycles worth Rs 500 each. How many cycles he will be able to buy if each cycle is costing Rs 125 more?
17. Raghu has enough money to buy 75 machines worth Rs 200 each. How many machines can he buy if he gets a discount of Rs 50 on each machine?
18. If x and y vary inversely as each other and
    (i) $x = 3$ when $y = 8$, find y when $x = 4$
    (ii) $x = 5$ when $y = 15$, find x when $y = 12$
    (iii) $x = 30$, find y when constant of variation $= 900$.
    (iv) $y = 35$, find x when constant of variation $= 7$.

ANSWERS

1. (i), (ii) 2. (i) 8, 24, 12, 384 (ii) 2, 8 (iii) 27,3 3. (i)

4. 45, $\frac{15}{8}$, 90, 0.9, 180, $\frac{9}{20}$ 5. 60 days 6. 2 months 7. 120 men 8. 480 men

9. 25 days 10. 12 km/hr 11. 300 soldiers 12. 36 minutes 13. 2 members

14. 88 cows 15. 42 men 16. 20 cycles 17. 100 machines

18. (i) $y = 6$ (ii) $x = \frac{25}{4}$ (iii) $y = 30$ (iv) $x = \frac{1}{5}$

11

TIME AND WORK

11.1 INTRODUCTION

In classes VI, VII you have learnt unitary method and in the previous chapter we have studied direct and inverse variations. In this chapter, we shall use unitary method to solve some problems on time and work. In fact, problems on time and work can also be solved by using variations. So, it is the choice of an individual to use either unitary method or variations or both of them in a mixed way.

11.2 TIME AND WORK

As we all know that the amount of work done by a person varies directly with the time taken by him (her) to complete it. Thus, if a man can complete a piece of work in 10 days, then by unitary method, we can say that in one day he will do only $\frac{1}{10}$ th part of the total work. On the other hand, if a man completes $\frac{1}{10}$ th of the work in one day, then he will take 10 days to complete the work. Thus, we obtain the following rules:

Rule 1 *If a person X completes a piece of work in n days, then work done by person X in one day is* $\left(\frac{1}{n}\right)^{th}$ *part of the work.*

Rule 2 *If a person X completes* $\left(\frac{1}{n}\right)^{th}$ *part of the work in one day, then person X will take n days to complete the work.*

In this chapter, we shall mainly discuss two types of problems on time and work.

(i) On finding the time required to complete a piece of work.

(ii) On finding the work done in a given period of time.

Following examples will illustrate the solutions of the above type of problems.

ILLUSTRATIVE EXAMPLES

Example 1 Amit can do a piece of work in 4 days and Sumit can do it in 6 days. How long will they take, if both Amit and Sumit work together ?

Solution We have,

Time taken by Amit to do the work = 4 days

Time taken by Sumit to do the work = 6 days

$\therefore$ Work done by Amit in 1 day $= \frac{1}{4}$

Work done by Sumit in 1 day $= \frac{1}{6}$

So, work done by Amit and Sumit in one day $= \frac{1}{4} + \frac{1}{6} = \frac{3+2}{12} = \frac{5}{12}$

Hence, Amit and Sumit can do the piece of work in $\frac{12}{5}$ days i.e., $2\frac{2}{5}$ days.

Example 2 Together, Chotu and Nitu plough a field in 4 days. Nitu alone takes 6 days to plough the same field. In how many days can Chotu alone plough the field?

Solution We have,

Time taken by Chotu and Nitu to plough the field together = 4 days

Time taken by Nitu to plough the field = 6 days.

$\therefore$ Chotu and Nitu's 1 day's work $= \frac{1}{4}$

Nitu's 1 day's work $= \frac{1}{6}$

Now,

Chotu's 1 day's work = (Chotu and Nitu's 1 day's work) – (Nitu's 1 day's work)

$$= \frac{1}{4} - \frac{1}{6} = \frac{3-2}{12} = \frac{1}{12}$$

Hence, Chotu can plough the field in 12 days.

Example 3 Kami, Karya and Kirti can together weave a carpet in 4 days. Kami by herself can weave the same sized carpet in 12 days and Kirti can do it in 10 days. How long will Karya take to do the work by herself?

Solution We have,

Time taken by Kami, Karya and Kirti to weave the carpet = 4 days.

Time taken by Kami to weave the carpet = 12 days

and, Time taken by Kirti to weave the carpet = 10 days.

$\therefore$ Kami, Karya and Kirti's 1 day's work $= \frac{1}{4}$

Kami's 1 day's work $= \frac{1}{12}$ and, Kirti's 1 day's work $= \frac{1}{10}$

Now,

Karya's 1 day's work = (Kami, Karya and Kirti's 1 day's work) – (Kami's 1 day's work) – (Kirti's 1 days work)

$$= \frac{1}{4} - \frac{1}{12} - \frac{1}{10} = \frac{15-5-6}{60} = \frac{4}{60} = \frac{1}{15}$$

Hence, Karya can weave the carpet in 15 days.

Example 4 A and B can do a piece of work in 12 days; B and C in 15 days; C and A in 20 days. In how many days will they finish it together and separately?

Solution We have,

A and B can finish the work in 12 days, B and C can finish the work in 15 days, C and A can finish the work in 20 days

$\therefore$ A and B's 1 day's work $= \frac{1}{12}$, B and C's 1 day's work $= \frac{1}{15}$

C and A's 1 day's work $= \frac{1}{20}$

Adding, we get

$$2\,(A + B + C)\text{'s 1 day's work} = \frac{1}{12} + \frac{1}{15} + \frac{1}{20} = \frac{5+4+3}{60} = \frac{12}{60} = \frac{1}{5}$$

$\therefore$ $(A + B + C)$'s 1 day's work $= \frac{1}{2 \times 5} = \frac{1}{10}$

Thus, A, B and C together can finish the work in 10 days.

Now,

A's 1 day's work = (A, B and C's 1 day's work) – (B and C's 1 day's work)

$$= \frac{1}{10} - \frac{1}{15} = \frac{3-2}{30} = \frac{1}{30}$$

So, A alone can finish the work in 30 days.

Now,

B's 1 day's work = (A, B and C's 1 day's work) – (A and C's 1 day's work)

$$= \frac{1}{10} - \frac{1}{20} = \frac{2-1}{20} = \frac{1}{20}$$

So, B alone can finish the work in 20 days.

C's 1 day's work = (A, B and C's 1 day's work) – (A and B's 1 day's work)

$$= \frac{1}{10} - \frac{1}{12} = \frac{6-5}{60} = \frac{1}{60}$$

So, C alone can finish the work in 60 days.

Example 5 P and Q together can do a piece of work in 10 days, Q and R can do the same work together in 12 days, while P and R can do together in 15 days. How long each will take to do it separately ?

Solution We have,

$(P + Q)$ can finish the work in 10 days, $(Q + R)$ can finish the work in 12 days

$(P + R)$ can finish the work in 15 days.

$\therefore$ $(P + Q)$'s 1 day's work $= \frac{1}{10}$, $(Q + R)$'s 1 day's work $= \frac{1}{12}$

$(Q + R)$'s 1 day's work $= \frac{1}{15}$

Adding, we get

$$2\,(P + Q + R)\text{'s 1 day's work} = \frac{1}{10} + \frac{1}{12} + \frac{1}{15} = \frac{6+5+4}{60} = \frac{15}{60} = \frac{1}{4}$$

$\therefore$ $(P + Q + R)$'s 1 day's work $= \frac{1}{2 \times 4} = \frac{1}{8}$

Now,

P's 1 day's work = $(P + Q + R)$'s 1 day's work − $(Q + R)$'s 1 day's work

$$= \frac{1}{8} - \frac{1}{12} = \frac{3-2}{24} = \frac{1}{24}$$

So, P alone can complete the work in 24 days.

Q's 1 day's work = $(P + Q + R)$'s 1 day's work − $(P + R)$'s 1 day's work

$$= \frac{1}{8} - \frac{1}{15} = \frac{15-8}{120} = \frac{7}{120}$$

So, Q alone can complete the work in $\frac{120}{7}$ days.

and, R's 1 day's work = $(P + Q + R)$'s 1 day's work − $(P + Q)$'s 1 day's work

$$= \frac{1}{8} - \frac{1}{10} = \frac{5-4}{40} = \frac{1}{40}$$

So, R alone can complete the work in 40 days.

Example 6 A can do a piece of work in 25 days and B can finish it in 20 days. They work together for 5 days and then A goes away. In how many days will B finish the remaining work?

Solution We have,

A can finish the work in 25 days, B can finish the work in 20 days.

∴ A's 1 day's work $= \frac{1}{25}$, B's 1 day's work $= \frac{1}{20}$.

So, $(A + B)$'s 1 day's work $= \frac{1}{25} + \frac{1}{20} = \frac{4+5}{100} = \frac{9}{100}$

∴ $(A + B)$'s 5 day's work $= 5 \times \frac{9}{100} = \frac{9}{20}$

Remaining work $= 1 - \frac{9}{20} = \frac{11}{20}$

The remaining work is done by B.

∴ Complete work is done by B in 20 days.

∴ $\frac{11}{20}$ of the work is done by B in $\left(20 \times \frac{11}{20}\right)$ days = 11 days.

Hence, the remaining work is done by B in 11 days.

Example 7 A and B can polish the floors of a building in 25 days. A alone can do $\frac{1}{3}$ of this job in 15 days. In how many days can B alone polish the floors of the building?

Solution It is given that A and B can polish the floors of the building in 25 days.

∴ $(A + B)$'s 1 day's work $= \frac{1}{25}$

Now, A alone can do $\frac{1}{3}$ of the work in 15 days.

∴ A alone can do the complete work in (3×15) = 45 days

$\Rightarrow$ A's 1 day's work $= \frac{1}{45}$

Now, B's 1 day's work $= (A + B)$'s 1 day's work $-$ A's 1 day's work

$$= \frac{1}{25} - \frac{1}{45} = \frac{9-5}{225} = \frac{4}{225}$$

Hence, B alone can polish the floor in $\frac{225}{4}$ days $= 56\frac{1}{4}$ days.

Example 8 Suneeta can embroider a saree in 15 days. Her sister-in-law Abha can do the job in 10 days. They start embroidering the saree together, but two days later Abha gives up the work and goes to her parents. In how many days will Suneeta finish the remaining work of embroidering the saree?

Solution Suneeta can embroider a saree in 15 days, Abha can embroider a saree in 10 days

$\therefore$ Suneeta's 1 day's work $= \frac{1}{15}$, Abha's 1 day's work $= \frac{1}{10}$

$\therefore$ (Suneeta + Abha)'s 1 day's work $= \frac{1}{15} + \frac{1}{10} = \frac{2+3}{30} = \frac{5}{30} = \frac{1}{6}$

$\Rightarrow$ (Suneeta + Abha)'s 2 day's work $= 2 \times \frac{1}{6} = \frac{1}{3}$

$\therefore$ Remaining work $= 1 - \frac{1}{3} = \frac{2}{3}$

Now,

Suneeta completes the work in 15 days

$\therefore$ Suneeta completes $\frac{2}{3}$ of the work in $15 \times \frac{2}{3}$ days $= 10$ days.

Hence, Suneeta will finish the remaining work of embroidering in 10 days.

Example 9 5 men can complete a job in 8 days. How many days will it take if 12 men do the job?

Solution It is given that:

5 men can complete a job in 8 days.

$\therefore$ 1 man can complete the same job in $(8 \times 5) = 40$ days

So, 12 men can complete the same job in $\frac{40}{12} = \frac{10}{3} = 3\frac{1}{3}$ days

Aliter Suppose 12 men complete the job in x days. Then, the given information can be put in the following tabular form.

Number of men	5	12
Number of days	8	x

Since more men can do the job in less number of days. So, it is a case of inverse variation.

$\therefore$ Ratio of number of men $=$ Inverse ratio of number of days

$\Rightarrow$ $5 : 12 = x : 8$

$\Rightarrow \quad \frac{5}{12} = \frac{x}{8}$

$\Rightarrow \quad 5 \times 8 = 12 \times x$

$\Rightarrow \quad x = \frac{5 \times 8}{12} = \frac{40}{12} = \frac{10}{3} = 3\frac{1}{3}$

Thus, 12 men can complete the job in $3\frac{1}{3}$ days.

Example 10 Seema weaves 25 baskets in 35 days. In how many days will she weave 110 baskets?

Solution Seema weaves 25 baskets in 35 days.

$\therefore$ Seema weaves 1 basket in $\frac{35}{25}$ days

So, Seema will weave 110 baskets in $\left(\frac{35}{25} \times 110\right) = 7 \times 22$ days $= 154$ days

Aliter Let Seema weave 110 baskets in x days. Then, the given information can be put in the following tabular form.

Number of baskets	25	110
Number of days	35	x

As the weaving of more baskets will require more days.

So, it is a case of direct variation.

$\therefore$ Ratio of number of baskets = Ratio of number of days

$\Rightarrow \quad 25 : 110 = 35 : x$

$\Rightarrow \quad \frac{25}{110} = \frac{35}{x}$

$\Rightarrow \quad 25 \times x = 110 \times 35$

$\Rightarrow \quad x = \frac{110 \times 35}{25} = 154$ days

Example 11 15 boys earn Rs 900 in 5 days, how much will 20 boys earn in 7 days?

Solution In 5 days 15 boys earn = Rs 900.

$\therefore$ In one day 15 boys earn = Rs $\frac{900}{5}$ = Rs 180

$\Rightarrow$ One boy earns in one day = Rs $\frac{180}{15}$ = Rs 12

$\Rightarrow$ One boy earns in 7 days = Rs $(12 \times 7) = 84$

$\Rightarrow$ 20 boys earn in 7 days = Rs (84×20) = Rs 1680

Example 12 Spinning 3 hours daily, Kanta can spin 2 kg cotton-balls in 12 days. Spinning 4 hours daily, how many days will she take to spin 10 kg cotton balls?

Solution Spinning 3 hours daily, Kanta can spin 2 kg cotton-balls in 12 days.

$\therefore$ Spinning 3 hours daily, Kanta can spin 1 kg cotton-balls in $\left(\frac{12}{2}\right) = 6$ days

$\Rightarrow$ Spinning 1 hour daily, Kanta can spin 1 kg cotton-balls in $6 \times 3 = 18$ days

$\Rightarrow$ Spinning 1 hour daily, Kanta can spin 10 kg cotton-balls in $(18 \times 10) = 180$ days

$\Rightarrow$ Spinning 4 hours daily, Kanta can spin 10 kg cotton-balls in $\frac{180}{4}$ days $= 45$ days.

Example 13 Somari sweeps 600 m long railway platform in $2\frac{1}{2}$ hours. His wife Imarati sweeps $\frac{2}{3}$ rd of the same platform in $1\frac{1}{2}$ hours. Who sweeps more speedily?

Solution We have,

Length of the platform $= 600$ m

$\therefore$ $\frac{2}{3}$ rd of the platform $= 600 \times \frac{2}{3}\text{ m} = 400\text{ m}$

In $2\frac{1}{2}$ hours, Somari sweeps 600 m.

$\therefore$ In 1 hour, Somari sweeps $\left(\frac{600}{2\frac{1}{2}}\right)\text{m} = \left(\frac{600}{5/2}\right)\text{m} = \left(600 \times \frac{2}{5}\right) = 240\text{ m}$

In $1\frac{1}{2}$ hours, Imarati sweeps 400 m.

$\therefore$ In 1 hour, Imarati sweeps $\left(\frac{400}{1\frac{1}{2}}\right)\text{m} = \left(\frac{400}{3/2}\right)\text{m} = \left(400 \times \frac{2}{3}\right)\text{m} = 266\frac{2}{3}\text{ m}$

Clearly, Imarati sweeps more length in 1 hour than Somari sweeps in the same time.

Hence, Imarati sweeps more speedily than Somari.

11.3 PIPES AND CISTERNS

As you know that a cistern or a water tank is always connected with two types of pipes. One which fills it up and the other which empties it out. The pipe which fills up the cistern is called an inlet and the one which empties it is called an outlet.

Let an inlet fill up a cistern in 8 hours. Then-in one hour it fills up $\frac{1}{8}$ th part of it. We can also say that the work done by inlet in 1 hour is $\frac{1}{8}$. Similarly, if an outlet empties out a cistern in 6 hours, then in one hour it empties out $\frac{1}{6}$ th part of the cistern i.e. the work done by the outlet in one hour is $\frac{1}{6}$.

NOTE: *The work done by the inlet is always positive whereas the work done by the outlet is always negative.*

We shall now discuss some problems on pipes and cisterns.

ILLUSTRATIVE EXAMPLES

Example 1 A cistern can be filled by one tap in 4 hours and by another in 3 hours. How long will it take to fill it if both taps are opened together?

Solution We have,

Time taken by the first tap to fill the cistern = 4 hours

Time taken by the second tap to fill the cistern = 3 hours

$\therefore$ Work done by the first tap in 1 hour $= \frac{1}{4}$

Work done by the second tap in 1 hour $= \frac{1}{3}$

Thus, work done by both the taps in 1 hour $= \frac{1}{4} + \frac{1}{3} = \frac{3+4}{12} = \frac{7}{12}$

$\therefore$ Both the taps together will fill the cistern in $\frac{12}{7}$ hours.

Example 2 Pipe A can fill an empty tank in 6 hours and pipe B in 8 hours. If both the pipes are opened and after 2 hours pipe A is closed, how much time B will take to fill the remaining tank?

Solution We have,

Pipe A can fill the tank in 6 hours, Pipe B can fill the tank in 8 hours.

$\therefore$ In one hour A can fill $\frac{1}{6}$th part of the tank.

In one hour B can fill $\frac{1}{8}$th part of the tank.

Thus,

In one hours A and B can fill $\left(\frac{1}{6} + \frac{1}{8}\right)$th $= \frac{7}{24}$th part of the tank.

$\Rightarrow$ In 2 hours A and B can fill $\left(2 \times \frac{7}{24}\right)$th $= \frac{7}{12}$th part of the tank.

Remaining part of the tank $= 1 - \frac{7}{12} = \frac{5}{12}$

Now,

B can fill the tank in 8 hours.

$\therefore$ $\frac{5}{12}$th part of the tank can be filled by B in $\frac{5}{12} \times 8 = \frac{10}{3}$ hrs $= 3\frac{1}{3}$ hrs.

Example 3 A cistern can be filled by a tap in 6 hours and emptied by an outlet pipe in 8 hours. How long will it take to fill the cistern if both the tap and the pipe are opened together?

Solution We have,

Time taken by the tap to fill the cistern = 6 hours

Time taken by the pipe to empty the cistern = 8 hours.

$\therefore$ In one hour the tap fills $\frac{1}{6}$ th part of the cistern

In one hour the pipe empties $\frac{1}{8}$ th part of the cistern.

Thus, in one hour $\left(\frac{1}{6}-\frac{1}{8}\right)$th $=\left(\frac{8-6}{48}\right)$th $=\left(\frac{1}{24}\right)$th part of the cistern is failed.

Hence, the cistern is filled in 24 hours.

Example 4 A pipe can fill a cistern in 6 hours. Due to a leak in the bottom it is filled in 7 hours. When the cistern is full, in how much time will it be emptied by the leak?

Solution When there is no leakage, the pipe can fill the cistern in 6 hours.

$\therefore$ The pipe fills $\frac{1}{6}$ th part of the cistern in one hour.

When there is leakage, the pipe can fill the cistern in 7 hours. Thus, in case of leakage, the pipe fills $\frac{1}{7}$ th part of the cistern in one hour.

Thus, in one hour due to leakage $\left(\frac{1}{6}-\frac{1}{7}\right)$th $=\frac{1}{42}$th part of the cistern is emptied out.

Hence, the cistern will be emptied by the leakage in 42 hours.

Example 5 A tank can be filled by two taps A and B in 12 hours and 16 hours respectively. The full tank can be emptied by a third tap in 8 hours. If all the taps be turned on at the same time, in how much time will the empty tank be filled up completely?

Solution We have,

Time taken by tap A to fill the tank = 12 hours

Time taken by tap B to fill the tank = 16 hours

Time taken by tap C to empty the tank = 8 hours

$\therefore$ Tap A fills up $\frac{1}{12}$th part of the tank in 1 hour,

Tap B fills up $\frac{1}{16}$th part of the tank in 1 hour,

Tap C empties out $\frac{1}{8}$th part of the tank in 1 hour.

Thus, in 1 hour $\left(\frac{1}{12}+\frac{1}{16}-\frac{1}{8}\right)$th part of the tank is filled.

We have, $\frac{1}{12}+\frac{1}{16}-\frac{1}{8}=\frac{4+3-6}{48}=\frac{1}{48}$

$\therefore$ In 1 hour $\frac{1}{48}$ th part of the tank is filled.

Hence, the tank will be filled completely in 48 hours, when all the three are opened together.

EXERCISE 11.1

1. Rakesh can do a piece of work in 20 days. How much work can he do in 4 days?
2. Rohan can paint $\frac{1}{3}$ of a painting in 6 days. How many days will he take to complete the painting ?
3. Anil can do a piece of work in 5 days and Ankur in 4 days. How long will they take to do the same work, if they work together?
4. Mohan takes 9 hours to mow a large lawn. He and Sohan together can mow it in 4 hours. How long will Sohan take to mow the lawn if he works alone?
5. Sita can finish typing a 100 page document in 9 hours, Mita in 6 hours and Rita in 12 hours. How long will they take to type a 100 page document if they work together?
6. A, B and C working together can do a piece of work in 8 hours. A alone can do it in 20 hours and B alone can do it in 24 hours. In how many hours will C alone do the same work?
7. A and B can do a piece of work in 18 days; B and C in 24 days and A and C in 36 days. In what time can they do it, all working together?
8. A and B can do a piece of work in 12 days; B and C in 15 days ; C and A in 20 days. How much time will A alone take to finish the work?
9. A, B and C can reap a field in $15\frac{3}{4}$ days; B, C and D in 14 days; C, D and A in 18 days; D, A and B in 21 days. In what time can A, B, C and D together reap it?
10. A and B can polish the floors of a building in 10 days. A alone can do $\frac{1}{4}$ th of it in 12 days. In how many days can B alone polish the floor?
11. A and B can finish a work in 20 days. A alone can do $\frac{1}{5}$ th of the work in 12 days. In how many days can B alone do it?
12. A and B can do a piece of work in 20 days and B in 15 days. They work together for 2 days and then A goes away. In how many days will B finish the remaining work?
13. A can do a piece of work in 40 days and B in 45 days. They work together for 10 days and then B goes away. In how many days will A finish the remaining work?
14. Aasheesh can paint his doll in 20 minutes and his sister Chinki can do so in 25 minutes. They paint the doll together for five minutes. At this juncture they have a quarrel and Chinki withdraws from painting. In how many minutes will Aasheesh finish the painting of the remaining doll ?
15. A and B can do a piece of work in 6 days and 4 days respectively. A started the work; worked at it for 2 days and then was joined by B. Find the total time taken to complete the work.
16. 6 men can complete the electric fitting in a building in 7 days. How many days will it take if 21 men do the job?
17. 8 men can do a piece of work in 9 days. In how many days will 6 men do it?
18. Reema weaves 35 baskets in 25 days. In how many days will she weave 55 baskets?
19. Neha types 75 pages in 14 hours. How many pages will she type in 20 hours?
20. If 12 boys earn Rs 840 in 7 days, what will 15 boys earn in 6 days?
21. If 25 men earn Rs 1000 in 10 days, how much will 15 men earn in 15 days?

22. Working 8 hours a day, Ashu can copy a book in 18 days. How many hours a day should he work so as to finish the work in 12 days?
23. If 9 girls can prepare 135 garlands in 3 hours, how many girls are needed to prepare 270 garlands in 1 hour?
24. A cistern can be filled by one tap in 8 hours, and by another in 4 hours. How long will it take to fill the cistern if both taps are opened together?
25. Two taps A and B can fill an overhead tank in 10 hours and 15 hours respectively. Both the taps are opened for 4 hours and then B is turned off. How much time will A take to fill the remaining tank?
26. A pipe can fill a cistern in 10 hours. Due to a leak in the bottom it is filled in 12 hours. When the cistern is full, in how much time will it be emptied by the leak?
27. A cistern has two inlets A and B which can fill it in 12 hours and 15 hours respectively. An outlet can empty the full cistern in 10 hours. If all the three pipes are opened together in the empty cistern, how much time will they take to fill the cistern completely?
28. A cistern can be filled by a tap in 4 hours and emptied by an outlet pipe in 6 hours. How long will it take to fill the cistern if both the tap and the pipe are opened together?

ANSWERS

1. $\frac{1}{5}$th 2. 18 days 3. $2\frac{2}{9}$ days 4. $\frac{36}{5}$ hours 5. $\frac{36}{13}$ hours 6. 30 hours
7. 16 days 8. 30 days 9. $12\frac{3}{5}$ days 10. $12\frac{12}{19}$ days 11. 30 days 12. $13\frac{1}{2}$ days
13. $21\frac{1}{9}$ days 14. 11 minutes 15. $3\frac{3}{5}$ days 16. 2 days 17. 12 days 18. $39\frac{2}{7}$ days
19. $107\frac{1}{7}$ pages 20. Rs 900 21. Rs 900 22. 12 hours 23. 54 girls 24. $2\frac{2}{3}$ hrs
25. $3\frac{1}{3}$ hours 26. 60 hours 27. 20 hours 28. 12 hours.

THINGS TO REMEMBER

1. *If a person A can finish a piece of work in n days, then the work done by A in 1 day* $= \frac{1}{n}$*th part of the work.*
2. *If a person A completes* $\frac{1}{n}$*th part of a work in one day, then the time taken by A to finish complete work in = n days*
3. *In a cistern, the pipe that fills it, is called an inlet and the pipe that empties it, is known as an outlet.*
4. *If an inlet fills up a cistern in n hours, then in 1 hour it will fill up* $\frac{1}{n}$*th part of the cistern.*
5. *If an outlet empties a full cistern in m hours, then in 1 hour* $\frac{1}{m}$*th part of the cistern will be emptied out.*

6. An angle of measure 360° is called
   (a) a zero angle (b) a straight angle (c) a reflex angle (d) a complete angle
7. An angle of measure 140° is
   (a) an acute angle (b) an obtuse angle
   (c) a straight angle (d) a complete angle
8. A reflex angle measures
   (a) more than 90° but less than 180° (b) more than 180° but less than 270°
   (c) more than 180° but less than 360° (d) None of these
9. The number of degrees in 2 right angles is
   (a) 90° (b) 180° (c) 270° (d) 360°
10. The number of degrees in 3 right angles is
   (a) 180° (b) 360° (c) 270° (d) 90°
11. If a bicycle wheel has 36 spokes, then the angle between a pair of adjacent spokes is
   (a) 10° (b) 15° (c) 20° (d) 12°

ANSWERS

1. (c) 2. (c) 3. (d) 4. (b) 5. (c) 6. (d) 7. (b)
8. (c) 9. (b) 10. (c) 11. (a)

THINGS TO REMEMBER

1. *An angle is a figure formed by two rays with the same initial point. The initial point is called the vertex and the two rays are called the arms of the angle.*
2. *The amount of rotation through which one of the arms of a given angle must be rotated about its vertex to bring it to the position of the other, is called the magnitude of the angle.*
3. *The standard unit of measurement of an angle is degree.*
   1 right angle = 90°, 1° = 60′, 1′ = 60″
4. *Two or more angles having the same magnitude are said to be equal.*
5. *A complete turn of a ray OA about O describes a complete angle.*
6. *A half turn of a ray OA about O describes a straight angle.*
   1 straight angle = 2 right angles = 180°
7. *A quarter turn of a ray OA about O describes a right angle,*
   1 right angle = 90°
8. *Zero angle = 0°, 0° < acute angle < 90°, 90° < obtuse angle < 180°.*

12

PERCENTAGE

12.1 INTRODUCTION

In previous class, you have studied the concept of percentage. You have also learnt to convert a percent into fraction, a ratio or decimal and vice-versa. In this chapter, we shall discuss some more problems on percentage.

12.2 A REVIEW OF WORK DONE EARLIER

PERCENT *The word percent is an abbreviation of the Latin phrase 'per centum' which means per hundred or hundredths.*

Thus, the term percent means per hundred or for every hundred.

By a certain percent we mean that many hundredths.

When we say that a man gives 30 percent of his income as income tax. This means that he pays Rs 30 out of every hundred rupees of his income as income tax.

The symbol % is used for the term percent.

PERCENT AS A FRACTION We have, 35% = 35 hundredths $= \frac{35}{100}$.

Thus, a fraction with its denominator 100 is equal to that percent as is the numerator.

So, $\frac{8}{100} = 8\%, \frac{12}{100} = 12\%, \frac{135}{100} = 135\%$ etc.

To convert a fraction into a percent we multiply the fraction by 100 and put the percent sign %.

Thus, $\frac{4}{5} = \left(\frac{4}{5} \times 100\right)\% = 80\%; \frac{9}{20} = \left(\frac{9}{20} \times 100\right)\% = 45\%$

To convert a percent into a fraction, we divide it by 100 and remove the percent sign %.

$\therefore$ $25\% = \frac{25}{100}, 13\% = \frac{13}{100}$ etc.

PERCENT AS A RATIO A percent can be expressed as a ratio with its second term 100 and first term equal to the given percent.

For example, $8\% = \frac{8}{100} = 8:100;\ 36\% = \frac{36}{100} = \frac{9}{25} = 9:25$

In order to convert a given ratio into a percent, we first convert the given ratio into the fraction and then multiply the fraction obtained by 100.

Thus, $6:5 = \frac{6}{5} = \left(\frac{6}{5} \times 100\right)\% = 120\%$ and, $3:12 = \frac{3}{12} = \left(\frac{3}{12} \times 100\right)\% = 25\%.$

To convert a given percent into a ratio, we first convert the percent into a fraction and then express it as a ratio.

For example, 52% $= \frac{52}{100} = \frac{13}{25} = 13:25$

PERCENT IN DECIMAL FORM To convert a given percent in decimal form, we express it as a fraction with denominator as 100 and then the fraction is written in decimal form.

For example, $65\% = \frac{65}{100} = 0.65, 7.4\% = \frac{7.4}{100} = 0.074$

In order to convert a given decimal into a percent, we move the decimal point on the right side by two digits and put the percent sign %.

For example, 0.122 = 12.2%, 0.275 = 27.5%, 0.037 = 3.7%.

EXERCISE 12.1

1. Write each of the following as percent:

   (i) $\frac{7}{25}$ (ii) $\frac{14}{625}$ (iii) $\frac{5}{8}$ (iv) 0.8 (v) 0.005 (vi) 3 : 25

   (vii) 11 : 80 (viii) 111 : 125 (ix) 13 : 75 (x) 15 : 16 (xi) 0.18 (xii) $\frac{7}{125}$

2. Convert the following percentages to fractions and ratios:

   (i) 25% (ii) 2.5% (iii) 0.25% (iv) 0.3 % (v) 125%

3. Express the following as decimal fractions:

   (i) 27% (ii) 6.3% (iii) 32% (iv) 0.25% (v) 7.5% (vi) $\frac{1}{8}\%$

ANSWERS

1. (i) 28% (ii) 2.24% (iii) 62.5% (iv) 80% (v) 0.5% (vi) 12%
   (vii) 13.75% (viii) 88.8% (ix) 17.33% (x) 93.75% (xi) 18% (xii) 5.6%

2. (i) $\frac{1}{4}$, 1 : 4 (ii) $\frac{1}{40}$, 1 : 40 (iii) $\frac{1}{400}$, 1 : 400 (iv) $\frac{3}{1000}$, 3 : 1000 (v) $\frac{5}{4}$, 5 : 4

3. (i) 0.27 (ii) 0.063 (iii) 0.32 (iv) 0.0025 (v) 0.075 (vi) 0.00125

12.3 FINDING A PERCENTAGE OF A NUMBER

To find a percent of a given number, we proceed as follows:

Step I *Obtain the number, say x.*

Step II *Obtain the required percent, say P %.*

Step III *Multiply x by P and divide by 100 to obtain the required P % of x*

i.e.,

$$P\% \text{ of } x = \frac{P}{100} \times x$$

Following examples will illustrate the above procedure.

ILLUSTRATIVE EXAMPLES

Example 1 Find:

(i) 12% of Rs 1200 (ii) 13% of Rs 6500 (iii) 20% of Rs 800

Solution (i) 12% of Rs 1200 $= \text{Rs} \frac{12}{100} \times 1200 = 144$

(ii) 13% of Rs 6500 $= \text{Rs}\ \frac{13}{100} \times 6500 = \text{Rs}\ 845$

(iii) 20% of Rs 800 $= \text{Rs}\ \frac{20}{100} \times 800 = \text{Rs}\ 160$

Example 2 If 23% of a is 46, then find a.

Solution We have,

$$23\% \text{ of } a = \frac{23}{100} \times a.$$

But, 23% of a is given as 46.

$$\therefore \quad \frac{23}{100} \times a = 46 \Rightarrow a = 46 \times \frac{100}{23} \Rightarrow a = 200$$

Example 3 72% of 25 students are good at Mathematics. How many are not good at it?

Solution We have,

Number of students who are good at Mathematics

$$= 72\% \text{ of } 25 = \frac{72}{\cancel{100}_4} \times \cancel{25}^1 = 18$$

$\therefore$ Number of students who are not good at Mathematics $= 25 - 18 = 7$.

Example 4 A football team won 10 games from the total they played. This was 40% of the total. How many games were played in all ?

Solution Let x be the total number of games played. Then,

$$40\% \text{ of } x = 10$$

$$\Rightarrow \quad \frac{40}{100} \times x = 10$$

$$\Rightarrow \quad \frac{2x}{5} = 10 \Rightarrow 2x = 50 \Rightarrow x = \frac{50}{2} = 25$$

Hence, in all 25 games were played.

Example 5 If Chameli had Rs 600 left after spending 75% of her money, how much did she have in the beginning ?

Solution Suppose Chameli had Rs x in the beginning. Then,

Money spent by Chameli $= 75\% \text{ of } x = \text{Rs}\ \frac{75}{100} \times x = \text{Rs}\ \frac{3x}{4}$

$\therefore$ Money left with Chameli $= \text{Rs}\ \left(x - \frac{3x}{4}\right) = \text{Rs}\ \frac{4x - 3x}{4} = \text{Rs}\ \frac{x}{4}$

But, it is given that she had Rs 600 left after spending 75% of her money.

$$\therefore \quad \frac{x}{4} = 600 \Rightarrow x = 600 \times 4 = 2400$$

Hence, Chameli had Rs 2400.

Example 6 78.8% of a common medicine for stomach-up sets is absolute alcohol; 3.3% of it is mentha oil; 0.07% spearmint oil, and 0.177% chloroform. How much of each of these compounds is there in a pack of 30 ml?

Solution We have,

Total quantity of the liquid in the pack = 30 ml.

$\therefore$ Amount of alcohol $= 78.8\%$ of 30 ml $= \frac{78}{100} \times 30$ ml $= 0.788 \times 30$ ml

$= 23.64$ ml

Amount of spearmint oil $= 0.07\%$ of 30 ml

$= \left(\frac{0.07}{100} \times 30\right)$ ml $= (0.0007 \times 30)$ ml $= 0.021$ ml

Amount of chloroform $= 0.177\%$ of 30 ml

$= \left(\frac{0.177}{100} \times 30\right)$ ml $= 0.00177 \times 30$ ml $= 0.0531$ ml

Example 7 A nursery has 5000 plants. 5% of the plants are roses and 1% are mango plants. What is the total number of other plants?

Solution We have,

Total number of plants = 5000

Number of rose plants $= 5\%$ of $5000 = \left(\frac{5}{100} \times 5000\right) = 250$

Number of mango plants $= 1\%$ of $5000 = \left(\frac{1}{100} \times 5000\right) = 50$

$\therefore$ Number of other plants $= 5000 - (250 + 50) = 4700$

Example 8 Malvika gets 98 marks in her exams. This amounts to 56% of the total marks. What are the maximum marks?

Solution Let the maximum marks be x. Then,

56% of $x = 98$ [Given]

$\Rightarrow \frac{56}{100} \times x = 98$

$\Rightarrow x = 98 \times \frac{100}{56}$

$\Rightarrow x = 175$

Hence, the maximum marks are 175

Example 9 A certain company has 80 employees who are engineers. In this company engineers constitute 40% of its work force. How many people are employed in the company?

Solution Let x people be employed in the company.

Since 40% of its work force are engineers. This means that 40% of x is equal to the total number of engineers.

$\therefore \frac{40}{100} \times x = 80 \Rightarrow x = \frac{100}{40} \times 80 = 200$

Hence, 200 people are employed in the company

Example 10 Kishan spends 30% of his salary on food and donates 3% of his salary in a temple. In a particular month, he spends Rs 231 on these two items. What is his total salary for this month?

Solution Suppose Kishan's total salary is Rs 100 per month.

Expenditure per month on food = 30% of Rs 100 = Rs 30

Donation per month to temple Rs. = 3% of Rs 100 = Rs 3.

Total expenditure = Rs (30 + 3) = Rs 33.

If expenditure is Rs 33, then total salary = Rs 100

If expenditure is Re 1, then total salary = Rs $\frac{100}{33}$

If expenditure is Rs 231, then total salary = Rs $\left(\frac{100}{33} \times 231\right)$ = Rs 700

Hence, Kishan's total salary for the given month is Rs 700.

Example 11 Out of her total income Mrs Sharma spends 20% on house rent and 70% of the rest on household expenditure. If she saves Rs 1800, what is the total income?

Solution Suppose total income of Mrs Sharma is Rs 100

Expenditure on house rent = 20% of Rs 100 = Rs 20

$\therefore$ Balance money = Rs (100 − 20) = Rs 80

Household expenditure = 70% of Rs 80 = Rs $\left(\frac{70}{100} \times 80\right)$ = Rs 56

Saving = Rs (80 − 56) = 24.

Now,

If saving is Rs 24, then total income = Rs 100

If saving is Re 1, then total income = Rs $\frac{100}{24}$

If saving is Rs 1800, then total income = Rs $\left(\frac{100}{24} \times 1800\right)$ = Rs 7500

Hence, total income of Mrs Sharma is Rs 7500

Example 12 Anushree has to pay 4% sales tax in addition to the price of a certain article. Find the price of her article, if she pays Rs 2.60 in all.

Solution Let the price of the article be Rs 100

Sales tax = 4% of Rs 100 = Rs 4

Total amount paid = Rs (100 + 4) = Rs 104

Now,

When she pays Rs 104, price = Rs 100

When she pays Re 1, price = Re $\frac{100}{104}$

When she pays Rs 2.60, price = Rs $\frac{100}{104} \times 2.60$ = Rs 2.50

Hence, price of the article is Rs 2.50

Example 13 A man loses 20% of his money. After spending 25% of the remainder, he has Rs 480.00 left. How much money did he originally have?

Solution Suppose, he originally had Rs 100

Amount lost = 20% of Rs 100 = Rs 20

Remainder $= \text{Rs}\,(100 - 20) = \text{Rs } 80$

Expenditure = 25% of the remainder

$= 25\% \text{ of Rs } 80 = \text{Rs}\left(\frac{25}{100} \times 80\right) = \text{Rs } 20$

Remainder $= \text{Rs}\,(80 - 20) = \text{Rs } 60$

If remainder is Rs 60, he originally had Rs 100

If remainder is Re 1, he originally had Rs $\frac{100}{60}$

If remainder is Rs 480, he originally had Rs $\left(\frac{100}{60} \times 480\right) = \text{Rs } 800$

Hence, the man had Rs 800

Example 14 An alloy contains 36% zinc, 40% copper and the rest is nickel. Find in grams the quantity of each of the contents in a sample of 1 kg alloy.

Solution We have,

Zinc in the alloy = 36%, Copper in the alloy = 40%

$\therefore$ Nickel in the alloy $= [100 - (36 + 40)]\% = 24\%$

Now,

Quantity of zinc in 1 kg of alloy = 36% of 1 kg

= 36% of 1000 grams

$= \left(\frac{36}{100} \times 1000\right) \text{grams} = 360 \text{ grams}$

Quantity of copper in the alloy = 40% of 1 kg

= 40% of 1000grams

$= \left(\frac{40}{100} \times 1000\right) \text{grams} = 400 \text{ grams}$

and,

Quantity of nickel in the alloy = 24% of 1 kg

= 24% of 1000 grams

$= \left(\frac{24}{100} \times 1000\right) \text{grams} = 240 \text{ grams}.$

Example 15 Rani's weight is 25% that of Meena's and 40% that of Tara's. What percentage of Tara's weight is Meena's weight?

Solution Let Meena's weight be x kg and Tara's weight be y kg. Then,

Rani's weight = 25% of Meena's weight $= \frac{25}{100} \times x$ ... (i)

Also, Rani's weight = 40% of Tara's weight $= \frac{40}{100} \times y$ ... (ii)

From (i) and (ii), we get

$$\frac{25}{100} \times x = \frac{40}{100} \times y$$

$\Rightarrow \quad 25x = 40y$ [Multiplying both sides by 100]

$\Rightarrow \quad 25x = 8y$ [Dividing both sides by 5]

$\Rightarrow \quad x = \frac{8}{5}y$ ... (iii)

We have to find Meena's weight as the percentage of Tara's weight i.e.,

$$\frac{x}{y}\times 100 = \frac{\frac{8}{5}y}{y}\times 100 = \frac{8}{5}\times 100 = 160 \quad \text{[Using (iii)]}$$

Hence, Meena's weight is 160% of Tara's weight.

Example 16 Rakesh's income is 25% more than that of Rohan. What percent is Rohan's income less than Rakesh's income?

Solution Let Rohan's income be Rs 100. Then,

Rakesh's Income = Rs 125

If Rakesh's income is Rs 125, Rohan's income = Rs 100

If Rakesh's income is Re 1, Rohan's income = Re $= \frac{100}{125}$

If Rakesh's income is Rs 100, Rohan's income = Rs$\left(\frac{100}{125}\times 100\right)$ = Rs 80

Hence, Rohan's income is 20% less than that of Rakesh.

Example 17 Rishi requires 40% to pass. If he gets 185 marks, falls short by 15 marks, what were the maximum marks he could have got?

Solution If Rishi had 15 marks more, he could have scored 40% marks.

Now, 15 marks more than 185 is 185 + 15 = 200

Let the maximum marks be x. Then,

40% of x = 200

$$\Rightarrow \quad \frac{40}{100}\times x = 200$$

$$\Rightarrow \quad x = \frac{200\times 100}{40} = 500$$

Thus, maximum marks = 500.

Example 18 The value of a machine depreciates every year by 10%. What will be its value after 2 years if its present value is Rs 50,000?

Solution Present value of the machine = Rs 50,000

Decrease in value after 1 year = 10% of Rs 50,000

$= \text{Rs}\left(\frac{10}{100}\times 50{,}000\right) = \text{Rs } 5000$

$\therefore$ Depreciated value after one year = Rs (50,000 – 5000) = Rs 45000

Decrease in value after 2 years = 10% of Rs 45000

$= \text{Rs}\left(\frac{10}{100}\times 45000\right) = \text{Rs } 4500$

$\therefore$ Depreciated value after 2 years = Rs (45000 – 4500) = Rs 40500

Thus, the value of the machine after 2 years = Rs 40500.

Example 19 The population of a town increases by 6% every year. If the present population is 15900, find its population a year ago.

Solution Let the population of the town be 100 a year ago. Then,

Increase in population = 6% of 100 = 6

∴ Present population = 106

If present population is 106, population a year ago = 100

If present population is 1, population a year ago = $\frac{100}{106}$

If present population is 15900, population a year ago = $\frac{100}{106} \times 15900 = 15000$

Hence, the population of the town a year ago was 15000.

Example 20 The price of sugar goes up by 20%. By how much percent must a house wife reduce her consumption so that the expenditure does not increase?

Solution Let the consumption of sugar originally be 100 kg and its price be Rs 100. Then,

New price of 100 kg sugar = Rs 120 [∵ Price increases by 20%]

Now, Rs 120 can fetch 100 kg sugar

∴ Rs 100 can fetch $= \left(\frac{100}{120} \times 100\right)$ kg sugar $= \frac{250}{3}$ kg sugar

∴ Reduction in consumption $= \left(100 - \frac{250}{3}\right)\% = \frac{50}{3}\% = 16\frac{2}{3}\%$

Example 21 A number is increased by 10% and then it is decreased by 10%. Find the net increase or decrease percent.

Solution Let the number be = 100

Increase in the number = 10% = 10% of 100 = 10

∴ Increased number = 100 + 10 = 110

This number is decreased by 10%.

∴ Decrease in the number = 10% of 110 $= \left(\frac{10}{110} \times 100\right) = 11$

∴ New number = 110 − 11 = 99

Thus, net decrease = 100 − 99 = 1

Hence net percentage decrease $= \left(\frac{1}{100} \times 100\right)\% = 1\%$

Example 22 The salary of an officer has been increased by 50%. By what percent the new salary must be reduced to restore the original salary?

Solution Let original salary be Rs 100. Then,

Increase in the salary = 50% of Rs 100 = Rs 50

Salary after increment = Rs 150

Now, in order to restore the original salary, a reduction of Rs 50 should be made on Rs 150.

Thus,

Reduction on Rs 150 = Rs 50

$\Rightarrow$ Reduction on Re 1 = Re $\dfrac{50}{150}$

$\Rightarrow$ Reduction on Rs 100 = Re $\left(\dfrac{50}{150}\times 100\right) = 33\dfrac{1}{3}$

Hence, reduction on new salary = $33\dfrac{1}{3}\%$

Example 23 Find the percent of pure gold in 22-carat gold, if 24 carat gold is hundred percent pure gold.

Solution In 22-carat gold pure gold is 22 parts out of 24 parts.

$\therefore$ Percent of pure gold in 22-carat gold $=\left(\dfrac{22}{24}\times 100\right)\% = 91\dfrac{2}{3}\%$

Example 24 If 60% people in a city like cricket, 30% like football and remaining like other games. What percent like the other games? If the total number of people is 56 lakhs, find the exact number who like each type of game.

Solution It is given that 60% people like cricket, 30% like football.

$\therefore$ Percentage of people who like other games $= (100 - 60 - 30)\% = 10\%$

Total number of people $= 56,00,000$

Number of people who like cricket $= 60\%$ of 5600000

$= \dfrac{60}{100}\times 5600000 = 33,60,000$

Number of people who like football $= 30\%$ of 5600000

$= \dfrac{30}{100}\times 5600000 = 16,80,000$

Number of people who like other games $= (10\%$ of $5600000) = 5,60,000$

EXERCISE 12.2

1. Find:
   (i) 22% of 120 (ii) 25% of Rs 1000 (iii) 25% of 10 kg
   (iv) 16.5% of 5000 metre (v) 135% of 80 cm (vi) 2.5% of 10000 ml
2. Find the number a, if
   (i) 8.4% of a is 42 (ii) 0.5% of a is 3 (iii) $\dfrac{1}{2}\%$ of a is 50
   (iv) 100% of a is 100
3. x is 5% of y, y is 24% of z. If $x = 480$, find the values of y and z.
4. A coolie deposits Rs 150 per month in his post office Savings Bank account. If this is 15% of his monthly income, find his monthly income.
5. Asha got 86.875% marks in the annual examination. If she got 695 marks, find the total number of marks of the examination.
6. Deepti went to school for 216 days in a full year. If her attendance is 90%, find the number of days on which the school was opened.
7. A garden has 2000 trees. 12% of these are mango trees, 18% lemon and the rest are orange trees. Find the number of orange trees.

8. Balanced diet should contain 12% of proteins, 25% of fats and 63% of carbohydrates. If a child needs 2600 calories in this food daily, find in calories the amount of each of these in his daily food intake.

9. A cricketer scored a total of 62 runs in 96 balls. He hit 3 sixes, 8 fours, 2 twos and 8 singles. What percentage of the total runs came in
(i) Sixes (ii) fours (iii) twos (iv) singles

10. A cricketer hit 120 runs in 150 balls during a test match . 20% of the runs came in 6's, 30% in 4's, 25% in 2's and the rest in 1's. How many runs did he score in
(i) 6's (ii) 4's (iii) 2's (iv) singles
What % of his shots were scoring ones?

11. Radha earns 22% of her investment. If she earns Rs 187, then how much did she invest?

12. Rohit deposits 12% of his income in a bank. He deposited Rs 1440 in the bank during 1997. What was his total income for the year 1997?

13. Gunpowder contains 75% nitre and 10% sulphur. Find the amount of the gunpowder which carries 9 kg nitre. What amount of gunpowder would contain 2.3 kg sulphur?

14. An alloy of tin and copper consists of 15 parts of tin and 105 parts of copper. Find the percentage of copper in the alloy?

15. An alloy contains 32% copper, 40% nickel and rest zinc. Find the mass of the zinc in 1 kg of the alloy.

16. A motorist travelled 122 kilometres before his first stop. If he had 10% of his journey to complete at this point, how long was the total ride?

17. A certain school has 300 students, 142 of whom are boys. It has 30 teachers, 12 of whom are men. What percent of the total number of students and teachers in the school is female?

18. Aman's income is 20% less than that of Anil. How much percent is Anil's income more than Aman's income?

19. The value of a machine depreciates every year by 5%. If the present value of the machine be Rs 100000, what will be its value after 2 years?

20. The population of a town increases by 10% annually. If the present population is 60000, what wll be its population after 2 years?

21. The population of a town increases by 10% annually. If the present population is 22000, find its population a year ago.

22. Ankit was given an increment of 10% on his salary. His new salary is Rs 3575. What was his salary before increment?

23. In the new budget, the price of petrol rose by 10%. By how much percent must one reduce the consumption so that the expenditure does not increase?

24. Mohan's income is Rs 15500 per month. He saves 11% of his income. If his income increases by 10%, then he reduces his saving by 1%, how much does he save now?

25. Shikha's income is 60% more than that of Shalu. What percent is Shalu's income less than Shikha's?

26. Rs 3500 is to be shared among three people so that the first person gets 50% of the second, who in turn gets 50% of the third. How much will each of them get?

27. After a 20% hike, the cost of Chinese Vase is Rs 2000. What was the original price of the object?

ANSWERS

1. (i) 26.40 (ii) Rs 250 (iii) 2.5 kg (iv) 825 metre (v) 1.08 metre (vi) 250 ml
2. (i) 500 (ii) 600 (iii) 10000 (iv) 100
3. $y = 9600, z = 40000$
4. Rs 1000
5. 800 marks
6. 240 days
7. 1400
8. 312, 650, 1638
9. (i) 29.03% (ii) 51.61% (iii) 6.45% (iv) 12.9%
10. (i) 24 (ii) 36 (iii) 30 (iv) 30, 38.67%
11. Rs 850
12. Rs 12000
13. 12 kg, 23 kg
14. 87.5%
15. 280 grams
16. 1220 km
17. $\frac{160}{3}\%$
18. 25%
19. Rs 90250
20. 72600
21. 20000
22. Rs 3250
23. $9\frac{1}{11}\%$
24. Rs1705, Same as before
25. 37.5%
26. Rs 500, Rs 1000, Rs 2000,
27. Rs 1666.67

THINGS TO REMEMBER

1. *Per cent means per hundred or for every hundred.*
2. *By a certain per cent, we mean that many hundredths.*
3. *A fraction with its denominator as 100 is called a per cent and is equal to that per cent as is the numerator.*
4. *A ratio with its second term 100 is also called a per cent.*
5. *To convert a fraction into a per cent, we multiply the fraction by 100.*
6. *To convert a ratio into a per cent, we write it as a fraction and multiply it by 100.*
7. *To convert a decimal into a per cent, we shift the decimal point two places to the right.*
8. *To convert a per cent into a fraction, we drop per cent sign (%) and divide the remainder by 100.*
9. *To convert a per cent into a ratio, we drop per cent sign (%) and form a ratio with the remaining number as the first term and 100 as the second term.*
10. *To convert a per cent into a decimal, we drop per cent sign (%) and shift the decimal point two places to the left.*
11. $\text{Increase\%} = \left(\frac{\text{Increase}}{\text{original value}} \times 100\right)\%$, $\text{Decrease \%} = \left(\frac{\text{Decrease}}{\text{original value}} \times 100\right)\%$

13

PROFIT, LOSS, DISCOUNT AND VALUE ADDED TAX (VAT)

13.1 INTRODUCTION

Upto class VII, we have learnt about the computation of profit and loss incurred in buying and selling goods. We have also learnt about profit and loss percent. In this chapter, we shall discuss more problems on profit and loss. At the end of the chapter, we shall introduce the notion of discount in buying and selling the goods. We shall also discuss problems on sales tax and value added tax (VAT). But, let us first review various concepts studied in earlier classes.

13.2 REVIEW OF CONCEPTS

COST PRICE *The amount paid to purchase an article or the price at which an article is made is known as its cost price.*

The cost price is abbreviated as C.P.

NOTE: *Generally, the overhead expenses like cartage, taxes, labour charges, etc. are included in the cost price. If overhead expenses are not included in the cost price, then*

Effective Cost Price = Payment made while purchasing the goods + Overhead expenses

SELLING PRICE *The price at which an article is sold is known as its selling price.*

The selling price is abbreviated as S.P.

PROFIT *If the selling price (S.P.) of an article is greater than the cost price (C.P.), the difference between the selling price and cost price is called profit.*

Thus, if S.P. > C.P., then

$$\text{Profit} = \text{S.P.} - \text{C.P.}$$
$$\Leftrightarrow \quad \text{S.P.} = \text{C.P.} + \text{Profit}$$
$$\Leftrightarrow \quad \text{C.P.} = \text{S.P.} - \text{Profit.}$$

PROFIT PERCENTAGE *The profit percent is the profit that would be obtained for a C.P. of Rs 100 i.e.,*

$$\text{Profit percent} = \frac{\text{Profit}}{\text{C.P.}} \times 100$$

Thus, in case of profit or gain (i.e., if S.P. > C.P.), we have

(i) Profit = S.P. – C.P.

(ii) S.P. = Profit + C.P.

(iii) C.P. = S.P. – Profit

(iv) $\text{Profit percent} = \dfrac{\text{Profit}}{\text{C.P.}} \times 100$

(v) $\text{Profit} = \dfrac{\text{C.P.} \times \text{Profit \%}}{100}$

(vi) S.P. = C.P. + Profit

$$\Rightarrow \text{S.P.} = \text{C.P.} + \frac{\text{Profit \%} \times \text{C.P.}}{100}$$

$$\Rightarrow \text{S.P.} = \left(\frac{100 + \text{Profit \%}}{100}\right) \times \text{C.P.}$$

(vii) $\text{C.P.} = \frac{100 \times \text{S.P.}}{(100 + \text{Profit \%})}$

LOSS *If the selling price (S.P.) of an article is less than the cost price (C.P.), the difference between the cost price (C.P.) and the selling price (S.P.) is called loss.*

Thus, if S.P. < C.P., then

$$\text{Loss} = \text{C.P.} - \text{S.P.}$$

$$\Leftrightarrow \quad \text{C.P.} = \text{S.P.} + \text{Loss}$$

$$\Leftrightarrow \quad \text{S.P.} = \text{C.P.} - \text{Loss}$$

LOSS PERCENTAGE *The loss percent is the loss that would be made for a C.P. of Rs* 100.

That is,

$$\text{Loss percent} = \frac{\text{Loss}}{\text{C.P.}} \times 100$$

Thus, in case of loss (i.e., when S.P. < C.P.), we have

(i) Loss = C.P. – S.P.

(ii) S.P. = C.P. – Loss

(iii) C.P. = S.P. + Loss

(iv) $\text{Loss \%} = \frac{\text{Loss}}{\text{C.P.}} \times 100$

(v) $\text{Loss} = \frac{\text{C.P.} \times \text{Loss \%}}{100}$

(vi) S.P. = C.P. – Loss

$$\Rightarrow \text{S.P.} = \text{C.P.} - \frac{\text{C.P.} \times \text{Loss \%}}{100}$$

$$\Rightarrow \text{S.P.} = \left(\frac{100 - \text{Loss \%}}{100}\right) \times \text{C.P.}$$

(vii) $\text{C.P.} = \frac{100 \times \text{S.P.}}{(100 - \text{Loss \%})}$

ILLUSTRATIVE EXAMPLES

Example 1 A shopkeeper buys a toy for Rs 250 and sells it for Rs 285. Find his gain and gain percent.

Solution We have,

C.P. of the toy = Rs 250

S.P. of the toy = Rs 285

Since S.P. > C.P. So, there is gain given by

Gain $= \text{S.P.} - \text{C.P.}$

$= \text{Rs } 285 - \text{Rs } 250 = \text{Rs } 35.$

Now, $\text{Gain \%} = \left(\frac{\text{Gain}}{\text{C.P.}} \times 100\right)\%$

$\Rightarrow \quad \text{Gain \%} = \left(\frac{35}{250} \times 100\right)\% = 14\%$

Hence, Gain = Rs 35 and Gain % = 14%.

Example 2 Rishi bought a wrist watch for Rs 2200 and sold it for Rs 1980. Find has loss and loss percent.

Solution We have,

C.P. of watch = Rs 2200

S.P. of watch = Rs 1980

Since S.P. < C.P. So, there is loss given by

Loss $= \text{C.P.} - \text{S.P.}$

$= \text{Rs } 2200 - \text{Rs } 1980 = \text{Rs } 220$

Now, $\text{Loss \%} = \left(\frac{\text{Loss}}{\text{C.P.}} \times 100\right)\% = \left(\frac{220}{2200} \times 100\right)\% = 10\%$

Hence, Loss = Rs 220 and Loss% = 10%.

Example 3 If the cost price of 18 mangoes is the same as the selling price of 16 mangoes, find the gain percent.

Solution Let the cost price of each mango be Re 1. Then,

C.P. of 16 mangoes = Rs 16

S.P. of 16 mangoes = Rs 18

$\therefore$ Gain $= \text{S.P.} - \text{C.P.} = \text{Rs } (18 - 16) = \text{Rs } 2.$

Now, $\text{Gain \%} = \left(\frac{\text{Gain}}{\text{C.P.}} \times 100\right)\%$

$\Rightarrow \quad \text{Gain \%} = \left(\frac{2}{16} \times 100\right)\% = 12.5\%$

Hence, Gain % = 12.5%

Example 4 If the C.P. of 25 chairs is equal to the S.P. of 30 chairs, find the loss percent.

Solution Let the C.P. of each chair be Re 1. Then,

C.P. of 30 chairs = Rs 30

It is given that,

S.P. of 30 chairs = C.P. of 25 chairs

$\Rightarrow$ S.P. of 30 chairs = Rs 25

Clearly, S.P. < C.P. So, there is loss given by

Loss $= \text{C.P.} - \text{S.P.} = \text{Rs } (30 - 25) = \text{Rs } 5$

Now, $\text{Loss \%} = \left(\frac{\text{Loss}}{\text{C.P.}} \times 100\right)\% = \left(\frac{5}{30} \times 100\right)\% = 16\frac{2}{3}\%$

Hence, $\text{Loss \%} = 16\frac{2}{3}\%$

Example 5 A girl buys lemons at 4 for Rs 3 and sells them at 5 for Rs 4. How much percent loss or gain does she make?

Solution It is given that the girl buys lemons at 4 for Rs 3 and sells them at 5 for Rs 4. Therefore, to avoid fractions assume that the girl buys and sells 4 times 5 = 20 lemons.

We have,

C.P. of 4 lemons = Rs 3

$\therefore$ C.P. of 1 lemon = Rs $\frac{3}{4}$

$\therefore$ C.P. of 20 lemons = Rs $\left(\frac{3}{4}\times 20\right)$ = Rs 15

S.P. of 5 lemons = Rs 4

$\therefore$ S.P. of 1 lemon = Rs $\frac{4}{5}$

$\therefore$ S.P. of 20 lemons = Rs $\left(\frac{4}{5}\times 20\right)$ = Rs 16

Clearly, S.P. > C.P.

$\therefore$ Gain = S.P. – C.P. = Rs (16 – 15) = Re 1

Hence, Gain % $=\left(\frac{\text{Gain}}{\text{C.P.}}\times 100\right)\% = \left(\frac{1}{15}\times 100\right)\% = 6\frac{2}{3}\%$

Example 6 A person sells an article for Rs 550, gaining $\frac{1}{10}$ of its C.P. Find gain percent.

Solution Let the C.P. of the article be Rs x. Then,

Gain $=\frac{1}{10}$ of Rs x = Rs $\frac{x}{10}$

Now, Gain % $=\left(\frac{\text{Gain}}{\text{C.P.}}\times 100\right)\%$

$\Rightarrow$ Gain % $=\left(\frac{\frac{x}{10}}{x}\times 100\right)\% = 10\%$

Example 7 200 kg of sugar was purchased at the rate of Rs 15 per kg and sold at a profit of 5%. Compute the profit and the selling price per kg.

Solution We have,

C.P. of 200 kg of sugar = Rs (200 × 15) Rs 3000

Profit % = 5%

$\therefore$ Profit = 5% of Rs 3000

$\Rightarrow$ Profit = Rs $\left(\frac{5}{100}\times 3000\right)$

$\Rightarrow$ Profit = Rs 150

Now, S.P. = C.P. + Profit

$\Rightarrow$ S.P. = Rs (3000 + 150) = Rs 3150

Hence, S.P. per kg = Rs $\left(\frac{3150}{200}\right)$ = Rs 15.75

Aliter

We have,

C.P. = Rs 3000 and Gain = 5%

$$\therefore \quad S.P. = \left(\frac{100 + \text{Gain}\,\%}{100}\right) \times C.P.$$

$$\Rightarrow \quad S.P. = Rs \left(\frac{100+5}{100}\right) \times 3000 = Rs\ 3150$$

Hence, S.P. per kg = Rs $\left(\frac{3150}{200}\right)$ = Rs 15.75

Example 8 A man buys a plot of agricultural land for Rs 300000. He sells one-third at a loss of 20% and two-fifths at a gain of 25%. At what price must he sell the remaining land so as to make an overall profit of 10%?

Solution We have,

C.P. of entire land = Rs 300000

Proposed overall profit = 10% of Rs 300000

$$= Rs \left(\frac{10}{100} \times 300000\right) = Rs\ 30000$$

$\therefore$ Proposed S.P. = Rs (300000 + 30000) = Rs 330000

Now, C.P. of one-third land = $\frac{1}{3}$ of Rs 300000 = Rs 100000

Loss = 20% of Rs 100000 = Rs $\left(\frac{20}{100} \times 100000\right)$ = Rs 20000

$\therefore$ S.P. = C.P. – Loss = Rs (100000 – 20000) = Rs 80,000

C.P. of two-fifths land = $\frac{2}{5}$ of Rs 300000 = Rs 120000

Gain = 25% of Rs 120000 = Rs $\left(\frac{25}{100} \times 120000\right)$ = Rs 30000

$\therefore$ S.P. = C.P. + Gain = Rs (120000 + 30000) = Rs 150000

Total S.P. of two parts of the land sold = Rs (80000 + 150000)

= 230000

$\therefore$ S.P. of the remaining land = Rs (330000 – 230000) = Rs 100000.

Example 9 A dishonest dealer professes to sell his goods at cost price, but he uses a weight of 960 grams for 1 kg. Find his gain percent.

Solution Let the C.P. of 1 gram of goods be Re 1. Then,

C.P. of 960 grams = Rs 960

S.P. of 960 grams = C.P. of 1 kg = Rs 1000

$\therefore$ Gain = S.P. – C.P. = Rs (1000 – 960) = Rs 40

Hence, Gain % $= \left(\frac{\text{Gain}}{\text{C.P}} \times 100\right)\% = \left(\frac{40}{960} \times 100\right)\% = 4\frac{1}{6}\%$

Example 10 A man purchases two fans for Rs 2160. By selling one fan at a profit of 15% and the other at a loss of 9% he neither gains nor losses in the whole transaction. Find the cost price of each fan.

Solution Let the cost price of first fan be Rs x. Then,

Cost price of second fan = Rs $(2160 - x)$

It is given that

In the whole transaction, the man neither gains nor loses.

$\therefore$ Gain on the sale of first fan = Loss in the sale of second fan

$\Rightarrow$ 15% of Rs x = 9% of Rs $(2160 - x)$

$\Rightarrow \frac{15}{100} \times x = \frac{9}{100} \times (2160 - x)$

$\Rightarrow 15x = 9(2160 - x)$

$\Rightarrow 5x = 3(2160 - x)$ [Dividing both sides by 3]

$\Rightarrow 5x = 6480 - 3x$

$\Rightarrow 5x + 3x = 6480 \Rightarrow 8x = 6480 \Rightarrow x = \frac{6480}{8} \Rightarrow x = 810$

$\therefore$ C.P. of first fan = Rs 810

C.P. of second fan = Rs $(2160 - x)$ = Rs $(2160 - 810)$ = Rs 1350.

Example 11 A man bought two T.V. sets for Rs 42500. He sold one at a loss of 10% and other at a profit of 10%. If the selling price of each T.V. set is same, determine the C.P. of each set.

Solution Let the C.P. of first T.V. set be Rs x. Then,

C.P. of second T.V. set = Rs $(42500 - x)$

Loss on first T.V. set = 10% of Rs x = Rs $\left(\frac{10}{100} \times x\right)$ = Rs $\frac{x}{10}$

S.P. of first T.V. set = Rs $\left(x - \frac{x}{10}\right)$ = Rs $\frac{9x}{10}$.

Gain on second T.V. set = 10% of Rs $(42500 - x)$

$= \text{Rs}\left\{\frac{10}{100} \times (42500 - x)\right\}$

$= \text{Rs}\left\{\frac{42500 - x}{10}\right\}$

$\therefore$ S.P. of second T.V. set = C.P. + Gain

$= \text{Rs}\,(42500 - x) + \text{Rs}\,\frac{42500 - x}{10}$

$= \text{Rs}\,(42500 - x) + \left(1 + \frac{1}{10}\right)$

$= \text{Rs}\,(42500 - x) + \frac{11}{10}$

It is given that S.P. of each T.V. set is same.

$$\therefore \quad \frac{9x}{10} = (42500 - x) \times \frac{11}{10}$$

$$\Rightarrow \quad 9x = (42500 - x) \times 11$$

$$\Rightarrow \quad 9x = 42500 \times 11 - 11x$$

$$\Rightarrow \quad 11x + 9x = 42500 \times 11$$

$$\Rightarrow \quad 20x = 42500 \times 11$$

$$\Rightarrow \quad x = \frac{42500 \times 11}{20} = 2125 \times 11 = 23375$$

Hence, C.P. of first T.V. set = Rs 23375

C.P. of second T.V. set = Rs (42500 − 23375) = Rs 19125

Example 12 If a man were to sell his hand-cart for Rs 720, he would lose 25%. What must he sell it for to gain 25% ?

Solution We have,

S.P. of the Cart = 720

Loss = 25%

$$\therefore \quad \text{C.P.} = \left(\frac{100}{100 - \text{Loss}} \times \text{S.P.}\right)$$

$$\Rightarrow \quad \text{C.P.} = \text{Rs}\left(\frac{100}{100 - 25} \times 720\right) = \text{Rs}\left(\frac{4}{3} \times 720\right) = \text{Rs } 960$$

Thus, C.P. of the cart = Rs 960.

Desired gain = 25%

$$\therefore \quad \text{S.P.} = \frac{100 + \text{Gain}\,\%}{100} \times \text{C.P.}$$

$$\Rightarrow \quad \text{S.P.} = \text{Rs}\left(\frac{100 + 25}{100} \times 960\right) = \text{Rs}\left(\frac{125}{100} \times 960\right) = \text{Rs}\left(\frac{5}{4} \times 960\right) = \text{Rs } 1200$$

Example 13 A man sold two articles at Rs 25920 each. These were sold at 8% gain and 4% loss respectively. Find the gain or loss percent in the whole transaction.

Solution *For first article:*

We have,

S.P. = 25920, Gain % = 8%

$$\therefore \quad \text{C.P.} = \left(\frac{100}{100 + \text{Gain}\,\%}\right) \times \text{S.P.}$$

$$\Rightarrow \quad \text{C.P.} = \text{Rs}\left(\frac{100}{100 + 8} \times 25920\right) = \text{Rs}\left(\frac{100}{108} \times 25920\right) = \text{Rs } 24000$$

For second article:

We have,

S.P. = Rs 25920, Loss % = 4%

$$\therefore \quad \text{C.P.} = \left(\frac{100}{100 - \text{loss}}\right) \times \text{S.P.}$$

$$\Rightarrow \quad \text{C.P.} = \text{Rs}\left(\frac{100}{100 - 4} \times 25920\right) = \text{Rs}\left(\frac{100}{96} \times 25920\right) = \text{Rs } 27000.$$

Now, total C.P. of two articles = Rs (24000 + 27000) = Rs 51000

Total S.P. of two articles = Rs (25920 + 25920) = Rs 51840

Clearly, S.P. > C.P.

Gain = S.P. – C.P. = Rs (51840 – 51000) = Rs 840

Hence, Gain % on the whole transaction = $\left(\frac{840}{51000}\times 100\right)\% = \frac{28}{17}\% = 1\frac{11}{17}\%$

Example 14 A toy was sold at a gain of 12%. Had it been sold for Rs 33 more, the gain would have been 14%. Find the cost price of the toy?

Solution Let the C.P. of the toy be Rs x.

Gain % = 12%

$\therefore$ Gain = 12% of Rs x = Rs $\frac{12x}{100}$ = Rs $\frac{3x}{25}$

$\therefore$ S.P. = C.P. + Gain = Rs $\left(x+\frac{3x}{25}\right)$ = Rs $\frac{28x}{25}$

New Gain % = 14%

$\therefore$ New Gain = 14% of Rs x = Rs $\frac{14x}{100}$ = Rs $\frac{7x}{50}$

$\therefore$ New S.P. = Rs $\left(x+\frac{7x}{50}\right)$ = Rs $\frac{57x}{50}$

It is given that difference between new S.P. and the original S.P. is Rs 33.

$$\therefore \quad \frac{57x}{50}-\frac{28x}{25}=33$$

$$\Rightarrow \quad \frac{57x-56x}{50}=33 \Rightarrow \frac{x}{50}=33 \Rightarrow x=33\times 50 \Rightarrow x=1650$$

Hence, the C.P. of the toy is Rs 1650

Example 15 A man bought an article and sold it at a gain of 10%. If he had bought it at 20% less and sold it for Rs 10 more, he would have made a profit of 40%. Find the C.P. of the article?

Solution Let the C.P. of the article be Rs x.

Gain = 10% of Rs x = Rs $\left(\frac{10}{100}\times x\right)$ = Rs $\frac{x}{10}$

$\therefore$ Original S.P. = Rs $\left(x+\frac{x}{10}\right)$ = Rs $\frac{11x}{10}$

New C.P. = {Rs x – 20% of Rs x} = Rs $\left(x-\frac{20x}{100}\right)$ = Rs $\frac{4x}{5}$

Gain percent = 40%

$\therefore$ New S.P. $=\frac{100+\text{Gain}\,\%}{100}\times\text{C.P.}$ = Rs $\left(\frac{100+40}{100}\times\frac{4x}{5}\right)$ = Rs $\frac{28x}{25}$

It is given that new S.P. is Rs 10 more than the original S.P

$\therefore$ New S.P. – Original S.P. = 10

$$\Rightarrow \frac{28x}{25} - \frac{11x}{10} = 10$$

$$\Rightarrow \frac{56x - 55x}{50} = 10 \Rightarrow x = 500$$

Hence, C.P. = Rs 500

Example 16 By selling a towel for Rs 126.90, a draper loses 6%. For how much should he sell the towel to gain 4%?

Solution We have,

S.P. of the towel = Rs126.90, Loss % = 6%

$$\therefore \text{ C.P. of the towel } = \left(\frac{100}{100 - \text{Loss\%}} \times \text{S.P.}\right)$$

$$= \left(\frac{100}{100-6} \times 126.90\right)$$

$$= \left(\frac{100}{94} \times 126.90\right) = \text{Rs}135$$

Now, C.P. of the towel = Rs135 and, Required gain% = 4%

$$\therefore \text{ S.P. } = \frac{100 + \text{Gain}}{100} \times \text{C.P.}$$

$$\Rightarrow \text{ S.P. } = \text{Rs}\left(\frac{100+4}{100} \times 135\right) = \text{Rs}\left(\frac{104}{100} \times 135\right) = \text{Rs}140.40$$

Hence, the drapper should sell the towel for Rs 140.40

Example 17 A dealer buys 50 chairs for Rs 50,000 but 20 of them are damaged. He decides to sell each damaged one at three fourths the price of the normal one. What should this price be in order that he may make a profit of 35% on the whole transaction?

Solution We have,

C.P. of 50 chairs = Rs50000

Required Profit percent = 35%

$$\therefore \text{ Overall profit} = 35\% \text{ of Rs}50000 = \text{Rs}\left(\frac{35}{100} \times 50000\right) = \text{Rs}17500.$$

$\therefore$ Desired S.P. of 50 chairs = Rs(50000 + 17500) = Rs67500

Let the S.P. of one good chair be Rs x. Then, the S.P. of one damaged chair is Rs $\frac{3}{4}x$.

S.P. of 30 good chairs = Rs $30x$

$$\text{S.P. of 20 damaged chairs} = \text{Rs}\left(20 \times \frac{3}{4}x\right) = \text{Rs}15x$$

$\therefore$ S.P. of 50 chairs = Rs $30x$ + Rs $15x$ = Rs $45x$.

But, S.P. of 50 chairs is Rs 67500.

$$\therefore 45x = 67500 \Rightarrow x = \frac{67500}{45} = 1500$$

$\therefore$ S.P. of a good chair = Rs 1500

$$\text{S.P. of a damaged chair} = \text{Rs}\left(\frac{3}{4} \times 1500\right) = \text{Rs}1125$$

Example 18 By selling a stool for Rs 67.50, a carpenter loses 10%. How much percent would he gain or lose by selling it for Rs 82.50?

Solution We have,

$$\text{S.P.} = \text{Rs}67.50 \text{ and Loss\%} = 10$$

$$\therefore \quad \text{C.P.} = \frac{100}{100-\text{Loss\%}} \times \text{S.P.}$$

$$\Rightarrow \quad \text{C.P.} = \text{Rs}\left(\frac{100}{100-10} \times 67.50\right) = \text{Rs}75$$

If S.P. = Rs82.50, then S.P. > C.P. So, there is gain given by

$$\text{Gain} = \text{S.P.} - \text{C.P.} = \text{Rs}82.50 - \text{Rs}75 = \text{Rs}7.50$$

$$\therefore \quad \text{Gain \%} = \left(\frac{\text{Gain}}{\text{C.P.}} \times 100\right) = \frac{7.50}{75} \times 100 = 10\%$$

Example 19 Three items are purchased at Rs 450 each. One of them is sold at a loss of 10%. At what price should the other two be sold so as to gain 20% on the whole transaction? What is the gain % on these two items?

Solution We have,

$$\text{C.P. of one item} = \text{Rs}450$$

$$\therefore \quad \text{S.P. of three items} = \text{Rs}(3 \times 450) = \text{Rs}1350$$

$$\text{Gain on the whole transaction} = 20\% \text{ of S.P.}$$

$$= 20\% \text{ of Rs}1350$$

$$= \text{Rs}\left(\frac{20}{100} \times 1350\right) = \text{Rs } 270$$

$$\therefore \quad \text{S.P. of three items} = \text{C.P.} + \text{Gain} = \text{Rs}1350 + \text{Rs}270 = \text{Rs}1620$$

It is given that first item is sold at a loss of 10%.

$$\therefore \quad \text{Loss on selling first item} = 10\% \text{ of Rs}450$$

$$= \text{Rs}\left(\frac{10}{100} \times 450\right) = \text{Rs } 45$$

$$\therefore \quad \text{S.P. of first item} = \text{C.P.} - \text{Loss} = \text{Rs}450 - \text{Rs}45 - \text{Rs}405$$

S.P. of three items is Rs 1620 and the S.P. of first item is Rs 405

$$\therefore \quad \text{S.P. of the remaining two items} = \text{Rs}1620 - \text{Rs } 405 = \text{Rs}1215$$

Thus, the other two items should be sold at Rs 1215

$$\text{C.P. of the remaining two items} = \text{Rs}(2 \times 450) = \text{Rs } 900$$

$$\therefore \quad \text{Gain on the remaining two items} = \text{S.P.} - \text{C.P.}$$

$$= \text{Rs}1215 - \text{Rs}900 = \text{Rs}315.$$

$$\therefore \quad \text{Gain \% on the remaining two items} = \left(\frac{315}{900} \times 100\right)\% = 35\%$$

Example 20 By reducing the selling price of an article by Rs 50, a gain of 5% turns into a loss of 5%. Find the original selling price of the article.

Solution Let the original selling price of the article be Rs x. It is given that on this S.P. there is a gain of 5%.

$$\therefore \quad \text{C.P.} = \left(\frac{100}{100+5}\right)x = \frac{20x}{21} \qquad \left[\text{Using: C.P.} = \frac{100}{100+\text{Gain\%}} \times \text{S.P.}\right] \quad \ldots \text{(i)}$$

When S.P. is reduced by Rs 50, there is loss of 5%.

$$\therefore \quad \text{C.P.} = \frac{100}{100-5}\times(x-50) = \frac{20}{19}(x-50) \left[\text{Using: C.P.} = \frac{100}{100-\text{Loss}\,\%}\times\text{S.P.}\right] \quad \ldots \text{(ii)}$$

From (i) and (ii), we get

$$\frac{20x}{21} = \frac{20}{19}(x-50)$$

$$\Rightarrow \frac{x}{21} = \frac{1}{19}(x-50) \quad \text{[Dividing both sides by 20]}$$

$$\Rightarrow 19x = 21(x-50) \quad \text{[Using cross multiplication]}$$

$$\Rightarrow 19x = 21x - 1050$$

$$\Rightarrow 21x - 19x = 1050$$

$$\Rightarrow 2x = 1050 \Rightarrow x = \frac{1050}{2} = 525$$

Hence, the original S.P. of the article is Rs 525

EXERCISE 13.1

1. A student buys a pen for Rs 90 and sells it for Rs 100. Find his gain and gain percent.
2. Rekha bought a saree for Rs 1240 and sold it for Rs 1147. Find her loss and loss percent.
3. A boy buys 9 apples for Rs 9.60 and sells them at 11 for Rs 12. Find his gain or loss percent.
4. The cost price of 10 articles is equal to the selling price of 9 articles. Find the profit percent.
5. A retailer buys a radio for Rs 225. His overhead expenses are Rs 15. If he sells the radio for Rs 300, determine his profit percent.
6. A retailer buys a cooler for Rs 1200 and overhead expenses on it are Rs 40. If he sells the cooler for Rs 1550, determine his profit percent.
7. A dealer buys a wristwatch for Rs 225 and spends Rs 15 on its repairs. If he sells the same for Rs 300, find his profit percent.
8. Ramesh bought two boxes for Rs 1300. He sold one box at a profit of 20% and the other box at a loss of 12%. If the selling price of both boxes is the same, find the cost price of each box.
9. If the selling price of 10 pens is equal to cost price of 14 pens, find the gain percent.
10. If the cost price of 18 chairs be equal to selling price of 16 chairs, find the gain or loss percent.
11. If the selling price of 18 oranges is equal to the cost price of 16 oranges, find the loss percent.
12. Ravish sold his motorcycle to Vineet at a loss of 28%. Vineet spent Rs 1680 on its repairs and sold the motor cycle to Rahul for Rs 35910, thereby making a profit of 12.5%, find the cost price of the motor cycle for Ravish.

13. By selling a book for Rs 258, a bookseller gains 20%. For how much should he sell it to gain 30%?
14. A defective briefcase costing Rs 800 is being sold at a loss of 8%. If the price is further reduced by 5%, find its selling price.
15. By selling 90 ball pens for Rs 160 a person loses 20%. How many ball pens should be sold for Rs 96 so as to have a profit of 20%?
16. A man sells an article at a profit of 25%. If he had bought it at 20% less and sold it for Rs 36.75 less, he would have gained 30%. Find the cost price of the article.
17. A dishonest shopkeeper professes to sell pulses at his cost price but uses a false weight of 950 gm for each kilogram. Find his gain percent.
18. A dealer bought two tables for Rs 3120. He sold one of them at a loss of 15% and other at a gain of 36%. Then, he found that each table was sold for the same price. Find the cost price of each table.
19. Mariam bought two fans for Rs 3605. She sold one at a profit of 15% and the other at a loss of 9%. If Mariam obtained the same amount for each fan, find the cost price of each fan.
20. Some toffees are bought at the rate of 11 for Rs 10 and the same number at the rate of 9 for Rs 10. If the whole lot is sold at one rupee per toffee, find the gain or loss percent on the whole transaction.
21. A tricycle is sold at a gain of 16%. Had it been sold for Rs 100 more, the gain would have been 20%. Find the C.P. of the tricycle.
22. Shabana bought 16 dozen ball bens and sold them at a loss equal to S.P. of 8 ball pens. Find
    (i) her loss percent
    (ii) S.P. of 1 dozen ball pens, if she purchased these 16 dozen ball pens for Rs 576.
23. The difference between two selling prices of a shirt at profits of 4% and 5% is Rs 6. Find
    (i) C.P. of the shirt (ii) the two selling prices of the shirt
24. Toshiba bought 100 hens for Rs 8000 and sold 20 of these at a gain of 5%. At what gain percent she must sell the remaining hens so as to gain 20% on the whole?

ANSWERS

1. Gain = Rs 10, Gain % = $11\frac{1}{9}\%$ 2. Loss = Rs 93, Loss % = 7.5% 3. Gain = $2\frac{3}{11}\%$
4. $11\frac{1}{9}\%$ 5. 25% 6. 25% 7. 25% 8. Rs 550, Rs 750
9. 40% 10. Gain 12.5% 11. $11\frac{1}{9}\%$ 12. Rs 42000 13. Rs 279.50
14. Rs 699.20 15. 36 16. Rs 175 17. $5\frac{5}{19}\%$ 18. Rs 1920, Rs 1200
19. Rs 1592.50, Rs 2012.50 20. Loss 1% 21. Rs 2500 22. (i) 4% (ii) Rs 34.56
23. (i) Rs 600 (ii) Rs 624, Rs 630 24. 23.75%

HINTS TO SELECTED PROBLEMS

20. Let the number of toffees bought be LCM of 9 and 11 i.e.; 99.

C.P. of 99 toffees bought at the rate of 11 for Rs 10 $= \text{Rs}\left(\frac{99}{11}\times 10\right) = \text{Rs } 90$

C.P. of 99 toffees bought at the rate of 9 for Rs 10 $= \text{Rs}\left(\frac{99}{9}\times 10\right) = \text{Rs } 110$

$\therefore$ C.P. of 198 toffees $= \text{Rs}\,(90+110) = \text{Rs } 200$

S.P. of 198 toffees $= \text{Rs}\,(198\times 1) = \text{Rs } 198$

Since C.P. > S.P.

$\therefore$ Loss $= \text{C.P.} - \text{S.P.} = \text{Rs } 200 - \text{Rs } 198 = \text{Rs } 2$

Hence, Loss % $= \frac{\text{Loss}}{\text{C.P.}}\times 100 = \left(\frac{2}{200}\times 100\right)\% = 1\%$

21. Let the C.P. of the tricycle be Rs x. Then,

$$\text{S.P.} = \text{Rs}\left(\frac{100+16}{100}\right)x = \text{Rs}\,\frac{116}{100} \quad \text{... (i)}$$

If the gain is 20%, then

$$\text{S.P.} = \text{Rs}\left(\frac{100+10}{100}\right)x = \text{Rs}\,\frac{120}{100}x \quad \text{... (ii)}$$

It is given that S.P. in (ii) is Rs 100 more than S.P. in (i).

$$\therefore \quad \frac{120x}{100} = \frac{116x}{100} + 100$$

$$\Rightarrow \frac{120x}{100} - \frac{116x}{100} = 100 \Rightarrow \frac{4x}{100} = 100 \Rightarrow \frac{x}{25} = 100 \Rightarrow x = 2500$$

13.3 DISCOUNT

You might have seen while buying goods that on every article there is a price marked. This price is known as the *marked price* (M.P.) of the article. In order to clear the stocks or to increase sales, sometimes shopkeepers offer a certain percent of rebate on the marked price for cash payments. This rebate is known as discount. The customer or buyer pays the difference between the marked price and the discount. Thus,

$$\text{S.P.} = \text{Marked price} - \text{Discount} \quad \text{... (i)}$$

Also,

$$\text{Rate of Discount} = \text{Discount \%} = \frac{\text{Discount}}{\text{M.P.}}\times 100 \quad \text{... (ii)}$$

Now,

$$\text{S.P.} = \text{M.P.} - \text{Discount}$$

$$\Rightarrow \quad \text{S.P.} = \text{M.P.} - \frac{\text{Discount \%}\times\text{M.P.}}{100} \quad \left[\text{From (ii), Discount} = \frac{\text{M.P.}\times\text{Discount \%}}{100}\right]$$

$$\Rightarrow \quad \text{S.P.} = \text{M.P.}\left(1 - \frac{\text{Discount \%}}{100}\right)$$

$$\Rightarrow \quad \text{S.P.} = \text{M.P.}\left(\frac{100 - \text{Discount \%}}{100}\right) \quad \text{... (iii)}$$

$$\Rightarrow \quad M.P. = \frac{100 \times S.P.}{(100 - \text{Discount }\%)} \quad \ldots \text{(iv)}$$

Again,

$$S.P. = M.P.\left(\frac{100 - \text{Discount }\%}{100}\right)$$

$$\Rightarrow \quad S.P. = M.P. - \frac{M.P. \times \text{Discount }\%}{100}$$

$$\Rightarrow \quad \frac{M.P. \times \text{Discount }\%}{100} = M.P. - S.P.$$

$$\Rightarrow \quad \text{Discount }\% = \left(\frac{M.P. - S.P.}{M.P.}\right) \times 100$$

Remark 1 *Electric goods, electronic and other things which are manufactured in a factory are marked according to the price list supplied by the factory, at which the retailer is supposed to sell them. This price is known as the list price.*

Remark 2 *For books, the printed price is the marked price.*

NOTE: *It should be noted that discount is given on the marked price only.*

Following examples will illustrate the computation of discount, selling price etc.

ILLUSTRATIVE EXAMPLES

Example 1 Find S.P. if

(i) M.P. = Rs 650 and Discount = 10%

(ii) M.P. = Rs 5450 and Discount = 5%

Solution (i) We have,

M.P. = Rs 650, Discount = 10%

$\therefore$ Discount $= 10\%$ of Rs 650 $= \text{Rs}\left(\frac{10}{100} \times 650\right) = \text{Rs } 65$

Hence, S.P. $= M.P. - \text{Discount} = \text{Rs } 650 - \text{Rs } 65 = \text{Rs } 585$

Aliter We have,

$M.P. = \text{Rs } 650$, Discount % = 10

$$\therefore \quad S.P. = M.P. \times \frac{(100 - \text{Discount }\%)}{100}$$

$$\Rightarrow \quad S.P. = \text{Rs}\left\{650 \times \left(\frac{100 - 10}{100}\right)\right\} = \text{Rs } (65 \times 9) = \text{Rs } 585$$

(ii) We have, M.P. = Rs 5450, Discount = 5%

$\therefore$ Discount $= 5\%$ of Rs 5450 $= \text{Rs}\left(\frac{5}{100} \times 5450\right) = \text{Rs } 272.50$

Hence, S.P. $= M.P. - \text{Discount} = \text{Rs } 5450 - \text{Rs } 272.50 = \text{Rs } 5177.50$

Aliter We have,

$M.P. = \text{Rs } 5450$, Discount = 5%

$\therefore \quad S.P. = M.P. \times \left(\dfrac{100 - \text{Discount}}{100} \right)$

$\Rightarrow \quad S.P. = \text{Rs} \left\{ 5450 \times \left(\dfrac{100 - 5}{100} \right) \right\} = \text{Rs} \left\{ 545 \times \dfrac{95}{10} \right\} = \text{Rs } 5177.50.$

Example 2 Find the M. P, if

(i) S.P. = Rs 3430 and, Discount = 2% (ii) S.P. = Rs 9250 and, Discount = $7\frac{1}{2}\%$

Solution (i) Let the M.P. be Rs 100

We have, Discount $= 2\% = 2\%$ of Rs 100 = Rs 2

$\therefore \quad S.P. = M.P. - \text{Discount} = \text{Rs } 100 - \text{Rs } 2 = \text{Rs } 98$

Now,

When S.P. is Rs 98, M.P. = Rs 100

When S.P. is Re 1, M.P. $= \text{Rs } \dfrac{100}{98}$

When S.P. is 3430, M.P. $= \text{Rs} \left(\dfrac{100}{98} \times 3430 \right) = \text{Rs } 3500$

Aliter We have,

S.P. = Rs 3430, Discount % = 2

$\therefore \quad M.P. = \dfrac{100 \times S.P.}{100 - \text{Discount } \%}$

$\Rightarrow \quad M.P. = \text{Rs} \left\{ \dfrac{100 \times 3430}{100 - 2} \right\} = \text{Rs } 3500$

(ii) Let the M.P. be Rs 100

We have,

Discount $= 7\frac{1}{2}\% = 7\frac{1}{2}\%$ of Rs 100 = Rs 7.5

$\therefore \quad S.P. = M.P. - \text{Discount} = \text{Rs } 100 - \text{Rs } 7.5 = \text{Rs } 92.5$

Now,

When S.P. is Rs 92.5, M.P. = Rs 100

When S.P. is Re 1, M.P. $= \text{Rs } \dfrac{100}{92.5}$

When S.P. is Rs 9250, M.P. $= \text{Rs} \left(\dfrac{100}{92.5} \times 9250 \right) = \text{Rs } 10000$

Example 3 Find discount in percent when

(i) M.P. = Rs 625 and S.P. = Rs 562.50

(ii) M.P. = Rs 1600 and S.P. = Rs 1180

Solution (i) We have,

M.P. = Rs 625 and S.P. = Rs 562.50

$\therefore$ Discount $= \text{M.P.} - \text{S.P.} = \text{Rs } 625 - \text{Rs } 562.50 = \text{Rs } 62.50$

Now,

When M.P. is Rs 625, discount = Rs 62.50

When M.P. is Re 1, discount $= \text{Re } \frac{62.50}{625}$

When M.P. is Rs 100, discount $= \text{Rs}\left(\frac{62.50}{625} \times 100\right) = \text{Rs } 10$

Hence, discount % = 10

<u>Aliter</u> We have,

M.P. = Rs 625 and S.P. = Rs 562.50

$\therefore$ Discount % $= \left(\frac{\text{M.P.} - \text{S.P.}}{\text{M.P.}}\right) \times 100$

$= \left(\frac{625 - 562.50}{625}\right) \times 100 = \frac{100 \times 62.50}{625} = 10$

Hence, discount % = 10

(ii) We have, M.P. = Rs 1600 and S.P. = Rs 1180

$\therefore$ Discount $= \text{M.P.} - \text{S.P.} = \text{Rs } 1600 - \text{Rs } 1180 = \text{Rs } 420$

Now,

When M.P. is Rs 1600, discount = Rs 420

When M.P. is Re 1, discount $= \text{Re } \frac{420}{1600}$

When M.P. is Rs 100, discount $= \text{Rs}\left(\frac{420}{1600} \times 100\right) = \text{Rs } 26.25$

Hence, discount = 26.25%

<u>Aliter</u> We have,

M.P. = Rs 1600 and S.P. = Rs 1180

$\therefore$ Discount % $= \left(\frac{\text{M.P.} - \text{S.P.}}{\text{M.P.}}\right) \times 100$

$\Rightarrow$ Discount % $= \left(\frac{1600 - 1180}{1600}\right) \times 100 = \frac{100 \times 420}{1600} = 26.25$

Example 4 At a clearance sale, all goods are on sale at 45% discount. If I buy a skirt marked Rs 600, how much would I need to pay ?

Solution We have,

M.P. = Rs 600, Discount = 45%

$\therefore$ Discount = 45% of Rs 600 $= \left(\text{Rs } \frac{45}{100} \times 100\right) = \text{Rs } 270$

$\therefore$ S.P. = M.P. − Discount

$\Rightarrow$ S.P. = Rs 600 − Rs 270 = Rs 330

Thus, the amount I need to pay is Rs 330.

Aliter We have,

$$\text{M.P.} = \text{Rs } 600, \text{Discount } \% = 45$$

$$\therefore \quad \text{S.P.} = \text{M.P.} \times \left(\frac{100 - \text{Discount } \%}{100}\right)$$

$$\Rightarrow \quad \text{S.P.} = \text{Rs}\left\{600 \times \left(\frac{100-45}{100}\right)\right\} = \text{Rs } 330$$

Example 5 After allowing a discount of 12% on the marked price of an article, it is sold for Rs 880. Find its marked price.

Solution Let the marked price be Rs 100.

Discount $= 12\%$ of Marked price $= 12\%$ of Rs 100 = Rs 12

$\therefore$ S.P. = M.P. – Discount = Rs 100 – Rs 12 = Rs 88

Now,

When S.P. is Rs 88, M.P. = Rs 100

When S.P. is Re 1, M.P. $= \text{Rs } \frac{100}{88}$

When S.P. is Rs 880, M.P. $= \text{Rs}\left(\frac{100}{88} \times 880\right) = \text{Rs } 1000$

Hence, the marked price of the article is Rs 1000

Aliter We have,

$$\text{S.P.} = \text{Rs } 880, \text{Discount} = 12\%$$

$$\therefore \quad \text{M.P.} = \frac{100 \times \text{S.P.}}{100 - \text{Discount } \%}$$

$$\Rightarrow \quad \text{M.P.} = \text{Rs}\left\{\frac{100 \times 880}{100-12}\right\} = \text{Rs}\left(\frac{88000}{88}\right) = \text{Rs } 1000$$

Example 6 A shopkeeper offers his customers 10% discount and still makes a profit of 26%. What is the actual cost to him of an article marked Rs 280?

Solution We have,

Marked price = Rs 280, Discount = 10%

$$\therefore \quad \text{S.P.} = \text{MP} \times \left(\frac{100 - \text{Discount } \%}{100}\right)$$

$$\Rightarrow \quad \text{S.P.} = \text{Rs}\left\{280 \times \left(\frac{100-10}{100}\right)\right\} = \text{Rs}\left\{\frac{280 \times 90}{100}\right\} = \text{Rs } 252$$

Now, S.P. = Rs 252 and Gain = 26%

$$\therefore \quad \text{C.P.} = \frac{100}{100 + \text{Gain } \%} \times \text{S.P.}$$

$$\Rightarrow \quad \text{C.P.} = \text{Rs}\left(\frac{100}{100+26} \times 252\right) = \text{Rs}\left(\frac{100}{126} \times 252\right) = \text{Rs } 200$$

Hence, the actual cost of the article is Rs 200

Example 7 A shopkeeper marks his goods at such a price that after allowing a discount of 12.5% for cash payment, he still makes a profit of 10%. Find the marked price of an article which costs him Rs 245.

Solution We have,

C.P. of the article = Rs 245, Gain = 10%

$$\therefore \quad \text{S.P.} = \frac{100 + \text{Gain }\%}{100} \times \text{C.P.}$$

$$\Rightarrow \quad \text{S.P.} = \text{Rs}\left(\frac{100+10}{100} \times 245\right) = \text{Rs}\left(\frac{110}{100} \times 245\right) = \text{Rs } 269.50$$

Let the marked price be Rs 100. Then,

Discount allowed = 12.5% of M.P. = Rs 12.5

∴ S.P. of the article = M.P. – Discount = Rs 100 – Rs 12.5 = Rs 87.5

Thus,

When S.P. is Rs 87.5, M.P. = Rs 100

When S.P. is Re 1, M.P. = $\text{Rs}\dfrac{100}{87.5}$

When S.P. is Rs 269.50, M.P. = $\text{Rs}\left(\dfrac{100}{87.5} \times 269.50\right) = \text{Rs } 308$

Hence, marked price of the article is Rs 308

<u>Aliter</u> We have,

C.P. = Rs 245 and Gain % = 10

$$\therefore \quad \text{S.P.} = \left(\frac{100 + \text{Gain }\%}{100}\right) \times \text{C.P.}$$

$$\Rightarrow \quad \text{S.P.} = \text{Rs}\left\{\frac{100+10}{100} \times 245\right\} = \text{Rs}\left(\frac{110}{100} \times 245\right) = \text{Rs } 269.50$$

Now,

S.P. = Rs 269.50, Discount % = 12.5

$$\therefore \quad \text{M.P.} = \frac{100 \times \text{S.P.}}{100 - \text{Discount }\%}$$

$$\Rightarrow \quad \text{M.P.} = \text{Rs}\left\{\frac{100 \times 269.50}{100 - 12.5}\right\} = \text{Rs}\left(\frac{269.50}{87.5}\right) = \text{Rs } 308$$

Example 8 A dealer buys an article for Rs 380. At what price must he mark it so that after allowing a discount of 5%, he still makes a profit of 25%?

Solution We have, C.P. of the article = 380, Gain = 25%

$$\therefore \quad \text{S.P. of the article} = \left(\frac{100 + \text{Gain }\%}{100} \times \text{C.P.}\right)$$

$$\Rightarrow \quad \text{S.P. of the article} = \text{Rs}\left(\frac{100+25}{100} \times 380\right) = \text{Rs}\left(\frac{125}{100} \times 380\right) = \text{Rs } 475$$

Now, suppose the dealer marks Rs 100 as the price of the article.

He allows 5% discount on it.

$\therefore$ Discount = Rs 5

$\therefore$ S.P. = M.P. − Discount = Rs 100 − Rs 5 = Rs 95

Thus,

If S.P. is Rs 95, then M.P. = Rs 100

If S.P. is Re 1, then M.P. = Rs $\frac{100}{95}$

If S.P. is Rs 475, then M.P. = Rs $\left(\frac{100}{95}\times 475\right)$ = Rs 500

Aliter We have,

C.P. = Rs 380 and Gain % = 25

$$\therefore \quad \text{S.P.} = \left(\frac{100+\text{Gain }\%}{100}\times \text{C.P.}\right)$$

$$\Rightarrow \quad \text{S.P.} = \text{Rs}\left\{\frac{100+25}{100}\times 380\right\} = \text{Rs}\left(\frac{125}{100}\times 380\right) = \text{Rs } 475$$

Now, S.P. = Rs 475, Discount % = 5

$$\therefore \quad \text{M.P.} = \frac{100\times \text{S.P.}}{100-\text{Discount }\%}$$

$$\Rightarrow \quad \text{M.P.} = \text{Rs}\left\{\frac{100\times 475}{100-5}\right\} = \text{Rs}\left(\frac{47500}{95}\right) = \text{Rs } 500$$

Example 9 A tradesman allows a discount of 15% on the written price. How much above the cost price must he mark his goods to make a profit of 19%?

Solution Let the C.P. be Rs 100

We have, Gain = 19% of C.P. = Rs 19

$\therefore$ S.P. = C.P. + Gain = Rs 100 + Rs 19 = Rs 119

The trader allows a discount of 15%. This means that when marked price is Rs 100, then S.P. is Rs 85.

Now,

If Rs 85 is the S.P., then marked price = Rs 100

If Re 1 is the S.P., then marked price = Rs $\frac{100}{85}$

If Rs 119 is the S.P. , then marked price = Rs $\left(\frac{100}{85}\times 119\right)$ = Rs 140

Hence, the trader must mark his goods 40% above the cost price.

Aliter Let C.P. be Rs x. Then,

$$\text{S.P.} = \frac{100+\text{Gain }\%}{100}\times \text{C.P.}$$

$$\Rightarrow \quad \text{S.P.} = \text{Rs}\left(\frac{100+19}{100}\times x\right) \qquad [\because \text{Gain} = 19\%]$$

$\Rightarrow \quad \text{S.P.} = \text{Rs}\,\frac{119}{100}\times x$

Now,

$\text{S.P.} = \text{Rs}\,\frac{119}{100}x$ and Discount % = 15

$\therefore \quad \text{M.P.} = \frac{100\times\text{S.P.}}{(100-\text{Discount }\%)}$

$\Rightarrow \quad \text{M.P.} = \text{Rs}\left(\frac{100\times\frac{119}{100}x}{100-15}\right) = \text{Rs}\,\frac{119}{85}x = \text{Rs}\,\frac{7}{5}x$

$\therefore \quad$ Required difference $= \text{M.P.} - \text{C.P.} = \text{Rs}\left(\frac{7x}{5}-x\right) = \text{Rs}\,\frac{2x}{5}$

$\Rightarrow \quad \text{Difference }\% = \left(\frac{\frac{2x}{5}}{x}\times 100\right) = 40$

Hence, the trader must mark his goods 40% above the cost price.

Example 10 I mark up the computers I am selling by 20% and sell them at a discount of 15%. What is my net gain percent?

Solution Let the cost price be Rs 100. Then,

Marked price $= 20\%$ more than the C.P.

$= \text{C.P.} + 20\%\text{ of C.P.} = \text{Rs }100 + \text{Rs }20 = \text{Rs }120$

Discount $= 15\%$ of M.P. $= 15\%$ of Rs 120

$\therefore \quad$ Net discount $= \text{Rs}\left(\frac{15}{100}\times 120\right) = \text{Rs }18$

$\therefore \quad \text{S.P.} = \text{M.P.} - \text{Discount} = \text{Rs }120 - \text{Rs }18 = \text{Rs }102$

Now,

Profit $= \text{S.P.} - \text{C.P.} = \text{Rs }102 - \text{Rs }100 = \text{Rs }2$

Hence, Gain % $= \left(\frac{2}{100}\times 100\right)\% = 2\%$

Aliter Let C.P. be Rs x. Then,

$\text{M.P.} = \text{C.P.} + 20\%\text{ of C.P.} = \text{Rs}\left(x + \frac{20}{100}x\right) = \text{Rs}\,\frac{6x}{5}$

Now,

$\text{M.P.} = \text{Rs}\,\frac{6x}{5}$ and, Discount % = 15

$\therefore \quad \text{S.P.} = \left(\frac{100-\text{Discount }\%}{100}\right)\times\text{M.P.}$

$\Rightarrow \quad \text{S.P.} = \text{Rs}\left(\frac{100-15}{100}\times\frac{6x}{5}\right) = \text{Rs}\,\frac{102}{100}x$

$\therefore$ $\quad \text{Gain } \% = \dfrac{\text{S.P.} - \text{C.P.}}{\text{C.P.}} \times 100$

$\Rightarrow$ $\quad \text{Gain } \% = \left(\dfrac{\frac{102}{100}x - x}{x} \times 100 \right) = 2$

Example 11 Articles are marked at a price which gives a profit of 25%. After allowing a certain discount, the profit reduces to $12\frac{1}{2}\%$. Find the discount percent.

Solution Let the C.P. of an article be Rs 100. Then, to attain a profit of 25%, marked price must be 25% more than the cost price.

$\therefore$ $\quad$ Marked price $=$ Rs 100 + Rs 25 = Rs 125

After allowing a certain discount the profit reduces to $12\frac{1}{2}\%$.

$\therefore$ $\quad$ Profit $= 12\frac{1}{2}\%$ of C.P. $= 12\frac{1}{2}\%$ of Rs 100 $=$ Rs $12\frac{1}{2}$

$\therefore$ $\quad$ S.P. = C.P. + Profit = Rs 100 + Rs $12\frac{1}{2}$ = Rs $112\frac{1}{2}$

Now,

M.P. = S.P. + Discount

$\Rightarrow$ $\quad$ Discount $=$ M.P. − S.P. $=$ Rs 125 − Rs $112\frac{1}{2}$ = Rs $12\frac{1}{2}$

$\therefore$ $\quad \text{Discount } \% = \left(\dfrac{\text{Discount}}{\text{M.P.}} \times 100 \right) = \left(\dfrac{12\frac{1}{2}}{125} \times 100 \right) = 10$

Hence, discount $= 10\%$.

Example 12 A cycle merchant allows 25% commission on his advertised price and still makes a profit of 20%. If he gains Rs 60 over the sale of one cycle, find his advertised price.

Solution Let the advertised price be Rs 100

Commission on advertised price $= 25\% =$ Rs 25

$\therefore$ $\quad$ S.P. = Advertised price − Commission $=$ Rs 100 − Rs 25 = Rs 75

We have, profit $= 20\%$

$\therefore$ $\quad \text{C.P.} = \dfrac{100}{100 + \text{Gain}\,\%} \times \text{S.P.}$

$\Rightarrow$ $\quad \text{C.P.} = \text{Rs}\left(\dfrac{100}{100+20} \times 75 \right) = \text{Rs}\left(\dfrac{100}{120} \times 75 \right) = \text{Rs } 62.5$

$\therefore$ $\quad$ Gain = S.P. − C.P. = Rs 75 − Rs 62.5 = Rs 12.5

Now,

If the gain is Rs 12.5, advertised price $=$ Rs 100

If the gain is Re 1, advertised price $= \text{Rs}\,\frac{100}{12.5}$

If the gain is Rs 60, advertised price $= \text{Rs}\,\frac{100}{12.5} \times 60 = \text{Rs } 480$

Hence, advertised price of the cycle is Rs 480

Example 13 The marked price of a shirt was Rs 165 and it was sold at a discount of 12%. Find the discount allowed on the shirt and also its selling price.

Solution We have,

Marked price of the shirt = Rs 165, Discount % = 12%

$\therefore$ Discount $= 12\%$ of Rs 165 $= \text{Rs}\left(\frac{12}{100} \times 165\right) = \text{Rs } 19.80$

S.P. of the shirt $= \text{M.P.} - \text{Discount} = \text{Rs } (165.00 - 19.80) = \text{Rs } 145.20$

Hence, discount allowed is Rs 19.80 and S.P. of the shirt is Rs 145.20

Example 14 A trader marks his goods 40% above the cost price and gives a discount of 20% on the marked price. Find his gain percent.

Solution Let the cost price be Rs x. Then,

$$\text{M.P.} = \{x + 40\% \text{ of Rs } x\} = \text{Rs}\left(x + \frac{40x}{100}\right) = \text{Rs}\left(x + \frac{2x}{5}\right) = \text{Rs}\,\frac{7x}{5}$$

Discount % = 20

$$\therefore \quad \text{S.P.} = \frac{100 - \text{Discount }\%}{100} \times \text{M.P.}$$

$$\Rightarrow \quad \text{S.P.} = \text{Rs}\left(\frac{100 - 20}{100} \times \frac{7x}{5}\right) = \text{Rs}\,\frac{28x}{25}$$

$$\text{Profit} = \text{S.P.} - \text{C.P.} = \left(\frac{28x}{25} - x\right) = \text{Rs}\,\frac{3x}{25}$$

$$\text{Profit }\% = \left(\frac{\text{Prifit}}{\text{C.P.}} \times 100\right)\% = \left(\frac{3x}{25 \times x} \times 100\right)\% = 12\%$$

Aliter Let the cost price be Rs 100. Then, M.P. = Rs 140

We have,

Discount % = 20%

$$\therefore \quad \text{Discount} = \text{Rs}\left(\frac{20}{100} \times 140\right) = \text{Rs } 28$$

$$\therefore \quad \text{S.P.} = \text{M.P.} - \text{Discount} = \text{Rs } (140 - 28) = \text{Rs } 112$$

Thus, Gain = S.P. − C.P. = Rs (112 − 100) = Rs 12.

Hence, Gain % = 12%

Example 15 How much percent more than the C.P. should a manufacturer mark his goods so that after allowing a discount of 20% on the marked price, he gains 10%?

Solution Let the C.P. be Rs 100

Gain percent required = 10%

$\therefore$ S.P. = Rs (100 + 10) = Rs 110

Discount allowed = 20%

Let the Marked price be Rs x. Then,

$$\text{Discount} = 20\% \text{ of Rs } x = \text{Rs}\left(\frac{20}{100}\times x\right) = \text{Rs }\frac{x}{5}$$

$$\therefore \quad \text{S.P.} = \text{M.P.} - \text{Discount} = \text{Rs}\left(x - \frac{x}{5}\right) = \text{Rs }\frac{4x}{5}$$

But, S.P. = Rs 110

$$\therefore \quad \frac{4x}{5} = 110 \Rightarrow x = \frac{550}{4} = 137.50$$

Thus, marked price = Rs 137.50

Hence, the manufacturer should mark 37.50% more than the C.P.

<u>Aliter</u> Let the C.P. be Rs x.

We have, gain % = 10

$$\therefore \quad \text{S.P.} = \left(\frac{100 + \text{Gain }\%}{100}\right)\times \text{C.P.}$$

$$\Rightarrow \quad \text{S.P.} = \text{Rs}\left(\frac{100+10}{100}\times x\right) = \text{Rs }\frac{11x}{10}$$

Now,

$$\text{S.P.} = \text{Rs }\frac{11x}{10} \text{ and, Discount } \% = 20$$

$$\therefore \quad \text{M.P.} = \frac{100\times \text{S.P.}}{100 - \text{Discount }\%}$$

$$\Rightarrow \quad \text{M.P.} = \text{Rs}\left(\frac{100\times\frac{11x}{10}}{100-20}\right) = \text{Rs }\frac{11x}{8}$$

$$\therefore \quad \text{Required }\% = \left(\frac{\text{M.P.} - \text{C.P.}}{\text{C.P.}}\times 100\right) = \left(\frac{\frac{11x}{8} - x}{x}\times 100\right) = \left(\frac{3}{8}\times 100\right) = 37.5$$

Example 16 A shopkeeper allows a discount of 10% to his customers and still gains 20%. Find the marked price of an article which costs Rs 450 to the shopkeeper.

Solution We have,

C.P. = Rs 450 and, Gain % = 20%

$$\therefore \quad \text{S.P.} = \frac{100 + \text{Gain }\%}{100}\times \text{C.P.}$$

$$\Rightarrow \quad \text{S.P.} = \text{Rs}\left(\frac{100+20}{100}\times 450\right)$$

$\Rightarrow \quad$ S.P. = Rs 540 ... (i)

Now,

S.P. = Rs 540 and, Discount = 10%

$$\therefore \quad \text{M.P.} = \frac{100 \times \text{S.P.}}{100 - \text{Discount }\%} = \text{Rs}\left(\frac{100 \times 540}{100 - 10}\right) = \text{Rs } 600$$

Hence, marked price of the article is Rs 600

Example 17 A trader buys certain items at 32% off the list price and he wants to make a profit of 25% after allowing a discount of 20%. At what percent above the list price should he mark the items?

Solution Let the list price be Rs 100 and suppose the trader marks the price $x\%$ above the list price. Then,

M.P. = Rs $(100 + x)$

Discount on list price = 32% = Rs 32

$\therefore \quad$ C.P. = Rs (100 − 32) = Rs 68

$\because \quad$ Profit percent = 25%

$$\therefore \quad \text{S.P.} = \text{Rs}\left(\frac{100 + 25}{100} \times 68\right) = \text{Rs } 85 \qquad \left[\because \text{S.P.} = \frac{100 + \text{Gain }\%}{100} \times \text{C.P.}\right]$$

We have,

M.P. = Rs $(100 + x)$, Discount percent = 20%

$$\therefore \quad \text{Discount} = 20\% \text{ of Rs } (100 + x) = \text{Rs}\left\{\frac{20}{100} \times (100 + x)\right\} = \text{Rs}\left(\frac{100 + x}{5}\right)$$

$$\therefore \quad \text{S.P.} = \text{M.P.} - \text{Discount} = \text{Rs}\left\{(100 + x) - \frac{100 + x}{5}\right\} = \text{Rs } \frac{4}{5}(100 + x) \qquad \text{... (ii)}$$

From (i) and (ii), we have

$$\frac{4}{5}(100 + x) = 85 \Rightarrow 400 + 4x = 425 \Rightarrow 4x = 25 \Rightarrow x = \frac{25}{4} = 6.25$$

Hence, the trader should mark the items at 6.25% above the list price.

<u>Aliter</u> Let the list price of the item be Rs x.

It is given that the trader buys the item at 32% off the list price.

$\therefore \quad$ C.P. = L.P. − 32% of L.P.

$$\Rightarrow \quad \text{C.P.} = \text{Rs}\left(x - \frac{32}{100} \times x\right) = \text{Rs}\left(x - \frac{8x}{25}\right) = \text{Rs } \frac{17x}{25}$$

Now,

$$\text{Gain }\% = 25 \text{ and C.P.} = \text{Rs } \frac{17x}{25}$$

$$\therefore \quad \text{S.P.} = \frac{100 + \text{Gain \%}}{100} \times \text{C.P.} = \text{Rs}\left\{\frac{100+25}{100} \times \frac{17x}{25}\right\} = \text{Rs}\ \frac{17x}{20}$$

Thus, we have

$$\text{S.P.} = \text{Rs}\ \frac{17x}{20} \text{ and, Discount \%} = 20$$

$$\therefore \quad \text{M.P.} = \frac{100 \times \text{S.P.}}{(100 - \text{Discount \%})} = \text{Rs}\left(\frac{100 \times \frac{17x}{20}}{100-20}\right) = \text{Rs}\ \frac{85}{80}x$$

$$\therefore \quad \text{Required \%} = \frac{\text{M.P.} - \text{L.P.}}{\text{L.P.}} \times 100 = \left(\frac{\frac{85}{80}x - x}{x} \times 100\right) = \frac{100}{16} = 6.25$$

Example 18 A dealer of scientific instruments allows 20 % discount on the marked price of the instruments and still makes a profit of 25 %. If his gain over the sale of an instrument is Rs 150, find the marked price of the instrument.

Solution We have,

Gain % = 25 and Gain = Rs 150

$$\therefore \quad \text{Gain \%} = \frac{\text{Gain}}{\text{C.P.}} \times 100$$

$$\Rightarrow \quad 25 = \frac{150}{\text{C.P.}} \times 100$$

$$\Rightarrow \quad \text{C.P.} = \text{Rs}\left(\frac{150 \times 100}{25}\right) = \text{Rs } 600$$

Thus, we have

Gain % = 25 and C.P. = Rs 600

Now,

$$\text{S.P.} = \frac{100 + \text{Gain \%}}{100} \times \text{C.P.}$$

$$\Rightarrow \quad \text{S.P.} = \text{Rs}\left(\frac{100+25}{100} \times 600\right) = \text{Rs}\left(\frac{125}{100} \times 600\right) = \text{Rs } 750$$

Thus, we have

S.P. = Rs 750 and, Discount % = 20

$$\therefore \quad \text{M.P.} = \frac{100 \times \text{S.P.}}{(100 - \text{Discount \%})}$$

$$\Rightarrow \quad \text{M.P.} = \text{Rs}\left(\frac{100 \times 750}{100-20}\right) = \text{Rs}\left(\frac{75000}{80}\right) = \text{Rs } 937.50$$

Hence, marked price of the instrument is Rs 937.50

EXERCISE 13.2

1. Find the S.P. if
   (i) M.P. = Rs 1300 and Discount = 10%
   (ii) M.P. = Rs 500 and Discount = 15%
2. Find the M.P. if
   (i) S.P. = Rs 1222 and Discount = 6%
   (ii) S.P. = Rs 495 and Discount = 1%
3. Find discount in percent when
   (i) M.P. = Rs 900 and S.P. = Rs 873
   (ii) M.P. = Rs 500 and S.P. = Rs 425
4. A shop selling sewing machines offers 3% discount on all cash purchases. What cash amount does a customer pay for a sewing machine the price of which is marked as Rs 650.
5. The marked price of a ceiling fan is Rs 720. During off season, it is sold for Rs 684. Determine the discount percent.
6. On the eve of Gandhi Jayanti a saree is sold for Rs 720 after allowing 20% discount. What is its marked price?
7. After allowing a discount of $7\frac{1}{2}$% on the marked price, an article is sold for Rs 555. Find its marked price.
8. A shopkeeper allows his customers 10% off on the marked price of goods and still gets a profit of 25%. What is the actual cost to him of an article marked Rs 250?
9. A shopkeeper allows 20% off on the marked price of goods and still gets a profit of 25%. What is the actual cost to him of an article marked Rs 500?
10. A tradesman marks his goods at such a price that after allowing a discount of 15%, he makes a profit of 20%. What is the marked price of an article whose cost price is Rs 170?
11. A shopkeeper marks his goods in such a way that after allowing a discount of 25% on the marked price, he still makes a profit of 50%. Find the ratio of the C.P. to the M.P.
12. A cycle dealer offers a discount of 10% and still makes a profit of 26%. What is the actual cost to him of a cycle whose marked price is Rs 840?
13. A shopkeeper allows 23% commission on his advertised price and still makes a profit of 10%. If he gains Rs 56 on one item, find his advertised price.
14. A shopkeeper marks his goods at 40% above the cost price but allows a discount of 5% for cash payment to his customers. What actual profit does he make, if he receives Rs 1064 after paying the discount?
15. By selling a pair of earings at a discount of 25% on the marked price, a jeweller makes a profit of 16%. If the profit is Rs 48, what is the cost price? What is the marked price and the price at which the pair was eventually bought?
16. A publisher gives 32% discount on the printed price of a book to booksellers. What does a bookseller pay for a book whose printed price is Rs 275?
17. After allowing a discount of 20% on the marked price of a lamp, a trader loses 10%. By what percentage is the marked price above the cost price?
18. The list price of a table fan is Rs 480 and it is available to a retailer at 25% discount. For how much should a retailer sell it to gain 15%?

19. Rohit buys an item at 25% discount on the marked price. He sells it for Rs 660, making a profit of 10%. What is the marked price of the item?

20. A cycle merchant allows 20% discount on the marked price of the cycles and still makes a profit of 20%. If he gains Rs 360 over the sale of one cycle, find the marked price of the cycle.

21. Jyoti and Meena run a ready-made garment shop. They mark the garments at such a price that even after allowing a discount of 12.5%, they make a profit of 10%. Find the marked price of a suit which costs them Rs 1470.

22. What price should Aslam mark on a pair of shoes which costs him Rs 1200 so as to gain 12% after allowing a discount of 16%?

23. Jasmine allows 4% discount on the marked price of her goods and still earns a profit of 20%. What is the cost price of a shirt for her marked at Rs 850?

24. A shopkeeper offers 10% off-season discount to the customers and still makes a profit of 26%. What is the cost price for the shopkeeper on a pair of shoes marked at Rs 1120?

25. A lady shopkeeper allows her customers 10% discount on the marked price of the goods and still gets a profit of 25%. What is the cost price of a fan for her marked at Rs 1250?

ANSWERS

1. (i) Rs 1170 (ii) Rs 425 2. (i) Rs 1300 (ii) Rs 500 3. (i) 3% (ii) Rs 15%
4. Rs 630.50 5. 5% 6. Rs 900 7. Rs 600 8. Rs 180 9. Rs 320
10. Rs 240 11. 1 : 2 12. Rs 600 13. Rs 800 14. Rs 264
15. C.P. = Rs 300, M.P. = 464, Final price = Rs 348 16. Rs 187 17. 12.5% 18. Rs 414
19. Rs 800 20. Rs 2700 21. Rs 1848 22. Rs 1600 23. Rs 680 24. Rs 800
25. Rs 900.

HINTS TO SELECTED PROBLEMS

20. Proceed as in Ex. 18

21. We have,

Gain % = 10 and C.P. = Rs 1470

$$\therefore \text{ S.P.} = \frac{100 + \text{Gain}}{100} \times \text{C.P.}$$

$$\Rightarrow \text{ S.P.} = \text{Rs}\left(\frac{100+10}{100} \times 1470\right) = \text{Rs } 1617$$

Now,

S.P. = Rs 1617 and discount % = 12.5

$$\therefore \text{ M.P.} = \frac{100 \times \text{S.P.}}{100 - \text{Discount } \%} = \text{Rs}\left(\frac{100 \times 1617}{100 - 12.5}\right) = \text{Rs } 1848$$

22. We have,

C.P. = Rs 1200, Gain % = 12 and Discount % = 16

$$\therefore \text{ S.P.} = \frac{100 + \text{Gain}}{100} \times \text{C.P.} = \text{Rs}\left(\frac{100+12}{100} \times 1200\right) = \text{Rs } 1344$$

Now,

$$\text{M.P.} = \frac{100 \times \text{S.P.}}{100 - \text{Discount } \%} = \text{Rs}\left(\frac{100 \times 1344}{100 - 16}\right) = \text{Rs } 1600$$

23. We have,

M.P. = Rs 850, Discount % = 4 and Gain % = 20

$$\therefore \text{ S.P.} = \left(\frac{100 + \text{Discount }\%}{100} \times \text{M.P.}\right)$$

$$\Rightarrow \text{S.P.} = \text{Rs}\left(\frac{100-4}{100} \times 850\right) = \text{Rs } 816$$

Now, S.P. = Rs 816 and Gain % = 20

$$\therefore \text{ C.P.} = \left(\frac{100 \times \text{S.P.}}{100 + \text{Gain }\%}\right) = \text{Rs}\left(\frac{100 \times 816}{100+20}\right) = \text{Rs } 680$$

24. We have,

M.P. = Rs 1120, and Discount % = 10

$$\therefore \text{ S.P.} = \text{M.P.}\left(\frac{100 - \text{Discount }\%}{100}\right) = \text{Rs}\left\{1120 \times \left(\frac{100-10}{100}\right)\right\} = \text{Rs } 1008$$

Now,

Gain % = 26 and S.P. = Rs 1008

$$\therefore \text{ C.P.} = \left(\frac{100 \times \text{S.P.}}{100 + \text{Gain }\%}\right) \Rightarrow \text{ C.P.} = \text{Rs}\left(\frac{100 \times 1008}{100+26}\right) = \text{Rs } 800$$

13.4 VALUE ADDED TAX (VAT)

The central government as well as every state government provides various types of facilities such as construction and maintenance of roads, safety measures, dispenseries, hospitals, schools etc. for the general public. In order to provide these facilities to the general public, the government has to spend a lot of money. To meet these expenditures, the government imposes different types of taxes. Value added tax (VAT) is one of these. Previously it was known as sales tax. It is levied at a specified rate on the sale price of the items and it differs from item to item and state to state. Value added tax (VAT) is calculated on selling price (S.P.) Thus, if discount is given, first discount is calculated and then VAT is calculated on the selling price of the article. If there is no discount, then VAT is calculated on the marked (list) price of the article.

Following examples will illustrate the computation of value added tax (VAT)

ILLUSTRATIVE EXAMPLES

Example 1 George bought a V.C.R. at the list price of Rs 18,500. If the rate of VAT was 8%, find the amount he had to pay for purchasing the V.C.R.

Solution List price of V.C.R. = Rs 18500, VAT = 8%

$$\therefore \quad \text{VAT} = 8\% \text{ of Rs } 18{,}500 = \text{Rs } \frac{8}{100} \times 18500 = \text{Rs } 1480.$$

So, total amount which George had to pay for purchasing the V.C.R.

$$= \text{Rs } 18500 + \text{Rs } 1480 = \text{Rs } 19980.$$

Example 2 The price of a T.V. set inclusive of VAT is Rs 13,530. If the rate of VAT is 10%, find its basic price.

Solution Let the basic price of T.V. set be Rs x. Then,

$$\text{VAT at the rate of 10\% on Rs } x = \text{Rs } \frac{10}{100} \times x = \text{Rs } \frac{x}{100}$$

$$\text{Thus, the sale price of the T.V. set} = \text{Rs}\left(x + \frac{x}{10}\right) = \text{Rs } \frac{11x}{10}$$

It is given that the sale price of the T.V. set is Rs 13,530.

$$\therefore \quad \frac{11x}{10} = 13530 \Rightarrow x = \frac{13530 \times 10}{11} = 12300$$

Hence, the basic price of the T.V. set is Rs 12300.

Example 3 Samir bought a shirt for Rs 336, including 12% VAT and a neck-tie for Rs 110 including 10% VAT. Find the printed price (without VAT) of shirt and neck-tie together.

Solution Let the printed price of the shirt be Rs x and that of neck-tie be Rs y. Then,

$$\text{VAT on shirt} = 12\% \text{ of Rs } x = \text{Rs } \frac{12x}{100} = \text{Rs } \frac{3x}{25}$$

$$\text{VAT on neck-tie} = 10\ \% \text{ of Rs } y = \text{Rs } \frac{10y}{100} = \text{Rs } \frac{y}{10}.$$

$$\therefore \quad \text{Selling price of shirt} = \text{Rs}\left(x + \frac{3x}{25}\right) = \text{Rs } \frac{28x}{25}$$

and,

$$\text{Selling price of neck-tie} = \text{Rs}\left(y + \frac{y}{10}\right) = \text{Rs } \frac{11y}{10}$$

But, selling prices of shirt and neck-tie are Rs 336 and Rs 110 respectively.

$$\therefore \quad \frac{28x}{25} = 336 \quad \text{and} \quad \frac{11y}{10} = 110$$

$$\Rightarrow \quad x = \frac{336 \times 25}{28} \quad \text{and} \quad y = \frac{110 \times 10}{11}$$

$$\Rightarrow \quad x = 300 \quad \text{and} \quad y = 100$$

Hence, the total printed price of the shirt and neck-tie = Rs (300 + 100)
= Rs 400

Example 4 Reena goes to a shop to buy a radio, costing Rs 2568. The rate of value added tax is 7%. She tells the shopkeeper to reduce the price of the radio to such an extent that she has to pay Rs 2568, inclusive of value added tax. Find the reduction needed in the price of the radio.

Solution Let the reduced price, excluding the value added tax, of the radio be Rs x. Then,

$$\text{VAT} = 7\% \text{ of Rs } x = \text{Rs } \frac{7x}{100}$$

$$\therefore \quad \text{Selling price of the radio} = \text{Rs}\left(x + \frac{7x}{100}\right) = \text{Rs } \frac{107x}{100}$$

But, the selling price of the set is Rs 2568.

$\therefore \quad \frac{107x}{100} = 2568 \Rightarrow x = \frac{2568 \times 100}{107} \Rightarrow x = \text{Rs } 2400$

Hence, the reduction needed in the price of the radio

$= \text{Rs } (2568 - 2400) = \text{Rs } 168$

Example 5 David purchased a pair of shoes for Rs 441 including value added tax. If the sales price of the shoes is Rs 420, find the rate of value added tax.

Solution Let the rate of value added tax be $x\%$. Then,

$$\text{Value added tax} = x\% \text{ of Rs } 420 = \text{Rs}\left(\frac{x}{100} \times 420\right) = \text{Rs } \frac{21x}{5}$$

$$\therefore \quad \text{Selling price of shoes} = \text{Rs}\left(420 + \frac{21x}{5}\right)$$

But, selling price of shoes is Rs 441.

$$\therefore \quad 420 + \frac{21x}{5} = 441 \Rightarrow \frac{21x}{5} = 21 \Rightarrow x = 5$$

Hence, the rate of value added tax is 5%

Example 6 Samir bought the following articles from a departmental store:

Item	*Quantity*	*Rate per item (Rs)*	*Rate of VAT*
Shirts	4	200.00	8%
Pair of shoes	2	350.00	10%
Television	1	10900.00	10%
Tea-set	1	750.00	8%

Calculate the total bill paid, including VAT, by Samir to the departmental store.

Solution We have,

C.P. of 4 shirts $= \text{Rs } 200 \times 4 = \text{Rs } 800$, Rate of VAT $= 8\%$

$$\therefore \quad \text{VAT} = 8\% \text{ of Rs } 800 = \text{Rs}\left(\frac{8}{100} \times 800\right) = \text{Rs } 64$$

So, amount paid for 4 shirts $= \text{Rs } (800 + 64) = \text{Rs } 864$

C.P. of 2 pairs of shoes $= \text{Rs } 350 \times 2 = \text{Rs } 700$

Rate of VAT $= 10\%$

$$\therefore \quad \text{VAT} = 10\% \text{ of Rs } 700 = \text{Rs}\left(\frac{10}{100} \times 700\right) = \text{Rs } 70$$

So, amount paid for 2 pairs of shoes $= \text{Rs } (700 + 70) = \text{Rs } 770$

C.P. of television set $= \text{Rs } 10,900$, Rate of VAT $= 10\%$

$$\text{VAT} = 10\% \text{ of Rs } 10,900 = \text{Rs}\left(\frac{10}{100} \times 10,900\right) = \text{Rs } 1090.$$

So, amount paid for television set $= \text{Rs } (10900 + 1090) = \text{Rs } 11990$

Example 7 Hamida visits a departmental store and purchases the following articles:

(i) one rain coat for Rs 300, VAT @ 10%

(ii) one pair of shoes for Rs 460, VAT @ 9 %

(iii) food articles for Rs 450, VAT @ 5%

(iv) clothes for Rs 800, VAT @ 1%

Calculate the total amount of the bill.

Solution We have,

(i) Cost of rain coat = Rs 300.00, Rate of VAT = 10%

$$\text{VAT} = 10\% \text{ of Rs } 300 = \text{Rs}\left(\frac{10}{100}\times 30\right) = \text{Rs } 30.00$$

So, amount paid for one rain coat = Rs (300 + 30) = Rs 330

(ii) Cost of one pair of shoes = Rs 460, Rate of VAT = 9%

$$\text{VAT} = 9\% \text{ of Rs } 460 = \text{Rs}\left(\frac{9}{100}\times 460\right) = \text{Rs } 41.40$$

So, amount paid for one pair of shoes = Rs (460 + 41.40) = Rs 501.40

(iii) Cost of food articles = Rs 450, Rate of VAT = 5%

$$\text{VAT} = 5\% \text{ of Rs } 450 = \text{Rs}\left(\frac{5}{100}\times 450\right) = \text{Rs } 22.50$$

So, amount paid for food articles = Rs (450 + 22.50) = Rs 472.50

(iv) Cost of clothes = Rs 800, Rate of VAT = 1%

$$\text{VAT} = 1\% \text{ of Rs } 800 = \text{Rs}\left(\frac{1}{100}\times 800\right) = \text{Rs } 8$$

So, amount paid for clothes = Rs (800 + 8) = Rs 808

Hence, total amount of the bill = Rs (330 + 501.40 + 472.50 + 808) = Rs 2111.90

Example 8 List price of a pair of shoes is Rs 450. If Amit paid Rs 45 as VAT for it, find the rate of VAT.

Solution Since VAT is paid on the list price.

$$\therefore \quad \text{Rate of VAT} = \left(\frac{45}{450}\times 100\right)\% = 10\%$$

Example 9 Nisha goes to a shop to buy a box costing Rs 981. The rate of the VAT is 9%. She tells the shopkeeper to allow a discount on the price of the box to such an extent that she pays Rs 981 inclusive of VAT. Find the discount in the price of the box.

Solution Let the reduced price of the box after discount be Rs x. Then,

$$\text{VAT} = 9\% \text{ of } x = \text{Rs } \frac{9x}{100}$$

$$\therefore \quad \text{S.P.} = \text{Rs}\left(x + \frac{9x}{100}\right) = \text{Rs } \frac{109x}{100}$$

It is given that the selling price should be Rs 981.

$\therefore \quad \frac{109x}{100} = 981 \Rightarrow x = 900$

Thus, reduced price of the box after discount = Rs 900.

Hence, reduction needed in the price of the box = Rs (981 − 900) = Rs 81.

Example 10 Amit purchases a motorcycle, having marked price Rs 46000 at a discount of 5%. If VAT is charged at the rate of 10%, find the amount Amit has paid to purchase the motorcycle.

Solution Marked price of motorcycle = Rs 46000

Discount $= 5\%$ of Rs 46000 $= \text{Rs}\left(\frac{5}{100} \times 46000\right) = \text{Rs } 2300$

$\therefore$ Net price of motorcycle = Rs 46000 − Rs 2300 = Rs 43700

VAT $= 10\%$ of Rs 43700 $= \text{Rs}\left(\frac{10}{100} \times 43700\right) = \text{Rs } 4370$

$\therefore$ S.P. of motorcycle = Rs (43700 + 4370) = Rs 48070

Hence, Amit has paid Rs 48070 to purchase the motorcycle.

EXERCISE 13.3

1. The list price of a refrigerator is Rs 9700. If a value added tax of 6% is to be charged on it, how much one has to pay to buy the refrigerator?
2. Vikram bought a watch for Rs 825. If this amount includes 10% VAT on the list price, what was the list price of the watch?
3. Aman bought a shirt for Rs 374.50 which includes 7% VAT. Find the list price of the shirt.
4. Rani purchases a pair of shoes whose sale price is Rs 175. If she pays VAT at the rate of 7%, how much amount does she poy as VAT? Also, find the net value of the pair of shoes.
5. Swarna paid Rs 20 as VAT on a pair of shoes worth Rs 250. Find the rate of VAT.
6. Sarita buys goods worth Rs 5500. She gets a rebate of 5% on it. After getting the rebate if VAT at the rate of 5% is charged, find the amount she will have to pay for the goods.
7. The cost of furniture inclusive of VAT is Rs 7150. If the rate of VAT is 10%, find the original cost of the furniture.
8. A refrigerator is available for Rs 13750 including VAT. If the rate of VAT is 10%, find the original cost of the furniture.
9. A colour TV is available for Rs 13440 inclusive of VAT. If the original cost of TV is Rs 12000, find the rate of VAT.
10. Reena goes to a shop to buy a radio, costing Rs 2568. The rate of VAT is 7%. She tells the shopkeeper to reduce the price of the radio such that she has to pay Rs 2568, inclusive of VAT. Find the reduction needed in the price of radio.
11. Rajat goes to a departmental store and buys the following articles:

Item	*Price per item*	*Rate of VAT*
2 Pairs of shoes	Rs 800	5%
1 Sewing machine	Rs 1500	6%
2 Tea-sets	Rs 650	4%

Calculate the total amount he has to pay to the store.

12. Ajit buys a motorcycle for Rs 17600 including value added tax. If the rate of VAT is 10%, what is the sale price of the motorcycle?
13. Manoj buys a leather coat costing Rs 900 at Rs 990 after paying the VAT. Calculate the rate of VAT charged on the coat.
14. Rakesh goes to a departmental store and purchases the following articles:
    (i) biscuits and bakery products costing Rs 50, VAT @ 5%,
    (ii) medicines costing Rs 90, VAT @ 10%,
    (iii) clothes costing Rs 400, VAT @ 1%, and
    (iv) cosmetics costing Rs 150, VAT @ 10%.
    Calculate the total amount to be paid by Rakesh to the store.
15. Rajeeta purchased a set of cosmetics. She paid Rs 165 for it including VAT. If the rate of VAT is 10%, find the sale price of the set.
16. Sunita purchases a bicycle for Rs 660. She has paid a VAT of 10%. Find the list price of the bicycle?
17. The sales price of a television, inclusive of VAT, is Rs 13,500. If VAT is charged at the rate of 8% of the list price, find the list price of the television.
18. Shikha purchased a car with a marked price of Rs 210000 at a discount of 5%. If VAT is charged at the rate of 10%, find the amount Shikha had paid for purchasing the car.
19. Shruti bought a set of cosmetic items for Rs 345 including 15% value added tax and a purse for Rs 110 including 10% VAT. What percent is the VAT charged on the whole transaction?
20. List price of a cooler is Rs 2563. The rate of VAT is 10%. The customer requests the shopkeeper to allow a discount in the price of the cooler to such an extent that the price remains Rs 2563 inclusive of VAT. Find the discount in the price of the cooler.
21. List price of a washing machine is Rs 9000. If the dealer allows a discount of 5% on the cash payment, how much money will a customer pay to the dealer in cash, if the rate of VAT is 10%?

ANSWERS

1. Rs 10,282 2. Rs 750 3. Rs 350 4. Rs 12.25, Rs 187.25 5. 8%
6. Rs 5486.25 7. Rs 6500 8. Rs 12500 9. 12% 10. Rs 168 11. Rs 4622
12. Rs 16000 13. 10% 14. Rs 720.50 15. Rs 150 16. Rs 600 17. 12500
18. Rs 219450 19. 13.75% 20. Rs 233 21. Rs 9405

HINTS TO SELECTED PROBLEMS

2. Let the list price of the watch be Rs x. Then,

$$x + \frac{10x}{100} = 825 \Rightarrow x = \frac{825 \times 10}{11} \Rightarrow x = 750$$

13. Let the rate of VAT be $x\%$. Then,

$$\text{VAT} = \text{Rs}\left(\frac{x}{100} \times 900\right) = 9x, \therefore\ 900 + 9x = 990 \Rightarrow x = 10.$$

THINGS TO REMEMBER

1. *If S.P. > C.P. i.e. in case of profit:*

   (i) $\text{Profit} = S.P. - C.P.$

   (ii) $\text{Profit}\ \% = \frac{\text{Profit}}{C.P.} \times 100$ or, $\text{Profit} = \frac{C.P. \times \text{Profit}\%}{100}$

   (iii) $S.P. = C.P.\left(\frac{100 + \text{Profit}\%}{100}\right)$

   (iv) $C.P. = \frac{100 \times S.P.}{(100 + \text{Profit}\%)}$

2. *If S.P. < C.P. i.e. in case of loss:*

   (i) $\text{Loss} = C.P. - S.P.$

   (ii) $\text{Loss}\ \% = \frac{\text{Loss}}{C.P.} \times 100$ or, $\text{Loss} = \frac{C.P. \times \text{Loss}\ \%}{100}$

   (iii) $S.P. = C.P.\left(\frac{100 - \text{Loss}\ \%}{100}\right)$

   (iv) $C.P. = \frac{100 \times S.P.}{100 - \text{Loss}\ \%}$

3. (i) $\text{Discount} = M.P. - S.P.$

   (ii) $\text{Rate of Discount} = \text{Discount}\ \% = \frac{\text{Discount}}{M.P.} \times 100$

   (iii) $S.P. = M.P.\left(\frac{100 - \text{Discount}\ \%}{100}\right)$

   (iv) $M.P. = \frac{100 \times S.P.}{(100 - \text{Discount}\ \%)}$

4. *Value added tax (VAT) is charged on the selling price of an article.*

14

COMPOUND INTEREST

14.1 INTRODUCTION

In Class VII, you have learnt about the simple interest and the formula for calculating simple interest and amount. In this chapter, we shall discuss the concept of compound interest and the method of calculating the compound interest and the amount at the end of a certain specified period. We shall also study about the population growth and depreciation of the value of movable and immovable assets.

14.2 COMPOUND INTEREST

In class VII, you have learnt that, if Principal = Rs P, Rate = R % per annum, and Time = T (in years), then the simple interest (S.I.) in Rs is given by

$$\text{S.I.} = \frac{P \times R \times T}{100}$$

For example, if principal = Rs 5000 and rate of interest = 10% per annum, then

$$\text{S.I. for 1 year} = \text{Rs}\left(\frac{5000 \times 10 \times 1}{100}\right) = \text{Rs } 500$$

$$\text{S.I. for 2 years} = \text{Rs}\left(\frac{5000 \times 10 \times 2}{100}\right) = \text{Rs } 1000$$

$$\text{S.I. for 3 years} = \text{Rs}\left(\frac{5000 \times 10 \times 3}{100}\right) = \text{Rs } 1500 \text{ and so on.}$$

Clearly, in computing S.I. the principal remains constant throughout.

But, the above method of computing interest is generally not used in banks, insurance corporations, post offices and other money lending and deposit taking companies. They use a different method for computing interest. In this method, the borrower and the lender agree to fix up a certain time interval, say a year or a half year or a quarter of a year for the computation of interest and amount. At the end of first interval the interest is computed and is added to the original principal. The amount so obtained is taken as the principal for the second interval of time. The amount of this principal at the end of the second interval of time is taken as the principal for the third interval of time and so on. At the end of certain specified period, the difference between the amount and the money borrowed i.e. the original principal is computed and it is called the *compound interest* (abbreviated as C.I.) for that period. Thus, we may define the compound interest as follows :

COMPOUND INTEREST *If the borrower and the lender agree to fix up a certain interval of time (say, a year or a half year or a quarter of a year etc) so that the amount (= Principal + Interest) at the end of an interval becomes the principal for the next interval, then the total interest over all the intervals, calculated in this way is called the compound interest and is abbreviated as C.I.*

Clearly, compound interest at the end of certain specified period is equal to the difference between the amount at the end of the period and the original principal i.e.

$$C.I. = Amount - Principal$$

CONVERSION PERIOD *The fixed interval of time at the end of which the interest is calculated and added to the principal at the beginning of the interval is called the conversion period.*

In other words, the period at the end of which the interest is compounded is called the conversion period.

When the interest is calculated and added to the principal every six months, the conversion period is six months. Similarly, the conversion period is 3 months when the interest is calculated and added quarterly.

NOTE: *If no conversion period is specified, the conversion period is taken to be one year.*

14.3 COMPUTATION OF COMPOUND INTEREST

In this section, we shall discuss some examples to explain the meaning and the computation of compound interest.

ILLUSTRATIVE EXAMPLES

Type I **COMPUTATION OF COMPOUND INTEREST WHEN INTEREST IS COMPOUNDED ANNUALLY**

Example 1 Find the compound interest on Rs 1000 for two years at 4% per annum.

Solution Principal for the first year = Rs 1000

$$\text{Interest for the first year} = \text{Rs}\left(\frac{1000 \times 4 \times 1}{100}\right) \quad \left[\text{Using: Interest} = \frac{P \times R \times T}{100}\right]$$

$$= \text{Rs } 40$$

Amount at the end of first year = Rs 1000 + Rs 40 = Rs 1040

$$\text{Interest for the second year} = \text{Rs}\left(\frac{1040 \times 4 \times 1}{100}\right) = \text{Rs } 41.60$$

Principal for the second year = Rs 1040

Amount at the end of second year = Rs 1040 + Rs 41.60 = Rs 1081.60

∴ Compound interest = Rs (1081.60 − 1000) = Rs 81.60

Example 2 Maria invests Rs 93750 at 9.6% per annum for 3 years and the interest is compounded annually. Calculate :

(i) The amount standing to her credit at the end of second year.

(ii) The interest for the third year.

Solution (i) We have,

Principal for the first year Rs 93750

Rate of interest = 9.6% per annum.

$$\therefore \quad \text{Interest for the first year} = \text{Rs}\left(\frac{93750 \times 9.6 \times 1}{100}\right) = \text{Rs } 9000$$

Amount at the end of the first year $= \text{Rs } 93750 + \text{Rs } 9000 = \text{Rs } 102750$

Principal for the second year $= \text{Rs } 102750$

Interest for the second year $= \text{Rs}\left(\frac{102750 \times 9.6 \times 1}{100}\right) = \text{Rs } 9864$

Amount at the end of second year $= \text{Rs } 102750 + \text{Rs } 9864 = \text{Rs } 112614$

(ii) Principal for the third year $= \text{Rs } 112614$

Interest for the third year $= \text{Rs}\left(\frac{112614 \times 9.6 \times 1}{100}\right) = \text{Rs } 10810.94$

Remark *The compound interest can also be computed by adding the interest for each year.*

Type II COMPUTATION OF COMPOUND INTEREST WHEN INTEREST IS COMPOUNDED HALF-YEARLY

It should be noted that, if the rate of interest is R % per annum and the interest is compounded half-yearly, then the rate of interest will be $\frac{R}{2}\%$ per half-year.

Example 3 Find the compound interest on Rs 8000 for $1\frac{1}{2}$ years at 10% per annum, interest being payable half-yearly.

Solution We have,

Rate of interest $= 10\%$ per annum $= 5\%$ per half-year.

Time $= 1\frac{1}{2}$ years $= 3$ half- years

Original principal $= \text{Rs } 8000$

Interest for the first half-year $= \text{Rs}\left(\frac{8000 \times 5 \times 1}{100}\right) = \text{Rs } 400$

Amount at the end of the first half-year $= \text{Rs } 8000 + \text{Rs } 400 = \text{Rs } 8400$

Principal for the second half-year $= \text{Rs } 8400$

Interest for the second half-year $= \text{Rs}\left(\frac{8400 \times 5 \times 1}{100}\right) = \text{Rs } 420$

Amount at the end of the second half-year $= \text{Rs } 8400 + \text{Rs } 420 = \text{Rs } 8820$

Principal for the third half-year $= \text{Rs } 8820$

Interest for the third half-year $= \text{Rs}\left(\frac{8820 \times 5 \times 1}{100}\right) = \text{Rs } 441$

Amount at the end of third half-year $= \text{Rs } 8820 + \text{Rs } 441 = \text{Rs } 9261$

$\therefore$ Compound interest $= \text{Rs } 9261 - \text{Rs } 8000 = \text{Rs } 1261$

Type III **COMPUTATION OF COMPOUND INTEREST WHEN INTEREST IS COMPOUNDED QUARTERLY**

It should be noted that, if the rate of interest is R % per annum and the interest is compounded quarterly, then it is $\frac{R}{4}\%$ per quarter.

Example 4 Find the compound interest on Rs 10000 for 1 year at 20% per annum compounded quarterly.

Solution We have,

Rate of interest $= 20\%$ per annum $= \frac{20}{4}\% = 5\%$ per quarter

Time $= 1$ year $= 4$ quarters.

Principal for the first quarter $=$ Rs 10000

Interest for the first quarter $= \text{Rs}\left(\frac{10000 \times 5 \times 1}{100}\right) = \text{Rs } 500$

Amount at the end of first quarter $=$ Rs 10000 + Rs 500 = Rs 10500

Principal for the second quarter $=$ Rs 10500

Interest for the second quarter $= \text{Rs}\left(\frac{10500 \times 5 \times 1}{100}\right) = \text{Rs } 525$

Amount at the end of second quarter $=$ Rs 10500 + Rs 525 = Rs 11025

Principal for the third quarter $=$ Rs 11025

Interest for the third quarter $= \text{Rs}\left(\frac{11025 \times 5 \times 1}{100}\right) = \text{Rs } 551.25$

Amount at the end of the third quarter $=$ Rs 11025 + Rs 551.25
$=$ Rs 11576.25

Principal for the fourth quarter $=$ Rs 11576.25

Interest for the fourth quarter $= \text{Rs}\left(\frac{11576.25 \times 5 \times 1}{100}\right) = \text{Rs } 578.8125$

Amount at the end of fourth quarter $=$ Rs 11576.25 + Rs 578.8125
$=$ Rs 12155.0625

$\therefore$ Compound interest $=$ Rs 12155.0625 − Rs 10000 = Rs 2155.0625
$=$ Rs 2155.06

EXERCISE 14.1

1. Find the compound interest when principal $=$ Rs 3000, rate $= 5\%$ per annum and time $= 2$ years.
2. What will be the compound interest on Rs 4000 in two years when rate of interest is 5% per annum?
3. Rohit deposited Rs 8000 with a finance company for 3 years at an interest of 15% per annum. What is the compound interest that Rohit gets after 3 years?
4. Find the compound interest on Rs 1000 at the rate of 8% per annum for $1\frac{1}{2}$ years when interest is compounded half-yearly.
5. Find the compound interest on Rs 160000 for one year at the rate of 20% per annum, if the interest is compounded quarterly.

6. Swati took a loan of Rs 16000 against her insurance policy at the rate of $12\frac{1}{2}\%$ per annum. Calculate the total compound interest payable by Swati after 3 years.
7. Roma borrowed Rs 64000 from a bank for $1\frac{1}{2}$ years at the rate of 10% per annum.

   Compute the total compound interest payable by Roma after $1\frac{1}{2}$ years, if the interest is compounded half-yearly.
8. Mewa Lal borrowed Rs 20000 from his friend Rooplal at 18% per annum simple interest. He lent it to Rampal at the same rate but compounded annually. Find his gain after 2 years.
9. Find the compound interest on Rs 8000 for 9 months at 20% per annum compounded quarterly.
10. Find the compound interest at the rate of 10% per annum for two years on that principal which in two years at the rate of 10% per annum gives Rs 200 as simple interest.
11. Find the compound interest on Rs 64000 for 1 year at the rate of 10% per annum compounded quarterly.
12. Ramesh deposited Rs 7500 in a bank which pays him 12% interest per annum compounded quarterly. What is the amount which he receives after 9 months.
13. Anil borrowed a sum of Rs 9600 to install a handpump in his dairy. If the rate of interest is $5\frac{1}{2}\%$ per annum compounded annually, determine the compound interest which Anil will have to pay after 3 years.
14. Surabhi borrowed a sum of Rs 12000 from a finance company to purchase a refrigerator. If the rate of interest is 5% per annum compounded annually, calculate the compound interest that Surabhi has to pay to the company after 3 years.
15. Daljit received a sum of Rs. 40000 as a loan from a finance company. If the rate of interest is 7% per annum compounded annually, calculate the compound interest that Daljit pays after 2 years.

ANSWERS

1. Rs 307.50 2. Rs 410 3. Rs 4167.00 4. Rs 124.86 5. Rs 34481 6. Rs 6781.25
7. Rs 10088 8. Rs 648 9. Rs 1261 10. Rs 210 11. Rs 6644.03
12. Rs 8195.45 13. Rs1672.72 14. Rs 1891.50 15. Rs 5796.

14.4 COMPUTATION OF COMPOUND INTEREST BY USING FORMULAE

In the previous section, we have discussed some problems on the computation of compound interest. As you have seen that the method of computing compound interest was very lengthy and cumbersome, specially when the period of time is very large. In this section, we shall obtain some formulae for the computation of compound interest by using the method discussed in the previous section. Using these formulae, the computation of compound interest becomes very easy.

FORMULA 1 *Let P be the principal and the rate of interest be R% per annum. If the interest is compounded annually, then the amount A and the compound interest C.I. at the end of n years are given by*

$$A = P\left(1+\frac{R}{100}\right)^n$$

$$\text{and, } C.I. = A - P = P\left\{\left(1+\frac{R}{100}\right)^n - 1\right\} \text{ respectively.}$$

Proof: We have,

P = Principal and rate of interest is R % per annum.

Since the interest is reckoned annually.

$\therefore$ Interest after one year $= \frac{PR}{100}$

$\Rightarrow$ Amount at the end of one year $= P + \frac{PR}{100} = P\left(1+\frac{R}{100}\right)$

Now, this amount is taken as the principal for the second year.

$\therefore$ Interest for the second year $= P\left(1+\frac{R}{100}\right) \times \frac{R}{100}$

$\Rightarrow$ Amount at the end of second year $= P\left(1+\frac{R}{100}\right) + P\left(1+\frac{R}{100}\right) \times \frac{R}{100}$

$$= P\left(1+\frac{R}{100}\right)\left(1+\frac{R}{100}\right) = P\left(1+\frac{R}{100}\right)^2$$

Considering this amount as the principal for third year, we have

Interest for the third year $= P\left(1+\frac{R}{100}\right)^2 \times \frac{R}{100}$

$\Rightarrow$ Amount at the end of third year $= P\left(1+\frac{R}{100}\right)^2 + P\left(1+\frac{R}{100}\right)^2 \times \frac{R}{100}$

$$= P\left(1+\frac{R}{100}\right)^2 \times \left(1+\frac{R}{100}\right)$$

$$= P\left(1+\frac{R}{100}\right)^3$$

Continuing in this manner, we have

Amount at the end of n years $= P\left(1+\frac{R}{100}\right)^n$

Q.E.D.

FORMULA 2 *Let P be the principal and the rate of interest be R % per annum. If the interest is compounded annually, then the amount A and the compound interest C.I. at the end of n years are given by*

$$A = P\left(1+\frac{R}{100k}\right)^{nk}$$

$$\text{and, } C.I. = A - P = P\left\{\left(1+\frac{R}{100k}\right)^{nk} - 1\right\} \text{ respectively.}$$

Proof: Since the rate of interest is R % per year and the interest is payable k times in a year, therefore the rate of interest is $\frac{R}{k}$ % per interval. Hence, the amount A of principal P at the end of n years or nk intervals is

$$A = P\left(1+\frac{R/k}{100}\right)^{nk} \text{ or, } A = P\left(1+\frac{R}{100k}\right)^{nk}$$

PARTICULAR CASES

CASE I *When the interest is compounded half-yearly.*

In this case, we have $k = 2$

$$\therefore \quad A = P\left(1+\frac{R}{200}\right)^{2n} \text{ and } C.I. = P\left\{\left(1+\frac{R}{200}\right)^{2n} - 1\right\}$$

CASE II *When the interest is compounded quarterly*

In this case, we have $k = 4$

$$\therefore \quad A = P\left(1+\frac{R}{400}\right)^{4n} \text{ and } C.I. = P\left\{\left(1+\frac{R}{400}\right)^{4n} - 1\right\}$$

FORMULA 3 *Let P be the principal and the rate of interest be R_1% for first year, R_2% for second year, R_3% for third year and so on and in the last R_n% for the nth year. Then, the amount A and the compound interest C.I. at the end of n years are given by*

$$A = P\left(1+\frac{R_1}{100}\right)\left(1+\frac{R_2}{100}\right)\cdots\left(1+\frac{R_n}{100}\right) \text{ and, } C.I. = A - P \text{ respectively.}$$

Proof: For the first year the rate of interest is R_1%.

$$\therefore \quad \text{Interest at the end of first year } = \frac{PR_1}{100}$$

$$\Rightarrow \quad \text{Amount at the end of one year } = P + \frac{PR_1}{100} = P\left(1+\frac{R_1}{100}\right)$$

This amount is taken as the principal for the second year.

$$\therefore \quad \text{Interest at the end of second year } = P\left(1+\frac{R_1}{100}\right)\cdot\frac{R_2}{100}$$

$$\Rightarrow \quad \text{Amount at the end of second year } = P\left(1+\frac{R_1}{100}\right)\frac{R_2}{100} + P\left(1+\frac{R_1}{100}\right)$$

$$= P\left(1+\frac{R_1}{100}\right)\left(1+\frac{R_2}{100}\right)$$

Continuing in this manner, we obtain

$$\text{Amount at the end of } n \text{ years } = P\left(1+\frac{R_1}{100}\right)\left(1+\frac{R_2}{100}\right)\cdots\left(1+\frac{R_n}{100}\right)$$

FORMULA 4 *Let P be the principal and the rate of interest be R% per annum. If the interest is compounded annually but time is the fraction of a year, say $5\frac{1}{4}$ years, then amount A is given by*

$$A = P\left(1+\frac{R}{100}\right)^5\left(1+\frac{\frac{R}{4}}{100}\right) \text{ and, } C.I. = A - P$$

Following examples will illustrate the use of the above formulae in the computation of compound interest.

ILLUSTRATIVE EXAMPLES

Type I **ON FINDING THE COMPOUND INTEREST AND THE AMOUNT WHEN INTEREST IS COMPOUNDED ANNUALLY**

Example 1 Find the compound interest on Rs 12000 for 3 years at 10% per annum compounded annually.

Solution We know that the amount A at the end of n years at the rate of R % per annum when the interest is compounded annually is given by

$$A = P\left(1+\frac{R}{100}\right)^n$$

Here,

$$P = \text{Rs } 12000,\ R = 10\% \text{ per annum and } n = 3$$

$\therefore$ Amount A after 3 years

$$= P\left(1+\frac{R}{100}\right)^3$$
$$= \text{Rs } 12000 \times \left(1+\frac{10}{100}\right)^3$$
$$= \text{Rs } 12000 \times \left(1+\frac{1}{10}\right)^3$$
$$= \text{Rs } 12000 \times \left(\frac{11}{10}\right)^3$$
$$= \text{Rs } 12000 \times \frac{11}{10} \times \frac{11}{10} \times \frac{11}{10}$$
$$= \text{Rs } (12 \times 11 \times 11 \times 11) = \text{Rs } 15972$$

Now,

Compound interest $= A - P$

$\Rightarrow$ Compound interest $= \text{Rs } 15972 - \text{Rs } 12000 = \text{Rs } 3972$

Example 2 Abhay lent Rs 8000 to his friend for 3 years at the rate of 5% per annum compound interest. What amount does Abhay get after 3 years?

Solution Here, $P = \text{Rs } 8000$, $R = 5\%$ per annum and $n = 3$.

$\therefore$ Amount after 3 year

$$= P\left(1+\frac{R}{100}\right)^3$$
$$= \text{Rs } 8000 \times \left(1+\frac{5}{100}\right)^3$$
$$= \text{Rs } 8000 \times \left(1+\frac{1}{20}\right)^3$$

$$= \text{Rs } 8000 \times \left(\frac{21}{20}\right)^3$$

$$= \text{Rs } 8000 \times \frac{21}{20} \times \frac{21}{20} \times \frac{21}{20} = \text{Rs } 9261$$

Thus, Abhay gets Rs 9261 at the end of 3 years.

Example 3 Vijay obtains a loan of Rs 64000 against his fixed deposits. If the rate of interest be 2.5 paise per rupee per annum, calculate the compound interest payable after 3 years.

Solution Here, $P = \text{Rs } 64000$, $n = 3$ years, and

$R = 2.5$ paise per rupee per annum

$\Rightarrow \quad R = (2.5 \times 100)$ paise per hundred rupees per annum

$\Rightarrow \quad R = \left(\frac{2.5 \times 100}{100}\right)$ Rs per hundred rupees per annum

$\Rightarrow \quad R = 2.5\%$ per annum.

$$\therefore \quad \text{Amount } A \text{ after 3 years } = P\left(1 + \frac{R}{100}\right)^3$$

$$= \text{Rs } 64000 \times \left(1 + \frac{2.5}{100}\right)^3$$

$$= \text{Rs } 64000 \times \left(1 + \frac{25}{1000}\right)^3$$

$$= \text{Rs } 64000 \times \left(1 + \frac{1}{40}\right)^3$$

$$= \text{Rs } 64000 \times \left(\frac{41}{40}\right)^3$$

$$= \text{Rs } 64000 \times \frac{41}{40} \times \frac{41}{40} \times \frac{41}{40} = \text{Rs } 68921$$

Hence, compound interest payable after 3 years $= \text{Rs } 68921 - \text{Rs } 64000$

$= \text{Rs } 4921$

Example 4 Find the compound interest at the rate of 10% per annum for four years on the principal which in four years at the rate of 4% per annum gives Rs 1600 as simple interest.

Solution Let Rs P be the principal.

This principal gives Rs 1600 as S.I. in four years at the rate of 4% per annum.

$$\therefore \quad P = \frac{\text{S.I.} \times 100}{R \times T}$$

$$\Rightarrow \quad P = \text{Rs } \frac{1600 \times 100}{4 \times 4} = \text{Rs } 10000$$

Now, we have

$P = \text{Rs } 10000$, $R = 10\%$ and $n = 4$

$\therefore$ Amount after 4 years $= P\left(1+\frac{R}{100}\right)^n$

$$= \text{Rs } 10000 \times \left(1+\frac{10}{100}\right)^4$$

$$= \text{Rs } 10000 \times \left(1+\frac{1}{10}\right)^4$$

$$= \text{Rs } 10000 \times \left(\frac{11}{10}\right)^4$$

$$= \text{Rs } 10000 \times \frac{11}{10} \times \frac{11}{10} \times \frac{11}{10} \times \frac{11}{10} = \text{Rs } 14641$$

$\therefore$ Compound interest $= \text{Rs } 14641 - \text{Rs } 10000 = \text{Rs } 4641$

Example 5 Simple interest on a sum of money for 3 years at $6\frac{1}{4}\%$ per annum is Rs 2400. What will be the compound interest on that sum at the same rate for the same period?

Solution Let the sum of money be Rs P.

This sum of money gives Rs 2400 as S.I. in 3 years at the rate of $6\frac{1}{4}\%$ per annum.

$$\therefore \quad P = \frac{\text{S.I.} \times 100}{R \times T}$$

$$\Rightarrow \quad P = \frac{2400 \times 100}{\frac{25}{4} \times 3} = 12800 \qquad \left[\because \text{S.I.} = 2400,\ R = 6\frac{1}{4}\% = \frac{25}{4}\% \text{ and } T = 3 \text{ years}\right]$$

Now, we have

$$P = 12800,\ R = \frac{25}{4}\% \text{ and } n = 3$$

$\therefore$ Amount after 3 years $= P\left(1+\frac{R}{100}\right)^n$

$$= \text{Rs}\left[12800 \times \left(1+\frac{25}{400}\right)^3\right]$$

$$= \text{Rs}\left[12800 \times \left(1+\frac{1}{16}\right)^3\right]$$

$$= \text{Rs}\left[12800 \times \left(\frac{17}{16}\right)^3\right]$$

$$= \text{Rs}\left[12800 \times \frac{17}{16} \times \frac{17}{16} \times \frac{17}{16}\right]$$

$$= \text{Rs}\left[\frac{25 \times 17 \times 17 \times 17}{8}\right] = \text{Rs } 15353.125$$

$\therefore$ Compound interest $= \text{Rs } 15353.125 - \text{Rs } 12800 = \text{Rs } 2553.125 = \text{Rs } 2553.13$

Type II COMPUTATION OF COMPOUND INTEREST WHEN THE INTEREST IS COMPOUNDED HALF-YEARLY

FORMULA $A = P\left(1+\frac{R}{200}\right)^{2n}$ *and C.I. = A − P, where*

P = *Principal*, R = *Rate percent per annum*, n = *number of years*

Example 6 Compute the compound interest on Rs 12000 for 2 years at 20% per annum when compounded half-yearly.

Solution Here, Principal P = Rs 12000, R = 20% per annum and $n = 2$ years.

$\therefore$ Amount after 2 years $= P\left(1+\frac{R}{200}\right)^{2n}$

$$= \text{Rs } 12000 \times \left(1+\frac{20}{200}\right)^{2\times 2}$$

$$= \text{Rs } 12000 \times \left(1+\frac{1}{10}\right)^{4}$$

$$= \text{Rs } 12000 \times \left(\frac{11}{10}\right)^{4}$$

$$= \text{Rs } 12000 \times \frac{11}{10} \times \frac{11}{10} \times \frac{11}{10} \times \frac{11}{10}$$

$$= \text{Rs } 12000 \times \frac{14641}{10000} = \text{Rs } 17569.20$$

$\therefore$ Compound interest = Rs 17569.20 − Rs 12000 = Rs 5569.20

Example 7 Find the compound interest on Rs 1000 at the rate of 10% per annum for 18 months when interest is compounded half-yearly.

Solution Here, P = Rs 1000, R = 10% per annum and, $n = \frac{18}{12}$ years $= \frac{3}{2}$ years

$\therefore$ Amount after 18 months $= P\left(1+\frac{R}{200}\right)^{2n}$

$$= \text{Rs } 1000 \times \left(1+\frac{10}{200}\right)^{2\times\frac{3}{2}}$$

$$= \text{Rs } 1000 \times \left(1+\frac{1}{20}\right)^{3}$$

$$= \text{Rs } 1000 \times \left(\frac{21}{20}\right)^{3}$$

$$= \text{Rs } 1000 \times \frac{21}{20} \times \frac{21}{20} \times \frac{21}{20} = \text{Rs } 1157.63$$

Hence, Compound interest = Amount − Principal

= Rs 1157.63 − Rs 1000 = Rs 157.63 = Rs 157.63

Example 8 How much would a sum of Rs 16000 amount to in 2 years time at 10% per annum compound interest, interest being payable half-yearly?

Solution Here, $P = \text{Rs } 16000$, $R = 10\%$ per annum and $n = 2$ years.

$$\therefore \text{ Amount after 2 years} = P\left(1+\frac{R}{200}\right)^{2n}$$

$$= \text{Rs } 16000 \times \left(1+\frac{10}{200}\right)^{2\times 2}$$

$$= \text{Rs } 16000 \times \left(1+\frac{1}{20}\right)^{4}$$

$$= \text{Rs } 16000 \times \left(\frac{21}{20}\right)^{4}$$

$$= \text{Rs } 16000 \times \frac{21}{20} \times \frac{21}{20} \times \frac{21}{20} \times \frac{21}{20} = \text{Rs } 19448.10$$

Hence, a sum of Rs 16000 amounts to Rs 19448. 10 in 2 years.

Type III **COMPUTATION OF COMPOUND INTEREST, WHEN INTEREST IS COMPOUNDED QUARTERLY**

FORMULA $A = P\left(1+\frac{R}{400}\right)^{4n}$, *C.I.* = *A* − *P*., *where P* = *Principal, R* = *Interest rate percent per annum and n* = *number of years.*

Example 9 Find the compound interest on Rs 320000 for one year at the rate of 20% per annum, if the interest is compounded quarterly.

Solution Here, $P = \text{Rs } 320000$, $R = 20\%$ per annum and $n = 1$ years.

$$\therefore \text{ Amount after 1 years} = P\left(1+\frac{R}{400}\right)^{4n}$$

$$= \text{Rs } 320000 \times \left(1+\frac{20}{400}\right)^{4\times 1}$$

$$= \text{Rs } 320000 \times \left(1+\frac{1}{20}\right)^{4}$$

$$= \text{Rs } 320000 \times \left(\frac{21}{20}\right)^{4}$$

$$= \text{Rs } 320000 \times \frac{21}{20} \times \frac{21}{20} \times \frac{21}{20} \times \frac{21}{20} = \text{Rs } 388962$$

$$\therefore \text{ Compound interest} = \text{Rs } 388962 - \text{Rs } 320000 = \text{Rs } 68962.$$

Example 10 Ramesh deposited Rs 7500 in a bank which pays him 12% interest per annum compounded quarterly. What is the amount which he receives after 9 months?

Solution Here, $P = \text{Rs } 7500$, $R = 12\%$ per annum and $n = 9$ months $= \frac{9}{12}$ year $= \frac{3}{4}$ year.

$$\therefore \text{ Amount after 9 months} = P\left(1+\frac{R}{400}\right)^{4n}$$

$$= \text{Rs } 7500 \times \left(1+\frac{12}{400}\right)^{4\times\frac{3}{4}}$$

$$= \text{Rs } 7500 \times \left(1 + \frac{3}{100}\right)^3$$

$$= \text{Rs } 7500 \times \left(\frac{103}{100}\right)^3$$

$$= \text{Rs } 7500 \times \frac{103}{100} \times \frac{103}{100} \times \frac{103}{100} = \text{Rs } 8195.45$$

Example 11 Shyam deposited in a bank Rs 7500 for 6 months at the rate of 8% interest compounded quarterly. Find the amount he received after 6 months.

Solution Here, $P = \text{Rs } 7500$, $R = 8\%$ per annum and $n = 6$ months $= \frac{6}{12}$ year $= \frac{1}{2}$ year.

$$\therefore \quad \text{Amount after 6 months} = P\left(1 + \frac{R}{400}\right)^{4n}$$

$$= \text{Rs } 7500 \times \left(1 + \frac{8}{400}\right)^{4 \times \frac{1}{2}}$$

$$= \text{Rs } 7500 \times \left(1 + \frac{1}{50}\right)^2$$

$$= \text{Rs } 7500 \times \left(\frac{51}{50}\right)^2$$

$$= \text{Rs } 7500 \times \frac{51}{50} \times \frac{51}{50} = \text{Rs } 7803.$$

Type IV **COMPUTATION OF COMPOUND INTEREST, WHEN INTEREST IS COMPOUNDED ANNUALLY BUT RATES BEING DIFFERENT FOR DIFFERENT YEARS**

FORMULA $A = P\left(1 + \frac{R_1}{100}\right)\left(1 + \frac{R_2}{100}\right)\ldots\ldots\left(1 + \frac{R_n}{100}\right)$, *where* $P =$ *Principal and* $R_1, R_2, \ldots, R_n$ *interest rates percent for different years.*

Example 12 Ram Singh buys a refrigerator for Rs 4000 on credit. The rate of interest for the first year is 5% and of the second year is 15%. How much will it cost him if he pays the amount after two years?

Solution Here, $P = \text{Rs } 4000$, $R_1 = 5\%$ per annum and $R_2 = 15\%$ per annum.

$$\therefore \quad \text{Amount after 2 years} = P\left(1 + \frac{R_1}{100}\right)\left(1 + \frac{R_2}{100}\right)$$

$$= \text{Rs } 4000 \times \left(1 + \frac{5}{100}\right)\left(1 + \frac{15}{100}\right)$$

$$= \text{Rs } 4000 \times \left(1 + \frac{1}{20}\right)\left(1 + \frac{3}{20}\right)$$

$$= \text{Rs } 4000 \times \frac{21}{20} \times \frac{23}{20} = \text{Rs } 4830$$

Thus, the refrigerator will cost Rs 4830 to Ram Singh.

Type V **COMPUTATION OF COMPOUND INTEREST WHEN INTEREST IS COMPOUNDED ANNUALLY BUT TIME BEING A FRACTION**

FORMULA *If* $P =$ *Principal,* $R =$ *Rate% per annum and Time* $= 3\frac{3}{4}$ *years (say), then*

$$A = P\left(1+\frac{R}{100}\right)^3 \times \left(1+\frac{\frac{3}{4}\times R}{100}\right)$$

Example 13 Find the compound interest on Rs 24000 at 15% per annum for $2\frac{1}{3}$ years.

Solution Here, $P = \text{Rs } 24000$, $R = 15\%$ per annum and Time $= 2\frac{1}{3}$ years.

$\therefore$ Amount after $2\frac{1}{3}$ years $= P\left(1+\frac{R}{100}\right)^2 \times \left(1+\frac{\frac{1}{3}\times R}{100}\right)$

$$= \text{Rs}\left\{24000 \times \left(1+\frac{15}{100}\right)^2 \times \left(1+\frac{\frac{1}{3}\times 15}{100}\right)\right\}$$

$$= \text{Rs}\left\{24000 \times \left(1+\frac{3}{20}\right)^2 \times \left(1+\frac{1}{20}\right)\right\}$$

$$= \text{Rs}\left\{24000 \times \left(\frac{23}{20}\right)^2 \times \left(\frac{21}{20}\right)\right\} = \text{Rs } 33327$$

$\therefore$ Compound interest $= \text{Rs } (33327 - 24000) = \text{Rs } 9327$

EXERCISE 14.2

1. Compute the amount and the compound interest in each of the following by using the formulae when :
   (i) Principal = Rs 3000, Rate = 5%, Time = 2 years
   (ii) Principal = Rs 3000, Rate = 18%, Time = 2 years
   (iii) Principal = Rs 5000, Rate = 10 paise per rupee per annum, Time = 2 years
   (iv) Principal = Rs 2000, Rate = 4 paise per rupee per annum, Time = 3 years
   (v) Principal = Rs 12800, Rate = $7\frac{1}{2}\%$, Time = 3 years
   (vi) Principal = Rs 10000, Rate 20% per annum compounded half-yearly, Time = 2 years
   (vii) Principal = Rs 160000, Rate = 10 paise per rupee per annum compounded half-yearly, Time = 2 years.
2. Find the amount of Rs 2400 after 3 years, when the interest is compounded annually at the rate of 20% per annum.
3. Rahman lent Rs 16000 to Rasheed at the rate of $12\frac{1}{2}\%$ per annum compound interest. Find the amount payable by Rasheed to Rahman after 3 years.
4. Meera borrowed a sum of Rs 1000 from Sita for two years. If the rate of interest is 10% compounded annually, find the amount that Meera has to pay back.
5. Find the difference between the compound interest and simple interest. On a sum of Rs 50,000 at 10% per annum for 2 years.

6. Amit borrowed Rs 16000 at $17\frac{1}{2}\%$ per annum simple interest. On the same day, he lent it to Ashu at the same rate but compounded annually. What does he gain at the end of 2 years?
7. Find the amount of Rs 4096 for 18 months at $12\frac{1}{2}\%$ per annum, the interest being compounded semi-annually.
8. Find the amount and the compound interest on Rs 8000 for $1\frac{1}{2}$ years at 10% per annum, compounded half-yearly.
9. Kamal borrowed Rs 57600 from LIC against her policy at $12\frac{1}{2}\%$ per annum to build a house. Find the amount that she pays to the LIC after $1\frac{1}{2}$ years if the interest is calculated half-yearly.
10. Abha purchased a house from Avas Parishad on credit. If the cost of the house is Rs 64000 and the rate of interest is 5% per annum compounded half-yearly, find the interest paid by Abha after one year and a half.
11. Rakesh lent out Rs 10000 for 2 years at 20% per annum, compounded annually. How much more he could earn if the interest be compounded half-yearly?
12. Romesh borrowed a sum of Rs 245760 at 12.5% per annum, compounded annually. On the same day, he lent out his money to Ramu at the same rate of interest, but compounded semi-annually. Find his gain after 2 years.
13. Find the amount that David would receive if he invests Rs 8192 for 18 months at $12\frac{1}{2}\%$ per annum, the interest being compounded half-yearly.
14. Find the compound interest on Rs 15625 for 9 months, at 16% per annum, compounded quarterly.
15. Rekha deposited Rs 16000 in a foreign bank which pays interest at the rate of 20% per annum compounded quarterly, find the interest received by Rekha after one year.
16. Find the amount of Rs 12500 for 2 years compounded annually, the rate of interest being 15% for the first year and 16% for the second year.
17. Ramu borrowed Rs 15625 from a finance company to buy a scooter. If the rate of interest be 16% per annum compounded annually, what payment will he have to make after $2\frac{1}{4}$ years?
18. What will Rs 125000 amount to at the rate of 6%, if the interest is calculated after every four months?
19. Find the compound interest at the rate of 5% for three years on that principal which in three years at the rate of 5% per annum gives Rs 12000 as simple interest.
20. A sum of money was lent for 2 years at 20% compounded annually. If the interest is payable half-yearly instead of yearly, then the interest is Rs 482 more. Find the sum.
21. Simple interest on a sum of money for 2 years at $6\frac{1}{2}\%$ per annum is Rs 5200. What will be the compound interest on the sum at the same rate for the same period?
22. Find the compound interest at the rate of 5% per annum for 3 years on that principal which in 3 years at the rate of 5% per annum gives Rs 1200 as simple interest.

ANSWERS

1. (i) C.I. = Rs 307.50, A = Rs 3307.50 (ii) A = Rs 4177.20, C.I. = Rs 1177.20
(iii) A = Rs 6050, C.I. = Rs 1050 (iv) A = Rs 2249.68, C.I. = Rs 249.68
(v) A = Rs 15901.40, C.I. = Rs 3101.40 (vi) C.I. = Rs 4641, A = Rs 14641
(vii) A = Rs 194481, Rs 34481

2. Rs 4147.20 3. Rs 22781.25 4. Rs 1210 5. Rs 500 6. Rs 490
7. Rs 4913 8. Rs 9261, Rs 1261 9. Rs 69089.06 10. Rs 4921
11. Rs 241 12. Rs 2163.75 13. Rs 9826 14. Rs 1951 15. Rs 3448.10
16. Rs 16675 17. Rs 21866 18. Rs 132651 19. Rs 12610 20. Rs 20.000 21. Rs 5369
22. Rs 1261.

14.5 INVERSE PROBLEMS ON COMPOUND INTEREST

In the earlier section, we have learnt to find the amount A and compound interest C.I., when P, R and n were given. In this section, we shall discuss how to compute each of the three quantities, namely P, R and T, when sufficient data is given. This is explained in the following illustrative examples.

ILLUSTRATIVE EXAMPLES

Type I **ON FINDING THE PRINCIPAL WHEN *A*, C.I., *R* AND *n* ARE GIVEN**

Example 1 Find the principal, if the compound interest compounded annually at the rate of 10% per annum for three years is Rs 331.

Solution Let the principal be Rs 100. Then,

$$\text{Amount after three years } = \text{Rs}\left[100\times\left(1+\frac{10}{100}\right)^3\right] = \text{Rs}\left[100\times\left(\frac{11}{100}\right)^3\right]$$

$$= \text{Rs } 133.10$$

$\therefore$ Compound interest $= \text{Rs } (133.10 - 100) = \text{Rs } 33.10$

Now,

If compound interest is Rs 33.10, principal $= \text{Rs } 100$

If compound interest is Re 1, principal $= \text{Rs } \frac{100}{33.10}$

If compound interest is Rs 331, principal $= \text{Rs}\left(\frac{100}{33.10}\times 331\right) = \text{Rs } 1000$

Hence, principal $= \text{Rs } 1000$

Example 2 What sum will become Rs 9826 in 18 months if the rate of interest is $2\frac{1}{2}\%$ per annum and the interest is compounded half-yearly?

Solution Let the required sum i.e. the principal, be Rs P.

We have,

$$\text{Principal} = P, \text{Amount} = \text{Rs } 9826,\ R = 2\frac{1}{2}\% \text{ per annum}$$

$$\text{and, } n = 18 \text{ months} = \frac{18}{12} \text{ years} = \frac{3}{2} \text{ years.}$$

$$\therefore \quad A = P\left(1+\frac{R}{200}\right)^{2n}$$

$$\Rightarrow \quad 9826 = P\left(1+\frac{\frac{5}{2}}{200}\right)^{2\times\frac{3}{2}}$$

$$\Rightarrow \quad 9826 = P\left(1+\frac{1}{80}\right)^{3}$$

$$\Rightarrow \quad 9826 = P\left(\frac{81}{80}\right)^{3} \Rightarrow P = 9826\times\left(\frac{80}{81}\right)^{3} = \text{Rs } 9466.54$$

Hence, required sum = Rs 9466.54

Aliter Let the required sum be Rs 100. Then, the amount after 18 months i.e. $\frac{3}{2}$ years at the rate of $2\frac{1}{2}\%$ compounded half-yearly, is given by

$$\text{Amount} = \text{Rs}\left\{100\times\left(1+\frac{\frac{5}{2}}{200}\right)^{2\times\frac{3}{2}}\right\} = \text{Rs}\left\{100\times\left(\frac{81}{80}\right)^{3}\right\} = \text{Rs }\frac{531441}{5120}$$

Now,

If amount is Rs $\frac{531441}{5120}$, then principal = Rs 100

If amount is Re 1, then principal = Rs $\left(\frac{100\times5120}{531441}\right)$

If amount is Rs 9826, then principal = Rs $\left(\frac{100\times5120}{531441}\times9826\right)$ = Rs 9466.54

Hence, required sum = Rs 9466.54

Example 3 The difference between the compound interest and simple interest on a certain sum of money at 10% per annum for 2 years is Rs 500. Find the sum when the interest is compounded annually.

Solution Let the sum be Rs 100.

Computation of compound interest:

We have, Principal = Rs 100, $R = 10\%$ per annum and $n = 2$ years.

$$\text{Amount} = \text{Rs}\left[100\times\left(1+\frac{10}{100}\right)^{2}\right] = \text{Rs}\left[100\times\left(\frac{11}{10}\right)^{2}\right] = \text{Rs } 121$$

$\therefore$ C.I. = Rs 121 − Rs 100 = Rs 21

Computation of simple interest:

We have, Principal = Rs 100, $R = 10\%$ and Time = 2 years.

$\therefore$ S.I. $= \text{Rs}\left(\frac{100\times10\times2}{100}\right) = \text{Rs } 20$

Thus, difference in C.I. and S.I. $= \text{Rs } (21-20) = \text{Re } 1$

Now,

If difference between C.I. and S.I. is Re 1, sum $= \text{Rs } 100$

If difference between C.I. and S.I. is Rs 500, Sum $= \text{Rs } (100\times500) = \text{Rs } 50000$.

Type II **ON FINDING THE TIME OR PERIOD OF INVESTMENT**

Example 4 In what time will Rs 800 amount to Rs 882 at 5% per annum compounded annually?

Solution Here, amount $A = \text{Rs } 882$, Principal $P = \text{Rs } 800$ and rate $R = 5\%$ per annum.

$$\therefore \quad A = P\left(1+\frac{R}{100}\right)^n$$

$$\Rightarrow \quad 882 = 800\left(1+\frac{5}{100}\right)^n$$

$$\Rightarrow \quad \frac{882}{800} = \left(1+\frac{1}{20}\right)^n$$

$$\Rightarrow \quad \frac{882}{800} = \left(\frac{21}{20}\right)^n$$

$$\Rightarrow \quad \frac{441}{400} = \left(\frac{21}{20}\right)^2 \Rightarrow \left(\frac{21}{20}\right)^n = \left(\frac{21}{20}\right)^2 \Rightarrow n = 2$$

Hence, required time is 2 years.

Example 5 In what time will Rs 64000 amount to Rs 68921 at 5% per annum, interest being compounded half-yearly?

Solution Here, Principal $P = \text{Rs } 64000$, Amount $A = \text{Rs } 68921$, rate $R = 5\%$ per annum.

Since the interest is compounded half-yearly.

$$\therefore \quad A = P\left(1+\frac{R}{200}\right)^{2n}, \text{ where } n \text{ is the number of years.}$$

$$\Rightarrow \quad 68921 = 64000\left(1+\frac{5}{200}\right)^{2n}$$

$$\Rightarrow \quad \frac{68921}{64000} = \left(\frac{41}{40}\right)^{2n}$$

$$\Rightarrow \quad \left(\frac{41}{40}\right)^3 = \left(\frac{41}{40}\right)^{2n} \Rightarrow 2n = 3 \Rightarrow n = \frac{3}{2} \text{ years} = 1\frac{1}{2} \text{ years}$$

Type III **ON FINDING THE INTEREST RATE PERCENT PER ANNUM**

Example 6 At what rate percent per annum, compound interest will Rs 10000 amount to Rs 13310 in three years?

Solution Let the rate be R% per annum.

We have, $P = \text{Principal} = \text{Rs } 10000$, $A = \text{amount} = \text{Rs } 13310$ and $n = 3$ years.

$$A = P\left(1+\frac{R}{100}\right)^n$$

$$\Rightarrow \quad 13310 = 10000\left(1+\frac{R}{100}\right)^3$$

$$\Rightarrow \quad \frac{13310}{10000} = \left(1+\frac{R}{100}\right)^3$$

$$\Rightarrow \quad \frac{1331}{1000} = \left(1+\frac{R}{100}\right)^3$$

$$\Rightarrow \quad \frac{11^3}{10^3} = \left(1+\frac{R}{100}\right)^3$$

$$\Rightarrow \quad \left(1+\frac{R}{100}\right)^3 = \left(\frac{11}{10}\right)^3$$

$$\Rightarrow \quad 1+\frac{R}{100} = \frac{11}{10}$$

$$\Rightarrow \quad \frac{R}{100} = \frac{11}{10} - 1 \Rightarrow \frac{R}{100} = \frac{1}{10} \Rightarrow R = \frac{100}{10} = 10$$

Hence, rate $= 10\%$ per annum.

Example 7 Reena borrowed from Kamal certain sum for two years at simple interest. Reena lent this sum to Hamid at the same rate for two years compound interest. At the end of two years she received Rs 110 as compound interest but paid Rs 100 as simple interest. Find the sum and rate of interest.

Solution Let the principal be Rs P and the rate of interest be R % per annum.

We have, C.I. $=$ Rs 110, S.I. $=$ Rs 100 and Time $= 2$ years.

$$\therefore \quad 110 = P\left(1+\frac{R}{100}\right)^2 - P \text{ and } 100 = \frac{P\times R\times 2}{100}$$

$$\Rightarrow \quad 110 = P\left\{\left(1+\frac{R}{100}\right)^2 - 1\right\} \text{ and } 100 = \frac{PR}{50}$$

$$\Rightarrow \quad 110 = P\left\{\left(1+\frac{R}{100}\right)^2 - 1\right\} \text{ and } PR = 5000$$

$$\Rightarrow \quad 110 = P\left\{1+\frac{2R}{100}+\frac{R^2}{10000} - 1\right\} \text{ and } PR = 5000$$

$$\Rightarrow \quad 110 = \frac{2PR}{100}+\frac{PR^2}{10000} \text{ and } PR = 5000$$

$$\Rightarrow \quad 110 = \frac{PR}{50}+\frac{PR}{10000}\times R \text{ and } PR = 5000$$

$$\Rightarrow \quad 110 = \frac{5000}{50} + \frac{5000}{10000} \times R \qquad \text{[Putting } PR = 5000\text{]}$$

$$\Rightarrow \quad 110 = 100 + \frac{R}{2} \quad \Rightarrow \quad 10 = \frac{R}{2} \quad \Rightarrow \quad R = 20$$

Putting $R = 20$ in $PR = 5000$, we get

$$20P = 5000 \Rightarrow P = 250$$

Hence, principal = Rs 250 and rate = 20% per annum.

EXERCISE 14.3

1. On what sum will the compound interest at 5% per annum for 2 years compounded annually be Rs 164?
2. Find the principal if the interest compounded annually at the rate of 10% for two years is Rs 210.
3. A sum amounts to Rs 756.25 at 10% per annum in 2 years, compounded annually. Find the sum.
4. What sum will amount to Rs 4913 in 18 months, if the rate of interest is $12\frac{1}{2}\%$ per annum, compounded half-yearly?
5. The difference between the compound interest and simple interest on a certain sum at 15% per annum for 3 years is Rs 283.50. Find the sum.
6. Rachana borrowed a certain sum at the rate of 15% per annum. If she paid at the end of two years Rs 1290 as interest compounded annually, find the sum she borrowed.
7. The interest on a sum of Rs 2000 is being compounded annually at the rate of 4% per annum. Find the period for which the compound interest is Rs 163.20.
8. In how much time would Rs 5000 amount to Rs 6655 at 10% per annum compound interest?
9. In what time will Rs 4400 become Rs 4576 at 8% per annum interest compounded half-yearly?
10. The difference between the S.I. and C.I. on a certain sum of money for 2 years at 4% per annum is Rs 20. Find the sum.
11. In what time will Rs 1000 amount to Rs 1331 at 10% per annum, compound interest?
12. At what rate percent compound interest per annum will Rs 640 amount to Rs 774.40 in 2 years?
13. Find the rate percent per annum if Rs 2000 amount to Rs 2662 in $1\frac{1}{2}$ years, interest being compounded half-yearly?
14. Kamala borrowed from Ratan a certain sum at a certain rate for two years simple interest. She lent this sum at the same rate to Hari for two years compound interest. At the end of two years she received Rs 210 as compound interest, but paid Rs 200 only as simple interest. Find the sum and the rate of interest.
15. Find the rate percent per annum, if Rs 2000 amount to Rs 2315.25 in an year and a half, interest being compounded six monthly.
16. Find the rate at which a sum of money will double itself in 3 years, if the interest is compounded annually.

17. Find the rate at which a sum of money will become four times the original amount in 2 years, if the interest is compounded half-yearly.
18. A certain sum amounts to Rs 5832 in 2 years at 8% compounded interest. Find the sum.
19. The difference between the compound interest and simple interest on a certain sum for 2 years at 7.5% per annum is Rs 360. Find the sum.
20. The difference in simple interest and compound interest on a certain sum of money at $6\frac{2}{3}$% per annum for 3 years is Rs 46. Determine the sum.
21. Ishita invested a sum of Rs 12000 at 5% per annum compound interest. She received an amount of Rs 13230 after n years. Find the value of n.
22. At what rate percent per annum will a sum of Rs 4000 yield compound interest of Rs 410 in 2 years?
23. A sum of money deposited at 2% per annum compounded annually becomes Rs 10404 at the end of 2 years. Find the sum deposited.
24. In how much time will a sum of Rs 1600 amount to Rs 1852.20 at 5% per annum compound interest?
25. At what rate percent will a sum of Rs 1000 amount to Rs 1102.50 in 2 years at compound interest?
26. The compound interest on Rs 1800 at 10% per annum for a certain period of time is Rs 378. Find the time in years.
27. What sum of money will amount to Rs 45582.25 at $6\frac{3}{4}$% per annum in two years, interest being compounded annually?
28. Sum of money amounts to Rs 453690 in 2 years at 6.5% per annum compounded annually. Find the sum.

ANSWERS

1. Rs 1600   2. Rs 1000   3. Rs 625   4. Rs 4096   5. Rs 4000   6. Rs 4000
7. 2 years   8. 3 years   9. $\frac{1}{2}$ year   10. Rs 12500   11. 3 years   12. 10% per annum
13. 20 % per annum   14. Rs 1000, 10% per annum   15. 10% per annum   16. 25.99%
17. 82.84%   18. Rs 5000   19. Rs 64000   20. Rs 3375   21. 2   22. 5%
23. Rs 10,000   24. 3 years   25. 5%   26. 2 years   27. Rs 40,000   28. Rs 4,00,000.

14.6 POPULATION GROWTH

In our day-to-day life we observe that there are things or entities like population of a city, the value of property, the height of a tree, weight and height of a child, the number of bacteria etc. which increase in magnitude over a period of time. The relative increase in a quantity or entity is called growth and growth per unit of time is called the rate of growth. In this section, we shall illustrate how the formulae for computing amount and compound interest are used to calculate the growth of population etc.

FORMULAE FOR POPULATION GROWTH

FORMULA 1 *Let P be the population of a city or a town at the beginning of a certain year and the population grows at a constant rate of R% per annum, then*

Population after n years $= P\left(1+\frac{R}{100}\right)^n$

FORMULA 2 *Let P be the population of a city or a town at the beginning of a certain year. If the population grows at the rate of R_1% during first year and R_2% during second year, then*

Population after 2 years $= P\left(1+\frac{R_1}{100}\right)\times\left(1+\frac{R_2}{100}\right)$

This formula may be extended for more than 2 years also.

FORMULA 3 *Let P be the population of a city or a town at the beginning of a certain year. If the population decreases at the rate of R% per annum, then*

Population after n years $= P\left(1-\frac{R}{100}\right)^n$

Following examples will illustrate the use of the above formulae.

ILLUSTRATIVE EXAMPLES

Example 1 The population of a town is increasing at the rate of 5% per annum. What will be the population of the town on this basis after two years, if the present population is 16000?

Solution Here, P = Initial population = 16000

R = Rate of growth of population = 5% per annum, n = Number of years = 2

$\therefore$ Population after 2 years $= P\left(1+\frac{R}{100}\right)^n$

$= 16000\times\left(1+\frac{5}{100}\right)^2$

$= 16000\times\left(1+\frac{1}{20}\right)^2$

$= 16000\times\left(\frac{21}{20}\right)^2 = 16000\times\frac{21}{20}\times\frac{21}{20} = 17640.$

Hence, population after 2 years $= 17640$.

Example 2 The population of a village is 20000. If the annual birth rate is 4% and the annual death rate 2%, calculate the population after two years.

Solution We have,

Annual birth rate = 4%, Annual death rate = 2%

$\therefore$ Annual growth $= (4-2)\% = 2\%$

Thus, we have

P = Initial population = 20000, R = Rate of growth = 2% per annum, n = 2 years

$\therefore$ Population after 2 years $= P\left(1+\frac{R}{100}\right)^n$

$$= 20000 \times \left(1+\frac{2}{100}\right)^2$$

$$= 20000 \times \left(1+\frac{1}{50}\right)^2$$

$$= 20000 \times \left(\frac{51}{50}\right)^2 = 20000 \times \frac{51}{50} \times \frac{51}{50} = 20808$$

Hence, population of the town after 2 years $= 20808$.

Example 3 The population of a town was 160000 three years ago. If it had increased by 3%, 2.5% and 5% in the last three years, find the present population of the town.

Solution Let P be the present population of the town. Then,

$$P = 160000 \times \left(1+\frac{3}{100}\right) \times \left(1+\frac{2.5}{100}\right) \times \left(1+\frac{5}{100}\right)$$

$$\Rightarrow \quad P = 160000 \times \frac{103}{100} \times \frac{41}{40} \times \frac{21}{20}$$

$$\Rightarrow \quad P = 2 \times 103 \times 41 \times 21 = 177366.$$

Hence, present population of the town $= 177366$.

Example 4 The population of a town 2 years ago was 62500. Due to migration to cities, it decreases every year at the rate of 4% per annum. Find its present population.

Solution We have,

Population two years ago $= 62500$

Rate of decrease of population $= 4\%$ per annum.

$\therefore$ Present population $= 62500 \times \left(1-\frac{4}{100}\right)^2$

$$= 62500 \times \left(1-\frac{1}{25}\right)^2$$

$$= 62500 \times \left(\frac{24}{25}\right)^2 = 62500 \times \frac{24}{25} \times \frac{24}{25} = 57600.$$

Hence, present population $= 57600$.

Example 5 The present population of a city is 9261000. If it has been increasing at the rate of 5% per annum, find its population 3 years ago.

Solution Let the population three years ago be P. Then,

Present population $= P \times \left(1+\frac{5}{100}\right)^3$

$$\Rightarrow \quad 9261000 = P \times \left(1 + \frac{1}{20}\right)^3$$

$$\Rightarrow \quad 9261000 = P \times \left(\frac{21}{20}\right)^3$$

$$\Rightarrow \quad P = 9261000 \times \left(\frac{20}{21}\right)^3$$

$$\Rightarrow \quad P = 9261000 \times \frac{20}{21} \times \frac{20}{21} \times \frac{20}{21} = 8000000.$$

Hence, the population 3 years ago = 8000000.

Example 6 In a factory the production of scooters rose to 48400 from 40000 in 2 years. Find the rate of growth per annum.

Solution Let the rate of growth be R% per annum.

We have, Present production $= 48400$ scooters.

Previous production $= 40000$ scooters, Number of years $= 2$.

$$\therefore \quad 48400 = 40000 \times \left(1 + \frac{R}{100}\right)^2$$

$$\Rightarrow \quad \frac{484}{400} = \left(1 + \frac{R}{100}\right)^2$$

$$\Rightarrow \quad \frac{121}{100} = \left(1 + \frac{R}{100}\right)^2$$

$$\Rightarrow \quad \left(1 + \frac{R}{100}\right)^2 = \left(\frac{11}{10}\right)^2$$

$$\Rightarrow \quad 1 + \frac{R}{100} = \frac{11}{10} \Rightarrow \frac{R}{100} = \frac{11}{10} - 1 \Rightarrow \frac{R}{100} = \frac{1}{10} \Rightarrow R = \frac{100}{10} = 10$$

Hence, required rate of growth = 10 % per annum.

Example 7 The bacteria in a culture grows by 10% in the first hour, decreases by 10% in the second hour and again increases by 10% in the third hour. If the original count of the bacteria in a sample is 10000, find the bacteria count at the end of 3 hours.

Solution We have,

$P =$ Original count of bacteria $= 10000$

$$\therefore \quad \text{Bacteria count after 3 hours} = 10000 \times \left(1 + \frac{10}{100}\right) \times \left(1 - \frac{10}{100}\right) \times \left(1 + \frac{10}{100}\right)$$

$$= 10000 \times \frac{11}{10} \times \frac{9}{10} \times \frac{11}{10}$$

$$= 10 \times 11 \times 9 \times 11 = 10890.$$

Example 8 Ashish opened a bookshop with an initial investment of Rs 32000. In the first year, he incurred a loss of 5%. However, during the second year, he earned a profit of 10% which in the third year rose to $12\frac{1}{2}$%. Calculate his net profit for the entire period of three years.

Solution We have,

Initial investment = Rs 32000, Loss in first year = 5%

Profit in second year = 10%, Profit in third year $= 12\frac{1}{2}\% = \frac{25}{2}\%$

$\therefore$ Ashish's assets at the end of three years are worth

$$= \text{Rs}\left\{32000 \times \left(1 - \frac{5}{100}\right) \times \left(1 + \frac{10}{100}\right) \times \left(1 + \frac{\frac{25}{2}}{100}\right)\right\}$$

$$= \text{Rs}\left\{32000 \times \left(1 - \frac{1}{20}\right) \times \left(1 + \frac{1}{10}\right) \times \left(1 + \frac{1}{8}\right)\right\}$$

$$= \text{Rs}\left\{32000 \times \frac{19}{20} \times \frac{11}{10} \times \frac{9}{8}\right\} = \text{Rs } 37620.$$

Hence, net profit = Rs 37620 – Rs 32000 = Rs 5620.

Example 9 10000 workers were employed to construct a river bridge in four years. At the end of first year, 10% workers were retrenched. At the end of the second year, 5% of the workers at that time were retrenched. However to complete the project in time, the number of workers was increased by 10% at the end of the third year. How many workers were working during the fourth year ?

Solution We have,

Initial number of workers = 10000

Reduction of workers at the end of first year = 10%

Reduction of workers at the end of second year = 5%

Increase of workers at the end of third year = 10%

$\therefore$ Number of workers working during the fourth year

$$= 10000\left(1 - \frac{10}{100}\right)\left(1 - \frac{5}{100}\right)\left(1 + \frac{10}{100}\right) = 10000 \times \frac{9}{10} \times \frac{19}{20} \times \frac{11}{10} = 9405.$$

Hence, the number of workers working during the fourth year was 9405.

Example 10 24000 blood donors were registered with a charitable hospital. The number of donors increased at the rate of 5% every six month. Find the time period at the end of which the total number of blood donors becomes 27783.

Solution We have,

P = Initial number of donors = 24000, A = Final number of donors = 27783

R = Rate of increase = 5% every six month = 10% p.a.

Let the total time be n years. Then,

$$A = P\left(1 + \frac{R}{200}\right)^{2n}$$

$$\Rightarrow \quad 27783 = 24000\left(1+\frac{10}{200}\right)^{2n}$$

$$\Rightarrow \quad 27783 = 24000\left(\frac{21}{20}\right)^{2n}$$

$$\Rightarrow \quad \frac{27783}{24000} = \left(\frac{21}{20}\right)^{2n} \Rightarrow \left(\frac{21}{20}\right)^{3} = \left(\frac{21}{20}\right)^{2n} \Rightarrow 2n = 3 \Rightarrow n = \frac{3}{2}$$

Hence, required time period $= \frac{3}{2}$ years.

Example 11 A factory increased its production of three wheelers from 80000 in 1999 to 92610 in 2002. Find the annual rate of growth of production of three wheelers.

Solution Let the annual rate of growth be $R\%$ per annum. Then,

$$92610 = 80000\left(1+\frac{R}{100}\right)^{3}$$

$$\Rightarrow \quad \frac{92610}{80000} = \left(1+\frac{R}{100}\right)^{3}$$

$$\Rightarrow \quad \left(\frac{21}{20}\right)^{3} = \left(1+\frac{R}{100}\right)^{3}$$

$$\Rightarrow \quad \frac{21}{20} = 1+\frac{R}{100} \Rightarrow \frac{1}{20} = \frac{R}{100} \Rightarrow R = 5$$

Hence, the annual rate of growth of production is 5% per annum.

Example 12 Given that Carbon$-14(C_{14})$ decays at a constant rate in such a way that it reduces to 50% in 5568 years. Find the age of an old wooden piece in which the carbon is only 12.5% of the original.

Solution Let the rate of decay be $R\%$ per annum and the age of wooden piece be n years. Let the original amount of carbon in the wooden piece be P. Then, in 5568 years the amount left is $\frac{P}{2}$.

$$\therefore \quad \frac{P}{2} = P\left(1-\frac{R}{100}\right)^{5568}$$

$$\Rightarrow \quad \frac{1}{2} = \left(1-\frac{R}{100}\right)^{5568}$$

After n years, the carbon left in the wooden piece is 12.5% of P i.e., $\frac{12.5P}{100} = \frac{P}{8}$.

$$\therefore \quad \frac{P}{8} = P\left(1-\frac{R}{100}\right)^{n}$$

$$\Rightarrow \quad \frac{1}{8} = \left(1-\frac{R}{100}\right)^{n}$$

$$\Rightarrow \left(\frac{1}{2}\right)^3 = \left(1 - \frac{R}{100}\right)^n$$

$$\Rightarrow \left\{\left(1 - \frac{R}{100}\right)^{5568}\right\}^3 = \left(1 - \frac{R}{100}\right)^n$$

$$\Rightarrow \left(1 - \frac{R}{100}\right)^{5568 \times 3} = \left(1 - \frac{R}{100}\right)^n$$

$$\Rightarrow n = 5568 \times 3 = 16704 \text{ years}.$$

Hence, the age of the wooden piece is 16704 years.

EXERCISE 14.4

1. The present population of a town is 28000. If it increases at the rate of 5% per annum, what will be its population after 2 years?
2. The population of a city is 125000. If the annual birth rate and death rate are 5.5% and 3.5% respectively, calculate the population of city after 3 years.
3. The present population of a town is 25000. It grows at 4%, 5% and 8% during first year, second year and third year respectively. Find its population after 3 years.
4. Three years ago, the population of a town was 50000. If the annual increase during three successive years be at the rate of 4%, 5% and 3% respectively, find the present population.
5. There is a continuous growth in population of a village at the rate of 5% per annum. If its present population is 9261, what it was 3 years ago?
6. In a factory the production of scooters rose to 46305 from 40000 in 3 years. Find the annual rate of growth of the production of scooters.
7. The annual rate of growth in population of a certain city is 8%. If its present population is 196830, what it was 3 years ago?
8. The populaticn of a town increases at the rate of 50 per thousand. Its population after 2 years will be 22050. Find its present population.
9. The count of bacteria in a culture grows by 10% in the first hour, decreases by 8% in the second hour and again increases by 12% in the third hour. If the count of bacteria in the sample is 13125000, what will be the count of bacteria after 3 hours?
10. The population of a certain city was 72000 on the last day of the year 1998. During next year it increased by 7% but due to an epidemic it decreased by 10% in the following year. What was its population at the end of the year 2000?
11. 6400 workers were employed to construct a river bridge in four years. At the end of the first year, 25% workers were retrenched. At the end of the second year, 25% of those working at that time were retrenched. However, to complete the project in time, the number of workers was increased by 25% at the end of the third year. How many workers were working during the fourth year?
12. Aman started a factory with an initial investment of Rs 100000. In the first year, he incurred a loss of 5%. However, during the second year, he earned a profit of 10% which in the third year rose to 12%. Calculate his net profit for the entire period of three years.

13. The population of a town increases at the rate of 40 per thousand annually. If the present population be 175760, what was the population three years ago.
14. The production of a mixi company in 1996 was 8000 mixies. Due to increase in demand it increases its production by 15% in the next two years and after two years its demand decreases by 5%. What will be its production after 3 years ?
15. The population of a city increases each year by 4% of what it had been at the beginning of each year. If the population in 1999 had been 6760000, find the population of the city in (i) 2001 (ii) 1997.
16. Jitendra set up a factory by investing Rs 2500000. During the first two successive years his profits were 5% and 10% respectively. If each year the profit was on previous year's capital, compute his total profit.

ANSWERS

1. 30870	2. 132651	3. 29484	4. 56238	5. 8000	6. 5%
7.156250	8. 20000	9. 14876400	10. 69336	11. 4500	12. Rs17040
13.156250	14. 10051	15. (i) 7311616 (ii) 6250000		16. Rs 387500	

14.7 DEPRECIATION

It is a well known fact that the constant use of any machine or any other article causes wear and tear due to which its value decreases with time. The relative decrease in the value of a machine over a period of time is called its *depreciation*. Depreciation per unit of time is called the *rate of depreciation*. The value at any time is called the depreciated value.

Result1 *If V_0 is the value of an article at a certain time and R% per annum is the rate of depreciation, then the value V_n at the end of n years is given by*

$$V_n = V_0\left(1-\frac{R}{100}\right)^n$$

Proof: Since the rate of depreciation is R % per annum.

$\therefore$ Depreciation in one year $= \dfrac{V_0 R}{100}$

$\Rightarrow$ Depreciated value at the end of a year $= V_0 - \dfrac{V_0 R}{100} = V_0\left(1-\dfrac{R}{100}\right)$

Now, Depreciation in the second year $= V_0\left(1-\dfrac{R}{100}\right)\times\dfrac{R}{100}$

$\therefore$ Depreciated value at the end of two years

$$= V_0\left(1-\frac{R}{100}\right) - V_0\left(1-\frac{R}{100}\right)\frac{R}{100}$$

$$= V_0\left(1-\frac{R}{100}\right)^2$$

Continuing in this manner, we get

$$V_n = V_0\left(1-\frac{R}{100}\right)^n$$

<u>Result 2</u> *If V_0 is the value of an article at certain time and the rate of depreciation is $R_1\%$ for first n_1 years, $r_2\%$ for next n_2 years and so on and R_k % for the last n_k years, then the value at the end of $n_1 + n_2 + \cdots + n_k$ years is given by*

$$V = V_0\left(1-\frac{R_1}{100}\right)^{n1}\left(1-\frac{R_2}{100}\right)^{n2} \ldots\ldots \left(1-\frac{R_k}{100}\right)^{nk}$$

ILLUSTRATIVE EXAMPLES

Example 1 The value of a residential flat constructed at a cost of Rs 100000 is depreciating at the rate of 10% per annum. What will be its value 3 years after construction ?

Solution We have,

V_0 = Initial value = Rs 100000, R = Rate of depreciation = 10% per annum

$$\therefore \quad \text{Value after 3 years} = V_0\left(1-\frac{R}{100}\right)^3$$

$$= \text{Rs}\left\{100000\times\left(1-\frac{10}{100}\right)^3\right\}$$

$$= \text{Rs}\left\{100000\times\left(1-\frac{1}{10}\right)^3\right\}$$

$$= \text{Rs}\left\{100000\times\left(\frac{9}{10}\right)^3\right\}$$

$$= \text{Rs}\left\{100000\times\frac{9}{10}\times\frac{9}{10}\times\frac{9}{10}\right\} = \text{Rs } 72900$$

Hence, value of the flat after 3 years = Rs 72900

Example 2 A new car costs Rs 360000. Its price depreciates at the rate of 10% a year during the first two years and at the rate of 20% a year thereafter. What will be the price of the car after 3 years ?

Solution We have,

Cost of the car = Rs 360000

Rate of depreciation in first two years = 10% per annum.

Rate of depreciation in the third year = 20%

$\therefore$ Price of the car after 3 years

$$= \text{Rs}\left\{360000\times\left(1-\frac{10}{100}\right)\times\left(1-\frac{10}{100}\right)\times\left(1-\frac{20}{100}\right)\right\}$$

$$= \text{Rs}\left\{360000\times\left(1-\frac{1}{10}\right)\times\left(1-\frac{1}{10}\right)\times\left(1-\frac{1}{5}\right)\right\}$$

$$= \text{Rs}\left\{360000\times\frac{9}{10}\times\frac{9}{10}\times\frac{4}{5}\right\} = \text{Rs } 233280$$

Hence, the price of the car after 3 years = Rs 233280.

Example 3 The present price of a scooter is Rs 7290. If its value decreases every year by 10%, then find its value before 3 years.

Solution Let the value of the scooter be P Rs before three years. Then, its present value is

$$\text{Rs } P\left(1-\frac{10}{100}\right)^3$$

But, the present value is given as Rs 7290.

$$\therefore \quad 7290 = P\times\left(1-\frac{10}{100}\right)^3$$

$$\Rightarrow \quad 7290 = P\times\left(1-\frac{1}{10}\right)^3$$

$$\Rightarrow \quad 7290 = P\times\left(\frac{9}{10}\right)^3$$

$$\Rightarrow \quad 7290 = P\times\frac{9^3}{10^3} \Rightarrow P = \frac{7290\times 10^3}{9^3} = 10000$$

Hence, the value before 3 years was Rs 10000.

Example 4 The value of a flat worth Rs 500000 is depreciating at the rate of 10% per annum. In how many years will its value be reduced to Rs 364500 ?

Solution We have,

Present value = Rs 500000, Depreciated value = Rs 364500

Rate of depreciation = 10% per annum.

Let the depreciation period be of n years. Then,

$$364500 = 500000\left(1-\frac{10}{100}\right)^n$$

$$\Rightarrow \frac{3645}{5000} = \left(\frac{9}{10}\right)^n$$

$$\Rightarrow \frac{729}{1000} = \left(\frac{9}{10}\right)^n \Rightarrow \left(\frac{9}{10}\right)^3 = \left(\frac{9}{10}\right)^n \Rightarrow n = 3$$

Hence, in 3 years the value of the flat be reduced to Rs 364500.

Example 5 The value of a property increases every year at the rate of 5%. If its value at the end of 3 years be Rs 411540, what was its original value at the beginning of these years ?

Solution Let the original value be Rs P.

It is given that

R = rate of increase = 5% per annum.

Present value = Rs 411540, n = Period = 3 years.

$$\therefore \quad A = P\left(1+\frac{R}{100}\right)^n$$

$$\Rightarrow \quad 411540 = P\left(1+\frac{5}{100}\right)^3$$

$$\Rightarrow \quad 411540 = P\left(\frac{21}{20}\right)^3$$

$$\Rightarrow \quad P = 411540 \times \left(\frac{20}{21}\right)^3 = \frac{411540 \times 8000}{9261} = 355503.72$$

Hence, the original value of the property was Rs 355503.72

Example 6 Afridi purchased an old scooter for Rs 16000. If the cost of scooter after 2 years depreciates to Rs 14440, find the rate of depreciation.

Solution Let the rate of depreciation be $R\%$ per year. Then,

$$14440 = 16000\left(1 + \frac{R}{100}\right)^2$$

$$\Rightarrow \quad \frac{1444}{1600} = \left(1 + \frac{R}{100}\right)^2$$

$$\Rightarrow \quad \frac{361}{400} = \left(1 + \frac{R}{100}\right)^2$$

$$\Rightarrow \quad \left(\frac{19}{20}\right)^2 = \left(1 + \frac{R}{100}\right)^2$$

$$\Rightarrow \quad \frac{19}{20} = 1 + \frac{R}{100} \Rightarrow \frac{R}{100} = \frac{1}{20} \Rightarrow R = 5$$

Hence, the rate of depreciation is 5% per annum.

EXERCISE 14.5

1. Ms. Cherian purchased a boat for Rs 16000. If the total cost of the boat is depreciating at the rate of 5% per annum, calculate its value after 2 years.
2. The value of a machine depreciates at the rate of 10% per annum. What will be its value 2 years hence, if the present value is Rs 100000? Also, find the total depreciation during this period.
3. Pritam bought a plot of land for Rs 640000. Its value is increasing by 5% of its previous value after every six months. What will be the value of the plot after 2 years ?
4. Mohan purchased a house for Rs 30000 and its value is depreciating at the rate of 25% per year. Find the value of the house after 3 years.
5. The value of a machine depreciates at the rate of 10% per annum. It was purchased 3 years ago. If its present value is Rs 43740, find its purchase price.
6. The value of a refrigerator which was purchased 2 years ago, depreciates at 12% per annum. If its present value is Rs 9680, for how much was it purchased ?
7. The cost of a T.V. set was quoted Rs 17000 at the beginning of 1999. In the beginning of 2000 the price was hiked by 5%. Because of decrease in demand the cost was reduced by 4% in the beginning of 2001. What was the cost of the T.V. set in 2001 ?
8. Ashish started the business with an initial investment of Rs 500000. In the first year he incurred a loss of 4%. However during the second year he earned a profit of 5% which in third year rose to 10%. Calculate the net profit for the entire period of 3 years.

ANSWERS

1. Rs 14440.00 2. Rs 81000, Rs 19000 3. Rs 706440.25 4. Rs 12656.25
5. Rs 60000 6. Rs 12500 7. Rs 17136 8. Rs 554400.

THINGS TO REMEMBER

1. *If the borrower and the lender agree to fix up a certain interval of time (say, a year or a half-year or a quarter of a year etc.) so that the amount at the end of an interval becomes the principal for the next interval, then the total interest over all the intervals calculated in this way is called the compound interest and is denoted by C.I. Also, C.I. = Amount – Principal.*
2. *The fixed interval of time at the end of which the interest is calculated and added to the principal at the beginning of the interval is called the conversion period.*
3. *Let P be the principal and the rate of interest be R % per annum. If the interest is compounded annually, then the amount A and the compound interest C.I. at the end of n years are given by*

$$A = P\left(1+\frac{R}{100}\right)^n$$

and, $$C.I. = A - P = P\left\{\left(1+\frac{R}{100}\right)^n - 1\right\} \text{ respectively.}$$

4. *Let P be the principal and the rate of interest be R % per annum. If the interest is compounded k-times in a year, then the amount A and the compound interest C.I. at the end of n years are given by*

$$A = P\left(1+\frac{R}{100k}\right)^{nk}$$

and, $$C.I. = A - P = P\left\{\left(1+\frac{R}{100k}\right)^{nk} - 1\right\} \text{ respectively.}$$

5. *Let P be the principal and the rate of interest be R_1% for first year, R_2% for second year, R_3% for third year and so on and in last R_n % for the nth year. Then, the amount A and the compound interest C.I. at the end of n years are given by*

$$A = P\left(1+\frac{R_1}{100}\right)\left(1+\frac{R_2}{100}\right)\cdots\left(1+\frac{R_n}{100}\right)$$

and, C.I. = A – P respectively.

6. *Let P be the principal and the rate of interest be R % per annum. If the interest is compounded annually but time is the fraction of a year, say $5\frac{1}{4}$ years, then amount A is given by*

$$A = P\left(1+\frac{R}{100}\right)^5\left(1+\frac{\frac{R}{4}}{100}\right)$$

and, $C.I. = A - P.$

7. *Let P be the population of a city or town at the beginning of a certain year and the population grows at a constant rate of R % per annum, then*

$$\text{Population after n years} = P\left(1+\frac{R}{100}\right)^n.$$

8. *Let P be the population of a city or a town at the beginning of a certain year. If the population grows at the rate of R_1% during first year and R_2% during second year, then*

$$\text{Population after 2 years} = P\left(1+\frac{R_1}{100}\right)\times\left(1+\frac{R_2}{100}\right).$$

This formula may be extended for more than 2 years also.

9. *Let P be the population of a city or a town at the beginning of a certain year. If the population decreases at the rate of R % per annum, then*

$$\text{Population after } n \text{ years} = P\left(1-\frac{R}{100}\right)^n$$

10. *If V_0 is the value of an article at a certain time and R % per annum is the rate of depreciation, then the value V_n at the end of n years is given by*

$$V_n = V_0\left(1-\frac{R}{100}\right)^n.$$

11. *If V_0 is the value of an article at certain time and the rate of depreciation is R_1% for first n_1 years, R_2% for next n_2 years and so on and R_k% for the last n_k years, then the value at the end of $n_1 + n_2 + \ldots\ldots n_k$ years is given by*

$$V = V_0\left(1-\frac{R_1}{100}\right)^{n1}\cdot\left(1-\frac{R_2}{100}\right)^{n2}\ldots\left(1-\frac{R_k}{100}\right)^{nk}$$

15

UNDERSTANDING SHAPES-I (Polygons)

15.1 INTRODUCTION

In our day-to-day life we come across various plane surfaces such as top of our study table, black board in a class room, a page of a note book, a drawing board etc.

(i)

These are perfect models for a plane surface.

Let us now do an activity on a plane surface.

ACTIVITY

Step I Take a sharp pencil.

Step II Take a note book and open a page of ...

Step III Mark a point A on the plane of the pa[illegible]

Step IV Move the pencil aimlessly without lifting [illegible] move your pencil in any direction [illegible] drawing other than single points.

Now look at the figure you get. It may be in an[illegible]

(i) (ii) (iv) (v)

Fig 15.2

15

UNDERSTANDING SHAPES-I (Polygons)

15.1 INTRODUCTION

In our day-to-day life we come across various plane surfaces such as top of our study table, black board in a class room, a page of a note book, a drawing board etc.

(i) (ii) (iii)

Fig. 15.1

These are perfect models for a plane surface.

Let us now do an activity on a plane surface.

ACTIVITY

<u>*Step I*</u> *Take a sharp pencil.*

<u>*Step II*</u> *Take a note book and open a page of it.*

<u>*Step III*</u> *Mark a point A on the plane of the paper and put the sharp tip of the pencil at A.*

<u>*Step IV*</u> *Move the pencil aimlessly without lifting the tip and reach to a point B. You may move your pencil in any direction you wish but do not retrace any portion of drawing other than single points.*

Now look at the figure you get. It may be in any one of the following shapes:

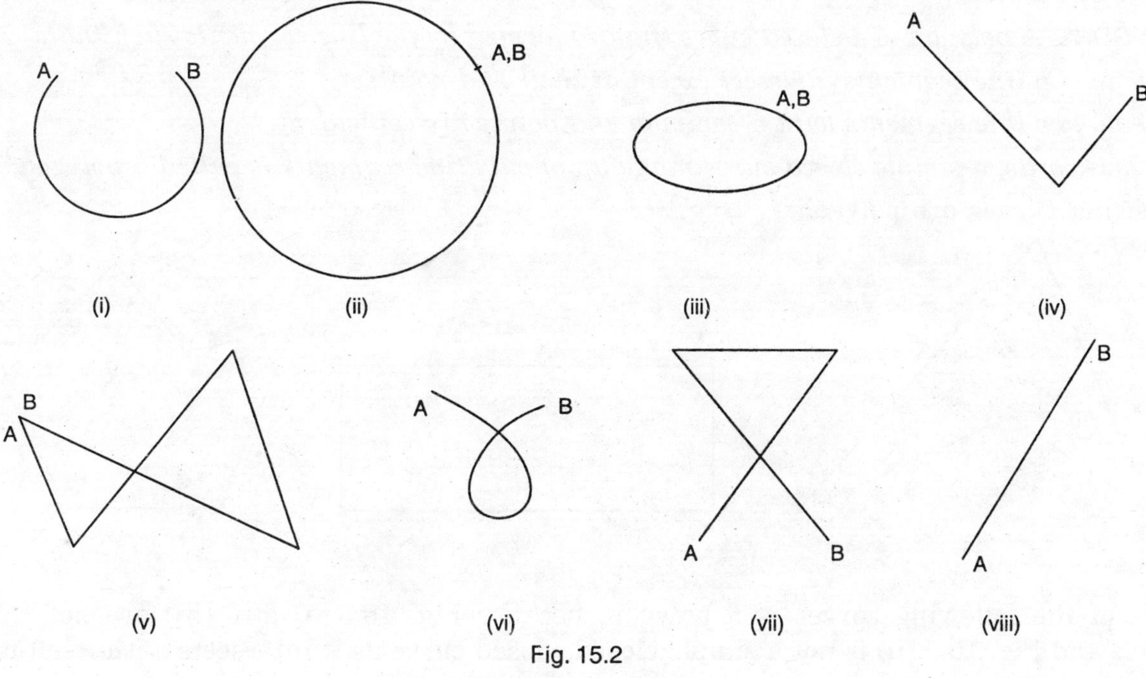

Fig. 15.2

Such figures are called curves. Similarly, if we take a piece of paper and it is just doodled. Then, the pictures obtained as a result of doodling are called curves. Thus, we may define a curve as follows:

CURVE *A plane figure formed by joining a number of points without lifting a pencil from the paper and without retracing any portion of the drawing other than single points is called a curve.*

In our day-to-day life the word 'curve' means 'not straight. However, in mathematics a curve can be straight as shown in fig 15.2 (viii).

OPEN CURVES *A curve which does not cut itself is called an open curve.*

In Fig. 15.2, curves (i), (iv), (vii) and (viii) are open curves.

CLOSED CURVES *A curve which cuts itself is called a closed curve.*

In Fig. 15.2, curves (ii), (iii), (v) and (vi) are closed curves.

SIMPLE CLOSED CURVE *A closed curve is called a simple closed curve, if it does not pass through one point more than once.*

In Fig. 15.2, curves (vi), (v) and (vii) are not simple closed curves whereas curves (ii) and (iii) are simple closed curves.

POSITION OF A POINT WITH RESPECT TO A CURVE If a closed curve is drawn on the plane of the paper, then it divides the plane into three disjoint parts:

(i) the points lying inside the curve or the interior of the curve.

(ii) the points lying on the curve or the boundary of the curve.

(iii) the points lying outside the curve or the exterior of the curve.

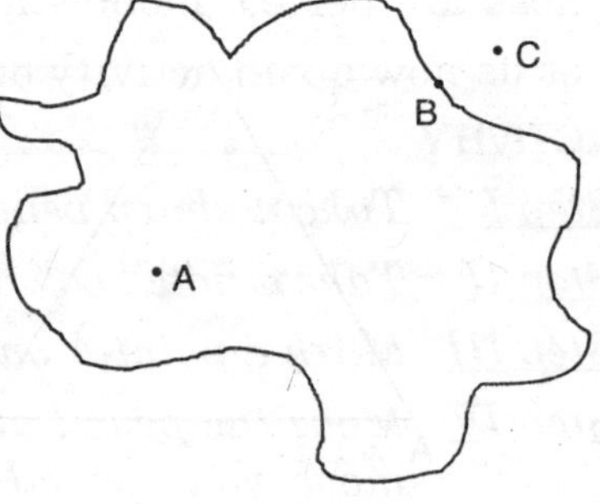

Fig. 15.3

The interior of a curve together with its boudary is called its "*region*". In the Fig. 15.3, A is in the interior, C is in the exterior and B is on the curve.

15.2 POLYGONS

POLYGONS *A polygon is a closed curve (figure) formed by the line segments such that:*

(i) no two line segments intersect except at their end-points.

(ii) no two line segments with a common end points are coincident.

In other words, a simple closed curve made up of only line segments is called a polygon.

Following curves are polygons.

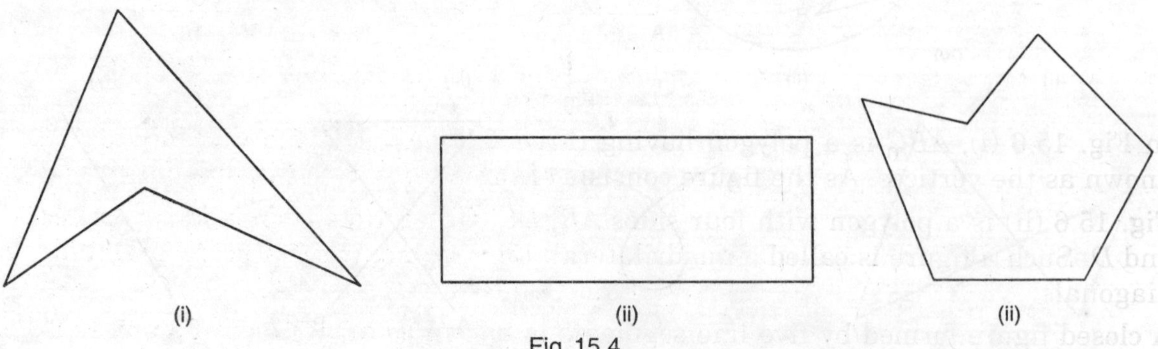

Fig. 15.4

None of the following curves is a polygon, because Fig. 15.5 (i) and (iii) are not closed curves and Fig. 15.5 (ii) is not a simple closed, closed curve as it intersects with itself more than once.

Fig. 15.5 (iv) is also not a polygon as *BC* is not a line segment.

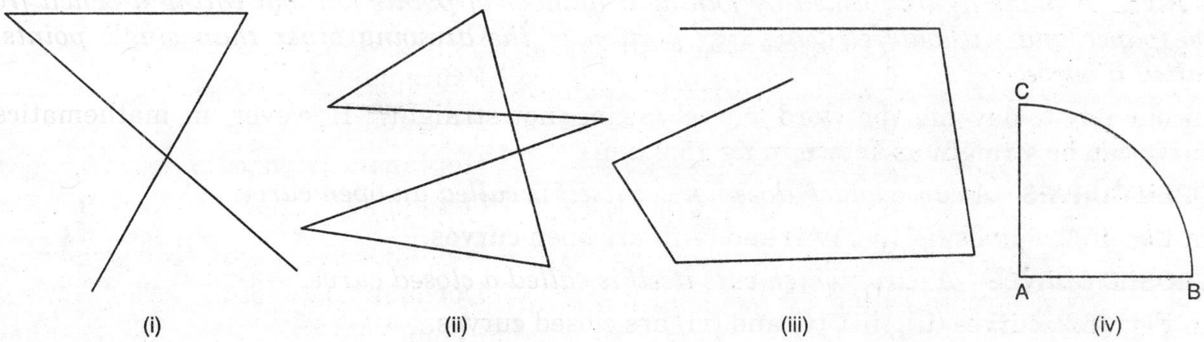

Fig. 15.5

The line segments forming a polygon are called its sides and the end-points of the line segments are called its vertices. In other words, the meeting point of a pair of sides is called a vertex of the polygon.

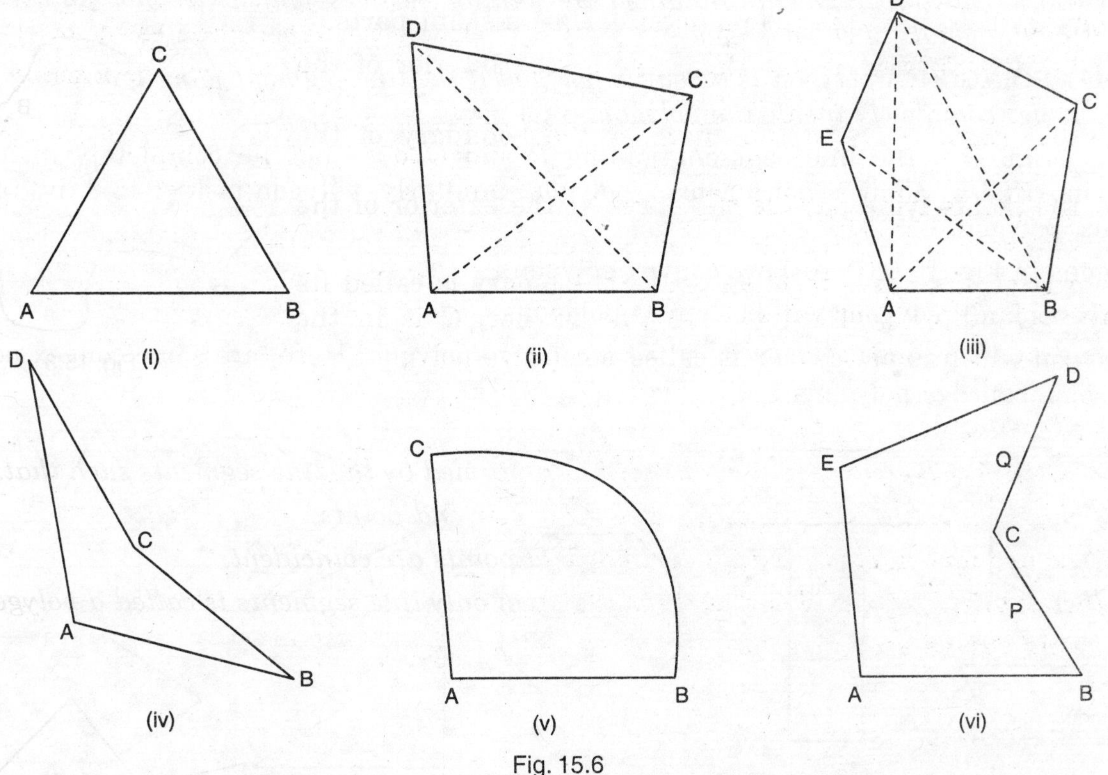

Fig. 15.6

In Fig. 15.6 (i), *ABC* is a polygon having three sides *AB*, *BC* and *CA*. Points *A*, *B*, *C* are known as the vertices. As the figure consists of three sides. So, it is called a triangle.

Fig. 15.6 (ii) is a polygon with four sides *AB*, *BC*, *CD* and *DA*. It has four vertices *A*, *B*, *C* and *D*. Such a figure is called a quadrilateral. Line segments *AC* and *BD* are known as the diagonals.

A closed figure formed by five line segments is known as a pentagon. Figure 15.6 (iii) is a pentagon with *AB*, *BC*, *CD*, *DE* and *EA* as five sides. *A*, *B*, *C*, *D* and *E* are five vertices of the pentagon. Line segments *AC*, *AD*, *BD* and *BE* are diagonals.

Fig. 15.6 (v) is not a polygon as *BC* is not a line segment.

Polygons are classified according to the number of sides (or vertices) as follows:

Number of sides or vertices	Name of the polygon
3	Triangle
4	Quadrilateral
5	Pentagon
6	Hexagon
7	Heptagon
8	Octagon
9	Nonagon
10	Decagon
n	n-gon

ADJACENT SIDES *Any two sides with a common end-point (vertex) are called the adjacent sides of the polygon.*

ADJACENT VERTICES *The end-points of the same side of a polygon are known as the adjacent vertices.*

DIAGONALS *The line segments obtained by joining vertices which are not adjacent are called the diagonals of the polygon.*

CONVEX POLYGON *A polygon is a convex polygon if the line segment joining any two points inside it lies completely inside the polygon.*

In Fig. 15.6 (vi), the line segment joining P and Q does not lie completely inside the polygon $ABCDE$. So, it is not a convex polygon. Similarly, polygon in Fig. 15.6 (iv) is not a convex polygon.

Polygons in Fig. 15.6 (i)–(iii) are convex polygons.

In this book all polygons will be convex polygons.

A polygon which is not convex is called a concave polygon. Here, are some convex polygon and some cancave polygons:

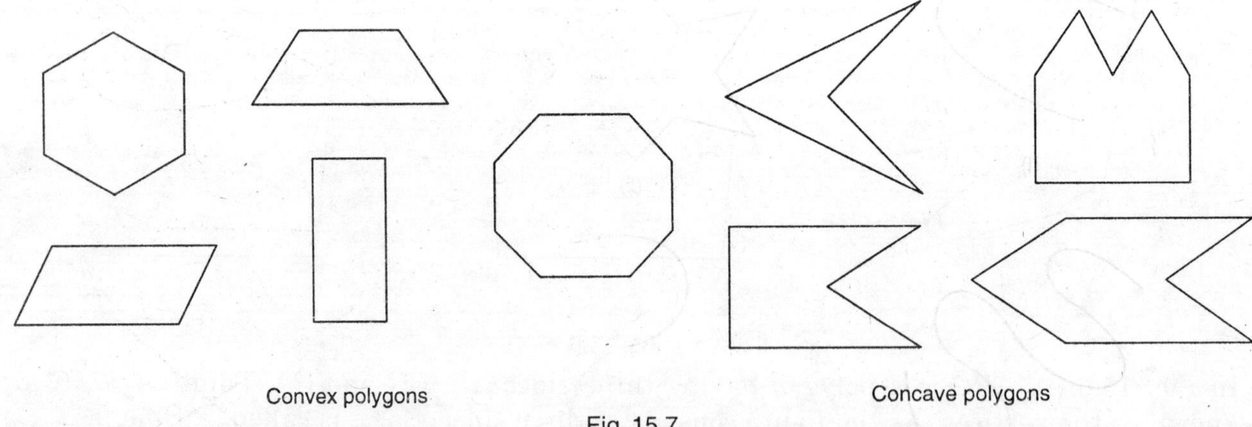

Fig. 15.7

Clearly, convex polygons have no portions of their diagonals in their exteriors which is not true in case of concave polygons.

If there are n-sides of a convex polygons and $n > 3$, then it has $\frac{n(n-3)}{2}$ diagonals. A triangle has no diagonals.

REGULAR POLYGON *A regular polygon is a polygon whose all sides and all angles are equal.*

Thus, a regular polygon is both equiangular and equilateral.

A square has all sides of equal length and each angle of measure 90°. So, it is a regular polygon. A rectangle has all angles equal each equal to 90° but its all sides need not be equal.

In fact, its opposite sides are equal. So, a rectangle is not a regular polygon.

Following are some polygons which are regular and some polygons that are not regular:

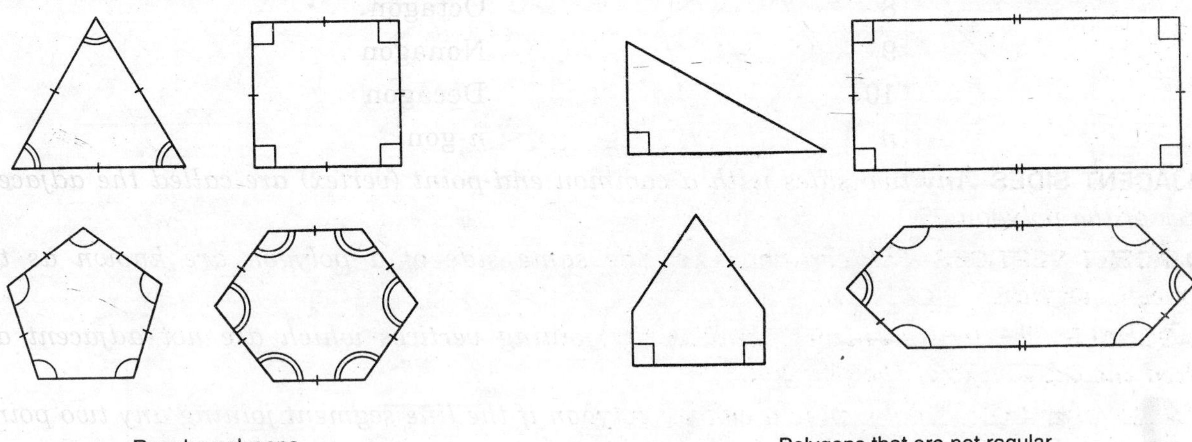

Fig. 15.8

EXERCISE 15.1

1. Draw rough diagrams to illustrate the following:

   (i) Open curve (ii) Closed curve

2. Classify the following curves as open or closed:

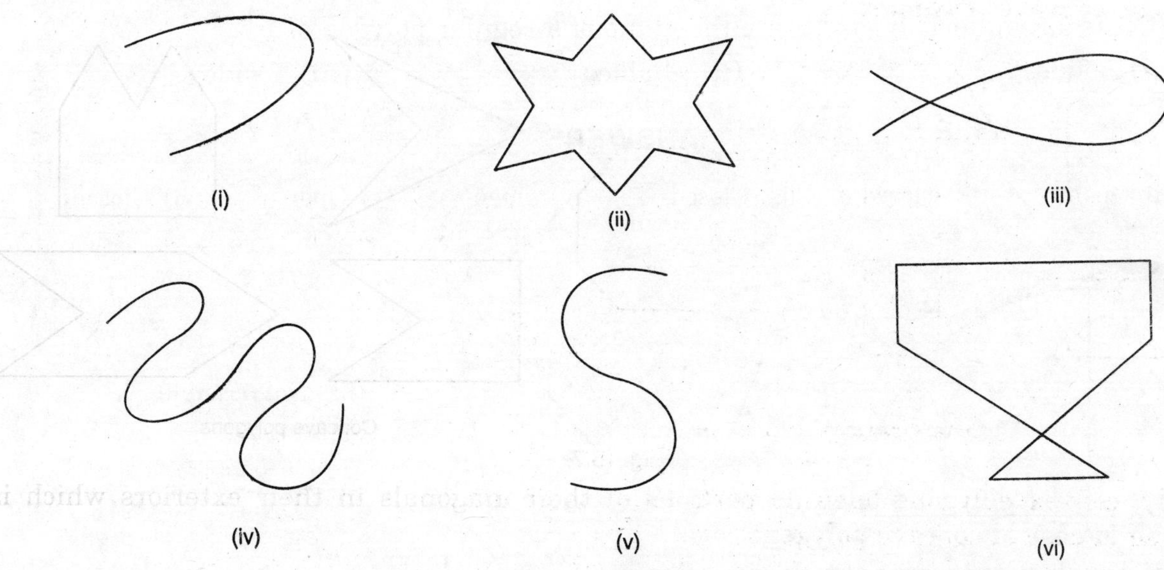

Fig. 15.9

3. Draw a polygon and shade its interior. Also draw its diagonals, if any.

4. Illustrate, if possible, each one of the following with a rough diagram:
   (i) A closed curve that is not a polygon.
   (ii) An open curve made up entirely of line segments.
   (iii) A polygon with two sides.
5. Following are some figures: Classify each of these figures on the basis of the following:
   (i) Simple curve (ii) Simple closed curve (iii) Polygon
   (iv) Convex polygon (v) Concave polygon (vi) Not a curve

(i)

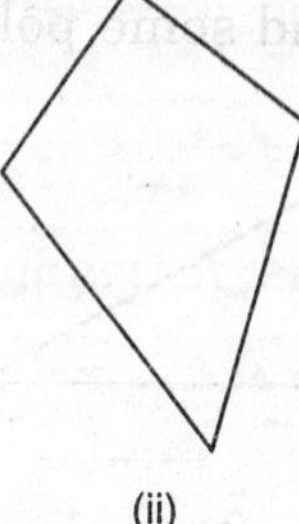
(ii)

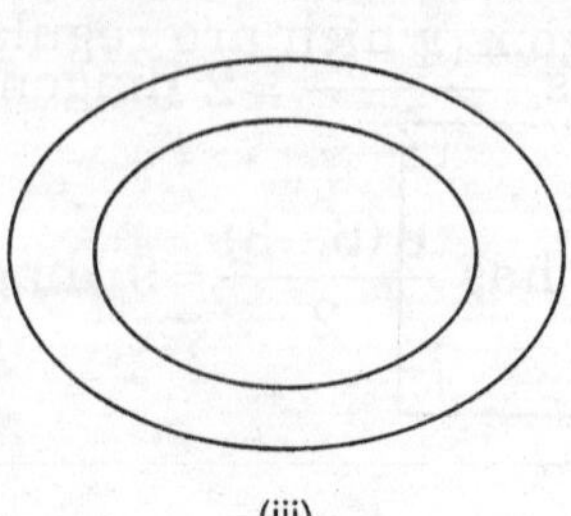
(iii)

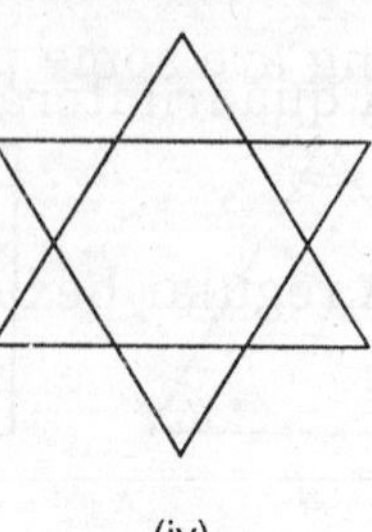
(iv)

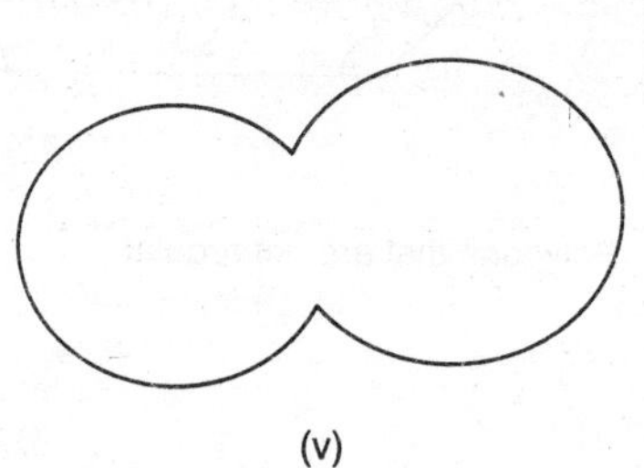
(v)

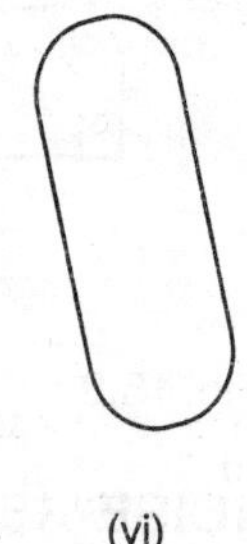
(vi)

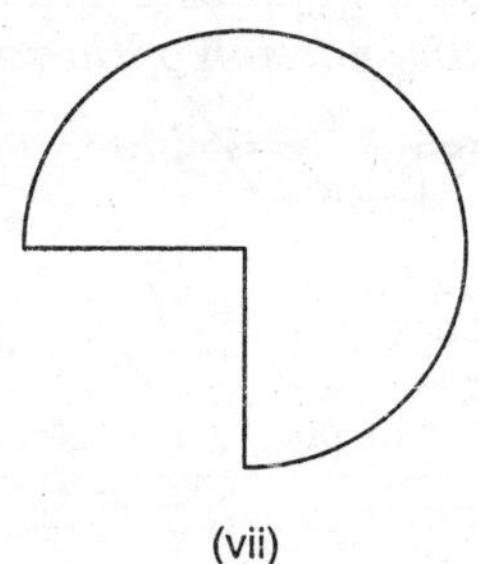
(vii)

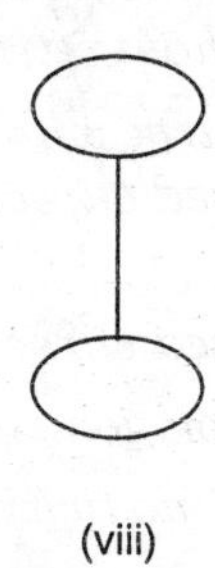
(viii)

Fig. 15.10

6. How many diagonals does each of the following have?
   (i) A convex quadrilateral (ii) A regular hexagon (iii) A triangle
7. What is a regular polygon? State the name of a regular polygon of
   (i) 3 sides (ii) 4 sides (iii) 6 sides

ANSWERS

2. (i) Open (ii) Closed (iii) Closed (iv) Open (v) Open (vi) Closed

4. (i)

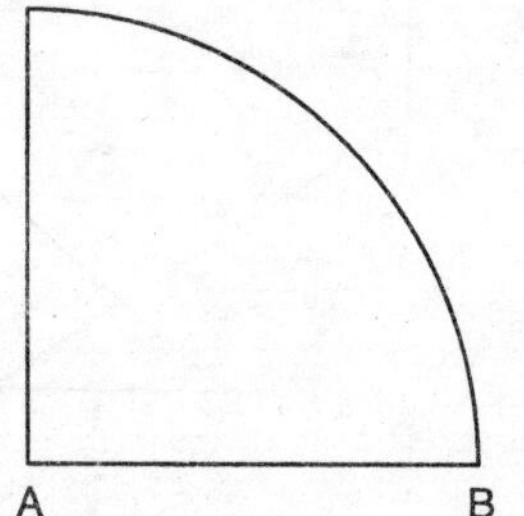

(ii)

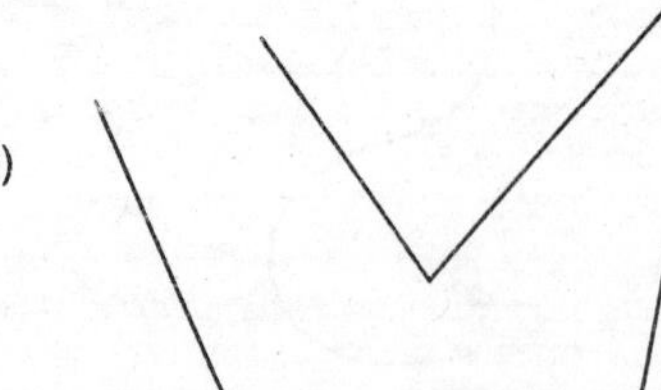

(iii) Not possible

5. (i) Simple closed curve and a concave polygon. (ii) Simple closed curve and a convex polygon.
(iii) Not a curve and hence it is not a polygon. (iv) Not a curve and hence it is not a polygon.
(v) Simple closed curve but not a polygon. (vi) Simple closed curve but not a polygon.
(vii) Simple closed curve but not a polygon. (viii) Simple closed curve but not a polygon.

6. (i) 2 (ii) 9 (iii) none
7. (i) Equilateral triangle (ii) Rhombus (iii) Regular hexagon

HINTS TO SELECTED PROBLEMS

6. An n-sided convex polygon has $\frac{n(n-3)}{2}$ diagonals.

$\therefore$ A quadrilateral has $\frac{4(4-3)}{2} = 2$ diagonals.

A regular hexagon has $\frac{6(6-3)}{2} = 9$ diagonals. A triangle has no diagonal.

THINGS TO REMEMBER

1. *A plane figure formed by joining a number of points without lifting a pencil from the paper and without retracing any portion of the drawing other than single points is called a plane curve.*
2. *A curve which does not cut itself is called an open curve and a curve which cuts itself is called a closed curve.*
3. *If a closed curve does not pass through one point more than once, then it is called a simple closed curve.*
4. *A polygon is a closed curve formed by the line segments such that:*
   (i) no two line segments intersect except at their end-points.
   (ii) no two line segments with a common end-point are coincident.
5. *The line segments forming a polygon are known as its sides and their end-points are known as the vertices of the polygon.*
6. *Any two sides of a polygon with a common end-point are called the adjacent sides of the polygon.*
7. *The end-points of the same side of a polygon are known as the adjacent vertices.*
8. *The line segments joining the non-adjacent vertices are called the diagonals of the polygon.*
9. *A polygon is a convex polygon if the line segment joining any two points inside it lies completely inside the polygon.*

16

UNDERSTANDING SHAPES-II (Quadrilaterals)

16.1 INTRODUCTION

In class VII, we have learnt the angle sum property of a triangle. The sum of the interior angles of a triangle is 180°. In this chapter, we shall learn the angle sum property of a quadrilateral and other polygons.

16.2 QUADRILATERAL

DEFINITION *Let A, B, C and D be four points in a plane such that:*

(i) no three of them are collinear

and, (ii) the line segments AB, BC, CD and DA do not intersect except at their and points.

Then, the figure made up of the four line segments is called the quadrilateral with vertices A, B, C and D.

Figure 16.1 (i), (ii) are quadrilaterals but (iii) is not a quadrilateral, because the line segments *AB*, *BC*, *CD* and *DA* intersect at points other than their end-points.

The quadrilateral with vertices *A*, *B*, *C* and *D* is generally called the quadrilateral *ABCD*.

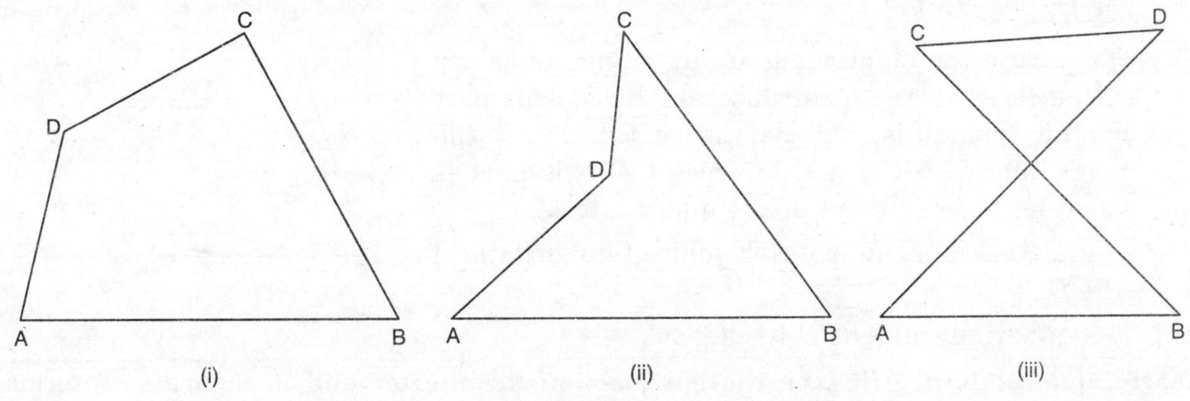

Fig. 16.1

SIDES *In a quadrilateral ABCD, the four line segments AB, BC, CD and DA are called its sides.*

ADJACENT SIDES *Two sides of a quadrilateral are called its adjacent sides, if they have a common end-point.*

In Fig. 16.1 (i), (ii), *AB*, *BC*; *BC*, *CD*; *CD*, *DA* and *DA*, *AB* are four pairs of adjacent sides of the quadrilateral *ABCD*.

OPPOSITE SIDES *Two sides of a quadrilateral are called its opposite sides, if they do not have a common end-point.*

In Fig. 16.1 (i), (ii), *AB*, *CD* and *AD*, *BC* are two pairs of opposite sides of the quadrilateral *ABCD*.

DIAGONALS *In the quadrilateral ABCD, the line segments AC and BD are called its diagonals*

ANGLES *In the quadrilateral ABCD, the angles,* $\angle DAB, \angle ABC, \angle BCD$ *and* $\angle CDA$ *are called its angles. These angles are denoted by* $\angle A, \angle B, \angle C$ *and* $\angle D$ *respectively.*

ADJACENT ANGLES *Two angles of a quadrilateral are called adjacent angles, if they have a common side as an arm.*

In Fig. 16.1 (i), (ii), $\angle A, \angle B; \angle B, \angle C; \angle C, \angle D$ and $\angle D, \angle A$ are four pairs of adjacent angles of the quadrilateral *ABCD*.

OPPOSITE ANGLES *Two angles of a quadrilateral which are not adjacent angles, are known as opposite angles of the quadrilateral.*

In Fig. 16.1 (i), (ii), $\angle A, \angle C$ and $\angle B, \angle D$ are two pairs of opposite angles of the quadrilateral *ABCD*.

We observe that a quadrilateral has four sides, four angles and two diagonals. However, a quadrilateral does not contain its diagonals, except for their end-points.

16.3 INTERIOR AND EXTERIOR OF A QUADRILATERAL

Consider a quadrilateral *ABCD*. Clearly, it is a plane figure. All points in the plane of quadrilateral *ABCD* are divided into following three parts:

(i) The part of the plane made up by all such points as are enclosed by quadrilateral *ABCD*. This part of the plane is called the interior of the quadrilateral *ABCD* and any point of this part is called an interior point of the quadrilateral.

In Fig. 16.2, *P* is an interior point of quadrilateral *ABCD*.

(ii) The part of the plane made up by all-points as are not enclosed by the quadrilateral *ABCD*. This part of the plane is called the exterior of the quadrilateral *ABCD* and any point of this part is called an exterior point of the quadrilateral.

In Fig. 16.2, *Q* is an exterior point of quadrilateral *ABCD*.

(iii) The quadrilateral *ABCD* itself.

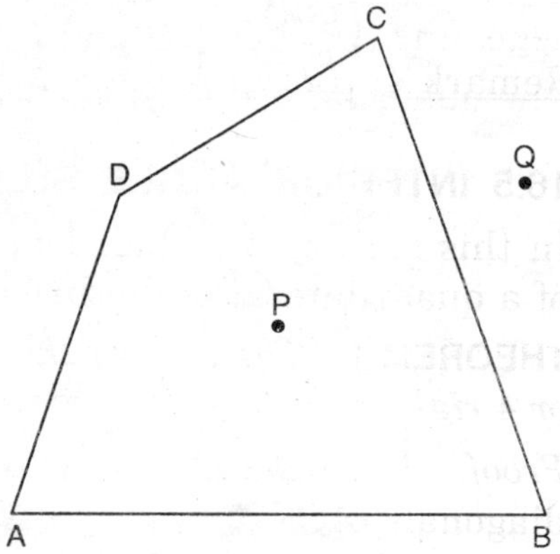

Fig. 16.2

Clearly, quadrilateral *ABCD* is the boundary of its interior and it separates interior of quadrilateral from its exterior.

QUADRILATERAL REGION *The interior of a quadrilateral ABCD, together with quadrilateral ABCD, is called the quadrilateral region ABCD.*

16.4 CONVEX QUADRILATERAL

DEFINITION *A quadrilateral is called a convex quadrilateral, if the line containing any side of the quadrilateral has the remaining vertices on the same side of it. In Fig. 16.3 (i), quadrilateral ABCD is a convex quadrilateral, because*

Vertices *A*, *B* lie on the same side of line *CD*, Vertices *B*, *C* lie on the same side of line *DA*,

Vertices *C*, *D* lie on the same side of line *AB*, and, Vertices *D*, *A* lie on the same side of line *BC*.

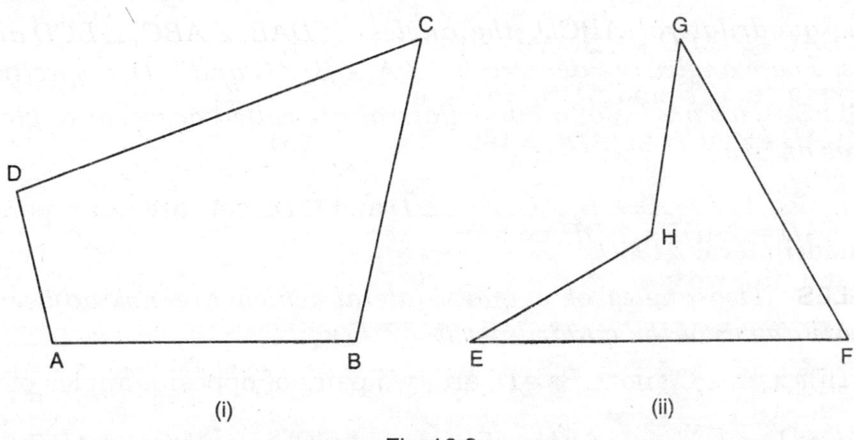

Fig. 16.3

The quadrilateral $EFGH$ shown in Fig. 16.3 (ii) is not a convex quadrilateral, because the vertices E and F lie on the opposite side of line GH.

Remark 1 *In a convex quadrilateral the line segment joining any two points in its interior lies completely in its interior.*

Remark 2 *In a convex quadrilateral the measure of each angle is less than* 180°.

Remark 3 *In this chapter, we shall be dealing with convex quadrilaterals only. Henceforth, the word 'quadrilateral' will be assumed to mean convex quadrilateral only.*

Remark 4 *Both the diagonals of a convex quadrilateral lie wholly in its interior.*

16.5 INTERIOR ANGLE SUM PROPERTY

In this section, we shall learn about an important property related to the interior angles of a quadrilateral and other polygons.

THEOREM 1 *The sum of the angles of a quadrilateral is* 360° *or* 4 *right angles.*

Proof: Let $ABCD$ be a quadrilateral. Draw one of its diagonals, AC.

Clearly, $\angle 1 + \angle 2 = \angle A$ and $\angle 3 + \angle 4 = \angle C$.

We know that the sum of the angles of a triangle is 180°.

Therefore,

In ΔABC, we have

$$\angle 1 + \angle 4 + \angle B = 180° \quad \text{... (i)}$$

and, in ΔACD, we have

$$\angle 2 + \angle 3 + \angle D = 180° \quad \text{...(ii)}$$

Fig. 16.4

Adding (i) and (ii), we get

$$(\angle 1 + \angle 4 + \angle B) + (\angle 2 + \angle 3 + \angle D) = 180° + 180°$$

$$\Rightarrow \quad (\angle 1 + \angle 2) + \angle B + (\angle 3 + \angle 4) + \angle D = 360°$$

$$\Rightarrow \quad \angle A + \angle B + \angle C + \angle D = 360° \quad [\because \angle 1 + \angle 2 = \angle A \text{ and } \angle 3 + \angle 4 = \angle B]$$

THEOREM 2 *Prove that the sum of the interior angles of pentagon is* 540°.

Proof: Let $ABCDE$ be a pentagon. Join AC and AD.

We have to prove that $\angle A + \angle B + \angle C + \angle D + \angle E = 540°$.

We know that the sum of the angles of a triangle is 180°. Therefore, in ΔABC, we have

$$\angle BAC + \angle ABC + \angle BCA = 180° \quad \text{... (i)}$$

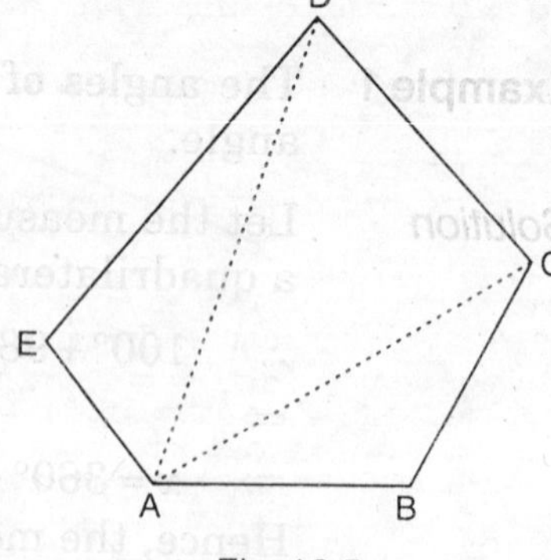

Fig. 16.5

Similarly, in triangles *ACD* and *ADE*, we have

$$\angle CAD + \angle ACD + \angle ADC = 180° \quad \text{... (ii)}$$

and,

$$\angle EAD + \angle ADE + \angle DEA = 180° \quad \text{... (iii)}$$

Adding (i), (ii) and (iii), we get

$$\angle BAC + \angle ABC + \angle BCA + \angle CAD + \angle ACD + \angle ADC$$
$$+\angle EAD + \angle ADE + \angle DEA = 180° + 180° + 180°$$

$\Rightarrow$ $(\angle BAC + \angle CAD + \angle EAD) + \angle ABC + (\angle BCA + \angle ACD) + (\angle ADC + \angle ADE) + \angle DEA = 540°$

$\Rightarrow$ $\angle BAE + \angle ABC + \angle BCD + \angle CDE + \angle DEA = 540°$

$\Rightarrow$ $\angle A + \angle B + \angle C + \angle D + \angle E = 540°$

THEOREM 3 *Thu sum of all the angles of a hexagon is* $720°$.

Proof: Let *ABCDEF* be a hexagon. Join *AC*, *AD* and *AE*.

We have to prove that $\angle FAB + \angle ABC + \angle BCD + \angle CDE + \angle DEF + \angle EFA = 720°$

In ΔABC, we have

$$\angle BAC + \angle ABC + \angle BCA = 180° \quad \text{... (i)}$$

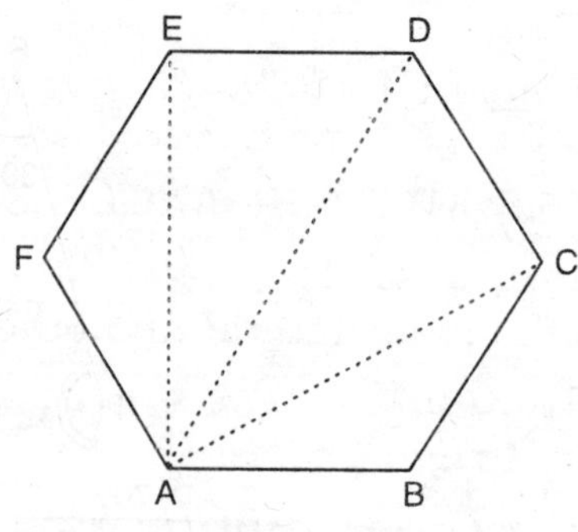

Fig. 16.6

In ΔADC, we have

$$\angle CAD + \angle ADC + \angle ACD = 180° \quad \text{... (ii)}$$

In ΔADE, we have

$$\angle DAE + \angle ADE + \angle DEA = 180° \quad \text{... (iii)}$$

In ΔAEF, we have

$$\angle EAF + \angle AEF + \angle AFE = 180° \quad \text{... (iv)}$$

Adding (i), (ii), (iii), (iv) and regrouping, we get

$$(\angle BAC + \angle CAD + \angle DAE + \angle EAF) + \angle ABC + (\angle BCA + \angle ACD)$$
$$+ (\angle ADC + \angle ADE) + (\angle DEA + \angle AEF) + \angle AFE = 720°$$

$\Rightarrow$ $\angle FAB + \angle ABC + \angle BCD + \angle CDE + \angle DEF + \angle EFA = 720°$

Remark 1 *It follows from the above two theorems that if there is a polygon of n sides* $(n \geq 3)$, *we can cut it up into* $(n-2)$ *triangles with a common vertex and so the sum of all the interior angles of a polygon of n sides would be*

$$(n-2) \times 180° = (n-2) \times 2 \text{ right angles } = (2n-4) \text{ right angles.}$$

Remark 2 *If there is a regular polygon of n sides* $(n \geq 3)$, *then its each interior angle is equal to* $\left(\frac{2n-4}{n}\right)$ *right angles i.e.,* $\left(\frac{2n-4}{n} \times 90\right)^{\circ}$.

ILLUSTRATIVE EXAMPLES

Example 1 The angles of a quadrilateral are respectively 100°, 98°, 92°. Find the fourth angle.

Solution Let the measure of fourth angle be $x°$. We know that the sum of the angles of a quadrilateral is 360°.

$\therefore \quad 100° + 98° + 92° + x = 360°$

$\Rightarrow \quad 290 + x = 360$

$\Rightarrow \quad x = 360° - 290° = 70°$

Hence, the measure of fourth angle is 70°.

Example 2 Find the value of x in each of the following:

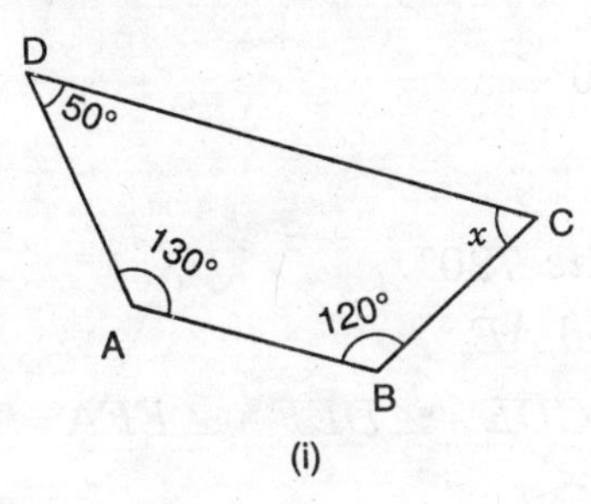

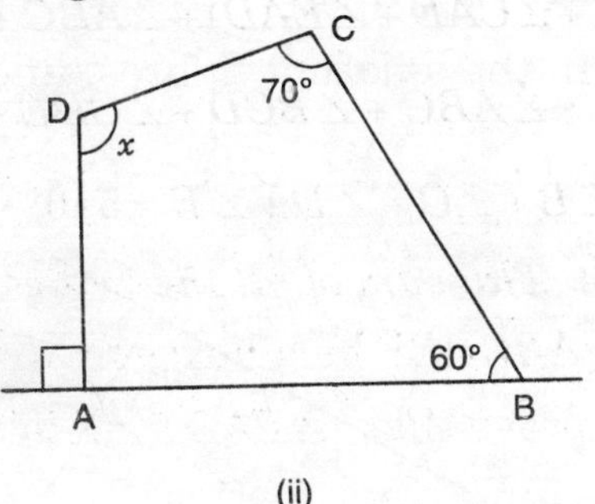

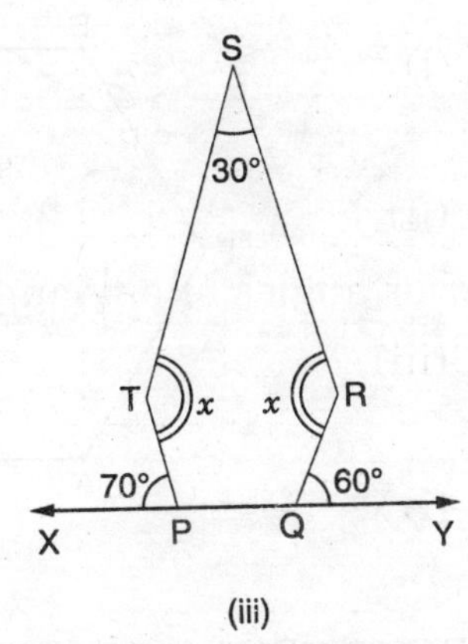

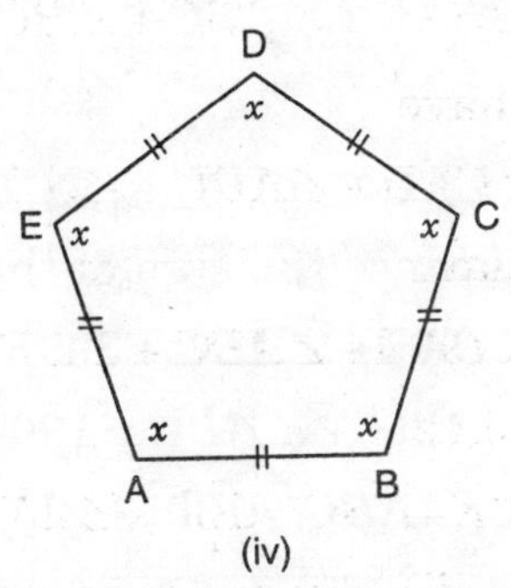

Fig. 16.7

Solution (i) We know that the sum of the interior angles of a quadrilateral is 360°.

$\therefore \quad 130° + 120° + x + 50° = 360°$

$\Rightarrow \quad x + 300° = 360°$

$\Rightarrow \quad x = 360° - 300° = 60°$

(ii) Clearly, ext $\angle A = 90°$ (given)

$\therefore \quad \angle A = 180° - 90° = 90°$

Since the sum of the measures of interior angles of a quadrilateral is 360°.

$\therefore \quad 90° + 60° + 70° + x = 360°$

$\Rightarrow \quad 220° + x = 360° \Rightarrow x = 360° - 220° = 140°$

(iii) We have, $\angle TPX = 70°$ and $\angle RQY = 60°$

$\therefore \quad \angle TPQ = 180° - \angle TPX = 180° - 70° = 110°$

and, $\angle PQR = 180° - \angle RQY = 180° - 60° = 120°$

Since the sum of the measures of interior angles of a pentagon is 540°

$\therefore \quad \angle TPQ + \angle PQR + \angle QRS + \angle RST + \angle STP + \angle TPQ = 540°$

$\Rightarrow \quad 110° + 120° + x + 30° + x = 540°$

$\Rightarrow \quad 2x + 260° = 540°$

$\Rightarrow \quad 2x = 540° - 260° = 280°$

$\Rightarrow \quad x = 140°$

(iv) Since the sum of the measures of a pentagon is 540°.

$\therefore \quad x + x + x + x + x = 540°$

$\Rightarrow \quad 5x = 540°$

$\Rightarrow \quad x = 108°$

Example 3 In the adjacent figures, find (i) $x + y + z$ (ii) $x + y + z + w$

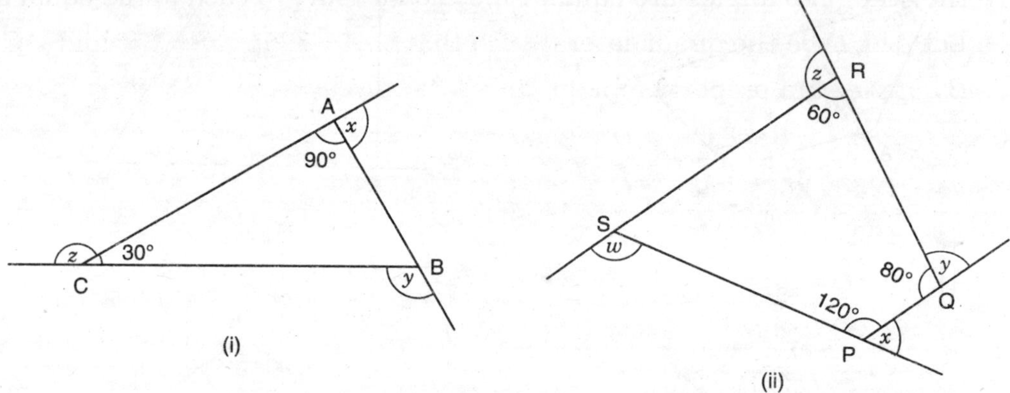

Fig. 16.8

Solution (i) Since the sum of the measures of interior angles of a triangle is 180°.

$\therefore \quad 90° + \angle ABC + 30° = 180°$

$\Rightarrow \quad 120° + \angle ABC = 180°$

$\Rightarrow \quad \angle ABC = 180° - 120° = 60°$

Now,

$z = 180° - \angle ACB = 180° - 30° = 150°, \quad y = 180° - \angle ABC = 180° - 60° = 120°$

and, $x = 180° - \angle BAC = 180° - 90° = 90°$

$\therefore \quad x + y + z = 90° + 120° + 150° = 360°$

(ii) Since the sum of the measures of interior angles of a quadrilateral is 360°.

$\therefore \quad 120° + 80° + 60° + \angle RSP = 360°$

$\Rightarrow \quad 260° + \angle RSP = 360° \Rightarrow \angle RSP = 360° - 260° = 100°$

Now,

$x = \text{ext} \angle SPQ = 180° - \angle SPQ = 180° - 120° = 60°$

Similarly,

$y = 180° - 80° = 100°$, $z = 180° - 60° = 120°$ and $w = 180° - 100° = 80°$

$\therefore \quad x + y + z + w = 60° + 100° + 120° + 80° = 360°$

Example 4 In a quadrilateral *ABCD*, the angles *A*, *B*, *C* and *D* are in the ratio 1 : 2 : 3 : 4. Find the measure of each angle of the quadrilateral.

Solution We have, $\angle A : \angle B : \angle C : \angle D = 1:2:3:4$

So, let $\angle A = x°$, $\angle B = 2x°$, $\angle C = 3x°$ and $\angle D = 4x°$

$\therefore \quad \angle A + \angle B + \angle C + \angle D = 360°$

$\Rightarrow \quad x + 2x + 3x + 4x = 360°$

$\Rightarrow \quad 10x = 360°$

$\Rightarrow \quad x = 36°$

Thus, the angles are:

$\angle A = 36°$, $\angle B = (2 \times 36)° = 72°$, $\angle C = (3 \times 36)° = 108°$ and, $\angle D = (4x)° = (4 \times 36)° = 144°$

Example 5 The measures of two adjacent angles of a quadrilateral are 125° and 35° and the other two angles are equal. Find the measure of each of the equal angles.

Solution Let *ABCD* be the quadrilateral such that $\angle A = 125°$, $\angle B = 35°$ and $\angle C = \angle D$

By angle sum property of a quadrilateral, we have

$\angle A + \angle B + \angle C + \angle D = 360°$

$\Rightarrow \quad 125° + 35° + \angle C + \angle C = 360° \quad [\because \angle C = \angle D]$

$\Rightarrow \quad 160° + 2\angle C = 360°$

$\Rightarrow \quad 2\angle C = 360° - 160°$

$\Rightarrow \quad 2\angle C = 200°$

$\Rightarrow \quad \angle C = \left(\dfrac{200}{2}\right)° = 100°$

Hence, $\angle C = \angle D = 100°$

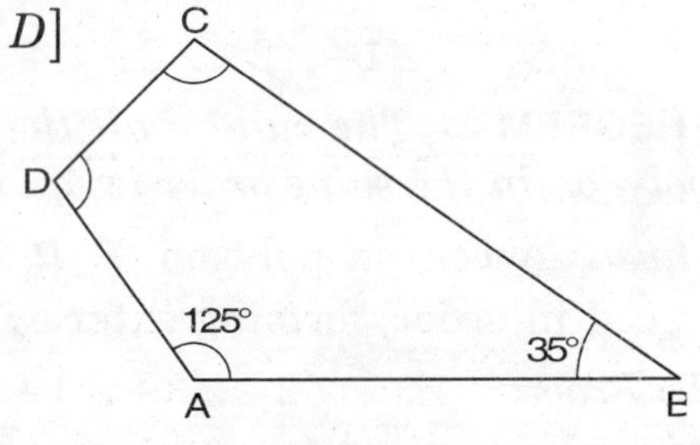

Fig. 16.9

Example 6 One angle of a quadrilateral is 108° and the remaining three angles are equal. Find the three equal angles.

Solution Let *ABCD* be a quadrilateral such that $\angle A = 108°$ and $\angle B = \angle C = \angle D$

Further, let $\angle B = \angle C = \angle D = x°$

Now, by angle sum property of a quadrilateral, we have

$\angle A + \angle B + \angle C + \angle D = 360°$

$\Rightarrow \quad 108° + x + x + x = 360°$

$\Rightarrow \quad 108 + 3x = 360°$

$\Rightarrow \quad 3x = 360 - 108°$

$\Rightarrow \quad 3x = 252°$

$\Rightarrow \quad x = \dfrac{252}{3} = 84°$

Hence, the measure of each of the remaining three equal angles is 84°.

16.6 EXTERIOR ANGLE PROPERTY

Consider a quadrilateral *ABCD*. The angles $\angle A$, $\angle B$, $\angle C$ and $\angle D$ of quadrilateral *ABCD* are called its interior angles.

If the sides of quadrilateral are produced in order as shown in Fig. 16.10, then $\angle 1$, $\angle 2$, $\angle 3$ and $\angle 4$ are called its exterior angles.

THEOREM 1 (*Exterior angle sum property*) *If the sides of a quadrilateral are produced in order, the sum of four exterior angles so formed is* 360°.

Proof: Let the sides of a quadrilateral *ABCD* be produced in order as shown in Fig. 16.10, forming exterior angles $\angle 1, \angle 2, \angle 3$ and $\angle 4$.

Since $\angle 1$ and $\angle A$ form a linear pair and the sum of the angles of a linear pair is 180°.

$\therefore \quad \angle 1 + \angle A = 180°$

Similarly, we have

$\angle 2 + \angle B = 180°$

$\angle 3 + \angle C = 180°$

and, $\angle 4 + \angle D = 180°$

Fig. 16.10

Adding the angles on either side, we get

$$(\angle 1 + \angle 2 + \angle 3 + \angle 4) + (\angle A + \angle B + \angle C + \angle D) = 180° + 180° + 180° + 180°$$

$\Rightarrow \quad \angle 1 + \angle 2 + \angle 3 + \angle 4 + 360° = 720° \qquad [\because \angle A + \angle B + \angle C + \angle D = 360°]$

$\Rightarrow \quad \angle 1 + \angle 2 + \angle 3 + \angle 4 = 720° - 360° = 360°$

THEOREM 2 *The sum of all the exterior angles formed by producing the sides of a convex polygon in the same order is equal to four right angles.*

Given: A convex polygon $P_1 P_2 P_3 P_4 P_5$. Its sides $P_1 P_2, P_2 P_3, P_3 P_4, P_4 P_5, P_5 P_1$ are produced in order, forming exterior angles $\angle 1, \angle 2, \angle 3, \angle 4$ and $\angle 5$.

To Prove: $\angle 1 + \angle 2 + \angle 3 + \angle 4 + \angle 5 = 4$ right angles.

Construction: Take any point *O*, outside the polygon. Draw OA_1, OA_2, OA_3, OA_4 and OA_5 parallel to and in the same sense as $P_1 P_2, P_2 P_3, P_3 P_4, P_4 P_5$, and $P_5 P_1$ respectively.

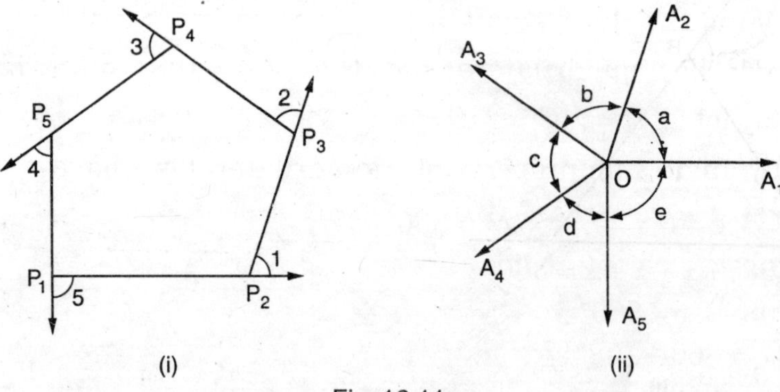

Fig. 16.11

Proof: Since the arms of $\angle 1$ and $\angle a$ are parallel and drawn in the same sense.

$\therefore \quad \angle 1 = \angle a$

Similarly, $\angle 2 = \angle b, \angle 3 = \angle c, \angle 4 = \angle d$ and $\angle 5 = \angle e$

$\therefore \quad \angle 1 + \angle 2 + \angle 3 + \angle 4 + \angle 5 = \angle a + \angle b + \angle c + \angle d + \angle e$

$= 360° \qquad$ [$\because$ Sum of the angles at a point is 360°]

$= 4 \times 90°$

$= 4$ right angles.

In the above theorems, we have proved that the sum of the measures of the exterior angles of a quadrilateral and a pentagon is 360°. In fact, this is true for any polygon whatever be the number of its sides.

Remark *Each exterior angle of a regular polygon of n sides is equal to* $\left(\frac{360}{n}\right)^\circ$

ILLUSTRATIVE EXAMPLES

Example 1 Find the value of x in the adjacent figure.

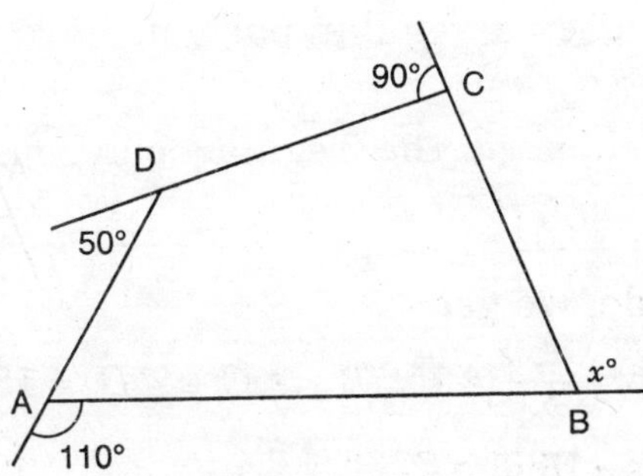

Fig. 16.12

Solution We know that the sum of the measures of exterior angles of a polygon is 360°.

$\therefore \quad x + 90° + 50° + 110° = 360°$

$\Rightarrow \quad x + 250° = 360°$

$\Rightarrow \quad x = 360° - 250°$

$\Rightarrow \quad x = 110°$

Example 2 Find the measure of x in each of the following figures:

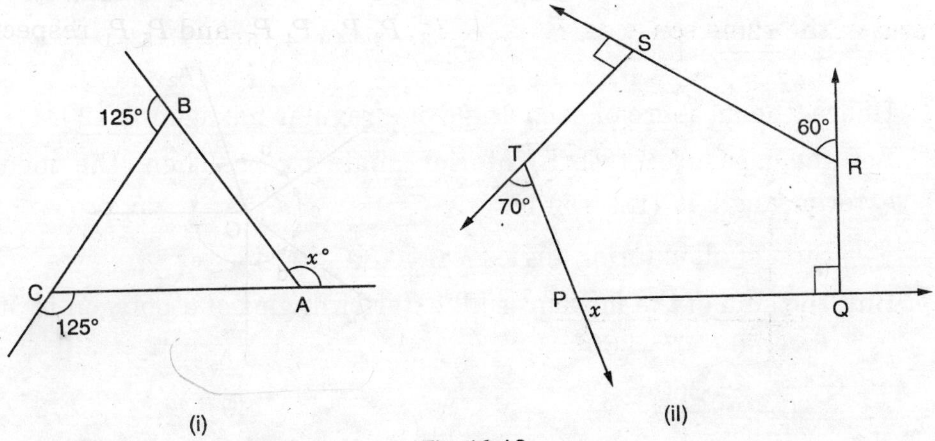

Fig. 16.13

Solution (i) Since the sum of the measures of exterior angles of a polygon is 360°.

$\therefore \quad 125° + x° + 125° = 360°$

$\Rightarrow \quad 250° + x° = 360°$

$\Rightarrow \quad x° = 360° - 250° = 110°$

(ii) Since the sum of the measures of exterior angles of a polygon is 360°.

$\therefore \quad x + 90° + 60° + 90° + 70° = 360°$ $[\because \angle Q = 90° \therefore \text{ ext } \angle Q = 180° - 90° = 90°]$

$\Rightarrow \quad x + 310° = 360°$

$\Rightarrow \quad x = 360° - 310° = 50°$

Example 3 Find the number of sides of a regular polygon whose each exterior angle has measure 45°.

Solution We know that the measure of each exterior angle of n-sided regular polygon is $\left(\frac{360}{n}\right)^\circ$.

$$\therefore \quad \frac{360}{n} = 45 \Rightarrow n = \frac{360}{45} = 8$$

Hence, there are 8 sides of the polygon.

Example 4 How many sides does a regular polygon have if the measure of an exterior angle is 24°?

Solution Let there be n sides of the regular polygon. Then, the measure of each exterior angle is $\left(\frac{360}{n}\right)^\circ$.

$$\therefore \quad \frac{360}{n} = 24 \Rightarrow n = \frac{360}{24} = 15$$

So, the polygon has 15 sides.

Example 5 What is the measure of each angle of a regular hexagon?

Solution Let the measure of each angle be $x°$. Then, sum of all the angles $= 6x°$.

We know that the sum of all interior angles of a polygon of n sides is $(2n - 4)$ right-angles.

$\therefore$ Sum of all interior angles of a hexagon $= (2 \times 6 - 4)$ right angles

$= 8$ right angles $= 8 \times 90° = 720°$

$\therefore \quad 6x° = 720°$

$\Rightarrow \quad x = \frac{720°}{6} = 120°$

Hence, the measure of each angle of a regular haxagon is 120°.

Aliter Let the measure of each interior angle be $x°$. Then, the measure of each exterior angle is $(180 - x)°$.

$\therefore$ Sum of all exterior angles $= 6 \times (180 - x)°$

But, the sum of the measures all exterior angles of a polygon is 360°.

$\therefore \quad 6 \times (180 - x)° = 360°$

$\Rightarrow \quad 180 - x = \frac{360}{6}$

$\Rightarrow \quad 180 - x = 60$

$\Rightarrow \quad x = 180 - 60 = 120$

Example 6 The interior angle of a regular polygon is 156°. Find the number of sides of the polygon.

Solution Let there be n sides of the polygon. Then, its each interior angle is equal to

$$\left(\frac{2n-4}{n} \times 90\right)^\circ$$

$$\therefore \quad \left(\frac{2n-4}{n} \times 90\right) = 156$$

$\Rightarrow \quad 180n - 360 = 156n$

$\Rightarrow \quad 24n = 360$

$\Rightarrow \quad n = 15$

Thus, there are 15 sides of the polygon.

Aliter Let there be n sides of the polygon. Then,

Measure of each exterior angle $= \left(\frac{360}{n}\right)^\circ$

It is given that the measure of each interior angle is 156°.

$\therefore$ Measure of each exterior angle $= (180 - 156)^\circ = 24^\circ$

$\therefore \quad \frac{360}{n} = 24 \Rightarrow n = \frac{360}{24} = 15$

Example 7 How many sides has a regular polygon, each angle of which is of measure 108° ?

Solution Let there be n sides of the polygon. Then, each interior angle is of measure $\left(\frac{2n-4}{n} \times 90\right)^\circ$.

$\therefore \quad \frac{2n-4}{n} \times 90 = 108$

$\Rightarrow \quad (2n-4) \times 90 = 108n$

$\Rightarrow \quad 180n - 360 = 108n$

$\Rightarrow \quad 180n - 108n = 360$

$\Rightarrow \quad 72n = 360$

$\Rightarrow \quad n = 5$

So, the polygon has 5 sides.

Aliter Let there be n sides of the regular polygon. Then, the measure of each exterior angle is $\left(\frac{360}{n}\right)^\circ$.

It is given that the measure of each interior angle is 108°.

$\therefore$ The measure of each exterior angle $= 180^\circ - 108^\circ = 72^\circ$

$\therefore \quad \frac{360}{n} = 72 \Rightarrow n = \frac{360}{72} = 5$

Example 8 Prove that the interior angle of a regular pentagon is three times the exterior angle of a regular decagon.

Solution A pentagon has five sides.

$\therefore$ Each interior angle of a regular pentagon

$$= \left(\frac{2 \times 5 - 4}{5} \times 90\right)^\circ = \left(\frac{6}{5} \times 90\right)^\circ = 108^\circ \qquad \left[\text{Putting } n = 5 \text{ in } \left(\frac{2n-4}{n} \times 90\right)^\circ\right]$$

A decagon has 10 sides.

$$\therefore \text{ Exterior angle of a regular decagon} = \left(\frac{360}{10}\right)^\circ = 36^\circ \qquad \left[\text{Putting } n = 10 \text{ in } \left(\frac{360}{n}\right)^\circ\right]$$

Clearly, each interior angle of a regular pentagon is three times the exterior angle of a regular pentagon.

Example 9 Two regular polygons are such that the ratio between their number of sides is 1 : 2 and the ratio of measures of their interior angles is 3 : 4. Find the number of sides of each polygon.

Solution Let the number of sides of the regular polygons be n and $2n$. Then, their interior angles are

$$\left(\frac{2n-4}{n}\times 90\right)^{\circ} \text{ and } \left(\frac{2(2n)-4}{2n}\times 90\right)^{\circ}$$

It is given that the ratio of measures of interior angles is 3 : 4.

$$\therefore \quad \frac{\frac{2n-4}{n}\times 90}{\frac{2(2n)-4}{2n}\times 90} = \frac{3}{4}$$

$$\Rightarrow \quad \frac{\frac{2n-4}{n}}{\frac{4n-4}{2n}} = \frac{3}{4}$$

$$\Rightarrow \quad \frac{2n-4}{n}\times\frac{2n}{4n-4} = \frac{3}{4}$$

$$\Rightarrow \quad \frac{2(n-2)}{1}\times\frac{2}{4(n-1)} = \frac{3}{4}$$

$$\Rightarrow \quad \frac{n-2}{n-1} = \frac{3}{4}$$

$$\Rightarrow \quad 4n-8 = 3n-3$$

$$\Rightarrow \quad 4n-3n = 8-3$$

$$\Rightarrow \quad n = 5$$

Thus, the number of sides of the polygons are 5 and 10 respectively.

Example 10 The exterior angle of a regular polygon is one-third of its interior angle. How many sides has the polygon?

Solution Let there be n sides of the polygon. Then,

Each exterior angle $= \left(\frac{360}{n}\right)^{\circ}$, Each interior angle $= \left(\frac{2n-4}{n}\times 90\right)^{\circ}$

We have,

Exterior angle $= \frac{1}{3}$ (Interior angle)

$$\Rightarrow \quad \frac{360}{n} = \frac{1}{3}\times\left(\frac{2n-4}{n}\times 90\right)$$

$$\Rightarrow \quad \frac{360}{n} = 60\left(\frac{n-2}{n}\right)$$

$$\Rightarrow \quad 360 = 60(n-2)$$

$$\Rightarrow \quad 6 = n-2 \qquad \text{[Dividing both sides by 60]}$$

$$\Rightarrow \quad n = 8$$

Thus, the polygon has 8 sides.

Example 11 In Fig. 16.14, determine $\angle P + \angle Q + \angle R + \angle S + \angle T$.

Solution We know that the sum of the exterior angles formed by producing the sides of a convex polygon in the same order is equal to four right angles.

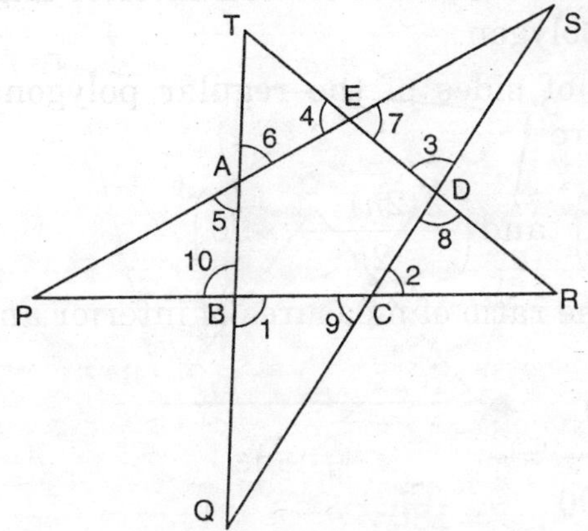

Fig. 16.14

$\therefore \quad \angle 1 + \angle 2 + \angle 3 + \angle 4 + \angle 5 = 4$ right angles

and, $\angle 6 + \angle 7 + \angle 8 + \angle 9 + \angle 10 = 4$ right angles

$\Rightarrow \quad \angle 1 + \angle 2 + \angle 3 + \angle 4 + \angle 5 + \angle 6 + \angle 7 + \angle 8 + \angle 9 + \angle 10 = 8$ right angles. ... (i)

The sum of the angles of a triangle is 2 right angles.

$\therefore \quad (\angle P + \angle 5 + \angle 10) + (\angle Q + \angle 1 + \angle 9) + (\angle R + \angle 2 + \angle 8) + (\angle S + \angle 3 + \angle 7)$
$+ (\angle T + \angle 4 + \angle 6) = 5 \times 2$ right angles.

$\Rightarrow \quad (\angle P + \angle Q + \angle R + \angle S + \angle T)$
$+ (\angle 1 + \angle 2 + \angle 3 + \angle 4 + \angle 5 + \angle 6 + \angle 7 + \angle 8 + \angle 9 + \angle 10) = 10$ right angles

$\Rightarrow \quad (\angle P + \angle Q + \angle R + \angle S + \angle T) + 8$ right angles $= 10$ right angles [Using (i)]

$\Rightarrow \quad \angle P + \angle Q + \angle R + \angle S + \angle T = 2$ right angles.

Example 12 *ABCDE* is a regular pentagon. The bisector of $\angle A$ of the pentagon meets the side *CD* in *M*. Show that $\angle AMC = 90°$.

Solution We know that the measure of each interior angle of a regular pentagon is $108°$.

$\therefore \quad \angle BAM = \frac{1}{2}(108°) = 54°$

Since the sum of the angles of a quadrilateral is $360°$. Therefore, in quadrilateral *ABCM*, we have

$\angle BAM + \angle ABC + \angle BCM + \angle AMC = 360°$

$\Rightarrow \quad 54° + 108° + 108° + \angle AMC = 360°$

$\Rightarrow \quad \angle AMC = 90°$

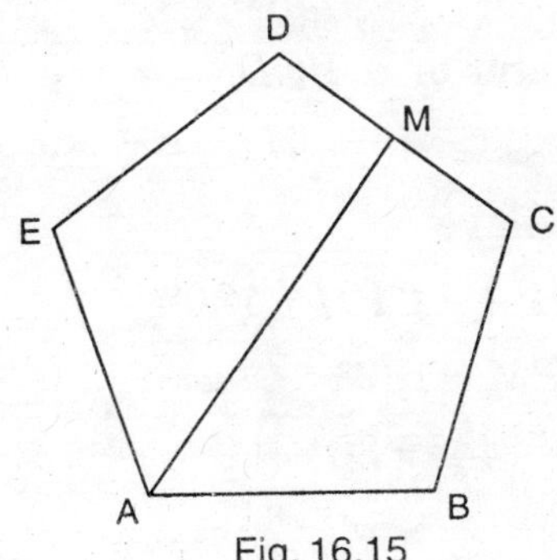

Fig. 16.15

Example 13 In a quadrilateral $ABCD$, AO and BO are the bisectors of $\angle A$ and $\angle B$ respectively. Prove that $\angle AOB = \frac{1}{2}(\angle C + \angle D)$.

Solution In ΔAOB, we have

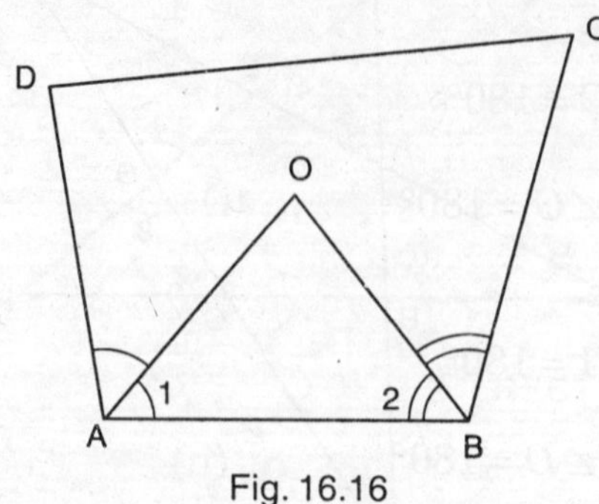

Fig. 16.16

$$\angle AOB + \angle 1 + \angle 2 = 180°$$

$$\Rightarrow \quad \angle AOB = 180° - (\angle 1 + \angle 2)$$

$$\Rightarrow \quad \angle AOB = 180° - \left(\frac{1}{2}\angle A + \frac{1}{2}\angle B\right) \qquad \left[\angle 1 = \frac{1}{2}\angle A \text{ and } \angle 2 + \frac{1}{2}\angle B\right]$$

$$\Rightarrow \quad \angle AOB = 180° - \frac{1}{2}(\angle A + \angle B)$$

$$\Rightarrow \quad \angle AOB = 180° - \frac{1}{2}[360° - (\angle C + \angle D)] \qquad \left[\begin{array}{l} \because \angle A + \angle B + \angle C + \angle D = 360° \\ \therefore \angle A + \angle B = 360° - (\angle C + \angle D) \end{array}\right]$$

$$\Rightarrow \quad \angle AOB = 180° - 180° + \frac{1}{2}(\angle C + \angle D)$$

$$\Rightarrow \quad \angle AOB = \frac{1}{2}(\angle C + \angle D).$$

Example 14 $ABCDE$ is a regular pentagon and bisector of $\angle BAE$ meets CD at M. If bisector of $\angle BCD$ meets AM at P, find $\angle CPM$.

Solution We know that the measure of each interior angle of a regular pentagon is 108°.

$$\therefore \quad \angle BAM = \frac{1}{2}(108°) = 54°$$

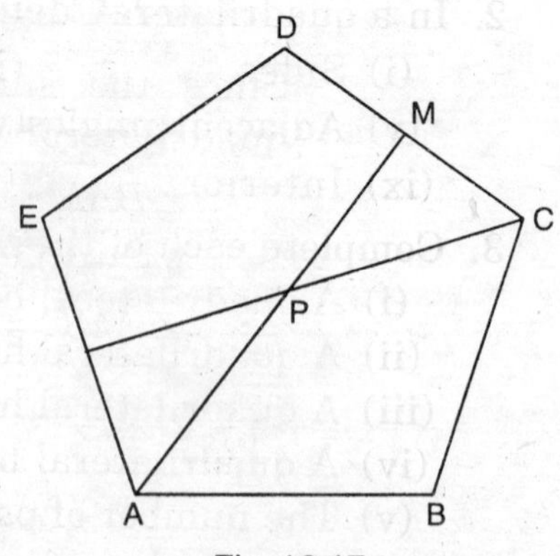

Fig. 16.17

Since the sum of the angles of a quadrilateral is 360°. Therefore, in quadrilateral $ABCM$, we have

$$\angle BAM + \angle ABC + \angle BCM + \angle CMA = 360°$$

$$\Rightarrow \quad 54° + 108° + 108° + \angle CMA = 360°$$

$$\Rightarrow \quad \angle CMA = 90° \qquad \text{... (i)}$$

Since CP is the bisector of $\angle BCD$.

$$\therefore \quad \angle PCM = 54°$$

Now, in ΔCPM, we have

$$\angle PCM + \angle CMP + \angle CPM = 180°$$

$$\Rightarrow \quad 54° + 90° + \angle CPM = 180° \qquad [\text{From (i) } \angle CMP = \angle CMA = 90°]$$

$$\Rightarrow \quad \angle CPM = 180° - 144° = 36°$$

Example 15 In Fig. 16.18, bisectors of $\angle B$ and $\angle D$ of quadrilateral $ABCD$ meet CD and AB produced at P and Q respectively. Prove that $\angle P + \angle Q = \frac{1}{2}(\angle ABC + \angle ADC)$.

Solution In ΔPBC, we have

$\therefore \quad \angle P + \angle 4 + \angle C = 180°$

$\Rightarrow \quad \angle P + \frac{1}{2}\angle B + \angle C = 180° \quad$ ... (i)

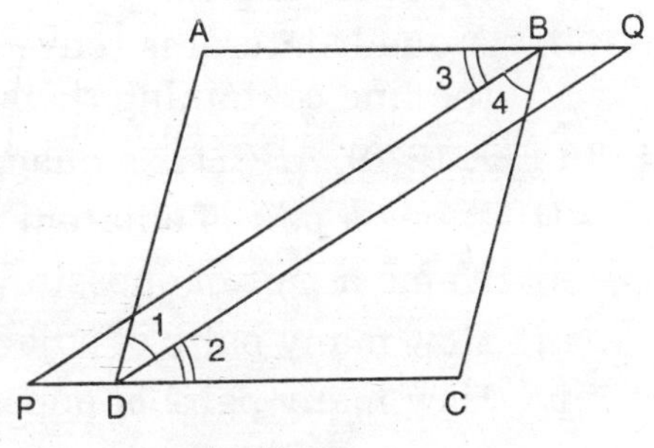

Fig. 16.18

In ΔQAD, we have

$\angle Q + \angle A + \angle 1 = 180°$

$\Rightarrow \quad \angle Q + \angle A + \frac{1}{2}\angle D = 180° \quad$ ... (ii)

Adding (i) and (ii), we get

$\angle P + \angle Q + \angle A + \angle C + \frac{1}{2}\angle B + \frac{1}{2}\angle D = 180° + 180°$

$\Rightarrow \quad \angle P + \angle Q + \angle A + \angle C + \frac{1}{2}\angle B + \frac{1}{2}\angle D = 360° \quad$ ...(i)

But, in quadrilateral $ABCD$, we have

$\angle A + \angle B + \angle C + \angle D = 360° \quad$ ...(ii)

From (i) and (ii), we have

$\angle P + \angle Q + \angle A + \angle C + \frac{1}{2}(\angle B + \angle D) = \angle A + \angle B + \angle C + \angle D$

$\Rightarrow \quad \angle P + \angle Q = \frac{1}{2}(\angle B + \angle D)$

$\Rightarrow \quad \angle P + \angle Q = \frac{1}{2}(\angle ABC + \angle ADC)$

EXERCISE 16.1

1. Define the following terms:
   (i) Quadrilateral (ii) Convex Quadrilateral
2. In a quadrilateral, define each of the following:
   (i) Sides (ii) Vertices (iii) Angles (iv) Diagonals
   (v) Adjacent angles (vi) Adjacent sides (vii) Opposite sides (viii) Opposite angles
   (ix) Interior (x) Exterior
3. Complete each of the following, so as to make a true statement:
   (i) A quadrilateral has .... sides.
   (ii) A quadrilateral has ...... angles.
   (iii) A quadrilateral has ..... vertices, no three of which are .....
   (iv) A quadrilateral has .... diagonals.
   (v) The number of pairs of adjacent angles of a quadrilateral is ....
   (vi) The number of pairs of opposite angles of a quadrilateral is ......
   (vii) The sum of the angles of a quadrilateral is ......
   (viii) A diagonal of a quadrilateral is a line segment that joins two ...... vertices of the quadrilateral.
   (ix) The sum of the angles of a quadrilateral is .... right angles.

(x) The measure of each angle of a convex quadrilateral is ..... 180°.

(xi) In a quadrilateral the point of intersection of the diagonals lies in ..... of the quadrilateral.

(xii) A point is in the interior of a convex quadrilateral, if it is in the ..... of its two opposite angles.

(xiii) A quadrilateral is convex if for each side, the remaining .... lie on the same side of the line containing the side.

4. In Fig. 16.19, *ABCD* is a quadrilateral.

(i) Name a pair of adjacent sides.

(ii) Name a pair of opposite sides.

(iii) How many pairs of adjacent sides are there?

(iv) How many pairs of opposite sides are there?

(v) Name a pair of adjacent angles.

(vi) Name a pair of opposite angles.

(vii) How many pairs of adjacent angles are there?

(viii) How many pairs of opposite angles are there?

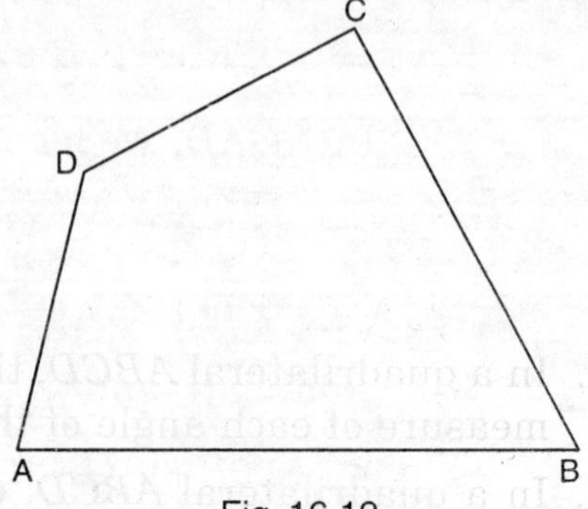

Fig. 16.19

5. The angles of a quadrilateral are 110°, 72°, 55° and x°. Find the value of x.

6. The three angles of a quadrilateral are respectively equal to 110°, 50° and 40°. Find its fourth angle.

7. A quadrilateral has three acute angles each measures 80°. What is the measure of the fourth angle?

8. A quadrilateral has all its four angles of the same measure. What is the measure of each?

9. Two angles of a quadrilateral are of measure 65° and the other two angles are equal. What is the measure of each of these two angles?

10. Three angles of a quadrilateral are equal. Fourth angle is of measure 150°. What is the measure of equal angles.

11. The four angles of a quadrilateral are as 3 : 5 : 7 : 9. Find the angles.

12. If the sum of the two angles of a quadrilateral is 180°. What is the sum of the remaining two angles?

13. In Fig. 16.20, find the measure of $\angle MPN$.

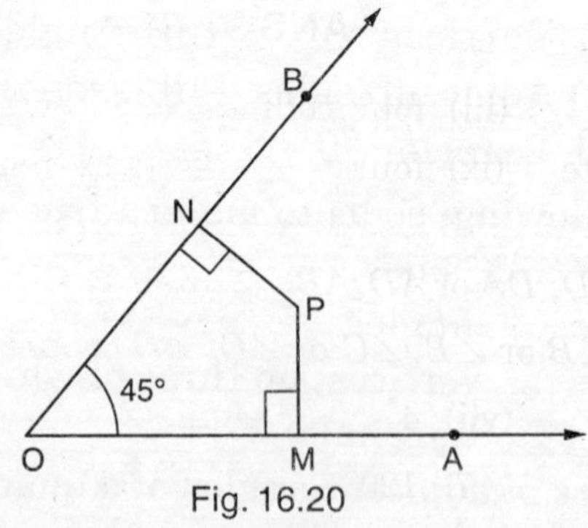

Fig. 16.20

14. The sides of a quadrilateral are produced in order. What is the sum of the four exterior angles?

15. In Fig.16.21, the bisectors of $\angle A$ and $\angle B$ meet at a point P. If $\angle C = 100°$ and $\angle D = 50°$, find the measure of $\angle APB$.

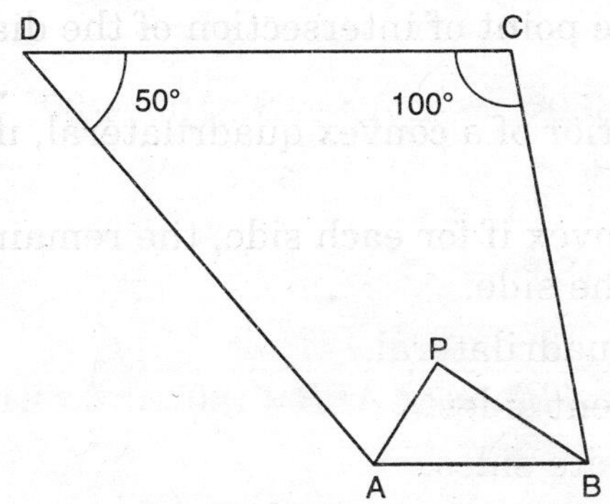

Fig. 16.21

16. In a quadrilateral $ABCD$, the angles A, B, C and D are in the ratio 1 : 2 : 4 : 5. Find the measure of each angle of the quadrilateral.
17. In a quadrilateral $ABCD$, CO and DO are the bisectors of $\angle C$ and $\angle D$ respectively. Prove that $\angle COD = \frac{1}{2}(\angle A + \angle B)$.
18. Find the number of sides of a regular polygon, when each of its angles has a measure of
    (i) 160° (ii) 135° (iii) 175° (iv) 162° (v) 150°
19. Find the number of degrees in each exterior angle of a regular pentagon.
20. The measure of angles of a hexagon are $x°$, $(x-5)°$, $(x-5)°$, $(2x-5)°$, $(2x-5)°$, $(2x+20)°$. Find the value of x.
21. In a convex hexagon, prove that the sum of all interior angle is equal to twice the sum of its exterior angles formed by producing the sides in the same order.
22. The sum of the interior angles of a polygon is three times the sum of its exterior angles. Determine the number of sides of the polygon.
23. Determine the number of sides of a polygon whose exterior and interior angles are in the ratio 1 : 5.
24. $PQRSTU$ is a regular hexagon. Determine each angle of ΔPQT.

ANSWERS

3. (i) four (ii) four (iii) four, collinear (iv) Two (v) four (vi) two (vii) 360° (viii) opposite (ix) four (x) less than (xi) the interior (xii) interiors (xiii) vertices

4. (i) AB, BC or BC, CD or CD, DA or AD, AB (ii) AB, CD or BC, DA (iii) 4 (iv) 2 (v) $\angle A, \angle B$ or $\angle B, \angle C$ or $\angle C, \angle D$ or $\angle D, \angle A$ (vi) $\angle A, \angle C$ or $\angle B, \angle D$ (vii) 4 (viii) 2

5. 123° 6. 160° 7. 120° 8. 90° 9. 115° 10. 70°

11. 45°, 75°, 105°, 135° 12. 180° 13. 135° 14. 360° 15. 75°

16. 30°, 60°, 120°, 150° 18. (i) 18 (ii) 8 (iii) 72 (iv) 20 (v) 12

19. 72° 20. 80 22. 8 23. 12 24. $\angle P = 90°$, $\angle Q = 60°$, $\angle T = 30°$

HINTS TO SELECTED PROBLEMS

15. We have,

$$\angle A + \angle B + \angle C + \angle D = 360^\circ \Rightarrow \angle A + \angle B + 100^\circ + 50^\circ = 360^\circ \Rightarrow \angle A + \angle B = 210^\circ$$

In ΔAPB, we have

$$\frac{1}{2}\angle A + \frac{1}{2}\angle B + \angle APB = 180^\circ$$

$$\Rightarrow \angle APB = 180^\circ - \frac{1}{2}(\angle A + \angle B) \Rightarrow \angle APB = 180^\circ - \left(\frac{1}{2} \times 210^\circ\right) = 75^\circ$$

22. We have,

$$\{(2n-4) \times 90^\circ\} = 3 \times \left(\frac{360}{n} \times n\right) \Rightarrow (n-2) \times 180 = 3 \times 360 \Rightarrow n - 2 = 6 \Rightarrow n = 8$$

23. Let there be n sides of the polygon. Let the exterior and interior angles be x° and $5x^\circ$. Since the sum of an interior and the corresponding exterior angle is 180°. Therefore, $x^\circ + 5x^\circ = 180^\circ \Rightarrow x = 30^\circ$.

The polygon has n sides.

So, sum of all exterior angles $= (30\,n)^\circ$

But, the sum of all exterior angles of a polygon is 360°. Therefore, $30n = 360 \Rightarrow n = 12$.

THINGS TO REMEMBER

1. *If A,B, C, D are four points in a plane such that (i) no three points are collinear, and (ii) the segments AB, BC, CD and DA do not intersect except at their end-points; then the figure made up of the four segments is called the quadrilateral with vertices A, B, C and D.*
2. *In a quadrilateral with vertices A, B, C and D. The four line segments AB, BC, CD and DA are called its sides.*

   If two sides have a common end-point, they are called adjacent sides.

   If two sides do not have a common end-point, they are called opposite sides.

   The line segments AC and BD are called its diagonals.

   The angles $\angle DAB$, $\angle ABC$, $\angle BCD$ and $\angle CDA$ are called its angles and are generally denoted by $\angle A$, $\angle B$, $\angle C$ and $\angle D$ respectively.

   The angles having a common arm are adjacent angles.

   The angles which are not adjacent are opposite angles.
3. *A quadrilateral is convex, if for any side of the quadrilateral, the line containing it has the remaining vertices on the same side of it.*
4. *The sum of the angles of a quadrilateral is 360°.*
5. *If the sides of a quadrilateral are produced, in order , the sum of the four exterior angles so formed is 360°.*
6. *The sum of all interior angles of an n sided polygon is (2n – 4) right angles.*
7. *Each interior angle of a regular polygon of n sides is* $\left(\frac{2n-4}{n} \times 90\right)^\circ$.
8. *The sum of exterior angles of a polygon is 360°.*
9. *The measure of each exterior angle of an n sided regular polygon is* $\left(\frac{360}{n}\right)^\circ$.

17

UNDERSTANDING SHAPES-III (Special Types of Quadrilaterals)

17.1 INTRODUCTION

In previous chapter we have learnt about a quadrilateral in general. In this chapter, we shall learn about some special types of quadrilaterals and their properties.

17.2 VARIOUS TYPES OF QUADRILATERALS

In this section, we shall define various types of quadrilaterals.

TRAPEZIUM *A quadrilateral having exactly one pair of parallel sides, is called a trapezium.*

In Fig. 17.1, $ABCD$ is a trapezium in which $AB \parallel DC$.

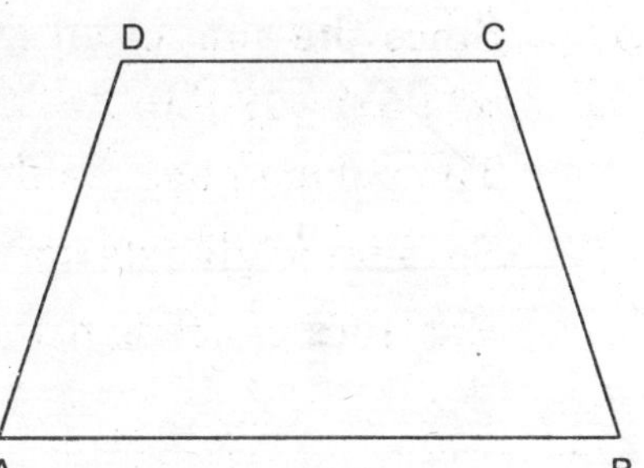

Fig. 17.1

ISOSCELES TRAPEZIUM *A trapezium is said to be an isosceles trapezium, if its non-parallel sides are equal.*

Thus, a quadrilateral $ABCD$ is an isosceles trapezium, if $AB \parallel DC$ and $AD = BC$.

Each of the following figures represents a trapezium:

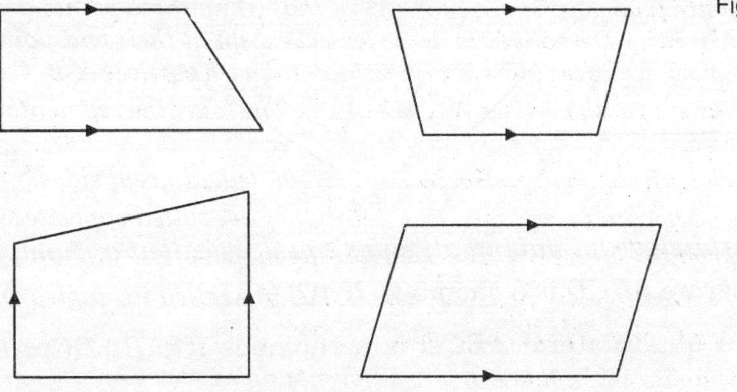
Fig. 17.2

None of these figures is a trapezium.

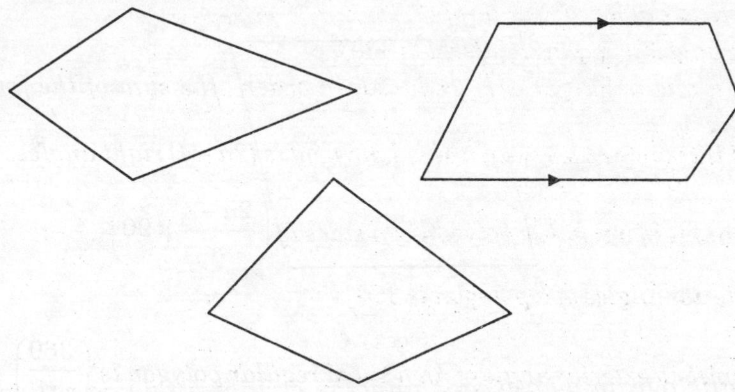
Fig. 17.3

PARALLELOGRAM *A quadrilateral is a parallelogram if its both pairs of opposite sides are parallel.*

In Fig. 17.4, quadrilateral $ABCD$ is a parallelogram, because $AB \parallel DC$ and $AD \parallel BC$.

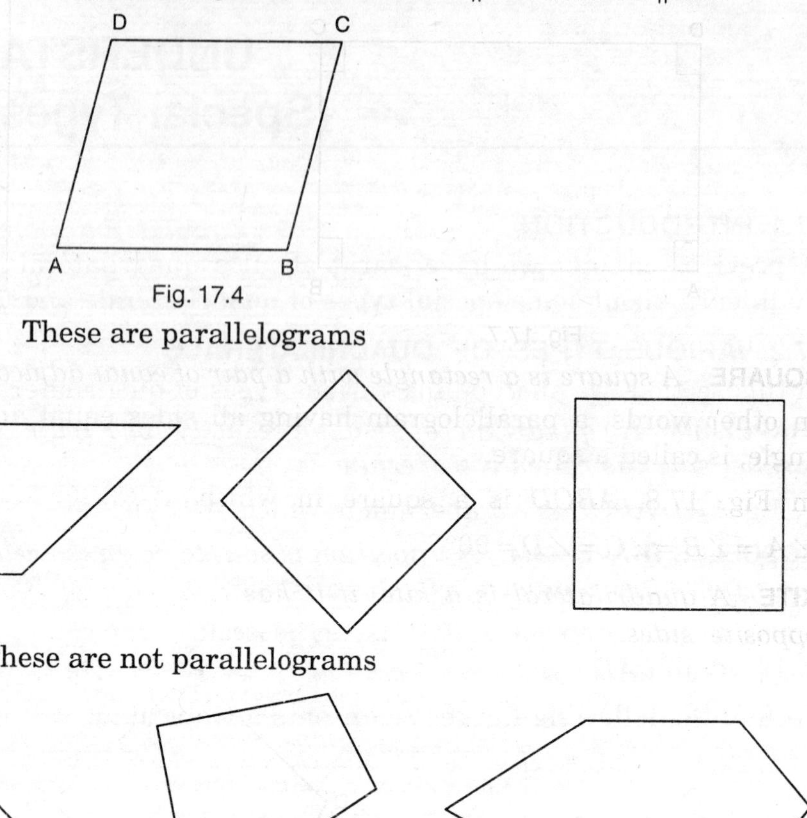

Fig. 17.4

These are parallelograms

These are not parallelograms

Fig. 17.5

RHOMBUS *A parallelogram having all sides equal, is called a rhombus.*

Thus, a parallelogram $ABCD$ is a rhombus, if $AB = AD$.

In other words, a quadrilateral $ABCD$ is a rhombus if $AB \parallel DC$, $AD \parallel BC$ and $AB = BC = CD = DA$.

In Fig. 17.6, $ABCD$ is a rhombus, since $ABCD$ is a parallelogram in which $AB = AD$.

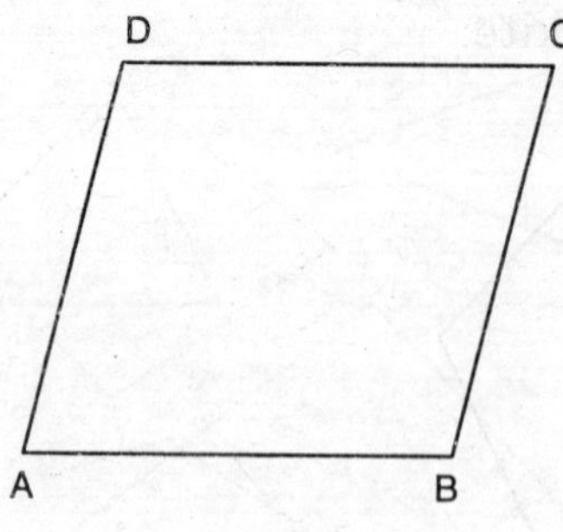

Fig. 17.6

RECTANGLE *A parallelogram whose each angle is a right angle, is called a rectangle.*

In Fig. 17.7, $ABCD$ is a rectangle in which $AB \parallel CD$, $AD \parallel BC$ and $\angle A = \angle B = \angle C = \angle D = 90°$.

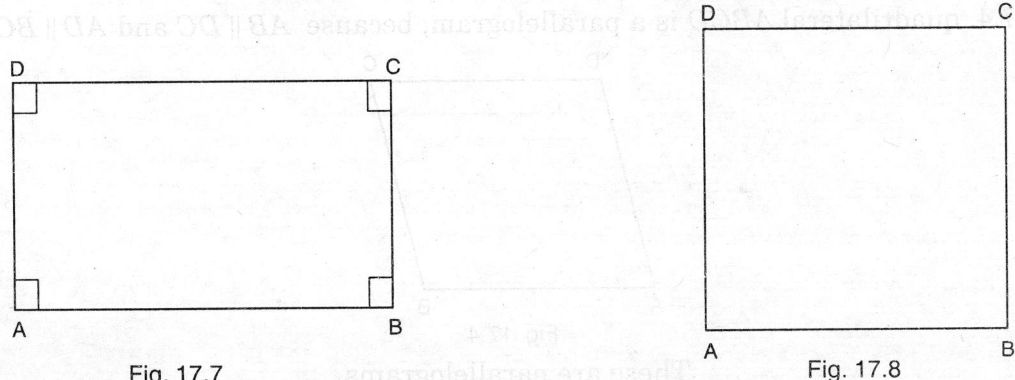

Fig. 17.7 Fig. 17.8

SQUARE *A square is a rectangle with a pair of equal adjacent sides.*

In other words, a parallelogram having all sides equal and each angle equal to a right angle, is called a square.

In Fig. 17.8, $ABCD$ is a square in which $AB \parallel DC$, $AD \parallel BC$, $AB = BC = CD = DA$ and $\angle A = \angle B = \angle C = \angle D = 90°$.

KITE *A quadrilateral is a kite, if it has two pairs of equal adjacent sides and unequal opposite sides.*

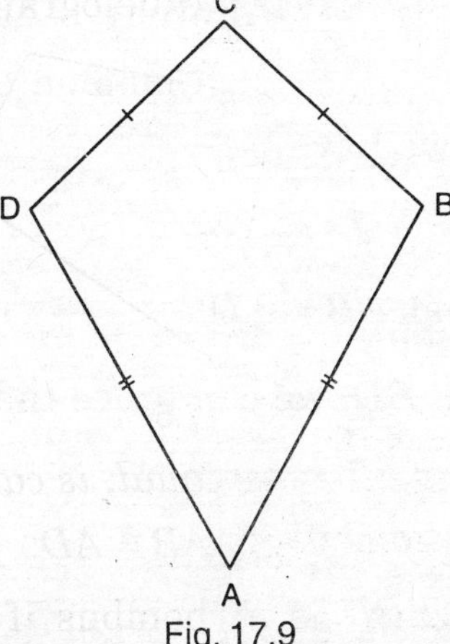

Fig. 17.9

Thus, a quadrilateral $ABCD$ is a kite, if

$AB = AD$, $BC = CD$ but $AD \neq BC$ and $AB \neq CD$.

Each of the following figures is a kite:

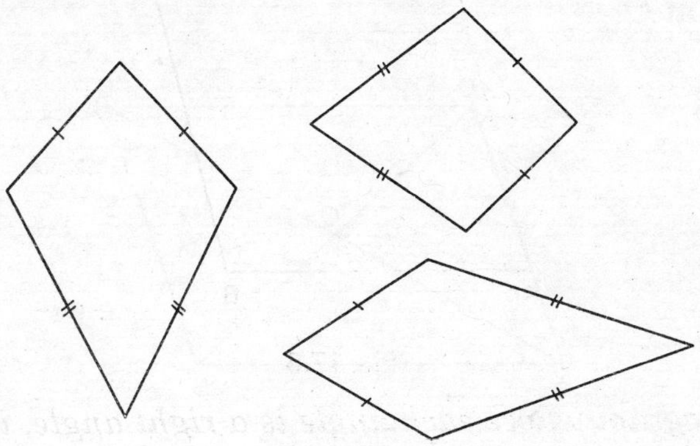

None of the following figures is a kite:

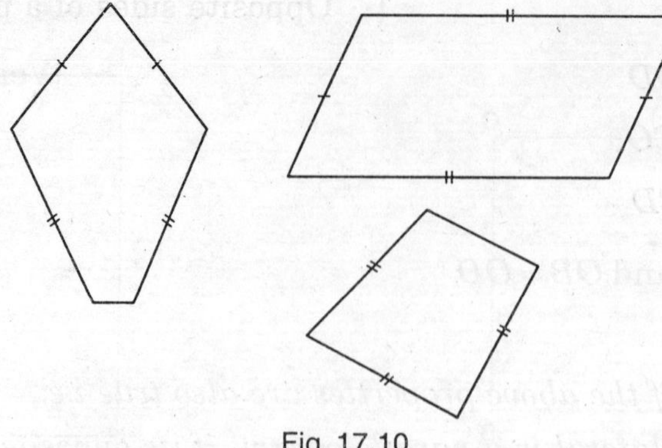

Fig. 17.10

17.3 PROPERTIES OF A PARALLELOGRAM

THEOREM: *In a parallelogram, prove that*

(i) the opposite sides are equal; *(ii) the opposite angles are equal;*

(iii) diagonals bisect each other.

Proof: Let $ABCD$ be a parallelogram. Draw its diagonal AC.

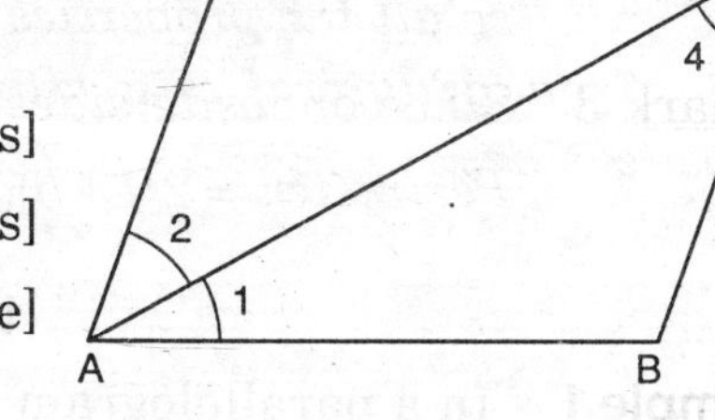

Fig. 17.11

In triangles ABC and CDA, we have

$\angle 1 = \angle 3$ [Alternate angles]

$\angle 2 = \angle 4$ [Alternate angles]

and, $AC = AC$ [Common side]

So, by ASA congruence criterion, we have

$\Delta ABC \cong \Delta CDA$

$\Rightarrow$ $AB = CD, BC = AD$ and $\angle B = \angle D$ [$\because$ Corresponding parts of congruent triangle are equal]

Similarly, by drawing the diagonal BD, we can prove that

$\Delta ABD \cong \Delta CDB$

$\Rightarrow$ $AD = BC$ and $\angle A = \angle C$

Hence, in parallelogram $ABCD$, we have

$AB = CD, AD = BC, \angle A = \angle C, \angle B = \angle D$

This proves (i) and (ii)

In order to prove (iii), consider a parallelogram $ABCD$. Draw its diagonals AC and BD, intersecting each other at O.

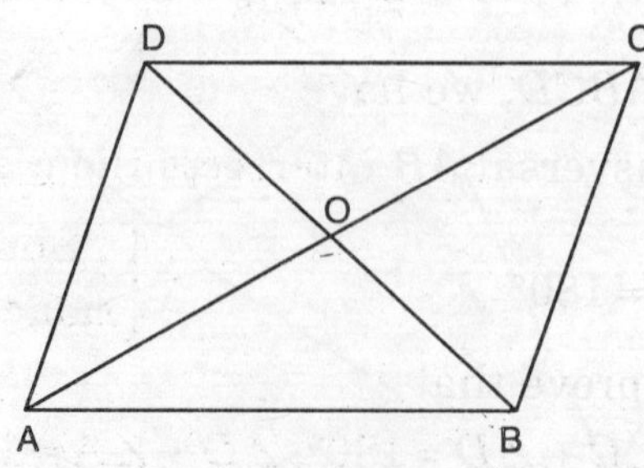

Fig. 17.12

In Δs AOB and COD, we have

$AB = CD$ [$\because$ Opposite sides of a parallelogram are equal]

$\angle AOB = \angle COD$ [Vertically opposite angles]

$\angle OAB = \angle DCO$ [Alternate angles]

$\therefore$ $\Delta OAB \cong \Delta OCD$

$\Rightarrow$ $OA = OC$ and $OB = OD$

This proves (iii).

Remark 1 *The converse of the above properties are also true i.e.,*

(i) A quadrilateral is a parallelogram, if its opposite sides are equal.

(ii) A quadrilateral is a parallelogram, if its opposite angles are equal.

(iii) A quadrilateral is a parallelogram, if it has one pair of opposite sides parallel and equal.

(iv) A quadrilateral is a parallelogram, if its diagonals bisect each other.

Remark 2 *Since a rhombus, a rectangle and a square are special types of parallelogram, so all the properties of a parallelogram are true for each of them.*

Remark 3 *Since opposite sides of a parallelogram are equal. Therefore,*

Perimeter $= 2(l + b)$, *where* l *and* b *are the lengths of its two adjacent sides.*

ILLUSTRATIVE EXAMPLES

Example 1 In a parallelogram the sum of any two adjacent angles is 180°.

OR

In a parallelogram, two adjacent angles are supplementary.

Solution Let $ABCD$ be a parallelogram. Then, $\angle A, \angle B$; $\angle B, \angle C$; $\angle C, \angle D$ and $\angle D, \angle A$ are four pairs of adjacent angles. We have to prove that

$\angle A + \angle B = 180°$; $\angle B + \angle C = 180°$, $\angle C + \angle D = 180°$, $\angle D + \angle A = 180°$

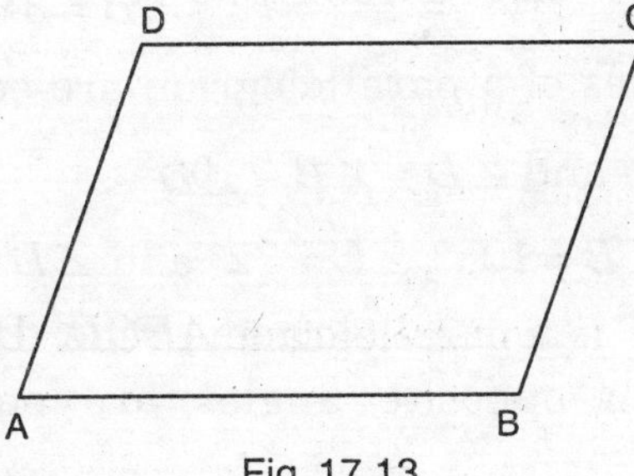

Fig. 17.13

In parallelogram $ABCD$, we have

$AD \parallel BC$ and transversal AB intersects them at A and B respectively.

$\therefore$ $\angle A + \angle B = 180°$ [$\because$ Sum of the interior angles on the same side of the transversal is 180°]

Similarly, we can prove that

$\angle B + \angle C = 180°$, $\angle C + \angle D = 180°$, $\angle D + \angle A = 180°$

Example 2 Two adjacent angles of a parallelogram are equal. What is the measure of each?

Solution Let the measure of each angle be $x°$. Since adjacent angles of a parallelogram are supplementary.

$$\therefore \quad x° + x° = 180° \Rightarrow 2x° = 180 \Rightarrow x° = \frac{180°}{2} = 90°$$

Hence, the measure of each angle is 90°.

Example 3 In a parallelogram $ABCD$, $\angle D = 115°$, determine the measure of $\angle A$ and $\angle B$.

Solution Since the sum of any two consecutive angles of a parallelogram is 180°.

$\therefore \quad \angle A + \angle D = 180°$ and $\angle A + \angle B = 180°$

Now,

$\angle A + \angle D = 180°$

$\Rightarrow \quad \angle A + 115° = 180°$ $\quad [\because \angle D = 115° \text{ (Given)}]$

$\Rightarrow \quad \angle A = 180° - 115° = 65°$

and, $\angle A + \angle B = 180° \Rightarrow 65° + \angle B = 180° \Rightarrow \angle B = 115°$

$\therefore \quad \angle A = 65°$ and $\angle B = 115°$

Example 4 Two adjacent angles of a parallelogram are as 2 : 3. Find the measures of all the angles.

Solution Let $ABCD$ be a parallelogram. Let $\angle A$ and $\angle B$ be its two adjacent angles such that $\angle A : \angle B = 2:3$.

Let $\angle A = 2x°$ and $\angle B = 3x°$

Since adjacent interior angles are supplementary.

$\therefore \quad \angle A + \angle B = 180°$

$\Rightarrow \quad 2x° + 3x° = 180°$

$\Rightarrow \quad 5x° = 180°$

$\Rightarrow \quad x° = \frac{180}{5} = 36°$

$\therefore \quad \angle A = 2x° = 72°, \angle B = 3x° = 108°$

Since opposite angles of a parallelogram are equal.

$\therefore \quad \angle C = \angle A = 72°$ and $\angle D = \angle B = 108°$

Hence, $\angle A = 72°, \angle B = 108°, \angle C = 72°$ and $\angle D = 108°$

Example 5 In Fig. 17.14, $BEST$ is a parallelogram. Find the values of x, y and z.

Solution In a parallelogram opposite angles are equal and adjacent angles are supplementary.

$\therefore \quad \angle S = \angle B$, and $\angle B + \angle T = 180°$

$\Rightarrow \quad x = 100°$ and, $100° + \angle T = 180°$

$\Rightarrow \quad x = 100°$ and, $100 + z = 180°$

$[\because \angle T = \angle E \Rightarrow \angle T = z]$

$\Rightarrow \quad x = 100°$ and, $z = 180° - 100° = 80°$

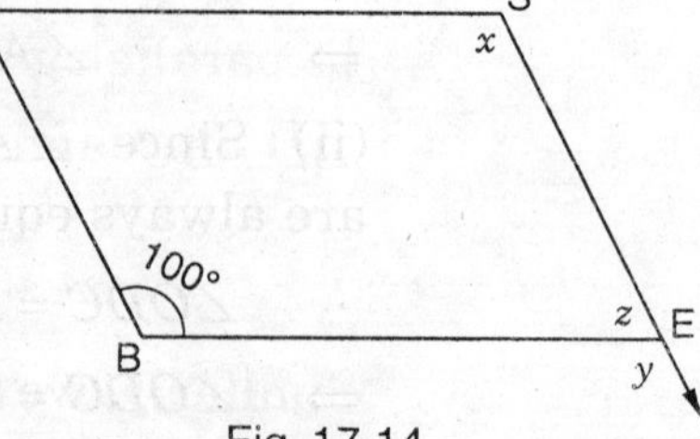

Fig. 17.14

Clearly,

$y + z = 180°$

$\Rightarrow \quad y + 80 = 180°$

$\Rightarrow \quad y = 180° - 80° = 100°$

Hence, $x = 100°$, $y = 100°$ and $z = 80°$

Example 6 In Fig. 17.15, *HELP* is a parallelogram. If $OE = 4$ cm and HL is 5 cm more than PE. Find OH.

Solution We have, $OE = 4$ cm

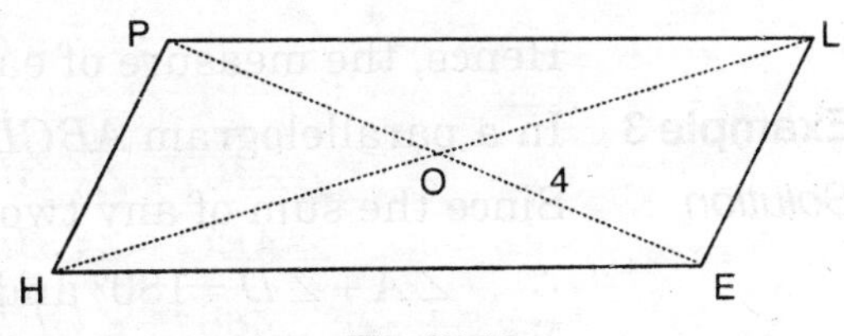

Fig. 17.15

$\therefore \quad PE = 2OE = 2 \times 4 \text{ cm} = 8 \text{ cm}$

It is given that

$HL = PE + 5$

$\Rightarrow \quad HL = (8 + 5) \text{ cm} = 13 \text{ cm}$

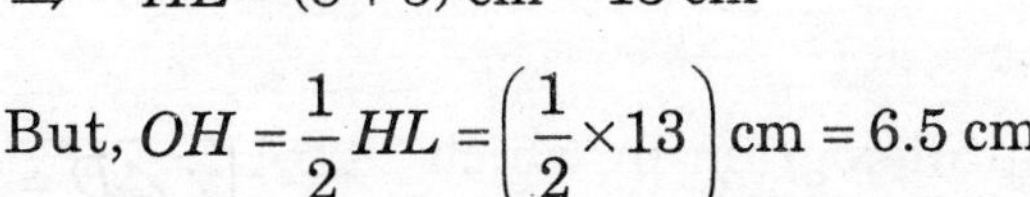

But, $OH = \frac{1}{2} HL = \left(\frac{1}{2} \times 13\right) \text{cm} = 6.5 \text{ cm}$

Example 7 In Fig. 17.16, *RING* is a parallelogram, if $\angle R = 70°$, find all other angles.

Solution Since adjacent angles in a parallelogram are supplementary.

$\therefore \quad \angle R + \angle I = 180° \text{ and } \angle R + \angle G = 180°$

$\Rightarrow \quad 70° + \angle I = 180° \text{ and } 70° + \angle G = 180°$

$\Rightarrow \quad \angle I = 110° \text{ and } \angle G = 110°$

Since opposite angles in a parallelogram are equal

$\therefore \quad \angle N = \angle R \Rightarrow \angle N = 70°$

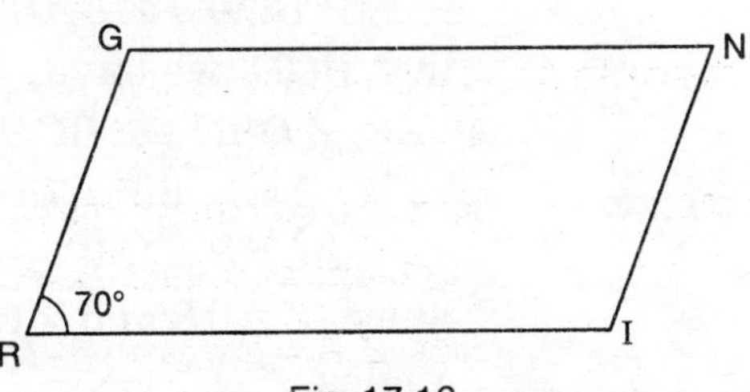

Fig. 17.16

Hence, $\angle G = \angle I = 110°$ and $\angle N = 70°$

Example 8 In Fig. 17.17, *ABCD* is a parallelogram in which $\angle DAO = 40°$, $\angle BAO = 35°$ and $\angle COD = 65°$. Find:

(i) $\angle ABO$ (ii) $\angle ODC$ (iii) $\angle ACB$ (iv) $\angle CBD$

Solution Since $\angle AOB$ and $\angle COD$ are vertically opposite angles.

$\therefore \quad \angle AOB = \angle COD$

$\Rightarrow \quad \angle AOB = 65°$

[$\because \angle COD = 65°$ (Given)]

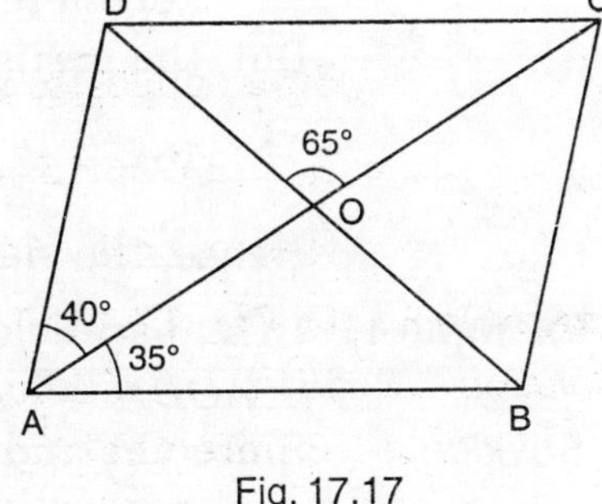

Fig. 17.17

(i) In ΔAOB, we have

$\angle OAB + \angle AOB + \angle ABO = 180°$

$\Rightarrow \quad 35° + 65° + \angle ABO = 180°$

$\Rightarrow \quad 100° + \angle ABO = 180°$

$\Rightarrow \quad \angle ABO = 180° - 100° = 80°$

(ii) Since $\angle ABO$ and $\angle ODC = \angle BDC$ are alternate interior angles which are always equal.

$\therefore \quad \angle ODC = \angle ABO$

$\Rightarrow \quad \angle ODC = 80°$ [Using (i)]

(iii) Since $\angle ACB$ and $\angle DAC$ are alternate interior angles.

$\therefore \quad \angle ACB = \angle DAC$

$\Rightarrow \quad \angle ACB = 40°$ [$\because \angle DAC = 40°$ (Given)]

(iv) Since $\angle A$ and $\angle B$ are adjacent interior angles of parallelogram $ABCD$ and adjacent interior angles are supplementary.

$\therefore \quad \angle A + \angle B = 180°$

$\Rightarrow \quad \angle B = 180° - \angle A$

$\Rightarrow \quad \angle B = 180° - (40° + 35°) = 105°$ [See Fig. 17.17]

$\Rightarrow \quad \angle ABD + \angle CBD = 105°$

$\Rightarrow \quad \angle ABO + \angle CBD = 105°$ [$\because \angle ABD = \angle ABO$]

$\Rightarrow \quad 80° + \angle CBD = 105°$ [Using (i), $\angle ABO = 80°$]

$\Rightarrow \angle CBD = 105° - 80° = 25°$

Example 9 In Fig. 17.18, $ABCD$ is a parallelogram in which $\angle DAB = 75°$, $\angle DBC = 60°$. Calculate $\angle CDB$ and $\angle ADB$.

Solution Since opposite angles of a parallelogram are equal.

$\therefore \quad \angle BCD = \angle DAB = 75°$

In ΔBCD, we have

$\angle DBC + \angle BCD + \angle CDB = 180°$

$\Rightarrow \quad 60° + 75° + \angle CDB = 180°$

$\Rightarrow \quad \angle CDB = 180° - (60° + 75°) = 45°$

Since $\angle ADB$ and $\angle CBD$ are alternate interior angles.

$\therefore \quad \angle ADB = \angle CBD = 60°$ [$\because \angle CBD = 60°$]

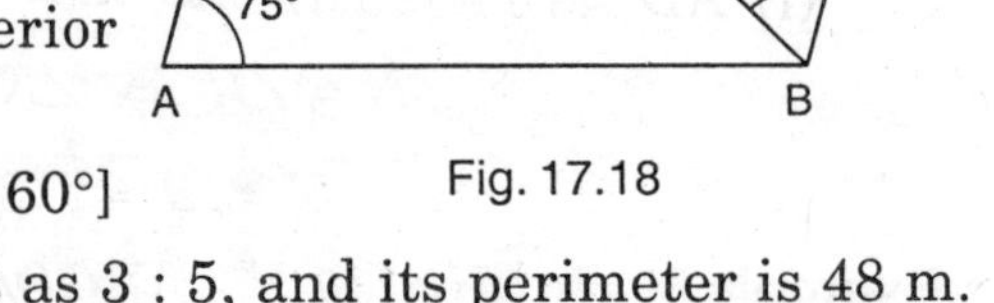

Fig. 17.18

Example 10 The ratio of two sides of a parallelogram is as 3 : 5, and its perimeter is 48 m. Find the sides of the parallelogram.

Solution Let the two sides of the parallelogram be $3x$ metres and $5x$ metres in length. Then,

$\Rightarrow$ Perimeter $= 2$ (Length + Breadth)

$\Rightarrow$ Perimeter $= 2\ (3x + 5x)$ metres $= 2 \times 8x$ metres $= 16x$ metres.

But, the perimeter is given as 48 metres.

$\therefore \quad 16x = 48 \Rightarrow \dfrac{16x}{16} = \dfrac{48}{16} \Rightarrow x = 3$

Hence, the sides of the parallelogram are 3×3 m $= 9$ m and 5×3 m $= 15$ m

Example 11 In a parallelogram $ABCD$, the bisectors of $\angle A$ and $\angle B$ meet at O. Find $\angle AOB$.

Solution Since OA and OB are the bisectors of $\angle A$ and $\angle B$ respectively.

$\therefore \quad \angle OAB = \frac{1}{2}\angle A$ and $\angle OBA = \frac{1}{2}\angle B$

In ΔAOB, we have

$\angle OAB + \angle AOB + \angle OBA = 180°$

$\Rightarrow \quad \frac{1}{2}\angle A + \angle AOB + \frac{1}{2}\angle B = 180°$

$\Rightarrow \quad \angle AOB = 180° - \frac{1}{2}(\angle A + \angle B)$

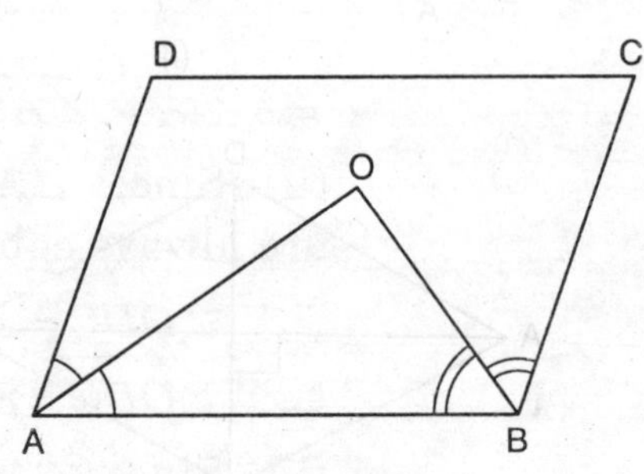

Fig. 17.19

$\Rightarrow \quad \angle AOB = 180° - \frac{1}{2}(180°)$ $\left[\because \angle A \text{ and } \angle B \text{ are adjacent angles of parallelogram } ABCD \therefore \angle A + \angle B = 180°\right]$

$\Rightarrow \quad \angle AOB = 180° - 90° = 90°$

Example 12 Draw a parallelogram $ABCD$ in which $AB = 8$ cm, $AD = 5$ cm and $\angle A = 60°$.

Solution We follow the following steps to construct the required parallelogram.

Steps of construction

Step I Draw $AB = 8\,cm$.

Step II At A, draw $\angle BAX = 60°$.

Step III With A as centre and radius equal to $AD = 5\,cm$, cut off an arc intersecting AX at D.

Step IV With B as centre and radius equal to $AD = 5\,cm$, cut off an arc.

Step V With D as centre and radius equal to $AB = 8\,cm$, cut off an arc intersecting the arc drawn in step IV at C.

Step VI Join DC and BC to obtain the required parallelogram.

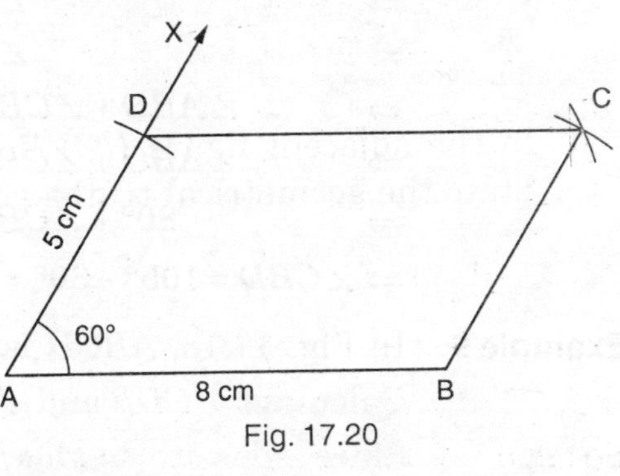

Fig. 17.20

EXERCISE 17.1

1. Given below is a parallelogram $ABCD$. Complete each statement along with the definition or property used.

(i) $AD =$ (ii) $\angle DCB =$ (iii) $OC =$ (iv) $\angle DAB + \angle CDA =$

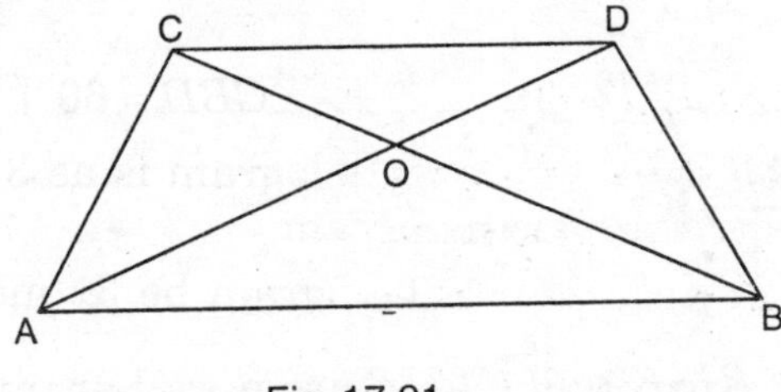

Fig. 17.21

2. The following figures are parallelograms. Find the degree values of the unknowns x, y, z.

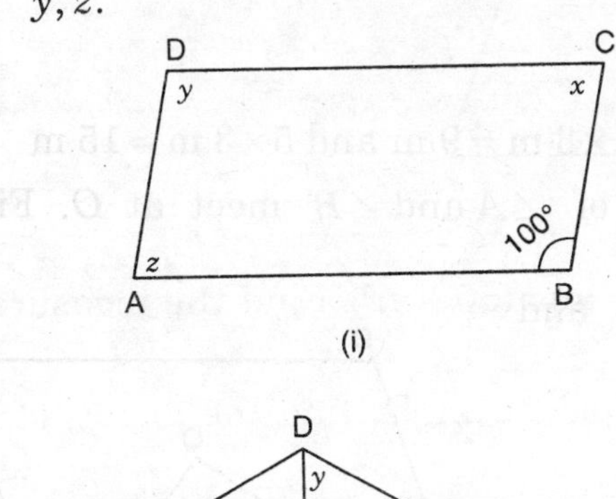

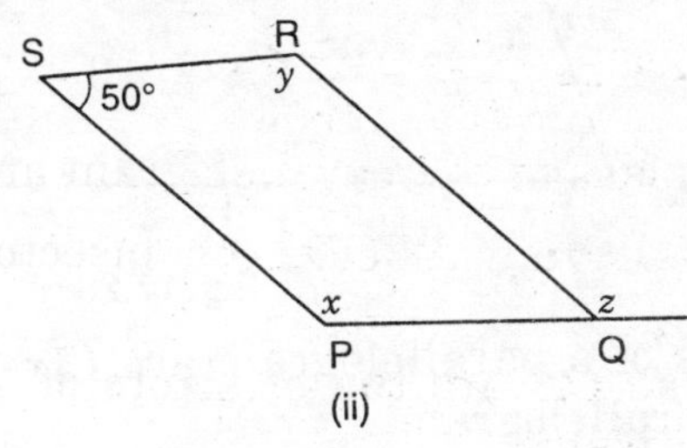

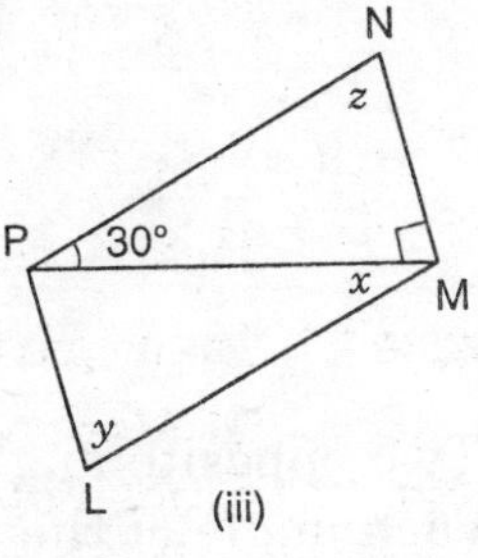

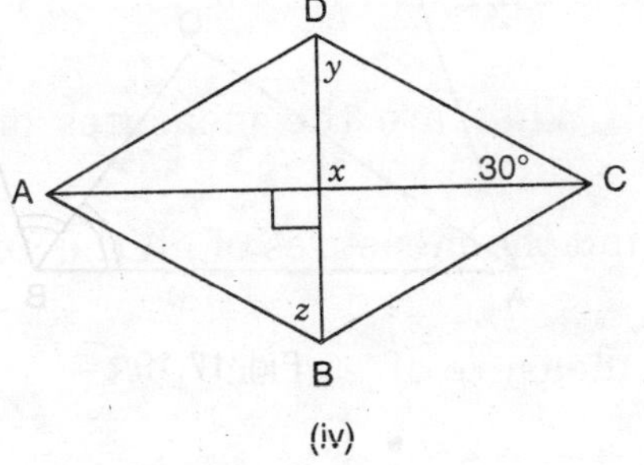

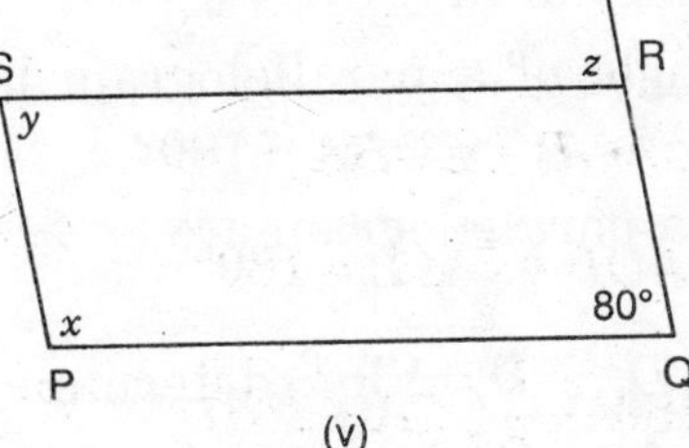

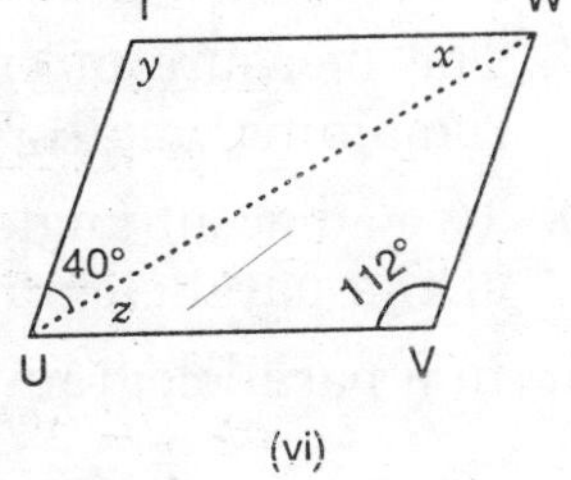

Fig. 17.22

3. Can the following figures be parallelograms. Justify your answer.

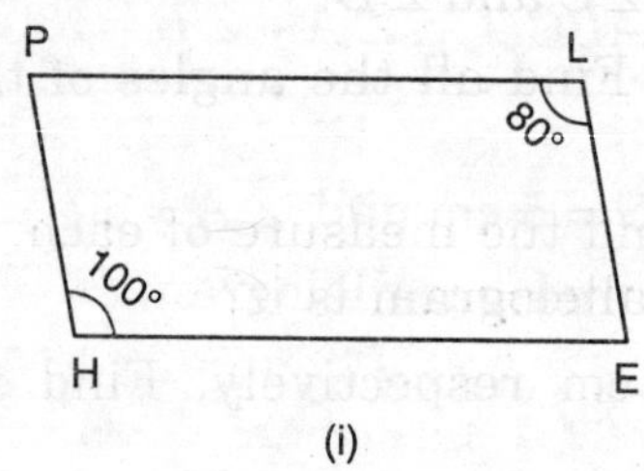

(i)

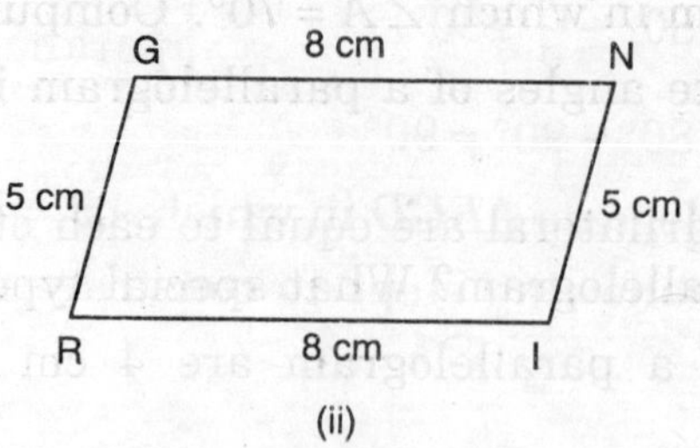

(ii)

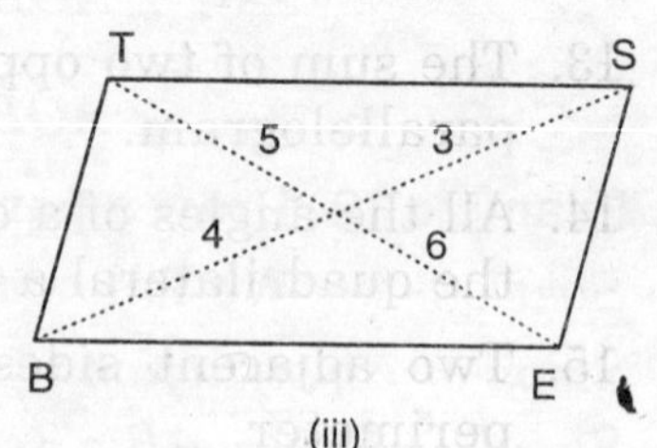

(iii)

Fig. 17.23

4. In the adjacent figure *HOPE* is a parallelogram. Find the angle measures x,y and z. State the geometrical truths you use to find them.

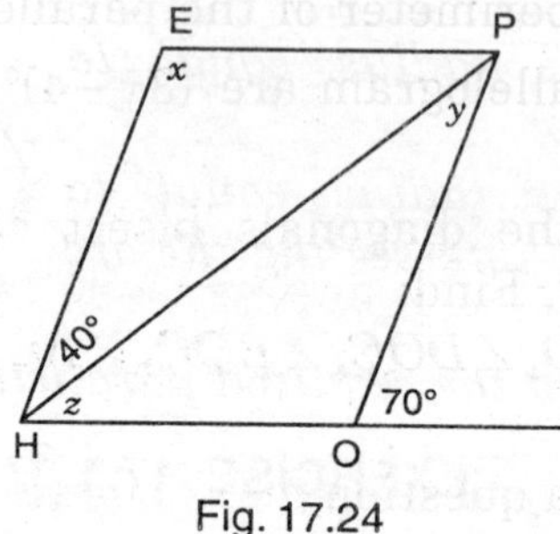

Fig. 17.24

5. In the following figures *GUNS* and *RUNS* are parallelograms. Find x and y.

(i)

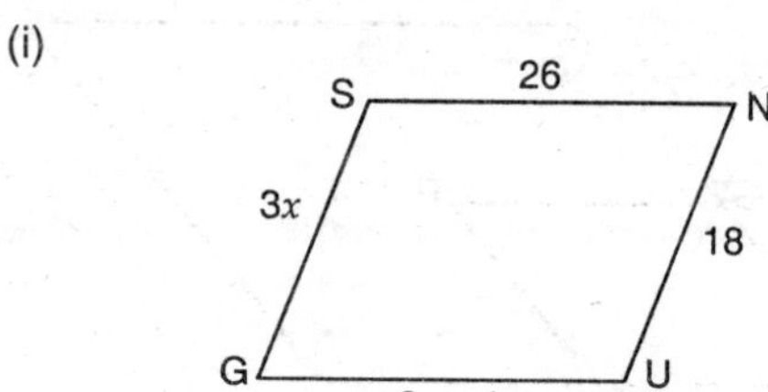

(ii)

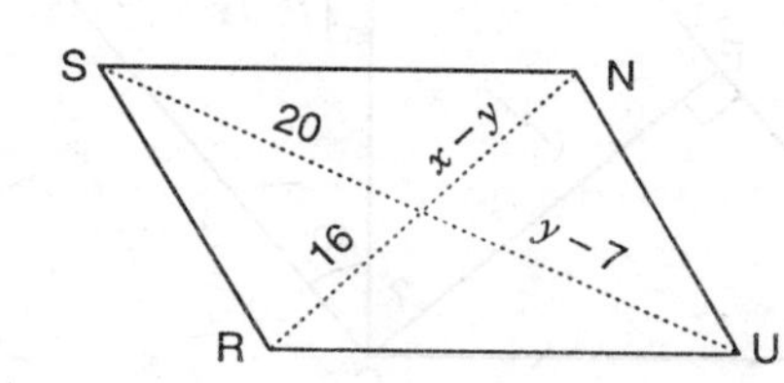

Fig. 17.25

6. In the following figure *RISK* and *CLUE* are parallelograms. Find the measure of x.

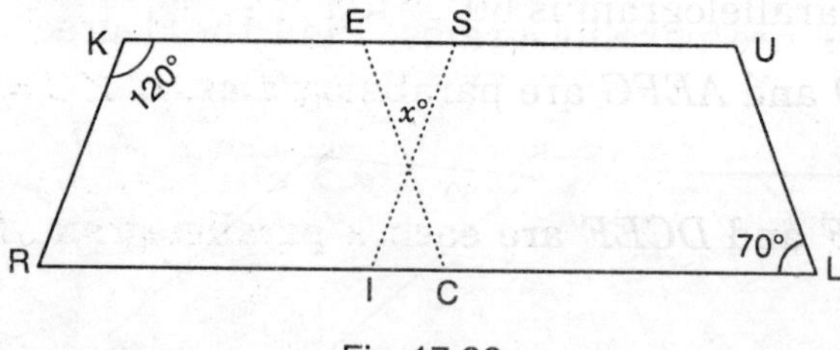

Fig. 17.26

7. Two opposite angles of a parallelogram are $(3x - 2)°$ and $(50 - x)°$. Find the measure of each angle of the parallelogram.
8. If an angle of a parallelogram is two-third of its adjacent angle, find the angles of the parallelogram.
9. The measure of one angle of a parallelogram is 70°. What are the measures of the remaining angles?
10. Two adjacent angles of a parallelogram are as 1 : 2. Find the measures of all the angles of the parallelogram.
11. In a parallelogram $ABCD$, $\angle D = 135°$, determine the measure of $\angle A$ and $\angle B$.

12. *ABCD* is a parallelogram in which $\angle A = 70°$. Compute $\angle B$, $\angle C$ and $\angle D$.
13. The sum of two opposite angles of a parallelogram is 130°. Find all the angles of the parallelogram.
14. All the angles of a quadrilateral are equal to each other. Find the measure of each. Is the quadrilateral a parallelogram? What special type of parallelogram is it?
15. Two adjacent sides of a parallelogram are 4 cm and 3 cm respectively. Find its perimeter.
16. The perimeter of a parallelogram is 150 cm. One of its sides is greater than the other by 25 cm. Find the length of the sides of the parallelogram.
17. The shorter side of a parallelogram is 4.8 cm and the longer side is half as much again as the shorter side. Find the perimeter of the parallelogram.
18. Two adjacent angles of a parallelogram are $(3x - 4)°$ and $(3x + 10)°$. Find the angles of the parallelogram.
19. In a parallelogram *ABCD*, the diagonals bisect each other at *O*. If $\angle ABC = 30°$, $\angle BDC = 10°$ and $\angle CAB = 70°$. Find:
$\angle DAB, \angle ADC, \angle BCD, \angle AOD, \angle DOC, \angle BOC, \angle AOB, \angle ACD, \angle CAB, \angle ADB,$
$\angle ACB, \angle DBC$ and $\angle DBA$.
20. Find the angles marked with a question mark shown in Fig. 17.27

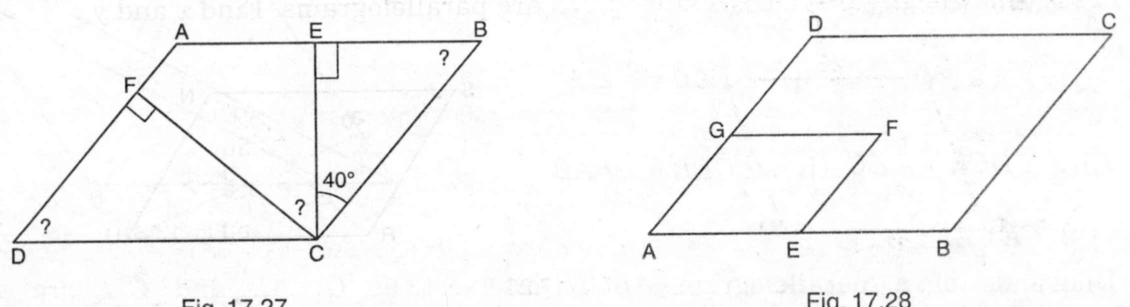

Fig. 17.27

Fig. 17.28

21. The angle between the altitudes of a parallelogram, through the same vertex of an obtuse angle of the parallelogram is 60°. Find the angles of the parallelogram.
22. In Fig. 17.28, *ABCD* and *AEFG* are parallelograms. If $\angle C = 55°$, what is the measure of $\angle F$?
23. In Fig. 17.29, *BDEF* and *DCEF* are each a parallelogram. Is it true that $BD = DC$? Why or why not?

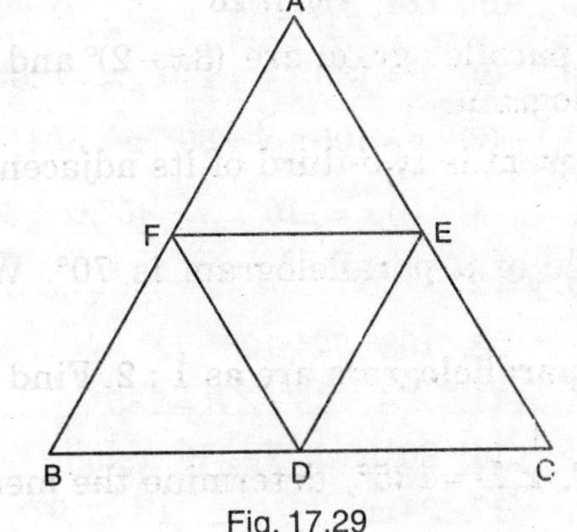

Fig. 17.29

24. In Fig. 17.29, suppose it is known that $DE = DF$. Then, is ΔABC isosceles? Why or why not?

25. Diagonals of parallelogram $ABCD$ intersect at O as shown in Fig. 17.30. XY contains O, and X, Y are points on opposite sides of the parallelogram. Give reasons for each of the following:

(i) $OB = OD$ (ii) $\angle OBY = \angle ODX$

(iii) $\angle BOY = \angle DOX$ (iv) $\Delta BOY \cong \Delta DOX$

Now, state if XY is bisected at O.

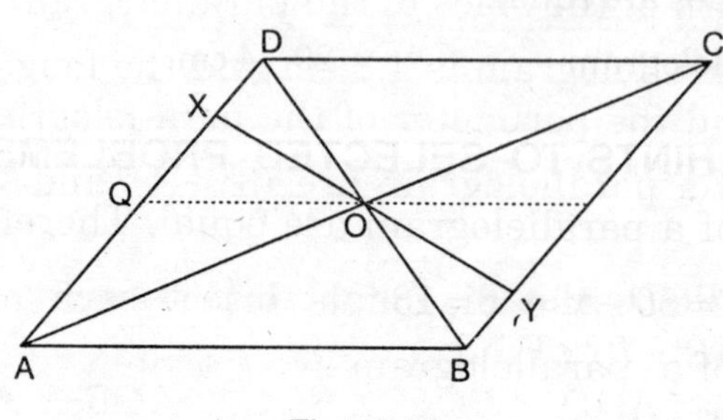

Fig. 17.30

26. In Fig. 17.31, $ABCD$ is a parallelogram, CE bisects $\angle C$ and AF bisects $\angle A$. In each of the following, if the statement is true, give a reason for the same:

(i) $\angle A = \angle C$ (ii) $\angle FAB = \dfrac{1}{2}\angle A$

(iii) $\angle DCE = \dfrac{1}{2}\angle C$ (iv) $\angle CEB = \angle FAB$

(v) $CE \parallel AF$

Fig. 17.31

27. Diagonals of a parallelogram $ABCD$ intersect at O. AL and CM are drawn perpendiculars to BD such that L and M lie on BD. Is $AL = CM$? Why or why not?

28. Points E and F lie on diagonal AC of a parallelogram $ABCD$ such that $AE = CF$. What type of quadrilateral is $BFDE$?

29. In a parallelogram $ABCD$, $AB = 10$ cm, $AD = 6$ cm. The bisector of $\angle A$ meets DC in E, AE and BC produced meet at F. Find the length CF.

ANSWERS

1. (i) BC (ii) $\angle BAD$ (iii) OA (iv) 180°

2. (i) $x = 80°, y = 100°, z = 80°$ (ii) $x = 130°, y = 130°, z = 130°$ (iii) $x = 30°, y = 60°, z = 60°$ (iv) $x = 90°, y = 60°, z = 60°$ (v) $x = 100°, y = 80°, z = 80°$ (vi) $x = 28°, y = 112°, z = 28°$

3. (i) No (ii) Yes (iii) No.

4. (i) $x = 110°$, $y = 40°, z = 30°$

5. (i) $x = 6, y = 9$, (ii) $x = 43, y = 27$

6. $x = 50°$

7. 37°, 143°, 37°, 143°

8. 108°, 72°, 108°, 72°

9. 110°, 70°, 110°

10. 120°, 60°, 120°, 80°

11. $\angle A = 45°, \angle B = 135°$

12. $\angle B = 110° = \angle D, \angle C = 70°$

13. 65°, 115°, 65°, 115°

14. 90° each, Yes, Rectangle

15. 14 cm

16. 50 cm, 25 cm

17. 24 cm

18. 97°, 83°

19. $\angle DAB = 150°$, $\angle ADC = 30°$, $\angle BCD = 150°$, $\angle AOD = 80°$, $\angle DOC = 100°$, $\angle BOC = 80°$, $\angle AOB = 100°$, $\angle ACD = 70°$, $\angle CAB = 70°$, $\angle ADB = 20°$, $\angle ACB = 80°$, $\angle DBC = 20°$ and $\angle DBA = 10°$ 20. $\angle EBC = 50°$, $\angle ADC = 50°$, $\angle FCE = 50°$

21. $60°, 120°, 60°, 120°$ 22. $55°$ 23. Yes 24. Yes 25. 1.5 cm

25. (i) Diagonals of a parallelogram bisect each other (ii) Alternate angles
(iii) Vertically opposite angles (iv) ASA congruence, yes

26. (i) T, Opposite angles of a parallelogram (ii) T, AF is the bisector of $\angle A$
(iii) T, CE is the bisector of $\angle C$ (iv) T, $\angle CEB = \angle DCE = \angle FAB$
(v) T, Corresponding angles are equal.

27. Yes 28. Parallelogram 29. 4 cm.

HINTS TO SELECTED PROBLEMS

7. Since opposite angles of a parallelogram are equal. Therefore,

$$3x - 2 = 50 - x \Rightarrow x = 13$$

8. Since adjacent angles of a parallelogram are supplementary.

$$\therefore \quad x + \frac{2}{3}x = 180° \Rightarrow x = 108°$$

11. $\angle C + \angle D = 180° \Rightarrow \angle C = 45°$

Now, $\angle A = \angle C$ and $\angle B = \angle D \Rightarrow \angle A = 45°; \angle B = 135°$

29. Construct parallelogram $ABFE$, where E is the point of intersection of AD produced and a line drawn through F parallel to AB. Now, ΔAFE is isosceles. Therefore, $AE = EF \Rightarrow AD + DE = 10 \Rightarrow DE = 4$ cm $\Rightarrow CF = 4$ cm.

17.4 PROPERTIES OF A RHOMBUS

In section 17.2, we have defined a rhombus as a parallelogram having a pair of adjacent sides equal. Thus, if $ABCD$ is a rhombus as shown in Fig. 17.32, then it is a parallelogram with $AB = AD$.

In the previous section, we have learnt about some properties of a parallelogram. Since every rhombus is a parallelogram, therefore if $ABCD$ is a rhombus, then it has the following properties:

(i) Opposite sides are equal i.e.

$AB = DC$ and $BC = AD$

(ii) Opposite angles are equal i.e.

$\angle A = \angle C$ and $\angle B = \angle D$

(iii) Diagonals bisect each other i.e.

$AO = OC$ and $BO = OD$

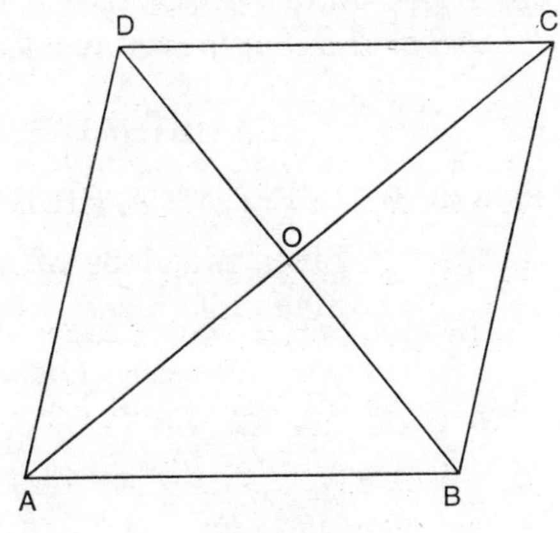

Fig. 17.32

Now, AB and AD are the two adjacent sides of rhombus $ABCD$ and adjacent sides of a rhombus are equal.

$\therefore \quad AB = AD$

Also, $ABCD$ is a parallelogram

$\therefore \quad AB = DC$ and $BC = AD$

Hence, $AB = AD = BC = DC$.

So, all the sides of a rhombus are equal.

In addition to the above properties, the diagonals of a rhombus possess an important property as given below.

THEOREM *(Diagonal property of a Rhombus) The diagonals of a rhombus bisect each other at right angles.*

Proof: Let $ABCD$ be a rhombus whose diagonals AC and BD intersect at O as shown in Fig. 17.33.

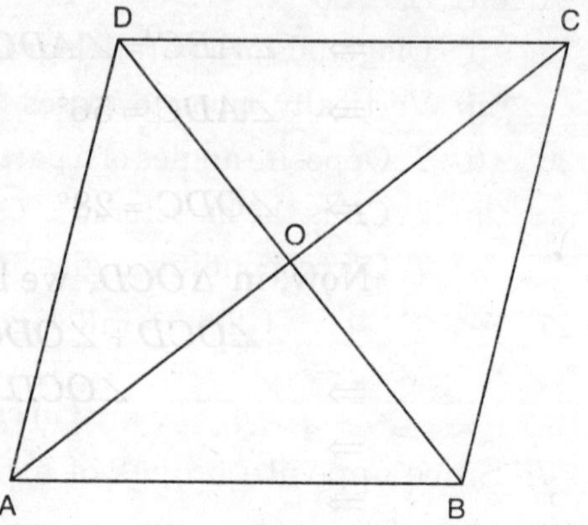

Fig. 17.33

Since every rhombus is a parallelogram and the diagonals of a parallelogram bisect each other.

$\therefore \quad OA = OC$ and $OB = OD$

Thus, diagonals of a rhombus bisect each other.

In order to prove that the diagonals of the rhombus $ABCD$ are perpendicular to each other, consider triangles AOB and AOD.

In Δs AOB and AOD, we have

$AB = AD$ [Sides of a rhombus are equal]

$OB = OD$ [O is the mid-point of BD]

and, $OA = OA$ [Common side]

$\therefore$ By SSS congruence criterion, we have

$\Delta AOB \cong \Delta AOD$

$\Rightarrow \quad \angle AOB = \angle AOD$

But, $\angle AOB + \angle AOD = 180°$ [Linear pair]

$\therefore \quad \angle AOB + \angle AOB = 180°$

$\Rightarrow \quad 2\angle AOB = 180° \Rightarrow \angle AOB = 90°$

Thus, $\angle AOB = \angle AOD = 90°$

Hence, the diagonals of a rhombus bisect each other at right angles.

SUMMARY *The properties of a rhombus can be summarized as under:*

(i) All the sides of a rhombus are equal.
(ii) The opposite angles of a rhombus are equal.
(iii) The adjacent angles of a rhombus are supplementary.
(iv) The diagonals of a rhombus bisect each other at right angles.

ILLUSTRATIVE EXAMPLES

Example 1 In Fig. 17.34, RICE is parallelogram. Find x, y, z.

Solution Since all sides of a rhombus are equal and its diagonals bisect each other.

$\therefore \quad RI = RE,\ OE = OI$ and $OR = OC$

$\Rightarrow \quad z = 13,\ x = 5$ and $y = 12$.

Hence, $x = 5$, $y = 12$ and $z = 13$.

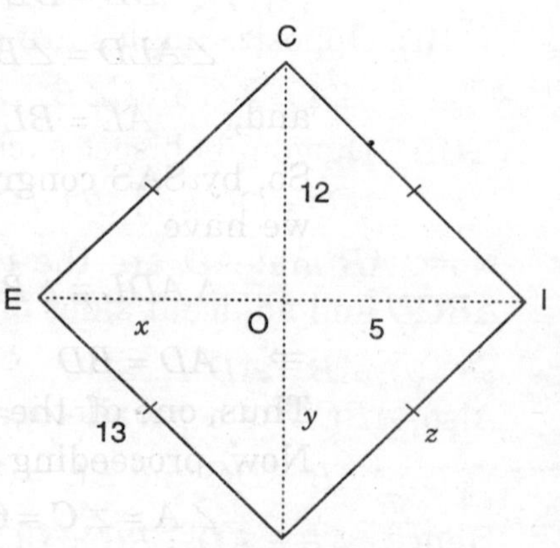

Fig. 17.34

Example 2 In Fig. 17.35, $ABCD$ is a rhombus with $\angle ABC = 56°$. Determine $\angle ACD$.

Solution $ABCD$ is a rhombus

$\Rightarrow$ $ABCD$ is a parallelogram

$\Rightarrow$ $\angle ABC = \angle ADC$ [Opp $\angle s$ of $\|_{gm}$ are equal]

$\Rightarrow$ $\angle ADC = 56°$ [$\because \angle ABC = 56°$ (Given)]

$\Rightarrow$ $\angle ODC = 28°$ $\left[\because \angle ODC = \frac{1}{2}\angle ADC\right]$

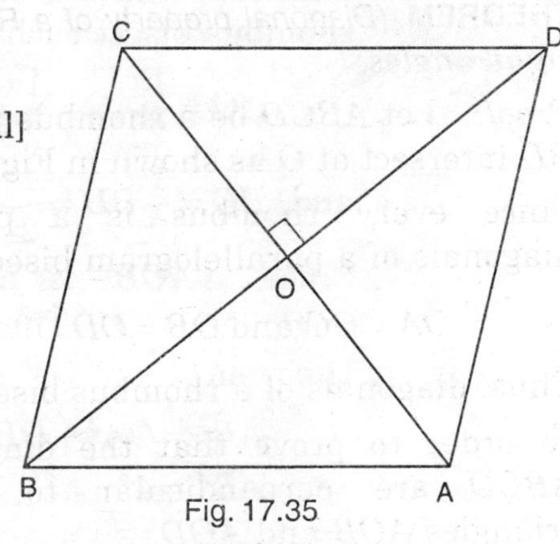

Fig. 17.35

Now, in ΔOCD, we have

$$\angle OCD + \angle ODC + \angle COD = 180°$$

$\Rightarrow$ $\angle OCD + 28° + 90° = 180°$

$\Rightarrow$ $\angle OCD = 62°$

$\Rightarrow$ $\angle ACD = 62°$

Example 3 One of the diagonals of a rhombus is equal to one of its sides. Find the angles of the rhombus.

Solution Let $ABCD$ be a rhombus such that its diagonals BD is equal to its sides.

That is, $AB = BC = CD = AD = BD$

$\Rightarrow$ $\Delta s\ ABD$ and BCD are equilateral

$\Rightarrow$ $\angle A = \angle C = 60°$

Now, $\angle A + \angle B$ $\left[\begin{array}{l}\because \text{adjacent angles} \\ \text{of a } \|_{gm} \text{ are supple.}\end{array}\right]$

$\Rightarrow$ $60° + \angle B = 180°$

$\Rightarrow$ $\angle B = 180° - 60° = 120°$

Hence, $\angle A = 60° = \angle C$ and $\angle B = \angle D = 120°$.

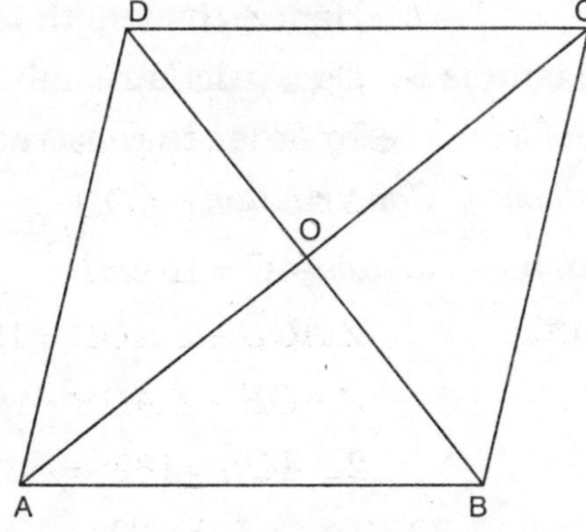

Fig. 17.36

Example 4 $ABCD$ is a rhombus in which the altitude from D to side AB bisects AB. Find the angles of the rhombus.

Solution Let DL be the altitude from D on side AB. It is given that L bisects AB i.e. $AL = BL$. Join BD.

In $\Delta s\ ADL$ and BDL, we have

$DL = DL$ [Common side]

$\angle ALD = \angle BLD = 90°$

and, $AL = BL$

So, by SAS congruence criterion, we have

$\Delta ADL \cong \Delta BDL$

$\Rightarrow$ $AD = BD$

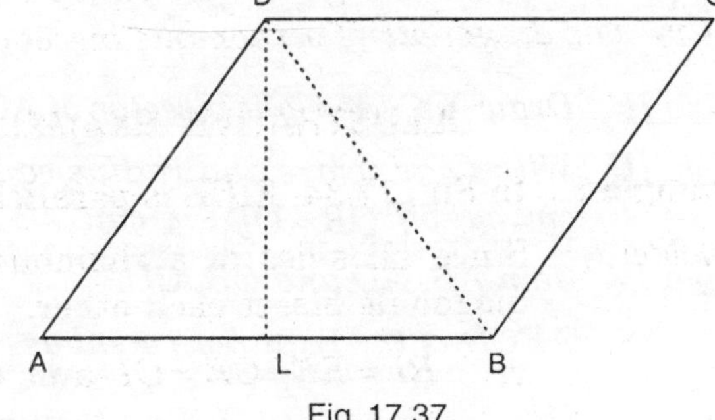

Fig. 17.37

Thus, one of the diagonals of rhombus $ABCD$ is equal to one of its sides.

Now, proceeding as in Example 3, we get

$\angle A = \angle C = 60°$ and $\angle B = \angle D = 120°$

Example 5 The diagonals of a rhombus are 6 cm and 8 cm. Find the length of a side of the rhombus.

Solution Let $ABCD$ be the rhombus whose diagonals AC and BD are of lengths 8 cm and 6 cm respectively. Let AC and BD intersect at O. Since the diagonals of a rhombus bisect each other at right-angles.

$$\therefore \quad AO = \frac{1}{2}AC = \frac{1}{2} \times 8 \text{ cm} = 4 \text{ cm}$$

and, $BO = \frac{1}{2}BD = \frac{1}{2} \times 6 \text{ cm} = 3 \text{ cm}$

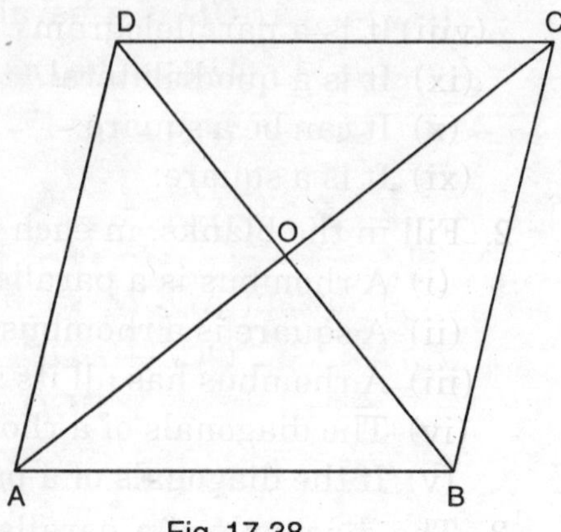

Fig. 17.38

Since ΔAOB is a right triangle, right angled at O. Therefore, by Pythagoras theorem

$$AB^2 = OA^2 + OB^2$$
$$\Rightarrow \quad AB^2 = 4^2 + 3^2$$
$$\Rightarrow \quad AB^2 = 16 + 9$$
$$\Rightarrow \quad AB^2 = 5^2$$
$$\Rightarrow \quad AB = 5$$

Hence, the length of each side of the rhombus is 5 cm.

Example 6 Construct a rhombus whose diagonals are 10 cm and 8 cm.

Solution In order to construct the given rhombus, we follow the following steps:

Steps of Construction

Step I *Draw* $AC = 10$ *cm.*

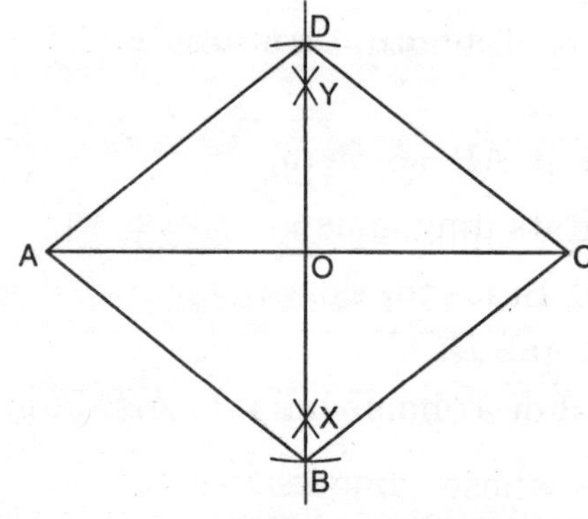

Fig. 17.39

Step II *Draw XY, the right bisector of AC meeting it at O.*

Step III *With O as centre and radius equal to half of the length of the other diagonal i.e. 4 cm, cut off* $OB = OD = 4$ *cm.*

Step IV *Join AB, AD and CB, CD.*

ABCD is the required rhombus.

EXERCISE 17.2

1. Which of the following statements are true for a rhombus?
   - (i) It has two pairs of parallel sides.
   - (ii) It has two pairs of equal sides.
   - (iii) It has only two pairs of equal sides.
   - (iv) Two of its angles are at right angles.

(v) Its diagonals bisect each other at right angles.
(vi) Its diagonals are equal and perpendicular.
(vii) It has all its sides of equal lengths.
(viii) It is a parallelogram.
(ix) It is a quadrilateral.
(x) It can be a square.
(xi) It is a square.

2. Fill in the blanks, in each of the following, so as to make the statement true:
   (i) A rhombus is a parallelogram in which ......
   (ii) A square is a rhombus in which ....
   (iii) A rhombus has all its sides of .... length.
   (iv) The diagonals of a rhombus ...... each other at ...... angles.
   (v) If the diagonals of a parallelogram bisect each other at right angles, then it is a ....
3. The diagonals of a parallelogram are not perpendicular. Is it a rhombus ? Why or why not?
4. The diagonals of a quadrilateral are perpendicular to each other. Is such a quadrilateral always a rhombus ? If your answer is 'No', draw a figure to justify your answer.
5. $ABCD$ is a rhombus. If $\angle ACB = 40°$, find $\angle ADB$.
6. If the diagonals of a rhombus are 12 cm and 16 cm, find the length of each side.
7. Construct a rhombus whose diagonals are of length 10 cm and 6 cm.
8. Draw a rhombus, having each side of length 3.5 cm and one of the angles as 40°.
9. One side of a rhombus is of length 4 cm and the length of an altitude is 3.2 cm. Draw the rhombus.
10. Draw a rhombus $ABCD$, if $AB = 6$ cm and $AC = 5$ cm.
11. $ABCD$ is a rhombus and its diagonals intersect at O.
   (i) Is $\Delta BOC \cong \Delta DOC$? State the congruence condition used?
   (ii) Also state, if $\angle BCO = \angle DCO$.
12. Show that each diagonal of a rhombus bisects the angle through which it passes.
13. $ABCD$ is a rhombus whose diagonals intersect at O. If $AB = 10$ cm, diagonal $BD = 16$ cm, find the length of diagonal AC.
14. The diagonals of a quadrilateral are of lengths 6 cm and 8 cm. If the diagonals bisect each other at right angles, what is the length of each side of the quadrilateral?

ANSWERS

1. (i) T (ii) T (iii) F (iv) F (v) T (vi) F
   (vii) T (viii) T (ix) T (x) T (xi) F
2. (i) adjacent sides are equal (ii) one angle is right angle (iii) equal
   (iv) bisect, right (v) rhombus
3. No, Diagonals must be perpendicular
4. No, Draw a quad. of side 8.5 cm each 5. 50° 6. 10 cm
11. (i) Yes, SSS (ii) Yes 13. 12 cm 14. 5 cm

HINTS TO SELECTED PROBLEMS

10. Draw ΔABC, with $AC = 5$ cm, $AB = BC = 6$ cm. Complete parallelogram $ABCD$.

17.5 PROPERTIES OF A RECTANGLE

In section 17.2, we have defined a rectangle as a parallelogram, whose one of the angles is a right angle. Thus, a rectangle has all the properties that a parallelogram possesses. In this section, we shall learn about some more properties of a rectangle.

Property 1 *Each angle of a rectangle is a right angle.*

Proof: Let $ABCD$ be a rectangle such that $\angle A = 90°$. We have to prove that each angle of the rectangle $ABCD$ is a right angle. For this, we have to show that $\angle B = \angle C = \angle D = 90°$.

Since $ABCD$ is a parallelogram.

$\therefore \quad AB = DC, BC = AD$ and $\angle A = \angle C, \angle B = \angle D$

$\Rightarrow \quad \angle C = 90°$ $\quad [\angle A = 90°]$

Now, $AB \parallel DC$ and AD intersects them at A and D respectively.

$\therefore \quad \angle A + \angle D = 180°$ $\quad$ [$\because$ Adjacent interior angles are supplementary]

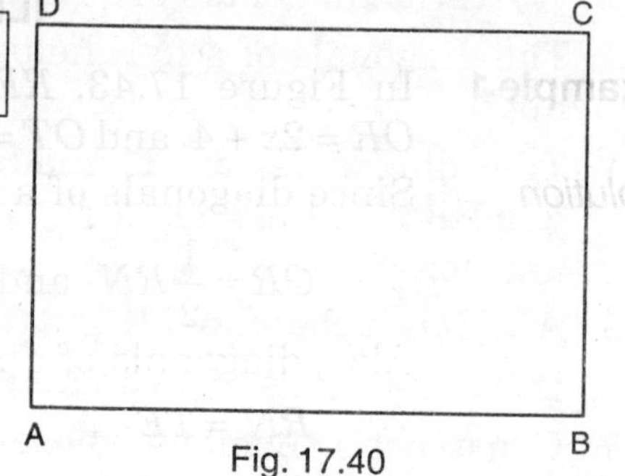

Fig. 17.40

$\Rightarrow \quad 90° + \angle D = 180°$ $\quad [\because \angle A = 90°]$

$\Rightarrow \quad \angle D = 180 - 90° = 90°$

But, $\angle B = \angle D$

$\therefore \quad \angle B = 90°$

Hence, $\angle A = \angle C = \angle B = \angle D = 90°$

Property 2 *The diagonals of a rectangle are equal.*

Proof: Let $ABCD$ be a rectangle with its diagonals AC and BD. (Fig. 17.41)

In triangles DAB and CBA, we have

$AD = BC$ $\quad$ [Opposite sides of a rectangle]

$\angle DAB = \angle CBA$ $\quad$ [Each equal to 90°]

and, $AB = BA$ $\quad$ [Common]

So, by SAS congruence criterion, we have

$\Delta DAB \cong \Delta CBA$

$\Rightarrow \quad BD = AC$

Fig. 17.41

Hence, the diagonals of a rectangle are equal.

NOTE: *Diagonals of a rectangle need not be perpendicular to one another.*

17.6 PROPERTIES OF A SQUARE

In section 17.2, we have defined a square as a rectangle whose adjacent sides are equal and in the previous section, we have learnt the properties of a rectangle. Thus, if $ABCD$ is a square, then

$$AB = BC, BC = CD, AD = CD \text{ and } AD = AB$$

$$\Rightarrow \quad AB = BC = CD = AD$$

Thus, all sides of a square are equal.

Also, each angle of a rectangle is a right angle and diagonals of a rectangle are equal.

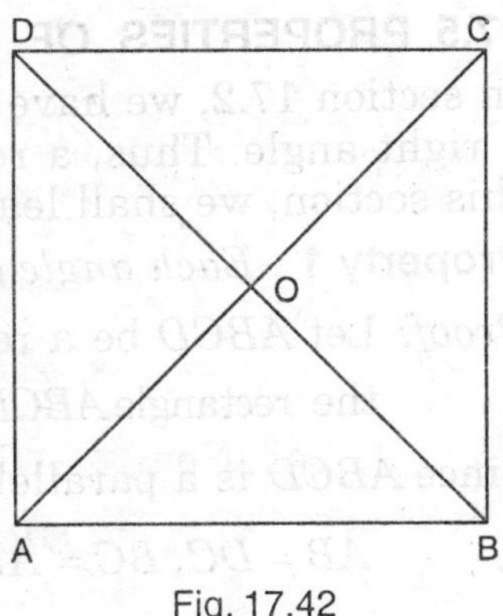

Fig. 17.42

Therefore, each angle of a square is a right angle and diagonals of a square are also equal.

Since all sides of a square are equal and opposite sides are parallel. So, it is a rhombus. But the diagonals of a rhombus bisect each other at right angles. Therefore, the diagonals AC and BD of a square bisect each other at right angles.

The above properties can be summarized as under :

SUMMARY *In a square:*

(i) all the sides are of the same length.

(ii) each of the angles is a right angle.

(iii) the diagonals are of equal length.

(iv) the diagonals bisect each other at right angles.

ILLUSTRATIVE EXAMPLES

Example 1 In Figure 17.43, $RENT$ is a rectangle. Its diagonals meet at O. Find x, if $OR = 2x + 4$ and $OT = 3x + 1$.

Solution Since diagonals of a rectangle bisect each other.

$$OR = \frac{1}{2}RN \text{ and } OT = \frac{1}{2}TE$$

Also, diagonals of a rectangle are equal.

$\therefore \quad RN = TE$

$\Rightarrow \quad \frac{1}{2}RN = \frac{1}{2}TE$

$\Rightarrow \quad OR = OT$

$\Rightarrow \quad 2x + 4 = 3x + 1$

$\Rightarrow \quad 3x - 2x = 4 - 1$

$\Rightarrow \quad x = 3.$

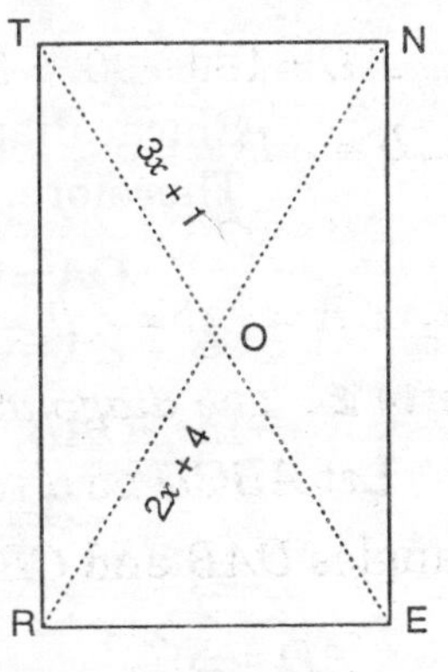

Fig. 17.43

Example 2 $PQRS$ is a square. PR and SQ intersect at O. State the measure of $\angle POQ$.

Solution Since the diagonals of a square intersect at right angle. Therefore,

$\angle POQ = 90°$

Example 3 In Fig. 17.44, $PQRS$ is a square. Determine $\angle SRP$.

Solution $PQRS$ is a square.

$\therefore \quad PS = SR$ and $\angle PSR = 90°$

In ΔPSR, we have

$PS = SR$

$\Rightarrow \quad \angle 1 = \angle 2$ [$\because$ Angles opp. to equal sides are equal]

But, $\angle 1 + \angle 2 + \angle PSR = 180°$

$\therefore \quad 2\angle 1 + 90° = 180° \quad [\because \angle PSR = 90°]$

$\Rightarrow \quad 2\angle 1 = 90°$

$\Rightarrow \quad \angle 1 = 45°$

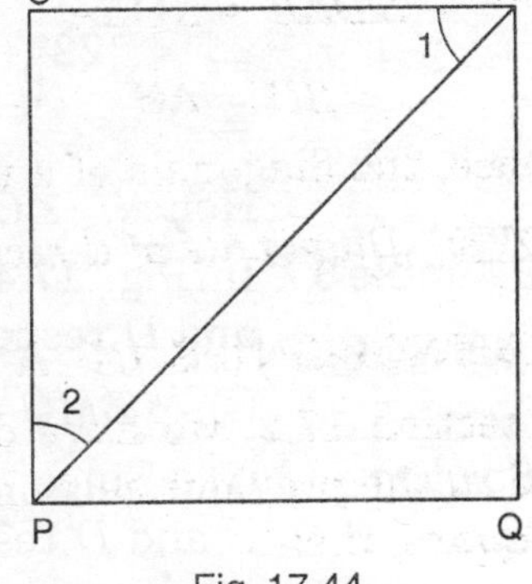

Fig. 17.44

Example 4 $ABCD$ is a rectangle with $\angle BAC = 32°$. Determine $\angle DBC$.

Solution Suppose the diagonals AC and BD intersect at O

In ΔOAB, we have

$OA = OB$ $\left[\because \text{Diagonals of a rectangle are equal and they bisect each other}\right]$

$\Rightarrow \quad \angle OAB = \angle OBA$

$\Rightarrow \quad \angle BAC = \angle DBA$

$\Rightarrow \quad \angle DBA = 32°$ $[\because \angle BAC = 32° \text{ (Given)}]$

Now, $\angle ABC = 90°$

$\Rightarrow \quad \angle DBA + \angle DBC = 90°$

$\Rightarrow \quad 32° + \angle DBC = 90°$

$\Rightarrow \quad \angle DBC = 90° - 32° = 68°$

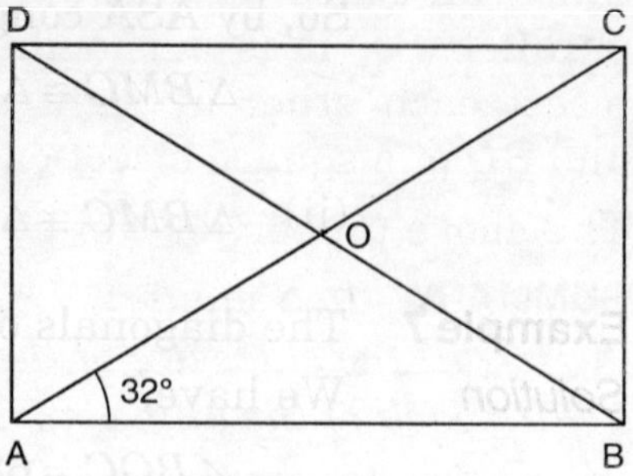

Fig. 17.45

Example 5 The diagonals of a rectangle $ABCD$ meet at O. If $\angle BOC = 44°$, find $\angle OAD$.

Solution We have,

$\angle BOC + \angle BOA = 180°$ [Linear pairs]

$\Rightarrow \quad 44° + \angle BOA = 180°$

$\Rightarrow \quad \angle BOA = 136°$

Since diagonals of a rectangle are equal and they bisect each other. Therefore, in ΔOAB, we have

$OA = OB$

$\Rightarrow \quad \angle 1 = \angle 2$ $[\because$ Angles opp. to equal sides are equal$]$

In ΔOAB, we have

$\angle 1 + \angle 2 + \angle BOA = 180°$

$\Rightarrow \quad 2\angle 1 + 136° = 180°$

$\Rightarrow \quad 2\angle 1 = 44°$

$\Rightarrow \quad \angle 1 = 22°$

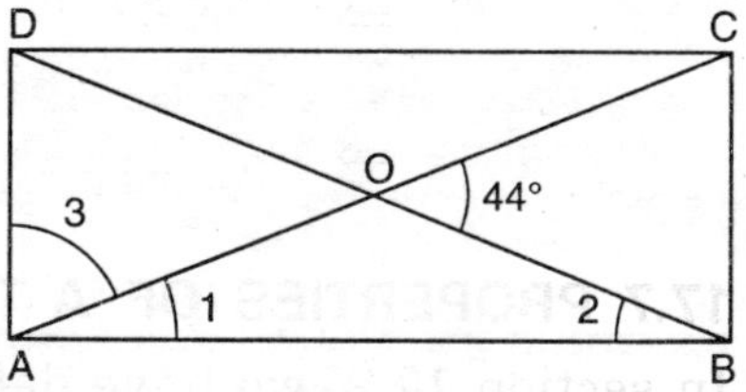

Since each angle of a rectangle is a right angle.

$\therefore \quad \angle BAD = 90°$

$\Rightarrow \quad \angle 1 + \angle 3 = 90°$

$\Rightarrow \quad 22° + \angle 3 = 90°$

$\Rightarrow \quad \angle 3 = 68°$

Hence, $\angle OAD = 68°$

Fig. 17.46

Example 6 In Fig. 17.47, $ABCD$ is a rectangle. BM and DN are perpendiculars from B and D respectively on AC. Prove that

(i) $\Delta BMC \cong \Delta DNA$ (ii) $BM = DN$

Solution (i) Since BM and DN are perpendiculars from B and D respectively on AC.

$\therefore \quad BM \parallel DN$

Also, $AD \parallel BC$

$\therefore \quad \angle ADN = \angle CBM$

In Δs ADN and BCM, we have

$\angle ADN = \angle CBM$

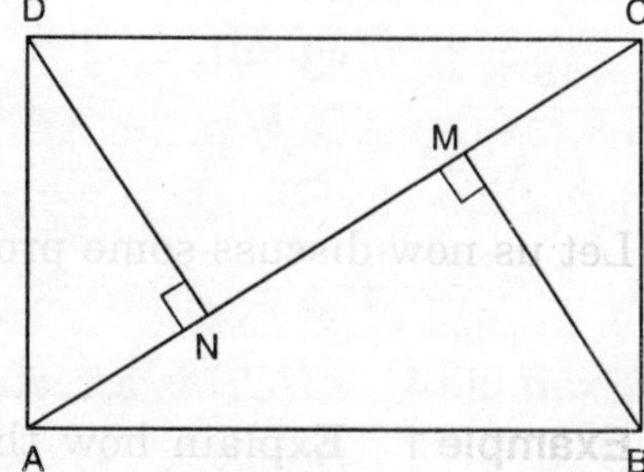

Fig. 17.47

$AD = BC$

$\angle DAN = \angle BCM$ [Alternate angles as $AD \parallel BC$]

So, by ASA congruence criterion, we have

$\Delta BMC \cong \Delta DNA$

(ii) $\Delta BMC \cong \Delta DNA \Rightarrow BM = DN$ [$\because$ Corresponding parts of congruent triangles are equal]

Example 7 The diagonals of a rectangle $ABCD$ intersect in O. If $\angle BOC = 68°$, find $\angle ODA$.

Solution We have,

$\angle BOC = 68°$

$\Rightarrow \angle AOD = 68°$ [Vertically opposite angles]

Since the diagonals of a rectangle are equal and they bisect each other.

$\therefore OA = OD$

Thus, in ΔAOD, we have

$OA = OD$ [Prove above]

$\Rightarrow \angle ODA = \angle OAD$ [$\angle s$ opp. to equal sides]

Fig. 17.48

But, $\angle ODA + \angle OAD + \angle AOD = 180°$ [By angle sum property in ΔAOD]

$\Rightarrow 2\angle ODA + 68° = 180°$

$\Rightarrow 2\angle ODA = 180° - 68°$

$\Rightarrow 2\angle ODA = 112°$

$\Rightarrow \angle ODA = \dfrac{112°}{2} = 56°$

17.7 PROPERTIES OF A TRAPEZIUM

In section 17.2, we have defined a trapezium as a quadrilateral having exactly one pair of parallel sides. Therefore, if $ABCD$ is a trapezium in which $AB \parallel DC$. Then,

(i) $\angle B + \angle C = 180°$ (ii) $\angle A + \angle D = 180°$

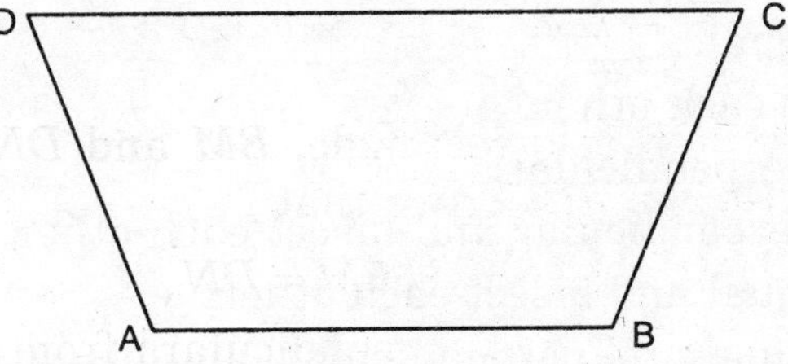

Fig. 17.49

Let us now discuss some problems based upon this property of a trapezium.

ILLUSTRATIVE EXAMPLES

Example 1 Explain how the following figure is a trapezium? Which of its two sides are parallel?

Solution We have,

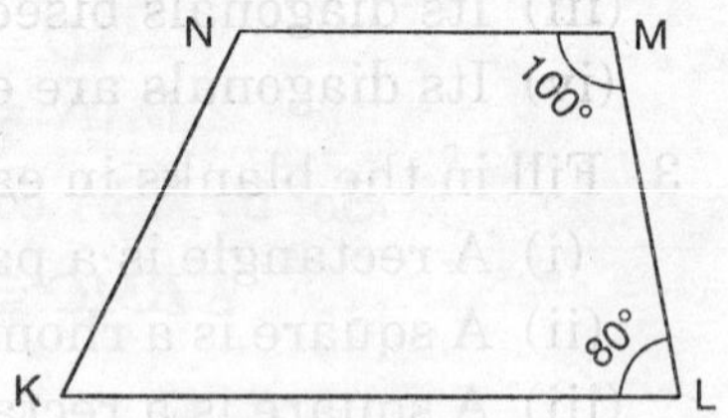

Fig. 17.50

$$\angle KLM + \angle NML = 80° + 100° = 180°$$

$\Rightarrow$ $\angle KLM$ and $\angle NML$ are supplementary

$\Rightarrow$ $KL \parallel NM$

$\Rightarrow$ $KLMN$ is a trapezium in which $KL \parallel NM$.

Example 2 In the following figure $ABCD$ is a trapezium in which $AB \parallel DC$. Find the measure of $\angle C$.

Solution It is given that $ABCD$ is a trapezium in which $AB \parallel DC$.

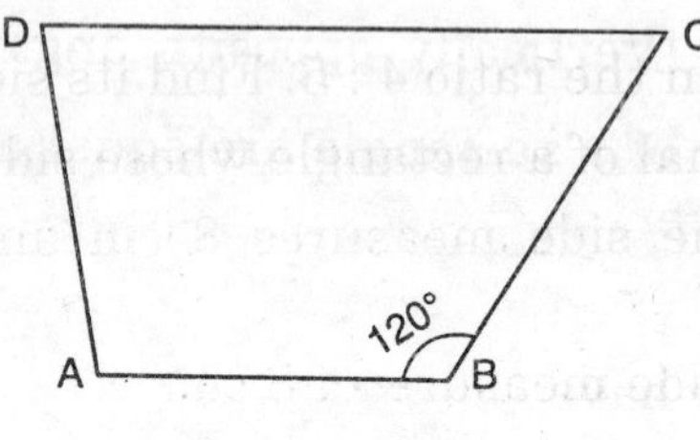

Fig. 17.51

$\therefore$ $\angle C + \angle B = 180° \Rightarrow \angle C + 120° = 180° \Rightarrow \angle C = 180° - 120° = 60°$

Example 3 The adjacent figure $PQRS$ is a trapezium in which $SP \parallel RQ$, find the measures of $\angle P$ and $\angle R$.

Solution Since $PQRS$ is a trapezium in which $SP \parallel RQ$.

$\therefore$ $\angle P + \angle Q = 180°$ and $\angle S + \angle R = 180°$

$\Rightarrow$ $\angle P + 130° = 180°$ and $90° + \angle R = 180°$

$\Rightarrow$ $\angle P = 180° - 130° = 50°$ and $\angle R = 180° - 90° = 90°$

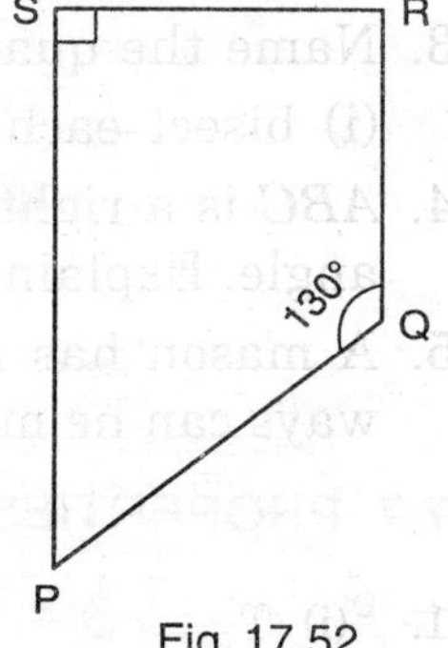

Fig. 17.52

EXERCISE 17.3

1. Which of the following statements are true for a rectangle?
   (i) It has two pairs of equal sides.
   (ii) It has all its sides of equal length.
   (iii) Its diagonals are equal.
   (iv) Its diagonals bisect each other.
   (v) Its diagonals are perpendicular.
   (vi) Its diagonals are perpendicular and bisect each other.
   (vii) Its diagonals are equal and bisect each other.
   (viii) Its diagonals are equal and perpendicular, and bisect each other.
   (ix) All rectangles are squares.
   (x) All rhombuses are parallelograms.
   (xi) All squares are rhombuses and also rectangles.
   (xii) All squares are not parallelograms.
2. Which of the following statements are true for a square?
   (i) It is a rectangle.
   (ii) It has all its sides of equal length.

(iii) Its diagonals bisect each other at right angle.
(iv) Its diagonals are equal to its sides.

3. Fill in the blanks in each of the following, so as to make the statement true :
   (i) A rectangle is a parallelogram in which .....
   (ii) A square is a rhombus in which ......
   (iii) A square is a rectangle in which ....
4. A window frame has one diagonal longer than the other. Is the window frame a rectangle ? Why or why not?
5. In a rectangle *ABCD*, prove that $\Delta ACB \cong \Delta CAD$.
6. The sides of a rectangle are in the ratio 2 : 3, and its perimeter is 20 cm. Draw the rectangle.
7. The sides of a rectangle are in the ratio 4 : 5. Find its sides if the perimeter is 90 cm.
8. Find the length of the diagonal of a rectangle whose sides are 12 cm and 5 cm.
9. Draw a rectangle whose one side measures 8 cm and the length of each of whose diagonals is 10 cm.
10. Draw a square whose each side measures 4.8 cm.
11. Identify all the quadrilaterals that have:
    (i) Four sides of equal length (ii) Four right angles
12. Explain how a square is
    (i) a quadrilateral? (ii) a parallelogram? (iii) a rhombus? (iv) a rectangle?
13. Name the quadrilaterals whose diagonals:
    (i) bisect each other (ii) are perpendicular bisector of each other (iii) are equal.
14. *ABC* is a right-angled triangle and *O* is the mid-point of the side opposite to the right angle. Explain why *O* is equidistant from *A*, *B* and *C*.
15. A mason has made a concrete slab. He needs it to be rectangular. In what different ways can he make sure that it is rectangular.?

ANSWERS

1. (i) T (ii) F (iii) T (iv) T (v) F (vi) F
   (vii) T (viii) F (ix) F (x) T (xi) T (xii) F
2. (i) T (ii) T (iii) T (iv) F
3. (i) one angle is a right angle (ii) one angle is a right angle (iii) adjacent sides are equal.
4. No, diagonals of a rectangle are equal 7. 20 cm, 25 cm 8. 13 cm
11. (i) Rhombus, square (ii) Rectangle, square
12. (i) By definition (ii) opposite sides are parallel and equal
    (iii) All sides are equal and opposite sides are parallel
    (iv) Opposite sides are equal and each angle is a right angle.
13. (i) Parallelogram, rectangle, rhombus, square (ii) Rhombus, square (ii) Square, rectangle
15. (i) By measuring each angle (ii) By measuring the lengths of diagonals.

HINTS TO SELECTED PROBLEMS

14. Construct a rectangle *ABCD* having *AC* as diagonal and vertex *D* opposite to the vertex *B*. Since diagonals of a rectangle are equal and they bisect each other. Therefore, *O* is the mid-point of *AC* and *BD* both

$\therefore \quad OA = OB = OC$

THINGS TO REMEMBER

1. *If A, B, C, D are four points in a plane, such that (i) no three points are collinear, and (ii) the segments AB, BC, CD and DA do not intersect except at their end-points ; then the figure made up of the four segments is called the quadrilateral with vertices A, B, C and D.*
2. *In a quadrilateral with vertices A, B, C and D : The four line segments AB, BC, CD and DA are called its sides.*

   If two sides have a common end-point, they are called adjacent sides.

   If two sides do not have a common end-point, they are called opposite sides.

   The line segments AC and BD are called its diagonals.

   The angles $\angle DAB$, $\angle ABC$, $\angle BCD$ and $\angle CDA$ are called its angles and are generally denoted by $\angle A$, $\angle B$, $\angle C$ and $\angle D$ respectively.

   The angles having a common arm are adjacent angles.

   The angles which are not adjacent are opposite angles.
3. *A quadrilateral is convex, if for any side of the quadrilateral, the line containing it has the remaining vertices on the same side of it.*
4. *The sum of the angles of a quadrilateral is 360°.*
5. *If the sides of a quadrilateral are produced, in order , the sum of the four exterior angles so formed is 360°.*
6. *A quadrilateral having exactly one pair of parallel sides is called a trapezium.*
7. *A quadrilateral with each pair of opposite sides parallel is called a parallelogram.*
8. *A parallelogram having all sides equal is called a rhombus.*
9. *A parallelogram with each angle a right angle is called a rectangle.*
10. *A rectangle with a pair of adjacent sides equal is a square.*
11. *In a parallelogram :*
    - *(i) opposite sides are equal.*
    - *(ii) opposite angles are equal.*
    - *(iii) diagonals bisect each other.*
12. *In a rhombus :*
    - *(i) all sides are equal.*
    - *(ii) diagonals bisect each other at right angles.*
13. *In a rectangle :*
    - *(i) each of the angles is a right angle.*
    - *(ii) diagonals bisect each other.*
    - *(iii) diagonals are equal.*
14. *In a square :*
    - *(i) all the sides are of the same length.*
    - *(ii) each of the angles is a right angle.*
    - *(iii) the diagonals are of equal length*
    - *(iv) the diagonals bisect each other at right angles.*

18 PRACTICAL GEOMETRY (Constructions)

18.1 INTRODUCTION

In earlier classes, we have learnt about the construction of triangles. We have seen that to construct a triangle we require three measurements of sides or angles (at least one of them is a side). Now a natural question arises whether four measurements would be sufficient to draw a quadrilateral. In fact a quadrilateral has 10 elements (four sides, four angles and two diagonals) and to draw a quadrilateral any five independent elements must be given. In this chapter, we will study construction of quadrilaterals.

18.2 CONSTRUCTION OF QUADRILATERALS

As we know that the shape and size of a polygon are defined by its elements. The elements that make up a polygon are its sides, enclosed angles and diagonals. A triangle is the simplest polygon. It does not have any diagonal. So, the elements that define a triangle are its three sides and three angles. It is possible to draw a triangle if the size of any three independent elements are given. In the previous class, we have learnt how to construct a triangle when :

(i) its three sides are given ;

or,(ii) its two sides and the angle included are given ;

or,(iii) its two angles and the included side are given ;

or,(iv) the hypotenuse and one side of a right triangle are given.

In case of a quadrilateral the elements are its four sides, two diagonals and its four angles. Thus, a quadrilateral has ten elements. It is possible to draw a convex quadrilateral if any five independent elements are given. To draw a non-convex quadrilateral, six independent elements are required.

In what follows, we shall learn to construct a convex quadrilateral in the following simple cases :

(i) when the lengths of four sides and one diagonal are given ;

(ii) when the lengths of three sides and the two diagonals are given ;

(iii) when the lengths of four sides and one angle are given ;

(iv) when the lengths of three sides and two included angles are given ;

(v) when three angles and two included sides are given.

18.2.1 CONSTRUCTING A QUADRILATERAL WHEN FOUR SIDES AND ONE DIAGONAL ARE GIVEN

When four sides and a diagonal of a quadrilateral are given, we consider the quadrilateral *ABCD* as a figure made of two triangles:

(i) ΔABC and ΔADC when diagonal AC as the common side is given.

or,(ii) ΔABD and ΔBCD when diagonal BD as the common side is given.

In order to draw the quadrilateral when four sides and one diagonal are given, we first draw a rough sketch of the quadrilateral and write its dimensions along the sides and then we divide it into two conveniently constructable triangles.

Following examples will illustrate the same.

ILLUSTRATIVE EXAMPLES

Example 1 Construct a quadrilateral *ABCD* in which $AB = 4.4$ cm, $BC = 4$ cm, $CD = 6.4$ cm, $DA = 2.8$ cm and $BD = 6.6$ cm.

Solution First we draw a rough sketch of the quadrilateral *ABCD* and write down its dimensions along the sides.

We may divide the quadrilateral *ABCD* into two constructible triangles *ABD* and *BCD*.

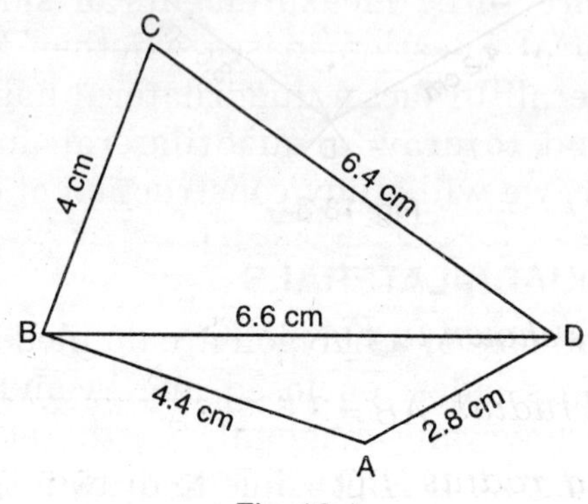

Fig. 18.1

Steps of Construction:

Step I *Draw $BD = 6.6$ cm.*

Step II *With B as centre and radius $BC = 4$ cm, draw an arc.*

Step III *With D as centre and radius $CD = 6.4$ cm, draw an arc, to intersect the arc drawn in step II at C.*

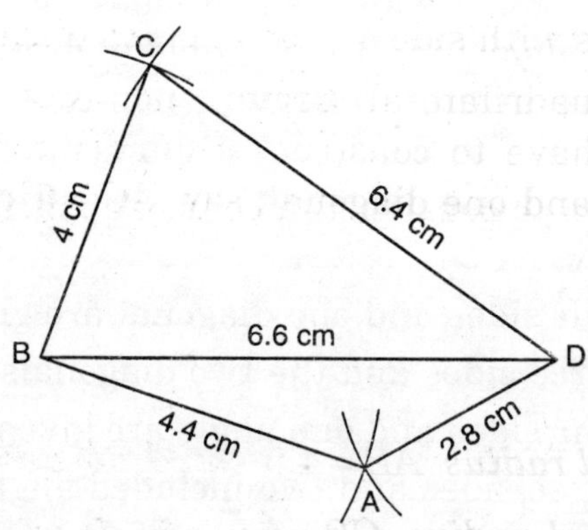

Fig. 18.2

Step IV *With B as centre and radius $BA = 4.4$ cm, draw an arc on the side of BD opposite to that of C.*

Step V *With D as centre and radius $AD = 2.8$ cm, draw another arc to intersect the arc drawn in step IV at A.*

Step VI *Join BA, DA, BC and CD.*

The quadrilateral *ABCD* so obtained is the required quadrilateral.

Example 2 Construct a parallelogram $ABCD$ where $AB = 3.6$ cm, $BC = 4.2$ cm and $AC = 6.5$ cm.

Solution In a parallelogram opposite sides are equal. Thus, we have to construct a quadrilateral $ABCD$ in which $AB = 3.6$ cm, $BC = 4.2$ cm, $CD = 3.6$ cm, $AD = 4.2$ cm and $AC = 6.5$ cm.

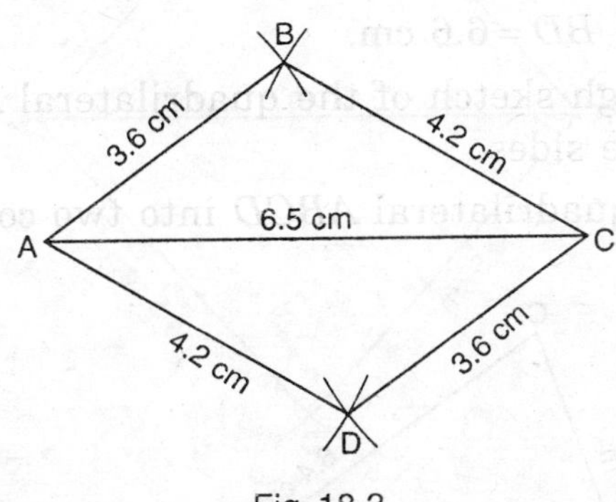

Fig. 18.3

Steps of Construction:

<u>Step I</u> *Draw* $AC = 6.5$ *cm as shown in Fig.* 18.3.

<u>Step II</u> *With A as centre and radius* $AB = 3.6$ *cm, draw an arc.*

<u>Step III</u> *With C as centre and radius* $BC = 4.2$ *cm, draw an arc, intersecting the arc drawn in step II at B.*

<u>Step IV</u> *With A as centre and radius* $AD = 4.2$ *cm, draw an arc on the side of AC opposite to that of B.*

<u>Step V</u> *With C as centre and radius* $CD = 3.6$ *cm, draw another arc to intersect the arc drawn in step IV at D.*

<u>Step VI</u> *Join AB, BC, AD and CD to obtain the required parallelogram ABCD.*

Example 3 Construct a rhombus with side 4.5 cm and one diagonal 6 cm.

Solution A rhombus is a quadrilateral having all sides equal and opposite sides parallel. Thus, we have to construct a quadrilateral $ABCD$ whose all sides are equal to 4.5 cm and one diagonal, say $AC = 6$ cm. To draw this, we follow the following steps.

Steps of Construction:

<u>Step I</u> *Draw* $AC = 6$ *cm.*

<u>Step II</u> *With A as centre and radius* $AB = 4.5$ *cm, draw an arc.*

<u>Step III</u> *With C as centre and radius* $CB = 4.5$ *cm, draw an arc intersecting the arc drawn in step II at B.*

<u>Step IV</u> *With A as centre and radius* $AD = 4.5$ *cm, draw an arc on the side of AC opposite to that of B.*

<u>Step V</u> *With C as centre and radius* $CD = 4.5$ *cm, draw another arc intersecting the arc drawn in step IV at D.*

<u>Step VI</u> *Join AB, BC, CD and AD to obtain the required rhombus.*

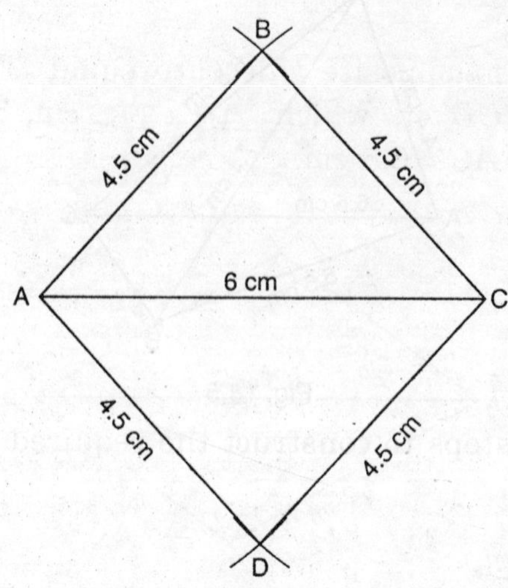

Fig. 18.4

EXERCISE 18.1

1. Construct a quadrilateral $ABCD$ in which $AB = 4.4$ cm, $BC = 4$ cm, $CD = 6.4$ cm, $DA = 3.8$ cm and $BD = 6.6$ cm.
2. Construct a quadrilateral $ABCD$ such that $AB = BC = 5.5$ cm, $CD = 4$ cm, $DA = 6.3$ cm and $AC = 9.4$ cm. Measure BD.
3. Construct a quadrilateral $XYZW$ in which $XY = 5$ cm, $YZ = 6$ cm, $ZW = 7$ cm, $WX = 3$ cm and $XZ = 9$ cm.
4. Construct a parallelogram $PQRS$ such that $PQ = 5.2$ cm, $PR = 6.8$ cm and $QS = 8.2$ cm.
5. Construct a rhombus with side 6 cm and one diagonal 8 cm. Measure the other diagonal.
6. Construct a kite $ABCD$ in which $AB = 4$ cm, $BC = 4.9$ cm and $AC = 7.2$ cm.
7. Construct, if possible, a quadrilateral $ABCD$ given $AB = 6$ cm, $BC = 3.7$ cm, $CD = 5.7$ cm, $AD = 5.5$ cm and $BD = 6.1$ cm. Give reasons for not being able to construct it, if you cannot.
8. Construct, if possible, a quadrilateral $ABCD$ in which $AB = 6$ cm, $BC = 7$ cm, $CD = 3$ cm, $AD = 5.5$ cm and $AC = 11$ cm. Give reasons for not being able to construct, if you cannot. (Not possible, because in triangle ACD, $AD + CD < AC$).

18.2.2 CONSTRUCTING A QUADRILATERAL WHEN ITS THREE SIDES AND THE TWO DIAGONALS ARE GIVEN

Similar to the previous sub-section, in this sub-section also we divide the quadrilateral into two conveniently constructible triangles as is illustrated in the following examples.

ILLUSTRATIVE EXAMPLES

Example 1 Construct a quadrilateral $ABCD$ in which $AB = 5.5$ cm, $AD = 4.4$ cm, $CD = 6.5$ cm, $AC = 6.5$ cm and $BD = 7.1$ cm.

Solution First we draw a rough sketch of quadrilateral $ABCD$. It is evident from the rough sketch that we have sufficient data to draw triangles ADC and ABD.

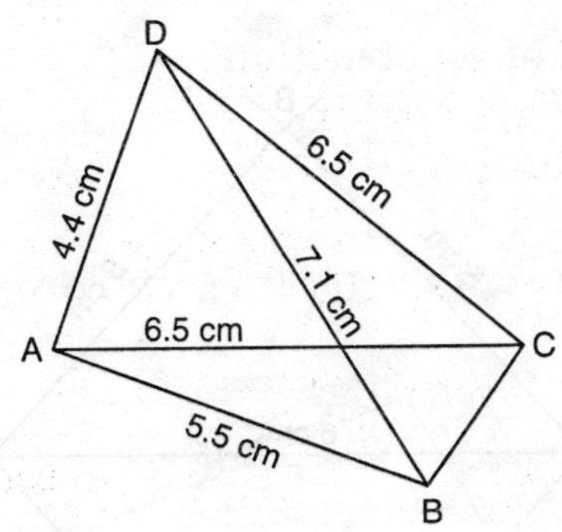

Fig. 18.5

Now, we follow the following steps to construct the required quadrilateral.

Steps of Construction:

<u>Step I</u> *Draw* $AC = 6.5$ *cm.*

<u>Step II</u> *With A as centre and radius* $AD = 4.4$ *cm, draw an arc.*

<u>Step III</u> *With C as centre and radius* $CD = 6.5$ *cm, draw an arc to intersect the arc drawn in step II at D.*

<u>Step IV</u> *With A as centre and radius* $AB = 5.5$ *cm, draw an arc on the side of AC opposite to that of D.*

<u>Step V</u> *With D as centre and radius* $BD = 7.1$ *cm, draw another arc to intersect the arc drawn in step IV at B.*

<u>Step VI</u> Join *AD, CD, AB* and *CB to obtain the required quadrilateral.*

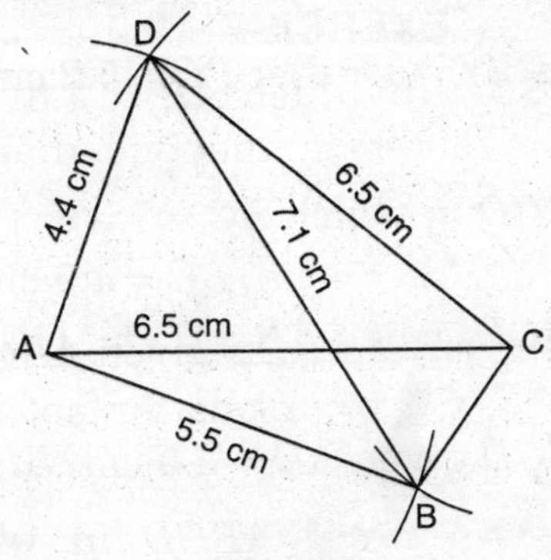

Fig. 18.6

Example 2 Construct a quadrilateral in which $AB = 5.4$ cm, $BC = 2.5$ cm, $CD = 4$ cm, $AC = 6.5$ cm and $BD = 5$ cm.

Solution It is evident from the rough sketch of quadrilateral *ABCD* that we have sufficient data for the construction of triangles *ABC* and *BCD*, with *BC* as common side.

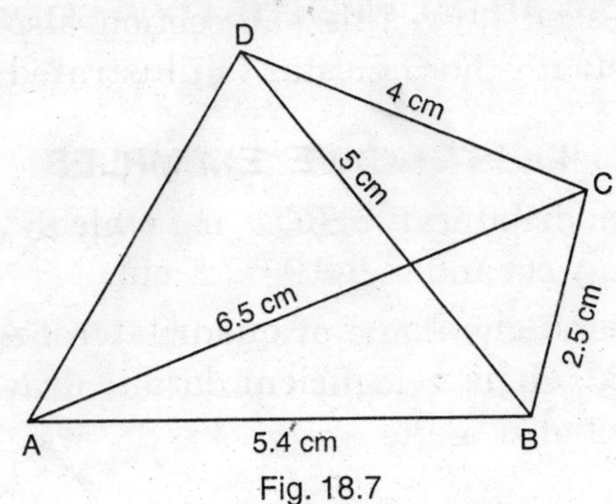

Fig. 18.7

So, we follow the following steps of construction:

Steps of construction:

Step I Draw $AB = 5.4$ cm.

Step II With A as centre and radius $AC = 6.5$ cm, draw an arc.

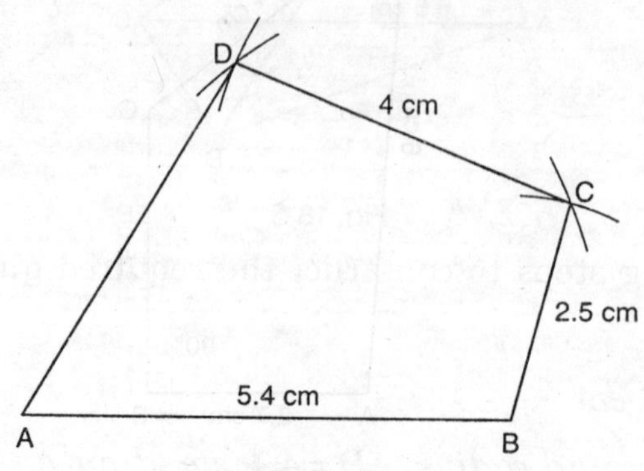

Fig. 18.8

Step III With B as centre and radius $BC = 2.5$ cm, draw an arc to cut the arc drawn in step II at C.

Step IV With B as centre and radius $BD = 5$ cm, draw an arc.

Step V With C as centre and radius $CD = 4$ cm draw another arc cutting the arc drawn in previous step at D.

Step VI Join BC, CD and AD to get the required quadrilateral.

EXERCISE 18.2

1. Construct a quadrilateral $ABCD$ in which $AB = 3.8$ cm, $BC = 3.0$ cm, $AD = 2.3$ cm, $AC = 4.5$ cm and $BD = 3.8$ cm.
2. Construct a quadrilateral $ABCD$ in which $BC = 7.5$ cm, $AC = AD = 6$ cm, $CD = 5$ cm and $BD = 10$ cm.
3. Construct a quadrilateral $ABCD$, when $AB = 3$ cm, $CD = 3$ cm, $DA = 7.5$ cm, $AC = 8$ cm and $BD = 4$ cm.
4. Construct a quadrilateral $ABCD$ given $AD = 3.5$ cm, $BC = 2.5$ cm, $CD = 4.1$ cm, $AC = 7.3$ cm and $BD = 3.2$ cm.
5. Construct a quadrilateral $ABCD$ given $AD = 5$ cm, $AB = 5.5$ cm, $BC = 2.5$ cm, $AC = 7.1$ cm and $BD = 8$ cm.
6. Construct a quadrilateral $ABCD$ in which $BC = 4$ cm, $CA = 5.6$ cm, $AD = 4.5$ cm, $CD = 5$ cm and $BD = 6.5$ cm.

18.2.3 CONSTRUCTING A QUADRILATERAL WHEN ITS FOUR SIDES AND ONE ANGLE ARE GIVEN

Following examples will illustrate the procedure of construction.

ILLUSTRATIVE EXAMPLES

Example 1 Construct a quadrilateral $ABCD$ in which $AB = 2.7$ cm, $BC = 3.5$ cm, $CD = 4$ cm, $AD = 6$ cm and $\angle B = 90°$.

Solution Here, four sides and one angle are given. We first draw the rough sketch as shown in Fig. 18.9. It is evident from the rough sketch that in ΔABC, two sides and the included angle are given. So, we first construct ΔABC. Now,

AC is known from ΔABC and AD and CD are given. So, ΔACD can also be drawn. Thus, to draw the quadrilateral $ABCD$, we follow the following steps.

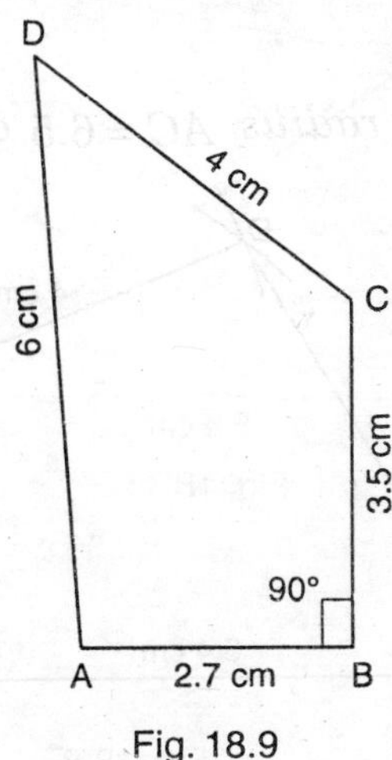

Fig. 18.9

Steps of Construction:

Step I — *Draw* $AB = 2.7$ *cm.*

Step II — *Construct* $\angle ABX = 90°$

Step III — *With B as centre and radius* $BC = 3.5$, *cut off* $BC = 3.5$ *cm along BX.*

Step IV — *Join AC.*

Step V — *With A as centre and radius* $AD = 6$ *cm draw an arc.*

Step VI — *With C as centre and radius* $CD = 4$ *cm draw an arc to cut the arc drawn in step V at D.*

Step VII — *Join CD and AD.*

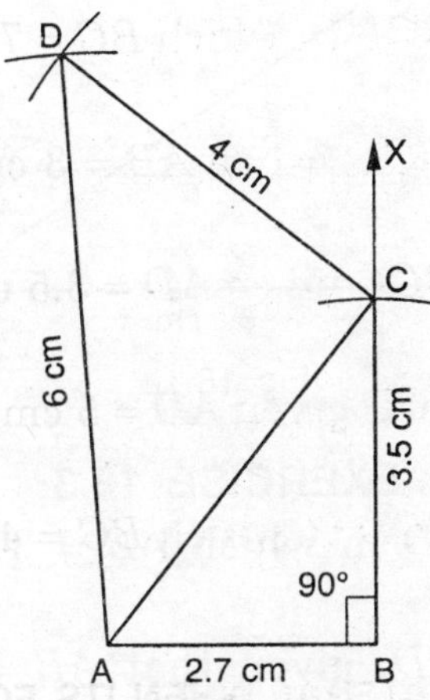

Fig. 18.10

The quadrilateral $ABCD$ so obtained is the required quadrilateral.

Example 2 Construct a quadrilateral $ABCD$ given $AB = 5.6$ cm, $BC = 4.1$ cm, $CD = 4.4$ cm, $AD = 3.3$ cm and $\angle A = 75°$.

Solution We first draw a rough sketch of the required quadrilateral and write down its dimensions along the sides. We can divide the construction of required quadrilateral into two parts (i). Construction of ΔABD (ii) Construction of ΔBCD.

The following steps are used to construct the required quadrilateral.

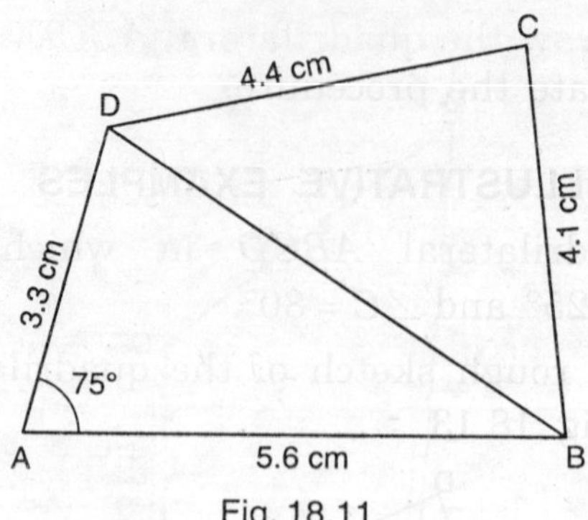

Fig. 18.11

Steps of Construction:

Step I Draw $AB = 5.6$ cm.

Step II Construct $\angle BAX = 75°$.

Step III With A as centre and radius $AD = 3.3$ cm, cut off $AD = 3.3$ cm along AX.

Step IV Join BD.

Step V With D as centre and radius $DC = 4.4$ cm, draw an arc.

Step VI With B as centre and radius $BC = 4.1$ cm, draw an arc to cut the arc drawn in step V at C.

Join BC, CD to obtain the required quadrilateral ABCD.

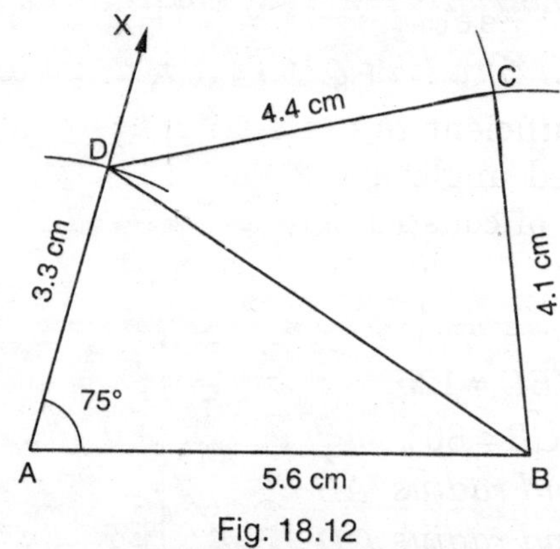

Fig. 18.12

EXERCISE 18.3

1. Construct a quadrilateral *ABCD* in which *AB* = 3.8 cm, *BC* = 3.4 cm, *CD* = 4.5 cm, *AD* = 5 cm and $\angle B = 80°$.
2. Construct a quadrilateral *ABCD*, given that *AB* = 8 cm, *BC* = 8 cm, *CD* =10 cm, *AD* =10 cm and $\angle A = 45°$.
3. Construct a quadrilateral *ABCD* in which *AB* = 7.7 cm, *BC* = 6.8 cm, *CD* = 5.1 cm, *AD* = 3.6 cm and $\angle C = 120°$.
4. Construct a quadrilateral *ABCD* in which *AB* = *BC* = 3 cm, *AD* = CD = 5 cm and $\angle B = 120°$.
5. Construct a quadrilateral *ABCD* in which *AB* = 2.8 cm, *BC* = 3.1 cm, *CD* = 2.6 cm and *DA* = 3.3 cm and $\angle A = 60°$.
6. Construct a quadrilateral *ABCD* in which *AB* = *BC* = 6 cm, *AD* = *DC* = 4.5 cm and $\angle B = 120°$.

18.2.4 CONSTRUCTION OF A QUADRILATERAL WHEN ITS THREE SIDES AND THEIR INCLUDED ANGLES ARE GIVEN

Following examples will illustrate the procedure.

ILLUSTRATIVE EXAMPLES

Example 1 Construct a quadrilateral $ABCD$ in which $AB = 3.6$ cm, $BC = 5.5$ cm, $CD = 5$ cm, $\angle B = 125°$ and $\angle C = 80°$.

Solution We first draw the rough sketch of the quadrilateral and indicate on it the data as shown in Fig. 18.13.

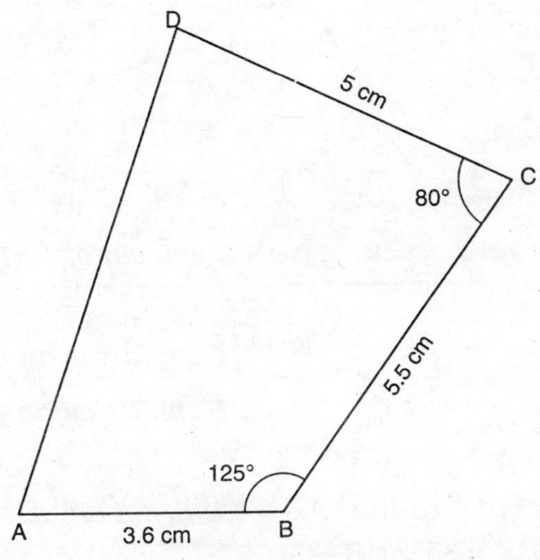

Fig. 18.13

We observe that the data is sufficient to draw triangles BCA and BCD. Because in each case two sides and the included angle are given. The side BC is common to both. This suggests us the following steps of construction.

Steps of Construction:

Step I *Draw* $BC = 5.5$ *cm.*

Step II *At B construct* $\angle XBC = 125°$.

Step III *At C construct* $\angle YCB = 80°$, *such that X and Y are on the same side of BC.*

Step IV *With B as centre and radius* $AB = 3.6$ *cm, draw an arc to intersect BX at A.*

Step V *With C as centre and radius* $CD = 5$ *cm, draw an arc to intersect CY at D.*

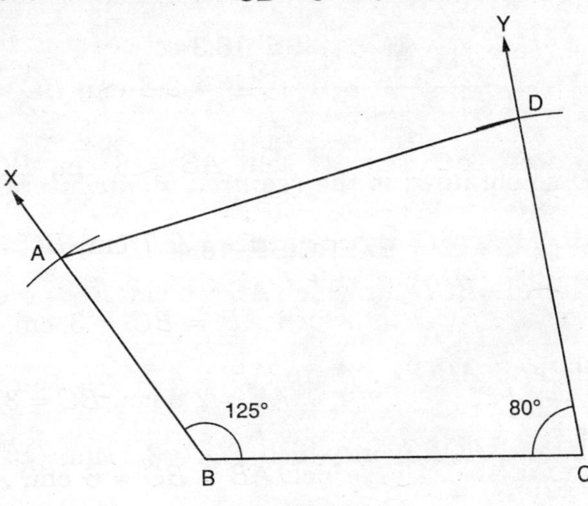

Fig. 18.14

Step VI *Join AD.*

The quadrilateral *ABCD* so obtained is the required quadrilateral.

Example 2 Construct a quadrilateral *ABCD* given $AB = 5.1$ cm, $AD = 4$ cm, $BC = 2.5$ cm, $\angle A = 60°$ and $\angle B = 85°$.

Solution First we draw the rough sketch of quadrilateral *ABCD* and indicate the data on it as shown in Fig. 18.15. We observe that the given data is sufficient to construct ΔABC and ΔABD. So, we follow the following steps of construction.

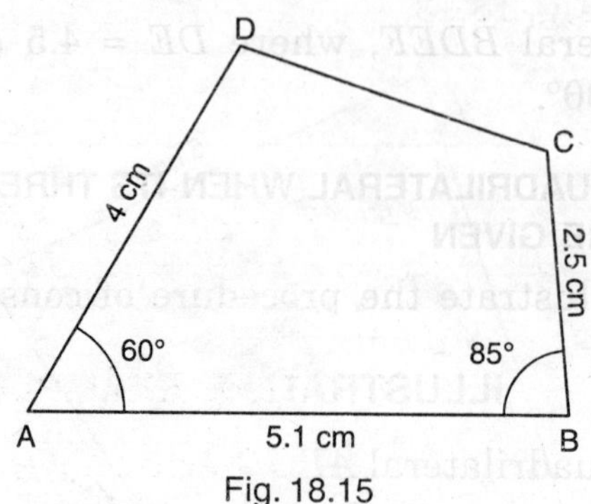

Fig. 18.15

Steps of Construction:

Step I *Draw* $AB = 5.1$ *cm.*

Step II *Construct* $\angle XAB = 60°$ at *A*.

Step III *With A as centre and radius* $AD = 4$ *cm, cut off* $AD = 4$ *cm along AX.*

Step IV *Construct* $\angle ABY = 85°$ at *B*.

Step V *With B as centre and radius* $BC = 2.5$ *cm, cut off* $BC = 2.5$ *cm along BY.*

Step VI *Join CD.*

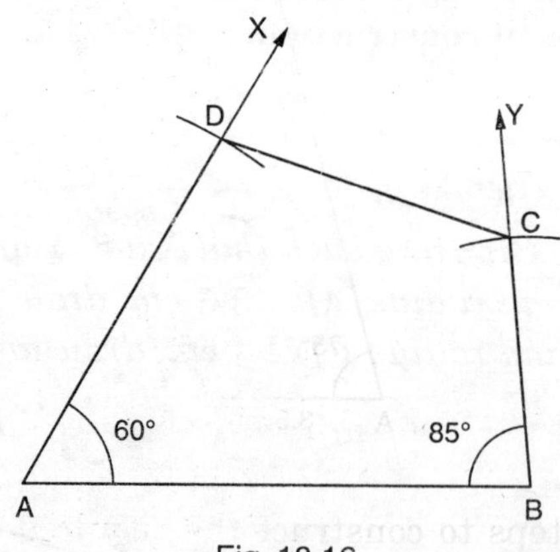

Fig. 18.16

The quadrilateral *ABCD* so obtained is the required quadrilateral.

EXERCISE 18.4

1. Construct a quadrilateral *ABCD,* in which $AB = 6$ cm, $BC = 4$ cm, $CD = 4$ cm, $\angle B = 95°$ and $\angle C = 90°$.
2. Construct a quadrilateral *ABCD,* where $AB = 4.2$ cm, $BC = 3.6$ cm, $CD = 4.8$ cm, $\angle B = 30°$ and $\angle C = 150°$.
3. Construct a quadrilateral *PQRS,* in which $PQ = 3.5$ cm, $QR = 2.5$ cm, $RS = 4.1$ cm, $\angle Q = 75°$ and $\angle R = 120°$.

4. Construct a quadrilateral *ABCD* given *BC* = 6.6 cm, *CD* = 4.4 cm, *AD* = 5.6 cm and $\angle D = 100°$ and $\angle C = 95°$.
5. Construct a quadrilateral *ABCD,* in which *AD* = 3.5 cm, *AB* = 4.4 cm, *BC* = 4.7 cm, $\angle A = 125°$ and $\angle B = 120°$.
6. Construct a quadrilateral *PQRS,* in which $\angle Q = 45°, \angle R = 90°$; *QR* = 5 cm, *PQ* = 9 cm and Rs = 7 cm.
7. Construct a quadrilateral *ABCD* in which *AB* = *BC* = 3 cm, *AD* = 5 cm, $\angle A = 90°$ and $\angle B = 105°$.
8. Construct a quadrilateral *BDEF*, where *DE* = 4.5 cm, *EF* = 3.5 cm, *FB* = 6.5 cm, $\angle F = 50°$ and $\angle E = 100°$.

18.2.5 CONSTRUCTING A QUADRILATERAL WHEN ITS THREE ANGLES AND THEIR TWO INCLUDED SIDES ARE GIVEN

Following examples will illustrate the procedure of construction.

ILLUSTRATIVE EXAMPLES

Example 1 Construct a quadrilateral *ABCD,* where $AB = 3.5$ cm, $BC = 6.5$ cm, $\angle A = 75°$, $\angle B = 105°$ and $\angle C = 120°$.

Solution Let us draw a rough sketch of the required quadrilateral and write down the given data as shown in Fig. 18.17.

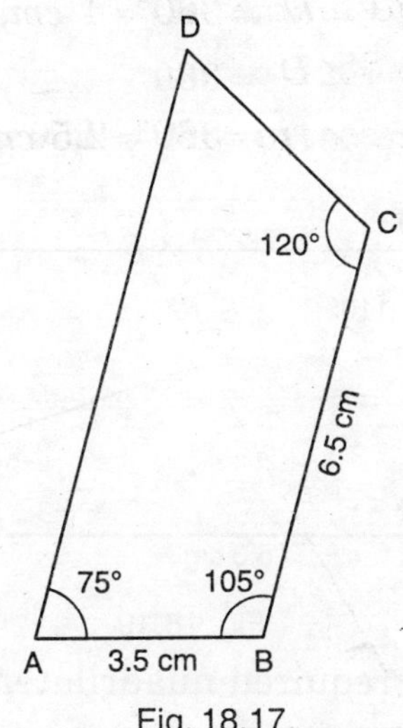

Fig. 18.17

We now follow following steps to construct the required quadrilateral.

Steps of Construction:

<u>*Step I*</u> *Draw* $AB = 3.5$ *cm.*

<u>*Step II*</u> *Draw* $\angle XAB = 75°$ *at A* and $\angle ABY = 105°$.

<u>*Step III*</u> *With B as centre and radius* $BC = 6.5$ *cm, draw an arc to intersect BY at C.*

<u>*Step IV*</u> *At C draw* $\angle BCZ = 120°$ *such that CZ meets AX at D.*

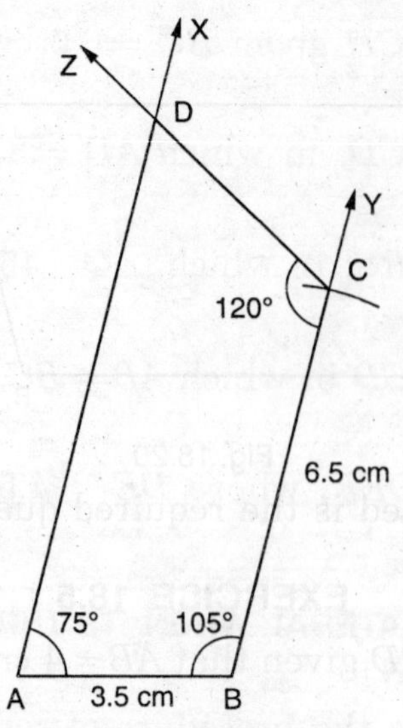

Fig. 18.18

The quadrilateral *ABCD* so obtained is the required quadrilateral.

Example 2 Construct a quadrilateral *ABCD* given $AB = 5.3$ cm, $AD = 2.9$ cm, $\angle A = 70°$; $\angle B = 95°, \angle C = 85°$.

Solution We know that the sum of the angles of a quadrilateral is 360°.

$$\therefore \quad \angle A + \angle B + \angle C + \angle D = 360°$$

$$\Rightarrow \quad 70° + 95° + 85° + \angle D = 360°$$

$$\Rightarrow \quad 250° + \angle D = 360°$$

$$\Rightarrow \quad \angle D = 360° - 250° = 110°$$

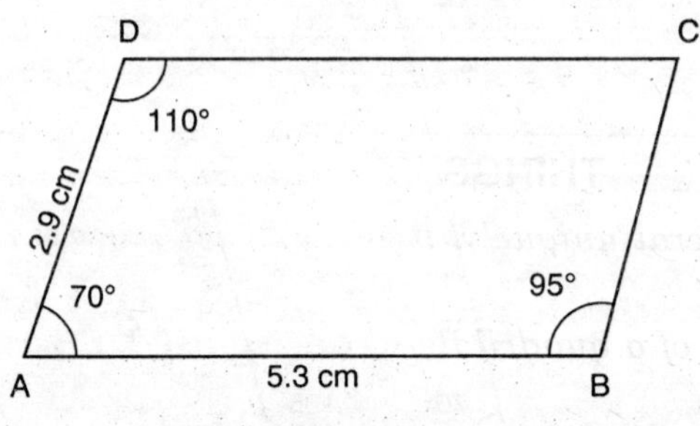

Fig. 18.19

Let us draw a rough sketch of the required quadrilateral *ABCD* and write down the given data as shown in Fig. 18.19.

We now follow the following steps of construction to construct the required quadrilateral.

Steps of Construction:

Step I Draw $AB = 5.3$ *cm.*

Step II At A draw $\angle XAB = 70°$.

Step III With A as centre and radius $AD = 2.9$ *cm draw an arc to cut AX at D.*

Step IV At D draw $\angle ADY = 110°$.

Step V At B draw $\angle ZBA = 95°$ *so that ZB intersects YD at C.*

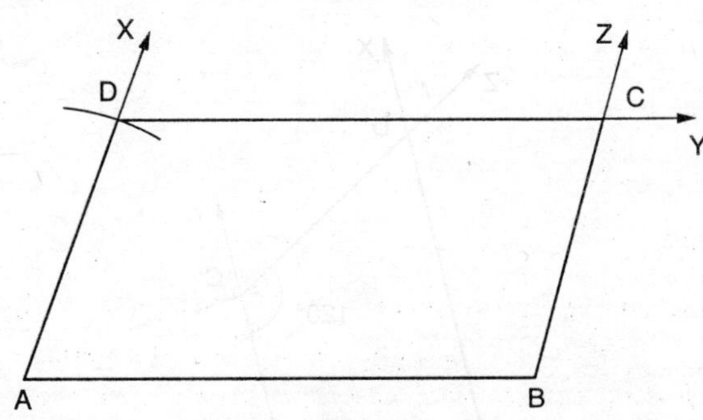

Fig. 18.20

The quadrilateral *ABCD* so obtained is the required quadrilateral.

EXERCISE 18.5

1. Construct a quadrilateral *ABCD* given that *AB* = 4 cm, *BC* = 3 cm, $\angle A = 75°$, $\angle B = 80°$ and $\angle C = 120°$.
2. Construct a quadrilateral *ABCD*, where *AB* = 5.5 cm, *BC* = 3.7 cm, $\angle A = 60°$, $\angle B = 105°$ and $\angle D = 90°$.
3. Construct a quadrilateral *PQRS*, where *PQ* = 3.5 cm, *QR* = 6.5 cm, $\angle P = \angle R = 105°$ and $\angle S = 75°$.
4. Construct a quadrilateral *ABCD* when *BC* = 5.5 cm, *CD* = 4.1 cm, $\angle A = 70°$, $\angle B = 110°$ and $\angle D = 85°$.
5. Construct a quadrilateral *ABCD*, where $\angle A = 65°, \angle B = 105°, \angle C = 75°, BC = 5.7$ cm and $CD = 6.8$ cm.
6. Construct a quadrilateral *PQRS*, in which *PQ* = 4 cm, *QR* = 5 cm, $\angle P = 50°$, $\angle Q = 110°$ and $\angle R = 70°$.

THINGS TO REMEMBER

1. *To construct a quadrilateral uniquely, it is necessary to have the knowledge of at least five independent elements.*
2. *Data about five elements of a quadrilateral are sufficient to construct a quadrilateral in the following cases :*
   - *(i) 4 sides and 1 diagonal;*
   - *(ii) 3 sides and both diagonals;*
   - *(iii) 4 sides and 1 angle ;*
   - *(iv) 3 sides and 2 included angles;*
   - *(v) 3 angles and their 2 included sides.*
3. *Data about five parts of a quadrilateral in order to be sufficient must also satisfy (i) the triangle inequality (ii) angle sum property of a triangle, wherever applicable.*
4. *It is possible to construct a quadrilateral with the sufficient data (other than five simple cases), where less than five parts but some other relations between them are given.*
5. *In all cases, it is convenient and helpful to draw rough sketch of the quadrilateral and indicate the data on it. This suggests the steps of construction.*

19

VISUALISING SHAPES

19.1 INTRODUCTION

In earlier classes, we have learnt that figures having length only are known as one dimensional figures. A line is a one dimensional figure. Figures having length and breadth are known as two dimensional figures. A polygon, a circle etc are two dimensional figures. Objects and shapes having length, breadth and height are known as three dimensional objects and shapes. Generally, two dimensional figures are known as 2-D figures. Similarly, three dimensional shapes are known as [illegible] visualise 3-D figures drawn on the plane of the [illegible] only. If a 3-D shape is represented by a figure [illegible] when the length, breadth and height of a 3-D [illegible] plane of the paper which is a two dimensional [illegible] the shape. Therefore, we must understand the [illegible] their two dimensional figures drawn on the [illegible] we will discuss visualisation of 3-D shapes from their [illegible] representation of three dimensional shapes on [illegible]

In class VII, we have discussed visualisation [illegible]

Fig. 19.1

Let us now visualise some more solid shapes called [illegible]

19.2 POLYHEDRA

The word polyhedra is the plural of word polyhedron [illegible]

POLYHEDRON A solid shape bounded by polygons is called a polyhedron.

FACES Polygons forming a polyhedron are known as its [illegible]

EDGES Line segments common to intersecting [illegible]

VERTICES Points of intersection of edges of a [illegible]

In a polyhedron three or more edges meet at a point [illegible]

19

VISUALISING SHAPES

19.1 INTRODUCTION

In earlier classes, we have learnt that figures having length only are known as one dimensional figures. A line is a one dimensional figure. Figures having length and breadth are known as two dimensional figures. A polygon, a circle etc are two dimensional figures. Objects and shapes having length, breadth and height are known as three dimensional objects and shapes. Generally, two dimensional figures are known as 2-D figures. Similarly, three dimensional shapes are known as 3-D shapes. It is very convenient to visualise 2-D figures drawn on the plane of the paper as they have length and breadth only. If a 3-D shape is represented by a figure drawn on the plane of the paper, that is when the length, breadth and height of a 3-D shape are represented by lines drawn on the plane of the paper which is a two dimensional figure, then it slightly difficult to visualise the shape. Therefore, we must understand the technique of visualising 3-D shapes from their two-dimensional figures drawn on the plane of the paper. In this chapter, we will discuss visualisation of 3-D shapes from their plane figures. We will also learn about the representation of three dimensional shapes on the plane of the paper.

In class VII, we have discussed visualization of following solid 3-D shapes.

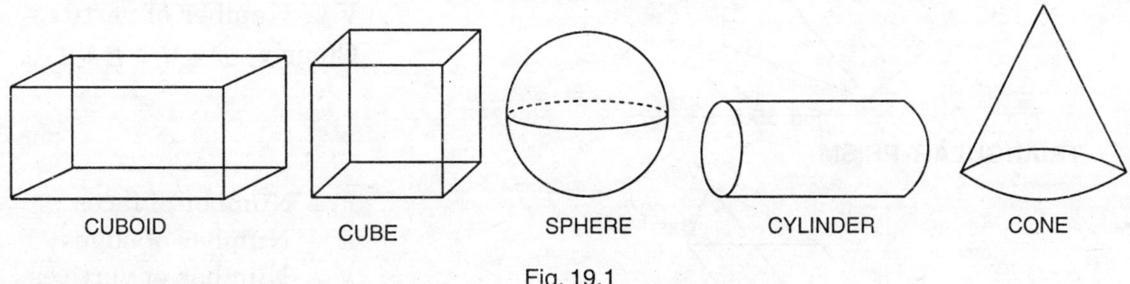

Fig. 19.1

Let us now visualise some more solid shapes called polyhedra.

19.2 POLYHEDRA

The word polyhedra is the plural of word polyhedron which may be defined as follows:

POLYHEDRON *A solid shape bounded by polygons is called a polyhedron.*

FACES *Polygons forming a polyhedron are known as its faces.*

EDGES *Line segments common to intersecting faces of a polyhedron are known as its edges.*

VERTICES *Points of intersection of edges of a polyhedron are known as its vertices.*

In a polyhedron three or more edges meet at a point to form a vertex.

Following are some polyhedrons:

(i) **CUBOID**

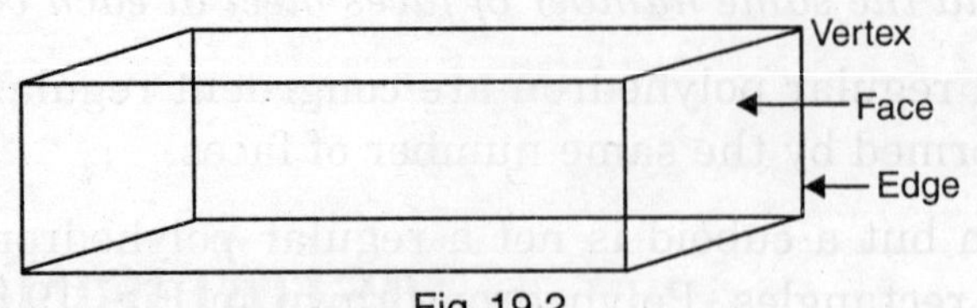

Fig. 19.2

F = Number of faces = 6
E = Number of edges = 12
V = Number of vertices = 8
Clearly, $F + V = E + 2$

(ii) **CUBE**

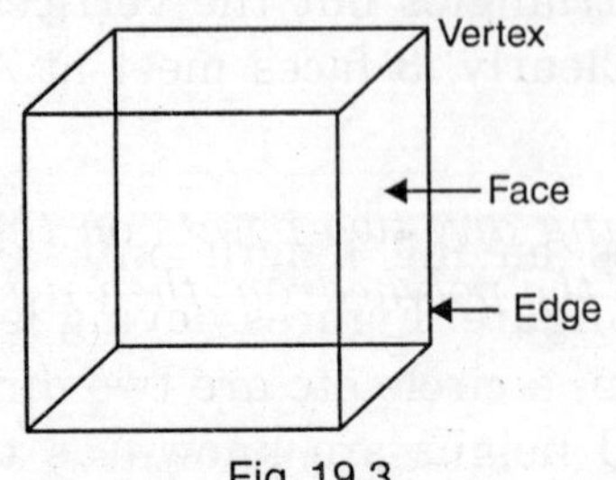

Fig. 19.3

F = Number of faces = 6
E = Number of edges = 12
V = Number of vertices = 8
Clearly, $F + V = E + 2$

(iii) **PYRAMID**

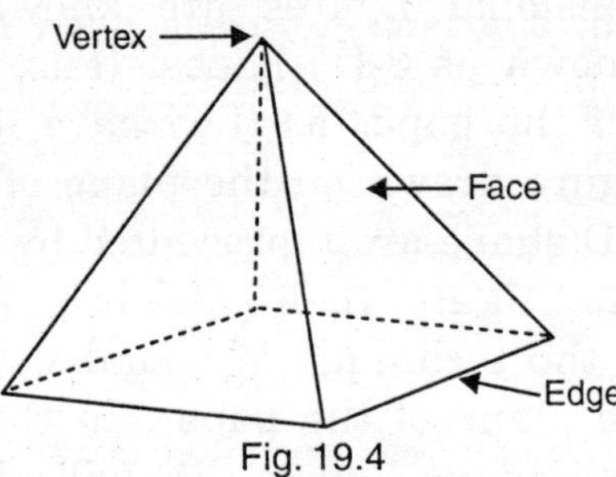

Fig. 19.4

F = Number of faces = 5
E = Number of edges = 8
V = Number of vertices = 5
Clearly, $F + V = E + 2$

(iv) **TRIANGULAR PYRAMID OR TETRAHEDRON**

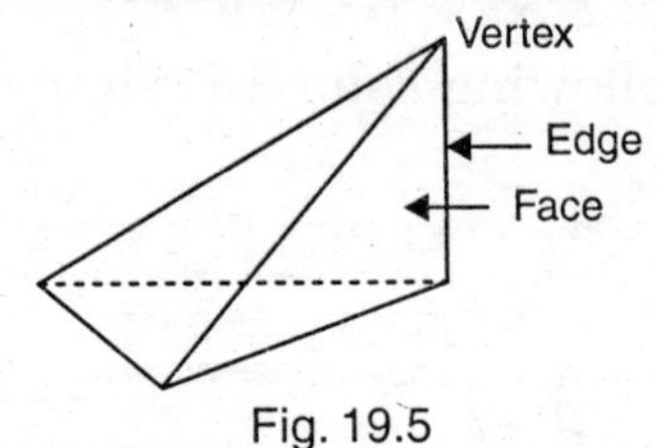

Fig. 19.5

F = Number of faces = 4
E = Number of edges = 6
V = Number of vertices = 4
Clearly, $F + V = E + 2$

(V) **TRIANGULAR PRISM**

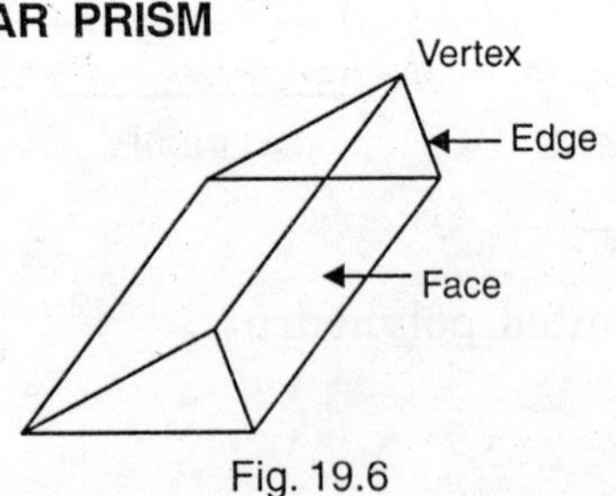

Fig. 19.6

F = Number of faces = 5
E = Number of edges = 9
V = Number of vertices = 6
Clearly, $F + V = E + 2$

Following solids are not polyhedrons as they are not made of polygons. In other words, their faces are not polygons.

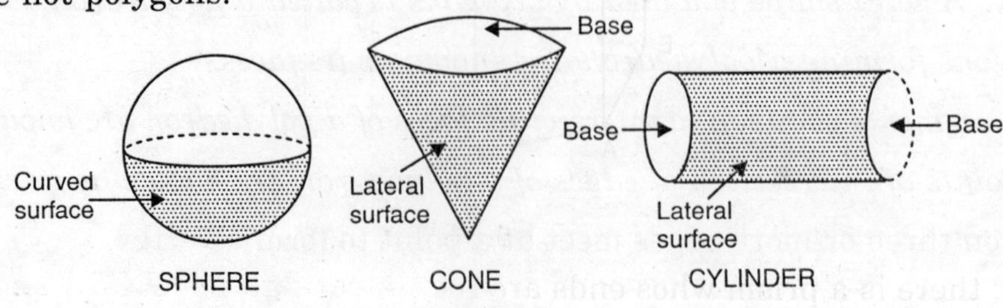

Fig. 19.7

REGULAR POLYHEDRON *A polyhedron is said to be a regular polyhedron if its faces are made up of regular polygons and the same number of faces meet at each vertex.*

This means that the faces of a regular polyhedron are congruent regular polygons and its vertices are formed by the same number of faces.

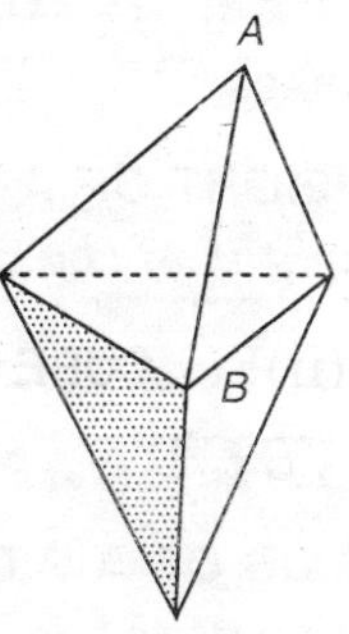

Fig. 19.8

A cube is a regular polyhedron but a cuboid is not a regular polyhedron as its faces are not congruent rectangles. Polyhedron drawn in Fig. 19.8 is not regular because its faces are congruent triangles but the vertices are not formed by the same number of faces. Clearly, 3 faces meet at A but 4 faces meet at B.

CONVEX POLYHEDRON *If the line segment joining any two points on the surface of a polyhedron entirely lies inside or on the polyhedron, then it is said to be a convex polyhedron.*

Otherwise, it is known as a concave polyhedron.

A cube, a cuboid, a tetrahedron, a pyramid, a prism etc are convex polyhedrons. In the following figures, (i) is a convex polyhedron but (ii) and (iii) are not convex polyhedrons.

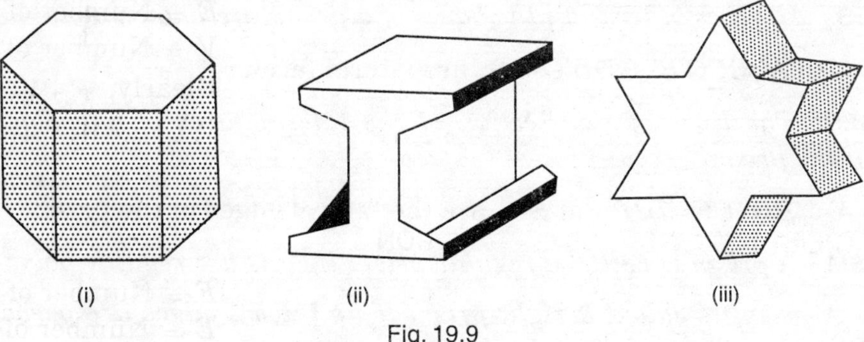

Fig. 19.9

19.2.1 PRISMS AND PYRAMIDS

Two important members of polyhedron family are prisms and pyramids. So, let us know about these two polyhedrons.

PRISM *A prism is a solid, whose side faces are parallelograms and whose ends (or bases) are congruent parallel rectilinear figures.*

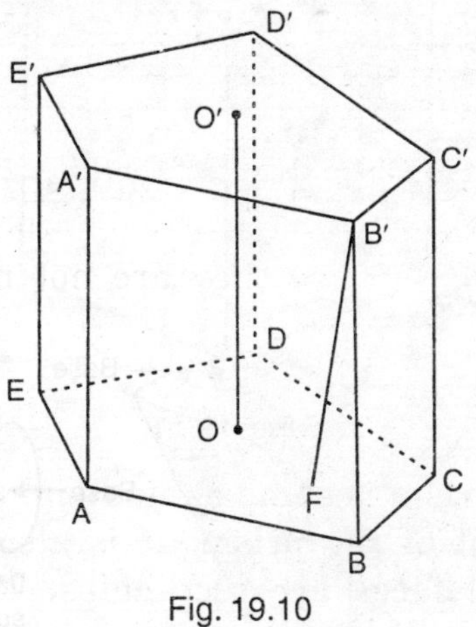

Fig. 19.10

In Fig. 19.10, there is a prism whos ends are rectilinear figures $ABCDE$ and $A'B'C'D'E'$.

BASE OF A PRISM *The end on which a prism may be supposed to stand is called the base of the prism.*

In Fig. 19.10, $ABCDE$ and $A'B'C'D'E'$ are the bases of the prism. Every prism has two bases.

HEIGHT OF A PRISM *The perpendicular distance between the ends of a prism is called the height of the prism.*

In Fig. 19.10, $B'F$ is the' perpendicular distance between the ends $ABCDE$ and $A'B'C'D'E'$. So, it is the height of the prism shown in Fig. 19.10.

AXIS OF A PRISM *The straight line joining the centres of the ends of a prism is called the axis of the prism.*

In Fig. 19.10, a straight line passing through O and O' is the axis of the prism.

LENGTH OF A PRISM *The length of a prism is the portion of the axis that lies between the parallel ends.*

In Fig. 19.10, OO' is the length of the prism.

LATERAL FACES *All faces other than the bases of a prism are known as its lateral faces.*

In Fig. 19.10, $ABB'A', BCC'B', CDD'C'$ etc. are lateral faces.

LATERAL EDGES *The lines of intersection of the lateral faces of a prism are called the lateral edges of the prism.*

In Fig. 19.10, AA', BB', CC', DD' and EE' are the lateral edges of the prism.

REGULAR PRISM *A prism is called a regular prism if ends are regular polygons.*

RIGHT PRISM *A prism is called a right prism if its lateral edges are perpendicular to its ends (bases). Otherwise it is said to be an oblique prism.*

The prism shown in Fig. 19.10 is an oblique prism whereas the prism shown in Fig. 19.11 is a right prism.

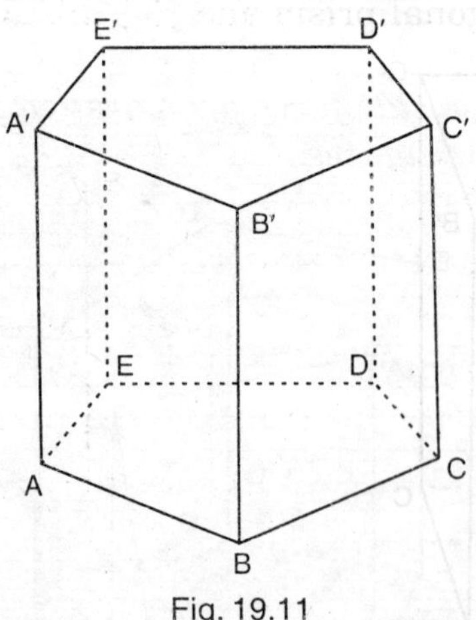

Fig. 19.11

In a right prism, length of the prism is same as its height. Also, all lateral edges are of the same length equal to the height of the prism. It is also evident from the definition of a right prism that its all lateral faces are rectangles. The number of lateral edges and lateral faces of a prism is same as the number of sides in the base of the prism.

TRIANGULAR PRISM *A prism is called a triangular prism if its ends are triangles.*

RIGHT TRIANGULAR PRISM *A right prism is called a right triangular prism if its ends are triangles.*

In other words, a triangular prism is called a right triangular prism if its lateral edges are perpendicular to its ends.

The prism shown in Fig. 19.12 is a triangular prism whereas the prism shown in Fig. 19.13 is a right triangular prism.

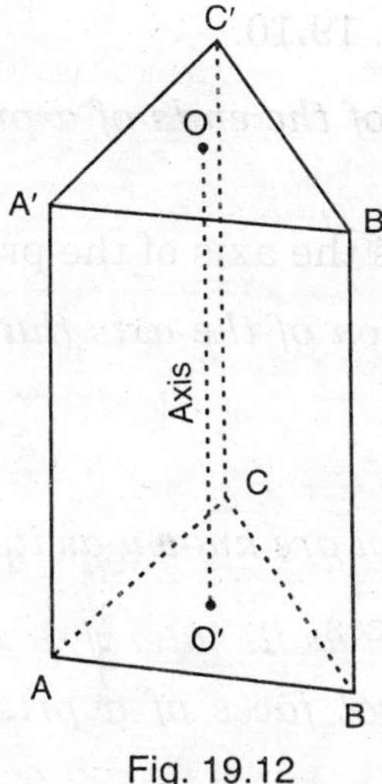

Fig. 19.12

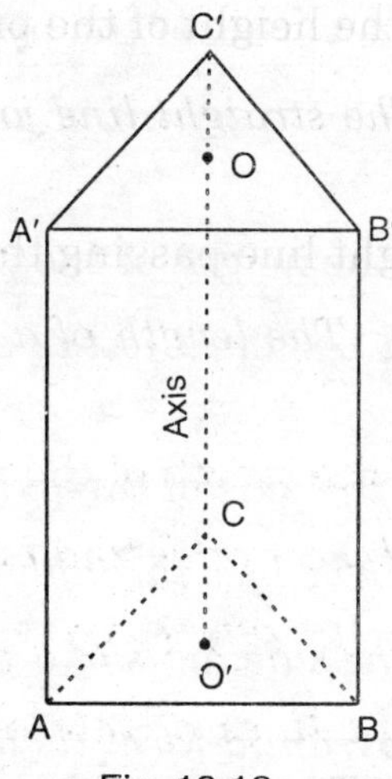

Fig. 19.13

A prism is said to be a quadrilateral prism or a pentagonal prism or a hexagonal prism etc according as the number of sides in the rectilinear figure forming the ends (bases) is four or five or six etc.

If the ends of a quadrilateral prism are parallelograms, then it is also known as a parallelopiped.

A quadrilateral prism with its ends as squares is called a rectangular solid or a cuboid.

Figure 19.14 shows a right pentagonal prism and Fig. 19.15 shows a rectangular solid.

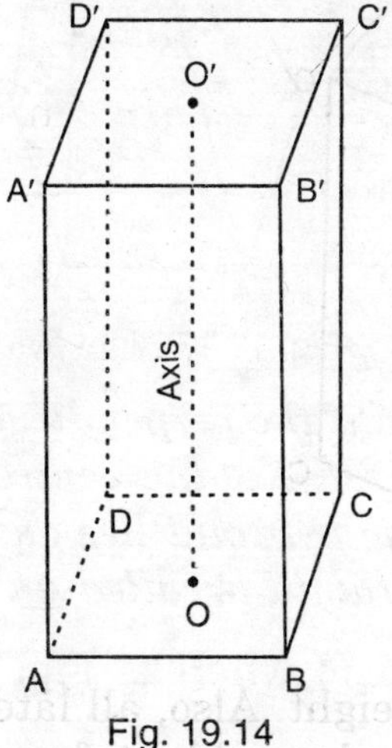

Fig. 19.14

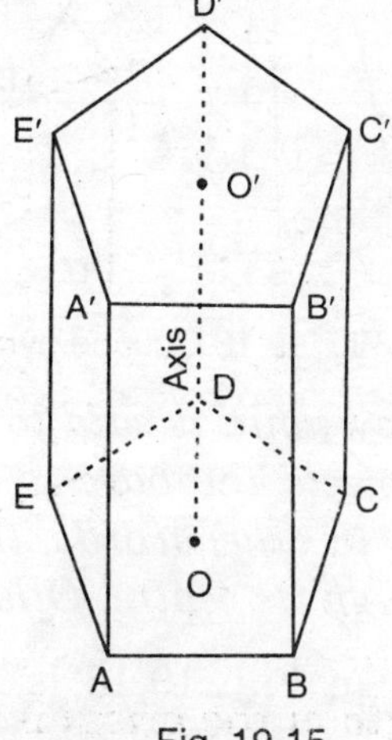

Fig. 19.15

Let us now learn about a polyhedron called pyramid that has fascinated human beings from ancient times. Pyramids of Egypt are one of the seven wonders of the world.

PYRAMID *A pyramid is a polyhedron whose base is a polygon of any number of sides and whose other faces are triangles with a common vertex.*

If all corners of a polygon are joined to a point not lying in its plane, we get a pyramid.

Figure 19.16 shows a pyramid *V, ABCDE*. The base of this prism is the pentagon *ABCDE* and triangles *VAB, VBC, VCD, VDE* and *VEA* are five faces.

VERTEX *The common vertex of the triangular faces of a pyramid is called the vertex of the pyramid.*

In Fig. 19.16, *V* is the vertex of the pyramid *V, ABCDE*.

HEIGHT *The height of a pyramid is the length of the perpendicular from the vertex to the base.*

In Fig. 19.16, *VP* is the height of the pyramid *V, ABCDE*.

AXIS *The axis of a pyramid is the straight line joining the vertex to the central point of the base.*

In Fig. 19.16, *VO* is the axis of the pyramid *V, ABCDE*.

LATERAL EDGES *The edges through the vertex of a pyramid are known as its lateral edges.*

LATERAL FACES *The side faces of a pyramid are known as its lateral faces.*

The side faces of a pyramid form its lateral surface.

If the base of a pyramid is a polygon of n sides then it has n lateral faces, each one of which is a triangle, and 2n edges.

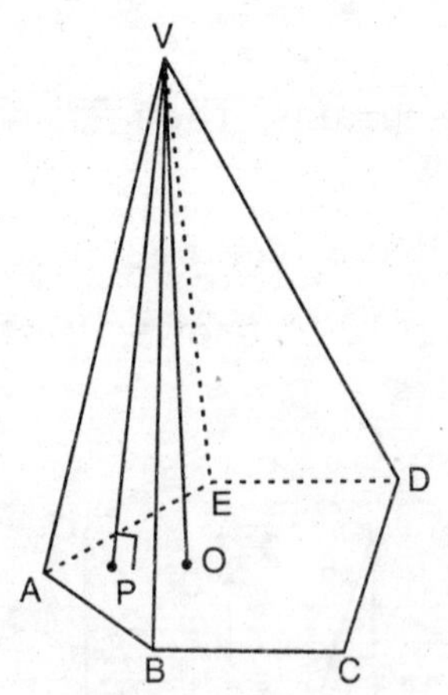

Fig. 19.16 Oblique pyramid

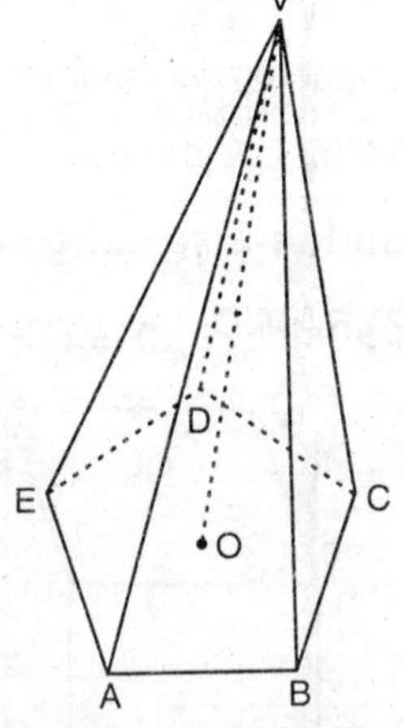

Fig. 19.17 Right pyramid

RIGHT PYRAMID *A pyramid is said to right pyramid if the perpendicular dropped from the vertex on the base meets the base at its central point i.e. the centre of the inscribed or circumscribed circle. In other words, the vertex of the pyramid lies on the perpendicular to the base drawn through its centre. Otherwise, the pyramid is called an oblique prism.*

The pyramid shown in Fig. 19.16 is an oblique prism whereas Fig. 19.17 shows a right prism.

REGULAR PYRAMID *A pyramid is said to be a regular pyramid if its base is a regular figure i.e. all sides of its base are equal.*

In case of a right regular pyramid the lateral edges are equal and the lateral faces are congruent triangles.

SLANT HEIGHT *The slant height of a regular right-pyramid is the line segment joining the vertex to the mid-point of anyone of the sides of the base.*

Figure 19.18 shows a right regular pyramid, in which O is the centre of the base and VM is the slant height.

Also, in right angled triangle VOM, we have

$$VM^2 = OM^2 + VO^2 \quad \text{[By Pythagoras theorem]}$$

$$\Rightarrow \quad VM = \sqrt{VO^2 + OM^2}$$

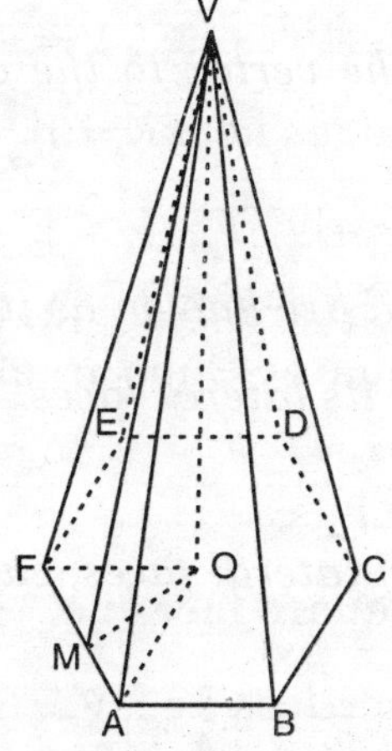

Fig. 19.18 Right regular pyramid

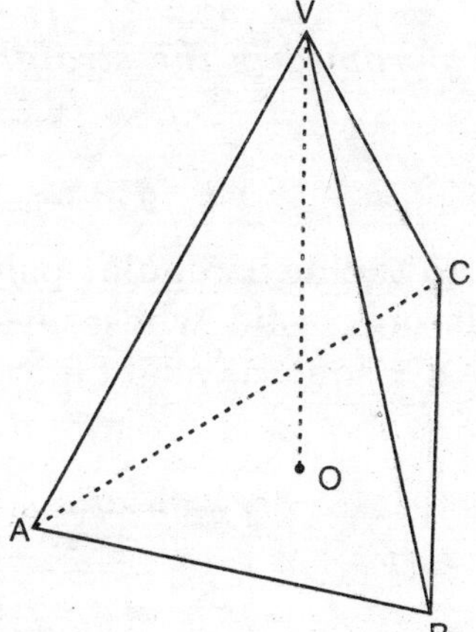

Fig. 19.19 Triangular pyramid (Tetrahedron)

TRIANGULAR PYRAMID *A pyramid is called a triangular pyramid if its base is a triangle.*

A triangular pyramid is also called a *tetrahedron*

QUADRILATERAL PYRAMID *A pyramid is called a quadrilateral pyramid if its base is a quadrilateral.*

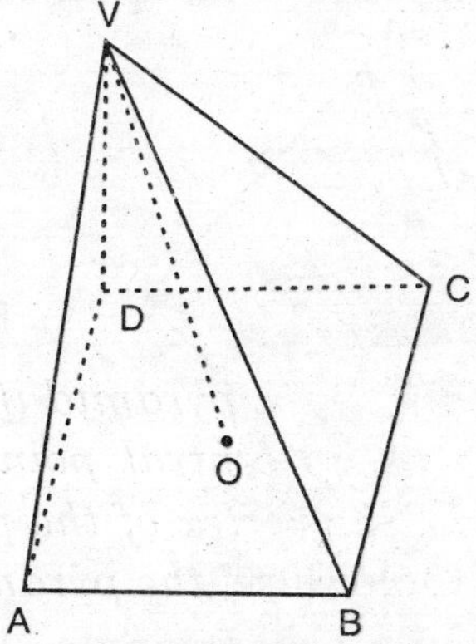

Fig. 19.20 Quadrilateral pyramid

If the base of a pyramid is a square, then it is called a square pyramid. Similarly, a pyramid is called a pentagonal, hexagonal, septagonal and octagonal according as the number of sides of the base is 5, 6, 7 or 8.

19.2.2 PLATONIC SOLIDS

A platonic solid is a polyhedron. It is interesting as well as surprising to know that there are exactly five platonic solids.

Note that in any polyhedron at least three polygons (called faces) must meet at a vertex to form a solid angle. Also, the sum of all plane angles forming the solid angle at a vertex must be less than 360°. Let us start with the simplest regular polygon forming the faces of a polyhedron. Clearly, such a regular polygon is an equilateral triangle. The polyhedron or platonic solid whose faces are congruent equilateral triangles is called the tetrahedron as shown in the following figure:

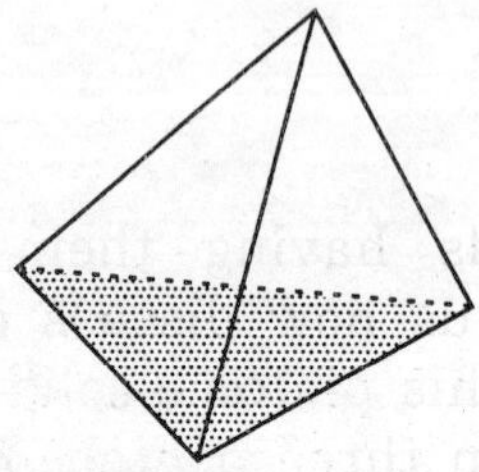
Fig. 19.21 Tetrahedron

A tetrahedron has:

4 triangular faces i.e., $F = 4$

4 vertices i.e., $V = 4$

6 edges i.e., $E = 6$

Clearly, $F + V = E + 2$

Let us now move on to the next regular polygon, that is, a square. Six squares form a cube. Cube is the only platonic solid whose every face is a square. Cube is also known as a hexahedron as it has six squares as its faces.

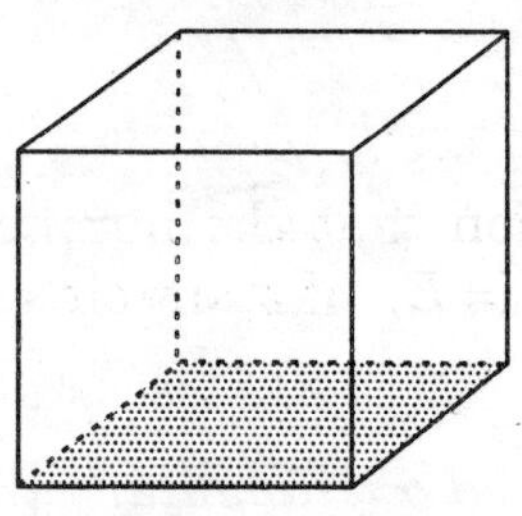
Fig. 19.22 Cube

A cube has:

6 square faces i.e., $F = 6$

8 vertices i.e., $V = 8$

12 edges i.e., $E = 12$

Clearly, $F + V = E + 2$

Tetrahedron and cube are platonic solids in which three faces (regular polygons) meet at a point to form a vertex. Let us now move on to a new platonic solid in which four regular polygons meet at a point to form a vertex. The platonic solid which has four equilateral triangles meeting at each vertex is known as the octahedron as shown in the following figure:

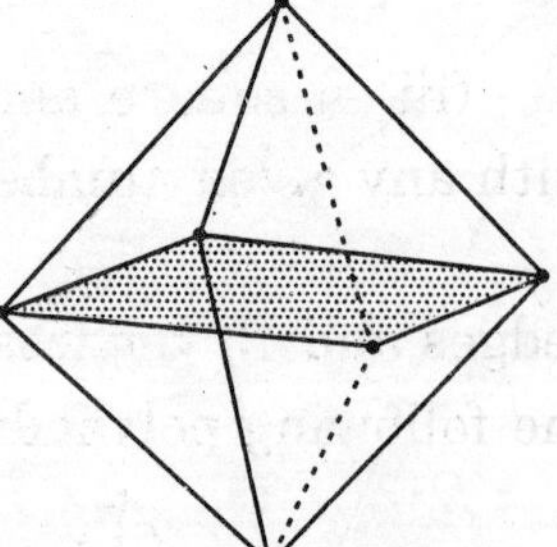
Fig. 19.23 Octahedron

An octahedron has:

8 triangular faces i.e., $F = 8$

6 vertices i.e., $V = 6$

12 edges i.e., $E = 12$

Clearly, $F + V = E + 2$

The platonic solid in which five equilateral triangles meet at a point to form a vertex, is known as an icosahedron as shown in the following figure:

An icosahedron has:

20 triangular faces i.e., $F = 20$

12 vertices i.e., $V = 12$

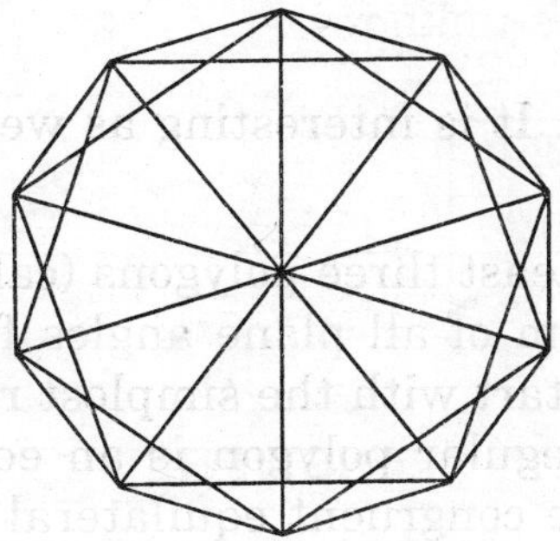

Fig. 19.24 An icosahedron

30 edges i.e., $E = 30$

Clearly, $F + V = E + 2$

We have learnt about platonic solids having their faces as equilateral triangles and squares. Let us now discuss a platonic solid whose every face is a pentagon. This platonic solid is known as the dodecahedron. In a dodecahedron three pentagons meet at every vertex and it has:

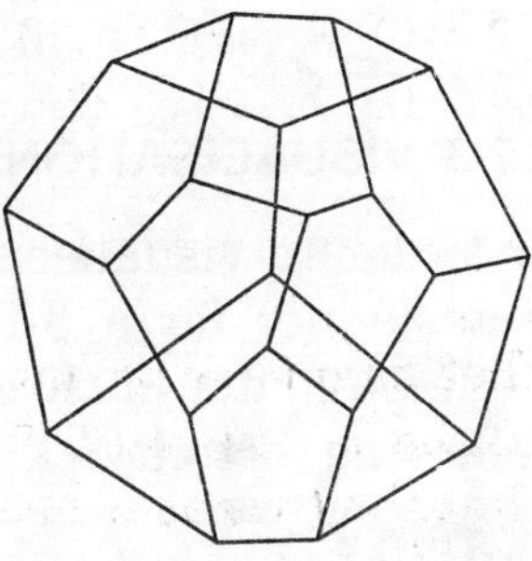

Fig. 19.25 Dodecahedron

12 pentagonal faces i.e., $F = 12$

20 vertices i.e., $V = 20$

30 edges i.e., $E = 30$

Clearly, $F + V = E + 2$

It is an evident from the above discussion that the number of faces $(= F)$, the number of vertices $(= V)$ and the number of edges $(= E)$ of a simple convex polyhedron are connected by the following formula:

$$F + V = E + 2$$

This relationship is known as *EULER'S Formula.*

EXERCISE 19.1

1. What is the least number of planes that can enclose a solid? What is the name of the solid?
2. Can a polyhedron have for its faces:

   (i) 3 triangles? (ii) 4 triangles? (iii) a square and four triangles?
3. Is it possible to have a polyhedron with any given number of faces?
4. Is a square prism same as a cube?
5. Can a polyhedron have 10 faces, 20 edges and 15 vertices?
6. Verify Euler's formula for each of the following polyhedrons:

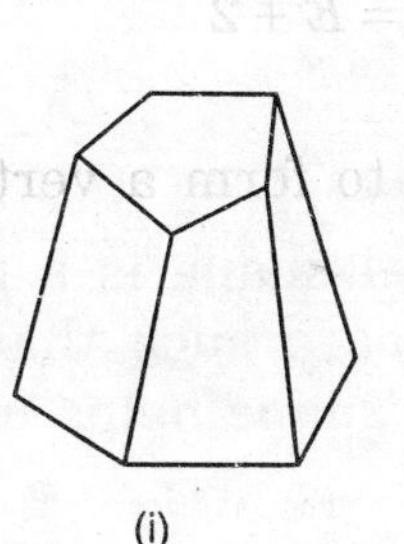

(i)

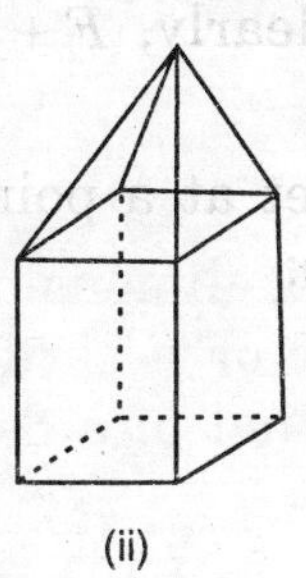

(ii)

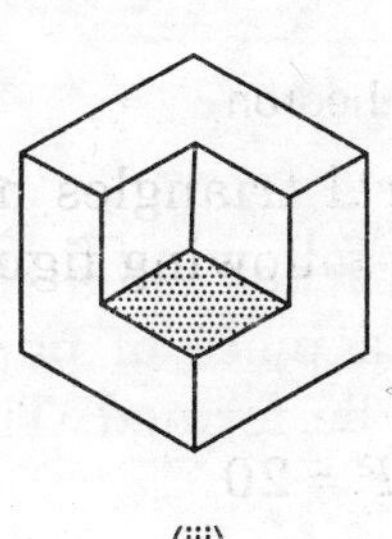

(iii)

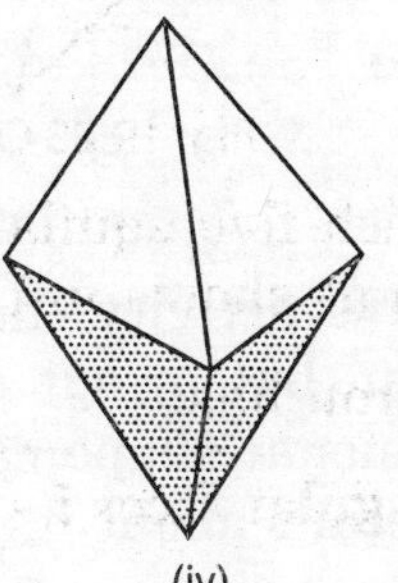

(iv)

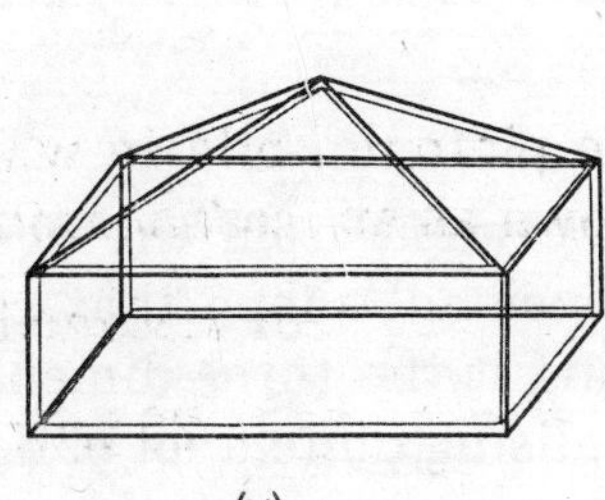

(v)

Fig. 19.26

7. Using Euler's formula find the unknown:

Faces	?	5	20
Vertices	6	?	12
Edges	12	9	?

ANSWERS

1. 4, Tetrahedron
2. (i) No (ii) Yes, A tetrahedron as 4 triangles as its faces
   (iii) Yes, A square pyramid has a square and four triangles as its faces.
3. Yes, if the number of faces is four or more. 4. Yes 5. No
7. (i) Faces 8 (ii) Vertices 6 (iii) Edges 30

19.3 VISUALISATION OF 3-D SHAPES THROUGH NETS

In order to visualise 3-D shapes more clearly, we try to form these shapes through their nets. A net for a 3-D shape is a sort of skelton-outline in two dimension which, when folded, results in three dimensional shape. In order to understand this let us perform the following activity:

ACTIVITY

Step I *Take a card-board box as shown in Fig. 19.27 (i).*

Step II *Cut the edges of the box as shown in Fig. 19.27 (ii).*

Step III *Open the box as shown in Fig. 19.27 (iii).*

Step IV *Lay the box flat as shown in Fig. 19.27 (iv) to get a net for the given card-board box..*

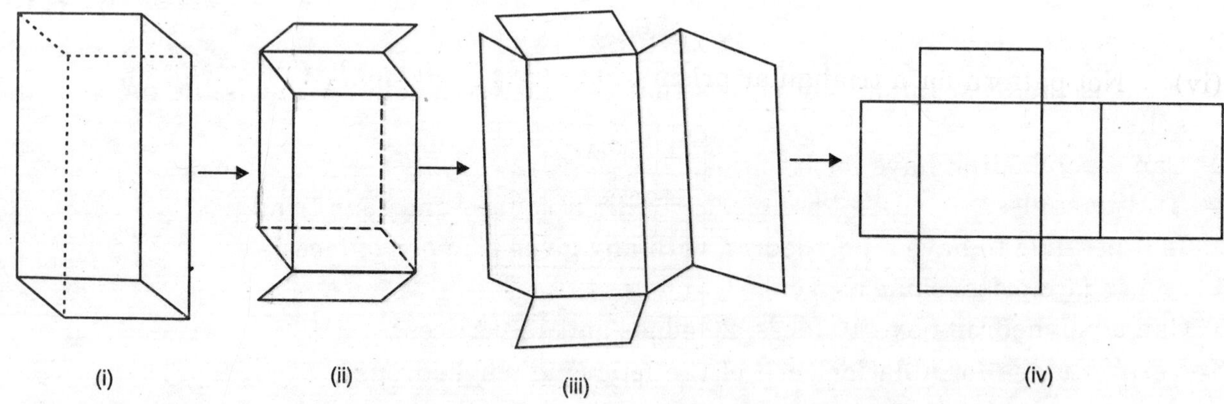

Fig. 19.27

It is evident from the above activity that a net for a three-dimensional shape is a two-dimensional shape that can be cut-out of a piece of paper or a card-board such that by folding it the three-dimensional shape can be formed. The net of a 3-D shape helps us in visualising quite a lot of details about it.

Following are net patterns for various polyhedrons:

(i) Net pattern for a cuboid:

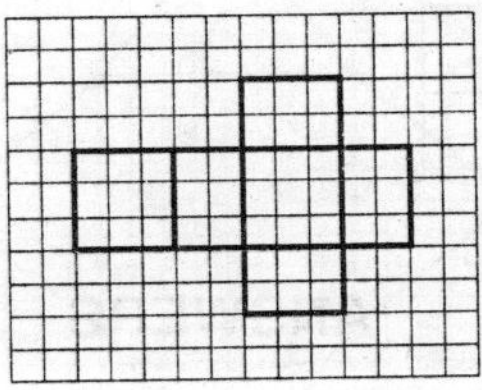

Fig. 19.28

(ii) Net pattern for a cube:

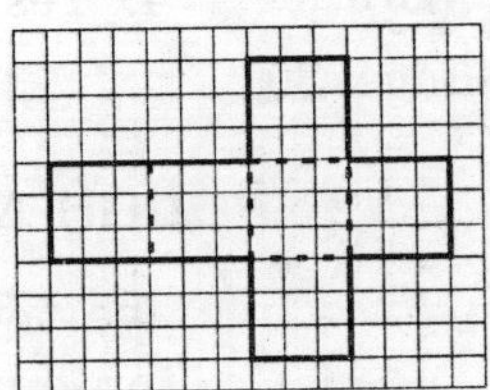

Fig. 19.29

(iii) Net pattern for a triangular prism, having base as a right triangle:

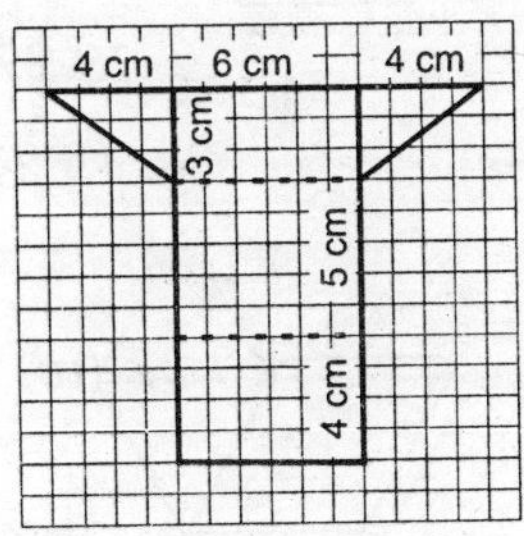

Fig. 19.30

(iv) Net pattern for a triangular prism whose base is an equilateral triangle:

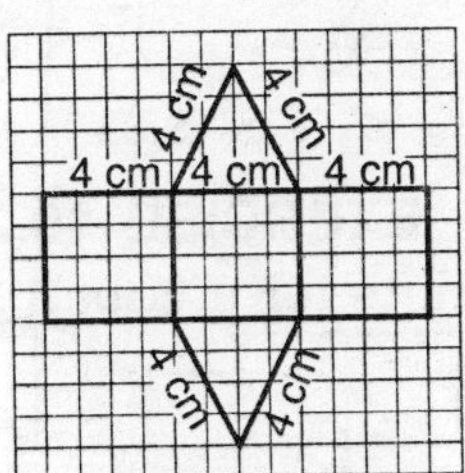

Fig. 19.31

(v) Net pattern for a tetrahedron:

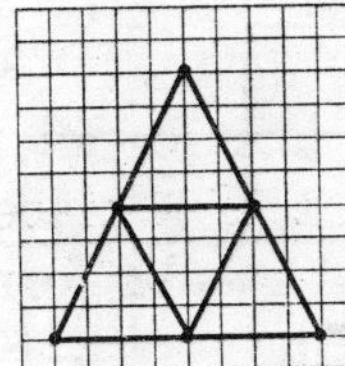

Fig. 19.32

(vi) Net pattern for a square pyramid:

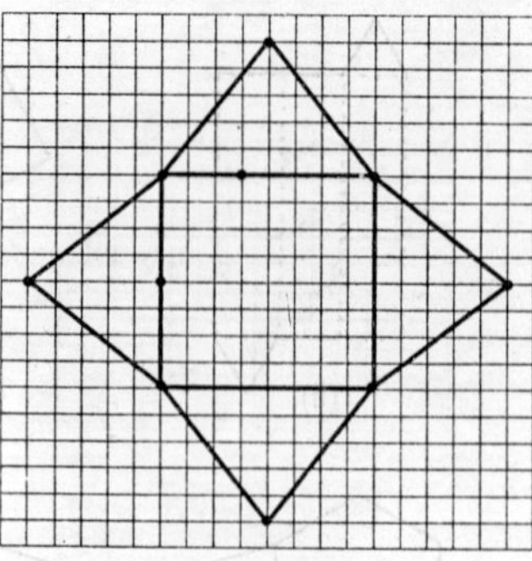

Fig. 19.33

(vii) Net pattern for a hexagonal pyramid:

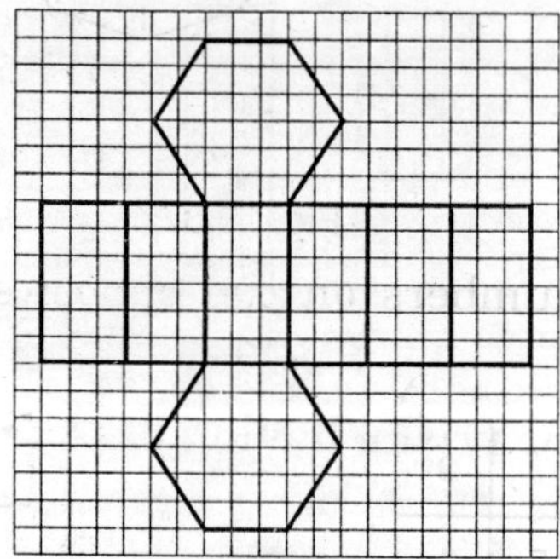

Fig. 19.34

(vi) Net pattern for a octahedron:

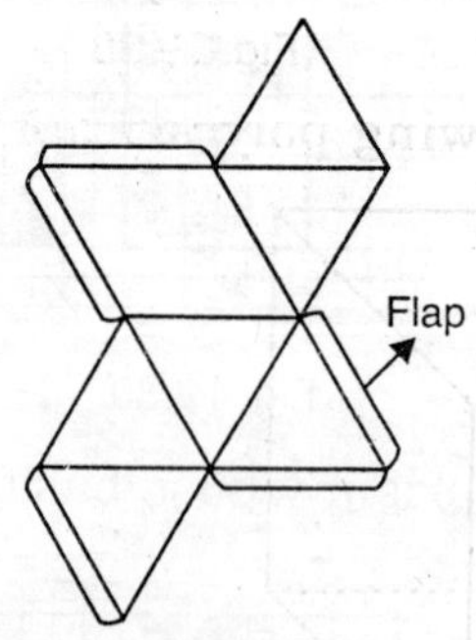

Fig. 19.35

EXERCISE 19.2

1. Which among the following are nets for a cube?

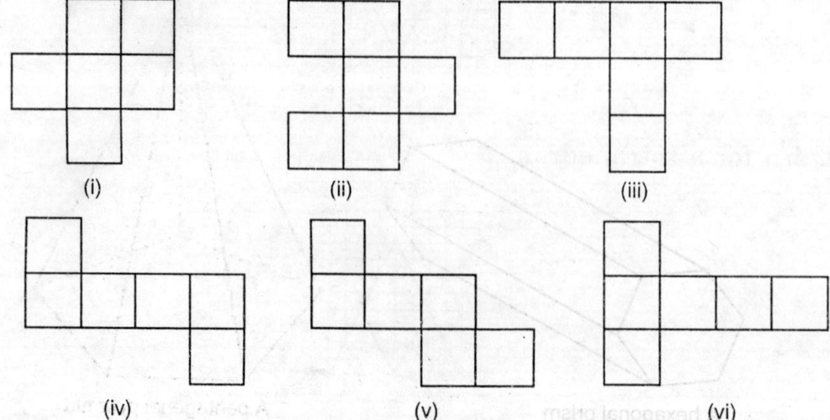

Fig. 19.36

2. Name the polyhedron that can be made by folding each net:

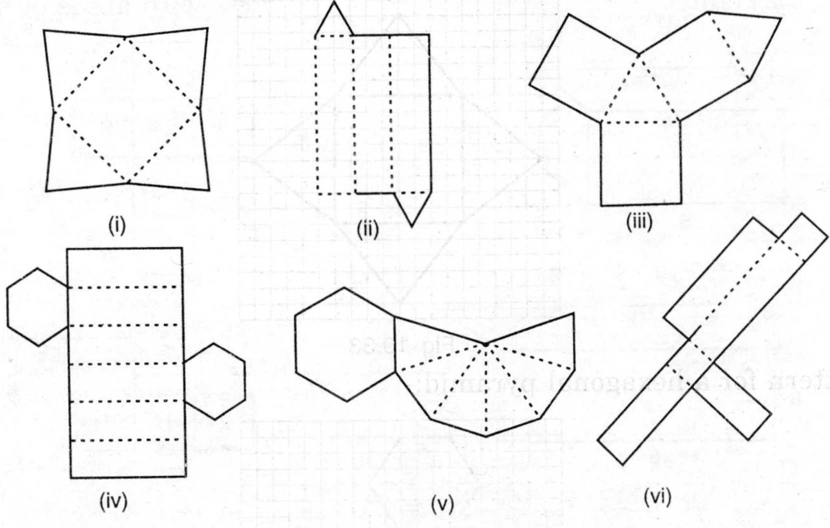

Fig. 19.37

3. Dice are cubes where the numbers on the opposite faces must total 7. Which of the following are dice?

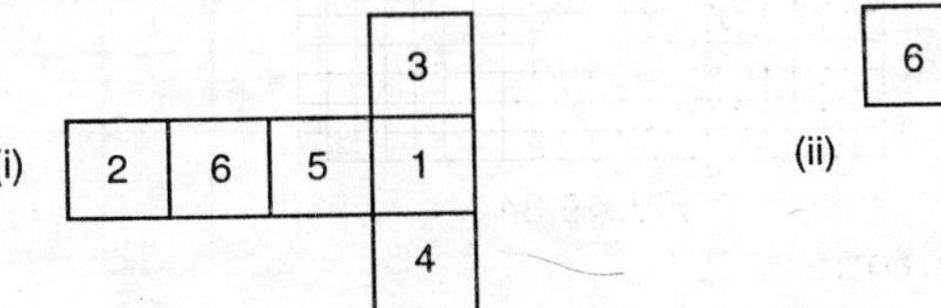

Fig. 19.38

4. Draw nets for each of the following polyhedrons:

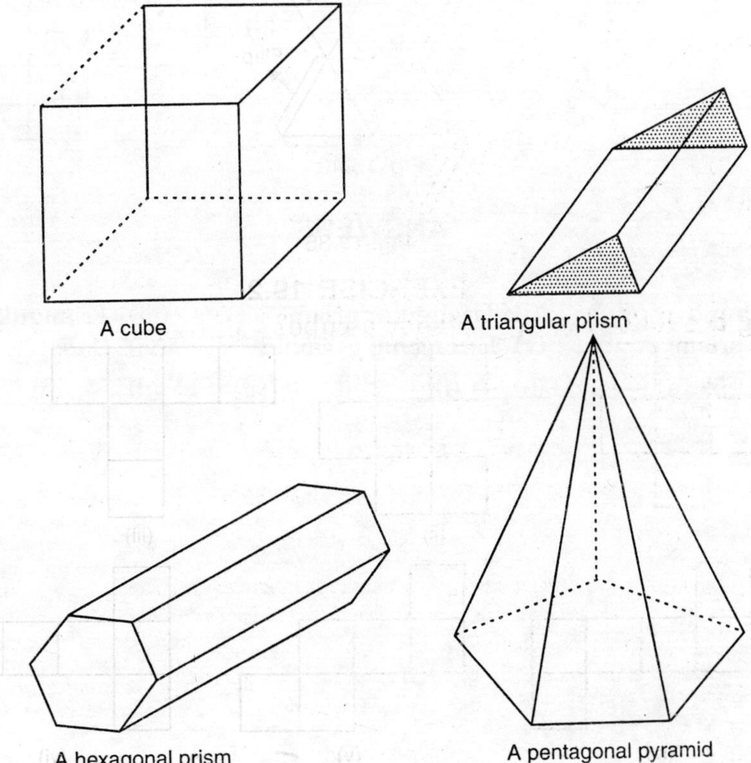

Fig. 19.39

5. Match the following figures:

Prisms | Nets with areas of faces

(a) 4 4 6

(i)

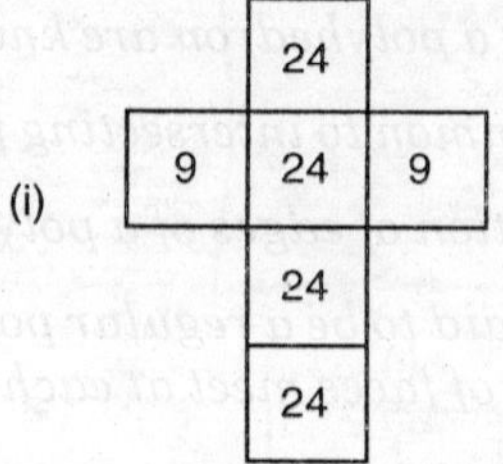

(b)

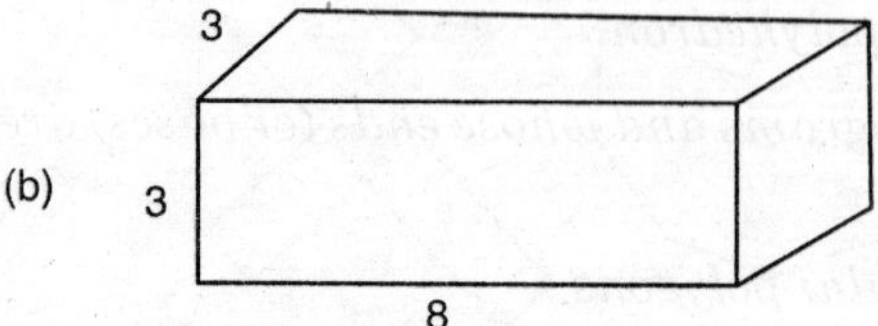

(ii)

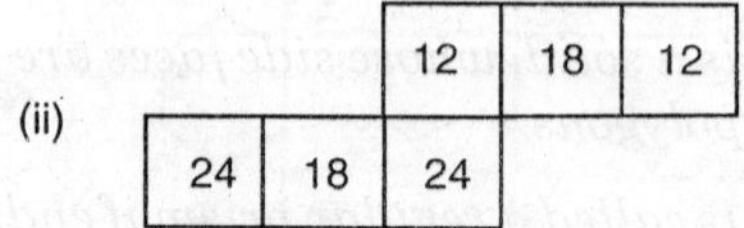

(c)

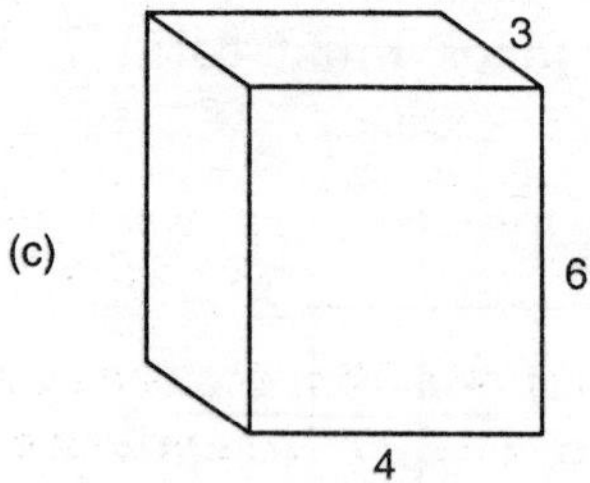

(iii)

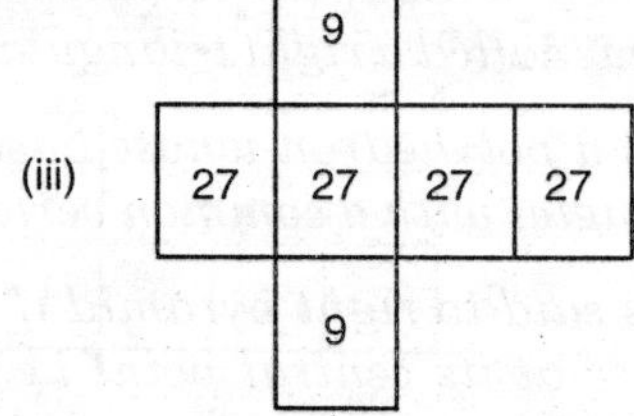

(d)

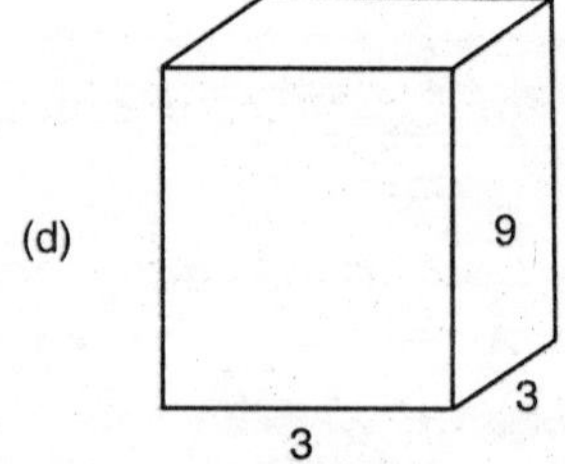

(iv)

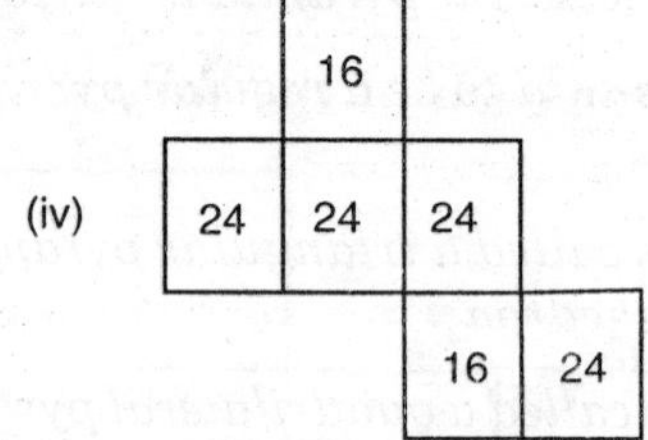

Fig. 19.40

ANSWERS

1. (d), (e), (f)
2. (i) Square pyramid (ii) Triangular prism (iii) Triangular prism
   (iv) Hexagonal prism (v) Hexagonal pyramid (vi) Cube
3. (i) 5. (a) — (iv) (b) — (i) (c) — (ii) (d) — (iii)

THINGS TO REMEMBER

1. *A solid shape bounded by polygons is called a polyhedron.*
2. *Polygons forming a polyhedron are known as its faces.*
3. *Line segments common to intersecting faces of a polyhedron are known as its edges.*
4. *Points of intersection of edges of a polyhedron are known as its vertices.*
5. *A polyhedron is said to be a regular polyhedron if its faces are made up of regular polygons and the same number of faces meet at each vertex.*
6. *If the line segment joining any two points on the surface of a polyhedron entirely lies inside or on the polyhedron, then it is said to be a convex polyhedron.*
7. *A prism is a solid, whose side faces are parallelograms and whose ends (or bases) are congruent parallel polygons.*
8. *A prism is called a regular prism if ends are regular polygons.*
9. *A prism is called a right prism if its lateral edges are perpendicular to its ends (bases). Otherwise it is said to be an oblique prism.*
10. *A prism is called a triangular prism if its ends are triangles.*
11. *A right prism is called a right triangular prism if its ends are triangles.*
12. *A pyramid is a polyhedron whose base is a polygon of any number of sides and whose other faces are triangles with a common vertex.*
13. *A pyramid is said to right pyramid if the perpendicular dropped from the vertex on the base meets the base at its central point i.e. the centre of the inscribed or circumscribed circle. In other words, the vertex of the pyramid lies on the perpendicular to the base drawn through its centre. Otherwise, the pyramid is called an oblique prism*
14. *A pyramid is said to be a regular pyramid if its base is a regular figure i.e. all sides of its base are equal.*
15. *A pyramid is called a triangular pyramid if its base is a triangle. A triangular pyramid is also called a tetrahedron*
16. *A pyramid is called a quadrilateral pyramid if its base is a quadrilateral.*
17. *A platonic solid is a polyhedron. There are exactly five platonic solids.*
18. *A net for a 3-D shape is a sort of skelton-outline in two dimension which, when folded, results in three dimensional shape.*

20

MENSURATION-I (Area of a Trapezium and a Polygon)

20.1 INTRODUCTION

In earlier classes, we have learnt about perimeters and areas of various plane figures such as squares, rectangles, parallelograms, rhombuses, triangles etc. In this chapter, we will study about methods of finding the area of a trapezium. We will also discuss problems on finding areas of some polygons (regular and non-regular both) by using the formulae for the area of a triangle and that of a trapezium.

20.2 REVIEW

We know that the part of the plane enclosed by a simple closed figure is called the region enclosed by it and the measurement of this region is its area. The area of the region enclosed by a square of side 1 cm is 1 square centimetre and is written as 1 cm². A square centimetre is a standard unit of area. Other standard units of area are square metre (m²), square decimetre (dm²), square decametre (dam²) or an are, square hectometre (hm²) or a hectare, square kilometre (km²) etc.

The inter-relationship between various units of measurement of area are listed below for ready reference:

$$1\,m^2 = 1\,m \times 1\,m$$

$$= 100\,cm \times 100\,cm$$

$$= 100 \times 100\,cm^2 = 10^4\,cm^2$$

Also, $1\,m^2 = 1\,m \times 1\,m = 10\,dm \times 10\,dm = 10 \times 10\,dm^2 = 100\,dm^2$

$$1\,dm^2 = 1\,dm \times 1\,dm$$

$$= 10\,cm \times 10\,cm$$

$$= (10 \times 10)\,cm^2 = 100\,cm^2$$

$$1\,dam^2 = 1\,dam \times 1\,dam$$

$$= 10\,m \times 10\,m$$

$$= (10 \times 10)\,m^2 = 100\,m^2$$

or, $1\,are = 100\,m^2$

$$1\,hm^2 = 1\,hm \times 1\,hm$$

$$= 100\,m \times 100\,m = 100 \times 100\,m^2 = 10000\,m^2$$

$$1\,hectare = 10000\,m^2$$

20

MENSURATION-I
(Area of a Trapezium and a Polygon)

20.1 INTRODUCTION

In earlier classes, we have learnt about perimeters and areas of various plane figures such as squares, rectangles, parallelograms, rhombuses, triangles etc. In this chapter, we will study about methods of finding the area of a trapezium. We will also discuss problems on finding areas of some polygons (regular and non-regular both) by using the formulae for the area of a triangle and that of a trapezium.

20.2 REVIEW

We know that the part of the plane enclosed by a simple closed rectilinear figure is called the region enclosed by it and the measurement of region is known as its area. The area of the region enclosed by a square of side 1 cm is called a square centimetre and is written as 1 cm^2. A square centimetre is a standard unit of area. Other standard units of area are: square metre (m^2), square decimetre (dm^2), square decametre (dam^2) or an are, square hectometre (hm^2) or a hectare, square kilometre (km^2) etc.

The inter-relationship between various units of measurement of area are listed below for ready reference:

$$1\,m^2 = 1\,m \times 1\,m$$

$$= 100\text{ cm} \times 100\text{ cm} \qquad [\because 1\,m = 100\text{ cm}]$$

$$= 100 \times 100\text{ cm}^2 = 10^4\text{ cm}^2$$

Also, $1\,m^2 = 1\,m \times 1\,m = 10\text{ dm} \times 10\text{ dm} = (10 \times 10)\text{ dm}^2 = 100\text{ dm}^2$

$$1\text{ dm}^2 = 1\text{ dm} \times 1\text{ dm}$$

$$= 10\text{ cm} \times 10\text{ cm} \qquad [\because 1\text{ dm} = 10\text{ cm}]$$

$$= (10 \times 10)\text{ cm}^2 = 100\text{ cm}^2$$

$$1\text{ dam}^2 = 1\text{ dam} \times 1\text{ dam}$$

$$= 10\,m \times 10\,m \qquad [\because 1\text{ dam} = 10\text{ m}]$$

$$= (10 \times 10)\,m^2 = 100\,m^2$$

or, $1\text{ are} = 100\,m^2$

$$1\,hm^2 = 1\,hm \times 1\,hm$$

$$= 100\,m \times 100\,m = 100 \times 100\,m^2 = 10000\,m^2 \qquad [\because 1\text{ hm} = 100\text{ m}]$$

$$1\text{ hectare} = 10000\,m^2$$

Also, $1\text{ hectare} = 100\text{ ares}$

$$1\text{ km}^2 = 1\text{ km} \times 1\text{ km}$$

$$= 1000\text{ m} \times 1000\text{ m} = (1000 \times 1000)\text{ m}^2 = 10^6\text{ m}^2$$

Also, $1\text{ km}^2 = 100\text{ hectares}.$

Following are the areas and perimeters of various plane figures which we have studied in earlier classes:

(i) Perimeter and area of a rectangle:

Let l and b denote respectively the length and breadth of a rectangle. Then,

(i) Perimeter $= 2(l + b)$

(ii) Area $= l \times b$

(iii) Length $= \dfrac{\text{Area}}{\text{Breadth}}$

(iv) Breadth $= \dfrac{\text{Area}}{\text{Length}}$

(v) Diagonal $= \sqrt{l^2 + b^2}$

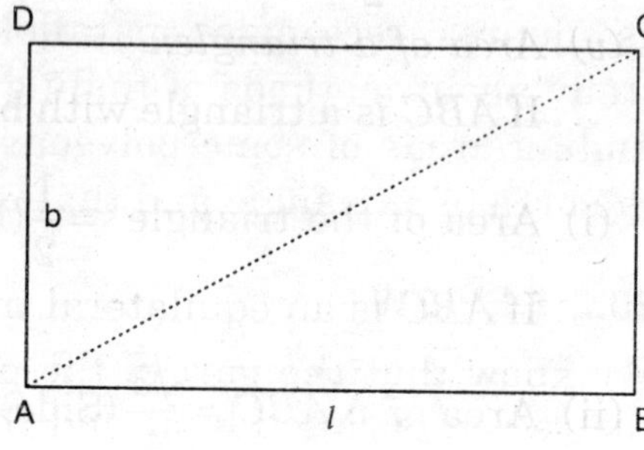

Fig. 20.1

(ii) Perimeter and area of a square:

Let a be the length of each side of a square. Then,

(i) Perimeter $= 4a$

(ii) Area $= a^2$

Also, Area $= \left(\dfrac{\text{Perimeter}}{4}\right)^2$

(iii) Side of the square $= \sqrt{\text{Area}}$

(iv) Diagonal $= \sqrt{2}\,a$

(v) Area $= \dfrac{1}{2}(\text{Diagonal})^2$

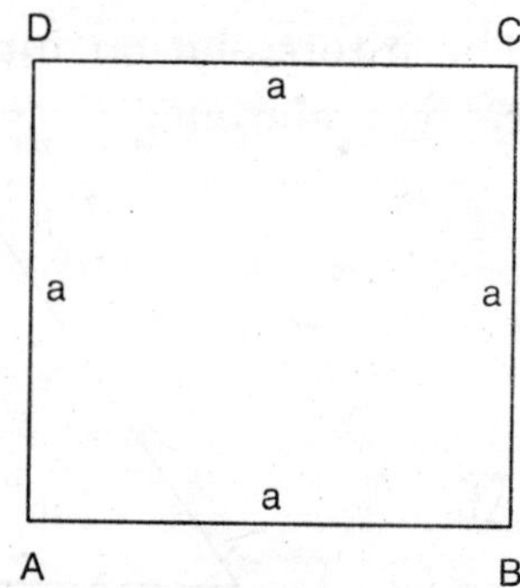

Fig. 20.2

(iii) Perimeter and area of a parallelogram:

Let *ABCD* be a parallelogram. Then,

(i) Area of the parallelogram $= \text{Base} \times \text{Height}$

(ii) Base of the parallelogram $= \dfrac{\text{Area}}{\text{Height}}$

(iii) Height of the parallelogram $= \dfrac{\text{Area}}{\text{Base}}$

(iv) Perimeter $= 2$ (Sum of two adjacent sides)

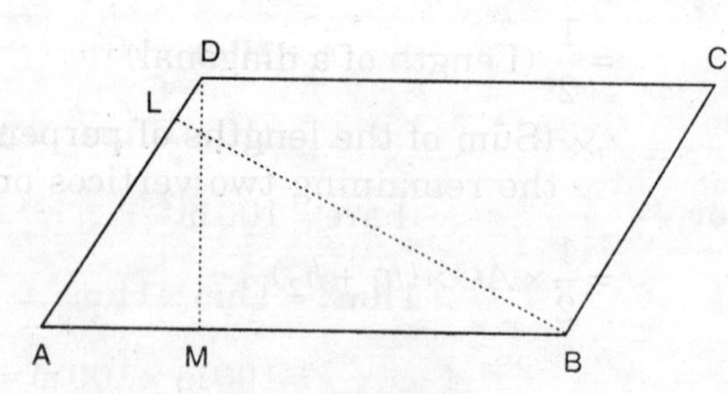

Fig. 20.3

NOTE: *In parallelogram ABCD shown in Fig.20.3, if AB is the base, then DM is the height and corresponding to the base AD, BL is the height.*

(iv) Perimeter and area of a rhombus:

If d_1 and d_2 are the lengths of the diagonals of a rhombus *ABCD*, then

(i) Side of the rhombus $= \frac{1}{2}\sqrt{d_1^2 + d_2^2}$

(ii) Perimeter $= 4 \times (\text{Side}) = 2\sqrt{d_1^2 + d_2^2}$

(iii) Area $= \frac{1}{2}(d_1 \times d_2)$

Fig. 20.4

(v) Area of a triangle:

If *ABC* is a triangle with base b and height h, then

(i) Area of the triangle $= \frac{1}{2}(\text{Base} \times \text{Height}) = \frac{1}{2}(b \times h)$

If *ABC* is an equilateral triangle each of whose side is a units in length, then

(ii) Area of $\Delta ABC = \frac{\sqrt{3}}{4}(\text{Side})^2$

(iii) Height or Altitude $= \frac{\sqrt{3}}{2}$ (Side)

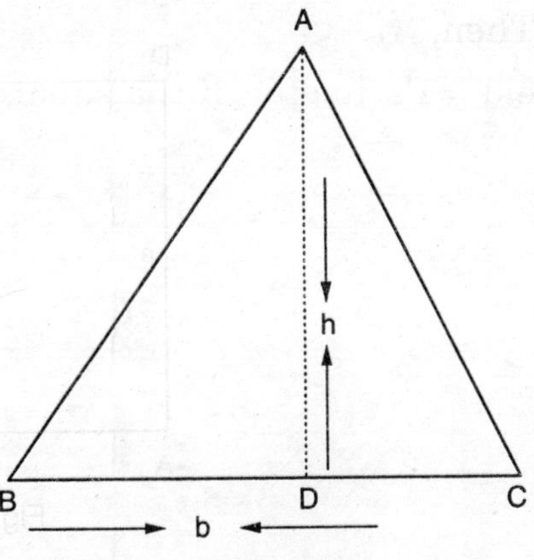

Fig. 20.5

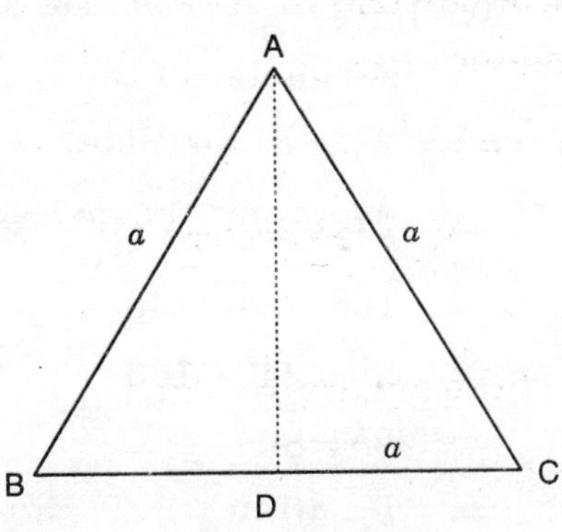

Fig. 20.6

(vi) Area of a quadrilateral: If *ABCD* is a quadrilateral, then

Area of quadrilateral *ABCD*

$= \frac{1}{2}$ (Length of a diagonal)

$\times$ (Sum of the lengths of perpendiculars from the remaining two vertices on it)

$= \frac{1}{2} \times AC \times (h_1 + h_2)$

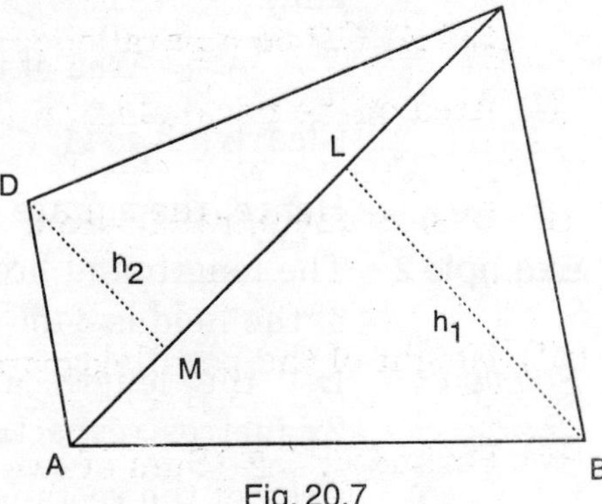

Fig. 20.7

(vii) Perimeter and area of a circle:

Let r be the radius of a circle. Then,

(i) Circumference (Perimeter) $= 2\pi r$

(ii) Area $= \pi r^2$

(iii) Diameter $= 2r$

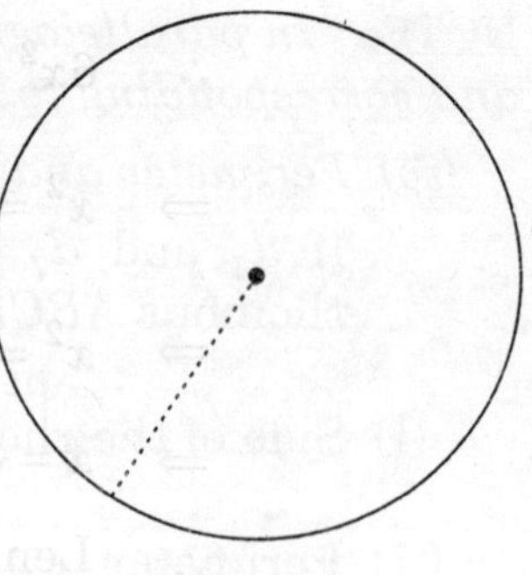

Fig. 20.8

Let us now discuss some examples to revise the applications of these formulae.

ILLUSTRATIVE EXAMPLES

Example 1 In Fig. 20.9, one square and one rectangular field have the same perimeter. Which field has a larger area?

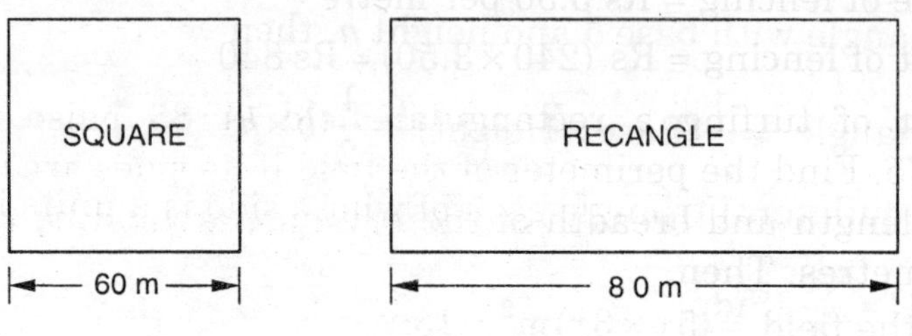

Fig. 20.9

Solution Let l be the length and b be the width of the rectangular field.

It is given that $l = 80$ m

We have,

Perimeter of the rectangular field = Perimeter of the square field

$\Rightarrow \quad 2(l + b) = 4$ (Side)

$\Rightarrow \quad 2(80 + b) = 4 \times 60 \qquad [\because \text{Side} = 60 \text{ m}]$

$\Rightarrow \quad 160 + 2b = 240$

$\Rightarrow \quad 2b = 240 - 160$

$\Rightarrow \quad 2b = 80$

$\Rightarrow \quad b = 40$ m

Now,

A_1 = Area of the square field $= (\text{Side})^2 = (60)^2 \text{ m}^2 = 3600 \text{ m}^2$

and,

A_2 = Area of the rectangular field $= l \times b = 80 \times 40 \text{ m}^2 = 3200 \text{ m}^2$

Clearly, $A_1 > A_2$

Hence, the square field has larger area.

Example 2 The length and breadth of a rectangular field are in the ratio 3 : 2. If the area of the field is 3456 m^2, find the cost of fencing the field at Rs 3.50 per metre.

Solution Let the length and breadth of the rectangular field be $3x$ metres and $2x$ metres respectively. Then,

Area of the rectangular field $= (3x \times 2x) \text{ m}^2 = 6x^2 \text{ m}^2$

It is given that the area of the rectangular field is 3456 m^2

$\therefore \quad 6x^2 = 3456$

$\Rightarrow \quad x^2 = \dfrac{3456}{6}$

$\Rightarrow \quad x^2 = 576$

$\Rightarrow \quad x = \sqrt{576} = 24$

$\therefore$ Length $= (3 \times 24)$ m $= 72$ m, Breadth $= (2 \times 24)$ m $= 48$ m

$\therefore$ Perimeter of the field $= 2 \times$ (Length + Breadth) $= [2 \times (72 + 48)]$ m $= 240$ m

We have,

Rate of fencing = Rs 3.50 per metre

$\therefore$ Cost of fencing = Rs (240×3.50) = Rs 840

Example 3 The cost of turfing a rectangular field at 85 paise per square metre is Rs 624.75. Find the perimeter of the field if its sides are in the ratio 5 : 3.

Solution Let the length and breadth of the rectangular field be respectively $5x$ metres and $3x$ metres. Then,

Area of the field $= (5x \times 3x)\,\text{m}^2 = 15x^2\,\text{m}^2$

The cost of turfing 1 square metre of the field $= 85$ paise $=$ Rs $\dfrac{85}{100} =$ Rs $\dfrac{17}{20}$

$\therefore$ Total cost of turfing the field $=$ Rs $\left(15x^2 \times \dfrac{17}{20}\right) =$ Rs $\left(3x^2 \times \dfrac{17}{4}\right) =$ Rs $\dfrac{51x^2}{4}$

But, the total cost of turfing the field is given as Rs 624.75

$\therefore \quad \dfrac{51x^2}{4} = 624.75$

$\Rightarrow \quad x^2 = \dfrac{624.75 \times 4}{51} \Rightarrow x^2 = 49 \Rightarrow x = \sqrt{49} = 7$

Hence, the sides of the rectangular field are

$5x = (5 \times 7)$ m $= 35$ m and $3x = (3 \times 7)$ m $= 21$ m

$\therefore$ Perimeter of the field $= 2\,(35 + 21)$ m $= 112$ m

Example 4 The shape of a garden is rectangular in the middle and semi-circular at the ends as shown in the diagram. Find the area and perimeter of this garden.

Solution We have,

Diameter of circular ends $= 7$ m

$\therefore \quad r =$ Radius of circular ends $= \dfrac{7}{2}$ m $= 3.5$ m

Also,

$l =$ Length of the rectangle $= \{20 - (3.5 + 3.5)\}$ m $= (20 - 7)$ m $= 13$ m

$b =$ Width of the rectangle $= 7$ m

Perimeter of the garden $= 2l + \pi r + \pi r$

$= 2l + 2\pi r$

$$= \left\{2\times 13 + 2\times\frac{22}{7}\times\frac{7}{2}\right\} \text{m} = (26+22)\,\text{m} = 48\,\text{m}$$

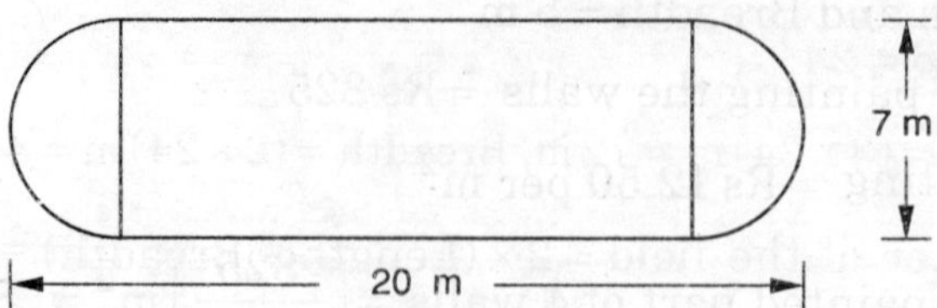

Fig. 20.10

Area of the garden = Area of rectangular part + Area of semi-circular ends

$$= l\times b + \frac{1}{2}(\pi r^2) + \frac{1}{2}(\pi r^2)$$

$$= l\times b + \pi r^2$$

$$= \left\{13\times 7 + \frac{22}{7}\times\left(\frac{7}{2}\right)^2\right\}\text{m}^2 = \left(91 + \frac{77}{2}\right)\text{m}^2 = 129.5\,\text{m}^2$$

Example 5 The dimensions of a room are $16\times 14\times 10$ metres. There are 4 windows of $1.3\,\text{m}\times 1.4\,\text{m}$ and 2 doors of $2\,\text{m}\times 1\,\text{m}$. What will be the cost of white washing the walls and painting the doors and windows, if the rate of white washing is Rs 5 per m^2 and the rate of painting is Rs 8 per m^2.

Solution We have,

Length $= 16\,\text{m}$, Breadth $= 14\,\text{m}$, and Height $= 10\,\text{m}$

$\therefore$ Area of four walls of the room $= [2\times(\text{Length} + \text{Breadth})\times \text{Height})]\,\text{m}^2$

$= [2\times(16+14)\times 10]\,\text{m}^2 = 600\,\text{m}^2$

Area of one door $= (2\times 1)\,\text{m}^2 = 2\,\text{m}^2$

$\therefore$ Area of two doors $= (2\times 2)\,\text{m}^2 = 4\,\text{m}^2$

Area of one window $= (1.3\times 1.4)\,\text{m}^2 = 1.82\,\text{m}^2$

$\therefore$ Area of 4 windows $= (4\times 1.82)\,\text{m}^2 = 7.28\,\text{m}^2$

Thus, the area to be white washed $= \{600 - (4+7.28)\}\,\text{m}^2 = 588.72\,\text{m}^2$

$\therefore$ Cost of white washing at the rate of Rs 5 per sq. metre = Rs (5×588.72)

= Rs 2943.6

Area to be painted $= (4+7.28) = 11.28\,\text{m}^2$

$\therefore$ Cost of painting the doors and windows = Rs $\{(8\times 11.28)\}$ = Rs 90.24

Hence, total cost of white washing and painting = Rs (2943.6×90.24)

= Rs 3033.84.

Example 6 A room is 7 metres long and 5 metres broad. It has one door measuring 2 m by 1.5 m and two windows, each measuring 1.5 m by 1 m. The cost of painting the walls at Rs 12.50 per square metre is Rs 825. Find the height of the room.

Solution Let the height of the room be h metres.

We have,

Length = 7 m and Breadth = 5 m

Total cost of painting the walls = Rs 825

Rate of painting = Rs 12.50 per m^2

$\therefore$ Area of painted part of 4 walls $= \left(\frac{825}{12.50}\right) m^2 = \left(825 \times \frac{2}{25}\right) m^2 = 66 \, m^2$

Now,

Area of one door $= (2 \times 1.5) m^2 = 3 m^2$

Area of 2 windows $= \{2 \times (1.5 \times 1)\} m^2 = 3 m^2$

$\therefore$ Area of one door and two windows $= (3+3) m^2 = 6 m^2$

So, total area of 4 walls $= (66+6) m^2 = 72 m^2$

Also,

Total area of 4 walls = 2 × (Length + Breadth) × Height

$= \{2 \times (7+5) \times h\} m^2 = 24 h \, m^2$

$\therefore$ $24h = 72 \Rightarrow h = 3$

Hence, height of the room is 3 metres.

Example 7 The area of square $ABCD$ is 16 cm^2. Find the area of the square joining the mid-points of the sides.

Solution We have,

Area of square $ABCD$ = 16 cm^2

$\therefore$ Each side of square $ABCD = \sqrt{16}$ cm = 4 cm

In ΔAPS, we have

$AP = \frac{1}{2} AB = 2$ cm and $AS = \frac{1}{2} AD = 2$ cm

Using Pythagoras theorem in ΔPAS, we have

Also, $PS^2 = AP^2 + AS^2$

$\Rightarrow$ $PS = \sqrt{2^2 + 2^2} = \sqrt{8} = 2\sqrt{2}$ cm

Thus, each side of square $PQRS$ is of length $2\sqrt{2}$ cm

$\therefore$ Area of the square $PQRS = (2\sqrt{2})^2$ cm^2 = 8 cm^2

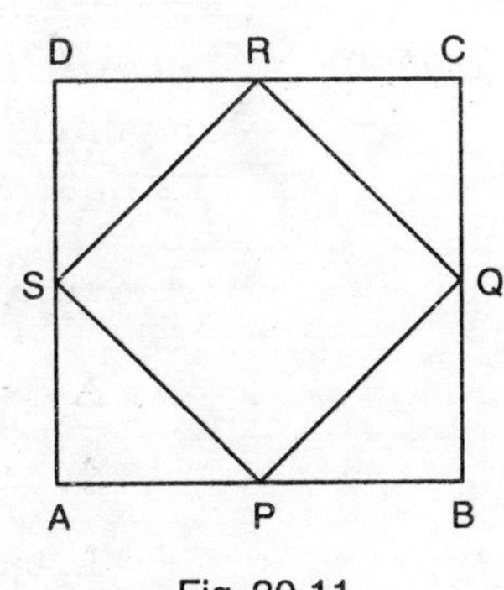

Fig. 20.11

Example 8 The base of a parallelogram is thrice its height. If the area is 867 cm^2, find the base and height of the parallelogram.

Solution Let the height of the parallelogram be x cm. Then, base $= 3x$ cm

$\therefore$ Area of the parallelogram $= (x \times 3x)$ $cm^2 = 3x^2$ cm^2

But, area of the parallelogram is given as 867 cm^2

$\therefore$ $3x^2 = 867 \Rightarrow x^2 = 289 \Rightarrow x = \sqrt{289} = 17$

$\therefore$ Height = 17 cm and Base $= (3 \times 17)$ cm = 51 cm

Example 9 Find the area of a rhombus having each side equal to 13 cm and one of whose diagonals is 24 cm.

Solution Let $ABCD$ be the given rhombus whose diagonals intersect at O.

We have,

$$AB = 13 \text{ cm and } AC = 24 \text{ cm}$$

Since the diagonals of a rhombus bisect each other at right angles. Therefore, ΔAOB is a right triangle, right angled at O such that $OA = \frac{1}{2}AC = 12$ cm and $AB = 13$ cm.

Using Pythagoras theorem, in ΔAOB, we have

$$AB^2 = OA^2 + OB^2$$

$$\Rightarrow \quad 13^2 = 12^2 + OB^2$$

$$\Rightarrow \quad OB^2 = 13^2 - 12^2$$

$$\Rightarrow \quad OB^2 = 169 - 144 = 25$$

$$\Rightarrow \quad OB^2 = 5^2$$

$$\Rightarrow \quad OB = 5 \text{ cm}$$

$$\therefore \quad BD = 2 \times OB = 2 \times 5 \text{ cm} = 10 \text{ cm}$$

Fig. 20.12

Hence, Area of rhombus $ABCD = \frac{1}{2} \times AC \times BD = \frac{1}{2} \times 24 \times 10 \text{ cm}^2 = 120 \text{ cm}^2$

Example 10 If the area of a rhombus be 24 cm^2 and one of its diagonals be 4 cm, find the perimeter of the rhombus.

Solution Let $ABCD$ be a rhombus such that its one diagonal AC = 4 cm. Suppose the diagonals AC and BD intersect at O.

We have,

$$\text{Area of rhombus } ABCD = 24 \text{ cm}^2$$

$$\Rightarrow \quad \frac{1}{2} \times AC \times BD = 24$$

$$\Rightarrow \quad \frac{1}{2} \times 4 \times BD = 24$$

$$\Rightarrow \quad 2 \times BD = 24$$

$$\Rightarrow \quad BD = 12 \text{ cm}$$

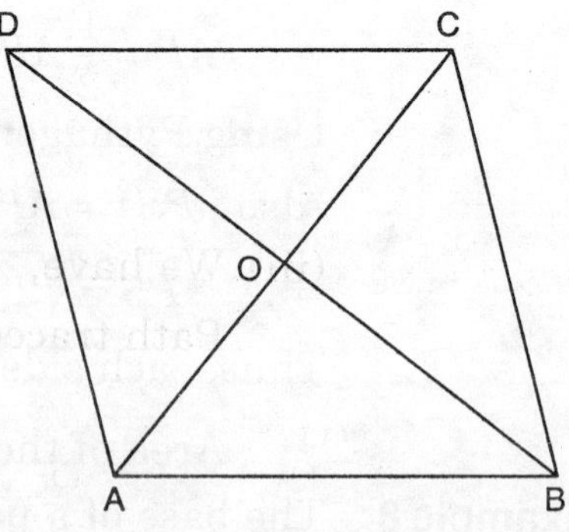

Fig. 20.13

Thus, we have $AC = 4$ cm and $BD = 12$ cm

$$\therefore \quad OA = \frac{1}{2}AC = 2 \text{ cm and } OB = \frac{1}{2}BD = 6 \text{ cm}$$

Since the diagonals of a rhombus bisect each other at right angle. Therefore, ΔOAB is right triangle, right angled at O.

Using Pythagoras theorem in ΔAOB, we have

$$AB^2 = OA^2 + OB^2$$

$$\Rightarrow \quad AB^2 = 2^2 + 6^2 = 40$$

$$\Rightarrow \quad AB = \sqrt{40} \text{ cm} = 2\sqrt{10} \text{ cm}$$

Hence, Perimeter of rhombus $ABCD = (4 \times 2\sqrt{10})$ cm $= 8\sqrt{10}$ cm

Example 11 An ant is moving around a few food particles of different shapes scattered on the floor. For which food particle would the ant have to take a longer round?

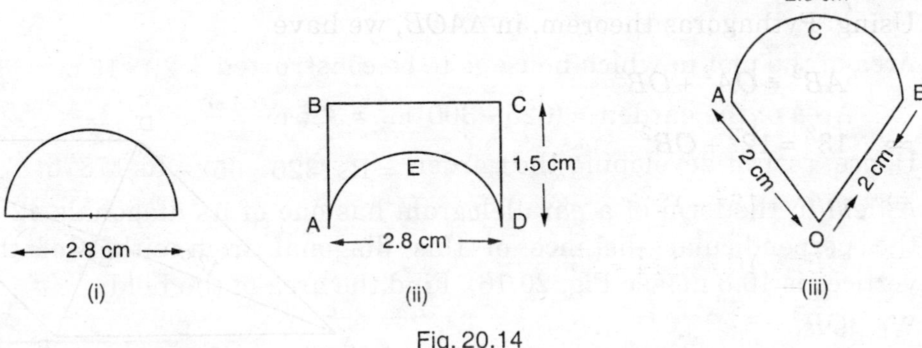

Fig. 20.14

Solution (i) We have,

Diameter of the semi-circular path $= 2.8$ cm

$\therefore \quad r =$ Radius of the semi-circular path $= 1.4$ cm

Path traced by the ant $= \pi r + 2r = \left(\frac{22}{7} \times 1.4 + 2 \times 1.4\right)$ cm

$= (22 \times 0.2 + 2.8)$ cm $= (4.4 + 2.8)$ cm $= 7.2$ cm

(ii) Clearly,

Path traced by the ant $= AB + BC + CD +$ arc AED

$= 1.5$ cm$+ 2.8$ cm$+ 1.5$ cm$+ \pi \times 1.4$ cm

$= \left(1.5 + 2.8 + 1.5 + \frac{22}{7} \times 1.4\right)$ cm

$= (5.8 + 4.4)$ cm $= 10.2$ cm

(iii) We have,

Path traced by the ant $= OA +$ arc $ACB + OB$

$= (2 + \pi \times 1.4 + 2)$ cm

$= \left(4 + \frac{22}{7} \times 1.4\right)$ cm $= (4 + 4.4)$ cm $= 8.4$ cm

Clearly, for (ii) food particle ant will have to take a longer round.

Example 12 Mrs Kaushik has a square plot as shown in Fig. 20.15. She wants to construct a house in the middle of the plot. A garden is developed around the house. Find the total cost of developing a garden around the house, if cost of developing a garden is Rs 55 per square metre.

Solution We have,

Area of the square plot $=(25)^2\ \text{m}^2 = 625\ \text{m}^2$

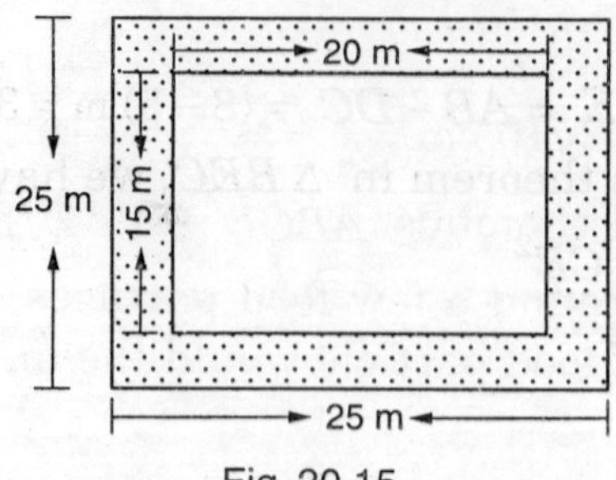

Fig. 20.15

Area of the plot in which house is to be constructed $= 20\times 15\ \text{m}^2 = 300\ \text{m}^2$

$\therefore$ Area of the garden $=(625-300)\ \text{m}^2 = 325\ \text{m}^2$

Hence, cost of developing the garden $=$ Rs $(325\times 55) =$ Rs 17875

Example 13 A field in the form of a parallelogram has one of its diagonals 42 m long and the perpendicular distance of this diagonal from either of the outlying vertices is 10.8 m (see Fig. 20.16). Find the area of the field.

Solution We have,

$AC = 42$ m and $DL = BM = 10.8$ m

$\therefore$ Area of the field $= 2\times$ Area of ΔACD

$$= 2\times\frac{1}{2}\times 42\times 10.8\ \text{m}^2$$

$$= 453.6\ \text{m}^2$$

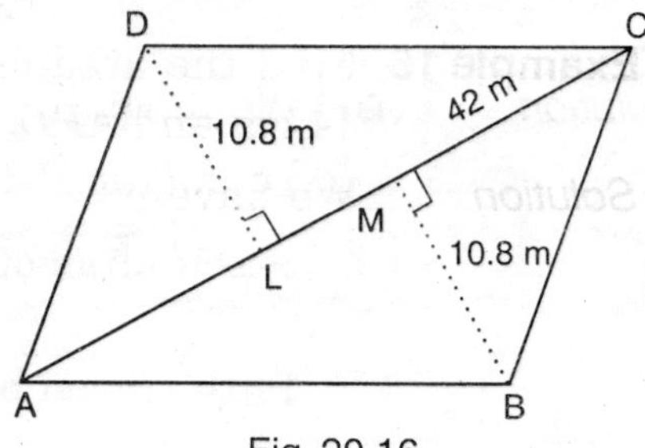

Fig. 20.16

Example 14 The diagonal of a quadrilateral is 20 m in length and the perpendiculars to it from the opposite vertices are 8.5 m and 11 m. Find the area of the quadrilateral.

Solution In quadrilateral $ABCD$, we have

$AC = 20$ m

Let $BL\perp AC$ and $DM\perp AC$ such that $BL = 8.5$ m and $DM = 11$ m

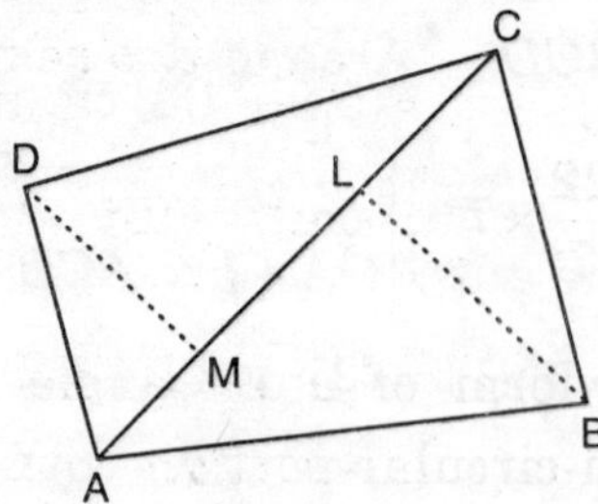

Fig. 20.17

$\therefore$ Area of quadrilateral $ABCD = \frac{1}{2}\times AC\times(BL+DM)$

$$= \left\{\frac{1}{2}\times 20\times(8.5+11)\right\}\text{m}^2$$

$$= (10\times 19.5)\ \text{m}^2 = 195\ \text{m}^2$$

Example 15 In quadrilateral $ABCD$ shown in Fig. 20.18, $AB \parallel DC$ and $AD \perp AB$. Also, $AB = 8\,\text{m}, DC = BC = 5\,\text{m}$. Find the area of the quadrilateral.

Solution We have,

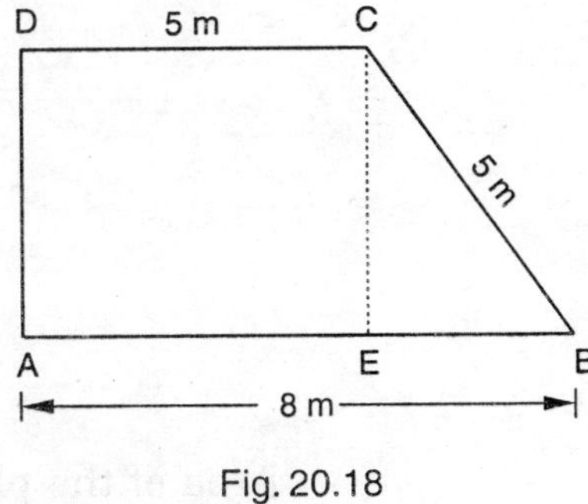

Fig. 20.18

$$BE = AB - AE = AB - DC = (8-5)\,\text{m} = 3\,\text{m}$$

Using Pythagoras theorem in ΔBEC, we have

$$BC^2 = BE^2 + CE^2$$

$$\Rightarrow \quad 5^2 = 3^2 + CE^2$$

$$\Rightarrow \quad CE^2 = 25 - 9$$

$$\Rightarrow \quad CE^2 = 16$$

$$\Rightarrow \quad CE = \sqrt{16}\,\text{m} = 4\,\text{m}$$

$\therefore$ Area of quadrilateral $ABCD$ = Area of rectangle $AECD$ + Area of ΔBEC

$$= AE \times CE + \frac{1}{2} \times BE \times CE$$

$$= (5 \times 4 + \frac{1}{2} \times 3 \times 4)\,\text{m}^2 = (20+6)\,\text{m}^2 = 26\,\text{m}^2$$

Example 16 Find the area of the shaded region in Fig. 20.19, if $ABCD$ is a square of side 14 cm and APD and BPC are semi-circles.

Solution We have,

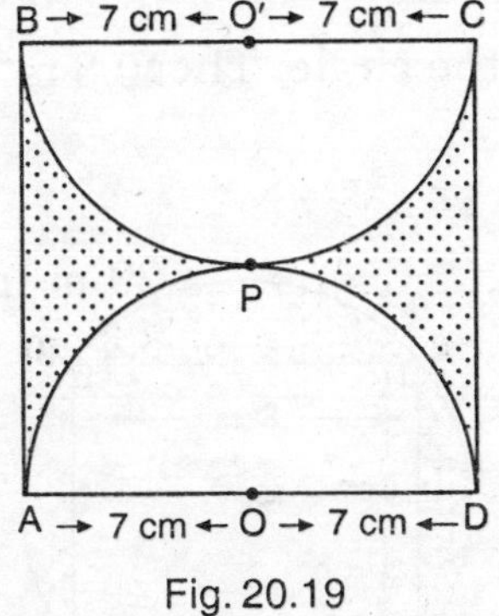

Fig. 20.19

Area of the shaded region

= Area of square $ABCD$ – Area of two semi-circles

$$= \left\{(14 \times 14) - 2\left(\frac{1}{2} \times \frac{22}{7} \times 7^2\right)\right\}\,\text{cm}^2 = (196 - 154)\,\text{cm}^2 = 42\,\text{cm}^2$$

Example 17 A paper is in the form of a rectangle $ABCD$ in which $AB = 20$ cm and BC = 14 cm. A semi-circular portion with BC as diameter is cut-off. Find the area of a remaining part.

Solution We have,

Length of the rectangle $ABCD$ = AB = 20 cm

Breadth of the rectangle $ABCD$ = BC = 14 cm

$\therefore$ Area of rectangle $ABCD = (20 \times 14)\,\text{cm}^2 = 280\,\text{cm}^2$

Diameter of the semi-circle $= BC = 14$ cm

$\therefore$ Radius of the semi-circle $= 7$ cm

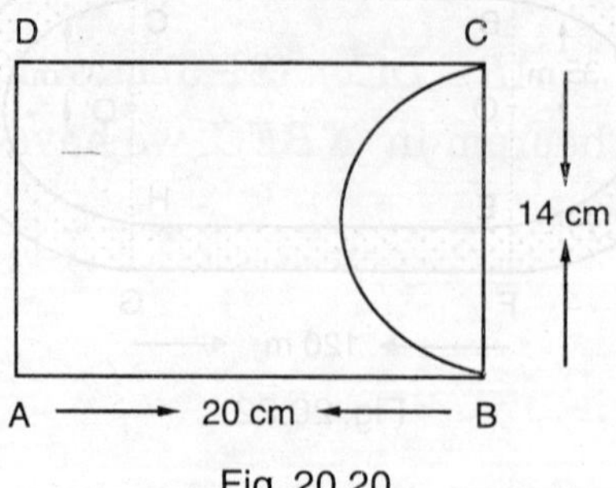

Fig. 20.20

Area of the semi-circular portion cut-off from the rectangle $ABCD$

$$= \frac{1}{2}(\pi r^2) = \left(\frac{1}{2} \times \frac{22}{7} \times 7^2\right) \text{cm}^2 = 77 \text{ cm}^2$$

$\therefore$ Area of the remaining part

= Area of rectangle $ABCD$ − Area of semi-circle $= (280 - 77)\,\text{cm}^2 = 203\,\text{cm}^2$

Example 18 In Figure 20.21, find the area of the shaded region [Use $\pi = 3.14$]

Solution Clearly, Diameter of the circle = Diagonal BD of rectangle $ABCD$

$\therefore$ Diameter $= BD = \sqrt{BC^2 + CD^2} = \sqrt{6^2 + 8^2}$ cm $= 10$ cm

Let r be the radius of the circle. Then,

$$r = \frac{10}{2} \text{ cm} = 5 \text{ cm}$$

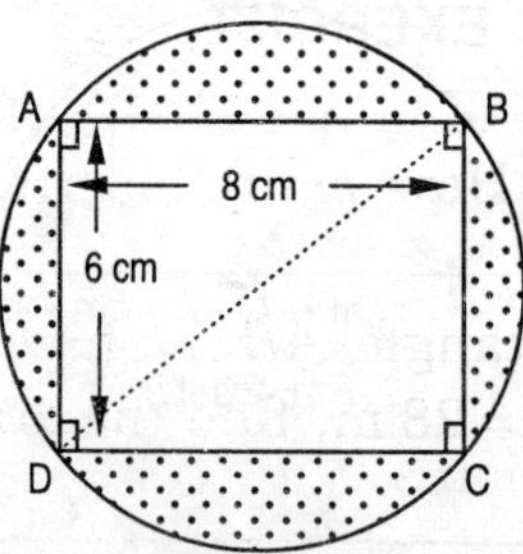

Fig. 20.21

Area of rectangle $ABCD = AB \times BC = (8 \times 6)\,\text{cm}^2 = 48\,\text{cm}^2$

Area of the circle $= \pi r^2 = 3.14 \times (5)^2\,\text{cm}^2 = 78.50\,\text{cm}^2$

Hence,

Area of the shaded region = Area of the circle − Area of rectangle $ABCD$

$= (78.50 - 48)\,\text{cm}^2 = 30.50\,\text{cm}^2$

Example 19 An athletic track 14 m wide consists of two straight sections 120 m long joining semi-circular ends whose inner radius is 35 m. Calculate the area of the shaded region.

Solution We have,

$OB = O'C = 35$ m and $AB = CD = 14$ m

$\therefore \quad OA = O'D = (35 + 14) \text{ m} = 49 \text{ m}$

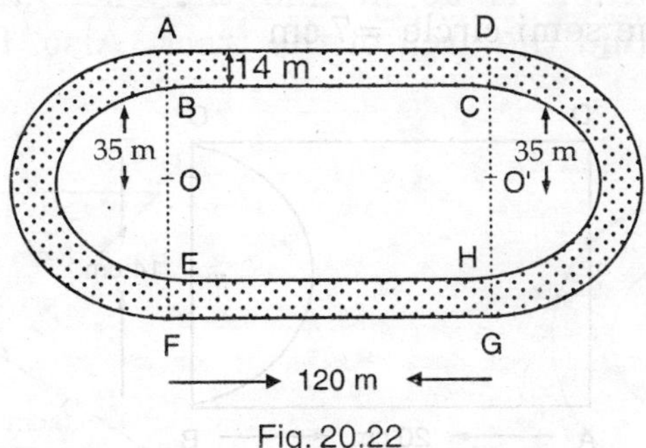

Fig. 20.22

Now,

Area of the shaded region
= Area of rectangle $ABCD$ + Area of rectangle $EFGH$
+ 2 {Area of the semi-circle with radius 49 m}
− 2 { Area of the semi circle with radius 35 m}

$$= (14 \times 120) + (14 \times 120) + 2\left\{\frac{1}{2} \times \frac{22}{7} \times (49)^2\right\} - 2\left\{\frac{1}{2} \times \frac{22}{7} \times (35)^2\right\} \text{ m}^2$$

$$= \left\{1680 + 1680 + \frac{22}{7}(49^2 - 35^2)\right\} \text{m}^2$$

$$= \left\{3360 + \frac{22}{7}(49 + 35)(49 - 35)\right\} \text{m}^2$$

$$= \left\{3360 + \frac{22}{7} \times 84 \times 14\right\} \text{m}^2 = \{3360 + 44 \times 84\} \text{m}^2 = 7056 \text{m}^2$$

Hence, the area of the shaded region is 7056 m^2.

EXERCISE 20.1

1. A flooring tile has the shape of a parallelogram whose base is 24 cm and the corresponding height is 10 cm. How many such tiles are required to cover a floor of area 1080 m^2?
2. A plot is in the form of a rectangle $ABCD$ having semi-circle on BC as shown in Fig. 20.23. If $AB = 60$ m and $BC = 28$ m, find the area of the plot.

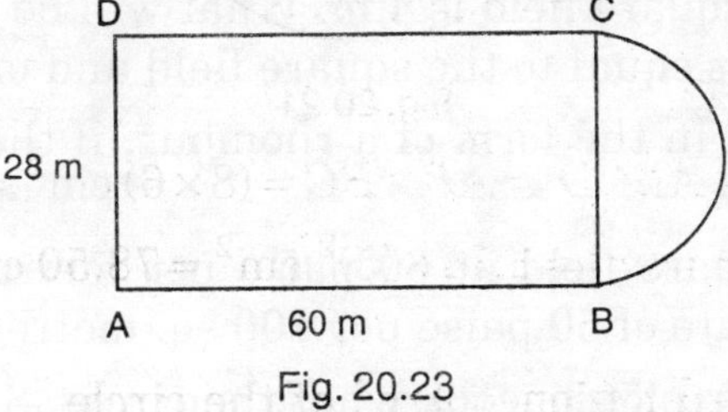

Fig. 20.23

3. A playground has the shape of a rectangle, with two semi-circles on its smaller sides as diameters, added to its outside. If the sides of the rectangle are 36 m and 24.5 m, find the area of the playground. (Take $\pi = 22/7$).
4. A rectangular piece is 20 m long and 15 m wide. From its four corners, quadrants of radii 3.5 m have been cut. Find the area of the remaining part.

5. The inside perimeter of a running track (shown in Fig. 20.24) is 400 m. The length of each of the straight portion is 90 m and the ends are semi-circles. If track is everywhere 14 m wide, find the area of the track. Also, find the length of the outer running track.

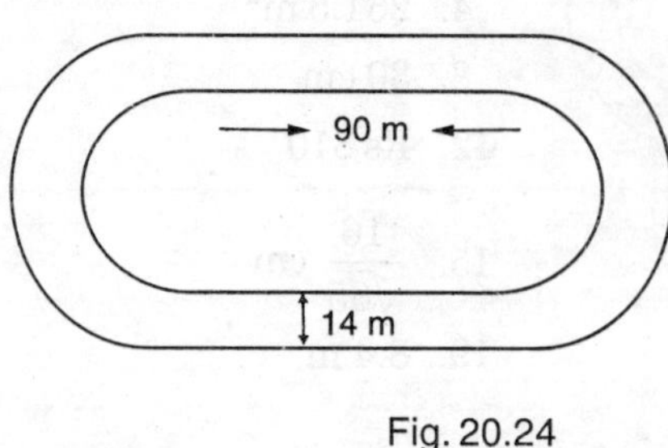

Fig. 20.24

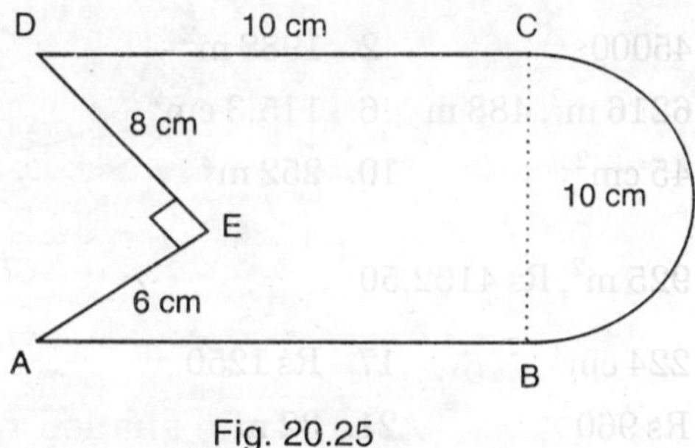

Fig. 20.25

6. Find the area of Fig. 20.25, in square cm, correct to one place of decimal. (Take $\pi = 22/7$)
7. The diameter of a wheel of a bus is 90 cm which makes 315 revolutions per minute. Determine its speed in kilometres per hour. [Use $\pi = 22/7$]
8. The area of a rhombus is 240 cm^2 and one of the diagonal is 16 cm. Find another diagonal.
9. The diagonals of a rhombus are 7.5 cm and 12 cm. Find its area.
10. The diagonal of a quadrilateral shaped field is 24 m and the perpendiculars dropped on it from the remaining opposite vertices are 8 m and 13 m. Find the area of the field.
11. Find the area of a rhombus whose side is 6 cm and whose altitude is 4 cm. If one of its diagonals is 8 cm long, find the length of the other diagonal.
12. The floor of a building consists of 3000 tiles which are rhombus shaped and each of its diagonals are 45 cm and 30 cm in length. Find the total cost of polishing the floor, if the cost per m^2 is Rs 4.
13. A rectangular grassy plot is 112 m long and 78 m broad. It has a gravel path 2.5 m wide all around it on the side. Find the area of the path and the cost of constructing it at Rs 4.50 per square metre.
14. Find the area of a rhombus, each side of which measures 20 cm and one of whose diagonals is 24 cm.
15. The length of a side of a square field is 4 m. What will be the altitude of the rhombus, if the area of the rhombus is equal to the square field and one of its diagonal is 2 m?
16. Find the area of the field in the form of a rhombus, if the length of each side be 14 cm and the altitude be 16 cm.
17. The cost of fencing a square field at 60 paise per metre is Rs 1200. Find the cost of reaping the field at the rate of 50 paise per 100 sq. metres.
18. In exchange of a square plot one of whose sides is 84 m, a man wants to buy a rectangular plot 144 m long and of the same area as of the square plot. Find the width of the rectangular plot.
19. The area of a rhombus is 84 m^2. If its perimeter is 40 m, then find its altitude.
20. A garden is in the form of a rhombus whose side is 30 metres and the corresponding altitude is 16 m. Find the cost of levelling the garden at the rate of Rs 2 per m^2.
21. A field in the form of a rhombus has each side of length 64 m and altitude 16 m. What is the side of a square field which has the same area as that of a rhombus?

22. The area of a rhombus is equal to the area of a triangle whose base and the corresponding altitude are 24.8 cm and 16.5 cm respectively. If one of the diagonals of the rhombus is 22 cm, find the length of the other diagonal.

ANSWERS

1. 45000	2. 1988 m^2	3. 1353.625 m^2	4. 261.5 m^2
5. 6216 m^2, 488 m	6. 115.3 cm^2	7. 53.46 km/h	8. 30 cm
9. 45 cm^2	10. 252 m^2	11. 24 cm^2, 3 cm	12. Rs 810
13. 925 m^2, Rs 4162.50		14. 384 cm^2	15. $\frac{16}{\sqrt{65}}$ cm
16. 224 cm^2	17. Rs 1250	18. 49 m	19. 8.4 m
20. Rs 960	21. 32 m	22. 18.6 cm	

20.3 AREA OF A TRAPEZIUM

A trapezium is a quadrilateral whose two sides are parallel. Fig. 20.26 is that of a trapezium $ABCD$ such that AB and CD are its two parallel sides while AD and BC are its non-parallel sides.

BASE *Each of the two parallel sides of a trapezium is called a base of the trapezium.*

HEIGHT OR ALTITUDE *The distance between the two bases (parallel sides) is called the height or altitude of the trapezium.*

Let h be the height of the trapezium $ABCD$. Then, $DL = h$.

Join AC. Clearly, AC divides the trapezium $ABCD$ into two triangles ABC and ACD.

$\therefore$ Area of trapezium $ABCD$ = Area of ΔABC + Area of ΔACD ...(i)

Since h is the altitude of trapezium $ABCD$. Therefore, it is also the altitude of ΔABC and ΔACD.

$\therefore$ Area of $\Delta ABC = \frac{1}{2} \times AB \times h$

and, Area of $\Delta ACD = \frac{1}{2} \times DC \times h$

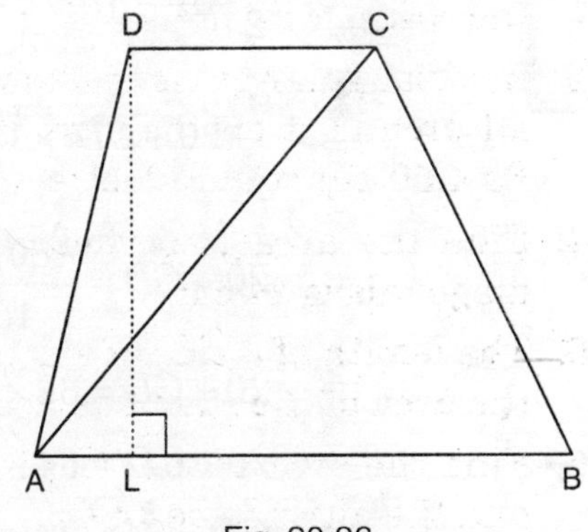

Fig. 20.26

Substituting these values in (i), we get

$$\text{Area of trapezium } ABCD = \frac{1}{2} \times AB \times h + \frac{1}{2} \times DC \times h$$

$$= \frac{1}{2} \times (AB + DC) \times h$$

$$= \frac{1}{2} \times (\text{Sum of the parallel sides}) \times (\text{Distance between parallel sides})$$

Hence, the area of a trapezium equals half the sum of parallel sides multiplied by the altitude.

Following examples will illustrate the use of the above formula.

ILLUSTRATIVE EXAMPLES

Example 1 Find the area of a trapezium whose parallel sides are of lengths 10 cm and 12 cm and the distance between them is 4 cm.

Solution We have,

Area of the trapezium $= \frac{1}{2} \times$ (Sum of the parallel sides) $\times$ (Distance between the parallel sides)

$$= \left\{\frac{1}{2} \times (10+12) \times 4\right\} \text{cm}^2 = \left(\frac{1}{2} \times 22 \times 4\right) \text{cm}^2 = 44 \text{ cm}^2$$

Example 2 The area of a trapezium is 440 cm^2. The lengths of the parallel sides are respectively 30 cm and 14 cm. Find the distance between them.

Solution Let the distance between the parallel sides be h cm. Then,

$$\text{Area} = 440 \text{ cm}^2$$

$$\Rightarrow \frac{1}{2} \times (30+14) \times h = 440$$

$$\Rightarrow \frac{1}{2} \times 44 \times h = 440 \Rightarrow 22 \times h = 440 \Rightarrow h = \frac{440}{22} = 20$$

Hence, the distance between the parallel sides is 20 cm.

Example 3 The area of a trapezium shaped field is 480 m^2, the height is 15 m and one of the parallel side is 20 m. Find the other side.

Solution We have,

$$\text{Area of trapezium } ABCD = 480 \text{ m}^2$$

$$\Rightarrow \frac{1}{2}(AB + CD) \times AL = 480$$

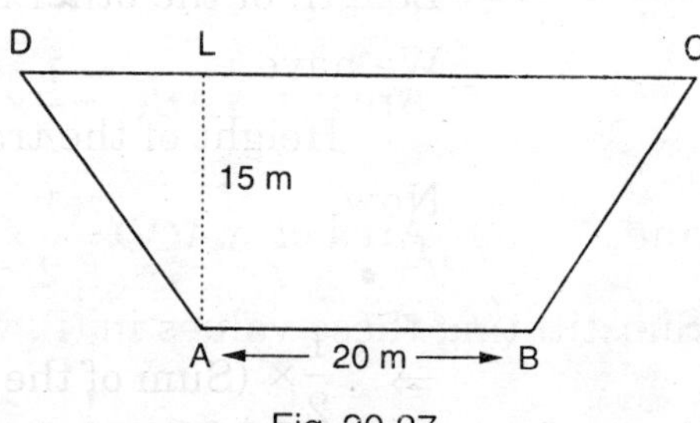

Fig. 20.27

$$\Rightarrow \frac{1}{2}(20 + CD) \times 15 = 480$$

$$\Rightarrow 20 + CD = \frac{480 \times 2}{15}$$

$$\Rightarrow 20 + CD = 32 \times 2$$

$$\Rightarrow 20 + CD = 64$$

$$\Rightarrow CD = 64 - 20 = 44$$

Hence, the other side of the trapezium is 44 m.

Example 4 Find the altitude of a trapezium, the sum of the lengths of whose bases is 6.5 cm and whose area is 26 cm^2.

Solution Let the altitude of the trapezium be h cm.

We have,

$$\text{Area of the trapezium} = 26 \text{ cm}^2$$

$$\Rightarrow \frac{1}{2} \times \text{(Sum of the bases)} \times \text{Altitude} = 26$$

$\Rightarrow \quad \frac{1}{2} \times 6.5 \times \text{Altitude} = 26$

$\Rightarrow \quad \text{Altitude} = \frac{26 \times 2}{6.5} \text{ cm} = 8 \text{ cm}$

Hence, the altitude of the trapezium is 8 cm.

Example 5 Find the sum of the lengths of the bases of a trapezium whose altitude is 11 cm and whose area is 0.55 m^2.

Solution We have,

$$\text{Altitude of the trapezium} = 11 \text{ cm} = \frac{11}{100} \text{ m},$$

$$\text{Area of the trapezium} = 0.55 \text{ m}^2$$

Now,

$$\text{Area} = 0.55 \text{ m}^2$$

$\Rightarrow \quad \frac{1}{2} \times (\text{Sum of the lengths of bases}) \times \text{Altitude} = 0.55$

$\Rightarrow \quad \frac{1}{2} \times \text{Sum of the lengths of bases} \times \frac{11}{100} = 0.55$

$\Rightarrow \quad \text{Sum of the lengths of bases} = \frac{0.55 \times 200}{11} \text{ m} = 10 \text{ m}$

Hence, the sum of the lengths of bases of the trapezium is 10 m.

Example 6 The area of the trapezium is 105 cm^2 and its height is 7 cm. If one of the parallel sides is longer than the other by 6 cm, find the two parallel sides.

Solution Let the length of the smaller parallel side be x cm. Then,

Length of the other side $= (x + 6)$ cm

We have,

$$\text{Height of the trapezium} = 7 \text{ cm, Area of the trapezium} = 105 \text{ cm}^2$$

Now,

$$\text{Area of the trapezium} = 105 \text{ cm}^2$$

$\Rightarrow \quad \frac{1}{2} \times (\text{Sum of the parallel sides}) \times \text{Height} = 105$

$\Rightarrow \quad \frac{1}{2} \times (x + 6 + x) \times 7 = 105$

$\Rightarrow \quad \frac{1}{2} \times (2x + 6) \times 7 = 105$

$\Rightarrow \quad 2x + 6 = \frac{105 \times 2}{7} \Rightarrow 2x + 6 = 30 \Rightarrow 2x = 24 \Rightarrow x = 12.$

Hence, the lengths of parallel sides are 12 cm and $(12 + 6)$ cm $= 18$ cm.

Example 7 The area of a trapezium is 180 cm^2 and its height is 12 cm. If one of the parallel sides is double that of the other, find the two parallel sides.

Solution Let the length of the smaller parallel side be x cm. Then, length of the larger parallel side is $2x$ cm.

We have,

Area of the trapezium $= 180 \text{ cm}^2$, Height of the trapezium $= 12$ cm

Now,

$$\text{Area of the trapezium} = 180 \text{ cm}^2$$

$\Rightarrow \quad \frac{1}{2} \times (\text{Sum of the parallel sides}) \times \text{Height} = 180$

$\Rightarrow \quad \frac{1}{2} \times (x + 2x) \times 12 = 180$

$\Rightarrow \quad 6(x + 2x) = 180$

$\Rightarrow \quad 18x = 180$

$\Rightarrow \quad x = \frac{180}{18} = 10 \text{ cm}$

Hence, the lengths of the parallel sides are 10 cm and 20 cm.

Example 8 The parallel sides of a trapezium are 20 cm and 10 cm. Its non-parallel sides are both equal, each being 13 cm. Find the area of the trapezium.

Solution Let $ABCD$ be a trapezium such that $AB = 20$ cm, $CD = 10$ cm and $AD = BC = 13$ cm.

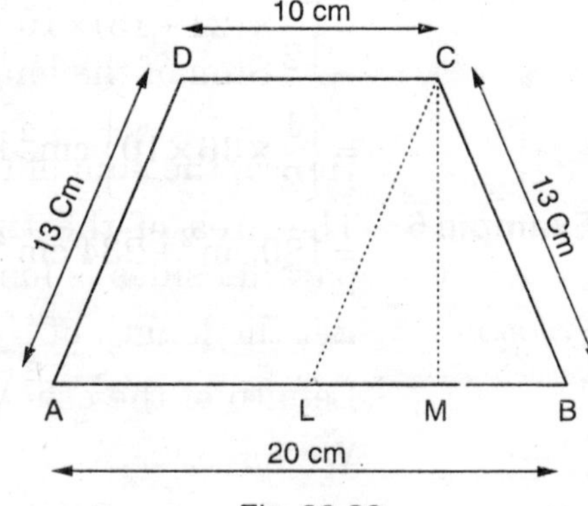

Fig. 20.28

Draw $CL \parallel AD$ and $CM \perp AB$.

Now, $CL \parallel AD$ and $CD \parallel AB$.

$\therefore \quad ALCD$ is a parallelogram.

$\Rightarrow \quad AL = CD = 10$ cm and $CL = AD = 13$ cm

In ΔCLB, we have

$CL = CB = 13$ cm

$\therefore \quad \Delta CLB$ is an isosceles triangle.

$\Rightarrow \quad LM = MB = \frac{1}{2} BL = \frac{1}{2} \times 10 \text{ cm} = 5 \text{ cm} \quad [\because BL = AB - AL = (20 - 10) \text{ cm} = 10 \text{ cm}]$

Applying Pythagoras theorem in ΔCLM, we have

$CL^2 = CM^2 + LM^2$

$\Rightarrow \quad 13^2 = CM^2 + 5^2$

$\Rightarrow \quad CM^2 = 169 - 25 = 144$

$\Rightarrow \quad CM = \sqrt{144} = 12$

$\therefore \quad \text{Area of } \Delta CLB = \frac{1}{2} \times BL \times CM = \frac{1}{2} \times 10 \times 12 \text{ cm}^2 = 60 \text{ cm}^2$

Area of parallelogram $ALCD = AL \times CM = (10 \times 12) \text{ cm}^2 = 120 \text{ cm}^2$

Hence,

Area of trapezium $ABCD =$ Area of parallelogram $ALCD$ + Area of ΔCLB

$$= (120 + 60) \text{ cm}^2 = 180 \text{ cm}^2$$

Example 9 If the perimeter of a trapezium be 52 cm, its non-parallel sides are equal to 10 cm each and its altitude is 8 cm, find the area of the trapezium.

Solution We have,

Perimeter of the trapezium $= 52$ cm, Altitude of the trapezium $= 8$ cm

$\Rightarrow$ Sum of the parallel sides + Sum of the non-parallel sides $= 52$ cm

$\Rightarrow$ Sum of the parallel sides $+ 2 \times 10 = 52$

$\Rightarrow$ Sum of the parallel sides $= (52 - 20)$ cm $= 32$ cm

$\therefore$ Area of the trapezium $= \frac{1}{2} \times$ (Sum of the parallel sides) $\times$ Altitude

$$= \frac{1}{2} \times 32 \times 8 \text{ cm}^2 = 128 \text{ cm}^2$$

Example 10 Find the area of Fig. 20.29.

Solution We have,

Area of the given figure

= Area of trapezium $ABCD$ + Area of trapezium $CDFE$

$$= \left\{\frac{1}{2} \times (21 + 15) \times 10\right\} \text{cm}^2 + \left\{\frac{1}{2} \times (15 + 24) \times 12\right\} \text{cm}^2$$

$$= \left\{\frac{1}{2} \times 36 \times 10\right\} \text{cm}^2 + \left\{\frac{1}{2} \times 39 \times 12\right\} \text{cm}^2$$

$$= 180 \text{ cm}^2 + 234 \text{ cm}^2 = 414 \text{ cm}^2$$

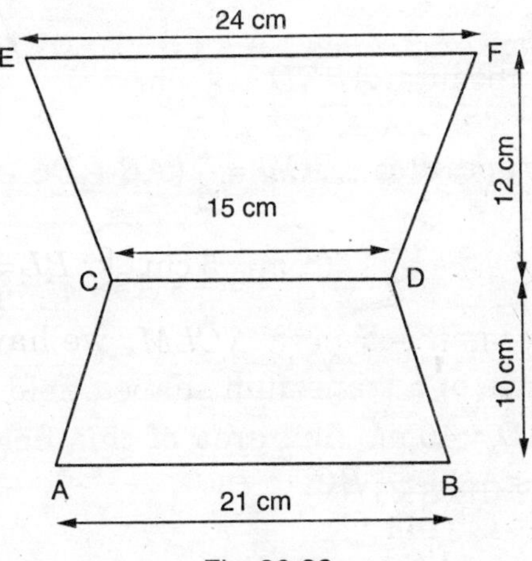

Fig. 20.29

Example 11 The area of a trapezium is 180 cm^2 and its height is 9 cm. If one of the parallel sides is longer than the other by 6 cm, find the two parallel sides.

Solution Let one of the parallel sides be of length x cm. Then, the length of the other parallel side is $(x + 6)$ cm.

$\therefore$ Area of the trapezium $= \left\{\frac{1}{2} \times (x + x + 6) \times 9\right\} \text{cm}^2$

$$= \left\{\frac{1}{2} \times (2x + 6) \times 9\right\} \text{cm}^2 = (9x + 27) \text{ cm}^2$$

But, area of the trapezium is given as 180 cm^2.

$\therefore \quad 9x + 27 = 180 \Rightarrow 9x = 180 - 27 = 153 \Rightarrow x = \dfrac{153}{9} = 17$

Thus, the two parallel sides are of lengths 17 cm and (17 + 6) cm = 23 cm

Example 12 In the adjoining figure $AB \parallel DC$ and DA is perpendicular to AB. Further, $DC = 7$ cm, $CB = 10$ cm and $AB = 13$ cm. Find the area of the quadrilateral $ABCD$.

Solution Draw CM perpendicular from C to AB. Clearly, $AMCD$ is a rectangle.

$\therefore \quad AM = DC$

$\Rightarrow \quad AM = 7 \text{ cm} \qquad [\because DC = 7 \text{ cm}]$

$\Rightarrow \quad AB - BM = 7$

$\Rightarrow \quad 13 - BM = 7$

$\Rightarrow \quad BM = (13 - 7) \text{ cm} = 6 \text{ cm}$

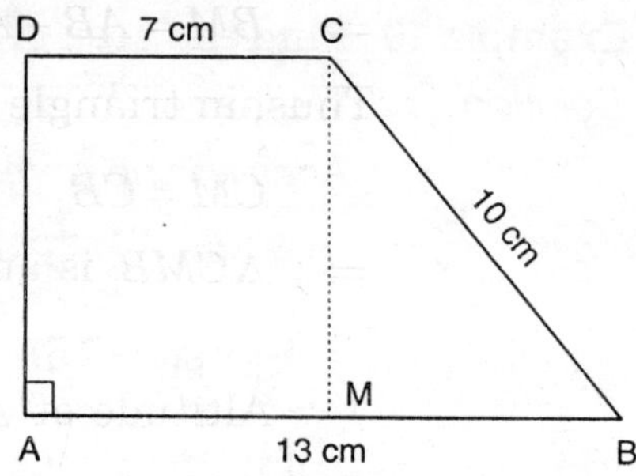

Fig. 20.30

Applying Pythagoras Theorem, in right angled triangle BMC, we have

$BC^2 = BM^2 + CM^2$

$\Rightarrow \quad 10^2 = 6^2 + CM^2$

$\Rightarrow \quad CM^2 = 100 - 36 = 64$

$\Rightarrow \quad CM = 8 \text{ cm}$

$\Rightarrow$ Height of trapezium $ABCD = 8$ cm

Hence, area of trapezium $ABCD = \dfrac{1}{2}(AB + DC) \times CM$

$= \dfrac{1}{2} \times (13 + 7) \times 8 \text{ cm}^2 = 80 \text{ cm}^2$

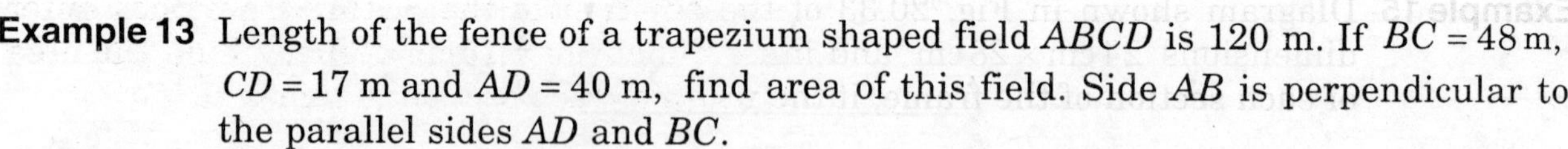

Example 13 Length of the fence of a trapezium shaped field $ABCD$ is 120 m. If $BC = 48$ m, $CD = 17$ m and $AD = 40$ m, find area of this field. Side AB is perpendicular to the parallel sides AD and BC.

Solution We have,

$AB + BC + CD + AD = 120 \text{ m}$

$\Rightarrow \quad AB + 48 + 17 + 40 = 120$

$\Rightarrow \quad AB + 105 = 120$

$\Rightarrow \quad AB = 120 - 105$

$\Rightarrow \quad AB = 15 \text{ m}$

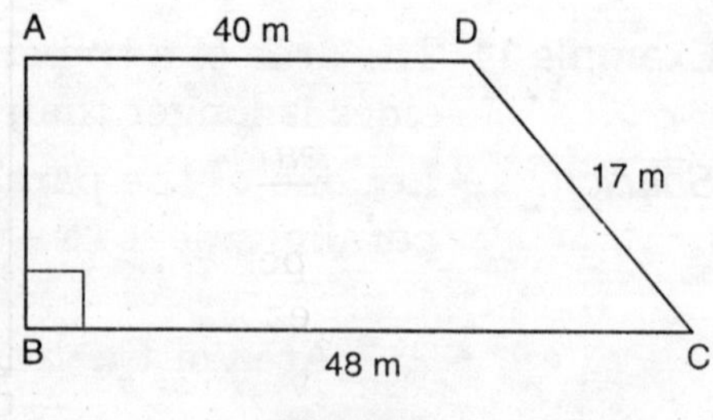

Fig. 20.31

Since AB is perpendicular to the parallel sides AD and BC. Therefore, AB is the altitude (height) of the trapezium.

Area of the field $= \frac{1}{2}(BC + AD) \times AB = \frac{1}{2}(48 + 40) \times 15\,\text{m}^2 = 44 \times 15\,\text{m}^2 = 660\,\text{m}^2$

Example 14 The parallel sides DC and AB of a trapezium are 12 cm and 36 cm respectively. Its non-parallel sides are each equal to 15 cm. Find the area of the trapezium.

Solution Through C, draw a line parallel to DA meeting AB in M.

Clearly, $AMCD$ is a parallelogram.

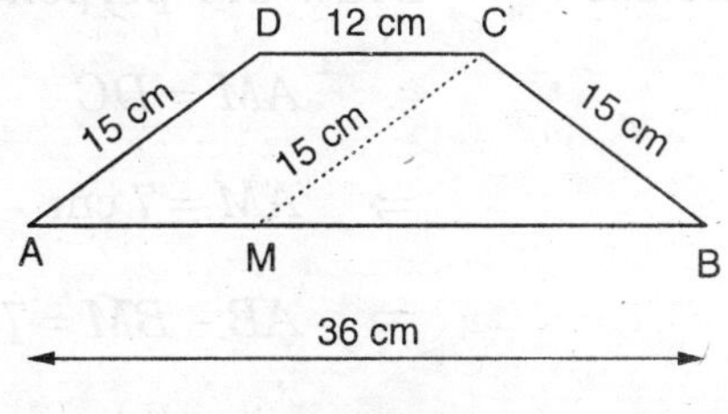

Fig. 20.32

$\therefore \quad CM = AD$ and $AM = DC$

$\Rightarrow \quad CM = 15$ cm and $AM = 12$ cm

$\Rightarrow \quad BM = AB - AM = (36 - 12)$ cm $= 24$ cm

Thus, in triangle CMB, we have

$CM = CB$

$\Rightarrow \quad \Delta CMB$ is an isosceles triangle.

$\therefore \quad$ Altitude of $\Delta CMB = \sqrt{(\text{Equal side})^2 - \left(\frac{1}{2} \times \text{base}\right)^2}$

$\Rightarrow \quad$ Altitude of $\Delta CMB = \sqrt{(15)^2 - \left(\frac{1}{2} \times 24\right)^2}$

$\Rightarrow \quad$ Altitude of $\Delta CMB = \sqrt{225 - 144} = \sqrt{81}$ cm $= 9$ cm

$\Rightarrow \quad$ Altitude of trapezium $ABCD = 9$ cm

Hence, area of trapezium $ABCD = \frac{1}{2} \times (AB + CD) \times \text{Altitude}$

$= \left\{\frac{1}{2} \times (36 + 12) \times 9\right\} \text{cm}^2 = (24 \times 9)\,\text{cm}^2 = 216\,\text{cm}^2$.

Example 15 Diagram shown in Fig. 20.33 of the adjacent of the picture frame has outer dimensions $24\,\text{cm} \times 28\,\text{cm}$ and inner dimensions $16\,\text{cm} \times 20\,\text{cm}$. Find the area of each section of the frame, if the width of each section is same.

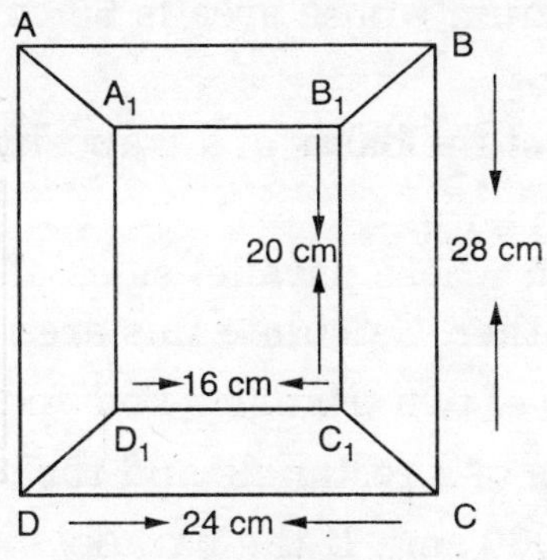

Fig. 20.33

Solution We have,

Area of section $AB\,B_1A_1$ = Area of section $CD\,D_1C_1$

$$= \frac{1}{2}(24+16)\times 4 \text{ cm}^2$$

$$= 20\times 4 \text{ cm}^2 = 80 \text{ cm}^2$$

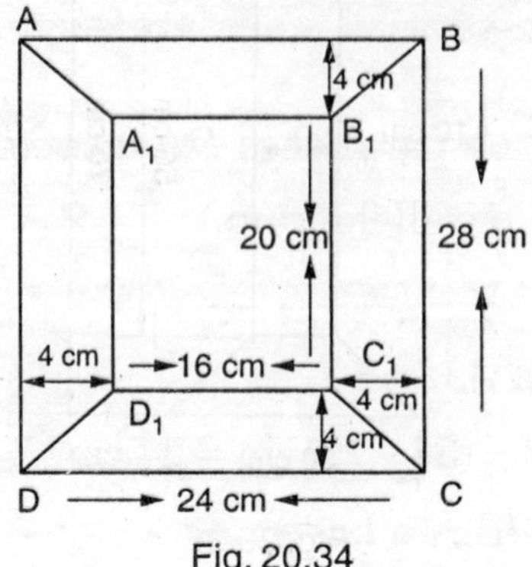

Fig. 20.34

Area of section $AD\,D_1A_1$ = Area of section $BC\,C_1B_1$

$$= \frac{1}{2}(28+20)\times 4 \text{ cm}^2 = 24\times 4 \text{ cm}^2 = 96 \text{ cm}^2$$

Area of section $A_1B_1C_1D_1 = A_1B_1 \times B_1C_1 = 16\times 20 \text{ cm}^2 = 320 \text{ cm}^2$

EXERCISE 20.2

1. Find the area, in square metres, of the trapezium whose bases and altitudes are as under:
   (i) bases = 12 dm and 20 dm, altitude = 10 dm
   (ii) bases = 28 cm and 3 dm, altitude = 25 cm
   (iii) bases = 8 m and 60 dm, altitude = 40 dm
   (iv) bases = 150 cm and 30 dm, altitude = 9 dm.
2. Find the area of trapezium with base 15 cm and height 8 cm, if the side parallel to the given base is 9 cm long.
3. Find the area of a trapezium whose parallel sides are of length 16 dm and 22 dm and whose height is 12 dm.
4. Find the height of a trapezium, the sum of the lengths of whose bases (parallel sides) is 60 cm and whose area is 600 cm^2.
5. Find the altitude of a trapezium whose area is 65 cm^2 and whose bases are 13 cm and 26 cm.
6. Find the sum of the lenghts of the bases of a trapezium whose area is 4.2 m^2 and whose height is 280 cm.
7. Find the area of a trapezium whose parallel sides of lengths 10 cm and 15 cm are at a distance of 6 cm from each other. Calculate this area as
   (i) the the sum of the areas of two triangles and one rectangle.
   (ii) the difference of the area of a rectangle and the sum of the areas of two triangles.
8. The area of a trapezium is 960 cm^2. If the parallel sides are 34 cm and 46 cm, find the distance between them.

9. Find the area of Fig. 20.35 as the sum of the areas of two trapezium and a rectangle.

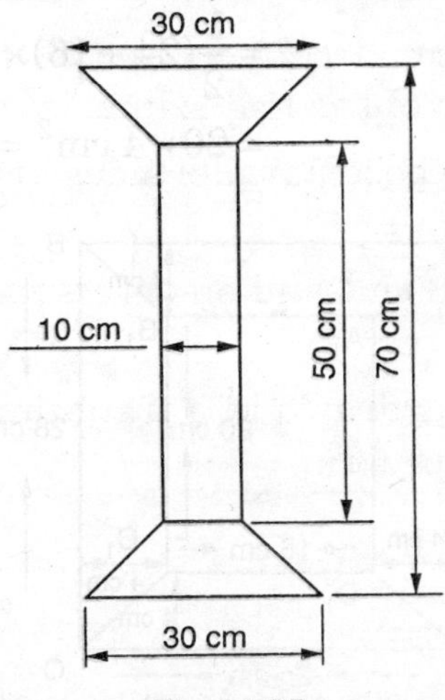

Fig. 20.35

10. Top surface of a table is trapezium in shape. Find its area if its parallel sides are 1 m and 1.2 m and perpendicular distance between them is 0.8 m.

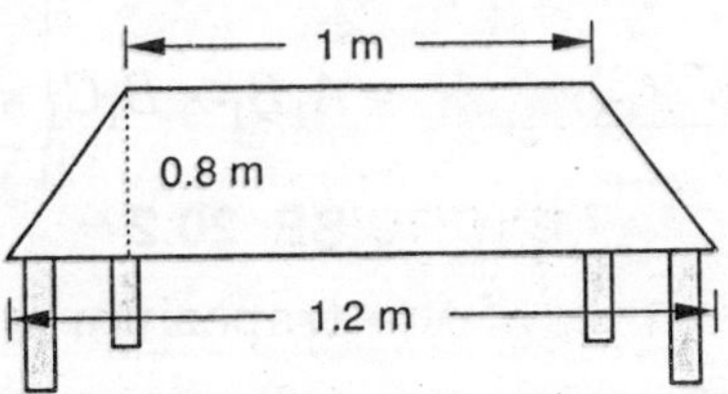

Fig. 20.36

11. The cross-section of a canal is a trapezium in shape. If the canal is 10 m wide at the top 6 m wide at the bottom and the area of cross-section is 72 m^2 determine its depth.

12. The area of a trapezium is 91 cm^2 and its height is 7 cm. If one of the parallel sides is longer than the other by 8 cm, find the two parallel sides.

13. The area of a trapezium is 384 cm^2. Its parallel sides are in the ratio 3 : 5 and the perpendicular distance between them is 12 cm. Find the length of each one of the parallel sides.

14. Mohan wants to buy a trapezium shaped field. Its side along the river is parallel and twice the side along the road. If the area of this field is 10500 m^2 and the perpendicular distance between the two parallel sides is 100 m, find the length of the side along the river.

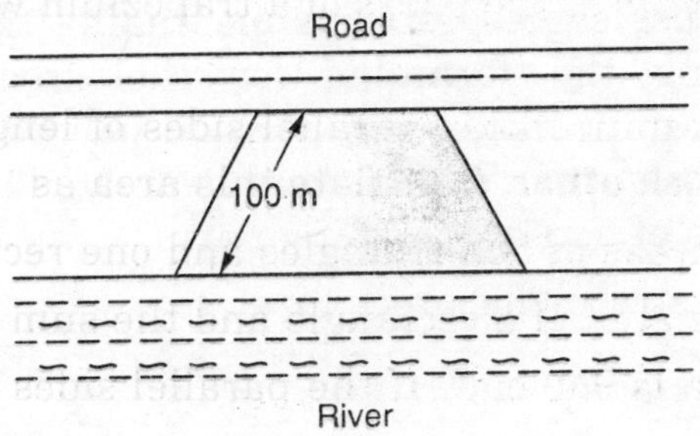

Fig. 20.37

15. The area of a trapezium is 1586 cm^2 and the distance between the parallel sides is 26 cm. If one of the parallel sides is 38 cm, find the other.
16. The parallel sides of a trapezium are 25 cm and 13 cm; its nonparallel sides are equal, each being 10 cm, find the area of the trapezium.
17. Find the area of a trapezium whose parallel sides are 25 cm, 13 cm and the other sides are 15 cm each.
18. If the area of a trapezium is 28 cm^2 and one of its parallel sides is 6 cm, find the other parallel side if its altitude is 4 cm.
19. In Fig. 20.38, a parallelogram is drawn in a trapezium, the area of the parallelogram is 80 cm^2, find the area of the trapezium.

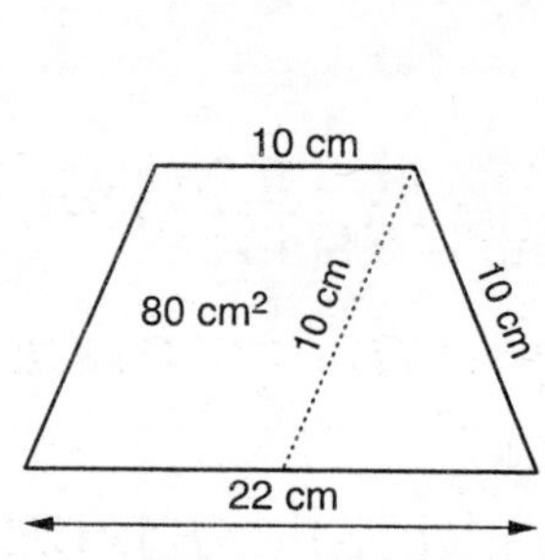

Fig. 20.38

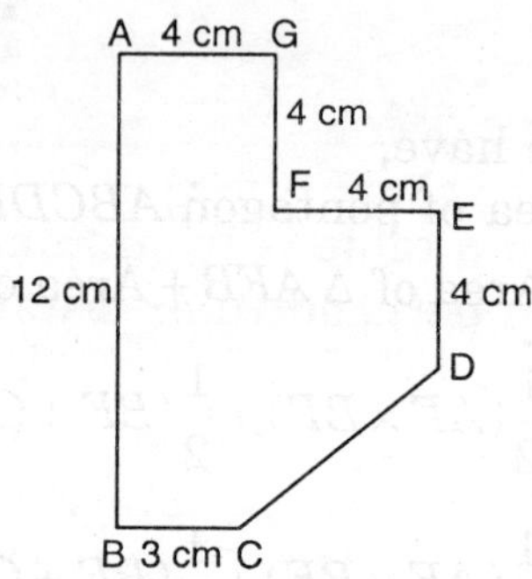

Fig. 20.39

20. Find the area of the field shown in Fig. 20.39 by dividing it into a square, a rectangle and a trapezium.

ANSWERS

1. (i) 1.6 m^2 (ii) 0.0725 m^2 (iii) 28 m^2 (iv) 2.025 m^2 2. 96 cm^2 3. 2.28 m^2
4. 20 cm 5. $\frac{10}{3}$ cm 6. 3 m. 7. 75 cm^2 8. 24 cm 9. 1300 cm^2
10. 0.88 m^2 11. 9 m 12. 17 cm, 9 cm 13. 24 cm, 40 cm
14. 140 m 15. 84 cm 16. 152 cm^2 17. $57\sqrt{21}$ cm^2
18. 8 cm 19. 128 cm^2 20. 70 cm^2

20.4 AREA OF A POLYGON

In this section, we will discuss some problems on finding the areas of some regular and irregular polygons by using the formulae for the areas of a triangle, rectangle, parallelogram and a trapezium. Infact, given polygon will be divided into non-overlapping rectilinear plane figures whose areas can be found easily. The area of the polygon will be equal to the sum of the areas of non-overlapping parts.

Following examples will illustrate the procedure.

ILLUSTRATIVE EXAMPLES

Example 1 Find the area of the pentagon $ABCDE$ shown in Fig. 20.40, if $AD = 8$ cm, $AH = 6$ cm, $AG = 4$ cm, $AF = 3$ cm, $BF = 2$ cm, $CH = 3$ cm and $EG = 2.5$ cm.

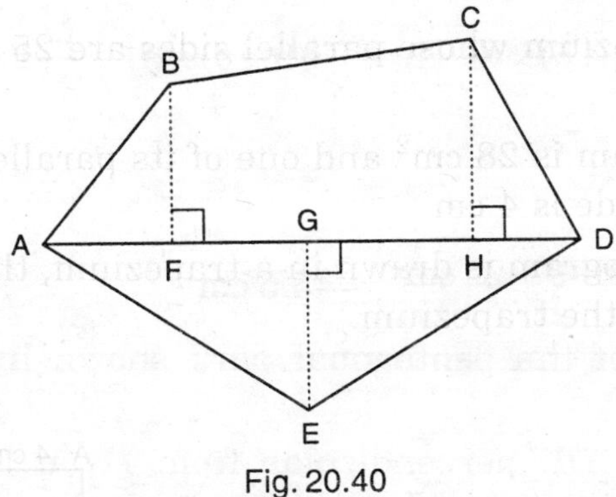

Fig. 20.40

Solution We have,

Area of pentagon $ABCDE$

$= \text{Area of } \Delta AFB + \text{Area of trapezium } FBCH + \text{Area of } \Delta CHD + \text{Area of } \Delta ADE$

$$= \frac{1}{2}(AF \times BF) + \frac{1}{2}(BF + CH) \times FH + \frac{1}{2}(DH \times CH) + \frac{1}{2}(AD \times GE)$$

$$= \frac{1}{2}(AF \times BF) + \frac{1}{2}(BF + CH) \times (AH - AF) + \frac{1}{2}\{(AD - AH) \times CH)\} + \frac{1}{2}(AD \times GE)$$

$$= \frac{1}{2}(3 \times 2) + \frac{1}{2}(2 + 3) \times (6 - 3) + \frac{1}{2}(8 - 6) \times 3 + \frac{1}{2}(8 \times 2.5)$$

$$= \left(3 + \frac{15}{2} + 3 + 10\right) \text{cm}^2 = \frac{47}{2} \text{cm}^2 = 23.5 \text{ cm}^2$$

Example 2 Find the area of the hexagon shown in Fig. 20.41 if $MP = 9$ cm, $MD = 7$ cm, $MC = 6$ cm, $MB = 4$ cm, $MA = 2$ cm, $AN = 3$ cm, $OC = 5$ cm, $DQ = 2$ cm and $BR = 4$ cm.

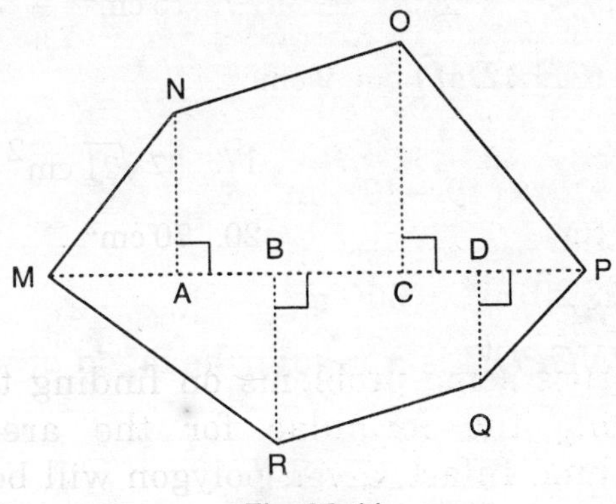

Fig. 20.41

Solution We have,

Area of hexagon $MNOPQR$

$= \text{Area of } \Delta MAN + \text{Area of trapezium } CONA + \text{Area of } \Delta PCO + \text{Area of } \Delta MBR$
$+ \text{Area of trapezium } BDQR + \text{Area of } \Delta PDQ$

$$=\frac{1}{2}(MA\times AN)+\frac{1}{2}(AN+OC)\times AC+\frac{1}{2}(PC\times CO)+\frac{1}{2}(MB\times BR)+\frac{1}{2}(BR+DQ)\times BD+\frac{1}{2}(DP\times DQ)$$

$$=\left[\frac{1}{2}(2\times 3)+\frac{1}{2}(3+5)\times(6-2)+\frac{1}{2}\{(9-6)\times 5\}+\frac{1}{2}(4\times 4)+\frac{1}{2}(4+2)\times(7-4)+\frac{1}{2}(9-7)\times 2\right]\text{cm}^2$$

$$=\left(3+16+\frac{15}{2}+8+9+2\right)\text{cm}^2=45.5\text{ cm}^2$$

Example 3 Find the area of the pentagonal park shown in Fig. 20.42 in two different ways:

Solution *Method I*: Draw DL perpendicular from D on AB. This divides the pentagonal park into two trapeziums.

$\therefore$ Area of the park

= Area of trapezium $ALDE$ + Area of trapezium $LBCD$

$=\frac{1}{2}(AE+DL)\times AL+\frac{1}{2}(DL+CB)\times LB$

$=\frac{1}{2}(20+40)\times AL+\frac{1}{2}(40+20)\times LB$

$=30AL+30LB$

$=30\,(AL+LB)$

$=30\times AB$

$=30\times 20\text{ m}^2$

$=600\text{ m}^2$

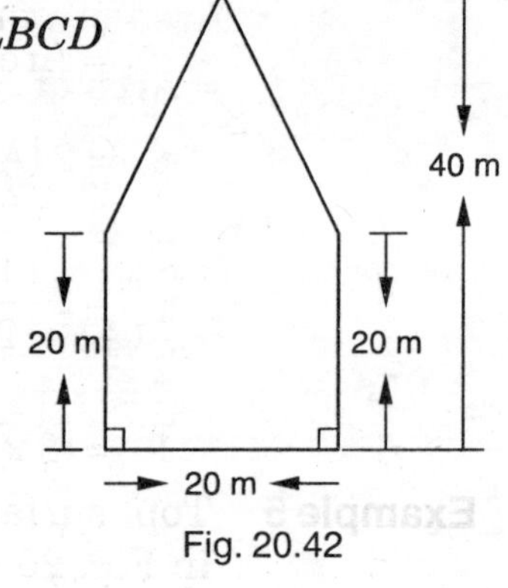

Fig. 20.42

Method II: Join CE. This divides the pentagonal park into two parts, a triangle and a square

$\therefore$ Area of the park

= Area of square $ABCE$ + Area of ΔCDE

$=(20)^2+\frac{1}{2}(CE\times DM)$

$=\left\{400+\frac{1}{2}\times 20\times(40-20)\right\}\text{m}^2$

$=(400+10\times 20)\text{m}^2=600\text{ m}^2$

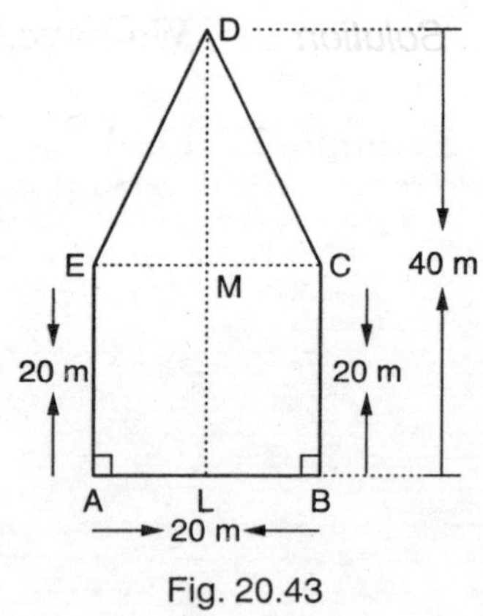

Fig. 20.43

Example 4 In fig. 20.44, $MNOPQR$ is a regular hexagon of side 5 cm. Find its area in two different ways:

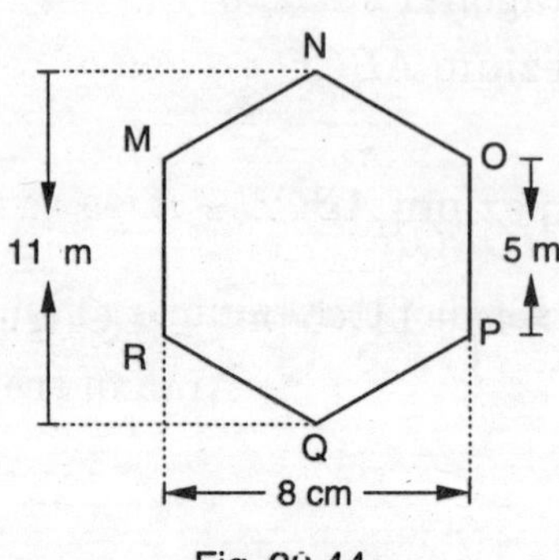

Fig. 20.44

Solution *Method I*: If we join NQ, it divides the hexagon into two trapeziums of equal area as shown in Fig. 20.45

$\therefore$ Area of hexagon $MNOPQR$

$= 2$ Area of trapezium $MNQR$

$$= 2\left\{\frac{1}{2}(MR + NQ)\ RS\right\}$$

$$= 2\left\{\frac{1}{2}(5 + 11) \times 4\right\} \text{cm}^2$$

$$= 16 \times 4 \text{ cm}^2 = 64 \text{ cm}^2$$

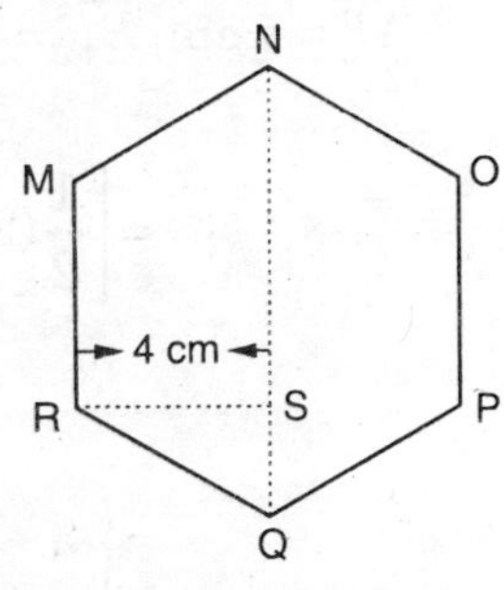

Fig. 20.45

Method II: Join MO and RP. The hexagon is divided into two triangles of equal area and a rectangle.

$\therefore$ Area of hexagon $MNOPQR$

$= $ Area of ΔMNO + Area of rectangle $MOPR$ + Area of ΔPQR

$= 2$ (Area of ΔMNO) + Area of rectangle $MOPR$

$$= 2\left\{\frac{1}{2}(OM \times NT)\right\} + MO \times OP$$

$$= (8 \times 3 + 8 \times 5) \text{ cm}^2 = 64 \text{ cm}^2$$

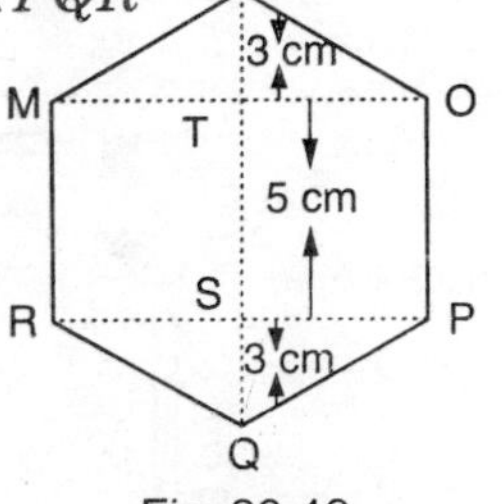

Fig. 20.46

Example 5 Top surface of a raised platform is in the shape of a regular octagon as shown in Fig. 20.47. Find the area of the octagonal surface?

Solution We have,

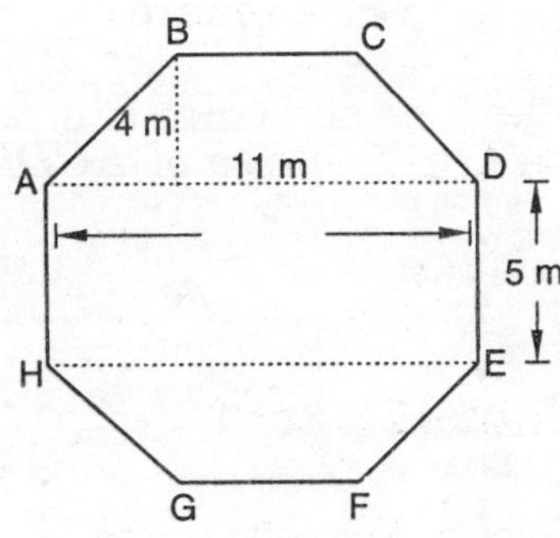

Fig. 20.47

Area of the octagonal surface

$= $ Area of trapezium $ABCD$ + Area of rectangle $ADEH$ + Area of trapezium $EFGH$

$= 2$ Area of trapezium $ABCD$ + Area of rectangle $ADEH$

$$= \left[2\left\{\frac{1}{2}(11 + 5) \times 4\right\} + 11 \times 5\right] \text{m}^2 = (16 \times 4 + 11 \times 5) \text{ m}^2 = (64 + 55) \text{ m}^2 = 119 \text{ m}^2$$

EXERCISE 20.3

1. Find the area of the pentagon shown in fig. 20.48, if $AD = 10$ cm, $AG = 8$ cm, $AH = 6$ cm, $AF = 5$ cm, $BF = 5$ cm, $CG = 7$ cm and $EH = 3$ cm.

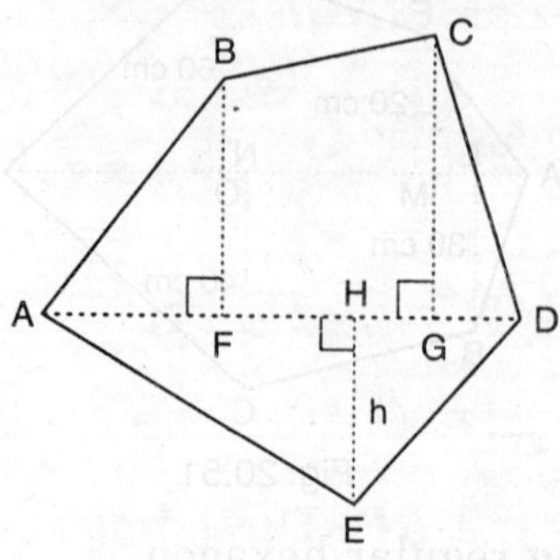

Fig. 20.48

2. Find the area enclosed by each of the following figures [Fig. 20.49 (i)-(iii)] as the sum of the areas of a rectangle and a trapezium:

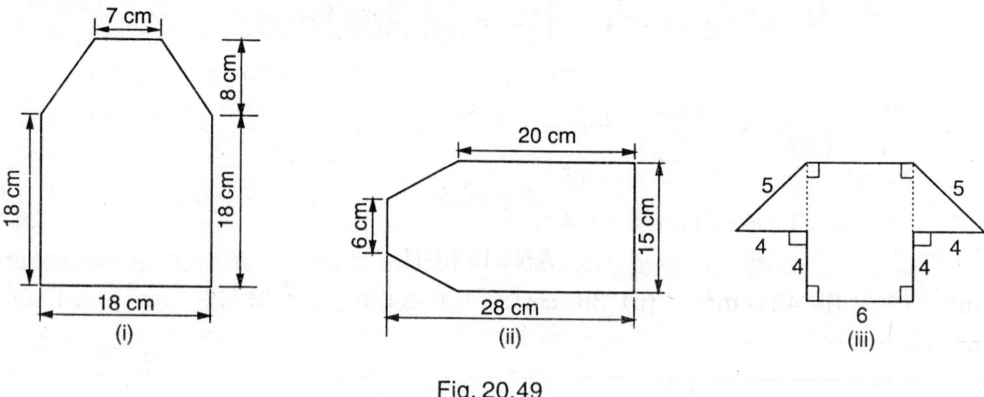

Fig. 20.49

3. There is a pentagonal shaped park as shown in Fig. 20.50. Jyoti and Kavita divided it in two different ways.

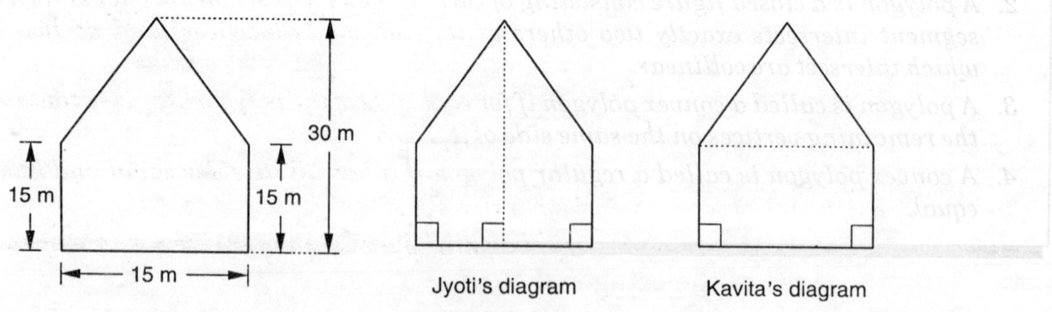

Fig. 20.50

Find the area of this park using both ways. Can you suggest some another way of finding its area?

4. Find the area of the following polygon, if $AL = 10$ cm, $AM = 20$ cm, $AN = 50$ cm, $AO = 60$ cm and $AD = 90$ cm.

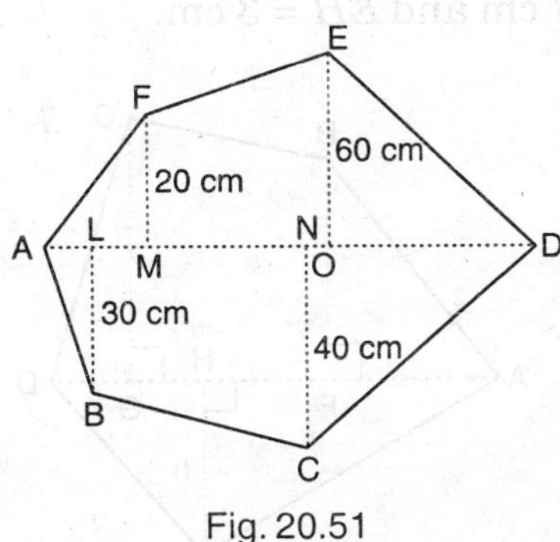

Fig. 20.51

5. Find the area of the following regular hexagon.

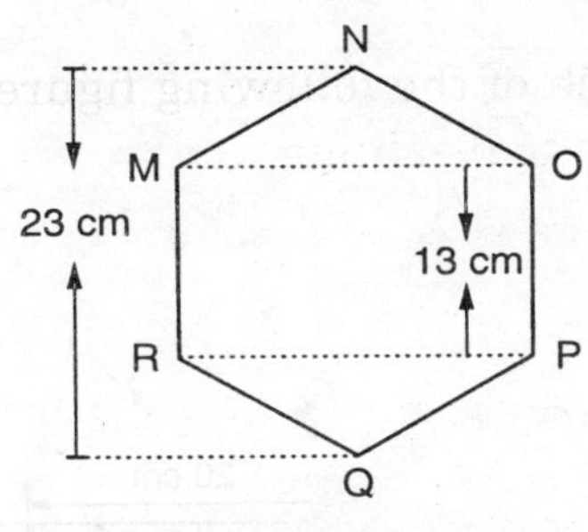

Fig. 20.52

ANSWERS

1. 52.5 cm^2 2. (i) 424 cm^2 (ii) 384 cm^2 (iii) 54 cm^2 3. 337.5m^2 4. 5050 cm^2
5. 432 cm^2

THINGS TO REMEMBER

1. *Area of a trapezium* $= \frac{1}{2} \times$ *(Sum of the parallel sides)* $\times$ *(Distance between the parallel sides)*
2. *A polygon is a closed figure consisting of three or more line segments (sides) such that each line segment intersects exactly two others at its end points (vertices) and no two line segments which intersect are collinear.*
3. *A polygon is called a convex polygon if for each side of the polygon, the line containing it has all the remaining vertices on the same side of it.*
4. *A convex polygon is called a regular polygon if it has all its sides equal and has all its angles equal.*

21

MENSURATION-II
(Volumes and Surface Areas of a Cuboid and a Cube)

21.1 INTRODUCTION

In this chapter, we shall learn about the volumes and surface areas of a cuboid and a cube. The formulae for the same will also be derived. Some applications of these formulae to solve some simple problems from every day life situations will also be discussed. In class VII, we have visualised some solid shapes including a cuboid and a cube. Let us first recall the same.

21.2 CUBOID

In our every day life, we come across objects like [illegible] chalk box, a dice, a book etc. All these objects [illegible] are made of six rectangular plane [illegible]

Fig. 21.1

These objects are in the shape of a cuboid [illegible]

CUBOID *A cuboid is a solid bounded by six* [illegible]

Fig. 21.2 represents a cuboid. It should be [illegible] drawn on a sheet of the paper.

We shall now explain some terms related to a cuboid.

FACES *Figure 21.2 is made of six rectangular* [illegible] AEHD, CGFB, AEFB and CDHG. *These six* [illegible] *cuboid shown in Fig. 21.2.*

The top face ABCD and the bottom face EFGH [illegible] ABFE, DCGH and DAEH, CBFG are pairs of [illegible]

Any two faces other than the opposite faces [illegible]

Clearly, a cuboid has six faces. ABCD and ABFE [illegible]

Similarly, ABCD and AEHD are adjacent faces.

21

MENSURATION-II
(Volumes and Surface Areas of a Cuboid and a Cube)

21.1 INTRODUCTION

In this chapter, we shall learn about the volumes and surface areas of a cuboid and a cube. The formulae for the same will also be derived. Some applications of these formulae to solve some simple problems from every day life situations will also be discussed. In class VII, we have visualised some solid shapes including a cuboid and a cube. Let us first recall the same.

21.2 CUBOID

In our every day life, we come across objects like a wooden box, a match box, a tea packet, a chalk box, a dice, a book etc. All these objects have similar shapes. In fact, all these objects are made of six rectangular plane regions as shown in Fig. 21.1.

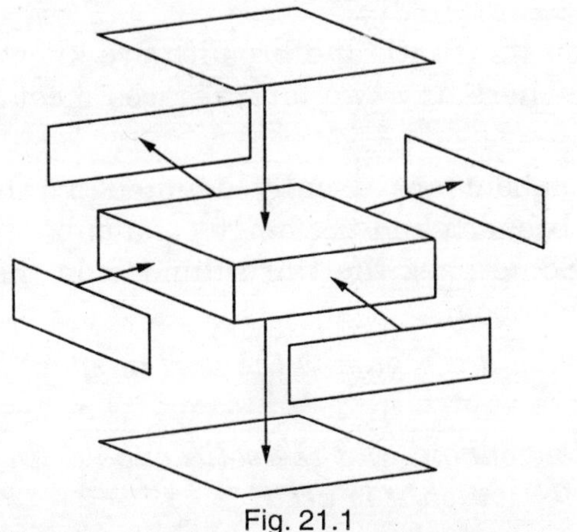

Fig. 21.1

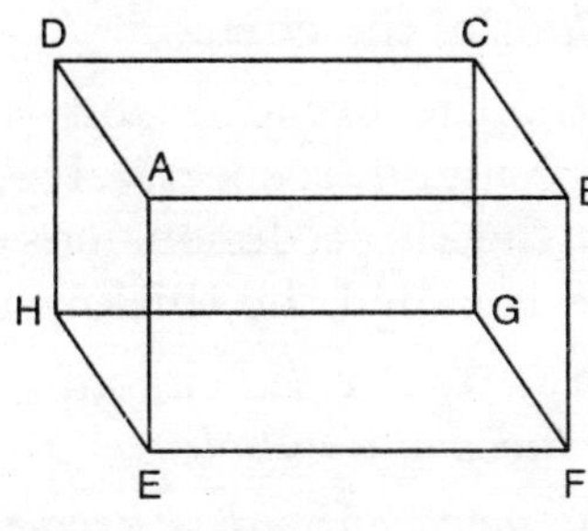

Fig. 21.2

These objects are in the shape of a cuboid which may be defined as follows:

CUBOID *A cuboid is a solid bounded by six rectangular plane regions.*

Fig. 21.2 represents a cuboid. It should be noted that it is not a plane figure, although it is drawn on a sheet of the paper.

We shall now explain some terms related to a cuboid.

FACES *Figure 21.2 is made of six rectangular plane regions, namely ABCD, EFGH, AEHD, CGFB, AEFB and CDHG. These six rectangular plane regions are six faces of the cuboid shown in Fig. 21.2.*

The top face *ABCD* and the bottom face *EFGH* form one pair of opposite faces. Similarly, *ABFE*, *DCGH* and *DAEH*, *CBFG* are pairs of opposite faces.

Any two faces other than the opposite faces are called adjacent faces.

Clearly, a cuboid has six faces. *ABCD* and *ABFE* are two adjacent faces.

Similarly, *ABCD* and *AEHD* are adjacent faces.

EDGES *Any two adjacent faces of a cuboid meet in a line segment, which is called an edge of the cuboid.*

In Fig. 21.2, *AB, AD, AE, HD, HE, HG, GF, GC, FE, FB, EF* and *CD* are 12 edges of the cuboid.

Since the opposite sides of a rectangle are equal, therefore

$$AB = CD = GH = EF, AE = DH = BF = CG \text{ and } EH = FG = AD = BC$$

VERTEX *For any two edges that meet at an end-point, there is a third edge, that also meets them at that end-point. This point of intersection of three edges of a cuboid is called a vertex of the cuboid.*

The vertices of the cuboid in Fig. 21.2 are: *A, B, C, D, E, F, G, H.*

Clearly, a cuboid has 8 vertices.

Thus, we see that the twelve edges of a cuboid can be grouped into three groups such that all edges in one group are equal in length. This means that twelve edges of a cuboid can have only three distinct lengths. Usually, the longest of these is called the length of the cuboid and out of the remaining two, one is called the breadth or width and the other height of the cuboid.

BASE AND LATERAL FACES *Any face of a cuboid may be called the base of the cuboid. In that case, the four faces which meet the base are called the lateral faces of the cuboid.*

In Fig. 21.2, the face *EFGH* is the base and the faces *FGCB, AEHD, GHDC* and *FEAB* are lateral faces.

When we take a face of a cuboid as the base, then its length and breadth are known as the length and breadth of the cuboid, and the edge where any two lateral faces meet is taken as the height of the cuboid.

The length, the breadth and the height of a cuboid are usually denoted by the letter symbols l, b and h, respectively. The length, the breadth and the height of a cuboid are also known as the three dimensions of the cuboid. Sometimes the third dimension (height) of the cuboid is called the thickness or depth of the cuboid.

SOLID CUBOID *A solid cuboid or a cuboid or a cuboidal region is the part of space bounded by the six faces of a cuboid.*

NOTE: *The word cuboid is used for both-the hollow cuboid and the solid cuboid. In any use of the word the context will always make it clear for which it is used.*

If all six faces of a cuboid are squares of the same size as shown in Fig. 21.3, then such a solid is called a cube as defined below.

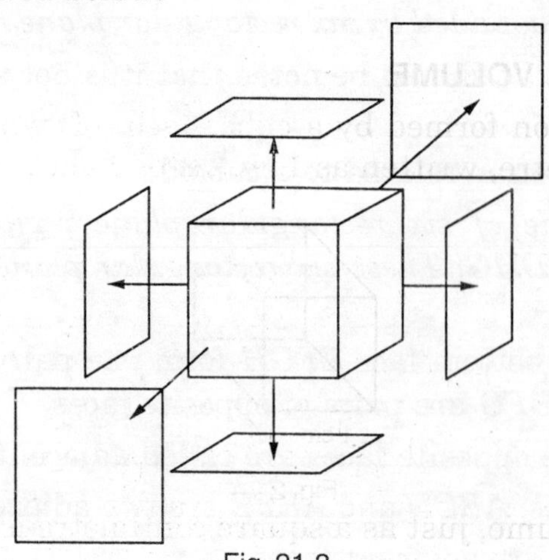

Fig. 21.3

CUBE *A cuboid whose length, breadth and height are all equal is called a cube.*

SOLID CUBE *A solid cube is the part of the space enclosed by the six faces of the cube.*

As with a cuboid, the wood 'cube' is also used for both the hollow cube and the solid cube. In any use of the word, the context in which it is used, will make the meaning clear.

Each edge of a cube is called its side.

21.3 SPACE REGIONS

In chapter 20, we have learnt about plane regions. As we have discussed that a plane figure together with its interior is called the region enclosed by it. In this chapter, we shall generalize the concept of plane region to space region.

The space occupied by a solid is known as its space region.

To understand the meaning of space region, let us consider a rectangular over head water tank. The part of the space enclosed by it is known as its space region. Since the tank is in the form of a cuboid, so the space enclosed by it is also called the *cuboidal region.*

Now consider a cylindrical tin box which is made to store oil.

Clearly, the interior of the cylindrical box occupies a certain part of the space which is known as its space region. Since the box is cylindrical, so the part of the space enclosed by it is known as the *cylindrical region.*

Similarly, in everyday life, we come across various forms of space regions such as spherical space region, conical space region etc.

In this chapter, we shall study about cuboidal and cubical space regions only.

21.4 VOLUME OF THE SPACE REGION FORMED BY A BODY

In the previous section, we have introduced the idea of the space region of a solid body. If two space regions are given, one can always talk of one being greater than or less than the other. Thus, space regions can be compared. In other words, a space region has a magnitude or size which is known as its volume as defined below.

VOLUME *The magnitude of the space region of a body is called its volume.*

In other words, the measure of the space occupied by a solid body is called its volume.

In particular, the magnitude of the cuboidal region of a cuboid is called its volume.

Remark *We often speak of the volume of a cuboid, in fact it is the volume of the cuboidal region i.e. the magnitude of the cuboidal region.*

In future, the term volume of a cuboid will always mean the magnitude of the cuboidal region.

21.5 A STANDARD UNIT OF VOLUME

The volume of the space region formed by a cube, each of whose sides (or edges) is 1 cm long, is called a cubic centimetre, written as 1 cu. cm or 1 cm^3.

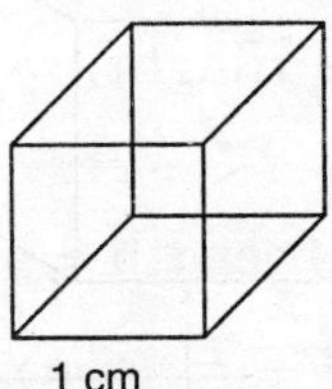

Fig. 21.4

This is a standard unit of volume, just as a square centimetre is a standard unit of area.

If a space region S contains V such cubes, then we say that its volume is V cm^3.

The cuboid shown in Fig. 21.5 contains 4 one-centimetre cubes. So, its volume is 4 cm^3.

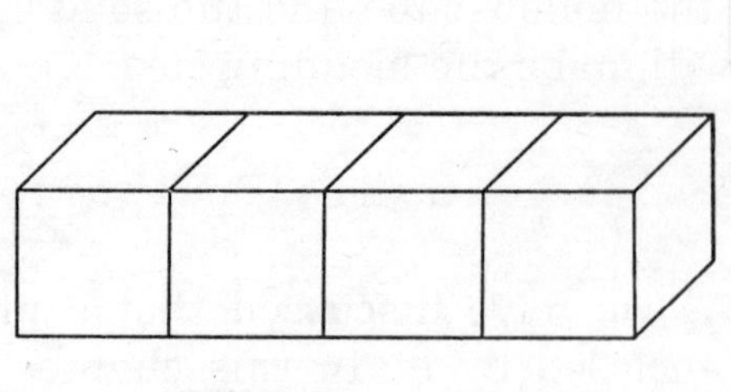

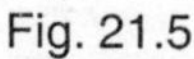

Fig. 21.5

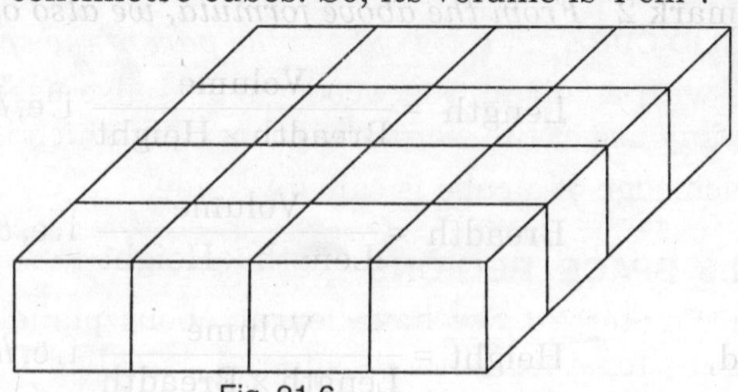

Fig. 21.6

The cuboid shown in Fig. 21.6 contains 16 one- centimetre cubes. So, its volume is 16 cm^3.

21.6 FORMULA FOR FINDING THE VOLUME OF A CUBOID

In this section, we shall derive a formula for finding the volume of a cuboid in terms of its length, breadth and height. For this, let us consider the following experiments:

<u>Experiment 1</u> Take five wooden or plastic cubical boxes of the same size, each 1 cm cube. Put them end-to-end in a row as shown in Fig. 21.7.

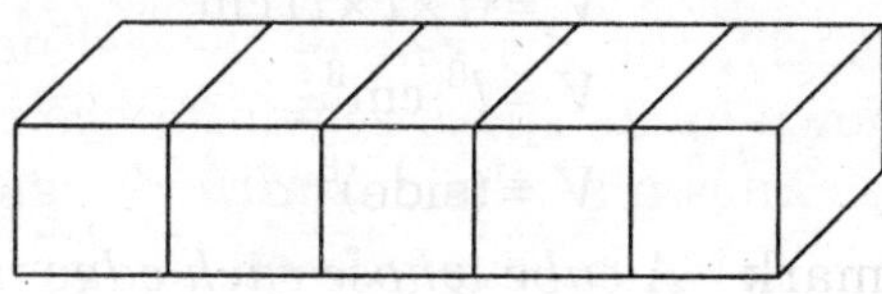

Fig. 21.7

We observe that the shape of the solid so formed is a cuboid. Since it contains 5 cubes, each one cm cube. So, the volume of this cuboid is 5 cm^3.

We observe that this cuboid has length $=5$ cm, breadth $=1$ cm and height $=1$ cm.

Also, $5 = 5\times1\times1$

$\therefore$ Volume of the cuboid $= (5\times1\times1)\ cm^3 = (\text{Length}\times\text{Breadth}\times\text{Height})\ cm^3$

<u>Experiment 2</u> Take 15 wooden or plastic cubical boxes of the same size, each 1 cm cube. Put then end-to-end in three rows, each row containing 5 cubes, as shown in Fig. 21.8.

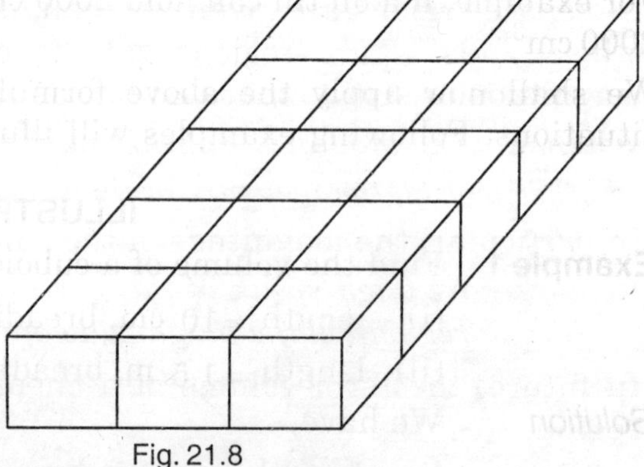

Fig. 21.8

In this case also the solid obtained is a cuboid. This cuboid contains 15 cubes, each 1 cm cube.

So, the volume of this cuboid is 15 cm^3.

We observe that this cuboid has length $=3$ cm, breadth $=5$ cm and height $=1$ cm.

Also, $15 = 5\times3\times1$

Thus, volume of this cuboid $= (5\times3\times1)\ cm^3 = (\text{Length}\times\text{Breadth}\times\text{Height})\ cm^3$

It has been observed that when the same activity is performed by taking more cubes and forming cuboids of different dimensions, the volume in each case is equal to

(Length × Breadth × Height)

Hence, we conclude that:

Volume V of a cuboid of length $=l$ cm, breadth $=b$ cm and, height $=h$ cm is given by

$$V = (l\times b\times h)\ cm^3$$

<u>Remark 1</u> *While finding the volume of a cuboid, its length, breadth and height must be expressed in the same units.*

Remark 2 *From the above formula, we also obtain that*

$$\text{Length} = \frac{\text{Volume}}{\text{Breadth} \times \text{Height}} \quad \text{i.e, } l = \left(\frac{V}{b \times h}\right)$$

$$\text{Breadth} = \frac{\text{Volume}}{\text{Length} \times \text{Height}} \quad \text{i.e, } b = \left(\frac{V}{l \times h}\right)$$

and,
$$\text{Height} = \frac{\text{Volume}}{\text{Length} \times \text{Breadth}} \quad \text{i.e, } h = \left(\frac{V}{l \times b}\right)$$

21.7 VOLUME OF A CUBE

We know that a cube is a special type of a cuboid whose length, breadth and height are all equal.

So, the volume V of a cube of edge $l cm$ is given by

$$V = (l \times l \times l) \text{ cm}^3$$

$\Rightarrow$ $$V = l^3 \text{ cm}^3$$

or, $$V = (\text{side})^3$$

Remark *A cube whose each edge is l cm long is generally referred to as a l-cm cube.*

VOLUME AND CAPACITY *Sometimes, word capacity is also used instead of word volume.* Even though there is no clear difference between these two words, however we will use:

(i) Volume when we will refer to the amount of space occupied by an object.

(ii) Capacity when will refer to the quantity that a container holds:

For example, if a oil tin can hold 2000 cm^3 of oil, then we may say that capacity of the tin is 2000 cm^3.

We shall now apply the above formulae for solving some problems from everyday life situations. Following examples will illustrate the same.

ILLUSTRATIVE EXAMPLES

Example 1 Find the volume of a cuboid whose

(i) length $= 10$ cm, breadth $= 8$ cm, height $= 3$ cm

(ii) length $= 1.5$ m, breadth $= 25$ cm, height $= 15$ cm

Solution We have,

(i) Length $= 10$ cm, breadth $= 8$ cm and height $= 3$ cm

$\therefore$ Volume of the cuboid $= (\text{Length} \times \text{Breadth} \times \text{Height})$

$$= (10 \times 8 \times 3) \text{ cm}^3 = 240 \text{ cm}^3$$

(ii) Length $= 1.5$ m $= 1.5 \times 100$ cm $= 150$ cm, breadth $= 25$ cm and height $= 15$ cm.

$\therefore$ Volume of the cuboid $= (\text{Length} \times \text{Breadth} \times \text{Height})$

$$= (150 \times 25 \times 15) \text{ cm}^3 = 56250 \text{ cm}^3$$

Example 2 Find the volume of a cube whose side is 7 cm

Solution We know that: Volume of a cube $= (\text{Side})^3$

$\therefore$ Volume of the given cube $= (7)^3 \text{ cm}^3 = 343 \text{ cm}^3$

Example 3 A cuboidal wooden block contains 189 cm^3 wood. If it be 7 cm long and 4.5 cm high, find its breadth.

Solution We have,

Volume of the wooden block $= 189\ cm^3$

Length of the wooden block $= 7$ cm , Height of the wooden block $= 4.5$ cm

$$\therefore \quad \text{Breadth of the wooden block} = \frac{\text{Volume}}{\text{Length} \times \text{Height}} = \frac{189}{7 \times 4.5}\ cm = 6\ cm$$

Example 4 Find the height of a cuboid whose volume is 275 cm^3 and base area is 25 cm^2?

Solution We have,

Volume of the cuboid $= 275\ cm^3$, Area of the base $= 25\ cm^2$

$$\therefore \quad \text{Height of the cuboid} = \frac{\text{Volume of the cuboid}}{\text{Area of the base}} = \frac{275}{25}\ cm = 11\ cm$$

Example 5 A cuboidal vessel is 10 cm long and 8 cm wide. How high must it be made to hold 480 cubic centimetres of a liquid?

Solution We have,

Volume of the cuboidal Vessel $= 480\ cm^3$

Length of the cuboidal Vessel $= 10$ cm , Breadth of the cuboidal Vessel $= 8$ cm

$$\therefore \quad \text{Height of the cuboidal Vessel} = \frac{\text{Volume}}{\text{Length} \times \text{Breadth}} = \frac{480}{10 \times 8}\ cm = 6\ cm$$

Example 6 How many 5 cm cubes can be obtained (cut-off) from a cube whose edge is 20 cm?

Solution The volume V of a cube is given by $V = (\text{Side})^3$

Here, Side $= 20$ cm

$\therefore \quad V = (20)^3\ cm^3 = 8000\ cm^3$

Also, the side of the smaller cube $= 5$ cm

$\therefore \quad$ Volume of the smaller cube $= (5)^3\ cm^3 = 125\ cm^3$

Hence, the number of cubes cut-off $= \frac{8000}{125} = 64$

Example 7 A match box measures 4 cm by 2.5 cm by 1.5 cm. What will be the volume of a packet containing 12 such match boxes? How many such packets can be placed in a cardboard box whose size is 60 cm × 30 cm × 24 cm?

Solution We have,

Volume of a match box $= (4 \times 2.5 \times 1.5)\ cm^3 = 15\ cm^3$

$\therefore \quad$ Volume of a packet containing 12 match boxes $= (12 \times 15)\ cm^3 = 180\ cm^3$

Now, Volume of cardboard box $= (60 \times 30 \times 24)\ cm^3 = 43200\ cm^3$

$\therefore \quad$ Number of packets that can be put in a cardboard $= \frac{43200}{180} = 240$

Example 8 What will happen to the volume of a cube if its edge is doubled?

Solution Let the edge of the cube be l cm. Then, its volume V is given by

$$V = l^3 \text{ cm}^3 \quad \ldots\text{(i)}$$

Let V_1 be the volume of the cube when its edge is doubled. Then,

$V_1 = (2l)^3 \text{ cm}^3$ [$\because$ Length of the edge of new cube $= 2l$ cm]

$\Rightarrow V_1 = 8l^3$

$\Rightarrow V_1 = 8V$ [Using (i)]

Hence, if each edge of the cube is doubled, then the volume becomes 8 times.

Example 9 Three cubes of sides 3 cm, 4 cm and 5 cm are melted and a new cube is formed. Find the side of the new cube.

Solution We have,

Total volume of three cubes $= (3^3 + 4^3 + 5^3) \text{ cm}^3$

$= (27 + 64 + 125) \text{ cm}^3 = 216 \text{ cm}^3$

Let the side of the new cube be l cm. Then,

Volume of the new cube $= 216 \text{ cm}^3$

$\Rightarrow l^3 = 216 \Rightarrow l^3 = 6^3 \Rightarrow l = 6$ cm [$\because$ Volume $= l^3 \text{ cm}^3$]

Example 10 A rectangular block of ice measures 40 cm by 25 cm by 15 cm. Calculate its weight in kg, if ice weighs $\frac{9}{10}$ of the weight of the same volume of water and 1 cm^3 of water weighs 1 gm.

Solution We have,

Volume of the rectangular block of ice $= 40 \times 25 \times 15 \text{ cm}^3 = 15000 \text{ cm}^3$

Now, weight of 1 cm^3 of water $= 1$ gm

and, weight of 1 cm^3 of ice $= \left(\frac{9}{10}\right)^{\text{th}}$ of the weight of 1 cm^3 of water

$\therefore$ Weight of 1 cm^3 of ice $= \left(\frac{9}{10}\right)$ gm

$\therefore$ Weight of the rectangular block of ice $= \frac{9}{10} \times 15000$ gm

$= 13500 \text{ gm} = 13.5 \text{ kg}$

Example 11 Eight identical cuboidal wooden blocks are stacked one on top of the other. The total volume of the solid so formed is 128 cm^3. If the height of each block is 1 cm and the base is a square, find the dimensions of each block.

Solution Let the length and breadth of the base of each wooden block be x cm each.

Since eight identical blocks are stacked one on top of the other and the height of each block is 1 cm.

So, height of the solid formed $= 8$ cm

$\therefore$ Volume of the solid formed $= (x \times x \times 8) \text{ cm}^3 = 8x^2 \text{ cm}^3$

But, the volume of solid formed is 128 cm^3 (given).

$$\therefore \quad 8x^2 = 128 \Rightarrow x^2 = \frac{128}{8} \Rightarrow x^2 = 16 \Rightarrow x^2 = 4^2 \Rightarrow x = 4 \text{ cm}$$

Hence, each wooden block is of dimension 4 cm × 4 cm × 1 cm

EXERCISE 21.1

1. Find the volume of a cuboid whose
   (i) length = 12 cm, breadth = 8 cm, height = 6 cm
   (ii) length = 1.2 m, breadth = 30 cm, height = 15 cm
   (iii) length = 15 cm, breadth = 2.5 dm, height = 8 cm.
2. Find the volume of a cube whose side is
   (i) 4 cm (ii) 8 cm (iii) 1.5 dm (iv) 1.2 m (v) 25 mm
3. Find the height of a cuboid of volume 100 cm^3, whose length and breadth are 5 cm and 4 cm respectively.
4. A cuboidal vessel is 10 cm long and 5 cm wide. How high it must be made to hold 300 cm^3 of a liquid?
5. A milk container is 8 cm long and 50 cm wide. What should be its height so that it can hold 4 litres of milk?
6. A cuboidal wooden block contains 36 cm^3 wood. If it be 4 cm long and 3 cm wide, find its height.
7. What will happen to the volume of a cube, if its edge is
   (i) halved (ii) trebled?
8. What will happen to the volume of a cuboid if its :
   (i) Length is doubled, height is same and breadth is halved?
   (ii) Length is doubled, height is doubled and breadth is same?
9. Three cuboids of dimensions 5 cm × 6 cm × 7 cm, 4 cm × 7 cm × 8 cm and 2 cm × 3 cm × 13 cm are melted and a cube is made. Find the side of cube.
10. Find the weight of solid rectangular iron piece of size 50 cm × 40 cm × 10 cm, if 1 cm^3 of iron weighs 8 gm.
11. How many wooden cubical blocks of side 25 cm can be cut from a log of wood of size 3 m by 75 cm by 50 cm, assuming that there is no wastage?
12. A cuboidal block of silver is 9 cm long, 4 cm broad and 3.5 cm in height. From it, beads of volume 1.5 cm^3 each are to be made. Find the number of beads that can be made from the block.
13. Find the number of cuboidal boxes measuring 2 cm by 3 cm by 10 cm which can be stored in a carton whose dimensions are 40 cm, 36 cm and 24 cm.
14. A cuboidal block of solid iron has dimensions 50 cm, 45 cm and 34 cm. How many cuboids of size 5 cm by 3 cm by 2 cm can be obtained from this block? Assume cutting causes no wastage.
15. A cube A has side thrice as long as that of cube B. What is the ratio of the volume of cube A to that of cube B?

16. An ice-cream brick measures 20 cm by 10 cm by 7 cm. How many such bricks can be stored in deep fridge whose inner dimensions are 100 cm by 50 cm by 42 cm?
17. Suppose that there are two cubes, having edges 2 cm and 4 cm, respectively. Find the volumes V_1 and V_2 of the cubes and compare them.
18. A tea-packet measures 10 cm × 6 cm × 4 cm. How many such tea-packets can be placed in a cardboard box of dimensions 50 cm × 30 cm × 0.2 m?
19. The weight of a metal block of size 5 cm by 4 cm by 3 cm is 1 kg. Find the weight of a block of the same metal of size 15 cm by 8 cm by 3 cm.
20. How many soap cakes can be placed in a box of size 56 cm × 0.4 m × 0.25 m, if the size of a soap cake is 7 cm × 5 cm × 2.5 cm?
21. The volume of a cuboidal box is 48 cm^3. If its height and length are 3 cm and 4 cm respectively, find its breadth.

ANSWERS

1. (i) 576 cm^3 (ii) 54000 cm^3 (iii) 3000 cm^3 (iv) 1728000 cm^3 = 1.728 m^3 (v) 15.625 cm^3
2. (i) 64 cm^3 (ii) 512 cm^3 (iii) 3375 cm^3
3. 5 cm
4. 6 cm
5. 10 cm
6. 3cm
7. (i) $\frac{1}{8}$ times (ii) 27 times
8. (i) same (ii) 4 times
9. 8 cm
10. 160 kg
11. 72
12. 84
13. 576
14. 2550
15. 27 : 1
16. 150
17. $V_1 = 8$ cm^3, $V_2 = 64$ cm^3 $V_2 = 8V_1$
18. 125
19. 6 kg
20. 640
21. 4 cm

21.8 OTHER STANDARD UNITS OF VOLUME

So far we have used cubic centimetre (cm^3) as a standard unit of measurement of volume. Since there are various units of measurement of length like metre, decimetre, decametre etc. Therefore, there are many other standard units of measurement of volume. Also, cubic centimetre is a very small unit for measuring volumes of water tanks, oil tanks etc. We shall now discuss other units of measurements of volume.

LITRE OR CUBIC DECIMETRE *The volume of the solid region formed by a cube of side 1 decimetre (dm) is called a litre or a cubic decimetre (1 dm^3).*

$\because$ 1 dm = 10 cm

$\therefore$ 1 dm^3 = 1 dm×1 dm×1 dm = (10×10×10) cm^3 = 1000 cm^3

or, 1 litre = 1000 cm^3

METRE CUBE AND CUBIC METRE *The solid region formed by a cube of side 1 m is called a metre cube and its volume is 1 cubic metre (1m^3).*

$\because$ 1 m = 100 cm

$\therefore$ 1 m^3 = (100×100×100) cm^3 = 1000000 cm^3

But, 1000 cm^3 = 1 litre

$$\therefore \quad 1\text{ m}^3 = \frac{1000000}{1000}\text{ litres} = 1000\text{ litres}$$

Now, $1l = 1000$ cm^3

$\therefore \quad 1\text{ cm}^3 = \frac{1}{1000}$ th of a litre.

This is generally called a millilitre (ml).

Thus, $1\,l = 1000$ ml

CUBIC MILLIMETRE *The volume of a solid cubical region of side 1 mm is called a cubic millimetre (mm^3).*

$\because \quad 1\text{ cm} = 10\text{ mm}$

$\therefore \quad 1\text{ cm}^3 = (10\times10\times10)\text{ mm}^3 = 1000\text{ mm}^3$

Remark $\quad 1\text{m}^3$ is also called a kilolitre. Thus,

$1 \text{ kilolitre} = 1\text{ m}^3 = 1000000\text{ cm}^3 = 1000\times1000\text{ cm}^3$

$= 1000$ litre $\quad [\because 1000\text{ cm}^3 = 1\text{ litre}]$

CONVERSION OF UNITS Each of the various standard units introduced above can be converted into the others by using the following table:

Units of Length	*Units of Volume*
(i) Millimetre (mm)	Cubic millimetre (mm^3)
(ii) Centimetre (cm)	Cubic centimetre or millilitre
$1\text{ cm} = 10\text{ mm}$	$1\text{ cm}^3 = (10\times10\times10)\text{ mm}^3$
(iii) Decimetre (dm)	Cubic decimetre or litre
$1\text{ dm} = 10\text{ cm}$	$1\text{ dm}^3\ (=1\text{ litre}) = (10\times10\times10)\text{ cm}^3$
	$= 1000\text{ cm}^3 = 1000\text{ ml} \quad [\because 1\text{ cm}^3 = 1\text{ ml}]$
(iv) Metre	Cubic metre (m^3)
$1\text{ m} = 10\text{ dm}$	$1\text{ m}^3 = (10\times10\times10)\text{ dm}^3 = 1000\text{ dm}^3 = 1000$ litre

We shall now use these units for finding the volumes of solid regions.

Following examples will illustrate the procedure.

ILLUSTRATIVE EXAMPLES

Example 1 Find the volume in cubic metre (cu. m) of each of the cuboids whose dimensions are:

(i) Length $= 10$ m, breadth $= 8$ m, height $= 2.5$ m

(ii) Length $= 2$ m, breadth $= 1.5$ m, height $= 25$ cm

(iii) Lenght $= 12$ m, breadth $= 35$ dm, height $= 50$ cm.

Solution We have,

(i) Length $= 10$ m, breadth $= 8$ m and height $= 2.5$ m

$\therefore$ Volume $= (10\times8\times2.5)\text{ m}^3 = 200\text{ m}^3$

(ii) Length $= 2$ m, breadth $= 1.5$ m

and, height $= 25\text{ cm} = \frac{25}{100}\text{ m} = 0.25\text{ m}$ $\quad [\because 1\text{ m} = 100\text{ cm}]$

$\therefore$ Volume $= (2\times1.5\times0.25)\text{ m}^3 = 0.75\text{ m}^3$

(iii) Lenght $= 12$ m,

Breadth $= 35$ dm $= 35 \times 10$ cm [$\because 1 \text{ dm} = 10 \text{ cm}$]

$= \dfrac{35 \times 10}{100}$ m $= 3.5$ m [$\because 1 \text{ m} = 100 \text{ cm}$]

and, Height $= 50 \text{ cm} = \dfrac{50}{100} \text{ m} = 0.5$ m

$\therefore$ Volume $= (12 \times 3.5 \times 0.5) \text{ m}^3 = 21 \text{ m}^3$

Example 2 Find the volume in cu dm of each of the cubes whose side is

(i) 1.2 m (ii) 25 cm (iii) 1 dm 5 cm

Solution (i) Length of the side of the cube $= 1.2$ m

$= (1.2 \times 10)$ dm $= 12$ dm [$\because 1 \text{ m} = 10 \text{ dm}$]

$\therefore$ Volume of the cube $= (\text{Side})^3 = (12)^3 \text{ dm}^3 = 1728 \text{ dm}^3$

(ii) We have,

Length of the side of the cube $= 25$ cm

$= \dfrac{25}{10}$ dm $= 2.5$ dm [$\because 10 \text{ cm} = 1 \text{ dm}$]

$\therefore$ Volume of the cube $= (2.5)^3 \text{ dm}^3 = 15.625 \text{ dm}^3$

(iii) We have,

Length of the side of the cube $= 1$ dm 5 cm

$= (1 \times 10 + 5)$ cm [$\because 1 \text{ dm} = 10 \text{ cm}$]

$= 15 \text{ cm} = \dfrac{15}{10}$ dm [$\because 10 \text{ cm} = 1 \text{ dm}$]

$= 1.5$ dm

$\therefore$ Volume of the cube $= (1.5)^3 \text{ dm}^3 = 3.375 \text{ dm}^3$

Example 3 The length, breadth and height of a room are 8 m, 6.5 m and 3.5 m respectively. Find the volume of the air contained in the room.

Solution We have,

Length of the room $= 8$ m, Breadth of the room $= 6.5$ m

Height of the room $= 3.5$ m

$\therefore$ Volume of the air in the room $=$ Volume of the room

$= (\text{Length} \times \text{Breadth} \times \text{Height})$

$= (8 \times 6.5 \times 3.5) \text{ m}^3 = 182 \text{ m}^3$

Example 4 A room is in the form of a cuboid of measures $60 \text{ m} \times 40 \text{ m} \times 30 \text{ m}$. How many cuboidal boxes can be stored in it if the volume of one box is 0.8 m^3?

Solution We have,

Volume of one box $= 0.8 \text{ m}^3$

Volume of room $= 60 \times 40 \times 30 \text{ m}^3 = 72000 \text{ m}^3$

∴ Number of boxes that can be stored in the room

$$= \frac{\text{Volume of the room}}{\text{Volume of one box}} = \frac{60 \times 40 \times 30}{0.8} = 90,000$$

Hence, the number of cuboidal boxes that can be stored in the room is 60,000.

Example 5 A rectangular water reservoir contains 42000 litres of water. Find the depth of the water in the reservoir if its base measures 6 m by 3.5 m.

Solution We have,

Volume of the reservoir $= 42000$ litres

$$= \frac{42000}{1000} \text{ m}^3 \quad [\because 1 \text{ m}^3 = 1000 \text{ litres}]$$

$$= 42 \text{ m}^3$$

Length of the reservoir $= 6$ m, Breadth of the reservior $= 3.5$ m

∴ Area of the base of the reservoir $= (6 \times 3.5)\text{ m}^2 = 21 \text{ m}^2$

But, (Area of the base × Height) = Volume of the reservoir

∴ Height or depth of the reservoir $= \dfrac{\text{Volume}}{\text{Area of the base}} = \dfrac{42}{21} \text{ m} = 2 \text{ m}$

Hence, the depth of the reservoir is 2 m.

Example 6 What will be the labour charges for digging a cuboidal pit 8 m long, 6 m broad and 3 m deep at the rate of Rs 20 per m^3?

Solution We have,

Volume of the pit $= (\text{Length} \times \text{Breadth} \times \text{Height}) = (8 \times 6 \times 3)\text{ m}^3 = 144 \text{ m}^3$

Since labour charges are at the rate of Rs 20 per m^3.

∴ Total labour charges = Rs (144 × 20) = Rs 2880

Example 7 How many bricks of size 22 cm × 10 cm × 7 cm are required to construct a wall 33 m long, 3.5 m high and 40 cm thick, if cement and sand used in the construction occupy $\frac{1}{10}$th part of the wall?

Solution We have,

Length of the wall $= 33$ m, Height of the wall $= 3.5$ m

Thickness of the wall $= 40 \text{ cm} = \dfrac{40}{100} \text{ m} = 0.4 \text{ m}$

∴ Volume of the wall $= (33 \times 3.5 \times 0.4)\text{ m}^3 = 46.2 \text{ m}^3$

Volume of the space occupied by the cement and sand

$$= \frac{1}{10}\text{th of the volume of the wall} = \frac{46.2}{10} \text{ m}^3 = 4.62 \text{ m}^3$$

∴ Volume of the bricks $= (46.2 - 4.62)\text{ m}^3$

$$= 41.58 \text{ m}^3$$

$$= 41.58 \times 1000000 \text{ cm}^3 = 41580000 \text{ cm}^3$$

Now,

Volume of a brick $= (22 \times 10 \times 7)\ \text{cm}^3 = 1540\ \text{cm}^3$

$\therefore$ Number of bricks $= \dfrac{\text{Volume of the bricks}}{\text{Volume of a brick}} = \dfrac{41580000}{1540} = 27000$

Example 8 A water tank built by a municipality of a town to supply water to its 25000 inhabitants at 125 litres per day per person is 40 m long and 31.25 m broad. The tank, when it is full, can supply water for two days to the inhabitants of the town. Find the depth of the tank.

Solution Water consumed by the inhabitants in one day

$= $ Number of inhabitants $\times$ Water consumed by an inhabitant in one day

$= (25000 \times 125)$ litres $= 3125000$ litres

$\therefore$ Water consumed by the inhabitants in two days

$= (3125000 \times 2)$ litres

$= 6250000$ litres $= \dfrac{6250000}{1000}\ \text{m}^3$ $\qquad [\because 1000 \text{ litres} = 1\ \text{m}^3]$

$= 6250\ \text{m}^3$

$\therefore$ Volume of the tank $= 6250$ litres

$\therefore$ Depth of the tank $= \dfrac{\text{Volume}}{\text{Length} \times \text{Breadth}} = \dfrac{6250\ \text{m}^3}{40\ \text{m} \times 31.25\ \text{m}} = \dfrac{6250}{1250}\ \text{m} = 5\ \text{m}$

Example 9 The earth taken out from a pit is evenly spread over a rectangular field of length 90 m, width 60 m. If the, volume of the earth dug is 3078 m^3. Find the height of the field raised.

Solution Let the height of the field raised be h metre. Then,

Volume of the earth dug $= 90 \times 60 \times h\ \text{m}^3$

$\Rightarrow \quad 3078 = 90 \times 60 \times h$

$\Rightarrow \quad h = \dfrac{3078}{90 \times 60}\ \text{m} = \dfrac{3078}{5400}\ \text{m} = \dfrac{3078}{5400} \times 100\ \text{cm} = \dfrac{3078}{54}\ \text{cm} = 57\ \text{cm}$

Example 10 A rectangular field is 154 m long and 121 m broad. A well of 14 m length and 11 m breadth is dug inside the field and mud taken out is spread evenly over the remaining part of the field to a thickness of 25 cm. Find the depth of the well.

Solution We have,

Length of the well $= 14$ m, Breadth of the well $= 11$ m

$\therefore$ Area of the base of the well $= (14 \times 11)\ \text{m}^2 = 154\ \text{m}^2$

Also, Area of the field $= (154 \times 121)\ \text{m}^2 = 18634\ \text{m}^2$

$\therefore$ Area of the field in which mud is spread $= (18634 - 154)\ \text{m}^2 = 18480\ \text{m}^2$

Thickness of the mud $= 25\ \text{cm} = \dfrac{25}{100}\ \text{m} = \dfrac{1}{4}\ \text{m}$

$\therefore$ Volume of the mud $= 18480 \times \frac{1}{4} \text{m}^3 = 4620 \text{ m}^3$

$\therefore$ Depth of the well $= \frac{\text{Volume of the mud taken out of the well}}{\text{Area of the base of the well}} = \frac{4620}{154} \text{ m} = 30 \text{ m}$

Example 11 If the rainfall on a certain day was 5 cm, how many litres of water fell on 1 hectare field on that day?

Solution We have,

Area of the field $= 1$ hectare $= 10000 \text{ m}^2$ $[\because 1 \text{ hectare} = 10000 \text{ m}^2]$

Depth of the water on the field $= 5$ cm $= \frac{5}{100} \text{ m} = \frac{1}{20} \text{ m}$

$\therefore$ Volume of water = Area of the field $\times$ Depth of water

$= 10000 \times \frac{1}{20} \text{m}^3 = 500 \text{ m}^3$

$= 500 \times 1000$ litres $= 500000$ litres $[\because 1 \text{ m}^3 = 1000 \text{ litres}]$

Example 12 The length, breadth and height of a cuboidal reservoir is 7 m, 6 m and 15 m respectively. 8400 litre of water is pumped out from the reservoir. Find the fall in the water-level in the reservoir.

Solution We have,

Volume of water pumped out from the reservoir

$= 8400 \text{ litres} = \frac{8400}{1000} \text{m}^3 = 8.4 \text{ m}^3$ $[\because 1000\, l = 1 \text{ m}^3]$

Area of the base of the reservoir $= (7 \times 6) \text{ m}^2 = 42 \text{ m}^2$

$\therefore$ Fall in water-level of the reservoir $= \frac{\text{Volume of water pumped out}}{\text{Area of the base}}$

$= \frac{8.4}{42} \text{ m} = 0.2 \text{ m}$

$= (0.2 \times 100) \text{ cm} = 20 \text{ cm}$

Example 13 What is the weight of a cubical block of ice 50 cm in length, if one cubic metre of ice weighs 900 kilograms?

Solution Length of an edge of the cubical block of ice $= 50 \text{ cm} = \frac{50}{100} \text{ m} = \frac{1}{2} \text{ m}$

$\therefore$ Volume of the block of ice $= \left(\frac{1}{2}\right)^3 \text{m}^3 = \frac{1}{8} \text{m}^3$

Since one cubic metre of ice weighs 900 kilograms.

$\therefore$ Weight of the cubical block $= \frac{1}{8} \times 900 \text{ kg} = 112.5 \text{ kg}$

EXERCISE 21.2

1. Find the volume in cubic metre (cu. m) of each of the cuboids whose dimensions are :
   (i) length = 12 m, breadth = 10 m, height = 4.5 m
   (ii) length = 4 m, breadth = 2.5 m, height = 50 cm.
   (iii) length = 10 m, breadth = 25 dm, height = 25 cm.
2. Find the volume in cubic decimetre of each of the cubes whose side is
   (i) 1.5 m (ii) 75 cm (iii) 2 dm 5 cm
3. How much clay is dug out in digging a well measuring 3 m by 2 m by 5 m?
4. What will be the height of a cuboid of volume 168 m^3, if the area of its base is 28 m^2?
5. A tank is 8 m long, 6 m broad and 2 m high. How much water can it contain?
6. The capacity of a certain cuboidal tank is 50000 litres of water. Find the breadth of the tank, if its height and length are 10 m and 2.5 m respectively.
7. A rectangular diesel tanker is 2 m long, 2 m wide and 40 cm deep. How many litres of diesel can it hold?
8. The length, breadth and height of a room are 5 m, 4.5 m and 3 m, respectively. Find the volume of the air it contains.
9. A water tank is 3 m long, 2 m broad and 1 m deep. How many litres of water can it hold?
10. How many planks each of which is 3 m long, 15 cm broad and 5 cm thick can be prepared from a wooden block 6 m long, 75 cm broad and 45 cm thick?
11. How many bricks each of size 25 cm × 10 cm × 8 cm will be required to build a wall 5 m long, 3 m high and 16 cm thick, assuming that the volume of sand and cement used in the construction is negligible?
12. A village, having a population of 4000, requires 150 litres water per head per day. It has a tank which is 20 m long, 15 m broad and 6 m high. For how many days will the water of this tank last?
13. A rectangular field is 70 m long and 60 m broad. A well of dimensions 14 m × 8 m × 6 m is dug outside the field and the earth dug-out from this well is spread evenly on the field. How much will the earth level rise?
14. A swimming pool is 250 m long and 130 m wide. 3250 cubic metres of water is pumped into it. Find the rise in the level of water.
15. A beam 5 m long and 40 cm wide contains 0.6 cubic metre of wood. How thick is the beam?
16. The rainfall on a certain day was 6 cm. How many litres of water fell on 3 hectares of field on that day?
17. An 8 m long cuboidal beam of wood when sliced produces four thousand 1 cm cubes and there is no wastage of wood in this process. If one edge of the beam is 0.5 m, find the third edge.
18. The dimensions of a metal block are 2.25 m by 1.5 m by 27 cm. It is melted and recast into cubes, each of the side 45 cm. How many cubes are formed?
19. A solid rectangular piece of iron measures 6 m by 6 cm by 2 cm. Find the weight of this piece, if 1 cm^3 of iron weighs 8 gm.

20. Fill in the blanks in each of the following so as to make the statement true :
   (i) $1\text{ m}^3 = ...\text{cm}^3$
   (ii) 1 litre = ... cubic decimetre
   (iii) $1\text{ kl} = ...\text{m}^3$
   (iv) The volume of a cube of side 8 cm is ....
   (v) The volume of a wooden cuboid of length 10 cm and breadth 8 cm is 4000 cm^3. The height of the cuboid is ......cm.
   (vi) 1 cu.dm = ... cu. mm
   (vii) 1 cu. km = ... cu. m
   (viii) 1 litre = ... cu. cm
   (ix) 1 ml = ... cu. cm
   (x) 1 kl = ... cu. dm = ...cu. cm.

ANSWERS

1. (i) 540 m^3 (ii) 5m^3 (iii) 6.25 m^3 2. (i) 3375 dm^3 (ii) 421.875 dm^3 (iii) 15.625 dm^3
3. 30 m^3 4. 6 m 5. 96000 litres 6. 2 m 7. 1600 litres 8. 67.5 m^3
9. 6000 litres 10 90 11. 1200 12. 3 days 13. 16 cm 14. 0.1 m
15. 0.3 m 16. 18×10^5 litres 17. 0.001 m 18. 10 19. 57.6 kg
20. (i) 10^6 (ii) 1 (iii) 1 (iv) 512 cm^3 (v) 50 (vi) 10^6
(vii) 10^9 (viii) 10^3 (ix) 1 (x) 1000, 10^6

HINTS TO SELECTED PROBLEMS

5. Use: $1\text{ m}^3 = 1000$ litres
6. Volume of the tank $= 50000\text{ litres} = 50\text{ m}^3$
7. Use: $1\text{ m}^3 = 1000$ litres.

21.9 SURFACE AREAS OF A CUBOID AND A CUBE

In section 21.2, we have seen that the surface of a cuboid consists of six rectangular faces. So, the surface area of a cuboid equals the sum of the areas of its six rectangular faces. Let us now derive the formula for the surface area of a cuboid.

Consider a cuboid whose length is l cm, breadth b cm and height h cm as shown in Fig. 21.9.

Area of face $ABCD$ = Area of face $EFGH = (l \times b)\text{ cm}^2$

Area of face $AEHD$ = Area of face $BFGC = (b \times h)\text{ cm}^2$

Area of face $ABEF$ = Area of face $DHGC = (l \times h)\text{ cm}^2$

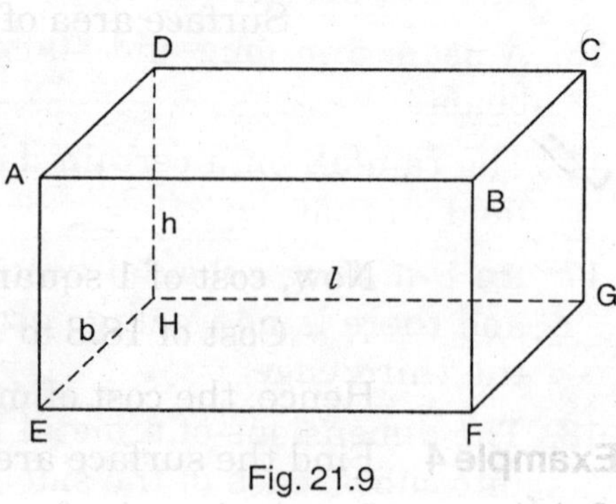

Fig. 21.9

∴ Total surface area of the cuboid

= Sum of the areas of all its six faces

$= 2\,(l \times b) + 2\,(b \times h) + 2\,(l \times h)\text{ cm}^2$

$= 2\,(l \times b + b \times h + l \times h)\text{ cm}^2$

$= 2\,(lb + bh + lh)\text{ cm}^2$

$= 2\,(\text{Length} \times \text{Breadth} + \text{Breadth} \times \text{Height} + \text{Length} \times \text{Height})\text{ cm}^2$

Remark *For the calculation of surface area of a cuboid, the length, breadth and height must be expressed in the same units.*

SURFACE AREA OF A CUBE Since all the six faces of a cube are squares of the same size i.e., for a cube, we have $l = b = h$.

Thus, if l cm is the length of the edge or side or a cube, then

$$\text{Surface area of the cube} = 2(l \times l + l \times l + l \times l) = 2 \times 3l^2 = 6l^2 = 6\,(\text{Edge})^2$$

ILLUSTRATIVE EXAMPLES

Example 1 Find the surface area of a chalk box whose length, breadth and height are 16 cm, 8 cm and 6 cm, respectively.

Solution Clearly, a chalk box is in the form of a cuboid.

Here, $l = 16$ cm, $b = 8$ cm and $h = 6$ cm.

$$\therefore \quad \text{Surface area of the cuboid} = 2(lb + bh + lh)$$
$$= 2(16 \times 8 + 8 \times 6 + 16 \times 6)\ \text{cm}^2$$
$$= 2(128 + 48 + 96)\ \text{cm}^2 = 544\ \text{cm}^2$$

Example 2 Find the surface area of a cube whose edge is 11 cm.

Solution We know that the surface area of a cube $= 6\,(\text{Edge})^2$

Here, Edge $= 11$ cm

$$\therefore \quad \text{Surface area of the given cube} = 6 \times (11)^2\ \text{cm}^2 = (6 \times 121)\ \text{cm}^2 = 726\ \text{cm}^2$$

Example 3 A cuboidal oil tin is 30 cm by 40 cm by 50 cm. Find the cost of the tin required for making 20 such tins if the cost of tin sheet is Rs 20 per square metre.

Solution The cost of tins depend upon their total surface area. It is given that a tin is in the shape of a cuboid such that

$$l = 30\ \text{cm},\ b = 40\ \text{cm and } h = 50\ \text{cm}$$

$$\therefore \quad \text{Surface area of one tin} = 2(lb + bh + lh)$$
$$= 2(30 \times 40 + 40 \times 50 + 30 \times 50)\ \text{cm}^2$$
$$= 2(1200 + 2000 + 1500)\ \text{cm}^2$$
$$= (2 \times 4700)\ \text{cm}^2 = 9400\ \text{cm}^2$$

$$\text{Surface area of 20 such tins} = (20 \times 9400)\ \text{cm}^2$$
$$= 188000\ \text{cm}^2$$
$$= \frac{188000}{10000}\ \text{m}^2 = 18.8\ \text{m}^2 \qquad [\because 10000\ \text{cm}^2 = 1\ \text{m}^2]$$

Now, cost of 1 square metre of tin sheet = Rs 20

$$\therefore \quad \text{Cost of } 18.8\ \text{m}^2 \text{ of tin sheet} = \text{Rs}\ (20 \times 18.8) = \text{Rs}\ 376$$

Hence, the cost of making 20 tins = Rs 376

Example 4 Find the surface area of a cube whose volume is 512 m^3.

Solution Let the length of an edge of the cube be l m. Then, its volume is l^3.

But, the volume is given as 512 m^3.

$$\therefore \quad l^3 = 512 \Rightarrow l^3 = 8^3 \Rightarrow l = 8\ \text{m}$$

$$\therefore \quad \text{Surface area} = 6l^2 = 6(8)^2\ \text{m}^2 = 6 \times 64\ \text{m}^2 = 384\ \text{m}^2$$

Example 5 Find the volume of a cube whose surface area is 54 cm^2.

Solution Let the length of an edge of the cube be l cm. Then, its surface area is $6l^2$ cm^2. But, the surface area is given as 54 cm^2.

$$\therefore \quad 6l^2 = 54 \Rightarrow l^2 = \frac{54}{6} = 9 \Rightarrow l^2 = 3^2 \Rightarrow l = 3\,\text{cm}$$

Now,

Volume of the cube $= l^3 \text{ cm}^3 = 3^3 \text{ cm}^3 = 27 \text{ cm}^3$

Example 6 An aquarium is in the form of a cuboid whose external measures are 80 cm × 30 cm × 40 cm. The bottom, side faces and back face are to be covered with a colour paper. Find the area of the paper needed?

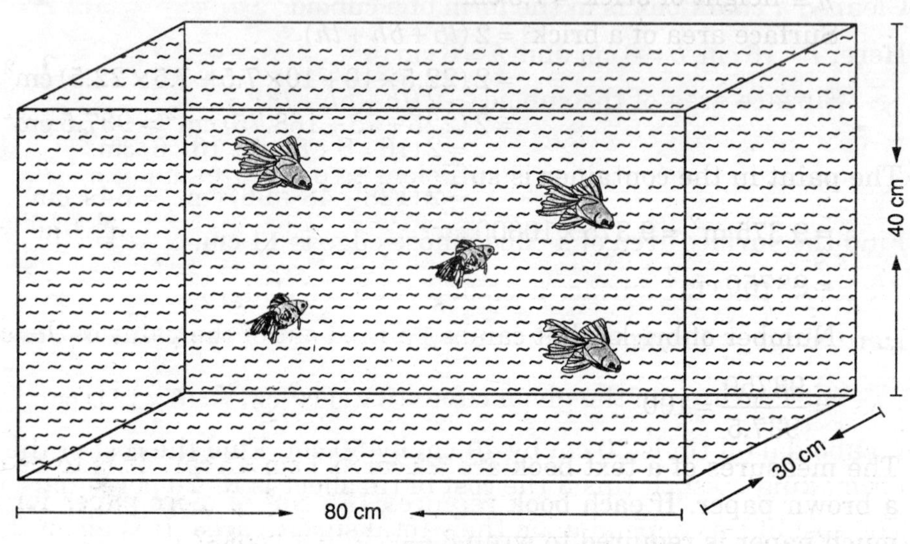

Fig. 21.10

Solution We have,

Length of the aquarium $= l = 80$ cm, Width of the aquarium $= b = 30$ cm

Height of the aquarium $= h = 40$ cm

$\therefore$ Area of the front face $= l \times h = 80 \times 40 \text{ cm}^2 = 3200 \text{ cm}^2$

Area of the top face $= l \times b = 80 \times 30 \text{ cm}^2 = 2400 \text{ cm}^2$

Total surface area of the aquarium $= 2\,(lb + bh + lh)$

$= 2\,(80 \times 30 + 30 \times 40 + 80 \times 40) \text{ cm}^2$

$= 13600 \text{ cm}^2$

$\therefore$ Area of the colour paper required

= Total surface area – (Area of the front face + Area of the top face)

$= 13600 - (3200 + 2400) = 8000 \text{ cm}^2$

Example 7 The dimensions of a cuboid are in the ratio of 1 : 2 : 3 and its total surface area is 88 m^2. Find the dimensions.

Solution Since the dimensions of the cuboid are in the ratio 1:2:3. So, let the dimensions be x, $2x$, $3x$ in metres.

Now,

Surface are $= 88 \text{ m}^2$

$\Rightarrow \quad 2\,(x \times 2x + 2x \times 3x + x \times 3x) = 88$

$\Rightarrow \quad 2\,(2x^2 + 6x^2 + 3x^2) = 88$

$\Rightarrow \quad 2 \times 11x^2 = 88$

$\Rightarrow \quad 22x^2 = 88 \Rightarrow x^2 = \frac{88}{22} \Rightarrow x^2 = 4 \Rightarrow x^2 = 2^2 \Rightarrow x = 2 \text{ m}$

$\therefore \quad 2x = 2 \times 2 = 4$ and $3x = 3 \times 2 = 6$

Hence, the dimensions are 2 m, 4 m and 6 m.

Example 8 The paint in a certain container is sufficient to paint an area equal to 9.375 m². How many bricks measuring 22.5 cm by 10 cm by 7.5 cm can be painted out of this container?

Solution We have,

$l =$ length of a brick $= 22.5$ cm, $b =$ breadth of a brick $= 10$ cm

$h =$ height of brick $= 7.5$ cm

$\therefore$ Surface area of a brick $= 2(lb + bh + lh)$

$= 2(22.5 \times 10 + 10 \times 7.5 + 7.5 \times 22.5)\text{ cm}^2$

$= 2(225 + 75 + 168.75)\text{ cm}^2 = 937.5\text{ cm}^2$

The paint in the container is sufficient to paint area

$= 9.375\text{ m}^2 = 9.375 \times 10000\text{ cm}^2$ $\quad [\because 1\text{ m}^2 = 10000\text{ cm}^2]$

$= 93750\text{ cm}^2$

$\therefore$ Number of bricks that can be painted out of the paint in the container

$= \frac{93750}{937.5} = 100$

Example 9 The measures of a text book are $22\text{ cm} \times 11\text{ cm} \times 3\text{ cm}$. It is to be covered with a brown paper. If each book requires 164 cm² of more paper for folding, how much paper is required to wrap 85 such text books?

Solution We have,

Length of a text book $= l = 22$ cm,

Width of a text book $= b = 11$ cm,

Height of a text book $= h = 3$ cm

The text book is covered with a paper only on three faces, that are bottom, top and back.

We have,

Area of the bottom $= l \times b = 22 \times 11\text{ cm}^2 = 242\text{ cm}^2$

Area of the top = Area of the bottom $= 242\text{ cm}^2$

Area of the back face $= l \times h = 22 \times 3 = 66\text{ cm}^2$

Area of the paper required for folding $= 164\text{ cm}^2$

$\therefore$ Area of the paper required for one text book

$= (242 + 242 + 66 + 164)\text{ cm}^2 = 714\text{ cm}^2$

b = 11 cm
Mathematics Unlimited – 2001 and Beyond
l = 22 cm
h = 3 cm

Fig. 21.11

Hence, Area of paper needed for 85 such text books $= 714 \times 85\text{ cm}^2 = 60690\text{ cm}^2$.

21.10 SURFACE AREA OF THE WALLS OF A ROOM

In previous section, we have learnt the formula for the surface area of a cuboid and a cube. In this section, we shall obtain a formula for the surface area of the walls of a room. For this, let us consider a room whose length, breadth and height are l cm, b cm and h cm respectively. Clearly, a room has four walls, two long and two short each in the rectangular shape. Size of each long wall is l cm by h cm and the size of each short wall is b cm by h cm.

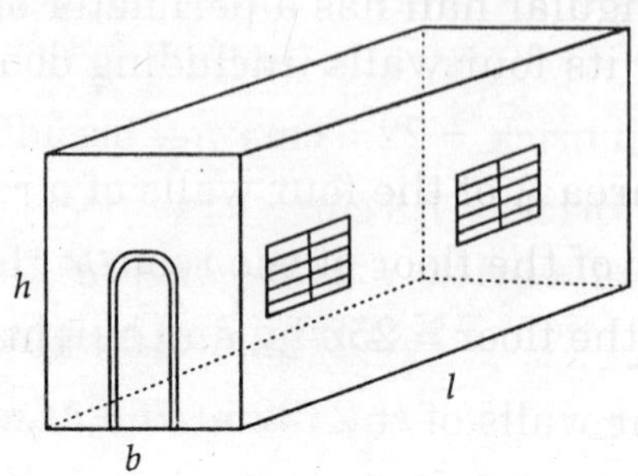

Fig. 21.12

$\therefore$ Surface area of the four walls $= \{2(l \times h) + 2(b \times h)\}$ cm^2

$= 2(l + b) \times h$ cm^2

$= 2 \times$(Length+ Breadth)$\times$Height

$=$ (Perimeter of the floor) $\times$ Height

[$\because 2(l + b) =$ Perimeter of the floor]

NOTE: *The above formula is also applicable to the lateral surface area of a cuboid.*

Following examples will illustrate the use of the above formula.

ILLUSTRATIVE EXAMPLES

Example 1 Find the area of the four walls of a room whose length is 6 m, breadth 5 m and height 4 m. Also, find the cost of white-washing the walls, if the rate of white washing is Rs 5 per square metre. (Doors, windows and other openings ignored).

Solution Here, $l = 6$ m, $b = 5$ m and $h = 4$ m

$\therefore$ Area of the four walls $= 2h(l + b) = [2 \times 4 \times (6 + 5)]$ m^2 $= (8 \times 11)$ m^2 $= 88$ m^2

Cost of white-washing of 1 square metre = Rs 5

$\therefore$ Cost of white-washing the walls = Rs (5×88) = Rs 440.

Example 2 A swimming pool is 20 m in length, 15 m in breadth, and 4 m in depth. Find the cost of cementing its floor and walls at the rate of Rs 12 per square metre.

Solution We have,

$l =$ Length of the swimming pool = 20 m,

$b =$ Breadth of the swimming pool = 15 m

$h =$ Height of the swimming pool = 4 m

$\therefore$ Area of the four walls of the swimming pool.

$= 2(l + b)h = [2 \times 4 \times (20 + 15)]\ m^2 = 8 \times 35\ m^2 = 280\ m^2$

Area of the floor of the swimming pool $= l \times b = 20 \times 15\ m^2 = 300\ m^2$

$\therefore$ Total area to be cemented $= (280 + 300)\ m^2 = 580\ m^2$

Cost of cementing of 1 square metre = Rs 12.

$\therefore$ Cost of cementing the floor and the walls = Rs (12×580) = Rs 6960

Example 3 The floor of a rectangular hall has a perimeter of 250 m. Its height is 6 m. Find the cost of painting its four walls (including doors, etc.) at the rate of Rs 6 per square metre.

Solution We know that the area A of the four walls of a room is given by

A = Perimeter of the floor of the room × Height

Here, Perimeter of the floor = 250 m, and height = 6 m

$\therefore$ Area of the four walls of the room $= (250 \times 6)\ m^2 = 1500\ m^2$

Cost of painting of 1 square metre = Rs 6

$\therefore$ Cost of painting the four walls = Rs (6×1500) = Rs 9000

Example 4 A cuboid has total surface area of 40 m^2 and its lateral surface area is 26 m^2. Find the area of its base.

Solution We have,

Total surface area = 2 (Surface area of base) + (Surface area of 4 walls)

$\Rightarrow$ 40 = 2 (Surface area of base) + (Lateral surface area)

$\Rightarrow$ 40 = 2 (Surface area of base) + 26

$\Rightarrow$ 14 = 2 (Surface area of base)

$\Rightarrow$ Surface area of base $= \frac{14}{2}\ m^2 = 7\ m^2$

Example 5 Length of a class-room is two times its height and its breadth is $1\frac{1}{2}$ times its height. The cost of white-wasing the walls at the rate of Rs 1.60 per m^2 is Rs 179.20. Find the cost of tiling the floor at the rate of Rs 6.75 per m^2.

Solution Let the height of the classroom be h metres. Then,

Length $= 2h$ metres and, Breadth $= \frac{3}{2}h$ metres

$\therefore$ Area of the four walls $= 2 \times \text{Height} \times (\text{Length} + \text{Breadth})$

$$= \left\{2 \times h \times \left(2h + \frac{3}{2}h\right)\right\} m^2$$

$$= \left\{2 \times h \times \left(\frac{4h + 3h}{2}\right)\right\} m^2 = \left\{2 \times h \times \frac{7h}{2}\right\} m^2 = 7h^2\ m^2$$

Cost of white-washing of 1 m^2 = Rs 1.60

$\therefore$ Cost of white-washing of the four walls = Rs $(1.60 \times 7h^2)$ = Rs $11.20\ h^2$

But, the cost of white-washing is given as Rs 179.20

$\therefore \quad 11.20h^2 = 179.20 \Rightarrow h^2 = \frac{179.20}{11.20} = 16 \Rightarrow h^2 = 4^2 \Rightarrow h = 4$

$\therefore$ Length of the classroom $= (2 \times 4)$ m $= 8$ m

Breadth of the classroom $= \frac{3}{2} \times 4$ m $= 6$ m

$\therefore$ Area of the floor of the room $= (8 \times 6)\ m^2 = 48\ m^2$

Cost of tiling of 1 m^2 of the floor = Rs 6.75

$\therefore$ Cost of tiling the floor = Rs (6.75×48) = Rs 324

EXERCISE 21.3

1. Find the surface area of a cuboid whose
   (i) length = 10 cm, breadth = 12 cm, height = 14 cm
   (ii) length = 6 dm, breadth = 8 dm, height = 10 dm
   (iii) length = 2 m, breadth = 4 m, height = 5 m
   (iv) length = 3.2 m, breadth = 30 dm, height = 250 cm.
2. Find the surface area of a cube whose edge is
   (i) 1.2 m (ii) 27 cm (iii) 3 cm (iv) 6 m (v) 2.1 m
3. A cuboidal box is 5 cm by 5 cm by 4 cm. Find its surface area.
4. Find the surface area of a cube whose volume is
   (i) 343 m^3 (ii) 216 dm^3
5. Find the volume of a cube whose surface area is
   (i) 96 cm^2 (ii) 150 m^2
6. The dimensions of a cuboid are in the ratio 5 : 3 : 1 and its total surface area is 414 m^2. Find the dimensions.
7. Find the area of the cardboard required to make a closed box of length 25 cm, 0.5 m and height 15 cm.
8. Find the surface area of a wooden box whose shape is of a cube, and if the edge of the box is 12 cm.
9. The dimensions of an oil tin are 26 cm × 26 cm × 45 cm. Find the area of the tin sheet required for making 20 such tins. If 1 square metre of the tin sheet costs Rs 10, find the cost of tin sheet used for these 20 tins.
10. A classroom is 11 m long, 8 m wide and 5 m high. Find the sum of the areas of its floor and the four walls (including doors, windows, etc.)
11. A swimming pool is 20 m long 15 m wide and 3 m deep. Find the cost of repairing the floor and wall at the rate of Rs 25 per square metre.
12. The perimeter of a floor of a room is 30 m and its height is 3 m. Find the area of four walls of the room.
13. Show that the product of the areas of the floor and two adjacent walls of a cuboid is the square of its volume.
14. The walls and ceiling of a room are to be plastered. The length, breadth and height of the room are 4.5 m, 3 m and 350 cm, respectively. Find the cost of plastering at the rate of Rs 8 per square metre.

15. A cuboid has total surface area of 50 m^2 and lateral surface area is 30 m^2. Find the area of its base.
16. A classroom is 7 m long, 6 m broad and 3.5 m high. Doors and windows occupy an area of 17 m^2. What is the cost of white-washing the walls at the rate of Rs 1.50 per m^2.
17. The central hall of a school is 80 m long and 8 m high. It has 10 doors each of size 3 m × 1.5 m and 10 windows each of size 1.5 m × 1 m. If the cost of white-washing the walls of the hall at the rate of Rs 1.20 per m^2 is Rs 2385.60, find the breadth of the hall.

ANSWERS

1. (i) 856 cm^2 (ii) 376 dm^2 (iii) 76 m^2 (iv) 5020 dm^2
2. (i) 8.64 m^2 (ii) 4374 cm^2 (iii) 54 cm^2 (iv) 216 m^2 (v) 26.46 m^2 3. 130 cm^2
4. (i) 294 m^2 (ii) 216 dm^2 5. (i) 64 cm^2 (ii) 125 m^2 6. 15 m, 9 m, 3 m
7. 4750 cm^2 8. 864 cm^2 9. 120640 cm^2, Rs 120.64 10. 278 m^2 11. Rs 12750
12. 90 m^2 14. Rs 528 15. 10 m^2 16. Rs 111 17. 48 m

21.11 MISCELLANEOUS PROBLEMS

In this section, we shall discuss some miscellaneous problems on volume and surface area of a cube and cuboid.

ILLUSTRATIVE EXAMPLES

Example 1 The volume of a cuboid is 440 cm^3 and the area of its base is 88 cm^2. Find its height.

Solution We have,

$$\text{Volume} = 440 \text{ cm}^3 \text{ and, Area of the base} = 88 \text{ cm}^2$$

$$\therefore \quad \text{Height} = \frac{\text{Volume}}{\text{Area of the base}} \Rightarrow \text{Height} = \frac{440}{88} \text{ cm} = 5 \text{ cm}$$

Example 2 The volume of a cube is 1,000 cm^3. Find its total surface area.

Solution Let the length of each edge of the cube be a cm. Then,

$$\text{Volume} = 1000 \text{ cm}^3 \Rightarrow a^3 = 1000 \Rightarrow a = 10 \text{ cm}$$

$$\therefore \quad \text{Surface area} = 6a^2 \text{ cm}^2 = 6 \times 10^2 \text{ cm}^2 = 600 \text{ cm}^2$$

Example 3 The dimensions of a metallic cuboid are: 100 cm × 80 cm × 64 cm. It is melted and recast into a cube. Find the surface area of the cube.

Solution Volume of the metallic cuboid $= 100 \times 80 \times 64 \text{ cm}^3 = 512000 \text{ cm}^3$

Since the metallic cuboid is melted and is recasted into a cube

$\therefore$ Volume of the metallic cuboid = Volume of the cube.

Let the length of each edge of the recasted cube be a cm. Then,

Volume of the cube = Volume of the cuboid

$$\Rightarrow \quad a^3 = 512000$$

$$\Rightarrow \quad a^3 = 8^3 \times 10^3$$

$$\Rightarrow \quad a = 8 \times 10 \text{ cm} = 80 \text{ cm}$$

$$\therefore \quad \text{Surface area of the cube} = 6a^2 \text{ cm}^2 = 6 \times (80)^2 \text{ cm}^2 = 38400 \text{ cm}^2$$

Example 4 How many 3 metre cubes can be cut from a cuboid measuring $18\text{ m}\times 12\text{ m}\times 9\text{ m}$?

Solution We have,

Edge of the each cube = 3 m

$\therefore$ Volume of each cube $=(\text{edge})^3=(3^3)\text{ m}^3=27\text{ m}^3$

Volume of the cuboid $=(18\times 12\times 9)\text{ m}^3=1944\text{ m}^3$

$$\therefore \quad \text{Number of cubes}=\frac{\text{Volume of the cuboid}}{\text{Volume of each cube}}=\frac{1944}{27}=72$$

Example 5 A cube of 9 cm edge is immersed completely in a rectangular vessel containing water. If the dimensions of the base are 15 cm and 12 cm, find the rise in water level in the vessel.

Solution We have,

Edge of the given cube = 9 cm

$\therefore$ Volume of the cube $=(9^3)\text{ cm}^3=729\text{ cm}^2$

If the cube is immersed in the vessel, then the water level rises. Let the rise in water level be x cm.

Clearly,

Volume of the cube = Volume of the water replaced by it.

$\Rightarrow$ Volume of the cube = Volume of a cuboid of dimension $15\text{ cm}\times 12\text{ cm}\times x\text{ cm}$.

$\Rightarrow \quad 729 = 15\times 12\times x$

$$\Rightarrow \quad x=\frac{729}{15\times 12}\text{ cm}\Rightarrow x=\frac{81}{20}\text{ cm}=4.05\text{ cm}.$$

Example 6 The length of a cold storage is double its breadth. Its height is 3 metres. The area of its four walls (including doors) is 108 m^2. Find its volume.

Solution Let length, breadth and height of the cold storage be l metres, b metres and h metres respectively. Then, $l=2b$ (given) and $h=3$ metres.

Now,

Area of four walls $=108\text{ m}^3$

$\Rightarrow \quad 2(l+b)h=108$

$\Rightarrow \quad 2(2b+b)\times 3=108$

$\Rightarrow \quad 18b=108 \Rightarrow b=6$ metres

$\therefore \quad l=2b\Rightarrow l=12$ metres

Hence, Volume of the cold storage $=(lbh)\text{ m}^3=(12\times 6\times 3)\text{ m}^3=216\text{ m}^2$

Example 7 Two cubes each of 10 cm edge are joined end to end. Find the surface area of the resulting cuboid.

Solution If two cubes are joined end to end, we get a cuboid such that

$l=$ Length of the resulting cuboid $=10\text{ cm}+10\text{ cm}=20\text{ cm}$,

$b=$ Breadth of the resulting cuboid $=10\text{ cm}$

$h=$ Height of the resulting cuboid $=10\text{ cm}$,

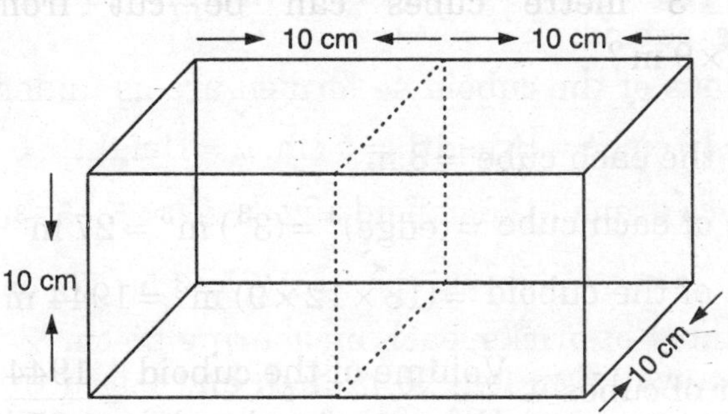

Fig. 21.13

$\therefore$ Surface area of the cuboid $= 2(lb + bh + lh)$

$$= 2(20 \times 10 + 10 \times 10 + 20 \times 10)\ \text{cm}^2 = 1000\ \text{cm}^2$$

Example 8 The sum of length, breadth and depth of a cuboid is 19 cm and the length of its diagonal is 11 cm. Find the surface area of the cuboid.

Solution Let the length, breadth and height of the cube be l cm, b cm and h cm respectively. Then, $l + b + h = 19$ ...(i)

Now,

Diagonal $= 11$ cm

$\Rightarrow \sqrt{l^2 + b^2 + h^2} = 11 \Rightarrow l^2 + b^2 + h^2 = 121$ ...(ii)

Now,

$l + b + h = 19$

$\Rightarrow (l + b + h)^2 = 19^2$

$\Rightarrow l^2 + b^2 + h^2 + 2(lb + bh + lh) = 361$

$\Rightarrow 121 + 2(lb + bh + lh) = 361$ [Using (ii)]

$\Rightarrow 2(lb + bh + lh) = 240$

Hence, the surface area of the cuboid is 240 cm^2.

Example 9 A plot of land in the form of a rectangle has a dimension 240 m $\times$ 180 m. A drainlet 10 m wide is dug all around it (on the outside) and the earth dug out is evenly spread over the plot, increasing its surface level by 25 cm. Find the depth of the drainlet.

Solution Let the depth of the drainlet be x metres. Width of the drainlet $= 10$ m.

$\therefore$ Volume of the drainlet

$$= (260 \times 10 \times x + 260 \times 10 \times x + 180 \times 10 \times x + 180 \times 10 \times x)\ \text{m}^3$$

$$= (5200x + 3600x)\ \text{m}^3 = 8800\,x\ \text{m}^3$$

When earth dug out is evenly spread over the plot, we get a cuboid whose base area is $240 \times 180\ \text{m}^3$ and height $= 25$ cm $= 0.25$ m.

$\therefore$ Volume of earth spread over the plot $= (240 \times 180 \times 0.25)\ \text{m}^3 = 10800\ \text{m}^2$

Clearly, Volume of earth spread over the plot $=$ Volume of the drainlet

$$\therefore \quad 10800 = 8800x \Rightarrow x = \frac{10800}{8800} = 1.227\ \text{m}$$

Example 10 Three cubes each of side 5 cm are joined end to end. Find the surface area of the resulting cuboid.

Solution The dimensions of the cuboid so formed are as under:

l = Length = 15 cm, b = Breadth = 5 cm, h = Height = 5 cm

So, the surface area of the cuboid $= 2(15\times5+5\times5+15\times5)\ \text{cm}^2$

$= 2(75+25+75)\ \text{cm}^2 = 350\ \text{cm}^2$

Example 11 Find the number of bricks, each measuring 25 cm $\times$ 12.5 cm $\times$ 7.5 cm required to construct a wall 6 m long, 5 m high and 0.5 m thick, while the cement and sand mixture occupies 1 / 20 of the volume of the wall.

Solution We have,

Volume of the wall $= (6\times5\times0.5)\ \text{m}^3 = 15\ \text{m}^3$

Volume occupied by the mortar $= \frac{1}{20}\times$ Volume of the wall

$= \left(\frac{1}{20}\times15\right)\text{m}^3 = 0.75\ \text{m}^3$

$\therefore$ Volume occupied by the bricks $= (15-0.75)\ \text{m}^3 = 14.25\ \text{m}^3$

Volume of each brick $= \left(\frac{25}{100}\times\frac{12.5}{100}\times\frac{7.5}{100}\right)\text{m}^3 = \frac{3}{1280}\ \text{m}^3$

So, required number of bricks $= \dfrac{\text{Volume occupied by the bricks}}{\text{Volume of each brick}}$

$= \dfrac{14.25}{3/1280}$

$= 14.25\times\frac{1280}{3} = \frac{1425}{100}\times\frac{1280}{3} = 6080$

Example 12 A metallic sheet is of the rectangular shape with dimensions 48 cm × 36 cm. From each one of its corners, a square of 8 cm is cut-off. An open box is made of the remaining sheet. Find the volume of the box.

Solution In order to make an open box, a square of side 8 cm is cut-off from each of the four corners and the flaps are folded up.

Thus, the box will have the following dimensions:

Length $= (48-8-8)$ cm $= 32$ cm, Breadth $= (36-8-8)$ cm $= 20$ cm, Height $= 8$ cm

$\therefore$ Volume of the box formed $= (32\times20\times8)\ \text{cm}^3 = 5120\ \text{cm}^3$

Example 13 How many planks each of which is 2 m long, 2.5 cm broad and 4 cm thick can be cut-off from a wooden block 6 m long, 15 cm broad and 40 cm thick?

Solution We have,

Length of wooden block $= 6$ m $= 600$ cm

Breadth of wooden block $= 15$ cm, Height of wooden block $= 40$ cm

$\therefore$ Volume of wooden block $= (600\times15\times40)\ \text{cm}^3$

Length of each plank $= 2$ m $= 200$ cm, Breadth of each plank $= 2.5$ cm and Height of each plank $= 4$ cm

$\therefore$ Volume of each plank $= (200\times2.5\times4)\ \text{cm}^2$

So, number of planks $= \dfrac{\text{Volume of wooden block}}{\text{Volume of each plank}} = \dfrac{600\times15\times40}{200\times2.5\times4} = 3\times15\times4 = 180$

Example 14 An agricultural field is in the form of a rectangle of length 20 m and width 14 m. A pit 6 m long, 3 m wide and 2.5 m deep is dug in a corner of the field and the earth taken out of the pit is spread uniformly over the remaining area of the field. Find the extent to which the level of the field has been raised.

Solution Let $ABCD$ be the field and let $A_1\ B_1\ C_1\ D_1$ be the part of the field where a pit is to be dug.

Volume of the earth dugout $= (6 \times 3 \times 2.5)\ \text{m}^3 = 45\ \text{m}^3$ ...(i)

Area of the remaining part of the field = Area of the field − Area of pit

$= (20 \times 14 - 6 \times 3)\ \text{m}^2 = 262\ \text{m}^2$

The earth taken out of the pit is spread uniformly over the remaining area of the field. Let h metres be the level raised over the field uniformly.

Clearly, the earth taken out forms a cuboid of base area 262 m^2 and height h.

Volume of the earth dugout $= (262 \times h)\ \text{m}^3$ (ii)

From (i) and (ii), we have

$$262\,h = 45$$

$$\Rightarrow \quad h = \frac{45}{262} = 0.1718\ \text{m} = 17.18\ \text{cm}$$

Hence, the level is raised by 17.18 cm.

Example 15 The length of a hall is 20 m and width 16 m. The sum of the areas of the floor and the flat roof is equal to the sum of the areas of the four walls. Find the height and the volume of the hall.

Solution Let the height of the hall be h m. Then,

Sum of the areas of four walls $= 2\,(l + b)\,h\ \text{m}^2 = 2\,(20 + 16)\,h\ \text{m}^2 = 72\,h\ \text{m}^2$

Sum of the areas of the floor and the flat roof $= (20 \times 16 + 20 \times 16)\ \text{m}^2 = 640\ \text{m}^2$

It is given that the sum of the areas of four walls is equal to the sum of the areas of the floor and roof.

$$\therefore \quad 72\,h = 640 \Rightarrow h = \frac{640}{72}\ \text{m} = \frac{80}{9}\ \text{m} = 8.88\ \text{m}$$

So, height of the hall = 8.88 m

$$\text{Volume of the hall} = 20 \times 16 \times \frac{80}{9}\ \text{m}^3 = \frac{25600}{9}\ \text{m}^3 = 2844.4\ \text{m}^3$$

Example 16 A room is half as long again as it is broad. The cost of carpeting the room at Rs 3.25 per m^2 is Rs 175.50 and the cost of papering the walls at Rs 1.40 per m^2 is Rs 240.80. If 1 door and 2 windows occupy 8 m^2, find the dimensions of the room.

Solution Let the breadth of the room be x m. Then,

$$\text{Length} = \left(x + \frac{x}{2}\right)\text{m} = \left(\frac{3x}{2}\right)\text{m}$$

$\therefore$ Area of the room $= \left(x \times \frac{3x}{2}\right) m^2 = \left(\frac{3x^2}{2}\right) m^2$

$\Rightarrow$ Cost of carpeting the room at the rate of Rs 3.25 per m^2 = Rs $\left(\frac{3x^2}{2} \times 3.25\right)$

But, the cost of carpeting is given as Rs 175.50

$\therefore \quad \frac{3x^2}{2} \times 3.25 = 175.50$ [$\because$ Cost of carpeting = Rs 175.50 (given)]

$\Rightarrow \quad x^2 = \frac{175.50 \times 2}{3 \times 3.25} = \frac{351}{3 \times 3.25} = \frac{351}{6.5} = \frac{3510}{65} = 36$

$\Rightarrow \quad x = 6$

$\therefore$ Breadth $= 6$ m and, Length $= \left(6 + \frac{6}{2}\right)$ m $= 9$ m

Let the height of the room be h metres. Then,

Area of 4 walls = 2 (Length + Breadth) × Height

$= 2(6+9) \times h \text{ m}^2 = 30\,h \text{ m}^2$

Area of 1 door and 2 windows $= 8 \text{ m}^2$

$\therefore$ Area to be papered = Area of 4 walls – Area of 1 door and 2 windows

$= (30\,h - 8) \text{ m}^2$

Cost of papering walls at Rs 1.40 per m^2 = Rs. $(30h - 8) \times 1.40$

But, the cost of papering the walls is given as Rs 240.80

$\therefore \quad (30\,h - 8) \times 1.40 = 240.80$

$\Rightarrow \quad (30h - 8) = \frac{240.80}{1.40}$

$\Rightarrow \quad 30h - 8 = \frac{24080}{140}$

$\Rightarrow \quad 30h - 8 = \frac{2408}{14} \Rightarrow 30\,h - 8 = 172 \Rightarrow 30\,h = 180 \Rightarrow h = 6$

$\therefore$ Height = 6 m

Hence, the dimensions of the room are: Length = 9 m, Breadth = 6 m and, Height = 6 m.

Example 17 A solid cube is cut into two cuboids of equal volumes. Find the ratio of the total surface area of the given cube and that of one of the cuboids.

Solution Let the edge of the solid cube be a units. Since the cube is cut into two cuboids of equal volumes. Therefore, the dimensions of each of the cuboid are:

Length $= a$ units, breadth = a units and, height $= \frac{a}{2}$ units

Now,

S = Total surface area of cube $= 6a^2$ sq. units

S_1 = Total surface area of one cuboid $= 2\left(a \times a + a \times \frac{a}{2} + \frac{a}{2} \times a\right) = 4a^2$ sq. units

$\therefore \quad S : S_1 = 6a^2 : 4a^2 = 3 : 2.$

Example 18 The external length, breadth and height of a closed rectangular wooden box are 18 cm, 10 cm and 6 cm respectively and thickness of wood is 1/2 cm. When the box is empty, it weights 15 kg and when filled with sand it weighs 100 kg. Find the weight of the cubic cm of wood and cubic cm of sand.

Solution We have,

Thickness of wood $= \frac{1}{2}$ cm

Internal length of wooden box $= 18 - \left(\frac{1}{2} + \frac{1}{2}\right) = 17$ cm

Internal breadth of wooden box $= 10 - \left(\frac{1}{2} + \frac{1}{2}\right) = 9$ cm

Internal depth of wooden box $= 6 - \left(\frac{1}{2} + \frac{1}{2}\right) = 5$ cm

$\therefore$ Internal volume of wooden box $= (17 \times 9 \times 5)\ \text{cm}^3 = 765\ \text{cm}^3$

External volume of wooden box $= (18 \times 10 \times 6)\ \text{cm}^3 = 1080\ \text{cm}^3$

Volume of wood = External volume – Internal volume

$= (1080 - 765)\ \text{cm}^3 = 315\ \text{cm}^3$

Weight of empty box = 15 kg

$\Rightarrow$ Weight of 315 cm^3 wood is 15 kg.

$\therefore$ Weight of 1 cm^3 of wood $= \left(\frac{15}{315}\right)$ kg $= \frac{1}{21}$ kg

Now,

Volume of sand = Internal volume of box $= 765\ \text{cm}^3$

Weight of sand = Weight of box filled with sand – Weight of empty box

$= (100 - 15)$ kg $= 85$ kg

Volume of sand $= 765\ \text{cm}^3$

$\therefore$ Weight of 1 cm^3 of sand $= \left(\frac{85}{765}\right)$ kg $= \frac{1}{9}$ kg

Example 19 The outer dimensions of a closed wooden box are 10 cm by 8 cm by 7 cm. Thickness of the wood is 1 cm. Find the total cost of wood required to make box, if 1 cm^3 of wood costs Rs. 2.00.

Solution The external dimension of the box are :

Length = 10 cm, Breadth = 8 cm, Height = 7 cm.

$\therefore$ External volume of the box $= (10 \times 8 \times 7)\ \text{cm}^3 = 560\ \text{cm}^3$

Thickness of the wood = 1 cm.

$\therefore$ Internal length $= 10 - 2 = 8$ cm, Internal breadth $= 8 - 2 = 6$ cm

Internal height $= 7 - 2 = 5$ cm .

$\therefore$ Internal volume $= (8 \times 6 \times 5)\ \text{cm}^3 = 240\ \text{cm}^3$

Volume of the wood = External volume – Internal volume

$= (560 - 240)\ \text{cm}^3 = 320\ \text{cm}^3$

Hence, total cost of wood required to make box = Rs (320×2) = Rs 640.

EXERCISE 21.4

1. Find the length of the longest rod that can be placed in a room 12 m long, 9 m broad and 8 m high.
2. If V is the volume of a cuboid of dimensions a, b, c and S is its surface area, then prove that

$$\frac{1}{V}=\frac{2}{S}\left(\frac{1}{a}+\frac{1}{b}+\frac{1}{c}\right)$$

3. The areas of three adjacent faces of a cuboid are x, y and z. If the volume is V, prove that $V^2 = xyz$.
4. A rectangular water reservoir contains 105 m^3 of water. Find the depth of the water in the reservoir if its base measures 12 m by 3.5 m.
5. Cubes A, B, C having edges 18 cm, 24 cm and 30 cm respectively are melted and moulded into a new cube D. Find the edge of the bigger cube D.
6. The breadth of a room is twice its height, one half of its length and the volume of the room is 512 cu. dm. Find its dimensions.
7. A closed iron tank 12 m long, 9 m wide and 4 m deep is to be made. Determine the cost of iron sheet used at the rate of Rs 5 per metre sheet, sheet being 2 m wide.
8. A tank open at the top is made of iron sheet 4 m wide. If the dimensions of the tank are 12 m × 8 m × 6 m, find the cost of iron sheet at Rs 17.50 per metre.
9. Three equal cubes are placed adjacently in a row. Find the ratio of total surface area of the new cuboid to that of the sum of the surface areas of the three cubes.
10. The dimensions of a room are 12.5 m by 9 m by 7 m. There are 2 doors and 4 windows in the room; each door measures 2.5 m by 1.2 m and each window 1.5 m by 1 m. Find the cost of painting the walls at Rs 3.50 per square metre.
11. A field is 150 m long and 100 m wide. A plot (outside the field) 50 m long and 30 m wide is dug to a depth of 8 m and the earth taken out from the plot is spread evenly in the field. By how much is the level of field raised?
12. Two cubes, each of volume 512 cm^3 are joined end to end. Find the surface area of the resulting cuboid.
13. Three cubes whose edges measure 3 cm, 4 cm, and 5 cm respectively are melted to form a new cube. Find the surface area of the new cube formed.
14. The cost of preparing the walls of a room 12 m long at the rate of Rs 1.35 per square metre is Rs 340.20 and the cost of matting the floor at 85 paise per square metre is Rs 91.80. Find the height of the room.
15. The length of a hall is 18 m and the width 12 m. The sum of the areas of the floor and the flat roof is equal to the sum of the areas of the four walls. Find the height of the wall.
16. A metal cube of edge 12 cm is melted and formed into three smaller cubes. If the edges of the two smaller cubes are 6 cm and 8 cm, find the edge of the third smaller cube.
17. The dimensions of a cinema hall are 100 m, 50 m and 18 m. How many persons can sit in the hall, if each person requires 150 m^3 of air?
18. The external dimensions of a closed wooden box are 48 cm, 36 cm, 30 cm. The box is made of 1.5 cm thick wood. How many bricks of size 6 cm × 3 cm × 0.75 cm can be put in this box?

19. The dimensions of a rectangular box are in the ratio of 2 : 3 : 4 and the difference between the cost of covering it with sheet of paper at the rates of Rs 8 and Rs 9.50 per m^2 is Rs. 1248. Find the dimensions of the box.

ANSWERS

1. 17 m 4. 2.5 m 5. 36 cm 6. 16 dm, 8 dm, 4 dm 7. Rs 960
8. Rs 1470 9. 7 : 9 10. Rs 1011.50 11. 8 cm 12. 640 cm^2 13. 216 cm^2
14. 6 m 15. 7.2 m 16. 10 cm 17. 600 18. 2970 19. 8 m, 12 m, 16 m

HINTS TO SELECTED PROBLEMS

1. Length of the longest rod = length of the diagonal

$= \sqrt{12^2 + 9^2 + 8^2}$ m.

2. We have, $V = abc$ and $S = 2(ab + bc + ca)$.

$\therefore$ R.H.S. $= \frac{2}{S}\left(\frac{1}{a} + \frac{1}{b} + \frac{1}{c}\right) = \frac{2}{S}\left(\frac{bc + ca + ab}{abc}\right) = \frac{1}{S}\frac{2(ab + bc + ca)}{abc} = \frac{1}{S} \times \frac{S}{V} = \frac{1}{V}$

3. Let l, b and h be the length, breadth and height of the cuboid. Then,

$x = lb$, $y = bh$ and $z = lh$.

Now, $V = lbh \Rightarrow V^2 = l^2b^2h^2 \Rightarrow V^2 = (lb)(bh)(lh) \Rightarrow V^2 = xyz$

4. Depth $= \frac{\text{Volume}}{\text{Area of the base}}$

6. Let, height $= x$ dm. Then, breadth $= 2x$ dm and length $= 4x$ dm.

$\therefore$ Volume $= 512$ cu. dm $\Rightarrow 4x \times 2x \times x = 512 \Rightarrow x = 4$

7. Here, $l = 12$ m, $b = 9$ m, $h = 4$ m

$\therefore$ Surface area of the tank $= 2(lb + bh + lh) = 2(12 \times 9 + 9 \times 4 + 4 \times 12)$ m^2 $= 384$ m^2

Width of iron sheet $= 2$ m $\therefore$ length $= 384/2 = 192$ m

Hence, Cost $=$ Rs. $(192 \times 5) =$ Rs. 960

8. Area of iron sheet $= \{2(l + b) \times h + l \times b\}$ m^2 $= 336$ m^2

$\therefore$ Length of the sheet $= \frac{\text{Area}}{\text{Width of the sheet}} = \frac{336}{4}$ m $= 84$ m

Hence, Cost $=$ Rs. $84 \times 17.50 =$ Rs 1470.

9. Let the length of the edge of three equal cubes be x cm. Then,

Sum of the surface areas of 3 equal cubes $= 3(6x^2)$ cm^2 $= 18x^2$ cm^2

Dimensions of the resulting cuboid are $3x$ cm, x cm, x cm.

$\therefore$ Surface area of the resulting cuboid $= 2(3x^2 + x^2 + 3x^2)$ cm^2

Required ratio $= 14x^2 : 18x^2 = 7 : 9$

13. Let the length of the edge of the new cube be a cm. Then,

Volume $= (3^3 + 4^3 + 5^3)$ cm^3 $\Rightarrow a^3 = 216 \Rightarrow a = 6$.

$\therefore$ Surface area of the new cube $= 6a^2 \text{ cm}^2$

14. Area of the floor $= \dfrac{\text{Cost of matting}}{\text{Rate per m}^2} = \left(\dfrac{91.80}{0.85}\right) \text{m}^2 = 108 \text{ m}^2$

$\therefore$ Breadth of the room $= \dfrac{\text{Area of floor}}{\text{length}} = \left(\dfrac{108}{12}\right) \text{m} = 9 \text{ m}$

Area of four walls of the room $= \dfrac{\text{Cost of preparing the walls}}{\text{Rate per m}^2} = \dfrac{340.20}{1.35} \text{m}^2 = 252 \text{ m}^2$

Also, Area of four walls $= 2$ (Length + Breadth) × Height $= 2(12+9) \times \text{height}$

$\therefore \quad 2(12+9) \times \text{height} = 252 \Rightarrow h = 6 \text{ m}$

16. Let the edge of the third smaller cube be x cm. Then,

$x^3 + 6^3 + 8^3 = 12^3 \Rightarrow x = 10 \text{ cm}$

17. Number of persons $= \dfrac{\text{Volume}}{\text{Space occupied by a person}} = \dfrac{100 \times 50 \times 18}{150}$

19. Let $l = 2x$, $b = 3x$ and $h = 4x$ in metres.

Surface area $= 2(lb + bh + lh) = 52x^2 \text{ m}^2$

Difference of costs at the two rates $= \text{Rs}\left\{52x^2 \times 9.5 - 52x^2 \times 8\right\} = 78x^2$

$\therefore \; 78x^2 = 1248 \Rightarrow x = 4$

THINGS TO REMEMBER

1. *The magnitude of a space region or solid region is called its volume.*
2. *A cubic centimetre is the volume of the region formed by a cube of side 1 cm.*
3. *Volume of a cuboid* = (length × breadth × height)

   or, $V = l \times b \times h$

   Height of a cuboid $= \dfrac{Volume}{(length) \times (breadth)}$

   or, $h = \dfrac{V}{l \times b}$

   Length of a cuboid $= \dfrac{Volume}{(breadth) \times (height)}$

   or, $l + \dfrac{V}{b \times h}$

   Breadth of a cuboid $= \dfrac{Volume}{(length) \times (height)}$

   or, $b = \dfrac{V}{l \times h}$
4. *Volume of a cube* $= (edge)^3$ *or* $(side)^3$

   or, $V = l^3$
5. *Standard units of volume and their relations:*

   (i) $1\ m^3 = 1000000\ cm^3$

   (ii) $1\ m^3 = 1000\ dm^3 = 1000$ *litres*

   (iii) $1\ dm^3 = 1000\ cm^3 = 1000$ *millilitre*

   (iv) 1 *kilo litre* = 1000 *litre* $= 10^6\ cm^3 = 1\ m^3$.

   (v) $1\ cm^3 = 1000\ mm^3$
6. *The sum of the areas of all the six faces of a cuboid is called the surface area of the cuboid.*
7. (i) *Surface area of a cuboid* $= 2\,(l \times b + b \times h + l \times h)$

   (ii) *Surface area of a cube* $= 6 \times (Side)^2$
8. *Area of the four walls of a room* $= 2 \times (l + b) \times h$ = *Perimeter of the floor × height.*

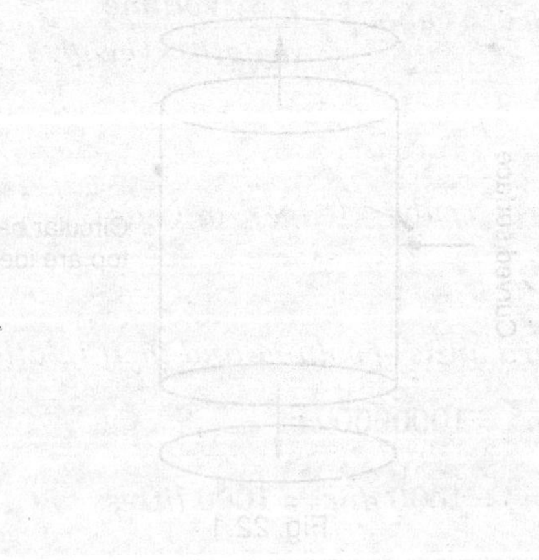

22

MENSURATION-III
(Surface Area and Volume of a Right Circular Cylinder)

22.1 RIGHT CIRCULAR CYLINDER

In our day to day life, we come across several solids like measuring jars, circular pillars, circular pipes, a garden roller, gas cylinder etc. These solids have a curved (lateral) surfaces with congruent circular ends. Such solids are right circular cylinders.

A right circular cylinder has two plane ends. Each plane end is circular in shape, and the two plane ends are parallel; that is, they lie in parallel planes. Each of the plane end is called a *base of the cylinder*.

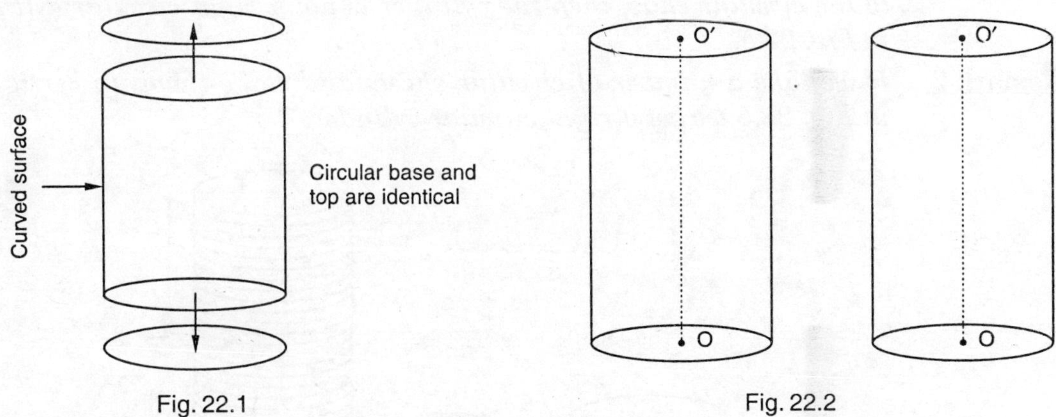

Fig. 22.1 Fig. 22.2

AXIS *The line segment joining the centres of two bases is called the axis of the cylinder.*

In Fig. 22.2, OO' is the axis of the cylinder.

Clearly, axis is perpendicular to the circular ends.

We observe that in a right circular cylinder both circular faces are parallel and congruent and curved surface is perpendicular to them as shown in Fig. 22.3.

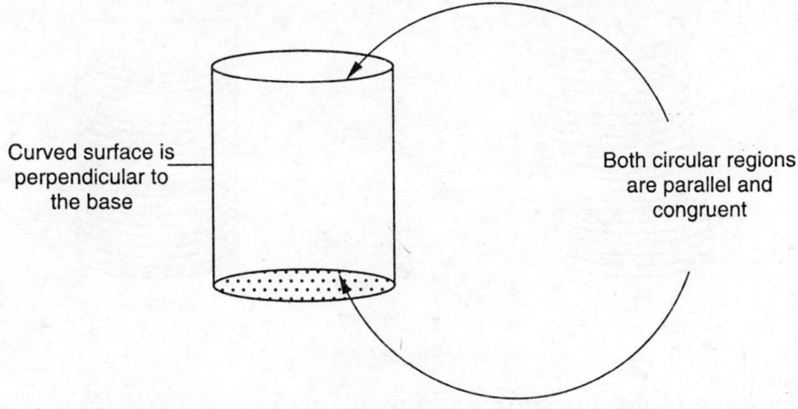

Fig. 22.3

AN ALTERNATIVE DEFINITION *A solid generated by the revolution of a rectangle about one of its sides is called a right circular cylinder.*

Consider a rectangle $OO'AB$ which revolves about its side OO' and completes a full round to arrive at its initial position. The revolution generates a right circular cylinder as shown in Fig. 22.4.

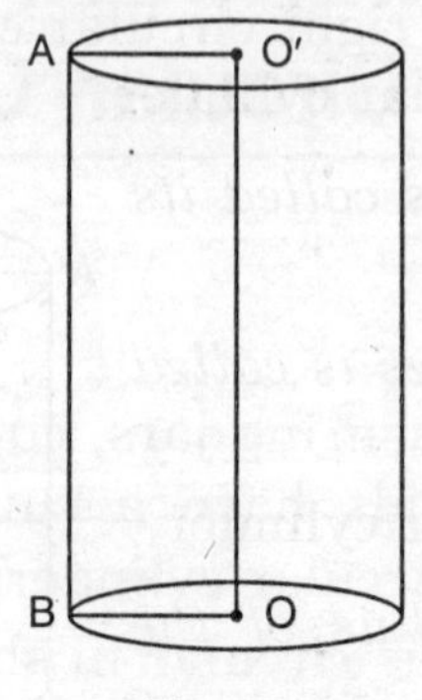

Fig. 22.4

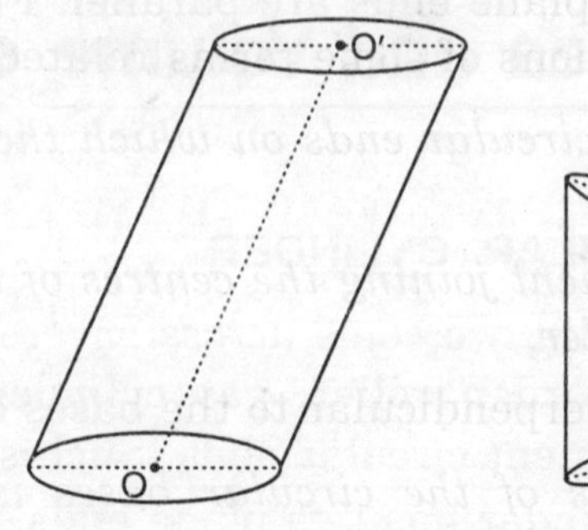

Fig. 22.5

Remark 1: *If the line joining the centres of circular ends of a cylinder is not perpendicular to the circular ends, then the cylinder is not a right circular cylinder as shown in Fig. 22.5.*

Remark 2: *If we take a number of circular sheets and stake them up vertically as shown in Fig. 22.6 we get a right circular cylinder.*

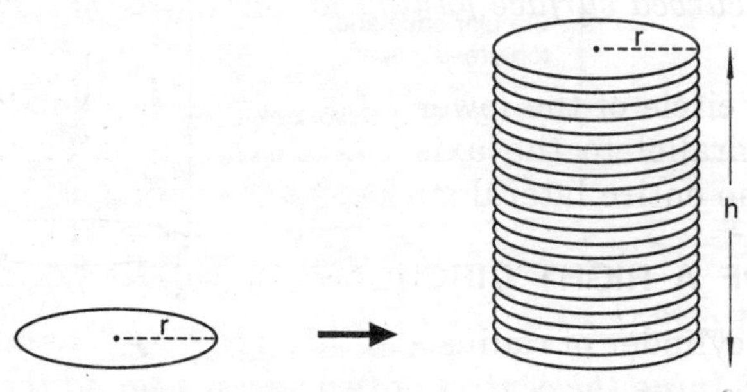

Fig. 22.6

In case circular sheets are not stacked up vertically as shown in Fig. 22.7 (i) then the cylinder is not a right circular cylinder. However, it is a circular cylinder but not a right circular cylinder.

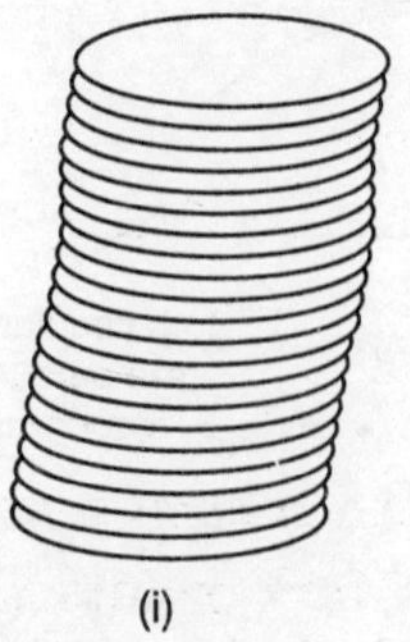

(i)

(ii)

Fig. 22.7

If the base is not circular as shown in Fig. 22.7 (ii) then, the cylinder with a non-circular base is a right cylinder but not a circular one.

<u>NOTE:</u> *From now onwards, in this chapter, the word 'cylinder' will always mean the right circular cylinder.*

22.2 DEFINITIONS OF SOME TERMS

As discussed earlier that a right circular has two plane ends. Each plane end is circular in shape, and the two plane ends are parallel. Fig. 22.8 shows a right circular cylinder. The following are definitions of some terms related to a right circular cylinder:

BASE *Each of the circular ends on which the cylinder rests is called its base.*

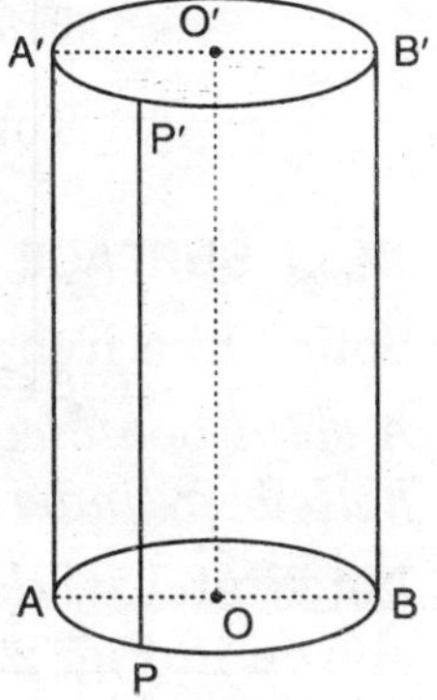

Fig. 22.8

AXIS *The line segment joining the centres of two circular bases is called the axis of the cylinder.*

The axis is always perpendicular to the bases of a right circular cylinder.

RADIUS *The radius of the circular bases is called the radius of the cylinder.*

HEIGHT *The length of the axis of the cylinder is called the height of the cylinder.*
In other words, the perpendicular distance between the two parallel plane ends or the altitude to either base from a point on the other is called the height of the cylinder.

LATERAL SURFACE *The curved surface joining the two bases of a right circular cylinder is called its lateral surface.*

For every point P on the circle of the lower base there is a point P' on the circle of upper base such that PP' is parallel to the axis OO'. As P goes around the circle, the line segment PP' generates the entire lateral surface of the cylinder.

22.3 SURFACE AREA OF A RIGHT CIRCULAR CYLINDER

Consider a right circular cylinder of radius r and height h as shown in the 22.9.

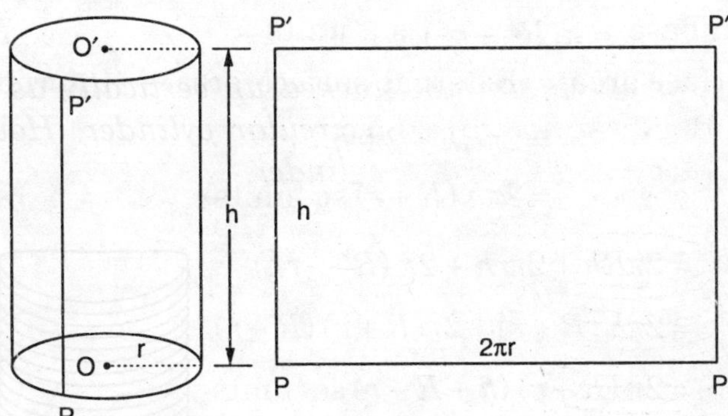

Fig. 22.9

Each of the bases is a circle of radius r. Therefore, length of each circular edge is $2\pi r$.

Now, take a rectangular strip of paper of width h. Mark points P and P' on the two circular bases such that PP' is parallel to the axis OO'. Place the edge of the strip of paper along PP' and hold it fast. Now, wrap the strip around the cylinder, till you reach PP' again. Now, cut-off the strip along PP'. Remove the piece of the strip so cut-off and spread it on a plane surface. You will find that the strip is a rectangle of length $2\pi r$ (equal to the length of the circular edge) and breadth h.

$\therefore$ Area of the lateral surface of the cylinder = Area of the rectangular strip of paper

$= $ Area of a rectangle of length $2\pi r$ and breadth h

$= 2\pi r \times h$ square units

$= 2\pi rh$ square units

Thus, for a cylinder of radius r and height h, we have

Lateral (curved) surface area $= 2\pi rh$ sq. units

Each base surface area $= \pi r^2$ sq. units

Total surface area $= (2\pi rh + 2\pi r^2)$ sq. units $= 2\pi r\,(h + r)$ sq. units

22.3.1 SURFACE AREA OF HOLLOW CYLINDER

Solids like iron pipes, rubber tubes etc. are hollow cylinders. Thus,

A solid bounded by two coaxial cylinders of the same height and different radii is called a hollow cylinder.

Let R and r be the external and internal radii of a hollow cylinder and h be its height as shown in Fig. 22.10. Then, we have the following results:

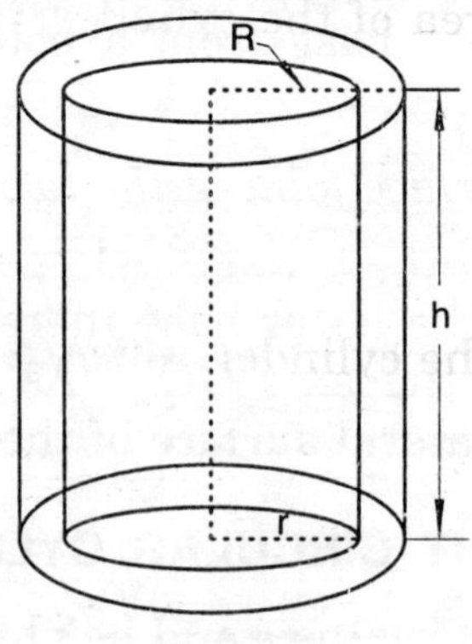

Fig. 22.10

(i) Surface area of each base $= \pi(R^2 - r^2)$ sq. units

(ii) Curved (lateral) surface area = (External surface area) + (Internal surface area)

$= 2\pi Rh + 2\pi rh$

$= 2\pi h\,(R + r)$ sq. units

(iii) Total surface area $= 2\pi Rh + 2\pi rh + 2\pi\,(R^2 - r^2)$

$= 2\pi h\,(R + r) + 2\pi(R + r)\,(R - r)$

$= 2\pi\,(R + r)\,(h + R - r)$ sq. units

ILLUSTRATIVE EXAMPLES

Example 1 Find the curved surface area and total surface area of a right circular cylinder whose height is 15 cm and the radius of the base is 7 cm. (Take $\pi = 22/7$)

Solution Here, r = Radius of the base of the cylinder = 7 cm

h = Height of the cylinder = 15 cm

$\therefore$ Curved surface area of the cylinder $= 2\pi rh$

$$= \left(2\times\frac{22}{7}\times 7\times 15\right) \text{cm}^2$$

$$= 2\times 22\times 15 \text{ cm}^2 = 660 \text{ cm}^2$$

Total surface area of the cylinder $= 2\pi r(h+r)$

$$= 2\times\frac{22}{7}\times 7\times(15+7) \text{ cm}^2$$

$$= 2\times 22\times 22 \text{ cm}^2 = 968 \text{ cm}^2$$

Example 2 The diameter of the base of a right circular cylinder is 42 cm and its height is 10 cm. Find the area of the curved surface and total surface area.

Solution We have,

Diameter of the base of the cylinder = 42 cm

$\therefore$ r = Radius of the base of the cylinder = 21 cm

h = Height of the cylinder = 10 cm

$\therefore$ Curved surface area of the cylinder $= 2\pi rh$

$$= 2\times\frac{22}{7}\times 21\times 10 \text{ cm}^2$$

$$= 2\times 22\times 3\times 10 \text{ cm}^2 = 1320 \text{ cm}^2$$

Total surface area of the cylinder $= 2\pi r\,(h+r)$

$$= 2\times\frac{22}{7}\times 21\times(10+21) \text{ cm}^2$$

$$= 2\times 22\times 3\times 31 \text{ cm}^2 = 4092 \text{ cm}^2$$

Example 3 Find the height of a cylinder whose radius is 7 cm and the total surface area is 968 cm^2?

Solution Let the height of the cylinder be h cm. It is given that

r = Radius of the cylinder = 7 cm

We have,

Total surface area = 968 cm^2

$\Rightarrow$ $2\pi r\,(h+r) = 968$

$\Rightarrow$ $2\times\frac{22}{7}\times 7\times(h+7) = 968$

$\Rightarrow$ $44\times(h+7) = 968$

$\Rightarrow$ $h+7 = \frac{968}{44}$

$\Rightarrow$ $h+7 = 22$

$\Rightarrow$ $h = 15$

Hence, the height of the cylinder is 15 cm.

Example 4 A closed cylindrical tank of radius 1.5 m and height 3 m is made from a sheet of metal. How much sheet of metal is required?

Solution Clearly, total area of the sheet of metal required in making closed cylindrical tank is equal to the total surface area of the cylinder of radius $r = 1.5$ m and height $h = 3$ m.

$\therefore$ Total area of metal sheet $= 2\pi r\,(h + r)$

$$= 2 \times \frac{22}{7} \times 1.5 \times (3 + 1.5)\ \text{m}^2$$

$$= 2 \times \frac{22}{7} \times 1.5 \times 4.5\ \text{m}^2 = 297\ \text{m}^2$$

Example 5 The curved surface area of a right circular cylinder of height 14 cm is 88 cm^2. Find the diameter of the base of the cylinder.

Solution Let r be the radius and h be the height of the cylinder. Then,

$2\pi rh = 88$ and $h = 14$ [Given]

$\Rightarrow\ 2 \times \frac{22}{7} \times r \times 14 = 88$

$\Rightarrow\ 88r = 88$

$\Rightarrow\ r = 1$

$\therefore$ Diameter of the base $= 2r = 2$ cm.

Example 6 Savitri had to make a model of a cylindrical Kaleidoscope for her science project. She wanted to use chart paper to make the curved surface of the Kaleidoscope. What should be the area of chart paper required by her, if she wanted to make a Kaleidoscope of length 25 cm with a 3.5 cm radius?

Solution We have,

r = Radius of the base of the cylindrical Kaleidoscope = 3.5 cm

h = Height (length) of Kaleidoscope = 25 cm

$\therefore$ Area of the chart paper required = Curved surface area of the Kaleidoscope

$$= 2\pi rh$$

$$= 2 \times \frac{22}{7} \times 3.5 \times 25\ \text{cm}^2 = 550\ \text{cm}^2$$

Example 7 The ratio between the curved surface area and the total surface area of a right circular cylinder is 1 : 2. Find the ratio between the height and radius of the cylinder.

Solution Let h be the height and r be the radius of the cylinder. Then,

$$\frac{2\pi rh}{2\pi rh + 2\pi r^2} = \frac{1}{2}$$

$$\Rightarrow\ \frac{2\pi rh}{2\pi r\,(h + r)} = \frac{1}{2}$$

$$\Rightarrow\ \frac{h}{h + r} = \frac{1}{2} \Rightarrow 2h = h + r \Rightarrow h = r \Rightarrow h : r = 1 : 1$$

Hence, the required ratio is 1 : 1.

Example 8 The radii of two right circular cylinders are in the ratio 2 : 3 and their heights are in the ratio 5 : 4. Calculate the ratio of their curved surface areas.

Solution Let the radii of the cylinders be $2r$ and $3r$ respectively, and their heights be $5h$ and $4h$ respectively. Let S_1 and S_2 be the curved surface area of two cylinders. Then,

S_1 = Curved surface area of the cylinder of height $5h$ and radius $2r$

$$\Rightarrow \quad S_1 = 2\pi \times 2r \times 5h = 20\,\pi rh$$

S_2 = Curved surface area of the cylinder of height $4h$ and radius $3r$

$$\Rightarrow \quad S_2 = 2\pi \times 3r \times 4h = 24\,\pi rh$$

$$\therefore \quad \frac{S_1}{S_2} = \frac{20\,\pi rh}{24\,\pi rh} = \frac{5}{6} \Rightarrow S_1 : S_2 = 5 : 6$$

Example 9 The radius of the base of a cylindrical waterdrum open at the top is 35 cm and height 1.3 m. Find the inner surface area of the waterdrum.

Solution We have,

r = Radius of waterdrum = 35 cm, h = Height of waterdrum = 1.3 m = 130 cm

$\therefore$ Inner surface area of the waterdrum = Curved surface area + Area of the base

$$= 2\pi rh + \pi r^2$$

$$= \pi r\,(2h + r)$$

$$= \frac{22}{7} \times 35 \times (2 \times 130 + 35)\ \text{cm}^2$$

$$= 22 \times 5 \times 295\ \text{cm}^2 = 32450\ \text{cm}^2$$

Example 10 In a temple there are 25 cylindrical pillars. The radius of each pillar is 28 cm and height 4 m. Find the total cost of painting the curved surface area of pillars at the rate of Rs 8 per m^2.

Solution We have,

$$r = \text{Radius of a cylindrical pillar} = 28\ \text{cm} = \frac{28}{100}\ \text{m}$$

$$h = \text{Height of a cylindrical pillar} = 4\ \text{m}$$

$$\therefore \quad \text{Curved surface area of a cylindrical pillar} = 2\pi rh = 2 \times \frac{22}{7} \times \frac{28}{100} \times 4\ \text{m}^2$$

$$\therefore \quad \text{Curved surface area of 25 pillars} = 2 \times \frac{22}{7} \times \frac{28}{100} \times 4 \times 25\ \text{m}^2 = 176\ \text{m}^2$$

Hence, total cost of painting at the rate of Rs 8 per m^2 = Rs (176×8) = Rs 1408

Example 11 A road roller takes 750 complete revolutions to move once over to level a road. Find the area of the road if the diameter of a road roller is 91 cm and length is 1.25 m.

Solution We have,

$$h = \text{Length of the road roller} = 1.25\ \text{m}$$

$$r = \text{Radius of the road roller} = \frac{91}{2}\ \text{cm} = \frac{91}{200}\ \text{m}$$

$\therefore$ Curved surface area of the road roller $= 2\pi rh$

$$= 2 \times \frac{22}{7} \times \frac{91}{200} \times 1.25 \text{ m}^2$$

$$= \frac{22 \times 13 \times 1.25}{100} \text{ m}^2$$

Hence,
Area of the road levelled by the road roller in 750 complete revolutions.

= 750 × Curved surface of the road roller

$$= 750 \times \frac{22 \times 13 \times 1.25}{100} \text{ m}^2 = 2681.25 \text{ m}^2$$

Example 12 The diameter of a roller 120 cm long is 84 cm. If it takes 500 complete revolutions to level a playground, determine the cost of levelling it at the rate of 30 paise per square metre.

Solution Clearly, the roller is a right circular cylinder of height $h = 120$ cm and radius of its base $= r = 42$ cm.

$\therefore$ Area covered by the roller in one revolution

= Curved surface area of the roller

$$= 2 \times \frac{22}{7} \times 42 \times 120 \text{ cm}^2 = 31680 \text{ cm}^2$$

So, area covered by the roller is 500 revolutions $= (31680 \times 500) \text{ cm}^2$

$$= \frac{31680 \times 500}{100 \times 100} \text{ m}^2 = 1584 \text{ m}^2$$

Hence, cost of levelling the playground $= \text{Rs } 1584 \times \frac{30}{100} = \text{Rs } 475.20$

Example 13 An iron pipe 20 cm long has exterior diameter equal to 25 cm. If the thickness of the pipe is 1 cm, find the whole surface of the pipe.

Solution We have,

R = External radius = 12.5 cm

r = Internal radius = (External radius – Thickness) = (12.5 – 1) = 11.5 cm

h = Length of the pipe = 20 cm

$\therefore$ Total surface area of the pipe

= (External curved surface) + (Internal curved surface) + 2 (Area of the base of the ring)

$$= 2\pi Rh + 2\pi rh + 2(\pi R^2 - \pi r^2)$$

$$= 2\pi (R + r) h + 2\pi (R^2 - r^2)$$

$$= 2\pi (R + r) h + 2\pi (R + r)(R - r)$$

$$= 2\pi (R + r)(h + R - r)$$

$$= 2 \times \frac{22}{7} \times (12.5 + 11.5) \times (20 + 12.5 - 11.5) \text{ cm}^2$$

$$= 2 \times \frac{22}{7} \times 24 \times 21 \text{ cm}^2 = 3168 \text{ cm}^2$$

Example 14 A rectangular sheet of paper 44 cm×18 cm is rolled along its length and a cylinder is formed. Find the radius of the cylinder.

Solution When the rectangular sheet is rolled along its length, we find that the length of the sheet forms the circumference of its base and breadth of the sheet becomes the height of the cylinder.

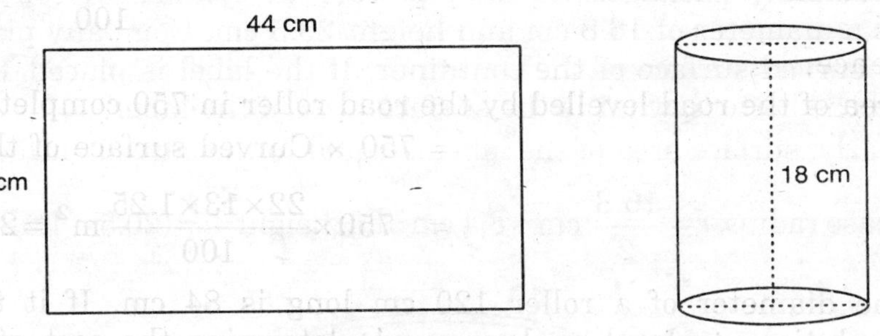

Fig. 22.11

Let r cm be the radius of the base and h cm be the height. Then, $h = 18$ cm

Now,

$$\text{Circumference of the base} = \text{Length of the sheet}$$

$$\Rightarrow \quad 2\pi r = 44$$

$$\Rightarrow \quad 2\times\frac{22}{7}\times r = 44 \Rightarrow r = 7 \text{ cm}$$

Hence, radius of the cylinder is 7 cm.

Example 15 The lateral surface area of a hollow cylinder is 4224 cm^2. It is cut along its height and formed a rectangular sheet of width 32 cm. Find the perimeter of rectangular sheet.

Solution We have,

$$h = \text{Height of the cylinder} = \text{Width of the sheet} = 32 \text{ cm}$$

Let r be the radius of the base of the hollow cylinder.

We have,

$$\text{Lateral surface area of the cylinder} = 4224 \text{ cm}^2$$

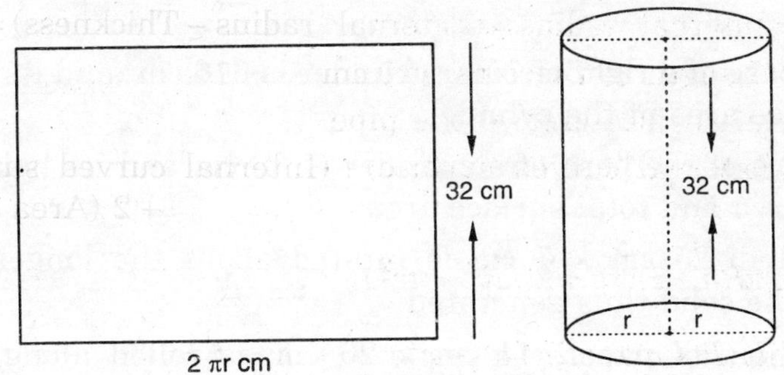

Fig. 22.12

$$\Rightarrow \quad 2\pi rh = 4224$$

$$\Rightarrow \quad 2\times\frac{22}{7}\times r\times 32 = 4224$$

$$\Rightarrow \quad r = \frac{4224\times 7}{2\times 22\times 32} \text{ cm} = 21 \text{ cm}$$

$\therefore$ Length of the sheet $= 2\pi r = 2\times\frac{22}{7}\times 21$ cm $= 132$ cm

Hence,

Perimeter of the sheet = 2 (Length + Width) = 2 (132 + 32) cm = 328 cm.

Example 16 A company packages its milk powder in cylindrical containers whose base has a diameter of 16.8 cm and height 20.5 cm. Company places a label around the curved surface of the container. If the label is placed 1.5 cm from the top and the bottom, what is the surface area of the label?

Solution Clearly, surface area of the label is equal to the curved surface area of a cylinder of base radius $r = \frac{16.8}{2}$ cm $= 8.4$ cm and, height $h = (20.5 - 1.5 - 1.5)$ cm $= 17.5$ cm.

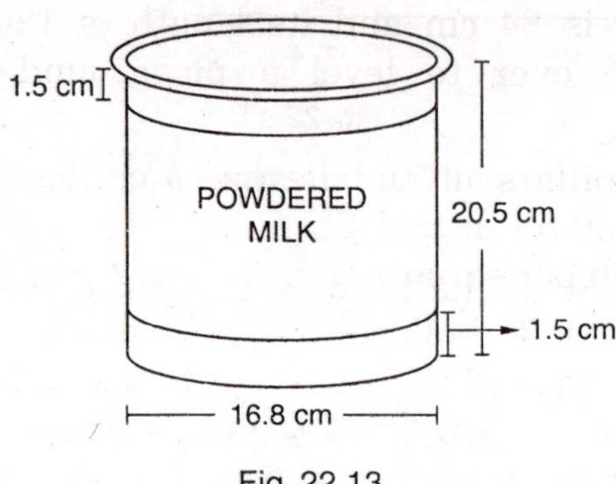

Fig. 22.13

$\therefore$ Surface area of the label $= 2\pi rh = 2\times\frac{22}{7}\times 8.4\times 17.5\ \text{cm}^2$

$= 2\times 22\times 1.2\times 17.5\ \text{cm}^2 = 924\ \text{cm}^2$

EXERCISE 22.1

1. Find the curved surface area and total surface area of a cylinder, the diameter of whose base is 7 cm and height is 60 cm.
2. The curved surface area of a cylindrical road is 132 cm^2. Find its length if the radius is 0.35 cm.
3. The area of the base of a right circular cylinder is 616 cm^2 and its height is 2.5 cm. Find the curved surface area of the cylinder.
4. The circumference of the base of a cylinder is 88 cm and its height is 15 cm. Find its curved surface area and total surface area.
5. A rectangular strip 25 cm × 7 cm is rotated about the longer side. Find the total surface area of the solid thus generated.
6. A rectangular sheet of paper, 44 cm × 20 cm, is rolled along its length to form a cylinder. Find the total surface area of the cylinder thus generated.
7. The radii of two cylinders are in the ratio 2 : 3 and their heights are in the ratio 5 : 3. Calculate the ratio of their curved surface areas.
8. The ratio between the curved surface area and the total surface area of a right circular cylinder is 1 : 2. Prove that its height and radius are equal.

9. The curved surface area of a cylinder is 1320 cm^2 and its base has diameter 21 cm. Find the height of the cylinder.
10. The height of a right circular cylinder is 10.5 cm. If three times the sum of the areas of its two circular faces is twice the area of the curved surface area. Find the radius of its base.
11. Find the cost of plastering the inner surface of a well at Rs 9.50 per m^2, if it is 21 m deep and diameter of its top is 6 m.
12. A cylindrical vessel open at the top has diameter 20 cm and height 14 cm. Find the cost of tin-plating it on the inside at the rate of 50 paise per hundred square centimetre.
13. The inner diameter of a circular well is 3.5 m. It is 10 m deep. Find the cost of plastering its inner curved surface at Rs 4 per square metre.
14. The diameter of a roller is 84 cm and its length is 120 cm. It takes 500 complete revolutions moving once over to level a playground. What is the area of the playground?
15. Twenty one cylindrical pillars of the Parliament House are to be cleaned. If the diameter of each pillar is 0.50 m and height is 4 m, what will be the cost of cleaning them at the rate of Rs 2.50 per square metre?
16. The total surface area of a hollow cylinder which is open from both sides is 4620 sq. cm, area of base ring is 115.5 sq. cm and height 7 cm. Find the thickness of the cylinder.
17. The sum of the radius of the base and height of a solid cylinder is 37 m. If the total surface area of the solid cylinder is 1628 m^2, find the circumference of its base.
18. Find the ratio between the total surface area of a cylinder to its curved surface area, given that its height and radius are 7.5 cm and 3.5 cm.
19. A cylindrical vessel, without lid, has to be tin-coated on its both sides. If the radius of the base is 70 cm and its height is 1.4 m, calculate the cost of tin-coating at the rate of Rs 3.50 per 1000 cm^2.

ANSWERS

1. 1320 cm^2, 1397 cm^2 2. 60 cm. 3. 220 cm^2 4. 1320 cm^2, 2552 cm^2
5. 1408 cm^2 6. 880 cm^2 7. 10 : 9 9. 20 cm 10. 7 cm 11. Rs 3762
12. Rs 5.97 13. Rs 440 14. 1584 m^2 15. Rs 330 16. $\frac{7}{29}$ cm 17. 44 m, 4620 m^3
18. 22 : 15 19. Rs 539

HINTS TO SELECTED PROBLEMS

5. By rotating the strip about the longer side, a solid cylinder of base radius 7 cm and height 25 cm is generated.

$\therefore$ Total surface area $= 2\pi r\,(h + r)$

6. By rolling the sheet along its length, a hollow cylinder of length 44 cm is generated such that the perimeter of its base is 20 cm.

22.4 VOLUME OF A CYLINDER

Let us take circular sheets of radius r and stack them up vertically as shown in Fig. 22.14 to form a right circular cylinder of height h. Then,

Volume of the cylinder = Measure of the space occupied by the cylinder
= The area of each circular sheet × Height
$= \pi r^2 h$

Thus, we have

Volume of a right circular cylinder = Area of the base × Height

Also, Volume of a right circular cylinder $= \pi r^2 h$

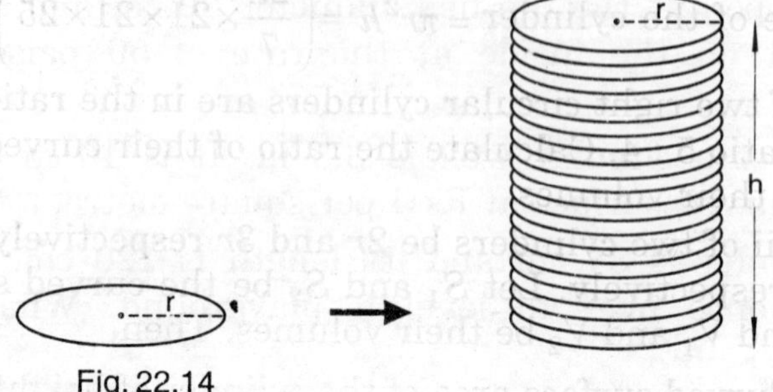

Fig. 22.14

22.5 VOLUME OF A HOLLOW CYLINDER

Solids like iron pipes, rubber tubes etc. are hollow cylinders. Thus,

A solid bounded by two coaxial cylinders of the same height and different radii is called a hollow cylinder.

Let R and r be the external and internal radii of a hollow cylinder and h be its height as shown in Fig.22.15. Then,

Volume of the material

= Exterior volume – Interior volume

$= \pi R^2 h - \pi r^2 h$

$= \pi h (R^2 - r^2)$

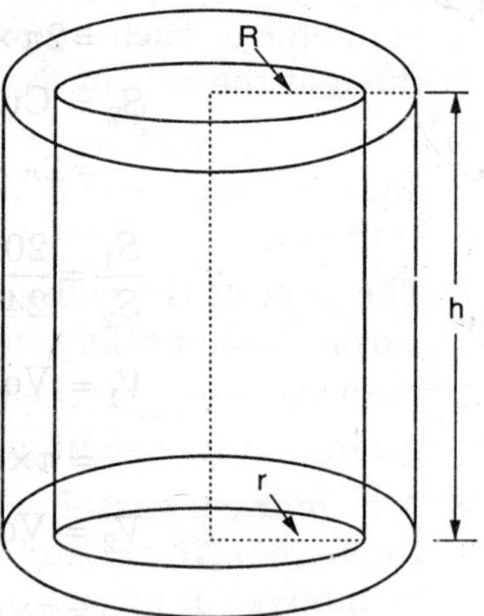

Fig. 22.15

ILLUSTRATIVE EXAMPLES

Example 1 Find the volume of a right circular cylinder, if the radius (r) of its base and height (h) are 7 cm and 15 cm respectively.

Solution We have, Volume of a cylinder $= \pi r^2 h$

Here, $r = 7$ cm and $h = 15$ cm

$\therefore$ Volume of the cylinder $= \frac{22}{7} \times (7)^2 \times 15 \text{ cm}^3 = 22 \times 7 \times 15 \text{ cm}^3 = 2310 \text{ cm}^3$

Example 2 The area of the base of a right circular cylinder is 154 cm^2 and its height is 15 cm. Find the volume of the cylinder.

Solution We have,

Volume of a cylinder = (Area of the base) × (height)

Here, area of the base $= 154$ cm^2 and height $= 15$ cm

$\therefore$ Volume of the cylinder $= (154 \times 15) \text{ cm}^3 = 2310 \text{ cm}^3$

Example 3 The circumference of the base of a cylinder is 132 cm and its height 25 cm. Find the volume of the cylinder.

Solution Let r cm be the radius of the cylinder. Then,

Circumference $= 132$ cm

$$\Rightarrow \quad 2\pi r = 132 \Rightarrow 2\times\frac{22}{7}\times r = 312 \Rightarrow r = \frac{132\times 7}{2\times 22}\text{ cm} \Rightarrow r = 21\text{ cm}$$

We have, $h =$ height of the cylinder $= 25$ cm

$$\therefore \quad \text{Volume of the cylinder} = \pi r^2 h = \left(\frac{22}{7}\times 21\times 21\times 25\right)\text{cm}^3 = 34650\text{ cm}^3$$

Example 4 The radii of two right circular cylinders are in the ratio 2 : 3 and their heights are in the ratio 5 : 4. Calculate the ratio of their curved surface areas and also the ratio of their volumes.

Solution Let the radii of two cylinders be $2r$ and $3r$ respectively, and their heights be 5 h and 4 h respectively. Let S_1 and S_2 be the curved surface areas of the two cylinders and V_1 and V_2 be their volumes. Then,

$S_1 =$ Curved surface area of the cylinder of height $5h$ and radius $2r$

$= 2\pi\times 2r\times 5h = 20\pi rh$ sq. units

$S_2 =$ Curved surface area of the cylinder of height $4h$ and radius $3r$

$= 2\pi\times 3r\times 4h = 24\pi rh$

$$\therefore \quad \frac{S_1}{S_2} = \frac{20\pi rh}{24\pi rh} = \frac{5}{6} \Rightarrow S_1 : S_2 = 5:6$$

$V_1 =$ Volume of the cylinder of height $5h$ and radius $2r$

$= \pi\times(2r)^2\times 5h = 20\pi r^2 h$ cubic units

$V_2 =$ Volume of the cylinder of height $4h$ and radius $3r$

$= \pi\times(3r)^2\times 4h = 36\pi r^2 h$, cubic units

$$\therefore \quad \frac{V_1}{V_2} = \frac{20\pi r^2 h}{36\pi r^2 h} = \frac{5}{9} \Rightarrow V_1 : V_2 = 5:9$$

Example 5 Two cylinder cans have bases of the same size. The diameter of each is 14 cm. One of the cans is 10 cm high and the other is 20 cm high. Find the ratio of their volumes.

Solution

	Can I	*Can II*
Base diameter	14 cm	14 cm
Base radius	$r_1 = 7$ cm	$r_2 = 7$ cm
Height	$h_1 = 10$ cm	$h_2 = 20$ cm
Volume	$V_1 = \pi r_1^2 h_1$	$V_2 = \pi r_2^2 h_2$
	$= \pi\times(7)^2\times 10\text{ cm}^3$	$= \pi\times(7)^2\times 20\text{ cm}^3$
	$= 490\,\pi\text{ cm}^3$	$= 980\,\pi\text{ cm}^3$

$$\therefore \quad \frac{V_1}{V_2} = \frac{490\pi}{980\pi} = \frac{1}{2} \Rightarrow V_1 : V_1 = 1:2$$

Example 6 A rectangular sheet of paper 44 cm × 18 cm is rolled along its length and a cylinder is formed. Find the volume of the cylinder. (Use $\pi = 22/7$)

Solution When the rectangular sheet is rolled along its length, we find that the length of the sheet forms the circumference of its base and breadth of the sheet becomes the height of the cylinder.

Let r cm be the radius of the base and h cm be the height. Then, $h = 18$ cm.

Now,

Circumference of the base = Length of the sheet

$\Rightarrow$ Circumference $= 44$ cm

$\Rightarrow$ $2\pi r = 44$

$\Rightarrow$ $2 \times \frac{22}{7} \times r = 44$

$\Rightarrow$ $r = 7$ cm

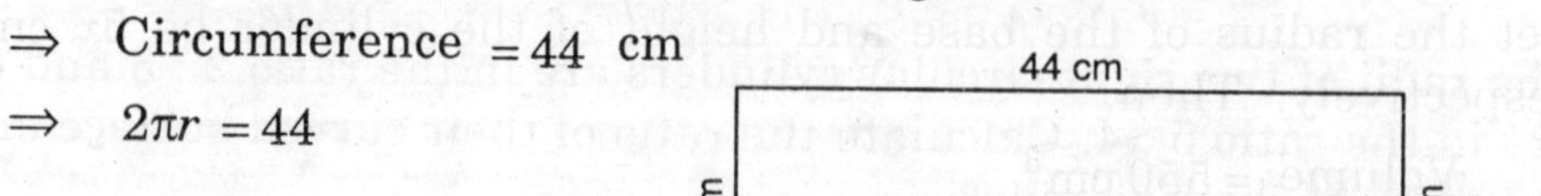

Fig. 22.16

$\therefore$ Volume of the cylinder $= \pi r^2 h$ cm^3

$$= \frac{22}{7} \times (7)^2 \times 18 \text{ cm}^3 = 2772 \text{ cm}^3$$

Example 7 A rectangular paper of length 20 cm and width 14 cm is revolved along its width and a cylinder is formed. Find the volume of the cylinder. (Take $\pi = 22/14$)

Solution A cylinder is formed by revolving the paper along its width: Hence the width of the paper becomes height and length of the paper becomes radius of the cylinder.

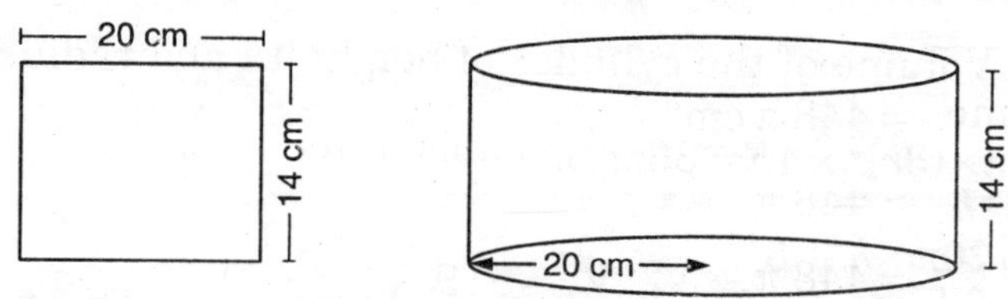

Fig. 22.17

Thus, we have

h = Height of the cylinder = 14 cm, r = Radius of the cylinder = 20 cm

$$\therefore \quad \text{Volume of the cylinder} = \pi r^2 h = \frac{22}{7} \times 20^2 \times 14 \text{ cm}^3 = 17600 \text{ cm}^3$$

Hence, the volume of the cylinder is 17600 cm^3.

Example 8 If the radius of the base of a right circular cylinder is halved, keeping the height same, what is the ratio of the volume of the reduced cylinder to that of the original.

Solution Let r be the radius of the base and h be the height of the given cylinder.

Then, radius of the base and the height of the reduced cylinder are $r/2$ and h respectively.

Let V_1 and V_2 be the volumes of the given cylinder and reduced cylinder respectively. Then,

$$V_1 = \pi r^2 h \text{ cubic units and, } V_2 = \pi\left(\frac{r}{2}\right)^2 h = \frac{\pi}{4} r^2 h \text{ cubic units}$$

$$\therefore \quad \frac{V_1}{V_2} = \frac{\pi r^2 h}{\frac{\pi}{4} r^2 h} = 4 \Rightarrow \frac{V_2}{V_1} = \frac{1}{4} \Rightarrow V_2 : V_1 = 1:4$$

Example 9 The radius and height of a cylinder are in the ratio 5 : 7 and its volume is 550 cm^3. Find its radius. (Use $\pi = 22/7$).

Solution Let the radius of the base and height of the cylinder be $5x$ cm and $7x$ cm respectively. Then,

$$\text{Volume} = 550 \text{ cm}^3$$

$$\Rightarrow \quad \pi r^2 h = 500$$

$$\Rightarrow \quad \frac{22}{7} \times (5x)^2 \times 7x = 550 \qquad [\text{Here, } r = 5x, h = 7x]$$

$$\Rightarrow \quad \frac{22}{7} \times 25x^2 \times 7x = 550$$

$$\Rightarrow \quad 22 \times 25x^3 = 550$$

$$\Rightarrow \quad 550x^3 = 550$$

$$\Rightarrow \quad x^3 = 1 \Rightarrow x = 1 \text{ cm}$$

Hence, radius of the cylinder $= 5x \text{ cm} = (5 \times 1) \text{ cm} = 5 \text{ cm}$.

Example 10 The volume of a cylinder is 448 π cm^3 and height 7 cm. Find its lateral surface area and total surface area.

Solution Let the radius of the base and height of the cylinder be r cm and h cm respectively. Then, $h = 7$ cm (Given)

Now,

$$\text{Volume} = 448\,\pi \text{ cm}^3$$

$$\Rightarrow \quad \pi r^2 h = 448\,\pi$$

$$\Rightarrow \quad \pi \times r^2 \times 7 = 448\,\pi \qquad [\because h = 7 \text{ cm}]$$

$$\Rightarrow \quad r^2 = \frac{448}{7} = 64 \Rightarrow r = 8 \text{ cm}$$

$$\therefore \quad \text{Lateral surface area} = 2\pi rh \text{ cm}^2 = 2 \times \frac{22}{7} \times 8 \times 7 \text{ cm}^2 = 352 \text{ cm}^2$$

$$\text{Total surface area} = (2\pi rh + 2\pi r^2) \text{ cm}^2$$

$$= 2\pi r (h + r) \text{ cm}^2$$

$$= 2 \times \frac{22}{7} \times 8\,(7 + 8) \text{ cm}^2 = \frac{5280}{7} \text{ cm}^2 = 754.28 \text{ cm}^2$$

Example 11 The thickness of a hollow wooden cylinder is 2 cm. It is 35 cm long and its inner radius is 12 cm. Find the volume of the wood required to make the cylinder, assuming it is open at either end.

Solution We have,

r = Inner radius of the cylinder = 12 cm, Thickness of the cylinder = 2 cm

$\therefore$ R = Outer radius of the cylinder $= (12 + 2)$ cm $= 14$ cm

h = Height of the cylinder $= 35$ cm

$\therefore$ Volume of the wood $= \pi (R^2 - r^2) h$

$$= \frac{22}{7} \times \{(14)^2 - (12)^2\} \times 35 \text{ cm}^3$$

$$= \frac{22}{7} \times (14 + 12) \times (14 - 12) \times 35 \text{ cm}^3$$

$$= 22 \times 26 \times 2 \times 5 \text{ cm}^3 = 5720 \text{ cm}^3$$

Example 12 The thickness of a metallic tube is 1 cm and the inner diameter of the tube is 12 cm. Find the weight of 1 m long tube, if the density of the metal be 7.8 gm/cm^3.

Solution We have,

Inner diameter of the tube $= 12$ cm

$\therefore$ r = Inner radius of the tube $= 6$ cm

Thickness of the tube $= 1$ cm

$\therefore$ R = Outer radius of the tube $= (6 + 1)$ cm $= 7$ cm

h = Length of the tube $= 1$ m $= 100$ cm

$\therefore$ Volume of the metal in the tube $= \pi (R^2 - r^2) h$

$$= \frac{22}{7} \times (7^2 - 6^2) \times 100 \text{ cm}^3$$

$$= \frac{22}{7} \times 13 \times 100 \text{ cm}^3$$

Density of the metal $= 7.8$ gm/cm^3

$\therefore$ Weight of the tube = Volume × Density

$$= \frac{22}{7} \times 13 \times 100 \times 7.8 \text{ gm}$$

$$= 31868.57 \text{ gm} = \frac{31868.57}{1000} \text{ kg} = 31.86857 \text{ kg} = 31.869 \text{ kg}$$

Example 13 A cylindrical road roller made of iron is 1 m wide. Its inner diameter is 54 cm and thickness of the iron sheet rolled into the road roller is 9 cm. Find the weight of the roller if 1 c.c. of iron weighs 8 gm.

Solution The width of the road roller is 1 m i.e., 100 cm.

So, Height (length) of the cylinder $= 100$ cm

Inner radius of the cylinder $= r = \frac{54}{2}$ cm $= 27$ cm

Thickness of the iron sheet $= 9$ cm

$\therefore$ Outer radius of the cylinder $= R = (27 + 9)$ cm $= 36$ cm

Hence,

$$\text{Volume of the iron sheet used} = (\pi R^2 h - \pi r^2 h)\ \text{cm}^3$$

$$= \pi (R^2 - r^2) h\ \text{cm}^3$$

$$= \{\pi (R + r)(R - r) h\}\ \text{cm}^3$$

$$= \{3.14 \times (36 + 27)(36 - 27) \times 100\}\ \text{cm}^2$$

$$= \frac{314}{100} \times 63 \times 9 \times 100\ \text{cm}^3 = 178038\ \text{cm}^3$$

$\therefore$ Weight of the roller $= 178038 \times 8$ gms $= 178038 \times \frac{8}{1000}$ kgs $= 1424.304$ kgs

Example 14 A well with 10 m inside diameter is dug 14 m deep. Earth taken out of it is spread all around to a width of 5 m to form an embankment. Find the height of embankment.

Solution Volume of the earth dug-out $= \pi r^2 h\ \text{m}^3 = \frac{22}{7} \times 5 \times 5 \times 14\ \text{m}^3 = 1100\ \text{m}^3$

Area of the embankment (shaded region) $= \pi (R^2 - r^2)$

$$= \pi (10^2 - 5^2)\ \text{m}^2 = \frac{22}{7} \times 75\ \text{m}^2$$

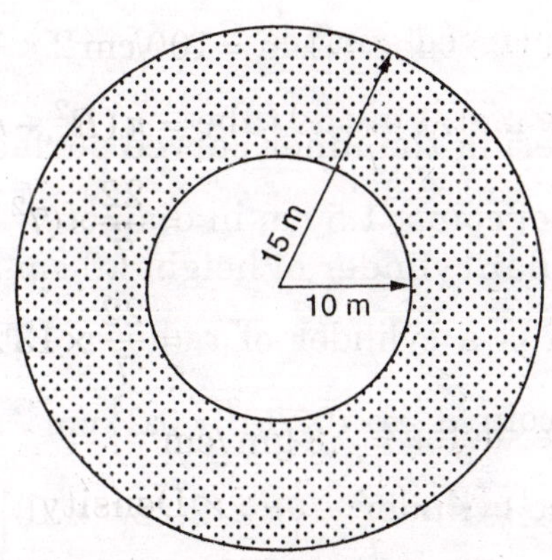

Fig. 22.18

$$\therefore \text{Height of the embankment} = \frac{\text{Volume of the earth dug-out}}{\text{Area of the embankment}}$$

$$= \frac{1100}{\frac{22}{7} \times 75} = \frac{7 \times 1100}{22 \times 75} = 4.66\ \text{m}$$

Example 15 A circular well of radius 3.5 m is dug 20 m deep and the earth so dug is spread on a rectangular plot of length 14 m and breadth 11 m. Find:

(i) Volume of the earth dug-out?

(ii) Height of the platform formed by spreading the earth on the rectangular plot.

Solution (i) We have,
r = Radius of the cylindrical well = 3.5 m, h = depth of the cylindrical well = 20 m

$\therefore$ Volume of the earth dug-out $= \pi r^2 h$

$$= \frac{22}{7} \times (3.5)^2 \times 20 \text{ m}^3 = \frac{22}{7} \times \left(\frac{7}{2}\right)^2 \times 20 \text{ m}^3 = 770 \text{ m}^3$$

(ii) Let h metre be the height of the platform formed by spreading out the earth dug-out of the well. Clearly, the platform is in the shape of a cuboid of length 14 m, breadth 11 m and height h metre.

Volume of the earth in platform = Volume of the earth dug-out

$$\Rightarrow \quad 14 \times 11 \times h = 770$$

$$\Rightarrow \quad h = \frac{770}{14 \times 11} \text{ m} = 5\text{m}$$

Example 16 How many cubic metres of earth must be dug-out to sink a well 22.5 m deep and of diameter 7 m? Also, find the cost of plastering the inner curved surface at Rs 3 per square metre.

Solution Volume of earth to be dug-out = Volume of the well

$$= \frac{22}{7} \times \frac{7}{2} \times \frac{7}{2} \times 22.5 \text{ m}^3 = 866.25 \text{ m}^3$$

Area of the inner curved surface $= 2\pi rh = 2 \times \frac{22}{7} \times \frac{7}{2} \times 22.5 \text{ m}^2 = 495 \text{ m}^2$

$\therefore$ Cost of plastering the inner curved surface $=$ Rs $(495 \times 3) =$ Rs 1485.

Example 17 Find the number of coins, 1.5 cm in diameter and 0.2 cm thick, to be melted to form a right circular cylinder of height 10 cm and diameter 4.5 cm.

Solution Clearly, each coin is a cylinder of radius r = 0.75 cm and height h = 0.2 cm.

Volume of a coin $= \{\pi \times (0.75)^2 \times 0.2\} \text{ cm}^3$

Volume of the cylinder $= \{\pi \times (2.25)^2 \times 10\} \text{ cm}^3$

$$\therefore \quad \text{Number of coins} = \frac{\text{Volume of the cylinder}}{\text{Volume of a coin}}$$

$$= \frac{\pi \times (2.25)^2 \times 10}{\pi \times (0.75)^2 \times 0.2} = \frac{2.25 \times 2.25 \times 10}{0.75 \times 0.75 \times 0.2} = 3 \times 3 \times 50 = 450$$

Example 18 A glass cylinder with diameter 20 cm has water to a height of 9 cm. A metal cube of 8 cm edge is immersed in it completely. Calculate the height by which water will rise in the cylinder. (Take π = 3.142).

Solution Suppose the water rises by h cm. Clearly, water in the cylinder forms a cylinder of height h cm and radius 10 cm.

$\therefore$ Volume of the water displaced = Volume of the cube of edge 8 cm

$$\Rightarrow \quad \pi r^2 h = 8^3$$

$$\Rightarrow \quad 3.142 \times 10^2 \times h = 8 \times 8 \times 8 \qquad [\because r = 10 \text{ cm}]$$

$$\Rightarrow \quad h = \frac{8 \times 8 \times 8}{3.142 \times 10 \times 10} \text{ cm} = 1.6 \text{ cm}$$

Example 19 Into a circular drum of radius 4.2 m and height 3.5 m, how many full bags of wheat can be emptied if the space required for wheat in each bag is 2.1 cu. m. (Take $\pi = 3.14$)

Solution Here, $r = 4.2$ m, $h = 3.5$ m

$\therefore$ Volume of the drum $= (\pi r^2 h)\ m^3 = \left(3.14 \times (4.2)^2 \times 3.5\right) m^3$

Volume of each bag of wheat $= 2.1$ cubic metre

$$\therefore \text{ Number of bags} = \frac{\text{Volume of drum}}{\text{Volume of a bag}} = \frac{3.14 \times 4.2 \times 4.2 \times 3.5}{2.1}$$

$$= 3.14 \times 8.4 \times 3.5 = 92.316 = 92 \text{ bags nearly}.$$

Example 20 The volume of a metallic cylindrical pipe is 748 cm³. Its length is 14 cm and its external radius is 9 cm. Find its thickness.

Solution We have,

$R =$ External radius of pipe $= 9$ cm, $h =$ Length of the pipe $= 14$ cm

$V =$ Volume of the pipe $= 748$ cm³

Let r be the internal radius in centimetres. Then,

Volume $= 748$ cm³

$$\Rightarrow \pi (R^2 - r^2) h = 748 \text{ cm}^3$$

$$\Rightarrow \frac{22}{7}(9^2 - r^2) \times 14 = 748$$

$$\Rightarrow 81 - r^2 = \frac{748}{44}$$

$$\Rightarrow 81 - r^2 = 17 \Rightarrow r^2 = 64 \Rightarrow r = 8 \text{ cm}$$

Hence, thickness of the pipe $= (R - r)$ cm $= (9 - 8)$ cm $= 1$ cm.

Example 21 The rain water that falls on a roof of area 6160 m² is collected in a cylindrical tank of diameter 14 m and height 10 m and thus the tank is completely filled. Find the height of rain water on the roof.

Solution Let the height of rain water on the roof be h metre. Clearly, rain water accumulated on the roof forms a cuboid of base area 6160 m² and height h metre.

$\therefore$ Volume of water accumulated on the roof $= 6160 \times h$ m³

This water completely fills a cylindrical tank of radius 7 m and height 10 m.

$\therefore$ Volume of water accumulated on the roof = Volume of the cylindrical tank

$$\Rightarrow 6160h = \frac{22}{7} \times 7^2 \times 10$$

$$\Rightarrow h = \frac{1540}{6160} \text{ m} = 0.25 \text{ m} = 25 \text{ cm}$$

Hence, the height of the rain water on the roof = 25 cm.

Example 22 2.2 cubic dm of brass is to be drawn into a cylindrical wire 0.50 cm in diameter. Find the length of the wire.

Solution Let the length of the wire be l cm

Clearly, wire forms a cylinder of radius 0.25 cm and height l cm

$\therefore$ Volume of the wire $= \frac{22}{7} \times (0.25)^2 \times l \text{ cm}^3$

But, Volume given $= 2.2 \text{ dm}^3 = (2.2 \times 10^3) \text{ cm}^3$ [$\because$ 1 dm = 10 cm]

$= (2.2 \times 1000) \text{ cm}^3 = 2200 \text{ cm}^3$

$$\therefore \quad \frac{22}{7} \times 0.25 \times 0.25 \times l = 2200$$

$$\Rightarrow \quad \frac{22}{7} \times \frac{25}{100} \times \frac{25}{100} \times l = 2200$$

$$\Rightarrow \quad \frac{22}{7} \times \frac{1}{4} \times \frac{1}{4} \times l = 2200 \Rightarrow l = \frac{2200 \times 4 \times 4 \times 7}{22} \text{ cm} = 11200 \text{ cm} = 112 \text{ m}$$

Hence, the length of the wire is 112 m.

Example 23 A solid iron rectangular block of dimensions 4.4 m, 2.6 m and 1 m is cast into a hollow cylindrical pipe of internal radius 30 cm and thickness 5 cm. Find the length of the pipe.

Solution Let the length of the pipe be l cm. Then, volume of iron in the pipe is equal to the volume of iron of the block.

We have,

Volume of the block $= (4.4 \times 2.6 \times 1) \text{ m}^3 = (440 \times 260 \times 100) \text{ cm}^3$

$r =$ Internal radius of the pipe $= 30$ cm

$R =$ External radius of the pipe $= (30 + 5)$ cm $= 35$ cm

$\therefore$ Volume of iron in the pipe = (External volume) – (Internal volume)

$$= \pi R^2 h - \pi r^2 h$$

$$= \pi(R^2 - r^2)\, h$$

$$= \pi\,(R + r)\,(R - r)\, h$$

$$= \pi \times (35 + 30) \times (35 - 30) \times h \text{ cm}^3$$

$$= \pi \times 65 \times 5 \times h \text{ cm}^3$$

Now,

Volume of iron in the pipe = Volume of iron in the block

$$\Rightarrow \quad \pi \times 65 \times 5 \times h = 440 \times 260 \times 100$$

$$\Rightarrow \quad \frac{22}{7} \times 65 \times 5 \times h = 440 \times 260 \times 100$$

$$\Rightarrow \quad h = \left(440 \times 260 \times 100 \times \frac{7}{22} \times \frac{1}{65} \times \frac{1}{5}\right) \text{ cm}$$

$$\Rightarrow \quad h = 11200 \text{ cm} = 112 \text{ m}$$

Hence, the length of the pipe is 112 m.

Example 24 A solid cylinder has total surface area of 462 square cm. Its curved surface area is one-third of its total surface area. Find the volume of the cylinder.

(Take $\pi = 22/7$)

Solution Let r be the radius of the base and h be the height of the cylinder. Then,

Total surface area $= 2\pi r\,(h + r) \text{ cm}^2$

Curved surface area $= 2\pi rh \text{ cm}^2$

We have,

Curved surface area $= \frac{1}{3}$ (Total surface area)

$\Rightarrow \quad 2\pi rh = \frac{1}{3}\{2\pi r\,(h+r)\}$

$\Rightarrow \quad 6\pi rh = 2\pi rh + 2\pi r^2$

$\Rightarrow \quad 4\pi rh = 2\pi r^2$

$\Rightarrow \quad 2h = r$

$\because$ Total surface area $= 462 \text{ cm}^2$

$\Rightarrow \quad 2\pi r\,(h+r) = 462$

$\Rightarrow \quad 2\pi r\left(\frac{r}{2}+r\right) = 462 \qquad \left[\because 2h = r \therefore h = \frac{r}{2}\right]$

$\Rightarrow \quad 2\pi r \times \frac{3r}{2} = 462$

$\Rightarrow \quad 2\times\frac{22}{7}\times\frac{3}{2}\times r^2 = 462$

$\Rightarrow \quad r^2 = 49$

$\Rightarrow \quad r = 7$ cm

Now, $2h = r \Rightarrow h = \frac{r}{2} = \frac{7}{2}$ cm

Hence, Volume of the cylinder $= \pi r^2 h = \left(\frac{22}{7}\times 7^2 \times \frac{7}{2}\right) \text{cm}^3 = 539 \text{ cm}^3$

Example 25 A hollow cylindrical pipe is 21 dm long. Its outer and inner diameters are 10 cm and 6 cm respectively. Find the volume of the copper used in making the pipe.

Solution We have,

$h =$ Height of the cylindrical pipe $= 21 \text{ dm} = 210 \text{ cm}$ $[\because 1 \text{ dm} = 10 \text{ cm}]$

$R =$ External radius $= \frac{10}{2}$ cm $= 5$ cm, $r =$ Internal radius $= \frac{6}{2}$ cm $= 3$ cm

Volume of the copper used in making the pipe

= Volume of the external cylinder – Volume of the internal cylinder

$= \pi R^2 h - \pi r^2 h$

$= \pi (R^2 - r^2)h$

$= \frac{22}{7}\times(5^2 - 3^2)\times 210 \text{ cm}^3$

$= \frac{22}{7} + 16 \times 210 \text{ cm}^3 = 10560 \text{ cm}^3$

Example 26 The difference between outside and inside surfaces of a cylindrical metallic pipe 14 cm long is 44 cm^2. If the pipe is made of 99 cu. centimetres of metal, find the outer and inner radii of the pipe.

Solution Let R cm and r cm be the external and internal radii of the metallic pipe.

We have, $h =$ Length of the pipe $= 14$ cm

It is given that

Outside surface area − Inside surface area $= 44\text{ cm}^2$

$\Rightarrow \quad 2\pi Rh - 2\pi rh = 44$

$\Rightarrow \quad 2\pi(R-r)h = 44 = 44$

$\Rightarrow \quad 2\times\frac{22}{7}(R-r)\times 14 = 44$

$\Rightarrow \quad R-r = \frac{1}{2}$ ... (i)

It is given that the volume of the metal used $= 99$ cubic centimetres.

$\therefore$ External volume − Internal volume $= 99$ cubic centimetres

$\Rightarrow \quad \pi R^2 h - \pi r^2 h = 99$

$\Rightarrow \quad \pi(R^2 - r^2)h = 99$

$\Rightarrow \quad \frac{22}{7}\times(R+r)(R-r)\times 14 = 99$

$\Rightarrow \quad \frac{22}{7}\times(R+r)\times\frac{1}{2}\times 14 = 99$ [Using (i)]

$\Rightarrow \quad R+r = \frac{99}{22}$

$\Rightarrow \quad R+r = \frac{9}{2}$ ... (ii)

Solving (i) and (ii), we get: $R = 2.5$ and $r = 2$.

Hence, Outer radius $= 2.5$ cm, and Inner radius $= 2$ cm.

Example 27 An iron pipe 20 cm long has exterior diameter equal to 25 cm. If the thickness of the pipe is 1 cm, find the whole surface of the pipe.

Solution We have,

$R =$ External radius $= 12.5$ cm

$r =$ Internal radius $=$ (External radius − Thickness) $= (12.5 - 1)$ cm $= 11.5$ cm

$h =$ Length of the pipe $= 20$ cm

$\therefore$ Total surface area of the pipe

= (External curved surface) + (Internal curved surface) + 2 (Area of the base of the ring)

$= 2\pi Rh + 2\pi rh + 2(\pi R^2 - \pi r^2)$

$= 2\pi(R+r)h + 2\pi(R^2 - r^2)$

$= 2\pi(R+r)h + 2\pi(R+r)(R-r)$

$= 2\pi(R+r)(h+R-r)$

$= 2\times\frac{22}{7}\times(12.5+11.5)\times(20+12.5-11.5)\text{ cm}^2$

$= 2\times\frac{22}{7}\times 24\times 21\text{ cm}^2 = 3168\text{ cm}^2$

Example 28 Find the weight of a lead pipe 3.5 m long, if the external diameter of the pipe is 2.4 cm and the thickness of the lead is 2 mm and 1 cubic cm of lead weighs 11 gm.

Solution We have,

$R =$ External radius of the pipe $= 1.2$ cm

$r =$ Internal radius of the pipe $=$ (external radius – thickness)

$= (1.2 - 0.2)$ cm $= 1$ cm

$h =$ Length of the pipe $= 3.5$ m $= 350$ cm

$\therefore$ Volume of lead $=$ External volume – Internal volume

$$= \pi R^2 h - \pi r^2 h$$

$$= \pi (R^2 - r^2) h$$

$$= \pi (R + r)(R - r) h$$

$$= \left\{\frac{22}{7} \times (1.2 + 1) \times (1.2 - 1) \times 350\right\} \text{cm}^3$$

$$= \left\{\frac{22}{7} \times 2.2 \times 0.2 \times 350\right\} \text{cm}^3 = 484 \text{ cm}^3$$

Since one cubic centimetre of lead weighs 11 gm.

$$\therefore \quad \text{Weight of the pipe} = (484 \times 11) \text{ gm} = \frac{484 \times 11}{1000} \text{ kg} = 5.324 \text{ kg}$$

Example 29 The barrel of a fountain-pen, cylindrical in shape, is 7 cm long and 5 mm in diameter. A full barrel of ink in the pen will be used up on writing 330 words on an average. How many words would use up a bottle of ink containing one fifth of a litre?

Solution Volume of barrel $= \left(\frac{22}{7} \times 0.25 \times 0.25 \times 7\right) \text{cm}^3 = 1.375 \text{ cm}^3$

Volume of ink in the bottle $= \frac{1}{5}$ litre $= \frac{1000}{5}$ cm^3 $= 200$ cm^3

$\therefore$ Total number of barrels that can be filled from the given volume of ink

$$= \frac{200}{1.375}$$

So, required number of wards $= \frac{200}{1.375} \times 330 = 48000$

Example 30 The cost of painting the total outside surface of a closed cylindrical oil tank at 60 paise per sq. dm is Rs 237.60. The height of the tank is 6 times the radius of the base of the tank. Find its volume correct to two decimal places.

Solution Let r dm be the radius of the base and h dm be the height of the cylindrical tank. Then, $h = 6r$ (given)

Total surface area $= 2\pi r(r + h) = 2\pi r(r + 6r) = 14\pi r^2$

$$\Rightarrow \quad \text{Cost of painting} = \text{Rs } (14\pi r^2) \times \frac{60}{100} = \text{Rs } \frac{42}{5}\pi r^2$$

It is given that the cost of painting is Rs 237.60

$$\therefore \quad \frac{42}{5}\pi r^2 = 237.60$$

$\Rightarrow \quad \frac{42}{5} \times \frac{22}{7} \times r^2 = 237.60$

$\Rightarrow \quad r^2 = 237.60 \times \frac{5}{42} \times \frac{7}{22} = 9$

$\Rightarrow \quad r = 3 \text{ dm}$

Hence, Volume of the cylinder $= \pi r^2 h = (\pi \times 3 \times 3 \times 18) \text{ dm}^3$

$= \left(\frac{22}{7} \times 9 \times 18\right) \text{dm}^2 = 509.14 \text{ dm}^2$

Example 31 A lead pencil consists of a cylinder of wood with a solid cylinder of graphite filled into it. The diameter of the pencil is 7 mm, the diameter of the graphite is 1 mm and the length of the pencil is 10 cm. Calculate the weight of the whole pencil, if the specific gravity of the wood is 0.7 gm/cm^3 and that of the graphite is 2.1 gm/cm^3.

Solution Diameter of the graphite cylinder $= 1 \text{ mm} = \frac{1}{10} \text{ cm}$

$\therefore$ Radius $= \frac{1}{20}$ cm

Length of the graphite cylinder $= 10$ cm

Volume of the graphite cylinder $= \left(\frac{22}{7} \times \frac{1}{20} \times \frac{1}{20} \times 10\right) \text{cm}^3$

Weight of graphite = Volume × Specific gravity

$= \left(\frac{22}{7} \times \frac{1}{20} \times \frac{1}{20} \times 10 \times 2.1\right) \text{gm}$

$= \left(\frac{22}{7} \times \frac{1}{20} \times \frac{1}{20} \times 10 \times \frac{21}{10}\right) \text{gm} = 0.165 \text{ gm}$

Diameter of pencil $= 7 \text{ mm} = \frac{7}{10}$ cm

$\therefore$ Radius of pencil $= \frac{7}{20}$ cm and, Length of pencil $= 10$ cm

$\therefore$ Volume of pencil $= \left(\frac{22}{7} \times \frac{7}{20} \times \frac{7}{20} \times 10\right) \text{cm}^3$

Volume of wood $= \left(\frac{22}{7} \times \frac{7}{20} \times \frac{7}{20} \times 10 - \frac{22}{7} \times \frac{1}{20} \times \frac{1}{20} \times \frac{1}{10}\right) \text{cm}^3$

$= \frac{22}{7} \times \frac{1}{20} \times \frac{1}{20} \times 10\,(7 \times 7 - 1) \text{ cm}^3$

$= \frac{11}{7} \times \frac{1}{20} \times 48 \text{ cm}^3$

$\therefore$ Weight of wood $= \left(\frac{11}{7} \times \frac{1}{20} \times 48 \times 0.7\right) \text{gm} = \left(\frac{11}{7} \times \frac{1}{20} \times 48 \times \frac{7}{10}\right) \text{gm} = 2.64 \text{ gm}$

Total weight $= (2.64 + 0.165) \text{ gm} = 2.805 \text{ gm}$

EXERCISE 22.2

Use $\pi = \frac{22}{7}$, unless otherwise indicated

1. Find the volume of a cylinder whose

   (i) $r = 3.5$ cm, $h = 40$ cm (ii) $r = 2.8$ m, $h = 15$ m

2. Find the volume of a cylinder, if the diameter (d) of its base and its altitude (h) are:

   (i) $d = 21$ cm, $h = 10$ cm (ii) $d = 7$ m, $h = 24$ m

3. The area of the base of a right circular cylinder is 616 cm^2 and its height is 25 cm. Find the volume of the cylinder.

4. The circumference of the base of a cylinder is 88 cm and its height is 15 cm. Find the volume of the cylinder.

5. A hollow cylindrical pipe is 21 dm long. Its outer and inner diameters are 10 cm and 6 cm respectively. Find the volume of the copper used in making the pipe.

6. Find the (i) curved surface area (ii) total surface area and (iii) volume of a right circular cylinder whose height is 15 cm and the radius of the base is 7 cm.

7. The diameter of the base of a right circular cylinder is 42 cm and its height is 10 cm. Find the volume of the cylinder.

8. Find the volume of a cylinder, the diameter of whose base is 7 cm and height being 60 cm. Also, find the capacity of the cylinder in litres.

9. A rectangular strip 25 cm × 7 cm is rotated about the longer side. Find the volume of the solid, thus generated.

10. A rectangular sheet of paper, 44 cm × 20 cm, is rolled along its length to form a cylinder. Find the volume of the cylinder so formed.

11. The volume and the curved surface area of a cylinder are 1650 cm^3 and 660 cm^2 respectively. Find the radius and height of the cylinder.

12. The radii of two cylinders are in the ratio 2 : 3 and their heights are in the ratio 5 : 3. Calculate the ratio of their volumes.

13. The ratio between the curved surface area and the total surface area of a right circular cylinder is 1 : 2. Find the volume of the cylinder, if its total surface area is 616 cm^2.

14. The curved surface area of a cylinder is 1320 cm^2 and its base has diameter 21 cm. Find the volume of the cylinder.

15. The ratio between the radius of the base and the height of a cylinder is 2 : 3. Find the total surface area of the cylinder, if its volume is 1617 cm^3.

16. The curved surface area of a cylindrical pillar is 264 m^2 and its volume is 924 m^3. Find the diameter and the height of the pillar.

17. Two circular cylinders of equal volumes have their heights in the ratio 1 : 2. Find the ratio of their radii.

18. The height of a right circular cylinder is 10.5 m. Three times the sum of the areas of its two circular faces is twice the area of the curved surface. Find the volume of the cylinder.

19. How many cubic metres of earth must be dug-out to sink a well 21 m deep and 6 m diameter?

20. The trunk of a tree is cylindrical and its circumference is 176 cm. If the length of the trunk is 3 m, find the volume of the timber that can be obtained from the trunk.
21. A well is dug 20 m deep and it has a diameter of 7 m. The earth which is so dug out is spread out on a rectangular plot 22 m long and 14 m broad. What is the height of the platform so formed?
22. A well with 14 m diameter is dug 8 m deep. The earth taken out of it has been evenly spread all around it to a width of 21 m to form an embankment. Find the height of the embankment.
23. A cylindrical container with diameter of base 56 cm contains sufficient water to submerge a rectangular solid of iron with dimensions 32 cm × 22 cm × 14 cm. Find the rise in the level of the water when the solid is completely submerged.
24. A rectangular sheet of paper 30 cm × 18 cm can be transformed into the curved surface of a right circular cylinder in two ways i.e., either by rolling the paper along its length or by rolling it along its breadth. Find the ratio of the volumes of the two cylinders thus formed.
25. The rain which falls on a roof 18 m long and 16.5 m wide is allowed to be stored in a cylindrical tank 8 m in diameter. If it rains 10 cm on a day, what is the rise of water level in the tank due to it?
26. A piece of ductile metal is in the form of a cylinder of diameter 1 cm and length 5 cm. It is drawnout into a wire of diameter 1 mm. What will be the length of the wire so formed?
27. Find the length of 13.2 kg of copper wire of diameter 4 mm, when 1 cubic cm of copper weighs 8.4 gm.
28. 2.2 cubic dm of brass is to be drawn into a cylindrical wire 0.25 cm in diameter. Find the length of the wire.
29. The difference between inside and outside surfaces of a cylindrical tube 14 cm long is 88 sq. cm. If the volume of the tube is 176 cubic cm, find the inner and outer radii of the tube.
30. Water flows out through a circular pipe whose internal diameter is 2 cm, at the rate of 6 metres per second into a cylindrical tank, the radius of whose base is 60 cm. Find the rise in the level of water in 30 minutes?
31. A cylindrical tube, open at both ends, is made of metal. The internal diameter of the tube is 10.4 cm and its length is 25 cm. The thickness of the metal is 8 mm everywhere. Calculate the volume of the metal.
32. From a tap of inner radius 0.75 cm, water flows at the rate of 7 m per second. Find the volume in litres of water delivered by the pipe in one hour.
33. A cylindrical water tank of diameter 1.4 m and height 2.1 m is being fed by a pipe of diameter 3.5 cm through which water flows at the rate of 2 metre per second. In how much time the tank will be filled?
34. A rectangular sheet of paper 30 cm × 18 cm can be transformed into the curved surface of a right circular cylinder in two ways i.e., either by rolling the paper along its length or by rolling it along its breadth. Find the ratio of the volumes of the two cylinders thus formed.
35. How many litres of water flow out of a pipe having an area of cross-section of 5 cm^2 in one minute, if the speed of water in the pipe is 30 cm/sec?
36. A solid cylinder has a total surface area of 231 cm^2. Its curved surface area is $\frac{2}{3}$ of the total surface area. Find the volume of the cylinder.

37. Find the cost of sinking a tubewell 280 m deep, having diameter 3 m at the rate of Rs 3.60 per cubic metre. Find also the cost of cementing its inner curved surface at Rs 2.50 per square metre.

38. Find the length of 13.2 kg of copper wire of diameter 4 mm, when 1 cubic cm of copper weighs 8.4 gm.

39. 2.2 cubic dm of brass is to be drawn into a cylindrical wire 0.25 cm in diameter. Find the length of the wire.

40. A well with 10 m inside diameter is dug 8.4 m deep. Earth taken out of it is spread all around it to a width of 7.5 m to form an embankment. Find the height of the embankment.

41. A hollow garden roller, 63 cm wide with a girth of 440 cm, is made of 4 cm thick iron. Find the volume of the iron.

42. What length of a solid cylinder 2 cm in diameter must be taken to recast into a hollow cylinder of length 16 cm, external diameter 20 cm and thickness 2.5 mm?

43. In the middle of a rectangular field measuring 30m × 20m, a well of 7 m diameter and 10 m depth is dug. The earth so removed is evenly spread over the remaining part of the field. Find the height through which the level of the field is raised.

ANSWERS

1. (i) 1540 cm^3 (ii) 369.6 cm^3 2. (i) 3465 cm^3 (ii) 924 m^3 3. 15400 cm^3 4. 9240 cm^3
5. 10560 cm^3 6. (i) 660 cm^2 (ii) 968 cm^2 (iii) 2310 cm^3 7. 13860 cm^3
8. 2310 cm^3, 2.31 litres 9. 3850 cm^3 10. 3080 cm^3 11. 5 cm, 21 cm 12. 20 : 27
13. 1078 cm^3 14. 6930 cm^3 15. 770 cm^2 16. 14 m, 6 m 17. $\sqrt{2}:1$ 18. 1617 m^3
19. 594 m^3 20. 0.74 m^3 21. 2.5 m 22. 53.3 cm 23. 4 cm 24. 5 : 3
25. 59.06 cm 26. 5 m 27. 125 m 28. 448 m 29. 1.5 cm, 2.5 cm
30. 3 metres 31. 704 cm^3 32. 4455 litres 33. 28 minutes 34. 5 : 3
35. 9 litres 36. 269.5 cm^3 37. Rs 7128, Rs 6600 38. 125 metres
39. 448 metres 40. 1.6 m 41. 107712 cm^3 42. 20.62 cm 43. 68.6 cm

HINTS TO SELECTED PROBLEMS

9. Solid generated is a cylinder with $r = 7$ cm and $h = 25$ cm

10. We have, $h = 20$ cm and $2\pi rh = 44$ cm

11. We have, $\pi r^2 h = 1650$, $2\pi rh = 660$

$$\therefore \frac{\pi r^2 h}{2\pi rh} = \frac{1650}{660} \Rightarrow \frac{r}{2} = 2.5 \Rightarrow r = 5$$

Now, $\pi r^2 h = 1650 \Rightarrow \frac{22}{7} \times 25 \times h = 1650$

13. We have, $\frac{2\pi rh}{2\pi r(h+r)} = \frac{1}{2} \Rightarrow \frac{h}{h+r} = \frac{1}{2} \Rightarrow h = r$

$$\therefore 2\pi r(h+r) = 616 \Rightarrow 4\pi r^2 = 616$$

14. $r = \frac{21}{2}$ cm,

$$\therefore 2\pi rh = 1320 \Rightarrow 2 \times \frac{22}{7} \times \frac{21}{2} \times h = 1320 \Rightarrow h = 20 \text{ cm}$$

Now, $V = \pi r^2 h = \frac{22}{7} \times \left(\frac{21}{2}\right)^2 \times 20$

15. Let $r = 2x$, $h = 3x$. Then,

Volume $= 1617 \Rightarrow \frac{22}{7} \times (2x^2) \times 3x = 1617 \Rightarrow x = \frac{7}{2}$

$\therefore$ radius = 7 cm and height $= \frac{21}{2}$ cm

16. $2\pi rh = 264$ and $\pi r^2 h = 924$

$\therefore \frac{\pi r^2 h}{2\pi rh} = \frac{924}{264} \Rightarrow r = 7$

17. $\pi r^2 h = \pi r^2 (2h) \Rightarrow r : R = \sqrt{2} : 1$

18. $3(2\pi r^2) = 2\pi r (10.5) \Rightarrow r = 7$

19. Volume of earth dugout = Volume of the well.

24. For first way; $h = 18$, $2\pi r = 30$.

For second way; $h = 30$, $2\pi r = 18$.

27. Obtain h in cm from the following: $\frac{22}{7} \times 0.2 \times 0.2 \times h \times \frac{8.4}{1000} = 13.2$

31. For first way: $h = 18$, $2\pi r = 30$. Now, find its volume V_1.

For second way: $h = 30$, $2\pi r = 18$. Now, find its volume V_2.

35. Obtain h in cm from the following: $\frac{22}{7} \times 0.2 \times 0.2 \times h \times \frac{8.4}{1000} = 13.2$.

THINGS TO REMEMBER

1. *The magnitude of a space (solid) region is called its volume.*
2. *Standard units of volume and their relations are:*

$$1 \text{ cm}^3 = 1000 \text{ mm}^3$$
$$1 \text{ m}^3 = 10^6 \text{ cm}^3$$
$$1 \text{ dm}^3 = 1000 \text{ cm}^3$$
$$1 \text{ m}^3 = 1000 \text{ dm}^3$$
$$1 \text{ km}^3 = 10^9 \text{ m}^3$$
$$1 \text{ l} = 1 \text{ dm}^3 = 1000 \text{ cm}^3$$
$$1 \text{ ml} = 1 \text{ cm}^3$$
$$\therefore \quad 1 \text{ l} = 1000 \text{ ml}^3$$
$$1 \text{ kl} = 1000\, l = 1 \text{ m}^3$$

3. *Formulae :*

(i) *Volume of a cuboid* = *length* × *breadth* × *height*

or, $V = l \times b \times h$

(ii) *Volume of a cube* = $(Side)^3$

or, $V = l \times l \times l = l^3$

(iii) *Surface area of a cuboid* = 2 (*length* × *breadth* + *breadth* × *height* + *height* × *length*)

or, $S = 2\,(lb + bh + lh)$

(iv) *Surface area of a cube* = $6 \times (Side)^2$

$S = 6l^2$

4. *Each plane end of a right circular cylinder is called its base.*
5. *The line segment joining the centres of the circular ends of a right circular cylinder is called its axis. The length of the axis is called the height of the cylinder.*
6. *The curved surface which joins two bases of a right-circular cylinder is called its lateral surface.*
7. *Formulae:*

(i) *Volume of a right circular cylinder* = (*Area of base*) × (*Height*)

or, $V = \pi r^2 h$

(ii) *Lateral surface area of a right circular cylinder* = (*Circumference of base*) × (*Height*)

or, $S = 2\pi rh$

(iii) *Total surface area of a right circular cylinder* = 2 (*Area of base*) + (*Area of lateral surface*)

or, Total surface area $= 2\pi r^2 + 2\pi rh = 2\pi r\,(r + h)$

DATA HANDLING-I
(Classification and Tabulation of Data)

23.1 RAW DATA

The word data means information (its exact dictionary meaning is: given facts). Collection of observations is the first step in statistical investigations. The numerical observations collected by an observer cannot be put to any use immediately and directly. That is why it is called a raw data. For example, look at the following list of marks (out of 100) scored by 30 students of class VIII in a test:

55, 65, 15, 40, 35, 70, 90, 92, 84, 85, 70, 75, 65, 72, 80,
78, 64, 88, 78, 76, 55, 54, 52, 72, 70, 90, 85, 75, 65, 80

We find that each entry in the above list is a numerical fact which is called an observation. Such a collection of observations gathered initially is called raw data.

23.2 PRESENTATION OF DATA

After collection of data, the investigator has to find ways to condense them in tabular form in order to study their salient features. Such an arrangement is called presentation of data.

The raw data can be arranged in any one of the following ways :

(i) Serial order or alphabetical order (ii) Ascending order
(iii) Descending order

The raw data when put in ascending or descending order of magnitude is called an array.

Let the marks obtained by 30 students of class VIII in a class test, out of 50 marks, according to their roll numbers be :

39, 25, 5, 33, 19, 21, 12, 41, 12, 21, 19, 1, 10, 8, 12, 17, 19, 17, 17, 41, 40, 12, 41, 33, 19, 21, 33, 5, 1, 21.

The data in this form are called raw data or ungrouped data. The above raw data can be arranged in serial order as follows:

Roll No.	*Marks*	*Roll No.*	*Marks*	*Roll No.*	*Marks*
1	39	11	19	21	40
2	25	12	1	22	12
3	5	13	10	23	41
4	33	14	8	24	33
5	19	15	12	25	19
6	21	16	17	26	21

Roll No.	Marks	Roll No.	Marks	Roll No.	Marks
7	12	17	19	27	33
8	41	18	17	28	5
9	12	19	17	29	1
10	21	20	41	30	21

Now suppose we wish to judge the standard of achievement of the students. The data in this form do not give us a clear picture of the group. If we arrange them in ascending or descending order, it gives us a slightly better picture. In ascending order, the data look as follows:

1, 1, 5, 5, 8, 10, 12, 12, 12, 12, 17, 17, 17, 19, 19, 19, 19, 21, 21, 21, 25, 33, 33, 33, 39, 40, 41, 41, 41.

In descending order, the data look as follows :

41, 41, 41, 40, 39, 33, 33, 33, 25, 21, 21, 21, 21, 19, 19, 19, 19, 17, 17, 17, 12, 12, 12, 12, 10, 8, 5, 5, 1, 1.

The raw data when put in ascending or descending order of magnitude is called an *array* or *arrayed data.*

If the number of observations is large, then arranging data in ascending or descending or serial order is a tedious job and it does not tell us much except perhaps the minimum(*s*) and maximum(*s*) of data. So, to make it easily understandable and clear, we can tabulate data in the from of a table given below.

Marks	*Tally marks*	*No. of students*
1	||	2
5	||	2
8	|	1
10	|	1
12	||||	4
17	|||	3
19	||||	4
21	||||	4
25	|	1
33	|||	3
39	|	1
40	|	1
41	|||	3

In the first column of the table, we write all marks from lowest to highest. We now look at the first value in the given raw data and put a bar (vertical line) in the second column opposite to it. Now we see the second value in the given raw data and put a bar opposite to it in the second column. This process is repeated till all observations in the given raw data are exhausted. The bars drawn in the second column are known as *tally marks* and to facilitate we record tally marks in bunches of five, the fifth tally mark is drawn diagonally across the first four. For example, 𝍸 || = 7. We finally count the number of tally marks corresponding to each observation and write in the third column.

This way of presentation of data is known as *frequency distribution*. Marks are called *variates* and the number of students who have secured a particular number of marks is called frequency of the variate. *The number of times an observation occurs in the given data, is called the frequency of the observation.*

The presentation of data can be further condensed into class groups. In this presentation all observations are divided into groups. These groups are called *classes* or class intervals.

We can arrange the above data into classes as follows:

Marks	*No. of students (Frequency)*
1-10	6
11-20	11
21-30	5
31-40	4
41-50	4

The class 1-10 means the marks obtained between 1 and 10 including both 1 and 10. The number of observations falling in a particular class is called the *frequency of that class or class frequency*.

Thus, the class 1-10 has frequency 6 and the class 11-20 has 11 as class frequency. In the class 1-10, we say that 1 is the lower limit and 10 is the upper limit of the class. Similarly, in class 11-20, 11 is the lower limit and 20 is the upper limit. This type of presentation of data is called *grouped frequency distribution.*

23.3 FREQUENCY DISTRIBUTION

Frequency table or frequency distribution is a method to present raw data in the form from which one can easily understand the information contained in the raw data.

Frequency distributions are of two types :

(i) Discrete frequency distribution. (ii) Continuous or grouped frequency distribution.

23.3.1 DISCRETE FREQUENCY DISTRIBUTION

The process of preparing this type of distribution is very simple. The construction of a discrete frequency distribution from the given raw data is done by the use of the method of tally marks. In the first column of the frequency table we write all possible values of the variable from the lowest to the highest.

We now look at the first value in the given raw data and put a bar (vertical line) in the second column opposite to it. Now, we see the second value in the given raw data and put a bar opposite to it in the second column. This process is repeated till all observations in the given raw data are exhausted. To facilitate counting blocks of five |||| are prepared and some space is left in between each block. We finally count the number of bars corresponding to each value of the variable and place it in the third column of frequency. The process will be clear from the following example of the number of children in 20 families :

1, 1, 2, 3, 4, 3, 2, 1, 1, 4, 5, 2, 4, 2, 2, 1, 3, 3, 2, 5

The data may be put in the form of a discrete frequency distribution as follows:

No. of children	*Tally bars*	*Frequency*
1	𝍸	5
2	𝍸 I	6
3	IIII	4
4	III	3
5	II	2

23.3.2 CONTINUOUS OR GROUPED FREQUENCY DISTRIBUTION

The above method of condensing the raw data is convenient only where the values in the raw data are largely repeating and the difference between the greatest and the smallest observations is not very large.

If the number of observations in data is large and the difference between the greatest and the smallest observations is large, then we condense the data into classes or groups. For example, let the marks obtained by 30 students of a class in a test be

39, 25, 5, 33, 19, 21, 12, 48, 13, 21, 9, 1, 10, 8, 12, 17, 19, 17, 41, 40, 12, 46, 37, 17, 27, 30, 6, 2, 23, 19.

We can arrange these marks as follows:

Marks (Class intervals)	*Tally bars*	*Number of students (frequency)*
0-10	𝍸 I	6
10-20	𝍸 𝍸 I	11
20-30	𝍸	5
30-40	IIII	4
40-50	IIII	4

Such a presentation of data is known as the *grouped frequency distribution*.

In the above example 30 observations have been divided into 5 groups. These groups are called *classes*. The class 0-10 means the marks obtained between 0 and 10 including 0 and excluding 10. The number of observations falling in a particular class is called the frequency of that class or class frequency. Thus, the class 0-10 has frequency 6 and the class 10-20 has 11 as class frequency. In the class 0-10, we say that 0 is the *lower limit* and 10 is the *upper limit* of the class. Similarly in the class 10-20, 10 is the lower limit and 20 is the upper limit. The span of the class i.e., the difference between the upper limit and the lower limit, is known as the *class interval*. For example, in the class 10-20 the class interval is 20 – 10 = 10.

There are two methods of classifying the data according to the class intervals, viz. (i) 'exclusive' method, and (ii) 'inclusive' method.

EXCLUSIVE METHOD When the class intervals are so fixed that the upper limit of one class is the lower limit of the next class it is known as the exclusive method of classification. In this method the upper limit of a class is not included in the class. Thus, in the class 0 – 10 of marks obtained by students, a student who has obtained 10 marks is not included in this class. He is counted in the next class 10-20.

INCLUSIVE METHOD In this method the classes are so formed that the upper limit of a class is included in that class. Following example illustrates the method.

Wages (Rs.)	*No. of workers*
1000-1099	125
1100-1199	150
1200-1299	200
1300-1399	250
1400-1499	175
1500-1599	100
	Total 1000

In the class 1000-1099 we include workers having wages between Rs. 1000 and Rs. 1099. If the income of a worker is exactly Rs. 1100 he is included in the next class 1100-1199.

Exclusive Method		*Inclusive Method*	
Wages (Rs.)	*No. of workers*	*Wages (Rs.)*	*No. of workers*
1000-1100	125	1000-1099	125
1100-1200	150	1100-1199	150
1200-1300	200	1200-1299	200
1300-1400	250	1300-1399	250
1400-1500	175	1400-1499	175
1500-1600	100	1500-1599	100
	Total 1000		Total 1000

It is evident from the above example that both the inclusive and exclusive methods give us the same class frequency, although the class intervals are apparently different in the two cases. In the above example in case of exclusive method the class interval is 100 whereas in case of inclusive method the class interval is 99. However, 99 is not the correct class interval. Whenever inclusive method is used it is necessary to make an adjustment to determine the correct class intervals and to have continuity. If $a - b$ is a class in inclusive method, then in exclusive method it becomes $a-\frac{h}{2}-b+\frac{h}{2}$, where

$$h=\frac{(\text{lower limit of a class})-(\text{upper limit of previous class})}{2}$$

In the above example on inclusive method the difference between the lower limit of a class and the upper limit of the preceding class is 1 i.e., $h = 1$. Therefore we subtract 1/2 from the lower limit of each class and add 1/2 in the upper limit of each class to make it continuous. The adjusted classes would then be as follows:

Wages (Rs.)	*No. of workers*
999.5-1099.5	125
1099.5-1199.5	150
1199.5-1299.5	200
1299.5-1399.5	250
1399.5-1499.5	175
1499.5-1599.5	100

It should be noted that before adjustment the class interval was 99 but after adjustment, it is 100.

The *mid-value* of a class is called the *class mark*. For example, the class-mark or mid-value of the class 1000-1100 is 1050. In fact

$$\text{Class mark} = \frac{\text{Lower limit} + \text{Upper limit}}{2}$$

or, $$\text{Class mark} = \text{Lower limit} + \frac{1}{2}\,(\text{Difference between the upper and lower limits})$$

23.4 CONSTRUCTION OF A DISCRETE FREQUENCY DISTRIBUTION

To prepare a discrete frequency distribution from the given raw data we use the following algorithm.

ALGORITHM

Step I — *Obtain the given raw data.*

Step II — *Prepare a table with three columns: first for variable under study such as marks, weight, height etc., second for 'Tally marks' and third for the total, representing corresponding frequency to each value or size of the variable.*

Step III — *Place all the values of the variable in the first column in ascending order.*

Step IV — *Take the first observation in the raw data and put a bar in the second column opposite to it. Then take the second observation in the given raw data and put a bar opposite to it. Continue this process till all the observations in the given raw data are exhausted. For the sake of convenience, record tally marks in bunches of five, the fifth is obtained by crossing diagonally the other four. Leave some space between each block of bars.*

Step V — *Count the number of bars (tally marks) in respect of each value of the variable and place it in the third column.*

Step VI — *Give a suitable title to the frequency distribution table so that it conveys exactly what the table is about.*

Following illustrations will clarify the above algorithm.

ILLUSTRATIVE EXAMPLES

Example 1 Given below are the ages of 25 students of class VIII in a school. Prepare a discrete frequency distribution.

15, 16, 16, 14, 17, 17, 16, 15, 15, 16, 16, 17, 15, 16, 16, 14, 16, 15, 14, 15, 16, 16, 15, 14, 15.

Solution Frequency distribution of ages of 25 students

Age	*Tally marks*	*Frequency*
14	IIII	4
15	~~IIII~~ III	8
16	~~IIII~~ ~~IIII~~	10
17	III	3
Total		25

Example 2 Form a discrete frequency distribution from the following scores :
15, 18, 16, 20, 25, 24, 25, 20, 16, 15, 18, 18, 16, 24, 15, 20, 28, 30, 27, 16, 24, 25, 20, 18, 28, 27, 25, 24, 24, 18, 18, 25, 20, 16, 15, 20, 27, 28, 29, 16.

Frequency distribution of scores

Variate	*Tally marks*	*Frequency*
15	||||	4
16	~~||||~~ |	6
18	~~||||~~ |	6
20	~~||||~~ |	6
24	~~||||~~	5
25	~~||||~~	5
27	|||	3
28	|||	3
29	|	1
30	|	1
Total		40

EXERCISE 23.1

1. Define the following terms :
   (i) Observations
   (ii) Raw data
   (iii) Frequency of an observation
   (iv) Frequency distribution
   (v) Discrete frequency distribution
   (vi) Grouped frequency distribution
   (vii) Class-interval
   (viii) Class-size
   (ix) Class limits
   (x) True class limits
2. The final marks in mathematics of 30 students are as follows:
   53, 61, 48, 60, 78, 68, 55, 100, 67, 90, 75, 88, 77, 37, 84,
   58, 60, 48, 62, 56, 44, 58, 52, 64, 98, 59, 70, 39, 50, 60
   (i) Arrange these marks in the ascending order, 30 to 39 one group, 40 to 49 second group etc.
   Now answer the following :
   (ii) What is the highest score ?
   (iii) What is the lowest score ?
   (iv) What is the range ?
   (v) If 40 is the pass mark how many have failed ?
   (vi) How many have scored 75 or more ?
   (vii) Which observations between 50 and 60 have not actually appeared ?
   (viii) How many have scored less than 50 ?
3. The weights of new born babies (in kg) in a hospital on a particular day are as follows:
   2.3, 2.2, 2.1, 2.7, 2.6, 3.0, 2.5, 2.9, 2.8, 3.1, 2.5, 2.8, 2.7, 2.9, 2.4
   (i) Rearrange the weights in descending order.
   (ii) Determine the highest weight.
   (iii) Determine the lowest weight.

(iv) Determine the range.

(v) How many babies were born on that day ?

(vi) How many babies weigh below 2.5 kg ?

(vii) How many babies weigh more than 2.8 kg ?

(viii) How many babies weigh 2.8 kg ?

4. Following data gives the number of children in 40 families:

1, 2, 6, 5, 1, 5, 1, 3, 2, 6, 2, 3, 4, 2, 0, 0, 4, 4, 3, 2, 2, 0, 0, 1, 2, 2, 4, 3, 2, 1, 0, 5, 1, 2, 4, 3, 4, 1, 6, 2, 2.

Represent it in the form of a frequency distribution.

5. Prepare a frequency table of the following scores obtained by 50 students in a test:

42, 51, 21, 42, 37, 37, 42, 49, 38, 52, 7, 33, 17,
44, 39, 7, 14, 27, 39, 42, 42, 62, 37, 39, 67, 51,
53, 53, 59, 41, 29, 38, 27, 31, 54, 19, 53, 51, 22,
61, 42, 39, 59, 47, 33, 34, 16, 37, 57, 43

6. A die was thrown 25 times and following scores were obtained:

1, 5, 2, 4, 3, 6, 1, 4, 2, 5, 1, 6, 2,
6, 3, 5, 4, 1, 3, 2, 3, 6, 1, 5, 2,

Prepare a frequency table of the scores.

7. In a study of number of accidents per day, the observations for 30 days were obtained as follows :

6, 3, 5, 6, 4, 3, 2, 5, 4, 2, 4, 2, 1, 2, 2,
0, 5, 4, 6, 1 6, 0, 5, 3, 6, 1, 5, 5, 2, 6

Prepare a frequency distribution table.

8. Prepare a frequency table of the following ages (in years) of 30 students of class VIII in your school :

13, 14, 13, 12, 14, 13, 14, 15, 13, 14, 13, 14, 16, 12, 14, 13, 14, 15, 16, 13, 14, 13, 12, 17, 13, 12, 13, 13, 13, 14

9. Following figures relate to the weekly wages (in Rs) of 15 workers in a factory :

300, 250, 200, 250, 200, 150, 350, 200, 250, 200, 150, 300, 150, 200, 250

Prepare a frequency table.

(i) What is the range in wages (in Rs) ?

(ii) How many workers are getting Rs 350 ?

(iii) How many workers are getting the minimum wages ?

10. Construct a frequency distribution table for the following marks obtained by 25 students in a history test in calss VIII of a school :

9, 17, 12, 20, 9, 18, 25, 17, 19, 9, 12, 9, 12, 18, 17, 19, 20, 25, 9, 12, 17, 19, 19, 20, 9

(i) What is the range of marks ?

(ii) What is the highest mark ?

(iii) Which mark is occurring more frequently ?

ANSWERS

2. (ii) 100 (iii) 37 (iv) 63 (v) 2 (vi) 8 (vii) 51, 54, 57 (viii) 5

3. (i) 3.1, 3.0, 2.9, 2.9, 2.8, 2.8, 2.7, 2.7, 2.6, 2.5, 2.4, 2.4, 2.3, 2.2, 2.1
   (ii) 3.1 kg (iii) 2.1 kg (iv) 1.0 kg (v) 15 (vi) 4 (vii) 4 (viii) 2

5.

Marks	*No. of students*	*Marks*	*No. of students*	*Marks*	*No. of students*
7	2	33	2	49	1
14	1	34	1	51	3
16	1	37	4	52	1
17	1	38	2	53	3
19	1	39	4	54	1
21	1	41	1	57	1
22	1	42	6	59	2
27	2	43	1	61	1
29	1	44	1	62	1
31	1	47	1	67	1

6.

Score	: 1	2	3	4	5	6
Number of times	: 5	5	4	3	4	4

7.

Number of accidents	: 0	1	2	3	4	5	6
Number of days	: 2	3	6	3	4	6	6

8.

Ages (in years)	: 12	13	14	15	16	17
Number of students	: 4	13	8	2	2	1

9. (i) 200 (ii) 1 (iii) 3 10. (i) 16 (ii) 25 (iii) 9

23.5 CONSTRUCTION OF A GROUPED FREQUENCY DISTRIBUTION

Following algorithm is used for the construction of a grouped frequency distribution

<u>Step I</u> *Determine the maximum and minimum value of the variate occurring in the data.*

<u>Step II</u> *Decide upon the number of classes to be formed. Note that the number of classes should be in range of 5 to 15.*

<u>Step III</u> *Find the difference between the maximum value and minimum value and divide this difference by the number of classes to be formed to determine the class interval. The difference between the maximum value and minimum value in a data is called range.*

<u>Step IV</u> *Be sure that there must be classes with us to include minimum and maximum occurring in the data.*

<u>Step V</u> *Take each item from the data, one at a time and put a tally mark (|) against the class to which the item belongs. If tally marks are more than 4, then record them in the bunches of five, the fifth one is marked by crossing diagonally the first four.*

<u>Step VI</u> *By counting determine the total number of tally marks in each class, which gives us the frequency of the class.*

<u>Step VII</u> *Check that the total of all frequencies is same as the total number of observations.*

<u>Step VIII</u> *Give a suitable title to the frequency table so that it conveys exactly what the table is about.*

Following illustrations will further clarify the above procedure.

ILLUSTRATIVE EXAMPLES

Example 1 The water tax bills (in rupees) of 30 houses in a locality are given below. Construct a grouped frequency distribution with class size of 10.

30, 32, 45, 54, 74, 78, 108, 112, 66, 76, 88, 40, 14, 20, 15, 35, 44, 66, 75, 84, 95, 96, 102, 110, 88, 74, 112, 14, 34, 44.

Solution Here, the maximum and minimum values of the variate are 112 and 14 respectively.

$\therefore \quad \text{Range} = 112 - 14 = 98$

It is given that the class size is 10, and $\frac{\text{Range}}{\text{Class size}} = \frac{98}{10} = 9.8$

So, we should have 10 classes each of size 10.

The minimum and maximum values of the variate are 14 and 112 respectively. So, we have to make the classes in such a way that first class includes the minimum value and the last class includes the maximum value. If we take the first class as 14-24 it includes the minimum value 14. If the last class is taken as 104-114, then it includes the maximum value 112. Here, we form classes by exclusive method. In the class 14-24, 14 is included but 24 is excluded. Similarly, in other classes, the lower limit is included and the upper limit is excluded.

In the view of above discussion, we construct the frequency distribution table as follows :

Bill (in rupees)	*Tally marks*	*Frequency*
14-24	||||	4
24-34	||	2
34-44	|||	3
44-54	|||	3
54-64	|	1
64-74	||	2
74-84	~~||||~~	5
84-94	|||	3
94-104	|||	3
104-114	||||	4
Total		30

Example 2 Form a grouped frequency distribution from the following data by inclusive method taking 4 as the magnitude of class intervals.

31, 23, 19, 29, 22, 20, 16, 10, 13, 34, 38, 33, 28, 21, 15, 18, 36, 24, 18, 15
12, 30, 27, 23, 20, 17, 14, 32, 26, 25, 18, 29, 24, 19, 16, 11, 22, 15, 17, 10

Solution Here, the minimum and maximum values of the variable are 10 and 38 respectively.

$\therefore$ Range = 38 − 10 = 28

Since magnitude of class intervals = 4 [Given]

$\therefore$ Number of class intervals $= \frac{28}{4} = 7$

We take 10 as the lower limit of first class interval. Since the frequency distribution is to be formed by inclusive method. So, the class intervals are 10-13, 14-17, 18-21, 22-25, 26-29, 30-33, 34-37, 38-41.

In view of the above, we obtain the following frequency distribution.

Frequency Distribution

Class interval	*Tally marks*	*Frequency*
10-13	~~IIII~~	5
14-17	~~IIII~~ III	8
18-21	~~IIII~~ III	8
22-25	~~IIII~~ II	7
26-29	~~IIII~~	5
30-33	IIII	4
34-37	II	2
38-41	I	1
Total		40

Example 3 The maximum temperatures (in degrees celcius) and relative humidity (in percent) for Delhi for the month of August 1998, as reported by Meteorological department, are given below. Construct a frequency table for each.

Maximum temperatures (in degree celcius) 32.5, 30.5, 33.8, 31.0, 28.6, 33.9, 33.3, 32.4, 30.4, 32.6, 34.7, 34.9, 31.9, 35.2, 35.3, 35.5, 36.4, 36.9, 37.0, 34.4, 32.5, 31.4, 34.4, 35.6, 37.3, 37.5, 36.9, 37.0, 36.3, 36.9, 36.7.

Relative humidity (in percent) 90, 97, 92, 95, 93, 95, 93, 85, 83, 85, 83, 77, 83, 77, 74, 60, 71, 65, 74, 80, 87, 82, 81, 76, 61, 63, 58, 58, 56, 57, 54.

Solution We have,

Highest temperature = 37.5°C, Lowest temperature = 28.6°C

$\therefore$ Range = 37.5 − 28.6 = 8.9°

Let the class size be 2°C. Then,

Number of classes = 5 $\left[\because \frac{\text{Range}}{\text{Class size}} = \frac{8.9}{2} = 4.95\right]$

Let the lower limit for the first class interval be 28°C. Then, the class intervals are: 28-30, 30-32, 32-34, 34-36, 36-38 and the frequency distribution by inclusive method is as given below.

Frequency Distribution for Maximum Temperature

Temperature (in degree celcius)	*Tally marks*	*Frequency*
28 - 30	|	1
30 - 32	~~||||~~	5
32 - 34	~~||||~~ |||	8
34 - 36	~~||||~~ ||	7
36 - 38	~~||||~~ ~~||||~~	10
Total		31

We have,

Maximum humidity $=97\%$, Minimum humidity $=54\%$

$\therefore$ Range $=97-54=43$

Let us choose the class size as 10. Then,

Number of classes $=5$ $\left[\because \frac{\text{Range}}{\text{Class size}}=\frac{43}{10}=4.3\right]$

Let the lower limit for the first class interval be 50. Then, various class intervals are: 50-60, 60-70, 70-80, 80-90, and 90-100 and the frequency distribution by inclusive method is as given below.

Frequency Distribution for Relative Humidity

Relative Humidity (in%)	*Tally marks*	*Frequency distribution*
50-60	~~||||~~	5
60-70	||||	4
70-80	~~||||~~ |	6
80-90	~~||||~~ ||||	9
90-100	~~||||~~ ||	7
Total		31

Example 4 The marks obtained by 40 students of class VIII in an examination are given below:

18, 8, 12, 0, 8, 16, 12, 5, 23, 2, 16, 23, 2, 10, 20, 12, 9, 7, 6, 5, 3, 5, 13, 21, 13, 15, 20, 24, 1, 7, 21, 16, 13, 18, 23, 7, 3, 18, 17, 16.

Present the data in the form of a frequency distribution using the same class size, one such class being 15-20 (where 20 is not included).

Solution The minimum and maximum marks in the given raw data are 0 and 24 respectively. It is given that 15-20 is one of the class intervals and the class size is same. So, the classes of equal size are: 0-5, 5-10, 10-15, 15-20 and 20-25.

Thus, the frequency distribution is as given below:

Frequency Distribution of Marks

Mark	*Tally marks*	*Frequency*
0-5	~~IIII~~ I	6
5-10	~~IIII~~ ~~IIII~~	10
10-15	~~IIII~~ II	7
15-20	~~IIII~~ IIII	9
20-25	~~IIII~~ III	8
Total		40

Example 5 The weights in grams of 50 oranges picked at random from a consignment are as follows:

131, 113, 82, 75, 204, 81, 84, 118, 104, 110, 80, 107, 111, 141, 136, 123, 90, 78, 90, 115, 110, 98, 106, 99, 107, 84, 76, 186, 82, 100, 109, 128, 115, 107, 115, 119, 93, 187, 139, 129, 130, 68, 195, 123, 125, 111, 92, 86, 70, 126

Form the grouped frequency table by dividing the variable range into intervals of equal width, each corresponding to 20 gms in such a way that the mid-value of the first class corresponds to 70 gms.

Solution We have,

Size of each class = 20, Mid-value of first class = 70

We know that if a is the mid-value of a class and h is the class size, then the lower and upper limits of the class are $a - \frac{h}{2}$ and $a + \frac{h}{2}$ respectively.

Here, $a = 70$ and $h = 20$

So, the lower limit of the first class interval $= 70 - 10 = 60$

and, the upper limit of the first class interval $= 70 + 10 = 80$

$\therefore$ First class interval is 60-80

In view of the above, we obtain the following frequency distribution.

Frequency Distribution of Weights of Oranges

Weight (in gms)	*Tally marks*	*Frequency*
60-80	~~IIII~~	5
80-100	~~IIII~~ ~~IIII~~ III	13
100-120	~~IIII~~ ~~IIII~~ ~~IIII~~ II	17
120-140	~~IIII~~ ~~IIII~~	10
140-160	I	1
160-180		0
180-200	III	3
200-220	I	1
Total		50

EXERCISE 23.2

1. The marks obtained by 40 students of class VIII in an examination are given below:

   16, 17, 18, 3, 7, 23, 18, 13, 10, 21, 7, 1, 13, 21, 13, 15, 19, 24, 16, 3, 23, 5, 12, 18, 8, 12, 6, 8, 16, 5, 3, 5, 0, 7, 9, 12, 20, 10, 2, 23.

   Divide the data into five groups, namely 0-5, 5-10, 10-15, 15-20 and 20-25 and prepare a grouped frequency table.

2. The marks scored by 20 students in a test are given below:

   54, 42, 68, 56, 62, 71, 78, 51, 72, 53, 44, 58, 47, 64, 41, 57, 89, 53, 84, 57.

   Complete the following frequency table:

(Marks in class intervals)	*Tally marks*	*Frequency (No. of children)*
40-50		
50-60		
60-70		
70-80		
80-90		

   What is the class interval in which the greatest frequency occurs?

3. The following is the distribution of weights (in kg) of 52 persons:

Weight in kg	*Persons*
30-40	10
40-50	15
50-60	17
60-70	6
70-80	4

   (i) What is the lower limit of class 50-60?

   (ii) Find the class marks of the classes 40-50, 50-60.

   (iii) What is the class size?

4. Construct a frequency table for the following weights (in gm) of 35 mangoes using the equal class intervals, one of them is 40-45 (45 not included):

   30, 40, 45, 32, 43, 50, 55, 62, 70, 70, 61, 62, 53, 52, 50, 42, 35, 37, 53, 55, 65, 70, 73, 74, 45, 46, 58, 59, 60, 62, 74, 34, 35, 70, 68.

   (i) What is the class mark of the class interval 40-45?

   (ii) What is the range of the above weights?

   (iii) How many classes are there?

5. Construct a frequency table with class-intervals 0-5 (5 not included) of the following marks obtained by a group of 30 students in an examination:

   0, 5, 7, 10, 12, 15, 20, 22, 25, 27, 8, 11, 17, 3, 6, 9, 17, 19, 21, 29, 31, 35, 37, 40, 42, 45, 49, 4, 50, 16.

6. The marks scored by 40 students of class VIII in mathematics are given below:

   81, 55, 68, 79, 85, 43, 29, 68, 54, 73, 47, 35, 72, 64, 95, 44, 50, 77, 64, 35, 79, 52, 45, 54, 70, 83, 62, 64, 72, 92, 84, 76, 63, 43, 54, 38, 73, 68, 52, 54.

   Prepare a frequency distribution with class size of 10 marks.

7. The heights (in cm) of 30 students of class VIII are given below:
155, 158, 154, 158, 160, 148, 149, 150, 153, 159, 161, 148, 157, 153, 157, 162, 159, 151, 154, 156, 152, 156, 160, 152, 147, 155, 163, 155, 157, 153.
Prepare a frequency distribution table with 160-164 as one of the class intervals.
8. The monthly wages of 30 workers in a factory are given below:
830, 835, 890, 810, 835, 836, 869, 845, 898, 890, 820, 860, 832, 833, 855, 845, 804, 808, 812, 840, 885, 835, 836, 878, 840, 868, 890, 806, 840, 890.
Represent the data in the form of a frequency distribution with class size 10.
9. Construct a frequency table with equal class intervals from the following data on the monthly wages (in rupees) of 28 labourers working in a factory, taking one of the class intervals as 210-230 (230 not included):
220, 268, 258, 242, 210, 268, 272, 242, 311, 290, 300, 320, 319, 304, 302, 318, 306, 292, 254, 278, 210, 240, 280, 316, 306, 215, 256, 236.
10. The daily minimum temperatures in degrees Celsius recorded in a certain Arctic region are as follows:
– 12.5, – 10.8,– 18.6, – 8.4, – 10.8, – 4.2, – 4.8, – 6.7, – 13.2, – 11.8, – 2.3, 1.2, 2.6, 0, – 2.4, 0, 3.2, 2.7, 3.4, 0, – 2.4, – 2.4, 0, 3.2, 2.7, 3.4, 0, – 2.4, – 5.8, – 8.9, – 14.6, – 12.3, – 11.5, – 7.8, – 2.9
Represent them as frequency distribution table taking – 19.9 to – 15 as the first class interval.

ANSWERS

2. 50-60 3. (i) 50 (ii) 45, 55 (iii) 10
4. (i) 42.5 (ii) 44 (iii) 9

THINGS TO REMEMBER

1. *Numerical observations collected by an observer, is called a raw data.*
2. *The number of times an observation occurs in the given data, is called the frequency of the observation.*
3. *A way of presenting data that exhibits the values of the variable and corresponding frequencies, is called a frequency distribution.*

24

DATA HANDLING-II
(Graphical Representation of Data as Histograms)

24.1 GRAPHICAL METHOD OF REPRESENTING A DATA

In the previous class, we have learnt how to draw bar graphs for representing the frequency distribution of ungrouped data. As we have seen that in a bar chart, the heights of rectangles are proportional to the frequencies and breadth does not matter at all. A well constructed bar chart is the quickest way to represent a frequency distribution pictorially. In this section, we shall learn how to represent a grouped frequency distribution graphically. The most common graphic representation is the histogram.

HISTOGRAM *A histogram or frequency histogram is a graphical representation of a frequency distribution in the form of rectangles with class intervals as bases and heights proportional to corresponding frequencies such that there is no gap between any two successive rectangles.*

A histogram is a two dimensional diagram. In this chapter, we shall discuss the contruction of a histogram for a continuous grouped frequency distribution with equal class-intervals only.

In drawing the histogram of a continuous grouped frequency distribution, we use the following algorithm.

ALGORITHM

Step I — *Take a graph paper and draw two perpendicular lines, one horizontal and one vertical, intersecting at O (say). Mark them as OX and OY.*

Step II — *Take horizontal line OX as X-axis and vertical line OY as Y-axis.*

Step III — *Choose a suitable scale for X-axis and along X-axis represent class - limits.*

Step IV — *Choose a suitable scale for Y-axis and mark frequencies along Y-axis.*

Step V — *Construct rectangles with class intervals as bases and respective frequencies as heights.*

NOTE: *It should be noted that the scale for X-axis may not be same as the scale for Y-axis. The selection of scale depends upon our convenience and the type of data.*

Following illustrations will clarify the above algorithm.

ILLUSTRATIVE EXAMPLES

Example 1 The following table gives the marks scored by 100 students in an entrance examination.

Marks:	0 – 10	10 – 20	20 – 30	30 – 40	40 – 50	50 – 60	60 – 70	70 – 80
No. of students (Frequency):	4	10	16	22	20	18	8	2

Represent this data in the form of a histogram.

Solution We represent the class limits along X-axis on a suitable scale and the frequencies along Y-axis on a suitable scale.

Taking class-intervals as bases and the corresponding frequencies as heights, we construct rectangles to obtain the histogram of the given frequency distribution as shown in Fig. 24.1.

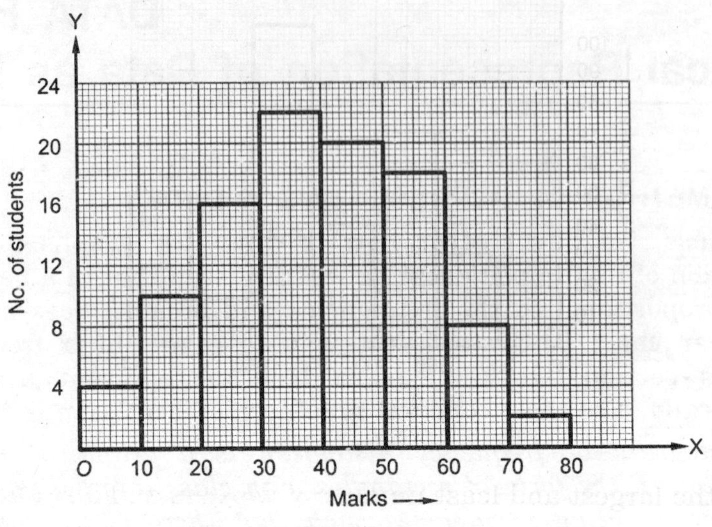

Fig. 24.1

Example 2 The following is the distribution of weights (in kg) of 50 persons :

Weight (in kg):	50 – 55	55 – 60	60 – 65	65 – 70	70 – 75	75 – 80	80 – 85	85 – 90
No. of persons:	12	8	5	4	5	7	6	3

Draw a histogram for the above data.

Solution We represent the class limits along X-axis on a suitable scale and the frequencies along Y-axis on a suitable scale.

Since the scale on X-axis starts at 50, a kink (break) is indicated near the origin to signify that the graph is drawn to scale beginning at 50, and not at the origin.

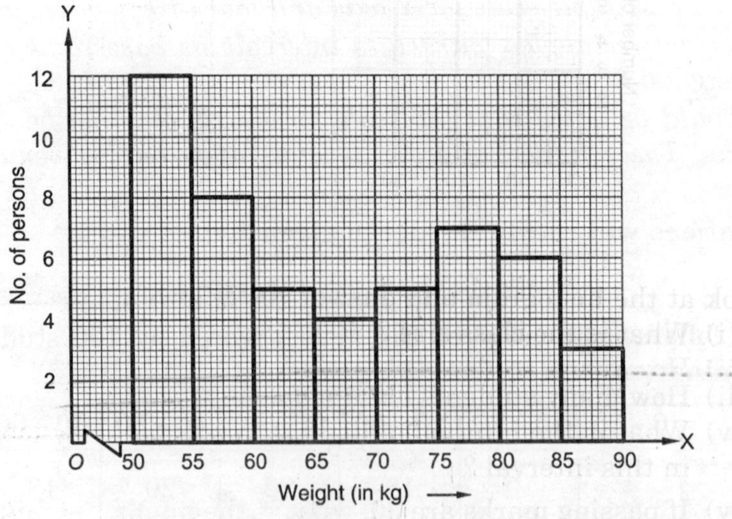

Fig. 24.2

Example 3 The following histogram shows the monthly wages (in Rs) of workers in a factory :

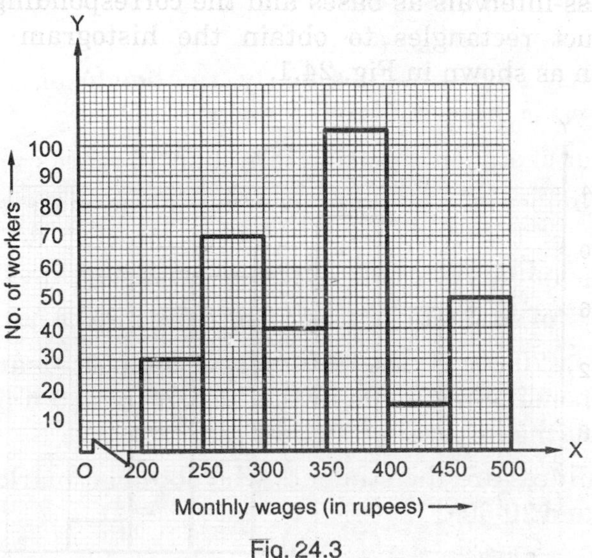

Fig. 24.3

Find the largest and least number of workers and also their wages in rupees.

Solution In the above histogram, we see that the highest rectangle corresponds to the largest number of workers, that is 105, and the wages from 350-400 rupees.

The rectangle of minimum height corresponds to the least number of workers, that is, 15 and their wages are between Rs 400 and Rs 450.

Example 4 The following histogram depicts the marks obtained by 45 students of a class:

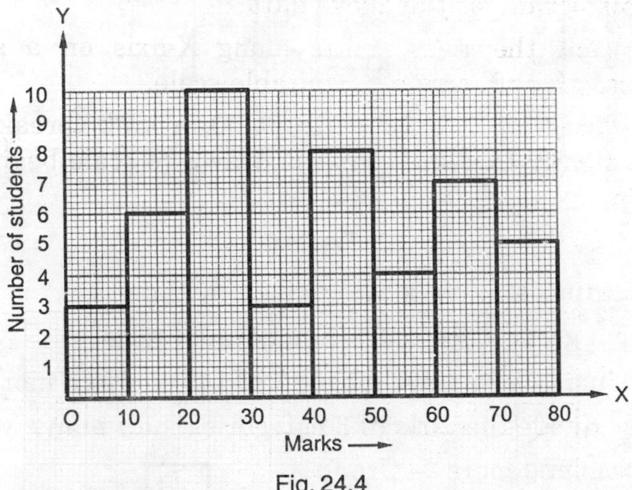

Fig. 24.4

Look at the histogram and answer the following questions :

(i) What is the class size ?

(ii) How many students obtained less than 10 marks ?

(iii) How many students obtained 30 or more marks but less than 40 ?

(iv) What is the interval of highest marks and how many students are there in this interval ?

(v) If passing marks are 30, what is the number of failures ?

Solution In the above histogram, the frequenices are represented by the heights of the rectangles whose bases are the class intervals.

(i) The class intervals are 0-10, 10-20, 20-30, ..., 70-80. So, class size = 10.

(ii) The number of students who obtained less than 10 marks is the frequency of class 0-10. Clearly, the height of the rectangle having base as the class interval 0-10 is 2 units.

$\therefore$ Number of students getting less than 10 marks = 2.

(iii) The number of students securing 30 or more marks but less than 40 marks is the frequency of class interval 30-40. The height of the corresponding rectangle in the given histogram is 3 units.

$\therefore$ Number of students getting 30 or more marks but less than 40 marks = 3.

(iv) Clearly, 70-80 is the interval of highest marks. The height of the corresponding rectangle in the histogram is 5 units. Thus, 5 students are there in the interval of highest marks.

(v) The failures are the students who obtained marks in the intervals 0 - 10, 10-20 and 20-30.

$\therefore$ Number of failures $= (2 + 6 + 10) = 18$

Example 5 Observe the following histogram and answer the questions given below:

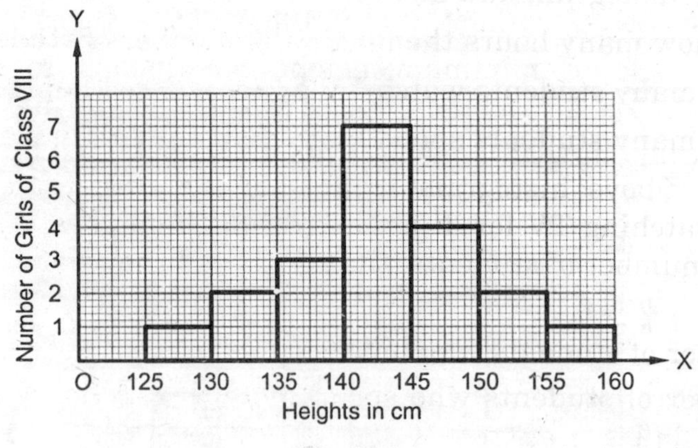

Fig. 24.5

(i) What information is being given by the graph?

(ii) Which group does contain maximum girls?

(iii) How many girls have a height of 145 cms and more?

(iv) If we divide the girls in 3 categories, how many would there be in each?

150 cm and more — Group *A*

140 cm to less than 150 cm — Group *B*

Less than 140 cm — Group *C*

Solution (i) Given hostogram depicts heights (in cm) of the girl students of class VIII.

(ii) The class interval 140-145 contains maximum number of girls. This means that maximum number of students have height between 140 cm and 150 cm.

(iii) Number of girls having the heights 145 cm and more $= 4 + 2 + 1 = 7$.

(iv) Number of girls in group $A = 2+1=3$

Number of girls in group $B = 7+4=11$

Number of girls in group $C = 1+2+3=6$

Example 6 The number of hours television watched in a day by the students of a particular class during holidays is shown in the following histogram:

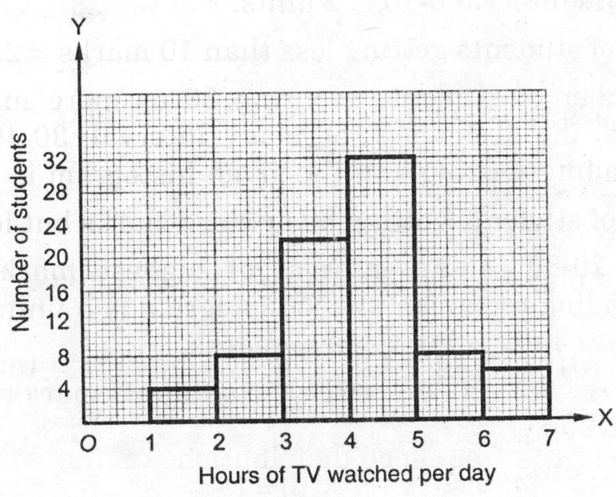

Fig. 24.6

Look at the histogram and answer the following questions:

(i) For how many hours the maximum number of students watch TV?

(ii) How many students watch TV for less than 4 hours?

(iii) How many students spend more than 5 hours in watching TV?

Solution (i) In the above histogram heights of the bars represent the number of students watching TV for different hours. The highest bar corresponds to the maximum number of students, that is 32, and they watch TV from 4 to 5 hours in a day.

(ii) Number of students watching TV less than 4 hours $= 4+8+22=34$

(iii) Number of students who spend more than 5 hours in a day in watching TV is $8+6=14$

EXERCISE 24.1

1. Given below is the frequency distribution of the heights of 50 students of a class :

Class interval:	140 – 145	145 – 150	150 – 155	155 – 160	160 – 165
Frequency:	8	12	18	10	5

Draw a histogram representing the above data.

2. Draw a histogram of the following data :

Class interval:	10 – 15	15 – 20	20 – 25	25 – 30	30 – 35	35 – 40
Frequency:	30	98	80	58	29	50

3. Number of workshops organized by a school in different areas during the last five years are as follows :

Years	No. of workshops
1995–1996	25
1996–1997	30
1997–1998	42
1998–1999	50
1999–2000	65

Draw a histogram representing the above data.

4. In a hypothetical sample of 20 people the amounts of money with them were found to be as follows :

114, 108, 100, 98, 101, 109, 117, 119, 126, 131, 136, 143, 156, 169, 182, 195, 207, 219, 235, 118.

Draw the histogram of the frequency distribution (taking one of the class intervals as 50-100).

5. Construct a histogram for the following data :

Monthly school fee (in Rs):	30 – 60	60 – 90	90 – 120	120 – 150	150 – 180	180 – 210	210 – 240
Number of schools:	5	12	14	18	10	9	4

6. Draw a histogram for the daily earnings of 30 drug stores in the following table :

Daily earnings (in Rs):	450 – 500	500 – 550	550 – 600	600 – 650	650 – 700
Number of stores:	16	10	7	3	1

7. Draw a histogram to represent the following data :

Monthly salary (in Rs)	*Number of teachers*
5600–5700	8
5700–5800	4
5800–5900	3
5900–6000	5
6000–6100	2
6100–6200	3
6200–6300	1
6300–6400	2

8. The following histogram shows the number of literate females in the age group of 10 to 40 years in a town:

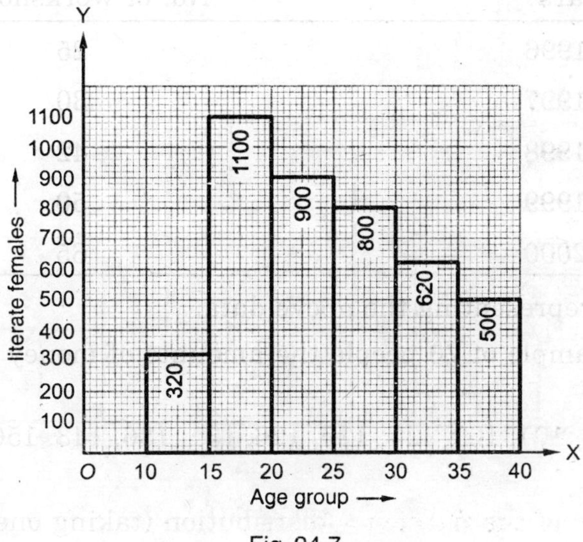

Fig. 24.7

(i) Write the age group in which the number of literate female is the highest.

(ii) What is the class width ?

(iii) What is the lowest frequency ?

(iv) What are the class marks of the classes ?

(v) In which age group literate females are the least ?

9. The following histogram shows the monthly wages (in Rs) of workers in a factory :

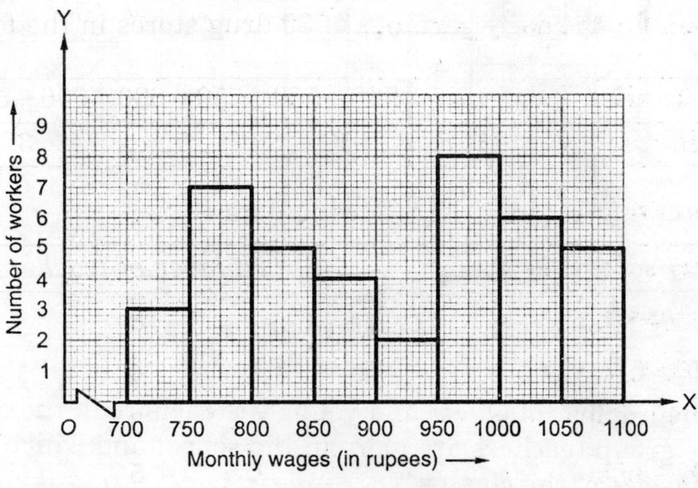

Fig. 24.8

(i) In which wage-group the largest number of workers are being kept ? What is their number ?

(ii) What wages are the least number of workers getting ? What is the number of such workers ?

(iii) What is the total number of workers ?

(iv) What is the factory size ?

10. Below is the histogram depicting marks obtained by 43 students of a class:
   (i) Write the number of students getting the highest marks.
   (ii) What is the class size ?

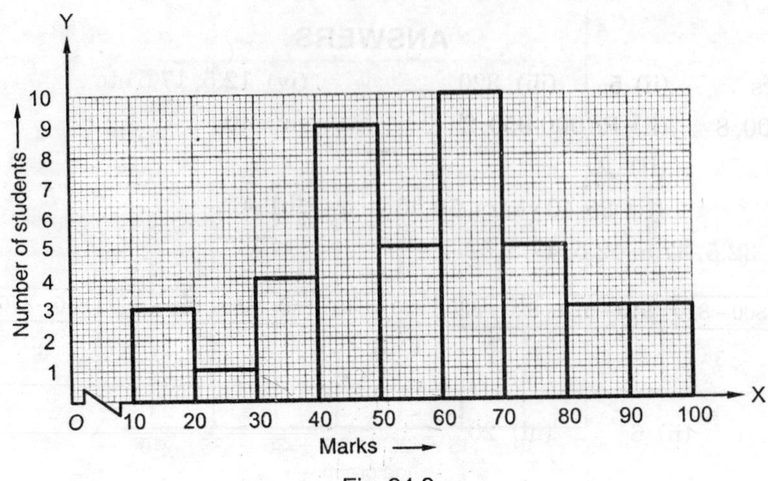

Fig. 24.9

11. The following histogram shows the frequency distribution of the ages of 22 teachers in a school:

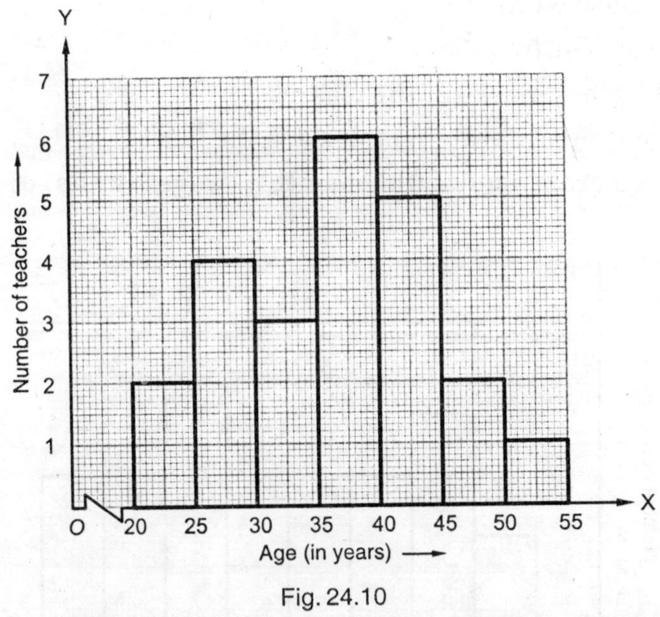

Fig. 24.10

   (i) What is the number of eldest and youngest teachers in the school ?
   (ii) Which age group teachers are more in the school and which least ?
   (iii) What is the size of the classes ?
   (iv) What are the class marks of the classes ?

12. The weekly wages (in Rs.) of 30 workers in a factory are given:

   830, 835, 890, 810, 835, 836, 869, 845, 898, 890, 820, 860, 832, 833, 855, 845, 804, 808, 812, 840, 885, 835, 835, 836, 878, 840, 868, 890, 806, 840

   Mark a frequency table with intervals as 800-810, 810-820 and so on, using tally marks.

Also, draw a histogram and answer the following questions:

(i) Which group has the maximum number of workers?

(ii) How many workers earn Rs 850 and more?

(iii) How many workers earn less than Rs 850?

ANSWERS

8. (i) 15-20 years (ii) 5 (iii) 320 (iv) 12.5, 17.5 etc (v) 10-15 years
9. (i) Rs 950-1000, 8 (ii) Rs 900-950, 2 (iii) 40 (iv) 50
10. (i) 3 (ii) 10
11. (i) 1, 2 (ii) 35-40 years, 50-55 years (iii) 6
    (iv) 22.5, 27.5, 32.5, 37.5, 42.5, 47.5, 52.5
12.

Wages (in Rs):	800 – 810	810 – 820	820 – 830	830 – 840	840 – 850	850 – 860	860 – 870	870 – 880	880 – 890
Number of workers :	3	2	1	9	5	1	3	1	1

(i) Rs 830-840 (ii) 6 (iii) 20

25

DATA HANDLING-III (Pictorial Representation of Data as Pie Charts or Circle Graphs)

25.1 INTRODUCTION

In chapters 23 and 24, we have learnt about classification and tabulation of data and their graphical representation by using histograms. In this chapter, we shall learn about the diagramatic representation of data. The diagramatic representation of data has preference over graphic representation because we don't need graph paper to draw a plane diagram whereas in graphic representation we generally require graph papers. Also diagrams are more attractive to the eye and they are better suited for publicity and propaganda.

In practice a very large variety of diagrams are used in diagramatic representation. In this chapter, we will discuss a particular type of diagrams, known as pie diagrams or pie-charts or circle graphs, to represent the given data.

25.2 PIE-DIAGRAMS OR PIE-CHARTS

DEFINITIONS A pie-diagram or a pie-chart is a pictorial representation of the numerical data by non-intersecting adjacent sectors of the circle such that the area of each sector is proportional to the magnitude of the data represented by the sector.

Figure 25.1, shows a pie-diagram of per capita incomes of four countries. In this figure a circle is sliced into four sectors such that the size of each sector is proportional to the per capita income of the country represented by the sector.

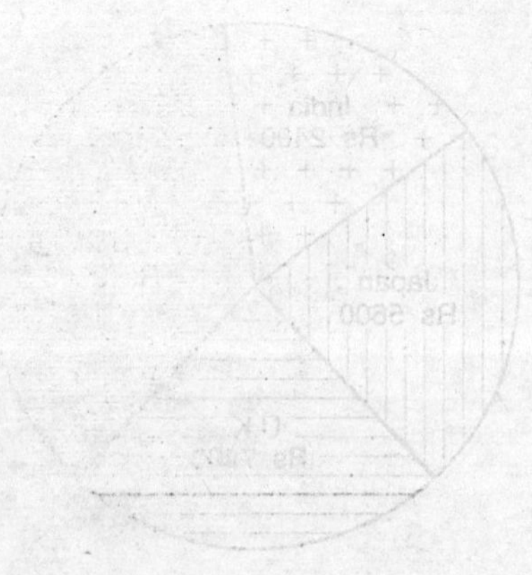

Fig. 25.1

This figure is called a pie-diagram or a pie-chart because the entire graph looks like a pie and the components resemble with slices cut from a pie.

25

DATA HANDLING-III
(Pictorial Representation of Data as Pie Charts or Circle Graphs)

25.1 INTRODUCTION

In chapters 23 and 24, we have learnt about classification and tabulation of data and their graphical representation by using histograms. In this chapter, we shall learn about the diagramatic representation of data. The diagramatic representation of data has preference over graphic representation because we can draw diagrams on a plain paper whereas in graphic representation we generally require graph paper. Also diagrams are more attractive to the eye and they are better suited for publicity and propaganda.

In practice a very large variety of diagrams are in use for diagramatic representation. In this chapter, we will discuss a particular type of diagrams, known as pie-diagrams or pie-charts or circle graphs, to represent the given data.

25.2 PIE-DIAGRAMS OR PIE-CHARTS

DEFINITIONS *A pie-diagram or a pie-chart is a pictorial representation of the numerical data by non-intersecting adjacent sectors of the circle such that area of each sector is proportional to the magnitude of the data represented by the sector.*

Figure 25.1, shows a pie-diagram of per capita income of four countries. In this figure a circle is sliced into four sectors such that the size of a sector is proportional to the per-capita income of the country represented by the sector.

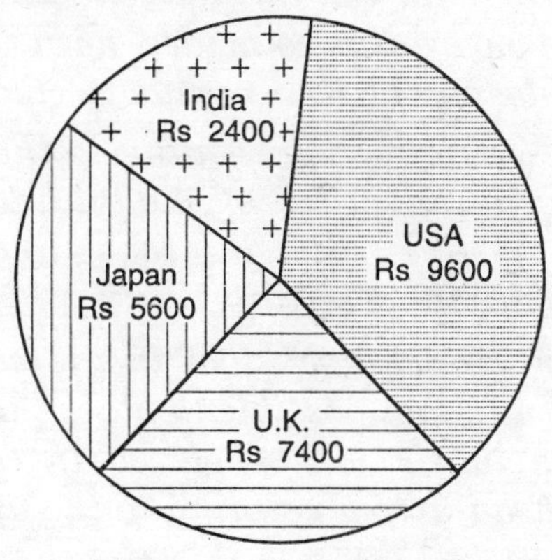

Fig. 25.1

This figure is called a pie-diagram or a pie-chart because the entire graph looks like a pie and the components resemble with slices cut from a pie.

Pie-diagrams are used to show percent breakdowns. For example, with the help of a pie-diagram we can show how the expenditure of the government is distributed over different heads like Defence, Commerce and Industry, Tourism, Agriculture and Irrigation etc. Using pie-diagrams we can also show how the expenditures incurred by an industry are divided under different heads like raw materials, wages and salaries, marketing etc.

25.3 CONSTRUCTION OF PIE-DIAGRAMS

In this section, we will discuss the construction of pie-diagrams.

In the previous section, we have seen that a pie-diagram consists of a circle which is divided into as many sectors as there are components of the data. In case of a frequency distribution the circle is divided into as many sectors as there are classes in the distribution. The area of each sector is proportional to the component value (relative frequency) of the component (class) represented by the sector. But, we know that the area of a sector is proportional to the angle subtended at the centre by its arc. Therefore, sector angles or central angles are proportional to the component values (relative frequencies) of the components (classes) represented by the sectors. Thus, we have

$$\text{Central angle of a component} = \left(\frac{\text{Value of the component}}{\text{Sum of the component values}} \times 360\right)^{\circ}$$

Following algorithm may be used for the construction of a pie-diagram of given data:

ALGORITHM

<u>Step I</u> *Obtain the data and find the sum of various component values.*

In case of a frequency distribution various component values are class frequencies (f_i) and their sum is total number of values i.e., $N\left(=\sum_i f_i\right)$

<u>Step II</u> *Divide each component value by the sum obtained in step I and multiply by 360 to obtain the sector angles (central angles) of the sectors represented by them.*

<u>Step III</u> *Draw a circle of appropriate size with a compass and a radius of it coinciding with 12 O′clock position of the two hands of the clock.*

<u>Step IV</u> *Select the component with the largest central angle and construct a sector in such a way that its one radius coincides with the radius drawn in step III and the other radius is below the first radius in clockwise direction.*

<u>Step V</u> *Construct other sectors representing other components in clockwise succession in descending order of magnitude of central angles, except for catch-all components like "Miscellaneous" and "all other" which are shown last, contrast with adjacent sectors.*

<u>Step VI</u> *Put explanatory or descriptive label inside each sector so that they can be easily identified. If it is not possible to place the labels inside the sectors due to lack of space, then labels can be placed in contiguous positions outside the circle, usually with an arrow pointing to the appropriate sector.*

Following examples will illustrate the above algorithm.

ILLUSTRATIVE EXAMPLES

Example 1 The number of students in a hostel speaking different languages is given below. Present the data in a pie-chart.

Language	Hindi	English	Marathi	Tamil	Bengali	Total
Number of students	40	12	9	7	4	72

Solution We know that

$$\text{Central angle of a component} = \left(\frac{\text{Value of the component}}{\text{Sum of the component values}} \times 360\right)^\circ$$

Here, total number of students = 72

$\therefore$ Central angle for a language

$$= \left(\frac{\text{Number of students speaking that language}}{\text{Total number of students}} \times 360\right)^\circ$$

The computation of central angles for different sectors representing different languages is shown in the following table.

Computation of central angles

Language	*Number of students*	*Central angles*
Hindi	40	$\left(\frac{40}{72} \times 360\right)^\circ = 200^\circ$
English	12	$\left(\frac{12}{72} \times 360\right)^\circ = 60^\circ$
Marathi	9	$\left(\frac{9}{72} \times 360\right)^\circ = 45^\circ$
Tamil	7	$\left(\frac{7}{72} \times 360\right)^\circ = 35^\circ$
Bengali	4	$\left(\frac{4}{72} \times 360\right)^\circ = 20^\circ$
Total	72	360°

Now to construct the pie-chart we follow the following steps:

<u>Step I</u> Draw a circle of an appropriate radius.

<u>Step II</u> Draw a vertical radius, coinciding with the 12 O'clock position of the hands of a clock, of the circle drawn in Step I.

<u>Step III</u> Choose the largest central angle. Here, it is 200°. Construct a sector of central angle 200° whose one radius coincides with the radius drawn in step II and the other radius is in clockwise direction to the vertical radius.

<u>Step IV</u> Construct other sectors representing other languages in clockwise sense in descending order of magnitudes of their central angles.

<u>Step V</u> Shade the sectors so obtained by different patterns or designs and label them as shown in Fig. 25.2.

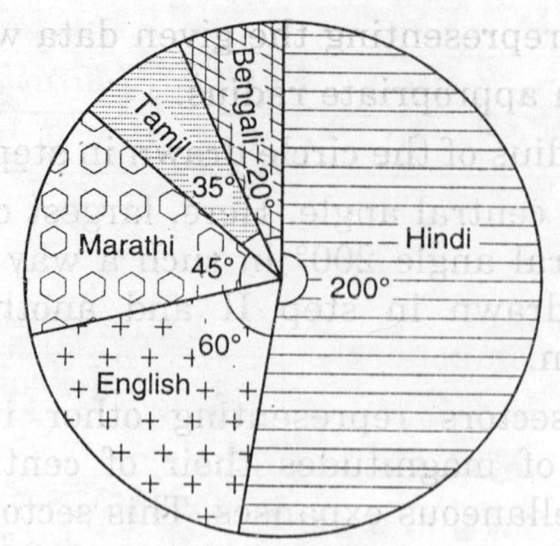

Fig. 25.2

Example 2 In the month of July 2004, a house holder spent his monthly salary amounting to Rs 7200 on different items as given below:

Items	*Clothing*	*Food*	*House Rent*	*Education*	*Miscellaneous*
Amount spent (in Rs)	600	4000	1200	400	1000

Represent the information in the form of a pie-chart.

Solution We know that

$$\text{Central angle of a component} = \left(\frac{\text{Component value}}{\text{Sum of the component values}} \times 360\right)^\circ$$

Here, total amount = Rs 7200

Computation of Central angles:

$$\therefore \quad \text{Central angle for an item} = \left(\frac{\text{Amount spent on the item}}{\text{Total amount}} \times 360\right)^\circ$$

The central angles of the sectors representing different items are computed in the following table:

Computation of central angles

Items	*Amount spent (In Rs)*	*Central angles*
Clothing	600	$\left(\frac{600}{7200} \times 360\right)^\circ = 30^\circ$
Food	4000	$\left(\frac{4000}{7200} \times 360\right)^\circ = 200^\circ$
House rent	1200	$\left(\frac{1200}{7200} \times 360\right)^\circ = 60^\circ$
Education	400	$\left(\frac{400}{7200} \times 360\right)^\circ = 20^\circ$
Miscellaneous	1000	$\left(\frac{1000}{7200} \times 360\right)^\circ = 50^\circ$
Total	7,200	360°

Now to construct the pie-chart representing the given data we follow the following steps:

Step I — Draw a circle of an appropriate radius.

Step II — Draw a vertical radius of the circle drawn in step I.

Step III — Choose the largest central angle. Here, largest central angle is of 200°. Draw a sector with central angle 200° in such a way that its one radius coincides with the radius drawn in step II and another radius is in its counter clockwise direction.

Step IV — Construct other sectors representing other items in clockwise sense in descending order of magnitudes their of central angles except the sector representing miscellaneous expanses. This sector is to be drawn in the last.

Step V — Shade the sectors so obtained by different designs and label them as shown in Fig. 25.3 to obtain the required pie-chart.

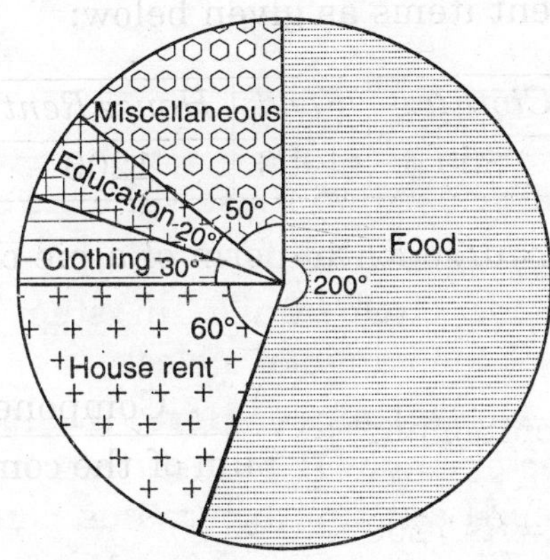

Fig. 25.3

Example 3 The number of students admitted in different faculties of a college are given below:

Faculty	*Science*	*Arts*	*Commerce*	*Law*	*Education*	*Total*
Number of students	1000	1200	650	450	300	3600

Draw a pie-chart to represent the above information.

Solution We know that

$$\text{Central angle of a component} = \left(\frac{\text{Value of the component}}{\text{Sum of the component values}} \times 360\right)^\circ$$

Here, total number of students $= 3600$

$$\therefore \quad \text{Central angle of a component} = \left(\frac{\text{Number of students in the faculty}}{\text{Total number of students}} \times 360\right)^\circ$$

The computation of central angles of the sectors representing different faculties is shown in the following table.

Computation of central angles

Faculty	*Number of students*	*Central angles*
Science	1000	$\left(\frac{1000}{3600}\times 360\right)^\circ = 100^\circ$
Arts	1200	$\left(\frac{1200}{3600}\times 360\right)^\circ = 120^\circ$
Commerce	650	$\left(\frac{650}{3600}\times 360\right)^\circ = 65^\circ$
Law	450	$\left(\frac{450}{3600}\times 360\right)^\circ = 45^\circ$
Education	300	$\left(\frac{300}{3600}\times 360\right)^\circ = 30^\circ$
Total	3,600	360°

In order to construct the pie-chart based on these values we follow the following steps:

Step I Draw a circle of convenient radius.

Step II Draw a radius of the circle drawn in step I such that it coincides with 12 O'clock position of the hands of a clock.

Step III Choose the largest central angle. Here, the largest central angle is of 120°. Draw a sector of sector angle 120° such that its one radius coincides with the radius drawn in step II and another radius is in the clocksidewise direction.

Step IV Draw other sectors in succession in descending order of magnitudes of central angles in clockwise direction such that each sector is adjacent to the previously drawn sector.

Step V Shade the sectors obtained by different designs and label them as shown in Fig. 25.4 to obtain the required pie-chart.

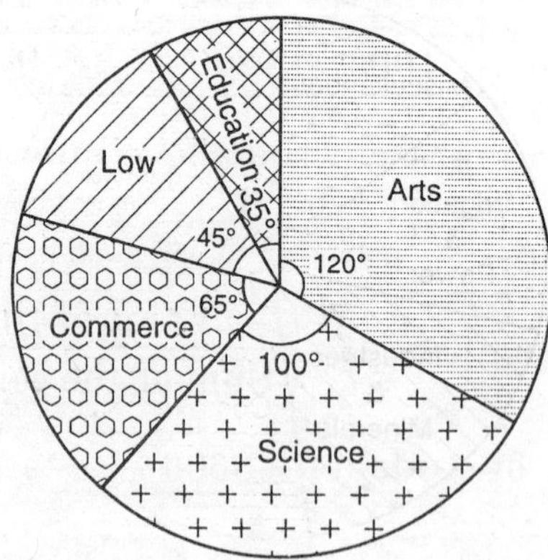

Fig. 25.4

Example 4 Draw a pie-diagram to represent the following data on the proposed outlay during the fourth Five-year plan.

Items	*Agriculture*	*Industries and Minerals*	*Irrigation and Power*	*Communi-cation*	*Miscella-neous*
Rupees (in crores)	6000	4000	2500	4500	3000

Solution We have,

Total outlay = Rs (6000 + 4000 + 2500 + 4500 + 3000) crores = Rs 20,000 crores

Computation of section angles

Items	*Amount (In crores of Rs)*	*Sector Angles*
Agriculture	6000	$\left(\frac{600}{20000} \times 360\right)^\circ = 108^\circ$
Industries and Minerals	4000	$\left(\frac{4000}{20000} \times 360\right)^\circ = 72^\circ$
Irrigation and Power	2500	$\left(\frac{2500}{20000} \times 360\right)^\circ = 45^\circ$
Communication	4500	$\left(\frac{4500}{20000} \times 360\right)^\circ = 81^\circ$
Miscellaneous	3000	$\left(\frac{3000}{20000} \times 360\right)^\circ = 54^\circ$
Total	20,000	360°

Now, draw a circle of an appropriate radius and a radius coinciding with 12 O'clock position of the hands of a clock. We observe that the largest sector angle is of 108°. So, we construct a sector in clockwise sense whose sector angle is 108° and whose one radius coincides with the vertical radius. Similarly, we construct other sectors representing other items in clockwise succession in descending order of magnitude of sector angles. The pie-diagram shown in Fig. 25.5 is the required pie-diagram.

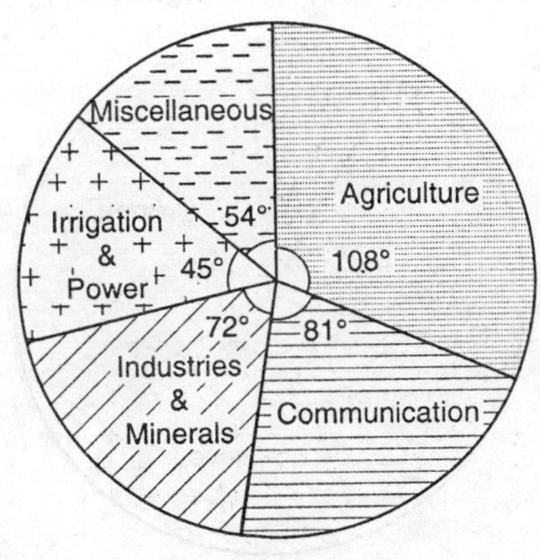

Fig. 25.5

Example 5 The following data relates to the cost of construction of a house in Delhi.

Items	*Cement*	*Steel*	*Bricks*	*Timber*	*Labour*	*Miscellaneous*
Expenditure	30%	10%	10%	15%	25%	10%

Draw a pie-diagram to represent the above data.

Solution *Computation of Central Angles*:

Items	*Expenditure (in percent)*	*Central angles*
Cement	30	$\left(\frac{30}{100}\times 360\right)^\circ = 108^\circ$
Steel	10	$\left(\frac{10}{100}\times 360\right)^\circ = 36^\circ$
Bricks	10	$\left(\frac{10}{100}\times 360\right)^\circ = 36^\circ$
Timber	15	$\left(\frac{15}{100}\times 360\right)^\circ = 54^\circ$
Labour	25	$\left(\frac{25}{100}\times 360\right)^\circ = 90^\circ$
Miscellaneous	10	$\left(\frac{10}{100}\times 360\right)^\circ = 36^\circ$
Total	100	360°

Now, draw a circle of an appropriate radius and also draw a radius coinciding with the 12 O'clock position of two hands of a clock. We observe that the largest sector angle is 108°. So, we construct a sector whose sector angle is 108° and whose one radius coincides with the vertical radius and the other radius is in clockwise direction. Draw other sectors in succession in descending order of magnitude of sector angles in clockwise direction.

The pie-diagram so obtained is shown in Fig. 25.6.

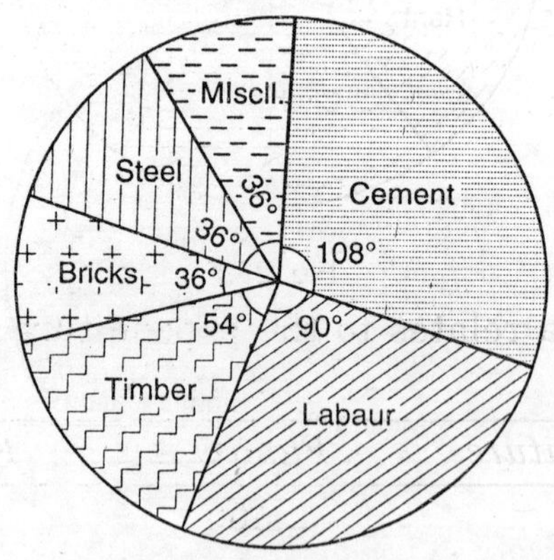

Fig. 25.6

Example 6 Draw a pie-diagram for the following data of expenditure pattern in a family:

Items	*Food*	*Clothing*	*Rent*	*Education*	*Miscellaneous*
Expenditure (in Rs)	4000	2000	1500	1500	1000

Solution

Computation of central angles

Items	*Expenditure*	*Central angles*
Food	4000	$\left(\frac{4000}{10000}\times 360\right)^\circ = 144^\circ$
Clothing	2000	$\left(\frac{2000}{10000}\times 360\right)^\circ = 72^\circ$
Rent	1500	$\left(\frac{1500}{10000}\times 360\right)^\circ = 54^\circ$
Education	1500	$\left(\frac{1500}{10000}\times 360\right)^\circ = 54^\circ$
Miscellaneous	1000	$\left(\frac{1000}{10000}\times 360\right)^\circ = 36^\circ$
Total	10,000	360°

Now, draw a circle of an appropriate radius and a radius of it which coincides with 12 O'clock position of the hands of a clock. Construct sectors in clockwise sense with descending order of magnitude of central angles as shown in Fig. 25.7.

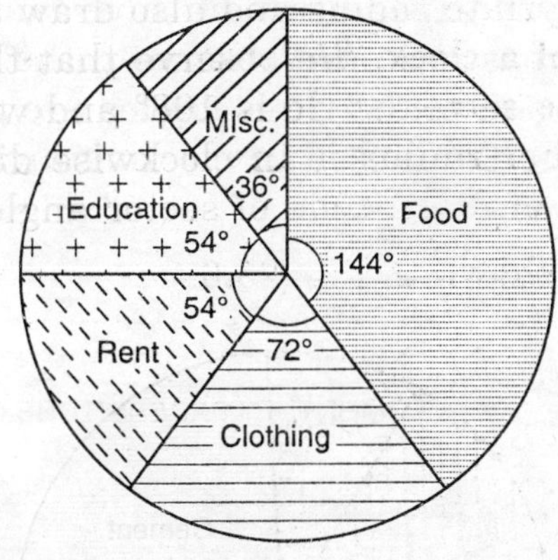

Fig. 25.7

Example 7 The following data relates to the expenditure of the families A, B and C per month:

Items of expenditure	*Family A*	*Family B*	*Family C*
Food	400	600	1600
Rent	200	400	1500
Clothing	200	300	1000
Education	100	400	800
Litigation	50	100	300
Miscellaneous	50	200	800

Represent this data by a pie-diagram.

Solution *Computation of sector angles*

Items of Expenditure	Family A Exp. in Rs	Family A Sector angles	Family B Exp. in Rs	Family B Sector angles	Family C Exp. in Rs	Family C Sector angles
Food	400	$\frac{400}{1000}\times 360^\circ = 144^\circ$	600	$\frac{600}{2000}\times 360^\circ = 108^\circ$	1600	$\frac{1600}{6000}\times 360^\circ = 96^\circ$
Rent	200	$\frac{200}{1000}\times 360^\circ = 72^\circ$	400	$\frac{400}{2000}\times 360^\circ = 72^\circ$	1500	$\frac{1500}{6000}\times 360^\circ = 90^\circ$
Clothing	200	$\frac{200}{1000}\times 360^\circ = 72^\circ$	300	$\frac{300}{2000}\times 360^\circ = 54^\circ$	1000	$\frac{1000}{6000}\times 360^\circ = 60^\circ$
Education	100	$\frac{100}{1000}\times 360^\circ = 36^\circ$	400	$\frac{400}{2000}\times 360^\circ = 72^\circ$	800	$\frac{800}{6000}\times 360^\circ = 48^\circ$
Litigation	50	$\frac{50}{1000}\times 360^\circ = 18^\circ$	100	$\frac{100}{2000}\times 360^\circ = 18^\circ$	300	$\frac{300}{6000}\times 360^\circ = 18^\circ$
Miscellaneous	50	$\frac{50}{1000}\times 360^\circ = 18^\circ$	200	$\frac{200}{2000}\times 360^\circ = 36^\circ$	800	$\frac{800}{6000}\times 360^\circ = 48^\circ$
Total	1,000	360°	2,000	360°	6,000	360°

In order to represent the monthly expenditure of three families by pie-diagrams, we draw three circles such that their areas are proportional to the total expenditures of the three families. This means that the radii of the three circles are proportional to the square roots of the total expenditures of three families. The pie-diagrams are shown in Fig. 25.8

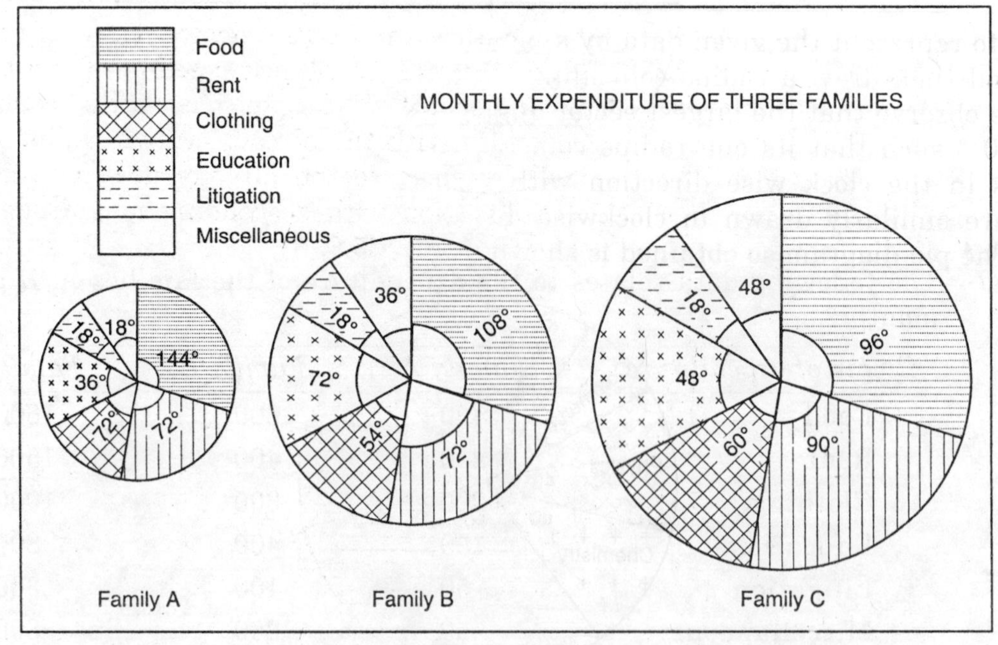

Fig. 25.8

Example 8 The following data shows the number of students opting different subjects in a college:

Subjects	*English*	*Maths*	*Physics*	*Chemistry*	*Economics*	*Commerce*
No. of Students	45	60	20	30	10	15

Construct a pie-diagram to represent the above data.

Solution

Computation of central angles

Subjects	*Frequency*	*Sector angles*
English	45	$\left(\frac{45}{180}\times 360\right)^{\circ} = 90^{\circ}$
Mathematics	60	$\left(\frac{60}{180}\times 360\right)^{\circ} = 120^{\circ}$
Physics	20	$\left(\frac{20}{180}\times 360\right)^{\circ} = 40^{\circ}$
Chemistry	30	$\left(\frac{30}{180}\times 360\right)^{\circ} = 60^{\circ}$
Economics	10	$\left(\frac{10}{180}\times 360\right)^{\circ} = 20^{\circ}$
Commerce	15	$\left(\frac{15}{180}\times 360\right)^{\circ} = 30^{\circ}$
Total	10,000	360°

In order to represent the given data by a pie-diagram, we first draw a circle of appropriate radius and then draw a radius coinciding with the 12 O'clock position of the hands of a clock. We observe that the largest sector angles is 120°. So, we construct a sector of sector angle 120 ° such that its one radius coincides with the already drawn radius and other radius is in the clock wise direction with respect to the already drawn radius. Other sectors are similarly drawn in clockwise direction with descending magnitude of sector angles. The pie-diagram so obtained is shown in Fig. 25.9.

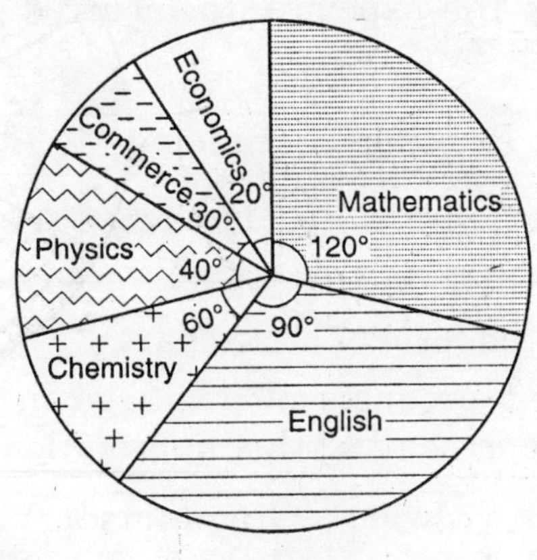

Fig. 25.9

EXERCISE 25.1

1. The number of hours, spent by a school boy on different activities in a working day, is given below:

Activities	Sleep	School	Home	Play	Others	Total
Number of hours	8	7	4	2	3	24

Present the information in the form of a pie-chart.

2. Employees of a company have been categorized according to their religions as given below:

Religions	Hindu	Muslim	Sikh	Christian	Total
Number of workers	420	300	225	105	1080

Draw a pie-chart to represent the above information.

3. In one day the sales (in rupees) of different items of a baker's shop are given below:

Items	Ordinary bread	Fruit bread	Cakes and Pastries	Biscuits	Others	Total
Sales (in Rs)	260	40	100	60	20	480

Draw a pie-chart representing the above sales.

4. The following data shows the expenditure of a person on different items during a month. Represent the data by a pie-chart.

Items of expenditure	Rent	Education	Food	Clothing	Others
Amount (in Rs)	2700	1800	2400	1500	2400

5. The percentages of various categories of workers in a state are given in the following table.

Categoies	Culti-vators	Agricultural Labourers	Industrial Workers	Commercial Workers	Others
% of workers	40	25	12.5	10	12.5

Present the information in the form a pie-chart.

6. The following table shows the expenditure incurred by a publisher in publishing a book:

Items	Paper	Printing	Binding	Advertising	Miscellaneous
Expenditure (in %)	35%	20%	10%	5%	30%

Present the above data in the form of a pie-chart.

7. Percentage of the different products of a village in a particular district are given below. Draw a pie-chart representing this information.

Items	Wheat	Pulses	Jwar	Grounnuts	Vegetables	Total
%	$\frac{125}{3}$	$\frac{125}{6}$	$\frac{25}{2}$	$\frac{50}{3}$	$\frac{25}{3}$	100

8. Draw a pie-diagram for the following data of expenditure pattern in a family:

Items	Food	Clothing	Rent	Education	Unforeseen events	Midicine
Expenditure (in percent)	40%	20%	10%	10%	15%	5%

9. Draw a pie-diagram of the areas of continents of the world given in the following table:

Continents	Asia	U.S.S.R	Africa	Europe	North America	South America	Australia
Area (in million sq.km)	26.9	20.5	30.3	4.9	24.3	17.9	8.5

10. The following data gives the amount spent on the construction of a house. Draw a pie diagram.

Items	Cement	Timber	Bricks	Labour	Steel	Miscellaneous
Expenditure (in thousand Rs)	60	30	45	75	45	45

11. The following table shows how a student spends his pocket money during the course of a month. Represent it by a pie-diagram.

Items	Food	Entertainment	Other expenditure	Savings
Expenditure	40%	25%	20%	15%

12. Represent the following data by a pie-diagram:

Items of expenditure	*Expenditure*	
	Family A	*Family B*
Food	4000	6400
Clothing	2500	480
Rent	1500	3200
Education	400	1000
Miscellaneous	1600	600
Total	10000	16000

13. Following data gives the break up of the cost of production of a book:

Printing	Paper	Binding charges	Advertisement	Royalty	Miscellaneous
30%	15%	15%	20%	10%	15%

Draw a pie-diagram depicting the above information.

14. Represent the following data with the help of a pie-diagram:

Items	Wheat	Rice	Tea
Production (in metric tons)	3260	1840	900

15. Draw a pie-diagram representing the relative frequencies (expressed as percentage) of the eight classes as given below:
 12.6, 18.2, 17.5, 20.3, 2.8, 4.2, 9.8, 14.7

16. Following is the break up of the expenditure of a family on different items of consumption:

Items	Food	Clothing	Rent	Education	Fuel etc.	Medicine	Miscellaneous
Expenditure (in Rs)	1600	200	600	150	100	80	270

Draw a pie-diagram to represent the above data.

17. Draw a pie-diagram for the following data of the investment pattern in a five year plan:

Agriculture	Irrigation and Power	Small Industries	Transport	Social service	Miscellaneous
14%	16%	29%	17%	16%	8%

25.4 READING OF PIE-CHARTS

In the previous section, we have learnt about construction of a pie-chart to represent the given data. In this section, we shall see how desired information can be ascertained from a given pie-chart. The process of obtaining various informations related to given data from the given pie-chart is known as reading of pie-chart. In the previous section, we have learnt that

$$\text{Central angle for a component} = \left(\frac{\text{Value of the component}}{\text{Sum of the component values}} \times 360\right)^\circ$$

$\Rightarrow$ Value of a component

$$= \left(\frac{\text{Central angle of the component} \times \text{Sum of the component values}}{360^\circ}\right)$$

and,

$$\text{Percentage value of a component} = \left(\frac{\text{Central angle of the component} \times 100}{360^\circ}\right)$$

These formulae will be used to find the values of various components of the data from its pie-chart.

ILLUSTRATIVE EXMAPLES

Example 1 The pie-chart given in Fig. 25.10, represents the expenditure on different items in constructing a flat in a metro city. Find the percentage expenditure on different items by reading the pie-chart. If the cost of flat is Rs 5,40,000. Find the following:

(i) The expenditure incurred on steel and cement separately.

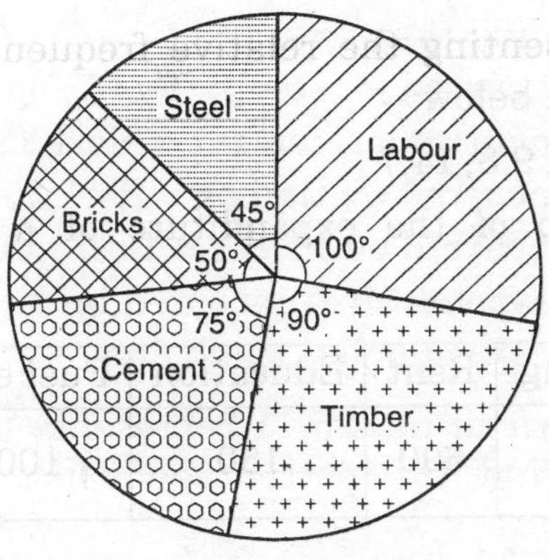

Fig. 25.10

(ii) Difference of expenditures incurred on timber and bricks.

Solution We know that in a pie-chart

Value of a component

$$= \left(\frac{\text{Central angle of the component} \times \text{Sum of the component values}}{360°}\right)$$

In this case, we have

Cost of the flat = Rs 5,40,000

Expenditure incurred on an item

$$= \frac{\text{Central angle of the corresponding sector} \times \text{Cost of the flat}}{360°}$$

$$= \frac{\text{Central angle of the corresponding sector} \times 540000}{360°}$$

and, Percentage expenditure on an item

$$= \frac{\text{Central angle of the corresponding sector} \times 100}{360°}$$

Using these formulae, the computations of expenditures incurred and percentage expenditures on different items are shown in the following table.

Items	*Central angles*	*Expenditures (in Rs)*	*Percentage Expenditures*
Labour	100°	$\frac{100° \times 5,40,000}{360°} = 1,50,000$	$\frac{100° \times 100}{360°} = \frac{250}{9}\%$
Timber	90°	$\frac{90° \times 5,40,000}{360°} = 1,35,000$	$\frac{90° \times 100}{360°} = 25\%$
Cement	75°	$\frac{75° \times 5,40,000}{360°} = 1,12,500$	$\frac{75° \times 100}{360°} = \frac{125}{6}\%$
Bricks	50°	$\frac{50° \times 5,40,000}{360°} = 75,000$	$\frac{50° \times 100}{360°} = \frac{125}{9}\%$
Steel	45°	$\frac{45° \times 5,40,000}{360°} = 67,500$	$\frac{45° \times 100}{360°} = \frac{25}{2}\%$

From the table we find that

(i) Expenditure incurred on steel = Rs 67,500
    Expenditure incurred on cement = Rs 1,12,500

(ii) Expenditure incurred on timber = Rs 1,35,000
    Expenditure incurred on bricks = Rs 75,000

$\therefore$ Difference of expenditures incurred on timber and bricks

$$= \text{Rs } 1,35,000 - \text{Rs } 75,000 = \text{Rs } 60,000$$

Example 2 The pie-chart shown in fig. 25.11 represents the expenditures of a family on different items. Find the percentage expenditures on different items by reading the pie-chart.

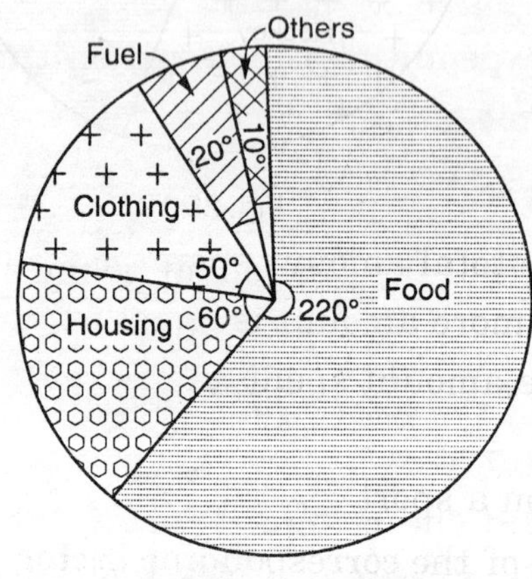

Fig. 25.11

Solution We know that

$$\text{Percentage value of a component} = \frac{\text{Central angle of the compoent}}{360°} \times 100$$

In this case, we have

Percentage expenditure on an item

$$= \left(\frac{\text{Central angle of the corresponding sector}}{360°} \times 100\right)$$

Percentage expenditures on various items are computed in the following table:

Items	*Central angles*	*Percentage expenditures*
Food	220°	$\frac{220° \times 100}{360°} = 61\%$
Housing	60°	$\frac{60° \times 100}{360°} = 16.7\%$
Clothing	50°	$\frac{50° \times 100}{360°} = 13.9\%$
Fuel	20°	$\frac{20° \times 100}{360°} = 5.5\%$
Others	10°	$\frac{10° \times 100}{360°} = 2.8\%$

Example 3 The following pie-chart represents the amount spent on different sports by a school administration in a calender year. If the money spent on football is Rs 9000, answer the following questions:

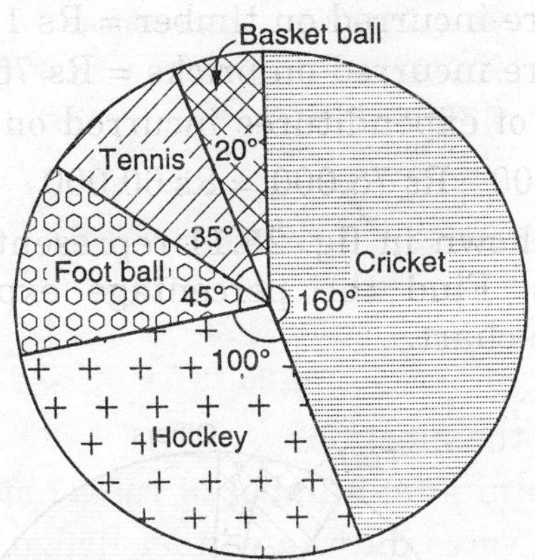

Fig. 25.12

(i) What is the total amount spent on sports?

(ii) How much more amount is spent on hockey than on football?

(iii) What is the amount spent on cricket?

Solution (i) We have,

Amount spent on a sport

$$= \frac{\text{Central angle of the corresponding sector}}{360°} \times \text{Total amount spent on all sports}$$

$\therefore$ Total amount spent on all sports

$$= \frac{360° \times \text{Money spent on a sport}}{\text{Central angle of the corresponding sector}}$$

It is given that money spent on football = Rs 9,000

$$\therefore \quad \text{Total amount spent on all sports} = \text{Rs}\left(\frac{360° \times 9{,}000}{45°}\right) = \text{Rs } 72{,}000$$

$$\text{(ii) Amount spent on hockey} = \text{Rs}\left(\frac{100° \times 72{,}000}{360°}\right) = \text{Rs } 20{,}000$$

$\therefore$ Amount spent on hockey – Amount spent on football

$= \text{Rs } 20{,}000 - \text{Rs } 9{,}000 = \text{Rs } 11{,}000$

Thus, amount spent on hockey is Rs 11,000 more than that on football.

$$\text{(iii) Amount spent on cricket} = \text{Rs}\left(\frac{160° \times 72{,}000}{360°}\right) = \text{Rs } 32{,}000$$

Example 4 The following pie-chart represents the total number of valid votes obtained by four students who contested for school leadership. The total number of valid votes polled was 720. Answer the following questions by reading the pie-chart:

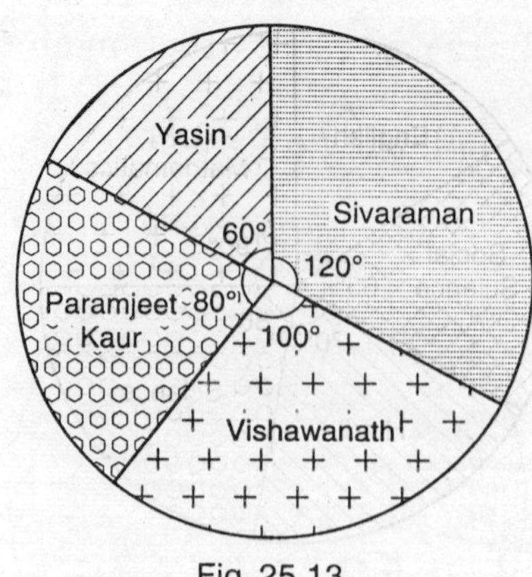

Fig. 25.13

(i) Who has won the election?

(ii) What is the minimum number of votes obtained by any candidate?

(iii) By how many votes did the winner defeat the nearest contestent?

Solution We have,

Total number of valid votes polled $= 720$

$\therefore$ Number of votes obtained by a candidate

$$= \frac{(\text{Central angle of the corresponding sector}) \times \text{Total number of votes}}{360^\circ}$$

$$= \frac{(\text{Central angle of the corresponding sector}) \times 720}{360^\circ}$$

$= 2 \times$ (Magnitude of the central angle of the corresponding sector)

Number of votes obtained by different candidates are given in the following table:

Candidates	*Central angles*	*Number of votes received*
Sivaraman	120°	$2 \times 120 = 240$
Vishwanath	100°	$2 \times 100 = 200$
Paramjeet Kaur	80°	$2 \times 80 = 160$
Yasin	60°	$2 \times 60 = 120$

(i) It is evident from the above table that Sivaraman received maximum number of votes. So, he won the election.

(ii) Yasin received minimum number of votes equal to 120

(iii) Votest received by Sivaraman $= 240$

Votest received by Vishwanath (nearest contestent) $= 200$

. Difference of votes $= 240 - 200 = 40$

Hence, the winner (Sivaraman) defeated the nearest contestent (Vishwanath) by 40 votes.

Example 5 The following pie-chart gives the marks scored in an examination by a student in various subjects. If the total marks obtained by the student were 540, answer the following questions.

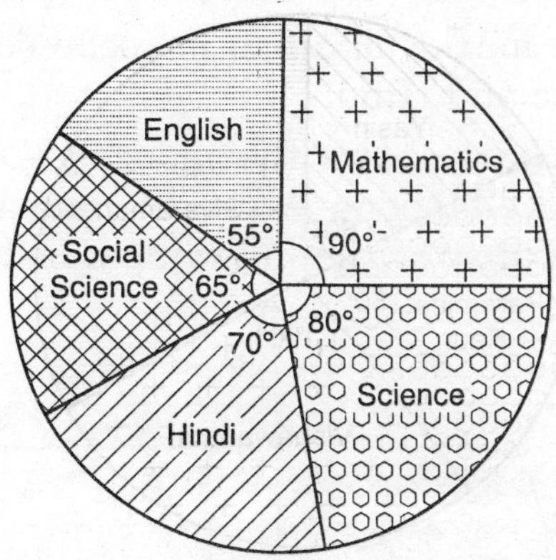

Fig. 25.14

(i) In which subject did the student score 105 marks?

(ii) How many more marks were obtained by the student in Mathematics than in Hindi?

(iii) Examine whether the sum of marks obtained in social Science and Mathematics is more than that in science and Hindi.

Solution We have,

Total marks $= 540$

Also, Marks obtained in a subject

$$= \frac{(\text{Central angle of the corresponding sector}) \times (\text{Total marks})}{360^\circ}$$

Marks obtained in various subjects by using the above formula are computed in the following table:

Subjects	*Central angles*	*Marks obtained*
Mathematics	90°	$\frac{90^\circ \times 540}{360^\circ} = 135$
Science	80°	$\frac{80^\circ \times 540}{360^\circ} = 120$
Hindi	70°	$\frac{70^\circ \times 540}{360^\circ} = 105$
Social Science	65°	$\frac{65^\circ \times 540}{360^\circ} = 97.5$
English	55°	$\frac{55^\circ \times 540}{360^\circ} = 82.5$

(i) From the table, we find that 105 marks are scored in Hindi.

(ii) Marks scored in Mathematics = 135, Marks scored in Hindi $= 105$

$\therefore$ Difference of marks scored in Mathematics and Hindi $= 135 - 105 = 30$

Hence, the student scored 30 marks more in Mathematics than that in Hindi.

(iii) Sum of the marks obtained in Social Science and Mathematics

$$= 97.5 + 135 = 232.5$$

Sum of the marks obtained in Science and Hindi $= 120 + 105 = 225$

Clearly, sum of the marks obtained in social science and Mathematics is more than that in Science and Hindi.

Example 6 The following pie-chart shows the monthly expenditure of a family on food, clothing, rent, miscellaneous expenses and savings. If the family spends Rs 825 on clothing, answer the following questions:

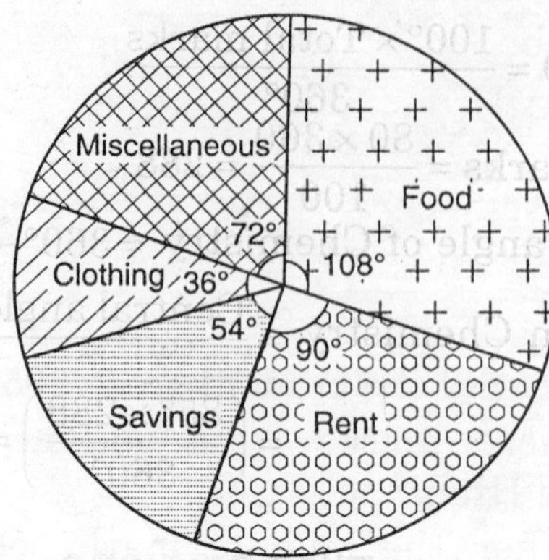

Fig. 25.15

(i) What is the total monthly income of the family?

(ii) What percent of the total income does the family save?

Solution (i) We have,

Amount spent on clothing

$$= \frac{\text{(Central angle of the corresponding sector} \times \text{Total monthly income}}{360°}$$

$$\therefore \quad \text{Total monthly income} = \frac{\text{Amount spent on clothing} \times 360°}{\text{Central angle of the corresponding sector}}$$

$$= \text{Rs}\left(\frac{825 \times 360°}{36°}\right) = \text{Rs } 8250$$

Hence, total monthly income $=$ Rs 8250

(ii) Central angle for savings $= 360° - (108° + 90° + 72° + 36°) = 54°$

$$\therefore \quad \text{Savings } \% = \left(\frac{\text{Central angle for savings}}{360°} \times 100\right)\% = \left(\frac{54}{360} \times 100\right)\% = 15\%$$

Example 7 The following pie-chart shows the marks secured by Rohit in different subjects. If he scored 80 marks in Mathematics, find the following:

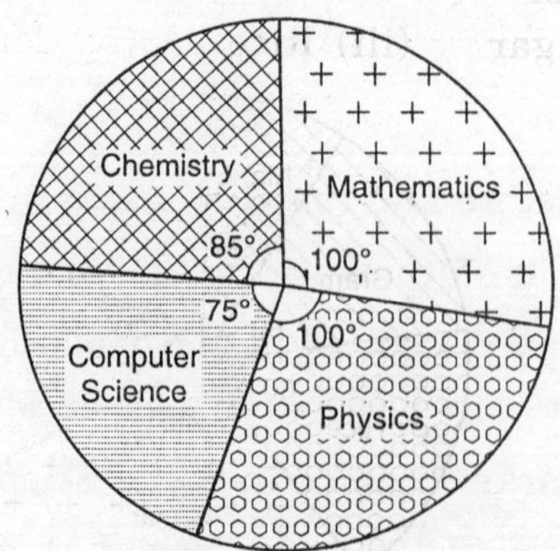

Fig. 25.16

(i) Total marks scored in all subjects.

(ii) Marks scored in Chemistry.

Solution (i) We have,

$$\text{Marks scored in Mathematics} = \frac{\text{Central angle of the corresponding sector} \times \text{Total marks}}{360^\circ}$$

$$\therefore \quad 80 = \frac{100^\circ \times \text{Total marks}}{360^\circ}$$

$$\Rightarrow \quad \text{Total marks} = \frac{80 \times 360}{100} = 288$$

(ii) $\text{Central angle of Chemistry} = 360^\circ - (100^\circ + 100^\circ + 75^\circ) = 85^\circ$

$$\text{Marks scored in Chemistry} = \frac{\text{Central angle for Chemistry} \times \text{Total marks}}{360^\circ}$$

$$= \left(\frac{85^\circ \times 288}{360^\circ}\right) = 68$$

EXERCISE 25.2

1. The pie-chart given in Fig. 25.17 represents the expenditure on different items in constructing a flat in Delhi. If the expenditure incurred on cement is Rs 112500, find the following:

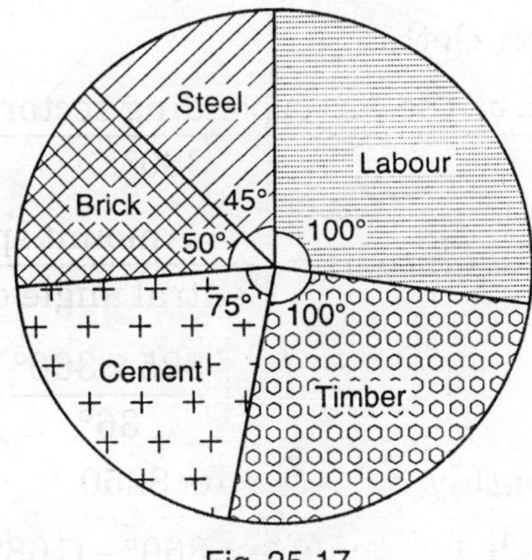

Fig. 25.17

(i) Total cost of the flat.

(ii) Expenditure incurred on labour.

2. The pie-chart given in Fig. 25.18 shows the annual agricultural production of an Indian state. If the total production of all the commodities is 81000 tonnes, find the production (in tonnes) of

(i) Wheat (ii) Sugar (iii) Rice (iv) Maize (v) Gram

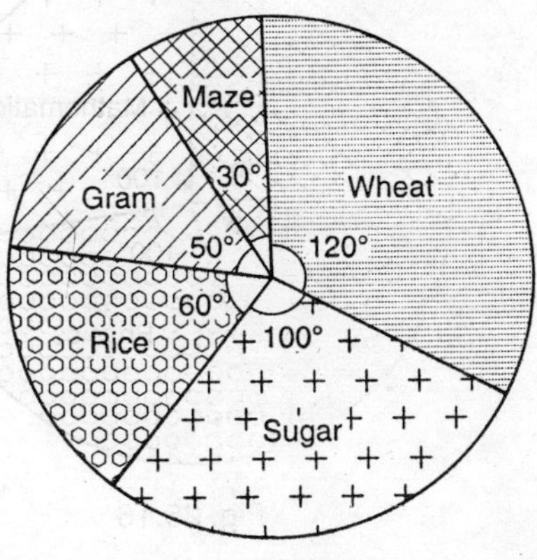

Fig. 25.18

3. The following pie-chart shows the number of students admitted in different faculties of a college. If 1000 students are admitted in Science answer the following:

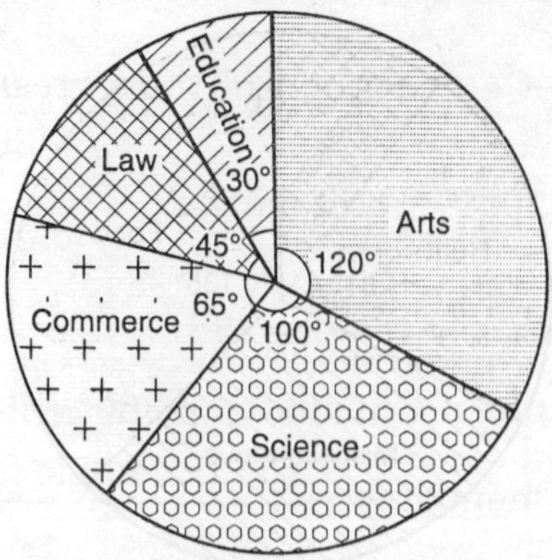

Fig. 25.19

(i) What is the total number of students?

(ii) What is the ratio of students in science and arts?

4. In Fig. 25.20, the pie-chart shows the marks obtained by a student in an examination. If the student secures 440 marks in all, calculate his marks in each of the given subjects.

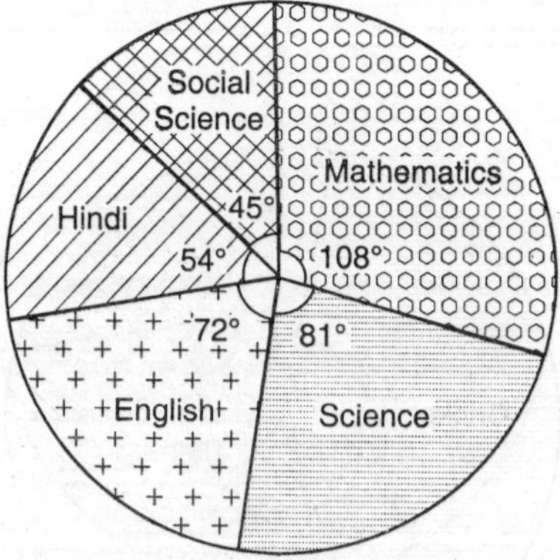

Fig. 25.20

5. In Fig. 25.21, the pie-chart shows the marks obtained by a student in various subjects. If the student scored 135 marks in mathematics, find the total marks in all the subjects. Also, find his score in individual subjects.

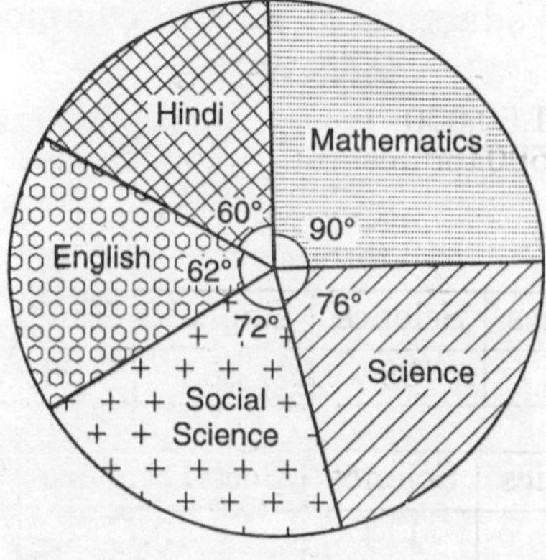

Fig. 25.21

6. The following pie-chart shows the monthly expenditure of Shikha on various items. If she spends Rs 16000 per month, answer the following questions:

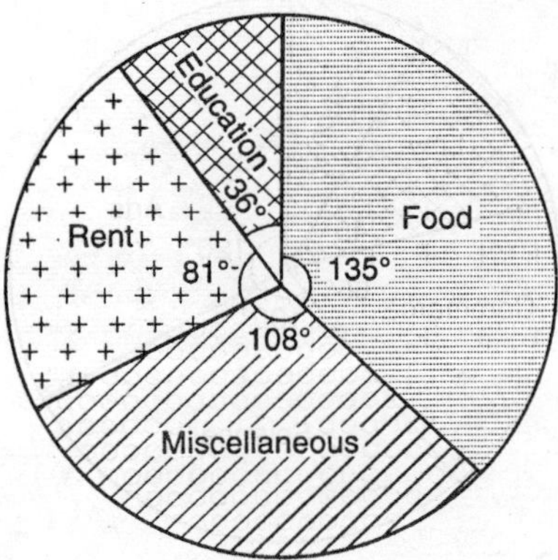

Fig. 25.22

(i) How much does she spend on rent?

(ii) How much does she spend on education?

(iii) What is the ratio of expenses on food and rent?

7. The pie chart (as shown in the figure 25.23) represents the amount spent on different sports by a sports club in a year. If the total money spent by the club on sports is Rs 1,08,000, find the amount spent on each sport.

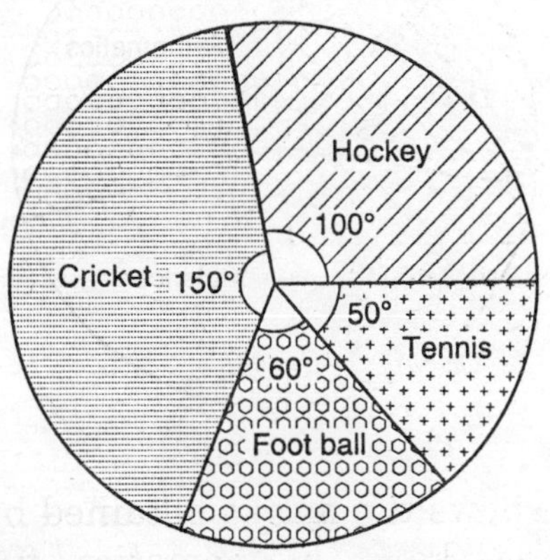

Fig. 25.23

ANSWERS

1. (i) Rs 5,40,000 (ii) Rs 1,50,000
2. (i) 27,000 tonnes (ii) 22,500 tonnes (iii) 13,500 tonnes (iv) 6,750 tonnes (v) 11,250 tonnes
3. (i) 3,600 (ii) 5 : 6.
4.

Subject	Mathematics	Science	English	Hindi	Social Science
Marks obtained	132	99	88	66	55

5.

Subject	Mathematics	Science	Social Science	English	Hindi
Marks obtained	135	114	108	93	90

6. (i) Rs 3,600 (ii) Rs 1,600 (iii) 5 : 3
7. (i) Hockey : Rs 30,000 Cricket : Rs 45,000 Football : Rs 18,000 Tennis : Rs 15,000

26

DATA HANDLING-IV (Probability)

26.1 INTRODUCTION

The word 'probability' is commonly used in our day-to-day conversation and we generally use this word even without going into the details of its actual meaning. Generally, people have a rough idea about its meaning. In our day-to-day life we come across statements like:

(i) Probably it may rain to day.

(ii) He may possibly join politics.

(iii) Indian Cricket team has good chances of winning world cup.

(iv) He is probably right.

In such statements, we generally use the terms possible, probable, chance, likely etc. All these terms convey the same sense that the event is not certain to take place. In other words, there is uncertainty about the occurrence or happening of the event in question. Thus, in layman's terminology the word 'probability' connotes that there is uncertainty about what has happened or what is going to happen. However, in the theory of probability we assign numerical value to the degree of uncertainty.

The concept of probability originated in the beginning of seventeenth century in problems pertaining to games of chance such as throwing a die, tossing a coin, drawing a card from a pack of cards etc. Starting with games of chance, probability today has become one of the basic tools of Statistics and has vide range of applications in science and engineering.

26.2 THEORETICAL APPROACH TO PROBABILITY

What we have learnt in the chapter on probability in class IX is known as experimental or impirical approach to probability. In this approach, as we have seen, the probabilities were based on actual experiments and adequate recording of the happening of events. In this chapter and in higher classes, we will study about theoretical approach to probability. The basic difference between these two approaches to probability is that in the experimental approach to probability, the probability of an event is based on what has actually happened while in theoretical approach to probability, we try to predict what will happen without actually performing the experiment.

It has been observed that the experimental probability of an event approaches to its theoretical probability if the number of trials of an experiment is very large.

In the theory of probability we deal with events which are outcomes of an experiment. The word 'experiment' means an operation which can produce some well-defined outcome(s). There are two types of experiments: (i) Deterministic (ii) Random or Probabilistic.

Deterministic experiments are those experiments which when repeated under identical conditions produce the same result or outcome. When experiments in science and Engineering are repeated under identical conditions, we obtain almost the same result every time.

26

DATA HANDLING-IV (Probability)

26.1 INTRODUCTION

The word 'probability' is commonly used in our day-to-day conversation and we generally use this word even without going into the details of its actual meaning. Generally, people have a rough idea about its meaning. In our day-to-day life we come across statements like:

(i) Probably it may rain to day.

(ii) He may possibly join politics.

(iii) Indian Cricket team has good chances of winning World-Cup.

(iv) He is probably right.

In such statements, we generally use the terms: possible, probable, chance, likely etc. All these terms convey the same sense that the event is not certain to take place or, in other words, there is uncertainty about the occurrence (or happening) of the event in question. Thus, in layman's terminology the word 'probability, connotes that there is uncertainty about what has happened or what is going to happen. However, in the theory of probability we assign numerical value to the degree of uncertainty.

The concept of probability originated in the beginning of eighteenth century in problems pertaining to games of chance such as throwing a die, tossing a coin, drawing a card from a pack of cards etc. Starting with games of chance, 'probability' today has become one of the basic tools of Statistics and has vide range of applications in Science and Engineering.

26.2 THEORETICAL APPROACH TO PROBABILITY

What we have learnt in the chapter on probability in class VII was experimental or impirical approach to probability. In this approach, as we have seen, the probabilities were based on actual experiments and adequate recording of the happening of events. In this chapter and in higher classes, we will study about theoretical approach to probability. The basic difference between these two approaches to probability is that in the experimental approach to probability, the probability of an event is based on what has actually happened while in theoretical approach to probability, we try to predict what will happen without actually performing the experiment.

It has been observed that the experimental probability of an event approaches to its theoretical probability if the number of trials of an experiment is very large.

In the theory of probability we deal with events which are outcomes of an experiment. The word 'experiment' means an operation which can produce some well defined outcome(s). There are two types of experiments: (i) Deterministic (ii) Random or Probabilistic.

Deterministic experiments are those experiments which when repeated under identical conditions produce the same result or outcome. When experiments in Science and Engineering are repeated under identical conditions, we obtain almost the same result every time.

If an experiment, when repeated under identical conditions, do not produce the same outcome every time but the outcome in a trial is one of the several possible outcomes, then it is known as a random or probabilistic experiment. For example, in tossing of a coin one is not sure if a head or a tail will be obtained, so it is a random experiment. Similarly, rolling an unbiased die and drawing a card from a well shuffled pack of cards are examples of a random experiment.

Throughout this chapter we shall be discussing random experiments and the term experiment will stand for random experiment.

Let us now discuss various terms associated with a random experiment. These terms will help us in introducing the theoretical concept of probability.

ELEMENTARY EVENT *An outcome of a random experiment is called an elementary event.*

Consider the random experiment of tossing of a coin. The possible outcomes of this experiment are head (H) or tail (T).

Thus, if we define

E_1 = Getting head (H) on the upper face of the coin,

and,

E_2 = Getting tail (T) on the upper face of the coin.

Then, E_1 and E_2 are elementary events associated with the experiments of tossing of a coin.

Let us now consider the random experiment of tossing two coins simultaneously. The possible outcomes of this experiment are as under:

Head on first and Head on second, Head on first and Tail on second,

Tail on first and Head on second, Tail on first and Tail on second.

If we define

HH = Getting head on both the coins, HT = Getting Head on first and tail on second,

TH = Getting tail on first and head on second, TT = Getting tail on both the coins.

Then, HH, HT, TH and TT are elementary events associated with the random experiment of tossing of two coins.

Similarly, if three coins are tossed simultaneously, then the elementary events associated with this experiment are HHH, HHT, HTH, THH, HTT, THT, TTH, TTT.

Let there be a cubical die marked with numbers 1, 2, 3, 4, 5 and 6 on its six faces. Consider now-the random experiment of throwing a cubical die. If the die is rolled, then any one of the six faces may come upward. So, there are six possible outcomes of this experiment, namely 1, 2, 3, 4, 5, 6.

Thus, if we define

E_1 = Getting a face marked with number 1

E_2 = Getting a face marked with number 2

$\vdots$

E_6 = Getting a face marked with number 6

Then, E_1, E_2 ...., E_6 are six elementary events associated to this experiment.

Now, consider the random experiment in which two six-faced dice are rolled together or a die is rolled twice, then possible outcomes of this experiment are:

$$\begin{matrix} (1,1), & (1,2), & (1,3), & (1,4), & (1,5), & (1,6) \\ (2,1), & (2,2), & (2,3), & (2,4), & (2,5), & (2,6) \\ (3,1), & (3,2), & (3,3), & (3,4), & (3,5), & (3,6) \\ (4,1), & (4,2), & (4,3), & (4,4), & (4,5), & (4,6) \\ (5,1), & (5,2), & (5,3), & (5,4), & (5,5), & (5,6) \\ (6,1), & (6,2), & (6,3), & (6,4), & (6,5), & (6,6) \end{matrix}$$

Clearly, these outcomes are elementary events associated with the random experiment of throwing two six faced dice together. The total number of these elementary events is 36.

If a card is drawn from a well shuffled pack of 52 cards, then any one of 52 cards can be the outcome. So, there are 52 elementary events associated to the random experiment of drawing a card from a pack of 52 playing cards.

COMPOUND EVENT *An event associated to a random experiment is a compound event if it is obtained by combining two or more elementary events associated to the random experiment.*

In a single throw of a die, the event "Getting an even number" is a compound event as it is obtained by combining three elementary events, namely, 2, 4, 6.

Similarly, "Getting an odd number" is a compound event obtained by combining elementary events 1, 3 and 5.

Consider the random experiment of tossing two coins simultaneously. If we define the event "Getting exactly one head", then *HT* and *TH* are two elementary events associated to it. So, it is a compound event.

Associated to the random experiment of tossing three coins simultaneously, we have following elementary events:

HHH, HHT, HTH, THH, TTH, HTT, THT and TTT.

If we define event

E = Getting exactly two heads

Then, *HHT, THH, HTH* are three elementary events associated to event E

So, it is a compound event.

Similarly,

F = Getting exactly one head and, G = Getting at least one head

are compound events.

OCCURRENCE OF AN EVENT *An event A associated to a random experiment is said to occur if any one of the elementary events associated to the event A is an outcome.*

Consider the random experiment of throwing an unbiased die. Let A denote the event "Getting an even number". Elementary events associated to this event are: 2, 4, 6. Now, suppose that in a trial the outcome is 4, then we say that the event A has occurred. In another trial, let the outcome be 3, then we say that the event A has not occurred.

Let a die be rolled and the outcome of the trial be 4. Then, we can say that each of the following events have occurred:

(i) Getting a number greater than or equal to 2,

(ii) Getting a number less than or equal to 5,

(iii) Getting an even number.

On the basis of the same outcome, we can also say that the following events have not occurred:

(i) Getting an odd number,

(ii) Getting a multiple of 3.

Let us now consider the random experiment of throwing a pair of dice. If (2, 6) is an outcome of a trial, then we can say that each of the following events have occurred.

(i) Getting an even number on first die.

(ii) Getting an even number on both dice

(iii) Getting 8 as the sum of the numbers on two dice.

However, on the basis of the same outcome, one can also say that the following events have not occurred:

(i) Getting a multiple of 3 on first die.

(ii) Getting an odd number on first die.

(iii) Getting a doublet.

FAVOURABLE ELEMENTARY EVENTS *An elementary event is said to be favourable to a compound event A, if it satisfies the definition of the compound event A.*

In other words, an elementary event E is favourable to a compound event A, if we say that the event A occurs when E is an outcome of a trial.

Consider the random experiment of throwing a pair of dice and the compound event A defined by "Getting 8 as the sum." We observe that the event A occurs if we get any one of the following elementary events as outcome:

$$(2, 6),\ (6, 2),\ (3, 5),\ (5, 3),\ (4,4)$$

So, there are 5 elementary events favourable to event A.

If two coins are tossed simultaneously and A is an event associated to it defined as "Getting exactly one head". We say that the event A occurs if we get either HT or TH as an outcome. So, there are two elementary events favourable to the event A.

NEGATION OF AN EVENT *Corresponding to every event A associated with a random experiment we define an event "not A" which occurs when and only when A does not occur. The event "not A" is called the negation of event A and is denoted by $\overline{A}$.*

Clearly, event A occurs if and only if $\overline{A}$ does not occur.

26.3 THEORETICAL PROBABILITY

DEFINITION *If there are n elementary events associated with a random experiment and m of them are favourable to an event A, then the probability of happening or occurrence of event A is denoted by P (A) and is defined as the ratio $\frac{m}{n}$.*

Thus, $$P(A) = \frac{m}{n} = \frac{\text{Favourable number of elementary events}}{\text{Total number of elementary events}}$$

Clearly, out of n elementary events, m are favourable to an event A.

$\therefore \quad 0 \le m < n$

$\therefore \quad 0 \le \frac{m}{n} \le 1$ [Dividing throughout by n]

$\Rightarrow \quad 0 \le P(A) \le 1$

If $P(A) = 1$, then A is called a certain event and event A is called an impossible event, if $P(A) = 0$.

If m elementary events are favourable to an event A out of n elementary events, then the number of elementary events which ensure the non-occurrence of A i.e. the occurrence of $\overline{A}$ is $n - m$.

$$\therefore \quad P(\overline{A}) = \frac{\text{Favourable number of elementary events to event } \overline{A}}{\text{Total number of elementary events}}$$

$$\Rightarrow \quad P(\overline{A}) = \frac{n-m}{n}$$

$$\Rightarrow \quad P(\overline{A}) = 1 - \frac{m}{n}$$

$$\Rightarrow \quad P(\overline{A}) = 1 - P(A)$$

$$\Rightarrow \quad P(A) + P(\overline{A}) = 1$$

i.e.,
Probability of occurrence of an event A + Probability of Non-occurrence of an event A = 1.

Let us now discuss some problems to illustrate the above definition.

ILLUSTRATIVE EXAMPLES

Example 1 An unbiased die is thrown. What is the probability of getting:

(i) an even number (ii) a multiple of 3

(iii) an even number or a multiple of 3

(iv) an even number and a multiple of 3 (v) a number 3 or 4

(vi) an odd number (vii) a number less than 5

(viii) a number greater than 3 (ix) a number between 3 and 6.

Solution In a single throw of a die we can get any one of the six numbers 1, 2, ..., 6 marked on its six faces. Therefore, the total number of elementary events associated with the random experiment of throwing a die is 6.

(i) Let A denote the event "Getting an even number"

Clearly, event A occurs if we obtain any one of 2, 4, 6 as an outcome.

$\therefore$ Favourable number of elementary events = 3

Hence, $P(A) = \frac{2}{6} = \frac{1}{3}$

(ii) Let A denote the event "Getting a multiple of 3"

We observe that the event A occurs if we obtain either 3 or 6 as an outcome.

$\therefore$ Favourable number of elementary events = 2

Hence, $P(A) = \frac{2}{6} = \frac{1}{3}$

(iii) An even number or a multiple of 3 is obtained if we obtain one of the numbers 2, 3, 4, 6 as an outcome.

$\therefore$ Favourable number of elementary events = 4

Hence, required probability $= \frac{4}{6} = \frac{2}{3}$

(iv) Let A denote the event "Getting an even number and a multiple of 3"
Clearly, event A happens if we get 6 as an outcome

$\therefore$ Favourable number of elementary events = 1

Hence, $P(A) = \frac{1}{6}$

(v) Let A denote the event "Getting 3 or 4 "
Clearly, A occurs when we get either 3 or 4 as an outcome

$\therefore$ Favourable number of elementary events = 2

Hence, $P(A) = \frac{2}{6} = \frac{1}{3}$

(vi) Let A denote the event "Getting an odd number"
We observe that the event A occurs when we get 1 or 3 or 5 as an outcome.

$\therefore$ Favourable number of elementary events = 3

Hence, $P(A) = \frac{3}{6} = \frac{1}{2}$

(vii) The event "Getting a number less than 5" will occur if we get one of the numbers 1, 2, 3, 4 as an outcome.

$\therefore$ Favourable number of outcomes = 4

Hence, required probability $= \frac{4}{6} = \frac{2}{3}$

(viii) The event "Getting a number greater than 3" will occur if we obtain one of the numbers 4, 5, 6 as an outcome.

$\therefore$ Favourable number of outcomes = 3

Hence, required probability $= \frac{3}{6} = \frac{1}{2}$

(ix) The event "Getting a number between 3 and 6" occurs if we obtain either 4 or 5 as an outcome.

$\therefore$ Favourable number of outcomes = 2

Hence, required probability $= \frac{2}{6} = \frac{1}{3}$

Example 2 Two unbiased coins are tossed simultaneously. Find the probability of getting:

(i) two heads (ii) one head
(iii) one tail (iv) at least one head
(v) at most one head (vi) no head

Solution If two unbiased coins are tossed simultaneously we obtain any one of the following as an outcome.

HH, HT, TH, TT

$\therefore$ Total number of elementary events = 4

(i) Two heads are obtained if the elementary event HH occurs.

$\therefore$ Favourable number of elementary events = 1

Hence, required probability $= \frac{1}{4}$

(ii) One head is obtained if any one of the following elementary events occurs: *HT*, *TH*

$\therefore$ Favourable number of elementary events = 2

Hence, required probability $= \frac{2}{4} = \frac{1}{2}$

(iii) One tail is obtained if any one of the following elementary events occurs: *TH*, *HT*

$\therefore$ Favourable number of elementary events = 2

Hence, required probability $= \frac{2}{4} = \frac{1}{2}$

(iv) At least one head is obtained if any one of the following elementary events happens:

$$HH, HT, TH$$

$\therefore$ Favourable number of elementary events = 3

Hence, required probability $= \frac{3}{4}$

(v) If one of the elementary events *HT*, *TH*, *TT* occurs, then we say that at most one head is obtained.

$\therefore$ Favourable number of elementary events = 3

Hence, required probability $= \frac{3}{4}$

(vi) No head is obtained if the elementary event *TT* occurs

$\therefore$ Favourable number of elementary events = 1

Hence, required probability $= \frac{1}{4}$

Example 3 Three unbiased coins are tossed together. Find the probability of getting:

(i) all heads (ii) two heads

(iii) one head (iv) at least two heads

Solution Elementary events associated to random experiment of tossing three coins are:

HHH, *HHT*, *HTH*, *THH*, *HTT*, *THT*, *TTH*, *TTT*

$\therefore$ Total number of elementary events = 8.

(i) The event "Getting all heads" is said to occur, if the elementary event *HHH* occurs i.e. *HHH* is an outcome.

$\therefore$ Favourable number of elementary events = 1

Hence, required probability $= \frac{1}{8}$

(ii) The event "Getting two heads" will occur, if one of the elementary events *HHT*, *THH*, *HTH* occurs.

$\therefore$ Favourable number of elementary events = 3

Hence, required probability $= \frac{3}{8}$

(iii) The events of getting one head, when three coins are tossed together, occurs if one of the elementary events *HTT*, *THT*, *TTH* happens.

∴ Favourable number of elementary events = 3

Hence, required probability $= \frac{3}{8}$

(iv) If any of the elementary events *HHH*, *HHT*, *HTH*, and *THH* is an outcome, then we say that the event "Getting at least two heads" occurs.

∴ Favourable number of elementary events = 4

Hence, required probability $= \frac{4}{8} = \frac{1}{2}$.

Example 4 Find the probability that a leap year selected at random will contain 53 Sundays.

Solution In a leap year there are 366 days.

We have, 366 days = 52 weeks and 2 days.

Thus, a leap year has always 52 Sundays.

The remaining 2 days can be:

(i) Sunday and Monday (ii) Monday and Tuesday

(iii) Tuesday and Wednesday (iv) Wednesday and Thursday

(v) Thursday and Friday (vi) Friday and Saturday

(vii) Saturday and Sunday.

Clearly, there are seven elementary events associated with this random experiment.

Let *A* be the event that a leap year has 53 Sundays.

Clearly, the event *A* will happen if the last two days of the leap year are either Sunday and Monday or Saturday and Sunday.

∴ Favourable number of elementary events = 2

Hence, required probability $= \frac{2}{7}$

Example 5 What is the probability that a number selected from the numbers 1, 2, 3, ..., 25 is a prime number, when each of the given numbers is equally likely to be selected?

Solution Out of 25 numbers 1, 2, 3, ..., 25 one number can be chosen in 25 ways.

∴ Total number of elementary events = 25

The number selected will be a prime number if it is chosen from the numbers 2, 3, 5, 7, 11, 13, 17, 19, 23.

∴ Favourable number of elementary events = 9

Hence, required probability $= \frac{9}{25}$

Example 6 Tickets numbered from 1 to 20 are mixed up together and then a ticket is drawn at random. What is the probability that the ticket has a number which is a multiple of 3 or 7?

Solution Out of 20 tickets numbered from 1 to 20, one can be chosen in 20 ways. So, total number of elementary events associated with the given random experiment is 20. Out of 20 tickets numbered 1 to 20, tickets bearing numbers which are multiple of 3 or 7 bear numbers 3, 6, 7, 9, 12, 14, 15 and 18.

$\therefore$ Favourable numbers of elementary events = 8

Hence, required probability $= \frac{8}{20} = \frac{2}{5}$

Remark *A pack of playing cards consists of 52 cards which are divided into 4 suits of 13 cards each. Each suit consists of one ace, one king, one queen, one jack and 9 other cards numbered from 2 to 10. Four suits are named as spades (♠), hearts (♥), diamonds (♦) and clubs (♣).*

Example 7 One card is drawn from a pack of 52 cards, each of the 52 cards being equally likely to be drawn. Find the probability that the card drawn is:

(i) an ace (ii) red

(iii) either red card or king (iv) red and a king

(v) a face card (vi) a red face card

(vii) '2' of spades (viii) '10' of a black suit

Solution Out of 52 cards, one card can be drawn in 52 ways.

So, total number of elementary events = 52.

(i) There are four ace cards in a pack of 52 cards. So, one ace can be chosen in 4 ways.

$\therefore$ Favourable number of elementary events = 4

Hence, required probability $= \frac{4}{52} = \frac{1}{13}$

(ii) There are 26 red cards in a pack of 52 cards. Out of 26 red cards one card can be chosen in 26 ways.

$\therefore$ Favourable number of elementary events = 26

Hence, required probability $= \frac{26}{52} = \frac{1}{2}$

(iii) There are 26 red cards, including two red kings, in a pack of 52 playing cards. Also, there are 4 kings, two red and two black. Therefore, card drawn will be a red card or a king if it is any one of 28 cards (26 red cards and 2 black kings).

$\therefore$ Favourable number of elementary events = 28

Hence, required probability $= \frac{28}{52} = \frac{7}{13}$

(iv) A card drawn will be red as well as king, if it is a red king. There are 2 red kings in a pack of 52 playing cards.

$\therefore$ Favourable number of elementary events = 2

Hence, required probability $= \frac{2}{52} = \frac{1}{26}$

(v) In a deck of 52 cards: aces, kings, queens, and jacks are called face cards. Thus, there are 12 face cards. So, one face card can be chosen in 12 ways.

∴ Favourable number of elementary events = 12

Hence, required probability $= \frac{12}{52} = \frac{3}{13}$

(vi) There are 6 red face cards 3 each from diamonds and hearts. Out of these 6 red face cards one card can be chosen in 6 ways.

∴ Favourable number of elementary events = 6

Hence, required probability $= \frac{6}{52} = \frac{3}{26}$

(vii) There is only one '2' of spades.

∴ Favourable number of elementary events = 1

Hence, required probability $= \frac{1}{52}$

(viii) There are two suits of black cards viz. spades and clubs. Each suit contains one card bearing number 10.

∴ Favourable number of elementary events = 2

Hence, required probability $= \frac{2}{52} = \frac{1}{26}$

Example 8 The king, queen and jack of clubs are removed from a deck of 52 playing cards and the well shuffled. One card is selected from the remaining cards. Find the probability of getting.

(i) a heart (ii) a king

(iii) a club (iv) the '10' of hearts.

Solution After removing king, queen and jack of clubs from a deck of 52 playing cards there are 49 cards left in the deck. Out of these 49 cards one card can be chosen in 49 ways.

∴ Total number of elementary events = 49

(i) There are 13 heart cards in the deck containing 49 cards out of which one heart card can be chosen in 13 ways.

∴ Favourable number of elementary events = 13

Hence, P (Getting a heart) $= \frac{13}{49}$

(ii) There are 3 kings in the deck containing 49 cards. Out of these three kings one king can be chosen in 3 ways.

∴ Favourable number of elementary events = 3

Hence, P (Getting a king) $= \frac{3}{49}$

(iii) After removing king, queen and jack of clubs only 10 club cards are left in the deck. Out of these 10 club cards one club card is chosen in 10 ways.

∴ Favourable number of elementary events = 10

Hence, P (Getting a club) $= \frac{10}{49}$

(iv) There is only one '10' of hearts.

$\therefore$ Favourable number of elementary events = 1

Hence, P (Getting the '10' of hearts) $= \frac{1}{49}$

Example 9 A bag contains 3 red and 2 blue marbles. A marble is drawn at random. What is the probability of drawing a blue marble?

Solution There are 5 marbles in the bag. Out of these 5 marbles one can be chosen in 5 ways.

$\therefore$ Total number of elementary events = 5

Since the bag contains 2 blue marbles. Therefore, one blue marble can be drawn in 2 ways.

$\therefore$ Favourable number of elementary events = 2

Hence, P (Getting a blue marble) $= \frac{2}{5}$

Example 10 It is known that a box of 600 electric bulbs contains 12 defective bulbs. One bulb is taken out at random from this box. What is the probability that it is a non-defective bulb?

Solution Out of 600 electric bulbs one bulb can be chosen in 600 ways.

$\therefore$ Total number of elementary events = 600

There are 588 (= 600 − 12) non-defective bulbs out of which one bulb can be chosen in 588 ways.

$\therefore$ Favourable number of elementary events = 588

Hence, P (Getting a non-defective bulb) $= \frac{588}{600} = \frac{49}{50} = 0.98$

Example 11 17 cards numbered 1, 2, 3, ..., 17 are put in a box and mixed thoroughly. One person draws a card from the box. Find the probability that the number on the card is:

(i) odd (ii) a prime

(iii) divisible by 3 (iv) divisible by 3 and 2 both

Solution Out of 17 cards, in the box, one card can be drawn in 17 ways.

$\therefore$ Total number of elementary events = 17

(i) There 9 odd numbered cards, namely, 1, 3, 5, 7, 9, 11, 13, 15, 17. Out of these 9 cards one card can be drawn in 9 ways.

$\therefore$ Favourable number of elementary events = 9

Hence, required probability $= \frac{9}{17}$

(ii) There are 7 prime numbered cards, namely, 2, 3, 5, 7, 11, 13, 17. Out of these 7 cards one card can be chosen in 7 ways.

$\therefore$ Favourable number of elementary events = 7

Hence, P (Getting a prime number) $= \frac{7}{17}$

(iii) Let A denote the event of getting a card bearing a number divisible by 3.

Clearly, event A occurs if we get a card bearing one of the numbers 3, 6, 9, 12, 15.

$\therefore$ Favourable number of elementary events = 5

Hence, P (Getting a card bearing a number divisible by 3) $= \frac{5}{17}$

(iv) If a number is divisible by both 3 and 2, then it is a multiple of 6. In cards bearing number 1, 2, 3, ..., 17 there are only 2 cards which bear a number divisible by 3 and 2 both *i.e.* by 6. These cards bear numbers 6 and 12.

$\therefore$ Favourable number of elementary events = 2

Hence, P (Getting a card bearing a number divisible by 3 and 2) $= \frac{2}{17}$

Example 12 Cards marked with the numbers 2 to 101 are placed in a box and mixed thoroughly. One card is drawn from this box. Find the probability that the number on the card is:

(i) an even number (ii) a number less than 14

(iii) a number which is a perfect square (iv) a prime number less than 20.

Solution There are 100 cards in the box out of which one card can be drawn in 100 ways.

$\therefore$ Total number of elementary events = 100

(i) From numbers 2 to 101, there are 50 even numbers, namely, 2, 4, 6, 8, ..., 100. Out of these 50 even numbered cards, one card can be chosen in 50 ways.

$\therefore$ Favourable number of elementary events = 50

Hence, P (Getting an even numbered card) $= \frac{50}{100} = \frac{1}{2}$

(ii) There are 12 cards bearing numbers less than 14 i.e. numbers 2, 3, 4, 5, ..., 13

$\therefore$ Favourable number of elementary events = 12

Hence, required probability $= \frac{12}{100} = \frac{3}{25}$

(iii) Those numbers from 2 to 101 which are perfect squares are 4, 9, 16, 25, 36, 49, 64, 81, 100 i.e. squares of 2, 3, 4, 5, ..., and 10 respectively. Therefore, there are 9 cards marked with the numbers which are perfect squares.

$\therefore$ Favourable number of elementary events = 9

Hence, P (Getting a card marked with a number which is a perfect square) $= \frac{9}{100}$

(iv) Prime numbers less than 20 in the numbers from 2 to 101 are 2, 3, 5, 7, 11, 13, 17 and 19. Thus, there are 8 cards marked with prime numbers less than 20. Out of these 8 cards one card can be chosen in 8 ways.

$\therefore$ Favourable number of elementary events = 8

Hence, P (Getting a card marked with a prime number less than 20) $= \frac{8}{100} = \frac{2}{25}$

Example 13 A bag contains 5 red balls, 8 white balls, 4 green balls and 7 black balls. If one ball is drawn at random, find the probability that it is:

(i) black (ii) red (iii) not green.

Solution Total number of balls in the bag $= 5 + 8 + 4 + 7 = 24$

$\therefore$ Total number of elementary events = 24

(i) There are 7 black balls in the bag.

$\therefore$ Favourable number of elementary events = 7

Hence, P (Getting a black ball) $= \frac{7}{24}$

(ii) There are 5 red balls in the bag.

$\therefore$ Favourable number of elementary events = 5

Hence, P (Getting a red ball) $= \frac{5}{24}$

(iii) There are $5 + 8 + 7 = 20$ balls which are not green.

$\therefore$ Favourable number of elementary events = 20

Hence, P (Not getting a green ball) $= \frac{20}{24} = \frac{5}{6}$

Example 14 Two dice are thrown simultaneously. Find the probability of getting:

(i) an even number as the sum

(ii) the sum as a prime number

(iii) a total of at least 10

(iv) a doublet of even number

(v) a multiple of 2 on one die and a multiple of 3 on the other

(vi) same number on both dice i.e. a doublet

(vii) a multiple of 3 as the sum.

Solution Elementary events associated to the random experiment of throwing two dice are:

(1,1), (1,2), (1,3), (1,4), (1,5), (1,6)
(2,1), (2,2), (2,3), (2,4), (2,5), (2,6)
(3,1), (3,2), (3,3), (3,4), (3,5), (3,6)
(4,1), (4,2), (4,3), (4,4), (4,5), (4,6)
(5,1), (5,2), (5,3), (5,4), (5,5), (5,6)
(6,1), (6,2), (6,3), (6,4), (6,5), (6,6)

$\therefore$ Total number of elementary events $= 6 \times 6 = 36$

(i) Let A be the event of getting an even number as the sum i.e., 2, 4, 6, 8, 10, 12

Elementary events favourable to event A are:

(1, 1), (1, 3), (3, 1), (2, 2), (1, 5), (5, 1), (2, 4), (4, 2), (3, 3), (2, 6), (6, 2), (4, 4), (5, 3), (3, 5), (5, 5), (6, 4), (4, 6) and (6, 6).

Clearly, favourable number of elementary events = 18

Hence, required probability $= \frac{18}{36} = \frac{1}{2}$

(ii) Let A be the event of getting the sum as a prime number i.e., 2, 3, 5, 7, 11

Elementary events favourable to event A are:

(1, 1), (1, 2), (2, 1), (1, 4), (4, 1), (2, 3), (3, 2), (1, 6), (6, 1), (2, 5), (5, 2), (3, 4), (4, 3), (6, 5) and (5, 6).

$\therefore$ Favourable number of elementary events = 15

Hence, required probability $= \frac{15}{36} = \frac{5}{12}$

(iii) Let A be the event of getting a total of at least 10 i.e, 10, 11, 12. Then, the elementary events favourable to A are:

(6, 4), (4, 6), (5, 5), (6, 5), (5, 6) and (6, 6).

$\therefore$ Favourable number of elementary events = 6

Hence, required probability $= \frac{6}{36} = \frac{1}{6}$

(iv) Let A be the event of getting a doublet of even number. Then, the elementary events favourable to A are (2, 2), (4, 4) and (6, 6)

$\therefore$ Favourable number of elementary events = 3

Hence, required probability $= \frac{3}{36} = \frac{1}{12}$

(v) Let A be the event of getting a multiple of 2 on one die and a multiple of 3 on the other. Then, the elementary events favourable to A are:

(2, 3), (2, 6), (4, 3), (4, 6), (6, 3), (6, 6), (3, 2), (3, 4), (3, 6), (6, 2), (6, 4).

$\therefore$ Favourable number of elementary events = 11

Hence, required probability $= \frac{11}{36}$

(vi) Let A be the event of getting the same number on both dice. Then, elementary events favourable to A are:

(1, 1), (2, 2), (3, 3), (4, 4), (5, 5) and (6, 6)

$\therefore$ Favourable number of elementary events = 6

Hence, required probability $= \frac{6}{36} = \frac{1}{6}$

(vii) Let A be the event of getting a multiple of 3 as the sum i.e., 3, 6, 9, 12.

Then, elementary events favourable to A are:

(1, 2), (2, 1), (1, 5), (5, 1), (2, 4), (4, 2), (3, 3), (3, 6), (6, 3), (5, 4), (4, 5), (6, 6).

$\therefore$ Favourable number of elementary events = 12

Hence, required probability $= \frac{12}{36} = \frac{1}{3}$

EXERCISE 26.1

1. The probability that it will rain tomorrow is 0.85. What is the probability that it will not rain tomorrow?
2. A die is thrown. Find the probability of getting:

   (i) a prime number (ii) 2 or 4 (iii) a multiple of 2 or 3

3. In a simultaneous throw of a pair of dice, find the probability of getting:
   (i) 8 as the sum (ii) a doublet
   (iii) a doublet of prime numbers (iv) a doublet of odd numbers
   (v) a sum greater than 9 (vi) an even number on first
   (vii) an even number on one and a multiple of 3 on the other
   (viii) neither 9 nor 11 as the sum of the numbers on the faces
   (ix) a sum less than 6 (x) a sum less than 7
   (xi) a sum more than 7 (xii) at least once
   (xiii) a number other than 5 on any dice.
4. Three coins are tossed together. Find the probability of getting:
   (i) exactly two heads (ii) at least two heads
   (iii) at least one head and one tail (iv) no tails
5. A card is drawn at random from a pack of 52 cards. Find the probability that the card drawn is:
   (i) a black king (ii) either a black card or a king
   (iii) black and a king (iv) a jack, queen or a king
   (v) neither a heart nor a king (vi) spade or an ace
   (vii) neither an ace nor a king (viii) neither a red card nor a queen.
   (ix) other than an ace (x) a ten
   (xi) a spade (xii) a black card
   (xiii) the seven of clubs (xiv) jack
   (xv) the ace of spades (xvi) a queen
   (xvii) a heart (xviii) a red card
6. An urn contains 10 red and 8 white balls. One ball is drawn at random. Find the probability that the ball drawn is white.
7. A bag contains 3 red balls, 5 black balls and 4 white balls. A ball is drawn at random from the bag. What is the probability that the ball drawn is:
   (i) white? (ii) red? (iii) black? (iv) not red?
8. What is the probability that a number selected from the numbers 1, 2, 3, ..., 15 is a multiple of 4?
9. A bag contains 6 red, 8 black and 4 white balls. A ball is drawn at random. What is the probability that ball drawn is not black?
10. A bag contains 5 white and 7 red balls. One ball is drawn at random. What is the probability that ball drawn is white?
11. A bag contains 4 red, 5 black and 6 white balls. A ball is drawn from the bag at random. Find the probability that the ball drawn is:
    (i) white (ii) red (iii) not black (iv) red or white
12. A bag contains 3 red balls and 5 black balls. A ball is drawn at random from the bag. What is the probability that the ball drawn is:
    (i) red (ii) black
13. A bag contains 5 red marbles, 8 white marbles, 4 green marbles. What is the probability that if one marble is taken out of the bag at random, it will be
    (i) red (ii) white (iii) not green

14. If you put 21 consonants and 5 vowels in a bag. What would carry greater probability? Getting a consonant or a vowel? Find each probability.
15. If we have 15 boys and 5 girls in a class which carries a higher probability? Getting a copy belonging to a boy or a girl. Can you give it a value?
16. If you have a collection of 6 pairs of white socks and 3 pairs of black socks. What is the probability that a pair you pick without looking is (i) white? (ii) black?
17. If you have a spinning wheel with 3-green sectors, 1-blue sector and 1-red sector. What is the probability of getting a green sector? Is it the maximum?
18. When two dice are rolled:
    (i) List the outcomes for the event that the total is odd.
    (ii) Find probability of getting an odd total.
    (iii) List the outcomes for the event that total is less than 5.
    (iv) Find the probability of getting a total less than 5?

ANSWERS

1. 0.15
2. (i) $\frac{1}{2}$ (ii) $\frac{1}{3}$ (iii) $\frac{2}{3}$
3. (i) $\frac{5}{36}$ (ii) $\frac{1}{6}$ (iii) $\frac{1}{12}$ (iv) $\frac{1}{12}$ (v) $\frac{1}{6}$ (vi) $\frac{1}{2}$
   (vii) $\frac{11}{36}$ (viii) $\frac{5}{6}$ (ix) $\frac{5}{18}$ (x) $\frac{5}{12}$ (xi) $\frac{5}{12}$ (xii) $\frac{11}{36}$
   (xiii) $\frac{25}{36}$
4. (i) $\frac{3}{8}$ (ii) $\frac{1}{2}$ (iii) $\frac{3}{4}$ (iv) $\frac{1}{8}$
5. (i) $\frac{1}{26}$ (ii) $\frac{7}{13}$ (iii) $\frac{1}{26}$ (iv) $\frac{3}{13}$ (v) $\frac{9}{13}$ (vi) $\frac{4}{13}$
   (vii) $\frac{11}{13}$ (viii) $\frac{7}{13}$ (ix) $\frac{12}{13}$ (x) $\frac{1}{13}$ (xi) $\frac{1}{4}$ (xii) $\frac{1}{2}$
   (xiii) $\frac{1}{52}$ (xiv) $\frac{1}{13}$ (xv) $\frac{1}{52}$ (xvi) $\frac{1}{13}$ (xvii) $\frac{1}{4}$ (xviii) $\frac{1}{2}$
6. $\frac{4}{9}$
7. (i) $\frac{1}{3}$ (ii) $\frac{1}{4}$ (iii) $\frac{5}{12}$ (iv) $\frac{3}{4}$
8. $\frac{1}{5}$
9. $\frac{5}{9}$
10. $\frac{5}{12}$
11. (i) $\frac{2}{5}$ (ii) $\frac{4}{15}$ (iii) $\frac{2}{3}$ (iv) $\frac{2}{3}$
12. (i) $\frac{3}{8}$ (ii) $\frac{5}{8}$
13. (i) $\frac{5}{17}$ (ii) $\frac{8}{17}$ (iii) $\frac{13}{17}$
14. Getting a consonant, $\frac{21}{26}, \frac{5}{21}$
15. Getting a copy belonging to a boy, $\frac{3}{4}$
16. (i) $\frac{2}{3}$ (ii) $\frac{1}{3}$
17. $\frac{3}{5}$, Yes
18. (i) (1, 2), (2, 1), (1, 4), (4, 1), (2, 3), (3, 2), (1, 6), (6, 1), (3, 4), (4, 3), (2, 5), (5, 2), (3, 6), (6, 3), (4, 5), (5, 4), (6, 5), (5, 6).
    (ii) $\frac{1}{2}$ (iii) (1, 1), (1, 2), (2, 1), (1, 3), (3, 1), (2, 2) (iv) $\frac{1}{6}$

THINGS TO REMEMBER

1. *If an experiment, when repeated under identical conditions, do not produce the same outcome every time but the outcome in a trial is one of the several outcomes, then it is known as a random experiment.*
2. *An outcome of a random experiment is called an elementary event.*
3. *An event obtained by combining two or more elementary events is known as a compound event.*
4. *An event, associated to a random experiment, is said to occur if any one of the elementary events associated to the event is an outcome.*
5. *An elementary event is said to be favourable to a compound event A, if it satisfies the definition of the compound event A.*
6. If there are *n elementary events associated to a random experiment such that m of them are favourable to an event A, then*

$$\text{Probability of happening of } A = \frac{m}{n} = \frac{\text{Favourable number of elementary events}}{\text{Total number of elementary events}}$$

7. For any event A, we have

$$P(A) + P(\overline{A}) = 1$$

27

INTRODUCTION TO GRAPHS

27.1 INTRODUCTION

In our day-to-day life, we come across many situations where we are given the values of a variable at different points of time. For example, the temperature of a patient taken at different times in a day, sales of a shopkeeper on various days of a week etc. Such an information can be presented conveniently with the help of graphs which indicate the positions of the variable at various intervals of time. In this chapter, we shall discuss the construction and reading of graphs. In order to draw graphs, we first plot various points and then they are joined by a free hand curve. So, let us first learn how to plot points in a plane.

27.2 CARTESIAN PLANE

Take a squared paper, known as graph paper and mark a point O on it. Draw a horizontal line OX and a vertical line OY through O in the plane of the graph paper as shown in Fig. 27.1. The point O is called the origin and the lines OX and OY are called the x-axis and y-axis respectively. The lines OX and OY taken together are known as the coordinate axes and the plane XOY is known as the Cartesian plane.

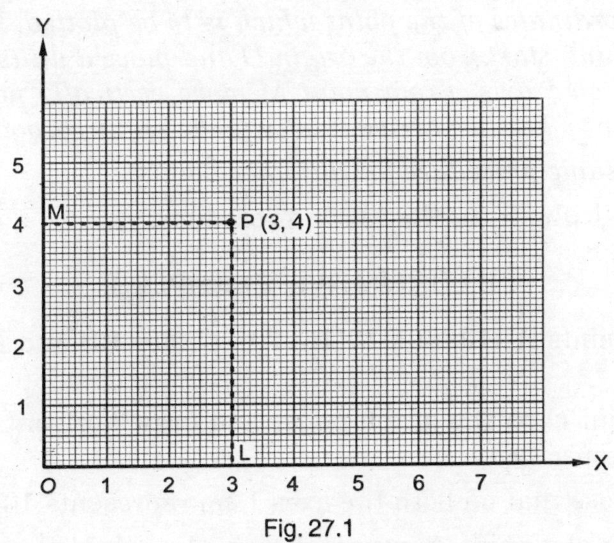

Fig. 27.1

Let P be any point in the plane of the graph paper. In order to locate the position of point P, let us draw PL perpendicular to OX and PM perpendicular to OY. Then, MP is the distance of P from the y-axis i.e. OY and LP is the distance of P from the x-axis i.e. OX. We call MP as the x-coordinate (or abscissa) of point P and LP as the y-coordinate (or ordinate of P). In Fig. 27.1, we have

$$MP = OL = 3 \text{ units and } LP = OM = 4 \text{ units}$$

So, x-coordinate of P is 3 and y-coordinate of P is 4. These two taken together constitute an ordered pair (3, 4) consisting of x-coordinate of P at first place and y-coordinate of P at second place. This ordered pair determines the coordinates of P and we say that the coordinates of P are (3, 4). Note that (3, 4) is an ordered pair in which the positions of 3 and 4 cannot be interchanged.

Thus, x and y coordinates of a point in the Cartesian plane are its distances from y-axis and x-axis respectively.

If we take a point on x-axis i.e. OX, then its distance from x-axis is zero and therefore, the y-ordinate of this point is O.

Thus, the y-coordinate of every point on x-axis i.e. OX is zero and the coordinates of a point on x-axis are of the form $(x, 0)$.

Similarly, if a point is taken on y-axis i.e. OY, then its distance from y-axis is zero and therefore, the x-coordinate of this point is zero.

Thus, the x-coordinate of every point on y-axis i.e. OY is zero and the coordinates of a point on y-axis are of the form (o, y).

The coordinates of the origin O are taken as (0, 0).

27.3 PLOTTING OF POINTS

In order to plot points in Cartesian plane, we may use the following procedure:

PROCEDURE

Step I *Mark a point O on the graph paper and draw a horizontal line OX and a vertical line OY through point O. The horizontal line OX is called x-axis and the vertical line OY is called y-axis.*

Step II *Choose a suitable scale on x-axis and y-axis and mark the points on both the axes.*

Step III *Obtain the coordinates of the point which is to be plotted. Let the point be P (a, b). To plot this point, start from the origin O and move a units along OX to arrive at a point M (say) on x-axis. From point M move vertically parallel to OY through b units. The point where we arrive finally is the required point.*

Continue the same procedure for all other points.

Following examples will illustrate the above procedure.

ILLUSTRATIVE EXAMPLES

Example 1 Plot the points A (10, 50), B (15, 20), C (40, 10) and D (60, 80) on the graph paper.

Solution Take a point O on the graph paper and draw horizontal and vertical lines OX and OY respectively.

Let us choose that on both the axes 1 cm represents 10 units.

In order to plot point A, we start from the origin O and move 1 cm along OX and then 5 cm vertical parallel to OY. The point where we arrive is point A (10, 50).

To plot point B, we first move 1.5 cm along OX and then 2 cm parallel to OY. The point where we arrive is the point B (15, 20).

Similarly, points C and D are plotted on the graph paper as shown in Fig. 27.2.

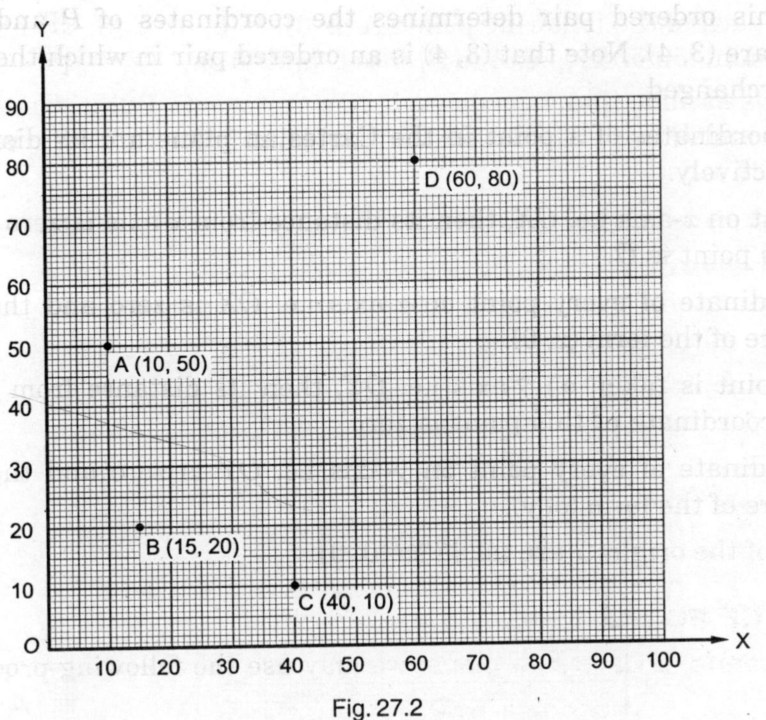

Fig. 27.2

Example 2 Plot the points A (3, 0), B (5, 0) and C (8, 0). What do you observe where do they lie? Also, plot the points P (0, 2), Q (0, 5) and R (0, 9). Do they lie on x-axis?

Solution Let us assume that 1 cm on each axis denote 1 unit. On this scale points A, B, C, P, Q and R plotted on the graph paper as shown in Fig. 27.3 Clearly, points A, B, and C lie on x-axis and points P, Q and R lie on y-axis.

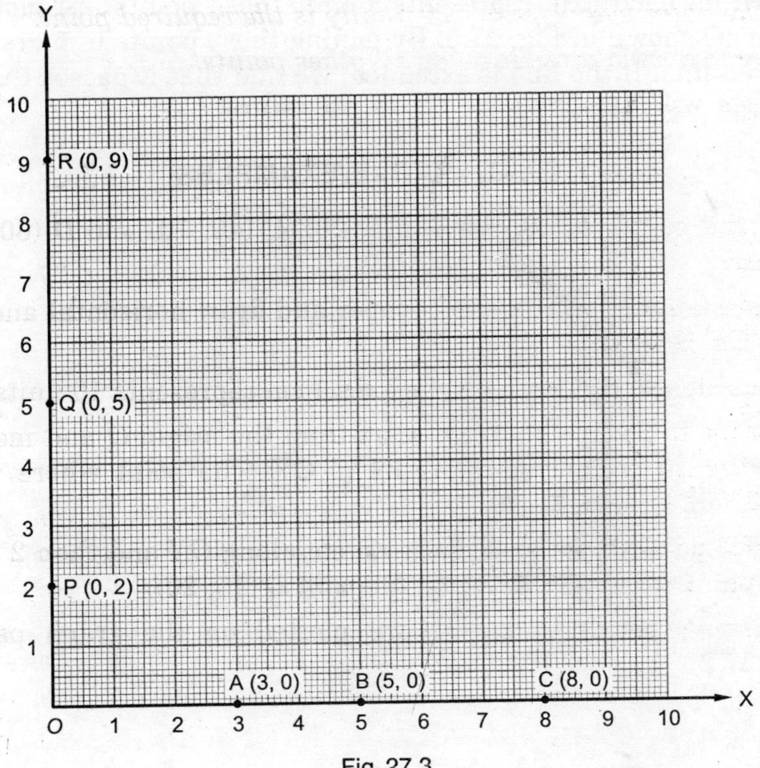

Fig. 27.3

Example 3 Plot each of the following points A (2, 3), B (5, 3), C (5, 5) and D (2, 5). Connect the points in order, i.e. A to B, B to C and so on.

Solution Let us assume that 1 cm on each axis represents 1 unit. On this scale points A, B, C and D are plotted and then joined in order to form a rectangle shown in Fig. 27.4.

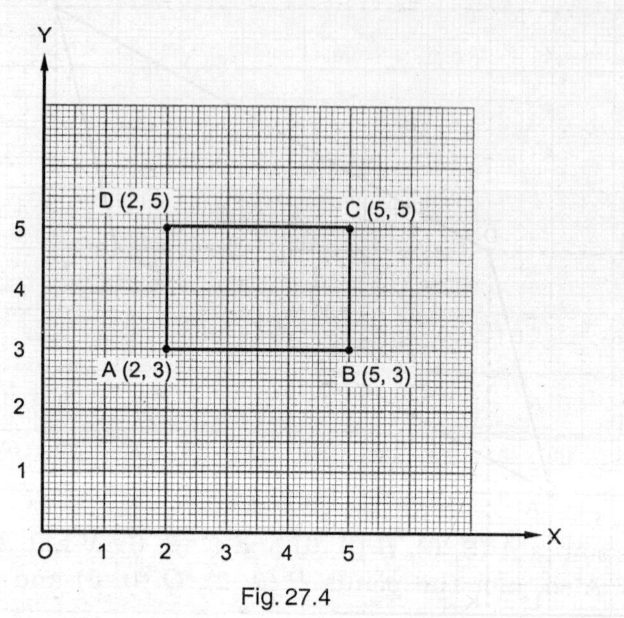

Fig. 27.4

Example 4 Plot any three points such that x-coordinate of each point is equal to its y-coordinate. Join these points in pairs. Do they lie on a line passing through the origin?

Solution Let us take the points as A (2, 2), B (5, 5) and C (8, 8). Assuming that 1 cm length on each axis represents 1 unit these points are plotted on the graph paper as shown in Fig. 27.5. By joining these points in pairs we find that they lie on a line. If the line is extended, we find that it passes through the origin.

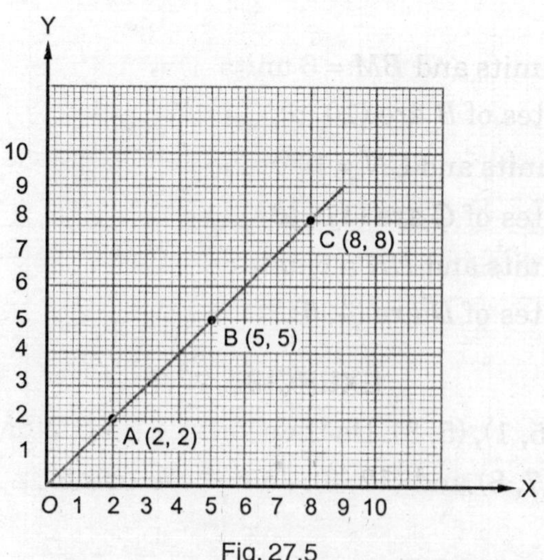

Fig. 27.5

Example 5 Write the coordinates of the vertices of the following figure:

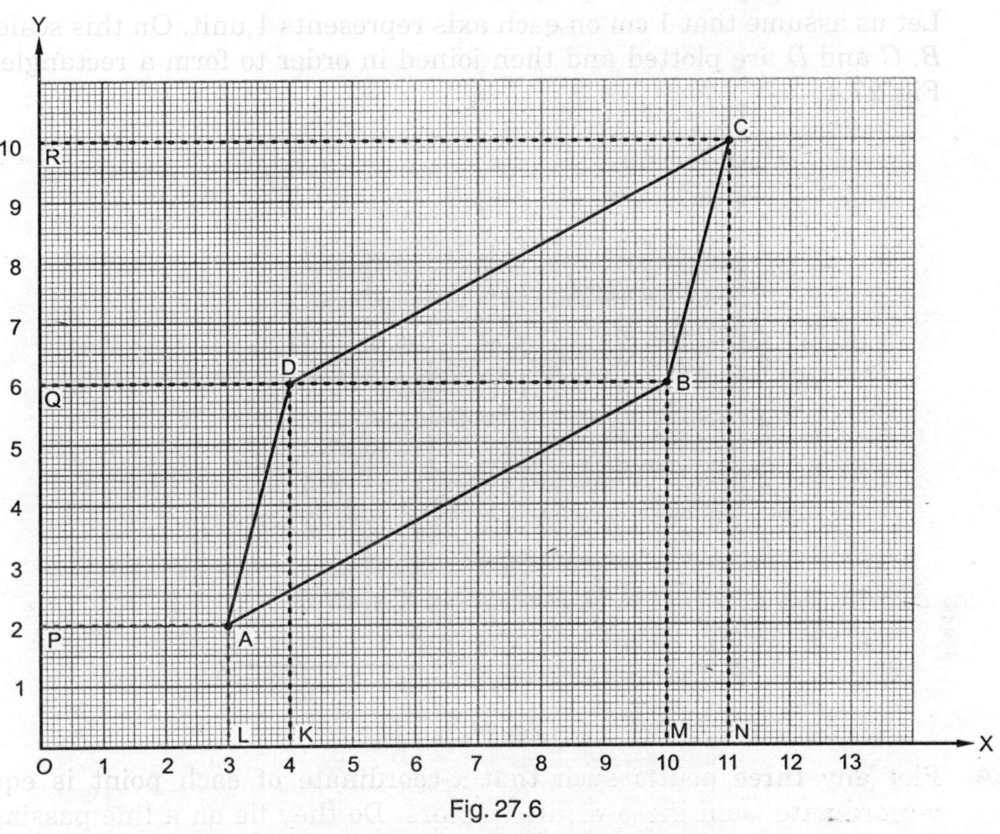

Fig. 27.6

Solution Draw perpendiculars AL, BM, CN and DK from A, B, C and D on x-axis. Also, draw perpendiculars AP, BQ, CR and DQ from these vertices on y-axis OY.

Clearly, $AP = 3$ units and $AL = 2$ units. That is the distance of vertex A from y-axis is 3 units and its distance from x-axis is 2 units. So, the coordinates of vertex A are (3, 2).

Similarly,

$BQ = 10$ units and $BM = 6$ units

$\therefore$ Coordinates of B are (10, 6)

$CR = 11$ units and $CN = 10$ units

$\therefore$ Coordinates of C are (11, 10)

and, $DQ = 4$ units and $DK = 6$ units

$\therefore$ Coordinates of D are (4, 6).

EXERCISE 27.1

1. Plot the points (5, 0), (5, 1), (5, 8). Do they lie on a line? What is your observation?
2. Plot the points (2, 8), (7, 8) and (12, 8). Join these points in pairs. Do they lie on a line? What do you observe?
3. Locate the points:

   (i) (1, 1), (1, 2), (1, 3), (1, 4) (ii) (2, 1), (2, 2), (2, 3), (2, 4)

   (iii) (1, 3), (2, 3), (3, 3), (4, 3) (iv) (1, 4), (2, 4), (3, 4), (4, 4).

4. Find the coordinates of points A, B, C, D in Fig. 27.7.

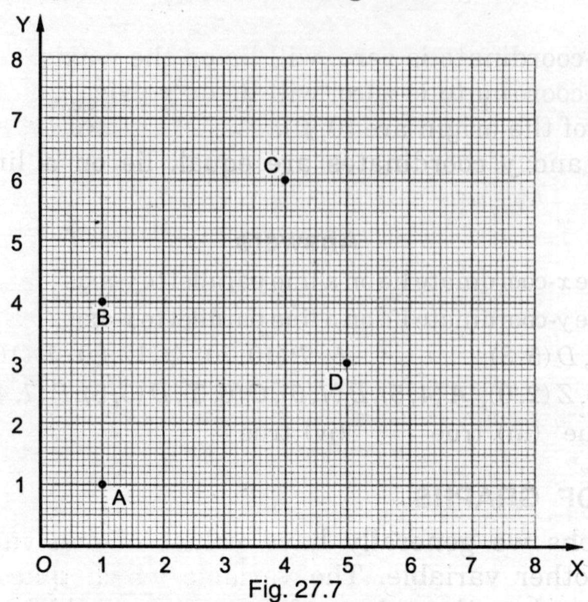

Fig. 27.7

5. Find the coordinates of points P, Q, R and S in Fig. 27.8.

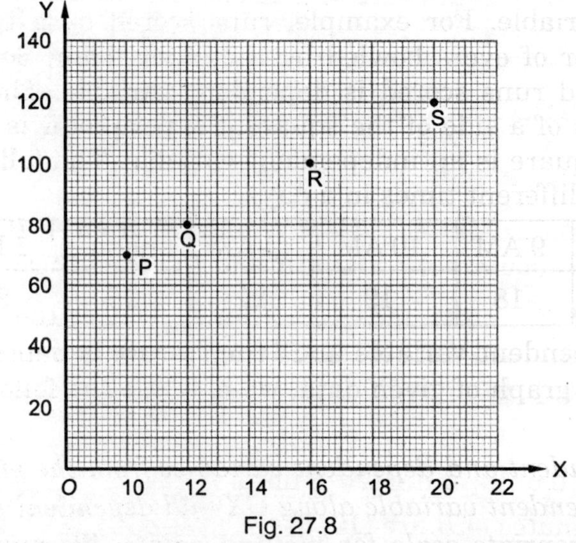

Fig. 27.8

6. Write the coordinates of each of the vertices of each polygon in Fig. 27.9.

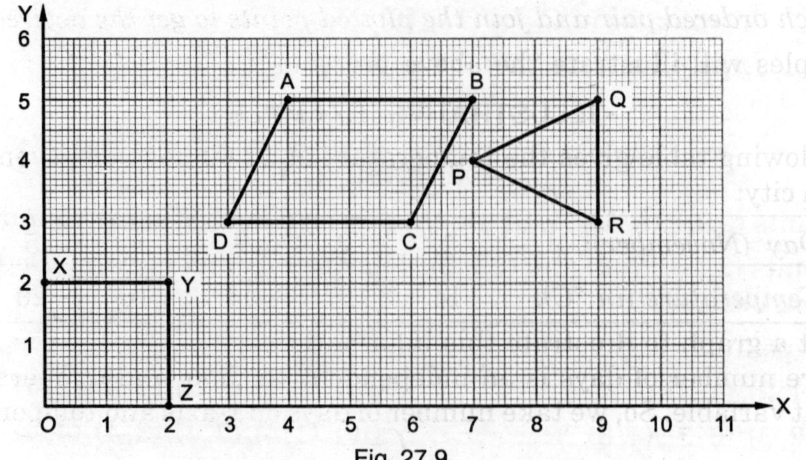

Fig. 27.9

7. Decide which of the following statements is true and which is false. Give reasons for your answer.
   (i) A point whose x-coordinate is zero, will lie on the y-axis.
   (ii) A point whose y-coordinate is zero, will lie on x-axis.
   (iii) The coordinates of the origin are (0, 0).
   (iv) Points whose x and y coordinates are equal, lie on a line passing through the origin.

Answers

1. Yes, points having same x-coordinate lie on a line parallel to y-axis
2. Yes, points having same y-coordinate lie on a line parallel to x-axis.
4. $A(1, 1), B(1, 4), C(4, 6), D(5, 3)$ 5. $P(10, 70), Q(12, 80), R(16, 100), S(20, 120)$
6. $O(0, 0), X(0, 2), Y(2, 2), Z(2, 0)$; $A(4, 5), B(7, 5), C(6, 3), D(3, 3)$; $P(7, 4), Q(9, 5), R(9, 3)$
7. (i) true (ii) true (iii) true (iv) true

27.4 CONSTRUCTION OF GRAPHS

While constructing graphs we generally have values of one variable corresponding to different values of the other variable. The variable which takes values freely, that is, whose values do not depend on the values of the other variable, is called an independent variable and the variable whose values depend on the values taken by the other variable is known as dependent variable. For example, runs scored by a cricket team in a match depend upon the number of overs bowled by the other team. So, number of overs is an independent variable and runs scored is dependent variable. The perimeter of a square depends upon the length of a side of the square. So, perimeter is dependent variable and length of a side of the square is an independent variable. The following table exhibits the temperature of a city at different times in a day:

Time:	9 AM	10 AM	11 AM	noon	1 PM	2 PM	3 PM
Temperature (in °C):	18	19	22	25	27	24	22

Clearly, time is an independent variable and temperature is dependent variable.
In order to construct the graph of given data, we may use the following prodedure:

PROCEDURE

Step I Identify independent and dependent variables from the given information.

Step II Label the independent variable along OX and dependent variable along OY.

Step III Choose an appropriate scale for plotting points. We may choose different scales along OX and OY.

Step IV Plot each ordered pair and join the plotted points to get the desired graph.

Following examples will illustrate the above procedure:

ILLUSTRATIVE EXAMPLES

Example 1 Following table gives the temperature at 12:00 noon on seven successive days in a city:

Day (November):	1	2	3	4	5	6	7
Temperature (in °C):	14	18	14	16	20	15	18

Plot a graph to illustrate this information.

Solution Here number of days is an independent variable and temperature is a dependent variable. So, we take number of days on x-axis and temperature on y-axis.

Let us choose the following scale:

On x-axis: 2 cm = 1 day, On y-axis: 1 cm = 2 °C

Now, we plot each ordered pair (1, 14), (2, 18), (3, 14), (4, 16), (5, 20), (6, 15) and (7, 18). These points are joined to get the graph representing the given information as shown in Fig. 27.10.

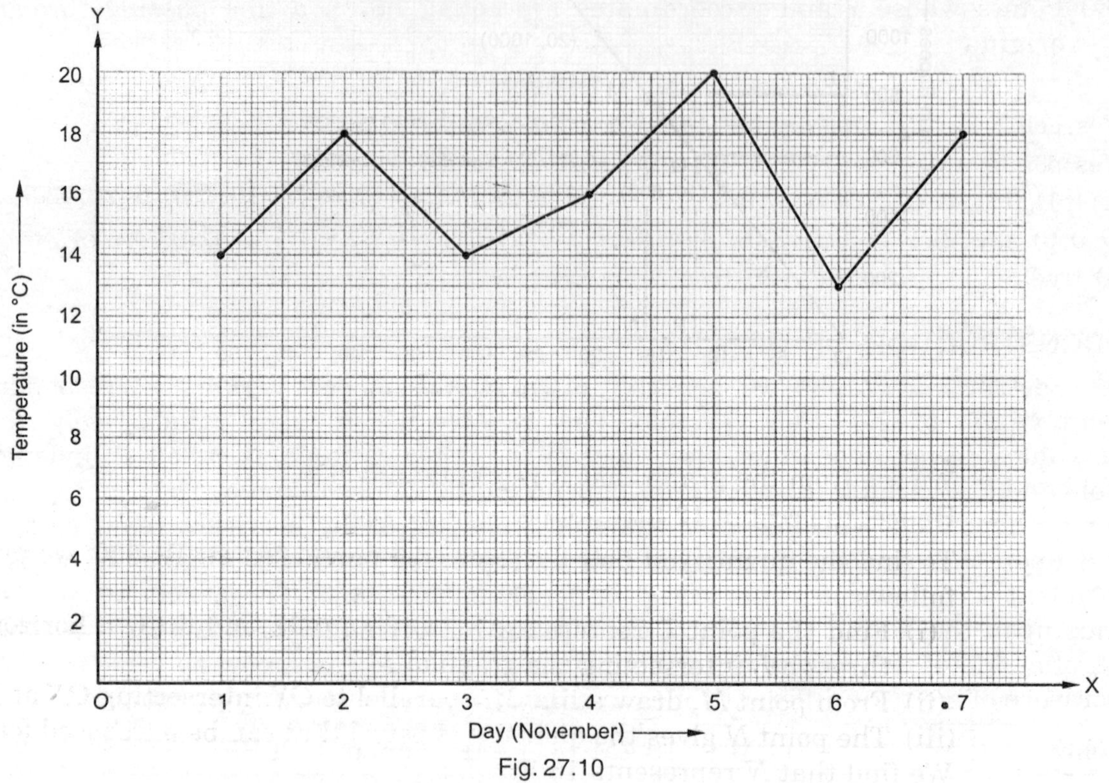

Fig. 27.10

Example 2 The quantity of petrol filled in a car and the cost of petrol are given in the following table:

Litres of petrol filled:	10	15	20	25
Cost of petrol:	500	750	1000	1250

Draw a graph representing the above data. Also, find the cost of 12 litres of petrol using the graph. How much petrol can be purchased for Rs 800?

Solution Let us take petrol filled in litres along x-axis and the cost of petrol along y-axis.

Let us choose the following scale:

On x-axis: 1 cm = 5 litres, On y-axis: 1 cm = Rs 200

Using this scale, we plot the ordered pairs (10, 500), (15, 750), (20, 1000) and (25, 1250) and join these plotted points to get the graph representing the given data.

Clearly, the graph is a straight line.

To find the cost of 12 litres of petrol using this graph, we proceed as follows:

(i) Find 12 on the horizontal axis representing the quantity of petrol in litres and mark it P.

(ii) At point P, draw a line perpendicular to OX intersecting the graph at point Q.

(iii) From point Q, draw a line QR parallel to OX meeting the vertical axis OY at R.

(iv) The point R gives the cost of 12 litres of petrol.

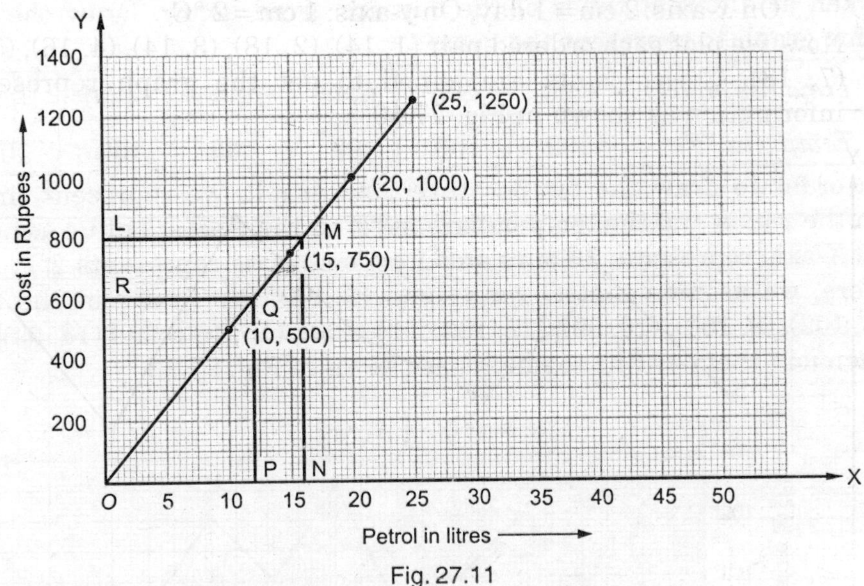

Fig. 27.11

We see from the graph that R represents Rs 600.

Hence, the cost of 12 litres of petrol is Rs 600.

To find the quantity of petrol that can be purchased for Rs 800, we proceed as follows:

(i) Find the point L representing Rs 800 on OY and draw a horizontal line through L intersecting the graph at M.

(ii) From point M, draw a line MN parallel to OY intersecting OX at N.

(iii) The point N gives the quantity of petrol that can be purchased for Rs 800.

We find that N represents 16 litres.

Hence, 16 litres of petrol can be purchased for Rs 800.

Example 3 The perimeter P and side s of a square are connected by the relation $P = 4s$. Draw the graph of this relation on the graph paper.

Solution The values of P for different values of s are given in the following table:

Sides (s):	1	2	3	4	5	6	7
Perimeter: $P = 4s$	$4\times1=4$	$4\times2=8$	$4\times3=12$	$4\times4=16$	$4\times5=20$	$4\times6=24$	$4\times7=28$

Let us take s on x-axis and P on y-axis.

Also, assume that 1 cm on x-axis represents 1 unit length of the side of the square and 1 cm on y-axis represents 4 units of perimeter.

Plot the points (ordered pairs) (1, 4), (2, 8), (3, 12), (4, 16), (5, 20), (6, 24) and (7, 28) on the graph paper and join them to get the graph representing the given relation as shown in Fig. 27.12.

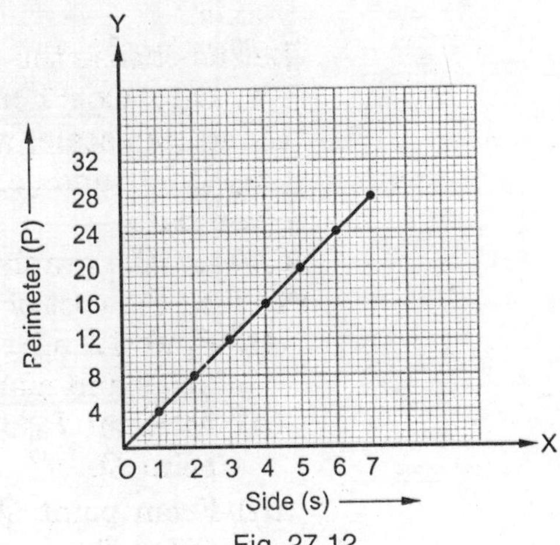

Fig. 27.12

Example 4 The temperature of a patient, admitted in a hospital with typhoid fever, taken at different times of the day are given below. Draw the temperature-time graph to represent the data:

Time (in hours):	6:00	8:00	10:00	12:00	14:00	16:00	18:00
Temp. (in °F):	102	100	99	103	100	102	99

Solution In order to draw the temperature-time graph, we represent time (in hours) on the x-axis and the temperature in °F on the y-axis. Let us assume that 1 cm on X-axis represents 2 hours and 1 cm on Y-axis represents 2°F.

Here, we assume that O represents (0, 96). We first plot the ordered pairs (6, 102), (8, 100), (10, 99), (12, 103), (14, 100), (16, 102) and (18, 99) as points and then join them by line segments as shown in Fig. 27.13.

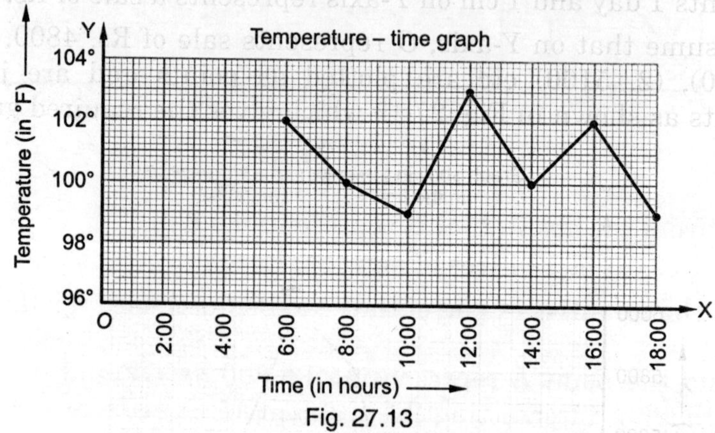

Fig. 27.13

Example 5 A car is going for a long journey of 16 hours, starting at 5:00 hrs. The speeds of the car at different hours are given below:

Time (in hours):	*5:00*	*7:00*	*9:00*	*11:00*	*13:00*	*15:00*	*17:00*	*19:00*	*21:00*
Speed (in km / hour):	40	50	60	80	70	65	75	60	50

Draw a velocity-time graph for the above data.

Solution Here, we represent time (in hr) on the x-axis and speed (in km/hr) on the y-axis. Let us assume that 1 cm on X-axis represents 2 hours and 1 cm on Y-axis represents speed of 10 km/hr. Also, assume that O represents the point (0, 30).

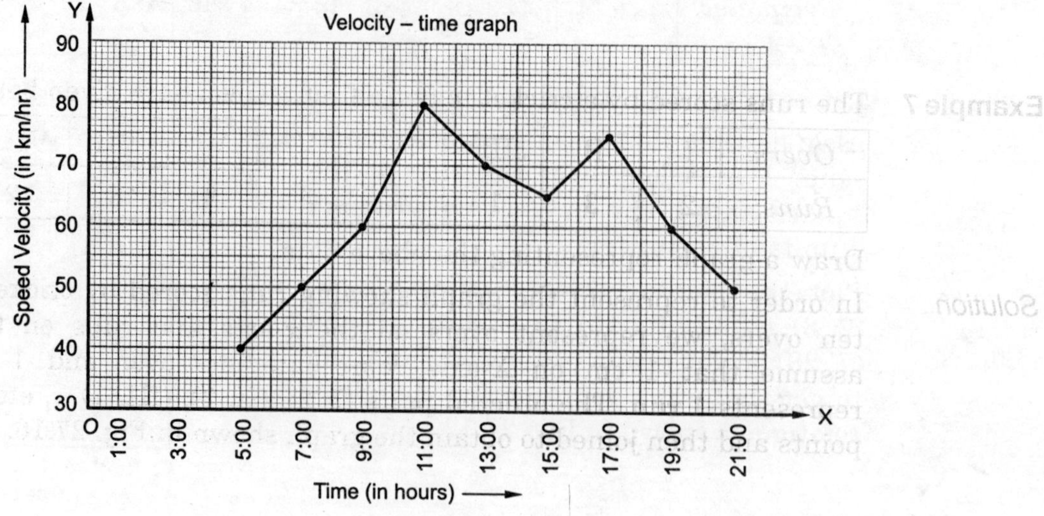

Fig. 27.14

We plot the ordered pairs (5, 40), (7, 50), (9, 60), ... (21, 50) etc. as points and join them by line segments to obtain the required graph as shown in Fig. 27.14.

Example 6 The sales of a shopkeeper in the first week of January 2002, are given below:

Date:	1	2	3	4	5	6	7
Sales (in Rs):	5000	5100	4900	5800	6000	5500	5200

Draw a graph representing the above data.

Solution In order to represent the above data graphically, we represent dates on x-axis and sales (in Rs) on y-axis. Let us assume that 1 cm on X-axis represents 1 day and 1 cm on Y-axis represents a sale of Rs. 200.

Also assume that on Y-axis, O represents sale of Rs. 4800. The ordered pairs (1, 5000), (2, 5100) etc are plotted as points and are joined by the line segments as shown in Fig. 27.15 which gives the required graph.

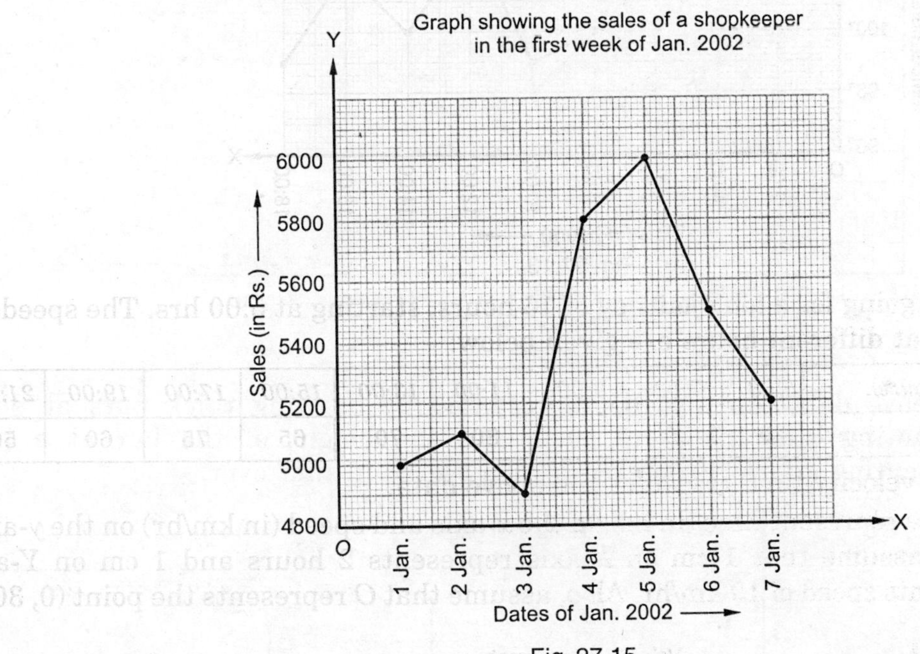

Fig. 27.15

Example 7 The runs scored by a cricket team in first 10 overs are given below:

Overs:	I	II	III	IV	V	VI	VII	VIII	IX	X
Runs:	2	3	1	6	4	3	8	12	4	10

Draw a graph representing the above data.

Solution In order to represent the graph showing runs scored by cricket team in first ten overs, we represent overs on the x-axis and runs on the y-axis. We assume that 1 cm on X-axis represents one over and 1 cm on Y-axis represents 1 run. The ordered pairs (I, 2), (II, 3), (III, 1)..., etc are plotted as points and then joined to obtain the graph shown in Fig. 27.16.

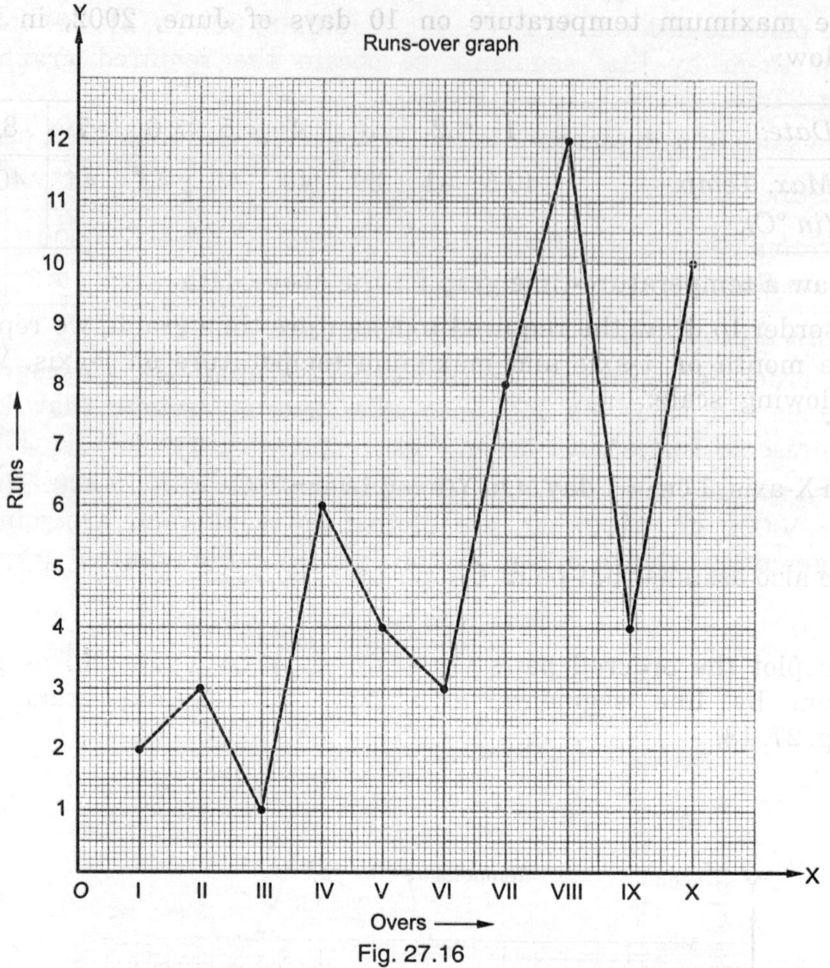

Fig. 27.16

The above data can also be represented by drawing thick bars at points representing different overs such that the height of the bar at a point (representing an over) represents runs scored in that over.

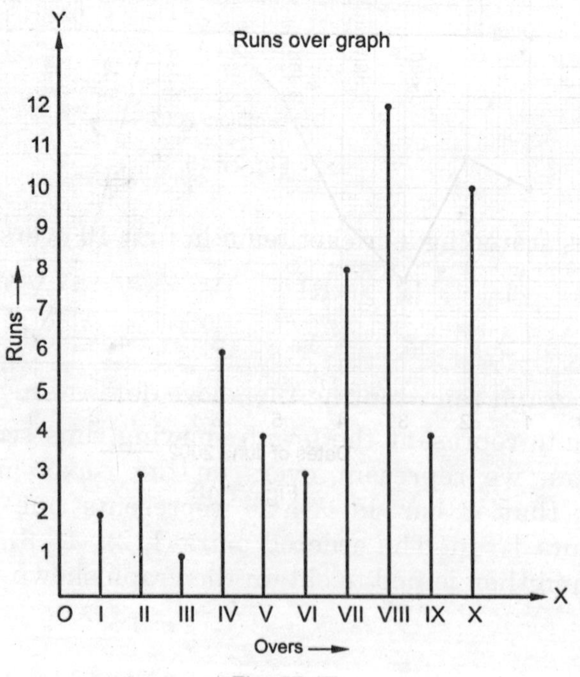

Fig. 27.17

Example 8 The maximum temperature on 10 days of June, 2002, in Delhi is given below:

Date:	1	2	3	4	5	6	7	8	9	10
Max. Temp. (in °C):	40.5	41	39	40	42	43	44	40	38	39

Draw a temperature-time grap for the above data.

Solution In order to draw the required temperature-time graph, we represent dates of the month on x-axis and maximum temperature on y-axis. We assume the following scale:

On X-axis, 1 cm = 1 day, On Y-axis, 1 cm = 1°C

We also assume that point O on Y-axis represents 37°C.

We plot the ordered pairs (1, 40.5), (2, 41), ..., (10, 39) as points and join them by line segments to obtain the required graph as shown in Fig. 27. 18.

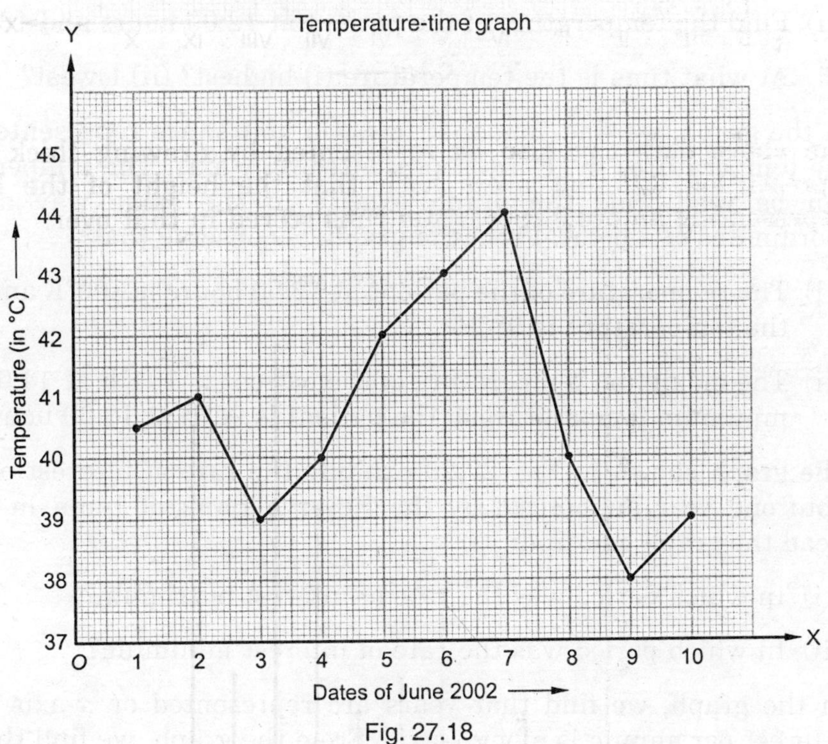

Fig. 27.18

Example 10 Given below is the temperature chart of a patient.

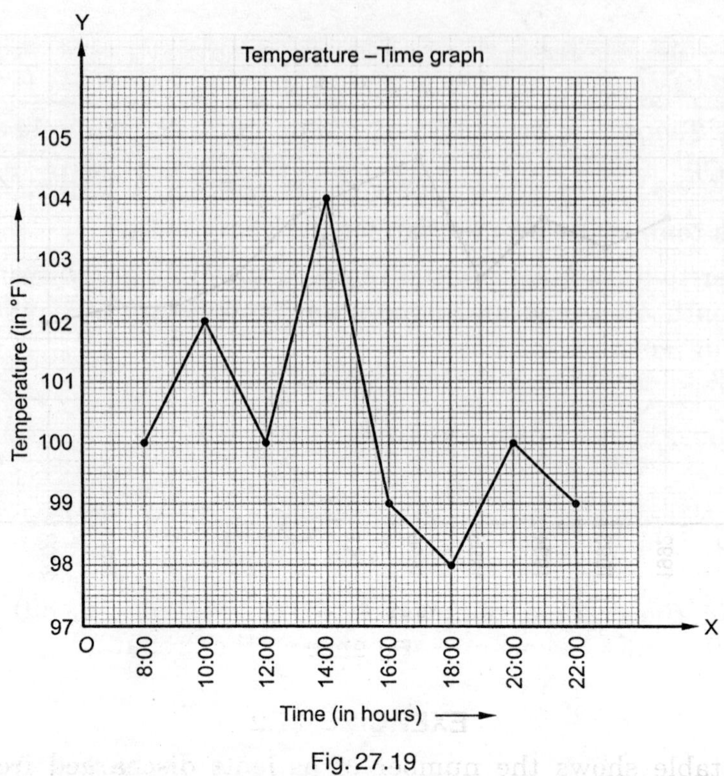

Fig. 27.19

(i) Find the temperature of the patient at 12:00 hours and 18:00 hours.

(ii) At what time is the temperature (i) highest? (ii) lowest?

Solution In the graph, we find that the times (in hours) are represented on x-axis and the temperatures in °F are represented on y-axis. The temperature at a time can be read from the graph exactly in the same way as we read the coordinates of a point. From the graph, we observe that:

(i) The temperature of the patient at 12:00 hours is 100°F and at 18:00 hours the temperature is 98°F.

(ii) The maximum temperature of the patient is 104°F at 14:00 hours and the minimum temperature of the patient is 98°F at 18:00 hours.

Example 11 The graph shown in Fig. 27.20 exhibits the rate of interest on fixed deposits upto one year announced by the Reserve Bank of India in different years. Read the graph and find:

(i) In which period was the rate of interest maximum?

(ii) In which period was the rate of interest minimum?

Solution In the graph, we find that years are represented on x-axis and the rate of interest per annum is along y-axis. From the graph, we find that

(i) The rate of interest was maximum (12%) in 1996.

(ii) The minimum rate of interest was 6.5% in the year 2002.

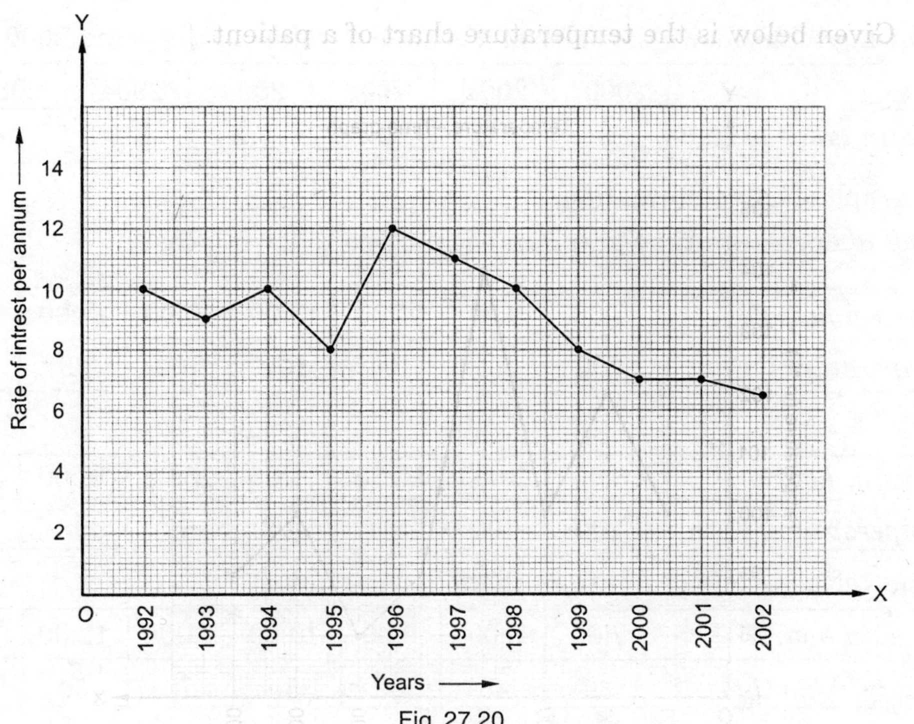

Fig. 27.20

EXERCISE 27.2

1. The following table shows the number of patients discharged from a hospital with HIV diagnosis in different years:

Years:	2002	2003	2004	2005	2006
Number of patients:	150	170	195	225	230

Represent this information by a graph.

2. The following table shows the amount of rice grown by a farmer in different years:

Years:	2000	2001	2002	2003	2004	2005	2006
Rice grown (in quintals):	200	180	240	260	250	200	270

Plot a graph to illustrate this information.

3. The following table gives the information regarding the number of persons employed to a piece of work and time taken to complete the work:

Number of persons:	2	4	6	8
Time taken (in days):	12	6	4	3

Plot a graph of this information.

4. The following table gives the information regarding length of a side of a square and its area:

Length of a side (in cm):	1	2	3	4	5
Area of square (in cm^2):	1	4	9	16	25

Draw a graph to illustrate this information.

5. The following table shows the sales of a commodity during the years 2000 to 2006.

Years:	2000	2001	2002	2003	2004	2005	2006
Sales (in lakhs of Rs):	1.5	1.8	2.4	3.2	5.4	7.8	8.6

Draw a graph of this information.

6. Draw the temperature-time graph in each of the following cases:

(i)

Time (in hours):	7:00	9:00	11:00	13:00	15:00	17:00	19:00	21:00
Temperature (°F) in:	100	101	104	102	100	99	100	98

(ii)

Time (in hours):	8:00	10:00	12:00	14:00	16:00	18:00	20:00
Temperature (°F) in:	100	101	104	103	99	98	100

7. Draw the velocity-time graph from the following data:

Time (in hours):	7:00	8:00	9:00	10:00	11:00	12:00	13:00	14:00
Speed (in km/hr):	30	45	60	50	70	50	40	45

8. The runs scored by a cricket team in first 15 overs are given below:

Overs:	I	II	III	IV	V	VI	VII	VIII	IX	X	XI	XII	XIII	XIV	XV
Runs:	2	1	4	2	6	8	10	21	5	8	3	2	6	8	12

Draw the graph representing the above data in two different ways as a graph and as a bar chart.

9. The runs scored by two teams A and B in first 10 overs are given below:

Overs:	I	II	III	IV	V	VI	VII	VIII	IX	X
Team A:	2	1	8	9	4	5	6	10	6	2
Team B:	5	6	2	10	5	6	3	4	8	10

Draw a graph depicting the data, making the graphs on the same axes in each case in two different ways as a graph and as a bar chart.

THINGS TO REMEMBER

1. *The x-coordinate of a point is its distance from y-axis.*
2. *The y-coordinate of a point is its distance from x-axis.*
3. *The coordinates of the origin are (0, 0).*
4. *The x-coordinate of every point on y-axis is zero.*
5. *The y-coordinate of every point on x-axis is zero.*